THE OXFORD HANDBOOK OF

JEWISH LAW

THE OXFORD HANDBOOK OF

JEWISH LAW

Edited by

ZEV ELEFF, ROBERTA ROSENTHAL KWALL

and

CHAIM SAIMAN

OXFORD
UNIVERSITY PRESS

OXFORD
UNIVERSITY PRESS

Oxford University Press is a department of the University of Oxford.
It furthers the University's objective of excellence in research, scholarship,
and education by publishing worldwide. Oxford is a registered trade mark of
Oxford University Press in the UK and certain other countries.

Published in the United States of America by Oxford University Press
198 Madison Avenue, New York, NY 10016, United States of America.

Library of Congress Cataloging-in-Publication Data
Names: Eleff, Zev, editor. | Rosenthal Kwall, Roberta, editor. | Saiman, Chaim, editor.
Title: The Oxford handbook of Jewish law / Zev Eleff, Roberta Rosenthal Kwall, and Chaim Saiman [editors].
Description: New York : Oxford University Press, 2025. | Series: Oxford handbooks series |
Includes index. | Identifiers: LCCN 2025002292 (print) | LCCN 2025002293 (ebook) |
ISBN 9780197508305 (hardback) | ISBN 9780197508329 (epub) | ISBN 9780197508336
Subjects: LCSH: Jewish law. | Mishpat Ivri.
Classification: LCC KBM524 .O94 2025 (print) | LCC KBM524 (ebook) |
DDC 296.1/274—dc23/eng/20250118
LC record available at https://lccn.loc.gov/2025002292
LC ebook record available at https://lccn.loc.gov/2025002293

DOI: 10.1093/oxfordhb/9780197508305.001.0001

Printed by Marquis Book Printing, Canada

Note to Readers

This publication is designed to provide accurate and authoritative information in regard to the subject matter covered. It is based upon sources believed to be accurate and reliable and is intended to be current as of the time it was written. It is sold with the understanding that the publisher is not engaged in rendering legal, accounting, or other professional services. If legal advice or other expert assistance is required, the services of a competent professional person should be sought. Also, to confirm that the information has not been affected or changed by recent developments, traditional legal research techniques should be used, including checking primary sources where appropriate.

(Based on the Declaration of Principles jointly adopted by a Committee of the American Bar Association and a Committee of Publishers and Associations.)

FSC
www.fsc.org
MIX
Paper | Supporting responsible forestry
FSC® C103567

Contents

PART II DISTINGUISHING CHARACTERISTICS OF JEWISH LAW

PART III JEWISH LAW AND PRACTICE IN MODERNITY

A. Movements and Denominations

Acknowledgments

The editors thank the Bill Bass Foundation and Mindy Jacobson for their generous financial support for this project. We are also grateful to Shprintza Block (DePaul Law, 2021), Azaria Jacobson, and Dov Karrol for administrative and other organizational assistance. Finally, we appreciate the outstanding efforts of our Oxford Project Editor, Lisa Butts, whose expertise facilitated the final stages of this publication, and to our initial Oxford Editor, Jamie Berezin, for his encouragement in the early stages of our work.

Editors' Introduction

We began this volume before the start of the COVID-19 pandemic, when the world was, in many ways, a very different place. We finished our work shortly before October 7, 2023, when the Jewish world was turned upside down. Throughout this unusually turbulent period, the one comfort we shared is that *halakhah* (Jewish law) has maintained the same functions as it has throughout the centuries: providing wisdom, guidance, and comfort to all those who dare to explore its riches.

The first two parts of this volume focus on the classical canon of Jewish legal texts. Part I, "Reading Foundational Jewish Texts and Law," displays sensitivity to the fact that the core documents of *halakhah* were produced throughout nearly two millennia, across multiple continents, and in innumerable different contexts. In other words, Jewish law is not a constant but developed and shifted significantly over time. This section considers the historical development of Jewish law as seen from the perspective of one who engages it via its textual tradition. It opens with a chapter on how classical *halakhic* sources understand the nature, origin, and authority of the oral law tradition that serves as the backbone of the Jewish legal system. In other words, how does Jewish law understand its own authority?

This section's chapter then explore the development of Jewish law by examining how each layer of sources read and reacted to the authoritative texts that stood before it. This starts with how the *tannaitic* rabbis of the early Common Era read the Torah, followed by how the rabbis of the Talmud read the Mishna, and then how scholars of the Middle Ages read the Talmud. The section then examines how different genres of *halakhic* writing approached the Talmudic materials: how rabbis restated the mass of Talmudic discussions into a leaner set of rules; how waves of commentators on these restatements transformed them into authoritative codes of binding law; and how the genre of *responsa* developed to address novel questions not yet covered in earlier material. Part I closes with a chapter that assesses how rabbis who were theologically orientated toward esotericism and mysticism read through the multifarious details of the *halakhic* tradition.

Part II, "Distinguishing Characteristics of Jewish Law," recesses the historical framework to offer more cross-temporal, conceptual, and phenomenological accounts of Jewish law as an ongoing tradition. These chapters primarily focus on the structural features that characterize the *halakhic* tradition and set it apart from other modes of law or thought. This includes an assimilative chapter on rabbinic modes of interpretation, the intermingling of *halakhah* and *Aggadah*, and the impact of the commandment to study Torah on the formation and content of Jewish law. Several chapters examine how authority manifests in a decentralized system that does not sustain coordinating bodies of political authority. These chapters explore how the practices derived from communal legislation and folk and pietistic practices interact with laws sourced to Talmudic points of origin. Other chapters rely on expressly comparative analysis to explore topics such as the degree to which Jewish law's reputation for formalism is warranted, how Jewish law's emphasis on duties contrasts with the Western legal orientation toward rights, and why issues of doubt, stringency, and leniency take on outsized importance in Jewish law.

Part III, "Jewish Law and Practice in Modernity," contains four subdivisions. Here, the volume transitions from centering on the classical canon of *halakhic* texts to exploring the modern period in which the authority and normativity of the Jewish legal tradition is no longer taken for granted. The chapters in the first section of this part, "Movements and Denominations," discuss how *halakhah* transitioned from a semiautonomous system of governance that competed with the state to one that covers a narrower set of practices understood explicitly as *religious*. This is followed by chapters about how Jewish law was adapted to serve as a system distinguishing Orthodoxy from the Reform and Conservative movements. The section concludes with how the emergence of Zionism has impacted the practice and interpretation of Jewish law.

The second section, "*Halakhic* Responses to Modernity," contains five case studies examining how Jewish law has confronted cultural, scientific, and economic settings far removed from the world envisioned by its classical texts. The chapters discuss shifts in the relationship between Jews and non-Jews, how new scientific understandings and paradigms impact *halakhah*, how Jewish law and culture have confronted the problems presented by *halakhah*'s strictures concerning divorce, how *halakhah* has responded to commercial and economic norms that differ substantially from Talmudic paradigms, and what we can learn from how *halakhists* responded to the acute crises wrought by the COVID-19 pandemic. Each chapter tells a different narrative about the often-fraught relationship between continuity and flexibility and how the boundary between these elements is managed.

The three chapters in the third section, "*Halakhah* and State," describe how *halakhah* interacts with modern state-based legal systems. This section is likely to be of particular interest to practicing lawyers. The chapters discuss how American courts conceptualize Jewish law, the *halakhic* doctrines that enable and limit how observant Jews participate in the state's legal system, and finally, how the State of Israel incorporates certain aspects of *halakhic* governance into the state's legal system.

The final section of Part III, "*Halakhah* and Personhood," opens with a chapter on the cultural shifts that have impacted the structure of the Jewish family such as rising divorce rates, intermarriage, and gay marriage. The second chapter features the highly relevant topic of abortion, and the book concludes with an exploration of matters related to organ donation and brain death. These chapters elaborate on the points of contention within and across denominations and enhance our understanding of how Jewish law is interpreted and practiced in religious, legal, and politically contested zones.

We are humbled by the ambition of this project and the remarkable set of the contributors who have made this project a reality. But we do not expect (or desire) this volume to be the final word on the subject. Instead, we hope that this *Handbook on Jewish Law* spurs deeper discussion on this and other topics and compels researchers to expand the range of scholarship on the history and legal aspects of *halakhah*. For example, we fervently hope that future works can include scholarship on how Sephardic rabbinic culture and religious practice has shaped the modern framework of *halakhah*. Other fertile ground for research might consider the relationship between *halakhah* and areas of common interest to civil legal systems such as contract, property, and commercial law. Of course, the fabric of Jewish tradition itself also provides ample opportunities for deeper explorations of legal discussion in connection with topics that are staples such as Shabbat, kashrut, and life-cycle events.

We wish to conclude by reciting the traditional formula used upon finishing a Jewish book: *Tam v'nishlam shevah le-El borei olam*—"This book is complete, praise be to God, Creator of the universe."

Zev Eleff, Roberta Rosenthal Kwall, and Chaim Saiman
July 2024, *Tammuz* 5784

PART I

READING FOUNDATIONAL JEWISH TEXTS AND LAW

CHAPTER 1

THE THEOLOGY OF CLASSICAL JEWISH LAW

The Written Torah and the Oral Torah—History, Theology, and Authority

BERACHYAHU LIFSHITZ

INTRODUCTION

ACCORDING to rabbinic literature there are two Torahs: The Written Torah (WT), the Pentateuch, and the Oral Torah (OT), or the Unwritten Torah. The definitions of the two Torahs and the relationship between them are of our interest here. WT was so defined because after being given orally to Moses at Sinai and afterward, he was ordered by God to write it down. It was meant to be written down. After being written down it lost its very short temporary oral origin and nature; it was read or recited punctiliously.[1] Thus, its definition seems to be simple.

On the other hand, the definition and the scope of contents of the "Oral Torah" are not so clear. The question has two aspects. Its central aspect is its substantive one: What is it and what does it include? Its secondary facet is procedural and involves the prohibition of writing down OT (after it has already been defined).[2] The scope of research throughout generations on the prohibition of writing down the OT occupies a wider expanse than discussion of the first aspect and is taken for something of mystery.[3] Naturally, from the standpoint of Jewish *Law*, the constitutive aspect is essential, while the procedural component trails along behind.[4] As we will propose ahead, both aspects are connected with each other and the mystery regarding the reason for the prohibition against writing OT can be solved.

Defining Oral Torah

Research has suggested several definitions of OT and their relation to the OT the Sages refer to. One theory suggests the OT is the unwritten background for the WT and elucidates its terminologies, expressions, and their connections. This framework can be reconstructed through tradition, historical data, comparative law and inner-biblical parallels. It is not, however, the OT the Sages spoke of. Another definition was proposed by Urbach: "It was not interpretive dialectics or discussion . . . rather ['Oral Torah' denotes] the authority of [Rabbinic] institutions. It is the institutional character of *halakha*."

There are those who compare the OT with the "Unwritten Law" Philo speaks of *Agrafos Nomos*, law not written in books but inscribed on the hearts of individuals and in a way it resembles Natural Law.[5] While this Torah as well is not written, it is also not the OT the Sages refer to; theirs is not assessed by its "naturalness" and fitness for human civilizations from the time of Creation onward and to the laws of most of the nations. On the contrary, it is uniquely directed to Israel and not binding on Gentiles whatsoever, who may even be prohibited from studying it and observing it.[6] It has specific content and the Sages claim they know how and when it originated—and it is not on the date of Creation. Also, one does not comply with it out of free will or volition; rather it is forced on the people.[7] OT is also not directly connected with arguments against Paul's doctrine of Christianity which annuls any need to keep Torah law.[8]

From an historical standpoint which is presented in Talmudic sources, it seems that the term and idea of OT are a rabbinic reaction to attacks on their claim that they are *authorized* to interpret and expound the WT, the Five Books of Moses. (If these are the "Word of God," their claim includes subsequent revelations as well, though the focus is on the Pentateuch.) The polemic included participants from various sects of Judaism and Christianity (which too began from a Jewish origin) and spanned generations. Its criticism was directed at the additions and detractions the Sages made in the course of their interpretation (*derashot*) of WT, contravening Deut. 4.2: "You shall not add to anything I command you nor take away anything from it."

The Rabbinic Innovation and Its Sectarian Opposition

The framework of the Sages' innovation was primarily theological, involving conceptions of divinity and revelation: Does God still directly reveal Himself? (This article does not deal with the question whether the WT was given by God at Mt. Sinai directly to Moses or not. It seems that the Talmudic tradition and the post-Talmudic authorities accepted the affirmative answer to that question.) Is there prophecy anymore? However, there is a jurisprudential consequence—the question of authority to interpret the WT and formulate innovations. An additional theological tension followed: as all concede the WT was given by the Divine from heaven, it is conceived as eternal and no alterations whatsoever can be made to it by human hands; to do so undermines the premise of a perfect Divine text and its Author. It undermines the canonicity of the WT which is not interpreted from within but rather by the human mind. The borderline between the rule of the Torah (*d'oraita*) and the ruling of the rabbis (*d'rabanan*) was blurred, especially when the rabbis were trying to unify their interpretations and the WT.

Based on our knowledge from Scripture, the opposition certainly had grounds to rely on. The people Moses elected (on Jethro's counsel) could arbitrate only when instructions were clear and simple to apply. Hard questions were brought to Moses who stood directly before God to receive His answers.[9] In the same manner, the judges who would serve after the Israelites entered the Land of Israel were instructed to arrive to the Temple to find out what the law is.[10] This way of adjudicating and making new laws can be traced through the days of Ezra and the era of the *Sofrim*.

Actually, this was the core of the dispute between the Sectarians and the Pharisees.[11] The Sectarians held that Torah commands are meant to be understood—and everyone can understand them—at face value[12] while God alone has authority to issue new law for changing times, for other reasons, or to clarify the current law. He did so by revealing Himself to the High Priest or to the *Doresh ha-Torah*. You may not add or change the text, but surely God may do so. When such an addition is revealed, it is written down and so preserved in the holy book. This was exactly the procedure while the Israelites were in the desert, and any question that arose was posed by Moses before God, who revealed the answer to him.

Qumran hidden scrolls incorporate the biblical terms (Deut. 29:28) "Revealed and Hidden." In their view "the revealed" is the portion of Torah first written on the Heavenly tablets which had already been revealed to all humans, while "the Hidden" marks the portions that has yet to be revealed and divulged, periodically, according to God's will.[13] "The Hidden" or "Oral Torah" is not written by our hands, nor is it created by our contemplation.

According to the Temple Scroll, this also applies to law unknown to judges after Moses's death: judges were to approach the place of God's choice (the Temple) and there the priests would reveal the law to them (Deut. 17:8–13) after it was revealed to the Priests by God.[14] One Qumranic source relays that in Temple times, the *Urim* and *Thummim* were used to resolve disputes or for elucidations from the Deity.[15] For such the High Priest would enter the Holy of Holies on the Day of Atonement (or any other time necessary) along with the incense, to welcome the coming King.[16] When the sect was distant from the Temple, they had a figure denominated as "inquirer of the Torah" (*doresh ha-Torah*), who would pose questions and wait until Torah *was revealed* to him (*darash* = reveal).[17] The instruction communicated was then written in a book,[18] and this accounts for many of the textual discrepancies found between the Masoretic version and that of the Scrolls (and between several differences within the Masoretic WT itself as well).[19]

Thus, the Sages were faced with a very serious problem: From where do they draw authority to depart from protocol determined by Torah? They struggled with this continuously and for quite some time. In a way, the Sages preferred the OT over the WT and denied an ongoing revelation. They said that the words of the Sages (*Sofrim*) are more cherished than the words of Torah[20] and that the Sinai covenant was made in order *to allow* the Israelites to accept the OT.[21] And though it is possible such statements were meant as persuasions intended to promote compliance with Oral Law instructions, they include a substantive element as well: The WT is interpreted by the OT and it determines the language's meaning and compass of its rules, fills in missing details (in the text) without which fulfillment of the commandments cannot be precise, which adds to it or detracts from it and, at times, uproots Scripture's command altogether.[22]

The Legal Power of an Unwritten Law

This claim encounters another legal difficulty: it was believed that an unwritten law cannot be binding since its content is not promulgated or subject to verification.[23]

The Sages claimed the *entire* Torah was already given from Heaven and nothing remained in Heaven to be revealed later on. Therefore, nothing was to be altered on claims of "revelation" as this was deemed false prophecy. For the rabbis, this is the true meaning of Deuteronomy's command, "You shall not add." For this reason, the prophet is altogether denied authority to prophesy on legal matters.[24] The final stage in this matter was the declaration that prophecy no longer exists. Authority for this is lent exclusively to the Sages since "the Sage is preferable to the prophet."[25] The Sages are not required to evince proof for their statements on *halakhic* matters and are relied on while a prophet must show signs and wonders to be believed.[26] This is the thrust of the Sages' claim against the Sadducees in *Megillat Ta'anit*, "[New] Laws are not to be written in the Book."[27] Therefore, the Sages, who were very strict about maintaining the accuracy of the WT to its letters, absolutely forbade emendations and ruled that *any* change invalidates it. If a change is found in a scroll, it is regarded as an unfit scroll for the formal reading. Another important reason for doing so was the need for exact books to use as an authentic basis for their *derashot*. They also absolutely forbade reading in the books of the *Minim* who used to add the new laws revealed to them into the scrolls.

The Concept of Two Torahs and Its Sources

In response to the argument that revelation was necessary to interpret or to renew Torah, the Sages tendered a claim which is also based on revelation: Two Torahs were given to Moses at the same time/contemporaneously at Sinai, one being the "Written

Torah" and the other the "Oral Torah" and he transferred them to Joshua (mAv.1:1) and so on through all generations. According to this perspective, the Sages do not innovate *any* Torah matter; rather they only *preserve* the tradition, cite it, and transfer it on.

Thus, the OT is designated as such as it was *given* verbally as opposed to the Torah *given* in writing; the WT.[28] The *Sifri* conveys this idea:

> ["They shall teach your laws to Jacob and your instructions [*toratcha*, read *torotech*, in the plural] to Israel" (Deut. 33:10)]:
>
> And Your Torah [*torot*] to Israel—this teaches us that two Torahs were given to Israel, one verbally another in writing
>
> Angitus Hagamun asked R. Gamliel, "How many Torahs were given to Israel?" He responded, "Two, one oral and one written."[29]

The idea is found in the *Sifra* as well:[30]

> These are the laws, and the rules, and the torahs (Lev. 26:46)—this teaches that two "torahs" were given to Israel—one in writing and one orally.

To the *Midrash*, the verses denote a literal and simple giving, from God's mouth to Moses. Other sources apply the miracle, glory, and mysteriousness of the WT's delivery to the giving of the OT as well. For example,

> "He showed him (*yevonenehu*)"—with the Ten Commandments. Teaching that when a commandment left God's mouth the Israelites saw [=*ro-im*] it and understood all its *midrash* and all its laws (*halacha*), each deduction and inference it included.[31]

Within the commandments all halakhic details were *discernable*; "*Yevonenehu*"—like the word "*hitbonenut*," observing and seeing rather than "understanding."

And so we read in another *derasha*,

> Like the sea, that between one great wave and the next is little waves, so between each commandment and commandment were the minutest details and refinements of Torah.[32]

In several sources, the Sages are sure to note that all components of the Sages' creation had (already) been relayed to Moses at Sinai:

> "The Tablets"—these are the Ten Commandments, "Torah"—this is *Mikra* (=Bible), and the "Mitzvah"—this is the *Mishna*, "Which I Wrote"—these are the Prophets and Scriptures (*ketuvim*), "To instruct them"—this is the *Gemara*. It teaches that all were delivered to Moses at Sinai.[33]
>
> Teaching that God showed Moses the finest details of Torah and the details of the *Sofrim* and what the *Sofrim* would innovate in the future.[34]

> The additions *(tosafot)* of Rabbi's academy . . . even they were given to Moses at Sinai, and of them it is said, "And the Lord gave me the two tablets of stone inscribed by the finger of God, with the exact words that the Lord had addressed to you" (Deut. 9:10):
>
> Scripture, Mishna, Halacha and Talmud, Tosafot and Aggadot, even what a seasoned scholar would say before his rabbi—all were given as law to Moses at Sinai.[35]
>
> The Torah, Mishna, Talmud and Aggadah, even what a seasoned scholar would instruct in the future were all said to Moses at Sinai. Why? "Sometimes there is a phenomenon of which they say, 'look this one is new'—it occurred long before" (Eccles. 1:10).[36]

In the latter *Midrash*, all details of the Torah and prophecies were impressed in the minds and hearts of each soul—prophets and Sages—standing present at Sinai. When the time was ripe, a particular prophet or Sage would arise and state a prophecy or Torah detail they already received at Sinai as souls.[37]

In this conception, Moses himself did not receive the entire Torah, rather each Sage received his portion at Sinai, and revelation transpired bit by bit. It includes a sort of response to the aforementioned Sectarian claim of new revelations at God's will. This mysterious and enigmatic understanding which speaks of innovations divulged far earlier also meets the claim that the OT was given at Sinai and the reality of new material devised in Rabbinic academies; only (very) limited material relayed in the academies did not involve dispute and could be classified as "Law (given) to Moses at Sinai," while the bulk was subject to disagreement and therefore difficult to ascribe to Sinai revelation. Likewise, the claim helps overcome the real difficulty with accepting that the tradition managed to preserve all the particulars from the moment of delivery at Sinai. It contends that it only *seems* the Sages innovate laws, while in actually they reveal what was "within them" from the time of Sinai and thus nothing was forgotten.

Criticism and Replies

This view raised criticism. Why the need for a strange, double rendition of Torah, one revealed the other hidden? Invariably, written texts are concise and require elaboration and after all, even in proximity to delivery at Sinai questions arose and were inquired of Moses? And why was the WT itself given in a way that called for such comprehensive interpretation and changes, at times even contravening its literal meaning? It is not the standard way of giving laws to the people. Nonetheless, the Sages stood their ground. And it seems they adopted this position owing to the intense polemics from outside, and for internal discord among some Jewish congregations.

The viewpoint that everything was given to Moses at Sinai was endorsed by the Babylonian *Geonim* as well, with Rav Sa'adia Ga'on (ninth–tenth centuries) at their lead. He polemicized with the Karaites who had strong sway at the time and claimed the Mishna was never given, but was a rabbinic creation.[38] Rav Sa'adia asserted the disputes touched minor issues alone. But Maimonides (thirteenth-century Egypt) who was involved in clashes with the large Karaite community in Egypt digressed in part from the sweeping view. In his understanding, only *tannaitic* material (*halakhic midrashim, Mishna, tosefta* and *b'raytot*)—and even here not all—composes what Moses received at Sinai. "They would write down the text and learn its tradition by-heart . . . all the mitzvoth were given with their principles, details and specifications at Sinai" (*Introduction to the Mishna's Commentary*, in his view, as the definition of the Oral Torah is the main statements which are found in the *tannaitic* sources). This is (readily) apparent in *Sefer ha-Mitzvot* and from his phraseology in *Mishne Torah* where he designates the material as "the Word of God." There were no disputes concerning its major substance, only disagreements touching secondary issues and these alone were determined by the Sages.[39] So, Maimonides partly conceded and limited the broad scope of the disputes and eased the pressure of Karaitic attack.

Although this stance was polemic and primarily targeted outward—though perhaps also directed at simpletons among the rabbis' circles and rejected their prevailing conception[40]—among themselves the Sages adopted an utterly different claim: the assertion that at Sinai they were *authorized* by God to interpret Torah!

There were those who replied the WT was deliberately written with ambiguities and contradictions, and the key to decrypting it was given uniquely to Israel to distinguish Israel from other nations claiming "We are Israel" (*Verus Israel*):

> When God told Moses "Write down these commandments," Moses asked for the Mishna to be in writing [too], but since God saw that in the future nations would translate the Torah and read from it in Greek and say "We are Israel!"—"until now the scales have been off (unbalanced)," God said to the Gentiles, "You say you are My children? I do not know, rather those who hold my secrets, these are my children." And what is it? It is the Mishna that was given orally, and all is to be learned from you.[41]

The Torah (Exod. 20.15) relays the nation "saw the sounds at Sinai." How can sound be seen? Rabbi Yehudah the Prince explains:

> To indicate Israel's praise . . . "He compassed him about, He made them understand (*yevonenehu*)" (Deut. 32.10), as they heard the commandment—they *interpreted* it.[42]

That is to say they comprehended and explained it to themselves. Seeing here means understanding by interpretation.[43] The need to interpret a text is essential and therefore authority to interpret it is just as critical—both were issued simultaneously when the text was given. OT was *not given* at Sinai as a closed body of knowledge; rather it is the outcome of Israel's process of interpretation. The Torah's words are fixed however they multiply and develop as a sapling.[44]

Authority and Its Basis

The question of *authority* is the focal point in the well-known story of the Gentile who wished to convert and asked Shamai, "How many Torahs do you have?" Shamai responded, "Two, the Written Torah and the Oral Torah," and drove him away when he said he only believed in one—the WT, but not the OT. The Gentile next turned to Hillel and through a rhetorical exercise Hillel caused him to admit that the WT cannot be understood without the aid of interpretation and as such he must rely on the Sages for the OT as well which marks an interpretation of the WT.[45] Hillel does not assume a philosophical or practical stance; he claims he has authority to interpret what is written in the Torah.[46]

As for *derashot*—though authority to expound is itself lent to dispute (making the solution somewhat circular)—the Sages also found it necessary to establish formal authority to expound:

> "But if you do not obey" (Lev. 26.14)—If you do not observe the sages' interpretation [of Torah]. One might erroneously conclude: ["Do not obey"] refers to [not observing] what is [actually] written in the Written Torah. But when it (Scripture) states: "and do not perform all of these commandments" behold, "what is written in Torah" has been stated already.
>
> How then should one understand [the expression]: "But if you do not obey"?—If you do not obey the sages' interpretation [of Torah].[47]

But this is precisely the issue: The rabbis' authority to expound the meaning of the words of the Torah lends the interpretation the status as though their words came from God Himself whose force we ultimately act on!

And another *derasha:*

> Words of the Scribes are more cherished than words of Torah . . . of the words of Scribes it's said, "According to the Torah they instruct you" (Deut. 17.11)—it is not written here "which the Torah instructs you" rather "*they* instruct you," and it is not written here "the law it [=the Torah] relays to you" rather "the law *they* relay to you" (ibid.).[48]

The same is true as well in a different episode, involving the well-known dispute between the Pharisees and the Sadducees on the start-date for counting the Omer "from the day after the Shabbat" (Lev. 23:16). The Sadducees claimed it refers to the Shabbat of Creation—the standard Sabbath—while the Sages interpreted it as the day following the first festive day of Passover. The Sages offered various explanations for their stance and among them:

> There is no need [for additional grounds]. After all it is written: "Count for yourself" (Deut. 16.9) [in singular]—counting is contingent on Rabbinic courts that *know how*

> *to innovate* "the day following the Sabbath"—(as) the day after the festive day. This precludes Sabbath of Creation as everyone counts it.[49]

Here the Sages somewhat concede it is an innovation of the Sages. But what is the meaning of "those who know how to innovate" and what knowledge is needed for this? "To know" has the same meaning it possesses in the following excerpt, "The Torah gave the Sages knowledge (da'at) to expound (the *Torah*) and to innovate new meaning";[50] "*da'at*" here means *authority*. That is, the Torah lent the Sages authority to expound, innovate, and determine that "the day following the Sabbath" is the day following the first festive day! We have no need for a justification on account of the verse's plain meaning, since the matter depends on the Sages' domain.

And so they said of Otniel who used his reasoning to restore all laws forgotten during the term spent mourning Moses,[51] and who conquered (again through reasoning) Kiryat Sefer, the city of the Book (Jud. 1.13), meaning the Book of Torah. This town is also named D'vir (Josh. 15.15), the site of the Holy of Holies, the place of revealing new laws.

The next analogy relays matters somewhat differently: a parable of a king who had two servants and gave each a measure of wheat and a bundle of flax. The wise made a cloth from the linen which he spread over the table and with the wheat he baked bread and placed it there. The simpleton did nothing. Naturally the first is appraised! "Likewise, when God gave Israel the Torah, He gave it as wheat to make flour from and as flax to transform into garments." In this sense also, the OT does derive from Heaven.[52] Torah laws are compared with nature which too does not accomplish its features rather humans must complete them.[53] In the delivery of Torah to humankind lies God's hidden expectation—and demand—that they use the raw materials given to them and draw on their intellectual powers to infer one matter through another using the thirteen principles of hermeneutics.

Rav Yanai identified a similar basis for the authority of commentary:

> Said Rabbi Yannai, had the Torah been given clear cut it would not have had a leg to stand on. For what reason? "And God spoke to Moses," He said before Him: Master of the World, inform me what the [exact ruling] is, He said, "Follow the many." If the majority acquit—acquit, if the majority rule liable—he is liable, so Torah might be expounded with forty-nine grounds to rule "impure" and forty-nine grounds to rule "pure."[54]

The Torah was given incomplete to allow for it to be interpreted in different directions according to need. Inhering in its very incompletion lies the authority to interpret.

Earlier we cited the opening of a *derasha* from the Sifra on the two Torahs given to Israel. Rabbi Akivah responds to it,

> "Does this mean that [only] two 'torahs' were given to Israel? Were not many '*torahs*' given to them? As it is stated [in Scripture]:" This is the "*torah*" of the burnt offering; this is the "*torah*" of the sin offering.[55]

There are no two Torahs, but one Torah! The OT is the creation of humans. Rabbi Akiva's view is also illustrated through the well-known episode of Moses who found God tying/lacing crowns (*tagim*) to the Torah's letters before delivering it. God explained to Moses that after several generations, Rabbi Akiva would expound profusions of laws (*halachot*) on each one. Moses descends to visit Rabbi Akiva's academy to see what transpires there, "and did not comprehend what they spoke." He returned and said before God, "You have an individual like this and yet? deliver the Torah through me?" God replied, "Silence! This is my plan!"[56]

Rabbi Akiva's teachings did not come directly from the Torah that would be (according to the story) given to Moses. The Torah of Rabbi Akiva is comprised of interpretations stemming from textual difficulties, from comparisons of its different components, from solutions to hard questions, and so on—these are the "crowns of the letters," the writing. And as for Moses's question—why God chose to deliver the Torah through him and not Rabbi Akivah, given both Rabbi Akivah and his Torah surpass Moses and his Torah—God's answer is that this is his decree. There are different qualities of Torah and from the outset God wished each would be realized at due time. So, Rabbi Akiva was authorized to do what he was doing.

Pluralism in *Halakha* and Majority

The famous story of Achnai's oven represents this notion as well.[57] Rabbi Joshua refuses to admit glaring miracles from Heaven as evidence for the *halakhic* opinion was to be accepted as binding in a disputed ruling in a given case—including the Divine Voice Rabbi Eliezer uses as proof for his ruling—but claims, "It is not in the Heavens" (Deut. 30.12). Rather, one adopts the majority ruling on earth. Rabbi Joshua relies on a homily (*derasha*) to prove his authority to expound although this is the very heart of the matter! In doing so he essentially declares the Sages' independence in *halakhic* matters. And the Talmud well knows how to describe God's wrath that followed until He accepted, as it were, his sons' victory.

Rabbi Joshua's proof from the rule "Follow the majority" derives from the decisive role the majority decision plays in resolving disputes. In the view claiming Divine authority is decisive, there is no possibility for dispute, since it is a given one cannot dispute words of the Revealing God. And therefore, neither in Torah nor in Qumran literature do we find disagreement over God's word. The Rabbi who opposed the Sages was Rabbi Eliezer who, as we are told, repeats only words he heard from his Rabbi, who heard from his Rabbi, tracing back to Law (given) to Moses at Sinai,[58] and he is willing to rely on Divine signals. Rabbi Eliezer belongs to Shammai's academy and they too seem to have held the OT is from Heaven and this was their disagreement with Hillel's academy. Each claimed *halacha* was according to them, that is, its very nature and into whose hands it is given.[59]

The Talmud institutes that *halacha* follows the academy of Hillel as they studied the rulings of Shammai's academy along with their own. That is, they accepted the natural existence of plurality of views and recognize the possibility of retracting their own and ruling like Shammai's academy when they are accepted through their own logic. In contrast, Shammai's academy did not include materials from that of Hillel in their studies and never rescinded and ruled like Hillel.[60] Therefore, "These and these are the words of a Living God, and law follows the academy of Hillel." The views of Shammai's academy reflect the earlier stance (Moses) and Hillel's academy the present view (Rabbi Akiva), as "This is the design as I planned it."

To the Sages, differences of opinion (*machloket*) mark an important indicator in the process of *halacha* and therefore much expanse is devoted to disputes, though it seems the theological signs featuring in the dispute afterward were excessive. On the other hand, the Sages also determined the High Court were to decide a single law for all Israel and in theory there was no need for disputes in *halacha*; rather they arose, so it is said, as disciples did not heed their rabbis as they should have[61] and hence "two Torahs developed."[62]

Essentially both of these different answers to what OT is are quite simple, but with time the Sages evaluated their coherence and enhanced them with various clarifications. Multiple answers which often did not distinguish between the two distinct views added to the difficulty, and hybrid positions emerged that tried to reconcile the two as one which reflected different relations to the WT and the OT. This process was rather dogmatic and unhistorical and therefore we will not deal with it here.[63]

Now we can reflect and consider—perhaps there are not really two answers, one of revelation and the other of authority; rather, the phraseology can be construed in either direction according to the reader. After all, even the expressions used in the expansive revelation view may be understood as construed to mean everything ultimately stems from Sinai owing to the authority then given to interpret and innovate Torah.[64] At times the alternate explanations rest alongside the other, hinting as it were at the connection between them.[65] One way or the other, apart from the radical views that preserve their purity, the two perceptions of the Oral Torah continue to exist one along with the other in a unique way in each generation: The more accepted assertion is that the OT was also given from Heaven, and belief in this is among the pillars of Judaism, but in practice, and as it always was, it is innovated by human hands and is not "in Heaven."

Writing Down the Oral Torah

Let's proceed to examine the question of recording the OT in writing.[66] On one hand, there are several statements of the Sages that prohibit documenting the OT in writing, for instance, such as: "Matters said orally you cannot say in writing. Words that are said by mouth are not permitted to be said in writing. Matters in writing you are not permitted to say but from what is written."[67] On the other hand, and as Sussmann extensively demonstrates all their *studies* were verbal and not from the book. It therefore seems this marks the parameters of the prohibition, but it cannot be understood without its *grounds*.[68] The basis appears to be a theological wish not to resemble the Boethusians mentioned, who write *halacha* in the book:[69] "The Boethusians would write *halachot* in book; [when] a person asked [the law], they *showed* him in the book."[70] Therefore, the core is the prohibition of instruction and study (teaching and studying) from the book: "The Sages rely on their version. And as there is forgetting, they write and set it aside. When something was forgotten, they looked in the book."[71]

From the sources, it is hard not to get the clear impression that the *Tannaim* and *Amoraim* had hidden scrolls in their homes, "Books of *Aggadah*" (*megilot s'tarim*),[72] which were written books of *halacha*(!), and while their *study and instructions* were only done verbally, it was possible to look at them as required to verify a correct version and as a refresher of their content, as Maimonides advances in his introduction to the *Mishne Torah*.[73] An upshot of this is that content which is not *halakha* but regulations made by the Sages (*takanot*) could be written down and read (from) in public.[74]

On the other hand, it is hard to imagine that in each and every place there was a library and in it the entire OT found in writing, rather than scrolls, were dispersed in assorted places. But since it was permitted to write a Megilla or keep a registry, the prohibition was not sweeping. Either way, against the backdrop of theological struggles with the Sadducees—though its intensity had already waned—the unique and exceptional phenomenon is properly understood, of the long-standing tradition of the Sages to educate verbally rather than from written works, a matter reflected in their continual references to oral study and their omission to mention any regular study from books, though living in a society that composes written works.[75] Only this profound ideological, binding framework can lead to such an unbelievable result.[76] This also accounts for the phenomenon of mysterious (and haphazard) sudden appearances of written versions of the OT in Gaonic times, without evoking any particular problem. If we presume that books were kept/there were books—however, their use was minimal and, at some point, study from them became an open, standard practice—the question loses its sharpness.[77]

Conclusion

This chapter deals with the theology of classical Jewish Law by examining the concepts of the Written Torah and the Oral Torah. It investigates the different relationship between these two Torahs, their definitions, and their underlying theological and authoritative functions.

Various historical and theological perspectives are presented regarding the nature of the OT. The debates between different sects of Judaism and early Christianity provide a context for understanding the evolution of these ideas. It seems that the original underlying issue was who is authorized to interpret the WT and by what method of interpretation. It is suggested that the original meaning of the OT was "those laws which were not written down explicitly in the WT." The other definitions are only secondary ones but have much more influence on rabbinic Judaism.

This question has bearing on questions like understanding of Divine revelation, touching upon questions of prophecy, authority, the interaction between humans and the Divine, and the tension between innovation and tradition.

This chapter sheds light on the interplay between the Written and Oral Torahs, the authority of the Sages, and the complex theological underpinnings that have shaped the development of Jewish legal thought throughout history.

NOTES

1. Cf. Shmuel Safrai, "Oral Tora," in *The Literature of the Sages*, First Part, ed. Shmuel Safrai et al. (Minneapolis, MN: Fortress Press, 1987); Benjamin D. Sommer, "Unity and Plurality in Jewish Canons: The Case of the Oral and Written Torahs," in *One Scripture or Many? Canons from Biblical, Theological and Philosophical Perspectives* (Oxford: Oxford University Press, 2004), esp. at 144ff; Steven D. Fraade, "Concepts of Scripture in Rabbinic Judaism; Oral Torah and Written Torah," in *Jewish Concepts of Scripture, A Comparative Introduction*, ed. Benjamin Sommer (New York: Yeshiva University, 2012), 31–46.
2. See Ephraim E. Urbach, *The Sages: Their Concepts and Beliefs* (Jerusalem: Magnes Press, 1975), 291: "The distinctive character of the 'Oral Torah' lies in the fact that it was not put in writing." It seems he did not distinguish between matters sufficiently. Likewise, Yaakov N. Epstein, *An Introduction to The Mishnah*, 2nd ed. (Jerusalem: Magnes Press, 1963), 698 [Hebrew]; Yaakov Sussmann, *Oral Law—Taken Literally: The Power of the Tip of a Yod* (Jerusalem: Magnes Press, 2019) [Hebrew]. See also Birger Gerhardson, *Memory and Manuscript* (Grand Rapids, MI: Eerdmans, 1998); E. S. Alexander, "The Orality of Rabbinic Writing," in *The Cambridge Companion to the Talmud*, ed. C. E. Fonrobert and M. S. Jaffee (Cambridge: Cambridge University Press, 2007), 39–46.
3. See Sussmann, *Oral Law*, 226 n. 1, 259 (and extensive bibliography he cites); Jacob Blidstein, "A Note on the Term Oral Torah," *Da'at* 4 (1979): 5 and Jacob Blidstein, "Transitions of the Term Oral Torah," *Tarbitz* 42 (1972): 496 [Hebrew]; Avraham Rosenthal, "The Oral Torah and Torah from Sinai: Law and Action," in *Mekhkerei Talmud* 2, ed. Moshe Bar-Asher et al. (Jerusalem: Magnes Press, 1993), 448–89 [Hebrew]; Channan Gafni, *Conceptions of the Oral Law in Modern Jewish Scholarship* (Jerusalem: Zalman Shazar Institutes, 2018) [Hebrew]; Nahman Danzig, "From an Oral Talmud to a Written Talmud: The Method of Transmitting the Babylonian Talmud and Its Study in Medieval Ages," in *Bar Ilan* 30–31 (2005): 49–112 [Hebrew]; Martin S. Jaffee, *Torah in the Mouth: Writing and Oral Traditions in Palestinian Judaism, 200 BCE–400 CE* (New York: Oxford University Press, 2001). The work of Yochanan D. Silman deals with the Oral Torah's essential aspect, *The Voice Heard at Sinai: Once or Ongoing?* (Jerusalem: Magnes Press, 1999) [Hebrew]; Shamma Friedman, "Transmission of the Talmud and the Computer Age," in *Printing the Talmud: From Bomberg to Schottenstein*, ed. Gabriel M. Goldstein and Sharon Liberman Mintz (New York: Yeshiva University Museum, 2006), 143–50.
4. See Sussmann, *Oral Torah*, 226 n. 2, on the importance of this question in research and the literature referenced in notes 3 and 8. See discussions noted by Berachyahu Lifshitz, *The Halakha—By God or by Man* (Jerusalem: Bialik Press, 2018) [Hebrew]. The *exact* contents

of each (written or oral) collection, their editors' intentions and editorial work (if at all), their time of being edited and their different characteristics, all these are not of our interest here. There is a large literature dealing with these matters, see, e.g., Safrai et al., *Literature of the Sages, Part One*; *The Classic Rabbinic Literature of Eretz Israel, Instructions and Texts*, Noam et al. (Jerusalem: Yad Ben Zvi, 2018), and the bibliography cited therein.

5. Philo, *The Special Laws, IV*, 149. See Urbach, *Sages*, 259; Christine Hayes, *What's Divine about Divine Law?* (Princeton, NJ: Princeton University Press, 2015).
6. A Gentile who observes the Sabbath is condemned to death (bSan. 58b); *The Cambridge Companion to the Talmud* (Cambridge: Cambridge University Press, 2007), 39–46; Aaron Lichtenstein, *The Seven Laws of Noah* (New York: Rabbi Jacob Joseph School Press, 1981); Maimonides, Laws of Kings 8:11.
7. Urbach, *Sages*, 259. He does not discuss the question of authority.
8. Urbach discusses this extensively. Ibid.; Yisrael I. Yuval, "The Orality of Early Jewish Law: from Pedagogy to Ideology," in *Judaism, Christianity, and Islam in the Course of History: Exchange and Conflicts*, ed. Lothar Gall and Dietmar Willoweit (Berlin: De Gruyter, 2010), 237–60.
9. Exod. 18:13–26; Exod. 33: 7–11; Exod. 34: 29–35; Lev. 24: 10–23; Num. 9: 6–10; Num. 15: 32–36; Num. 27: 1–8; Num. 36: 1–12.
10. Deut. 17.
11. For elaboration, see Lifshitz, *Halakha*.
12. See b.Kiddushin 66b. See Lifshitz, *Halakha*, from 382 onward.
13. The Community Rule, *The Dead Sea Scrolls; the Hebrew Writings*, vol. 1, ed. Elisha Qimron (Jerusalem: Ben Zvi Institute, 2010), 218, 224, 226.
14. The Temple Scroll, *The Dead Sea Scrolls*, vol. 1, 195.
15. *The Dead Sea Scrolls*, vol. 2, 312; Lifshitz, *Halakha*, 75. [urim and tummim = "elements of the *hoshen*, the breastplate worn by the High Priest attached to the ephod. They are connected with divination in general, and cleromancy in particular. Most scholars suspect that the phrase refers to a set of two objects used by the high priest to answer a question or reveal the will of God"—Wikipedia].
16. Lifshitz, *Halakha*, 259 onward.
17. Ibid., 118 onward.
18. The Damascus Covenant, *The Dead Sea Scrolls*, vol. 1, 12–13.
19. See, for instance, the introduction of Ba'al Sefer Mitzvoth Gadol to his work. And see Numbers Rabbah 14, 12: "For your love is sweeter than wine" (Song of Songs 1:2)—"Words of the beloved are sweeter than the wine of Torah. One cannot instruct properly (accurately) from the words of Torah, since they are vague/obstructed . . . however from one can instruct properly from the Sages' words, as they lay (spread) out the Torah."
20. j.Sanhrdrin 11.3, 30a; Song of Songs Rabbah, 1, 18.
21. b.Gittin. 70b; b.Shv'ot 39a; Urbach, *Sages*, 270.
22. j.Kiddushin 1.2, 59d; b.Sottah 16a. See as well the issues of the "Rebellious Son" and the "Subverted Town," b.Sanhedrin 71a.
23. See b.Eruvin 21b: "Lest you say, if they have substance why weren't they written?" Scripture clarified, "The making of many books is without limit" (Eccles. 12:12). See Saul Lieberman, *Greek in Roman Palestine*, 2nd ed. (New York: Feldheim Press, 1965), 238ff., who tried to contend with the issue of promulgation. He makes the note that there is evidence to both: no teaching from books and the existence of books; Lifshitz, "The 'Aggadah' and Its Role in the History of the Oral Law," *Diné Israel* 24 (2007): 11–28.

24. b.Tamid16a.
25. b.Bava Batra 12b; Seder Olam Rabbah 27 (98): "Until now the prophets would prophesy through the Divine Spirit. From here on, 'Incline your ear and listen to the words of the sages.'"
26. j.Avodah Zarah 2.8, 41c. See Maimonides, Foundations of the Torah 9:1.
27. Vered Noam, *The Scroll of Ta'anit: The Versions, Meanings and Backgrounds* (Jerusalem: Ben Zvi Institute, 2003), 77: "The Boethusians would write *laws* (*halakhot*) in books, when someone would ask (the rule), they would show him in the book. The Sages said to them: But Scripture says, 'for in accordance (*al pi =on the mouth*) with these commandments I make a covenant with you and with Israel' (Exod. 34:27); 'You shall act in accordance with (*al pi*) the instruction given you' (Deut. 17.11)—instructing that *laws* (*halakhot*) are not to be written in books." And see there from 206 onward. See b.Tamid 14b, "Those who write *laws* (*halakhot*) are like those who burn Torah, whoever studies from them receive no reward." This is almost the exact wording of *Scroll of Ta'anit*.
28. Urbach, *Sages*, 259. Urbach well accentuates this point. He claims that what is unique about the Oral Torah is that it is not written, rather is transmissions that were not written. See, as well, Yaakov N. Epstein, *Introductions to Tannaitic Literature* (Jerusalem: Magnes Press, 1957), 16: "Laws of our fathers" rather than "Your laws" in Ezr. 14:21 contra Ezr. 4:23 Traditions of Fathers or Transmissions of the Elders, "which is not written, this precisely constitutes the Oral Torah." This statement needs to be qualified however, as mentioned.
29. Sifre on Deuteronomy, *Piska* 351, trans. Reuven Hammer (New Haven, CT: Yale University Press, 1986), 363–64. Note the different version there, some rendered "Your Torahs" (*ve'torotecha*) to suit the homily, and the letters without vowels can be read this way as well.
30. Sifra, Behukotai, Chapter 8 trans. Howard Apothaker (Cincinnati, OH: Hebrew Union College Press, 2002), 229–30.
31. *Sifre* on Deuteronomy, 313. And see Rosenthal, "Oral Torah," 463, on what is included and what was transmitted from Sinai.
32. j.Sot. 8.3, 22d. In this conception, the Oral Torah is quite similar to the Written Torah since it too could be seen.
33. Eccles. Rabbah 5.8.
34. b.Megilah 19b.
35. Eccles. Rabbah 5.8.
36. j.Pe'ah 2.4, 17a.
37. Exodus Rabbah 28.6: "R. Isaac said: Everything the prophets would prophesy in the future they received at Mount Sinai, as Moses tells them, tells Israel, 'Both with those who are standing here with us this day . . . and those who are not with us here' (Deut. 29.14)—these are the souls of those that would be created in the future, not actual persons, as the word 'standing' is absent, even though they were not present that moment, each one received his portion. . . . And not only the prophets, even the Sages who will be in the future . . . each and every one received his portion at Sinai."
38. Simkha Assaf, "Early Karaite Polemics against the Rabbis," *Tarbitz* 4 (1932): 35, 193 [Hebrew]; *Saadia's Commentary on Genesis*, Zuker ed. (New York: Jewish Theological Seminary, 1983), 187; *Sefer Ha-Qabbalah by Ibn Daud*, Cohen ed. (Philadelphia: Jewish Publication Society, 1967), 1.
39. See also Otzar Ha-G'eonim, b.Gittin 60b, Ha-Perushim, 131. See also tHagigah 2.9, which states in passing that there are laws which were not transmitted in tradition. See also Nachmanides on Deut. 17.20.

40. b.Menakhot 65b. See Amram Troper, "The Meaning of the Phrases 'You set them aside with a reed' and 'It is impossible to turn you away empty' in Rabbinic Literature," *Netu'im* 16 (2009): 9–31 [Hebrew].
41. *Midrash* Tanhuma, *Ki Tisa*, 34. And the *Midrash* continues in this line: "R. Yehuda Bar Shalom said: God said to Moses: Why do you ask for the Torah to be in writing? What difference (will there be) between Israel and Gentile? As Scripture says, 'I will write for him many [not all] of my teachings' otherwise 'they were considered alien' (Hos. 8.12)? Rather give them Scripture in writing and the Mishna verbally." See Mark Bergman, "Mishna as Myster," in Mekhkerei Talmud, 3rd ed. David Rosenthal et al. (Jerusalem: Magnes Press, 2004), 101–10 [Hebrew].
42. Mekhilta d'Rabbi Ishmael, *Bahodesh*, 9. Urbach believed Sinai revelation included the Torah, its interpretations and conferral of authority to interpret. *Sages*, 267. But it seems interpretations were not given at all, just the WT and the authority to interpret it.
43. See Berachyahu Lifshitz, *Law and Action* (Jerusalem: Bialik Institute, 2001) [Hebrew], roughly "saw."
44. tSotah 6:10–12; b.Hagigah 3b.
45. b.Shabbat 31a. In Avot de-R. Natan he is a Jew (but not rabbinic) who wished to learn only the Written Torah. See *Sefer Mitzvot Gadol*, in the introduction, "Likewise with the mitzvah of *tzizit*, it would not be understood how many strings to attach, how many knots to tie and the proportion between the strings and their knots. Also, the mitzvah of phylacteries, it would not be clear what *totafot* are, the content of their chapters, where and how to set the boxes, or how to fulfill the mitzvah of *mezuzah*, its content, the place to fix it, whether on the right or the left, whether towards the top of the doorpost or towards the bottom. Had God not explained these to Moses [their meaning] would not be known."
46. Believes = Relies on.
47. Sifra *BeHuqotai*, 2 (Apothaker ed.), 195.
48. Song of Songs Rabbah 1.2. This homily includes a hidden polemic against the Boethusians, who point in the book and (next) the book itself teaches the law (*halakha*).
49. b.Menakhot 65b. In several sugyot the Talmud mentions things that were transmitted to the Sages, see Lifshitz, *Halacha*, 238 and onward. See as well near note 34, that authority to interpret was given to Israel to distinguish it from other nations who only had the book.
50. Sifre on Numbers, 134. See Nahum Bronznik, "The Meaning of 'Knowledge' (*da'at*) in Rabbinic Language," *Hama'ayan* 46 (2005): 48 [Hebrew].
51. b.Tamid 16a.
52. Genesis Rabbah, 11.
53. Seder Eliyahu Zuta, 2. Ish-Shalom edition, 171–72.
54. j.Sanhedrin 4.2, 22a. See *Hidushei ha'Ritva* on b.Eruvin 13b:

> These and these are the living words of God. They asked the Rabbis of France, How can it be both these and these are the living words of God when one prohibits and the other permits? And they answered that when Moses went up to the heavens to receive the Torah they showed him for each and every matter forty-nine angles to prohibit and forty-nine angles to permit. And he asked God about this, and He said, so it will be transmitted to the Sages and in each and every generation their determinations will be decisive.

55. Sifra, Behukotai (Apothaker ed.) 230. See Song of Songs Rabbah (1.51) as well.
56. b.Menakhot. 29b. See as well b.Sanhedrin 38b. See *Sifre* Devarim 48 and Avot d'Rabbi Natan B.12, 15a: "Matters that had been hidden and concealed from creation were brought

to light by Rabbi Akivah"; Leviticus Rabbah 19.6: "Matters that were not revealed to Moses were revealed to Rabbi Akivah and his fellows."

57. b.Bava Metzi'a 59b.
58. b.Succah 28a. See Urbach, *Sages*, 268.
59. b.Eruvin 13b.
60. j.Succah 2.7, 53b.
61. tSanhedrin 1.1.
62. tSottah 14.9. On the dispute, see the sources compiled by Hanina Ben Menahem, Neil S. Hecht, and Shai Wosner, *Controversy and Dialogue in Halakhic Sources* (Boston: Boston University, Institute of Jewish Law, 2005) [Hebrew] and the literature referenced there. For an elaboration see Lifshitz, *Law and Action*, 220 and onward. The start point of the dispute may well signify the beginning of the rabbinic process.
63. Silman, *Voice Heard at Sinai*, deals with question of essence in this way. See also Shalom Rosenberg, "Ongoing Revelation—Three Directions," in *Revelation, Faith, Wisdom: Collected Lectures* (Ramat Gan: Bar Ilan University, 1975) [Hebrew], 131. For a traditional view see Joshua Inbal, *The Oral Torah: Its Authority and Methods* (Jerusalem: Rav Kook Institute, 2015); Shmuel Ariel, *Planted in Us: Foundations of the Oral Torah* (Otniel: Gilluy, 2018) [Hebrew].
64. *Derashot Ha-Ran*, 11: "And it seen they agree on one matter, which is what Moses was commanded from the Almighty."
65. Sifra Behukotai (ibid. n. 55); Exod. Rabbah 41:6 presents two stances: Moses learned everything at Sinai, or learned only principles to further (enable) independent (self-) study. If these in fact are two distinct views, each perceives homilies differently: if everything was given at Sinai—homilies affirm existing laws. If only the Written Torah was given—homilies create law; see Epstein, *Introduction to the Mishna*. [See j.Naz.7.b, 56b: "מאי כדון, וכי המדרשות אמנה," —are the derashot to be relied upon?] see Berachyahu Lifshitz, *Asmachta (Promise)—Obligation and Property in Jewish Law* (Jerusalem: Magnes Press, 1988), 172 [Hebrew]. In Rabbi Eliezer's traditional view homilies are only permitted when they enforce laws from Sinai, m.Negilah 9.3; 11.7.
66. This question has to be distinguished from the issue of the *collection* of the OT. Collections could be made in an oral stage as well and be studied by heart. For possible reasons, for such a compilation, see Catherine Hezser, "Rabbis as Intellectuals in the Context of Graeco-Roman and Byzantine Christian Scholasticism," in *Scholastic Culture in the Hellenistic and Graeco-Roman Eras* (Berlin: De Gruyter, 2019), 169–86, and bibliography cited therein. It should also be distinguished from the issue of the practical ability to write down the OT. Prohibiting writing the OT suggests that even if it is possible, it is still prohibited. Cf. Catherine Hezser, "Bookish Circles? The Use of Written Texts in Rabbinic Oral Culture," *Temas Medievales* 25 (2017): 63–81. One should be aware of the meaning of "arach," "habr," and "sadar" in biblical and rabbinical Hebrew—all mean "to collect" and "to put together" side by side and not "to redact."
67. b.Tamid 14b: "to instruct from what is written." Some render the *reisha* "you are not permitted to write them," but as we shall see shortly, it seems the prohibition is only partial; when owing to concern of forgetting, writing is permitted, only *instructing* from what's written is prohibited as teaching (study) must be done orally. See as well *Midrash* Tanhuma (Buber) *Vayera* 6; see Exod. Rabbah Chap. 47.3, "'In accordance with (*al pi*) these commandments' (Exod. 34.27)—the Written Torah and the Oral Torah. 'I make a covenant with you'—and if you alter it, and make what is oral written and what is written

oral—you receive no reward. Why? As this is how I gave it, a Written Torah and an Oral Torah" (and Tanhuma Buber *Ki Tisah*, 18); j.Meg. 4.5 until "Matters said verbally—[are to remain] verbal, matters said in writing—are to be written" (and so in j.Peah 2.6, 17a). According to Epstein, there was no such prohibition, and the evidence—books were written, in his view. As mentioned, the prohibition is partial.

68. See the critical review of Natalie B. Dohrmann, "Can 'Law' Be Private? The Mixed Message of Rabbinic Oral Law," in *Public and Private in Ancient Mediterranean Law and Religion*, ed. Clifford Ando and Jörg Rüpke (Berlin: De Gruyter, 2015), 187–216. Dohrman's own suggestion is just as speculative as are the others mentioned there.

69. The Mishnah [and all *tannaitic* materials on law] is a book of rulings, of decrees, of laws (see Lifshitz, *Law and Action*, on the terms "*gazar*," "*halach*," and "*shanna*"; Sussmann, *Oral Torah*, 332 n. 4), and therefore its not to be written, to reference halacha from, or to instruct from. Written scrolls were not kept or stored inside rabbinic academies (houses of study); one had to leave it to look in them (Sussmann, *Oral Torah*, 242), find what was necessary and return to the house of study to report what was noted verbally, and perhaps even in whisper (Lifshitz, "Aggada," 11)!

70. Megillat Ta'anit, Noam ed., 77. Sussmann believes the issue of "whether writing laws in books was among the core disagreements between Second Temple sects" has yet to be determined (*Oral Torah*, 332, and see appendix 12). In my view (as explained in Lifschitz, *Law and Action*) the question was answered in the positive. See as well R' Yerahmiel, *Seder ha'Hahamim* I, 171: "When students of Shammai and Hillel had increased . . . they returned to study from the written [scrolls], even Oral Torah. But beforehand they would not write, only the Sadducees [wrote]."

71. b.Tamid 14b. See Rashi: "Hidden Scrolls—they were hidden as they were not to be written, and when they heard a new opinion that wasn't studied in the *beit midrash* they would write it so it wouldn't be forgotten, and hide the scroll" (b.Shabbat 6b; 96b). See Sussmann, *Oral Torah*, 228 n. 15, on Rashi's stance which rejects all writing. See also Lifshitz, "*Aggada*." And as well Maimonides's introduction to his Commentary on the Mishna: "The students made notes of what they studied and wrote them." Sussmann, *Oral Torah*, 334, takes this to be a later episode; however it seems to reflect the past.

72. Lifshitz, "Aggadah." See also Otzar Ha-Geonim b.Gittin, 67b, Ha-Perushim, 142.

73. Authorities of Sefarad and Ashkenaz disagreed over this, and research has clashed over this question as well, see Epstein, *Introduction to the Mishna*, 673 and onward; Shraga Abramson, "Writing the Mishna (Views of the Geonim and Rishonim)," in *Culture and Society in the History of Medieval Jewry* (Jerusalem: Zalman Shazar Institute, 1988), 17 [Hebrew]; Sussmann, *Oral Torah*. All agree they studied orally, and disagree over whether there was *also* a written book. That is, even Epstein who believes there were written books, and the *Geonim*, who clearly had written books studied, rendered versions and memorized only orally. See *Iggeret R. Shrirah Ga'on* at 71—they were cautious to render versions only orally, not from writings (אבל לא מנוסחי, aval lo minuschei). See as well *Otzar ha'Ge'onim le'Shabbat, Ha'Teshuvot*, 310.

74. They did not disagree with the Boethusians on this point; see Lifshitz, "Aggadah." This is why the books of *Aggadah*, the Haggadah (interpretations of biblical verses which do not deal with *halakhic* issues), the Scroll of Ta'anit (which is a decree), and court rulings were written.

75. See Sussmann, 334 and onward.

76. Rabbi Yosef Albo (*Sefer Ha-Ikarim*), for instance, believes one couldn't write the bulk of OT in a book. But if so, why not write up the Mishna—its text is shorter than Scripture. There were those who suggested a need for in-person explanations, absent from written texts. Later generations advanced that in remaining oral, the law could more readily adopt innovations required for changing times than written law. But this claim is also difficult, as ultimately the Oral Torah made serious changes to laws of the Written Torah. And further: A good portion of the Oral Torah can't be justified by a need to respond to changing times (new situations). Anyhow, all these explanations are 'practical' and therefore can't account for a *prohibition* to record in writing, nor for the fact that books were (indeed) written the times of the *Geonim* while they continued to study the tradition orally.
77. Sussmann, *Oral Torah*, 319 onward. His theory that material was put in writing during the Inquisition is difficult. On the contrary, according to *Pirkoi Ben Bavuye*, several books of Mishnah and Talmud already hidden were later salvaged.

CHAPTER 2

HOW DO THE *TANNAIM* READ THE TORAH?

ELIZABETH SHANKS ALEXANDER

INTRODUCTION

THE legal portions of the Torah constitute the core and foundation of all subsequent Jewish law. The legal scholars and jurists featured throughout this volume do not, however, inherit the Torah's legal content as an independent source. Torah law is not, for them, a *tabula rasa*, subject to whatever manipulation and interpretation their legal imaginations see fit. Rather, the legal materials of the Torah reach the hands of later scholars of rabbinic and Jewish law through the framing and mediation of Sages who lived and worked during the *tannaitic* period (*c.* 70–250 CE).

The term *tanna* is Aramaic and means "one who repeats [a teaching]." In post-*tannaitic* academies and learning circles, the *tanna* was an official functionary whose job it was to memorize and repeat tradition upon request.[1] The major accomplishment of the *tannaitic* period was the consolidation of tradition into a form amenable to repetition, retrieval, and preservation following the destruction of the Second Temple (70 CE) when much was at risk for loss. The Sages who lived and worked following the Temple's destruction are called *Tannaim* (= pl., sing. = *Tanna*) not because they themselves served as memorizers, but to link them with the overriding collective project of their generation, the rendering of tradition into repeatable form. This chapter examines the *tannaitic* literary corpus for what it can tell us about the *tannaitic* framing of the biblical legal heritage. How did the scholarly efforts of the *Tannaim* mold the biblical inheritance? And how are those efforts manifest in the literary texts that the *Tannaim* bequeathed to subsequent generations?

Tannaitic legal thinking is preserved in two distinct genres of writing, each of which orients differently toward biblical scripture. *Midrash* adopts the form of a commentary to those portions of the Pentateuch that are rich sources for law. Mishnah,[2] on the other hand, collects discrete *halakhic* (legal) dicta and organizes them topically for ease of memorization and convenient retrieval. Where *Midrash* is typically explicit about the relationship between its legal traditions and biblical verses, Mishnah tends to obscure the biblical roots of its traditions and foreground the topical rubrics that facilitate ordering tradition. Following the cue of these generic conventions, scholars generally regard *Midrash* as the preferable site for excavating *tannaitic* practices of interpreting the biblical legal heritage. In my view, scholars overly rely on the generic conventions of *Midrash* to imagine what *tannaitic* reading looks like.

Another approach assumes interpretation has occurred when one encounters its effects. That is, the existence of an interpretative framing to biblical materials indicates an interpretative process has transpired. James Kugel devises a scholarly method he calls "reverse engineering" to illuminate interpretation that is known only from its effects. The researcher starts with a product and reconstructs the process that (plausibly) led to its creation.[3] The products that Kugel seeks to reverse engineer are fanciful narrative expansions (*Aggadah*) that *Midrash* represents as part and parcel of the biblical narrative.

Legal *Midrash* contains a comparable phenomenon, which I call "the *tannaitic* framing of biblical legal materials." The *Tannaim* view biblical legal materials through the lens of terms and concepts that they regard as innate to the biblical text. The discerning eye, however, observes a gap between the terms and concepts that *Tannaim* impute to biblical law and the terms and concepts suggested by a close reading of the biblical text on its own terms. Clearly an interpretative practice moved ancient readers from raw biblical materials to the fully formed *tannaitic* framing. If scholars want to understand how the *Tannaim* read the Torah, they must attend not only to that which is explicitly marked as scriptural interpretation by the generic conventions of *Midrash*. They must also investigate the unmarked interpretative activity that yields the *tannaitic* framing of biblical legal materials.

Daniel Boyarin's work demonstrates how productive it can be to set aside the implicit claims that midrashic rhetoric makes about where reading happens. He eschews the cues of midrashic rhetoric and focuses on reconstructing an unmarked reading practice.[4] Specifically, Boyarin reconstructs intertextual readings practices that produce fanciful expansions of biblical narrative from the patterns of biblical citation in *Midrash*. *Tannaitic* legal writings can likewise be analyzed with a view to reconstructing unmarked reading practices.[5] Interestingly, both genres of *tannaitic* legal writing, *Midrash* and Mishnah, accept the *tannaitic* framing as a starting point in their discussion of biblical legal topics. Any serious investigation of *tannaitic* practices of scriptural reading in the legal domain must engage data from both *Midrash* and Mishnah.

Scholars by and large overlook the Mishnah as a site for illuminating *tannaitic* scriptural interpretation.[6] They generally follow the cues of the generic conventions of both *Midrash* and Mishnah when deciding where to look for evidence of *tannaitic* scriptural interpretation.[7] In the first section, I review the generic conventions of both *Midrash* and Mishnah, highlighting how each genre signals to its audience a distinct view of the relationship between *tannaitic* and biblical legal tradition. As commentary, *Midrash* displays the interconnectedness of *tannaitic* and biblical legal tradition.

As a legal compendium, Mishnah calls attention to its own structuring categories and obscures the biblical origins of its contents. Notwithstanding the strength of these rhetorical codes, the relationship between *tannaitic* and biblical tradition in *tannaitic* legal writings is multifaceted and complex. The commentarial format of *Midrash* reveals less about *tannaitic* reading practices than is typically assumed. Conversely, Mishnah's reticence about its dependence on biblical sources does not controvert the centrality of scriptural interpretation to its project.[8]

Evidence of unmarked interpretative activity exists in both *Midrash* and Mishnah. In the second section, I reconstruct the interpretative process that gives rise to the terms and concepts that constitute the *tannaitic* framing of biblical legal topics. I argue that the *tannaitic* framing emerges from a reading practice driven by jurisprudential concerns. Readers with jurisprudential interests approach the Torah's legal contents as a set of precedents that must be fully understood if they are to guide future decisions. Such readers identify and characterize cases in the biblical text, clarify the principles informing their legal resolution, imagine new and related cases, and establish criteria for resolving them. In my view, this jurisprudentially driven reading practice has a more formative impact on *tannaitic* legal tradition than that which is explicitly marked as interpretation in midrashic discourse. This jurisprudentially driven reading practice produces the terminological and conceptual framing of biblical law that is taken for granted throughout *tannaitic* discussions of biblical law.

In the third section, I integrate observations about the generic conventions of *Midrash* and Mishnah (from the first section) with insights into the interpretative process that generates the *tannaitic* framing of biblical legal materials (from the second section). Recognizing that the midrashic form foregrounds the relationship between *tannaitic* and biblical tradition, I ask why *Midrash* concomitantly obscures the interpretative process that underwrites the *tannaitic* project as a whole. Broadening the scope of inquiry, I consider what the generic conventions of *Midrash* and Mishnah accomplish, if not transparently reflecting the process that generated the *tannaitic* framing. I propose that both sets of rhetorical conventions serve pedagogical purposes. They engage their readers in different modalities of integrating and mastering *tannaitic* legal tradition.

Generic Conventions of *Midrash* and Mishnah

This section reviews the generic conventions of *Midrash* and Mishnah, highlighting how each prompts its audience to think about the relationship between *tannaitic* and biblical legal tradition. The impressions created by *Midrash*'s and Mishnah's generic conventions are, however, unrelated to the unmarked reading practice that produces the *tannaitic* framing of the biblical legal materials. Both midrashic and mishnaic discourse are grounded in a shared vocabulary of legal terms and concepts. *Midrash*, though generically marked as scriptural interpretation, is surprisingly opaque about the reading practices that yield this vocabulary.[9] Alternatively, though Mishnah is presented as something other than scriptural interpretation, its reflexive adoption of the *tannaitic* framing indicates how central scriptural interpretation is to its project.

Midrash: Tannaitic *Tradition alongside Pertinent Biblical Verses*

Tannaitic Midrash adopts the format of a verse-by-verse commentary to major portions of the Pentateuch.[10] Each pericope pairs a citation (a phrase or word) from the biblical passage, the lemma, with a rabbinic comment that can be loosely understood as interpretation. The term *Midrash* is Hebrew, from the three-letter root *d.r.sh.* meaning "to inquire." Paul Mandel explains that while the root originally referred to an oracle-like inquiry of God, by the time the *tannaitic* collections of *Midrash* were compiled, the term indicated interpretative inquiry into the scriptural text.[11] I use the term *Midrash* (= sing.; pl. = *midrashim*) in two distinct senses: to indicate (1) a textual unit comprised of a biblical lemma and a *tannaitic* comment thereon, or (2) the genre that characterizes such textual units collectively. According to Menahem Kahana, the extant *tannaitic* midrashic compilations date to approximately "the generation or two following the redaction of the Mishnah, that is, in the middle of the third century CE."[12]

Tannaitic Midrash is sometimes called "*halakhic Midrash*," on account of the centrality of legal materials to the corpus. *Tannaitic* Sages generally focus their interpretative energy on those portions of the Pentateuch that are rich sources for law. For example, there is no *tannaitic Midrash* extant for the book of Genesis.[13] On the same principle (at least) one *tannaitic Midrash* to Exodus begins with chapter 12,[14] which the rabbis regard as the site of the Bible's first legal instruction. Notwithstanding the prominence of law in *tannaitic Midrash*, considerable parts of the extant compilations comment on nonlegal verses and/or offer comments without legal content. Though the legal interests of this volume dictate a focus on legal parts of the corpus, I follow the convention of describing the corpus according to chronological criteria ("*tannaitic Midrash*").

Two Schools of Midrashic Production

One of the most important achievements of modern scholarly research on *tannaitic Midrash* involves the detection of two schools of midrashic production. In the late nineteenth century, David Hoffmann observed that the traditionally transmitted *Midrash* collections exhibit two distinct patterns with respect to technical terms, the hermeneutic operations they employ, and the Sages they cite. These data form the basis for the now universally accepted theory that the compilations derive from two distinct schools.[15] Hoffmann associated the commentaries on Leviticus and Deuteronomy with

Table 2.1 Schools of Midrashic Interpretation

Pentateuchal Book	Commentaries from School of R. Ishmael	Commentaries from School of R. Akiba	Possible Second Strand within School of R. Akiba
Exodus	MEKHILTA OF R. ISHMAEL	Mekhilta of R. Shimon bar Yohai	
Leviticus	(material interwoven into Sifra)	SIFRA	
Numbers	SIFRE NUMBERS		Sifre Zuta Numbers
Deuteronomy	Mekhilta Deuteronomy	SIFRE DEUTERONOMY	Sifre Zuta Deuteronomy

Note. The Pentateuchal books subject to *tannaitic* midrashic commentary and the schools with which each commentary is associated. ALL CAPS indicates collections reaching modern readers through traditional chains of transmission.

the school of Rabbi Akiba, and those on Exodus and Numbers with school of Rabbi Ishmael. As scholars have discovered and reconstructed additional compilations, a picture is emerging in which it appears that each school produced its own legal commentary on each of the four law-centric books of the Pentateuch (see table 2.1).[16]

While the schools differ on a number of points, they take part in what is recognizable as a single endeavor.[17] *Tannaitic* midrashic compilations work through the biblical text sequentially, taking up verses, phrases, and often individual words according to the order in which they appear in the biblical text. A question-and-answer format is often employed.[18] The dialectic of question-and-answer often includes reference to other verses. Sample comments from each of the two schools illustrate features of *tannaitic Midrash* in general, as well as distinctive features of each school. Together with a sample text from Mishnah discussed shortly thereafter, these comments form a case study. The case study reveals the difficulty of relying exclusively on the evidence of *Midrash*'s and Mishnah's generic conventions to reconstruct the reading practices that generate the *tannaitic* framing of biblical legal materials.

School of Rabbi Ishmael

This *Midrash*, from the school of R. Ishmael, comments on a verse from Exodus that discusses a father's sale of his daughter into a type of servitude known as "maidservice." The verse differentiates the maidservant's protocol of manumission from that of the (male) Hebrew slave,[19] who is discussed in the immediately preceding verses (Exod. 21:2–6).

> [7]When a man sells his daughter as a maidservant, she is not manumitted in the manner that slaves are manumitted.
>
> (Exodus 21:7)

Like much biblical law, this verse is formulated casuistically. A first clause, the protasis ("when a man . . .") establishes the case being treated, and a second clause, the apodosis ("she is not . . .") provides legal instruction. The midrashic commentary begins by focusing on the first substantive word of the protasis ("man").

> ***When a man sells.*** A man sells his daughter, but a woman does not sell her daughter. [Scripture makes this point explicit] since the following deduction is reasonable [but wrong]:
> Given the fact that a son, whose father is *not* authorized to sell him, can go ahead and sell his daughter [when he himself becomes a father],
> Isn't it logical that a daughter, whose father *is* authorized to sell her, can likewise go ahead and sell her own daughter [when she herself becomes a mother]?
> [To refute this reasonable, but erroneous conclusion]
> Scripture states, ***When a man sells.***
>
> (Mekhilta of R. Ishmael, Nezikin [Mishpatim], Parasha 3.2)[20]

The *Midrash* first cites the lemma and offers an interpretation: a father, not a mother, is authorized to sell their daughter as a maidservant. The gender-restrictive framing of the biblical verse appears as an interpretative comment juxtaposed to the lemma.

Next, the *Midrash* articulates a warrant to interpret the lemma. The interpretation is justified by noting a problematic understanding that would have emerged had scripture failed to use the word "man." The *Midrash* envisions a legal thinker familiar with the institution of maidservice, but lacking access to the biblical text with its gender-specific designation of the key subject ("man"). This in itself is a striking premise, as the institution of maidservice derives from the very verse whose legal implications the reader is presumed to be unfamiliar with. The imagined reader is familiar with the verse's general normative implications (the institution of maidservice), but not its detailed specifications (fathers, not mothers, act as sellers).

The *Midrash* establishes its warrant by reasoning with the only resources available to it: knowledge of related legal provisions and formal logic. The deductive process starts from the premise that daughters, but not sons, can be sold by their father. The *Midrash* does not establish how or from where it knows this provision. Again, the *Midrash* envisions readers with selective knowledge of the law at hand: they know who can be sold (daughters, not sons), but not who can do the selling (fathers, not mothers). Reasoning from this premise will, in any event, lead the hypothetical reader to misunderstand maidservice. The *Midrash* conceives a logical sequence that concludes with a mother being authorized to sell her daughter. The importance of the lemma, according to this view, is that it refutes the plausible but incorrect conclusion one reaches when reasoning from established legal premises. Were it not for the likelihood of reaching this incorrect conclusion, the lemma (per the *Midrash*'s understanding) would serve no purpose.

The next segment of midrashic commentary focuses on the direct object of the protasis ("his daughter") and makes a formally identical argument. The *Midrash* first asserts a gender-restrictive interpretation of the lemma ("his daughter" = daughters, not sons) and then establishes a warrant for its interpretation.

> A man may sell his daughter, but may not sell his son.
> [Scripture makes this point explicit] since the following deduction is reasonable [but wrong]:
> Given the fact that a daughter, who *cannot* be sold to resolve a debt incurred by theft, can be sold by her father,
> Isn't it logical to conclude that a son, who *is* sold to resolve a debt incurred by theft, should also be able to be sold by his father?
> [To refute this reasonable, but erroneous conclusion]
> Scripture states, ***When a man sells [his daughter].***
>
> (Mekhilta of R. Ishmael, Nezikin [Mishpatim], Parasha 3.2)

Though the lemma is not re-invoked, it appears that the *Midrash* proceeds to the next lexeme in the sequence ("his daughter"). What was granted as a premise in the previous segment (daughters, not sons, are sold) is now derived from the text. That is, it is no longer accepted as a premise of the argument. Though the gender-restrictive interpretation (daughters, not sons) is justified, again the *Midrash* does not argue for it. The midrashic argument limits itself to establishing a warrant for interpretation. Once again, the warrant is imagined in terms of deferring the problematic legal conclusion that emerges when reasoning from established legal premises. Here the premise is that males ("sons"), but not females ("daughters"), are sold into slavery to repay a punitive debt incurred by theft. Granting this premise, the *Midrash* reasons that sons can be sold by their fathers, a conclusion the *Midrash* knows to be normatively false. This exercise justifies scripture's word choice for the direct object ("daughter"). Indirectly, it validates the gender-restrictive interpretation (daughters, not sons). Again, the *Midrash* reasons from a premise without establishing from where or how it is known.

The two segments together function as an extended comment on the lemma. The *Midrash* reads both the grammatical subject of the protasis ("father") and its direct object ("daughter") in a gender-restrictive manner. It is interesting to consider whether and how this extended comment functions as interpretation. Formally, the proffered interpretations are juxtaposed to, not derived from, the lemma. At no point does the *Midrash* make an argument in favor of one reading over another. The arguments, to the extent that they exist, counter the errant conclusions achieved when reasoning from known premises. The hitch is that the premises are constantly shifting. What is known and established in the first segment (sons are not sold by fathers) must itself be determined in the second segment. Furthermore, the *Midrash* seems to know in advance which legal conclusions are to be eschewed. Interpretative activity clearly lies behind both the premises of midrashic reasoning and its confidence that certain legal conclusions are unacceptable. The *Midrash* does not, however, disclose the process that generates its working assumptions.

The passage's rhetoric constructs scripture itself as an active agent. Scripture nudges the reader away from problematic conclusions and toward appropriate ones. Azzan Israel-Yadin argues that the figure of scripture as an active agent directing interpretation is distinctive to the school of R. Ishmael.[21] Notably, scripture proffers its interventions into a legal system that is, for the most part (save each newly proposed provision), pretty much fully formed. At each juncture, the only provision that is contingent is the one currently being investigated. Ishay Rosen-Zvi describes the hermeneutic at work in midrashim like these as driven by the idea that no individual word of scripture is extraneous. Every lexical unit in scripture is potentially capable of making a seismic shift in our legal understanding.[22] But we must keep in mind that this hermeneutic explains only that which *Midrash*'s generic conventions represent as interpretation. It does not illuminate the unmarked interpretative practice that supplies the argument's operative premises.

School of Rabbi Akiba

A second example of midrashic discourse is drawn from the school of R. Akiba. This *Midrash* comments on a verse from the laws concerning impure skin affections.

> 44He is a leprous man; he is impure. The priest shall pronounce him unclean; his affection is on his head.
> 45As for the leprous person, his clothes shall be rent and his head shall be left bare.
>
> (Lev. 13:44–45)

Verse 44 concludes a paragraph (Lev. 13:40–44) on skin affections that appear on a (male) bald head. The verse confirms the impure status of the bald man, following the priest's pronouncement. Verse 45 begins a new paragraph (Lev. 13:45–46), which returns to provisions that are relevant for individuals impure from assorted manifestations of skin affections (not only the bald head).[23] All individuals impure from skin affections must tear their clothes and bare their heads.

As in the example from the school of R. Ishmael, the Akiban *Midrash* treats each lexeme in the lemma in serial fashion. The English translation ("he is a leprous man") misrepresents the original word order. In Hebrew, the sequence is (1) grammatical subject ("man," *'ish*), (2) adjectival participle ("leprous," *tzarua'*), and (3) predicate ("he is," *hu'*). A literal translation is "a man, leprous, he is." The *Midrash* starts its treatment of the lemma by focusing on the first word, "man."

> ***Man.*** I have only a "man." From where [in scripture do I know to] include a "woman" and a "minor"?
> Scripture states, ***leprous***. Irrespective of whether a man, a woman or a minor.
> If so, why does scripture state ***man***?
> It relates to the [scriptural] clause below, [about which I conclude:]

A [leprous] man bares [his head] and rends [his garment], but a [leprous] woman does not bare [her head] or rend [her garment].

(Sifra, Tazria, Perek 12)

The *Midrash* begins by limiting the law about skin affections on a bald head's applicability to men only ("I have only man"). As in the Ishmaelian *Midrash*, the exegetical focus is on an atomized lexeme ("man"). But establishing the gender-restrictive sense of the first lexeme raises a question. The *Midrash* knows from elsewhere (and again it does not specify how or from where) that women and minors are also subject to this provision. The *Midrash* seeks a basis for including them as subjects ("from where . . ."). As above, the *Midrash* has extensive familiarity with legal provisions related to the topic (here, skin affections) that precede its encounter with the verse. But knowledge of the legal provisions deriving from this verse is selective. Previously unknown provisions (women and minors are also subjects of the law) are said to derive from the same verse that supplies prior knowledge (men are subjects). The imagined reader knows some, but not all, of the normative implications of this verse.

Having effectively established the law's broad constituency, the *Midrash* returns to the restrictive language that first elicits interest ("if so, why does scripture state 'man'?"). In its final move, the *Midrash* explains that the exclusive language from verse 44 ("man") anticipates a gender-restrictive provision in the next verse ("it relates to the clause below"). Recall, verse 45 instructs the confirmed leprous person to bare their head and rend their garment. According to the *Midrash*, this provision (not the prior one about bald heads) applies to men, but not women. This interpretation overturns the plain sense meaning of the verses. The provision of verse 44 (on bald heads) is read as relevant to men, women and minors even though its plain sense relates to men only. And the provision of verse 45 is read restrictively (men only), even though its plain sense relates to *all* affected by skin affections (i.e., men, women and children).[24] The midrashic interpretation inverts the straightforward sense of the biblical text! We might conjecture that an unmarked reading process gives rise to the interpretation,[25] but the *Midrash* does not preserve it.

Finally, this Akiban *Midrash* is recognizable as such by the technical term it uses ("include") to expand the legal subject from "man only" to "man, woman and minor." The *Midrash* asks "from where do I know to *include* a woman and a minor?" Using this term to extend the legal ramifications of a scriptural provision is a signature move of the school of R. Akiba.[26]

In sum, *Midrash* from both schools is typified by the formal feature of correlating *tannaitic* legal tradition (*halakhic* dicta) with biblical lexemes. The examples we saw show *Midrash* to be more formal scriptural commentary than explication of interpretative practice.[27] Though it attests to and includes much scriptural interpretation, the basis for interpretation remains unclear and is not typically argued for. While the commentary form of *Midrash* presents the proffered traditions as interpretation (and in the school of R. Ishmael the interpretative process is directed and authorized by scripture itself), the form does not preserve the reading practices that yield interpretation.[28]

In the next section, we continue to challenge the transparency of generic conventions as a window onto *tannaitic* reading practices. Though the generic conventions of Mishnah construct it as something other than reading, mishnaic discourse attests to deep engagement with scriptural interpretation.

Mishnah: *Halakhic* Dicta Organized Topically

The word *Mishnah* comes from the three-letter Hebrew root *sh.n.h.* meaning "to repeat," a cognate of the Aramaic *t.n.*ʾ. that gives us the term *tanna* ("one who repeats").[29] Mishnah, according to this paradigm, is tradition that has been formulated in order to be repeated, that is, for ease of a presumably oral transmission. A unit of tradition thus formulated is called "a mishnah" (lowercase, pl. = "*mishnayot*"). "The Mishnah" (uppercase) indicates the edited compilation of many such traditions. *Geonic* historiography credits Rabbi Judah the Patriarch with editing the Mishnah *c.* 200 CE, though as with many ancient documents the modern notion of strong editorial oversight by a great mind at a single moment in time is probably inaccurate. Modern scholars have suggested that multiple Mishnah collections circulated both before and after the compilation of "our Mishnah."[30]

Halakhic dicta not included in the Mishnah eventually came to be known as *baraita*, from the Aramaic word *bara*ʿ, meaning outside. A *baraita* is a dictum that was preserved outside the Mishnah (pl. = *baraitot*). The Tosefta (lit., "addition" or "addendum") is a companion document to the Mishnah, consisting of excluded but related legal traditions. The terminological distinction between *Mishnah* and *baraita* reflects a post-mishnaic sensibility when some traditions were "inside" and others were "outside" the Mishnah. Modern scholars debate the chronological relationship between individual traditions found in and the redacted compilations of the Mishnah and the Tosefta.[31] Both Mishnah and Tosefta are structured according to the same topical divisions, with each tractate focusing on a relatively narrow area of law (marriage, divorce, agricultural gifts to priests, blessings, menstrual impurity, etc.). The sixty-three tractates are further clustered into six broad groups (Agriculture, Holidays, Women, Civil Damages, Holy Things, and Purities). While foregrounding the topical conception of the Mishnah's contents, this organizational structure obscures the scriptural origins of many of its legal topics and traditions. Furthermore, the scriptural bases for law are rarely cited explicitly in the Mishnah (more so in the Tosefta).[32]

Collecting and Sorting *Halakhic* Tradition

The project of collecting legal traditions into transmissible form is said to have begun shortly after the destruction of the Second Temple in 70 CE. The following story is one of the earliest records of the impulse to preserve tradition into what eventually became the Mishnah.

When the sages entered the vineyard at Yavneh, they said:
The time is coming when a person will seek a word
From the teachings of the Torah, but will not find it,
From the teachings of the scribes, but will not find it.
. . .
They said: Let us begin with [by collecting the traditions of] Hillel and Shammai.
(t.Eduyot 1.1)

In this source, scholarly efforts are undertaken to stave the loss of tradition following the destruction of the central cultic and scribal center. Tradition is organized according to tradents' names, Hillel and Shammai, transitional figures bridging the Second Temple and the *tannaitic* periods. The source confirms that a substantial portion of tradition has roots in the Torah ("a person will seek a word from . . . Torah"). Nonetheless, the organizational strategy of grouping traditions according to tradents masks those roots.

A later text envisions a different stratagem for organizing tradition. This text depicts the academic activities of Rabbi Akiba (d. *c.* 135 CE) who is credited with compiling an early Mishnah-like collection.

As for Rabbi Akiba, they called him a "stuffed treasure chest."
To what can Rabbi Akiba be likened?
To a worker who took a basket and went outside.
He found wheat, he put it in.
He found barley, he put it in,
Spelt, he put it in,
Lentils, he put them in.
When he got home, he sorted:
The wheat, by itself,
The barley, by itself,
The beans, by themselves,
The lentils, by themselves.
In like manner, Rabbi Akiba processed (*'asah*) the whole Torah with a series of bands.
(Fathers of R. Natan A, ch. 18)

This source understands Rabbi Akiba's intellectual achievement by analogy to an agricultural worker. The laborer performs two discrete tasks. First, he collects diverse types of grain and throws them indiscriminately into a single basket. When he returns home, he sorts them according to type. The grains are valuable only after being organized. Then they can be retrieved in sufficient quantity to be used. The passage's final line, which correlates the laborer's agricultural work to Rabbi Akiba's intellectual project, relates only to the second of the laborer's tasks. Like the laborer who arranges the collected grains according to type, Rabbi Akiba processes what he gathers by means of "a series of bands" or rings. Once organized and sorted according to type, collected traditions are useful. Like the grains, now they can be retrieved. As in the previous source, the traditions subject to collection, collation, and organization are envisioned as fully formed. The grains and legumes of the analogue are mature and ready for harvesting. The laborer's contribution is to take fully formed units and arrange them in user-friendly configurations.

Highlighting Legal Categories

The image of an agricultural worker collecting and sorting grains aptly captures the intellectual activity represented by Mishnah's generic conventions. The Mishnah rehearses *halakhic* dicta in a manner that brings together teachings from diverse sources and highlights latent categorical affinities among them.[33] Consider the following Mishnah. Bolded text indicates fully formed traditions that we already encountered in our review of *Midrash*.

> What is the difference between man and woman?
> **A man [leper] bares [his head] and tears [his garment], but a woman [leper] does not bare [her hair] or tear [her garment].**
> A man may submit his son to a Nazirite vow, but a woman may not submit her son to a Nazirite vow.
> A man may shave [as a means of bringing] his father's Nazirite vow to a conclusion, but a woman may not shave [as a means of bringing] her father's Nazirite vow to a conclusion.
> **A man may sell his daughter [as a maidservant], but a woman may not sell her daughter [as a maidservant].**
> A man may betroth his daughter, but a woman may not betroth her daughter.
> A man is stoned naked, but a woman is not stoned naked.
> A man is hung, but a woman is not hung.
> **A man is sold [as a slave] to repay what he stole, but a woman is not sold [as a slave] to repay what she stole.**
>
> (m.Soṭah 3:8)

The Mishnah begins by announcing the legal categories it wishes to clarify. Its project is to establish "man" and "woman" as distinct types of legal subjects. The Mishnah achieves its understanding by compiling a list of rulings drawn from diverse areas of law (leprosy, Nazirite vows, maidservant sale, betrothal, execution, and debt slavery). In each arena, men and women are subject to different legal requirements.

The intellectual work that lies behind this Mishnah is easily imagined in terms of the agricultural analogy. *Tannaitic* Sages (akin to Rabbi Akiba) survey a large swath of legal traditions ("went outside"),[34] identify those that treat men and women differently ("found wheat and put it in"), and collate the list ("sorted the wheat by itself"). The fact that the collated traditions have midrashic parallels suggests that one aspect of the surveying process entails engaging tradition in connection with scripture. But when the traditions are collated in the Mishnah, their scriptural associations are obscured.

What moves to the foreground from in this presentation is the coherence of "man" and "woman" as distinct legal categories. Though the intellectual exercise that lies behind the Mishnah involves surveying traditions of scriptural interpretation, whatever scriptural interpretation contributed to the formation of these traditions remains unremarked upon. Case studies like this one demonstrate the difficulty of relying on the generic conventions of *Midrash* and/or Mishnah to illuminate *tannaitic* practices of reading scripture.

Jurisprudential Reading Practices Attested by Both *Midrash* and Mishnah

As observed in the previous section, both *Midrash* and Mishnah take for granted a particular framing of the biblical legal sources. The *tannaitic* framing of biblical legal sources manifests in the premises of midrashic argumentation and the fully formed interpretations presented as known legal traditions in the Mishnah.

In this section, I reconstruct an interpretative process—more immediately recognizable as interpretation than *Midrash*'s baldly asserted connections between lemma and legal tradition—that plausibly accounts for the emergence of the *tannaitic* framing of biblical legal sources. At its core, the interpretative process I document here is jurisprudential, engaging biblical text as points of access to a legal system comprised of cases, rulings and principles. The unmarked interpretative practice that I reconstruct is similar to a practice that Michael Fishbane calls "rationalization."[35] Legists working with early biblical legal sources inherited a corpus that was incomplete in terms of "the scope and precision necessary for viable juridical decisions."[36] The inner-biblical interpretative practice of rationalization sought to fill in missing elements so that the corpus would be adequate to "viable juridical decisions." I argue that a similar interest, probably in an academic context, in understanding biblical legal sources as adequate for the making of "viable juridical decisions" drove the unmarked reading process to which *tannaitic* sources attest.

Case Study in *Tannaitic* Legal Vocabulary

The legal concepts featured in the next case study are widely regarded as biblical. Notwithstanding their dependence on biblical materials, the operative *tannaitic* terms for discussing the topic differ substantially from those in the biblical source.

Tannaitic law envisions four arrangements by which one person's property (the owner's) comes to be in the domain of another (the guardian). "Guardianship" is the technical term the *Tannaim* devise for the arrangement.[37] The Mishnah offers a clear, concise overview of the categories by which the liability of guardians is determined in the event of loss or damage to the owner's property.

> There are four types of guardian: (1) the unpaid guardian, and (2) the borrower, (3) the wage-bearer, and (4) the renter.
> (1) The unpaid guardian swears for everything,
> (2) And the borrower pays for everything.
> (3) The wage-bearer and (4) the renter swear regarding the injured, the captured and the dead [animal], and they pay for loss and theft.
>
> (m.Baba Metzia 7:8)

The four situations wherein one person's property resides in another's domain are distinguished by who benefits from the arrangement and whether a fee is paid. The first two arrangements differ in who benefits and are offered without payment: (1) the owner benefits when the unpaid guardian takes care of their property without a charge; (2) the borrower benefits when the owner allows use of their property without a charge. The final two arrangements involve the same services (and benefits) to owner and guardian, respectively, but are predicated upon payment; (3) the owner pays a fee to the wage-bearer to take care of their property; and (4) the renter pays a fee to use the owner's property.

The second half of the Mishnah states the financial liability that each guardian bears in the event of loss or damage. The Mishnah envisions five circumstances in which the owner's property is not returned intact. The property may be (1) lost, or (2) stolen, and if the property is an animal, it may (3) be injured, (4) be captured, or (5) die. The unpaid guardian bears the least responsibility for loss or damage. Under all circumstances of damage (loss, theft, injury, capture, and death), the unpaid guardian is released from liability by swearing to no foul play on their part ("swears for everything"). The borrower, on the other hand, bears the highest degree of culpability. Under all circumstances (loss, theft, injury, capture, and death), the borrower compensates the owner for the loss ("pays for everything"). The wage-bearer and renter each bear partial culpability. They can swear to no foul play and be released from responsibility for circumstances beyond their control (injury, capture, and death), but they are required to pay for circumstances they could have prevented (loss and theft).

The mishnaic synopsis of these laws is streamlined, succinct, and marked by simple symmetries. The four guardians are understood to be engaged in comparable transactions, distinguished by whether the arrangement benefits the owner or the guardian and whether or not a fee is paid. The number four has a symbolic value of completeness, lending the impression of a comprehensive treatment of the issue.[38] The unpaid guardian and borrower represent the two poles of financial liability (entirely on owner vs. entirely on guardian). The wage-bearer and the renter represent intermediate levels of liability (shared between owner and guardian). The Mishnah's structural organization forefronts cases where liability lies exclusively with one party and secondarily introduces cases of shared liability.

From Biblical Source to *Tannaitic* Schematization

The mishnaic summary of the degrees of the guardians' liability derives from a strategic reading of Exodus 22:6–14. The biblical passage on which the Mishnah's categories are based is sprawling compared to the concise mishnaic summary. The layout of the biblical materials below highlights elements that are central to the mishnaic schematization alongside elements that are eschewed or suppressed in the *tannaitic* framing. Biblical terms that supply language for *tannaitic* categories appear in **bold**. The paragraphing anticipates the Mishnah's four categories, with each paragraph corresponding to one of the *tannaitic* "guardians." A quick visual scan of the biblical passage, with its vastly different scales of treatment in the first two versus last two paragraphs, suggests that the elegant symmetry of the *tannaitic* categories is artificially imposed on the biblical materials. The native categorical interests of the biblical passage are evident in its subcases (indicated by an arrow, "→"). Parallel elements in the first two paragraphs (indicated by *italics*) hint at additional categories at play in the biblical presentation.

> 6 *When a man gives silver or vessels to his fellow* **to guard**, and it is **stolen** from the man's house –
> →if the thief is found, he shall pay double.
> →7 If a thief is not found,
> the owner of the house shall **depose before God** whether or not he has not laid his hand upon his fellow's property,
> 8 In all charges of misappropriation—*pertaining to an ox, a sheep, a garment or any other* **loss**, *whereof the party alleges "This is it!"*—the case of both parties shall come before God,
> he whom God declares guilty shall **pay** double to the other.
>
> 9 *When a man gives an ass, an ox, a sheep or any other animal to his fellow* **to guard**,
> →and **it dies or is injured or is captured**, and no one sees,
> 10 An **oath before the Lord** shall confirm between them whether or not he laid his hand upon his fellow's property;
> the owner must acquiesce, and no restitution shall be made.
> →11 But if it was stolen from him, he shall **pay** its owner.
> →12 If it was torn by beasts, he shall bring it as evidence; he need not replace what has been torn by beasts
>
> 13 If a man **borrows** [an animal] from his fellow and **it is injured or dies**,
> →Its owner not being with it, he must **pay**.
> →14a If its owner was with it, he does not pay;
>
> 14b But if [the animal] was **rented**, he is entitled to its rental fee.

The first thing to note is the bolded terms, which are deployed as core legal categories in *tannaitic* discourse. The term "guardian," which underwrites the *tannaitic* conception, appears in the protasis of the first two cases as a verbal infinitive ("when a man gives . . . to his fellow **to guard**," vv. 6, 9). The *tannaitic* scheme extends the term's applicability to the borrower and renter (vv. 13, 14b). The five *tannaitic* categories of loss and damage to the property (loss, theft, death, injury, and capture) also come directly from biblical language ("it is **stolen**," v. 6; "any other **loss**," v. 8; "it **dies**, is **injured** or **carried** off," v. 9, see also v. 13). Finally, terms for two of the four guardians (borrower and renter) appear in the passage ("if a man **borrows**," v. 13; "if it was **rented**," v. 14b). On the other hand, the biblical passage contains no language that anticipates the *tannaitic* terms "unpaid guardian" or "wage-bearer." These categories correlate with the first two longer paragraphs (unpaid guardian = first paragraph; wage-bearer = second paragraph), but the *Tannaim* supply the language and associated concepts.

A second thing to note is the schematic organization that structures it. Each of the first three paragraphs includes a number of subcases (each indicated by→). The subcases present factors deemed relevant when determining liability.

Central to the first paragraph is whether the party responsible for the loss (the thief) is located. When the thief is found, they are liable; when the thief is not found *and* an oath before God reveals the guardian to have misappropriated the property, the guardian is treated like a thief (they pay double, as a thief would). The passage implies, without stating explicitly, that if the oath affirms the guardian did *not* misappropriate the property, they are not liable and the owner bears the loss. Notably, the *tannaitic* schematization does not consider the possibility of finding the thief (the primary concern in the biblical passage). The Mishnah attends to an eventuality not explicitly mentioned in the biblical passage (i.e., the guardian swears to no foul play and the owner takes the loss).

In the second paragraph, liability is determined by the conditions under which the property is lost or damaged, which tracks more closely with the *tannaitic* scheme. The second paragraph imagines animals only as the property guarded by the guardian. The paragraph envisions three contexts in which damage and loss occurs. When the circumstances are beyond the guardian's control (death, injury, capture), the guardian takes an oath to confirm no foul play and is released from liability. When the circumstances are preventable (theft), the guardian must compensate the owner. Finally, in cases where evidence indicates the animal was torn by beasts, the owner bears the cost. The *tannaitic* schematization includes four of these conditions (theft vs. death, injury, capture), but not the last (torn by beasts). The second paragraph links the guardian's liability to the whether the circumstances of loss were preventable. The correlation between un/preventable circumstances and liability becomes a structuring motif for assessing liability for all four of the guardians in the *tannaitic* schematization.

Returning to the biblical passage, liability in the third paragraph turns on whether the owner is present when the damage/loss occurs. Consideration of this issue is altogether absent in the *tannaitic* schematization. The final half verse of the passage (14b) is not a full paragraph, though I represent it as such to anticipate its role as a source for the *tannaitic* "renter." According to David Wright, this provision stipulates that "the loss of the animal does not negate the requirement to pay the full rental fee."[39] This consideration is not reflected in the *tannaitic* schematization at all.

Just as the *tannaitic* schematization drops structuring concerns evident in the biblical passage, it adds structuring elements that are absent in the biblical passage. First, the Mishnah reorders the presentation of the guardians. Unlike the biblical sequence, the Mishnah clusters guardianships where one of the parties bears full liability for loss/damage (unpaid guardian, borrower) and where they share the cost of the loss (wage-bearer, renter). We can speculate that the Mishnah emphasizes full versus shared liability because the different degrees of liability correlate with an unarticulated but implicit issue. The cases where one party bears full financial liability are also cases where the responsible party benefits, at the expense of the other party, from the arrangement. The owner benefits from both the service provided by the unpaid guardian, and the fact that it is provided *gratis*. Correspondingly, the owner is financially liable in all cases of damage/loss. The borrower also enjoys a double benefit from the arrangement: use of the property without having to pay a fee. Correspondingly, the borrower also bears full liability. On the other hand, when money is exchanged between the two parties, the benefit—and the liability—is shared. The wage-bearer provides a service, but benefits from the collected fee. Likewise, the renter benefits from use of the property but confers benefit in paying a fee. Both the wage-bearer and the renter pay for preventable loss/damage, and swear to no foul play in unpreventable cases. The Mishnaic ordering in its list of the guardians hints that it links the degree of liability to the extent to which one benefits.

In sum, the *tannaitic* schematization levels much of the complexity in the biblical passage. It foregrounds some categories suggested by biblical language and obscures others. It also introduces new concerns and produces its own concise and internally consistent account.

Jurisprudential Reading Practices

We can speculatively reconstruct several reading practices that could have led interpreters from the sprawling biblical presentation to the *tannaitic* framing. One reading practice is "extension," or transfer. Issues that, in the biblical passage, are relevant in only one or two of the four paragraphs are extended or transferred to other cases. I have already noted that the *tannaitic* schematization treats all four arrangements as instances of guarding, even though the language of guarding is used in only the first two paragraphs.

Another instance of extension results when the Mishnah evaluates liability for the five of the types of damage/loss mentioned for each of the four guardians. Four types of damage (death, injury, capture, theft) are mentioned in conjunction with the second paragraph (i.e., wage-bearer), but only two (theft and loss) are mentioned in the first paragraph (i.e., unpaid guardian). The *tannaitic* schematization, however, regards all five types of damage as relevant to both the unpaid guardian and the wage-bearer. Likewise, all five categories of damage/loss are relevant to the borrower even though only two (death and injury) are explicitly mentioned in the biblical verses (vv. 13–14a). Perhaps most striking is that all five categories of damage/loss are relevant for the renter even though not one is mentioned in their half verse (v. 14b). The work of extension or transfer has the effect of creating cases (e.g., a renter who loses the property) that are not explicitly attested in the biblical passage. Insofar as this reading practice introduces new cases for consideration, it is jurisprudentially driven. It tries to impose a uniformity on the categories implied by biblical language, connecting it to what Fishbane calls "rationalization."[40]

A second reading practice involves discerning the principles operative in biblically attested cases in order to redeploy them to resolve the biblically unattested cases. Consider the case of the renter, of whom the biblical passage says only that the rental fee is not waived when the rented animal is lost or damaged.[41] Above we noted that practice of extension or transfer has the effect of creating the case where a renter loses the property. How is the renter's liability to be assessed? The Mishnah regards the renter's liability as comparable to that of the wage-bearer.

> The wage-bearer *and the renter* swear regarding the injured, the captured and the dead [animal], and they pay for loss and theft (emphasis added).
>
> (m.Baba Metzia 7:8)

The renter, like the wage-bearer, has the option to swear to no foul play in the event of circumstances beyond their control (injury, capture, death) but must compensate the owner in the event of circumstances they are reasonably expected to guard against (loss and theft). The extent of the wage-bearer's responsibilities is stated explicitly in the biblical passage. The wage-bearer has the option to swear to no foul play and be released of liability in the case of injury, capture and death (vv. 9–10), but must compensate the owner in the case of theft (v. 11) On what basis does the *tannaitic* scheme treat the renter like the wage-bearer?

There is a telltale trace of the principle that guides the *tannaitic* ruling. As previously noted, the Mishnah's ordering of the guardians does not mirror the biblical sequence. The Mishnah first lists the unpaid guardian, who provides a service to the owner without remuneration, and then lists the borrower, who uses the property without a rental fee. (In contrast, the biblical arrangement features the unpaid guardian first, followed by the paid guardian.) In each of the Mishnah's first two cases, liability for damage/loss is borne solely by the party that benefits from the arrangement. We can speculate that the Mishnah clusters the renter together with the wage-bearer on the assumption that they too are alike in how they distribute benefit between the owner and guardian. In the *tannaitic* framing, rental and paid guardian are understood to be arrangements that distribute benefit between owner and guardian. The *tannaitic* scheme follows the biblically attested principle for the paid guardian (second paragraph) when it rules that the liability for damage during rental is shared between owner and the guardian.

Finally, a third reading practice involves extrapolating the conceptual basis or rationale for a legal resolution and expanding its significance. This reading practice accounts for the technical terms ("unpaid guardian" and "wage-bearer") that the *tannaitic* scheme uses to describe the arrangement in the first (vv. 6–8) and second (vv. 9–12) paragraphs. One can imagine a process like the following:

1. Reader notes parallel language in the protasis of the first and second paragraphs (see italicized text in vv. 6 and 9).
2. Reader notes a difference in the opening lines: in the first case the owner leaves *silver or vessels* (movable property) for safekeeping; in the second case the owner leaves *an animal.*
3. Reader notes the distinction between the two cases is not absolute. Verse 8 in the first paragraph reiterates the types of property subject to guarding, and animals appear on the list though they are absent from the original list in verse 6.
4. Reader wonders why the paragraphs lead with a distinction that is not absolute.
5. Reader further observes that the guardian of the second paragraph bears greater financial liability than that of the first.
6. Reader now wonders what in the second case occasions greater liability, given that both cases can involve guarding an animal.
7. Reader links greater liability to greater responsibility, and seeks evidence for the fact that the guardian in the second case has greater responsibility.
8. Reader speculates that the first guardian offers their service as a favor (gratis), which accounts for why they bear no liability for loss. Reader speculates that the second guardian offers their services for a fee, explaining why they bear some financial liability.
9. Reader retroactively understands that the opening sentence in the protasis of first paragraph describes the typical case of an unpaid guardian. While one might ask someone to watch "silver or vessels" as a favor, one would not expect them to care for an animal, which involves considerable labor, as a favor. The mention of animals in verse 8 no longer appears as an inconsistency because the first two guardians are distinguished by whether they are paid, not by the type of property they guard (vessels vs. animal).

This admittedly speculative reconstruction produces the technical terms for and legal concepts associated with the guardians in first and second paragraphs: "unpaid guardian" and "wage-bearer." Note that the process that yields these terms engages paragraphs, which attest to cases and principles, as analytic units.

In sum, we can make several general remarks about the reading practices that yield the *tannaitic* schematization.[42] First, they *precede* the composition of the Mishnah. By the time the pithy Mishnah before us was formulated, the technical terms for the guardians and types of damage had already been coined and the legal concept that correlates liability with benefit had already been worked out. The Mishnah accepts these terms and concepts as givens. Second, this reading is driven by jurisprudential, rather than literary, interests, and concerns. The unit of analysis in this reading is "the case," not the phrase or word. Paragraphs are regarded as literary attestations of discrete legal cases. The interpretative process is driven by questions related to legal protocol (what is the rationale for a given ruling? are there other relevant, related cases? how should one rule in related cases?). Interpretation involves comparison across different paragraphs and sections of the passage, thought of as cases. Disparate pieces of information are integrated into a coordinated and consistent whole. The ultimate concern of the exercise is to understand the rationale for the attested rulings rather than to account for the language used in the passage. Finally, the *tannaitic* reading is not narrated or marked as such. That such reading practices took place at all is known only from the resulting product, the *tannaitic* schematization of legal categories, and its vocabulary of technical terms and legal concepts.

Circling Back to the Generic Conventions

In this final section, I return to the generic conventions of *Midrash* and Mishnah. Given that both *Midrash* and Mishnah take the *tannaitic* framing of the biblical legal heritage as a point of departure, what is at stake when they represent the relationship between *tannaitic* and biblical legal tradition so differently? What compels the genres to present a shared interpretative heritage (the *tannaitic* framing) in such disparate ways? What is at stake when they adopt distinct generic conventions? I argue that the generic conventions are best thought of as a means to rehearse or process the newly emergent interpretative tradition represented by the *tannaitic* framing. Each set of generic conventions rehearses tradition for a distinct set of pedagogical or scholastic purposes.[43] Midrashic discourse affirms connections between the newly emergent interpretative tradition and the language of biblical text. Mishnaic discourse, on the other hand, presses the newly emergent terms and concepts for greater jurisprudential clarity. It seeks to clarify, articulate, and further develop legal categories and principles. Where *Midrash* grounds the newly emergent legal tradition in the authority of biblical scripture, Mishnah grounds it in the authority of the *tannaitic* Sages.[44]

Midrashic Presentation of the Newly Emergent Interpretative Tradition

Midrash attests to its acceptance of the unmarked interpretative process when it adopts the *tannaitic* framing of the four-guardians passage. Consider a midrashic commentary to one of the subcases (indicated by→) from the second paragraph. The leading protasis of the second paragraph concerns damage or loss brought about by an unwitnessed death, injury, or capture (v. 9: "and it dies or is injured or is captured, and no one sees"). The leading case is resolved when the guardian swears to no foul play and is relieved of responsibility. The subcase from which the lemma is drawn posits a different type of damage/loss and proffers a different resolution: "But if it [the animal] was stolen from him, he shall pay its owner" (v. 11). The *Midrash* comments:

> *And if it is stolen from him* (Exodus 21:11). This [paragraph] refers to the guardian who accepts a wage and the above [paragraph] refers to the unpaid guardian.
> Or perhaps this [paragraph] refers to the unpaid guardian and the above [paragraph] refers to the guardian who accepts a wage?
> You must reason as follows:
> Given that the borrower is liable and the guardian [spoken of in this paragraph] is liable:
> [We must infer that] just as borrower benefits [from the arrangement], so too the guardian spoken of in this paragraph benefits [from the arrangement].
> This precludes the unpaid guardian, since they do not benefit [from the arrangement].
> Therefore, you must conclude in accordance with the first proposal, and not the second proposal:
> This paragraph refers to the guardian who accepts a wage and the above [paragraph] refers to the unpaid guardian.
>
> (Mekhilta of R. Ishmael, Nezikin, Parasha 16)

This midrashic unit seeks to determine the identity of the "mystery guardian" who is the subject of the paragraph in which the subcase (v. 11) appears. Is the second paragraph about the unpaid guardian or "the guardian who accepts a wage" ("wage-bearer" per the Mishnah's parlance)? Constructing an argument from established and known premises, the unit concludes that the paragraph concerns the guardian who accepts a wage (the wage-bearer). In the sequence of its deductive reasoning, the *Midrash* takes for granted terms and concepts that are not biblical givens but part of the *tannaitic* framing. (Terms: "guardian who accepts a wage," "unpaid guardian." Concept: that the borrower benefits from the arrangement.)

The argument proceeds as follows. First, the Midrash establishes the borrower as a fitting comparandum for the mystery guardian. Both the borrower and the mystery guardian bear liability for (some) cases of loss/damage. This premise is drawn directly from the biblical text. Verse 13 establishes the borrower's liability ("if a man borrows . . . its owner not being with it, *he must pay*") and verse 11 establishes the mystery guardian's liability ("if it is stolen . . ., *he shall pay its owner*").

Having established a comparandum for the mystery guardian, the *Midrash* recalls a known attribute: the borrower benefits from the arrangement. This concept is not explicitly stated in the biblical passage. It is a product of the jurisprudentially driven reading process reconstructed in the previous section. Recognizing that the comparandum (borrower) benefits from the arrangement (free use of the animal), the *Midrash* infers the same of the mystery guardian. They too benefit from the arrangement.

The final step of the argument eliminates the unpaid guardian—as one who does not benefit from the arrangement—from being the mystery guardian. These terms and concepts also derive from the interpretative process outlined above. A central premise of the argument is that the unpaid guardian does not benefit from the arrangement. But recall, neither the term "unpaid guardian" nor the concept of benefit being correlated with the obligation to pay are invoked explicitly in the biblical passage. In its back and forth, and its consideration of multiple solutions, the midrashic passage is much more dialogical than its mishnaic counterpart (m.Baba Metzia 7:8), though both versions rely upon and rehearse the same interpretative tradition.

An interesting feature of the *Midrash* is its selective withholding of insights from the jurisprudentially driven interpretation. We saw something similar in the Ishmaelian *Midrash* examined in the first section. The reading process that supplies the argument's working vocabulary of terms and concepts entails *integrating all four paragraphs into a single legal paradigm*: comparing and contrasting them, transferring attributes associated with one case to others, and articulating the principles that govern the explicitly stated rulings in order to apply them to cases for which no ruling is explicitly stated. This interpretative process is at base integrative. The *Midrash*, however, acts as if each lexical unit bears decoding independently of the others. Little is known about the guardian from the second paragraph at the same time that much is known about the borrower and the unpaid guardian. The technical terms "unpaid guardian" and "paid guardian" and the legal concept that correlates liability to benefit, once derived, are assumed to exist in the ether of legal conceptual space independently of their textual attestation.

Interpretative Process vs. Rhetoric of Interpretation

We are now in a position to appreciate the difference between the interpretative process that supplies the working legal vocabulary for both *Midrash* and Mishnah, and the "rhetoric of interpretation" cued by the generic conventions of *Midrash*. I have argued that *Midrash* and Mishnah employ a (fairly) stable vocabulary of technical terms and legal concepts.[45] I have further argued that this vocabulary emerges from a jurisprudential reading process that engages the biblical text as record of legal cases. The reading practice is concerned with the principles that govern jurisprudence. It seeks to understand individual cases within a network of related cases. This jurisprudentially driven interpretation yields what I have been calling a "*tannaitically* conceived version of the biblical legal heritage." Though deeply grounded in biblical sources, the vocabulary of technical terms and legal concepts is *tannaitic*, not biblical.

The jurisprudential interpretative process that yields the premises from which both mishnaic and midrashic discourse operate differs from the *Midrash*'s representation of interpretation in important ways. *Midrash* rehearses a connection between discrete biblical lexical units and an interpretation that *has already been achieved.*[46] Where the interpretative process that yields the legal categories, technical terms, and legal concepts is intertextual and integrative across the paragraphs, the midrashic rhetoric of interpretation focuses on atomized lexical units that are considered independently of one another. It correlates fully made legal categories (paid and unpaid guardians) with discrete lexical units (first and second paragraphs).

Mishnaic Rhetoric

Though both midrashic and mishnaic discourse draw upon the same set of legal premises, they rehearse the shared interpretative tradition to different effects. Midrashic rhetoric, as noted, correlates the legal traditions expressing newly emergent categories, principles, and concepts with discrete lexical units of biblical text. What about mishnaic rhetoric? What does performance of the shared interpretative tradition in a mishnaic key achieve?

Mishnaic discourse exercises the robustness of the conceptual underpinnings of the legal system as newly conceived.[47] As noted, the Mishnah's vocabulary of technical terms and legal concepts attests to its acceptance of the results of the (unmarked) jurisprudential reading process. Within the context of a legal system implied by these terms and concepts, the Mishnah presses the newly emergent categories, principles, and terms for greater clarity. Though unmarked as such, this activity constitutes another type of biblical interpretation.[48] For example, the mishnaic ordering of the guardians highlights three levels of liability: no liability under any conditions (unpaid guardian), complete liability (borrower), and liability for preventable circumstances (paid guardian/renter). The Mishnah's opening juxtaposition of the borrower and the unpaid guardian (where the arrangement favors one party at the expense of the other), on one hand, with the paid guardian and the renter (where the two parties share the benefit of the arrangement), on the other hand, evinces awareness of the connection between liability and benefit.

The mishnaic rehearsal of tradition also pushes for greater clarity of legal principles assumed to be operative. The jurisprudential interpretative process that underwrites the *tannaitic* project entails conceiving cases by extension or transfer from the biblically attested cases. The Mishnah participates in and extends this project by conceiving new cases that force clarity of the legal principles assumed to be operative.[49] For example, underlying the five categories of damage and loss is a distinction between avoidable and unavoidable circumstances. Guardians that benefit in some measure from the arrangement (paid guardian, renter, and borrower) are liable for loss and theft, which they can reasonably be expected to prevent. Underlying the Mishnah's rulings that the unpaid guardian, the paid guardian, and the renter take an oath to be released from liability if the animal dies is an assumption that the death is unpreventable. To test this principle, the Mishnah conceives cases that challenge this assumption.

> If [the animal] died of its own accord—this is considered unavoidable.
> If [the guardian] mistreated it and then it died—this is not considered unavoidable.
> If [the animal] went up to cliffs [of its own accord], and then fell—this is considered unavoidable.
> If [the guardian] took it up to the cliffs and it fell and died—this is not considered unavoidable.
>
> (m.Baba Metzia 7:10)

The Mishnah considers circumstances in which the guardian's behavior contributes to the animal's death: the guardian mistreats the animal or leads it to the top of a dangerous cliff.

The Mishnah's boundary cases force a refined understanding of the principle that death constitutes an unavoidable circumstance. The cases demonstrate that the guardian's behavior can support or undermine the animal's well-being. Death, it turns out, is not an unconditionally "unavoidable circumstance." The principle that imposes liability in avoidable circumstances extends to include death following mistreatment. The effect of the Mishnah's boundary cases is to foreground the legal concept of "avoidable circumstances" that lies behind the two biblically attested examples (theft and loss). The Mishnah's interest in liminal cases follows from its engagement with legal taxonomy and the concepts that underwrite the biblical passage.

Conclusion

Scholars have spilled much ink asking which mode of rehearsing tradition (Mishnah or *Midrash*) arose first.[50] There is general agreement that the redacted text of the Mishnah is earlier than the redacted collections of *tannaitic Midrash*, but Second Temple sources demonstrate the antiquity of both modes of presenting legal tradition. A more interesting question, which I have tried to answer in this chapter, is how the two genres complement each other, both rhetorically and pedagogically.

Regardless of how the relationship between the two genres is conceived, whether chronologically, rhetorically, or pedagogically, the fact remains that both genres emerge in the aftermath of an interpretative process that needs to be differentiated from the interpretative rhetoric of the *Midrash*. Scholars of an earlier generation described the interpretative process that yields the premises of *tannaitic* legal writings as an early, simple form of *Midrash* in contrast to the later, more complex *Midrash* regularly featured in *tannaitic Midrash*.[51] This approach supports the conclusion that *Midrash* preceded Mishnah. In my view, such an approach muddles matters in unhelpful ways. It associates an intellectual activity (jurisprudential interpretation) that was central to both the *Midrash* and Mishnah with *Midrash* exclusively.

For the purposes, of this chapter, it is not necessary to resolve the question of which genre came first. When regarded as alternate approaches to integrating one's command of newly emergent traditions, the two modalities of rehearsing tradition can be seen as complementary and mutually reinforcing. Each way of rehearsing the newly emergent tradition consolidates one's grasp in a distinct way. *Midrash* affirms the links between the newly emergent tradition and relevant scripture sources. Mishnah continues the jurisprudential line of questioning that drives the emergence of the newly emergent tradition.

The case studies in this chapter represent an admittedly limited data set. They are intended to illustrate the merit of an alternate approach to the question of how the *Tannaim* read the Torah. The dominant scholarly approach has been to engage the question primarily in light of evidence from *Midrash*, by parsing *Midrash*'s generic conventions as commentary. In contrast, this chapter uses the case studies to demonstrate the value in turning to *both* Mishnah and *Midrash*, and focusing on the unmarked interpretation that supplies the legal premises of both genres of *tannaitic* legal writing.

In sum, jurisprudential interpretation sets the terms for, and in a sense precedes, both *Midrash* and Mishnah as formal literary endeavors. The kind of interpretative work that has been reconstructed in this chapter should regarded as analogous to other jurisprudential interpretative endeavors of the Second Temple period, especially those attested at Qumran which are likewise focused on the law-dense portions of the Pentateuch. Following Michael Fishbane, I understand the kind of jurisprudential interpretative work reconstructed here to have its roots early in the Second Temple period, before the text of the Pentateuch was fixed.[52] In its *tannaitic* iteration, the signature moves of this kind of interpretative work are:

1. Reading biblical texts as records of case law.
2. Formalizing technical terms.
3. Introducing new cases related to those that are attested in the biblical passage.
4. Generating new rulings for biblically unattested cases.
5. Extracting governing principles from the rulings provided in the biblical passage.

Recognizing this type of interpretative work as distinct from the midrashic project of tying *tannaitic* legal traditions to biblical lexemes has an added advantage for the study of *Midrash*. Often, uninitiated students of *tannaitic Midrash* have difficulty making sense of *Midrash* as interpretative literature. The analytic framework of this chapter—which distinguishes the *interpretative process* that supplies the working premises of *Midrash* from the *commentarial rhetoric* represented by the generic conventions of *Midrash*—allows us to disentangle two distinct orientations to the biblical text in *Midrash*. Formally, midrashic discourse correlates units of rabbinic tradition with the biblically appropriate lexical units. While that way of rehearsing rabbinic tradition formally assigns newly emergent tradition a biblical origin, it leaves unmarked the interpretative work that yields the technical terms and legal concepts that constitute the *tannaitic* framing, which *Midrash* takes for granted. The astute reader senses that the interpretative process is more complex than midrashic rhetoric allows. This chapter explains how and why. If we are to understand how the *Tannaim* read the Torah, we should not focus exclusively on the moves marked explicitly as biblical interpretation. We must also explain how the repertoire of technical terms and legal concepts that are taken for granted in discussion of biblical legal topics throughout the *tannaitic* corpus came to be.

Notes

1. See Saul Lieberman, "The Publication of the Mishnah," in *Greek in Jewish Palestine/Hellenism in Jewish Palestine* (New York: Jewish Theological Seminary of America, 1994), 83–99.

2. Throughout this chapter, I use the term "Mishnah" as shorthand to refer to *halakhic* texts, a category that includes Tosefta as well as Mishnah.
3. James L. Kugel, *In Potiphar's House: The Interpretive Life of Biblical Texts*, 1st ed. (San Francisco: Harper San Francisco, 1990), 251–53.
4. Daniel Boyarin, *Intertextuality and the Reading of Midrash* (Bloomington: Indiana University Press, 1990), esp. 22–23.
5. Assaf Rosen-Zvi offers a valuable model for how to use the telltale traces of interpretative practice in legal texts to reconstruct unmarked, legal reading practices. See Assaf Rosen-Zvi, "Text Version, Redaction and Hermeneutics in the Mekhilta of Rabbi Ishmael, Masekhta D'kaspa" (PhD diss., Hebrew University, 2016), esp. 77–96 [Hebrew].
6. Important exceptions include Mira Balberg, *Purity, Body, and Self in Early Rabbinic Literature* (Berkeley: University of California Press, 2014); Mira Balberg, *Blood for Thought: The Reinvention of Sacrifice in Early Rabbinic Literature* (Oakland: University of California Press, 2017); and Chaya T. Halberstam, *Law and Truth in Biblical and Rabbinic Literature* (Bloomington: Indiana University Press, 2009). See also Tzvi Novick, "The Mishnah and the Bible," in *What Is the Mishnah? The State of the Question*, ed. Shaye J. D. Cohen (Cambridge, MA: Harvard University Press, 2023); and Alexander Samely, *Rabbinic Interpretation of Scripture in the Mishnah* (New York: Oxford University Press, 2002).
7. Recent explorations of *tannaitic* legal interpretation by means of *Midrash*'s rhetorical conventions include Azzan Yadin-Israel, *Scripture and Tradition: Rabbi Akiva and the Triumph of Midrash* (Philadelphia: University of Pennsylvania Press, 2014); Azzan Yadin-Israel, *Scripture as Logos: Rabbi Ishmael and the Origins of Midrash* (Philadelphia: University of Pennsylvania Press, 2004), and Ishay Rosen-Zvi, *Between Mishna and Midrash: The Birth of Rabbinic Literature* (Tel Aviv: Open University, 2020) [Hebrew].
8. See, e.g., m.Hagigah 1:8.
9. I associate the "hermeneutical rules" (*middot*) of interpretation (seven attributed to Hillel, thirteen to R. Yishmael) with the midrashic rhetoric of interpretation. I do not view the rules as central to the production of the *tannaitic* framing of biblical legal materials (technical terms and concepts).
10. On the generic conventions of commentary of *Midrash*, see Steven D. Fraade, *From Tradition to Commentary: Torah and Its Interpretation in the Midrash Sifre to Deuteronomy* (Albany: State University of New York Press, 1991), esp. 1–23 and Yakir Paz, *From Scribes to Scholars: Rabbinic Biblical Exegesis in Light of the Homeric Commentaries* (Tübingen, Germany: Mohr Siebeck, 2022).
11. Paul D. Mandel, *The Origins of Midrash: From Teaching to Text* (Leiden, The Netherlands: Brill, 2017), 289–94.
12. Menahem Kahana, "The Halakhic Midrashim," in *The Literature of the Sages Second Part: Midrash and Targum, Liturgy, Contracts, Inscriptions, Ancient Science and the Languages of Rabbinic Literature*, ed. Shmuel Safrai et al. (Leiden, The Netherlands: Brill Academic, 2006), 60.
13. Although, on the possibility of such a collection, see Aharon Mirsky, *A Tannaitic Midrash to Genesis* (Jerusalem: Mossad Harav Kook, 2000) [Hebrew].
14. The Mekhilta of R. Ishmael begins its exposition at Exodus 12:1. The Mekhilta of R. Shimon bar Yohai contains sporadic interpretation (of an *aggadic* nature) on the verses preceding Exodus 12:1. The interpreted verses are: Exodus 3:2, 3:7–8 and 6:2. W. David Nelson speculates that the *aggadic* material preceding Exodus 12:1 may not be *tannaitic*. W. David Nelson, *Mekhilta De-Rabbi Shimon Bar Yoḥai* (Philadelphia: Jewish Publication Society, 2006), xviii–xix.

15. For summary of scholarship, see Christine Hayes, "Intertextuality and Tannaic Literature," in *The Literature of the Sages: A Re-Visioning*, ed. Christine Hayes (Leiden, The Netherlands: Brill, 2022), 124–37, 61–62.
16. Collections associated with both schools appear to draw on a single common source of *aggadic* material. See Kahana, "Halakhic Midrashim," 44–46.
17. See ibid., 17–47.
18. See Steven D. Fraade, *Legal Fictions: Studies of Law and Narrative in the Discursive Worlds of Ancient Jewish Sectarians and Sages* (Leiden, The Netherlands: Brill, 2011), 408; and Paz, *Scribes to Scholars*, 167–226.
19. Scholars debate whether the previous paragraph concerns both male and female indentured servants, or only male ones. See summary in Hilary Lipka, "Women, Children, Slaves, and Foreigners," in *The Oxford Handbook of Biblical Law*, ed. Pamela Barmash (New York: Oxford University Press, 2019), 67–68.
20. All citations of rabbinic text are drawn from Ma'agrim (https://maagarim.hebrew-academy.org.il/Pages/PMain.aspx) and translated by the author.
21. Yadin-Israel, *Scripture as Logos*, esp. 11–69.
22. Rosen-Zvi, *Mishna and Midrash*, 272–338.
23. Jacob Milgrom, *Leviticus 1-16: A New Translation with Introduction and Commentary* (New York: Doubleday, 1991), 802.
24. Ibid., 800–2. Milgrom establishes the gender specificity of v. 44 in contrast to the broad relevance (gender and otherwise) of v. 45.
25. Rosen-Zvi, "Mekhilta Hermeneutics," 77–96 offers a paradigm for reconstructing this reading practice.
26. On the terminology associated with each school, see Kahana, "Halakhic Midrashim," 27.
27. See Fraade, *Tradition to Commentary*, and Paz, *Scribes to Scholars*.
28. Fraade, *Legal Fictions*, 392 distinguishes the *process that generates interpretation* from the *formal representation of interpretation in rabbinic commentary.*
29. Martin S. Jaffee, *Torah in the Mouth: Writing and Oral Tradition in Palestinian Judaism, 200 BCE-400 CE* (New York: Oxford University Press, 2001), 4.
30. Hermann Leberecht Strack and Günter Stemberger, *Introduction to the Talmud and Midrash* (Minneapolis, MN: Fortress Press, 1992), 145–56.
31. See Hayes, "Intertextuality," 165–96.
32. See Novick, "Mishnah and Bible," and Samely, *Interpretation in Mishnah*.
33. There are important, but not nearly as extensive, precedents in late Second Temple sources for organizing law by topical rubrics. See summary in Steven D. Fraade, *The Damascus Document* (New York: Oxford University Press, 2021), 7–8.
34. In addition to the midrashic parallels indicated in bold, the Mishnah includes parallels from elsewhere in Mishnah and *Midrash*. See m.Nazir 4:6–7, m.Sanhedrin 6:3–4, and Sifre Deuteronomy 231.
35. Michael A. Fishbane, *Biblical Interpretation in Ancient Israel* (New York: Oxford University Press, 1985), 230–77.
36. Ibid., 95.
37. Yael Landman, *Legal Writing, Legal Practice: The Biblical Bailment Law and Divine Justice* (Providence, RI: Brown Judaic Studies, 2022), uses the English legal term "bailment" to describe the arrangement.
38. Throughout the Mishnah, the number four functions as a structuring motif to indicate a complete paradigm. See m.Shabbat 1:1, m.Rosh Hashanah 1:1, 1:2, m.Baba Kamma 1:1,

m.Sanhedrin 7:1, m.Shevuot 1:1, 2:1, 3:1, 8:1, m.Eduyot 3:7, 3:9, 5:6, 5:7, m.Avot 5:10-15, m.Kelim 12:6, m.Negaim 1:1, 1:3, m.Taharot 6:2, m.Niddah 1:3.

39. David P. Wright, *Inventing God's Law: How the Covenant Code of the Bible Used and Revised the Laws of Hammurabi* (New York: Oxford University Press, 2009), 278. See also William Henry Propp, *Exodus 19–40: A New Translation with Introduction and Commentary* (New York: Doubleday, 2006), 252.
40. Fishbane, *Biblical Interpretation*, 239.
41. Following Wright, *Inventing God's Law*, 278.
42. On other, earlier stages in the theorization of the four guardians, see David Henshke, *An Early Iteration of Later Tannaitic Teaching: Passages in the Laws of Guardianship* [Mishnah Rishonah Be-Talmudam Shel Tana'im Aḥaronim: Sugyot Be-Dine Shomrim] (Ramat Gan: Universiṭat Bar-Ilan, 1997) [Hebrew].
43. Building on Elizabeth Shanks Alexander, *Transmitting Mishnah: The Shaping Influence of Oral Tradition* (New York: Cambridge University Press, 2006).
44. See Paz, *Scribes to Scholars*, 41–102; and Azzan Yadin-Israel, "The Halakhic Midrashim and the Canonicity of the Mishnah," in *What Is the Mishnah? The State of the Question: The Proceedings of a Conference at Harvard University*, ed. Shaye J. D. Cohen (Cambridge, MA: Harvard University Press, 2023), esp. 427–34.
45. Though, note the slight variation between the Mishnah's "wage-bearer" and the *Midrash*'s "guardian who accepts a wage." The terms differ slightly in the details, but reflect the same conceptual considerations and should be regarded as synonymous terms. See Alexander, *Transmitting Mishnah*, 64–73.
46. See Paz, *Scribes to Scholars*, 80–101. Paz describes a practice wherein the commentary links a freestanding, independent tradition to the biblical or Homeric text as "re-scripturizing tradition" This essay documents a related phenomenon: "re-scripturizing *interpretation*." In this case, the commentary correlates a newly emergent *interpretative* tradition with the biblical text.
47. See Alexander, *Transmitting Mishnah*, 117–73.
48. Balberg, *Purity, Body and Self*; and Balberg, *Blood for Thought*, demonstrate the interpretative depth of unmarked biblical interpretation in the Mishnah.
49. See Alexander, *Transmitting Mishnah*, 117–73.
50. See Hayes's review in "Intertextuality," 155–67.
51. For example, Dayid Halivni, *Midrash, Mishnah, and Gemara: The Jewish Predilection for Justified Law* (Cambridge, MA: Harvard University Press, 1986), 18–55.
52. Fishbane, *Biblical Interpretation*, 230–77.

CHAPTER 3

HOW DOES THE TALMUD READ THE MISHNAH?

LEIB MOSCOVITZ

INTRODUCTION: THE MISHNAH AND THE TALMUDS

THE Mishnah[1] is the central work of Jewish law (*halakhah*) stemming from the so-called *tannaitic* period[2] (see Shanks Alexander, this volume)—approximately the first two centuries of the Common Era and the beginning of the third century. This work, which was written in Hebrew and compiled in the land of Israel, where it was apparently edited by Rabbi Judah the Prince and/or his circle in the beginning of the third century CE, includes the legal rulings—for the most part, without explanation or justification—of numerous rabbis from multiple generations regarding virtually all aspects of Jewish law, both ritual and nonritual (civil and criminal law, etc.). The Mishnah also includes a relatively small amount of nonlegal material. Rulings in the Mishnah are often disputed, and thus the Mishnah is actually a compilation or anthology of the teachings of multiple scholars, although the precise nature and chronology of its redaction remain unclear. The work is organized thematically (with occasional deviations of various sorts from strict thematic organization), and it is divided into six "orders," each of which deals with different legal themes: (a) *Zera'im* ("seeds"), which deals primarily with agricultural law; (b) *Mo'ed* ("festival"), on the Jewish holidays; (c) *Nashim* ("women"), on marriage and divorce law, although various other topics are also discussed here; (d) *Nezikin* ("damages"), primarily on civil, criminal, and procedural law—in short, those aspects of *tannaitic* law which have parallels in modern legal systems; (e) *Kodashim* ("sacred matters"), primarily about the laws of sacrifices; and (f) *Tohorot* ("purities"), primarily about the laws of ritual purity and impurity. Each of these orders consists of multiple tractates (*massekhtot*), and each tractate deals with a particular area of law relevant to the specified order (e.g., Tractate *Pesahim*, which appears in Order *Mo'ed*, the order dealing with the festivals, discusses the laws of the Passover holiday). These tractates consist of multiple chapters, each of which consists of *mishnayot* ("paragraphs" or "subsections"). An individual subsection of this sort is also called a "Mishnah," so this term may denote either the mishnaic corpus as a whole (capitalized) or a subsection thereof (lowercase), depending upon the context. The work contains 524 chapters and close to 4,200 subsections, totaling close to 200,000 words, and was apparently composed and transmitted orally for centuries before finally being committed to writing (precisely when this happened is not clear).

As may be inferred from the list of themes treated by the Mishnah, some of the Mishnah's teachings were of practical import to its authors and their assumed audience (e.g., mishnaic discussions of the Sabbath laws), although others were not (e.g., the laws of sacrifices, since the Jerusalem Temple, where such sacrifices had previously been offered, was no longer in existence when the Mishnah was redacted). In addition, the Mishnah contains elements which would presumably render its use as a legal code problematic, notably the presence of internal contradictions and unresolved disputes between different rabbis. The aim of the Mishnah's compilation is thus unclear: among other possibilities,[3] the Mishnah may have been intended to serve as a study book or as a scholarly compilation with essentially theoretical and scholastic value, or perhaps as an authoritative legal code, even though the internal contradictions and unresolved disputes it contains would presumably render this problematic (but note that similar phenomena obtain in Justinian's *Digest*, which was meant to serve as an authoritative legal text). In any event, the Mishnah seems to have been conceived of as canonical and authoritative in at least some sense of these terms by many, and perhaps most, post-mishnaic Sages,[4] and its teachings, at least as interpreted by the Talmuds, form the basis for accepted Jewish legal praxis in subsequent generations.[5]

After the redaction of the Mishnah, two major works of rabbinic law—again, compilatory works, whose composition spanned the course of centuries and which include the teachings of numerous rabbis from multiple geographical centers—were produced: the Babylonian and Palestinian Talmuds ("Talmud" = "study" or "learning"). These works, which were written in a combination of Hebrew and Aramaic, were redacted in Babylonia and Palestine, respectively,[6] during the so-called Amoraic[7] period. Both of the Talmuds take the Mishnah as their principal point of departure,[8] and function in large measure as commentaries on that work, interpreting it section by section[9] from multiple perspectives, as set forth at length in this chapter. That said, mishnaic interpretation is by no means the sole component of the Talmuds; they also engage in such matters as biblical interpretation and homiletics, narrative (often nonlegal in character), legal decision-making (at times), and dialectical discussion of various types of legal issues.

While the Talmuds deal at length with matters of Jewish law generally and the Mishnah specifically, they differ significantly from both modern legal codes and classical commentaries on other works of Jewish literature, whether legal or nonlegal. Thus, the Talmuds are not collections of legal decisions, and they do not attempt to resolve all unresolved mishnaic disputes. Indeed, final and authoritative legal rulings do not occur that frequently in the Talmuds.[10] To be sure, the rulings of specific authorities are often quoted in the Talmuds, but these rulings are frequently disputed by other Sages, without any attempt to determine the legal "bottom line." Moreover, a great deal of the Talmuds is devoted to theoretical and scholastic legal analysis. This analysis is frequently formulated dialectically and discursively, and it takes the form of discussion and argumentation between different rabbis—questions and answers, objections and solutions, and so on—rather than straightforward commentary on the texts being discussed, whether the Mishnah or other texts. Accordingly, when we speak of "Talmudic law" in this chapter, we refer to all components of the Talmuds which deal with legal matters, even if these components are dialectical, analytical, or theoretical in nature and do not present the actual legal "bottom line."

The Mishnah and Its Interpretation

Regardless of what the purpose of the Mishnah's composition may have been—whether it was meant to serve as the basis for issuing legal rulings or for theoretical *halakhic* discussion (see the previous section), or something else—the Mishnah would have been largely useless without interpretation. This need for interpretation stems from a variety of factors. Aside from the fact that texts, and certainly legal texts, almost invariably require interpretation, certain characteristics specific to the Mishnah, as well as rabbinic ideas about how to read texts generally, made Mishnah exegesis[11] a necessity. These factors include the frequent brevity, obscurity, and ambiguity of the mishnaic text, which accordingly necessitated clarification of problematic passages, as well as the need to resolve seeming contradictions between mishnaic teachings and other rabbinic sources, including internal contradictions found in the Mishnah. This essay accordingly seeks to survey mishnaic exegesis in both Talmuds, presenting a taxonomy of the different types of Talmudic Mishnah interpretation and analyzing them from a variety of perspectives—chronological, geographical, legal, and hermeneutic—all of which, to be sure, are ultimately interrelated.

It should be noted that while this chapter focuses on how the Talmudic rabbis read the Mishnah, the phenomena surveyed here seem to be equally applicable to how these rabbis read other *tannaitic* sources.[12] Even though the Mishnah generally seems to have been considered more authoritative than other *tannaitic* sources, this does not seem to have prompted the development of different exegetical approaches to these different types of sources.

The Role of Mishnah Interpretation in the Talmuds

Mishnah exegesis plays a significant role in the Talmuds. Indeed, the Talmuds sometimes analyze aspects of the Mishnah which seem to have no legal or other substantive implications (e.g., stylistic features of the Mishnah, such as the order of items in a mishnaic list), although at times such exegesis might ultimately prove to have legal ramifications. Thus, Mishnah exegesis was frequently a textual activity no less than a legal one, although the boundaries between these two types of activity can obviously be blurry at times.

The academic and scholastic character of Talmudic Mishnah exegesis finds expression in other ways as well. For example, much Talmudic Mishnah exegesis deals with issues which had no practical import during Talmudic times,[13] such as the laws of sacrifices or ritual purity. Similarly, where multiple interpretations of mishnaic rulings were proposed, the Talmuds frequently make no attempt to determine which interpretation is correct or legally binding. Moreover, even mishnaic teachings which were rejected (e.g., minority viewpoints which were rejected because they were disputed by the majority of Sages, or the viewpoints of particular *tannaitic* Sages or schools which were deemed inauthoritative), were analyzed by the Talmuds in exactly the same way that accepted mishnaic teachings were.

At the same time, much Mishnah interpretation is clearly law-oriented. Thus, the application of legal rulings in the Mishnah obviously depends upon how those rulings are interpreted. The legal significance of Mishnah exegesis also finds expression in Talmudic passages where the Mishnah is adduced in order to support or challenge a particular legal ruling, since such a mishnaic statement, once reinterpreted, might no longer provide valid support for or grounds for objection to the viewpoint which it had initially meant to support or challenge. At the same time, it should be kept in mind that not all Talmudic legal discussion, whether theoretical or practical, was based on Mishnah interpretation. Other factors and types of material, including custom, court rulings, and especially extra-mishnaic *tannaitic* teachings and Mishnah-independent Amoraic dicta, also played a significant role in the development of Talmudic law.

Finally, it should be emphasized that from the perspective of most post-Talmudic Jewish legal sources[14]—and, presumably,[15] of the Talmuds themselves—it is the Talmudically interpreted Mishnah which was deemed authoritative for legal purposes and not the Mishnah according to its plain sense, and as noted elsewhere in this chapter (see, e.g., the end of the section "Intertextual Interpretation and Harmonistic Exegesis"), these readings of the Mishnah often differ. That said, the "plain sense" Mishnah was studied, mainly for theoretical and academic purposes, in various times, places, and circles, both academic and traditional, during the post-Talmudic period.[16]

Frameworks of Talmudic Mishnah Exegesis

Talmudic Mishnah exegesis took place in various frameworks. The most prominent of these is the direct explanation of mishnaic passages which serve as the basis for the local Talmudic discussion, whether in the form of direct comments on the Mishnah (e.g.,

"The mishnah applies in case X") or in response to rhetorical questions (e.g., "What is the reason for this [Mishnaic ruling]?"). However, due to the Talmuds' dialectical and discursive character, Mishnah interpretation also took place in other types of contexts—essentially, secondary contexts, in which a mishnaic ruling was adduced, and frequently reinterpreted, in the course of analyzing other rulings, e.g., in the course of attempting to support or challenge such a ruling based on a mishnaic statement.[17] For example, the Babylonian Talmud states (b.Mo'ed Qatan 18b):

1. Samuel said, It is permitted to betroth a woman during the intermediate days of a festival, lest someone else precede him [and betroth the woman before he does].
2. Shall we say that this [m.Mo'ed Katan 3:3] supports him: "These may be written on the intermediate days of a festival: *kiddushin* [literally 'betrothal'] of women"?
3. No, [the mishnah refers to] documents of stipulation [which record how much parents agree to pay as dowries for their children].

In 2, the Talmud asks whether support for the ruling in 1 (attributed to the Babylonian Amora Samuel) permitting betrothal of a woman on the intermediate days of a festival may be adduced from the Mishnah's statement that one may write documents of betrothal (*kiddushin*) then, which would seem to imply that such betrothal is permitted. However, the Talmud rejects this possibility (in 3) by offering a new interpretation of the Mishnah, suggesting that it refers not to "betrothal" (which is the plain meaning of the Mishnah cited), but to documents which specify dowries. Thus, the Talmud's interpretation of the Mishnah cited in 2 was not offered in the course of attempting to clarify its meaning *ab initio*, but rather in the course of analyzing a later, Amoraic ruling—specifically, attempting to determine whether the Mishnah provides valid support for the ruling cited in 1.

Finally, Talmudic Mishnah interpretation sometimes finds expression in the Talmuds' citation of explanatory *Baraitot*, viz., extra-mishnaic sources composed during the *tannaitic* period which interpret mishnaic teachings (e.g., by stating "When does this [Mishnaic statement] apply? When . . ."). And while such *baraitot*, in contrast to most of the material on which this chapter focuses, were themselves composed during the *tannaitic* period, the Talmuds' decision to cite these sources is presumably the handiwork of the Talmuds' authors or redactors. Accordingly, the inclusion of such sources in the Talmuds may rightfully be considered part of the Talmudic project of interpreting the Mishnah.

Unity and Diversity in Mishnah Interpretation

Considerable diversity obtained with regard to how the Talmudic rabbis read the Mishnah: these Sages were far from a uniform or monolithic body, a phenomenon which also finds expression with regard to numerous other aspects of rabbinic literature. Thus, particular mishnayot are often interpreted in different ways by different rabbis. Moreover, different approaches to Mishnah interpretation are apparently found in rabbinic literature (see the section "Geographical and Chronological Aspects of Mishnaic Interpretation").

This diversity notwithstanding, the principal types of Mishnah exegesis, as well as a considerable common core of exegetical approaches, seem to have been shared by rabbinic interpreters of the Mishnah throughout the Talmudic period in both Palestine and Babylonia. Hence, this chapter generally speaks of Mishnah interpretation by the Talmudic rabbis or the Talmuds without distinguishing between particular Sages or groups of Sages, although such distinctions will be noted where relevant; see especially the section "Geographical and Chronological Aspects of Mishnaic Interpretation."

Previous Scholarship and Desiderata for Future Research

Virtually all aspects of Mishnah exegesis treated in this chapter have been discussed by scholarly, and at times traditional, writers from a variety of perspectives—philological, historical, hermeneutic, and ideological-theological (although the scope, focus, and quality of these discussions obviously varies). Even so, there is still room for further discussion of various aspects of Talmudic Mishnah exegesis, and two principal themes in this connection should be noted here.[18] First, more detailed and nuanced description and characterization of the different approaches to Mishnah interpretation adopted by different Sages, in different periods and geographical centers, is necessary. Second, the phenomenon of forced Talmudic interpretation of the Mishnah, which has admittedly been the subject of considerable previous discussion (see the section "Hermeneutic Aspects of Talmudic Mishnah Interpretation"), requires further consideration, in order to better clarify its exact scope, character, and hermeneutic basis.

Types of Mishnah Interpretation

Various types of Mishnah interpretation are found in the Talmuds.[19] Here we address each of these separately, although the boundary lines between them are sometimes fuzzy, and at times they are interrelated or overlap. Moreover, the legal conclusions which emerge from Talmudic analysis of the Mishnah often stem from the combination of multiple modes of Mishnah interpretation.

Textual Interpretation

Various types of textual interpretation are found in the Talmuds, and, as is well-nigh inevitable with a legal text, almost all of these types of interpretation may have legal ramifications. Moreover, analysis of these types of Mishnah interpretation can sometimes shed light on such fundamental issues as the sources of Talmudic Mishnah interpretation, the type and degree of authority which the Talmudic rabbis attributed to the mishnaic text, and the like.

Lexical Interpretation

Many Talmudic passages present lexical interpretations of mishnaic words or expressions—frequently, translations or dictionary definitions of obscure or unfamiliar mishnaic terminology (e.g., words of foreign extraction, especially words of Greek or Latin origin).

Significantly, these Talmudic interpretations do not always reflect the meaning of the relevant expressions as understood by modern philology. In such instances the Talmudic interpretations were presumably based on conjecture, rather than on historically accurate traditions about the meaning of the mishnaic text.[20]

"Ordinary" Textual Exegesis

The Talmuds include various types of ordinary textual exegesis. These include[21] clarifying the referents of obscure or ambiguous mishnaic phrases and illuminating the scope of mishnaic teachings. For example, where a list of cases appears in the Mishnah, the Talmuds may discuss whether the list should be taken as exhaustive or exemplary: sometimes the Mishnah was interpreted expansively and sometimes restrictively. In short, any aspect of the Mishnah which is unclear is likely to be the subject of textual exegesis of this sort.

Textual Criticism and Emendation

The Talmudic Sages engaged in various types of text-critical activities. These include attempts to determine the correct reading of the Mishnah, as this was not always clear[22] (e.g., "what shall we teach,[23] [reading X] or [reading Y?]"); citation and analysis of variant readings of the mishnaic text (e.g., "there is one Tanna who teaches [reading X] and one Tanna who teaches [reading Y]; according to the first Tanna . . . according to the second Tanna . . ."); and, at times, emendation of the mishnaic text.[24] Such emendations often entail modification of the substance of the Mishnah and not just its style.

The motivations behind and text-critical character of Talmudic emendations of the Mishnah vary from Sage to Sage and from passage to passage. These emendations were often motivated by textual and interpretative difficulties of various sorts, whether artificial or bona fide, or under the influence of alternative *tannaitic* traditions. In cases of the latter sort, emendation entails the de facto rejection of mishnaic rulings in favor of competing traditions (cf. the following section), at the same time maintaining pro forma adherence to the Mishnah (for the hermeneutic basis of this tactic, see the section "Hermeneutic Aspects of Talmudic Mishnah Interpretation"). It should be stressed that Talmudic emendations of the Mishnah often (generally?) seem to be conjectural, and they are nowhere supported in the Talmuds by reference to alternative, written texts of the Mishnah.[25]

Rejection of Mishnaic Teachings

Even more radical than emendations of the types considered in the previous section are Amoraic assertions—usually, from the earlier Amoraic generations—which explicitly reject mishnaic teachings as inauthoritative.[26] It should be stressed, however, that these statements do not reject mishnaic authority as a whole, but only particular mishnaic statements. Accordingly, such assertions function in a manner which is ultimately similar, though not identical, to emendation of the Mishnah.

Source Criticism of the Mishnah

As noted in the introductory section of this chapter, the Mishnah is an anthological work which contains the teachings of numerous Sages, even if we assume that its final redaction was the work of a single scholar, R. Judah the Prince. Thus, rulings in the Mishnah, even if they are anonymous, do not necessarily reflect the view of all mishnaic Sages. Accordingly, one of the modes of Mishnah interpretation practiced by the Talmudic rabbis was mishnaic source criticism—determining the identity of the Sages whose viewpoints presumably underlay particular mishnaic rulings (generally anonymous rulings). For example, the discussion of m.Megillah 2:4 in the Babylonian Talmud (b.Megillah 19b) states:

1. [Mishnah] Everyone is acceptable to read the Megillah [=the biblical book of Esther read on the festival of Purim], except for one who is deaf...
2. [Talmud] Who taught that someone who is deaf is not acceptable...?
3. Rav Mattanah said, It is Rabbi Yose, as we have learned [m.Berakhot 2:3]: "One who read the *Shema* [Deuteronomy 6:4ff.] inaudibly (literally, "not made it heard by his ear") has fulfilled his obligation. Rabbi Yose said, He has not fulfilled his obligation."

Here the Talmud suggests that the anonymous ruling in 1, which disqualifies deaf people from reading the Megillah, actually reflects the view of a single *Tanna*, Rabbi Yose (cited in 3). To be sure, Rabbi Yose does not deal with reading the Megillah, but with an entirely different issue: reciting the *Shema*.[27] Nevertheless, the Talmud assumes that the legal issue underlying both rulings is identical—is recitation in ritual frameworks which was not heard by the reciter legally acceptable. Hence the Talmud concludes that the ruling of Mishnah Megillah reflects the view of Rabbi Yose, even though his ruling appears in a different literary context and seemingly addresses a different issue, viz., inaudible recitation of the *Shema*.

Mishnaic source criticism serves multiple functions.[28] At times it seems to be an essentially technical and philological endeavor—analysis of the Mishnah's sources for its own sake. Of course, such source criticism could have legal ramifications: if an anonymous and seemingly undisputed Mishnah was shown (or claimed) to reflect the view of a Sage which was rejected (e.g., because his was a minority opinion), the ruling of the relevant Mishnah would have to be rejected.

Elsewhere, Talmudic source criticism of the Mishnah served as a tool for legal exegesis. Thus, at times the Tanna whose viewpoint is claimed by the Talmuds to underlie a particular mishnaic statement ("the mishnah is in accordance with Tanna X, who says/holds . . .") deals with a different case, as in the example from b.Megillah 19b discussed earlier in this section. In such instances, identification of this *Tanna* ultimately serves as an explanatory technique, whereby the legal principle underlying the relevant Mishnah is identified as that espoused by the aforementioned *Tanna*, whether explicitly or implicitly. In such instances, then, Talmudic source criticism of the Mishnah serves as a legal tool no less than a philological tool.

Stylistic Aspects of the Mishnah

Many Talmudic discussions of the Mishnah address stylistic aspects of the work, under the assumption that the Mishnah is formulated with tremendous and perhaps even absolute precision and concision (see further the end of this section). At times these Talmudic treatments of the Mishnah analyze it in much the same way as other rabbinic sources, especially the *halakhic* Midrashim composed during the *tannaitic* period, interpreted the biblical text.[29] Such interpretation apparently assumes that the Mishnah's formulation is so precise that extraordinarily close readings of its text are justified, including the discovery of deeper textual meanings which seem far removed from its plain sense (see also the sections "Different *Amoraim*: Abbaye and Rava" and "Hermeneutic Aspects of Talmudic Mishnah Interpretation"). Among the various types of stylistic analysis of the Mishnah appearing in the Talmuds we may note the following:[30]

1. Often statements in the Mishnah seem superfluous, whether because their content seems obvious on logical grounds or because they repeat ideas found elsewhere, whether explicitly or implicitly, in the Mishnah or other *tannaitic* sources. Hence the Talmuds, and particularly the Babylonian Talmud, frequently attempt to account for the inclusion of such material in the Mishnah.

Two principal techniques were employed to account for the inclusion of seemingly superfluous mishnaic teachings. Sometimes the Talmuds maintain that this material is in fact superfluous, and its inclusion is accordingly explained on the basis of literary or stylistic considerations. Thus, the Talmud assumes that the Mishnah was not formulated with absolute concision in such cases.

Elsewhere, though—and this technique seems to be far more common—the Talmuds claim that the Mishnah included material which, though seemingly superfluous, was in fact necessary, because it was intended to teach us something (usually, by implication) which we might otherwise not have known. This approach, in contrast to the previous one, assumes that the Mishnah does not contain superfluous material, although the significance of the Mishnah's statements may lie more in what they imply (as understood by the Talmuds) than in what they state explicitly. For example, the discussion of m.Berakhot 3:3 in the Babylonian Talmud (b.Berakhot 20b) states:

1. [Mishnah] Women . . . are exempt from reciting the *Shema*.
2. [Talmud] This is obvious! [For reciting the *Shema*] is a positive commandment with a fixed time, and women are exempt from all positive commandments with fixed times [see m.Kiddushin 1:7]!
3. Lest you say: Since [the *Shema*] entails [acceptance of] the yoke of Heaven—[therefore the Mishnah] teaches us [that women are exempt from reciting the *Shema*].

The Mishnah's statement in 1 that women are exempt from reciting the *Shema* seems superfluous, at least to a reader familiar with the rest of the Mishnah, since another mishnaic passage (m.Kiddushin 1:7) states that women are exempt from all commandments with fixed times, and recitation of the *Shema* falls under this category, as may be readily inferred from other passages in m.Berakhot (not cited here). The Talmud accordingly explains in 3 that the Mishnah's ruling in 1 was necessary to prevent a potential error. For without the ruling in 1 we might have thought that recitation of the *Shema* is an exception to the general rule exempting women from time-bound commandments, since recitation of the *Shema* entails "acceptance of the yoke of Heaven," which, due to its special importance, would presumably devolve upon women as well, even though this is a time-bound obligation. Hence the Mishnah's inclusion of 1 was necessary to prevent the reader from drawing such an erroneous conclusion.

2. The Talmuds frequently draw inferences from the choice of words in the Mishnah (*diyyuk*; see especially Melamed, 1973, 370–72), even where this choice of words could be attributed to stylistic considerations rather than to the Mishnah attempting to imply some substantive conclusion. Among the types of *diyyuk* found in the Talmuds are inferences from the Mishnah's choice of examples; its use of a particular phrase rather than another, seemingly synonymous expression (e.g., "I am liable [to pay] *compensation for* its damage," rather than just "liable for its damage"; see Melamed, 1973, 371); and especially inferences affirming that the inverse of a conditional mishnaic statement is correct (e.g., if the Mishnah states "If X then Y," then we may infer that "if not X, then not Y"), even though such inferences are not valid under classical logic. Presumably, the Talmuds' willingness to draw such inferences is predicated on the assumption that the Mishnah was formulated with such great precision that deductions of this sort were considered exegetically viable.

Legal Interpretation

The Mishnah frequently fails to supply the reasons for its rulings.[31] Hence one of the most important types of Talmudic Mishnah interpretation entails determining the legal basis of mishnaic rulings. Such interpretation not only enables us to understand the reasoning behind the relevant mishnaic rulings, but it facilitates application of the law to other cases which are not discussed in the Mishnah.

Various types of reasons for mishnaic rulings are proposed in the Talmuds. These include biblical exegesis, often based on *halakhic* midrashim from the *tannaitic* period; rabbinic decrees prescribing or proscribing a particular action,[32] generally with the aim of furthering various types of policy-related goals; and logical reasoning of various sorts (*sevara*), including abstract and wide-ranging legal principles (e.g., "there is retrospective determination of reality," "designation is [legally] significant").[33] Abstract principles of this sort facilitate application of the law to cases from multiple legal domains even where such cases seem unrelated, and perhaps even based on totally different considerations.

Geographical and Chronological Aspects of Mishnaic Interpretation

Different approaches to Mishnah interpretation seem to have been adopted by different Sages and groups of Sages, and in different geographical centers and chronological periods. Here we survey some of the most prominent phenomena of this sort without attempting to be exhaustive; as noted earlier in this chapter, this issue requires further research. In any event, it should be stressed that these approaches were not always implemented with absolute consistency, as they often reflect general tendencies rather than universally adopted methodologies.

Between the Babylonian and Palestinian Talmuds

Scholars have noted various differences between the approaches to Mishnah interpretation in the Palestinian and Babylonian Talmuds.[34] These include the Palestinian Talmud's more widespread tendency to explain the Mishnah according to its plain sense (although forced explanations of the Mishnah are also found in this Talmud);[35] the Babylonian Talmud's stronger inclination to interpret mishnaic teachings as reflecting abstract and wide-ranging legal principles;[36] the Babylonian Talmud's tendency to explain mishnaic prohibitions as rabbinic decrees aimed at preventing the inadvertent violation of Torah precepts, rather than as independent, "first-order" prohibitions;[37] and the Babylonian Talmud's tendency to engage in certain types of forced stylistic inference.[38]

How are we to account for these differences? Two complementary possibilities may be considered. Perhaps these differences are attributable to geographical considerations, as different interpretative approaches developed, or were adopted or dominant, in the different centers. These differences might also be rooted in chronological factors: the

Amoraic period in the Babylonian Talmud lasted much longer than the Amoraic period in the Palestinian Talmud, and the Babylonian Talmud seems to contain a redactional stratum of post-Amoraic provenance which had no parallel in the Palestinian study centers. Thus, different approaches to Mishnah interpretation in the two Talmuds might be attributable to the later Sages of the Babylonian Talmud, whose exegetical approaches differed from those of the earlier scholars cited in the Palestinian Talmud.

Attributed and Anonymous Material in the Babylonian Talmud

A widely, though by no means universally, accepted view among contemporary Talmud scholars attributes much of the anonymous material in the Babylonian Talmud to post-Amoraic Sages,[39] and it has been suggested that the differences between these strata of the Talmud find expression, inter alia, in their approaches to Mishnah interpretation. In particular, Avinoam Cohen[40] has argued that attributed Amoraic material in the Babylonian Talmud focuses on analysis of the substance of mishnaic teachings (e.g., eliminating seeming contradictions between this material and other sources). In contrast, the anonymous and supposedly later material deals more with the style of the Mishnah than its content—in particular, attempting to justify the inclusion of seemingly superfluous teachings in the Mishnah, an issue which, it has been argued, was of comparatively little concern to the *Amoraim*.[41]

Different *Amoraim*: Abbaye and Rava

Scholars have noted that two of the most prominent *Amoraim* in the Babylonian Talmud, the fourth-generation scholars Abbaye and Rava, frequently disagree about how to interpret the Mishnah.[42] More specifically, Abbaye tended to emend problematic mishnaic teachings, whereas Rava tended to accept the mishnaic text as is, resolving its difficulties by subjecting it to innovative and often forced exegesis. David Henshke saw this dispute as reflective of a wider difference of opinion about the Mishnah's status, with Rava maintaining that the Mishnah enjoys quasi-canonical status (a view which Abbaye rejected), and hence he considered the mishnaic text unalterable.[43] At the same time, precisely because its text was deemed unalterable, the mishnaic text could be interpreted creatively and in forced fashion, in much the same way as the rabbis interpreted the biblical text.[44]

Saboraic Interpretation of the Mishnah

Certain passages in the Babylonian Talmud were attributed by medieval rabbis to a group of post-Amoraic scholars, the so-called *Sabora'im* or "explainers." While the exact chronology, nature, and scope of the *Sabora'im*'s contribution to the Talmud is not fully clear,[45] some of the passages explicitly attributed or at least plausibly attributable to these figures—often, the opening sections of Talmudic tractates[46]—interpret the Mishnah in fashions largely unattested in the rest of the Talmuds—for example, through grammatical analysis of the Mishnah's wording in a fashion which has no impact on the meaning of the text (e.g., analyzing the gender of nouns in the Mishnah). Accordingly, it has been suggested[47] that this approach to Mishnah interpretation—which, admittedly, is comparatively rare—should be attributed to the Saboraim's putative audience, which might have been less concerned with substantive issues and more interested in peripheral aspects of mishnaic formulation, although this claim requires further analysis.

Intertextual Interpretation and Harmonistic Exegesis

The rabbis read the Mishnah intertextually, constantly comparing it to other sources. These could be *tannaitic* sources, whether found elsewhere in the Mishnah or outside the Mishnah (including *halakhic* Midrashim, which were sometimes adduced as a source for mishnaic legal rulings), or Amoraic sources. Sources of all these sorts, as well as other types of legal sources, notably a priori legal reasoning and actual legal praxis, often contradicted mishnaic teachings, and the Talmudic rabbis frequently attempted to resolve such contradictions.

A variety of strategies were employed toward this aim. (Why a particular tactic was adopted in any given case is not always clear; this may reflect the general exegetical approach of a particular Sage, the agenda of the redactors of a particular Talmudic passage, or other considerations.) At times the Talmudic rabbis openly admitted the existence of contradictions, stating that the different passages reflect the views of different Sages (e.g., "[the Sage] who taught this did not teach that," "it is [the teaching of] two Tannaim"), even where there is no explicit indication of this in the mishnaic text and where such an interpretation might seem unlikely (e.g., where both of the contradictory statements appear together in the same Mishnah and both are anonymous, suggesting that both are attributable to a single, if unnamed authority). This approach, which assumes that not all statements in the Mishnah reflect a single and universally accepted point of view, coheres well with the fact noted in the section "Source Criticism of the Mishnah" that *tannaitic* literature is not compositionally or legally monolithic. Likewise, the Talmudic rabbis sometimes emended problematic sources in order to resolve contradictions and other types of difficulties.

Far more often, however, the Talmudic Sages attempted to resolve contradictions between the Mishnah and other sources through harmonistic exegesis of various sorts. Thus, contradictions were sometimes resolved through the use of factual or legal distinctions between seemingly contradictory rulings. For example, the Babylonian Talmud's discussion (b.Bava Metzi'a 37a) of m.Bava Metzi'a 3:3 states:

1. [Mishnah] If someone said to two people: I stole from one of you a *maneh* [an amount of money], and I don't know [from] which of you . . . he gives this one a *maneh* and that one a *maneh*.
2. [Talmud] Hence, [we may infer that] in [cases of] uncertainty, we expropriate property [i.e., the additional *maneh*, since the thief only stole one *maneh* but must nevertheless pay two]! An objection was raised [m.Bava Metzi'a 3:4]: "If two people deposited something with one person, this one a *maneh* and the other one two *maneh*—he gives this one a *maneh* and that one a *maneh*, and leaves the rest alone!" . . .
3. They said, Can you compare theft to deposit? In [a case of] theft, where one violated a prohibition, the rabbis fined him; in [a case of] deposit, where one did not violate a prohibition, the rabbis did not fine him.

The Talmud attempts to resolve a contradiction between two mishnaic passages. According to the first passage, if someone who stole money is uncertain about the identity of the victim, he must fully reimburse both of the people from whom he might have stolen, whereas according to the second passage, if a bailee is uncertain about how much money each person deposited with him, he need not provide maximum compensation to both of the possible depositors. The Talmud's solution, like many other solutions to contradictions from the Mishnah, is based on a legal distinction: expropriation in cases of uncertainty is only required where the person who owes money is guilty of a crime (theft), but not in other cases—for example, where he was a bailee. Such a distinction, though not explicit in the mishnaic text, certainly seems plausible, and the same applies to many other Talmudic distinctions which are used to resolve contradictions.

Elsewhere, however, the Talmuds adopt a different tack: problematic sources were subjected to various types of reinterpretation. In particular, the Talmuds frequently subject the Mishnah and related texts to restrictive interpretation, whereby one or more of the sources was claimed to apply only in a particular case, even though there is no indication of this in the texts under consideration. For example, the discussion of m. Makkot 2:2 in the Babylonian Talmud (b.Makkot 8a) states:

1. [Mishnah] One who throws a stone into a public domain and killed [someone there] is exiled [exile being the punishment prescribed by Jewish law for unintentional killing; see e.g. Numbers 35:11].
2. [Talmud] [Throwing a stone] into a public domain—this is intentional! [And intentional murder is subject under Jewish law to capital punishment, not exile!]
3. Rav Samuel Bar Isaac said, [The Mishnah refers] to someone who is tearing down his [stone] wall.
4. Then [the person who tore down the wall] should have looked [to make sure that no one would be hurt]! –

5. [The Mishnah refers to a case] where one tore down his wall at night [when it is rare that people are in the public domain, and hence the killing is deemed unintentional].
6. At night he should also have looked! –
7. [The Mishnah refers to a case] where he tore down his wall at night into a scrap heap [and then it is almost certain that no one is present, so the killing is deemed unintentional].

According to the Mishnah's ruling in 1, someone who killed another person by throwing a stone into a public domain is deemed guilty of manslaughter rather than first-degree murder. However, the Talmud (2) objects that this makes no sense: since people are presumably present at all times in a public domain, and this is obvious to anyone who throws stones there, throwing a stone into such an area should presumably be treated as first-degree murder! The Talmud resolves this difficulty by reinterpreting the statement in 1 as referring to someone who demolished a stone wall, as a result of which a stone fell upon someone and killed him, but not to a case where someone actually threw a stone into the public domain, as implied by the plain sense of the Mishnah. Yet even this radical reinterpretation of the Mishnah does not satisfy the Talmud: it argues (in 4) that this sort of killing should also be treated as intentional, since the person demolishing the wall failed to exercise proper caution when doing so. The Talmud accordingly claims that the Mishnah refers to a case where a stone fell in the course of demolishing a wall at night, when presumably no one else would be present, but there is not the slightest indication of any of this in the Mishnah.

The exegetical plausibility of the various interpretative techniques discussed here, and of the use of restrictive interpretation in particular, varies from case to case. At times such approaches seem plausible, but in other instances (such as the example from b.Makkot 8a just considered) the harmonistic exegesis found in the Talmud seems strained, and the Talmuds' reading of the Mishnah seems like a poorly disguised attempt to forcibly harmonize the Mishnah with contradictory literary sources or legal assumptions. Accordingly, the motivation behind and hermeneutic basis of such interpretations require further analysis, and we discuss these issues at greater length in the next section.

Hermeneutic Aspects of Talmudic Mishnah Interpretation

A fundamental question arises in connection with almost every Talmudic reading of the Mishnah: to what extent does it reflect the original intent of the Mishnah's authors? Similarly, to what extent are Talmudic interpretations of the Mishnah based on earlier traditions about the meaning of the Mishnah to which the post-mishnaic Sages had access, and to what extent are these interpretations conjectural, even if they accurately reflect the original meaning of the Mishnah?

In fact, the exegetical validity of Talmudic Mishnah interpretations apparently varies from case to case. Some of these interpretations seem to reflect the plain sense of the Mishnah and hence, presumably, the original intention of its authors, while other interpretations—mainly, forced interpretations of the sorts described in the previous section—do not. Of course, it is not always possible to reliably assess the exegetical validity of any particular interpretation of the Mishnah found in the Talmuds.

As for the dependence of Talmudic interpretations of the Mishnah on earlier interpretative traditions, the fact that the Talmudic rabbis often disagreed about how to interpret the Mishnah suggests that many of their interpretations were the product of conjecture rather than tradition. Nevertheless, it is possible that at least some interpretations of the Mishnah were based on tradition.

We now return to what is probably the most problematic aspect of Talmudic Mishnah interpretation, hermeneutically speaking: the frequent appearance in the Talmuds of forced interpretations of the Mishnah. In many of these cases it is evident that these interpretations contradict the plain sense of the Mishnah (see, e.g., the passage from b.Makkot 8a discussed at the end of the previous section), and it is inconceivable that the Sages who offered these interpretations could not have been aware of this.[48] How then could the rabbis have suggested such explanations?[49] And while the *motivation* behind such exegesis generally seems clear—the need to resolve problems with the mishnaic text, including but not limited to the need to bring it into conformance with other legal rulings or approaches which seemed superior on a priori grounds, or which reflected actual *halakhic* praxis—the question remains: why not simply emend the Mishnah in such cases or reject its rulings outright? What value was there in paying mere lip service to the Mishnah? And if the Mishnah was truly considered authoritative, on what basis was its real meaning rejected in favor of other "meanings" which the Mishnah itself clearly never intended?

These issues have been addressed by scholars of various sorts—traditional students of rabbinic literature, academic Talmudists, and students of hermeneutic theory—who have suggested a variety of possible solutions.[50] These solutions—all unpersuasive, to my mind—include such notions as the possibility of adopting a mystical approach toward Mishnah interpretation; treating Mishnah interpretation as a sort of "language game"; interpreting the Mishnah as referring to an ideal world (in the Platonic sense), whose realization in the actual world is only possible through the use of restrictive interpretation; and so on.

More likely, to my mind, is the possibility that the rabbis who interpreted the Mishnah in this fashion adopted a more flexible, expansive and, perhaps, pre-modern, conception of the authority and meaning of texts, one ostensibly at odds with classical or modern approaches to textual interpretation. Specifically, the Talmudic rabbis might have considered such texts substantively malleable, with their meaning ultimately dependent upon text-independent "legal truth" and similar considerations.[51] Hence these texts were deemed capable of exegetical transformation where necessary. On this approach, the authority of the Mishnah was not violated and its meaning was not misconstrued when the work was subjected to creative reinterpretation of the sort found in the Talmuds. That said, this suggestion, offered here tentatively, requires considerable further consideration.

CONCLUSION

The Talmuds serve in large measure as textual and legal commentary on the Mishnah. In particular, Talmudic law in both its theoretical-analytic and practical expressions is frequently based on Mishnah study and interpretation, even though these were admittedly not the sole source of Talmudic law. The Talmuds did not study the Mishnah in isolation, as a self-contained document, but in light of other Jewish legal sources, whether other literary sources, especially other mishnaic passages or other *tannaitic* sources, or a priori logical reasoning (*sevara*); as with rabbinic biblical exegesis, intertextual reading was the order of the day. The result, quite frequently, was harmonistic interpretation of the Mishnah (or emendation of the Mishnah), which generated new, and at times forced, interpretations—actually, reinterpretations—of this text. And while the Mishnah seems to have been conceived of as canonical and authoritative in at least some sense of the word by many, and perhaps most, post-mishnaic Sages, in the final analysis the Mishnah's authority was by no means absolute, as it—or, more precisely, its plain meaning—was often trumped by external legal and exegetical considerations, with the plain sense of its text yielding to the force of interpretation.

NOTES

1. The best introduction to the Mishnah is Ishay Rosen-Zvi, "Mavo La-Mishnah," in *Sifrut Hazal Ha-Eretz Yisre'elit, Mevo'ot U-Mehkarim*, ed. Menahem Kahana et al., 1:1–64 (Jerusalem: Yad Yitzhak Ben-Zvi, 2018). For an extremely brief but nevertheless helpful and up-to-date scholarly description of the Mishnah's most prominent characteristics, see Shaye J. D. Cohen and Hayim Lapin, "Introduction," in *The Oxford Annotated Mishnah*, ed. Shaye J. D. Cohen, Robert Goldenberg, and Hayim Lapin, 1:1–6 (Oxford: Oxford University Press, 2022); the three volumes of this work present an annotated translation of the entire Mishnah. In addition, openly accessible texts, commentary, and English translation of the Mishnah are available online at https://www.sefaria.org/texts/Mishnah, although these are not scholarly editions.
2. The term "*tannaitic*" is derived from the Hebrew *tanna'im* ("teachers" or, somewhat more literally, "reciters"), and designates the rabbinic Sages who flourished during the first two centuries of the Common Era and the beginning of the third century. Many of their teachings are cited in the Mishnah, while other teachings of these Sages are found in other rabbinic compilations from this period.
3. For a comprehensive survey, see Yaakov Elman, "Order, Sequence, and Selection: The Mishnah's Anthological Choices," in *The Anthology in Jewish Literature*, ed. David Stern (Oxford: Oxford University Press, 2004), 53–80.

4. See generally Shlomo Zalman Havlin, "'Al 'Ha-Hatimah Ha-Sifrutit' Ki-Ysod Ha-Halukkah Li-Tekufot Ba-Halakhah," in *Mehkarim Be-Sifrut Ha-Talmudit, Yom Iyyun Le-Regel Melot Shemonim Shanah Le-Shaul Lieberman*, 148–92 (Jerusalem: Israel Academy of Sciences and Humanities, 1983); David Halivni, "The Reception Accorded to Rabbi Judah's Mishnah," in *Jewish and Christian Self-Definition, Vol. 2: Aspects of Judaism in the Graeco-Roman Period*, ed. E. P. Sanders with A. I. Baumgarten and Alan Mendelson (London: S.C.M. Press, 1981), 204–12; and cf. Menahem I. Kahana, "*Mippenei Tikkun Ha-Olam*": *Talmud Bavli Massekhet Gittin Perek Revi'i* (Jerusalem: Magnes, 2020), 19 n. 4. See also Isaac M. Landes, "The Transmission of the Mishnah and the Spread of Rabbinic Judaism, 200 CE–1200 CE" (PhD diss., Princeton University, 2023), chs. 1–3, passim.
5. See the section "The Role of Mishnah Interpretation in the Talmuds."
6. Precisely when, how, why, and by whom are the subjects of much scholarly debate. Here I eschew further discussion of these issues, which in any case are of minimal importance for the discussion in this chapter.
7. From the word *amora* ("expounder"), the term used to describe those post-*tannaitic* Sages who are identified by name in the Talmuds. Both Talmuds also include anonymous teachings, whose chronological provenance may differ from that of the attributed Amoraic teachings. See further in the section "Attributed and Anonymous Material in the Babylonian Talmud."
8. While extra-mishnaic teachings of various sorts undoubtedly played a major role in the formation and composition of the Talmuds; see, e.g., the literature surveyed in Hanan Mazeh, "Massekhet Demai Ba-Talmud Ha-Yerushalmi: Parshanut, Halakhah Ve-Tahalikhim Hevratiyyim Bi-Tekufat Ha-Amora'im" (PhD diss., Ben-Gurion University of the Negev, 2020, 47–49; this work deals primarily with the Palestinian Talmud), the primacy of the Mishnah in this regard cannot be denied.
9. However, not all mishnaic passages were explained by the Talmuds, even where such passages were ostensibly in need of interpretation, and it is not clear why this is the case. In addition, no Talmuds are extant on entire orders of the Mishnah (orders *Kodashim* and *Tohorot* in the Palestinian Talmud, except for part of one tractate, and orders *Zera'im* and *Tohorot* in the Babylonian Talmud, except for one tractate). Precisely why there are no Talmuds on these orders is an issue which requires further analysis and lies beyond the purview of this chapter; for further discussion, see mainly Yaakov Sussmann, "Sugyot Bavliyyot Li-Sedarim Zera'im Ve-Taharot" (PhD diss., Hebrew University, 1969); David Rosenthal, "Arikhot Kedumot Ha-Meshukka'ot Ba-Talmud Ha-Bavli," *Mehkerei Talmud* 1 (1990): 155–204.
10. Indeed, some rulings of this sort found in our texts of the Talmud might actually be later additions of post-Talmudic provenance; see, e.g., the references in Barak Shlomo Cohen, "'Amar Shemuel: Hilkheta': Li-Vehinat Derekh Pesikat Ha-Halakhah Shel Shemuel Ba-Talmudim," *JSIJ* 12 (2013): 1–32, esp. 19–20 n. 125, https://jewish-faculty.biu.ac.il/files/jewish-faculty/shared/cohen.pdf. To be sure, some scholars have suggested that careful reading between the lines of Talmudic discussions can suggest which viewpoints the editors of these passages accepted; see especially Yuval Blankovsky, *Ma'amar Al Parshanut Ha-Talmud* (Jerusalem, 2013), https://www.daat.ac.il/daat/vl/belan-talmud/belan-talmud01.pdf; Kahana, "*Mippenei Tikkun Ha-Olam*," 15–18. While this viewpoint seems fundamentally correct (even if particular analyses embodying this approach may seem questionable), such a "between the lines" approach to determining Talmudic legal decisions is clearly not a standard form of legal decision-making or codification, and hence we do not consider it at greater length here.

11. For the sake of convenience, I use the expressions "Mishnah exegesis," "Mishnah interpretation," and "how the rabbis/Talmuds read the Mishnah" interchangeably in this chapter.
12. To a certain extent this claim is impressionistic, insofar as previous scholarship focused more on how the Talmuds interpreted the Mishnah than on how they interpreted other *tannaitic* sources. However, this impression seems to emerge quite clearly from even rudimentary study of the Talmuds.
13. In this respect, the Talmuds follow the approach taken by the Mishnah itself, which, as noted earlier (see the introductory section of this chapter), often treats matters of no direct practical consequence. See most recently Chaim Saiman, *Halakhah: The Rabbinic Idea of Law* (Princeton, NJ: Princeton University Press, 2018), ch. 2.
14. Although we occasionally find exceptions; see, e.g., Amnon Bazak, *Nitzehuni Banai: She'elot Yesod Be-Limmud Torah She-Be-Al Peh* (Rishon Lezion: Miskal, 2020), 337–38.
15. I say "presumably" due to the paucity of explicit, final rulings in the Talmuds.
16. See Hanan Gafni, *Peshutah Shel Mishnah: Iyyunim Be-Heker Sifrut Hazal Ba-Et Ha-Hadashah* (Tel-Aviv: Hakibbutz Hameuchad, 2011). And while the Mishnah was often interpreted according to its plain sense in Talmudic times, the point here is that explicit, systematic focus on the Mishnah's plain sense accompanied by the principled rejection of forced Mishnah interpretation is apparently unique to, and at the very least far better attested during, the post-Talmudic period.
17. Significantly, in such instances the Mishnah adduced is not necessarily the "local" Mishnah (i.e., the mishnaic passage which serves as the point of departure for the local Talmudic discussion); this Mishnah might stem from a different literary or legal context, and sometimes even from a different Talmudic tractate.
18. Theoretically, one more desideratum might be considered: the relationship between Talmudic interpretation of the Mishnah and rabbinic interpretation of other texts, mainly the Bible. Likewise, it might prove illuminating to compare how the Talmuds interpreted the Mishnah (and other *tannaitic* sources) with how interpreters from non-rabbinic cultures interpreted authoritative/canonical/central/sacred texts from these cultures. However, such comparative analysis requires systematic study of the other modes of interpretation, which has not always been carried out by previous scholars, and which must obviously be pursued before any sort of comparative analysis can be undertaken. That said, various illuminating comparative observations of this sort have recently been made by Moulie Vidas, *The Rise of Talmud* (Oxford: Oxford University Press, 2025), 68–75, 228–36, 245–48; my thanks to Prof. Vidas for letting me examine a preliminary version of this extremely important study.
19. See especially E. Z. Melamed, *Pirkei Mavo Le-Sifrut Ha-Talmud* (Jerusalem, 1973), 330–94; Yehiel Yaakov Weinberg, "Ha-Parshanut Ha-Talmudit La-Mishnah," in *Seridei Esh, Hikrei Halakhah, Hiddushim, Be'urim U-Ma'amarim* (Jerusalem: Mossad Harav Kook, 1977), 4:235–49.
20. At times, Talmudic explanations of obscure mishnaic terms seem to reflect folk etymologies which do not reflect the original meaning of the Mishnah. (Similar phenomena obtain with regard to some rabbinic interpretations of the Bible, although this latter issue lies beyond the purview of this chapter.) It is not clear whether the authors of these etymologies (mis)construed them as accurate explanations of the Mishnah, or whether they were intended to reflect an additional level of meaning—a sort of midrashic interpretation of the mishnaic text, as it were. Indeed, it is possible that not all etymologies of this sort were intended the same way, and the matter requires further analysis.

21. These types of exegesis are difficult to categorize precisely, and hence I make no attempt to do so here. Indeed, I use the term "'ordinary' textual exegesis" as a kind of catch-all phrase to include all types of interpretation which do not fall under the other categories considered here.
22. The text of the Mishnah was fluid during Talmudic times (which is perhaps not surprising in light of the fact that the mishnaic text was apparently transmitted orally during this period; see especially Yaakov Sussmann, "*Torah She-Be-Al Peh*" *Peshutah Ke-Mashma'ah, Koho Shel Kutzo Shel Yod* [Jerusalem: Magnes, 2019], passim), although the precise extent and nature of this fluidity is the subject of considerable scholarly discussion. See especially Yaakov Nahum Halevi Epstein, *Mavo Le-Nosah Ha-Mishnah*, 3rd ed. (Jerusalem: Magnes, 2000), passim; Sussmann, "*Torah She-Be-Al Peh*"; and see now Vidas, *Rise of Talmud*, 6.
23. The term "teach" (rather than "read") is frequently used by the Talmuds to refer to a particular reading, as is the case here; since the Mishnah was transmitted orally during the Talmudic period, the Mishnah's text is generally described as "teaching" (viz., oral teaching), rather than by a term which denotes a written text.
24. See Epstein, *Mavo Le-Nosah Ha-Mishnah*, esp. chs. 2, 3, 6, 7; Vidas, *Rise of Talmud*, 7.
25. Presumably because no such text existed during the Talmudic period; see Sussmann, "*Torah She-Be-Al Peh.*"
26. See, e.g., the references in Epstein, *Mavo Le-Nosah Ha-Mishnah*, 1417, 1423 (indexes), s.v. *einah mishnah, let kan, leta le-matninin*, viz., "it is not a [valid] Mishnah," "[the Mishnah] is not here" = it is not valid, and "the Mishnah is not [accepted]," respectively.
27. In addition, though perhaps less significant, the ruling in 1 deals with people who are deaf, whereas Rabbi Yose's statement deals with people who can hear, but who recited the *Shema* inaudibly.
28. Cf. Vidas, *Rise of Talmud*, 35–36.
29. This point has been made by numerous scholars, both traditional and academic, some dating as far back as the medieval period. See, e.g., the references in Itamar Brenner, *Okimta: Siah Hermeneuti, Siah Parshani U-Mashma'ut Te'ologit Ba-Talmud Ha-Bavli* (Jerusalem: Carmel, 2022), 169–70 n. 9, 193 n. 1; Christine Hayes, *Between the Babylonian and Palestinian Talmuds: Accounting for Halakhic Difference in Selected Sugyot from Tractate Avodah Zarah* (New York: Oxford University Press, 1997), 92–93, 105, and the literature cited there; David Henshke, "Abbaye Ve-Rava—Shtei Gishot Le-Mishnat Ha-Tanna'im," *Tarbiz* 49 (1980): 187–93, esp. 191–93; Kahana, "*Mippenei Tikkun Ha-Olam*," 19; Yosef Marcus, "Derishah Aggadit Shel Mishnayot Hilkhatiyyot Be-Sifrut Ha-Amora'it," *Netu'im* 22 (2020): 1–12. Perhaps also relevant in this connection is the rabbinic tendency to interpret the Mishnah intertextually, in much the same way as the rabbis did when interpreting the Bible; see, e.g., Blankovsky, *Ma'amar Al Parshanut Ha-Talmud*, 72–77.
30. See also the section "Saboraic Interpretation of the Mishnah."
31. See especially Leib Moscovitz, *Talmudic Reasoning: From Casuistics to Conceptualization* (Tübingen, Germany: Mohr Siebeck, 2002), 217, with references to earlier literature.
32. See especially Leib Moscovitz, "Le-Heker Ha-'Gezerah Shema' Ba-Yerushalmi," *Sidra* 24–25 (2010): 215–36.
33. See Moscovitz, *Talmudic Reasoning*.
34. See especially Zechariah Frankel, *Mevo Ha-Yerushalmi* (Breslau, Germany: Schlatter, 1870), 28b–31a.
35. See, e.g., ibid., 29b–30a.

36. See Moscovitz, *Talmudic Reasoning*, esp. 351–52.
37. See especially Avraham Goldberg, "Le-Hitpattehut Ha-Sugya Ba-Talmud Ha-Bavli (Ha-Shimush Be-Vituyim 'Gezerah Shema', 'Gezerat Dilma' U-'Gezerah Mi-Shum')," in *Sefer Ha-Yovel Le-Rabbi Hanokh Albeck* (Jerusalem: Mossad Harav Kook, 1963), 101–13; Moscovitz, "Le-Heker Ha-'Gezerah Shema' Ba-Yerushalmi." To be sure, this aspect of Babylonian Mishnah interpretation might ultimately be just another manifestation of the Babylonian Talmud's tendency to interpret the Mishnah in a fashion which does not accord with its plain sense; see Moscovitz, "Le-Heker Ha-'Gezerah Shema' Ba-Yerushalmi," 233–34.
38. See, e.g., Abraham Goldberg, "The Babylonian Talmud," in *The Literature of the Sages*, vol. 1, ed. Shmuel Safrai (Assen/Maastricht: Van Gorcum, 1987), esp. 331–32.
39. See most recently the survey of previous scholarship in Yoel Kretzmer-Raziel, "Stam Ha-Talmud Ke-Tofa'ah Hitpattehutit: Sugyot Ha-Petihah Le-Massekhet Nedarim Ba-Yerushalmi U-Va-Bavli," *Tarbiz* 86 (2019): esp. 611–14.
40. See Avinoam Cohen, "Bikkoret Hilkhatit Le'ummat Bikkoret Sifrutit Be-Sugyot Ha-Talmud," *Asuppot* 3 (1989): 331–46, and note also the brief but important observations of David Weiss Halivni, *Peshat and Derash: Plain and Applied Meaning in Rabbinic Exegesis* (New York: Oxford University Press, 1991), 37–39, 46–47.
41. Although such an approach does seem to be attested to a certain degree in the Palestinian Talmud, which is presumably contemporaneous with the attributed material in the Babylonian Talmud, so this issue requires further consideration. Cf., e.g., Hayes, *Between the Babylonian and Palestinian Talmuds*, 94 (and compare chapter 3 there generally); Kretzmer-Raziel, "Stam Ha-Talmud Ke-Tofa'ah Hitpattehutit," 653 n. 186; Vidas, *Rise of Talmud*, 271–75, 278–79.
42. See especially Henshke, "Abbaye Ve-Rava."
43. According to Henshke, ibid., 192–93, Rava's view about the quasi-canonicity of the Mishnah stemmed from the fact that the Mishnah had been committed to writing. However, the Mishnah might have enjoyed quasi-canonical status even if it was still an oral document (as scholars currently tend to assume); see especially the discussion in Sussmann, "*Torah She-Be-Al Peh.*"
44. For this idea that canonicity leads, perhaps somewhat paradoxically, to greater freedom of interpretation, cf. Moshe Halbertal, *People of the Book: Canon, Meaning, and Authority* (Cambridge, MA: Harvard University Press, 1997), 29, 32–33, but note that the discussion there refers specifically to a sacred or Divine text.
45. See Robert Brody, *The Geonim of Babylonia and the Shaping of Medieval Jewish Culture* (New Haven: Yale University Press, 1998), 4–11.
46. For the characteristic features of such passages, see, e.g., Kretzmer-Raziel, "Stam Ha-Talmud Ke-Tofa'ah Hitpattehutit," 623 n. 44 and the literature cited there.
47. See Yaakov Elman, "The World of the 'Sabboraim': Cultural Aspects of Post-Redactional Additions to the Bavli," in *Creation and Composition: The Contribution of the Bavli Redactors (Stammaim) to the Aggada*, ed. Jeffrey L. Rubenstein (Tübingen, Germany: Mohr Siebeck, 2005), 383–415.
48. While some passages in both Talmuds challenge particular Mishnah interpretations on exegetical rather than substantive grounds—to wit, these interpretations seem strained, and not just that they are contradicted by other legal sources—such passages are comparatively rare. Moreover, it remains to be determined which Sages were committed to plain-sense interpretation, to what extent and under what circumstances. (Significantly,

the Talmuds contain little reflection on the exegetical character of their interpretations and their approaches to interpretation in general.) See generally Brenner, *Okimta*, 78–158 (on interpretations explicitly identified in the Babylonian Talmud as forced; Brenner does not discuss such phenomena in the Palestinian Talmud, due to the focus of his study), and see now Vidas, *The Rise of Talmud*, 280–83 (on certain types of forced interpretations in the Palestinian Talmud).

49. A similar question, which has been addressed at length by both traditional writers and academic scholars, arises in connection with rabbinic interpretation of Scripture, which frequently deviates from the plain sense of the biblical text. However, it is questionable how relevant analysis of forced rabbinic approaches to scriptural exegesis is to the question of forced rabbinic interpretation of the Mishnah (but see Brenner, *Okimta*), due to the fundamental difference between the nature of these texts—a Divine text in the case of Scripture, which the rabbis accordingly assumed to have multiple and at times hidden meanings, in contrast to a human text in the case of the Mishnah. Interestingly, though, a recent study by Shamma Friedman suggests that a creative and nonliteral approach to the interpretation of legal documents of human origin might have been adopted during the *tannaitic* period. If this suggestion is correct, it provides a much closer parallel to the phenomenon of forced Amoraic Mishnah exegesis discussed here. See Shamma Yehudah Friedman, "'Hotzi'u Li Ketubbat Immoteikhem': Ma'aseh Hillel Ha-Zaken U-Venei Alexandriah U-Derishat 'Leshon Hedyot,'" in *Semitic, Biblical, and Jewish Studies in Honor of Richard C. Steiner*, ed. Aaron J. Koller, Mordechai Z. Cohen, and Adina Moshavi (Jerusalem: Mossad Bialik, 2020), 176–255, passim, esp. 222–28.

50. See generally Bazak, *Nitzehuni Banai*, ch. 6 (mainly traditional approaches) and Brenner, *Okimta*, chs. 1–5, and note particularly the very concise but comprehensive survey in *Okimta*, 170 n. 10.

51. This suggestion seems to resemble and might in fact be conceptually equivalent to that proffered by Bazak, *Nitzehuni Banai*, 294–98. Such a flexible conception of the status of canonical legal sources might also underlie other aspects of rabbinic approaches to religious law; see generally Christine Hayes, *What's Divine about Divine Law? Early Perspectives* (Princeton, NJ: Princeton University Press, 2015), Part III.

References

Bazak, Amnon. *Nitzehuni Banai: She'elot Yesod Be-Limmud Torah She-Be-'Al Peh*. Rishon Lezion: Miskal, 2020.

Blankovsky, Yuval. *Ma'amar 'Al Parshanut Ha-Talmud*. Jerusalem, 2013. http://www.daat.ac.il/daat/vl/belan-talmud/belan-talmud01.pdf.

Brenner, Itamar. *Okimta, Siah Hermeneuti, Siah Parshani U-Mashma'ut Te'ologit Ba-Talmud Ha-Bavli*. Jerusalem: Carmel, 2022.

Brody, Robert. *The Geonim of Babylonia and the Shaping of Medieval Jewish Culture*. New Haven and London: Yale University Press, 1998.

Cohen, Avinoam. "Bikkoret Hilkhatit Le'ummat Bikkoret Sifrutit Be-Sugyot Ha-Talmud." *Asuppot* 3 (1989): 331–46.

Elman, Yaakov. "Order, Sequence, and Selection: The Mishnah's Anthological Choices." In *The Anthology in Jewish Literature*, ed. David Stern (Oxford: Oxford University Press, 2004), 53–80.

Elman, Yaakov. "The World of the 'Sabboraim': Cultural Aspects of Post-Redactional Additions to the Bavli." In *Creation and Composition: The Contribution of the Bavli Redactors (Stammaim) to the Aggada*, ed. J. L. Rubenstein (Tübingen: Mohr Siebeck, 2005), 383–415.

Epstein, J. N. *Mavo Le-Nosah Ha-Mishnah*, 3rd ed. Jerusalem: Magnes, 2000.

Frankel, Zechariah. *Mevo Ha-Yerushalmi*. Breslau: Schlatter, 1870.

Gafni, Hanan. *Peshutah Shel Mishnah: Iyyunim Be-Heqer Sifrut Hazal Ba-Et Ha-Hadashah*. Tel-Aviv: Hakibbutz Hameuchad, 2011.

Goldberg, Abraham. "The Babylonian Talmud." In *The Literature of the Sages*, vol. 1, ed. Shmuel Safrai (Assen/Maastricht and Philadelphia: Van Gorcum and Fortress Press, 1987), 323–45.

Goldberg, Avraham. "Le-Hitpattehut Ha-Sugya Ba-Talmud Ha-Bavli (Ha-Shimush Be-Vituyim 'Gezerah Shema', 'Gezerat Dilma' U-'Gezerah Mi-Shum')." In *Sefer Ha-Yovel Le-Rabbi Hanokh Albeck* (Jerusalem: Mossad Harav Kook, 1963), 101–13.

Halivni, David Weiss. *Peshat and Derash: Plain and Applied Meaning in Rabbinic Exegesis*. New York and Oxford: Oxford University Press, 1991.

Halivni, David. "The Reception Accorded To Rabbi Judah's Mishnah." In *Jewish and Christian Self-Definition, Vol. 2: Aspects of Judaism in the Graeco-Roman Period*, ed. E.P. Sanders with A. I. Baumgarten and Alan Mendelson (London: S.C.M. Press Ltd, 1981), 204–12.

Havlin, S. Z. "'Al 'Ha-Hatimah Ha-Sifrutit' Ki-Ysod Ha-Halukkah Li-Tekufot Ba-Halakhah." In *Mehkarim Be-Sifrut Ha-Talmudit, Yom 'Iyyun Le-Regel Melot Shemonim Shanah Le-Shaul Lieberman* (Jerusalem: Israel Academy of Sciences and Humanities, 1983), 148–92.

Hayes, Christine. *Between the Babylonian and Palestinian Talmuds: Accounting for Halakhic Difference in Selected Sugyot from Tractate Avodah Zarah*. New York: Oxford University Press, 1997.

Henshke, David. "Abbaye Ve-Rava—Shtei Gishot Le-Mishnat Ha-Tanna'im." *Tarbiz* 49 (1980): 187–93.

Kahana, Menahem I. '*Mippenei Tikkun Ha-Olam': Talmud Bavli Massekhet Gittin Perek Revi'i*. Jerusalem: Magnes, 2020.

Melamed, E.Z. *Pirkei Mavo Le-Sifrut Ha-Talmud*. Jerusalem, 1973.

Moscovitz, Leib. "Le-Heker Ha-'Gezerah Shema' Ba-Yerushalmi." *Sidra* 24–25 (2010): 215–36.

Moscovitz, Leib. *Talmudic Reasoning: From Casuistics to Conceptualization*. Tübingen: Mohr Siebeck, 2002.

Sussmann, Yaakov. *'Torah She-Be-Al Peh' Peshutah Ke-Mashma'ah, Koho Shel Kutzo Shel Yod*. Jerusalem: Magnes, 2019.

Vidas, Moulie. *The Rise of Talmud*. Oxford: Oxford University Press, 2025.

Weinberg, Yehiel Yaakov. "Ha-Parshanut Ha-Talmudit La-Mishnah." In *Seridei Esh, Hikrei Halakhah, Hiddushim, Be'urim U-Ma'amarim*, 4: 235–49 (Jerusalem: Mossad Harav Kook, 1977).

CHAPTER 4

HOW DO THE *RISHONIM* READ THE TALMUD AND THE *GEONIM*?

EPHRAIM KANARFOGEL

INTRODUCTION

THIS chapter surveys the interpretative methods and textual interconnectedness of a representative sample of leading medieval Talmudists known traditionally as the *Rishonim*. Their approaches to apostasy and reversion are analyzed in order to chart how they read the text of the Talmud and the literature of the *Geonim* as a means of shaping *halakhic* policy and practice.[1] The *Rishonim* occupy the period between the *Geonim*, who flourished in Babylonia and especially in Baghdad during the ninth through the mid-eleventh centuries, and the period of the *Aharonim*, which began with the resettlements that followed the expulsion of the Jews from Spain and Portugal at the end of the fifteenth century, and the efflorescence of the Jewish communities in Eastern Europe *c.* 1550.[2]

Talmudic discussion concerning an apostate, a Jew who has left the community and adopted the beliefs and practices of another religion, is relatively sparse. However, a number of *Geonim* and *Rishonim* dealt extensively with this issue, both in terms of how apostates should be considered and treated when they are living outside the Jewish community and what requirements if any were to be imposed following their decision to return. As was their wont, post-Talmudic authorities from different periods and geographic areas sought to anchor their *halakhic* analyses and interpretations in the Talmudic corpus.[3]

The issue of apostasy in the Jewish communities of northern European became more prominent beginning with the period of the First Crusade in 1096. At that time, significant numbers of Jews were forcibly converted to Christianity, while others accepted Christianity willfully in light of the dominant role enjoyed by the societal majority.

Jacob Katz maintained that the approach taken toward apostates by Rashi (1040–1105) occupies a central place in the thinking of his rabbinic successors in northern France and Germany through the thirteenth century and beyond. Although Rashi does not formulate his larger position within his Talmudic commentary (which only rarely takes decisive *halakhic* stands), his treatment of these issues in several responsa stemmed from his understanding of a *memra* of R. Abba bar Zavda (Bavli Sanhedrin 44a) that was based on Joshua 7:11 (*hata Yisra'el*, a Jew has grievously sinned): "Even though he has sinned, he remains a Jew (*'af 'al pi she-hata Yisra'el hu*)."

Based on this Talmudic passage, Rashi rules that "if an apostate (*meshummad*) betroths (*she-kiddesh*) a woman, his kiddushin are binding."[4] He concludes in another responsum that a childless woman whose husband has died must receive *halitzah* from his apostate brother if he was the only brother available for this purpose.[5] *Halitzah* is the ceremonial act by which the childless wife of her deceased husband is released from the levirate bond established according to the Torah between this wife and one of her husband's surviving brothers. Rashi rejects the view of the *Geonim*, who held that the apostate must perform *halitzah* only if he apostatized after the couple was married, in accordance with a Talmudic principle that the potential levirate relationship between the wife and the brother is established at the time of the wedding (*nissu'in mappilim*).[6]

Rashi considered the *geonic* position to be flawed. If the apostate is not required to perform *halitzah* when he apostatized prior to the wedding since his status as a Jew is now compromised, he should also not be required to do so if the apostasy occurred after the wedding; and his *kiddushin* should not be binding either. Rejecting these possibilities, Rashi defines an apostate as a *Yisra'el hashud le-khol davar*, who is nonetheless a Jew. Rashi rules similarly in yet another responsum that it is prohibited for a Jew to lend money to an apostate at interest. Although he may not currently be part of the community, an apostate is still considered to be "your brother," and taking interest from him is prohibited according to Deuteronomy 23:21 (*ve-'et 'ahikha lo tashikh*).[7]

Katz suggests that the Talmudic linchpin which anchored Rashi's view is the ruling found in Bavli Yevamot (47b and Bekhorot 30b), that the *kiddushin* of a *Yisra'el mumar* is valid. In his commentary to Yevamot 47b, Rashi defines a *mumar*, whose betrothal is nonetheless effective, as a *Yisra'el rasha*. Indeed, both these *sugyot* also conclude that a convert to Judaism who subsequently slipped back into his prior behavior as a non-Jew is also considered a *Yisra'el mumar*. Rashi's conflation and sustained use of the principle of *'af 'al pi she-hata Yisra'el hu* was also intended to convey the notion that baptism did not diminish the apostate's Jewish status in any way, even if he was no longer observing Jewish law, a particularly relevant approach for the period of the First Crusade and its aftermath which coincided with the last decade of Rashi's life.[8]

A corollary of Rashi's approach, expressed already by his predecessor Rabbenu Gershom b. Judah of Mainz (d. 1028), is that an apostate who sincerely sought to revert to Judaism should be welcomed. If the apostate was prepared to return fully to Jewish communal and religious life, he should be encouraged to do so immediately, without undergoing ritual immersion, admitting his misdeeds, or otherwise accepting his recommitment to Judaism in a public way. Katz ascribes the echoes of the need for immersion, which he detected in less than a handful of thirteenth- and fourteenth-century rabbinic sources, to a "popular view, which did not accept the view that baptism did not affect the Jew's character qua Jew," noting that immersion was also not required during the *geonic* period.[9]

Immersion for Reverting Apostates

In fact, however, several responsa and rulings found in manuscript (and occasionally reflected in published texts) by the leading northern French Tosafist in the late twelfth century (and Rashi's great-grandson), Isaac b. Samuel of Dampierre (*Ri ha-Zaken*, d. *c.* 1190), and by two of his outstanding students, the brothers Isaac b. Abraham of Dampierre (*Ritzba*, d. 1209) and Samson b. Abraham (*Rash*) of Sens (d. 1214 in Israel), recognize the existence of a requirement for ritual immersion by a returning apostate. As opposed to their teacher *Ri*, however, the brothers R. Isaac and R. Samson sought more concrete ways to verify a reverting (former) apostate's sincerity, as will be seen shortly.

Although *Ri* of Dampierre's name is mentioned on virtually every folio page of the standard *Tosafot* glosses to the Babylonian Talmud in both interpretational and *halakhic* contexts, he also composed responsa and other rulings (*pesakim*). These texts contain significant amounts of high-level Talmudic analysis and comparative efforts that *Ri* offered when addressing questions that came before him, and must be taken into account when assessing the contribution of the Tosafists to Talmudic interpretation. Manuscript passages record what appear to be different versions of *Ri*'s response to the same case: an apostate went to a neighboring country or region (which was often done to avoid the wrath of the local Christian authorities), where he once again conducted himself in accordance with the Jewish religion (*ke-dat yehudit*). He then touched wine belonging to Jews; one version of *Ri*'s responsum notes that the former apostate became a servant in a Jewish household. However, it was not known whether he had immersed himself or reaccepted his Jewish faith in the presence of three (i.e., a rabbinic tribunal), even though he professed to two Jews who confronted him that he had indeed repented.

Ri rules that the wine touched by the former apostate is permitted for Jewish consumption, characterizing the apparently customary immersion for a reverting apostate as a proper act (a *mitzvah*), which was meant to "cleanse and purify him" (*mishum nekiyyut ve-toharah*, a form of expiation or even an un-baptism), but not as a *hovah*, an act mandated by Jewish law. He also notes an otherwise unidentified *geonic* responsum, which states that there is no requirement whatsoever for a reverting apostate to undergo immersion.[10]

Regarding the need for a returning apostate to reaccept Judaism before a rabbinic tribunal, *Ri* points out that an *'am ha-'aretz* who wishes to be relied upon in matters of ritual purity (as a *haver*) is required to appear before such a body (*Bekhorot* 30b) because up to that point, the *'am ha'aretz* had never been deemed trustworthy in these matters. A former apostate, however, who had been a member of the Jewish religious community prior to his apostasy, and "can easily return to his Creator (and his prior observances) when he regrets his religious waywardness" is not required to have his re-recommitment verified before a rabbinic tribunal (especially since many of those who apostatized did so only for venal reasons, such as the pressures of poverty or debt). Although a convert to Judaism who is later suspected of intentional neglect of particular Torah precepts is required to reaccept those precepts before a rabbinic tribunal (*Bekhorot* 30b, *'Avodah Zarah* 7a), a returning apostate is not the same as a convert, who as a non-Jew had not been bound by the Torah's laws and restrictions. The convert is similar in this regard to an *'am ha-'aretz*, who had was never before been entrusted with matters of ritual purity and only now wishes to become a *haver*.[11]

Ri's students, Isaac b. Abraham of Dampierre and his brother, Samson b. Abraham of Sens, composed their own responses to a similar case. These are recorded briefly in *Sefer Or Zarua'* (by Isaac b. Moses of Vienna, d. 1255, who studied in Paris with yet another important student of *Ri*, Judah b. Isaac Sirleon, d. 1224) and in a variant *Tosafot* text (to *Bekhorot* 31a),[12] and are found more expansively in manuscript.[13]

As noted, *Ri*'s students were more concerned than their teacher about the need for verification. Like *Ri*, *Ritzba* permitted the wine touched by a reverting apostate who claimed that he had repented on his own volition and had fully rejoined the Jewish community and its observances. However, this particular apostate was not required to make representation before a rabbinic court for the wine to be permitted because he appeared to now be observing Jewish law and indeed, he had entrusted his purse to *Ritzba* for safekeeping over the Sabbath. *Ritzba* felt that this was a more significant indicator of his commitment than immersion (*va-'afilu lo taval*, based on *Shabbat* 69b, *ha-meshammer shivto ba-shuq*). *Ritzba* asserts that the former apostate can now be considered a *ba'al teshuvah*, "since he had abandoned all forms of Christian worship (*heniah kol tarfutam*) and returned to his Creator." Although the Talmud (Bavli Sanhedrin 25b) requires a penitent to also right the wrongs that he had done to others (e.g., a moneylender must return any interest that he had taken), the renouncing of Christianity by returning to Jewish practice is what makes the former apostate a *ba'al teshuvah*. In this respect, he is similar to a convert (*ve-domeh ketzat la-ger*) who has renounced his former religious life. While the former apostate must continue to perfect his Jewish observances, his repentance is not compromised by his past indiscretions and the wine that he touched after his return to the Jewish community is permitted.

Samson of Sens, however, ruled that wine which a former apostate touched cannot be permitted to other Jews without more specific proof of his intentions. Indeed, this is no different than the Talmudic ruling about an *'m ha-aretz* who wished to become a *haver*, which requires verification by a rabbinic court. R. Samson cites a responsum attributed to Rav Tzemah Gaon (late ninth century) that while immersion is not required, a reverting apostate must arise publicly (*be-farhesya bifnei ha-tzibbur*) to confess what he did (along with listing the opportunities that had been available to him to violate Jewish law) while outside the Jewish community and its observances. Only then are other Jews permitted to eat and drink with him. R. Samson notes that *Ritzba*'s confirmation of the former apostate's Sabbath observance is inadequate, since he had apostatized "against the entire Torah," adding that reliance on the former apostate's own word that he had immersed himself is worthless. R. Samson concludes that "if he was truly sincere [*ve-'im hayah libbo le-shem shamayim*], would he not have presented himself before *haverim* (observant Jews, if not Torah scholars) so that they could ascertain and acknowledge his repentance? The fact that he did not do this indicates that in his heart, he has not yet recanted (*she-'ein be-libbo 'adayin*)."

For their part, contemporary German Tosafists adduced additional Talmudic sources to support and even strengthen the practice that a returning apostate must undergo immersion. Simhah b. Samuel of Speyer (d. *c.* 1230), author of a large but no longer extant Jewish legal tome entitled *Seder 'Olam*, points to a passage in *Avot de-Rabbi Nathan* which recounts the case of a young woman who had been captured by non-Jews. She was immersed following her rescue, "because during all the days that she was detained by the non-Jews she consumed their food and drink; she was immersed in order to be purified."[14] R. Simhah does not refer to the similar explanation about the purpose of immersion given by *Ri*, although this is likely the result of a separation between the Tosafist centers in northern France and Germany that occurred between 1175 and 1215. Pieces of *Ri*'s teachings reached Germany during that time, but much of what he wrote did not. At the same time, Simhah of Speyer, a major German Tosafist teacher, is barely mentioned in the standard *Tosafot* to the Babylonian Talmud, the vast majority of which were composed in northern France.[15]

R. Simhah's Rhineland colleague, Eli`ezer b. Joel ha-Levi (*Rabiah*) of Cologne (d. *c.* 1225), went even further. In a passage found in an early fourteenth-century compilation, *Ha-Semak mi-Zurich*, *Rabiah* requires an apostate who sought to revert to shave his head and immerse himself just as a convert to Judaism must (*ka-ger*). This immersion does not have to take place during the day as it does for a conversion, since conversion is overseen by a rabbinic court which must formally convene by day. However, the apostate's reacceptance of Judaism and Jewish practice (*ha-kabbalah*) before a rabbinic tribunal must be done by day.[16]

Unlike Simhah of Speyer, *Rabiah* was also focused, as was Samson of Sens (whose view is again not cited by the German Tosafists), on verifying the sincerity of the returning apostate before a rabbinic tribunal, similar to what a convert to Judaism must do. With regard to immersion, a passage in a Tosafist commentary to *Sifra* (incorrectly attributed to Samson of Sens but composed in fact by a German Tosafist contemporary of *Rabiah* and R. Simhah) also maintains that the accepted procedure for a penitent apostate is to shave his head and pare his nails prior to immersion, and the reverting apostate is referred to in that passage as a convert.[17]

A student of Simhah of Speyer, Avigdor b. Elijah *Kohen Tzedek* (Katz) of Vienna, assumed that a married couple who were both returning apostates must be immersed prior to their reacceptance into the community, and they must also shave their hair before this immersion as a symbolic removal of the impurities of idolatry. The only question for R. Avigdor was whether they also had to be separated for a period of three months (*havhanah, Yevamot* 41a–42a), as was required of a female convert to Judaism.

R. Avigdor's responds that while a returning female apostate (like a convert) is required to abstain from sexual relations during this period in order to ascertain whether she is pregnant with the child of a non-Jewish father, a period of separation is not needed in this instance because it is assumed that this married couple who had apostatized together continued to live only with each other during their period of apostasy.[18]

An otherwise unidentified "late *Tosafot*" (*Tosafot 'aharonot*), cited in the *hiddushim* of the Spanish *Rishon*, Yom Tov b. Abraham Ishvilli (*Ritva*, d. *c.* 1325) to *Bavli Yevamot*, identifies a Talmudic source for the immersion of a returning apostate.[19] The intent of this *Tosafot* passage was to more firmly anchor within the Talmudic corpus the Ashkenazic practice of having a returning apostate immerse. Rectifying religious customs and practices was yet another goal of the Tosafist *oeuvre*, beyond providing close textual readings and comparative analyses of the text of the Talmud (and Rashi's commentary), and deriving *halakhic* conclusions.[20]

Bavli Yevamot (47b) outlines the requirement for the immersion of a Canaanite slave who had been freed. Although he was immersed when he initially became an *'eved kena'ani* (as mandated by Torah law), which obligated him in a limited number of commandments, a freed slave transitions to a higher Jewish status and must now fulfill the same *mitzvot* as every other Jewish male. Several *Tosafot* texts maintain that the second immersion of an *'eved kena'ani* is required according to rabbinic law, and does not have to be overseen by a rabbinic court as his initial immersion did.[21] Indeed, both Moses b. Nahman (*Ramban*) of Gerona (d. 1270) and Solomon b. Abraham ibn Adret (*Rashba*) of Barcelona (d. *c.* 1310) attribute this position to "the rabbis of northern France" (*rabbotenu ha-Tzarefatim*).[22] A variant *Tosafot* to Bavli Yevamot characterizes this rabbinic requirement as a means of delineating between slavery and freedom (*le-hakkir bein 'avdut le-herut*).[23] But none of these *Tosafot* passages refers to the case of a returning apostate.

There is, however, a passage labeled *Tosafot Shitah* in a gloss to a manuscript version of *Sefer Mordekhai* (whose author, Mordekhai b. Hillel, died a martyr's death in Germany in 1298) which comports precisely with the Tosafist formulation cited by *Ritva*. In all likelihood, *Tosafot Shitah* represents a type or genre of *Tosafot* that was produced in the study hall of Evreux (led by the brothers Moses, Samuel and Isaac b. Shne'ur) during the mid-thirteenth century, or perhaps in the study hall of their direct student, Rabbenu Peretz b. Elijah of Corbeil (d. 1297).[24] According to this *Tosafot* passage, ritual immersion for a reverting apostate serves as a demarcation or sign (*la'asot hekkera*) for the penitent of his new status and (restored) responsibilities just as it does for the freed *'eved kena'ani*, rather than as an act of penance (as had been suggested by Simhah of Speyer and others). This formalizes what one version of *Ri* of Dampierre's treatment had assumed, that the immersion is intended to sensitize the returning apostate to his renewed commitment to Jewish observance. In any case, the *Tosafot Shitah* passage succeeds in rooting the immersion for a returning apostate, which was also required by other earlier Tosafists as noted, within a clear Talmudic formulation.[25]

In the matter of medieval rabbinic responses to apostasy, leading Talmudists and *halakhists* in southern Europe largely responded to the positions put forward by

Ashkenazic authorities, as has just been seen regarding the explanation provided by *Ritva* on the requirement for a reverting apostate to immerse. This is not often the case in matters of Talmudic interpretation and *halakhic* decision-making, in which distinct Sefardic methods and patterns are typically expressed alongside those of their Ashkenazic counterparts. Concerning apostasy, however, it would seem that Spanish Jewish society began to experience waves of apostasy only in the late thirteenth century and beyond (and culminating with the calamitous century between 1391 and 1492), at which point the Ashkenazic positions had already been fully developed and could be easily considered along with the views of *Geonim* (even as apostasy during the *geonic* period often involved Islam rather than Christianity).

In any case, the first significant discussion by a Provencal Talmudist about ritual immersion for a returning apostate is found in a response penned by Solomon b. Abraham of Montpellier (*min ha-Har*, d. c. 1240), to a question put to him by Nahmanides.[26] Solomon of Montpellier requires a returning apostate to "publicly repent without coercion . . . and remain among us and perform the *mitzvot* as he once did." These commitments entitle the returning apostate to be considered a *ba'al teshuvah*, without immersion or any form of self-abnegation (*belo tevillah uve-lo yissur*). However, to again be considered completely reliable (*kasher le-gamrei*) in all matters of *'issur ve-heter* and to be trusted as a witness, the former apostate must undergo a prescribed regimen of afflictions and display full remorse, "in accordance with what is prescribed by the *beit din* in his city. Once he has accepted those afflictions and has regretted his sin, he is considered to be fully reliable in all matters." However, at no point in this process does R. Solomon mandate immersion.

Although significant pieces of Tosafist materials had reached southern France by this time (including teachings of *Ri* of Dampierre), Provencal Talmudists did not always look to the north for their rulings.[27] Indeed, R. Solomon's position in this and other matters having to do with returning apostates is largely consonant with the *geonic* view, which he mentions toward the end of his responsum. Immersion was not required, but public (re)acceptance of the *mitzvot* (through both word and deed) was. In addition, the returning apostate must undergo forms of physical affliction—some *geonic* texts advised that lashes be given—in order to achieve a full measure of both credibility and expiation.[28] No other post-Talmudic authorities are mentioned by R. Solomon in this context, although Maimonides is cited, inter alia, with respect to the treatment of full-fledged apostates and heretics (*minim*). For Solomon of Montpellier (as for the *Geonim* and Samson of Sens, who is not cited), immersion did not achieve sufficient verification on behalf of the Jewish community, nor was it part of an expiation process.

Two similar *geonic* responsa regarding the requirements for a returning apostate are preserved in *Rashba* of Barcelona's extensive responsa collection.[29] These *geonic* texts make no mention of immersion for a returning apostate but require instead a public confession and expression of regret (along with lashes, according to one formulation). As we have seen, however, *Rashba*'s student *Ritva*, who also notes the *geonic* view, cites a Tosafist formulation in his *hiddushim* which supports immersion on the basis of a distinct Talmudic source. *Ritva*'s point is that this requirement (and approach) is better documented within the Talmudic corpus than that of the *Geonim*.[30]

APOSTATES AND *HALITZAH*

Rashi required an apostate to perform *halitzah* (as unlikely as that might be) if he was the only brother available to do so, whether he had apostatized prior to his brother's marriage or subsequently;[31] and most Ashkenazic authorities supported this approach. Meir b. Barukh of Rothenburg (Maharam, d. 1293), one of the last of the Tosafists, considered adopting the *geonic* view (which held that if the apostasy occurred prior to the brother's marriage the apostate is not obligated to perform *halitzah*) based on a passage toward the end of Bavli Bava Kamma (110b–111a), in which the Talmud raises the possibility that a woman can stipulate at the time of her marriage that she will not be subject to a levirate *zikah* involving a brother who has pronounced physical blemishes. Maharam ultimately concludes, however, that he cannot disagree with the approach of Rashi that the apostate brother must perform *halitzah* in all circumstances.[32]

However, two German Tosafists at the turn of the twelfth century took a position against Rashi, and went even further in exempting the apostate from performing *halitzah* than the *Geonim* had. Several early manuscripts of *Sefer Mordekhai to* Bavli Yevamot record the following: "I have found written in the name of R. Abraham [b. Moses] of Regensburg regarding a *yevamah* who falls before a *yavam* who is an apostate that it is a wonderment [*ki tema*] that she should even require *halitzah* from him. For this constitutes a forbidden sexual relationship [*ha-lo be-makom 'ervah hu*], and 'zealots are bidden to kill such a person in the act [*ve-kanna'im pog'im bo*].' A woman who has sexual relations with a non-Jew [lit. an *'aramaei*] would be subject to [the rule of] *kanna'im pog'in bah*."[33]

For Abraham of Regensburg, the point at which the apostate accepted Christian observances relative to his brother's marriage is irrelevant. An apostate is excluded from performing *halitzah* in all instances, inasmuch as he has the same status as a non-Jew with whom the widow cannot live. R. Abraham does not cite any Talmudic proof texts. His view appears to emerge from an application of the biblical episode involving Phineas (Pinhas), son of Eleazar *ha-Kohen* (Nu. 25:1–11), which graphically demonstrates that forbidden sexual relations cannot be countenanced as a matter of *halakhic* policy.[34]

At the same time, however, there is a conceptual distinction between the *kiddushin* and *get* of an apostate, which Abraham of Regensburg rules are both valid[35] and participation in *halitzah*, from which the apostate is excluded. *Gittin* and *kiddushin* are initiated by the apostate, and his inherent and ongoing status as a Jew allows them to be effective. Although he also technically initiates the decision to perform *halitzah* (as opposed to *yibbum*), eligibility for *halitzah* (and *yibbum*) is caused by his brother's marriage which creates the *zikah*. As such, the apostate's actions are not solely determinative in this matter, and *halakhic* interventions are possible.

The Tosafist Barukh b. Samuel of Mainz (d. 1221) bases his conclusion that an apostate may not perform *halitzah* on a reassessment of the Talmud's position concerning the point at which the *zikah* between a potential *yavam* and *yevamah* is established. R. Barukh, who served as the head judge of the Mainz rabbinical court, composed a voluminous work of Jewish law, *Sefer ha-Hokhmah* (containing his responsa and legal decisions, Talmudic interpretations, and even *Tosafot* to selected tractates), which is no longer extant.[36] His position on *halitzah* by an apostate is recorded in a gloss to *Sefer Mordekhai* on Bavli Yevamot which is further clarified by later rabbinic works.[37]

Unlike the *Geonim* (and Rashi), Barukh of Mainz maintains that the *zikah* between the other brothers and the widowed brother's wife is established not at the time of their wedding (*nissu'in mappilim*) but rather at the point at which the brother dies (*mitah mappelet*), which renders the issue of whether a potential *yavam* had already apostatized by the time of the marriage moot. At the time of his brother's death, the brother in question is surely an apostate, and as such, no *zikah* is created between him and his deceased brother's wife.

The question of *mitah mappelet* or *nissu'in mappilim* is discussed twice within *Yevamot* (13a and 30b, in a somewhat more muted context). Two early Sefardic *Rishonim*, Rabbenu Hanan'el b. Hushi'el of Kairwan (d. 1056) and Isaac b. Jacob Alfasi (*Rif*, d. 1103 in Lucena), ruled that *mitah mappelet* (following the view of the *Amoraim*, Rava, and Rav Ashi), although this remains a minority opinion among subsequent *Rishonim*.[38] In this instance, Barukh of Mainz and another of his rabbinic colleagues in central Europe made use of this Sefardic approach to solve the thorny problem of eliminating the need for *halitzah* where the only brother available was an apostate.

Indeed, as far as I can tell, no Ashkenazic rabbinic figure before Barukh of Mainz espoused this view, despite the fact that Tosafists frequently cited (and accepted) the views of Rabbenu Hanan'el.[39] R. Barukh presents additional support for this approach, adducing a proof from a *sugya* not mentioned by Rabbenu Hanan'el. Bavli Yevamot (108b–109a) questions whether a woman, whose husband divorced her and subsequently remarried her (*mahzir gerushato*, which is permitted only when she had not married another in between), can live with her husband's brother if he performs *yibbum* following the husband's death, since she and her husband are presently together only as the result of the remarriage. The Talmud suggests that this question depends on when the *zikah* was created: at the time of (the initial) marriage, or only when the husband dies. The Talmud rules that *yibbum* is possible in such a case (as codified also by Alfasi), suggesting that the position of *mitah mappelet* is normative. In light of this, Barukh of Mainz concludes, like Abraham of Regensburg albeit via a rather different interpretational strategy, that an apostate does not perform *halitzah*.

At the end of a lengthy passage, Isaac b. Moses of Vienna also appears to support the position taken by R. Barukh. The passage begins with citations from several *geonic* texts including *Sefer Basar 'al Gabbei Gehalim*, a *geonic* collection cited only by Ashkenazic authorities, which also contains a smattering of eleventh-century Ashkenazic material.[40] The conclusion of this portion of Isaac b. Moses's presentation is that if the brother apostatized prior to his brother's marriage, no *halitzah* is required. R. Isaac notes that even though the various *geonic* texts cited do not adduce Talmudic proofs to support their view, he is prepared to accept it, and he provides a proof of his own.

However, Isaac of Vienna adds that if the brother in question had been an apostate at the time of his brother's wedding but subsequently reverted (and remained in that state until his brother's death), a *zikah* between the widow and the penitent former apostate is created, which can then lead to either *halitzah* or *yibbum* if the brother dies, even though the now-penitent brother had been an apostate at the time of the marriage itself. R. Isaac supports this ruling with a *sugya* in Bavli Yevamot noted above (30b), in which Rava and Rav Ashi maintain that the death of the brother is what creates the *zikah* (*mitah mappelet*) rather than the marriage, noting also that Rabbenu Hanan'el had decided in favor of this view.

Isaac of Vienna further extends the scope and impact of Rabbenu Hanan'el's ruling: "For Rabbenu Hanan'el who rules that *mitah mappelet*, if he was an apostate when his brother died [even if he had been an observant Jew at the time of his wedding], he does not perform *halitzah* or *yibbum*, since the death creates the *zikah*. And at the time of his brother's death, he was not a Jew [*ubi-she'at mitah lo hayah yehudi*]." This application, which is ultimately the same as the one made by Barukh of Mainz (who is not cited here), moves beyond the allowance provided by the *Geonim*. Isaac *Or Zarua'* does not mean to say that an apostate is literally considered to be a non-Jew in terms of his personal religious status. Rather, the apostate is excluded from performing *halitzah* as if he were a non-Jew, since the widow cannot live with him.[41]

In his abridgement of *Sefer Or Zarua'* (known as *Simmanei Or Zarua'* or *Or Zarua' Katzar*), Isaac of Vienna's son, Hayyim Eli`ezer, reduces the lengthy passage just described to a few lines, in which the position of Rabbenu Hanan'el is equal (in terms of the space devoted to it and its weight) to the ruling of the *Geonim*. Indeed, in at least one version of the passage in *Or Zarua' Katzar*, R. Hayyim, when presenting his father's approach, rules explicitly in accordance with Rabbenu Hanan'el.[42] In a responsum, R. Hayyim was asked to clarify his father's stance. Did he rule in this matter like the "view of our northern French teachers" who, following the approach of Rashi, required an apostate to perform *halitzah* in all situations; or did R. Isaac agree with those who "ruled leniently (*ke-divrei ha-mattirim*)," that the apostate does not do *halitzah* at all?[43]

In a missive sent to Isaac of Vienna, Isaiah b. Mali of Trani (*RiD*, d. *c.* 1240), who had studied together with R. Isaac under Simhah of Speyer, implores R. Isaac not to side with those who ruled that a *yevamah* who had fallen before an apostate does not require *halizah*. *RiD* also chides R. Isaac for being swayed by the *geonic* view, which according to RiD appears to be against talmudic law: "Do not be one of the lenient ones (*min ha-mekilim*) who permits a Torah prohibition with impunity (*be-yad ramah*), without any proof from the Talmud."[44] In defense of some of his earlier remarks, *RiD* asserts that "even though an apostate has done evil and blasphemed and given himself to idolatry, he cannot be stripped of his *kedushat Yisra'el*."[45]

Following up on a formulation in *Sefer Yerei'im* by his teacher, Eli`ezer b. Samuel of Metz (d. 1198), Simhah of Speyer considered taking the step of largely disqualifying the *kiddushin* and *get* of an apostate on the basis of a *sugya* in Bavli Yevamot (16b), which suggests that doubts concerning the Jewish status of a husband render these acts less than fully effective. For R. Eli'ezer and R. Simhah, the *kiddushin* of an apostate would thus be valid only *le-humra*, meaning that while a *get* is required to retract such a marriage, the marriage itself is not completely valid. R. Simhah notes that in addition, an apostate may not be capable of authorizing and delivering a *get* according to Jewish law.

However, R. Simhah's student, R. Bonfant (Samuel *ha-Levi* of Worms) writes that his teacher found a *geonic* responsum in the name of Rav Kohen Tzedek Gaon (of Sura, ninth century), in which he rules that an apostate may effectively give his wife a *get* since marriage and divorce are inextricably linked by Talmudic exegesis (*makshinan havayah li-yetzi'ah*, based on Leviticus 27:19 and Deuteronomy 24:2, as per Bavli Kiddushin 5a and 41a).[46] R. Simhah's German Tosafist contemporary, *Rabiah* of Cologne, was aware of the view which held that the *get* of an apostate is ineffective because it is comparable to one given by a husband who was initially sound but is now unbalanced (*'ashfuye venishtateh*; Bavli Yevamot 112b, and Gittin 71b). However, *Rabiah* does not endorse this position, noting that Rabbenu Tam (d. 1171) reports in a responsum that he executed (*'asah*) *gittin* for more than twenty apostates in his day in northern France.[47] In any case, a restrictive approach with regard to the effectiveness of the *kiddushin* and *get* of an apostate would move well beyond the assignment of a lower Jewish status to an apostate (only) with respect to levirate marriage, as Abraham of Regensburg, Barukh of Mainz, and Isaac of Vienna had advocated.

Moneylending at Interest

Consistent with his overall view, Rashi ruled that interest cannot be taken from an apostate on a loan extended to him by a Jew (except in instances where the apostate sought an unfair advantage), just as an apostate cannot charge a Jew interest. Based on the principle of *'af 'al pi shehata Yisra'el hu*, Rashi held that an apostate is considered to be "your brother" with respect to the verses in the Torah (Lev. 25:36, and Deut. 23:20–21) that regulate the charging of interest.[48] Although several Tosafists ratified Rashi's approach, others raised questions based on a number of Talmudic *sugyot*.

Commenting on the *sugya* in Bavli Bava Metzia (70b–71a) which establishes the parameters of taking interest from non-Jews, the mid-twelfth-century German Tosafist (and maternal grandfather of *Rabiah*), Eli`ezer b. Nathan (*Raban*) of Mainz, also prohibited the taking of interest from an apostate because *'af 'al pi she-hata yisra'el hu*. In the same comment, however, *Raban* prohibits a Jews from selling improperly slaughtered animals (or sickly animals even if slaughtered properly, *terefot*) to an apostate because of the prohibition against placing a stumbling block before the blind (Lev. 19:14, *lifnei 'ivver lo tittein mikhshol*).[49]

In a passage from his (no longer extant) *Sefer ha-Hokhmah*, Barukh of Mainz writes that he heard (from someone identified only as "my relative and teacher") that Jews in northern France were permitted to lend money to apostates and to borrow from them at interest. These allowances were based on a *sugya* in Bavli 'Avodah Zarah (26a–b), which asserts that neither heretics nor informants are to be rendered economic support. R. Barukh maintains, however, that it prohibited for a Jew to borrow from or lend to an apostate at interest, because "who allowed him [*mi hitter lo*] to transgress these commandments?" Since the apostate is himself prohibited by Jewish law from being involved in a usurious transaction, other Jews cannot participate with him in such a transaction either, due to the prohibition of *lifnei 'ivver*.[50]

The "teacher and relative" to whom R. Barukh refers is Eli'ezer of Metz, who studied with Rabbenu Tam in northern France. R. Eli`ezer concludes in his *Sefer Yere'im* that "when a person pushes away permitted items and eats prohibited ones (*hekha de-shavik hetera ve-'akhil 'isura*)," he is considered to be a heretic (*min*) and must be treated accordingly. In Leviticus 25:35, the Torah instructs a Jew to support and strengthen his brother if he becomes needy. As indicated in the next verse, money lent to him for this purpose cannot be at interest because he is a brother who must be sustained. Since an apostate is not considered to be a brother because of his heresy, charging him interest is permitted (as per Bavli Avodah Zarah 26a–b).[51]

Another of Rabbenu Tam's students, *Ri* of Dampierre, based this allowance on Bavli Bava Metzia 62a, which understands Leviticus 25:36 to mean that not taking interest from a brother is crucial to his being sustained. For *Ri*, this means that an apostate, "who cleaves to the ways of the nations, practicing idolatry and forsaking the Torah, is rendered completely as a non-Jew (*ke-goy gamur*), even with respect to the obligation to sustain them." *Ri* also adduces a passage from the Yerushalmi ('Avodah Zarah 5:3), which permitted the taking of interest from the Cutheans of Caesarea after they had apostatized.[52]

According to *Ri*, since a Jew is permitted to lend at interest to an apostate, the apostate is permitted to pay that interest. However, *Ri* insists that an apostate still cannot not lend at interest to Jews, just as an apostate is not permitted to steal from or cheat them; and they are likewise not permitted to borrow money from the apostate at interest. Although this aspect of *Ri*'s position undercuts the full leniency put forward by Eli'ezer of Metz and Rabbenu Tam, *Ri* is still quite distant from the view of Barukh of Mainz (and Rashi), which does not allow any interest to be taken by either side.[53]

Rabiah also cites the Yerushalmi passage that allowed Jews to lend at interest to an apostate, and he further notes a responsum by Nathan b. Yehi'el of Rome (d. 1103), author of the *'Arukh*, that the talmudic notion of *'af 'al pi she-hata Yisra'el hu* was enunciated only with regard to an apostate's *get*, or his involvement with *halitzah*. However, when it comes, to monetary matters (*mamona*, which includes the taking of interest), it is appropriate to fine an apostate (*ra'ui le-konso*), just as the Tanna R. Meir exempted a Jew from making payment if his ox gored that of a Cuthean (Bavli Bava Kamma 38b).[54]

Moving forward in northern France, Moses b. Jacob of Coucy (d. *c.* 1255), author of *Sefer Mitzvot Gadol* (and a student of *Ri*'s student, Judah Sirleon of Paris), cites Eli`ezer of Metz in his *Sefer Yere'im* (as he often does), that one may lend money to an apostate at interest (and borrow from him at interest), along with the view of a Tosafist colleague, Samuel b. Solomon of Falaise (d. *c.* 1245), that one may not lend money to an apostate at interest because of the *lifnei ʿivver* issue that had been raised by Barukh of Mainz (whose name is not mentioned). Even though a Jew is not obligated to support an apostate (and he therefore should be permitted to lend to the apostate with interest), lending to him at interest causes the apostate to violate a prohibition for which he remains responsible. Moses of Coucy cites the Yerushalmi passage noted above in support of Eli`ezer of Metz's view, that there is no problem of *lifnei ʿivver* when lending money at interest to an apostate. It seems, however, that Moses of Coucy was not prepared to allow a Jew to borrow from an apostate at interest, in accordance with the distinction offered by *Ri* (whose name is also not mentioned).[55]

As *Rabiah* did, Moses of Coucy stresses that the possibility of treating the apostate like a non-Jew is limited only to moneylending at interest, since the Torah specifically associates this prohibition with brotherhood (*she-harei le-gabbei ribbit ʾahvah ketiv beh*). However, when it comes to initiating marriage and divorce, about which terms of brotherhood are not mentioned by the Torah, Moses of Coucy asserts that these religious acts when performed by an apostate are fully effective, a position maintained elsewhere in *Semag*.[56]

When asked whether it is permitted to lend to an apostate at interest, the Tosafist Yehiʾel b. Joseph of Paris (d. *c.* 1260; he too studied with Judah Sirleon) cites the permissive ruling of Rabbenu Tam, although as with *Sefer Mitzvot Gadol*, some of R. Yehiʾel's supporting talmudic texts are those of *Ri* of Dampierre. R. Yehiʾel adds that while the Talmud in Bavli Bavli Bava Kamma (119a) prohibits confiscating the money of a Jewish informant because he is still within the Jewish community and may yet have worthy descendants, the assets of an apostate, who lives among the Christians and is "submerged" (*nishka*) among them, can be confiscated even via theft and certainly through the taking of interest. However, R. Yehiʾel rules (again, like *Ri*) that a Jew cannot borrow from an apostate at interest, since this accrues to the apostate's benefit (*le-hashbiho*). The reason given here by R. Yehiʾel's reason is different from the one provided by *Ri* (that the apostate remains culpable for lending at interest to a Jew), which perhaps reflects a harsher view of the apostate in real terms.[57]

Among the *Rishonim* of Spain, *Ramban*, in his *hiddushim*, cites the northern French Tosafist position (in the name of Rabbenu Tam) that a Jew is permitted to lend to an apostate at interest (based on *ʿAvodah Zarah* 26b, and on the Yerushalmi passage), although *Ramban* also concludes that borrowing money from an apostate at interest may be prohibited.[58] In a responsum, Nahmanides asserts that an apostate is considered as a Jew with regard to his ability to affect *kiddushin* and a *get*, and to be involved with *halitzah*. *Ramban* informs his questioner that "this is my view in this matter, although nothing from the *Rishonim* has reached me. You should search within the responsa of the *Geonim* and the works of R. Judah [b. Barzilai of Barcelona, c. 1100], and let me know if even a kernel of material is found there." In this instance, *Ramban* does not refer to northern European rabbinic sources.[59]

Citation patterns similar to that of *Ramban* in his *hiddushim* can still be detected in Sefardic responsa from the late medieval period. Solomon b. Simeon Duran of Algiers (*Rashbash*, d. 1467) cites the *hiddushim* of Ramban's student, *Rashba* (to Bavli Yevamot

22a) that the *kiddushin* of an apostate are valid. He then cites "the students of Rashi" that interest cannot be taken from an apostate, noting that Rabbenu Tam, on the other hand, allowed it. *Rashbash* concludes by citing (in the name of *rabbanei Tzarefat*) the responsum of Isaac b. Abraham of Dampierre (*Ritzba*), that a returning apostate requires neither immersion nor an act of reacceptance before a rabbinic tribunal.[60] In a responsum about immersion for returning apostates (*'anusim*) from Islam, David ibn Zimra (*Radbaz*, d. 1573) mentions only the names of Simhah of Speyer and *Riba* of Speyer. Although immersion is meant to achieve a state of repentance and is thus not an obligatory ritual, it should nonetheless be done because these *'anusim* are now moving from a state of impurity (in which they live as non-Jews), to a state of purity.[61]

In another responsum about lending money at interest to the children of apostates (*bnei mumarim*, referring to *conversos* who fled from Spain or Portugal to Turkey and then traveled to Alexandria to conduct business), *Radbaz* begins with Rashi's responsum that this is prohibited. He then cites *Ri* who permitted this because apostates are not considered to be "your brethren (*'ahikha*)," based on the Yerushalmi passage, adding (as *Ri* did) that a Jew may not borrow from an apostate at interest. *Radbaz* notes that Moses of Coucy accepted *Ri*'s allowance in his *Sefer Mitzvot Gadol* (even as this is not the case for *gittin* and *kiddushin*), as Ramban and *Rashba* did in their *hiddushim*.[62] Here again in these *halakhic* aspects of apostasy, the indebtedness of Sefardic rabbinic authorities to their Ashkenazic colleagues remains firmly in evidence.

By the late medieval period, Ashkenazic rabbinic authorities as well did not express their Talmudic analyses in systematic commentaries, but rather in their responsa and other *halakhic* rulings. The leading rabbinic figure in fifteenth-century Austria and Germany, Israel Isserlein, laments that there is no shortage of "derelicts and scoundrels (*rekim u-pohazim*)" who seek to return to the Jewish community with less than complete contrition and sincerity, in order to benefit in some personal way from their reversion.[63] In addition, there were a series of persecutions in 1420–21 in Vienna and its environs that led to the apostasy of a number of men and women.[64]

Isserlein held that it is permitted to charge apostates interest because "even where permitted foods are available, they eat prohibited foods."[65] His student, Israel Bruna of Regensburg, offers a broader Talmudic proof that an apostate who "denies the God of the Jews and accepts idolatry" is not considered to be a Jew.[66] At the same time, however, both Isserlein and Israel Bruna openly reject the approach of Abraham of Regensburg and Isaac *Or Zarua*' that removed an apostate from the performance of *halitzah*.[67] Nonetheless, Israel Bruna elsewhere notes that Isserlein allowed a groom whose brother was an apostate to stipulate that his marriage would be valid only if it did not result in the apostate brother serving as a *levir*. If it turned out that the apostate was the only *levir* available, the marriage is retroactively annulled and the widow does not require *halitzah* in order to remarry.[68] In this way, these rabbinic figures took advantage of the leniency of the German Tosafists concerning an apostate and *halitzah*, while not running afoul of the majority view among the Tosafists (and that of Rashi) that an apostate brother is required to perform *halitzah*.[69]

Conclusion

Throughout this study, we have seen that when seeking the interpretations of the *Rishonim*, it is necessary to consult not only their Talmudic glosses and other direct comments, but also their responsa and rulings, which are often quite rich in Talmudic analyses. Awareness of the transmission of rabbinic texts from one period to another and (geographically) within the same period is also necessary. It cannot be assumed that everything written in an earlier century was known to all subsequent Talmudic interpreters, or that everything composed in northern Europe was known in southern Europe and vice versa. Nonetheless, texts and ideas traveled, and the possible pathways for such exchanges must be considered.

Notes

1. See Ephraim Kanarfogel, *Brothers from Afar: Rabbinic Approaches to Apostasy and Reversion in Medieval Europe* (Detroit, MI: Wayne State University Press, 2021), for the full range of rabbinic issues and views and their contextualization, including related trends in Christian society. The present study focuses on textual methods and strategies.
2. For a geographic and chronological survey of the *Rishonim* who flourished in Europe, see Ephraim Kanarfogel, "Talmudic Studies," in *The Cambridge History of Judaism, Vol. 6: The Middle Ages: The Christian World*, ed. R. Chazan (Cambridge: Cambridge University Press, 2018), 582–619. On the beginning of the period of the *Aharonim* (including the role that printing played), see Jay Berkovitz, "Rabbinic Culture and the Historical Development of *Halakhah*," in *The Cambridge History of Judaism, Vol. 7: The Early Modern World, 1500–1815*, ed. J. Karp and A. Sutcliffe (Cambridge: Cambridge University Press, 2018), 349–61 (and the literature cited in 359 n. 44).
3. See Gerald Blidstein, "Who Is Not a Jew? The Medieval Discussion," *Israel Law Review* 11, no. 3 (1976): 369–90. Apostasy during the *geonic* period typically involved Islam, while conversion away from Judaism in medieval Europe was to Christianity. See Uriel Simonsohn, "Are Geonic Responsa a Reliable Source for the Study of Jewish Conversion to Islam? A Comparative Analysis of Legal Sources," in *Jews, Christians and Muslims in Medieval and Early Modern Times*, ed. A. Franklin et al. (Leiden, The Netherlands: Brill, 2014), 119–38.
4. See *Teshuvot Rashi*, ed. I. Elfenbein (New York: 1943), 192 (171).
5. Ibid., 173.
6. On *nissu'in mappilin*, see *Otzar ha-Geonim*, vol. 7 [*Yevamot*], ed. B. M. Lewin (Jerusalem: Hebrew University Press, 1936), 37 (sec. 85), 305 (sec. 32); *Hilkhot ha-Rif li-Yevamot* 13a (fol. 3a) and 30b (fol. 8b); and cf. *Sefer ha-Miktzo'ot*, ed. S. Assaf (Jerusalem: Mossad ha-Rav Kook, 1947), 11; *Tosafot Yevamot* 13a, s.v. *nissu'in*; *Tosafot Yevamot* 30a, s.v. *ne'esrah*; *Tosafot* 84b, s.v. *ve-khi*; and Blidstein, "Who Is a Not a Jew?," 380 n. 39.
7. *Teshuvot Rashi*, 175. Rashi characterizes the apostate here as a *Yisra'el meshummad ve-hote*.
8. See J. Katz, "'Af 'al pi she-Hata Yisra'el Hu," *Tarbiz* 27 (1958): 203–17; J. Katz, *Halakhah ve-Kabbalah* (Jerusalem: Magnes Press, 1986), 255–69.

9. See J. Katz, *Exclusiveness and Tolerance* (Oxford: Oxford University Press, 1961), 69–70, esp. 73; J. Katz, *Bein Yehudim le-Goyim* (Jerusalem: Mossad Bialik, 1960), 76–77, esp. 80. See also *Teshuvot Rashi*, 168, that the wine of a former apostate is immediately available for Jewish consumption following his reversion, even if his apostasy had not been coerced; and cf. Avraham Grossman, *Hakhmei Tzarefat ha-Rishonim* (Jerusalem: Magnes Press, 1995), 152–53.
10. R. Natronai, R. 'Amram, and R. Paltoi are among the *Geonim* associated with this position; see *Teshuvot R. Natronai b. Hilai Gaon*, ed. R. Brody (Jerusalem: Ofek, 1994), 469 (sec. 315), and n. 6. Sefer Or Zarua, ed. Y. Farbstein (Jerusalem: Machon Yerushalayim, 2010), attributes this position to Rav Nahshon Gaon.
11. See ms. Oxford 566, fols. 60b–61a (Simcha Emanuel, *Teshuvot Maharam va-Haverav* (Jerusalem: World Union of Jewish Studies, 2012), 489–90, sec. 188); and ms. Vercelli C1, fol. 292a (Emanuel, *Teshuvot Maharam*, 487 n. 2). In ms. Vercelli, Ri distinguishes between becoming a *haver*, which cannot be accomplished absent the verification of a rabbinic tribunal, and the reversion of an apostate who recognizes that without immersing himself and reaccepting membership within the Jewish community and its observances, he will still be considered like a non-Jew (*muhzaq ke-goy*).
12. See *Sefer Or Zarua'*, 1:387 (sec. 448, end); and *Shitah Mekubbetzet 'al Massekhet Bekhorot*, ed. Y. D. Ilan (Bnei Brak, 1992), 149. *Sefer Or Zarua'* is a rich source for Tosafist texts from northern France, including versions of the *Tosafot* of Samson of Sens that are not found as clearly or completely in the standard editions of the Talmud. See, e.g., *Tosafot 'Eruvin* 72a, s.v. *u-modin*; *Sefer Or Zarua'*, 2:248–49 (sec. 172, end). Cf. A. R. Reiner, "From Rabbenu Tam to R. Isaac of Vienna: The Hegemony of the French Talmudic School in the Twelfth Century," in *The Jews of Europe in the Middle Ages*, ed. C. Cluse (Turnhout, Belgium: Brepols, 2004), 273–82.
13. See ms. Oxford 844, fols. 82d–83a (Emanuel, *Teshuvot Maharam*, 487–88).
14. See *Teshuvot u-Pesakim*, ed. E. Kupfer (Jerusalem: Mekitse Nirdamim, 1973), 290–91 (sec. 173); and *Sefer Or Zarua'*, 1:105–6 (sec. 112). Isaac *Or Zarua* was also a student of Simhah of Speyer, residing for a time in his home; see *Sefer Or Zarua'*, 3:667 (*piskei 'avodah zarah*, sec. 271).
15. See Ephraim Kanarfogel, "From Germany to Northern France and Back Again: A Tale of Two Tosafist Centers," in *Regional Identities and Cultures of Medieval Jews*, ed. J. Castano et al. (London: Littman Library, 2018), 149–71.
16. See Moses of Zurich, *Ha-Semak mi-Zurich*, vol. 2, ed. Y. Y. Har-Shoshanim (Jerusalem: Alef-Bet Press, 1977), 49 (*mitzvah* 156). The passage likely originated in *Rabiah*'s lost *halakhic* work, *Sefer Avi'asaf*. See also *Kitzur Sefer Mitzvot Gadol le-R. Avraham b. Ephraim*, ed. Y. Horowitz (Jerusalem: Mekitse Nirdamim, 2005), 194, where this passage appears without specific attribution (*'omrim*).
17. See *Perush ha-Sifra ha-Meyuhas le-R. Shimshon mi-Shantz* (Jerusalem: Safra Press, 1959), *pararshat Emor, parsheta* 14 (fol. 110b), in the context of the individual of mixed Jewish identity who blasphemed the Almighty (Lev. 24). The teacher of the author of this commentary was the German rabbinic scholar, David b. Kalonymus of Muenzberg; see E. E. Urbach, *Ba'alei ha-Tosafot* (Jerusalem: Mossad Bialik, 1984), 1:366.
18. See *Perushim u-Pesakim le-R. Avigdor b. Eliyyahu* (Brooklyn, NY: Machon Harerei Kedem, 1996), 410–11; R. Avigdor's ruling appears at the beginning of *parashat Ki Tetze*, in connection with *'eshet yefat to'ar*. Samson of Sens also presumed that a married couple who

had apostatized together did not stray; see *Haggahot Maimuniyyot, hilkhot 'issurei bi'ah*, 18:2 [1].

19. See *Hiddushei ha-Ritva le-Massekhet Yevamot* (47b), ed. A. Jofen (Jerusalem: Mossad ha-Rav Kook, 1988), 330–32.
20. See, e.g., Ephraim Kanarfogel, "*Halakhah* and *Metzi'ut* (Realia) in Medieval Ashkenaz: Surveying the Parameters and Defining the Limits," *The Jewish Law Annual* 14 (2003): 193–201.
21. See *Tosafot* and *Tosafot ha-Rosh* to *Yevamot* 47b, s.v. *sham ger ve-'eved tovlim*, ed. Y. D. Bar-Ilan (Jerusalem: Mossad ha-Rav Kook, 2016), 464–65; and cf. *Tosafot Kiddushin* 62b, *'ela me-'attah*, and Isaac of Corbeil, *Sefer Mitzvot Katan* (Constantinople, 1510), sec. 159. Maimonides rules that the immersion of a freed slave also requires the presence of three. See *Mishneh Torah, hilkhot 'issurei bi'ah* 13:12; and *Maggid Mishneh*, ad loc.
22. See *Hiddushei ha-Ramban*, and *Hiddushei ha-Rashba* to *Yevamot* 47b (end).
23. See *Tosafot Maharam ve-Rabbenu Peretz 'al Massekhet Yevamot*, ed. H. Porush (Jerusalem: Self-published, 1991), 129–30 (48a), *s.v. ki tanya ha-hi.*
24. See Ephraim Kanarfogel, "Rabbinic Conceptions of Marriage and Matchmaking in Medieval Europe," in *Entangled Histories*, ed. E. Baumgarten et al. (Philadelphia: University of Pennsylvania Press, 2017), 271 (n. 28). On *Ritva*'s use of these particular Tosafist collections, see Ephraim Kanarfogel, "Between Ashkenaz and Sefarad: Tosafist Teachings in the Talmudic Commentares of *Ritva*," in *Between Rashi and Maimonides*, ed. E. Kanarfogel and M. Sokolow (New York: KTAV, 2010), 250–73.
25. See ms. Vercelli C1, fol. 291v. The Torah compilation *Hizzekuni*, produced by Hezekiah b. Mahoah in northern France *c.* 1275, presents the explanation of Moses *ha-Darshan* of Narbonne, as cited by Rashi (Nu. 8:7), that the Levites immersed themselves and shaved their entire bodies as they entered into the service of the Tabernacle because the idolatry associated with the sin of the golden calf is equated with spiritual death, and the Levites' appointment signifies the renewal of life in the service of God. The *Hizzekuni* passage concludes: "And for that reason, penitents [from apostasy] are required to shave themselves [prior to their immersion]." To be sure, this is not a *halakhic* derivation for these practices, which by this time had apparently become widespread in northern France as well, although R. Israel Isserlein cites the interpretation of Moses *ha-Darshan* as support for these practices in late medieval Ashkenaz. See Israel Isserlein, *Terumat ha-Deshen*, ed. S. Abbitan (Jerusalem: Self-published, 1991), 1:76–77, esp. 86.
26. Solomon of Montpelier was a teacher of Ramban's cousin, Rabbenu Jonah b. Abraham of Gerona, and Ramban refers to him as a colleague (*haveri*). Nahmanides's question is not extant, but R. Solomon's response has been published no fewer than three times during the past century, most recently by H. S. Sha'anan in *Moriah* 9/11–12 (1980), 3–4.
27. See Israel Ta-Shma, *R. Zerahyah he-Levi u-Bnei Hugo* (Jerusalem: Mossad ha-Rav Kook, 1992), 27, 106–12, 148–49, 165–66; and Kanarfogel, "Talmudic Studies," 598–602.
28. See also *Shibbolei ha-Leket le-R. Zidkiyyah b. Avraham ha-Rofe mi-Romi*, part 2, ed. S. Hasida (Jerusalem: Ha-Segulah, 1988), 198 (sec. 147).
29. See *She'elot u-Teshuvot ha-Rashba*, 5:66, 7:411.
30. See *Hiddushei ha-Ritva le-Massekhet Yevamot* (47b), 330–32. Cf. Joseph Shatzmiller, "Converts and Judaizers in the Early Fourteenth Century," *Harvard Theological Review* 74 (1981): 63–77.
31. See *Teshuvot Rashi*, 171, 173.

32. See *Sefer Mordekhai 'al Massekhet Yevamot*, sec. 30; and *Teshuvot Maimuniyyot le-hilkhot 'ishut*, 29.
33. See *Sefer Mordekhai ha-Shalem*, ed. S. Rubin (Jerusalem: Machon Yerushalayim, 2021), 2:28–29 (sec. 29, to *Yevamot* 39a; in several manuscripts and in the printed edition, the reference is to R. Abraham *ha-Gadol*). On Abraham b. Moses as a Tosafist, see Urbach, *Ba'alei ha-Tosafot*, 207–8, 434–47; and Simcha Emanuel, *Shivrei Luhot* (Jerusalem: Magnes Press, 2006), 83–84 n. 147, esp. 109 n. 31, 224 n. 24.
34. Cf. Avraham Grossman, *Hakhmei Ashkenaz ha-Rishonim* (Jerusalem: Magnes Press, 1981), 154–57, 430–31.
35. See *Teshuvot u-Pesakim*, 296 (sec. 176).
36. See Urbach, *Ba'alei ha-Tosafot*, 425–29; and Emanuel, *Shivrei Luhot*, 104–53.
37. See *Haggahot Mordekhai 'al Massekhet Yevamot*, sec. 107; *She'elot u-Teshuvot Mahari Mintz*, ed. A. Siev (New York: Yeshiva University, 1995), 12 (fols. 46a, 47b); and *She'elot u-Teshuvot R. Eliyyahu Mizrahi* (Constantinople, 1560), 68 (fols. 231a, 232a).
38. See *Otzar ha-Geonim*, 37 (sec. 85), 305 (sec. 32); *Hilkhot ha-Rif li-Yevamot* 13a (fol. 3a) and 30b (fol. 8b); and cf. *Sefer ha-Miktzo'ot*, ed. S. Assaf (Jerusalem: Mossad ha-Rav Kook, 1947), 11; *Tosafot Yevamot* 13a, s.v. *nissu'in*; *Tosafot Yevamot* 30a, s. v. *ne'esrah*; *Tosafot* 84b, s.v. *ve-khi*; and Blidstein, "Who Is Not a Jew?," 380 n. 39.
39. See Israel Ta-Shma, *Knesset Mekarim*, vol. 1 (Jerusalem: Mossad Bialik, 2004), 43–49.
40. Cf. Simcha Emanuel, *Me-Ginzei Eiropah*, vol. 2 (Jerusalem: Mekitse Nirdamim, 2019), 62–69.
41. See *Sefer Or Zarua'*, 1:494–96 (sec. 605); and see also *Haggahot Mordekhai 'al Massekhet Yevamot*, sec. 108. *Sefer Or Zarua'* mentions Barukh of Mainz less than a handful of times; see Emanuel, *Shivrei Luhot*, 141.
42. See *Sefer Or Zarua'*, 1:494b, in the margin [*Piskei Or Zarua le-Rabbenu Hayyim b. Yitzhak me-Vienna*, ed. M. Y. Blau, 1:117, sec. 18]; *Haggahot Mordekhai 'al Massekhet Yevamot*, sec. 107; and *She'elot u-Teshuvot Mahari Mintz.*
43. See *Teshuvot Maharah Or Zarua*, ed. M. Abbitan (Jerusalem: Self-published, 2002), 106–7, esp. 116; and Blidstein, "Who Is Not a Jew?," 380–81 n. 42.
44. See *Teshuvot ha-RiD le-R. Yeshayah di Trani ha-Zaken*, ed. A. Y. Wertheimer (Jerusalem: Ha-Machon ha-Talmud ha-Yisraeli ha-Shalem, 1975), 326, 64. On R. Isaiah's presence in the Rhineland, see Ta-Shma, *Knesset Mehkarim*, vol. 3 (Jerusalem: Mossad Bialik, 2005), 20–25, 40–43.
45. See *Teshuvot ha-RiD*, 486 (sec. 99).
46. See *Sefer Yere'im ha-Shalem*, ed. A. A. Schiff (Vilna, 1892–1902), fol. 74a (sec. 156, end); *Teshuvot u-Pesakim*, 295–96 (sec. 176); and Blidstein, "Who Is Not a Jew?," 369, 372 n. 12, 377 n. 24.
47. See *Sefer Rabiah*, ed. A. Aptowitzer, vol. 1 (Jerusalem: Self-published, 1983), 158–59 (sec. 151); *Sefer Mordekhai 'al Massekhet 'Avodah Zarah*, sec. 814; *Teshuvot Maimuniyyot le-hilkhot 'ishut*, 12.
48. See *Teshuvot Rashi*, 175.
49. See *Sefer Raban*, ed. D. Deblitzky (Bnei Brak: Self-published, 2012), 3:159 (sec. 457).
50. See *Shitah Mekubbetzet, Hiddushei Bava Metzia*, ed. Oz Ve-Hadar, vol. 2 (Jerusalem: Self-published, 1996), fols. 553b–554a.
51. See *Sefer Yere'im ha-Shalem*, fols. 72a–74a (sec. 156). Cf. Alyysa Gray, "R. Eliezer of Metz's Exclusion of Charity of the Jewish *'Avaryan be-Mezid* ('Deliberate Transgressor')," in *Approaches to Poverty in Medieval Europe*, ed. Sharon Farmer (Turnhout, Belgium:

Brepols, 2016), 67–92. *Ri* of Dampierre (in *Teshuvot R. YitzhaK b. Shmu'el mi-Dampierre*, ed. P. Roth and A. R. Reiner [Jerusalem: Mekitse Nirdamim, 2020]) indicates that this was also the position of Rabbnu Tam. No *Geonim* permitted charging an apostate interest. See Blidstein, "Who Is Not a Jew?," 385–87; and Simcha Emanuel, "Teshuvot ha-Geonim ha-Ketzarot," in *'Atarah le-Hayyim*, ed. D. Boyarin et al. (Jerusalem: Magnes Press, 2000), 447–49.

52. See *Teshuvot R. YitzhaK b. Shmu'el mi-Dampierre*, 94–98 (sec. 61); this approach is recorded anonymously in *Tosafot 'Avodah Zarah* 26b, s.v. *'ani*. On the penetration of the Yerushalmi into northern Europe during this period, see Urbach, *Ba 'alei ha-Tosafot*, 703–12; and cf. A. R. Reiner, "The Yerushalmi in Rabbenu Tam's Library," *Revue des etudes juives* 178 (2019): 357–89.
53. To be sure, Rashi prohibits moneylending at interest because an apostate is considered to be a Jew, while R. Barukh does not allow this because even though Jews are not required to support an apostate, the apostate's personal religious identity as a Jew remains and he is still culpable for participating in a usurious transaction. R. Barukh's exclusion of an apostate from *halitzah* (see Urbach, *Ba'alei ha-Tosafot*, 425–29; Emanuel, *Shivrei Luhot*, 104–53; *Haggahot Mordekhai 'al Massekhet Yevamot*, sec. 107; *She'elot u-Teshuvot Mahari Mintz*; and *She'elot u-Teshuvot*) is predicated on the apostate's diminished status from the perspective of other Jews.
54. See *Sefer Rabiah*. The essence of this distinction appears already in Eli ' ezer of Metz's *Sefer Yere'im*.
55. See *Sefer Mitzvot Gadol* (Venice, 1547), vol. 2, fol. 207b (*'aseh* 162, on giving charity). The name of Samuel b. Solomon of Falaise's is also recorded in this context in *Kitzur Sefer Mitzvot Gadol*, 131, and in a number of manuscripts of *Sefer Mordekhai 'al Massekhet 'Avodah Zarah*. In the printed *Sefer Mordekhai*, however, this position appears in the name of Eli ' ezer b. Solomon, who posed a question to Rabbenu Tam (and was the author of two *selihot*); see Urbach, *Ba 'alei ha-Tosafot*, 61–62.
56. See *Sefer Mitzvot Gadol*, vol. 2, fol. 125b (*'aseh* 48: *Yisra'el meshummad she-kidesh 'af 'al pi she-'avad 'avodah zarah me-retzono harei 'elu kiddushin gemurin u-tzerikha mimmenu get*).
57. See Emanuel, *Teshuvot Maharam mi-Rothenburg va-Haverav*, 796 (sec. 413). Isaiah di Trani again espouses Rashi's position, that no interest may be collected from an apostate or paid to him. See *Shibbolei ha-Leket*, pt. 2, 185–86, sec. 46; and *Teshuvot ha-RiD*, 486 (sec. 99). R. Isaiah tended to follow Rashi in these matters, as seen also above in RID's position that an apostate is capable of performing *halizah*.
58. See *Hiddushei ha-Ramban le-Massekhet Bava Metzia* (71b), ed. E. R. Hishrik (Jerusalem: Mossad ha-Rav Kookn, 2002), 461–64. *Ramban* also notes (and seemingly rejects) Rashi's prohibitive view. See also *Hiddushei ha-Ritva 'al Massekhet Bava Metzia* (71b), ed. S. Raphael (Jerusalem: Mossad ha-Rav Kook, 1992), 590–91. On *Ramban*'s extensive use of Tosafist materials in his *hiddushim*, see Israel Ta-Shma, *Ha-Sifrut ha-Parshanit la-Talmud*, vol. 2 (Jerusalem: Magnes Press, 2000), 38–50.
59. See *Teshuvot ha-Ramban*, ed. S. Assaf (Jerusalem: n.p., 1935), 56–58 (sec. 2); and Ta-Shma, *Ha-Sifrut ha-Parshanit la-Talmud*, 49.
60. See *She'elot u-Teshuvot ha-Rashbash*, ed. M. Sobel (Jerusalem: Self-published, 1998), 71–71, esp. 89. For Ritzba's responsum, see *Sefer Or Zarua*, 1:387 (sec. 448, end); and *Shitah Mekubbetzet 'al Massekhet Bekhorot*, 149.
61. See *She'elot u-Teshuvot ha-Radbaz*, 3:858 (sec. 415), where the answer begins: *Katuv be-shem Rabbenu Simhah z"l de-kol ba 'alei teshuvah tzerikhin tevilah*. See also *Teshuvot Zikhron*

Yehudah le-R. Yehudah b. ha-Rosh, ed. A. Y. Havazelet (Jerusalem: Machon Yerushalayim, 2005), 159 (sec. 16), for a related text composed by a fifteenth-century Spanish authority; see *Teshuvot Zikhron Yehudah le-R. Yehudah b. ha-Rosh*, 153; and the editor's introduction, 44.

62. See *She'elot u-Teshuvot ha-Radbaz*, 4:1086 (sec. 12).
63. See Isaac Isserlein, *Terumat ha-Deshen*, ed. S. Abbitan, 2:420 (*pesakim*, 221; and 2:379–80, sec. 138).
64. See Isserlein, *Terumat ha-Deshen*, 1:194–97 (*teshuvot*, 241); and see *Sefer Yere'im ha-Shalem*, fols. 72a–74a (sec. 156).
65. See *Leket Yosher*, ed. J. Freimann (Berlin, 1903), *Yoreh De'ah*, 15.
66. See *She'elot u-Teshuvot R. Yisra'el Bruna*, ed. M. Hershler (Jerusalem: Self-published, 1960), 93 (sec. 135).
67. See *Terumat ha-Deshen*, ed. Abbitan, 1:161–63, esp. 223; and *She'elot u-Teshuvot R. Yisra'el Bruna*, 54–58 (secs. 66–68).
68. See *She'elot u-Teshuvot R. Yisra'el Bruna*, 112 (sec. 184).
69. This strategy was not uncommon in late medieval Ashkenaz; see, e.g., Yedidya Dinari, *Hakhmei Ashkenaz be-Shilhei Yemei ha-Benayim* (Jerusalem: Mossad Bialik, 1984), 34–40. For much the same reason, Isserlein (*Terumat ha-Deshen*, 1:76–77, esp. 86) cites the interpretation of Moses *ha-Darshan* of Narbonne, as preserved by Rashi, to justify immersion for a reverting apostate.

CHAPTER 5

HOW DO THE CODES READ EARLIER RABBINIC TEXTS?

TIRZA Y. KELMAN

Introduction: Codification in the Context of Jewish Law

STATES and empires undertake codification projects as an act of legislative sovereignty. Though a new code is always rooted in earlier writings and customs, it inevitably builds a new concept of law[1] and tends to neglect, change, or thoroughly reorganize the existing legal structure. The code's provisions might be questioned or debated, but as an act of the sovereign power, its legitimacy is not assured. The code *is* the law.

In the Jewish context, the term "Code of law" does not meet these characteristics, and the use of the term is somewhat confusing. Works referred to as "codes" contain broad collections of normative rulings of *halakha*—Jewish religious law. The rabbinic authorities composing these works were not sovereign authorities, nor was their acceptance based on state power. Although each book of Jewish law[2] contained innovations, these codification projects did not intend to replace former laws, but rather to synthesize, organize, and clarify existing law. Their texts were presented as reframing the earlier sources and interpreting them, even when specific rulings were acknowledged as innovative. Finally, while codes are often assumed to be an essential feature of Jewish Law, ever since the first code was written, they have been frequently criticized and questioned. The relationship between the code work and its sources, were a significant issue all authors of such works of Jewish law addressed. While each author introduced his work as a fresh answer to the challenges the existing texts presented, both code authors and their critics assumed they were fully obligated to the earlier texts and prior *halakhic* source material, even as they may disagree about the outcome.[3] Therefore, while often referred to as "codes of law," this term has somewhat different connotations in the *halakhic* context, as these works are closer to how *Restatements* function in modern American law.

Can the Blind Lead Public Prayer?

This chapter focuses on one example of a discrete *halakhic* question to introduce and demonstrate the characteristics and features of the different codes: Is a blind person permitted to lead the public in a specific prayer that accompanies the recitation of the Shema verses, which praise God for creating the heavenly? The issue itself is not particularly significant, yet tracing the history of this ruling offers an interesting prism to analyze the evolution of the legal discourse in premodern *halakhic* codes.

The classic Jewish tradition did not distinguish between religious and civil law. The same biblical chapter can include rules for Temple sacrifices, commandments regulating permitted and forbidden foods, and rules governing commerce. Although some of the fields of law deal with private issues between man and God, and others involve public institutions such as the courts, Jewish law addresses all fields of personal and social life without differentiation. Although citizen-adherents and the authorities have long needed clear guidance to follow religious law properly, none of the fundamental legal texts of Jewish law: the Bible, the Mishnah, and the Talmud, neatly codify or classify practical rulings.

In order to understand the medieval discussion regarding the law of a blind leader of the prayer, we must start from the mishnaic and Talmudic building blocks, that serve as the foundation of all subsequent legal texts referring to this topic.

The primary source is found in the third chapter of the tractate Megillah, where the Mishnah records rules of public prayer and ceremonial Torah reading, cited alongside the rules of reading the megillah. The Mishnah lists three categories of people whose ability to serve as the public leader of the ritual is in question: The minor, the "*Pokheakh*"—one who is not fully dressed (perhaps because he is unaware of proper behavior in public), and, most relevant to our discussion, the blind. The first part of the text focuses on the first two categories in light of four acts:

1. Public ritual reading of the Torah.
2. Translating of the biblical text to the public as part of the reading ritual.
3. Leading the reading of "*Shema*" as part of the prayer, including the blessings before and after the biblical chapters. The first of these blessings is one focusing on praising God for creating the sun, moon, and stars.
4. If the underaged or the "*Pokheakh*" are "*Kohanim*" (priests), can they be part of the priestly ritual of blessing the people?

The final part of the Mishnah is dedicated to the case of the blind, but only two of the four questions above (2 and 3) are addressed directly and permitted: leading the reading of "*Shema*" and translating the biblical text for the public. This latter section of the Mishnah also differs from the previous one citing not only a rule but a legal dispute. With respect to the reading of Shema, a dissenting opinion is brought in the name of R. Judah, stating that "one who never saw the luminaries in his life cannot lead the reading of '*Shema*.'" His opinion reflects an inseparable link between the blind man's ability to accept the leadership role and the content of the first blessing of the "*Shema*" focusing on God's creation of the luminaries (sun, moon, and stars).

The Babylonian Talmud on this Mishnah draws out the conceptual difference of opinion between the anonymous voice of the Mishnah (the "Rabbis"), who permit the blind to hold the leadership role, and R. Judah, who forbids it. This conceptual discussion is built using two additional *tannaitic* sources not recorded in the Mishnah. The first is a response to R. Judah's opinion, comparing the possibility of the blind to lead the prayer including a blessing focusing on the existence of the luminaries to the exposition of metaphysical texts in the bible, an area in which all persons are effectively "blind" for having never seen the mystery of the Divine Chariot (described in the first chapter of Ezekiel)[4]:

> They said to R. Judah: Many have sought to expound upon the Divine Chariot although they have never seen it.
>
> And R. Judah? There, [regarding the Divine Chariot] the matter depends upon the heart's comprehension, and one can concentrate and understand. Here [in the case of the blessing on the luminaries] the issue is whether he benefits, and the blind has no benefit.

According to the Talmud, the reaction to R. Judah's opinion could be answered by highlighting the fundamental difference between the metaphysical perception, subject to inner perception, and blessing the existence of the luminaries, which reflects the gratitude of appreciating the benefit of light—which a blind person never could enjoy. This theoretical exchange emphasizes the close connection between fitting the role of leading the public in the prayer of Shema and benefiting from the actual light.

The Talmudic discussion continues citing another *tannaitic* source to prove that even one who never saw light with his own eyes could nevertheless benefit from it. The text originally explains a metaphor found in the biblical phrase. Within a long list of punishments that God threatens to send to disobeying humans, the verse in Deuteronomy 28:29 reads: "You shall grope at noon as the blind grope in the dark." In the *tannaitic* text quoted in the Talmud, R. Yossi states he initially did not understand the biblical imprecation emphasizing a blind person groping in the dark—as the amount of light should be immaterial to the blind person. R. Yossi reports that the meaning became clearer when he met a blind person walking while carrying a torch. When asked, the blind person explained that holding light makes it possible for others to help him out. The Talmud uses this teaching to accept the argument of the first opinion in the Mishnah above, arguing that because even a blind person can benefit from the light, he should be permitted to lead the prayer praising God for the luminaries. This discussion serves as the foundation of all later legal texts regarding participation of the blind in prayer.

Rearranging Legal Information

In the centuries after its formation, Jews around the world accepted the Babylonian Talmud both as the foundation for scholarly discourse and as the central obliging legal text. Yet, the multidimensional nature of the text complicated the use of the collection as a source of law. An early attempt to structure a book of rulings confronting this challenge was R. Yitzhak Alfasi's "*Halkhot Rabati*" known as "the Rif" (being the pronunciation of the Hebrew acronyms of the author's name), written in eleventh-century North Africa, which became the starting point for all future codifying projects. The connection between Rif's work and its sources is obvious and explicit as most of the text is an abridged version of the Babylonian Talmud, with relatively few additional phrases that originate from Rif's own pen. Rif preserved the original wording of the Talmudic text along with its ambiguities,[5] as well as the meandering flow of Talmudic discussion. His methodological innovation was that the final text includes only the sections of the Talmud relevant to issuing *halakhic* rulings in the exilic period. In some geographical eras, this condensed version of the Talmud was the main text learned by Jewish scholars, and works written as commentarial glosses to Rif's book became a genre of their own.[6] As a result, Rif's work had a profound effect on how the Talmud came to be perceived by readers embracing his assumption that the Talmud can be divided into sections that are either relevant or irrelevant to legal discourse. While Rif separated the normative topics from other parts of the Talmudic text, he retained the textual logic of the Talmud—such as it is—and the work follows the Talmudic division of tractates, which encodes the Talmudic practice of scattering related topics in different tractates. Rif did not provide systematic tools to link associated discussions, or offer those not acquainted with the Talmudic structure the ability to locate related topics.

In Rif's abridgment of the Talmudic text about the capability of the blind to lead prayer, we find only some of the underlying Talmudic source material:

> Rabbi Judah says one how never in his life saw the lights etc. And the rule follows the Rabbis who say that the blind can lead the saying of "*Shema*" because even if he never saw the luminaries, he derives benefit from them as in the story of R. Yossi who said "I was once walking in the absolute darkness of the night, and I saw a blind man walking on his way with a torch in his hands. I said to him: 'My son, why do you need this torch?" "He said to me: 'As long as I have a torch in my hand, people see me and save me from the pits and the thorns and the thistles.'"[7]

Though it only paraphrases the Mishnah and the Talmud, Rif's text is new in three ways. First, it offers a legal conclusion: the majority opinion is accepted. Second, it includes condensed arguments of the Mishnah and the Talmud. Third, the story about R. Yossi meeting the blind person is edited to state that blind people can benefit from light but is delinked from the biblical verse and its hermeneutic interpretation. Finally, the *tannaitic* text comparing the blind to the human failure to see the Divine Chariot is altogether left out. The outcome is a text both very similar and very different from the Talmudic source.

Maimonides and His *Mishneh Torah*

R. Moses son of Maimon, known as Maimonides (or *Rambam*), is one of the most important, influential, and famous Jewish scholars in the rabbinic tradition.[8] His rich literary output in diverse fields of scholarship and knowledge had a dramatic impact on many different disciplines.

Maimonides was born in Cordova (Spain) in 1135. His education and early work took place within the school of Rif and his direct pupil R. Joseph Halevi ibn Migash, the teacher of Maimon, Maimonides's father.[9] His later works, which were broadly distributed, generated new forms and genres and have redefined Jewish law ever since.

For several decades, from his twenties onward,[10] Maimonides dedicated much of his attention to writing three different works on Jewish law: (1) a commentary on the Mishnah, (2) *Sefer HaMitzvot* (literally: "The Book of Commandments"), and finally (3) his magnum opus—The *Mishneh Torah*. All three projects were planned in advance as stages of an ongoing process, as presented in the preface of *Sefer HaMitzvot*, where Maimonides explained the relationship between the three parts of his larger project.

The initial step in accounting for all rabbinic literature was writing a commentary on the Mishnah. The second main project Maimonides took upon himself was *Sefer HaMitzvot* (literally: "The Book of Commandments").[11] According to a Talmudic saying (b.Makkot 23:b), there are 613 biblical commandments divided into 365 negative forbidden actions ("*Mitzvot Lo Ta'ase*" or "thou shalt nots") and 248 positive commandments ("*Mitzvot Ase*" the "thou shalt"). In fleshing out these numbers, Maimonides articulated the full list of the commandments, listed all the existing topics of Jewish law, and established a conceptual system of what counts as a separate commandment and what is a subdepartment of an existing commandment. The third and final part of the project was the "*Mishneh Torah.*" Literally meaning "Repetition of the Torah" as well as "Deputy of the Torah"—the name hints to its ambitious scope.

When editing the Mishnah around the year 220 CE, Rabbi Judah Nasi created the first corpus of Jewish law divided into tractates according to themes. Earlier literary forms of *Midrash* were organized according to the order of the relevant biblical text. The mishnaic categorization became the organizing platform of rabbinic writings, as other works of that era such as the *Tosefta*, the two Talmuds in the next centuries, and all the books written around them, preserved Rabbi Judah Nassi's structure. Maimonides, in his *Mishneh Torah*, departed from this structure, creating a unique and original thematical categorization of the Jewish law. He divided the work into fourteen "books" in an altogether novel system. Introducing the new concept in his introduction, Maimonides explained his division of Jewish law into fourteen "books" at length, reflecting his awareness of the methodological innovation of this project.

Maimonides's ambitions were broader than any other individual author of Jewish law. He incorporated all aspects of biblical and rabbinic law and thought, including those that had not been implemented for many generations. Hence, the laws of the Temple (that had not existed since the year 70 CE) and those governing a theoretical Jewish kingdom were dealt with in the same manner as the laws of prayer, Shabbat, or tort liability. Similarly, topics such as correct beliefs, ways to keep healthy, and the rules of repentance that were not previously subject to *halakhic* cofidication are all included as codified laws in the same format used for the technical instructions on classically legal topics. These aspects of the Maimonian categorization not only differed from the works created in the prior centuries but would not be repeated by later scholars, as explained below. Finally, while Maimonides's work was studied by scholars in the generations to come, not all parts of his work received the same attention. In the sixteenth century, R. Joseph Karo reported that only one or two scholars in a generation studied the more recondite sections of Maimonides's code which focused on the laws of the Temple.[12]

Each of the fourteen books comprising *Mishneh Torah* contained smaller thematical subcategories. Maimonides opens each book listing the biblical commandments included under this topic which parallels his presentation in "*Sefer HaMitzvot.*" *Mishneh Torah* divides the subcategories into distinct topics (such as "*Hilkhot of Prayer*" or "*Hilkot of Reciting Shema*"), which in turn are divided into chapters and then into short *halakhot* (in plural). Each paragraph or unit is called *halakha*, corresponding to the name of the field of Jewish law in both earlier and later texts.

Maimonides's formulation of these individual *halakhot* was unique too. They were composed as short decisive rulings, which did not indicate their source text. After centuries of rabbinic writing organized around earlier works, this choice was perceived as rebellious and provoked criticism.[13] Creating a brand-new thematic categorization that does not explicitly reveal its sources is not the only aspect in which Maimonides followed the footprints of R. Judah Nassi, the editor of the Mishnah. Maimonides's works were written using the cleaner *tannaitic* Hebrew, rather than biblical Hebrew or the mix of Aramaic and Hebrew found in the Talmud and later rabbinic works.[14] Maimonides's affinity to the Mishnah was not random or coincidental, as he saw himself engaged in a similar project and facing similar challenges. His description of R. Judah Nassi's decision to write the Mishnah indicates this. While most of the chain of tradition from Moses at Sinai to contemporary time listed in the preface to the *Mishneh Torah* is only mentioned briefly, R. Judah Nassi and his time receive an extensive description, drawing a picture that shares elements with the way Maimonides describes his own era, later in the same text. Referring both to the historical decision to write the Mishnah in the third century CE and to his current project, the decision to create a code of Jewish law is presented as a desperate necessity concluding from the threat that the harsh times will disrupt the continuity of tradition.[15]

Maimonides employed a wide range of sources in the Mishneh Torah. These include all the rabbinic writings from the *tannaitic* and Amoriac times: the Mishnah, *Tosefta*, both Talmuds, and the entire corpus of *Midrash*, alongside *geonic* materials and writings of scholars such as the Rif.[16] While some of these sources were standard, others were not typically used as sources of authoritative *halakha* either before or following Maimonides's time.

The tremendous effort of collecting, arranging, and weighing earlier sources was elegantly hidden from the main text and observable only to scholars aware of the tradition Maimonides was recasting. Moreover, as its name suggests, the simplified *Mishneh Torah* was designed to replace earlier sources. From Maimonides's point of view, once a neat, categorized, and harmonized list of conclusions was available, there was no need to bother with earlier sources or how they were transformed. The lean and styled text could become the final text of Jewish law.

Going back to our example of the blind man's qualifications to lead *Shema*, the *Book of Adoration*, the second of the fourteen books that comprise the *Mishneh Torah*, focuses on aspects of Jewish law that display the love for or adoration of God, in a new categorization that did not exist earlier in the history of Jewish law. Chapter 8:12 records as follows:

> A blind man may publicly lead the reading of *Shema* and be appointed to lead the prayer. But one whose shoulders are bare, though he may publicly recite the blessings before the *Shema*, does not lead the prayer unless he is properly clad.

While those familiar with the earlier sources will recognize how Maimonides combines and rephrases the diverse rules in this *halakha*, which all originate in tractate of *Megillah*, there is no indication in the text itself revealing its origins. The law approving a blind person as the leader of the blessings of *Shema* is simply cited as part of the longer list of those who may or may not lead the prayers without any explanation of its complexities or why it might be debated. The order of the rules, as well as the specific wording, are innovative and not derivative of any prior source.

The Mediaeval *Halakhic* Trio: Maimonides, Semag, *Tur*

Despite the influential position quickly granted to Maimonides as one of the most important scholars of any discussion of Jewish law, his effort to obscure his sources and sweep aside the different opinions was generally rejected. His code was thus increasingly subjected to works tracing the sources and legal foundations of his rulings.[17]

In addition to Maimonides's code, the advent of printing in the fifteenth century brought two other medieval "Jewish books of code" to the forefront, following centuries when they were only available as manuscripts. These works, known as *Semag* and *Tur* as will be described below, were both strongly influenced by Maimonides as well as by critics of his work. Because early printing in this era was expensive, texts that did not have a clear market did not justify the economic risk of printing. The repeated publication of Maimonides, Semag, and *Tur* in this era offers clear evidence of their influence and wide distribution.

While the *Tur*, as demonstrated below, became a major link in the chain of history of Jewish law, the Semag was highly influential in Medieval times but became peripheral in modern literature. Long before printing was invented in the mid-fifteenth century, the "Great Book of Commandments" known as "the Semag" (the pronunciation of the Hebrew acronyms of the name the of the book: "*Sefer Mitzvot Gadol*") became the most influential *halakhic* work in medieval Europe of the thirteenth century.[18] In contrast to Maimonides, R. Moses of Coucy's *Semag* did not list all the commandments singly but structured his book in two mirroring parts, one of the positive commandments ("*mitzvot ase*") and one of the negative commandments ("*mitzvot lo-tease*"). Semag made thorough use of the decisions of the *Mishneh Torah*, while reformatting it to suit the traditions of French Jewry.[19] R. Moses of Coucy was a wandering preacher, and this perspective shaped his work. Moving from the Iberian Peninsula to the French area, the considerable use of the *Mishneh Torah* in the Semag was an important channel through which Jews in the Franco-Germany areas became acquainted with Maimonides's work. This was especially significant in places where the Semag became influential, whereas Maimonides did not. Part of the power of the text in the French-German areas was based on R. Moses of Coucy, not only including opinions of scholars from these areas but also references to the Talmudic discussions, making the book interesting not only for laypeople but also for scholars seeking complex textual study.[20] Like the work of Maimonides, the Semag did not limit himself to topics relevant to immediate implementation.[21] Nevertheless, the nature of the Semag and its style of embedding preaching and law while selecting his topics based on his educational perspective is far from covering each and every rule and topic of Jewish law. Like many other issues, the question of the blind leading public rituals does not appear at all in this work.

Arba Turim of "the Laws in Practice"

The Semag had been in distribution for less than a century when R. Asher, son of Yehiel, usually referred to as the Rosh (again, the pronunciation of the Hebrew acronyms of his name), arrived in Castalia at the opening of the fourteenth century. He was an important Rabbi in the Ashkenazi region that became Germany, as well as a student of the Tosefists in Southern France and thus deeply connected to the Ashkenazi traditions. He fled to the Iberian Peninsula owing to riots against the Jewish community in the Ashkenazi lands, and was welcomed with great honor and appointed as head of the rabbinic court and yeshiva in Toledo. Rosh became a unique figure, combining traditions and knowledge from both the Ashkenazi world of his birth and his adopted home in the Sephardi milieu.[22]

The Rosh himself had written different texts of Jewish law, that were structured as commentary to and summaries of the Babylonian Talmud, closer to the conceptual framework of the Rif on the one hand and of the Tosefists on the other than to Maimonides.[23] This was an obstacle for most local rabbinic authorities in the Iberian Peninsula, who held only a basic level of literacy in texts formulating Jewish law,[24] and therefore used Maimonides's *Mishneh Torah* as their textbook. Once the authority of the Rosh for the Castilian Jews increased, however, the need for an adequate textbook became pressing. This challenge motivated the work of R. Jacob, son of the Rosh, who joined his father in fleeing to the Iberian Peninsula in 1304. R. Jacob's literary output, "*Arba Turim*" (literally meaning "four columns") or in short "The *Tur*" (as *Tur* is the single of Turim and means one column), was not only one of the most popular books of Jewish law in the next centuries but also created a novel influential structure for categorizing Jewish law that remains in use to this day.

R. Jacob aimed to offer his readership, which had previously been dependent on the *Mishneh Torah*, a new textbook that did not contain only conclusions, as did the Maimonidean text, but held a variety of opinions, especially those emphasized by his father, the Rosh. Nevertheless, with the exception of Rosh, Maimonides remains the most cited writer in the four volumes of the *Tur*, and the text devotes considerable attention to differences between the rulings of Maimonides and those of the Rosh.

R. Jacob, however, accepted some of the basic characteristics Maimonides established. He did not cite the Talmudic sources for the laws he presented, nor did he cite sources of uncontroversial rulings. He did not follow the mishnaic and Talmudic division of topics and, like Maimonides, offered a thematic categorization. Thus, his primary innovation was a new division of his text that was not based on any of the earlier codification projects.

The scope of Tur's project, however, was far more limited than Maimonides's all-encompassing code. It followed Rif's compilation that was limited only to "the laws in practice" (*dinim ha-nohagim*) in the exilic era, leaving out many Talmudic discussions codified by Maimonides. Moreover, the four volumes of the "*Arba Turim*," named after the biblical description of the stones on the breastplate worn by the high priest,[25] were not designed as such in advance—the various volumes were written separately and not as part of a preplanned whole.[26] The four volumes constitute two pairs of volumes, each addressing a different readership. The first pair: "*Orah Haim*" (literally meaning way of life) and "*Yore De'ah*" (literally meaning teacher of knowledge) were written for rabbis and guided the reader through fields of everyday life. The first volume contains almost seven hundred chapters (called "*simanim*," functioning as chapters) starting with the daily cycle from waking up in the morning through bedtime, including prayers and blessings for food. The second cycle is dedicated to the rules regarding the Shabbat, while the third cycle focuses on all holidays of the year. The second volume contains all other topics of life relevant to an observant Jew, from the rules of kosher food to the rules of honoring parents to grief.[27] These volumes were sufficient to guide local rank-and-file rabbinic authorities in leading everyday aspects of the personal and communal religious routine. The latter two volumes of the *Tur* also formed a pair and were written for more learned experts of Jewish law that operated in Jewish courts. "*Even Ha-Ezer*" (literally the stone of support) presents all issues regarding marriage, divorce, family law, and personal status. The final volume of "*Hoshen Mishpat*" (literally "breastplate of the trial" as the biblical breastplate is described in some verses) focuses on court process and civil law. The imagined readership of these volumes is not the populace coming before the court but the judges themselves. The level of literacy expected of the reader is higher than in the first two volumes, and compared to Maimonides, they include a lot of information about the history of the legal discussions until that point. Nevertheless, they do not contain explicit citations to the relevant Talmudic discussion.

While the new *Tur* did not completely replace the use of Maimonides—and each of the works was dominant in specific places and times—its popularity changed the way Maimonides was read. *Halakhic* scholars often used the trio of Maimonides, Semag, and *Tur* in parallel, with comparisons between these works enriching the legal discourse.[28] Based on R. Jacob's unique familiarity with both the Franko-German Ashkenazi traditions and the Iberian Sephardi ones, the text of the *Tur* offered a comparison between customs and embedded the sources of schools from both spaces. In turn, the *Tur* gained influence in diverse corners of the Jewish world, which increased the impact of its innovative method. The range of hand-copied manuscripts of the *Tur* found in different geographic areas, indicates the wide distribution of the *Tur* crossing the usual borders, long before print made the work more affordable and available.

The laws we have been following about the blind leading public ritual acts appear in chapter 53 of volume 1 (*Orah Haim*) of the *Tur*. This chapter, "The Blessings of the Morning and Related Blessings," is dedicated to rules governing the person appointed to lead the public in prayer ("*Shliah Tzibur*"). Like all chapters of the *Tur*, it is not divided into smaller parts. As part of the flow, the *Tur* reads: "The blind may lead the prayer so long as he does not also read the Torah [ritually], because it is forbitten to read from the Torah by heart."

To readers familiar with the earlier sources, the origins of this sentence are clear, as is the connection between leading the prayers and ritually reading from the Torah. The text, however, gives no clue to the sources it is based on; nor does it emphasize the question regarding the blessing of the luminaries. By this point, the Talmudic dispute has faded into the background and has been recast as a general rule implying that the blind person is equal to the seeing person with respect to leading the public in prayer, the sole exception being for Torah reading because that requires an act which is technically impossible for a blind person to perform.

R. Joseph Karo: Early Modern Reframing of Jewish Law

The *Shulhan Arukh*, first published in Venice in 1565, became the central platform of the discourse of Jewish law shortly after its publication,[29] and the term "*Shulhan Arukh*" became synonymous with Jewish law. Due to its significance, it is frequently described as the transition point between different eras in the history of Jewish law. R. Joseph Karo (1488–1575) and his major *halakhic* works, namely, the *Beit Yosef* and the *Shulhan Arukh*, are often marked as the border between the era of the "*Rishonim*" (literally meaning "the first ones")—the scholars since the beginning of the second millennium—and the "*Ahronim*" (literally meaning "the last ones") from the early modern era and onward.

Like the Maimonidean *Mishneh Torah*, the *Shulhan Arukh* (literally meaning "the set table") does not refer to any of its sources explicitly and contains only short paragraphs of normative rulings in imperative language. However, unlike the *Mishneh Torah*, R. Joseph Karo's influential work was not intended to stand alone. Though it became R. Joseph Karo's most famous work, from the author's point of view, this short *Shulhan Arukh* was neither the pinnacle of his legal writing nor meant to be studied in isolation. In the introduction to the first edition, the *Shulhan Arukh* is described as a collection of highlights of his earlier magnum opus, the *Beit Yosef*, which was printed around the *Tur* in four separate volumes throughout the previous decade. According to R. Joseph Karo, the *Shulhan Arukh* could serve as a starting point for the young and the unlearned audience and as a memorization mechanism to help accomplished scholars familiar with the *Beit Yosef* review the highlights of the entire corpus of practiced law every thirty days. By contrast, the earlier *Beit Yosef* demanded much more of its readers, as three decades of intense work led to a long and detailed book of Jewish law which aimed to cover existing debates and resolutions to all matters of practical Jewish law.

R. Joseph Karo's goal to rearrange all existing opinions explains why in the *Beit Yosef* he chose to use the *Tur* as a platform for his *halakhic* work. R. Karo explains that he had considered writing his work around the Maimonides *Mishneh Torah*, yet preferred framing it around *Tur* since it already contained some of the relevant sources.[30] This explanation, however, seems incomplete. It not only overlooks the presumption that his magnum opus should be arranged around a preexisting work but also ignores the significant impact of limiting his project to the practiced matters of *halakha* covered in the Arba Turim as opposed to encompassing the full ambit of Jewish law and thought as codified by Maimonides.

Writing the work was not the end of the process, as R. Joseph Karo was highly aware of how the new medium of print presented and modified understanding, preservation, and distribution of knowledge. He saw the publication via Italian printing houses as the final but essential part of his project. The first of the four volumes of the *Beit Yosef*, which R. Karo began writing in 1522 in Edirne, was sent to be printed in Venice in 1550. By that time, R. Karo was living in Ottoman Safed. The next volumes were published in 1551, 1553, and 1559 in Italy, as was the *Shulhan Arukh* in 1565.

Other aspects of the historical context in which R. Joseph Karo operated can help us comprehend the importance he attributed to shaping *halakhic* decisions. For example, as a member of a rabbinic family originating in Castile, attention must be given to the impact of the explosion from Spain in 1492. This is true although the Karo family was already living in Portugal when Joseph was born in 1488, before they moved on to the Ottoman Empire when he was a young scholar. At the time, the Ottoman Empire was at the height of its power. The conquest of large territories was followed by massive migration, partially forced by the Ottoman system and partially consisted of many Iberian Jews seeking to reestablish their communities. These immigrants were encouraged by the benefits offered by the Ottoman Empire, embedding the capital and manpower of the Jews fleeing to the east in the growing Empire. This situation brought together people from separate Jewish communities who had originated in different parts of the Iberian Peninsula, historically holding separate *halakhic* traditions. In the new locations in the Ottoman Empire, they were all labeled "Sephardi."[31] Conflicts between Iberian traditions occurred when various Jewish communities, with traditions rooted in diverse geographic and cultural backgrounds, met. The prosperity of the Ottoman Empire during this period was not only military and political but also included considerable preoccupation with legal aspects. Suliman the Great was not only a powerful military ruler. He was also deeply engaged in formulating a new legal codex rearranging the imperial Muslim hierarchy.[32]

Hints to these contexts can be traced in the introduction to the *Beit Yosef*. Though the short introduction to the first edition of the *Shulhan Arukh* quoted above was rarely printed again in the numerous editions of the code from the sixteenth century to the twenty-first, the introduction to the earlier *Beit Yosef*, along with an authorial note explaining that the book could not be understood absent the introduction, has been reprinted in nearly every edition of *Beit Yosef*. Throughout the centuries it has been perceived as a key to reading not only to the *Beit Yosef*, as the author originally intended, but for the later *Shulhan Arukh* as well.[33] In this introduction, R. Joseph Karo explained his motivations and methodology in creating the *Beit Yosef* (literary meaning "House of Joseph") described as "my estate in this world and the next [world]," and therefore his "house."

The introduction describes the pressing need to handle the information explosion and achieve certainty in the field of Jewish law, in the face of the multitude opinions existing in the various books. From R. Joseph Karo's point of view, the *halakhic* system is the pinnacle of all human achievements. The flow of information is presented not as an opportunity but as a danger that threatens the goal of clear and unified *halakhic* rulings, which he perceives as crucial for the sake of the universe. On this basis, R. Karo criticizes all the attempts to write books of Jewish law in the prior centuries.[34] His criticism is based on the dubious assumption that all prior authors shared his concept of the ideal form of Jewish legal literature. He complains that they did not trace the thread of scholarship leading from the Talmudic discussion to their conclusions; they related only to specific topics; and they did not clarify the relationship between their works and earlier or parallel writings. R. Joseph Karo perceived the *halakhic* body of knowledge as one whole, expecting a uniform conclusion to emerge when all the various interpretive or *halakhic* options are placed side by side to create a decision. However, reading the works he criticized, it is clear their authors did not oppose writing only about limited topics and hoped to add their unique voice as one of many. From their point of view, addressing readers not necessarily aware of other methods was not a problem.

From between the lines of his introduction to the *Beit Yosef*, R. Karo's view of the proper study of a *halakhic* topic becomes clear. He expects all scholars to understand the flow of the legal discussion from its Talmudic foundations as well "all the differing opinions . . . [so that] none are missing." This should be done for each and every topic, adding the challenge of remembering all the texts as well as retrieving the information. The new *Beit Yosef* which would accompany the learner and assist in the process of learning "everything," by collecting the different texts as parts of a greater sum, was meant to address these challenges.[35] The metaphor reflected in the title is of the biblical Joseph, who provided food for the masses by saving grain in his house in Egypt from the years of satiety for the years of hunger. This image empowers the illusion that minimizes the significance of R. Karo's personal contribution as an author, despite the fact that he was editing massive data and intending that his work end with decisions on all topics of practical law. Nonetheless, the style of the text of the *Beit Yosef*, which includes explicit decisions in only about a thousand cases out of tens of thousands of paragraphs, reinforces this illusion.

Most of the text of the *Beit Yosef* does not present explicit imperative phrases but rather hints to conclusions the reader should understand based on the rules he is expected to be aware of. Building his text to enable such reading, R. Joseph Karo often cited the opinions of the Rif, Maimonides, and the Rosh in one paragraph, immediately after citing the relevant Mishnah, Talmud, and commentary of Rashi and Tosefists.[36] The opinion of the Rif is brought into the *Beit Yosef* almost only in these paragraphs, whether opposed or affirmed by Maimonides and or the Rosh that each receive much more attention not only as part of the trio. Maimonides plays a unique role in the *Beit Yosef*, as many paragraphs of Maimonides's *Mishneh Torah* receive detailed discussion in the work.[37] As mentioned above, the opinion of the Rosh was emphasized in his son's book of the *Tur*. Since it is built according to the structure of the *Tur*, *Beit Yosef* inevitably includes many of the texts written by the Rosh.

Over the centuries much attention has been granted to the section of the introduction to the *Beit Yosef* focusing on the decision emerging from the range of opinions presented in the text, introducing sets of rules. The most famous rule, commonly referred to as "the *Beit Yosef* rule" or the "Three Pillars of Ruling," is to follow the majority of the "Three Pillars of Ruling" (i.e., Rif, Maimonides, and the Rosh). This rule confronts one of the major motivations of R. Karo's *halakhic* work. The differing traditions of the Iberian-originated communities, some leaning on the authority of Maimonides while others leaned on the Rosh, became a significant issue once the reestablished communities were united in new geographical spaces labeled "Sephardi." R. Joseph Karo himself, born to a Castilian family but educated also in Egypt, was son to both traditions. Many readers of the *Beit Yosef* perceived the rule as a declaration of the conclusion method, and R. Karo was later criticized because he did not follow it fully. Nonetheless, close reading of R. Joseph Karo's texts teaches that it is merely a description of the keys he wishes for the reader to use to identify the correct decision from the range of opinions cited, when there is no explicit conclusion, as is the case in most of the work. Obviously, the "three pillars of ruling" are far from being the only authorities cited in the *Beit Yosef*, or even the ending point of *halakhic* discussion. The introduction lists a few dozen *halakhic* collections, Responsa and commentary on existing codes are listed in the as sources,[38] and the list of actual works cited in the *Beit Yosef* is much longer. A bird's-eye view determines that the thread of the discourse usually runs from texts originating in the school of the thirteenth-century Catalan Nahmanedies and his students, such as the Rashba or the Ran. Nevertheless, works from many schools and geographic origin are included[39] and form part of the plan to create a text that holds "all the differing opinions" preforming different patterns of learning and discussing Jewish law.

Rema Confronting and Establishing the *Shulhan Arukh*

In following generations, many readers of the *Beit Yosef* took his statement about citing "everything" literally, as if sources excluded from the work were unfamiliar to R. Joseph Karo. Discussions about the scope of his library, his awareness of one book or another, and a study of the text of the *Beit Yosef* in light of such questions appear in *halakhic* texts from the early modern period onward,[40] as well as in modern research.[41] While some books were not in R. Joseph Karo's possession as he was writing,[42] a close reading of the *Beit Yosef* demonstrates the importance of the editorial choices made regarding which sources are cited and which are left out. These decisions set downstream precedents as to what became part of the primary discourse of Jewish law from the 1550s onward.

One of the first scholars to claim R. Joseph Karo was unaware of important works because "he had not seen them ever in his life" was R. Moses Isserles, known as Rema (the pronunciation in Hebrew of the abbreviations of his name), an active rabbinic authority in the sixteenth century in Krakow (Poland). He started writing the first version of a work named *Darkhei Moshe* after having once forgotten a relevant source dealing with a practical question. This motivated him to compose a new *halakhic* book that used *Tur* as a platform, which collected all *halakhic* discussions on each topic, similar to the yet to be published *Beit Yosef.* Nevertheless, as opposed to R. Joseph Karo's approach of presenting all opinions in the hope of reaching a unified decision that would turn them redundant, Rema perceived the increased flow of information as a blessing which called for new tools to contain the great abundance of knowledge. When Rema got hold of the new *Beit Yosef* fresh from the Venetian printing houses, he was both deeply impressed but also devastated realizing he had been preempted by Karo's text. Rema described in length how depressed he became when he saw the wonderful *Beit Yosef,* understanding that his effort would not be appreciated once R. Joseph Karo's work was distributed. In the introduction to his revised work, Rema drafted a critique of the *Beit Yosef* to justify the need for his project. This critique became a main prism through which the *Beit Yosef* and the *Shulhan Arukh* were later read. Rema's two main criticisms were that R. Joseph Karo did not follow his own decision-making rules and that there was a paucity of certain Ashkenazi works in the text of the *Beit Yosef*.[43]

In 1565, R. Joseph Karo published the *Shulhan Arukh*, only six years after the last of the four volumes of the *Beit Yosef* was published. Though structured to be parallel to the *Tur* and the *Beit Yosef* in the numbering of the chapters and topics, the short new work was written in a different genre. The *Shulhan Arukh* was divided into small sections of declarative do and do-not-do normative rulings, which contrasted with the more discursive style of the *Tur*. The text eliminated the sources and inner logic of the rules that are elaborated in *Beit Yosef*. Within a few generations, the new *Shulhan Arukh*, quickly gained popularity and became the central text that scholarship of Jewish law focused around. Paradoxically, part of its success in attaining authority beyond the communities of Ottoman- or Iberian-originated Jews and bringing into the European Ashkenazi realm was due to the Rema's "*Mapah*."

Rema chose *Mapah* as the name for his gloss, which literally means tablecloth and suggests the image of Rema beautifying R. Karo's set table (following the literal meaning of the title *Shulhan Arukh* in Hebrew) for Ashkenazi learners. Rema's notes, simultaneously confront R. Joseph Karo rulings but also establish their authority.[44] In numerous editions since the end of the sixteenth century, they were incorporated directly into the text of the *Shulhan Arukh* in a different font. Soon after, Eastern European rabbis started composing works of scholarship that would be published with the *Shulhan Arukh*, as commentary printed on the marginalia. These "*Nose'i Kelim*" (literally meaning arms bearers but a general name for the phenomenon of books written and published around an existing book)[45] undermined the *Shulhan Arukh* as a final conclusion of Jewish law and turned it into the new foundation for the ongoing discussion of Jewish law. Here too, works can become influential and authoritative, even as their author's specific intentions for writing the book is ignored.

R. Joseph Karo and Rema on Leading the Prayer by the Blind

Just as in *Tur*, the rule concerning the blind leader of prayer is found in chapter 53 of *Orah Haim* both in the *Beit Yosef* and in the *Shulhan Arukh* following the organizational scheme that R. Jacob established in his *Arba Turim*. In the *Beit Yosef*, R. Joseph Karo traces the sources to the rule presented in *Tur*.

> "The blind can lead the prayer": A Mishnah [in the fourth chapter of the tractate of Megillah was mentioned earlier in the text]: "A blind can lead the reading of *Shema* and translate the biblical text to the public. Rabbi Judah says one who never in his life saw the lights does not lead the reading of *Shema*." The authorities ruled in accord with the first opinion.

While this first part of the text of the *Beit Yosef* presents the most fundamental source to the sentence in the *Tur*, R. Joseph Karo continues the paragraph with a medieval discussion about the topic. Before citing the opinions of Maimonides and the Rosh in support of Tur's ruling, he quotes an opposing opinion in the work of another Provencal/Iberian rabbi of the fourteenth century, Rabeynu Yeruham, himself a student of the Rosh:

> And Rabeynu Yeruham wrote he does not lead the [central *Amida*] prayer. It seems that he explained the Mishnah as referring specifically to *Shema* that he can lead. But Maimonides wrote in chapter 8 of the laws of prayer "A blind man may publicly lead the reading of *Shema* and be appointed to lead the prayer." It seems he explains the rule is the same for *Shema* and leading [the Amida] prayer that was explicitly mentioned to contradict the opinion of R. Judah. And so wrote Rosh in responsa # 4 that the blind are obligated to keep all the commandments and also enjoy light, therefore even if he never saw light, he can lead *Shema* and the prayer as long as he does not read the ritual reading of the Torah. End of quote.

In the Talmud it is clear that there is a specific uncertainty regarding whether the blind may lead the blessing of luminaries, but when extracted from their original context, the logic might be presented in the opposite way, allowing R. Karo to explain Rabeynu Yeruham as permitting only the action that was explicitly discussed because there was a reason to think it should be prohibited. Similarly, we meet the reasoning in the responsa of the Rosh which contains two separate justifications: "that the blind are obligated to keep all the commandments and also enjoy light." While the second justification linking the possibility to lead the prayer to enjoying the light has been part of the Talmudic discussion and the medieval sources following, here it appears shortly, unexplained and as an addition. The first justification links a different debate to the question of leading the prayer. In Qidushin 31A there is a debate about the obligation of the blind to all the commandments. The same R. Judah who, in the Mishnah we read in chapter 4 of Megillah, holds that the blind cannot lead *Shema* appears there as arguing that altogether the blind are not obligated like other adults. The Rosh referred to both Talmudic discussions, ruling that the blind can lead all parts of prayer except reading the Torah.[46] R. Joseph Karo only quotes him, with no additional explanation or explicit decision in the paragraph. Nevertheless, using the key "Three Pillars of Ruling" rule, the reader is expected to know that presenting opinions of both Maimonides and the Rosh agreeing on the same opinion makes it the binding law permitting the blind to lead the ritual.

Moving on to the *Shulhan Arukh*, we will find this rule, adding a slight explanation to the similar ruling of *Tur*. Technically it is not only a sentence in the chapter, but a numbered clause, number 14:

> The blind may lead prayer as long as he does not read the Torah [ritually], because of the rule "written words you may not say orally."

This last sentence is a quote from the Talmud (Gitin 60B, Tmura 14B) forbidding ritual reading without the physical action of seeing and reading the words, even if one could recite it orally. Since the blind cannot do so, they may not lead the public in the ritual reading. This same rule appears again in chapter 139 of the *Shulhan Arukh*, which contains the rules of ritual Torah reading. In the end of clause 3 we find a sentence of R. Joseph Karo's pen: "The blind does not read for it is prohibited to read even one letter not from the scroll."

In the numerous editions of the *Shulhan Arukh* since the seventeenth century, this sentence is followed by Rema's gloss, elaborating by adding the Ashkenazi custom, which flows from changes to the practice of ritual Torah reading. The Talmudic custom was for those selected for the honor to read the Torah portion themselves. Centuries before the *Shulhan Arukh* was written, the custom shifted, whereby a designated reader performed the actual reading while the person honored with the reading merely recited the blessings and stood beside him. Although this process took place around the world, Sephardi communities preserved more of the original ritual while in the Ashkenazi realm the shift was total. Thus Maharil (R. Moshe Molin), one of the most influential Ashkenazi scholars and rabbinic authorities in the last quarter of the fourteenth century and the first quarter of the fifteenth century, is quoted by Rema as permitting the blind to "read" the Torah. Because the custom had changed, and no person called to Torah actually read from it, there was no reason to prevent the blind from receiving the honor. Rema thus writes: "And Maharil wrote that now since the blind reads like we read to the unlearned." The circle has been closed as none of the rituals in which the Mishnah in Megillah questioned whether the blind may participate remain off-limits to blind persons.

Conclusion

As is clear from this chapter, the term "code" in Jewish law is not only different than it is in other legal contexts but it also unifies a range of works that, despite common aspects, differ from one another. The history of books of code is a constant negotiation between different methods and approaches regarding the earlier sources that lay before the writers. From the pioneering project of Rif and on down, Jewish books of code always reacted to the existing texts and rearranged the knowledge the other books contained. Each medieval work referred to as a "classic work of halakhic code" chose a different approach to this question. Maimonides sought to make using the books that preceded his superfluous by creating a clear and authoritative text that could be used without the need for additional sources. While his impressive *Mishneh Torah* changed the way Jewish law was written and learned, his attempt to create a final text that reduced the study of more ancient sources did not. Later codes reacted to Maimonides's approach and created different textual models. Authors like R. Moses of Coucy or R. Jacob son of the Rosh adopted parts of Maimonides's method while criticizing others, creating their own approach toward integrating sources in the *halakhic* text they produced. Like Maimonides, R. Joseph Karo's *Shulhan Arukh* also contains rulings without explicit sources. But the connection between the text of this work and his much larger *Beit Yosef* makes it possible—and expected—for scholars to trace the thread of scholarly discussion.

While R. Karo's rulings became universally authoritative, they were not—and are still not—the final ruling. Rather they have become the new starting point for all early modern and modern *halakhic* discussion and decision making.

Like many of the works discussed, the *Beit Yosef* was received and used in a different way than its author intended. Written as a book of code, it was adopted as a supposably objective description of the flow of legal discourse until his times, and became a reference book for later scholars. It changed the way earlier works were studied, as learners used the condensed and adapted version of Rif, Maimonides, Semag, Rosh, *Tur*, and others incorporated within the *Beit Yosef* instead of resorting to the original works, thereby embracing R. Joseph Karo's lenses to guide their learning. Thus R. Karo's editorial decisions and—that which he edited in and edited out was often overlooked and not appreciated as a work of curation and interpretation. Moreover, the comprehensive text of the *Beit Yosef* legitimized the short formulation of the *Shulhan Arukh*, establishing its authority as the book of code rather than a memory aid or a pedagogical tool. The complementary work of the Rema both opposed some of the rulings and emphasized the authority of the text, while broadening the geographical area of influence of the combined new works. Finally, the increasing power of print technology boasted the scope of distribution and shortened the time frame required to complete the change of curriculum, as the *Shulhan Arukh* became the modern platform for learning and legal discourse and the cornerstone for new genres of Jewish legal texts.

The example we followed in this chapter is one of numerous rules of Jewish law. The different books of code throughout the centuries consistently discussed the rule by referring to the earlier texts. Commitment to the previous discourse allowed the law to be recited in the same contexts as in earlier works, even when there were no longer any special laws for the blind.

NOTES

1. See Jansen Nils, *The Making of Legal Authority Non-Legislative Codifications in Historical and Comparative Perspective* (e-book: Oxford University Press, 2010), 14–19.
2. As will be presented below, this topic combines different subgenres. In his famous work, Menachem Elon, *Jewish Law: History, Sources, Principles* (Philadelphia, PA: Jewish Publication Society, 1994), 3: 139–40, makes a clear cut between what he calls "books of *halakhot*" versus "books of *Psakim*." Nonetheless, this chapter presents a less dichotomous approach, indicating the range of literary formats, and the variety of connections between Jewish law books and their sources. Thus, this chapter will concentrate only on books that have been perceived as "classic books of code," ignoring most of the Jewish scholars in the Medieval times, even in the *halakhic* sphere, that is itself only one of the fields of Jewish intellectual activity. For an updated discussion on the notion of *halakha*, see Chaim N. Saiman, *Halakha: The Rabbinic Idea of Law* (e-book: Princeton University Press, 2018).
3. The considerable debate regarding the publishing of *Shulhan Arukh* in the early modern era offers a good example. See Joseph Davis, "The Reception of the *Shulhan Arukh* and

the Formation of the Ashkenazic Jewish Identity," *AJS Review* 35, no. 2 (2002): 251–66, esp. 255–59; Edward Fram, "Jewish Law from the *Shulhan Arukh* to the Enlightenment," in *An Introduction to the History of Jewish Law*, ed. N. S Hecht et al. (Oxford: Clarendon Press, 1996), 362–66; Moshe Halbertal, *People of the Book: Canon, Meaning, and Authority* (Cambridge, MA: Harvard University Press, 1997), 74–81; Asher Siev, *Rabeynu Mosheh Isserles (Rema)* (New York: Yeshiva University, 1972), 286–96; Hanina Ben-Menahem, Neil S. Hecht, and Shai Wosner, *Ha-Maḥaloḳet Ba-Halakhah*, vol. 2 (Boston: University of Boston Law School, 1991) [Hebrew], 513–85; Edward Fram, *Codification of Jewish Law on the Cusp of Modernity* (e-book: Cambridge University Press, 2022).

4. b. Megillah 24b.
5. R. Joseph Karo in the *Beit Yosef* faces this ambiguity (*Orah Haim* 196): "And regarding the Rabbi saying that was the Rif's understanding, I do not know where he learned that from, for the Rif only wrote the words of the Babylonian Talmud, and any possible explanation of the wording of the Talmud can be explained in the Rif too."
6. See Israel M. Ta-Shma, *Ha-Sifrut Ha-Parshanit La-Talmud Be-Eropah Uvi-Tsefon Afriḳah: Ḳorot, Ishim Ṿe-Shiṭot*, vol. 1 (Jerusalem: Magness, 1997), 153 [Hebrew]; Ezra Chwat, "Studies in the Alfasi Gloss-Supplements" (PhD diss., Bar Ilan University, 1995) [Hebrew]; Isadore Twersky, *Introduction to the Code of Maimonides (Mishneh Torah)* (New Haven, CT: Yale University Press, 1980), 89.
7. Rif Megillah 39a.
8. Twersky, *Introduction to the Code of Maimonides*, 1.
9. Ibid., 8–10.
10. Earlier, he composed a classic response to Rif and moved on to hermeneutic projects based on the Talmud that were never widely published and vanished over the years. See ibid., 8–10.
11. On the importance of this project as a theoretical foundation toward establishing a coherent body of Jewish law, see Moshe Halbertal, "'*Sefer Ha-Miẕwot*' of Maimonides—His Architecture of Halakha and Theory of Interpretation," *Tarbiz* 59, no. 3–4 (1990): 457–80 [Hebrew].
12. In *Beit Yosef* to *Orah Haim* 3, to explain why a specific clause from Maimonides was overlooked.
13. This was only one minor and maybe least controversial issue among some that put Maimonides's work in the midst of broad conflicts, especially in Europe. See Isadore Twersky, "The Beginnings of *Mishneh Torah* Criticism," in *Biblical and Other Studies*, ed. A. Altmann (Cambridge, MA: Harvard University Press, 1963), 161–83.
14. This was an explicit and intentional decision, as described in the introduction to *Sefer HaMitzvot*: "And I also saw fit not to write it in the parlance of the books of prophecy (Biblical Hebrew), because that parlance is too limited, in order for us to use it in explaining all the content of the laws. And I will also not write it in the parlance of the Talmud, since only a few among the people of our nation would understand it; and since some of its words are foreign or difficult even for those who are experts in Talmud. Rather I will write it in the parlance of the Mishnah, in order to make it simpler for most people." The modern revival of the Hebrew as an everyday language used the *tannaitic* Hebrew as a basis too; therefore, to modern Hebrew speakers, the language of the *Mishneh Torah* is very close to spoken modern Hebrew.
15. On the question of the extent of this discourse as a reflection of actual historical circumstances, see Omer Michaelis, "Crisis Discourse and Framework Transition in Maimonides' *Mishneh Torah*," *Open Philosophy* 3 (2020): 664–80.

16. Twersky, *Introduction to the Code of Maimonides*, 49–61. It is important to note that once Maimonides based his ruling on these peripheral texts, their paraments became part of the discourse through his lens, though left out of the syllabus in most times and places.
17. In the following centuries, when *Mishneh Torah* was reprinted, more of these projects reacting to the Maimonian text were printed around it and soon became a standard part of a volume *Mishneh Torah*. The first prints of the *Mishneh Torah* in the fifteenth and sixteenth centuries already included commentary. In the 1570s, a new edition was published, including R. Joseph Karo's *Kessef Mishneh* commentary and others. The standard page of Maimonides's magnum opus has been stable since the early modern times, but commentaries have been written in the twentieth century too. On the importance of Maimonides work in modern discourse, see David Berger, "The Uses of Maimonides by Twentieth-Century Jewry," in *Cultures in Collision and Conversation: Essays in the Intellectual History of the Jews* (e-book: Academic Studies Press, 2011), 190–202.
18. See Judah D. Galinsky, "The Significance of Form: R. Moses of Coucy's Reading Audience and His *Sefer Ha-Mitzvot*," *AJS Review* 35, no. 2 (2011): 293–321, esp. 293.
19. Galinsky, "Significance of Form," 302–3. Jeffry R. Woof, "Maimonides Revised: The Case of the 'Sefer Miswot Gadol,'" *The Harvard Theological Review* 90 (1997): 175–203.
20. Galinsky, "Significance of Form," 320–21.
21. Coucy's motivation was explained in different ways. Some researchers pointed to the Messianic approach in his texts, while others claimed the Maimonidean resemblance was the relevant prism, and it was linked to the concept of learning the whole body of Torah (see Galinsky, "Significance of Form," 295 and n. 12 there). It is important to note that these two options don't necessarily contradict.
22. This became especially important once his authority became the one Castilian Jews were most committed to. So was the case not only until the exile from Spain almost a century later but also in the different new locations where these communities were reestablished. See Yehuda Dov Galinsky, "The Four Turim and the Halakhic Literature of Fourteenth-Century Spain" (PhD diss., Bar Ilan University, 1999), 294–95 [Hebrew].
23. It must be noted that in other aspects the Rif and Tosefists were very different, and offered contrasting concepts of studying Talmud and writing about it. See Saiman, *Halakha*, 146–52.
24. Galinsky, *Four Turim*, 56–62.
25. Exod. 28:15.
26. Galinsky, *Four Turim*, 10.
27. The eclectic nature of the topics was explained by the intention to refer to all needed issues that were not included in the first volume. See Galinsky, *Four Turim*, 8.
28. Isaia Sonne, "*Tiyulim Be-Makom She-Hametziut Vehasefer- Historiya Ubibliographia-Noshkim Ze Et Ze*," in *Sefer Ha-Yovel Likhvod Alexander Marx* (New York: Jewish Theological Seminary of America, 1950), 209–32 [Hebrew].
29. Fram, "Jewish Law from the *Shulhan Arukh* to the Enlightenment," 62–366; Halbertal, *People of the Book*, 74–81, Noam Samet, "'Ketsot ha-choshen': The Beginning of 'Lamdanut': Features & Tendencies" (PhD diss., Ben Gurion University, 2016), 41–45.
30. R. Joseph Karo did face the challenge of finding the sources of the *Mishneh Torah* too, composing his "*Kessef Mishneh*" published with the Maimonian work since the 1570s. See Tirza Kelman, "'I Wrote in My Commentary': The Kesef Mishneh and the Commentary of Maimonides in the *Beit Yosef*, as a Prism to R. Joseph Karo's Work Process," *Oqimta* 9 (2023): 133–53.

31. R. Joseph Karo dealt with this issue directly in his responsa, and this is one of the contexts explaining his high motivation to create a text that would enable unified rulings. See Tirza Kelman, "'*I Shall Create Halakhic Ruling . . . For That Is the Objective': The Dimension of Halakhic Ruling in Joseph Karo's Beit Yosef*," PhD diss., Ben Gurion University, 2018, 89–119 [Hebrew].
32. On the impact of this process on R. Karo's work see ibid., 114–19; Roni Weinstein, *Joseph Karo and Shaping of Modern Jewish Law: The Early Modern Ottoman and Global Settings* (New York: Anthem Press, 2022).
33. For examples of this phenomenon, see Elon, *Jewish Law: History, Sources, Principles*, 1319–22; Mor Altshuler, *The Life of Rabbi Yoseph Karo* (Tel Aviv: Tel Aviv University Press, 2016), 324–25 [Hebrew].
34. Due to the limits of the scope of this chapter, other genres are not introduced here. Nevertheless, it should be noted that diverse genres of *halakhic* writing flourished in the high medieval times, and the more influential works also became sources R. Joseph Karo included in his writings. Although he criticized practical rulings regarding a specific topic of Jewish law, he made much use of them. This genre flourished mostly in Ashkenazi areas (which later became Northern France and Germany).
35. This kind of "library awareness" I claim R. Joseph Karo held, is close to what Avriel Bar-Levav defines as the thought of the "comprehensive library." See Avriel Bar-Levav, "The Sacred Space of the Portable Homeland: An Archeology of Unseen Libraries in Jewish Culture from the Medieval Period to the Internet," in *Ut videant et Contingant: Essays on Pilgrimage and Sacred Space in Honor of Ora Limor*, ed. Yitzhak Hen and Iris Shagrir (Ra'anana: Open University Press, 2011), 297–320, esp. 312–15 [Hebrew].
36. This reflects the basic Talmud learning process, linked to the format of printed Talmud editions from their first beginnings. As mentioned above, in the *Tur* itself different opinions are cited, but only of rabbis later than the Talmud. Rashi or Tosefists are rarely quoted as a text, though their opinion or the opinion of a specific Tosefist (e.g., Rabaynu Tam) appears in the text from time to time.
37. Some of these paragraphs are almost identical to the "*Kessef Mishneh*" published in the 1670s by R. Joseph Karo as a commentary to the *Mishneh Torah*, while some are different. See Kelman, "I Wrote in My Commentary." On some occasions, Maimonides is quoted in the *Beit Yosef* also from his commentary of the Mishnah, but it is not used consistently.
38. Elon, *Jewish Law: History, Sources, Principles*, 1315 n. 19. Ta-Shma saw this paragraph as significant too. See Israel M. Ta-Shema, "Rabbi Joseph Caro and His *Beit Yosef*: Between Spain and Germany," in *Moreshet Sepharad: The Sephardi Legacy*, vol. 2, ed. Haim Beinart (Jerusalem: Magnes Press, 2010), 192–206. Close investigation of the lists in the different volumes of the first edition of the *Beit Yosef* showed major differences in the parallel passage of lists that were overseen. See Kelman, "'*I Shall Create Halakhic Ruling*,'" 36–38.
39. Mostly books that have been printed. See Tirza Kelman, "'Written with Iron and Lead Letter in Print': The Print Revolution and the Creation of the *Beit Yosef*," *Pe'amim: Studies in Oriental Jewry* 148 (2017): 9–25 [Hebrew].
40. Many legal problems can occur following the notion that any opinion not cited in the *Beit Yosef* can be a reason to reopen the discussion, and therefor this question has been delicately handled by *halakhic* scholars through the generations. A selection of examples from the twentieth century can be found in *Yabia Omer* part 1 OH 17, *Shevet Halevi* part 11 chapter 175, *Tziz Eliezer* Part 5 chapter 18.

41. See Tirza Kelman, "'All of the Differing Opinions of the *Poskim*, No One Fails to Appear': The Use of Ashkenazi Works in R. Joseph Karo's *Beit Yosef*," in *Sephardim and Ashkenazim*, ed. Sina Rauschenbach (Berlin: De Gruyter, 2020), 89–101.
42. This dynamic can teach us a lot about the timing of different part of the book. See Kelman, "'*I Shall Create Halakhic Ruling*,'" 156–65.
43. Though he definitely quotes others. See Kelman, "All of the Differing Opinions."
44. See Davis, "Reception of the *Shulhan Arukh*"; Elchanan Reiner, "The Ashkenazi Élite at the Beginning of the Modern Era: Manuscript versus Printed Book," *Polin* 10 (1997): 85–98, esp. 96–98.
45. These works will be the center of Chapter 6.
46. The link to the debate in Qidushin continued to be part of the modern discourse brought in the "*Nose'i Kelim*" such as the Magen Avraham Orah Hayim 53.

CHAPTER 6

HOW DID THE *NOS'EI KELIM* ("ARMS-BEARERS") READ *SHULHAN ARUKH*?

NOAM SAMET, TRANSLATED BY ELLI FISCHER

Introduction

> The sages of the generation undertook and resolved to observe and act in accordance with everything stated in the concise formulation of *Shulhan Arukh* and the glosses of Rema. In my opinion, there is no doubt that all that was written is from God, guiding their hand.[1]

This is how Rabbi Yonatan Eybeschutz, the rabbi of Prague in the mid-eighteenth century, described the reception of *Shulhan Arukh* (first published in 1565) by the *halakhic* decisors of his generation. The "concisely formulated" work, which includes the basic text of Rabbi Yosef Karo—*Shulhan Arukh*—along with *Mapah*, the Ashkenazic glosses of Rabbi Moshe Isserles ("Rema") included in every edition of *Shulhan Arukh* since 1578, became the binding, comprehensive legal corpus, and it was not possible to decide *halakhah* in accordance with views not mentioned therein. Rabbi Eybeschutz's ruling was not merely a legal decision; it is coupled with the assertion that this book, together with Rema's glosses, was written with Divine inspiration, "from God, guiding their hand."

This far-reaching description is one of the high points in the reception of *Shulhan Arukh* as the central, definitive *halakhic* code—a process that began 150 years earlier. The canonization of *Shulhan Arukh* found expression not only through the acceptance of its *halakhic* rulings as authoritative but also, and primarily, through the consolidation of a secondary literature on *Shulhan Arukh*—a series of works that, over time, became known as the *nos'ei kelim*, the "arms-bearers."

The term "*nos'ei keli*" originates in the Bible,[2] where it describes a young man tasked with carrying the weapons and armor of a king or warrior. The term is commonly used in reference to commentaries printed alongside the canonic *halakhic* codes—Maimonides's *Mishneh Torah*, Rabbi Yaakov ben Asher's *Arba'ah Turim*, and *Shulḥan Arukh*. Underlying the use of this military metaphor is a conception of the Torah as a battlefield, the arena where decisors and commentators wage war. Moreover, the position of an arms-bearer vis-à-vis a king, general, or knight is subservient and defensive; it is his job to shield and protect his liege and to help him repel attacks. This image, which certainly has a medieval ring, corresponds to the position that the *Aharonim* assume with respect to the *Rishonim*.[3] Simply understood, the various commentators are the arms-bearers of the central text and are seen as its defenders in battle.[4] In reality, things are more complicated. Not infrequently the battle is waged between the central text and the arms-bearers—which do not merely explain or support its positions but oppose and challenge it.

This chapter surveys the development of the *nos'ei kelim* literature that developed around *Shulhan Arukh*, primarily between the seventeenth and nineteenth centuries, and addresses the relationship between this literature, the central text itself, and the objectives that its author, Rabbi Yosef Karo, articulated for it. The chapter begins by introducing several of the major commentators and their methods. It describes the different stages in the development of the *nos'ei kelim* literature, its main characteristics, and the complex relationship of the various commentaries to *Shulhan Arukh* itself.

The chapter concludes by examining how the *nos'ei kelim* literature consolidated into an exegetical and graphical whole in printed versions of *Shulhan Arukh* and considering how this literary whole, which emerged during the nineteenth century, relates to Rabbi Karo's original goals for *Shulhan Arukh*.

Rabbi Yosef Karo and the Purpose of *Shulhan Arukh*

After the printing of *Shulhan Arukh* in 1565 and on through the seventeenth and eighteenth centuries, a vast, eclectic literature sprung up around it, which includes *halakhic* objections, presentation of sources, interpretations, and scholarly notes. During these centuries, *Shulhan Arukh* became the main focus of *halakhic* writing.[5]

The first works of *nos'ei kelim* address the text of *Shulhan Arukh* itself: explaining its formulations, citing relevant sources, invoking alternate views, and ruling on disputes and on new issues not addressed in the text of *Shulhan Arukh*.[6] As the second stage coalesced, it included super-commentaries—which commented on the first layer of commentaries—alongside various anthologies.[7]

Over the years, printers placed these different commentaries around the base text of *Shulhan Arukh*, producing the traditional format of printed canonical works,[8] with the text of *Shulhan Arukh* in the center, surrounded by the various *nos'ei kelim*. This format, whose classic arrangement was completed during the nineteenth century, made *Shulhan Arukh* the central *halakhic* work and the formal and symbolic focus of modern *halakhic* culture.[9]

This ostensibly fulfilled the (almost messianic) expectations that the author of the book, Rabbi Yosef Karo, placed in it, as he wrote in its introduction:

> I have faith in the grace of the Most High that through this book the land will be filled with knowledge of the Lord; small and great alike; novices along with the wise, the skilled craftsman, and the clever speaker.

Yet R. Karo's expectations for *Shulhan Arukh* were not really met. In his preface, R. Karo presents *Shulhan Arukh* as an abridgment of a different, much larger work: *Beit Yosef*. In his programmatic introduction to *Beit Yosef*, R. Karo sets out his agenda.[10] He explains that, owing to historical traumas that left *halakhic* literature in a scattered state, his goal was to re-assemble the *halakhic* corpus, gather the vast material into one place, and decide the *halakhah* from among the various opinions: "**For this is the objective—that we have one Torah and one law.**"

R. Karo's did not complete his broader project with *Beit Yosef*, so several years later he complemented it with *Shulhan Arukh*, a shorter, more popular work, "so that the Lord's perfect Torah is fluent in the mouth of every Jewish person." In his introduction, he even suggests reviewing the entire work multiple times: "Divide it into thirty parts to study one part every day; thus, each month he reviews his learning, and it will be said of him, 'Fortunate is the man who arrives here with his learning in his hand.'" R. Karo's faith "in the grace of the Most High," which animates his efforts, also emphasizes the popular dimension of the book, through which "the land will be filled with knowledge of the Lord."

At first glance, the commentaries that developed around *Shulhan Arukh* opposed both aforementioned goals. Each of the *nos'ei kelim*, densely arranged around the *Shulhan Arukh* base text, has a unique reference marker, be it a font or another graphical feature, repeatedly sending the reader from the center to the margins of the page. The overcrowding of the base text with reference markers makes *Shulhan Arukh* almost impossible to read consecutively. Rather, using it demands familiarity, professionalism, and skill (Figure 6.1).

The technical complexity also reflects how the contents of these works are structured; as opposed to the "one Torah" to which R. Karo aspired, *Shulhan Arukh* and its *nos'ei kelim* became a crowded, complex, labyrinthine text that does not settle *halakhic* debates, but, to the contrary, opens and broadens them.

Thus, a deeper understanding of the *nos'ei kelim* literature also demands an examination of their complicated relationship with the text on which they comment: What do they seek in it? What are they trying to add to it? What is the relationship between their commentaries and R. Karo's original intent?

מאירת עינים חשן משפט עז הלכות טוען ונטען שפתי כהן ריח באר הגולה

FIGURE 6.1 A sample page from the *Shulchan Arukh,* Jerusalem 1931

Three Ashkenazic Responses to *Shulhan Arukh*

Before surveying the commentary produced around *Shulhan Arukh*, it is worth understanding the how R. Karo's efforts were initially received among Ashkenazic Sages in the generations prior to the development of the *nos'ei kelim* literature.

R. Karo's *halakhic* enterprise faced harsh criticism upon publication. *Beit Yosef*, his monumental commentary on *Arba'ah Turim* (or "*Tur*"), was criticized for privileging Sephardic tradition over Ashkenazic and for deciding the *halakhah* using a mechanism with a built-in preference for Sephardic practice. Criticism of *Shulhan Arukh* centers on another important point: the *halakhic* rulings of *Beit Yosef* appear in *Shulhan Arukh* without explanation or citation of sources, precluding further deliberation or criticism[11]—a shift that undermined the basic mechanisms of the Ashkenazic transmission of *halakhah*. The criticism also led to an explosion of *halakhic* creativity, as Ashkenazic Sages added their perspectives to R. Karo's enterprise from.

The first response is reflected in the work of Rabbi Shlomo Luria. Maharshal, as he was known, was a veteran figure in the traditional Torah world of mid-sixteenth-century Poland and the author of *Yam Shel Shlomo*, an Ashkenazic work organized according to the order of the Babylonian Talmud. This work grounds *halakhic* conclusions in exegetical discussions of Talmud passages against the background of traditional Ashkenazic interpretation and custom. Despite its power and scope, it never managed to compete with R. Karo's works. It remained in manuscript form until the eighteenth century, and even then, it was only published in part.[12]

Maharshal's younger cousin, Rabbi Moshe Isserles of Krakow, offered a bolder, second approach: He incorporated his glosses as a "tablecloth"—a "*mapah*"—over *Shulhan Arukh* (which means "set table"), adding the accepted rulings in Ashkenazic communities to the concise rulings of R. Karo. The "tablecloth" is an intriguing metaphor; on one hand, it covers and hides the table, but on the other hand, it beautifies the table and allows it to be used respectably. It was Rema himself who gave his work its name, writing in his introduction:

> I have come . . . **to spread a tablecloth (*mapah*) over the set table (*Shulhan Arukh*)** that he composed. . . . Without this, the table that he prepared before the Lord has not yet been offered to the people in these countries, as most practices of these countries are not in accordance with him.

Rema's words sharpen the meaning of his imagery. The tablecloth is not merely a decoration on the table; without the tablecloth, Ashkenazim could not access R. Karo's table, because its customs differ. The Ashkenazic tablecloth is what allows Rema's community to feast at the table.[13]

A few years after *Shulhan Arukh* was first printed in Venice (in 1565), an edition of the *Orah Hayim* section of *Shulhan Arukh* with Rema's glosses was published in Krakow (in 1578). From that point forward, this format became the standard and near-exclusive format for printing *Shulhan Arukh*. Rema's work altered the place of *Shulhan Arukh* within the Ashkenazic academy, making it a shared focus of *halakhic* discourse from that point forward.

Special attention should be given not only to Rema's *halakhic* rulings but also his method of writing. Prior to the emergence of print culture, the conventional mode of Ashkenazic commentary was to compose glosses that intrude into the text itself, to explain or disagree with it. In Ashkenazic manuscript culture—also reflected in printed Ashkenazic works like *Mordekhai* and *Piskei Ha-Rosh*—readers through the centuries added their views and novel insights to the text before them. The text of an Ashkenazic manuscript was dynamic and living, continuing to develop even after its initial commitment to writing.[14] Rema continues this tradition by interpolating his glosses directly into the text of *Shulhan Arukh*, embedding his own *halakhic* work in R. Karo's.

An example can illustrate how Rema's interpolations into the text of *Shulhan Arukh* can alter the meaning of the former. In *Orah Hayim* 206:6, *Shulhan Arukh* states:

> If one takes a fruit in hand and recites a blessing over it, and it then falls from his hand and is lost or becomes repulsive, he must repeat the blessing, even if other fruits of the same species were present before him when he recited the initial blessing.

Rema adds a brief gloss: "as long as he did not have in mind to eat of it." Rema is not merely clarifying or explaining the ruling of *Shulhan Arukh*, but significantly limiting its application.

At issue is the following: In discussing the obligation to recite a blessing immediately prior to eating a foodstuff, R. Karo rules that if one takes an apple in hand, recites a blessing, and something happens to the apple before one tastes it, they must recite a new blessing, even over another apple from a basket in front of them. Rema disagrees and rules that if one had initially planned to eat more than one apple, they should not recite a new blessing. Yet Rema's words are not framed as a disagreement, but simply continue the sentence of *Shulhan Arukh*. If not for the fact that the printers decided to preface the statement with the *hagah* ("gloss") and print it in a different or smaller font, they would be indistinguishable from the text of *Shulhan Arukh* itself, and the reader would conclude that the view of Rema is actually the view of *Shulhan Arukh*.

A third response to *Shulhan Arukh* appeared several years later, in the person of Rabbi Mordechai Jaffe, a disciple of both Rema and Maharshal. He found Rema's work insufficient because, though it brought the Ashkenazic tradition to bear, it did not cite the sources of his rulings from the Talmud and *Rishonim*, precluding a fulsome *halakhic* discussion. R. Jaffe chose to compose a parallel work, *Levush*,[15] which he intended to "moderates the extremes": It is shorter than *Beit Yosef*—a dense, lengthy, encyclopedic work—but longer than *Shulhan Arukh*, allowing for the citation of the law's sources rather than merely offering a summary ruling.

Despite R. Jaffe's criticisms of R. Karo and Rema, his *Levush* continues their project as *Beit Yosef*, *Shulhan Arukh*, and *Mapah* are the main texts on which it is based. Like Rema, who saw the text before him as being open and dynamic, *Levush* expands the text of *Shulhan Arukh* and, as it were, rewrites it as it ought to have been written.[16]

These three Ashkenazic reactions—*Yam Shel Shlomo*, *Ha-mapah*, and *Levush*—all composed shortly after the publication of *Beit Yosef* and *Shulhan Arukh*, exemplify the process by which R. Karo's works found their way into the Ashkenazic academy. Both Rema's enterprise and, in a certain sense, R. Jaffe's, reflect the rapid and dramatic assimilation of *Shulhan Arukh* into the Ashkenazic scholarly and *halakhic* program.

The Turning Point: *Sefer Me'irat Einayim*, the First Commentary on *Shulhan Arukh*

Following the publication of *Levush*, the first commentary on *Shulhan Arukh, Sefer Me'irat Einayim* ("*Sma*"),[17] by R. Yehoshua Falk Katz, was published on the *Hoshen Mishpat* section of *Shulhan Arukh*.[18] Unlike his predecessors, R. Falk did not gloss the *Shulhan Arukh* or write an alternative work. Rather, his commentary runs alongside the source text, with small symbols in the main text referring the reader to the relevant section of commentary. R. Falk explains in his introduction that this graphical choice was conscious, an explicit contrast with Rema's method of interpolation or R. Jaffe's method of reorganizing and rewriting *Shulhan Arukh*.

This choice reflects an important turning point, when *Shulhan Arukh*, together with Rema's glosses, gains acceptance as the textual infrastructure through which the *halakhic* creative enterprise would relate from that point forward. Additional commentators would follow *Sma* by engaging with the text of *Shulhan Arukh*, cumulatively producing the broad literary project that would become known as the *nos'ei kelim*. In this sense, *Sma* was the first of the *nos'ei kelim*.

In his preface to *Sma*,[19] R. Falk explains how he reached his decision, ascribing it to a surprising source, as it is not part of standard *halakhic* discourse: the introduction of Rabbi Yehudah Ibn Tibbon, a twelfth-century Spanish translator, to his translation of *Hovot Ha-levavot*.[20] Ibn Tibbon criticizes those who alter the works before them and meddle with them. He considers the views of the copyist or translator to be problematic, since they can "damage and alter"—disrupting and corrupting the text's original order.

> One who writes his own work, if he errs on a matter or stumbles in his words or is too brief, his fault is not so great, for this is what his mind has comprehended, and his wisdom penetrated only this far. The greater fault is with one who translated a book or work over which its author toiled, taking care in all its matters and arranging

> its chapters. . . . Then he comes to damage and alter, and he says "this is it," and those who study it will ascribe every error to the author.[21]

Ibn Tibbon's words exemplify how the Sephardic academy viewed the text. Unlike the Ashkenazic view of the text as something living and developing, the Sephardic academy strove to preserve the precise original text and safeguard the ancient traditions it contains from outside interference. In Ibn Tibbon's view, the model for safeguarding canonic texts is found in the Scripture, Mishnah, and Talmud—whose numerous commentators dared not alter the base text. Canonical texts must be closed to enable the wealth of translation and interpretation to grow around the text without defiling it.

R. Falk's decision to part ways with his teachers and write a commentary on *Shulhan Arukh* reflects his espousal of a "closed" view of the text. He finds precedent for this view in the words of Ibn Tibbon, a manifestly Sephardic exegete and translator. Here, *Shulhan Arukh* attains the status of a fundamental work whose textual integrity must be maintained. To that end, he modeled his commentaries on medieval commentaries on Scripture and Talmud, with clear demarcations between the canonized base text and its commentary.

It seems that we can identify two factors which together motivated R. Falk to deviate from the approach of his predecessors toward the text of *Shulhan Arukh* and to present his work as a commentary that stands external to the original text. The first, which *Sma* identifies expressly, is the *halakhic* gravity and authority of R. Karo and Rema, which caused R. Falk to be wary of meddling in their joint enterprise, lest he "be burnt by their embers." The second is that the print revolution and the spread of the printed book[22] produced changes in how people thought about knowledge itself, causing a basic shift in the conception of a text.[23]

The *Shulhan Arukh* that lay before R. Falk at the end of the sixteenth century was already a printed, complete, and bound book, which, unlike a manuscript, was a finished product. Print fixes and stabilizes the text, leaving no room for a dynamic view of the text or exegetical interpolations into it. The optimal way to respond to a printed text is as a critic and commentator. These factors shifted the conception of the text and the authority of *Shulhan Arukh* and led to the growth of the exegetical enterprise around it.[24]

The Return to Intensive Talmud Study

The revolution wrought by R. Falk vis-à-vis *Shulhan Arukh* requires going beyond merely considering the graphic form of the book and analyzing the exegetical nature of the work. As is typical of commentators and glossators, *Sma* reflects the reception of *Shulhan Arukh* as the organizing focus of *halakhic* writing while simultaneously challenging its primacy and diverting *halakhic* literature from the course charted by *Shulhan Arukh*.

R. Falk's preface to *Sma* includes a detailed criticism of R. Karo's (and Rema's!) decision to follow Maimonides and formulate a code free of sources and references. Paralleling Maharshal's earlier critique. R. Falk is concerned that people unqualified to render *halakhic* decisions—those who "have not attained [the expertise required to issue] rulings, yet rule"—will use *Shulhan Arukh* without any deeper familiarity with its sources and consequently issue mistaken rulings. Of course, this debate is not only about the process of *halakhic* decision-making; rather, the debate reflects conflicting conceptions of *halakhah* and Torah study. *Shulhan Arukh*, even if R. Karo and Rema did not initially intend as such, had become a stand-alone *halakhic* code that did not contain any sources. Since this threatened to alter the way *halakhah* was decided.[25] *Sma* supplied both a commentary on *Shulhan Arukh* as well as a necessary supplement and corrective.

R. Falk describes the goals of his commentary in its preface as follows:

> A commentary on *Shulhan Arukh*, I have titled it *Sefer Me'or Einayim* [lit. "*The Light of the Eyes*"] because it truly brightens the eyes of those who study *Shulhan Arukh* with [Rema's] glosses, which are vague and opaque, such that without this commentary, it is forbidden to issue rulings from it.[26]

The declared goal of the work is, in a sense, to make up for the defects of *Shulhan Arukh* as a legal code. According to R. Falk, **one should not issue rulings based on *Shulhan Arukh* unless one has supplemented it with the study of his own work.** The purpose of his commentary is to present the student with the background of the ruling and enable him to issue rulings through the study of primary *halakhic* sources instead of issuing facile rulings based on R. Karo's compendium. R. Falk further explains that his work is also addressed to the advanced scholar who wishes not only to know the bottom-line *halakhah* but to engage in penetrating study of the foundations of the *halakhic* discussion. *Sma* therefore contains references to the other major *halakhic* works—*Mishneh Torah* and *Tur*—as well as to novel legal rulings that stem from close study of the *halakhic* source.

Sma and *Bayit Hadash*—Between Analysis and Legal Decision-Making

This last point—the fact that R. Falk included novel legal rulings in *Sma*—drew the ire of his younger contemporary, R. Yoel Sirkis, author of *Bayit Hadash* ("*Bah*").[27] Though R. Sirkis composed his work as a commentary on *Tur*, in many respects it belongs among the *nos'ei kelim* on *Shulhan Arukh*; it constantly addresses the views of R. Karo and Rema, as well as later commentators *Levush* and *Sma*. In his introductions to various parts of his work, R. Sirkis repeatedly attacks the rulings of *Sma*. The introduction to *Bah* on *Hoshen Mishpat* states:

> Since, in our time, the great and pious Rabbi Falk Cohen, of blessed memory, arose and composed a lengthy commentary on *Shulhan Arukh*, and from his explanations and elucidations there occasionally emerged various legal rulings that the *Rishonim* never imagined. I am therefore compelled to alert and caution those who study *halakhah* for the purpose of practice that they issue proper rulings . . .

The novel legal rulings of which R. Falk was so proud in his introduction are precisely what unnerve R. Sirkis. It is evident from his other writings that R. Sirkis was not opposed to novel *halakhic* decisions generally, but rather took a principled stance against the type of *halakhic* discussion that characterizes R. Falk's works. In his preface to *Even Ha-Ezer*, R. Sirkis attacks *Sma* for using an excessively complex and casuistic mode of interpretation, which intensively scrutinizes the subtleties of the text but does not strive for the simple clarification of the *halakhic* tradition. This method of study, legitimate in the realm of rabbinic study, is ill suited for *halakhic* decision-making and should not be committed to print.

Debate over this method of study was not new. R. Sirkis's criticism perfectly echoes the criticism of casuistry ("*pilpul*"), a familiar mode of study since the early fifteenth century.[28] Even if the specific methods of *pilpul* did not remain constant throughout two centuries, the central claims against them remained the same: Its subtle inferences and hairsplitting belong in the study hall but should not be used to decide *halakhah*. Rather, *halakhah* should emerge clearly and directly from textual sources, not as the product of casuistic study.

The debate between the authors of *Bah* and *Sma* reflects an old debate within the Ashkenazic academy between two opposing conceptions of *halakhic* decision-making. From R. Sirkis's perspective, the main objective of a *halakhic* decisor is to analyze the *halakhic* discussion as it developed until his time. He is not expected to innovate anything, but on the contrary, should extract the *halakhic* truth by analyzing the views of his predecessors.

R. Falk's view was the exact opposite. It represents the elitist and scholastic world of the Polish rabbinic academy in which *halakhah* is a dynamic realm tightly linked to the world of the scholar in the study hall. The law is the product of the scholar's creativity, and distinctions that the scholar invents to resolve exegetical questions become *halakhic* novellae.[29]

R. Sirkis's criticism sharpens the significance of *Sma* as a commentary on *Shulhan Arukh* and its impact of the further development of the *nos'ei kelim* literature. *Sma* is the initial bridge from the casuistic world of the Ashkenazic study hall to the literature of canonic legal codes. R. Falk, operating within the analytic mindset of the *yeshivah*,[30] is not willing to accept R. Sirkis's disciplinary bifurcation of *halakhic* decision-making from academic study.[31] According to R. Falk, novel interpretations that emerge from *yeshivah*-style *pilpul* are part of the very fiber of *halakhic* literature, and any independent scholar may innovate after studying the sources. Debates, hairsplitting, and casuistry give rise to novel rulings, which appear in commentaries to *Shulhan Arukh* and ultimately become an integral part of *halakhic* literature.

To be sure, the openness to reconsidering rules, restoration of the Talmud as a source text, and casuistic circumlocutions are diametric opposites of R. Karo's basic agenda for *Shulhan Arukh*, which sought to unify and consolidate the *halakhic* system. Though *Sma* reinforces the centrality of *Shulhan Arukh*, it dismantles the framework it produced and presents a different conception of *halakhah*.

The curriculum at the rabbinic study hall of the late sixteenth century centered on two canonic texts—the Babylonian Talmud (or "Bavli") and *Shulhan Arukh*.[32] The literature of the *nos'ei kelim*—and especially *Sma*—reinforced this dual canonization.[33] On one hand, it continues the Ashkenazic analytic tradition of intensive engagement with the Talmud and its commentaries.[34] On the other hand, it acknowledges and preserves the status of *Shulhan Arukh* at the heart of *halakhic* literature. The result is a literature that, though it exists within the *halakhic* realm, in the margins of the pages of *Shulhan Arukh*, it imports the world of the study hall into the realm of *halakhic* decision-making.

Sma and the vast literature that flourished in its wake can be seen as complementing Rema's enterprise. It is not only Ashkenazic rulings, but also the spirit of the Ashkenazic study hall and analytic tradition find their way into *Shulhan Arukh*, thus completing the work while consciously upending its primary objectives.

Broadening the Scope

The foundations laid by *Sma* and *Bah* quickly inspired a literature that reinforced, the dual structure and the tension between analysis and *halakhic* decision-making, between the Talmud and *Shulhan Arukh*.

In 1646, about fifteen years after R. Sirkis published *Bah*, his son-in-law, R. David Segal,[35] published his commentary on *Shulhan Arukh*, known as *Turei Zahav* ("*Taz*"). Echoes of the revolution wrought by the *nos'ei kelim* vis-à-vis *Shulhan Arukh* are discernible in his preface:

> After I saw in the preface to *Beit Yosef* that [the author] was concerned that the Torah had become several *Torot*, due to the differences of opinion among decisors, so he pondered and sought out a proper home for clarifying the matters. Yet in our generation, this concern has returned, for after him giants arose in Israel, the one and only among our people, the great and eminent R. Shlomo Luria, of blessed memory, and after him, the eminent R. Falk, of blessed memory, and my teacher and father-in-law, R. Yoel, of blessed memory. They composed works, each according to his understanding. This one builds. and that one tears down; this one dreams, and that one interprets it, etc.

The introduction to *Taz* describes well the tension between R. Yosef Karo's initial goal—unifying legal rulings and gathering the material into a "proper home"—and the situation in the Polish study hall in the mid-seventeenth century, where the works of

Maharshal, *Sma*, and *Bah* breached the borders of *halakhic* discourse anew. Later, R. Segal declares that his goal is to repair the breach and reassert the words of *Shulhan Arukh*; and yet, in fact, his comments joined the burgeoning field of Ashkenazic commentary on *Shulhan Arukh*.

One factor producing this state of affairs was the conflict between R. Segal and his younger contemporary, Rabbi Shabbetai Cohen ("Shakh"),[36] who published his own work, *Siftei Kohen* (also called "*Shakh*"), the very same year that *Taz* appeared. Shakh grew up in the Polish rabbinic academy and belongs to the scholarly tradition of Maharshal's study hall.[37] Traces of this tradition are discernible in the character of his bold, innovative work, which emphasizes novel interpretation.[38] His work on the *Yoreh De'ah* section of *Shulhan Arukh*, which he published in Krakow in 1646, at the age of just 24 (!), is adorned with many approbations, the common theme of which is their attestation of the work's astounding innovations. Thus, for example, the approbation of Rabbi Mendel of Szydłów:

> I have considered some of his words in their place, and I found words that are worthy of the one who uttered them; they are <u>innovative words that those of early and later generations did not consider . . .</u> He delved into deep waters and found pearls, <u>words that no ear ever heard</u>.

The boldness and intellectual independence of Shakh's scholarly methods stand out. He does not hesitate to disagree with *Rishonim* and *Aharonim*, and rather than work through the intermediate apparatus of the codes and medieval commentaries, he proves his views directly from passages of Talmud.[39]

Alongside his extensive commentary on *Shulhan Arukh*, Shakh also published a small work called *Nekudot Ha-kesef* containing numerous objections against *Taz*.[40] R. Segal responded to Shakh's objections, and the debate between these two Sages intensified. The basic stance of *Taz*, as noted, was to defend the views of the earlier decisors and restore the honor of *Shulhan Arukh*; in contrast, Shakh's rulings often deviated from the line set forth by *Shulhan Arukh* and Rema in favor of a novel, independent ruling. Thus, the conflict between Shakh and R. Segal further developed the discussion around *Shulhan Arukh*.

The impetus to produce commentary on *Shulhan Arukh* included all four parts of the work. The first two parts to garner commentaries were *Hoshen Mishpat* and *Yoreh De'ah*, but commentaries on the *Orah Hayim* and *Even Ha-ezer* sections appeared soon after. The centrality of *Shulhan Arukh* led other writers to seek ways to stake their claim and place their works alongside *Shulhan Arukh*. Thus, Rabbi Shmuel of Fuerth,[41] in the preface to his *Beit Shmuel* in 1689, describes his aspiration to "build a home" for himself—that is, to compose a work that would make him famous within the field of *halakhic* literature. He directs his efforts to the *Even Ha-ezer* section of *Shulhan Arukh*, which, he suggests, has been neglected by commentators and has not yet merited a suitable commentary.[42] Thus, commentary on *Shulhan Arukh* became a phenomenon that fed on its own momentum. The wide distribution of the first commentaries encouraged additional writers to walk the same path and add their commentaries to the central work.

Rabbi Avraham Abele Gombiner's *Magen Avraham*,[43] a commentary on the *Orah Hayim* section of *Shulhan Arukh*, presents a similar phenomenon. This commentary, published at the end of the seventeenth century, became a significant source of *halakhic* rulings in the areas of his engagement. The author's son attests in his preface to the work that his father composed it "at the request of friends, who asked him for novellae on the four columns [i.e., sections of *Shulhan Arukh*], and he replied to them . . . that three have already been explained and elucidated, but I will not leave them emptyhanded vis-à-vis the fourth, as there is still no commentary on the column [i.e., section] of *Orah Hayim*." The fact that the other three sections of *Shulhan Arukh* had already garnered commentary drove R. Gombiner to complete the task and offer a commentary on the fourth section as well, *Orah Hayim*.[44]

Nevertheless, the objectives of these works are not always limited to just commenting and issuing rulings. In the preface to *Beit Shmuel* on *Even Ha-ezer*, the author describes his agenda as follows:

> It is not my intention to build the house of Shmuel ("*Beit Shmuel*") as a permanent structure for establishing the practical *halakhah*, for as I worked there was no one with me, neither friend nor disciple; I built it only to stroll in a lucid structure and a tower floating in air that makes one wise. Builders and the sons of builders will look out through its open windows, to sharpen, to debate.

It seems that the goals of this work differ somewhat from those of its predecessors. The "building" includes not only explanations and rulings but also sophisticated casuistic elaboration. The burgeoning writing around *Shulhan Arukh* expanded the horizons of debate and moved beyond the practical *halakhic* bottom line. R. Shmuel of Fuerth openly declares the theoretical objectives of his work, and he invites the Sages to stroll within it, to engage in scholastic debate, and to sharpen their thinking.

This broadening of horizons is also discernible in the works of Rabbi Yonatan Eybeschutz,[45] who, in the second half of the eighteenth century, composed wide-ranging commentaries on *Yoreh De'ah* (called *Kereti U-feleti*[46]) and *Hoshen Mishpat* (called *Urim Ve-tumim*[47]). In his preface to *Kereti U-feleti*, he describes his objectives as follows:

> There, great and small will seek to know the deed they shall do and the path on which they shall walk. There, scribes, saints, and ascetics will nest; its house is a meeting house for sages. . . . And there will lodge those who linger in the gardens, companions who listen to the voice of the Lord . . . wisely debating all the words of the *Rishonim* and *Aharonim*, wisely probing the judgments that the early sages, of blessed memory, uttered, even that right is left, etc.

R. Eybeschutz explains that his book is intended for broad audiences: First, it is a book of *halakhah* from which "great and small" can learn the correct *halakhic* rulings. Additionally, it is intended for "companions who listen to the voice of the Lord" (a paraphrase of Song of Solomon 8:13), who are invited to lodge in R. Eybeschutz's Torah and to seek wisdom there. His objective is exegetical as well, and thus he explains "the multitude of questions of the Tosafists and Maharsha." But in addition to these academic objectives, the book also has a didactic goals; it is intended for "novices in wisdom" to be taught "the straight path of Torah."

Like R. Falk in his commentary to *Tur*, R. Eybeschutz chose to divide his work into two parallel sections:

> I saw fit to compose a work with two sections: one short and one long. The first (short) section will contain, in the utmost brevity, all legal rulings uttered by the *Rishonim* and *Aharonim*, in addition to what has emerged from my study, whether deciding [between different views] or adding my own innovations. All who want to know the principles of the laws in brief will find satisfaction here. And the second section will provide all of the casuistry and the debates of Abaye and Rava; nothing is absent or too exalted.

Though he is introducing a commentary on *Shulhan Arukh*, R. Eybeschutz no longer views his composition merely as a book of *halakhah*, but as a work whose didactic goals return to the study hall. The distinction between the two parts of the work helps us understand two aspects of the *nos'ei kelim* literature, which function simultaneously as a practical *halakhic* literature and as an intellectual, analytic, casuistic literature whose objectives are didactic and academic. Not only does the study hall impact the literature of *Shulhan Arukh*, but the latter itself returns to impact the study hall.[48]

This brief historical survey of the *nos'ei kelim* returns us to the statement of R. Yonatan Eybeschutz that opens this chapter, which holds that *Shulhan Arukh* was composed with Divine inspiration.[49] R. Eybeschutz goes further, explaining:

> For many questions that later sages posed to [the authors of *Shulhan Arukh* and Rema's gloss] them have been answered profoundly and sharply, and likewise, they incorporated in their sweet, concise words numerous laws; there is no doubt that they did not intend everything, for how would it be possible given the abundance of work—the work of heaven—that was their duty? [. . .] Rather, the spirit of the Lord was manifest within them, so that their words corresponded to the *halakhah* even without the writer's intent; the will of the Lord prospered at their hand.

According to R. Eybeschutz, the clearest evidence of the holy spirit that rested on R. Karo and Rema is the paradoxical fact that the words they wrote made possible the many works that accumulated around it to debate their words, to make inferences from them, and to ascribe questions and answers to them—even those that are far from the straightforward meaning of the words and certainly never crossed the minds of the authors. The assumption that each word of a text contains multiple possible inferences and interpretations is a key property attributed to all works of Rabbinic Judaism's sacred canon; here, then, *Shulhan Arukh* is included in that class of texts.

As R. Eybeschutz attests, the many works around *Shulhan Arukh* stray very far from the original intent of the authors when they anchored complex analysis in its text and in peculiarities of its language. At the same time, this dynamic itself attests to the power and uniqueness of the book. From R. Eybeschutz's perspective, it is precisely the deconstruction of the *Shulhan Arukh* text and its being made to bear a heavy intellectual load that prove that it was written under Divine inspiration—and ultimately lead to its demarcation as the basic work of *halakhic* literature and the signifier of its boundaries.

To be sure, the canonization of a text is always a function of its reception. What comes into focus here is that the reception of *Shulhan Arukh* necessarily entailed the opposite trend as well: its deconstruction and the undermining of its primary objectives. Further reflection raises the idea that this is true of the canonization of *halakhic* literature more generally: the reception of a text as canonic grants it validity while simultaneously opening it up to commentary and interpretation that enable subsequent scholars to use it to nurture new horizons of deliberation.[50]

In his discussion of commentary, Michel Foucault addresses the paradoxical structure of all commentary, which always upholds its original text while profoundly negating it. In his words, the role of commentary is

> to say at last what was silently articulated "beyond," in the text. . . . [T]he commentary must say for the first time what had, nonetheless, already been said, and must tirelessly repeat what had, however, never been said.[51]

According to Foucault, the paradoxical relationship between commentary and its source text is built-in; commentary always develops ideas implicit in its source text while dismantling its framework.

This insight invites another, deeper perspective on the relationship between the *nos'ei kelim* and *Shulhan Arukh*, and between R. Karo's objectives for *Shulhan Arukh* and the final product as it consolidated over the centuries, and now stands before us. In a certain sense, at least, it seems that here, too, the consolidation of commentary on *Shulhan Arukh*, despite straying far from the original character of the work, expresses "what was silently articulated."

Shulhan Arukh as a Whole and the Consolidation of the Page Format

Contemporary versions of *Shulhan Arukh* include numerous commentaries around the main text, which developed over the three centuries between the initial printing of *Shulhan Arukh* until the latter half of the nineteenth century. Most commentaries address only one or two of its four sections. Consequently, when first published, they circulated as separate titles under various names, not as editions of *Shulhan Arukh*, even if they included the text of *Shulhan Arukh*. (This is much like the twentieth-century *Mishnah Berurah*, a commentary on *Orah Hayim*, which is not regarded as an edition of *Shulhan Arukh*.)

When printers began to gather commentaries on *Shulhan Arukh* in a single volume, the various commentaries on a particular section of *Shulhan Arukh* were generally printed together under a separate title, not as parts of a whole called "*Shulhan Arukh*." In 1677, a volume titled *Ashlei Ravrevi* was published which included the *Shakh* and *Taz* commentaries on *Yoreh De'ah*. Similarly, *Torat Kohanim*, published in 1692, got its name because it included commentaries by two men of priestly pedigree: R. Yehoshua Falk Cohen's *Sma* and R. Shabbetai Cohen's *Shakh*, both on *Hoshen Mishpat*. That same year, *Maginei Eretz* was also published, which included two commentaries on *Orah Hayim*: R. Gombiner's *Magen Avraham* and R. David Segal's *Magen David*.[52] The *Even Ha-ezer* section was printed relatively late, under the title *Apei Ravrevi*, and included the commentaries *Helkat Mehokek* and *Beit Shmuel*. The library of the eighteenth-century scholar did not contain a set of *Shulhan Arukh* as we have it today, but rather a variety of works, with different titles that relate mainly to the *nos'ei kelim* of *Shulhan Arukh*, rather than the work itself.[53]

The names of these volumes further demonstrate the importance of the *nos'ei kelim* in shaping the contours of *Shulhan Arukh*. It is evident that *Shulhan Arukh* itself was not always the real focus of this literature; even though it served as the fulcrum around which these works were organized. The *nos'ei kelim* do not only explain *Shulhan Arukh* but occasionally use it to produce more expansive *halakhic* works.

The next step in the graphic development of the traditional page format of *Shulhan Arukh* is tied to the emergence of secondary literature around the earlier commentaries. Three main types of secondary literature can be described: One consists of works that directly engage earlier commentators and expand, explain, and debate them. Such works include *Peri Megadim* and *Mahatzit Ha-shekel*, which deal extensively with the comments of *Magen Avraham*, *Shakh*, and *Taz*. The second type consists of works that aim to gather more *halakhic* material into the emerging volumes of *Shulhan Arukh*. *Ba'er Heitev*, *Sha'arei Teshuvah*, and *Pit'hei Teshuvah* anthologize *halakhic* rulings from the responsa literature of the sixteenth through eighteenth centuries, organizing and presenting them according to the order of *Shulhan Arukh*. The third type consists of works with a greater emphasis on analysis and casuistry, like *Ketzot Ha-hoshen* and *Netivot Ha-mishpat*.

The decision by these authors to add their works to the emerging literature around *Shulhan Arukh* demonstrates the centrality and significance of the earlier *nos'ei kelim* as major *halakhic* works. It also reinforces the utility of the printed *Shulhan Arukh* to the scholar, hence the desire to gather still more *halakhic* material into the volumes of *Shulhan Arukh*. Some of these writers explicitly describe their mission as the completion of R. Karo's task in writing *Shulhan Arukh*. For instance, in the preface to *Sha'arei Teshuvah*, its author, Rabbi Ephraim Zalman Margolis of Brody (d. 1828), describes his objectives as follows:

> The giants of the generations who produced novel *halakhic* rulings and tens of thousands of responsa—our master, [author of] *Beit Yosef*, prepared and examined them in his lengthy book; and in order to teach the students a concise method, he adopted brevity and went back to include it all in the four [sections of] *Shulhan Arukh*. And akin to his deeds were this Torah that Moshe . . . our master, Rema, of blessed memory . . . who after [R. Karo] collected from the books of the sages of the generation and responsa upon which the eye of *Beit Yosef* never shone. And upon them the sages of every generation set commentaries, elucidations, and innovations that are renewed each morning. And by these the set table ("*shulhan arukh*") will be carried ("*nisa*"), with all its utensils ("*kelav*") and for all its tasks.

R. Margolis begins with a description of what he finds before him: *Shulhan Arukh* and Rema gathered all *halakhic* material into their canonic works. The Sages of subsequent generations added their commentaries and novellae to *Shulhan Arukh*, but much *halakhic* material began to accumulate in the responsa literature as well. The proliferation of material posed a challenge to scholars, so R. Margolis, as he describes it, sought to collect this vast corpus and "brighten the eyes of those waiting to understand the clarified laws."

R. Margolis's words here strongly recall R. Karo's preface to *Beit Yosef*. He undertakes this great (in fact, impossible) task of reviewing and organizing the entire responsa literature. Thus, R. Margolis further completes the task of R. Karo, as his work distills ongoing *halakhic* creativity and centers it around *Shulhan Arukh*.

Alongside the burgeoning density of works by commentators, the printers also continued to include as many works as possible in volumes of *Shulhan Arukh*. Bringing these works together was meant to facilitate study, as Rabbi Avraham Yosef Madpis, who published a new edition of *Shulhan Arukh* in Lviv between 1860 and 1864, described:

> Rabbis will be glad and students will rejoice when they see the craftsmanship of this pure table ("*shulhan*") in its magnificent perfection, its ornaments bound upon it, buttons and almond-shaped flowers extending from its sides. And for the person who could not afford to gather everything into the chamber from which he issues instruction, or for whom it was too burdensome to keep them all before him—these works have now been gathered together for him on one page.

The organization of all the material around *Shulhan Arukh* makes things easier for students who cannot afford all the books individually. Moreover, the new format eases the task; the student no longer had to keep many books open on his desk, because they had all been gathered around *Shulhan Arukh* itself.[54]

Of course, no less than the concern shown for the interests of scholars, this edition also manifests competition between printers to produce the most extensive and comprehensive editions.[55] Either way, the consolidation of this secondary literature produced graphical density on the pages of *Shulhan Arukh*, as the number of works and commentaries added to its volumes continued to grow.

At this time, printers also began to reprint the volumes of *Shulhan Arukh* together, in complete editions that included all four sections of the work as well as several commentaries on each section.

The density of commentary produced over three centuries from when *Shulhan Arukh* was first printed in Venice in the sixteenth century found its way into the printed edition, resulting in the total product familiar to us as "*Shulhan Arukh.*" These editions, designed in Lviv and Vilnius (Vilna) in the latter half of the nineteenth century, became primary and were reprinted photographically numerous times over the past century and a half. These editions also determine which commentaries would continue to be printed with *Shulhan Arukh* to this day.[56]

Improvements and enhancements in print technology that allowed for easier and cheaper printing of large, multivolume sets of books certainly contributed to the shaping of these late nineteenth-century editions. Beyond this, it seems that the return to printing *Shulhan Arukh* as a complete set of all four of its sections and with numerous commentaries expresses the attitudes of printers and the potential target audience toward the work. From the publishers' perspective, a volume of *Shulhan Arukh* should be the only book that a decisor needs when deciding a *halakhic* question. It should therefore contain all relevant material. This, of course, is not only a marketing or graphical choice; printing *Shulhan Arukh* in complete editions, packed with commentaries, expresses the notion that *halakhah* in its entirety is concentrated within the volumes bearing the title *Shulhan Arukh*.

Nevertheless, the cost of this approach is that the original *Shulhan Arukh*, penned by R. Karo, is almost completely lost as an independent work. The crowding of *Shulhan Arukh* with references and markers made the original text almost unreadable. Today, the *Shulhan Arukh* mainly serves as the organizing focus of the *halakhic* and exegetical writing of subsequent centuries. The canonization of the work sidelined its status as an independent work of practical *halakhah* yet transformed it into the core around which modern *halakhic* writing aggregated.

Conclusion: "One Law" or a Literary Whole?

Discussion of *Shulhan Arukh* and its *nos'ei kelim* would not be complete without returning to address R. Karo's objectives. While perhaps counterintuitive, in some ways the set of *Shulhan Arukh* that stands before us may actualize R. Karo's aspirations for his enterprise.

More than three decades ago, Eliav Shochetman challenged the classical conception of *Shulhan Arukh* as a concise book of *halakhic* rulings and proposed that it should be viewed as a literary abridgement of *Tur*.[57] His view relies primarily on *Shulhan Arukh*'s lack of *halakhic* decisiveness: R. Karo included in *Shulhan Arukh* hundreds of *halakhic* disputes, and his words often contradict one another. It is hard to understand why a work meant to be a concise book of *halakhah* leaves so much unresolved.[58]

Maoz Kahana[59] follows this view to emphasize the tension between the practical aspiration toward discrete *halakhic* decisions and R. Karo's other fundamental aspiration—the desire for gather into one place the totality of *halakhic* literature. As elaborated in the introduction to *Beit Yosef*, R. Karo's central objective was encyclopedic: to centralize and incorporate all existing material in a single work. This aspiration contains a broad, inclusive aspect that contradicts, to an extent, the goal of creating "one *halakhah*, one law." Kahana suggests viewing the establishment of one resolute law as a utopian aspiration that finds concrete expression only with the formation of a *halakhic*-literary framework where all *halakhic* traditions can be gathered. In this reading, the goal of deciding the *halakhah* is a mission statement and an expression of a more basic necessity: maintaining the cohesiveness of *halakhic* discourse by gathering its expanding literary corpus into a single platform that would become the new center of focus, even if it does not unambiguously resolution every *halakhic* question.

This bears on our understanding of the relationship between *Shulhan Arukh* and its *nos'ei kelim*. Even acknowledging the tension between presenting discrete *halakhic* decisions and the expansive, analytic tendencies of the *nos'ei kelim*, their gathering around *Shulhan Arukh* seems to resonate deeply with R. Karo's aspiration to refocus and reorganize *halakhic* material. Placing *Shulhan Arukh* at the center of *halakhic* discourse accepts R. Karo's goals and uses his work as the new focus of *halakhic* literature. The *nos'ei kelim* went far beyond *Shulhan Arukh* in continuing the expansive *halakhic* discourse that predates *Shulhan Arukh*, delving back into the Talmud and its commentaries and giving expression to scholarly methods, *halakhic* traditions, and local custom. Yet this discourse was now reorganized around *Shulhan Arukh*, which served both as the textual focus to which the *nos'ei kelim* relate and as the published set in which all of these works appear together, as part of a single whole.

From this perspective, we can claim that the modern set of *Shulhan Arukh* fulfilled its author's expectations, even if not in the way R. Karo had hoped. *Shulhan Arukh* does not function as an accessible, popular *halakhic* code as its author intended, but to a large degree, the material collated in the printed set establishes the boundaries of *halakhah* in the modern era.

Hence the image of a "*Shulhan Arukh* Jew" serves as a familiar description of someone fully committed to *halakhah*. Beyond that, the map of the *halakhic* world is shaped by the chapters of *Shulhan Arukh* in its modern format, with all of the textual and graphic overcrowding it entails. Every modern *halakhic* discussion begins with a reference to the source of the ruling in *Shulhan Arukh* and its commentaries. The encounter between *Shulhan Arukh* and its commentators became the primary arena of *halakhic* literature, until *Shulhan Arukh* ultimately became the symbolic and literary heart of *halakhah* in the modern era. Even *halakhic* works beyond the boundaries of *Shulhan Arukh*—the responsa literature and commentary on the Talmud—continue to be gathered and reorganized into the topical *halakhic* framework demarcated by the sections of *Shulhan Arukh*. Many modern works of responsa are divided topically according to the sections of *Shulhan Arukh* and organized in the order of its chapters. The culmination of this process is when specific *halakhic* subjects are discussed and characterized with reference to the chapter in *Shulhan Arukh* in which they appear. For instance, every student of *halakhah* knows that the laws of cooking on Shabbat are addressed in chapter 318 of *Orah Hayim*, while the laws of mixing meat and dairy begin in chapter 87 of *Yoreh De'ah*. This, it seems, is very much in keeping with R. Karo's aspirations for his work.

Paradoxically, and as R. Eybeschutz emphasized long ago, it is precisely the extensive exegetical efforts devoted to *Shulhan Arukh* that transformed it into the text that reorganizes the modern *halakhic* corpus, providing an anchor around which its contents accumulate and consolidate. Even if this process strays far from the straightforward agenda of *Shulhan Arukh*, it simultaneously gives expression to R. Karo's deeper agenda, manifesting what was latent in *Shulhan Arukh* as a *halakhic* work.

Notes

1. Rabbi Yonatan Eybeschutz, *Urim Ve-Tumim*, §25.
2. See, for instance, Judg. 9:54; 1 Sam. 14:1–7, 16:21, 31:3–5; 2 Sam. 18:15.
3. It seems that the expression was first used in a rabbinic context in the early sixteenth century. See *Responsa Mahari Berab* §59; *Responsa Maharalbah* §§36 and 42. However, in these two sources, the "arms-bearers" are not specifically the commentaries printed on the page, but rather successors to the way of thinking of one of the Rishonim (*Responsa Maharalbah* §42 refers to "Rabbenu Tam and the arms-bearers of his thinking"). The expression first appears among Ashkenazic writers about a century later; see *Responsa Be'er Sheva* §20.
4. A slightly different meaning can be found in Rabbi Ephraim Zalman Margolis's preface to *Sha'arei Teshuvah* (discussed next to note 53 and below), where he paraphrases the verses that describe the carrying of the showbread table from the Tabernacle: "And by these the set table ('*shulhan*') will be carried ('*nisa*') with all its utensils ('*kelav*')." In his imagery, the "*kelim*" are not weapons of war but the accessories that serve the table. The various commentaries around *Shulhan Arukh* thus bear it and raise it up.
5. See the hyperbolic formulation in Chaim Tchernowitz (Rav Tzair), *Toledoth Ha-poskim: History of the Jewish Codes*, vol. 3 (New York: Jubilee, 1947), 158 [Hebrew]: "The entire literature of these later generation was limited to the circle of *Shulhan Arukh* and its commentaries..." There are grounds to claim that the formation of the *nos'ei kelim* literature reflects and demarcates the transition from the period of the *Rishonim* to the period of the *Aharonim*: Whereas the Talmud maintained pride of place as the basic *halakhic* text during the era of the *Rishonim*, beginning in the sixteenth century, *Shulhan Arukh* began its ascent to become the focus of *halakhic* writing. See S. Z. Havlin, "On Literary Closure as the Basis for Periodization in Halakhah," in *Researches in Talmudic Literature: A Study Conference in Honour of the Eightieth Birthday of Saul Lieberman*, ed. Samuel Re'em (Jerusalem: Israel Academy of Sciences and Humanities, 1983), 148–92 [Hebrew]; Mosheh Lichtenstein, "The Period of the *Aharonim*: Trends and Directions," *Netuim* 16 (2008): 137–38 [Hebrew]. Lichtenstein (p. 150 in that article) discerned that this is particularly true in the early modern period, and indeed, during the nineteenth and twentieth centuries, with the rise of the Lithuanian *yeshivot*, the Talmud reclaimed pride of place at the center of rabbinic writing.

6. The more prominent of these commentaries include:

   ***Sefer Me'irat Einayim* ("*Sma*")**: A commentary on the *Hoshen Mishpat* section of *Shulhan Arukh*, on rabbinic jurisprudence and civil and monetary law, by Rabbi Yehoshua Falk Katz (or Cohen; d. Lviv, 1614) and first published in 1614;

   ***Siftei Kohen* ("*Shakh*")**: A commentary on the *Hoshen Mishpat* and *Yoreh De'ah* (ritual law) by Rabbi Shabbetai Cohen (d. 1662, Holesov). The commentary on *Yoreh De'ah* was first printed in 1646.

   Magen Avraham: A commentary on the *Orah Hayim* (laws of daily routine, the Sabbath, and festivals) by Rabbi Avraham Abele Gombiner (d. Kalisz, 1682), first published in 1692.

   ***Turei Zahav* ("*Taz*")**: A commentary on all four sections of *Shulhan Arukh* by Rabbi David Segal (d. Lviv, 1667), first printed (on *Yoreh De'ah*) in 1646.

   Helkat Mehokek: A commentary on the *Even Ha-ezer* section of *Shulhan Arukh*, on laws pertaining to marriage and divorce, by Rabbi Moshe Lima (d. Brest-Litovsk, 1670).

   Beit Shmuel: A commentary on *Even Ha-ezer* by Rabbi Shmuel of Furth (d. Szydlow, 1706), first published in 1689.

7. Among the most prominent exemplars of this stage are:

   Ba'er Heitev: a succinct summary of *halakhic* rulings from earlier works, composed on all four sections of *Shulhan Arukh* by Rabbi Shmuel Ashkenazi and first published in Amsterdam in 1742.

   Peri Megadim: a super-commentary on *Taz*, *Shakh*, and *Magen Avraham* on *Yoreh De'ah* and *Orah Hayim*, by Rabbi Yosef Teomim (d. Frankfurt a. d. Oder, 1792), first published in 1785.

   Mahatzit Ha-shekel: a super-commentary on *Magen Avraham* by Rabbi Shmuel Loew of Kolin (d. Boskovice, 1806), first published in 1807.

   Sha'arei Teshuvah: a collection of rulings from the responsa literature pertaining to the *Orah Hayim* section, compiled by Rabbi Hayim Mordechai Margolioth (d. Dubno, 1823), first published in 1820.

   Pit'hei Teshuvah: a collection of rulings from the responsa literature pertaining to the *Yoreh De'ah*, *Hoshen Mishpat*, and *Even Ha-ezer* sections of *Shulhan Arukh*, compiled by Rabbi Avraham Tzvi Eisenstadt (d. Kaliningrad, 1868), first published in 1836.

8. This is the format, for example, of the Rabbinic Bible (*Mikra'ot Gedolot*) published in Venice in 1518, and later, of the Mishnah with the commentaries of Maimonides and Rabbi Ovadiah of Bertinoro (Venice, 1559).
9. On the rapid acceptance and symbolic status of *Shulhan Arukh*, see Meir Benayahu, Meir, "Why and for Whom Did R. Joseph Karo Write *Shulhan Arukh*?," *Asufot* 3 (1989): 263–74 [Hebrew]; Joseph Davis, "The Reception of the 'Shulhan Arukh' and the Formation of Ashkenazic Jewish," *AJS Review* 26 (2002): 251–76; Hagai Pely et al., *Rabbi Joseph Karo: History, Halakhah, Kabbalah* (Jerusalem: Shazar, 2021); Amnon Raz-Krakotzkin, "Legislation, Messianism, and Censorship: Printing the Shulkhan Aruch as the Beginning of Modernity," in *Tov Elem: Memory, Community, and Gender in Medieval and Early Modern Jewish Societies*, ed. E. Baumgarten et al. (Jerusalem: Bialik, 2011), 306–35 [Hebrew].
10. For an extensive discussion of this introduction and its meanings, see Tirza Kelman, "'I Shall Create *Halakhic* Ruling . . . for that is the Objective': The Dimension of *Halakhic*

Ruling in Joseph Karo's *Beit Yosef*" (PhD diss., Ben-Gurion University, 2018), 31–63 [Hebrew]. More recently, see Maoz Kahana, "A Universe Made of Words: Bibliography and Utopia in the *Halakhic* Project of Rabbi Yosef Karo," *Shenaton ha-Mishpat Ha-ivri* 30 (2019): 79–127. See also Kelman, this volume.

11. A condensed version of this criticism can be found in Rabbi Shlomo Luria (Maharshal)'s preface to *Yam Shel Shlomo*. On this preface and its different versions, see Meir Raffeld, *HaMaharshal Ve-sifro Yam Shel Shlomo* (Merkaz Shapira, Israel: private publication, 2022). On Maharshal's critique, see also Tchernowitz, *Toledoth Ha-poskim*, 74–91.
12. See Elchanan Reiner, "Beyond the Realm of Haskalah: Changing Learning Patterns in Jewish Traditional Society," *Simon Dubnow Institute Yearbook* 6 (2007): 123–33.
13. See, in this respect: Tchernowitz, *Toledoth Ha-poskim*, 47: "It should not be deemed paradoxical if we conclude that it was precisely Rema, the great opponent of *Shulhan Arukh*, who made *Shulhan Arukh* what it is, namely, a **set table** with a tablecloth spread upon it, ready for a banquet. For without the tablecloth, this table would have remained bare, a mere slab of wood."
14. For more on this process in the Ashkenazic context, see Elchanan Reiner, "The Ashkenazi Elite at the Beginning of the Modern Era: Manuscript versus Printed Book," *Polin* 10 (1997): 85–98.
15. First published in Lublin, 1590.
16. In the case of *Levush*, as that of *Yam Shel Shlomo*, the fact that the work was not attached to *Shulhan Arukh* impaired its eventual reception. Though cited relatively often, it does not garner the same accord as *Shulhan Arukh* and its *nos'ei kelim*.
17. First published in Prague, 1614.
18. On R. Katz, see Salomon Buber, *Anshei Shem* (Krakow: Joseph Fischer, 1895), 80 [Hebrew]; Tchernowitz, *Toledoth Ha-poskim*, 12–20; Menachem Elon, *Jewish Law: History, Sources, Principles*, vol. 3 (Philadelphia: Jewish Publication Society, 1994), 1408–12.
19. This introduction is actually the preface to *Beit Yisrael*, the collective name for all three of R. Falk's *halakhic* works: *Perishah* and *Derishah* commentaries on *Tur*, and *Sma* on *Shulhan Arukh*. The preface was printed together with the first edition of *Sma* in 1614. For more on *Perishah* and *Derishah*, see the discussion in Noam Samet, "'Ketsot Ha-choshen': The Beginning of 'Lamdanut'—Features and Tendencies" (PhD diss., Ben-Gurion University, 2016), esp. on 18 [Hebrew]. The fact that he wrote on both *Tur* and *Shulhan Arukh* illustrates the gradual transition from *Tur* to *Shulhan Arukh* as the central text of study in the Ashkenazic rabbinic academy. Later in the seventeenth century, Rabbi Yoel Sirkis (who we will discuss below) opted to devote his major work to *Tur*, even though he writes in his introduction that he is also working on a commentary to *Shulhan Arukh*—a work that was never published and is not extant.
20. This introduction was first printed in the Mantua 1559 edition of *Hovot Ha-levavot*.
21. *Hovot Ha-levavot* (Mantua: 1559), 4a.
22. For more on the link between *Shulhan Arukh* and the print revolution, see Raz-Krakotzkin, "Legislation, Messianism, and Censorship."
23. See Tamara Morsel Eisenberg, this volume.
24. In a certain sense, and as we will see at greater length below (next to note 52), the format of the page of *Shulhan Arukh* as it developed in the seventeenth through nineteenth centuries restores, somewhat, the sense of a living text, as it brings together different commentators who converse "over" the text of *Shulhan Arukh*.
25. R. Falk defends the intentions of the authors and blames readers for their failure to supplement their reading of *Shulhan Arukh* with concomitant study of the sources detailed in

Beit Yosef. However, based on R. Karo's description of his goals, as articulated in his introduction to *Shulhan Arukh*, it seems that his original intent was to produce a clear, popular work, not a book that demands supplementation with professional knowledge.

26. *Sefer Me'or Einayim* (Prague: 1614), 3b.
27. First printed in Krakow, 1631. For more on R. Sirkis and *Bah*, see Pinhas Sirkis, *Sefer Habah* (Tel Aviv: unknown publisher, 1984); Tchernowitz, *Toledoth Ha-poskim*, 112–20; Elon, *Jewish Law*, 1412–14.
28. For instance, these are the arguments of fifteenth-century Rabbi Yaakov Weil (Mahari Weil) against Rabbi Yisrael Isserlein, a leading rabbi of the generation:

    > I am further astonished by the outstanding rabbi . . . for certainly when we engage in casuistry and sharpness, as in the time of the Tosafists, we commonly discuss inferences and subtle distinctions, like passing an elephant through the eye of a needle. But to decide the law or permit the forbidden? One may not decide the law and one may not permit the forbidden without clear, lucid, resolute evidence.
    >
    > (*Responsa Mahari Bruna* §29)

    Later, David Gans, a contemporary of R. Falk, describes Rabbi Yaakov Pollack, considered the founder of the Polish rabbinic academy, as someone who "in his abundant sharpness and acuity, was the first to invent the *pilpul* of distinctions, which the heads of the rabbinic academies in these countries use to sharpen the minds of the students," even though his methods sparked the opposition of "all the sages and upright of heart"; David Gans, *Tzemah David* (Prague: 1592), 138.

    On R. Pollack and his rabbinic academy, see Elchanan Reiner, "Rabbi Ya'akov Pollack of Cracow: First and Foremost among Cracow's Scholars," in *Kroke-Kazimierz-Cracow: Studies in the History of Cracow Jewry*, ed. E. Reiner (Tel Aviv: Tel Aviv University, 2001), 43–68 [Hebrew]; Elchanan Reiner, "Transformations in the Polish and Ashkenazic Yeshivot during the Sixteenth and Seventeenth Centuries and the Dispute over Pilpul," in *Studies in Jewish Culture in Honor of Chone Shmeruk*, ed. I. Bartal, E. Mendelsohn, and C. Turniansky (Jerusalem: Shazar Center, 1993), 9–80.
29. Elsewhere in his preface to *Sma*, R. Falk describes legal innovations as the explicit purpose of one who studies the text in depth. In his description of the development of the oral Torah, R. Falk explains why the Torah was initially given only orally. In his view, the textual burden weighs down the scholar; oral transmission allows for the preservation of the knowledge without tethering it to a text. Scholars can thus produce, "many laws from their minds and their reason."
30. For more on the debate between R. Falk and R. Sirkis, and on R. Falk's decision to forego his station as a communal rabbi in order to serve exclusively as head of a yeshiva, see my dissertation: Samet, "'Ketsot Ha-choshen,'" 45–50.
31. Another manifestation of this duality within R. Falk's *halakhic* works is the dual structure of his works on *Tur*: *Perishah* and *Derishah*. Whereas *Perishah* is a brief, concise, and practical commentary on *Tur*, *Derishah* is a complicated, dense analytic commentary.

    The dual structure that R. Falk fashioned later influenced the further development of the *nos'ei kelim*; the works *Urim Ve-tumim* and *Netivot Ha-mishpat* are structured similarly. The same feature recurs in the twentieth-century commentaries of Rabbi Yisrael Meir Ha-Kohen of Radun, *Mishnah Berurah* and *Bi'ur Halakhah*.
32. It is important to mention two other central texts with canonic status in *halakhic* literature: Maimonides's *Mishneh Torah* and Rabbi Yaakov ben Asher's *Arba'ah Turim* (or "*Tur*").

Upon the publication of *Shulhan Arukh*, these two works were sidelined, and most early modern commentary centers on *Shulhan Arukh*.

33. Reiner, "Transformations," in *Kroke-Kazimierz-Cracow*, 58, suggests something similar when he describes the decline of the Ashenazic library. However, he emphasizes the perspective that distinguishes between the *halakhic* decisor ("*posek*") and the scholar, whereas I wish to identify a phenomenon that takes place within the world of the scholar, who, from this point forward, has two canonic texts before him.
34. This conception of *halakhah* characterizes the outstanding figures of the sixteenth-century Polish study halls—Rabbi Shalom Shachna and Maharshal.

    The preface to *Vikuʻah Mayim Hayim* and *Responsa Rema* §25 document R. Shalom Shachna's refusal to compose *halakhic* works, out of concern that they would become binding and restrict subsequent decisors. R. Shalom Shachna viewed *halakhah* as a local product, placed in the hands of the scholar and the communal rabbi charged with balancing between *halakhic* tradition with the concrete situation.

    See Maharshal's formulation in his preface to *Yam Shel Shlomo* on *Hullin*:

    > From the days of Ravina and Rav Ashi there has been no resolution to rule in accordance with any of the *Geonim* or *Aharonim*. Rather, one whose words meet approval, in that they are based on clear demonstration, based on the [Babylonian] Talmud, and the Jerusalem [Talmud] and the Tosefta when there is no decision in the [Babylonian] Talmud.

35. On R. Segal, see Shevach Knobil, *Toledot Gedolei Ha-horaʻah* (New York: Doubinsky, 1955), 75–84 [Hebrew]; Tchernowitz, *Toledoth Ha-poskim*, 139–41; Elon, *Jewish Law*, 1423–28.
36. On Rabbi Shabbetai Cohen, see Bernhard Friedberg (Hayim Dov), *Keter Kehuna* (Drohobych: Zupnik, 1898) [Hebrew]; Tchernowitz, *Toledoth Ha-poskim*, 146–58; Feiglin Yehezkel, "Rabbi Shabbetai Katz: Bio-Bibliography" (MA thesis, Ben-Gurion University, 2015) [Hebrew].
37. See Samet, "'Ketsot Ha-choshen,'" 83–85.
38. For further description of Shakh's methods, see Emanuel Warhaftig, "The Shakh—Rabbi Shabtai Katz—And His Scholarly-*Halakhic* Method" (PhD diss., Bar-Ilan University, 2019) [Hebrew]; Samet, "'Ketsot Ha-choshen,'" 56–57.
39. For one example among many, see *Shakh* to *Hoshen Mishpat* 66:126:

    > It is obvious that we do not follow the majority of decisors when it is evident from the Talmud that the truth is with the minority, especially since these decisors only reached that ruling by virtue of their proofs; once the matter is disproven, the structure collapses.

    Furthermore, in 87:38 of that work, he takes issue with R. Karo and Rema:

    > So wrote Maharik [= R. Yosef Colon] . . . and [Rema] and other *Aharonim* followed him. Yet I say that Maharik and those who follow him erred about an explicit teaching.

40. First published in Frankfurt, 1677.
41. On Rabbi Shmuel of Fuerth, see Tchernowitz, *Toledoth Ha-poskim*, 161–63; Elon, *Jewish Law*, 1430.
42. Although Rabbi Moshe Lima had already published his *Helkat Mehokek*, a popular commentary on *Even Ha-ezer*, in 1670, R. Shmuel viewed it as an incomplete and defective work, evidently because the work does not encompass *Even Ha-ezer* in its entirety. R. Shmuel also does not address *Nahalat Tzvi*, a commentary on *Shulhan Arukh* by Rabbi Tzvi Katz, published in 1661. Perhaps he did not see it or did not consider it a significant work.

43. On R. Gombiner and his *Magen Avraham*, see Knobil, *Toledot Gedolei Ha-hora'ah*, 99–104; Tchernowitz, *Toledoth Ha-poskim*, 169–71; and, at greater length, Eliezer Brodt, "Halachic Commentaries to the Shulchan Aruch on Orach Chayim from Ashkenaz and Poland in the Seventeenth Century" (PhD diss., Bar Ian University, 2015) [Hebrew].
44. We know of at least two other works on *Orah Hayim* from that period: Rabbi Shmuel bar Yosef's *Olat Tamid*, printed in 1681, and Rabbi Yair Hayim Bachrach's *Mekor Hayim*, which remained in manuscript. Neither of these works managed to compete with *Taz* and *Magen Avraham*, which occupied pride of place among commentaries on *Orah Hayim*. Nevertheless, they illustrate the efforts to explicate *Orah Hayim* during the seventeenth century.
45. R. Eybeschutz was a unique and multifaceted figure about whom much has been written. See Moshe Samet, "Eybeschütz, Yonatan," in YIVO Encyclopedia of Jews in Eastern Europe (http://www.yivoencyclopedia.org/article.aspx/Eybeschutz_Yonatan). Regarding his commentaries on *Shulhan Arukh*, see Tchernowitz, *Toledoth Ha-poskim*, 223–45. R. Eybeschutz's works were extremely lengthy and therefore were not printed with the other commentaries that came to comprise the standard format of *Shulhan Arukh*. Nevertheless, they were studied as major commentaries on *Shulhan Arukh* and impacted both *halakhic* rulings and ongoing *halakhic* discussion.
46. First published by the author himself in Altona, 1763.
47. First published in Karlsruhe, 1775.
48. Another aspect that should be mentioned here is the tension between the legal functions of *halakhic* literature and its status as part of the Torah and as the object of the commandment to study Torah. One of the declared objectives of R. Karo for *Shulhan Arukh* is "so that the Lord's perfect Torah is fluent in the mouth of every Jewish person." Emphasizing the academic-theoretical aspect as against the legal-statutory aspect dovetails with a broader view of law and the prominence of literary wholeness as one of the main objectives of the work. On this, see Chaim Saiman, *Halakhah: The Rabbinic Idea of Law* (Princeton, NJ: Princeton University Press, 2018), 174–76.
49. See Rabbi Yonatan Eybeschutz, *Urim Ve-Tumim*, §25.
50. On this process, see Moshe Halbertal, *People of the Book: Canon, Meaning, and Authority* (Cambridge, MA: Harvard University Press, 1997), 11–44.
51. Michel Foucault, "The Order of Discourse," in *Untying the Text: A Post-Structuralist Reader*, ed. R. Young (Boston: Routledge, 1981), 58.
52. In this case, the name *Magen Avraham* is what caused the printer to call the volume *Maginei Eretz*, and for the sake of uniformity, R. Segal's commentary on *Orah Hayim* was called *Magen David* (and not *Turei Zahav*, the name of his commentary on the other sections of *Shulhan Arukh*).
53. Even when the various sections of *Shulhan Arukh* were reprinted together, some printers continued to use the different names of the works on the title pages of the different sections. One can even find such title pages in offset editions that are produced today.
54. Ultimately, the contemporary student is likely to find using the book difficult precisely because of the crowdedness and graphical density of the text. Over the past thirty years, this has led to less crowded editions of *Shulhan Arukh*, which moved some of the *nos'ei kelim* from alongside the *Shulhan Arukh* text to the end of the volume. Yet all of these editions preserve the commentaries that were added to the classic editions, printed during the latter half of the nineteenth century. Some even retain the exact page format.
55. On the competition between printers in Lviv, see Samet, "'Ketsot Ha-choshen,'" 30–33.
56. The "sealing" of the nineteenth-century editions is related to the dearth of new commentaries on *Shulhan Arukh* from that period. Consequently, even the few works

that were written did not significantly impact the *halakhic* tradition. The center of gravity shifted to other genres: responsa and analytical works on the Talmud.

An exception to this trend is *Mishnah Berurah*, which has become a major practical *halakhic* work, even though it was published as a stand-alone work and was not added to the standard *Shulhan Arukh* page.

57. Eliav Schochetman, "On the Contradictions in *Shulhan Arukh* and on the Essence and Goals of the Work," *Asufot* 3 (1989): 323–30 [Hebrew]; see also Kelman, "'I Shall Create Halakhic Ruling . . . for that is the Objective,'" who addressed the profound links between *Shulhan Arukh* and *Tur*.
58. The lack of clear *halakhic* decisiveness led to the formulation of second order rules for reaching decisions where R. Karo cited different and contradictory views. However, this development transpired in the eighteenth century and thus only offers further evidence of the original work's lack of decisiveness.
59. Kahana, "A Universe Made of Words," 123–28.

CHAPTER 7

QUESTIONS OF LAW

The Significance of Rabbinic Responsa for Jewish Law

TAMARA MORSEL-EISENBERG

INTRODUCTION

RESPONSA, or *She'elot u-Teshuvot*, literally "questions and answers," are written rabbinic responses to questions posed, usually in a letter, concerning concrete questions of Jewish law. As a source of legal writing, responsa uniquely combine Jewish religious life and scholarship. The text of a responsum is, first, a temporal document; the material embodiment of communication meant to solve a real problem, of which later readers are seeing the remnant (or, more often an emended copy thereof). At the same time, responsa are legal opinions, intellectual products that scholars of Jewish law can study long after. This chapter examines both aspects of responsa and the transitions between them for clues about the genre's specific contribution to *halakha*.

Responsa are one of the oldest continuous forms of *halakhic* writing. Hints at the existence of responsa can already be found in the Talmud. We learn, for instance, of scholarly correspondence between Rabbi Yohanan in the Land of Israel, and Rav, in Babylonia (third century).[1] Responsa are among the most prominent surviving genres from the early medieval *Geonim*.[2] Later medieval rabbis in Sepharad and Ashkenaz wrote and exchanged responsa, within their geographic areas and from one such location to another. Those writings became an important part of the rabbinic corpus. Responsa collections often numbered hundreds, even thousands, of entries.[3] With the early modern invention of movable type, responsa—first those of earlier authorities, then those of contemporaries—were ushered into print.[4] By the eighteenth century, responsa collections often were the publication par excellence for which a rabbi became known.[5] Responsa writing persists to this day, both in its traditional form and in modern media such as text messages and websites.[6]

These writings were not necessarily meant to be published. Responsa were put to paper first and foremost for the purpose of real-time consultation and communication, not for posterity. They are poised in a liminal zone between the private correspondence of specific parties and published writing available to all, between a communication about the case of the moment and an intellectual contribution meant for future scholarship. This liminality extends to the legal relevance of responsa: are responsa universally binding precedents or remnants of ephemeral communications? Although their degree of institutional authority varies, responsa as a genre have been compared to *fatwas* in Islam, to the *Responsa Prudentium* in Rome, to legal *consilia* written by canon lawyers and civil law jurists, and to case law in a common-law system.[7] In Judeo-Arabic, Jews referred to responsa as "*fatwa*," and to the responding rabbi as a *mufti*.[8] Like *halakhic* responsa, *consilia* were a staple of legal writing.[9] The pontiffs of republican Rome dispensed responsa, and some may have received the authoritative status to do so from the emperor.[10] Medieval law in Europe reserved a prominent place for *quaestiones*, fictional cases formulated as concrete occurrences, often employed pedagogically.[11] The genre reappears with the renaissance of Roman law in Europe,[12] as the professional legal opinion of *juris doctors* was requested by local judges regarding cases brought before their court. *Consilia pro parte*, commissioned and paid for by one of the parties, emerged in the fourteenth century. Almost all the major commentators of the fourteenth and fifteenth centuries either personally or through their successors, collected and diffused their *consilia*, which were later published.[13] Like rabbinic responsa, the reasons prompting these writings varied from didactic exercises to scholarly correspondence to concrete professional advisory.[14] As in rabbinic responsa, these questions were sometimes fictional and sometimes factual, but almost always concerned with analyzing concrete cases.[15]

The potential of responsa, perhaps more than any other *halakhic* text, to preserve concrete details from the lived life of Jews, has always acted as a strong draw for historians, sometimes at the expense of appreciating their legal contributions. *Mishpat Ivri* scholarship has looked to *halakha* to inspire contemporary Israeli law and has long recognized responsa's importance as a legal source of case law. Responsa have also been prominent in digital projects like the Bar Ilan Responsa Project, the first full-text digitalized, searchable, database of responsa, and more recently Elijah Lab's *Mapah*-project, which collects and maps data that can be extracted from responsa about rabbis, correspondence, and Jewish communities.[16]

All too often, responsa are mined either as a trove of information about Jewish life and realia or as a transparent repository of legal opinions. Though responsa have featured as sources for some of the most important contributions to Jewish intellectual and cultural history, there has been to date no thorough reflection on the genre itself as an intellectual enterprise and a form of law.[17] The current chapter will attempt the latter by examining the creation and afterlife of these writings. The invention of print changed the trajectory of writing and publishing responsa, which altered the relationships between the initial creation of a responsum for its own time and its eventual publication. Those changes affected how the legal authority of this genre was understood by both its authors and readers. Insights drawn from the difference between responsa in the manuscript versus print eras can stimulate questions about such legal texts in the digital era. Studying how changes in publication affect the dynamics of legal authority for responsa reveals significant insights about their nature and their unique contribution to legal thought.

The three sections of this chapter address three questions about responsa: "Questions of Communication" treats responsa as the immediate product of *halakhic* activity and communication, given their origins in consultations and letters. How do responsa's roots in such communication affect them as *halakhic* writings? "Questions of Transmission" addresses the afterlife of responsa as *halakhic* sources. How has their emergence from lived rabbinic activity shaped their transmission? "Questions of Authority" examines how responsa's occupation with concrete questions rather than abstract principles made for a genre that was difficult to organize and therefore challenging to consult systematically, a difficulty that complicates the genre's legal authority. The final section, "Legal Questions," emphasizes the significance of responsa for Jewish legal thinking despite—or perhaps even because of—those same characteristics that cause their inherent ambiguity as legal texts.

Questions of Communication

In most cases, the problem requiring a response is a difficult legal question that demands an experienced rabbi. Responsa mostly relate to concrete cases, and even responsa not taken from real-life occurrences, are usually formulated in concrete terms, as a question about a case. A minority of responsa address theoretical questions, far-fetched hypotheticals, abstract textual explications, or nonlegal religious issues, from theology to pedagogy. Some responsa were not written as answers to questions, such as a rabbi noting down decisions he made in the context of a rabbinical court, questions posed to him orally, or a conundrum he himself concocted. But most often, questions were written from one individual, usually a rabbi, to another, more senior rabbi, about a concrete case.

Responsa frequently generate an extended written conversation between the correspondents. When more than one rabbi was consulted or the case was particularly controversial, multiple copies of a question and the responses could circulate to different rabbis, each of whom expressed their opinion.[18] Sometimes, questioners solicit support in larger disputes, seeking the rabbi's social standing and religious capital more than his *halakhic* acumen.

Responsa preserve hints about the practical aspects of letter-writing, such as the scribes tasked with copying a rabbi's letter, sending the recipient a neat copy and preserving a record for the rabbi;[19] the couriers (employed by merchants) who sometimes carried early modern responsa;[20] or the high price of medieval parchment, indicated by the rabbi responding on the reverse of the questioner's letter, left blank for that purpose.[21] In modern times, letterheads and digital time-stamps serve as similar reminders that responsa originate in rabbinic communication of a particular kind.

We tend to think of letters as private communication between two individuals. But studies of epistolarity have shown that this is not always the case. In reality, multiple persons could be involved in writing the letter, and the audience often extended beyond the addressee. This certainly holds for responsa. Babylonian *Geonim* co-wrote their answers, and many rabbis employed scribes. Manuscript evidence from Maimonides's son in Egypt suggests that for some simpler questions, assistants would prepare their own drafts formulating answers for the rabbi.[22] In Moravia, R. Israel Bruna (d. 1480) mentioned temporarily replacing his professional staff of responsa copiers with youths, "for everyone is preoccupied with the harvest."[23]

It was equally rare for responsa to have but one reader. At times, responsa were deliberately collected from and distributed to multiple rabbis, similarly to early modern circular letters.[24] One such collection of sixteenth-century responsa about a business dispute morphed into a decades-long international rabbinical controversy replete with mutual excommunications.[25] Other responsa were explicitly aimed for the general community. Maimonides addressed his "Epistle to Yemen" about messianism and religious persecution to the community leader, but he also requested it be publicly disseminated.[26] There is also evidence that responsa were sometimes read out loud on Sabbath in the recipients' synagogues.[27]

Even when clearly addressing one person, responsa often implied several readers. In one sixteenth-century exchange, R. Shlomo Luria notices that a letter he received from R. Moshe Isserles was "smudged and open . . . all the eyes of the readers have plowed and navigated through it." While R. Isserles's attacks offended R. Luria, he was not surprised by the additional readers, and even fought back by the same means, having his reply "copied by one person and then sent by another . . . so that the matter should be made public."[28] Both rabbis knew full well that their readership extended beyond the addressee. Similar expectations concerning privacy or rather, lack thereof can be observed in early modern humanist correspondence.[29]

The contents of letters, too, can have various purposes simultaneously. Reading and circulating a responsum may have been a scholarly matter for some, an act of solidarity for others, a legal matter, a form of evidence for a rabbinical court, or proof of marital status to present potential matches. An inner circle of scholars and a wider communal audience each read responsa in its own ways. Social aspects shaped conventions of status, hierarchy, and learned practices of letter writing. Many responsa feature praise-filled greetings to the addressee, often in rhyme and filled with literary allusions; clever uses of Biblical verses and numerical values to mark the date; declarations of humility before signing; or personal regards to the addressee and relatives.

Although these trappings were later considered extraneous and were often the first to be removed, they illustrate how the correspondence of responsa contributed to the construction of the rabbinic social circle and the determination of relationships and hierarchies within. Friendships were initiated and carried out across distances, and correspondents kept each other informed of their whereabouts, family life, health, and employment. A letter to Rabbi Meir of Padua (d. 1564), included two distinct parts—one *halakhic*, the other social—which were intended as a single communication.[30] Conversely, a rabbi who received a request made by Rabbi Yosef Katz (d. 1591) indirectly, was reported to be "angry and fuming" at being denied the social recognition of a personal letter.[31]

Benedict Anderson showed how communications media constructs community. Here too, sending and receiving responsa was a social act that created a scholarly community.[32] This networked community functions as a semipublic sphere, or forum. Responsa were simultaneously public and private, accessible yet elite. Scholars have shown how figures like the seventeenth-century R. Ḥayim Bacharach constructed their self-image as rabbis and adjudicators via responsa.[33]

Responsa thus did not circulate *within* a preexistent network; they *created* the social ties that constituted this community. As scholarly correspondence addressing an implied audience beyond the individual recipient, responsa are performative—even theatrical.[34] Responsa communications established a language both internally stratified and particular to the community. The genre also carried out educational functions through study, pedagogical remarks (sometimes playful) tests, and moral guidance for students (or former students).[35]

In addition to solving a legal problem, responsa, in their epistolary function, effectively established, negotiated, and supported a discursive community, including its own sociability, paradigms, language, and modes of reasoning.[36]

Questions of Transmission

In its first instance, as a letter responding to an acute request, the responsum is self-explanatory. Once read by the recipient, the letters lost their urgency and immediacy but retained importance as *halakhic* literature. The afterlife of these responsa varied, with significant consequences for their reception.

Overwhelmingly, responsa were kept deliberately by both author and recipient. Preserving correspondence was a common activity of lawyers, administrators, religious leaders, and others; rabbis fit well alongside these occupations.[37] The *geonic* yeshivot kept records of their responsa, as is evidenced by their remarks that certain questions had already been posed, sometimes copying the earlier answer. Communities receiving the answers often kept them in location-specific collections. Maimonides describes this, "the people of every town ask many questions to every *gaon* who lived in their days . . . and collect these responsa, making books out of them."[38] Various semipublic archives of responsa may have existed, but, as a question to the twelfth-century R. Yosef Ibn Migash about the practice of consulting such collections of responsa reveals, "not all in the same condition" of meticulous preservation or authorial accuracy.[39] In one responsum, R. Shlomo b. Adret (d. 1310) tells the questioners to "search in my responsa and questions located in your city."[40] When asked to send a copy of an earlier decision, the fourteenth-century R. Ytẓḥak b. Sheshet Perfet (Rivash) in Barcelona replied that he had indeed written a long responsum on this issue, but since the matter was urgent, he had not been able to keep a copy for his records, "as is my usual way with all my responsa."[41]

Correspondents kept responsa as part of a working archive, for the purpose of continuing their discussion, or for future consultation. Students and colleagues would sometimes copy from those records into their own manuscript collections. This stage was distinct from widespread scholarly publication of responsa collections, which was not a given.

How responsa are published can provide us with information on the place of responsa within the larger *halakhic* canon: Were the responsa thoughtfully arranged alongside the corresponding Talmudic commentary, thrown in as an appendix with no editorial input, or published as a stand-alone work? Such an attitude may depend on whether the authors of responsa and their circles considered these writings scholarly literature worthy of publication. The Ashkenazic Sages before the mid-thirteenth century may have copied responsa for themselves, but did not systematically publish these. When such responsa survived, their transmission was hardly intentional. A cluster of responsa is included in R. Tam's *Sefer ha-Yashar*, but the other *halakhic* writings in the work overshadow these entries, as do the hundreds of R. Tam's extant responsa excluded from *Sefer ha-Yashar*.[42]

Individual responsa copied for scholars' own personal archives would sometimes survive in miscellaneous manuscripts to be haphazardly copied and inherited by students and children, and eventually published. These examples of small responsa assemblages collected for individual consultation contrast sharply with other genres of *halakhic* works intended for publication.

The Sephardic orbit exhibited more prevalent practices of creating deliberate responsa collections from one particular rabbi. Sephardic responsa between the years 1000 and 1500 count far fewer authors of responsa (twenty-four) compared to the Ashkenazic equivalent (sixty). Yet most of those Sephardi authorities had a known, circulating responsa collection to their name (thirteen), whereas less than half of the Ashkenazim mentioned boasted such collections, and even those had been circulating in dispersed units and few manuscript copies, to be assembled and printed only in modern times.[43]

By and large, Sephardic collections featured a selection of the author's responsa. Maimonides and his son had a scribe copy selected responsa,[44] as did R. Nissim (Ran, 1315–1375) in Barcelona. Copies of their responsa discovered in the Cairo *genizah* suggest that neither Maimonides nor his son kept all their responsa. Ran likely wrote many more responsa than the roughly ninety he preserved.[45] While medieval Sages in Provençe tended not to keep responsa, a collection centered on Lunel and the *av beit din* (head of its Jewish court) denotes a circle that did deliberately assemble responsa.[46] R. Isaiah di Trani, an Italian tosafist (d. 1250), refers to his own responsa in his other writings using section numbers, indicating that he did not simply preserve all his correspondence. He consciously selected, numbered, and revised a distinct collection of these writings, probably ordered by correspondent.[47]

In the thirteenth century, R. Meir (Maharam) of Rothenburg represented a turning point for Ashkenazic responsa collection and transmission practices. Unlike his predecessors, Maharam consciously collected and copied their responsa and his own, as did his students. The collections titled *Responsa of Maharam Rothenburg* therefore contain responsa from earlier and later rabbis.[48] This indicates interest in collecting a corpus of responsa for study and reference. Maharam's student, R. Asher b. Yeḥiel (Rosh)'s successors deliberately collected, edited, and organized Rosh's responsa after he had fled from Worms to Toledo.[49]

In the beginning of the early modern period, some Ashkenazi rabbis evidently planned collections of their own responsa. R. Ya'acov Weil, for instance, copied responsa and other material from his teachers, and added his own writings, including responsa. In a responsum, R. Bruna, who was married to R. Weil's granddaughter, hints at a manuscript collection that had belonged to R. Weil and circulated in the family.[50] After R. Moellin's death, his sons inherited and divided their father's responsa, which prevented their survival as a unified collection, despite R. Moellin's wish that a scribe collect and copy all his responsa.[51]

With the invention of movable type, the dynamics of writing, preserving, and publishing responsa shifted. The first century of print saw the publication of the responsa from earlier periods. Rashba's is the first responsa collection—and possibly even the first Hebrew book—to be printed (Rome, *c.* 1470).[52] It represented but one fragmentary collection of Rashba's thousands of responsa circulating in manuscript. Over the years, additional collections of his responsa would be printed, many of the contents overlapping, and none of the collections complete.[53]

Throughout the sixteenth century, responsa collections left presses from Venice to Constantinople to Prague. In some ways, they resembled their manuscript precursors; in other ways, they harnessed the innovations—and fell prey to the pitfalls—typical of printed works. Print allows for greater standardization and stability compared to the vicissitudes of scribal copying. A responsum from 1565 speaks both to the wide circulation of a printed work and to the unprecedented effects of standardization: When a rabbi in Jerusalem mentioned R. Colon's responsum, he felt no need to quote it: "I will not quote the exact language here, because the responsa of . . . Rabbi Colon, are found in every learned person's home, go read it there."[54] Less than half a century after the book was first printed, it had become so widespread that rabbis could confidently assume that "every learned person" owned a near-identical copy for reference.

Print's expanded reading audience and textual stability made finding aids (discussed below) more necessary, useful, and worthwhile. Tables advertised a work's contents to prospective buyers and aided consultation, more crucial when the work being consulted is not one's personal manuscript. Indexes linked to specific pages rise in convenience for identically paginated copies. Yet printed works are prone to their own kind of errors, which proliferate further and faster. Among the responsa collections printed by Daniel Bomberg's press in Venice was one volume of Rashba's responsa mistakenly attributed to Naḥmanides. In *Beit Yosef*, R. Yosef Karo surprisingly stated that he would continue referring to this work by its wrong title, because that wrong title is the one under which it was printed, and "the printed books are found with every man."[55]

In sharp contrast to the flourishing Italian world that facilitated Hebrew printing, the Ottoman Empire boasted no such infrastructure. Hebrew books printed in the Ottoman realm were sometimes produced and sold in installments in order to raise funds. One rabbi in sixteenth-century Constantinople mentions responsa distributed on Sabbath in the synagogue, to be paid later.[56] Responsa's nature as smaller stand-alone units made them well-suited for such piecemeal distribution.

Despite the steady sixteenth-century growth of printed *halakhic* works, far fewer responsa collections were printed between 1470 and 1599 than other *halakhic* genres.[57] This may be a consequence of responsa's dispersed and unplanned manuscript transmission, as opposed to the deliberate, unified state of other *halakhic* works.

After the responsa of their predecessors had been printed, early modern responsa began to be published. These collections were overwhelmingly printed posthumously or close to the author's death. Responsa researcher Shmuel Glick mentions the "resistance among respondents to print their responsa,"[58] due to the fear of appearing brazen, or apprehension in the face of criticism. R. Binyamin Ze'ev of Arta, the first to publish his responsa in his lifetime as a stand-alone work, was indeed criticized for doing so.[59] This was not only the case for rabbis. Aldus Manutius, too, encountered difficulties when trying to print works of living authors.[60]

Responsa might suffer from an additional difficulty regarding print, related to their thematic heterogeneity and indeterminate afterlife. Printing a work required it to be complete, but without any definite parameters for their future use and purpose, when is a collection of responsa "complete"? Collections of past figures could be printed as an all-inclusive heterogeneous *Nachlass*, a posthumous collection of all the paperwork and letters from an intellectual's life. However, within one's lifetime, these texts presented no overall logic or any natural point when writing ceased and publication imposed itself.

Even rabbis who were by no means print-shy could not control their own responsa, which constantly grew as their professional lives continued. R. Karo and R. Isserles, authors of perhaps the most important *halakhic* works printed in their day and highly astute users of print, both left their responsa unpublished. R. Isserles's haphazard collection was printed in 1640, decades after his death. R. Karo's responsa, *ShUT Avkat Rokhel*, was similarly printed posthumously by his son (Salonica, 1597–1598), who printed only a part of the work due to the lack of any organized collection left behind by his father.[61]

This phenomenon is not unique to Jewish law. Non-Jewish genres saw similar trajectories of personal collections transmitted to students in manuscript, who eventually printed them "as is." Other legal genres related to real-life cases, including common law, similarly feature collections of legal notes from a lifetime that were not published by its authors. In the common-law world, as legal historian J. H. Baker explains, "reporting . . . was the life-long occupation of certain individuals," who started reporting as students and continued until their deaths.[62] Despite this intense activity, Edmund Plowden (1571–1578) was the only figure to publish his own reports in the sixteenth century. James Dyer's (d. 1582) reports were published posthumously from his notebooks (*Ascuns Novel cases*, 1585).[63]

The fate of responsa in their afterlife (or lack thereof) can indicate different attitudes toward this genre. Some historians consider the lack of preservation of medieval Ashkenazic responsa as evidence that this culture did not regard responsa as authoritative precedent; in Sepharad, by contrast, where a more centralized approach prevailed, responsa were considered normative legal decisions and carefully preserved.[64] Others emphasize that even if Ashkenazic responsa collections as such were not preserved, the contents of responsa would be dissected and discussed in compilations, alongside other *halakhic* material.[65] The very survival of such collections can thus not be read simply as evidence for a culture's attitude toward these sources. It can, at most, provide some hints.

Even once preservation and publication became easily possible with print, there are precious few hints whether printing them meant their endorsement as binding precedent. The ease of assuring responsa's survival made the significance of their persistence beyond the initial correspondence, if anything, *less* obvious than before. Even responsa published and introduced by their author do not formulate clear intentions for its purpose. R. Katz is the first Ashkenazi to print his own responsa collection, *ShUT She'erit Yosef* (Cracow, 1590). Rather than formulating a coherent goal for the work's publication, his introduction simply listed the circumstances that prompted the initial creation of the responsa, such as his role as a rabbinical judge.[66] Making sure responsa did *not* survive became a more telling action than printing one's responsa: the fifteenth-century R. Ya'akov Pollak was said to have deliberately *not* written anything, or even kept copies of his outgoing responsa, to avoid determining precedent.[67]

R. Bacharach published his responsa *Ḥavot Ya'ir* (Frankfurt am Main, 1699). In a notebook that served as an index of sorts to his own archives, he noted which responsa, among his many written materials, he had selected to publish.[68] But even this well-contemplated collection opens with R. Bacharach's declaration that he had, in truth, hoped to print his larger works. After giving up on his grand plans he decided, close to death, to at least publish his responsa, "to take from what is readily available to me, things as they were written."[69] Responsa could be printed with no larger scheme, making them easier to publish, but also more of an afterthought, without addressing their authoritative legal status.

Responsa continued to be generated mainly by real cases as they emerged throughout rabbinic careers, but rabbis increasingly viewed their records with the explicit goal of publication in mind. At certain points, responsa collections became the primary genre of *halakhic* creativity and expression, and a rabbi's main claim to fame. In some cases, this is expressed by a tendency toward longer, more theoretical responsa, in which the issues function more like invitations to write legal essays than acute problems in need of local solutions. As a sign of this change, one scholar notes that the most prominent seventeenth- and eighteenth-century rabbis (such as R. Tzvi Hirsch Ashkenazi, R. Yehuda Landau, and R. Moshe Sofer) were known by the title of their responsa (respectively, *Ḥakham Ẓevi*, *Nodah biYehuda*, and *Ḥatam Sofer*.) By contrast, sixteenth-century authors of responsa titled these collections after their names, such as *Responsa Maharshal* or *Responsa Rema* (respectively, R. Luria and R. Isserles's acronyms).[70] While titles may hint at the rising importance of responsa, it could simply be a function of whether these works were printed while their authors were alive to provide creative titles rather than the generic "responsa + acronym."[71] Of course, the rabbi's decision to create such a collection may reflect the status of responsa collections in the first place.

The rabbi's personal involvement in printing his works encouraged some to interpret printed responsa as endorsement to use these as legal precedents. For instance, when a controversial practice surrounding circumcision was attributed to a responsum by *Ḥatam Sofer*, others were quick to counter that the responsum was not published by the author, who thus did not intend it as precedent. Others disagreed, claiming that not so much should be read into the responsum's omission: perhaps he simply forgot to copy it.[72] In modern times, the gradual and nonchronological publication of Rabbi Moshe Feinstein's responsa (including, for instance, two responsa written simultaneously in 1959, but published in two volumes, 1963, and 1979) has elicited the hypothesis that he published his more controversial responsa later in his career.[73]

Our interpretation of the significance behind responsa and their trajectories must incorporate several layers of analysis. The significance of different publishing decisions varies as the mechanisms and realities of communications media shift. Where more deliberate action is required for publication, certain decisions can be interpreted meaningfully, but if survival is more arbitrary, the selection of published responsa need not carry significance. This rationale is not bound to any particular historical directionality: For instance, as digital preservation becomes ever cheaper and easier, responsa's very survival comes to mean less, given the lower degree of deliberate action required to preserve texts.

Alongside the technological possibilities for keeping and publishing texts are other factors, such as different approaches to precedent, varying expectations of legal consistency, and institutional practices. These factors impact one another. As the tools, possibilities, and conventions for keeping and disseminating responsa collections shift, so does the consciousness of rabbis when creating their responsa. If sixteenth-century rabbis gradually began publishing their responsa, later rabbis already authored responsa with a published collection in mind. Their expectations as to who would read these responsa and how inevitably inform their writing, which, in turn, can produce texts that indeed are more deliberately planned for a broader audience and are formulated to be used as a precedent. However, collections of responsa that too closely resemble this ideal form are sometimes seen as inauthentic for precisely that reason (as the case of *Terumat ha-Deshen*, in the next section, demonstrates).

In sum, precisely because of the genre's concrete origins and obvious practical functions, the initial purpose for writing down responsa is exceedingly obvious, while the significance of its afterlife is, by the same token, ambiguous. Responsa are created as part of a rabbi's daily function, then circulated as a form of communication, preserved as a mode of record keeping, and copied by individuals for their personal archives. There was little consistency in whether and how responsa were transmitted, and such collections do not evidence much conscious consideration of the matter. This lack of intentionality frustrates our understanding of the legal import of responsa beyond their initial moment.

Questions of Organization

A legal work's organization informs us as to how it should be consulted, hinting at the work's authority and function. Aspects of the Mishna and Talmud's organization remind us of its oral mode of transmission and the importance of mnemonic tactics. Commentaries or glosses follow the succession of the texts being glossed, since they are meant as companions for studying those texts. Maimonides designed the structure of his code, *Mishne Torah*, for maximum rational order and systematic coherence. The sixteenth-century code *Shulḥan Arukh* employed the well-known four-volume division and thematic sequence of its fourteenth-century predecessor *Arba Turim*, making it especially helpful for locating laws. A publication patterned after the structure of a canonic *halakhic* book indicates that it should be studied together with that work, as a study aid, a commentary, or an update. Inasmuch as the publication presents itself as part of that earlier book, it may also seek to share the legal authority enjoyed by that work. A *halakhic* text's significance can also change if its organization suggests a theoretical versus a more practical approach.

Responsa have no traditional order of publication, and, being made up of smaller stand-alone units, no obvious overarching organizational logic. The lack of organization in responsa collections exacerbates their confusing legal status as texts. Does their authority stem from the personal or communal status of the rabbi who authored it, from the questioner's agreement to follow the decision, from the respondent's superior intellect and convincing arguments, from the nature or canonic status of the texts invoked? Depending on the kind of authority undergirding a responsum, its status can also change from the text's birth to its later dissemination.

Forms of Authority

The reasons advanced to legitimize responsa are remarkably inconsistent. Berachyahu Lifshitz surveyed such arguments: Some rabbis present responsa as binding rabbinic adjudication (*psak*), or judicial decisions; others consider responsa nonbinding personal advice; and still others frame responsa as theoretical analysis; practical insight; or expert opinions.[74] Elon compared responsa to the pronouncements of a central court, an explanation that seems forced for most periods of Jewish history. Although there are instances of rabbis who both sat on religious courts and wrote responsa, as can be evidenced from R. Katz's mention of his years as a judge in the introduction to his responsa collection, or the dual role held by R. Aryeh Leib Günzburg in eighteenth-century Metz, the two forms of legal text and the types of legal authority buttressing them are essentially distinct.[75]

Although responsa are replete with concrete detail and represent a rabbi's *halakhic* decision, the genre should not be mistaken for rabbinical court records. Jay Berkovitz has contrasted rabbinical court writings to responsa. The respective legal texts they produced and the legal authority of those texts varied in different historical and legal surroundings, depending on such factors as communal stability and surrounding legal culture. Edward Fram differentiated between courts, whose authority was circumscribed by location, versus responsa, which could be written for anyone anywhere. Courts followed majority opinion, while responsa could defend whatever position the author supported. Responsa took the facts of the case as reported, often hearing only one side of a case (a problematic practice that responsa authors defended by declaring that they were respondents, not judges).[76] By contrast, courts were expected (and authorized) to hear both sides and carry out factual investigations. The constricted time frame of a court, tasked with resolving cases speedily, contrasts with the relative leisure of a respondent, who, even if they did sometimes need to respond urgently, could always "rework their views in preparation for eventual copying . . . or, in the era of print, for publication."[77]

The act of reworking a responsum prior to publication highlights its various stages and how authority changes along with these shifts. As far as the court was a community institution, it enjoyed recourse to whatever executive tools the community could muster, whereas an individual respondent's authority would depend on individual status and reputation alone. Even if a rabbi's decision was accepted as binding by the responsum's recipient, this authority did not necessarily inhere in the responsum when consulted thereafter. As Eliav Shochetman emphasizes regarding legal rationales in *halakha*, the bulk of most responsa, unlike rabbinical court decisions, is devoted to explaining the rabbi's opinion.[78] The convention to include rationales relates to a responsum's legal authority. Rabbinical courts can prescribe behavior on the basis of their decision alone. Explaining themselves could weaken that authority. Rabbinical judges often explicitly refused to write their rationales to avoid the risk of one party submitting the decision for review with another rabbi.[79] Often, the responsa author's reputation (built in no small measure by his corpus of carefully crafted responsa) compels a questioner to follow the decision.[80] Yet responsa may also be persuasive on the strength of their arguments.[81] While rabbinic courts thus enjoy stronger institutional legal authority, rabbis deployed legal authority of a different kind in their responsa. As Berkovitz puts it, judges were seen as having less judicial freedom than a rabbi in a responsum. While judges were expected to adhere to particular rulings a respondent could "set himself free through argumentation."[82]

When the text passes from correspondence to a collection consulted centuries later, the nature of its authority evolves. Does the author's intention regarding his responsum's afterlife matter? Different respondents could have dissimilar expectations about the authority of their texts beyond its immediate situation; sometimes the same respondent could have intended for only some of his responsa to remain valid for posterity. Some responsa may have been preserved for their intellectual value, but not necessarily as legal precedent. Court decisions, according to Shochetman, were barely preserved because their *halakhic* value was limited and "nothing can be learned from them at all."[83] The lack of explanation meant that the decision could not be adopted in the future on the basis of any legal arguments. Unlike in case law systems, evidence of a past rabbinic court decision was apparently not a compelling *halakhic* authority and thus not worthy of preservation.

To further complicate matters, responsa vary in the degree to which their rationale is developed, with some *halakhic* cultures displaying more elaborate explanations whereas others contain little beyond the decision itself. More investment in explanations tends to correlate with eras when publication, and thus survival, were more likely; responsa grew in length from the print era onward. As Elon remarks, early modern responsa became longer, added more theoretical discussion, and cited more extraneous sources than did responsa in prior eras (he blames the rise of casuistry).[84] Shochetman suggests that responsa contain explanations because they represent the individual opinion of a rabbi rather than a binding court decision, and persuasion is thus required. However, he also remarks that some responsa eschewed rationales, as their authors may have relied on their personal authority and thus saw no need to explain themselves. Moreover, these characterizations do not hold true for responsa in all times and locations. Ultimately, there is no unified theory for the binding authority of responsa and we can, at most, glean hints from *halakhists*' pronouncements and from the ways in which these texts were preserved and presented.

The basis of authority for responsa in non-Jewish contexts likewise varies. The degree to which *fatwa* were binding, and whether they were meant to be authoritative beyond the initial cases, is a matter of scholarly discussion in which issues of editing and record keeping play an important role.[85] In Republican Rome, *responsa prudentium* were not binding. Later, emperor Augustus may have granted some jurists who wrote responsa imperial authority.[86] The question of the *consilium*'s authority is discussed in *ius commune* doctrinal writing. Since *consilia*, not unlike responsa, were frequently commissioned by one of the disputing parties, they were considered biased. Yet others considered *consilia* more reliable precisely because they were commissioned, meaning that jurists devoted attention to their writing.[87] Since the financial motivation highlights suspicions that such *consilia* are likely to be biased, this appears counterintuitive. Comparison to rabbinic responsa, where financial remuneration was not a feature, clarifies that the distinctive type of authority undergirding these texts may be the important factor. The individual respondent's personality and subjective approach are key features of these legal texts, a source of their subjectivity and, by the same token, of their authority.[88] An author's standing influenced the success of his *consilia* and, vice versa, *consilia* were a way of gaining renown and authority. This dynamic also holds for rabbinic respondents, whose authority stems from their personal perspective and expertise.

The type of individual rabbinic legal authority behind responsa can be taken to an extreme, to preclude its validity beyond that unique pronouncement in the responsum. In early modern Ashkenaz, this idea accompanied an aversion to codification, or even to creating *halakhic* texts altogether. R. Ḥayim Friedberg, a contemporary of R. Isserles, strongly objected to his colleague's contribution to *Shulḥan Arukh*. R. Ḥayim admitted that consistent adjudication required *halakhic* writings, but considered inconsistency unproblematic. *Halakha*, R. Ḥayim insisted, need not be consistent, and even individual scholars could change their minds, "a person's opinion is not always the same, and perhaps his mind tends not to rule a case as he ruled yesterday, and there is nothing wrong or lacking with this . . . On the contrary, this is the way of the Torah."[89] English jurists who opposed generalized law books defended the disordered and voluminous state of their legal literature not only by insisting that the myriad detail contained an inherent system, but mainly by expressing a particular preference for this lack of unification. Not unlike R. Ḥayim, who viewed the rabbi as generating the law anew in every decision-making instance, Blackstone's apologetics for common law called judges "living oracles of the law."[90]

If justifying the binding force of responsa at their writing is problematic, the legal authority of these texts after the fact is even more puzzling. Some assert the primacy of responsa above other *halakhic* writings as *halakha le-ma'aseh* (practical); being forged in the furnace of actual cases endows them with stronger validity.[91] Others emphasize old responsa as foolproof sources for adjudication compared to the risks of independent decision-making by uneducated judges. For instance, R. Ibn Migash was asked whether adjudicating according to one's *halakhic* knowledge is preferable to applying *geonic* responsa. He favored responsa: "he who does not rely on himself, if he depends on the *geonic* responsa and their rulings . . . is more praiseworthy than those who think themselves to be deciding from the Talmud."[92] A statement by R. Moellin reveals both the distrust of others toward responsa and his own wholehearted endorsement of responsa for coming out of concrete action: "concerning . . . that one should not rely on responsa—on the contrary, they are halakha *le-ma'aseh*, and we rely on them more than from the words of adjudicators that did not take place at the time of instruction."[93] Statements by R. Sofer reveal his faith in special Divine guidance that directed the worthy respondent when presented with a question. His understanding of this oracle-like role led him to answer questions without second-guessing them, to permit his intuition, which he considered divinely guided, to provide infallible legal decisions.[94]

Rabbis who diminished the authority of responsa equally call upon their emergence from real life as reason for their inferior authority. One eighteenth-century rabbi explained that the urgent circumstances surrounding responsa induce errors. Comprehensive scholarly works are more reliable, "because these are words written with more quiet . . . and there was no one rushing him to collect the responsum, for sometimes a person cannot inquire properly due to his hurry to respond."[95] Even later, anxiety about the acute circumstances of responsa prompts a nineteenth-century rabbi to forbid his sons from publishing his responsa.[96] The reassurance offered to these sons when they did publish invoked a special brand of Divine inspiration granted when responding to cases.

Order and Authority

Are responsa authoritative as part of the *halakhic* textual canon? The authority of a textual canon functions better with distinct, well-edited, comprehensive books. Responsa collections are notoriously disorganized and lacked editorial input. R. Israel Isserlein produced a defined collection of his own responsa. He died in Wiener Neustadt, *c.* 1460, before Hebrew print. Bomberg printed this collection, titled *Terumat ha-Deshen*, in 1519. The collection evidenced a high level of uniformity and order, atypical for the fifteenth-century responsa collections being printed around that time. At the time of its publication, *Terumat haDeshen* was the most deliberately organized, planned, and well-edited collection of Ashkenazic responsa. Enhanced with an index, the work exuded deliberate planning so atypical that some would later consider the work inauthentic, claiming that the author must have written his own questions rather than taking them from real life.[97] Disorder is a marker that the collection is the product of concrete questions, while superior organization indicates lack of authenticity.

Some rabbis prefer the more authentic writings, while others express stronger faith in edited collections. Bomberg printed another collection of R. Isserlein's writings, a disordered miscellany with far less editorial involvement. When R. Karo noted a legal contradiction between the works, he favored *Terumat ha-Deshen*, "because a person is more meticulous about that which he writes in a book."[98] Both works were based on responsa, but the superior editing and order raised the work's degree of *halakhic* authority in R. Karo's eyes.

Superior organization is associated with canonicity. Rosh's thirteenth-century responsa sometimes contradict his Talmud commentaries (*Piskei ha-Rosh*). The author's son instructed readers to disregard such responsa, since the commentaries were written later in his father's career. R. di Trani disbelieved the idea that *all* the responsa predated the commentaries. He presents both commonsensical reasons—"did [Rosh] place a gatekeeper at the gate of the house of study, so that nobody ask him a halakhic question!?"—as well as textual proof—Rosh refers to his commentaries in his responsa.[99] R. di Trani's skepticism aligns with the view of responsa-writing as a lifelong activity, which is also how he explains their inferior authority: A rabbi would update his organized work, correcting things "in their place" even if new issues came up while writing responsa "in the moment of action, but not vice versa."[100]

R. Benvenişti explicitly connects *not* being "in the moment of action" with organization and reliability, which he relates to larger *halakhic* works, and contrasts with responsa:

> When a halakhic decisor is busy answering a responsum . . . he does not hesitate to consult his larger work . . . However, when a person is writing a work [*ḥibur*], he does not revisit all his responsa to see what he decided, because it is a great hassle to search where he wrote this specific thing in his responsa, since they are not organized as in a work that is planned and prepared before him; whereas, whenever he wants to see what his opinion is in a work, he opens it to the tractate where this law is mentioned.[101]

Structured, comprehensive, and complete works imply deliberate and continuous editing, enhancing the sense that the author stood behind his ideas. Responsa were at a distinct disadvantage in this respect.

In part, organization and authority are intertwined for technical reasons. The spontaneous circumstances that give rise to responsa makes them less likely to reflect a rabbi's final, comprehensive opinion. Moreover, proclaiming sources as legally authoritative for posterity obligates future legists to consult these sources when adjudicating. In that case, one would expect to see these sources being collected and organized in ways that make systematic consultation possible. Disorganization, on the other hand, implies that disregarding these sources is likely—and acceptable.

Transmission and Authority

The triple connection between assured transmission, supreme organization, and *halakhic* authority is expressed as part of a principle of adjudication in a fifteenth-century responsum. The principle of *hilkheta ke-batra'i*, "the law follows the later authorities," declares more recent *halakhic* interpretations superior. Later authorities prevail because they were exposed to their predecessors' teachings and thus presumably either agreed with, or satisfactorily countered, those teachings.[102] If a later source contradicted an earlier source without explicitly noting the disagreement, the later authority must have had its reasons for dissenting. Allowing for the possibility that the latter authority was ignorant of preceding sources would dismantle the principle.

In a responsum, R. Colon explained that *hilkheta ke-batra'i* does not apply to all genres. While some kinds of sources are indeed well-transmitted, others quite plausibly get lost. While knowledge of "well-known and famous" books is assumed, R. Colon considers responsa differently, "However, if the source is written *in the responsa* of some sage, and unrecorded in a known book . . . we can presume that this later [dissenting] sage never heard of that opinion."[103]

R. Colon excludes responsa from the presumption about canonical texts that animates *hilkheta ke-batra'i*. Unless they are absorbed into other genres, R. Colon argues, we cannot assume responsa to be common knowledge in the same way as other texts. This exclusion of responsa reflects the genre's lack of deliberate, organized transmission. The absorption of responsa into a larger work enhances its chances of survival. But such absorption does more than simply provide heft for responsa to prevent them from getting lost. Inserting responsa within a larger work enhances their organizational position. Better organization makes for more systematic consultation, which is crucial if responsa are to be considered as canonical as other *halakhic* texts. Prima facie, responsa appear as perfect candidates for *hilkheta ke-batra'i*, because ruling according to the most recent authority makes sense especially in concrete cases, where the details are more likely to resemble current situations. Nevertheless, their up-to-date character also hinder responsa's organization into canonical works. [104]

R. Isserles authored the Ashkenazic glosses on *Shulḥan Arukh*, arguably the most popular *halakhic* code ever. In the introduction to *Darkhei Moshe*, he describes what had jolted him into doing so. In the past, R. Isserles explained, he would refer to a set number of *halakhic* works: Talmud, the authorities of the early and high middle ages, and select newer works from the thirteenth century and onward. R. Isserles's initial modus operandi was brusquely interrupted, "when others came with hidden scrolls, contradicting me *from responsa*."[105] Recent scholars have wondered how R. Isserles had ventured to adjudicate without responsa. Glick exclaims: "could it be that it occurred to R. Isserles, the rabbi of the Ashkenazic Diaspora, to compose a book of *halakhic* decisions without taking the responsa into consideration?!"[106] The answer may relate to responsa's origins in particular cases; and to their resulting vagaries in the afterlife of this literature, which was not preserved systematically. As R. Colon assumed when he excluded responsa from *hilkheta ke-batra'i*, and as R. Isserles unproblematically admitted was the situation in his early days: unless included in a larger work, we cannot assume that rabbis saw every responsum from their precursors. As "hidden scrolls," in R. Isserles's words—privately circulating letters—responsa's authority was limited. Exhaustively covering this literature was impossible, and rabbis were not expected to do so. Once mentioned in "known books," as R. Colon called them, their status shifted. Finding aids and organized works, such as R. Isserles's glosses, made systematically consulting responsa possible. Only then did these sources become uncontrovertibly authoritative.

The arbitrary ways of keeping and transmitting responsa is more than a technical challenge; it weakens their authority. Some thinkers organized legal sources to establish the rationality of their legal system, thus buttressing its authority. This can be said of Gottfried Wilhelm Leibniz's project to create a scientific codification of civil law, or even of William Blackstone's attempt to organize common law.[107] But systematizing knowledge also enhances its authority in a pragmatic sense: if a legal source is authoritative and may not be ignored, there must be mechanisms in place for the jurist to find these sources.[108] Rabbis like R. Colon respected the authoritative nature of responsa as a source but nevertheless excluded responsa from the usual principles of canonic transmission unless they were part of a systematic work.

Lack of organization thus limits the authority of these texts for the future. Elon declared the "complete lack of system in the arrangement of the responsa" as one of the "problems"[109] of the genre, and initiated a project to systematize responsa, which he deemed crucial to promote this literature.[110] Without practical ability to systematically consult responsa, it is difficult to argue for their authoritative status.

Legal Questions

Different tactics of knowledge organization[111] were used to attempt systematizing past responsa. These include indices, finding aids, and incorporating of responsa into codes. These attempts at effectively organizing responsa material would prove problematic, as any true systematization of responsa is doomed either to fail or to undo essential elements that make responsa what they are.

In medieval Ashkenaz, responsa were sometimes appended to the appropriate Talmudic sections. A similarly rudimentary arrangement is the thirteenth-century R.

Meir Kohen's *Hagahot Maimuniot*, a *halakhic* collection arranged by general topics corresponding to the books in Maimonides's work, which also included clusters of tosafist responsa at the end of sections. Rosh's successors subjected their master's responsa to more thorough organization by dividing them into one of more than a hundred *halakhic* topics, even splitting up individual responsa if they addressed a succession of different subjects.[112] R. Ḥiya had rearranged the responsa in the printed *Terumat ha-Deshen* to follow a *halakhically* intuitive order.[113]

An alternative to rearranging the responsa themselves is creating tables of contents, thus reproducing the work in a manageable format and providing an overview of the contents. An index lists the entries not in order of appearance but following some sensible scheme. Printers often added indices listing *halakhic* topics in an intuitive, associative, or otherwise familiar order, thus making the work easier to consult. But these are incomplete methods at best.

Since adequately addressing a *halakhic* situation often demands combining divergent legal topics, responsa can only truly be organized when taken apart. However, doing so destroys the characteristics that make responsa what they are. Editors attempted to solve this conundrum in various ways. Rosh's students divided his responsa and rearranged their order by *halakhic* topic. This made the collection easier to consult and emphasized the responsa's general import, but dividing what had been one long responsum meant losing their concrete traces. When R. Ḥiya edited R. Colon's responsa, the table of contents listed the "root," or legal principle, derived from every responsum, in addition to their "branches" or subtopics, in order of appearance. Doing so organizes and highlights the responsa's general applications without needing to split any responsa. Isaac de Lattes, who printed Ran's responsa (Rome, 1545), numbered not just the pages but even the lines of the work, allowing him to separate the responsa's elements for consultation, even where disparate fields of *halakha* were interwoven:

> Because . . . several individual legal topics [*dinim*] can emerge in even a single responsum . . . we decided to add an index [*mar'eh makom*] organized according to each of the legal topics . . . indicating for the researcher [*ha-me'ayen*] the number of the responsum, the page, and the line [*shitah*] so that he not weary nor tire himself in locating what he wants and is looking for.[114]

Incorporating a responsum into a code or other systematic work made it easier to find, more likely to survive, and associated it with the authoritative power of the code, thus also making it impossible to ignore the source when adjudicating. R. Isserles and R. Karo had inserted responsa into their codes, as had many works before them, such as *Mordekhai* in Ashkenaz, *Arba Turim* in Spain; and as many later works would do, including the commentaries on *Shulḥan Arukh* composed in the century after its publication and finding aids such as *Pitḥei Teshuva*.

With the growing dominance of *Shulḥan Arukh*, finding aids for responsa would become ever more standardized. Elon decried the lack of system in the arrangement of earlier responsa, but remarked with relief that after *Shulḥan Arukh* was published, "a substantial change for the better in the organization of compilations of responsa occurred."[115] Printed collections of responsa after the sixteenth century would increasingly follow *Shulḥan Arukh*'s structure. For instance, the first collection of Rabbi Yoel Sirkis's responsa (1561–1640), published in 1697, was in arbitrary order with a thematic index. An additional collection was printed in 1775, this one featuring the contents themselves in order of the *Shulḥan Arukh*'s four volumes. R. Bacharach, the first Ashkenazi post-*Shulḥan Arukh* to fully collect, select, organize, and print his responsa in his own lifetime, arranged his index on the pattern of *Shulḥan Arukh*. By the nineteenth century, reference tools in *Shulḥan Arukh* (such as Rabbi Ḥayim Mordehkai Margalioth's *Sha'arei Teshuva* and Rabbi Avraham Ẓvi Hirsch Eisenstadt's *Pitḥei Teshuva*) would systematically list the relevant responsa for each entry. These references soon became standard, thus permitting consultation from the code to the responsa literature, and cementing the expectation that rabbis would consult these sources.[116]

Despite their use in facilitating consultation, these organizing tactics failed to completely solve the disorder of responsa. For one, the topics covered in responsa extend past the horizons of any standard *halakhic* scheme. R. Bacharach's near-exhaustive index patterned on *Shulḥan Arukh* is followed by a shorter index serving, as its title proclaimed, as an aid to find those "questions . . . that do not have a legal consequence," by which he meant questions not mentioned in the code.[117] The second edition of R. Colon's responsa (Cremona, 1557) tried ordering them on the pattern of Maimonides's comprehensive *halakhic* code. Yet several entries were impossible to place, inducing the editors to come up with new categories such as *minhagim ve-takanot* (customs and ordinances) and *yishuvim u-peshatim* (justifications and explanations).

Recent responsa collections, such as the multivolume present-day *Minḥat Asher* by Rabbi Asher Weiss (1953–), arrange the contents by volume of *Shulḥan Arukh*, yet present additional responsa under headings that were nonexistent in the early modern code, such as "halakha and medicine."[118] It would have been possible to subsume individual contemporary responsa in various sections of *Shulḥan Arukh* (for instance, medicine-related responsa were traditionally found among laws of desecrating Shabbat to save lives, or in the context of magic and divination). The addition of a new topic to the organizational structure indicates the emergence of new categories of Jewish law that were previously not considered coherent independent rubrics.

Elon's relief at responsa's improved organization post-*Shulḥan Arukh* is thus short-lived. Ultimately, the chronically incomplete, insufficiently comprehensive, and constantly shifting nature of these finding aids proves how essentially unfit for thorough organization responsa are. Responsa's tendency toward disorder is an essential characteristic of this genre. The direct connection to reality caused the nature of responsa—their sheer variety, detail, dynamism, and multifariousness—which makes them near-impossible to systematize.

Finding aids provide only rudimentary support in navigating responsa. These limitations result from the unbounded range of topics covered by responsa, the fact that they connect and combine multiple *halakhic* topics, and the open-ended nature of the collection, given its roots in correspondence carried out throughout the rabbi's lifetime.

Any tactics of systematization are incompatible with the particularity and dynamism that defines responsa. To permit insertion into larger works, responsa must be distilled or abstracted. While such conclusions preserve the legal upshot, they remove precisely those characteristic elements—its engagement with particulars, its representation of an individual perspective, and its unique combination of sources from different areas of *halakha*. The intervention required to make a responsum systematically findable transforms it in ways that may shift its authority. As R. Colon would have defined it, rabbis can be assumed to know all "the responsa of some sage, *recorded in a known book*." The book where it is recorded becomes the determining category. Adding a finding aid for responsa to *Shulḥan Arukh* enhances the consultation of responsa, but also the source of their authority, to the universe of that code, rather than establishing the authority of responsa as a genre.

Despite the many advantages of rendering responsa better organized, be it by summarizing their bottom lines in another genre or by writing responsa with an eye toward their ultimate publication (rather than their initial creation), the contention that responsa were written for a concrete case remained a crucial part of this genre's unique significance. Even responsa that were heavily edited (or altogether created) with publication in mind continued to be formulated in this tenor. At its core, then, the unique authority of responsa derives from those roots in the concrete, even as that very element complicates the eventual systematization of these sources.

Notwithstanding all these challenges, responsa boast distinct advantages as legal sources, practically, stylistically, morally, and as a mode of thought. Compared to the slower, more elaborate medium of published books, responsa's letter format made them especially nimble for quick and targeted reactions, and particularly flexible for adaptation to new circumstances and cases. When R. Isserles was criticized by local colleagues for officiating at a wedding on Sabbath, he wrote an "open-letter"-style responsum to defend his action.

Fearing that postponing the wedding would lead to its eventual annulment, R. Isserles controversially proceeded with a poor orphan's wedding on Sabbath. His responsum detailed the urgency of the matter in an engrossing narrative:

> There once was a man . . . the daughter remained, bereft and lonely . . .when the days of . . . her marriage came to pass . . . she saw no sign of the dowry . . . except for a voice telling her to immerse and prepare herself for her wedding. . . . And this maiden did as commanded by her female neighbors. . . .They also covered her on Friday with a veil as is the way of the maidens. . . . And as the evening shadows lengthened and the day was almost over . . . the relatives closed their fists . . .time was passing by . . . when the groom agreed to come to the marriage canopy, and so as not to humiliate an upright daughter of Israel, I stood up and officiated the marriage.[119]

The lyrical and dramatic language includes countless details and powerful biblical allusions, introducing emotional elements and rendering the bride completely innocent, her impending humiliation all the more unbearable.

Comparing the above description with R. Isserles's own reference to this case in *Shulḥan Arukh* illustrates the intense transformation necessary to include such a responsum in a codification, and, by extension, responsa's uniqueness. First, the statement is abstracted and generalized, better to allow the case to serve as a prescriptive legal statement beyond the one occurrence. *Shulḥan Arukh* states that weddings are forbidden on Shabbat. R. Isserles adds, "and there are those who permit . . . because human dignity is important." The gloss could have stopped here. Only in the rest of the sentence does it becomes clear that this is a generalized version of the responsum above, "as it is sometimes the habit that, when one could not agree about the dowry on Friday until nightfall, that one performs the *ḥuppa* and marriage on the night of Sabbath."[120]

Some of the emotive details in the responsum have *halakhic* relevance, such as the bride's potential embarrassment. By the time these elements make it into the codification however, they are scrubbed of all emotion. Responsa's adaptability allowed R. Isserles to describe the young bride's plight evocatively, but doing so had no place in the code. One historian presented *consilia* as a model for early modern justice that balanced theoretical coherence and legal-mindedness, on the one hand, with the concrete, on the other.[121] This same "midpoint" between practical focus and theoretical commitment informs responsa.

When brought into the legal conversation, responsa add the perspective of "thinking in cases," a mode of thought that typifies certain branches of science and medicine—and, of course, law—which reasons not through general principles but from specifics to specifics via cases and exemplars.[122] R. Isserles's addition of the occurrence into the codes is prefaced by the strange formulation "as it is sometimes the habit." This expression turns the responsum from an occurrence ("sometimes") into something more general ("the habit") thus justifying its place in the code: the responsum becomes a "case." If the problem is too standard, asking a question is unnecessary, but if the particular complexities are too distinctive, the responsum will likewise be useless. Conceiving of responsa as cases highlights their importance as exempla that allow for a degree of particularity which nevertheless has general implications. Moral and political arguments centered on extreme urgency have been considered a form of "thinking in cases" that balances overly rule-based moral thinking. R. Isserles's emotional description in the responsum displays the urgency that propelled his case-generated legal decision, which ultimately enters the code.

Conclusion

Responsa arise from *halakha* meeting particular situations. These origins result in peculiarities for the responsa corpus as legal material: they are haphazardly kept, collected unsystematically, and transmitted incompletely, making them difficult to consult comprehensively. The vagaries and disorder of their transmission result from responsa's roots in real-life situations. But responsa's troublesome nature is also the source of their unique strength. It is certainly why responsa are found at the forefront of historical change, the preferred genre for tackling traumatic incidents and unprecedented innovations; life in Nazi ghettos, COVID-19 restrictions, in vitro fertilization, and electricity are all treated first in responsa.[123] The necessity of asking questions speaks for itself, and responsa are the best genre to do so, for the agility of writing a stand-alone responsum versus a larger systematic work, and because responsa can be formulated in ways that do not fit the given order of *halakhic* works.

Conversely, responsa do not make for ideal books. The same elements that complicate responsa are the source of their unique value and power. Responsa contribute something crucial to law by engaging profoundly with life's particulars, which makes them such unruly legal sources. They superbly characterize rabbinic legal activity as both adjudicators and scholars by representing a dynamic scholarly archive—the rabbi's working records, notes, and communications. Prior to print, responsa that were not intentionally meant for publication often disappeared. Once print established the longevity and broad audience of responsa, writings were frequently already composed for this double role. In our digital age, when publication is once again more fluid than it had been in the print era, on the one hand, but their survival is far more assured than in the manuscript world, on the other, this dynamic shifts once more. Responsa can now find a broad audience long before appearing in a printed collection, and digital search methods render the thematic organization that characterized earlier collections less urgent. However, these changes also mean less control over what gets published and how, raising new questions about the authority of responsa.

No matter what forms responsa take in their afterlives, their unique kind of legal authority is drawn from its origins. Codes may well derive their authority from the objectivity, stability, and generality that the impersonal, summarizing style and fixed structure of such writings exude.[124] Responsa, by contrast, represent another kind of authority, not that of text as a finished product but as an active discourse. Responsa evoke the rabbi's persona, and the intellectual virtuosity exuding from a well-crafted response, both important sources of *halakhic* authority. Moreover, inasmuch as the responsum belongs to an ecosystem of correspondence beyond its individual author, the implied "invisible college"[125] of *halakhists* that participated in shaping and verifying this discourse adds a unique layer of authority bestowed by mutual supervision and dispute.

Organization, even of the least interventionist kind, is never entirely neutral. Scholars of modern legal research have established that organizational systems express a particular vision of the legal material they organize. This is obvious for agenda-driven programmatic projects, such as Blackstone's attempts to prove the internal rationality of English law, but even pragmatic projects aimed merely at facilitating practical reference work (such the key in West's *Digest*) incorporate assumptions of how legal sources should be used and determine the "universe of thinkable thoughts."[126] Shaping responsa into the mold of a code makes them easier to consult, but also confines these sources.

Recent digital tools have made it possible to consult vast swaths of responsa literature. Bar Ilan's *Responsa Project* has enabled online access to thousands of collections since 2006. *Otzar ha-Ḥokhma*'s hundreds of thousands of e-books, including responsa, are OCR-searchable. While such consultation is comprehensive, it is not truly systematic, since it does not employ any structured scheme of *halakhic* knowledge. Although such programs facilitate sifting through all the (digitalized) material at a speed unattainable to humans, the responsa remain untouched. The original texts are not distilled, abstracted, or schematized. In a sense, resorting to this comprehensive search method makes it possible to practically consult all responsa without addressing the issues that emerge in systematizing this corpus.[127] Giving up on more invasive finding aids also means avoiding any decision about responsa's subsequent use, place, and significance within the legal system. Despite technological and organizational innovations, responsa collections, be they printed with an index or enabled for digital search, are not meant to function in the same way as systematic *halakhic* works. Rather than seeking to resolve this impossibility, contemplating and appreciating this issue—as this chapter has sought to do—helps us ask crucial questions about different modes of *halakhic* thinking.

Perhaps the most important contribution of responsa as precedent is that it allows us to think in cases. Poised between complete abstraction and overwhelming concreteness, thinking in cases allows for reasoning with the multifariousness of reality in ways that pure generalities and syllogisms cannot offer. Such thinking can, to some extent, leave the law as a unified whole untheorized. But what responsa lack in systematicity they make up for in the ability to take incompatible data into consideration, to stand outside the given parameters of the system, and to tackle a broader range of phenomena. With the ascent of case-based-reasoning that guides so many current modes of digital algorithmic reasoning often not transparent to its users, it will become ever more important to consider how, why, and whether thinking in cases functions as legally authoritative.

Notes

1. These opened with the greeting "to our Master, who is in Babylonia." Babylonian Talmud, Tractate Hulin 95b. Often rabbis are said to "send" a question to another rabbi, such as in Sabbath, 108b, and Gittin, 89b (without explicitly mentioning if this was done in writing or orally, by messenger), but occasionally a written question is explicitly involved.
2. Robert Brody, *The Geonim of Babylonia and the Shaping of Medieval Jewish Culture* (New Haven: Yale University Press, 1998), 20.
3. The total amount of such responsa is in the hundreds of thousands. See Menachem Elon, "Preface," in *Digest of the Responsa Literature of Spain and North Africa*, ed. Menachem Elon (Jerusalem: Magnes Press, 1981), 15 [Hebrew] and Menachem Elon, "Preface," in *Digest of the Responsa Literature of Germany France and Italy*, ed. Berachyahu Lifshitz and Eliav Shochetman (Jerusalem: Hamakhon Leheker Hamishpat Ha'ivry, 1997) [Hebrew].
4. Shmuel Glick, *Kuntres ha-teshuvot he-ḥadash: Otzzar bibliografi le-sifrut ha-she'elot ve-ha teshuvot mi-reshit ha-dfus ve-ad shenat 2000*, 4 vols., ed. Shmuel Glick (Ramat Gan: Bar Ilan Law Library Press, 2006), 1:96–99 [Hebrew].
5. Moshe Lichtenstein, "The Period of the Aharonim: Trends and Directions," *Netu'im* 16 (2009): 131–74, here 151 [Hebrew].
6. Oren Z. Steinitz, "Responsa 2.0.: Are Q&A Websites Creating a New Type of Halachic Discourse?" *Modern Judaism* 31, no. 1 (2011): 85–102.

7. For more on *consilia*, see Mario Ascheri, Ingrid Baumgärtner, and Julius Kirshner, eds., *Legal Consulting in the Civil Law Tradition* (Berkeley: University of California Press, 1999).
8. See Shlomo D. Goitein, *A Mediterranean Society: The Jewish Communities of the Arab World as Portrayed in the Documents of the Cairo Geniza 2: The Community* (Berkeley: University of California Press, 1971), 325; Mordechai Akiva Friedman, "Fatwas for Abraham Maimonides," *Maarav* 21, nos. 1–2 (2014): 340–46; Wael B. Hallaq, "From Fatwas to Furu: Growth and Change in Islamic Substantive Law," *Islamic Law and Society* 1, no. 1 (1994): 29–65.
9. Norman Zacour, *Jews and Saracens in the Consilia of Oldradus de Ponte* (Toronto: Pontifical Institute of Mediaeval Studies 1990), 3.
10. Kaius Tuori, "The *ius respondendi* and the Freedom of Roman Jurisprudence," *Révue Internationale des droits de l'Antiquité LI* 51 (2004): 295–337.
11. Antonio Padoa-Schioppa, *A History of Law in Europe: From the Early Middle Ages to the Twentieth Century* (Cambridge: Cambridge University Press, 2017), 83–84.
12. For Italy, Osvaldo Cavallar and Julius Kirshner, eds., *Jurists and Jurisprudence in Medieval Italy* (Buffalo: University of Toronto Press, 2020).
13. Padoa-Schioppa, *History of Law*, 144–45.
14. For a taxonomy of the types of legal consilia, see Auweele and Oosterbosch, "Consilia Iuridica," 124–27.
15. For instance, ibid., 109.
16. HaMapah: Quantitative Analysis of Rabbinic Literature, https://blog.hamapah.org/about/.
17. Yizḥak Zev Kahana, *Studies in Responsa Literature* (Jerusalem: Mosad ha-Rav Kook, 1973), 97–107 [in Hebrew]. More recently, Tirza Kelman, "What Makes a Text Responsa? R. Israel Isserlein's Trumat Hadeshen as a Case Study," *Jewish Law Association Studies* 30 (2022): 99–110 addressed issues of genre with one responsa collection (*Terumat ha-Deshen*, discussed below) as her case study.
18. For instance, Isserles, *ShUT Rema*, §12–16; Luria, *ShUT MaharShaL*, §33. See also Alexander Marx, "A Jewish *Cause Célèbre* in Sixteenth-Century Italy," in *Abhandlungen zur Erinnerung an Hirsch Perez Chajes*, ed. V. Aptowitzer and A. Z. Schwartz (Vienna: Alexander Kohut Memorial Foundation, 1933), 150–93.
19. As did the fifteenth-century R. Jacob Moellin of Worms, for instance: Dinari, Yedidya. *The Sages of Ashkenaz in the late Middle Ages* (Jerusalem: Mossad Bialik, 1984), 278 n. 51 [Hebrew]; see also *Minhagei* Maharil. Sabbioneta: Tobias Foa, 1556, 105b.
20. See, for instance, Francis W. Carter, *Trade and Urban Development in Poland: An Economic Geography of Cracow, from Its Origins to 1795* (Cambridge: Cambridge University Press, 1994), 107. Carter set the pace for a courier carrying only mail at 100km/24h on average. See Isserles, *ShUT Rema*, ed. Siev, 498 n. 2; and Isserles, *ShUT Rema*, no. 128.
21. Israel M. Ta-Shma, *Collection of Studies: Inquiries into the Rabbinic Literature of the Middle Ages* (Jerusalem: Mossad Bialik, 2004), I:117 [Hebrew].
22. Mordechai Akiva Friedman, "Responsa of R. Abraham Maimonides from the Cairo Geniza a Preliminary Review," *Proceedings of the American Academy for Jewish Research* 56 (1990): esp. 45; Mordechai Akiva Friedman, "Responsa from R. Abraham Maimonides on a Debtor's Travails," in *Genizah Research after 90 years: The Case of Judeo Arabic*, ed. Joshua Blau and Stefan Reif (Cambridge: Cambridge University Press, 1992), 85.
23. Bruna, *Responsa* §34, cited in Yaakov Shmuel Spiegel, *Chapters in the History of the Jewish Book* (Ramat-Gan: Bar Ilan University Press, 2005), II:235 [Hebrew].

24. James Daybell, *The Material Letter in Early Modern England: Manuscript Letters and the Culture and Practices of Letter-Writing, 1512–1635* (New York: Palgrave Macmillan, 2012), 25, 176.
25. Marx, "A Jewish *Cause Célèbre*," 149–50.
26. Maimonides's letters are often divided into formulaic *halakhic* responsa versus general epistles, but boundaries between the two kinds of writing are blurry in practice. See, for instance.Yitzchak Shilat, "Introduction," in Maimonides, *Epistles of Maimonides* [Hebrew], ed. Yitzchak Shilat (Ma'ale Adumim: Shilat, 1995), 8–9.
27. Maimonides, *Responsa*, §297: "And when this instruction arrived they read it on Sabbath in the synagogue in public." See Yehoshua Blau, "Introduction," in Maimonides, *Responsa* (1960), ed. Yehoshua Blau (Jerusalem: Reuven Mas, 2014), 1:xl, 269.
28. Isserles, *ShUT Rema* §67.
29. See Dirk Van Miert, "Confidentiality and Publicity in Early Modern Epistolography: Scaliger and Casaubon," in *For the Sake of Learning: Essays in Honor of Anthony Grafton*, ed. Ann Blair and Anja-Silvia Goeing, vol. 1 (Leiden, The Netherlands: Brill, 2016), 18–19; Judith Rice-Henderson, "Humanist Letter Writing: Private Conversation or Public Forum?," in *Self-Presentation and Social Identification: The Rhetoric and Pragmatics of Letter Writing in Early Modern Times*, ed. Toon van Houdt et al. (Leuven, Belgium: Leuven University Press, 2002), 18.
30. Katz, *ShUT She'erit Yosef* §1.2.
31. Ibid., §19.
32. Elisheva Carlebach emphasizes the importance of responsa as "a conduit for some of the most enterprising minds in the early modern period." Elisheva Carlebach, "Letter into Text: Epistolarity, History, and Literature," in *Jewish Literature and History: An Interdisciplinary Conversation*, ed. Eliyana Adler and Sheila Jelen (Bethesda: University Press of Maryland, 2008), 115–16.
33. Lisa Jardine, *Erasmus, Man of Letters; The Construction of Charisma in Print* (Princeton, NJ: Princeton University Press, 2015); Jay R. Berkovitz, "The Persona of a *Poseq*: Law and Self-Fashioning in Seventeenth-Century Ashkenaz," *Modern Judaism: A Journal of Jewish Ideas and Experience* 32, no. 2 (2012): 251–69.
34. On the connection between public sphere, "theater," and oral, argumentative transparent discourse, Marcel Hénaff and Tracy B. Strong, "Introduction: Vision, Speech, Theatricality," in *Public Space and Democracy*, ed. Marcel Hénaff and Tracy B. Strong (Minneapolis: University of Minnesota Press, 2001), 5–6.
35. See, for instance, Isserles, *ShUT Rema*, §38–39, 95, 132, 7, 9. *Shir ha-ma'alot le-David* (Cracow, 1571), 8a; Simḥa Goldin, "'Companies of Disciples' and 'Companies of Colleagues': Communication in Jewish Intellectual Circles," in *Vox Iudaica, Communication in the Jewish Diaspora: The Pre-Modern World*, ed. Sophia Menache (Leiden, The Netherlands: Brill, 1996), 127–39.
36. Languages and discourses are often compared to games, whose rules are taught, enforced, and clarified through communal use. Wittgenstein and Foucault think of discourses as games, and so do "speech act" theorists such as J. L. Austin. See Tamara Morsel-Eisenberg, "The Organization of Halakhic Knowledge in Early Modern Ashkenaz" (PhD diss., University of Pennsylvania, 2018), ch. 5.3.
37. Daybell, *Material Letter*, 178; Ta-Shma, *Collection*, 119.
38. Maimonides, *Mishneh Torah*, introduction.
39. Yosef ibn Migash, *Responsa* §114.

40. Rashba, *Responsa* IV:116.
41. Rivash, *Responsa*, §153.
42. Ta-Shma, "Introduction," in *Digest*, IX. A few other tosafists appended small collections of responsa to their more comprehensive *halakhic* writings, such as the twelfth-century works of R. Eliezer b. Nathan of Mainz (Ravan) and R Eliezer b. Yoel haLevy (Raviyah), or *Zarua* on the Talmud. See Avraham (Rami) Reiner, *Rabbenu Tam: Parshanut, Halakha, Pulmus* (Ramat Gan: Bar Ilan University Press, 2021), 279–303 [Hebrew].
43. Ta-Shma, "Introduction," in *Digest*, 11. There are, of course, some exceptions: The eleventh-century Spanish authority, R. Izḥak Alfasi (Rif), wrote hundreds of responsa, many in Arabic. No collection by the author himself remains.
44. Goitein, *Mediterranean Society*, 326; Blau, "Introduction," 1:xl.
45. For hypotheses of why this was the case, see Aryeh Feldman, "Introduction," in R. Nissim Gerondi, *Responsa*, ed. Moshe Herschler (Jerusalem: Moznayim 1984), 15–16. See Bernard Cooperman, "Organizing Knowledge for the Jewish Market: An Editor/Printer in 16th Century Rome," in *Perspectives on the Hebraic Book: The Myron M. Weinstein Memorial Lectures at the Library of Congress*, ed. Peggy K. Pearlstein (Washington, DC: Library of Congress, 2012), 79–129.
46. Ta-Shma, *Collection*, 124.
47. See Ya'akov Shemu'el Spiegel, *Chapters in the History of the Jewish Book, vol 2: Scholars and their Annotations* (Ramat Gan: Bar Ilan University Press, 1996), 232 [Hebrew].
48. Simḥa Emanuel, "Introduction," in *The Responsa of Rabbi Meir Rothenburg and His Circle*, ed. Simḥa Emanuel (Jerusalem: World Union of Jewish Studies 2012), 179 [Hebrew].
49. Ta-Shma, *Collection*, 121. The responsa themselves also stem overwhelmingly from Rosh's (shorter) life in Spain. Ta-Shma considers this a Sephardic mode of treating an Ashkenazi rabbi's responsa.
50. R. Weil's collection was passed on to his son, whose son-in-law, R. Bruna, later inherited it, until it was printed in 1549. Israel Bruna, *Responsa*, §254: "Thus ends the quote in his book which is in the hand of his son, my brother-in-law."
51. Copied in Israel Yuval, *Sages in Their Generation: The Spiritual Leadership of German Jewry at the End of the Middle Ages* (Jerusalem: Magnes Press, 1989), 111–13 [Hebrew]. (First published in *ha-mazkir* 9 [1869]: 23.)
52. David Simonsen, "Zur Bücherkunde," in *Festschrift zum achtzigsten Geburtstage Moritz Steinschneiders* (Leipzig, Germany: Otto Harrassowitz, 1896), 166.
53. Shlomo Zalman Havlin, "Introduction," in *Responsa of the RaShbA* (Jerusalem: National Library, 1977), 3–44.
54. Published in Simḥa Assaf, "From the Archives of the Jerusalem Library," in *Minḥa le-David: Jubilee Volume for David Yelin* (Jerusalem: Reuven Mas, 1935), 233–35. Concerning Rabbi Yeḥiel Ashkenazi, see Eliezer Rivlin, *A Book of the History of the Sages of Jerusalem* (Jerusalem: Salomon Press, 1927–1930), 108 [Hebrew].
55. Yosef Karo, *Beit Yosef* (Venice, 1950), introduction (not paginated). Tirtẓa Kelman, "Written in Metal and Lead Letters in Print: The Print Revolution and the Creation of the Work Bet Yosef," *Peamim* 148 (2016): 9–27 [Hebrew].
56. See Joseph R. Hacker, "Authors, Readers and Printers of the Hebrew Book in the Sixteenth-Century Ottoman Empire," in *Perspectives on the Hebraic Book* (Washington, DC: Library of Congress, 2012), 38–39.
57. Shmuel Glick, ed., *The New Handbook of Responsa: A Bibliographic Anthology for Responsa Literature from the Beginning of Print to the Year 2000*, 4 vols. (Ramat Gan: Bar Ilan Law Library Press, 2006), 1:99–100 [Hebrew].

58. Glick, *New Handbook*, 1:91.
59. *ShUT Binyamin Ze'ev*, 1539. Meir Benayahu, *Prolegomenon to Sefer Benyamin Ze'ev* (Jerusalem: Yad HaRav Nissim, 1989), 55–61 [Hebrew]; and Benyamin Ze'ev of Arta, *Responsa*, §59.
60. Martin Lowry, *The World of Aldus Manutius: Business and Scholarship in Renaissance Venice* (Ithaca: Cornell University Press, 1979), 218–19; Ernst Philip Goldschmidt, *Medieval texts and Their First Appearance in Print* (London: Oxford University Press, 1943), 13, 23 (on commercial incentives for prioritizing printing older works).
61. According to his son, R. Karo instructed before his death "that all his responsa to questions be collected . . . and . . . arranged for print." Yosef Karo, "Introduction," in *Avkat rokhel* (Salonica), 1597–98.
62. J. H. Baker, *Introduction to English Legal History* (Oxford: Oxford University Press, 2019), 190. Peter Riesenberg, "Consilia Literature: A Prospectus," *Manuscripta* 6, no. 1 (1992): 3–22, esp. 5. On collecting, organizing, and publishing *fatwa*, Guy Burak, "Şeyhulislâm Feyzullah Efendi, the Ḥanafī Mufti of Jerusalem and the Rise of the Provincial Fatāwā: Collections in the Eighteenth Century," *Journal of the Economic and Social History of the Orient* 64 (2021): 377–403, here 382.
63. Baker, *Collected*, 654–55.
64. Hayim Soloveitchik, *Pawnbroking in the Middle Ages: A Study in the Interrelationship between Halakhah, Economic Activity, and Self-Image* (Jerusalem: Magnes Press, 1985), 83 [Hebrew]. He argues that so few medieval French Ashkenazic responsa survive because they were considered ephemera, "when these adjudicators approached the creation of books, these teachings did not take a central place in their consciousness . . . Questions were asked and responses were written, but these creations were seen as *livres des circonstance*."
65. Emanuel concludes this after finding various manuscripts in which the same responsa were copied and paraphrased in disparate ways without any particular effort to mention explicitly that this was a copy from a responsum. Many responsa were probably copied in this manner, meaning that they were preserved, but difficult to identify as responsa. See Simha Emanuel, *Fragments of the Tablets: Lost Books of the Tosafists* (Jerusalem: Magnes Press, 2006), 271–72 [Hebrew].
66. Some of the writings were created during his forty-nine years as a rabbinical judge; others were the result of the "questions that arose from all the praised communities of Israel, near and far." Katz, *ShUT She'erit Yosef*, introduction.
67. Isserles, *ShUT Rema* §25: R. Pollak said: "I know that they will no longer rule differently from what I will write, since the law is like the later authorities . . . And for that reason, the sage, our master, Ya'akov Pollak wrote no book, nor even a responsum that was sent from afar did they copy, these sages."
68. One of these volumes is at the NLI: MS Heb 38°5220.
69. R. Yair Bacharach, *Shut Ḥavot Ya'ir* (Frankfurt am Main, 1699), introduction.
70. He ascribes this shift to internal scholarly processes by which other *halakhic* genres were intellectually saturated, leading rabbis to responsa as a genre that permitted creativity. Moshe Lichtenstein, "The Period of the Aḥaronim: Trends and Directions," *Netu'im* 16 (2009): 151 [Hebrew]. Most recently, Elli Fischer, "The Responsa Literature in Galicia and Bukovina," in *Historical Atlas of the Jewry of Galicia and Bukovina*, ed. Levi Cooper, Judith Kalik, and Nathan Shifriss (forthcoming).
71. R. Katz, who, unlike his contemporaries, did print his own responsa, also coined a title for the collection (*She'erit Yosef*). The fifteenth-century R. Isserlein probably prepared his own

responsa collection for manuscript circulation, and he is often known by the work's title, *Terumat ha-Deshen*. See also Dinari, *Sages,* 303 n. 221.

72. For a discussion of this disagreement: Spiegel, *Chapters*, 239. Rabbi Moshe (Maharam) Shick (1807–1879) suggested that lack of copying a responsum is evidence that the decision was valid only for that moment. See Shick, *Responsa*, OḤ:§152 (Muncacz, 1880), 50a. The opposing opinion is mentioned by Rabbi Klonimus Weiss in Rabbi Shlomo Tzvi b. Nathan Shick, *Responsa*, OḤ §145 (Muncacz, 1900), I:110b.
73. https://blog.hamapah.org/responsa/what-we-can-and-cant-learn-from-our-data-on-rav-moshe-feinstein/.
74. Berachyahu Lifshitz, "The Legal Status of the Responsa Literature," *Shenaton ha-Mishpat ha-Ivri* 9–10 (1982–1983): 265–300 [Hebrew]; "The Legal Status of the Responsa Literature," in *Authority, Process and Method, Studies in Jewish Law*, ed. H. Ben-Menahem and N. Hecht (Canberra, Australia: Harwood Academic, 1998), 59–100 [English version].
75. Jay Berkovitz, "Competing Perspectives on Legal Decision-making in Early Modern Ashkenaz," *Jewish History* 31 (2017): 154 n. 14; Jay Berkovitz, *Protocols of Justice* (Leiden, The Netherlands: Brill, 2014).
76. Moellin, *Responsa*, §193.
77. Edward Fram, *A Window on their World: The Court Diary of Rabbi Ḥayyim Gundersheim, Frankfurt am Main, 1773–1794* (Cincinnati: Hebrew Union College Press, 2012), 73 n. 285.
78. Eliav Shochetman, "The Obligation to State Reasons for Legal Decisions in Jewish Law," *Shenaton haMishpat haIvri* 6–7 (1979–1980): 338.
79. Moshe S. Bacharach, *Responsa Ḥut haShani* (Frankfurt am Main, 1699), §27.
80. See, for instance, the argument that the title *Nodah bi-Yehuda* ("famous in Judah") was deliberately chosen because its author was hoping to build a reputation with this responsa collection. Fischer makes this claim in "The Responsa Literature in Galicia and Bukovina," citing David Katz, "A Case Study in the Formation of a Super-rabbi: The Early Years of Rabbi Ezekiel Landau, 1713–1754." (PhD diss., University of Maryland, 2004), 497–508.
81. For an attempt to address this question empirically in the American law system, see Brian N. Larson, "Precedent as Rational Persuasion," *Legal Writing* 135 (2021): 135–212.
82. Berkovitz, "Competing Perspectives," 162.
83. Shochetman, "Obligation to State Reasons for Legal Decisions in Jewish Law," 347.
84. Menachem Elon, *Jewish Law: History, Sources, Principles* (Jerusalem: Magnes, 1973), 3:1485.
85. Hallaq, "From Fatwas to Furu," 35.
86. Barry Nicholas, *An Introduction to Roman Law* (1962; repr. (Oxford: Oxford University Press, 2008), 31–34.
87. Padoa-Schioppa, *History of Law*, 145 n. 34, referring to Luigi Lombardi, *Saggio sul diritto guirisprudenziale* (Milan: Giuffre, 1967).
88. On rabbis' status and responsa, see Lifshitz, "Legal Status," 265–300; and Lifshitz, "Chapters in the Legal Procedure of Jewish Law," *Leshonenu* 67 (2017): 268–98 [Hebrew]. See also Jay R. Berkovitz, "Competing Perspectives on Legal Decision Making in Early Modern Ashkenaz," in "New Perspectives on Jewish Legal History," special issue, *Jewish History* 31, nos. 1–2 (2017): 149–71.
89. Ḥayim b. Beẓalel of Friedberg, *Vikkuaḥ Mayim Ḥayim* (Amsterdam, 1722), 1b.
90. See Gerald Postema, "Law's System: The Necessity of System in Common Law," *New Zealand Law Review* no. 1 (2014), on kinds of system, and why structural/organizational systematicity does not necessarily contribute most to the rule of law; William Blackstone,

Commentaries on the Laws of England in Four Books (Philadelphia: J. B. Lippincott, 1753), I:§3.

See also Tamar Herzog, *A Short History of European Law* (Cambridge: Harvard University Press, 2018), 137–41; John P. Dawson, *The Oracles of Law* (Ann Arbor: University of Michigan Law School, 1968), 65–80; Margaret McGlynn, "Idiosyncratic Books and Common Learning Readings on Statutes at the Inns of Court," in *The Oxford Handbook of English Law and Literature, 1500–1700*, ed. Lorna Hutson (Oxford: Oxford University Press, 2017), 43–60.

91. Berachyahu Lifshitz, "Custom and Its Place in the History of the Oral Law," *Shenaton ha-Mishpat ha-Ivri* 24 (2006–2007): 123–64 [Hebrew].
92. Yosef Ibn Migash, *Responsa,* §114 (translation from Judeo-Arabic, Makhon Yerushalaim edition, ed. Nehorai Yosef Oḥana, 2017).
93. Moellin, *Responsa*, §72 (referencing R. Asher ben Yeḥiel's writings, discussed in detail later on). The term *poskim* is used here in the sense of a book (a collection of legal decisions).
94. Maoz Kahana, "The Chatam Sofer: A Decisor in His Own Eyes," *Tarbiz* 66, nos. 3–4 (2007): 541–55.
95. Rabbi Yonah Navon (Jerusalem, 1713–1760), *ShUT Neḥpah ba-kesef, Even ha-ezer*, §27.
96. Rabbi David ha-Levi Bamberger, in the responsa of Rabbi Naftali Ẓvi Yehuda Berlin (*Neẓiv*, 1816–1893), *ShUT Meshiv davar*, Oraḥ ḥayim, §24, cited in Kahana, *Meḥkarim*, 10
97. Shabtai ha-Kohen, *Siftei kohen* on *Yoreh de'ah* §196:1, 20; David ha-Levi, *Turei zahav* on *Yoreh de'ah* §328:2; Yoel Sirkis, *Bait ḥadash* on *Yoreh de'ah* §196.
98. Karo, *Beit Yosef, Tur Oraḥ ḥayim*, §263:16.
99. Rabbi Yosef Di Trani, *ShUT Morenu ha-Rav Yosef mi-Trani*, I: *Ḥoshen mishpat*, §7.
100. Di Trani, *ShUT Morenu*, I: *Ḥoshen mishpat*, §7.
101. Ḥayim Benvenisti in *ShUT Ba'ei ḥayei*, 1: *Ḥoshen mishpat*, §61.
102. Meir Rafeld, "The Halakha Follows the Later Sages," *Sidra: A Journal for the Study of Rabbinic Literature* 8 (1992): 119–40 [Hebrew]; Israel Ta-Shma, "The Law Is Like the Later Authorities: Historical Aspects of a Legal Principle," *Shenaton ha-mishpat ha-ivri* (1979): 405–23 [Hebrew]; Israel I. Yuval, "Rishonim and Aḥaronim, *Antiqui et Moderni*: Periodization and Self-Awareness in Ashkenaz," *Zion* 57, no. 4 (1992): 369–94 [Hebrew]. Shay Wozner, "Hilkheta ke-Batra'i: A New Perspective," *Shenaton ha-Mishpat ha-Ivri* (1995): 151–67 [Hebrew]; among others.
103. Colon, *Responsa*, § 94.
104. On this dynamic, see my article: Tamara Morsel-Eisenberg, "Anxieties of Transmission," *Journal for the History of Ideas* 82, no. 3 (2021): 377–404.
105. All the works R. Isserles names there are indeed responsa. Isserles, *Darkhei Moshe*, introduction (emphasis mine): "when others came with hidden scrolls and showed from the responsa of the sages after whom we follow."
106. Glick, *Kuntres*, 1:9 n. 333.
107. Roger Berkowitz, *The Gift of Science: Leibniz and the Modern Legal Tradition* (Cambridge: Harvard University Press, 2005); Richard A. Danner, "Writings on the Form and Structure of Published Law," in *Legal Information and the Development of American Law*, ed. Richard A. Danner and Frank G. Houdek (St. Paul, MN: Thomson/West, 2008).
108. See Postema, "Law's System."
109. Menachem Elon, *Jewish Law: History, Sources, Principles* (Jerusalem: Magnes, 1973), 3:1485.
110. See Elon's seven-volume *Digest of Responsa Literature by the Sages of Sepharad and North Africa*, [Hebrew] ed. Menachem Elon (Jerusalem: The Institute for *Mishpat ivri*,

1981–1987) and *Digest of Responsa by the sages of Ashkenaz, France, and Italy*, ed. Eliav Shoḥetman and Berachyahu Lifshitz (Jerusalem: The Institute for *Mishpat ivri*, 1997).

For a description of Elon's enterprise and the place of responsa therein, see Aryeh Edrei, "Menachem Elon and Misphat Ivri: Milestones," in *Studies in Law and Halakhah: Menachem Elon Memorial Volume* [Hebrew]; eds. Arye Edrei, David Gliksberg, Aviad haCohen, Berachyahu Lifschutz, and Benjamin Porat (Zafririm: Nevo, 2018), 13–23. (Specifically, on responsa, 18–20.)

111. Ann Blair, *Too Much to Know: Managing Scholarly Information before the Modern Age* (New Haven, CT: Yale University Press, 2010).
112. See Ephraim E. Urbach, "The Responsa of Rosh in Manuscripts and Printed Books," *Shenaton ha-mishpat ha-ivri* 2 (1975): 1–153 [Hebrew].

     Judah D. Galinsky, "Ashkenazim in Sefarad: The ROSh and the Tur on the Codification of Jewish Law," *Jewish Law Annual* 16 (2006): 3–23.
113. Edward Fram, "On the Order of the Responsa in the Printed Edition of *Terumat ha-Deshen*," *Ale sefer* 20 (2008): 81–96 [Hebrew]; Pinchas Roth, "The Missing Entry in the Book *Terumat ha-Deshen*," *Ale Sefer* 21 (2010): 179–81.
114. Nissim Gerondi, *Responsa* (Rome, 1545), introduction. Translation taken from Cooperman, "Organizing Knowledge," 39.
115. Elon, *Jewish Law*, 3:1522–23. Elon mentions the *Turim* alongside *Shulḥan Arukh*. He means the *printing* of these works, not their manuscript publication, as the fourteenth-century *Turim* preceded the change that Elon mentions. The nineteenth-century Rabbi Avraham Ẓvi Eisenstadt created *Pitḥei teshuva* (Vilna, 1836; Lemberg, 1876), a finding aid for the *Shulḥan Arukh*, which inserted *halakhic* conclusions of almost two hundred works of responsa in their correct location in the code.
116. Ḥayim Mordehkai Margoliouth, *Sha'arei Teshuva* on *Orakh Ḥayim* (Dubno, 1820); Avraham Ẓvi Hirsch Eisenstadt, *Pitḥei Teshuva* on *Yoreh De'ah* (Vilna, 1836), on *Even ha'Ezer* (Johannesburg, 1861) and on *Ḥoshen Mishpat* (Vilna, 1871).
117. Bacharach, *Ḥavot Yair* (Frankfurt am Main, 1699), 255a.
118. Asher Weiss, *Responsa Minḥat Asher*, part I (Jerusalem, 2013), 1–386, divided according to the *Shulḥan Arukh*'s sections, versus 393–413, eight additional responsa under the header "halakha and medicine."
119. Isserles, *ShUT Rema*, §125.
120. Isserles, *Mapah* on *Shulḥan Arukh, OḤ*, §339:4.
121. Thomas Kuehn, "The Renaissance Consilium as Justice," *Renaissance Quarterly* 59 no. 4 (2006): 1058–88. On a similar tension between R. Isserles's responsa and his code, see Saul Berman, *Boundaries of Loyalty: Testimony Against Fellow Jews in Non-Jewish Courts* (New York: Cambridge University Press, 2016), 176–81.
122. John Forrester, "If P, Then What? Thinking in Cases," *History of the Human Sciences* 9 (1996): 1–25.
123. Ephraim Oshri, *Responsa from the Depths* (New York: Modern Line-type Camp, 1959) [Hebrew]; Asher Weiss, *Minḥat Asher: A Compilation of Lessons, Responsa, Letters, and Articles Related to the Corona Epidemic* (Yerushalaim: Makhon Minḥat Asher, 2020) [Hebrew]; Shlomo Zalman Auerbach, *Minḥat Shelomo* (Jerusalem: Makhon Sha'arei Ziv, 1999), vol. 2, §27 [Hebrew]; Eliezer Yehuda Waldenberg, *Tzitz Eliezer* (Jerusalem: Hamul, 1983), vol. 15 §45 [Hebrew].
124. Nils Jansen, *The Making of Legal Authority: Non-Legislative Codifications in Historical and Comparative Perspective* (Oxford: Oxford University Press, 2010).

125. Oscar Schachter, "The Invisible College of International Lawyers," *Northwestern University Law Review* 72, no. 2 (1977): 217–66.
126. Robert C. Berring, "Legal Research and the World of Thinkable Thoughts," *Journal of Appellate Practice and Process* 2 (2000): 305–18.
127. Peter Burke, *A Social History of Knowledge: From the Encyclopedia to Wikipedia* (Cambridge: Polity Press, 2012), 56.

CHAPTER 8

RENDERING THE INFINITE

Law, Meaning, and Ritual in Classical and Early Modern Jewish Mysticism

ARIEL EVAN MAYSE

Introduction

THE many reflections on the nature and purpose of *halakhah* found in Jewish mystical sources are not immediately comprehensible to lawyers or members of the legal academy today.[1] These religious sources rest upon bedrock of assumptions about world, text, tradition, sociopolitical organization, and human subjectivity that differ profoundly from those undergirding Western jurisprudence. The very notion that a legal system dealing with the stuff of crimes, contracts, and torts could be described as religious, Divine, or spiritually significant is far removed from contemporary discourse. But these quotidian elements are key to the commandments (*mitzvot*) of classical rabbinic Judaism, which represent holistic patterns of ritual and daily practice. Reflections on the purpose of these obligations rest at the heart of Kabbalah, a cluster of esoteric teachings that emerged in medieval Provence and Spain, and in Hasidism, a pietistic movement of spiritual renewal that drew on Kabbalah and swept across eastern Europe in the late eighteenth century. These mystics refer to *halakhah* as a system of divinely revealed norms, assigning vast cosmic and personal significance to the *mitzvot*.[2] Law moves the universe, they argue, because these actions reveal God's presence and heal fractures within the Divine.[3] At the same time, Jewish mystics made a counterintuitive claim: the divinity of their law is expressed in *halakhah*'s dynamism and constant evolution rather than its static immutability.[4]

The present chapter focuses on two interrelated themes that can shed light on the religious dimensions of Jewish law. First, I examine how these sources describe the origin and aim of the *mitzvot*, considering which features make *halakhah* "Divine" in their eyes. Second, I turn to kabbalistic and Hasidic depictions of legal evolution and their attempts to grapple with the diversity of rulings and opinions. If, as these mystical thinkers insisted, *halakhah* is the word of God revealed at Sinai and faithfully transmitted from Moses down to his rabbinic successors, why has it transformed dramatically over time and how can there be so many disagreements about its proper execution? How can mystical theology explain why scholars and jurists come to different conclusions when presented with the same precedential materials and fact patterns? In both domains we shall see that kabbalistic and Hasidic teachings offer an alternative to the understandings of law presented by those who separate law from morality, or, in the religious context, who seek to divide spiritual experience from the formulation and practice of law.

These sources consistently refer to *halakhah* as unfolding diversely through legislation, interpretation, and adaptive or situational application. Jewish mystics were grappling with a textural feature of the Jewish legal tradition, one in which disagreement (called *mahloket*) is necessary and essential rather than the result of competing interests or commitments.[5] It is striking, then, that their reflections on continuous interpretative creativity were rarely translated into major shifts in the way Jewish law was actually practiced. The zones of disagreement between the mystical thinkers and their opponents were relatively minor, although even slight changes to communal custom regarding liturgy, ritual slaughter, and so forth were considered significant by all parties. The horizons of kabbalistic and mystical innovation were confined by many factors: social norms and convention, intellectual opposition, and, perhaps most importantly, their internal commitment to normative Jewish practice.

Jewish mystical texts also suggest that law ought to be interpreted, formulated, and applied independent of purely legal considerations, placing these writers close to legal realists like Karl Llewellyn and Jerome Frank.[6] To be sure, the Kabbalists did not claim *halakhah* to be an empirical science or logical discourse; the commandments emerge from Divine sovereign and do not need to conform to human rationality. Unlike Hobbes, Locke, or Rousseau (and the contemporary orientations that emerge from their works), Jewish mystics do not see law as preserving social order or individual rights: they portray *halakhah* as a transformative and cosmically significant form of action. Hence, Jewish mystical writings offer an alternative to essentially all forms of contemporary legal thought: strict construction, liberal construction, legal positivism, legal formalism, and even legal realism. Though they share some superficial similarities with the latter, Jewish mystics come at the issue from a very different lens, grounded in a piety that transmutes legal decision-making from the realm of the political and social into the spiritual.

Origins and Aims of the Law

Classical Jewish sources suggest that *halakhah*, rooted in the written Torah and developed by the oral Torah, was revealed in some form to the Jewish people at Sinai (see

Lifshitz, this volume).[7] Mystical sources go further in describing this as an act Divine self-disclosure, a moment in which God's will emerged from silence and became clothed in the mantle of human language. This attempt to anchor Jewish law in God's personal revelation affords these precepts a sense of gravitas, timelessness, and transcendence. "The 613 commandments were emanated from the blessed divine essence," claimed one eighteenth-century Hasidic scholar. "God is eternal and exists forever, spanning past, present and future, and so, too, God's commandments are eternal."[8] Scripture, too, is far more than a book of narrative and rituals; the Torah, and the legal system to which it gave rise, both discloses—and conceals—God's Divine self. The legal scholar Arthur J. Jacobson described religious law as duties made known to a community of commanded subjects through a process of revelation that entails more than the transfer of knowledge. In bestowing statutes and prohibitions, claimed Jacobson, "God necessarily reveals a personality."[9] This holds implications for the law's execution as well as its origin. "Persons do not obey law so much as they reenact revelation," claims Jacobson. "By obeying law they walk with God."[10] Similarly, Jewish mystics recast the commandments as the obligations through which one recounts the moment of Sinai and experiences God's presence.

Kabbalists describe God as simultaneously transcendent and immanent, possessing both female and male qualities. This paradoxical combination is justified by recourse to the *sefirot*, a set of ten emanations that bridge between the unknowable *Ein Sof*, the "endless" or "limitless One," and the immanent or worldly manifestations of God's presence. These emanations are part of God, yet they are susceptible to human action; at present, they are said to be disconnected and damaged and thus in need of repair through the *mitzvot*. Because these legal precepts are rooted in Scripture and in God's self, performing the law ensures the flow of blessing into the cosmos.[11] "All the commandments are connected to the divine structure," claimed Me'ir ibn Gabbai, a prominent sixteenth-century Kabbalist. "The 613 commandments are connected to the Ten Commandments, the ten *sefirot*, roots from which all [other] commandments branch forth."[12] Jewish mystics thus refer to performing the *mitzvot* to fulfill a "divine need," uniting the *sefirot* and healing the fractured or defiled world.[13] The Kabbalists claim this extraordinary power for every facet of the law. "There is no part or whole from among the *mitzvot*," argued Meir ibn Gabbai, "that is not intended for the purpose of the soul's felicity and unifying God."[14] All elements of *halakhah*, from prayer and sacred study to torts and contract negotiation, are tools in this religious project.[15]

These mystics acknowledged that *halakhah*'s authority rests in God's absolute sovereignty, but they generally rejected the notion that the *mitzvot* should be treated as decrees that lack any reasons. Like many post-biblical Jewish thinkers, they ascribed "rationales" or "reasons" to each of the biblical and rabbinic commandments (called *ta'amei ha-mitzvot*). The famed Nahmanides, a thirteenth-century kabbalist and jurist, argued that every commandment holds a vast array of "purposes" (*to'elot*) that shape one's body and soul.[16] Shlomo ben Aderet, his intellectual descendant, suggested that these reasons are "endless" (*ein sof*) and inexhaustible; each particular rationale is but "a drop among the aims and intentions" of each commandment.[17] These rationales for God's law are often hidden, however, even from the most assiduous scholars.[18] This conception of seeking to understand the law's true intent shares something with contemporary secular notions of originalism, but with an important distinction: as in living constitutionalism, kabbalistic texts charge human interpreters with actively developing—sometimes described as "uncovering"—*new* or innovative explanations for those ancient laws.

The commandments are said to do far more than stabilize society and bring human culture into alignment with God's will. *Halakhah* heals intradivine fracture while refining body and soul, and thus every detailed aspect of the law is critical: "If one omits even a single commandment of Torah, one inflicts a defect where there must be none . . . Scripture's precepts enable one to complete spirit and soul in this world and in the world that is coming."[19] Every *mitzvah* transforms the body into a dwelling place for God, purifying the human form of its coarse materiality and healing Divine.[20] Here, too, we see the vast gulf that separates Western conceptions of law and the descriptions of self-transformation and theurgy, the capacity of human action to impact God, commonly found in kabbalistic sources.

These reflections on the interrelationship of law and cosmos took an experiential turn in eighteenth-century Hasidism, where *halakhah* was generally described as the obligations and duties by which the worshipper becomes bound to the Divine.[21] Hasidic sources often homiletically link the word *mitzvah* with the term *tzavta*, "connection" or "togetherness," a fanciful interpretation that highlights their power bind one to God.[22] Ya'akov Yosef ben Yehudah of Ostrog (1738–1790) argued that intention and commitment turn the *mitzvot* into technologies for experiencing the majesty of an otherwise hidden God. "God and Torah are one; by studying Torah and doing commandments both in deed and in desire of the heart, you draw Shekhinah [i.e., the divine Presence] upon yourself. . . . The commandments are the visitations (*pikudim*) of God."[23] Such actions, claimed Ya'akov Yosef, stitch the fabric of God's Presence into an mythic "tabernacle" (*mishkan*) composed of world, body, and self. Rather than limiting this dynamic to biblical commandments, he expanded this connective power to the totality of *halakhah* and Jewish ritual including rabbinic rules rooted in tradition or exegesis as well as later customs.

Classical Kabbalists assigned a unique purpose to each commandment or law.[24] These precepts are often described as a single integrated framework; "a single knot, for one [*mitzvah*] cannot exist without the other, much like a woven garment in which each and every thread is connected to and sustained by its neighbor."[25] This presentation of the *mitzvot* differed significantly from rationalist jurists such as Maimonides, who understood specific commandments as means to specified ends (i.e. imparting virtue, shaping correct belief, creating a stable society). One cryptic passage in Maimonides's *Commentary to the Mishnah* suggests that there is but one aim for all commandments—achieving life in the World to Come—and that this single goal may be reached through any *mitzvah* if it is executed for its own sake and out of love for God.[26] While Maimonides left the notion of a unified aim for the *mitzvot* by the wayside, not including it in his systematic restatement of rabbinic law, countless versions of his teaching tradition are variously quoted by innumerable Hasidic sources. While Maimonides may have assumed a very different view of the purpose of the *mitzvot*, this did not preclude Hasidic teachings from reinterpreting his writings toward their own view. They argued that the single goal to which all *mitzvot* incline is the experiential and emotional bond of communion with God (called *devekut*):

> Because each of the commandments contains all 613 commandments within it. In doing a single *mitzvah*, you are doing all 613 . . . I have seen commentators say in the name of Maimonides that it is only when you perform the *mitzvah* in joy that all 613 are included within it . . . Now "prayer without inner direction is like a body without a soul." The letters of Torah and prayer, as well as the fulfilled commandment, are all the body; the soul is the inner direction and joyous thought you have in doing your Maker's will.[27]

Uziel Meisels, the author of this text, argues that worshippers can attain the goal of the *mitzvot* by correctly executing even a single precept. Every commandment is connected to the others, and within the system of praxis, these actions function as a collective gateway into God's presence. But this power is inaccessible to one observing the commandments as an oppressive yoke and without inward intention, since, just as the soul unifies and animates the physical body, the worshipper's joyous interiority vitalizes that commandment's external form: "In the joyous thought of fulfilling God's commandment they are all one," he claimed. "They are united in the oneness of the Creator."[28] This devotional élan of a single *mitzvah* can propel the worshipper toward the Divine unity undergirding this vast web of seemingly isolated actions. In a sense, then, Hasidic teachings share Maimonides's utilitarian reading of the commandments and represent a staggering rupture with the Kabbalists and their *taamei ha-mitzvot* which traced the specific meaning of each and every detail of the *halakhah*.

Hasidic sources mitigate the particularity of various commandments, reminding us of the need to stretch for a broader, more expansive conception of law when considering religious sources. It would be foolish to suggest that one can reach the telos of American common law, if one can even speak of such a thing, by obeying a single federal law or state regulation. If one observes traffic laws, may one steal with impunity? Similarly, in the kingdom of *halakhah*, one cannot eat non-kosher food simply because one keeps the Sabbath; the commandments stand as independent obligations that cannot be exchanged or traded. Yet Hasidic teachings, reinterpreting the words of Maimonides, suggest that within each *mitzvah* the experiential aim of Jewish ritual can be attained in all its fullness. These processes of religious distillation, as vast networks of ideas and practices are reduced to a single burst of religious intensity, exist alongside a total commitment to *halakhah*, but Hasidic sources daringly suggest that the theurgic, cosmic, and existential goals of such religious law can be achieved through a single moment of illuminated praxis.

Legal Evolution

Spiritual reflections on the law's purpose were rarely translated into practical jurisprudence, and the impact of kabbalistic doctrine or custom on normative legal scholarship was fraught—even for these mystics.[29] While they emphasized interpretative creativity, they did not significantly alter the norms of Jewish practice. The mismatch between a practical conservatism and the potentially radical Hassidic constitutional theologies marks another key difference between *halakhah* and American law. Nevertheless, as Kabbalistic and Hasidic scholars were aware that Jewish law has changed significantly over time, they sought to conceptualize these shifts and understand why *halakhah* evolves, despite the fact that it comes entirely from God. Along the same lines, they grappled with the fact that different Sages or legal adjudicators offered divergent—even mutually exclusive opinions—based on similar cases or precedents.[30] Modern legal scholarship explores the political, intellectual, and social differences reflected in divergent formulations of the law, but Hasidic and kabbalistic sources see disagreement as essential to the nature of Jewish law.

Mystical thinkers claim that legal transformation is both possible and laudable precisely because the *mitzvot* are part of the ever-unfolding Divine will and founded in God's personhood rather than the immutable manifestation of static Divine reason often ascribed to Divine law.[31] To employ the frame of Karl N. Llewellyn, a prominent American legal scholar associated with legal realism, Jewish mystics sought to understand how the Jewish canon includes both sides of a series of contested values. Rather than seeking to conform to some abstract notion of an ideal *halakhah*, they were interested, in Llewellyn's words, in "the sense which *can be quarried out of it* in the light of the new situation."[32] The law's divinity is manifest in its living vitality as a body of sacred legislation that is constantly being revised, reapplied, and reinterpreted.

Here the Jewish mystics built upon an ethos of legal flexibility, found already in the Hebrew Bible and receiving fuller treatment in the many Talmudic and Midrashic passages which speak to issues of innovation and human interpretative agency.[33] This emphasis on the creative license of legal scholars is complemented, and complicated, by an important strain of pluralism within Jewish literature best expressed by the Talmudic dictum: "these and those are the words of the living God."[34] This statement allows two different legal positions to be verified as expressions of the Divine word, even if only one of them defines normative practice.[35] Another tradition claims that even opposing rulings, both those that permit something and those that prohibit it, were given to Israel by God.[36] There are said to be forty-nine reasons to permit each thing, but also forty-nine reasons to prohibit it.[37] Not only were opposite rulings given on certain issues, but God layered the opposing views directly into the system regarding every point of law. Llewellyn stressed the rhetoric rather than the substantive nature of this dialectic, but Jewish legal sources offer a framework for conceptualizing dramatic shifts in the legal praxis.

Questions of interpretative freedom and restraint arose in the constant push between traditions of summarizing codification and dialectic interpretations that have long characterized Jewish jurisprudence, a long-standing dialectic to which Jewish mystics contributed significantly.[38] Legal codes generally seek to curtail creativity by establishing norms that are universal, abstract, and hence often at variance with local practice or custom. Beginning in the rabbinic period and continuing into the present day, attempts by Jewish scholars to systematize and to standardize a normative *halakhah* were often met with criticism and challenged by commentaries or the situationally determined rulings found in responsa.[39] In justifying their efforts, many authors of Jewish codes attempted to explain why *halakhah* has changed over time. Ya'akov ben Asher (d. *c.* 1340), author of the famed code *Arba'ah Turim*, claimed that he sought to clarify the many doubts that had arisen regarding the proper modes of Jewish conduct.[40] Ben Asher represents a line of thinking which assumes that the revelation at Sinai contained every detail of *halakhah*; disagreement or controversy represents a breakdown in transmission introduced by negligence, and scholars must work toward restoring that pristine ideal.[41] Other scholars like Maimonides, took a minimalist approach, suggesting that only a small number of laws were issued at Sinai. Later Sages used logic, inference, and exegesis to develop this kernel into a full—and divergent—set of norms. The aim of his *Mishneh Torah*, the chef-d'œuvre of Jewish codes, was to clarify, unify, and arrange the laws that were rooted in Divine revelation but augmented and expanded by human interpretation.[42]

A particularly important source for Kabbalistic understandings of the counter-positioning riven into Jewish law was authored by Yom Tom Assevilli (Ritva), a noted Kabbalist in the school of Nahmanides who flourished in Barcelona and Saragossa in the thirteenth and fourteenth centuries.[43] Asked by the Sages of France to explain why Jewish legal works include contradictory opinions, Assevilli argued:

> Moses ascended to receive the Torah, seeing the forty-nine faces of impurity and forty-nine faces of purity for every issue. This matter was given over to the sages of each and every generation; the decisions ought to follow their [rulings]. This is correct according to the homiletical interpretation—and, according to the way of truth, there is an [even] deeper secret in this matter.[44]

Perhaps alluding to kabbalistic portrayals of a mythic God whose revelation of law is never-ending, Assevilli underscored the necessity of judicial discretion in reforming *halakhah*. He argued that scholars in every age ought render their own judgment by "quarrying" some new possible meaning from the inexhaustible store of Divine revelation.

Jewish mystical thinkers generally approached legal change neither as the result of forgetfulness nor as the inevitable drift of human interpretative efforts, but as a natural feature of a system of law given by—and rooted in—an ever-dynamic God. The thirteenth-century Moses de Leon, for example, refers to divergent opinions as being refracted through the matrix of the *sefirot* and grounded in the multivocal revelation at Sinai.[45] Many suggested that the Torah and its laws have taken on different forms in various historical periods, as divergent legal interpretations are drawn from the endless possibility.[46] Each form of practice and law thus represents the continuing echo of Sinai, an ongoing revelation of Divine law that changes across the generations:

> That font [of revelation] is the source from which [the law] flows endlessly . . . giving rise to all the different and opposite rulings, the faces [of law] that change and shift, to render impure or pure, to forbid or to permit, to rule as unfit or fit, as is known to scholars of tradition. The mighty voice [of revelation] never ended; it is [still] drawn from that place and surges forth from it, including within it all those different [opinions].[47]

The continuous movement of Jewish legal discourse is rooted in the experience of Sinai, developed throughout the ages as human scholars continue the work of revelation through interpretation. Opposing legal rulings are all rooted in that deeper realm of Divine wisdom in which mutually exclusive legal rulings can coexist.[48] While these potential opinions cannot all be manifest or enacted into legislation at the same time, the corpus of Jewish legal thought includes multitudes and can take different shapes and forms across the generations.

Questions about the processes through which *halakhah* may shift feature prominently in early Hasidism, much as this spiritual movement was concerned with issues of renewal. They appear, for example, in the sermons of Rabbi Dov Ber Friedman, an important Hasidic figure better known as the *Maggid* or "Preacher" of Mezritsh (d. 1772). One sermon begins with the classic disagreement between Beit Hillel and Beit Shammai over whether or not an egg laid on a Jewish holiday may be eaten on that same day.[49] He explains that their lack of consensus in this specific case is the key to understanding a broader phenomenon:

> "These and those are the words of the living God," both those that forbid and those that permit.[50] "With knowledge (*da'at*) chambers are filled" [Proverbs 24:4]. All of the [divine] attributes come from [God's] mind (*da'at*). . . . Each person draws forth [a ruling] from Mind, combining the words in this way or that. This one draws love from *da'at*, meaning that the egg is permitted. Another draws awe from *da'at*, and the egg is forbidden.[51] When one wants to change the halakhah, like Rabbi Joshua, who said that "we pay no attention to a heavenly voice,"[52] one returns the ruling to the attribute of Mind from there draws it forth through a different attribute. The enlightened will understand.
>
> Another explanation of "these and those are the words of the living God." The oral Torah is the adornments of the bride. One person says that the adornment must be like this, and another says that this is not so pleasing, and another way is more beautiful. The king receives great pleasure in their disagreement over the adornments, since both of them wish to adorn the king.[53]

In God's mind the law is yet unformed and exists as pure potential without precise stipulations. Human scholars must work to decide the practical application of the *halakhah* by drawing upon this reservoir of latent possibility, purposefully refracting the ruling through certain Divine attributes (*sefirot*) to reach a particular conclusion. Each position taken by various judges are the "words of the living God" since each is an authentic manifestation of the different potentialities included in God's mind.

But Friedman also claims, perhaps even prescriptively, that any rulings can be overturned by returning it to its ultimate source in the Divine mind, where the various other possibilities remain eternally valid and intact. The jurist may thus manifest a different legal decision as required by the hour. The seven lower *sefirot*, reservoirs of Divine energy here called "chambers," that emerge from God's mind are filled with Divine knowledge through human legal scholarship. His sermon builds on the kabbalistic geography of the Divine superstructure, but in this case, Friedman is also referring to the correlate elements of the human psyche. *Da'at* refers to both the infinite pool of potential legal rulings as well as the mystical interior connection to the Divine mind.[54] Retracing a particular judicial decision into this abstract realm, claims Friedman, is comparable to revelation because new law is legislated in the process.

This teaching may be read as suggesting that scholars possess a legal intuition that determines their vision of the law, perhaps akin to the intellectual or political commitments that govern Western jurisprudence, though often in subtle and unacknowledged ways. But Friedman may have been describing something even more radical: the intentional process of decision-making through which judges actively seek to change the law by drawing out or "quarrying" new legal possibilities from amid the multiple possibilities expressed within the legal canon. In the Maggid's religious framework, this is described as tapping into the unformed potential of God's mind. Secular legal scholars might describe this process as aligning one's ruling with the law's or the framer's original intent, or, through the lens of legal realism, as a demonstration of the flexibility of jurisprudential interpretation. Though its adherents ardently deny it, in both originalist and realist legal thinking the judge must look beyond the law as it has been applied and seek to understand the moral, philosophical, or other ideational commitments that undergird it.

We lack the textual evidence to see if such conceptualizations may have affected Friedman's legal rulings, but his teaching provides an interesting mystical justification for why different scholars will reach different verdicts when confronted by the same facts.[55] The rabbinic tale of the "oven of Akhnai," to which Friedman refers, is a tale in which two Sages argue over using Divine inspiration as legal authority. In that Talmudic tale, the heavenly voice is said to broadcast the current version of the *halakhah*, which accords with opinion of Rabbi Eliezer, but Rabbi Joshua reaches a different conclusion and, ignoring the Divine judgment, changes the law to accord with his own ideal. This rabbinic story famously emphasizes the importance of human agency in determining the *halakhah*, but Friedman's reading of Rabbi Joshua as deliberately rejecting the heavenly voice to alter the law is a fascinating interpretation, and not at all the obvious meaning of the Talmudic passage.

Friedman's second reading of "these and those are the words of the living God" differs markedly from the explanation that immediately precedes it. Kabbalistic sources often play on the similarity between the words *kallah* ("bride") and *halakhah* ("law"), describing innovative legal interpretations as "adornments of the Bride" [i.e., Shekhinah]. Friedman suggests that, much like standards of beauty, creative legal rulings have an inherently subjective dimension.[56] He illustrates this point with a parable of two Sages who disagree over which version of the law is most fitting for the king (surely referring to God, the King of kings in Jewish literature). But it is striking that neither scholar justifies their position as being the more rationally or logically compelling argument. The validity—or authority—of a line of legal reasoning is grounded instead in its aesthetic power and perhaps even in its rhetorical heft.

This suggests that even diametrically opposed decisions about points of *halakhah* bring God joy, as does the process of earnest legal argumentation. Each decision is appealing in the eye of the beholder and pleasing to the Divine, even if they are mutually exclusive. We should note that this embrace of legal dispute motivated by a good-faith desire to do what the scholar believes to be right in the eyes of God is quite different than the legal realist's view of law as an exercise of political power and discretion. As a non-state system, *halakhah* can sustain a divergence of practice and interpretation precisely because questions of fairness, uniformity, and governance are not at its center. At the same time, Friedman's framework shares the legal realist's commitment to legal argumentation as subjective, situational, and interpretative.[57]

Perhaps the aesthetic analogy to sartorial ornaments is to be taken less literally, since surely each proponent must have their own legal reasons (or precedent) in addition to a perception that their interpretations are more beautiful. Pure subjectivity, after all, is not integrity. Legal aesthetics may have its own inner logic and rules which define the nature of beauty, though such standards are surely flexible and inclusive of a great range of possibilities. Friedman describes God as delighting in the multiplicity, suggesting that the Divine has no interest in a legal system that is monochromatic, homogeneous, or resistant to change across the generations. The novelty Friedman's affective, subjective theory of law is thrown into relief when compared to a non-Hasidic source (printed *c.* 1800), that engages with similar questions from a strikingly different conceptional framework:

> No commandment is [fully] explicated in the Torah along with all of the details by which it is to be performed. Therefore, disagreements abound among the early rabbinic sages, and in every generation new responsa (*she'elot u-teshovut*) are generated [to address these ambiguities or new concerns]. But the sages of each generation disagree, for how are we to know God's mind, knowing how to act? . . . Pride may cause scholars to clarify the law out of a desire to defeat others. . . and they err in judgment. . . . But if they fear God . . . the blessed Holy One's mind is revealed to them.[58]

Eliezer Lipman, the author of this source, agrees with Friedman in describing *halakhah* as evolving through constant reinterpretation. No code of religious law can be exhaustive in spelling out the myriad details of *halakhah.* The particulars are threshed out as new cases arise and judges apply their mind to seeing how the ancient law might work in their present situation. But Lipman is adamant that God's will may only be discovered through fearful piety, whereas the Maggid's view of law empowers scholars to rule by tracing the law back to its origins in God and then reformulating the law in light of their own subjective consideration and commitments.

Community, Authority, and Change

Western legal theorists generally split over the degree to which a judge's personal intellectual or ideological commitments can—or should—factor into their ruling on a particular case. Some acknowledge that individual or interpretative factors ought to shape one's application of the law's ideals; they claim that judges rule in accord with their political interest or, structure legal doctrine to enable or restrict outcomes consistent with their political alignments. Other scholars depict the consummate legal authority as one whose dispassionate expertise enables them to determine the correct course of action. Both types of judges are sometimes accused of encoding their contested worldviews, into the law perhaps deciding issues judicially that might better be determined through the political process.

It is noteworthy, then, that Jewish mystical sources offer a surprising array of teachings on the subjective aesthetics of legal scholarship or decision-making as well as the diachronic transformation of *halakhah* across generations said to reflect the different "soul-roots" of the law's mystical adjudicators. For example, one of Friedman's teachings offers a creative reinterpretation of Exodus 23:2, long cited in Jewish legal texts as mandating the principle of majority rule,[59] and suggests that the *halakhah* must follow the strongest *sefirot*. He portrays the biblical King David as the ideal adjudicator whose rulings are indeed based on the cosmic root of his individual soul.[60] King David (*David ha-Melekh*) was the embodiment of *malkhut*, the last of the ten *sefirot* and the receptive pool into which all cosmic vitality flows. He was uniquely able to grasp the vast possibilities of the law and to choose among them and rule in accord with the particular situational needs of the hour:

> It is written, "incline after the majority" (Ex. 23:2), meaning whatever the preponderance may be, whether for kindness (*hesed*), strict judgment (*din*),or compassion (*rahamim*), which mediates [between them]. Whatever it may be, this is called "inclining after the majority."... although the other [opinions] are also the "words of the living God," they are subsumed within the majority. King David came from the attribute of *malkhut*, where everything is included and things reach completion.
>
> Thus, David could align the law and decide the tradition according to the [ideal] *halakhah*. This attribute is called *halakhah*, since it is the conclusion of all the "cosmic ways" (*halikhot olam*; Hab. 3:6) ... *Malkhut* is also called the oral Torah ... and the

> *halakhah* follows whichever attribute is victorious above. [David] aligned the truth in accord with how it concluded above in the root of his soul.[61]

The scholar charged with adjudicating the way he has to be attentive to cosmic processes, for the practice that is to become the legal norm is the result of the interface (*halikhot*) between the *sefirot*. King David's legal prowess seems to be based on his metaphysical investigation—which would seem to leave far less room for personal autonomy in deciding the *halakhah* than the teaching cited above. But Friedman adds another important piece to the puzzle by explaining that the root of a judge's soul is the lens that governs his internal process of deliberation, even determining the outcome of the decision-making process.[62] The biblical monarch is the ideal legal Sage because he embodied *malkhut* and was attuned to cosmic processes. His legal decisions reflect the way the *halakhah* had already been determined on high, and while both Saul's and David's rulings are the "words of the living God," only the latter was attuned to the higher legal truth.[63]

In the American legal tradition, law is restored to its origins for many reasons: to correct mistakes in interpretation along the way, to countermand modern developments that may deviate from the original meaning, or to apply the original meaning to new circumstances. The conception of *halakhah* advanced by Friedman here seems to align more closely with the idea that courts should interpret the original intent of a statute rather than flexibly reinterpreting its many dynamic and potential meanings. There appears to be an ultimate legal truth beyond the subjective decision of the individual scholar; this stance differs markedly from that of contemporary realists, but it also contradicts Friedman's own portrayal the judge proactively change the *halakhah* by "returning" the ruling to its origin and drawing forth another possibility. The present teaching suggests something akin to originalism, in that courts or judges should revisit both past precedent and the literal language of a law if there are mistakes or if the prevailing conception of that law does not accord with the intent with which it was originally drafted. But Friedman's mechanism for restoration is quite different: the proper *halakhah* is determined not by the scholar's logic, but through his perception—or perhaps better, his intuition, described as "the root of his soul"—regarding how the matter has already been decided above.[64] Perhaps Friedman meant that a Sage's legal reasoning would instinctively lead in that direction, such that ruling in accordance with the heavenly *halakhah* is not inherently inconsistent with the notion that the law can also be transformed. This approach supposes something close to originalism, with King David intuiting the mind of God much as contemporary judges recall the public meaning of the laws established by the founders and framers of the Constitution.

Theoretical interest in the interface of legal change and personal authority abounds in the works of early Hasidic leaders. All of the movement's charismatic and spiritual teachers were much concerned with the idea of religious law, but some of the most daring Hasidic reflections on legal reasoning and divergence were delivered by figures who served as community rabbis, judges, heads of rabbinic academies, and authors of legal texts and responsa. Levi Yitzhak of Barditshev, a well-regarded rabbinic scholar as well as a Hasidic teacher, addressed the subjective elements of legal decision-making quite openly:

> Regarding the disagreement between Beit Shammai and Beit Hillel, we have said that, "these and those are the words of the living God."[65] A person understands the plain-sense meaning of the holy Torah according to his own attribute (*behinah*). If he comes from the world of kindness [i.e., the *sefirah hesed*], everything is ritually pure, permitted and kosher, according to the ruling his mind deduces from the holy Torah. The reverse is also true. If he is from attribute of judgment [i.e., the *sefirah hesed*], then everything is the opposite. The attribute of Beit Hillel was kindness, and therefore they offered lenient rulings. Beit Shammai were of the attribute of judgment, and were therefore stringent. But the truth is that each of these, according to their level, are "the words of the living God." . . . The sages that came after Beit Shammai and Beit Hillel saw that the world needed to be run with kindness, and they established the *halakhah* to follow the leniencies of Beit Hillel in every case.[66]

Modern legal theories often assume that actors come to their ideas and conclusions because of different political, social, or intellectual commitments, but Levi Yitzhak suggests that each scholar rules in light their soul's cosmic root, which guides a judge's intuition and shapes their cognitive framework. The homily offers an interesting justification regarding why the particular decisions of the school of Hillel were adopted as the normative practice, an explanation that runs counter to Talmud's own suggestion that the opinions of Hillel were accepted because they were humble and were willing to teach the opinions of the opposing side before introducing their own.[67] Elsewhere Levi Yitzhak offered an even more programmatic vision acknowledging the continuous evolution of *halakhah* in the present:

> The oral Torah changes according to the sages of the generation. This one says such-and-such, and another says something different. The conduct of the *halakhah* accords with the generations. Rashi decided that tefillin should be donned in one way, and Rabbenu Tam decided that it be done in a different manner.[68]
>
> The truth is that the *halakhah* follows the attribute (*middah*) with which the blessed One directs the world [in that particular age]. If it is conducted by means of [divine] love [i.e., *hesed*], then the *halakhah* accords with the sage whose position reflects that. If it is splendor (*tif'eret*), then the *halakhah* follows that one. This explains why Israel lovingly desired to receive the Torah [at Sinai]. . . but balked at accepting the oral Torah. . . . It was difficult for them [to grasp] that the oral Torah would change in accord with the *tzaddik* of each generation. He causes the world to be directed by a certain [divine] attribute, and so too is it with *halakhah* of the oral Torah.[69]

Levi Yitzhak begins by asserting that Jewish law changed because it responds to the dynamic manner in which God directs the world. The judge must be attuned to these constant fluctuations, determining the particular Divine attribute that characterizes their age and should therefore be the lens through which he interprets the law. The *tzaddik* or righteous individual decides the correct form of the *halakhah* based on this cosmic knowledge. Thus Levi Yitzhak has turned Friedman's theoretical description of *halakhah* following with judge's soul-root into an account of the history of Jewish law. By the end of his sermon, however, Levi Yitzhak has arrived at a different message. He suggests that the *tzaddik* first determines the *halakhah*, with God responding to the Sage's ruling and directing the world in accord with their decision. This notion is indeed radical, but it is very much in keeping with a cornerstone of Levi Yitzhak's theology: through revelation God ceded interpretative power to the Jewish people, who now possess an exegetical duty to reformulate the *halakhah* in each generation.[70]

Surely Levi Yitzhak—the official rabbi and court-head of important communities in Pinsk and Barditshev—was not advocating religious-legal anarchy, a free-for-all in which autonomy enables each leader to develop his own unique version of the *halakhah*. He was more cautious, suggesting that change begins with *tzaddikim*, the spiritual aristocracy, rather than the whims of private individuals. Levi Yitzhak's model is elitist: only the *tzaddik*, a term that came to refer exclusively to Hasidic leaders, understands the different attributes with which God engages the world, and, more importantly, only the *tzaddik*, has been entrusted with the power to command these qualities. Charismatic authority—coupled with the scholarly excellence—defines who may revise the law.

Such teachings paved the way for Hasidic communities coming to see the *tzaddik* as a source of oracular and even prophetic authority whose words are, in many respects, an echo of revelation at Sinai.[71] These leaders rarely used mystical values or doctrine in their legal reasoning, but the reconfiguration of religious authority in the *tzaddik*'s spiritual personage did not always remain abstract.[72] There are testaments of Hasidic leaders deciding the law through Divine inspiration in responsa and legal sources as well as in their homilies; they are said to use the Holy Spirit to settle matters of debt, to clear the name of women suspected of prostitution, and even to permit the remarriage of women whose husbands' whereabouts were unknown (*agunot*).[73] Similarly, hagiographical tales depict founding Hasidic figures determining the law through clairvoyance, intuition, and revelation rather than jurisprudential logic.

It should be noted that this new type of normative religious authority was largely wielded to strengthen traditional commitments.[74] But the notion of the *tzaddik* as the ultimate arbiters of matters of ritual and praxis set the stage for a new kind of religious leadership—and a throwback to pre-rabbinic modes of prophecy—grounded in spiritual presence and charisma rather than scholarship or official rabbinic post. This flexible and individualistic impulse, radical even as it was embedded within the established traditional and communal structures, became a fundamental aspect of later Hasidic thought and culture that sets these mystics apart from their kabbalistic forebears.

Personal Situation

Abstract legal rules creak mightily when applied to specific situations, a fact that is readily acknowledged by general legal theorists as well as classical scholars of *halakhah*.

That a specific ruling issued for a person or situation cannot necessarily be generalized is widely discussed in both traditions, but Hasidic and kabbalistic sources go further in suggesting that legal consideration of one's individual circumstances may lead to opposite conclusions: intensification of the law through stringency (called *humrah*) on one hand, and temporary transgression or deviance on the other. Hasidic teachings were alert to the antinomian potential of such thinking, and they sought to understand how, and when, the law ought to be shifted in light of personal, spiritual, and extralegal considerations, and who is licensed to make such changes challenges each system.

Jewish mystical sources distinguish between a temporary exemption or break from the law (called *hora'at sha'ah* or *sha'at ha-dehak*) on one hand, and claims that the norm must be radically altered on the other. While the lines between them are sometimes blurry, Hasidic sources focus on the individual circumstances suggesting that no law code can address every situation, and, more strikingly, that what God asks of that person may not conform to legal precedent. These sources argue that devotion must be expressed through commitment and fealty, but also affirm that individuals must occasionally break with normative mandates. "Hasidism will always examine deeds in the light of the will of God and the instinctive inclination of the individual," argued the late Yehoshua Mondshine, "both of which change according to the circumstances of time and place."[75] Only the individual can know when such audacity is needed, however. No one else, not even a dear teacher or close friend, can identify such moments with total certainty or clarity.[76]

Hasidic visions of religious law involve *both* moments of transgression as well as striving for higher degrees of piety. Striving for God's will may lead one to break with communal or codified norms.[77] They acknowledge that pietism or legal stricture can become a vicious master, distracting one from the genuine obligations levied by God and derailing spiritual growth by causing guilt, sadness, and contrition.[78] Other Hasidic sources, however, remind their readers that, in some cases, permissiveness should give way to supererogatory obligation and a stricter interpretation of the law or practice may indeed be warranted. The urge to perform acts of devotion that go beyond the normative tradition emerges from an intimate connection with God: "When you devote your mind to the blessed Creator, God will send you thoughts regarding what you must do, as it says, 'Cast your burden upon God, [and He will sustain you]' (Psalms 55:23). If you truly want, desire and long [to perform] some pious practice (*davar hasidut*), presumably it must be necessary—for God has delivered it into your thoughts."[79] In such cases the longing for stringency is cast as an instance of sublime Divine revelation and a specific, immediate Divine command.

Thus the question of whether or not to follow such a stringent interpretation rests solely upon the individual worshiper and his inner devotional and spiritual sensibility; it cannot be cross-applied to all moments or an entire community. Correctly fulfilling religious law holds tremendous cosmic significance in the eyes of the Jewish mystics, and the flipside of this is that both outright transgression and blind adherence can contribute to the world's entropy. Ya'akov Yitzhak Horowitz of Lublin (1745–1815), for example, distinguished between those who correctly execute the commandments, and those who seek "solely to bring pleasure to the Creator."[80] The former are free of sin yet static and immobile, unable to imagine serving God beyond the boundaries of *halakhah*. The latter, by contrast, must constantly shift their mode of practices in accordance with the ever-changing Divine will. They are willing to engage in "a temporary injunction (*hora'at sha'ah*) . . . a sin for the sake of heaven,"[81] since formulating a response to God's call leaves room for temporary deviance or breaches in the nomos when performed for a higher purpose.

God's will, however, is often said to be unknowable, impenetrable, and opaque. Rather than seeking to understand and conform to some original Divine intent, Hasidic and kabbalistic sources call one to strive to fulfill it to the best of one's ability, remembering always that it is not simply obedience to *halakhah* that God has commanded of us. Of all the Hasidic communities, the dynasty of Izhbits has given this ethos the fullest treatment. Sources such as the following homily by Mordecai Yosef Leiner (1800–1854) describe the type of individual who trains their eyes upon God's will rather than the textual code or legal precedent:

> Even though one may know which way the law tends to lean, nonetheless this person turns to God to instruct him regarding the hidden truth in this particular situation. . . . He does not want to rely upon himself [i.e. his interpretation of the law]; rather, he seeks God's renewed enlightenment to comprehend His will. At times this approach may necessitate taking action contrary to the *halakhah*, since it is a "time to act for the Lord."[82]

For this Hasidic community, the possible anarchy embedded in this perspective was tempered by piety and a tremendous emphasis on personal integrity. Furthermore, any action contrary to classical *halakhah* was to be performed only when the worshiper achieved a level of clarity that *this* move—and not the words of conventional *halakhah*—indeed reflected the Will of God. One's experience of the cosmos and of one's inner world is governed by a degree of perpetual uncertainty, and rare indeed are these moments of illumination, divinely revealed sparks of lucidity in which the clouds depart and the light of conviction shines through. The question, of course, is what to do in the meanwhile: obey or break free? According to such teachings, *halakhah* becomes a human enterprise, one that is at least potentially at odds with the Divine will. A higher Torah indeed dwells in the heavens, and remains an ever-present basis for appeal or revisiting precedent. Even if we interpret Leiner's words to mean that *halakhah* is fundamentally correct but for certain exceptional situation, God's will can always yield an omnipresent veto power over any law.

This point introduces into the concept of law a radical subjectivity utterly foreign to any contemporary legal theory, though cognates abound in other religious legal traditions. This complicated jostling of values recalls Shahab Ahmed's discussion of Sufi poets and practitioners whose devotion seems to skirt the boundaries of *'al-sharī'a* and who, at times, flagrantly transgress the norms of Islamic piety. Ahmed argues that "we should conceive of the self-conception of these trajectories not as *anti*-nomian—*against* the law, but as *para*-nomian—that is, *beside* the law, or as *supra*-nomian—that is, above the law."[83] The "plurality of norms" found in these Islamic sources, claims Ahmed, include modes of thinking that contest "the epistemological authority of the law" by complementing and contrasting it to other modes of spiritual attainment. Likewise, Hasidic sources cut against the hegemony of *halakhah* while simultaneously underscoring the importance of ritual and the *mitzvot* that form the basis of *halakhah*.

We should not, of course, fall prey to the assumption that transgression is the heart of Hasidic spirituality. Rather than describing such texts as antinomian in the sense of being "against" or even "counter to" the framework of *halakhah*, Hasidic sources regarding moments of nonconformity do not call for overturning or breaking through the law, but for reaching the law's deeper or inner aim—attaining *devekut*—through extra-legal means.[84] Even as Hasidic thinkers contravene the normative dictates of *halakhah*, they do so without setting themselves "against" or "contra" to the law.[85] Hasidic sources argue that, unless there is compelling evidence to the contrary, one must act in accord with the terms of our covenant with God as classically understood in the normative *halakhah*. At the same time, they acknowledge that God's will takes on different forms—at different times, and for different people. Rather than suggesting that the goals of *halakhah* have changed or that its obligations have become irrelevant, Hasidic teachings justify temporary deviance through appeal to a higher spiritual call. The *mitzvot* are described as a supple, flexible, and dynamic system of rituals whose ultimate aim is not compliance with a written code but living and vital connection with God expressed in mind, body, and spirit.

Conclusion

This chapter has illustrated the many ways in which kabbalistic and Hasidic sources, central bodies in Jewish thought, present a vision of *halakhah* as a cosmically significant form of legal, social, and religious praxis. The proper formulation of Jewish law and execution of its obligations or precepts brings God's presence into the universe, aligning the *sefirot* while transforming the body and mind of the worshipper. Though largely conservative in the domain of actual jurisprudence and reticent to apply mystical dogma as a paradigm for real-world legal change, kabbalistic and Hasidic teachings are radical in their theorization of law as a theurgic force.

To be more specific, they embrace an ethos of constant development and interpretation while also placing limitations on that interpretation and thus articulate an alternative to the central streams of modern legal thought: strict construction, liberal construction, legal positivism, legal formalism, and even legal realism. Hasidic and kabbalistic teachings spell out an understanding of *halakhah* that is situationally applied and imbricated within a broader system of ethical, communal, personal, and theological values; legal and ritual obligations are socially embedded yet also treated as sources of personal meaning and spiritual significance.

Acknowledgments

My thanks to Jonathan Canel, Avraham Oriah Kelman, and Chaim Saiman for their extremely helpful feedback on earlier drafts of this work.

Notes

1. For additional discussion of these and related themes, see Ariel Evan Mayse, *Laws of the Spirit: Ritual, Mysticism, and the Commandments in Early Hasidism* (Stanford, CA: Stanford University Press, forthcoming).
2. See Yitzhak Heineman, *The Reasons for the Commandments in Jewish Literature* (rev. and expanded ed.) (Jerusalem: Horev, 1993) [Hebrew]; Jeremy Brown and Marc Herman, eds., *Accounting for the Commandments in Medieval Judaism* (Leiden, The Netherlands: Brill, 2021); Isadore Twersky, *Introduction to the Code of Maimonides (Mishneh Torah)* (New Haven, CT: Yale University Press, 1980), 374–514; Isadore Twersky, "Reasons for the Commandments (*Ta'amei ha-mitzvot*) in the Mishneh Torah," in Twersky, *Law and Spirit in Medieval Jewish Thought*, ed. Carmi Horowitz (Jerusalem: Zalman Shazar Center, 2020), 228–239 [Hebrew]; Christine Hayes, *What's Divine about Divine Law?: Early Perspectives* (Princeton, NJ: Princeton University Press, 2015), 265–80; Moshe Idel, *Kabbalah: New Perspectives* (New Haven, CT: Yale University Press, 1988), xii–xvi; Moshe Idel, "Maimonides and Kabbalah," in *Studies in Maimonides*, ed. Isadore Twersky (Cambridge, MA: Harvard University Press, 1992), 31–82; Elliot R. Wolfson, "Mystical Rationalization and the Commandments in *Sefer ha-Rimmon*," *Hebrew Union College Annual* 59 (1988): 217–51; Josef Stern, *Problems and Parables of Law: Maimonides and Nahmanides on Reasons for the Commandments (Ta'amei Ha-Mitzvot)* (Albany: State University of New York, 1998), esp. 67–76; Moshe Hallamish, *Kabbalistic Ritual: The Integration of Theory and Practice* (Tel Aviv: Idra, 2016), 134–38 [Hebrew]; Yair Lorberbaum, "On Rules and Reasons in Law and in Halakhah—A Fresh Conceptual Framework for the Study of the Rationale of the Commandments," *Jerusalem Studies in Jewish Thought* 26 (2021): 1–76 [Hebrew]; Yair Lorberbaum, "The Rise of Halakhic Religiosity of Mystery and Transcendence," *Diné Israel* 34 (2020): 1–49; Don Seeman, "Reasons for the Commandments as Contemplative Practice in Maimonides," *The Jewish Quarterly Review* 103, no. 3 (2013): 298–327; Yakov M. Travis, "Kabbalistic Foundations of Jewish Spiritual Practice: Rabbi Ezra of Gerona—On the Kabbalistic Meaning of the Mitzvot" (PhD diss., Brandeis University, 2002); and Leore Sachs-Shmueli, "The Rationale of the Negative Commandments by R. Joseph Hamadan: A Critical Edition and Study of Taboo at the Time of the Composition of the Zohar" (PhD diss., Bar-Ilan University, 2019) [Hebrew].
3. See Gershom Scholem, *Major Trends in Jewish Mysticism* (New York: Schocken, 1974), 29–30; Idel, *Kabbalah*, 157–268; Daniel C. Matt, "The Mystic and the Mizwot," in *From the Bible through the Middle Ages: Vol. 1. Jewish Spirituality*, ed. Arthur Green (New York: Crossroad, 1988), 367–404; Elliot R. Wolfson, *Venturing Beyond: Law and Morality in Kabbalistic Mysticism* (New York: Oxford University Press, 2006); and Maurizio Mottolese, *Bodily Rituals in Jewish Mysticism: The Intensification of Cultic Hand Gestures by Medieval Kabbalists* (Los Angeles: Cherub Press, 2016), 5–47 and 308–9.
4. Rémi Brague, *The Law of God: The Philosophical History of an Idea*, trans. Lydia G. Cochrane (Chicago: University of Chicago Press, 2007), 18. See also Hayes, *What's Divine*;

and, more broadly, David C. Flatto and Benjamin Porat, eds., *Law as Religion, Religion as Law* (Cambridge: Cambridge University Press, 2022).

5. See Shaul Magid, "The Intolerance of Tolerance: *Mahaloket* (Controversy) and Redemption in Early Hasidism," *Jewish Studies Quarterly* 8, no. 4 (2001): 326–68.
6. See Ronald Dworkin, *Law's Empire* (Cambridge, MA: The Belknap Press of Harvard University Press, 1986), esp. 47–52; and Mark D. Rosen, "Beyond Interpretation: the 'Cultural Approach' to Understanding Extra-Formal Change in Religious and Constitutional Law," *Journal of Law, Religion & State* 2 (2013): 200–33.
7. Gershom Scholem, "Revelation and Tradition as Religious Categories in Judaism," in *The Messianic Idea in Judaism and Other Essays on Jewish Spirituality* (New York: Schocken Books, 1971), 282–303.
8. Ya'akov Yosef Katz, *Toledot Ya'akov Yosef* (Jerusalem, 2011), *terumah*, 1:446. On the *mitzvot* as Divine emanations, see Elliot R. Wolfson, *Book of the Pomegranate: Moses de Leon's Sefer ha-Rimmon* (Atlanta, GA: Scholars Press, 1988), 57–59 (introduction).
9. Arthur J. Jacobson, "Hegel's Legal Plenum," *Cardozo Law Review* 10 (1989): 893. See also Suzanne Last Stone, "In Pursuit of the Counter-Text: The Turn to the Jewish Legal Mode in Contemporary American Legal Theory," *Harvard Law Review* 106, no. 4 (1993): 813–94; Brague, *Law of God*, 58; Hayes, *What's Divine*, 43; and Moshe Halbertal, *Nahmanides: Law and Mysticism*, trans. Daniel Tabak (New Haven, CT: Yale University Press, 2020), 49.
10. Jacobson, "Hegel's Legal Plenum," 894.
11. See Moshe Cordovero, *Pardes Rimmonim* (Jerusalem, 1998), 8:135a–35b.
12. Me'ir ibn Gabbai, *Tola'at Ya'akov* (Jerusalem, 1996), 19.
13. See, inter alia, *Perush ha-Ramban 'al ha-Torah*, ed. Chayim Dov Chavel (Jerusalem: Mossad Ha-Rav Kook, 1968) on Ex. 29:46; Bahye ben Asher ibn Halawa (Jerusalem: Mossad Ha-Rav Kook, 2006) on that same verse, as well as his comments on Ex. 13:8 and 20:1; and *Emek ha-Melekh* (Jerusalem, 2003), 1:1, 112.
14. Me'ir ibn Gabbai, *'Avodat ha-Kodesh* (Warsaw, 1883), 2:3, 47; Matt, "Mystic and the Mizwot," 395.
15. Moshe Cordovero, *Or Yakar* (Jerusalem, 1963), vol. 2, 181.
16. On Exod. 20:23, 411. See also *Torat Hashem Temimah*, in Moshe ben Nahman (Nahmanides), *Kitvei Ramban*, ed. Chayim Dov Chavel (Jerusalem: Mossad Ha-Rav Kook, 1961), 1:165; and his comments on Deut. 22:6, 2:448–49.
17. Shlomo ben Aderet, *She'elot u-Teshuvot ha-Rashba*, vol. 1 (Jerusalem, 1997), 1:94.
18. See the comments of *Nahmanides* on Lev. 19:19, 2:120.
19. Zohar 2:165b–166a; based on Matt, *Pritzker Zohar*, vol. 5, 459. See also Nahmanides' comments to Deut. 22:6, in *Perush ha-Ramban*, 2:448–449; *Tola'at Ya'akov*, 17; Elijah de Vidas, *Reshit Hokhmah, sha'ar ha-kedushah* (Jerusalem, 1984), ch. 4, 2:37; and *Tikkunei Zohar*, ed. Reuven Margoliot (Jerusalem: Mossad Ha-Rav Kook, 1978), no. 70, 132a.
20. See *Sha'arei Kedushah* (Jerusalem, 2005), 1:1. See also ibid, 1:3–4 and 2:3; *'Emek ha-Melekh* 6:6, 186; and *Toledot Ya'akov Yosef, hakdamah*, 1:1.
21. See Tanya M. Luhrmann, *How God Becomes Real: Kindling the Presence of Invisible Others* (Princeton, NJ: Princeton University Press, 2020), x–xi; and cf. Robert A. Orsi, *History and Presence* (Cambridge, MA: The Belknap Press of Harvard University Press, 2016), esp. 6–8, 21–24.
22. See Moshe Hayim Efrayim of Sudilkov, *Degel Mahaneh Efrayim* (Benei Brak, 2013), *korah*, 438; *Tif'eret 'Uziel (New York, 2016), shir ha-shirim*, 68; and *Isaiah Horowitz, Shenei Luhot ha-Berit* (Jerusalem, 2020), *'asarah ma'amarot, ma'amar shelishi u-revi'i, no.* 47; ibid, *yoma, derekh hayim tokhehat mussar*, no. 163; interpreting b.Berakhot 6b.

23. *Rav Yeevi*, 1:100; trans. Arthur Green et al., *Speaking Torah: Spiritual Teachings from around the Maggid's Table* (Woodstock, VT: Jewish Lights, 2013), 1:241.
24. *Ta'amei ha-Mitzvot le-Ha-Rav Rabbenu Menahem Recanati* (Basel, 1580), 3a.
25. El'azer Azikri, *Sefer Haredim* (Venice, 1601), *hakdamah*, 9a.
26. *Perush ha-Mishnah: Mekor u-Targum*, ed. and trans. Yosef Kafih (Jerusalem: Mossad Ha-Rav Kook, 1963–1969) on m.Makkot 3:16, 247: See also Maimonides, *Guide of the Perplexed*, 3:51; *Mishneh Torah* (Jerusalem, 2015), *hilkhot sukkah ve-lulav* 8:15 and *hilkhot teshuvah* 10:2; and Moshe Hallamish, "Everyone, One Commandment and One Letter," *Daat: A Journal of Jewish Philosophy & Kabbalah* 71 (2011): 25–52.
27. *Tif'eret 'Uziel, ki tavo*, 190; Arthur Green et al., *Speaking Torah*, 1:128–29.
28. Ibid.
29. See R. J. Zwi Werblowski, *Joseph Karo: Lawyer and Mystic* (rev. ed.) (Philadelphia: Jewish Publication Society of America, 1977); Jacob Katz, *Divine Law in Human Hands: Case Studies in Halakhic Flexibility* (Jerusalem: Magnes Press, 1998); Israel Ta-Shma *Ha-Nigle She-Banistar: The Halachic Residue in the Zohar* (Tel Aviv: Ha-Kibbutz ha-Me'uhad, 2001) [Hebrew]; and Hallamish, *Kabbalistic Ritual*.
30. See Ariel Evan Mayse, "Ever-Changing Path: Visions of Legal Diversity in Hasidic Literature," *Conversations: The Journal of the Institute for Jewish Ideas and Ideals* 23 (2015): 84–115; Maoz Kahana and Ariel Evan Mayse, "Hasidic Halakhah: Reappraising the Interface of Spirit and Law," *AJS Review* 41, no. 2 (2017): 397–408.
31. Hayes, *What's Divine*, 2–3, 17–19.
32. Karl N. Llewellyn "Remarks on the Theory of Appellate Decision and the Rules or Canons about How Statutes Are to Be Construed," *Vanderbilt Law Review* 3 (1949): 400 (emphasis in the original).
33. Hayes, *What's Divine*, 21. On the difference between human and Divine modification of the law, Hayes, *What's Divine*, 31; and below. See also Hayes, *What's Divine*, 286–327 and 336–37; and Aaron Panken, The *Rhetoric of Innovation: Self-Conscious Legal Change in Rabbinic Literature* (Lanham, MD: University Press of America, 2005).
34. b.Eruvin 13b.
35. To name but a few studies of this, see Avi Sagi, *The Open Canon: On the Meaning of Halakhic Discourse*, trans. Batya Stein (London: Continuum, 2007); Christine E. Hayes, "Legal Truth, Right Answers and Best Answers: Dworkin and the Rabbis," *Diné Israel* 25 (2008): 73–121; Moshe Sokol, "What Does a Jewish Text Mean?: Theories of '*Elu ve-Elu Divrei Elohim Hayim*' in Rabbinic Literature," *Daat: A Journal of Jewish Philosophy & Kabbalah* 32–33 (1994): xxiii–xxxv.
36. b.Hagigah 3b.
37. y.Sanhedrin 4:2.
38. See Moshe Halbertal, *People of the Book: Canon, Meaning, and Authority* (Cambridge, MA: Harvard University Press, 1997); and *Shemot Rabbah* 30:9.
39. See Chaim Saiman, *Halakhah: The Rabbinic Idea of Law* (Princeton, NJ: Princeton University Press, 2018), esp. 11, 99, 158, and 228.
40. See *'Arba'ah Turim, OH, hakdamah*.
41. See Halbertal, *Nahmanides*, 12–14 and the literature cited on 332–33 n. 4.
42. *Hakdamot la-Mishnah*, ed. Shailat, 40–41; *Guide of the Perplexed*, III:41; *Nahmanides*, 14–66; and Tchernowitz, *Toledot ha-Halakhah* 1:88. Cf. the presentation in his introduction to *Mishneh Torah*, based on t.Sanhedrin 7:1 and t.Sotah 14:9.
43. See Halbertal, *Nahmanides*, 59.

44. See Yom Tov Assevilli, *Hiddushei ha-Ritva* (Jerusalem: Zikhron Yaakov, 2002) to b.Eruvin 13b.
45. Moses de Leon, *Sefer ha-Rimmon*, 366–367; and cf. *Pardes Rimmonim* 9:2.
46. *Sefer ha-Temunah* (Lviv, 1892), *hakdamah le-temunah shelishit*, 27a.
47. *'Avodat ha-Kodesh* 3:23; and Scholem, "Revelation and Tradition."
48. See *Pardes Rimmonim* 9:2; and Hallamish, *Kabbalistic Ritual*, 126–34.
49. m.Beitzah 1:1.
50. b.Eruvin 13b, and see above.
51. Referring, respectively, to the sefirot *hesed* and *gevurah*.
52. b.Bava Metsi'a 59b.
53. *Maggid Devarav le-Ya'akov*, ed. Rivka Schatz-Uffenheimer (Jerusalem: Magness Press, 1976), no. 58, 86–87.
54. See *Maggid Devarav le-Ya'akov*, no. 87, 152; Ariel Evan Mayse, *Speaking Infinities: God and Language in the Teachings of Rabbi Dov Ber of Mezritsh* (Philadelphia: University of Pennsylvania Press, 2020), 148–54; and Arthur Green, "*Da'at*: Universalizing a Hasidic Value," in *Religious Truth: Towards a Jewish Theology of Religion*, ed. Alon Goshen-Gottstein (London: Littman Library of Jewish Civilization, 2020), 83–107. See also Elliot R. Wolfson, "The Hermeneutics of Visionary Experience: Revelation and Interpretation in the Zohar," *Religion* 18, no. 4 (1988): esp. 388; Elliot R. Wolfson, *Circle in the Square: Studies in the Use of Gender in Kabbalistic Symbolism* (Albany: State University of New York Press, 1995), 3, 8–9, 14–15.
55. See Mayse, *Speaking Infinities*, 239.
56. Katz, *Divine Law*, 56–87; and Daniel C. Matt, "Adorning the 'Bride' on the Eve of the Fest of Weeks," *Judaism in Practice: From the Middle Ages through the Early Modern Period*, ed. Lawrence Fine (Princeton, NJ: Princeton University Press, 2001), 74–80.
57. Hanina ben-Menahem, *Legal Deviation in Talmudic Law* (New York: Routledge, 1990).
58. Eliezer Lipman, *Beit Shlomo* (Zolkva, 1800), *petah habayit*, 3, 1–2; and Mendel Piekarz, *Beginning of Hasidism* (Jerusalem: Mossad Bialik, 1978), 416 [Hebrew].
59. Quoted in the story on b.Bava Meẓi'a 59b. Cf. Deuteronomy 17:11; y.Mo'ed Katan 3:1, 9a; y.Sanhedrin 1:4, 6a-b; b.Ḥullin 11a; *Derashot ha-Ran*, no. 7; Zohar 2:117a. See Itzhak Englard, "Majority Decision vs. Individual Truth: The Interpretation of the 'Oven of Achnai' Aggadah," in *Jewish Law and Legal Theory*, ed. Martin Golding (New York: New York University Press, 1993), 353–68; Ephraim E. Urbach, "'Al ha-kelal ''aḥarei rabim le-hatot,'" in *Studies in Jewish Thought*, ed. Moshe David Har and Jonah Fraenkel (Jerusalem: Magnes, 1998), 503–9.
60. See b.Eruvin 53a: "David decided the tradition according to the *halakhah*, but Saul did not." Cf. b.Sanhedrin 93b. See also b.Berakhot 3b; and Maoz Kahana, *Me-ha-Noda' bi-Yehudah le-ha-Ḥatam Sofer* (Jerusalem: Zalman Shazar Center, 2015), 428–30.
61. Dov Ber of Mezritsh, *Maggid devarav le-Ya'akov*, no. 189, 291. Ariel Evan Mayse, "The Ever-Changing Path: Visions of Legal Diversity in Hasidic Literature," *Conversations: The Journal of the Institute for Jewish Ideas and Ideals* 23 (2015): 84–115.
62. Here we might recall the debate about the role of intuition in legal decision-making more broadly; see Joseph C. Hutcheson, Jr., "The Judgment Intuitive: The Function of the 'Hunch' in Judicial Decision," *Cornell Law Quarterly* 14 (1928–29): 274–88; Richard A. Wasserstrom, *The Judicial Decision: Toward a Theory of Legal Justification* (Stanford, CA: Stanford University Press, 1961), esp. 20–21, 89–115.
63. See Halbertal, *Nahmanides*, 376 n. 47.

64. Another reading of this same sermon, however, yields a description of deciding the *halakhah* as a theurgic practice.
65. b.Eruvin 13b.
66. *Kedushat Levi, likkutim*, 2:479.
67. b.Eruvin 13b
68. b.Menaḥot 34b.
69. *Kedushat Levi, purim*, 1:237.
70. See also his formulation in *Kedushat Levi*, vol. 2, *likkutim*, 463–465; and Arthur Green, Defender *of the Faithful: The Life and Thought of Rabbi Levi Yitshak of Berdychiv* (Waltham, MA: Brandeis University Press, 2022), 100–31, 177–90.
71. See Arthur Green, "The Hasidic Homily: Mystical Performance and Hermeneutical Process," in *As a Perennial Spring: A Festschrift Honoring Rabbi Dr. Norman Lamm*, ed. Benzi Cohen (New York: Downhill, 2013), 237–65; Ariel Evan Mayse, "Voices of Moses: Theologies of Revelation in an Early Hasidic Circle," *Harvard Theological Review* 112, no. 1 (2019): 101–25; and, regarding prophecy, see Scholem, *Major Trends*, 334; Moshe Idel, "ha-Besht ce-navie u-kemagikhon talismany," in *Ma'ase sipur: mehkarim ba-siproet ha-yehudit mugashim le-Yo'av Elshtain* (Ramat Gan: Bar-Ilan University, 2006), 124–26; and Moshe Idel, "On Prophecy and Early Hasidism," in *Studies in Modern Religions, Religious Movements and the Bābī-Bahāī Faiths* (Boston: Brill, 2004), 43–45.
72. Maimonides sought to disentangle prophecy from legal authority, but the influential Kabbalist Nahmanides tied connection to God with clarity of judgement rendered by means of the Holy Spirit; see b.Bava Batra 12a; b.Nedarim 38a; *Sefer ha-Mitzvot*, 10–11; and *Perush ha-Ramban* on Deut. 17:11 and Num 11:16; Halbertal, *Nahmanides*, 23–25 and 62–64; Halbertal, Moshe *Maimonides: Life and Thought*, trans. Joel Linsider (Princeton, NJ: Princeton University Press, 2014), 126–27. See the thirteenth-century collection of responsa by the tosafist R. Ya'akov of Marvège, discussed in Israel Ta-Shma, "She'elot u-Teshuvot min ha-Shama'im," *Tarbiz* 57, no. 1 (1988): 51–66; Hayes, *What's Divine*, 18–19; LeFebvre, *Collections, Codes, and Torah: The Re-characterization of Israel's Written Law* (New York: T & T Clark, 2006), esp. 40–44.
73. See Yoav ben Yirmiyah, *Zeved Tov* (Zolkiev, 1806) *kuntres aharon*, 169b (unpaginated); Yitzhak Ze'ev Kahana, *Mehkarim be-Sifrut ha-Teshuvah* (Jerusalem: Mossad Harav Kook, 1973), 416. Cf. Yisra'el Hapstein, *She'erit Yisra'el* (Lublin, 1895), 23a; *Tanna de-ve Eliyahu 'im Perush Ramatayim Tsofim, seder eliyahu zuta* (Jerusalem, 1966), no. 17, 32b.
74. See Max Weber, "Politics as a Vocation," in *The Vocation Lectures*, ed. David Owen and Tracy B. Strong, trans. Rodney Livingston (New York: Hacket, 2004), 32–94; and Martin Krygier, "Law as Tradition," *Law and Philosophy* 5, no. 2 (1986): 237–62.
75. See Yehoshua Mondshine, "The Fluidity of Categories in Hasidism: *Averah Lishmah* in the Teachings of R. Zevi Elimelekh of Dynow," in Hasidism Reappraised, ed. Ada Rapaport-Albert (London: Littman Library of Jewish Civilization, 1997), 309–10.
76. In this, the supple flexibility in light of one's personal condition should be distinguished from the more systematic rebuilding of a category of *halakhah* or specific praxis in light of a different ethical mandate or religious value.
77. This seems to run counter an important vein of biblical thinking that emphasizes the validity of Torah and the *mitzvot* precisely because these actions and injections are manifestations of God's personal will; Hayes, *What's Divine*, 14–16; Moshe Greenberg, "Some Postulates of Biblical Criminal Law," in *Yehezkel Kaufmann Jubilee Volume*, ed. Menahem Haran (Jerusalem: Magnes Press, 1960) [Hebrew], 22. See also Piekarz, *Beginning of Hasidism*, 175–203; and, on the search for God's will in earlier Jewish

mysticism, Haym Soloveitchik, "Three Themes in the *Sefer Hasidim*," *AJS Review* 1 (1976): 312–25.

78. *Likkutim Yekarim*, no. 23, 4b.
79. Ibid, no. 11, 2b.
80. Ya'akov Yitzhak Horowitz, *Zot Zikaron* (Jerusalem, 2015), *va-yehi*, 18; See *Likkutei Moharan* 2:78, suggesting that, although "sometimes the nullification of Torah is its fulfillment," one who yearns for God would never forsake Torah even momentarily. Cf. *Likkutei Moharan* 1:76.
81. Ya'akov Yitzhak Horowitz, *Divrei Emet* (Jerusalem, 2015), *'ekev*, 423. See also Menachem Lorberbaum, *Before Hasidism* (Jerusalem: Mossad Bialik, 2022), 96–100; Rachel Elior, *Mystical Origins of Hasidism* (Oxford: Littman Library of Jewish Civilization, 2008), 152–60; and Uriel Gellman, *The Emergence of Hasidism in Poland* (Jerusalem: Zalman Shazar Center, 2018) [Hebrew], 91 and 167–69.
82. Based on Herzl Hefter, "'In God's Hands': The Religious Phenomenology of R. Mordechai Yosef of Izbica," *Tradition* 46, no. 1 (2013): 49, citing *Mei ha-Shiloah*, *va-yeshev*. There is an extensive scholarly literature about Mordechai Yosef Leiner; see Joseph Weiss, "Late Jewish Utopia of Religious Freedom," in *Studies in East European Jewish Mysticism and Hasidism*, ed. David Goldstein (London: Vallentine Mitchell, 1997), 209–48; Morris M. Faierstein, *All Is in the Hands of Heaven: The Teachings of Rabbi Mordecai Joseph Leiner of Izbica* (rev. ed.) (Piscataway, NJ: Gorgias Press, 2005); Shaul Magid, *Hasidism on the Margin: Reconciliation, Antinomianism, and Messianism in Izbica/Radzin Hasidism* (Madison: University of Wisconsin Press, 2005); Benjamin Brown, "Theoretical Antinomianism and the Conservative Function of Utopia: Rabbi Mordekhai Yosef of Izbica as a Case Study," *The Journal of Religion* 99, no. 3 (2019): 312–40; and the recently published Abraham Joshua Heschel, *Heavenly Torah as Refracted through the Generations*, ed. Dror Bondi (Jerusalem: Magid, 2020), 1044, and 1162–63 [Hebrew].
83. Shahab Ahmed, *What Is Islam? The Importance of Being Islamic* (Princeton, NJ: Princeton University Press, 2016), 96–97, See also ibid., 454–55.
84. See Wolfson, "Ascesis, Hypernomianism," esp. 248, referring to "the grounding of the law in the ground that exceeds the law as the hypernomian foundation of the cosmos." See also Wolfson, *Venturing Beyond*, 196–240, 269–85; Maoz Kahana, "Shabbatai Zvi: Halakhic Man," *Zion* 81, nos. 3/4 (2016): 391–433; Maoz Kahana, "Cosmos and Nomos: Sacred Space and Legal Action, from Rabbi Yosef Karo to Shabbatai Tsevi," *El Prezente* 10 (2016): 143–53.
85. Jay Michaelson, "Conceptualizing Jewish Antinomianism in the Teachings of Jacob Frank," *Modern Judaism* 37, nos. 3 (2017): 338–62; and Pawel Maciejko, *The Mixed Multitude: Jacob Frank and the Frankist Movement, 1755–1816* (Philadelphia: University of Pennsylvania Press, 2011), 82; and Brague, *Law of God*, on "factual transgression" versus the more radical position he describes as "anominiasm."

PART II

DISTINGUISHING CHARACTERISTICS OF JEWISH LAW

CHAPTER 9

CLOSE, YET CREATIVE, READING

Understanding Rabbinic Interpretative Strategies

ELANA STEIN HAIN

Introduction

From ancient times to the present, rabbinic authorities have been reading canonical *halakhic* (legal) texts closely while interpreting them against their plain contextual meaning. This combination is surprising, as fealty to a textual canon suggests obedience to the authority of the text, whereas interpretations that diverge from the plain meaning of a text reflect the authority of the interpreter. Yet, rabbinic Judaism posited that attentive reading of text expands interpretative possibilities rather than narrowing them.

This counterintuitive approach has been used for nearly two millennia to bring new meaning and coherence to vast and often internally contradictory corpora; in so doing, it has maintained the continued relevance of the Jewish canon amid ever-changing realities. The original focus on textual interpretation was born of the rabbinic emphasis on Torah study as a, if not the, central activity of Jewish life after the fall of the Temple in Jerusalem. The prominent place of exegesis grounded the authority and responsibility of the rabbinic establishment in shaping Jewish law.

Four Iterations of "Close-Yet-Creative" Reading

In this chapter we examine four iterations of rabbinic "close-yet-creative" textual reading which remain relevant for today's student of Jewish law: (1) *Midrash halakhah*—ancient rabbinic legal interpretation of the Bible; (2) *okimta*—a strategy for Talmudic interpretation of earlier rabbinic material; (3) *Tosafot's* commentary—medieval interpretation of Talmudic cases; and (4) *Brisker* methodology—nineteenth-century conceptualization of Jewish law. Each iteration emerged at a different chronological stage of the rabbinic intellectual tradition, and each bears its own contours and contributions. Yet, despite the differences and (temporal and geographical) distance between each iteration, each stage offered precedent and mental models for its successor(s). That all four of these models remain integral to the study of Jewish law today bespeaks the centrality of the strange synthesis of creative, yet rooted hermeneutics.

Midrash Halakhah—Ancient Scriptural Interpretation

Jewish law was profoundly shaped by ancient rabbinic interpretation ("exegesis") of biblical—and especially pentateuchal—verses. Some interpretation is found in early rabbinic anthologies known specifically as *Midrash halakhah* (legal exegesis), from the first centuries CE, but legal *Midrash* continued to develop later in both Talmuds as well. In this chapter we refer to both earlier and later legal exegesis of Scripture as *Midrash halakhah*. Legal *Midrash* reflects the following three commitments: (1) belief in the coherence of the entire Pentateuch (Torah); (2) belief in the significance of each word and even letter in the Torah; and (3) belief that Scripture could be interpreted without the constraints of context or syntactical rules.[1] The first two, (1) and (2), lead *Midrash* to identify "surface irregularities" in the biblical text. Some irregularities challenge scriptural coherence—such as a contradiction between two or more biblical passages. Other irregularities—such as an extraneous letter or a rare word—trigger the belief in the omnisignificance of the text. In response, rabbinic *Midrash* works to smooth out these irregularities, turning a "grain of sand which so irritates the *midrashic* oyster" into a pearl.[2] And often the resolutions diverge from, or even contradict, the plain contextual meaning of the texts themselves.

Biblical Coherence

A major indication of rabbinic commitment to the unity of the biblical text[3] is the role played by intertextuality in *Midrash halakhah* (i.e., explaining verses throughout the Bible in light of one another). This is especially true where the Torah distributes information about the same law or theme in several disparate places. Sometimes the citations contradict each other. For example, Exodus 12:5 specifies that the paschal sacrifice may be brought only of sheep or goats. However, Deuteronomy 16:2 says the paschal sacrifice may be brought from sheep *or cattle*. *Midrash halakhah* will not allow the Torah to contradict itself. To resolve the *apparent* contradiction, multiple rabbis suggest that the word "cattle" in Deuteronomy 16:2 does not refer to the paschal sacrifice but to another offering given on the holiday, known as the *ḥagigah*.[4] This is, however, an interpretative reach, given the fact that the verse clearly describes the paschal sacrifice.

Intertextual exegesis might also be prompted by the fragmentary nature of how a ruling is broken up in several places in the Torah. In such cases, rabbinic exegesis links citations throughout the Torah that describe aspects of the same law. For example, the laws of the sabbatical year are mentioned in Exodus 23, Leviticus 25, and Deuteronomy 15. However, in the first two citations, the sabbatical year ruling is about letting the land lie fallow, while in Deuteronomy 15, the sabbatical year ruling is about canceling debts that year. Rabbinic texts connect these different aspects of the sabbatical year by suggesting that Deuteronomy 15:2 alludes to the agricultural laws as well by using the word for sabbatical twice (once as a noun and once as a verb) in a row when introducing debt remission: "And this is the matter of *shemittah* (remission): *shamot* (remit)." While the plain meaning of the verse speaks of debt remission exclusively, exegetes explain the two uses of the root *sh.m.t.* as referring to the two different rules of the sabbatical—letting the land lie fallow and canceling debts. This allows for the following linkage: "And this is the matter of *shemittah*: *shamot*—when the (agricultural) sabbatical applies biblically, remitting debts applies biblically whether inside or outside the land of Israel."[5] In other words, Deuteronomy's presentation is not disconnected from Exodus and Leviticus; rather, it builds upon them, suggesting that the legal contours of debt remission are determined by the legal contours of letting the land lie fallow. When letting the land lie fallow is considered a biblical requirement, so is debt remission.[6]

Alternatively, intertextual exegesis might be founded on something shared by multiple passages—a word, a phrase, or even a date. For instance, because both Passover and Sukkot begin on the fifteenth of a Hebrew calendar month (*Nissan* and *Tishrei*), respectively, eating in the sukkah is required on the first night of Sukkot just as eating *matzah* is required[7] on the first night of Passover.[8]

Omnisignificance

Rabbinic commitment to the unity of the Torah sits alongside a commitment to the significance of each phrase, word, and even letter in the Torah. None are extraneous; each teaches something relevant. Thus, repetition within a given section, or the recurrence of the same law in different parts of the Torah is not simply literary flourish. Instead, each citation carries a distinct meaning. For instance, the Torah thrice mentions the prohibition of "You shall not cook a goat in its mother's milk."[9] *Midrash halakhah* derives three separate prohibitions from the repetition: cooking milk and meat together, eating them together, and deriving benefit from their combination.[10]

Believing that discrete meaning is embedded in each word and even letter of the Torah means that legal *Midrash* often identifies irregularities that are not considered problematic for ordinary language. For example, the fifth of the Ten Commandments, "Honor your father and your mother,"[11] employs the Hebrew word *et* before mentioning each parent: "Honor *et* your father and *et* your mother." The word *et* in Hebrew has no independent lexical meaning; it merely points to the direct object of the command to bestow honor (similar to how "the" might function in English). Thus, the verse simply means, "Honor your father and your mother." In ordinary language, this locution would not stand out. And yet, *Midrash* claims the repetition of *et* as an irregularity, and interprets each *et* as adding another family member to the list of whom one must honor. The word *et* modifying "your father" adds the requirement to honor one's stepmother; the word *et* modifying "your mother" adds the requirement to honor one's stepfather.

Rabbis even ascribe meaning to the conjunction letter *vav*, used to mean "and" in the clause "and your mother." Rather than simply being a conjunction that tells one to honor both father and mother, rabbinic interpretation asserts that "and" adds a requirement to honor one's older brother as well.[12] The fact that the verse does not command honor for both parents as a single unit, for example, "Honor your parents," but instead separates them out as discrete units is the foundational irregularity detected by the rabbis. In everyday speech, this would not be considered irregular, just idiomatic; today's readers might not even notice it. But *Midrash halakhah* actively seeks textual irregularities and generates new meanings from them.

While exegesis might expand and add new (dimensions of) law, sometimes rabbinic commitment to omnisignificance narrows the scope of a biblical rule through hyperliteral readings. Deuteronomy 21:18 introduces the criteria for putting one's rebellious son (*ben sorer u-moreh*) to death: "If a man has a wayward and defiant *son* who does not listen to the voice of his father or to the voice of his mother, and they discipline him, but he will not listen to them." First, rabbis read "son" not as offspring but as exclusively a son, not a daughter. Further, rabbis also read "son" as only someone who is not yet a father or a full adult himself;[13] they conclude that the permission only applies to boys between the age of exactly 13 and 13.25 because they are old enough to be commanded without yet being full adults themselves.[14] Rabbis continue to narrow the application of the law of the rebellious son based on other clauses in that biblical section: if either parent has a physical disability, they may not put their child to death because they will be unable to literally "take hold of him and bring him out to the elders of the town,"[15] as required in the biblical text.[16]

Reading against the Grain

The reading of the rebellious son foregoes the constraints of Scripture's contextual meaning. Another potent example of this is the rabbinic transformation of the biblical law of *lex talionis*, measure-for-measure punishment, into monetary compensation instead. In four instances the Torah commands commensurate corporal punishment of "an eye for an eye" for one who causes physical harm to another.[17] The rabbis, however, generally assert that most of these instances refer instead to charging the assailant money.[18] Rabbinic texts offer various justifications for this radical interpretation.[19]

Each justification uses the verses proximate to *lex talionis* for support. For instance, one points to the mention of injuring animals in the verse immediately following one citation of *lex talionis*. Leviticus 24:19–21 reads:

> *(19) If any party maims another [person]: what was done shall be done in return—(20) fracture for fracture, eye for eye, tooth for tooth. The injury inflicted on a human being shall be inflicted in return. (21) One who kills a beast shall make restitution for it; but one who kills a human being shall be put to death.*

The rabbinic reading goes as follows: verses 19 and 20 actually refer to monetary payment similar to the monetary payment one pays for injuring or even killing an animal mentioned in verse 21. This reading is bold, given that Leviticus 24:21 itself specifically emphasizes the *difference* between corporal punishment for one who kills a person, and monetary payment for one who kills an animal. In other words, Leviticus 24:21 should reinforce the idea of *lex talionis* as corporal punishment for injuring another person. Yet, rabbis reread it to apply the penalty of compensation for one who injures another person, focusing on the first half of verse 21 and linking it to the preceding verses. This is just one of several such creative and intertextual exegeses used to transform verses that clearly require "an eye for an eye" corporal punishment into a demand for monetary compensation instead.

Torah and Rabbinic Authority

The centrality of *Midrash halakhah* should be understood in context of the importance of Torah study and the growth of rabbinic authority after the destruction of the Temple in Jerusalem (70 CE). Shaping Jewish life after the fall of the Temple, the nascent and small rabbinic movement shifted the focus of Judaism from Temple worship to Torah study: "Torah study is equivalent to them all"[20]—that is, all the commandments, or at least those listed in the Mishnah preceding that statement (for more on this topic, see Hoffmann Libson, this volume). In that period, rabbis—who understood Scripture and could interpret it for others—became the leadership class. Rabbinic texts reflect an awareness of this authority and license this near-absolute status from within Torah itself, based on the verse, "You shall not deviate from what they teach you to the right or to the left."[21] This means that rabbinic ruling should be followed even if they "show in your eyes that what is right is left or what is left is right, listen to them."[22] Occasionally, rabbis consciously seek appreciation of their role in shaping how Scripture is understood. For instance, the talmudic Sage Rava laments that some stand in reverence for a passing Torah scroll, but not for a Sage. He finds this foolish because it is the Sages who hold authority over how the Torah is understood.

Rabbinic literature generally presents scriptural exegesis as emerging from the biblical text itself rather than being motivated by a desire to source received traditions, to conceal historical development, or to respond to moral challenges. Nonetheless—or perhaps as a result—much ink has been spilled over what motivated this idiosyncratic scriptural exegesis:[23] did rabbis believe they were discovering the true meaning of Scripture by using the reading tools of their day? Did they employ received reading methods passed down from Sinai? Were they (sometimes) motivated by ethical or public policy concerns, leading them to stretch or change the meaning of the biblical text? Were they trying to harmonize received or developed traditions with the text of the Bible to maintain the relevance of both Scripture and their own practice? Likely no single suggestion fully captures the background of such unique rabbinic interpretative practices.

The Contributions of *Midrash Halakhah*

The commitments of *Midrash halakhah* to the coherence of the Torah and the significance of every letter, alongside transcending the contextual constraints of ordinary language, served as a foundation for the Jewish intellectual tradition. In transforming problematic textual irregularities into exegetical opportunities, legal *Midrash* offered an important precedent for the role of creative interpretation in Jewish law and literature. Moreover, the rabbinic penchant not to justify their exegesis as responding to anything but the text itself strengthened their bold methodology as self-evident and not requiring justification. Thus, the rabbis' intertwined focus on Torah study and rabbinic interpretative authority became a cornerstone of Judaism for the next two millennia.

Okimta—Rabbinic Rereading of *Tannaitic* Materials

The flexibility of the rabbis' approach to scriptural exegesis is echoed in how talmudic texts interpret earlier rabbinic corpora. Rabbinic literature spans many centuries, with the earliest period ("*tannaitic*") lasting from the first through the mid-third century CE and later periods ("*Amoraic*" and "*stammaitic*") extending into the seventh century. Much talmudic discourse consists of the named rabbis ("*Amoraim*") or anonymous editors ("*stammaim*") from the later periods analyzing the earlier *tannaitic* material (known as Mishnah, *tosefta*, or *baraita*). Often, later rabbis/editors find that a *tannaitic* text contradicts either (a) an explicit ruling found elsewhere in the *tannaitic* corpus, or (b) an operative legal principle presumed by these later interpreters themselves.

Just as *Tannaim* and *Amoraim* do not accept incoherence within the Torah, *Amoraim* and *stammaim* do not accept contradictions within *tannaitic* literature.[24] And just as *Midrash halakhah* interprets texts inventively to maintain biblical coherence, *Amoraim* and *stammaim* do the same for the *tannaitic* corpus they inherited: they apply scriptural reading practices to the tannaitic canon.

To be sure, Scripture and *tannaitic* texts are fundamentally different, in that the former were transmitted in writing, while the latter were transmitted orally. Moreover, some strategies employed to resolve *tannaitic* contradictions could never be used in reference to scriptural contradictions. For instance, the Talmud sometimes attributes contradictory texts to different *Tannaim* or *tannaitic* schools. Alternatively, sometimes the Talmud alters a problematic *tannaitic* text, using the term "*teni*," meaning "recite" or "repeat" to change existing words in the text. Similarly, the Talmud proclaims *ḥasurei meḥasra ve-hakhi ke-tani*, "there is something missing, and this is how it reads," to add new words/phrases which change the meaning of the *tannaitic* text. Rabbis would never use such strategies to resolve scriptural contradictions due to their belief in the Pentateuch's singular Divine authorship.

Yet there is an iconic strategy used to resolve contradictions among *tannaitic* texts that applies the ingenuity of scriptural interpretation to *tannaitic* corpora. It is called *okimta*. From the Aramaic root *q.w.m.* meaning "to refer to" or "to establish," the word *okimta* is the second-person conjugation meaning "you explain" or "you interpret." Generally, an *okimta* narrows a *tannaitic* text's applicability, and its apparent indifference to the plain meaning of the texts it claims to interpret rivals early scriptural exegesis. *Okimtot* (pl.) often depart from the plain meaning of an original ruling, sometimes in the extreme.

The following illustrations from tort law exhibit how *okimtot* work. It is important to note that that an *okimta* seeks to resolve either of two types of contradictions raised by a *tannaitic* text: one is the contradiction between the explicit ruling of one *tannaitic* text and the explicit ruling of another *tannaitic* text. An *okimta* that resolves this kind of contradiction seeks *systematic coherence* within the *tannaitic* legal corpus. Another type of contradiction that an *okimta* seeks to resolve is the contradiction between a *tannaitic* text and a legal principle that the interpreters themselves presume to be binding on all texts. An *okimta* that resolves this kind of contradiction seeks *normative validity* on behalf of the *tannaitic* texts.[25]

The two *okimtot* will illustrate each type, respectively. The first example attempts to preserve the systematic coherence of the *tannaitic* corpus by resolving a contradiction between two *tannaitic* texts. The second example attempts to preserve the normative validity of a *tannaitic* text by rereading it to correspond to the assumed legal principle.

Example 1—Resolving a Contradiction between Two *Tannaitic* Texts

The Talmud in Bava Kamma[26] describes this scenario: someone entered private property and was accidentally killed by a projectile belonging to the landowner/host. The Talmud cites a *baraita* to determine whether the host should be exiled on account of this accidental death:[27]

> *If one enters a carpenter's shop without permission, and a chip [of wood] flies off and mortally wounds the intruder, the carpenter is not liable [to go into exile]. But if the person had entered with permission the carpenter is liable.*

According to this *baraita*, the key variable determining the carpenter's liability is whether the victim had permission to enter the land: if so, the carpenter is liable, and if not, the carpenter is exempt. This distinction is logical: hold a host accountable for invited guests but not for trespassers.[28] The Talmud, however, cites a contradictory *tannaitic* passage which absolves a host from liability even for those who entered with permission:

> *One who entered the blacksmith's shop and sparks flew and the one who entered was mortally wounded on the face, the blacksmith is not liable, even if [the victim] entered with permission.*

At this point, the Talmud confronts systematic incoherence, as two anonymous *tannaitic* texts plainly contradict each other: one rules that permitted entry makes the host liable, while the other releases the host from liability even when the victim entered with permission.

To resolve this, the talmudic editors (*stammaim*) offer an *okimta*:

> *What is the case we are dealing with here (i.e., where the blacksmith is not liable even having given permission for entry)?*
>
> *With the blacksmith's apprentice.*
>
> *Does the blacksmith's apprentice stand to be killed?*
>
> *The [case is where] the instructor pressures the apprentice to leave but the apprentice still does not leave.*
>
> *And because the instructor pressures the apprentice to leave, does the apprentice stand to be killed?*
>
> *If so, does this also apply to someone else?*
>
> *Someone else does not feel the fear/awe of their instructor, whereas this one (=the apprentice) feels the fear/awe of their instructor.*

The *okimta* runs as follows: generally, as the first *baraita* states, a host is responsible for their invited guest's safety. However, the second *baraita* offers a narrow exception to this general rule: where the host is an instructor who has pressed their apprentice to leave. In this case, *and only in this case*, the host (instructor) should not be liable for the death of the guest (apprentice). Why? Because an instructor who pressed their apprentice to leave can reasonably assume that the apprentice has left. Thus, the host (i.e., the instructor) cannot be considered negligent for not taking the precautions needed when another person is present.

This *okimta* narrows the case described in the second *baraita* to only an instructor and apprentice even though the wording of the *baraita* presented its ruling as generally applicable to anyone who walks into the blacksmith's shop. Thus, the *okimta* takes license in narrowing the *baraita* despite the *baraita*'s own language. It does not contradict the wording of the *baraita*, but it does offer a narrowing and counterintuitive reading.

Additionally, this *okimta* employs a distinctly talmudic form: back-and-forth discussion to pin down the parameters and logic of the case. The first stage of the argument transforms the "guest" into an apprentice and the "blacksmith" into the instructor. But the editors worry that this is unfair ("*Does the blacksmith's apprentice stand to be killed?*"). This leads to the next stage of the argument: adding the detail that the apprentice was instructed to leave. Again, the editors worry that this is unfair ("*And because the instructor pressures the apprentice to leave, does the apprentice stand to be killed? If so, then does this also apply to someone else?*"). This leads to the final state of the argument: asserting that an instructor who pressured their apprentice to leave can assume that the apprentice has left. And ultimately, this absolves the blacksmith instructor of legal liability.

This *okimta* constructs two intertwined narratives: the scenario of the apprentice and the instructor and the story of anonymous editors arguing over what is fair. In offering these narratives, the Talmud does more than just resolve a contradiction: it expands the discussion of the issues at hand, drawing the learner into the conversation in new ways.[29] Such dialectical discussion belongs to the general back-and-forth format for which talmudic discourse is well known. Thus, what begins as an attempt to harmonize contradictions within the *tannaitic* corpus becomes a rich narrative discussion about the application of Jewish law.

Example 2—Resolving a Contradiction between a *Tannaitic* Text and a Legal Principle

Our second *okimta* comes from tort law as well, but its goal is different. Rather than trying to resolve the contradiction between two *tannaitic* texts, this *okimta* sets out to resolve a contradiction between the ruling in a *tannaitic* text and the legal principles held by later interpreters.

The third chapter of Tractate Bava Kamma opens with the following Mishnah:

> *If one leaves a vessel in the public thoroughfare, and someone else slips on it and breaks it, the one who slipped is exempt; if the person who slipped was hurt, the owner of the vessel is obligated to pay damages.*

The *Mishnah* rules that one who leaves a vessel in the public thoroughfare is responsible for harm caused to others and for damage caused to the vessel: it is the owner's fault for leaving the vessel there in the first place. But the talmudic editors think the pedestrian who breaks the vessel should be held responsible:

> *Why is [the person who slipped on the vessel and broke it] exempt [from damages]? The pedestrian should have checked [the path] and then walked!*[30]

Unlike the Mishnah, the editors believe that the pedestrian should compensate the owner of the vessels because the pedestrian has a duty to pay attention to where they are walking. This is stated as a principle: "One should have checked [the path] and then walked!" Its Aramaic formulation suggests that this principle does not stem expressly from within *tannaitic* literature itself. Likely, it is what the later interpreters themselves believed should obtain, whether based on their understanding of earlier texts or their own legal/moral logic. But rather than rejecting the Mishnah or rejecting the legal principle, the Talmud tries to bridge the gap between them by offering three *Amoraic okimtot*:

- This Mishnah refers to a case where the entire path is full of vessels which the pedestrian cannot avoid. (per Rav)
- This Mishnah refers to a case when it is dark, and the pedestrian cannot see the vessel. (per Samuel)
- This Mishnah refers to a case where the vessel was in the corner, and the pedestrian turning could not see it. (per R. Yoḥanan)

Each *okimta* reinterprets the Mishnah as an exceptional case where the pedestrian could not have been more diligent—because the vessels were unavoidable, or because their sightline was compromised (due to darkness or a physical blind spot). But in all other cases, the pedestrian is liable for not being more careful.[31] Thus, the normative validity of the Mishnah is preserved.

This type of *okimta* makes explicit the legal principle with which the *Amoraim* and *stammaim* expect the *tannaitic* text to comport. But where does this principle come from? As mentioned above, it is reasonable to assume (even if not in all cases) that *Amoraim* or *stammaim* themselves hold certain legal principles, and they expect the earlier texts not to contravene those principles. Thus, the *okimta* may provide a prototypical example of later interpreters bridging the gap between their own assumptions and those reflected in earlier texts. This speaks to two sources of authority that must be reconciled. On the one hand, the *tannaitic* text clearly has authority; otherwise, why would *Amoraim* or *stammaim* need their legal principle to comport with it? But on the other hand, their legal principle must have authority too; otherwise, why would they want to bend the Mishnah to its ruling?

There are those who disagree with this explanation of *okimtot*, instead attempting to reduce the dissonance between *Amoraic/stammaitic* principles and the original *tannaitic* texts with which they seem to clash. Marshaling the rabbinic principle that *Amoraim* do not have the authority to argue with *Tannaim*, some advise not to take the tension between the *Amoraim/stammaim* and the *tannaitic* texts at face value. They also advise not to assume that anyone offering an *okimta* believes that it accurately describes what the *tannaitic* text meant. Rather, the *tannaitic* text expresses an abstract legal principle by offering a case, as rabbinic law is often expressed casuistically rather than in the form of abstract principles. For example, the Mishnah cited in the second *okimta* example above states that one who leaves their vessels in the public thoroughfare is responsible for them if they are broken. The notion that one who owns vessels is responsible for where they are placed is a theoretical principle that the Mishnah, the *Amoraim*, and the *stammaim* all agree with.

However, in practice, there are other variables that interfere with applying this abstract principle: in this case, the fact that the pedestrian should be more aware of the path makes it impossible to hold the vessel owner accountable. When the *stammaim* bring up this factor, they are not disagreeing with the theoretical principle offered by the Mishnah per se. Rather, they are bringing up an additional variable—the responsibility of the pedestrian—as something that interferes with the theoretical principle in practice. As a follow-up to this recognition of the gap between theory and the practice, *Amoraim* offer three scenarios that will provide laboratory-like conditions where the mishnah's theoretical principle can be applied in practice because pedestrian responsibility will not be an issue: there is nowhere else to walk, it is dark, or there is a sharp corner. The *okimtot* are not suggesting that the Mishnah truly refers to such narrow situations; rather the *okimtot* offer the situations where the principle stated in the Mishnah can be applied.

This process of claiming a general theoretical principle and then having to find the right conditions for it to apply in practice is known from the world of science: even true scientific rules require certain conditions that minimize interfering variables to be applicable in practice. For example, Newtonian physics might offer a formula for determining how much force is exerted on an object. While the formula may be theoretically true under ideal conditions, in practice, variables such as electric charge or friction might interfere. This does not mean that the original formula is false, only that it applies when other interfering variables are removed—in other words in laboratory conditions. *Okimtot* are the rabbinic version of laboratory-like conditions.[32]

As is the case with scriptural exegesis as well, there is no conclusive way to prove which of these explanations of *okimta* is correct: are the later rabbis disagreeing with the earlier texts but in a more concealed form? Or are they buttressing the earlier texts in ways that the purveyors of those texts would have fully agreed with? This is precisely the question facing all creative-yet-close reading.

The Contributions of *Okimtot*

Like biblical exegesis, rabbinic *okimtot* seek to harmonize textual problems. When *tannaitic* texts contradict each other, or when they contradict the legal presumptions of later rabbis and editors, they can be understood in new ways to retrieve coherence. Also, like scriptural exegesis, rabbinic *okimtot* are only minimally constrained by the plain meaning of the text they interpret. These similarities suggest a rabbinic belief in/desire for coherence of *tannaitic* texts that parallels their belief in/desire for the coherence of Scripture itself.

Beyond the ambition for coherence among *tannaitic* texts, *okimtot* that address normative validity introduce a new type of contradiction. Rather than focusing solely on the opposition between texts, such *okimtot* recognize the opposition between text and abstract legal principle. This recognition marks a more evolved stage of rabbinic jurisprudence, in which casuistic case law has given way to general legal principles.[33]

Tosafot—Medieval Dialectics to Resolve Talmudic Contradiction

Our next plot-point in the creative exegetical tradition of resolving textual problems moves hundreds of years forward to twelfth-century northern France with *Tosafot* (lit., "additions"), a commentary to the Babylonian Talmud. Initially, the Tosafists Rabbi Yaakov ben Meir (known as Rabbenu Tam) and Rabbi Yitzhak ben Shmuel of Dampier (known as *R"I Ha-Zaken*) wished to *add* to the talmudic explanations of their teacher, *Rashi* (R. *Shlomo Yitzḥaki*) in his definitive gloss on most of the *Bavli*. As time went on, however, *Tosafot*'s additions became far more voluminous than *Rashi's* commentary, and in time, spread to Germany, England, Eastern Europe, and ultimately Spain.

Midrash halakhah resolves contradictions in the Bible, *okimtot* resolve contradictions raised by *tannaitic* materials, and *Tosafot* resolve contradictions between different talmudic passages. *Tosafot*'s assumptions about the Babylonian Talmud play off the assumptions of earlier rabbinic exegetes and lead them to read the entire Babylonian Talmud as a coherent intertextual canon. Theirs is by far the boldest assumption of the three, given the length and variegation of the Babylonian Talmud, an enormous corpus that spans myriad topics and was edited variably over time. *Tosafot* also manifest another bold ambition: unlike earlier exegetes, *Tosafot* are often explicit about bridging gaps between the talmudic text and the way their communities practiced Jewish law. In these cases, *Tosafot* will often reinterpret rabbinic texts rather than condemn the actions of their communities.

Tosafistic methodology contains three steps: (1) gathering sources on a particular topic from throughout the Talmud, (2) noting contradictions/inconsistencies among said sources, and (3) suggesting the different variables among the sources that can resolve the seeming contradictions.[34]

Example—Contested Property

One example of *Tosafot*'s method arises in context of ownership of contested property/possessions. Rulings about contested property appear throughout the Babylonian Talmud. For example, Tractate Bava Metzia begins:

> *If two people are holding a garment. This one says, "I found it," that one says, "I found it"; this one says, "It's completely mine," and that one says, "It's completely mine": this*

> *litigant should swear that he does not own less than half of it, and that litigant should swear that he does not own less than half of it, and they should split (the value) of the garment.*

Two people clutch the same garment, and while neither has proof, both claim it as their own. The Mishnah rules: give each litigant half (the value) of the garment once they each swear to at least half ownership. *Tosafot*[35] note that this ruling contradicts a different case in Tractate Bava Batra,[36] where two people claim ownership of the same riverboat. In that case, rather than having them take oaths and split the value of the boat, the Talmud rules that whichever litigant is stronger (by argument or by force) takes the boat. Ostensibly, the garment and boat cases seem legally identical: two people, neither with better proof of ownership than the other, claim the same item as their own. Yet, the ruling differs in the two cases. Here we find the first two steps of tosafistic methodology: gathering case law and identifying a contradiction.

Tosafot resolve the inconsistency by asserting that physical possession differentiates the two cases. They write:[37]

> *. . . clutching [the garment] differs [from arguing over a boat] because [in the former case] it is as though each person definitely owns half, for we all see that what the person is physically holding belongs to them.*

Tosafot employ a principle that physically holding an item indicates ownership.[38] That principle explains the conflict between the two cases: in the garment case, each person physically holds the item, leading each to have a credible claim of ownership. But in the boat case, no one physically holds the boat, so the ruling differs.

However, *Tosafot* do not stop there. There are more cases to collate. The Talmud[39] explicitly compares the garment case to another scenario of contested ownership:

> *If two people deposited money with the same person, and one of them deposited a maneh (100 zuz) and the other deposited two hundred zuz: this one said, the two hundred are mine, and the other said likewise, the two hundred are mine: he must give one maneh (=100 zuz) to each, while the rest lies until Elijah comes.*[40]

In this case, a third party holds a sum of three hundred coins deposited by two people but does not know who deposited two hundred and who deposited one hundred. If both litigants claim to have deposited two hundred, the Mishnah rules that each depositor retrieves only one hundred, while the remaining contested one hundred is held in escrow until the messianic prophet Elijah will arrive in some distant future to determine whose money it is. In other words, the one hundred contested coins will be sitting in escrow for a long time. *Tosafot* note the Talmud's comparison between the deposit case and the garment case. They suggest that the commonality between the two is the principle of physical possession indicating credible ownership. *Tosafot* suggest that the third party is "holding" the contested money on behalf of each litigant:

> *it is considered as though the person holding the deposit is actually holding the money on behalf of each of them, as though they (=the depositors) themselves are actually physically holding the money.*

Tosafot expand the application of physical possession to the deposit case. Just as the litigants in the garment case physically hold the contested garment, in the deposit case, the third party physically holds the deposit on behalf of the litigants. Legally, it is as though the litigants themselves are holding it!

Having described both the garment and deposit cases as involving physical possession, *Tosafot* must reckon with a new contradiction: the ruling in the deposit case diverges from the the garment case by holding the contested one hundred *zuz* in escrow rather than splitting it! If both involve physical possession by/on behalf of the litigants, why is the ruling different in the deposit case from the garment case? *Tosafot* therefore suggest a distinction between the two cases that invokes another legal principle:

> *. . . dividing the remaining 100 zuz would be a false ruling. Therefore, allow it to rest (until Elijah comes). However, regarding the garment, since it is possible that it does belong to both of them, they should split its worth.*

Tosafot resolve the contradiction by suggesting a differentiating variable between the two cases: because it is certain that one person deposited one hundred and the other deposited two hundred, splitting the one hundred coins would lead to a demonstrably false of unjust result. On the other hand, since it is possible that both claimants do in fact own the garment (e.g., if they lifted it at precisely the same time), splitting its value might contain a true result. *Tosafot* hereby suggest another legal principle: that the ruling of the court should not patently contradict reality.[41]

Citing the deposit case complicated things precisely because of both its similarity to and differences from the garment case. Nonetheless, *Tosafot* include it owing to their ambition to explain how cases across the entire Talmud can be understood as part of a coherent legal system. They are beholden to the full gamut of rabbinic discussion of cases of contested ownership and thus incorporate other talmudic scenarios of contested ownership, fitting them all together into a legal schema that treats physical possession as a central variable while adding other subsidiary principles along the way.

Figure 9.1 maps our excerpt from *Tosafot*, with the legally significant variables bolded.

The Contributions of Tosafot

Tosafot, like the *Amoraim* and *stammaim* who offered *okimtot* before them, seek to harmonize legal rulings by distinguishing among those that contradict each other. However, while the *okimta* strategy resolved contradictions typically by narrowing the scope of a given case, *Tosafot* identify fine distinctions among cases and draw out corresponding

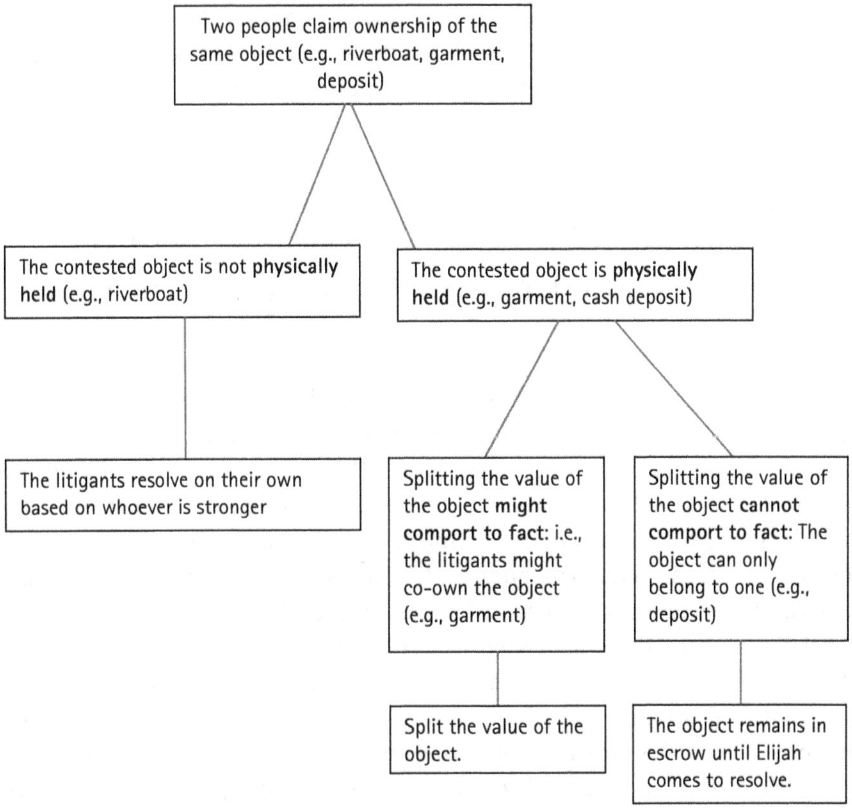

FIGURE 9.1 A visual map of Tosafot b.Bava Metzia 2a s.v., *ve-yaḥloku.*

legal principles. Additionally, while *Tosafot* may have used similar methods to scriptural exegesis and *okimtot*, as a commentarial style on the Talmud, it was considered innovative. From the close of the Talmud, the goal of talmudic learning in Europe was to absorb rabbinic law and customs without relating to the intra-canonical contradictions within rabbinic literature in a consistent way.[42] In contrast, *Tosafot* offered the dialectical approach of making fine distinctions between cases to tell a coherent story about the seeming contradictions in talmudic law. Their method is often known as *pilpul*, Hebrew for "sharp."[43]

Beyond resolving intra-talmudic contradictions, *Tosafot* explicitly harmonize conflicts between talmudic law and the communal practice of their day. Already on the very first page of the Talmud, *Tosafot* note a discrepancy between the mishnaic ruling that the evening *shema* should be recited after nightfall and common practice.[44] But rather than suggesting that the community change its practice to recite *shema* later, *Tosafot* offer somewhat contorted suggestions for how the community's practice actually corresponds to mishnaic/talmudic rulings, a pattern that recurs in a number of sections of their talmudic commentary.[45] To be sure, sometimes *Tosafot* refuse to justify the legally divergent actions of their community.[46] Nonetheless, they generally manifest deep respect for the pious character of their community.[47] They use their *pilpulistic* thinking in real time to keep a changed/ing Jewish reality rooted in the authority of the Talmud itself. This highlights the role played by flexible interpretation in ensuring continuity alongside change.

Brisker Methodology—Nineteenth-Century Conceptualization of Law

Our fourth and final example synthesizing close reading and creative interpretation is known as the Brisker method. Developed in the nineteenth century, this methodology is named for the Eastern European city of Brisk (Brest-Litovsk) where the movement's founder, R. Hayyim Soloveitchik, taught after the Yeshiva of Volozhin (1803–1892) closed. Reb Hayyim, as he is known, had many direct students, and his method of study continues to this day in centers of talmudic learning (*yeshivot*) around the world.

The Brisker method (also known as "Brisker Torah"[48]) employs dialectical thinking like *Tosafot*. However, there are two major differences between Brisker methodology and the other exegetical methods discussed in this chapter. First, all three earlier legal methodologies focused on determining or justifying the *halakhic* rules that are implemented in practice. Brisker Torah does not. It aims instead at developing a conceptual world which animates all *halakhic* views, including those that were not accepted into practice. Second, for scriptural exegetes, *okimtot* and *Tosafot*, resolving contradictions was likely the primary desideratum. For the Brisker method, the goal is not to resolve contradictions but to develop a conceptual or analytic account of the law. Through analysis, the Brisker method asserts that all legitimate *halakhic* positions—whether theoretical or applied in practice—are rooted in abstract frameworks of legal concepts.

Proponents of the Brisker method focus on a legal topic ("*sugya*"), by analyzing the character of the law it discusses. This analysis gives rise to central conceptual frameworks and/or distinctions. Typically, an analytic distinction, known as a *ḥakirah* ("investigation"),[49] proposes two (or more) dimensions of a legal rule or divergent ways of understanding how a rule functions. The *ḥakirah* elucidates different ways of understanding a single rule, or explains disputes/contradictions within talmudic literature or later legal corpora:[50] each side reflects a different side of the *ḥakirah* (i.e., a different understanding of the character of the law at hand).

Comparing a Brisker treatment to a *tosafistic* treatment of the same subject exposes its novelty. As described above, the opening Mishnah of Bava Metzia describes two people holding the same garment, each arguing that it is completely theirs. The resolution between them is that they split (the value) of the garment. *Tosafot* reacts to this case by citing other cases of contested possessions which rule differently and noting subtle distinctions between them to resolve these contradictions. A Brisker approach, however, begins by trying to conceptualize the mishnah's ruling of splitting the garment on its own. Brisker Torah might offer the following *ḥakirah*: should we understand splitting the garment as being a result of each litigant having clear (even if conflicting) ownership of the garment, such that no one can take the garment away without clear evidence? Or should we understand the splitting of the garment as being a result of neither litigant having clear ownership of the garment? In other words, is the garment split because it is the closest way to vindicate each party's claim of complete ownership, or is it split because in the absence of any certainty, the law merely splits the difference between the parties?

This *ḥakirah* theorizes what the ruling of splitting the garment means conceptually. But regardless of which approach is correct, the ruling is the same: the garment is split. The goal of offering the *ḥakirah* is not to resolve a contradiction or even necessarily to explain a debate, but to understand the theoretical depth of the legal position articulated in the Mishnah.[51]

Ḥakirot (pl.) are often used to analyze legal debate. Possibly the most well-known Brisker *ḥakirah* questions whether a particular rule focuses on an object (*ḥeftza*) or on the legal actor (*gavra*).[52] And this might have practical consequences for how one rules about a given issue. For example, Jewish law requires that Jews rid themselves of leavened food (*ḥametz*) prior to Passover. Reb Hayyim investigates whether this requirement focuses on the *ḥametz* (the *ḥeftza*) having to be destroyed or upon the legal actor (*gavra*) having to rid themselves of *ḥametz*. He suggests that the object/actor distinction explains an argument between R. Judah and the other Sages about how to properly rid oneself of *ḥametz*: Rabbi Judah requires that one destroy *ḥametz* only by burning it, while the Sages allow for other methods such as grinding the *ḥametz* to crumbs and allowing the wind to sweep it away or throwing it into the sea.[53] Reb Hayyim understands their argument as follows: For R. Judah, the commandment is for the *ḥametz*, the object, to be destroyed, as emphasized by insisting on a particular way to destroy the *ḥametz*. However, the Sages stress the fact that a person must rid themselves of *ḥametz* while the precise means are less relevant.[54] Unlike the previous example, here the *ḥakirah* does in fact explain a dispute: R. Judah rules one way due to his conceptualization, while the Sages rule a different way due to their conceptualization. Though Reb Hayyim does not rule which opinion should be followed, his analysis adds theoretical depth to each position.

Conceptual distinctions can also be used to explain disputes between medieval commentators. Reb Hayyim considered the relationship between the essential character of a ruling and its practical application to analyze a medieval debate about the evening prayer, *'arvit*. While this prayer originated in Jewish law as voluntary (*reshut*), subsequent generations of Jews accepted its daily recitation upon themselves as obligatory (*ḥovah*). The evolution of this prayer is ripe for Brisker analysis: is *'arvit* still considered voluntary in its essence even if practically it has become obligatory, or is the essence of *'arvit* now obligatory like the other daily prayers? Reb Hayyim identifies this as a matter of debate between the twelfth-century scholars, Maimonides and the *Ra'avad* (Rabbi Abraham ben David), whose debates Reb Hayyim often chooses as the site of his conceptual analysis. Here, Reb Hayyim analyzes an argument between them regarding what to do if one is reciting the *'arvit* prayer and realizes that one has already done so.

In his legal tome, *Mishneh Torah*, in the Laws of Prayer,[55] Maimonides rules:

> *One who was standing in prayer and remembered having already prayed stops even in the middle of a blessing; but if it was the evening prayer ('arvit), one does not stop, for at the outset one prayed it with the awareness that it is not a requirement.*

Yet, *Ra'avad*, who glossed and frequently critiqued Maimonides, writes: "This does not sit well."

Maimonides distinguishes between the *'arvit* prayer and those recited in the morning or afternoon. In that latter, if one becomes aware of duplicating their prayer one must stop praying mid-sentence so as not to recite an unnecessary blessing. The reasoning is as follows: rabbinic Judaism does not recognize the notion of offering an extra or voluntary prayer unless one intends from the outset of the prayer to be offering something extra. In the case of becoming aware of duplicating morning or afternoon prayer in the middle, the first part of the prayer was not recited with the intention of being a voluntary additional offering; rather, it was recited with the intention of fulfilling one's obligation. Once the mistake is noticed, one cannot simply switch midway: there is no such thing as a hybrid prayer that is half obligation/half voluntary offering.

If, however, one becomes aware of duplicating *'arvit,* Maimonides writes that one should continue praying through the end because *'arvit* itself is not obligatory. Since it was a voluntary prayer to begin with, one may simply continue the voluntary prayer as an additional voluntary offering. The *Ra'avad,* however, stressing that *'arvit* has been accepted by Jews for centuries upon themselves as obligatory, disagrees with Maimonides's ruling and holds that *'arvit* is just as obligatory as morning and afternoon prayers. All three are daily requirements in Jewish law.

Reb Hayyim offers a conceptual understanding of this argument as it relates to the essential character of *'arvit.* Maimonides still sees *'arvit* in its essence as a voluntary prayer (*reshut*) even though practically people are obligated to pray *'arvit* every night. While in practice it is obligatory,[56] since it was not legislated by the talmudic rabbis it can still be considered voluntary in its essential character. Thus, Reb Hayyim separates out two dimensions of this law of *'arvit*: (1) the practical requirement to recite it, and (2) the ideational understanding that *'arvit* is still voluntary in its essence. *Ra'avad,* on the other hand, holds that accumulated practice has shifted the essence of *'arvit* to become obligatory. Once again, Reb Hayyim's goal is not to rule what to do in practice, but to move the debate away from a technical understanding (i.e., should one stop midsentence or not) to a deeper conceptual understanding. In suggesting that a law might differ in its essence from its practical application, Reb Hayyim adds new layers of meaning to the law itself: its character is to be understood as more than simply the way it is practiced. This illustration is a microcosm of Brisk's influence: concrete rules of Jewish law rest on analytically abstract properties.

Contributions of Brisker Methodology

The examples above illustrate how Brisker analysis both echoes and diverges from earlier rabbinic interpretative strategies. First is the matter of the relationship between textual difficulties and conceptual ideas. Like interpreters before him, Reb Hayyim employs a dialectical method to distinguish between conflicting rulings or disagreements among decisors. However, Brisker Torah moves beyond resolving contradictions to focus on conceptual frameworks as a way to understand the depth of the law.[57] For this reason, Brisker methodology not only deals with contradictions but also with understanding disputes in *halakhic* literature as well as simply conceptualizing a ruling even in the absence of contradiction or dispute. Relatedly, whereas *okimtot* and the Tosafists often resolved contradictions by asserting a concrete or technical difference between two cases, Briskers place divergent conceptual understandings at the heart of their analysis.[58]

This relates to another major difference between the Briskers and earlier rabbinic creativity: the goal of Torah *lishmah*, Torah study for its own sake reflected in the Briskers' valuing of abstract ideas over practical legal conclusions. Reb Hayyim, for example, does not weigh in about whose opinion should be followed in practice, Maimonides or the *Ra'avad*, R. Judah or the Sages. His focus is not legal decision-making but on elevating Jewish law to a discussion of ideals by enriching legal positions with conceptual orientation.[59]

For the Briskers, the ideas behind the law are their own immersive world, and this world stands above (though not in place of) the world of concrete religious practice. As Rabbi Joseph B. Soloveitchik, a descendant of Reb Hayyim and a major exemplar of Brisker methodology in the twentieth-century United States, expresses it:

> *Suddenly the pots and the pans, the eggs and the onions disappeared from the laws of meat and milk; the salt, the blood and the spit disappeared from the laws of salting. The laws of kashrut were taken out of the kitchen and removed to an ideal halakhic world... constructed out of the complexes of abstract concepts.*[60]

In the long history of the mind-body distinction, Brisker Torah clearly emphasizes the importance of the mind. This nonpractical orientation was born at the Yeshiva of Volozhin—the first "academic" yeshiva founded not to train rabbinic functionaries but to train philosophers of Jewish law. In one sense, this approach might be understood as the ultimate fulfillment of the ancient rabbinic focus on the study of Torah. But in another sense, the Briskers' nonpractical orientation drives a wedge between the act of Torah study and the daily practice of Judaism which had traditionally been the goal of previous rabbinic exegesis.[61]

There are those who have suggested that the Brisker method was developed to rival the Jewish enlightenment (*haskalah*) movement which rejected rabbinic Judaism as benighted.[62] In fact, some trace the word "*ḥakirah*" to the word for research used often by *maskilim*, that is, proponents of Jewish enlightenment. Brisker methodology would seek to prove that Torah has undeniable depth and sophistication. There are some who also point to the similarities between Brisker methodology and nineteenth-century Classical legal thought in Roman and common law, as they all posit the centrality of analytical concepts and core legal principles in understanding law.[63] Regardless of the provenance and motivation of this movement, however, it has had an indelible impact on yeshiva study to this day.

In his day, Reb Hayyim's detractors referred to his method of study as "chemistry" because he and his followers established a scientific method of breaking down a law into its component parts. But the heart of their argument against him is that he was bringing concepts into the study of Jewish law that were not explicit in the texts themselves. Reb Hayyim and his followers, however, asserted that they were uncovering the abstract system underlying Jewish law and merely trying to understand what earlier decisors and even the Talmud itself truly meant.[64] This debate brings the Brisker method into the orbit of the earlier approaches discussed in this chapter. Like *Midrash halakhah*, *okimtot*, and *Tosafot*, the Briskers were both bound by an inherited canon yet more unconstrained than expected in interpreting that canon.

Conclusion

This chapter examined four movements in which canonical literature was understood creatively by successive rabbinic generations to shape and/or understand Jewish law. On the one hand, each set of rabbis was constrained by the texts and the rulings that they inherited. But on the other hand, they interpreted what came before them flexibly, fusing the new with the old, the innovative with the established.

Despite this similarity, each movement contributed new precedents and approaches. *Midrash halakhah* introduced the concept of turning a textual aberration into an opportunity for creativity. It asserted the coherence of the complete biblical canon and its intertextuality; the significance of every letter of the pentateuchal corpus; and the rabbinic authority to read verses, phrases, words, and even letters against their contextual meaning. In many ways, this laid the groundwork for the unfolding of the rabbinic legal tradition by placing rabbinic interpretation at the center of determining Jewish law.

Amoraim and *stammaim* who used *okimtot* transposed the claim of coherence assumed for Scripture to the *tannaitic* canon, a bold assertion in and of itself. Moreover, they applied the kind of against-the-grain reading practices of *Midrash halakhah* in resolving *tannaitic* contradictions. They also developed the idea of contradiction beyond conflicting texts to conflicts between earlier text and their own presumed legal principles. This marked a more sophisticated stage of jurisprudence, the move from casuistic case studies to principles. It also may indicate an *Amoraic/stammaitic* interest in bridging the gap between their own legal principles and the texts they inherited. And, finally, *okimtot* regularly offered rich back-and-forth discussion that could pull the reader/listener into the conundrums of a case in a distinctly talmudic way.

The boldness of *okimtot* in asserting coherence within *tannaitic* literature and between *tannaitic* literature and their own presumed legal principles pales in comparison to *Tosafot*'s assertion of coherence across the entirety of the Babylonian Talmud. *Tosafot* offered a watershed *pilpulistic* (dialectical) methodology in a post-talmudic intellectual milieu that focused more on simply anthologizing the rulings of the Talmud. Their dialectics offered principles that could be used to identify similarities and differences among various talmudic cases and to determine law in new situations. Perhaps most daringly, *Tosafot* explicitly attempted to resolve contradictions between talmudic texts and the practices of their own communities, and often by reexamining the meaning of the former rather than trying to change the behavior of the latter. Thus, they made explicit some aspects of earlier exegesis that may have been implicit—trying to bridge the gap between the opinions and experience of the exegetes and the meanings of the texts that were meant to be authoritative. In so doing, they reinforced their belief in the piety of their constituencies and the ability to connect the past texts to current life.

And lastly, the Briskers brought to bear the same creativity in reading texts as early movements, but with a distinctly conceptual focus. They were and are not interested in determining a bottom-line ruling but in revealing a deep ideational structure beneath what appear to be technical legal debates. In this way, they took the original focus of Torah study asserted by early post-Temple rabbinic authorities to new places. They asserted that Jewish law must be about more than bottom-line rulings, emphasizing instead the theoretical analysis of each legal opinion. This became the deeper meaning of Jewish law: the concrete reflects more profound abstract ideas.

Even while noting differences among these four interpretative movements, our comparison between them surfaced their similarities and exposed how each served as a foundation for its successor(s). Some threads running through these various movements include the centrality of Torah study; the commitment to intertextuality within a single corpus; appreciation for the potential for ingenuity latent in contradictions and even disputes; and the development of principles, coherence, and meaning within a sprawling, decentralized canon.

Describing this ongoing rabbinic phenomenon of close-yet-creative reading is not just an academic or historically oriented exercise; rather, it serves as the background for understanding the push-and-pull that animates the formation of Jewish law even today. As rabbinic interpretation offers the dual impressions of continuity and change, its students must be tethered to the past as well as the present. This has significant implications for shaping Jewish law in each generation. Here, we will mention three such implications. First, despite possible creativity, close reading of the text still acts as a constraint, resulting often in only partial amelioration of challenges that arise in each generation or employing creative strategies that circumvent the law rather than changing it. These are attempts to maintain the received texts while responding to new circumstances. Second, the creative dimension of the interpretative method raises significant questions about both validity and authenticity. Who is authorized to interpret texts, for what reasons, and using what guiding rules of interpretation? These questions continue to be debated between Jewish communities and within them. And third, Jewish legal tradition might be imagined as a snowball: the original texts are the core, and interpretations accrue around them. As the snowball continues to travel, the interpretations of previous generations become the layer of text for the next generation to interpret. This layering of text upon text, interpretation upon interpretation relies on the notion that each text is essential to the next layers. On the one hand, Torah is self-contained because interpreters throughout return to the same texts over and over, but on the other hand, the canon is ever-expanding.

Notes

1. See Martin Lockshin, "Does Halakhah Really Uproot Peshat?'" *Diné Israel* 32 (2018): 211–26. By contrast to the rabbinic movement, sectarians at Qumran hewed much closer to the contextual understanding of biblical verses. Sometimes this difference resulted in rabbinic law being more lenient than Qumran law, but not always. Additionally, it is possible that rabbis un/consciously polemicized against sectarian readings through decontextualized exegesis. See Vered Noam, "Stringency in Qumran: A Reassessment," *Journal for the Study of Judaism in the Persian, Hellenistic, and Roman Period* 40, no. 3 (2009): 342–55; Vered Noam, "Embryonic Legal Midrash in the Qumran Scrolls," in *The Hebrew Bible in Light of the Dead Sea Scrolls*, ed. Nóra Dávid et al. (Göttingen, Germany: Vandenhoeck & Ruprecht, 2011), 237–62.
2. Kugel, James. "Two Introductions to Midrash," *Prooftexts* 3, no. 2 (May 1983): esp. 145.
3. References to the Bible in this chapter mostly refer to the Pentateuch, as this is the main focus of *Midrash halakhah*.
4. *Mekhilta de-Rabbi Yishmael Masekhta de-Pisḥa, Bo* 4
5. See, e.g., j.Shevi'it 10:3, 39c; b.Kiddushin 38b
6. The question of when the sabbatical applies biblically and when its status is "only" rabbinic is discussed in a number of places in rabbinic literature. See, e.g., *Sifra Behar* 2, j.Gittin 4:3, 45d; b.Gittin 36a.
7. Per Exod. 12:18.
8. b.Sukkah 27a.
9. Exod. 23:19, 34:26, Deut. 14:21.
10. *Mekhilta de-Rabbi Yishmael Masekhta de-Kaspa, Mishpatim* 20. This *Midrash* also lists alternative explanations for the appearance of this phrase thrice in the Pentateuch.
11. Exod. 20:11.
12. See b.Ketubot 103a.
13. *Sifre* Deut. 218.
14. b.Sanhedrin 71a
15. Deut. 21:19.
16. *Sifre* Deut. 219. In a rabbinic rarity, R. Simon suggests a moral motivation behind narrowing the law. He does so in context of suggesting that the permission to execute a rebellious son was never applied. Rather, it is only present in the Torah to give people merit for studying and interpreting it (b.Sanhedrin 71a).
17. Exod. 21:23–25; Lev. 24:20; Deut. 19:21, 25:11–12.
18. The citation in Deuteronomy 19 of false witnesses is slightly more complicated and not the subject of this chapter.

19. See *Mekhilta de-Rabbi Yishmael Masekhta de-Nezikin, Mishpatim* 8 and b.Bava Kamma 83b–84a.
20. m.Pe'ah 1:1.
21. Deut. 17:11; see *Sifre Deut.* 154:11.
22. *Sifre* Deut. 154:11.
23. For example, in *How Do We Know This? Midrash and the Fragmentation of Modern Judaism* (Albany: State University of New York Press, 1995), Jay M. Harris details the various ways Jews from the Middle Ages to the modern period have understood the rabbinic interpretative project. And in *Commentary Revolutions in the Making: Values as Interpretative Considerations in Midrashei Halakhah* (Jerusalem: Magnes Press, 1997), Moshe Halbertal discusses the role that moral evaluation of Scripture plays in the creativity of rabbinic exegesis. In *Nitsḥuni Banai* (*Fundamental Questions in the Study of the Oral Law*) (*Rishon le-Tsiyon: Yedi'ot aḥaronot*, 2020), Amnon Bazak offers multiple ways of understanding rabbinic scriptural exegesis from the perspective for observant Jews bound by rabbinic law.
24. There are also examples of rabbinic reading which assert the omnisignificance of words within *tannaitic* texts, another assumption taken from scriptural exegesis. For example, the Talmud might ask why a Mishnah includes phrasing such as "this is the rule (*zeh haklal*)" after giving examples of said rule. While in ordinary language, this might be expected as a summation, the Talmud often extrapolates new rulings from it (see, e.g., b.Shabbat 103a).
25. See Ronen Reichman, "The Talmudic Okimta and Its Logical Structure: A Contribution to the Systematic Research into Talmudic Legal Hermeneutics," *Jewish Studies Quarterly* 12, no. 2 (2005): 129–47.
26. 32b.
27. Per Numbers 35b–33a and Deuteronomy 19:1–10, one who commits manslaughter must be exiled to a designated city of refuge.
28. For debates about the relationship between landlord liability and the category of person on the property in the common law tradition, see Keith N. Hylton, "Tort Duties of Landowners: A Positive Theory," *44 Wake Forest Law Review* 1049 (2009); James A. Henderson, Jr., "The Status of Trespassers on Land," *44 Wake Forest Law Review* 1071 (2009); Stephen D. Sugarman, "Land-Possessor Liability in the *Restatement (Third) of Torts*: Too Much and Too Little," *44 Wake Forest Law Review* 1079 (2009).
29. See Sarah Wolf, "The Rabbinic Legal Imagination: Narrativity and Scholasticism in the Babylonian Talmud" (PhD diss., Northwestern University, 2018). She argues that this narrativity betrays a more porous boundary between law (*halakhah*) and narrative (*Aggadah*) than previously acknowledged. She also argues that sometimes the editors create the need for an *okimta* where there is none, as the story format takes on an importance of its own.
30. b.BK 27b.
31. See Bava Kamma 27b *Tos. s.v., Amai* regarding whether the owner of the vessel would have to pay restitution if the pedestrian was injured in such cases.
32. For a fuller exposition of this perspective, see R. Michael Avraham, "A Platonic Perspective on *Okimtot* (Hebrew)," *Akdamot* 28 (5773): 115–41.
33. For more on this evolution, see Leib Moscovitz, *Talmudic Reasoning: From Casuistics to Conceptualization* (Tübingen, Germany: Mohr Siebeck, 2002).
34. These steps parallel the methodology of medieval Christian scholastics; scholars debate the scope of their influence on tosafistic thinking. See E. E. Urbach, *The Tosaphists:*

Their History, Writings and Methods (Jerusalem: Bialik Institute, 1986); E. Kanarfogel, *The Intellectual History and Rabbinic Culture of Medieval Ashkenaz* (Detroit: Wayne State University Press, 2013). While step (3) resembles *okimta* methodology, *Tosafot* are less prone to take untethered license in making assumptions about legal cases. Instead, they analyze contradictory cases carefully to identify subtle distinctions that already differentiate them. Additionally, using this analytical approach, *Tosafot* sometimes identify variables common to cases that at first appear dissimilar. In resolving contradictions, *Tosafot* introduce legal principles that can then be used to understand different cases and even to rule in new cases.

35. b.Bava Metzia 2a s.v., *ve-yaḥloku.*
36. 34b.
37. *Tosafot* wrote as a group, sometimes offering interpretations anonymously, other times listing the approach(es) of a (few) Tosafist(s) on a given issue.
38. See b.BB 33b where the legal significance of physically holding as evidence of ownership is indicated.
39. b.BM 3a.
40. m.Bava Metzia 3:4.
41. See b.BM 3a for the legal significance of the possibility that both litigants could be telling the truth.
42. See, e.g., *Ma'aseh ha-geonim* and *Sifrei de-bei rashi.*
43. The term is used in the Talmud in reference to debate (e.g., b.Bava Batra 145b) and sharp reasoning (e.g., b.Temurah 16a). "*Pilpul*" is also the name of a specific movement in Talmud study that originated in Eastern Europe in the fifteenth century and continued through the eighteenth century. While this movement also engaged dialectical thinking and creative interpretation, unlike the examples in this chapter, it is no longer widely practiced today. See Haim Zalman Dimitrovsky, "The Method of Pilpul (Hebrew)," in *Salo Wittmayer Baron Jubilee Volume*, vol. 1, ed. Saul Lieberman and Arthur Hyman (Jerusalem: American Academy for Jewish Research, 1975), 111–81.
44. b.Berakhot 2a s.v., *me-eimatai.*
45. For a general overview, see Haym Soloveitchik, "Religious Law and Change: The Medieval Ashkenazic Example," in *Collected Essays: Vol. 1*, ch. 9 (Oxford: Littman Library of Jewish Civilization, 2013); and Haym Soloveitchik, "'Religious Law and Change' Revisited," in *Collected Essays: Vol. 1*, ch. 10 (Oxford: Littman Library of Jewish Civilization, 2013).
46. E.g., b.Hullin 47a Tos. s.v., *hayyenu* regarding dietary law.
47. Particularly in situations that require sacrifice, *Tosafot* do their best to justify the actions of the community based on original readings of Talmudic law. See Soloveitchik, "'Religious Law and Change' Revisited."
48. While we used the word "Torah" in the first section of this chapter to refer to the Pentateuch, the term "Torah" here is used more expansively to refer to the study of or instruction (the literal meaning of the word "Torah") in Jewish matters. In this case, Brisker Torah is Brisk-generated ideas about Jewish legal texts.
49. While the term "*ḥakirah*" is popular in defining Brisker methodology, it was not used by Reb Hayyim himself as a descriptor and only entered the lexicon as a noun later.
50. Reb Hayyim's written manuscript, *Ḥiddushei Rabbeinu Hayyim Ha-Levi,* focuses on the legal writings of twelfth-century scholar Maimonides/*Rambam* and disputes between him and his chief glossator, Rabbi Abraham ben David/*Ra'avad.* The writings of his students expand this method to many other aspects of the Talmud and its commentarial literature.

51. However, a *ḥakirah* used to explain a given talmudic ruling might be used at a different point to theorize other debates among rabbinic positions in the Talmud or in later commentators, with different sides of the *ḥakirah* leading to different practical outcomes.
52. To compare this *ḥakirah* and the Roman distinction between *actio in rem* and *actio in personam*, see Norman Solomon, 123–24; Chaim Saiman, "Legal Theology: The Turn to Conceptualism in Nineteenth-Century Jewish Law," *Journal of Law and Religion* 21, no. 1 (2005/2006): 53.
53. m.Pesaḥim 2:1.
54. See *Ḥiddushei Reb Hayyim Hilkhot Ḥametz U-Matzah* [Laws of Leavened and Unleavened Bread] 1:3. The debate about *tashbitu*, in turn, may reflect a conceptual understanding of another biblical command, the command not to own *ḥametz* on Passover (Exod. 12:19, 13:7). And while, in this example, the *ḥeftza* refers to an actual physical object, the Briskers understood the category of *ḥeftza* more broadly. For example, an action or a phenomenon might be considered a *ḥeftza* as well.
55. 10:6.
56. *Mishneh Torah*, Laws of Prayer 1:6.
57. Some of the Brisker method's leading twentieth-century exponents explicitly emphasized the primacy of the project of mapping and definition of law over resolving difficulties or disputes within the text. For example, R. Aharon Lichtenstein insisted that even for Reb Hayyim, debates and contradictions served only as the springboard for the real goal: conceptual mapping and definition of a given law. But not all agree with this understanding, as some Brisk proponents remain focused on the resolution of textual difficulties as an important end goal. Others eschewed the sharp distinction between the focus on conceptual ideas and resolving textual difficulties, suggesting that Brisker methodology incorporates a sliding scale from the textual to the conceptual. See Avraham Walfish, "The Brisker Method and Close Reading-Response to R. Elyakim Krumbein," in *The Conceptual Approach to Jewish Learning*, ed. Yosef Blau (New York: MSYU, 2006), 299–312. Aharon Lichtenstein, "The Conceptual Approach to Torah Learning: the Method and its Prospects," in *Leaves of Faith I* (New York: Ktav, 2003), 19–60; Avraham Wein, "From the Micro to the Meta: Rabbi Michael Rosensweig's Unique Contribution to *Torat Brisk*" (Honors thesis, Yeshiva College, Yeshiva University, May 2018).
58. Briskers likewise reject historical and/or psychological explanations of positions, disputes or contradictions. See Daniel Wolf, "Hiddush Within the Beit Midrash," *Tradition* 47, no. 4 (2015): 113–25, p. 116.
59. Perhaps the strongest indication of this non-practical orientation is the centrality of Maimonides's code of law *Mishneh Torah* to Brisker analysis. Maimonides intended for the *Mishneh Torah* to be a bottom-line code of practice that allowed people to bypass the ins and outs of talmudic discussion. The Briskers, however, used Maimonides's streamlined text to distill (and construct) concepts from Talmudic discussion. See Mosheh Lichtenstein, "What Hath Brisk Wrought: The Brisker Derekh Revisited," *Torah U-Madda Journal* 9 (2000): 1–18, p. 3; Marc Shapiro, "The Brisker Method Reconsidered," *Tradition* 31, no. 3 (1997): 78–102.
60. Soloveitchik, *BeSod haYahid ve-haYahad*, 227 (trans. Lawrence Kaplan ["Rabbi Joseph B. Soloveitchik's Philosophy of Halakha"]), in *Jewish Law Annual 7*, ed. Bernard Jackson (New York: Harwood Academic, 1988), 139–97.
61. To consider the difference perhaps between a Brisker mindset and a talmudic mindset, for instance, see the argument cited in the Talmud over study or action is greater. The

conclusion is "Study is greater, *for* it leads to action" (b.Kiddushin 40b). Despite the preference for study, the force of study is as an impetus to Jewish practice.

62. See Paul E. Nahme, "Wissen und Lomdus: Idealism, Modernity, and History in some Nineteenth Century Rabbinic and Philosophical Responses to the Wissenschaft des Judentums," *Harvard Theological Review* 110, no. 3 (2017): 393–420; Normon Solomon, *The Analytic Movement: Hayyim Soloveitchik and his Circle* (Atlanta, GA: Scholars Press, 1993).
63. See Saiman, "Legal Theology."
64. See Marc Shapiro, "The Brisker Method Reconsidered: Review Essay," *Tradition* 31, no. 3 (1997): 78–102. On the question the significance of original intent to Brisker methodology, see Aharon Lichtenstein, "Torat Hesed and Torat Emet: Methodological Reflections," in *Leaves of Faith: The World of Jewish Learning* (Jersey City, NJ: KTAV, 2003), 61–87.

CHAPTER 10

HALAKHAH AND *AGGADAH* IN THE TALMUD AND POST-TALMUDIC LITERATURE

SUZANNE LAST STONE

Introduction

The relationship of Jewish law (*halakhah*) to other expressions of Jewish culture, including *Aggadah* (the early rabbinic "literary" tradition), philosophy, and *kabbalah* (the Jewish mystical tradition) is complex. Traditionally, these various cultural expressions have been viewed as accompaniments to the law. Each in diverse ways provided an explanatory system for the law and rationales for the commandments, imbuing the commandments with spiritual, ethical, and intellectual meaning. But these cultural expressions do not, according to the traditional viewpoint, intrude on the law's autonomy.

Aggadah's relationship to *halakhah* is far tighter than that of philosophy or *kabbalah* and therefore presents additional complexity. *Aggadah* is often the product of the very same scholastic circles that engaged in the legal disputations recorded in the Mishnah and Talmud, the formative texts of Jewish law, and *Aggadot* are freely interwoven with the legal discussion. Indeed, from 25 to 40 percent of the Babylonian Talmud (the *Bavli*) consists of material classifiable as *Aggadah*. The *Bavli* is regarded, moreover, as a canonical body of work and the authority granted to the *Bavli* arguably extends to the *Aggadah* contained in it. Most importantly, the very division of the early rabbinic and Talmudic output into two separate bodies of knowledge, the one, *halakhah*, concerned with clearly delineated rules of conduct or decision-making and the other, *Aggadah*, concerned with speculations about God, man, and the world, is a post-talmudic development.

The question persists, therefore, whether *Aggadah* plays a legal role in the Talmudic tradition. This question is all the more pertinent today because there has been a notable turn to *Aggadah* (as well as biblical narratives) as legal sources in contemporary *halakhic* writings, particularly in areas where there is a paucity of more conventional *halakhic* sources. Recently, there has been an explosion of academic scholarship exploring the connection between *Aggadot* and the legal material. Academic scholarship highlights both the *Aggadah*'s role as subtle critique of a legal ruling (i.e., a legal dissent in the form of a narrative) and the *Aggadah*'s role as a repository of principles and values that informs the legal discussion.[1] Scholars contend that both the traditional and academic resistance to acknowledging *Aggadah*'s legal role has suffered from narrowly viewing *halakhah*—and law in general—through the prism of both positivism and formalism.[2] Various developments, they contend, have contributed to this unduly narrow prism, such as the codificatory movement in law and *halakhah*, the hardening of the idea of law as rule governance rather than norm guidance, as well as the rise of religious styles within Judaism that placed conceptual legal analysis at the heart of the religious quest.[3]

This chapter explores how familiar jurisprudential debates about "what is law?" have implicitly shaped attitudes internal to the tradition toward *Aggadah* as a legal source. The first part of this chapter unpacks several key ideas by describing *Aggadah* in more detail, drawing comparisons between *halakhah* and *Aggadah* in the Talmudic tradition to the combination of law and narrative in the Hebrew Bible. The second part focuses on the jurisprudential and theological arguments marshaled by the post-talmudic *Geonim* against the authority of the *Aggadah*. The third part turns to the classical Anglo-American common law as a way of clarifying the role of narratives in legal reasoning, including in the Talmudic corpus. The fourth part of the chapter returns to the tradition's internal viewpoint, focusing on *halakhic* writings that reintroduce *Aggadah* as a legal source. Finally, the last part of this chapter outlines some of the theological and cultural aspects of the long-standing division between *halakhah* and *Aggadah*.

The Contested Relationship of *Halakhah* and *Aggadah*

The *Aggadah* reflects the world and thought of the Talmudic Sages. The ideas of the *Aggadah* are presented in a wide variety of narrative forms such as homilies, legends about biblical figures, myths, fables, stories of the doings of rabbis, folk sayings, and theological speculation. Because *Aggadah* is so diverse and eclectic in both literary form and subject matter, by far the most common modern definition of *Aggadah* has simply been the following negative one articulated by the nineteenth-century academic scholar Leopold Zunz (1794–1886): *Aggadah* is "that which is not *halakhah*."[4]

Halakhah and *Aggadah* appear together in all the early rabbinic collections: Mishnah, Tosefta, the *halakhic midrashim*, and the two Talmuds. The Hebrew Bible itself is a mix of legal prescriptions, historical narratives, poetry, prophetic speeches, and parables, and thus the Bible provides a model and explanation for this free-wheeling combination of disparate genres in a single work.[5]

Whether the legal and narrative material of the Hebrew Bible can be meaningfully separated from one another is a question often raised internally within the Jewish tradition and externally by academic scholars. While the standard internal rabbinic viewpoint is that the narrative material of the Bible, like *Aggadah*, is not "law," there is an extremely close connection between the two genres. The Book of Genesis and the first portion of the Book of Exodus are almost exclusively narrative. They detail the history of Israel before the giving of the law at Sinai. Yet, from the outset, Genesis assumes a world of law: Cain is punished for murder, the generation of the flood is obliterated for wrongdoing, and various forms of contracts are made. And both the Talmudic rabbis and later authorities squeezed norms, especially with respect to the laws incumbent on all societies (known as the Noahide laws), out of the narratives. Moreover, there is a deep thematic interplay between biblical law and biblical narrative.[6] For example, the sabbatical laws, and even the time period in which a Hebrew slave may remain enslaved, are tied to the account of God's creation while laws about proper treatment of strangers and foreign slaves are tied to the account of Israel's exodus from Egypt. As the academic biblical scholar Edward Greenstein put it, "law and narrative remain two separate genres but in a general way they teach the same values and the same principles can be deduced out of and underlie both."[7]

This deep connection between law and narrative continues in the Mishnah and Talmud, the formative sources of Jewish law codified in the early centuries of the Common Era. The Talmudic tradition, like the Hebrew Bible, evinces a commitment to communicate and discuss norms in two very different ways: through relatively clear, apodictic statements (i.e., rules) and logical argumentation and through concrete, contextual, personal—and sometimes, fantastical—examples or stories. For example, academic studies have shown how the details of the laws of execution are worked out against the background of theosophic assumptions revealed in the narrative material about the respect due to the body of humans created in the image of God. An *aggadic* parable tells of twins, one a robber and the other a king. The robber is executed and the crowd exclaims: "The king is hanged." In the parable, the king is a figure for God and the robber is a human. The parable implies that executing a human being, in effect, harms God because of the close connection between God and humans who are created in the image of God. This connection also finds expression in the laws of execution by fire, which requires a method that preserves the outer form of the human body.[8]

A concrete example of the close relationship of *halakhah* and *Aggadah*, especially useful for those unfamiliar with *Aggadah*, is one of the most cited narratives in the Babylonian Talmud, known as the story of the Oven of Akhnai. The *Aggadah* tells about a momentous event that occurred during the convocation of Sages at Yavneh:

> We learned . . . If one cut [the oven] into separate tiles and placed sand between each tile, Rabbi Eliezer declared it clean, and the Sages unclean. This was the oven of Akhnai [= snake]. Why Akhnai? Said Rabbi Judah in the name of Samuel: It is because they encircled it with arguments like a snake, and declared it unclean.

> It was taught: On that day Rabbi Eliezer replied with all the arguments in the world, but they did not accept them from him. He said to them: "If the halakhah agrees with me, this carob tree will prove it!" The carob tree was uprooted a hundred cubits from its place—and some say four hundred cubits. They said to him: "No proof may be brought from a carob tree." He then said to them: "If the halakhah agrees with me, the aqueduct will prove it!" The water thereupon flowed backwards. "No proof may be brought from an aqueduct," they said to him. Said he in turn: "If the halakhah agrees with me, the walls of the house of study will prove it!" The walls of the house of study started to fall. However, Rabbi Joshua rebuked them, saying: "If scholars debate one another about the halakhah, what concern is it of yours?" They did not fall down out of respect for Rabbi Joshua, but did not stand up straight out of respect for Rabbi Joshua. They are still inclining. Then he said to them: "If the halakhah agrees with me, Heaven will prove it!" A voice [*bat qol*] went forth and said: "What have you against Rabbi Eliezer, for the halakhah agrees with him everywhere." Then Rabbi Joshua stood up on his feet and said: "It is not in heaven!" [Deuteronomy 30:12]. What does "It is not in heaven" mean? Said Rabbi Jeremiah: "The Torah has already been given at Mount Sinai and one pays no attention to a voice from heaven; for You have already written on Mount Sinai in Your Law, 'after the majority must one incline' [Exodus 23:2]."
>
> Rabbi Nathan met Elijah and asked him: "What did the Holy One, blessed be He, do in that hour?" He replied: "He smiled and said, 'My children have defeated Me, My children have defeated Me.'"[9]

The above passage is a small section of a longer unit.[10] The *Aggadah* makes its appearance immediately after a discussion about whether in the time of the Sages the gates of heaven are now closed. In other words, is direct communication with the Divine still possible? One opinion states that only the gates of wounded feelings remains open and this statement introduces the *Aggadah*. In the continuation of the story, the *Aggadah* relates that Rabban Gamliel excommunicated Rabbi Eliezer for continuing to rule in accordance with his views, despite the majority decision of the Sages. Rabban Gamliel is nearly swept away at sea and saved in the last instance when he cries to heaven that he excommunicated R. Eliezer "so that disputes would not multiply in Israel." The coda of the narrative returns to the theme of wounded feelings. R. Eliezer's wife (who is also Rabban Gamliel's sister) is reported to go to great lengths to prevent her husband from crying out about his wounded feelings but she is unfortunately distracted for a moment and in that instant, R. Eliezer cries out and Rabban Gamliel is struck dead.

The literary elements of the *Aggadah* are remarkable,[11] but what concerns us here is its legal elements. The precise legal question posed is whether prophecy—Divine communication about the law—can be taken into account in *halakhic* decision-making. R. Eliezer, elsewhere in the Talmudic corpus, is portrayed as a Sage who bases his legal opinions on received legal tradition and in accordance with his received tradition, the oven was ritually clean. The majority of Sages held the view, most likely based on logical argumentation, that the oven was unclean. At this point, R. Eliezer invokes a variety of miracles to persuade the Sages that he is correct, culminating in the proclamation by a voice from heaven itself that R. Eliezer's opinion is the correct *halakhah*. In the face of this declaration, R. Joshua replies, citing a scriptural verse, the law "is not in heaven." And R. Jeremiah later explains the meaning now given to this scriptural citation: Once the Torah was revealed, the law was handed over for human deliberation and controversies about the law are settled by majority consensus.

Stripped of all the miraculous doings and God's laughing acquiescence, elements so characteristic of *Aggadah*, the passage presents a succinct statement about legal truth and validity. The passage is a clear jurisprudential cornerstone of the *halakhah*. Maimonides, the prominent twelfth-century Torah scholar, codifies the basic principle that prophecy has no role in *halakhic* deliberation and reasoning both in the Introduction to his Commentary to the Mishnah and in his Code of Law, the Mishneh Torah, citing the same scriptural proof texts invoked in the *aggadic* passage and giving them the same nonliteral interpretation.[12]

Yet, whether this *Aggadah* is a legal source remains unclear. This *Aggadah* could be understood in two different ways: as the legal source of rabbinic authority to disregard prophecy or, instead, as a marvelous account of a preexisting rule delineating rabbinic authority. In other words, the *Aggadah* could be understood as a statement *of* law, or as a statement *about* the law and thus legal theory rather than law. This is only one of a series of related jurisprudential puzzles *Aggadah* presents. Consider *aggadic* tales of the conduct of exemplary figures. For example, the Talmud specifies that the obligation to give charity may not be coerced by the court.[13] Yet, the Talmud also reports that Rava, a preeminent Talmudic judge and communal leader, once coerced someone to give charity.[14] The story of Rava could be viewed in several ways: as an implicit dissent to the rule; as a limitation on the rule permitting communal leaders, as opposed to the court, to coerce charity; or as a narrative precedent, from which a rule can be extracted that would allow the court to coerce charity.

Yet another jurisprudential puzzle is raised by the numerous *aggadic* passages (as well as scriptural verses) that convey broad-based, open-ended values and principles, such as "creation in the image of God" (*b'tzelem Elohim*) or "respect for human dignity" (*k'vod habriyyot*). Do these principles have independent legal force or are they simply general expressions of the purpose behind detailed, preexisting rules?[15] Pursuant to the second view, that the principles are merely explanations of concrete rules, the stipulated rules exhaust the scope of the principle. Pursuant to the first view, that principles have independent legal force, one could theoretically generate new rules from the principles and values the *Aggadot* convey and one could cite these principles to overcome specific rules in situations where the principles and rules point in different directions. For example, the idea of creation in the image of God, a biblical principle enhanced and elaborated on in countless *aggadic* passages, provides the conceptual underpinning of a set of rules about the respect accorded to corpses. The concrete rules setting out obligations of respect due to the creation of humans in the image of God are quite few, however. Can the principle of creation in the image of God serve as a basis for generating entirely new norms of respect to humans that extend beyond the body or override preexisting norms that conflict with the principle?[16]

That *Aggadah* is "not law" was first articulated in the post-talmudic, *geonic* period. Since then, the refrain "we do not learn *halakhah* from the *aggadah*" has become a convention within internal Jewish legal practice. Today, for example, in traditional yeshiva circles devoted to the study of *halakhah*, the *Aggadah* is hardly studied. Before engaging in a reassessment of the legal status of *Aggadah*, it is important to understand the basis for the *geonic* denial of legal authority to *Aggadah*.

"We Do Not Derive Law from *Aggadah*": A Second Look

The distinction between *halakhah* and *Aggadah* is only hinted at within the Talmudic corpus itself. In the Jerusalem Talmud,[17] Rabbi Zera in the name of Shmuel is quoted as saying that one does not make a decision on the basis of the *halakhot, haggadot, and tosafot*. This statement recognizes that there are a plurality of genres relevant to decision-making but does not relegate the *Aggadah* to a secondary status. According to another Talmudic statement, however, "the *aggadist* does not forbid or permit, proclaim unclean or proclaim clean."[18]

In the *geonic* period, the dictum attributed to Saadya Gaon (882–942 CE) that "one does not rely on *aggadah*" gained currency. The post-talmudic *Geonim* asserted, quoting "our rabbis," that *haggadah* should neither be relied on nor questioned.[19] According to the preeminent twentieth-century scholar of *Aggadah*, Joseph Heinemann, since the days of the rabbinic Talmudist and poet Shmuel HaNagid (993–1056 CE), the negative definition of *Aggadah* was accepted. Heinemann, notably, included in the definition of *Aggadah* any material with narrative qualities such as aphorisms, long stories, and fables.[20]

The *Geonim* articulated both jurisprudential and theological rationales for this view. The jurisprudential objection takes aim at the narrative form of the *Aggadah*, while the theological objection is directed toward the actual content of *Aggadah*. Those who articulated a jurisprudential objection identified the defect of the *Aggadah* in its departure from a rule-like form. The *Aggadah* is fluid in its details, often conveying multiple perspectives. It utilizes more free-wheeling interpretative canons when interpreting scripture, and, as a result, the singular quality of rules in which outcomes follow rules in relatively straightforward and predictable fashion is lacking. In the words of R. Hai Gaon: "It should be known that the words of the aggadah do not have the status of oral tradition (*shemuah*) and each person conjectures as he pleases, employing such terms as 'perhaps' and 'it could be said,' so that the issues are not clearly defined. For that reason we cannot rely upon them."[21]

The theological objection to the *Aggadah* as a source of law or legal reasoning is aimed primarily at the anthropomorphic conception of God appearing in numerous *Aggadot*. For example, God laughs and concedes defeat, God learns Torah and dons phylacteries.[22] Thus, Shmuel ben Hofni Gaon (920–1013 CE) remarked: "Where the words of the early authorities contradict intellectual perception, we are not obliged to accept them."[23] In a certain way, the theological objection cuts even deeper than the jurisprudential one, because it denies *Aggadah* authority even as theology. As the academic scholar Yair Lorberbaum notes, "*halakhah* and *aggadah* (especially the 'obscure' *aggadah*) are no longer seen as occupying the same ideational world."[24] According to this view, the *Aggadah* cannot even serve as an explanatory system accompanying the *halakhah*.

Yet, if the primary objection is theological, only *Aggadot* that are concerned with the nature of God and God's doings are disqualified as sources of law. In an intriguing study, Berachyahu Lifshitz argues that the term "*aggadah*" in the Talmud refers to narratives about God's nature,[25] as evidenced by Sifre Deuteronomy: "Dorshei Haggadot say: 'If you wish to know Him who spoke and the world came into being, study *haggadah*, for thereby you will come to know Him and cling to His ways.'"[26] According to this statement, *Aggadah* is concerned with metaphysical matters such as knowledge of God and His ways.

The distinction between *Aggadah* and *halakhah* in the early rabbinic layer, according to Lifshitz, is as follows: narratives concerned with the actions and obligations of God are *Aggadah* while narratives about human obligations are part of the *halakhic* corpus. In other words, the division between *halakhah* and *Aggadah* rests *not on its narrative form but on its content*. Put otherwise, normative guidance is the function of *halakhah* while metaphysics and ontology are the concern of *Aggadah*. If this thesis is correct, much of what we classify as *Aggadah* today based on its narrative form was not classified as *Aggadah* in the early rabbinic corpus. Consequently, narratives concerning human obligations were never intended by the Talmudic rabbis to be excluded from the legal corpus. These narratives are simply an unusual genre of reflection on human obligations from which legal knowledge and normative guidance could be extracted.

But the *geonic* objection directed toward the form of *Aggadot*, specifically their lack of framing in rule-like form and failure to offer clear-cut guidance, is not so easily dismissed. We expect law to speak with a large degree of clarity and precision. Expressing law in clear rules is part and parcel of the ideal of the modern Western rule of law, an ideal that cabins judicial whim by insisting that judges follow the rules laid down and that preserves individual freedom by insisting that law clearly demarcate between authorized and nonauthorized conduct. If law is a closed system of rules, decision-making becomes a formal operation.[27] Judges, in applying rules, do not exercise discretion because the rules do the work and thus the law, and not the judge, governs.

While the Jewish legal system vests far more trust in judges than modern legal systems and accords them far more authority to depart from rules, other aspects of the *halakhah* heighten the need for rules. As Israeli jurist Moshe Silberg long ago pointed out, the *halakhah* primarily addresses ordinary people who are performing the law on a daily and even hourly basis without court intervention or judicial instruction.[28] To perform the law, to know what are one's obligations, requires that the law be stated with precision and clarity. Since the post-Talmudic *geonic* period, the paradigm picture of *halakhah* is a set of rules, a picture that culminated in the project of codification. Thus, modern researchers who thought about the question of *halakhah* and *Aggadah* did so within a setting in which positivism—law as a pedigreed set of rules embodying authoritative directives hierarchically arranged within a unified state—increasingly dominated the landscape.

Nevertheless, rules can be embedded in stories and squeezed out or inferred from them. The classical common law, which consists almost entirely of judicial cases, is one example. And theories of law emanating from common law legal traditions, especially those that insist law is not restricted to rules but also encompasses principles, have opened up new ways to understand and describe how *Aggadah* at times functions as law in Talmudic literature, and increasingly as a legal source in the contemporary period.

Common law is not simply the name of a particular legal tradition such as the Anglo-American legal tradition. Common law is a style of legal thought and reasoning that characterizes many legal systems that have not been absorbed into the apparatus of the state.[29] The grounds for conceptual comparison of the Talmudic tradition and common law lie in in a variety of structural similarities.[30] The most important, for current purposes, is the role of narratives in legal reasoning. It is worth exploring a bit more deeply the common law style of legal reasoning in the hope that it can provide an analytic category for assessing the role of narratives in rabbinic legal reasoning.

Narrative Jurisprudence

Common Law Styles of Legal Reasoning

Classical Anglo-American common law consists entirely of cases that are extended narratives of social interaction. This jurisprudence of stories serves as a vehicle for reasoning about unwritten rules. Rules are extracted from a story of social interaction and even applied to the very case from which they have been extracted. Often a rule extracted from one narrative is reformulated in light of comparison to other stories, whether actual cases or hypotheticals. The classical common law viewed prior cases (and even parliamentary legislation) as no more or less authoritative than hypotheticals.[31] Both actual cases and hypotheticals are a means to explore the ambit of a rule. Rules are taken up, set aside, or revised in light of the concreteness that the narratives provide. This style of legal reasoning, of testing generally formulated rules against particulars provided by stories of social interaction, is preserved in the modern legal classroom, which is dominated by hypotheticals often framed around stories that border on the absurd and that are designed to test the limits of a rule's application. It is also preserved in the characteristic common law genre known as Restatements of the Law, which consists of a rule, followed by a series of cases intended to pinpoint when the rule breaks down.

Strikingly, the defects of the *Aggadah* as a source of law identified by the *Geonim* are echoed in the charges that Thomas Hobbes and Jeremy Bentham slung at the historical—and persisting—Anglo-American common law. According to Hobbes, the common law is a philosophy, not law.[32] Bentham went even further, describing the common law as "a thing merely imaginary."[33] If one believes, as does Hobbes, that "it is not Wisdom, but Authority that makes a Law,"[34] or agrees with Bentham that law must consist of commands, then common law is not law. For, "common law denies that command, sanction, authorized institutions, or even clarity is theoretically central to law."[35] According to the common law, the central aspect of law is norm guidance, and the common law seeks to provide that through an institutionalized, collaborative argument about norms.

The legal philosopher Ronald Dworkin remains the best articulator of the theory of law and style of legal reasoning that characterize the common law. Dworkin's first major intervention in legal theory draws on the common law in asserting that principles, and not solely rules, are sources of law.[36] In a later work, Dworkin described the judicial process of weighing principles along with rules as interpretative.[37] In describing law as an interpretative concept, Dworkin directs our attention away from positivism's idea of law as an authoritative text (such as a code, a statute, or a binding precedent) and toward the idea of law as a social practice in which participants argue about the content of norms in light of the larger purposes of the law. These purposes are not external to the law; rather, they are embedded in the accumulated past of the legal tradition.

The next section takes a fresh look at several *aggadic* passages as illustrative of common law styles of legal reasoning.

Aggadah and *Halakhah* Revisited: Two Talmudic Examples

Two *aggadic* passages, summarized below, highlight different aspects of common law styles of legal reasoning: the first deals with extracting and reformulating rules in light of narratives; the second, with the interaction of rules and principles.

The first example draws on a well-known *Aggadah* about a first-century figure, Honi The Circle-Drawer, who today is remembered primarily as a miracle worker who drew a circle and refused to leave it until God produced rain.[38] The tale appears several times in Talmudic literature in different versions, but its first appearance is in the mishnaic tractate dealing with the laws of public prayer in response to calamities that befall the community. In the third chapter, the Mishnah states: "They sound the ram's horn because of any public distress—may it never befall—but not because of too great an abundance of rain."[39] This rule is followed immediately by a story detailing how Honi at first refused to pray for the rain to cease, despite the entreaties of the people who had fled to the Temple portico seeking shelter, but eventually relented when the rain threatened to turn into a flood. The relationship of the Honi story to the rule in the Mishnah is complex because the rule Honi performs in the narrative is slightly ambiguous, as narratives tend to be. Attention to the details of the story, however, reveals the rule Honi enacted: One may pray for the ceasing of torrential rain but not rain that is merely burdensome. Although it may be perfectly sensible to pray for the cessation of torrential rain, this conduct is a clear violation of the literal terms of the mishnaic rule.

In the mishnaic account, it is unclear whether the narrative is functioning as a legal dissent cast in narrative form because the story contains conflicting assessments of Honi. He is a holy man—a member of God's household—yet the head of the High Court, Shimon ben Shetach, censures him. The role of the story in the later Talmudic discussion of the mishnaic rule is easier to pinpoint. The Jerusalem Talmud adopts a literal reading of the original mishnaic rule, forbidding praying for rain to cease even in cases of torrential rain that poses a danger to life.[40] The Jerusalem Talmud also supplies a theological rationale for this rule: God promised never to revisit a flood and so praying for rain to cease is tantamount to impugning God's promise. A version of the story of Honi is then cited, but in this version, through subtle alterations and interpolations, Honi is portrayed as a villain.

By contrast, the *Bavli*[41] completely reworks the mishnaic rule so that it is in conformity with the rule performed by Honi. Here the *Aggadah* is doing legal work. Thus, the *Bavli* explains the Mishnah's rule as follows: "Because one does not pray over an excess of good." The *Bavli*'s reformulation is completely contrary to the Jerusalem Talmud. The object of the mishnaic rule is no longer rain per se; rain is merely an example of an excess of good. The clear implication, however, is that torrential rain, unlike ordinary rain, is not an excess of good; torrential rain poses a danger to life and is a potential calamity. Accordingly, the *Bavli* adopts the rule Honi performed: one may not pray for merely burdensome rain to cease but one may pray for torrential rain to cease. And in the version of the Honi narrative appearing in the *Bavli*, Honi is praised. As this discussion demonstrates, throughout the course of the citation of the Honi narrative in the Talmudic corpus, the intimate connection between the rule and narrative is preserved through a subtle rewriting of the facts of the narrative, just as prior cases are subtly revised and retold in the common law to emerge as precedents for a reformulated rule.

The second example turns to the topic of rules and principles and is drawn from the *Bavli*'s commentary on a chapter in the Second Book of Samuel of the Hebrew Bible.[42] This text recounts the hanging of Saul's sons at the demand of the Gibeonites, a minority group living on the land who charged that King David's predecessor, Saul, had caused their death.[43] The biblical narrative is a story of three reconciliations: between God and Israel; between the people of Israel and the Gibeonites (a strife within the polity); and between the House of David and the House of Saul (a strife within the Israelite community). The story begins with a famine, moves to the dramatic moment when David acquiesces in the Gibeonites' demand for enacting retribution against the sons of Saul since Saul is already dead, and ends with David's burial of Saul's bones, at which point the famine is lifted.

The passage in the *Bavli* is morally complex and multifaceted.[44] My focus here is on the *Bavli*'s evaluation of King David's decision to hand over Saul's sons for execution. That decision goes against the grain of the *Bavli*'s general antipathy toward collective punishment and its efforts to establish individual punishment as the norm.[45] Yet, the *Bavli* is committed here to the correctness of David's decision. After all, the Bible reports that in the end, the Divine anger was appeased. Moreover, in the Talmudic tradition, David is a figure of one who exercises "righteous judgment." In this sense, the biblical narrative is akin to a judicial precedent: an account of social interaction that includes an evaluation or judgment of the action. Indeed, as will be discussed later, this biblical narrative along with the Talmudic commentary also functions as a legal source in contemporary *halakhic* writing.

The *Bavli* justifies David's decision to surrender Saul's sons for execution by commenting as follows: "Better that a letter of the Torah should be uprooted than profanation of the Name occur." The phrase "letter of the Torah" signifies that the rule allows only individual punishment. David uprooted the rule because it clashed with the often-cited Talmudic principle to uphold the public honor of God. The *Bavli* proceeds to explain that, as a result of David's decision, onlookers were now marveling at the punishment meted out to princes to avenge a wrong committed against a bedraggled minority population. Thus, God's public honor was enhanced. The importance of the narrative is that it makes the tension between rules and principles explicit and seems to treat both as components of a legal decision, with principles having weight and therefore able to overcome rules. Indeed, the narrative is set within a larger Talmudic analytic unit discussing the rabbinic power to uproot Torah law. Given this larger context, the narrative offers a classroom lesson on the process of legal reasoning and decision-making (with the decision projected onto King David) in a system composed of interacting rules and principles.

Thus far, we have concentrated on academic reassessments of the legal role of *Aggadah* in the Talmudic corpus. But do *halakhic* decisors themselves acknowledge *Aggadah* as a legal source? Put otherwise, did the model of *halakhah* as a collection of rules, implicitly advanced by the *Geonim*, persist as the exclusive model of *halakhah*? This question—how was *halakhah* tacitly theorized or pictured over the ages among differing *halakhists*—is far too large to tackle in this chapter. But citation to *Aggadah* as a legal source often offers an important clue bearing on this larger jurisprudential question.

Breaching the *Geonic* Wall from Within

The *geonic* viewpoint was followed by most medieval and later decisors, but not all. This section will briefly review the contested role of *Aggadah* in the work of Maimonides and then take a closer look at citations of *Aggadah* as a legal source in contemporary *halakhic* writings.

In his early work, Maimonides, who often took issue with the *Geonim*, seems to have set out to reunify the *halakhah* and *Aggadah* and reintroduce *Aggadah* into the scholastic curriculum. Maimonides asserted that once properly understood, *Aggadah* was philosophy. While Maimonides had precisely the same negative attitude to anthropomorphic understandings of God as did the *Geonim*, he contended that the Sages who composed the *Aggadah* were communicating philosophic truths in parables and riddles.

In his monumental Code of Jewish Law, the Mishneh Torah, Maimonides attempted to distill the vast Talmudic corpus into a succinct, practical statement of the law. He announced that he wished to present the *halakhic* material "pruned of the associative discussion, digression, and indeterminate debate"[46] that plagues the Talmudic corpus. Despite this commitment to brevity and the elimination of whatever is nonessential, Maimonides still incorporated *Aggadah* into the Code. But it is less than clear whether *Aggadah* is a source of legal ruling in the Mishneh Torah, or an explanatory accompaniment to the *halakhah*. Certainly, Maimonides held that the law is purposive; there are reasons for all the commandments. Thus Maimonides's citations to *Aggadah* in the Mishneh Torah most often serve to clarify the rationale of the *halakhic* rule.

Maimonides's extensive reliance on *Aggadah* in the Epistle on Martyrdom is equally ambiguous and hotly debated by academic scholars. The Epistle offers a legal opinion about a concrete situation and, as such, functions in substance as a responsum. It was received and cited as a legal opinion by several later rabbinic jurists. In this Epistle, which has been extensively analyzed from a jurisprudential perspective by Yair Lorberbaum and Haim Shapira,[47] Maimonides addresses a crisis situation: a period of intense persecution of Jews under the Almohad regime in the twelfth century when Jews were given the choice to recite the Islamic confession of faith or die. The question at hand is whether a Jew who confesses in these circumstances may still perform Jewish religious commandments in secrecy. A prior rabbinic jurist had ruled that there was no value in such religious performance, noting that the individual had a *halakhic* obligation to martyr himself rather than publicly confess Islam. Maimonides vehemently disagrees and makes extensive use of scripture and the *Aggadah* to show that biblical figures and Talmudic Sages behaved as if they were violating the *halakhah*, and that under extreme circumstances of duress, God rewards the good deeds of sinners. The Epistle ends with an analysis of the Talmudic rules subsumed under the principles of sanctifying and not desecrating the Divine Name.

The free use of the *Aggadah* by Maimonides in arriving at his opinion, as well as his departure from the thrust of Talmudic law (and even from his own statements in his Code), led the noted historian of *halakhah*, Haym Soloveitchik, to contend that the Epistle on Martyrdom was not intended as a legal ruling. Soloveitchik instead claimed it was "rhetoric," a political statement issued in Maimonides's role as a communal leader.[48] The academic debate about the nature of the Epistle on Martyrdom as law or rhetoric returns us to the problem of how intertwined the status of *Aggadah* is with particular understandings of law. Thus, Soloveitchik contends that the concept of law consists of a nested system of rules. Moral or political principles are not part of the *halakhah* unless already concretized in a rule; they are extra-*halakhic*. Soloveitchik also implicitly is claiming that this is the concept of law that Maimonides (and, indeed, all *halakhists*) hold. By contrast, Soloveitchik's interlocutor, David Hartman, argued that *halakhic* rules and moral and political values inferred from the *Aggadah* interact; the *halakhic* decisor (ideally) and Maimonides, in particular, weighs rules in light of principles, including principles drawn from scripture and the *Aggadah*. As Lorberbaum and Shapira detail, this debate between Soloveitchik and Hartman over the status of the Epistle as law or rhetoric reprises the classic one between Hart and Dworkin on the question "what is law?"

Lorberbaum notes that at the time the Epistle was written, Maimonides still esteemed the *Aggadah*. Later in life, Maimonides seems to have changed his position on the *Aggadah*. He never wrote his promised tract on the philosophic meaning of the *Aggadah*. As Lorberbaum points out, in the end, Maimonides adopted the jurisprudential objection of the *Geonim*.[49] He wrote to his student Pinchas Ben Meshullam HaDayyan, quoting the language of the *Geonim*, that we do not rely on legal matters on the *Aggadah*. Moreover, Maimonides goes one step further than the *Geonim* because they were silent on the status of *Aggadah* found in the *Bavli*. The reception of the *Bavli* as canonical gave a cloak of legitimacy to all material within it. But Maimonides makes clear here that even the *Aggadot* in the *Bavli* should not be given weight.

Yet, *Aggadah* and biblical narratives make a startlingly large appearance in contemporary *halakhic* writings, especially those authored within religious Zionist circles. As in the case of the Epistle on Martyrdom, many of these writings are a response to crisis. The return of Jews to sovereignty in the twentieth century after a nearly two-thousand-year hiatus posed considerable challenges for Jewish legal decisors. For example, Jews had no continuous legal tradition addressing the laws of war, the obligations of a sovereign Jewish government, or even the legitimacy of a secular Jewish parliament and court system (see Resnicoff, this volume).[50] Long-neglected legal sources, such as Maimonides's Code of Law on the topics of war and the laws of kings, were resuscitated and applied to present-day warfare and modern state sovereignty. The laws relevant to these modern-day dilemmas were sparse. Moreover, there was no *halakhic* tradition of continuous application, testing, and refinement of the rules in concrete circumstances.

Legal decisors in Israel responded to this challenge in very different ways.[51] Ultra-traditionalists adhered to older patterns of *halakhic* thought and largely neglected the new topics. From an ideological perspective, ultra-traditionalists do not assign independent religious value to the creation of a Jewish sovereign state. Nor do ultra-traditionalists, by and large, serve in the army. Therefore, the development of *halakhah* in light of modern warfare and battlefield ethics was not pressing. The question of the legitimacy of the state and its institutions could be settled by drawing on familiar patterns developed when living in exile under non-Jewish rulership. Military matters could be analyzed, however impracticably, by subsuming war to *halakhic* rules on individual aggression and defense. From a jurisprudential perspective, ultra-traditionalists assign great weight, even a transcendent force, to the continuous spiral of argument within the legal tradition. A subject lacking such a continuous spiral is best avoided. More significantly, ultra-traditionalists were not prepared to recognize the Jewish state as a *halakhic* entity, a collective subject to distinct obligations and rights.

In sharp contrast, rabbis within the religious Zionist segment treated the novel reality as a paradigm shift. They sought to fashion new collective obligations and rights that could be applied to the new entity of a Jewish sovereign state. Moreover, they insisted that the *halakhah* must be a part of the general Jewish cultural renaissance. Thus, they often rejected other proposed *halakhic* solutions that rested on the incorporation by reference of international or foreign law.[52] Rather, the *halakhah* must supply an indigenous and innovative solution, a culturally specific, Jewish response to the novel questions raised by Jewish sovereignty.

In this context, *halakhic* decisors have increasingly turned to novel sources, as well. A famous sermon by the prominent fourteenth-century Talmudic commentator Rabbi Nissim Gerondi that had become a focus for contemporary debate about the *halakhic* legitimacy of separating religion and state in a contemporary Jewish state is cited and redescribed by the early twentieth-century leader of the ultra-traditionalist community in Vilnius, Lithuania, R. Haim Grodzinski, as a *responsum* (a legal source).[53] Most often, rabbis within the religious Zionist camp have turned to *Aggadah* and biblical narratives to fashion law.[54] Many of these biblical narratives are set within the context of the biblical polity, and therefore provide a rough analogy for the modern Jewish state. As noted above, biblical narratives about the actions of kings of Israel are often accompanied by details in the narrative of Divine approval or disapproval. The narratives, in this sense, are no different from common law precedents: both are narratives of social interaction with a judgment attached, indicating whether the parties' actions are proper or improper. As with judicial cases, rules of conduct can be extracted from them.

The *Aggadah* as well as biblical narratives also appear prominently in religious Zionist attempts to fashion laws of war and battlefield ethics. Writings on this subject in particular illustrate both the benefit and risks of relying on fluid and ambiguous narratives and open-ended principles such as "be holy," as opposed to clearly delineated rules. The moderate camp tends to interpret the relevant narratives and principles such as "be holy," in ways that demand heightened ethical sensibilities. But more militant streams within religious Zionism ascribe a completely different meaning to the idea of holiness, valorizing extreme aggression.

The story of the Gibeonites provides another example of the contemporary fashioning of rules of conduct from *Aggadah*. The biblical narrative of the Gibeonites' demand for justice in light of King Saul's role in their destruction, as well as the *Bavli*'s commentary on it, form the centerpiece of a *responsum* authored by Rabbi Hayyim David HaLevi in 1985, who was then Chief Rabbi of Tel Aviv. This *responsum* outlines the obligations owed by the government of Israel to minority populations.[55] The Talmud questions how we know that Saul perpetrated a crime against the Gibeonites since scripture does not report one. It supplies the following answer: the Gibeonites were the servants of the priests of Nov whom Saul slayed for shielding David, then a usurper to the throne. As a result, the Gibeonites lost their means of sustenance and, observes the Talmud, "Scripture regards it as if he himself had killed them." HaLevi stresses that it was the responsibility of the government and indeed all Israel to sustain the Gibeonites, an obligation sworn to in a treaty inaugurated in the days of Joshua and binding on all later leaders. HaLevi also relies on the two principles invoked in the Talmudic discussion to justify overriding of the "letter of the law" regarding forbidding intergenerational punishment: the obligation to sanctify and the requirement to avoid desecrating the Divine Name. Together, they point to the clear obligation of a Jewish government to provide subsistence toward vulnerable minorities, "whether they are permanent residents or strangers."

The most striking feature of R. HaLevi's *responsum* is his sympathetic portrayal of the Gibeonites. In the biblical account, the Gibeonites are portrayed as a people with a just claim who demand satisfaction in an extraordinarily cruel manner. David is reported to have tried but failed to persuade them to accept money in place of blood. In the *aggadic* commentary, the cruelty of the Gibeonites is emphasized. They failed to act mercifully because they stood on their rights when they should have relinquished them. Indeed, the entire thrust of the *aggadic* passage is to explain a mishnaic law excluding the Gibeonites from converting and joining the community of Israel. In Maimonides Mishneh Torah, the Gibeonites are a figure of the "way of cruelty" that Israel must avoid.[56] In contrast, R. HaLevi dwells on the pitiful circumstances of the Gibeonites and justifies their demand to exact punishment on the sons of Saul: "The matter pained them greatly and justifiably so, and they were not able to forgive the injustice that was thereby perpetrated against them."[57]

These rabbinic writings are a far cry from the formal analysis that so characterizes most *halakhic responsa*. The same questions directed at Maimonides's Epistle could be, and have been, directed here. Thus, David Ellenson, who has written extensively on the jurisprudence of HaLevi, contends that principles play a large role throughout his *halakhic* writings.[58] Ellenson compares HaLevi to Dworkin's ideal judge who scours the legal tradition for the principles implanted in its base.

One might dismiss this turn to *Aggadah* as a transitory response to a moment of crisis. Still, the *Aggadah* always seems to resurface within *halakhic* writings whenever there is a historic shift perceived to be a change of paradigmatic proportions, regardless of whether that shift truly constitutes a crisis. Paradigmatic changes, such as those potentially posed by new technologies such as artificial intelligence, reveal the limits of the law's usual method of proceeding by precedent and analogy. Here, too, we see *halakhic* writings address the new technologies through the prism of Talmudic *Aggadah* in which rabbis clone cows and conjure robots. There seems to be two related instincts at work here. First, it is inconceivable that the *halakhah* has, to use Dworkin's term, simply run out. Second, there is a drive to squeeze out *halakhic* information from any available source, including *Aggadah*.

Theological and Cultural Aspects of the Division of *Halakhah* and *Aggadah*

The authority ostensibly denied to *Aggadah* (as well as philosophy and *kabbalah*) is not merely a technical question within Jewish law or a jurisprudential puzzle. Rather, it is a symbol of a much larger debate both over Judaism as a religion of law, and not spirit, and over the nature of Judaism in modernity. While *halakhah* has always occupied a central role in the definition of the Jewish religion, *halakhah* has not always been the exclusive definition of the Jewish religious quest. In the Talmudic literature itself, the study of *Aggadah* is described as the means to attain knowledge of God. In the medieval period, Maimonides declared that knowledge of God was the primary religious aim and philosophy the means to attain it. The later Lithuanian yeshiva movement declared that the conceptual study of the details of *halakhah* was itself a spiritual expression,[59] and largely removed *Aggadah* from the curriculum. This turn was presaged in the Talmudic dictum: "After the destruction of the Temple, God is confined to the four cubits of *halakhah*."[60] By contrast, the rise of a modern Jewish cultural identity has breathed new life into *Aggadah* as literature (and into Jewish philosophy and *kabbalah*). For the first time, these cultural expressions stand on their own. They are no longer explanatory systems of the *halakhah* but, rather, independent means to achieve a Jewish cultural identity.[61]

In his classic essay, "*Halakhah and Aggadah*" (1916), the Hebrew poet Haim Nahman Bialik sought to achieve a reintegration of *halakhah* and *Aggadah*. He wrote that *halakhah* and *Aggadah* are "two faces of the same creature." *Halakhah*, he affirmed, is the "crystallization" of *Aggadah*. It relates to *Aggadah* as "speech" is related to "thought" and "emotion," or as "the fruit" is to "the flower."[62] In other words, *Aggadah* is *halakhah in potentia*. But he also describes the two as a study in contrasts. The *halakhah* is "severe, strict, hard as iron"; it is "piety, fossilized, duty and yoke." The *Aggadah*, in contrast, is "compliant, merciful, softer than oil"; it is "eternal renewal, freedom, and leniency." For Bialik, *halakhah* and *Aggadah* served as heuristic devices intended to capture two cultural models Jews inherited. He called on Hebrew literature to retrieve both the practical, concrete, model concerned with the here and now as well as the other, joyous, imaginative, abstract model concerned with the eternal. Bialik emphasized that neither model—the dry, legalistic Judaism concerned with the ritual status of pots and pans nor the imaginative life represented by the *Aggadah*—existed in a vacuum. Rather, the two were in productive tension with one another and paradoxically interdependent.

Nearly a century later, on a separate continent, the American legal scholar Robert Cover penned a remarkable essay, *Nomos and Narrative*,[63] which breathed new life into Bialik's evocation of *halakhah* and *Aggadah* as in tension with one another yet paradoxically interdependent. Cover was speaking about the American legal tradition and not the Talmudic tradition, although the Jewish tradition was an intellectual resource for him.[64] In this essay, Cover outlined two models of law—the imperial and the paideic—and he portrayed them as studies in contrast and interdependent. The imperial model was concerned with law as a means to preserve social order through enforcement of clearly delineated rules of conduct. The paideic model was culturally specific, expressive, aspirational, and perfectionist. Not surprisingly, the paideic model of law drew its strength from the culture's narratives. These narratives were the more transparent repository of the principles and values of the community embedded in the law that legal interpretation aimed to achieve. Some readers of *Nomos and Narrative* understood its title to be a reference to Bialik's *Halakhah and Aggadah*, using the standard negative definition of *Aggadah*: that which is not law.[65] But Cover's paideia is a model of law. And this returns us to the central question this chapter has grappled with: does *Aggadah* have a role to play beyond the intellectual, spiritual, or aesthetic as a this-worldly resource for fashioning *halakhah*?

Notes

1. For an excellent overview, see Yair Lorberbaum, "Reflections on the *Halakhic* Status of *Aggadah*," *Dine Israel* 24 (2007): 29–64. See also Steven Fraade and Simon-Shoshan Moshe, "*Halakha* and *Aggadah* in Tannaitic Sources," in *The Literature of the Sages, Compendia Rerum Judaicarum ad Novum Testamentum*, ed. Christine Hayes (Leiden, The Netherlands: Brill Press, 2022), 463–543. Moshe Simon-Shoshan, *Stories of the Law: Narrative Discourse and the Construction of Authority in the Mishnah* (Oxford: Oxford University Press, 2012).
2. See Suzanne Last Stone, "On the Interplay of Rules, 'Cases,' and Concepts in Rabbinic Legal Literature: Another Look at the *Aggadot* on Honi thc Circle-Drawer," *Dine Israel* 24 (2007): 125–55.
3. See Lorberbaum, "Reflections on the *Halakhic* Status of *Aggadah*"; Stone, "Interplay of Rules, 'Cases,' and Concepts in Rabbinic Legal Literature."
4. See Maren R. Neihoff, "Zunz's Concept of *Haggadah* as an Expression of Jewish Spirituality," in *The Leo Baeck Institute Year Book* 43 (1998): 3–24.
5. While *Aggadah* and biblical stories share a common narrative genre, the term "*Aggadah*" is reserved for post-biblical, rabbinic material.
6. See Fraade and Shoshan, "*Halakha* and *Aggadah* in Tannaitic Sources."
7. Edward Greenstein, "*The Relationship between Law and Narrative in the Pentateuch,*" https://www.academia.edu/39002185/The_Relation_between_Law_and_Narrative_in_the_Pentateuch_lecture_2001_.
8. See Yair Lorberbaum, *In God's Image: Myth, Theology, and Law in Classical Judaism* (New York: Cambridge University Press, 2015), 61–88. For another example of framing laws of prayer around theosophic assumptions embedded in the narrative material, see Shlomo Naeh, "Creates the Fruit of Lips: A Phenomenological Study of Prayer According to Mishnah *Berakhot* 4:3, 5:3," *Tarbiz* 63 (1994): 185–218 [Hebrew].
9. b.Bava Metzia 59a–b.
10. For a fuller account, see Suzanne Last Stone, "In Pursuit of the Countertext: The Turn to the Jewish Legal Model in Contemporary Legal Theory," *Harvard Law Review* 106, no. 4 (February 1993): 813–94.
11. On the literary elements of the story, see Jeffrey Rubinstein, *Talmudic Stories: Narrative Art, Composition, and Culture* (Baltimore, MD: John Hopkins University Press, 1999), 34–63.
12. See Samuel J. Levine, "Halacha and Aggada: Translating Robert Cover's Nomos and Narrative," *Utah Law Review* 1998, no. 4 (June 1998): 465–504.
13. b.Hullin 110b.
14. b.Bava Batra 8b.
15. See Gerald Blidstein, "Greater Is the Dignity of Humans: Studies in the Unfolding of *Halakhah*," *Shenaton Ha-Mishpat Ha-Ivri* 9–10 (1982–83): 128–85 [Hebrew]. See also Benjamin Brown, "From Principles to Rules and from Musar to Halakhah," *Dine Israel* 25 (2008): 171–256.
16. Cf. Chayyim David HaLevi, "Ways of Peace in the Relations Between Jews and Non-Jews," *Tehumin* 9 (1958): 71–78 [Hebrew] (implying that the principle of creation in the image of God has generative force).

17. j.Hagiga 1:8, j.Peah 2:4.
18. j.Horayot 3:8.
19. Harkavy, *Teshuvot Ha-Geonim*, #353, 179 (quoted and translated in Lorberbaum, "Reflections on the *Halakhic* Status of *Aggadah*," 33).
20. See Joseph Heinemann, *Aggadah and Its Development* (Jerusalem: Keter Press, 1974), 7 [Hebrew].
21. *Otzar HaGeonim*, Hagigah 67 (quoted in and translated by Lorberbaum, "Reflections on the *Halakhic* Status of *Aggadah*," 33).
22. See David Stern, "*Imitatio Hominis*: Anthropomorphism and the Character(s) of God in Rabbinic Literature," Prooftexts vol 12, no. 2 (1992), 151–74.
23. *Otzar HaGeonim*, Hagigah 5 (quoted and translated in Lorberbaum, "Reflections on the *Halakhic* Status of *Aggadah*," 33).
24. See Lorberbaum, "Reflections on the *Halakhic* Status of *Aggadah*," 34.
25. See Berachyahu Lifshitz, "*Aggadah* and Its Role in the History of the Oral Law," *Shenaton HaMishpat HaIvri* 22 (2003): 232–328 [Hebrew].
26. Sifre Deuteronomy 49. *Dorshei Haggadot* refers to the expounders of *Aggadah*.
27. On the relationship of open and closed legal systems to formalism, see Frederick Schauer, *Yale Law Journal* 97 (March 1988): 509–48.
28. See Moshe Silberg, "Law and Morals in Jewish Jurisprudence," *Harvard Law Review* 75, no. 2 (December 1961): 306–31.
29. Legal anthropologist Lawrence Rosen, for example, identified Islamic law with common law, stressing its decentralized form, the concentration of power in a jurist class, resistance to becoming an arm of the state, and capacity to absorb local practices into the system. See Lawrence Rosen, *Law as Culture: An Invitation* (Princeton, NJ: Princeton University Press, 2006), 39–42.
30. Other structural similarities the classical common law and the Talmudic tradition share include a strong judiciary/jurist class; social institutions that have all the features of a gerontocracy (students sit at the feet of their masters and absorb the technique of innovation within tradition); and the argumentative and discursive structure of legal practice. The common law's distinctive approach to the nature of law and legal reasoning has yet to be fully mined as a conceptual comparison by those who study rabbinic texts. In particular, the common law conception of rules as only presumptively binding until tested in the course of their application, in light of their congruence with social propositions, may provide a useful means for analyzing the distinction between "theoretical law" (*halakhah*) and "law to be applied" (*halakhah le-ma'aseh*.)
31. On the absence of the doctrine of precedent in the classical common law, see A. W. B. Simpson, "The Common Law and Legal Theory," in *Oxford Essays*, ed. A. W. B. Simpson (Oxford: Clarendon Press, 1973), 77–99. On the use of hypotheticals in the common law, see Arthur J. Jacobson, "Death of the Hypothetical," *Stanford Literature Review* 9 (1992): 125–38. For a masterful account of the philosophy of the classical common law, see Gerald J. Postema, "The Philosophy of the Common Law," in *Oxford Handbook of Jurisprudence and Legal Philosophy*, ed. Jules Coleman and Scott Shapiro (New York: Oxford University Press, 2002), 558–662.
32. Thomas Hobbes, *A Dialogue between a Philosopher and a Student of the Common Laws of England*, ed. Joseph Cropsey (Chicago: University of Chicago Press, 1971), 55, quoted in Postema, "Philosophy of the Common Law," 616.

33. Jeremy Bentham, *A Comment on the Commentaries and a Fragment on Government*, ed. J. H. Burns and H. L. A. Hart (Oxford: Oxford University Press, 1977), 119, quoted in Postema, "Philosophy of the Common Law," 616.
34. Postema, "Philosophy of the Common Law," 616.
35. See Postema, "Philosophy of the Common Law," 617.
36. See Ronald Dworkin, "The Model of Rules I," in *Taking Rights Seriously* (Cambridge, MA: Harvard University Press, 1977), 14–45.
37. See Ronald Dworkin, *Law's Empire* (Cambridge, MA: Harvard University Press, 1986).
38. See Stone, "On the Interplay of Rules, 'Cases,' and Concepts in Rabbinic Legal Literature." See also Suzanne Last Stone, "Rabbinic Legal Magic: A New Look at Honi's Circle as the Construction of Legal Space," *Yale Journal of Law & the Humanities* 17 (March 2005): 97–123.
39. m.Ta'anit 3:8.
40. p.Ta'anit 3:10.
41. b.Ta'anit 22b–23a.
42. 2 Sam. 21.
43. b.Yevamot 78a–b.
44. The *Aggadah* is launched in response to a Mishnah that excludes the Netinim (identified with the Gibeonites) from the community of Israel. The Talmud locates the source of the mishnaic ruling in King David's decree. And the *Bavli* exploits this tradition to make a point of the differing expectations and obligations of Israel toward all the citizens in a polity (providing justice for wrongs) and of members of a covenantal community toward one another (exercising mercy and waiving rights).
45. The early rabbis inherited an equivocal legacy from the Hebrew Bible, but the trend of the Talmudic tradition is to uphold individual accountability as the norm. See Moshe Halbertal, "Halakha and Morality: The Case of the Apostate City," *S'vara* 3 (1993): 67–72.
46. See Isadore Twersky, *Introduction to the Code of Maimonides* (New Haven: Yale University Press, 1984).
47. Yair Lorberbaum and Haim Shapira, "Maimonides' Epistle on Martyrdom in the Light of Legal Philosophy," *Dine Israel* 25 (2008): 123–69.
48. Haym Soloveitchik, "Maimonides' *Iggeret Ha-Shemad*: Law and Rhetoric," in *Rabbi Joseph H. Lookstein Memorial Volume*, ed. Leo Landman (New York: KTAV, 1980), 271–318.
49. See Yair Lorberbaum, "Transformations in Maimonides's Approach to the Midrashim of the Sages," *Tarbiz* 78 (2009): 122–81 [Hebrew].
50. See Suzanne Last Stone, "Truth and Government in the Jewish Tradition," in *Ethical Perspectives on Truth and Governance*, ed. William Galston and Tom G. Palmer (Washington, DC: Brookings Institution Press, 2021), 66–90; Suzanne Last Stone, "Law without Nation or Law without State: The Case of *Halakhah*," in *Law without Nations*, ed. Austin Sarat, Laurence Douglas, and Martha Humphrey (Stanford, CA: Stanford University Press, 2010), 101–37. On the interpretative dilemmas created by the absence of a continuous legal tradition addressing the laws of war, see Arye Edrei, "Law, Interpretation, and Ideology: The Renewal of the Jewish Laws of War in the State of Israel," *Cardozo Law Review* 28, no. 1 (2006): 187–227; Suzanne Last Stone, "The Jewish Law of War: The Turn to International Law and Ethics," in *Just Wars, Holy Wars, and Jihad*, ed. Sohail Hashmi (New York: Oxford University Press, 2012), 342–63. See also in this volume Steven Resnicoff, "Dina De-Malkhuta Dina and Arkaot."
51. For a fuller discussion, see Edrei, "Law, Interpretation, and Ideology."

52. See Stone, "Jewish Law of War."
53. As reported by Isaac Halevi Herzog, "Toward a Jewish State," in *Be'Tzomet HaTorah ve-HaMedinah*, ed. Y. Shaviv (Jerusalem: Tzomet Press, 1991), 3–9 [Hebrew]. The citation of Rabbi Nissim of Gerondi's sermon by Grodzinski and elevation of the sermon to the status of a responsum is telling.
54. See Edrei, "Law, Interpretation, and Ideology."
55. See Chayyim David HaLevi, *Aseh Lecha Rav* 7:70–71, translated in David Ellenson, "Jewish Legal Interpretation and Moral Values," *CCAR Journal: A Reform Jewish Quarterly* (Summer 2011): 8–16.
56. Maimonides, *Mishneh Torah*, Laws of Repentance 2.
57. See Ellenson, "Jewish Legal Interpretation and Moral Values," 15.
58. See ibid.
59. See in this volume Chaim Saiman, "Is Jewish Law Formalistic? A Survey of the Dispute and Why it Matters."
60. b.Berachot 8a.
61. See Roberta Kwall, *The Myth of the Cultural Jew: Culture and Law in the Jewish Tradition* (New York: Oxford University Press, 2015).
62. Chaim Nachman Bialik, *Revealment and Concealment: Five Essays* (Jerusalem: Ibis, 2000), 46–47. Also quoted in Lorberbaum, "Reflections on the *Halakhic* Status of *Aggadah*," 36.
63. Robert Cover, "Nomos and Narrative," *Harvard Law Review* 97, no. 4 (September 1983): 4–68.
64. See Stone, "In Pursuit of the Countertext."
65. For a comparison of Bialik and Cover, see Levine, "Halacha and Aggada."

CHAPTER 11

TALMUD TORAH

The Paramount Value of Study in Jewish Law

AYELET HOFFMANN LIBSON

Introduction: Torah Study as a Paramount Value

From its very beginnings, rabbinic Judaism was a movement centered on Torah. In this it differed from its source of inspiration and authority in the Hebrew Bible. The Bible is concerned with a grand narrative of God as creator of the world, who chose the people of Israel from among the nations and commanded them to worship one God and to observe God's laws. Those laws focus on a limited cluster of themes, such as idolatry, sexual morality, and justice for the weak and oppressed. The Divine-human relationship finds expression through temple worship and the political institutions delineated for regulating and controlling the land of Israel: priesthood, prophecy, and monarchy. Rabbinic Judaism, however, was forged in a transformed reality. The Jerusalem temple had been destroyed and Jews were no longer politically autonomous in their land, but rather lived under the rule of the Roman, and later the Persian empires. As such, the rabbis were called upon to infuse new significance into the covenant between God and Israel, which they redirected to center on the mechanism of law.[1] The centrality of temple worship as a communal framework for preserving the covenant, maintaining the Divine presence, and attaining atonement was gradually replaced with the importance of law as a practice governing all aspects of human life. Whereas the general themes of biblical law are preserved in the legal writings of the Qumran sect, which regulate purity, festivals, and sacral law, rabbinic literature reflects an explosion of legal minutiae regulating the intricacies of all areas of everyday life, including property law, family law, criminal law, agricultural law, employment law, and more. As the focus of Israel's devotion to the Divine will shifted from the temple to the sphere of law, law became imbued with sacred authority and the performance of law was transformed into the paramount religious activity.

The rabbis worked to minimize this discontinuity and to present their novel legal program as continuing a direct and unbroken line from the biblical past. To do so they relied on the idea of the Oral Torah, given alongside the Written Torah at the revelation at Sinai, and transmitted from master to disciple in an uninterrupted chain until the time of the rabbis (see Lifshitz, this volume). Some rabbinic sources maintain that the Oral Torah was given in its entirety at Sinai, while others suggest that it developed gradually over centuries, guided by the application of a particular set of interpretative rules. All rabbinic sources, however, view it as an essential part of the Divine command.[2]

The significance of the law as the foremost vehicle of the relationship between God and the Jewish people led to a new conception of the law as a system not only to be performed but also to be studied intensively. Whereas the biblical verse "If, then, you faithfully keep all this instruction that I command you, loving the Lord your God, to walk in all his ways and to cleave to him" (Deuteronomy 11:22) clearly stresses the observance of the commandments as the sole path to drawing near to God, the Sifre, a rabbinic *Midrash* to Deuteronomy, emphasizes study rather than performance of the commandments as the sole path to "come to know the one who spoke and the world came into being and cleave to His ways."[3] It is study—rather than performance of the commandments—that leads a person to draw close to God.[4]

Torah thus came to be seen as the ultimate value in the rabbinic world. Mishnah Pe'ah famously describes study as the pinnacle of those commandments that benefit a person in this world and continue to offer rewards in the world to come:

> These are the things that have no [defined quantitative] measure: the amount left in the corner [of the field, to be left for the poor to collect], the first fruits, and the [offerings to be brought for] pilgrimage appearance, and acts of loving-kindness (*gemilut ḥasadim*) and study of Torah. These are the things that a person eats of their fruits in this world and the principal remains for the world to come: Honoring father and mother; acts of loving-kindness, bringing peace between a person and his friend; but the study of Torah is equivalent to them all.
>
> (m.Pe'ah 1:1)

This Mishnah first lists a select group of commandments focusing on care for the needy and acts of devotion to God. The second list, however, focuses more strongly on interpersonal commandments (the subject of tractate Pe'ah is gifts for the needy) but then surprisingly concludes by maintaining that Torah study is more important than any of these noble behaviors.

Torah study was viewed as an all-consuming occupation, to be engaged at every possible moment. Some extreme statements found particularly in the Babylonian Talmud may be understood as rhetorical arms in a battle to encourage absolute dedication to Torah study. We find, for example, Rava's teaching that "Whoever occupies himself with the study of Torah needs no burnt-offering or sin-offering, no meal-offering nor guilt-offering" (b.Menahot 110a) and Rabbi Yosef even proclaims that "Greater is the study of the Torah than the saving of lives" (b.Megillah 16b).[5] Several sources underscore this outlook by pitting Torah study against particular commandments. For example, a maxim appearing in four narratives in the Babylonian Talmud suggests that those who neglect Torah study "forsake eternal life and occupy themselves with temporal life." In two of these narratives the dictum is applied to people concerned with mundane activities such as plowing the earth or engaging in business (b.Shabbat 33b and b.Ta'anit 21a, respectively). On b.Betzah 15b, however, R. Eliezer criticizes those of his students who depart to celebrate the festival meal—itself a religious obligation. And on b.Shabbat 10a, Rava criticizes his colleague Rav Hamnuna's lengthy prayers on the grounds that "he forsakes eternal life and occupies himself with temporal life!" One might be justified in thinking that prayer represents the ultimate spiritual pursuit, yet in comparison to Torah study, Rava views it as merely "temporal life" because it takes away from the constant pursuit of Torah study. Other rabbinic sources reflect on the tensions caused by such extreme dedication to Torah study: for instance, when will one have time to work and provide a livelihood (Sifre Deuteronomy 42, b.Taanit 21a) or how to balance family life with the need to study intensively at an academy away from home (b.Ketubot 61–63a).

Study or Deeds?

Several rabbinic sources not only labor to portray Torah study as the paramount value, but also intentionally set it in contrast to performance of righteous deeds. The age-old debate between the *vita contemplativa* and the *vita activa* is a universal one found in many cultures,[6] yet it is startling to find against the backdrop of the pre-rabbinic tradition that centrally foregrounds the performance of the commandments and righteous deeds. As the biblical text does not appear to privilege the ideal of study, the rabbis were compelled to offer creative interpretations of biblical verses that emphasize the centrality of observing the commandments. The Sifre, for instance, contrasts the verse "And it shall come to pass, if you shall listen unto my commandments" (Deuteronomy 11:13) with an earlier verse, "That you may learn them and observe to do them" (Deuteronomy 5:1) and juxtaposes the verbs "listen" and "observe":

> Is it possible that they [the people of Israel] were not obligated to study (*talmud*) until they were obligated to observe deeds (*ma'aseh*)? Scripture says, "And it shall come to pass, if you shall listen unto my commandments" (11:13)—that indicates that they were immediately obligated to study.
>
> (Sifre Deuteronomy 41)

The *Midrash* reads the distinction between the verbs "listen" and "observe" in the respective verses as positing that the study of law was commanded to begin on the very day it was given, in contrast to the obligations of performing the deeds that became binding only at a later point. The study of the law is not merely a handmaiden in the service of improved observance, but rather a commandment in its own right that stands independent of action and is not contingent on immediate performance. The Sifre subsequently records a famous debate over the relative merits of study or deed:

> And it happened that Rabbi Tarfon and Rabbi Yose the Galilean and Rabbi Akiva were reclining (dining) at the house of Ares in Lydda. A question was raised before them: Which is greater, study or deed?
>
> Said Rabbi Tarfon: Great is deed.
>
> Rabbi Akiva says: Great is study.
>
> They all [the assembled] answered and said: Great is study for it leads to deed.
>
> Rabbi Yose the Galilean said: Great is study that preceded the giving of [the commandent to offer] dough [to the priest] by forty years, the tithes by fifty-four, and the sabbatical years by sixty, and the Jubilee years by one hundred and three [i.e. these commandments could be performed only upon entering the land of Israel, which occurs much later in the biblical narrative].

This passage asks the question in plain terms: Is it the study of God's Torah that is the ultimate objective or is it the execution of the many commandments put forth by that same Torah that holds paramount significance? Starting from the last opinion in this passage, Rabbi Yose maintains that study is greater than several commandments which could only be fulfilled when entering the land of Israel, as they are dependent on possession of that land. The implication of the timeline he draws is that the commandment to study Torah was given at the foundational moment of revelation at Sinai and is thus fundamental to God's covenant with his people. Moreover, the structure of the whole passage directs the reader to the preference for study over deed. Notice that the opinions of the three Sages are not presented in the same order as are the characters in the exposition of the narrative: Rabbi Tarfon, Rabbi Yose, Rabbi Akiva. Rather, two rabbis—Rabbi Tarfon and Rabbi Akiva—are presented symmetrically as promoting the value of either study or action. The opinion of Rabbi Yose is deferred until after the unanimous resolution of this weighty debate with the paradoxical compromise that "Great is study for it leads to deed." This compromise would seem to privilege deed, for study serves only as deed's maidservant. However, as Marc Hirshman has noted, the editor of this passage in the Sifre sandwiched this resolution between the opinions of Rabbi Akiva and Rabbi Yose, thereby bracketing the resolution of the majority between the two opinions promoting the primacy of study.[7] Although the original debate between the rabbis of the second century may have been concluded in favor of the primacy of deeds, the debate over the respective merits of study and deed endured. This fact is reflected in the Sifre's editorial process itself, which recasts the original debate favoring deeds so that the final redacted form of the passage appears to favor study.

Later scholars grappled with the tension found in this passage and in others like it.[8] Medieval Jewish decisors argued over the true meaning of the statement "great is study for it leads to deed": some insisted that study remained fundamentally superior to practice, while others reinterpreted it to mean "study is preferred" and distinguished between circumstances where study is to be favored and those where practice is to be preferred.[9] For instance, a scholar who had already attained great knowledge would be encouraged to continue to prefer study over deeds, while action would be encouraged as the correct path for minors or those unable to become scholars.[10]

Evaluating the relative merits of study and practice was also the subject of major philosophical arguments in the Middle Ages and reemerged later in Jewish history as one of the major bones of contention between Hasidim and Mitnagdim in the eighteenth century.[11] As in every intellectual culture, the scholars of every generation prized study over all else. Yet within the bounds of a religious community bound by its practices, theoretical study that did not lead to enhanced performance was frequently critiqued as excessively abstract. These recurring debates reflect the tension between a religion focused on performing practical commandments and the adoption of a contemplative ethos centered on study.

From the Valorization of Study to Nonapplied Law

If a person's highest calling is not (or, not only) performing the law, but rather engaging in Torah study for its own sake, by extension the idea of Torah study must undergo a radical metamorphosis. The practice of Torah study can no longer be limited to practical questions and implementation, but rather encourages theoretical and even hypothetical study of nonapplied law. One of the implications of the valorization of study was the paradoxical result that beginning with the foundational rabbinic compilation of the Mishnah, all parts of the law were treated with the same significance and import, despite the irrelevance of some portions of the law due to political and historical conditions. The political disruption that followed the destruction of the Jerusalem temple and the Bar Kokhba revolt rendered the political institutions of priesthood, monarchy, and prophecy inoperative. Nonetheless, the rabbis continued to study and occupy themselves with the minutiae of many of these institutions and rituals. For instance, of the six orders of the Mishnah, two orders (Qodashim and Tohorot), consisting of twenty-three tractates among them, are concerned with the laws of temple sacrifices and purity laws that were no longer in effect following the destruction of the temple. Some scholars have argued that in the *tannaitic* period this form of study was a way of expressing faith that the temple would soon be rebuilt.[12] Yet the Mishnah also discusses many cases of inapplicable law that have nothing to do with the temple at all, addressing them in the same terms as laws that could potentially be relevant at the time of the rabbis. Thus, the seventh chapter of tractate Sotah begins by discussing certain verbal formulae that may be recited in any language (and not only in Hebrew, the "sacred tongue"), such as the *shema* and *amidah* prayers, grace after meals, and various court-administered oaths (m.Sotah 7:1). The Mishnah then lists other ritual phrases that must be recited in Hebrew, while nearly all these are recitations related to biblical institutions no longer in effect at the time of the rabbis, such as bringing first fruits to the temple, the blessings recited by the high priest, the Torah portion read by the king at the conclusion of the sabbatical year, and the priestly address to the nation before going out to battle (m.Sotah 7:2). One of the items on this list is the ceremony of the blessings and curses to be declared on Mount Gerizim and Mount Ebal when the Israelites entered the land of Israel (Deuteronomy 28; Joshua 8), a one-time historical event, never to be repeated at all! As legal scholar Chaim Saiman writes, "in these cases, the Mishnah is not preserving rules for future reapplication—they will never apply again. Rather, it is recasting biblical events into the language of law where they are analyzed alongside practices that apply in the present."[13]

Even hundreds of years after the demise of the Temple and the dispersion of most of world Jewry to the new center of learning in Babylonia, the rabbis of the Talmud, known as the *Amoraim*, continued to study in intricate detail topics that could not be applied in their communities. Nevertheless, some practical considerations do seem to have directed the creation (or preservation) of certain tractates in the Talmudic period: for instance, the Babylonian Talmud lacks the order of Seeds, which is applicable only in the Land of Israel. It also lacks the order related to temple purity, while the Jerusalem Talmud lacks the order of Holy Things relating to temple offerings. As a whole, though composed by rabbis living far away from the land of Israel and hundreds of years later, the Babylonian Talmud contains hundreds of discussions that continue to elaborate on all areas of law, whether applicable or not.[14]

The valorization of study over practical application reached new heights in the Babylonian Talmud, which is full of discursive material focusing on the "give and take" of the discussion and exploring minority positions which have no bearing on practical law.[15] Indeed, the Talmud frequently offers lengthy explanations even for those positions that are explicitly rejected, such as the views of Shammai, which per the statement "the teaching of the house of Shammai in the place of the house of Hillel is no teaching," are not normatively guiding (*mishnat beit shammai einah mishnah*).[16] Lengthy dialectical debates investigate various Amoraic views, probing, hypothesizing, and testing different possibilities, finally concluding where they began, often without any resolution at all.[17] Similarly, the Talmud regularly narrows the applicability of an earlier ruling, often without any decision (see Stein Hain, this volume). A classic instance of this phenomenon is the Talmud's reading of the biblical injunction regarding the rebellious and wayward son (Deuteronomy 21:18–21). According to the biblical verses, a son who neither listens to his parents nor receives the rebuke of the congregations' elders must be put to death. By gradually narrowing the application of each clause of the biblical verses, the rabbis ultimately declare that in fact, the law of the rebellious son was never implemented. If so, however, why was the law written at all? The rabbis answer that it was included for no practical reason, but solely to grant merit to those who study the law (b.Sanhedrin 71a). The rabbis thus reduce the importance of examining Torah law with an eye to its application and instead elevate the significance of study in and of itself.

At times, the rabbis show express awareness of this gap between the law and its application. Several Talmudic phrases signal a gap between the law and the law as it should be instructed to the public, for instance, "this is the law but it is not instructed" (*halakhah ve-ein morin ken*)[18] or "one who comes to ask is not instructed" (*haba limalekh ein morin lo*).[19] These phrases indicate that the rabbis were mindful of reasons not to instruct the public about the established law. The rabbis' awareness of the distinction between theoretical law and applied law is found in a baraita cited on b.Bava Batra 130b: "one does not learn *halakhah* neither from study nor from a story [told of a rabbi], until one is told: '[this is] law in practice (*halakhah le-ma'aseh*),'" a ruling ironically supported in the Talmud by a story in which Rabbi Asi asks his master Rabbi Yohanan: "when our master tells us this is the law, may we act upon it?," to which the master responds: "do not act until I tell you it is law in practice." This story clearly distinguishes between theoretical law and law in practice, underscoring that a teaching may be considered "law" for the purposes of study, yet nonetheless should not be implemented.

The distinction between law on the books and law in practice could sometimes lead to confusion, as we find in the following account:

> Rabbi Yohanan expounded the law to the people of Tiberias in accordance with the view of Rabbi Shimon ben Eleazar. He intended to expound the [theoretical] law (*le-halakhah*), but they understood him as teaching the law to be applied (*uvda*). Some say he expounded the law to be applied, but when they [the Tiberians] approached him and inquired about his teaching he expounded the theoretical law. When he repeated his exposition, they did not know whether he meant it to be taken theoretically or as law to be applied.
>
> (j.Betzah 2:1; 61b)

In this rabbinic tragicomedy, Rabbi Yohanan engages in a lecture to a crowd of people in Tiberias, but the ultimate goal of theoretical Torah study for its own sake (*torah li-shmah*) is subverted when the people misunderstand the homily as applied law. Theoretical law (*le-halakhah*) and applied law (*uvda*) are presented as two distinct genres, despite engaging the same content.

Once introduced in the Talmud, the distinction between theoretical study and practical law became central to the responsa literature, which emerged from a tradition of questions sent to and answers given by prominent *halakhic* authors. The genre of responsa arose soon after the Talmudic period, when the *Geonim*—scholars who led the Babylonian academies of the ninth and tenth centuries—responded to queries directed to them from all over the Jewish world on matters ranging from interpretation of Talmudic passages to issues of theology to practical matters of ritual and monetary law. Responsa attained dominance as one of the central styles of *halakhic* writing in the fifteenth century, when most rabbis wrote for a more geographically limited community. Although this period saw most responsa come to focus on civil disputes, this literature also engages at length in Talmudic analysis and commentary on a variety of rabbinic texts. As such, this period saw the introduction of the distinction between *halakhah* (applied law) and *halakhah ve-lo le-ma'aseh* (law that is not to be implemented), by which scholars indicated that a particular responsum presented an exercise in academic Torah study and should not be taken as law for the general public.[20]

Practical and Scholastic Modes of Torah Study

Subsequent to the Talmudic period, the centrality of the value of *talmud Torah* owes much to the hegemony attained by the Babylonian Talmud throughout the Jewish world. The political conditions in Byzantine Palestine led to the early demise of the Jewish community and the incomplete compilation of the Jerusalem Talmud. The anonymous scholars who wove together the traditions in the Babylonian Talmud were able to create a more cohesive redaction of the Talmudic text, which led to its enhanced accessibility. As the Jewish world witnessed the Arab conquest of 638 and came under the influence of the caliphate of Bagdhad, the rabbis of Babylonia quickly became the leaders of world Jewry, exercising the authority of the state to benefit the enforcement of rabbinic law and to promote the traditions of the Babylonian Talmud. The *Geonim*—the leaders of Babylonian Jewry—viewed the Talmud as a completed work and lionized it as the focus of the academic curriculum of the great academies of the time. Students flocked to these *yeshivot* (academies), and there imbibed the centrality of the Talmud. The result was the authority of the Babylonian Talmud as the absolute source of Jewish law and the main object of scholarly study.[21] Although early sources from the *tannaitic* period as well as the Jerusalem Talmud were conflicted regarding the primacy of study or practice, the Babylonian Talmud's view that study is of ultimate value held great sway over the entirety of the Jewish world.

By the eleventh century, most of the Talmud had reached several distinct Jewish communities in Germany, Spain, and Provence, and by the twelfth and thirteenth centuries, scholars in these communities had produced commentaries in various legal genres, such as the responsa mentioned above, but also comprehensive codes of Jewish law, commentaries on vast portions of the Talmud, and anthologies of local customs. As these genres emerged, the tension between practical law and theoretical study led to two distinct forms of study in the Jewish world. Although not fully consistent, in general terms this division overlaps geographical divisions: scholars of Islamic countries focused primarily on the legal and applied aspect of Torah, and wrote commentaries focused on the practical side of Talmudic study.[22] Four classical digests of Jewish law were produced in the middle ages—Rabbi Isaac Alfasi's *Hilkhot ha-Rif*, Maimonides's *Mishneh Torah*, Rabbi Jacob ben Asher's *Arbaah Turim* and Rabbi Yosef Caro's *Shulkhan Arukh*—and it is no accident that all four were composed in Spain or in Sephardic communities. By contrast, among the Jews of France and Germany, the religious ideal of Torah study reigned supreme, and they included in their curriculum those talmudic tractates that no longer held practical applicability in their extended commentaries.

Study for the sake of applied Jewish law certainly held an important role, but the paramount goal was study for its own sake.[23]

The two modes of studying the Talmud had far-reaching implications beyond their respective geographical locales. As noted above, reading the Talmud for its practical legal conclusions was the characteristic mode of scholars in Spain and other Sephardic communities. A paradigmatic and influential exemplar of this tradition is Rabbi Isaac Alfasi (1013–1103, Fez), known by his Hebrew acronym *Rif.* His commentary, *Hilkhot ha-Rif,* is an impressive digest that proceeds according to the order of the Talmudic text. Indeed, *Rif* employs the very language of the Talmudic discussion and adheres to it closely, while omitting most of the extended dialectic back-and-forth, thus producing a more focused and serviceable text. Moreover, *Rif*'s commentary addresses only those legal sections of the Talmud applicable in his day, purging any non-legal portions of the Talmud from discussion, removing associative tangents, and discarding whole sections focused on Temple-related concerns. The result is an abbreviated Talmud that offers a condensed summary of legal rules.

Rif's practice of separating the wheat of legal rulings from the chaff of Talmudic give-and-take was embraced by the most renowned medieval codifier of Jewish law, Maimonides, in his fourteen-part work, the *Mishneh Torah.* Maimonides, however, went one step further than *Rif* in creating a method for classifying and systematizing the Talmudic rules, thereby leaving behind the original order and flow of the Talmudic text. Indeed, Maimonides himself writes that his intent was for his code to replace the central role of the Talmud in Jewish study.[24] The very title of the work, *Mishneh Torah*—a "reiteration" of the Torah—makes this clear, as do Maimonides's words in the Introduction to the code when he writes that the purpose of the *Mishneh Torah* is to employ "clear language and concise form so that the entirety of the oral Torah is presented before all without the need for questions, answers or debates."[25] As part of this ambitious goal, however, Maimonides codifies all aspects of Talmudic rulings, including those parts of the Talmud that deal with sacrifices or ritual purity, in contrast to *Rif* and other codifiers who engaged only those aspects that were applicable to their time. Although Maimonides not only intended to comment on the Talmud but strove to replace it, paradoxically he retained the Talmud's typical combination of practical and idealized law. In the long term, Maimonides revolutionized *halakhic* study but was unsuccessful in his goal of eclipsing the Talmud.

While the Sephardi *halakhists* studied the Talmud with an eye to extracting its legal rulings, in Ashkenaz a very different style of studying the Talmud developed.[26] Similarly to the way in which the rabbis of the Talmud had studied the biblical and earlier rabbinic texts, the medieval commentators sought out the contradictions and tensions between different Talmudic texts, and suggested resolutions to those inconsistencies. The most influential exemplar of this tradition is the collection of commentaries known as the *Tosafot* (additions or glosses), written by several rabbinic authorities in the twelfth- and thirteenth-century communities of France and Germany. The *Tosafists* read the Talmud as a holistic work, drawing together two or more passages from entirely different parts of the Talmud into dialogue with one another. If the passages contradict one another, the inconsistency offers the commentators the opportunity for creative interpretation, as they seek to harmonize the two texts by offering a conceptual distinction between them.[27]

Beginning in the thirteenth century, *Tosafot* attained recognition as one of the foremost commentaries on the Talmud, and when the entire Talmud was first printed in the late fifteenth century, the *Tosafot* occupied the influential position of the margin alongside the main text, where their commentary continues to be printed to this day.[28] Students of Talmud begin with the Talmudic text, progress to the literal-textual commentary of *Rashi* on the inner margin and the conceptual analysis on the outer margin, and only then turn to the conclusive summary of the discussion in the writings of the *Rif*, generally located at the end of each volume of Talmud, or the legal codification of Maimonides, printed in other volumes entirely.

Both the *Rif* and the *Tosafot* proceed according to the order of the Talmudic text, favoring close commentary to the text over conceptual codification (see Kanarfogel, this volume, and Stein Hain, this volume). However, whereas the *Rif* offered a condensed version of the Talmud's legal conclusions, the *Tosafot* engaged in close commentary to every word of the Talmud, whether applied law or speculative detour. One might say that the *Tosafot* "Talmudized" the Talmud, namely, just as the Talmud sought out contradictions between two or more authoritative texts and went to great lengths to resolve those contradictions, so too the *Tosafot* developed a method of seeking out discrepancies between Talmudic sources and dedicated their labors to reconciling or harmonizing those disparities. Whereas for *Rif*, the Talmud was a text to be studied with the purpose of eliciting the directives needed for living according to Jewish law, for the *Tosafot*, the Talmud presents a web of ideas to be studied for their conceptual value. Due to the *Tosafot*'s influential position, very soon after their own time a group of commentators began to study each line of the *Tosafot* with the same method of close reading that *Tosafot* themselves had employed in reading the Talmud. Some of these commentaries continued to develop the *Tosafot*'s conceptual analysis, subjecting their commentaries to the same method of harmonizing inconsistencies. Other commentaries, however, read the Tosafot through the more practice-oriented lens of the *Rif*, aiming to cull the applied legal rulings from the unwieldy conceptual discourse. Ultimately, *Tosafot*'s reading of a Talmudic discussion is often at the basis of accepted legal practice to this day, and in some cases holds the keys to understanding how medieval Ashkenazi customs superseded what seems to be the bottom line of a Talmudic *sugya*.

While most of medieval *halakhic* writings can be divided into the practically-oriented tradition of the *Rif* and Maimonides on the one hand, and the scholastic tradition of the *Tosafot* on the other, some approaches produced blends between these two points on the spectrum. In the twelfth century, Zekhariah Halevi of Gerona (known eponymously as *Baal ha-Maor*) and Rabbi Avraham ben David (known by his acronym as the *Raavad*) provided a critique of *Hilkhot ha-Rif* defending the back-and-forth of talmudic dialectics. Several preeminent Sephardi Rishonim of the thirteenth and fourteenth centuries wrote their commentaries primarily on tractates of practical relevance, yet also embraced the *Tosafot*'s style of drawing various sources from throughout the Talmud into conversation with one another.[29] Most famous of these is Naḥmanides, known by his Hebrew acronym *Ramban* (1194–1270), who spawned a school of scholars who frequently engaged in the same style of the *Tosafot*'s analysis. As a result, in both Ashkenazi and Sephardi academies, Talmud study came to be viewed not only as *halakhic* interpretation directed toward applied relevance, but also as a singular conceptual effort aimed at analytic brilliance and coherence.

Raising *Talmud Torah* to a Higher Power

Because the Tosafists and their followers required consistency among *halakhic* sources, they were often pressed to introduce very fine distinctions into Talmudic study. For instance, if two sources appeared to conflict, one might be understood to represent the general rule while the other would be presented as an exception. Alternatively, one source might be identified as referring to a very specific and narrow circumstance bearing no relevance to other cases. Over time, many additional techniques were employed, leading to a methodology of Talmud study in which the importance of bringing discordant opinions into agreement frequently overrode the actual wording and simple meaning of the text. Within the rabbinic yeshivot, the practice of using the text as a steppingstone for conceptual questions was also sometimes understood as an analytical exercise intended to sharpen the minds of students. When referring to the clever analysis of inconsistencies in earlier texts, this approach of careful reading and incisive resolution of contradictions came to be known as *pilpul*, from the root indicating "peppering" or "spicing" an examination.

Though the term *pilpul* is found already in the Talmud and throughout medieval commentaries, at the end of the fifteenth century in Eastern Europe it came to denote an entirely new way of analyzing and thinking about the Talmud.[30] The focus of this methodology, often attributed to Rabbi Jacob Pollak (1460–1541), was on challenging any inconsistent deductions that might be made on the basis of different stages of the Talmudic *sugya* and using a dialectic method to resolve the difficulties. In truth, the term *pilpul* was used to refer to two related but distinct ways of learning: *pilpul* as a method of commentary on the Talmud, and *pilpul* as the goal of instruction in the rabbinic academy (yeshiva).

In the sixteenth century, the curriculum of the yeshiva increasingly focused on two distinct techniques: *ḥiluk* (distinction) or *pilpul*. Although both methods had their roots in medieval Spain and Germany, they were introduced into Poland with the founding of the yeshiva of Lublin, and from there spread to many Eastern European centers of study. *Pilpul* was different from other methods of study in that it was characterized by study of the text with one colleague or more (*ḥevruta*). Secondly, in stark contrast to the harmonizing methodology of the Tosafot, *pilpul* focused on one passage of the Talmud, with no concern for other passages that might hold relevance to its interpretation. Most importantly, the method of *pilpul* glorified the student's ability to comprehend the text independently, offering novel interpretations that went beyond that of earlier commentators. However, as one could not turn to other talmudic passages to illuminate the text at hand, to produce a new interpretation the only way forward was to engage in hyper-textual analysis of every possible detail in the language, form, and structure of the passage. For instance, one might ask why a particular phrase was used, when a briefer one could have been employed. The superfluous words were then interpreted to demonstrate a new legal detail, which could not have been otherwise derived, often resulting in the creation of novel and sometimes highly abstract categories. The method of *pilpul* investigated every passage, unit, line, or word, investing each with significance. As part of the yeshiva curriculum, teachers would sometimes invent imaginary cases or difficulties to train their students in the analytical skills required to resolve these legal riddles.[31]

Champions of *pilpul* touted the dazzling insights that the method produced, while its critics ridiculed the strained readings that relied on contrived textual difficulties. The historical work *Yeven Metzulah* (1653) composed by Rabbi Nathan of Hannover offers a lively description of the way pilpul was perceived in seventeenth-century Ashkenaz: "[One who engages in pilpul] starts out asking a question on the Talmud or on *Rashi* or *Tosafot*. He then points out a contradiction between them. He then shows how all the answers to the contradiction still lead to contradictions in some other texts. Finally, after asking a few different kinds of questions, he provides an answer that explains all of the seeming contradictions."[32] The new methods of Torah study garnered strong opposition. Leading authorities argued that the method of *pilpul* had become no more than sophistry, with students valuing the art of proving their creativity over and above offering a reasonable interpretation of the *sugya* at hand. The great Rabbi Judah Loewe of Prague, known by his Hebrew acronym *Maharal* (d. 1609), rejected not only the long hours students spent engaged in *pilpul*, but also the fact that the yeshivot no longer saw the acquirement of basic study skills as the goal of yeshiva study.[33] Shlomo Luria of Lublin (1510–1573) called for reinstating a focus on the text of the Talmud and the traditional commentators, rejecting the development of intellectual dexterity in favor of understanding the text of the Talmud with the goal of applying it to practical *halakhah*. Rabbi Yeshayahu Horwitz—known by his acronym, *Shelah* (1558–1630)—and several of his contemporaries criticized the method of *pilpul* as contrasting with *derekh ha-yashar*, "the straight path" of study, which was the only way to gain a true understanding of the text. They argued that the path of *pilpul* as a means to sharpening the minds of students had come to take precedence over the very content of what was to be learned. The only way to lead students back to the text of the Talmud as the focus of the true curriculum was to eliminate the use of *pilpul* within the rabbinic academy. These critics were unsuccessful, however, and *pilpul* continued to enjoy great prominence into the eighteenth century. At the same time, competing methods of Talmud study began to emerge, particularly as medieval commentaries that had been unknown in most communities began to be published and enjoyed new prominence in Europe.

Torah Li-Shmah in the Lithuanian Yeshivot

By the late eighteenth century, Torah study in Eastern Europe had returned to a focus on classical Talmud study. This shift was initiated by Rabbi Elijah ben Solomon, the Vilna Gaon (1720–1797), who maintained that Talmud study required a more systematic approach, beginning with the study of Bible and grammar, moving on to the study of the Mishnah and other early rabbinic collections, and only then embarking on study of the two Talmuds, with a unique focus on establishing the correct version of textual manuscripts.[34] The Gaon espoused a two-pronged approach, examining all available manuscripts to establish the correct version of the Talmudic text, while simultaneously giving meaning to the passage at hand as a harmonious part of the larger canon of rabbinic literature.

The Gaon's leading disciple was Rabbi Ḥayyim Isaac of Volozhin (1749–1821), who founded the celebrated Yeshivat *Etz Ḥayyim* of Volozhin in 1802, where it quickly became the center of the Lithuanian school of Talmud study. At Volozhin, Torah study was valued beyond its role as a means to practicing Jewish law or as a devotional path to cleaving to God. Rather, the goal of Torah study was to engage in the intellectual activity of study for its own sake (*Torah li-shmah*).[35] According to Rabbi Ḥayyim, the Torah emerged from the same supernal origins as its author. Consequently, only by engaging in Torah study can one transcend the soul and develop a relationship with God: "There is no way to attain the sparks of the light of the soul other than by sacred toil and by cogitation and contemplation of the holy Torah. For both [the soul and the Torah] have one source, as the discerning are well-aware."[36] Yet Rabbi Ḥayyim goes a step further in maintaining that, due to the transcendent origins of the Torah, one who engages in Torah study requires no particular consciousness or spiritual experience to achieve these aims; rather, the very practice of engaging in the intellectual act of study is itself sufficient for cleaving to the Divine.[37]

The new mode of Torah study had a profound impact on the institution of the yeshiva. Study was not directed at the practice of *halakhah*, although strict compliance with the law was accepted as a fundamental condition for all who entered the halls of the rabbinic academy. Furthermore, unlike earlier institutions, at Volozhin teachers were not communal rabbis or legal decisors, but rather academic deans, fully immersed in the world of study which existed in parallel to the reality outside its halls. Students, too, were not trained to become pulpit rabbis but rather were challenged to attain the status of a scholar and to develop brilliant Torah novellae (*ḥiddushim*). Students flocked to Volozhin from all over Eastern Europe and were urged to see themselves as part of the yeshiva community, rather than as emissaries of their local community who would return to it when their education was complete.

The ethos of a world of study unto its own, characterized by intense intellectual concentration and uninterrupted by the demands of mundane living, yielded the ideal of toil in Torah (*amal Torah*), which was demanded by Rabbi Ḥayyim as part of the elite culture of Volozhin but subsequently spread to other nineteenth-century *yeshivot*. Rabbi Ḥayyim valued the effort of intellectual toil over the knowledge gained in the process, and repeatedly exhorted his disciples that "the main thing is the act of learning; the knowledge is secondary to it."[38] The focus on the diligence required to attain Torah, based on a recurring emphasis on those sources discussed earlier in this chapter that equated the value of Torah study with all other commandments, produced another concept formative to the yeshiva: *bittul Torah*, or neglect of Torah. Complete dedication to Torah study produced the complementary notion that any time not dedicated to Torah study is neglectful of the Torah and constitutes a transgression.[39] Even the highest of spiritual pursuits—prayer—could not compete with Torah study; spending too much time in prayer was viewed as a form of neglecting Torah study, the paramount religious charge.

The primacy of Torah study in the Lithuanian yeshivot was heatedly contested by followers of the Ḥasidic movement. Ḥasidism championed the ability of every individual to forge a direct relationship with God through personal piety and particularly through prayer. Despite their veneration of Torah, Ḥasidim rejected the centrality of the intellectual study of Torah as the only religious path to God.[40] Many Ḥasidic leaders demonstrated this approach to their followers in their own practice, preferring lengthy prayer and self-reflective seclusion (*hitbodedut*) over concerted efforts of study.[41] And while Ḥasidic teachers sustained the existing normative requirement to study some Torah every day, they rejected Torah study as the sole and ultimate route to God.

The focus on *Torah li-shmah*, study for its own sake, paved the way for a new method of conceptual Torah study at the end of the nineteenth century. Rabbi Ḥayyim Soloveitchik (1853–1918), one of the deans of the Volozhin Yeshiva, developed together with his students an analytic approach to the study of the Talmud, often known as the Brisker method, after the Yiddish name of the town of Brest-Litovsk to which Rabbi Ḥayyim moved later in life. Rabbi Ḥayyim and his followers perceived *halakhah* as a system of ideal constructs, bearing an a priori logic that needed to cohere internally but not with other thought systems. The Brisker method thus did not focus on legal decision-making, but rather treated the legal rulings of the Talmud as raw material to be analyzed and systematized through a near-scientific approach of reconstructing the inner coherence of legal categories. Scholars sought to define, describe, and formulate *halakhic* phenomena, but rarely saw the need to rationalize or offer explanations for *halakhic* positions.[42]

Previous medieval and early modern scholars had generally focused narrowly on solving difficulties emerging from the Talmudic text, and their analytical distinctions were introduced to resolve a particular conundrum, although the conceptual solution then occasionally took on a life of its own and was introduced by later scholars in their own commentaries. By contrast, nineteenth-century Talmudists responded to problems or ambiguities in the text by seizing the opportunity to develop novel analytic frameworks that would shed new light on broader issues. Rabbi Ḥayyim himself developed his written *ḥiddushim* (novellae) through a close examination of

Maimonides's legal code, the Mishneh Torah, observing discrepancies between two or more legal rulings and resolving the conflict by attributing each ruling to opposing conceptualizations. For instance, in one chapter Maimonides rules that intention is required throughout all the silent daily prayer (*Amidah*), while in another chapter he rules that intention is required only during the first blessing. Whereas earlier scholars might have resolved this discrepancy by suggesting that each of Maimonides's rulings refers to a different case, R. Ḥayyim infers the existence of two different concepts of intention: one category of intention entails awareness of standing before God (and is thus necessary throughout the silent prayer) while the other type of intention requires comprehension of the meaning of the text (limited to the first blessing alone).[43]

This school of Torah study became known as the Brisker method, or simply as *lomdus*. This method brought two of the characteristics of Torah study that have been described throughout this chapter to their zenith. First, the Brisker school views Torah study as the paramount charge of the rabbinic legal system and the primary form of religious devotion. And second, Torah study is not directed merely toward practical application of the law but rather to an intellectual project of harmonizing the entire body of the law. The systematic, "scientific" method of approaching the text in pursuit of internal legal coherence spread to most Lithuanian yeshivot and continues to be the dominant form of study in traditional yeshivot to this day.[44]

From the Academy to the Courtroom

If the theoretical nature of Torah study is at the core of rabbinic culture, how did this affect the application of law in a practical setting? Was there a firm separation between the study hall and the courtroom or did the academic nature of Torah study spill over into attempts to apply it?

The very first Mishnah of tractate Avot records the appeal of the Men of the Great Assembly to rabbinic leaders: "They said three things: Be patient in [the administration of] justice, raise many disciples and make a fence around the Torah."[45] These instructions encompass three realms of responsibility: adjudication, instruction, and legislation, presenting the ideal rabbinic scholar as one engaged in all areas of Torah, both theoretical and practical. This almost certainly idealized depiction nonetheless reveals the rabbis' aspirations to command both study and regulation.[46] While the historical reality of the classical rabbinic period is frequently shrouded in mist, scholars suggest that academic study and adjudication in this period were indeed often intertwined. In the *tannaitic* period, rabbis did not study in consolidated institutional structures but rather in "disciple circles" formed around a particular master.[47] These instructors occasionally served as judges in individual disputes, and their disciples learned from them as they aided their masters in court.[48] In the Babylonian Talmud, hundreds of court cases are cited, demonstrating that rabbinic academies did not focus on theoretical study alone, but rather served the broader Jewish community as the locus of the Jewish judicial system.[49] In particular, Isaiah Gafni has shown that a large majority of cases presented in the Talmud were adjudicated by the heads of the Babylonian yeshivot.[50] For instance, b.Bava Metzia 35a relates a case of two litigants who came before Rav Naḥman for a judgment. The Talmud then adds that this occurred during a theoretical discussion of a particular issue, leading Rava to question his master concerning the case at hand. This example and others indicate that disciples would sit before their masters at the time of adjudication, and this was viewed as a form of apprenticeship that complemented and enhanced the academic study with the master. The academy and the court were not seen as two separate and independent forums, but rather as one unified system, in which law simultaneously developed in both the academy and the courtroom.[51]

As the ideal of *Torah li-shmah* consolidated, however, it profoundly impacted the regulation of Jewish life. The tension between theoretical study and practical application (and the need for religious leadership to be involved in adjudication) led to significant differences between medieval Jewish communities. Many rabbinic scholars preferred to serve their communities by focusing on creative scholarship and interpretation; in some communities, however, religious leaders served as both head of the academy and communal judges.[52] Historians have demonstrated that the differences in leadership style track the distinct attitudes toward Torah study in different parts of the Jewish world. In Islamic countries, where practical Torah study was the norm, the yeshiva was closely tied to the local courthouse, and the head of the academy was often also the head of the court (*av beit din*).[53] In Jewish communities under Christian rule, the historical record is more complex, and practices varied between different areas. Ephraim Kanarfogel has argued that one of the defining variances between the Tosafists of France and Germany was in their attitude to this issue. In many German cities and towns, leading Tosafists served as judges on the local courts, adjudicating, handling appeals, and frequently exchanging written communiques with courts in other towns. Scholarship was understood to be in service of the community, and scholars were required to participate in rabbinical courts. By contrast, in France, the academy encouraged virtuosic scholarship, and rabbinic scholars often preferred to focus on their own creative scholarship, regarding the role of communal judge as a necessary evil to be taken on only if no one else could do so. Thus, Cologne Judge R. Ḥayyim b. Yeḥiel Ḥefes Zahav states, "If it were up to me, I would prefer that no case should come before me."[54] These differences reflect the tensions implicit in rabbinic sources from their earliest times: is the ideal rabbinic role that of the judges in the courtroom, applying practical law, or does rabbinical leadership derive from a scholar's capacity to engage in Torah study at the highest level, proposing innovative readings of the ancient sources? In medieval France and Germany, these two models of religious leadership existed side by side.[55]

As theoretical study gained cultural capital in rabbinic *yeshivot*, it also led to a reticence on behalf of some rabbinical scholars to take community posts or engage in rendering judicial decisions. Thus, the Briskers who valued "pure" Torah study over all else occupied themselves with the academic examination of such idealized legal concepts as "intention," "causality," or "ownership," and to them, engaging in the material realities of real litigants and criminals was only a sullied form of law which did not reflect true *halakhah*. This tradition has reached its culmination in contemporary yeshivot, particularly in the United States and Israel, where thousands of students aspire to study in the yeshiva throughout the duration of their adult lives, with the sole purpose of magnifying and enlarging the Torah (*lehagdil Torah u-lehaadirah*).

The academy and the courtroom, however, were not always in competition, but rather regularly complemented one another. A rabbinic court sitting in judgment on a complex legal case might send an inquiry to a leading rabbinic authority, who would take the opportunity to develop a lengthy responsum that touched on many theoretical issues not directly part of the particular court case. Complicated real-life cases might also require the respondent to deviate from an accepted interpretation to well-known sources and offer an innovate interpretation to a particular text to bring it into agreement with the desired legal ruling based on other rabbinic sources. Some scholars wore more than one hat, issuing practical rulings for the community's real-life problems while also engaging in sophisticated academic study. For example, the Austrian scholar Rabbi Israel Isserlein (1390–1460) earned his reputation as the author of *Terumat haDeshen*, a lengthy and learned collection of essays famously written in response to his own questions, yet he also issued brief practical responsa.[56]

Nonetheless, outside the halls of the academy legal decisions had to be made. Ever since the classical rabbinic period, debates had raged over the relative importance of answers to real-life questions versus rulings based on theoretical inferences. For instance, the Talmudic *sugya* mentioned earlier as to whether the teaching of a rabbi or his actions were to be preferred (b.Bava Batra 130b) was explained by Rabbi Samuel ben Meir of Northern France, known as the Rashbam (1160), as indicating that legal rulings given in the context of real-life questions carried more weight than those reached in an academic setting.[57] This issue gained even greater force with the emergence of the influential codes of Jewish law. One of the great comprehensive collections of legal rulings was written in the early fourteenth century by the eminent Rabbi Asher ben Yeḥiel, known by his Hebrew acronym as the Rosh (1250–1327), and this collection became one of the foundations of the influential code *Arba'ah Turim*, written by his son Rabbi Jacob ben Asher, and later, of Rabbi Joseph Caro's *Shulkhan Arukh*. However, Rabbenu Asher composed not only legal rulings, but also a compilation of responsa, and many contradictions can be found between the two. This incongruity stimulated a lively debate that continued for several generations, with some decisors arguing that an answer given in a responsa should be given precedence due to its practical, applied nature, while other scholars vehemently argued that the Rosh's legal rulings should be relied upon precisely because they were detached from a particular scenario and represented a purer ideal of the law.[58] Yet assuming that R. Asher himself was aware of the discrepancies between his varying rulings leads to the conclusion that the goals of his two works were distinct: one representing the ideal law untarnished by practical considerations, and the other reflecting the particular circumstances of a specific case.

Conclusion

At the beginning of his aptly titled *People of the Book*, Moshe Halbertal relays what one of his teachers told him regarding heaven and hell in the Jewish tradition: "Don't think that hell is where people are consumed by fire for their sins or that heaven is where they are rewarded with pleasures for their piety. What really happens is that God gathers everybody in one large hall. Then He gives them the Talmud and commands them to start studying. For the wicked, studying Talmud is hell. For the pious, it's heaven."[59] As Halbertal notes, the centrality of Torah study is so essential to Jewish life that even the afterlife cannot be envisioned without it. In this world too, rabbinic sources describe Torah as essential for life, so much so that one *Midrash* muses that when the Torah was given at Sinai, people should have received two mouths, so that even while one mouth was eating, the other would be free to study Torah.[60] An examination of the ideal of *talmud Torah* demonstrated that its significance throughout all periods and layers of rabbinic tradition serves to explain many of the unique characteristics of the Jewish legal system. Moreover, the ideal of Torah study complicates the very notion of "Jewish law," as the role of study as a foundational religious and devotional practice competes with the regulatory impulse of legal systems.[61] The complicated dance between practical application and theoretical study goes a long way toward explaining why matters of theology, philosophy, and ethics are often discussed in the form of legal texts, underscoring the wealth of meanings denoted by the rabbinic concept of *halakhah*.

Notes

1. Early precursors to the centrality of the law are found in occasional biblical hints, such as the use of the term "seeking God's teaching" (from the root *d-r-sh*) in Ezra 7:10 or I Chronicles 28:8. The importance of studying the law may be hinted at in Psalms 119, probably the only place in the Hebrew Bible where this idea is emphasized. See Avi Hurvitz, "Continuity and Innovation in Biblical Hebrew—The Case of 'Semantic Change' in Post Exilic Writings," in *Studies in Ancient Hebrew Semantics* (Supp. Ser. 4), ed. Takamitsu Muraoka and Abr Nahrain (Leuven, Belgium: Peeters, 1995), 1–10.
2. For the view of the Mishnah, *Midrash*, and Talmuds as revealed in full at Sinai, see j.Hagigah 1:8, 79d; b.Berakhot 5a. For a perspective implying gradual development, see Sifre Deuteronomy 313; m.Avot 5:22; b.Megillah 19b. For a discussion of the rabbinic conceptualization of the Oral Torah, see Martin S. Jaffee, *Torah in the Mouth: Writing and Oral Tradition in Palestinian Judaism* (New York: Oxford University Press, 2001).
3. Sifre Deuteronomy 49.
4. See Menachem Hirshman, "What Is the Place of Aggadah and Who Were the Baalei Aggadah," in *Meḥqerei Talmud* III, ed. Yaakov Sussman and David Rosenthal (Jerusalem: Magnes Press, 2005), 205–6 [Hebrew].
5. As Jeffrey Rubenstein has observed, such extreme expressions are virtually unparalleled in Palestinian sources, and demonstrate the "scholastic mentality and academic

preoccupations of the Bavli." See Jeffrey L. Rubenstein, *The Culture of the Babylonian Talmud* (Baltimore, MD: John Hopkins University Press, 2003), 31–35. For a detailed discussion, see E. E. Urbach, *The Sages: Their Concepts and Beliefs*, trans. Israel Abrahams (Jerusalem: Magnes Press, 1979), 608–16.

6. The distinction between these categories was foundational to the classical philosophical tradition beginning with Aristotle, and strongly influenced the Christian contemplative tradition best represented by Thomas Aquinas. For an examination of the centrality of these categories to the Western philosophical tradition, see Hannah Arendt, *The Human Condition* (Chicago: Chicago University Press, 1958).
7. Marc Hirshman, *The Stabilization of Rabbinic Culture, 100 C.E.–350 C.E.* (New York: Oxford University Press, 2009), 35.
8. This tension existed already in the Talmudic period between the rabbinic centers of Babylonia and the land of Israel. As an example, on b.Bava Batra several *Amoraim* dispute the meaning of Psalms 17:15, with the rabbis from the land of Israel interpreting it to refer to charity while the Babylonian Rav Naḥman bar Yitzḥak uses it to emphasize the importance of Torah study. These positions illustrate a broader ideological difference between the Palestinian and Babylonian attitudes toward study versus other commandments. See Alyssa Gray, *Charity in Rabbinic Judaism: Atonement, Rewards, and Righteousness* (New York: Routledge, 2019), 96.
9. *Tosfot* to b.Bava Kamma 17a, s.v. *ve-ha-amar mar*; *Tosfot* to b.Kiddushin 40b, s.v. *talmud gadol*; *Pnei Yehoshua* to b.Bava Kamma 17a.
10. *Tosfot* to b.Kiddushin 40b, s.v. *talmud gadol.*
11. For a summary of these debates, see Norman Lamm, *Torah Lishmah: Torah for Torah's Sake in the Worlds of Rabbi Hayyim of Volozhin and His Contemporaries* (Hoboken, NJ: Ktav, 1989), 140–152.
12. For a summary of this position as well as other explanations for the Mishnah's continued interest in temple-related law, see Naftali S. Cohn, *The Memory of the Temple and the Making of the Rabbis* (Philadelphia: University of Pennsylvania Press, 2013), 2–4 and literature cited therein. For an initial attempt to offer a comprehensive theory of the areas of law chosen by the rabbis for concerted elaboration, see David Kraemer, *Rabbinic Judaism: Space and Place* (London: Routledge, 2016).
13. Chaim Saiman, *Halakhah: The Rabbinic Idea of Law* (Princeton, NJ: Princeton University Press, 2020), 37.
14. On the study of Tohorot in Babylonia, see Yaakov Sussman, "Babylonian *Sugiyot* to the Orders *Zerai'm* and *Tohorot*" (PhD diss., Hebrew University of Jerusalem, 1969) [Hebrew].
15. See David Weiss Halivni, *Midrash, Mishnah and Gemara: The Jewish Predilection for Justified Law* (Cambridge, MA: Harvard University Press, 1986), 76–77.
16. b.Betzah 11b.
17. For more on the theoretical nature of Talmud study, see David Kraemer, *The Mind of the Talmud: An Intellectual History of the Bavli* (New York: Oxford University Press, 1990), 87–112; Daniel Boyarin, *Socrates and the Fat Rabbis* (Chicago: Chicago University Press, 2009), 133–67; Rubenstein, *Culture of the Babylonian Talmud*, 39–51.
18. b. Shabbat 12b; b.Eruvin 13a; b.Betzah 28b; b.Bava Kama 30b; b.Avodah Zarah 37b.
19. b.Sanhedrin 82a.
20. Haym Soloveitchik, "Responsa: Literary History and Basic Literacy," *Association of Jewish Studies Review* 24, no. 2 (1999): esp. 352–53. As Soloveitchik writes, "this phrase has been common currency in *halakhic* literature for well over seven hundred years, ever since the

days of R. Solomon Ibn Aderet (*Rashba*, d. 1315). How ubiquitous it is may be seen from the Bar-Ilan Responsa Project. The project's data bank yields no less than eighty-seven instances of its use in the sixteenth century alone."

21. See Robert Brody, *The Geonim of Babylonia and the Shaping of Medieval Jewish Culture* (New Haven, CT: Yale University Press, 1998), esp. 35–48, 113–34, 161–66, 333–35.
22. See Israel M. Ta-Shma, *Talmudic Commentary in Europe and North Africa: Literary History*, I (Jerusalem: Magnes Press, 1999), 16–21. It is true that many interpretative works were written by scholars from these countries, such as the commentaries of Rabbi Ḥananel and Rabenu Nissim in North Africa, and the commentaries of Rabbi Samuel Hanagid, Rabbi Itzhak ibn Giyat, and Rabbi Joseph ibn miGash in Spain, but these works had a clear *halakhic* orientation, unlike the commentaries from Ashkenaz and France. Similarly, even works of Jewish philosophy from this period reflect this more practical orientation. For instance, for Rabbi Yehuda Halevi (1075–1141), observance of the mitzvot was valued as the highest ideal and the principal path to God, while Hasdai Crescas (1340–1410) viewed the large number of commandments as the only route to spiritual perfection.
23. It is important to note that even within Ashkenaz the ideal of study for its own sake was not unanimously accepted. Scholars known as "the pious of Ashkenaz" (*ḥasidei Ashkenaz*) criticized the valorization of study as producing religious and moral distortions. See Haym Soloveitchik, "Three Themes in *Sefer Hasidim*," *Association of the Jewish Studies Review* 1 (1976): esp. 343–44.
24. Maimonides, *Introduction to Mishneh Torah*. For an exploration of Maimonides's intentions regarding the role of *Mishneh Torah* in the Jewish curriculum, see Moshe Halbertal, *Maimonides: Life and Thought* (Princeton, NJ: Princeton University Press, 2014), 164–96.
25. Maimonides, *Introduction to Mishneh Torah*.
26. In Germany and France, students of Torah held an important role in the community, even among those who could not themselves delve into the depth of Torah study. The fact that social hierarchy was structured around the importance of Torah study goes a long way toward explaining why it is precisely in Germany and France that the tradition of commentaries on the Talmud developed, a tradition that was not concerned with the practical implications of Torah study, and therefore also studied those tractates found in Seder Qodashim and Taharot that were entirely theoretical for the diasporic Jewish community. See Ephraim Kanarfogel, "What Do They Study in Your Yeshivah? The Scope of Talmudic Commentary in Europe during the High Middle Ages," in *Printing the Talmud: From Bomberg to Schottenstein*, ed. Sharon Lieberman Mintz and Gabriel M. Goldstein (New York: Yeshiva University Museum, 2005), 43–52.
27. The dialectical method of the *Tosafot* was instituted by Rabbenu Tam (1100–1171) and primarily carried on by his nephew, Rabbi Isaac of Dampierre (d. 1189). On Rabbenu Tam, see E. E. Urbach, *Baalei ha-Tosafot* (Jerusalem: Bialik, 1954), repr. 1980, 60–113; Avraham (Rami) Reiner, *Rabbenu Tam: Interpretation, Halakhah, Controversy* (Ramat Gan: Bar Ilan University Press, 2021). On Rabbi Isaac, see *Responsa of Rabbi Isaac ben Samuel of Dampierre: A Critical Edition*, ed. Avraham (Rami) Reiner and Pinchas Roth, with Introduction and Notes (Jerusalem: Magnes Press, 2019), 1–38.
28. See Edward Fram, "In the Margins of the Text: Changes in the Page of Talmud," in *Printing the Talmud: From Bomberg to Schottenstein*, ed. Sharon Lieberman Mintz and Gabriel M. Goldstein (New York: Yeshiva University Museum, 2005), 91–96.

29. Preeminent among these scholars were Naḥmanides, Rabbi Shlomo ibn Aderet (*Rashba*, 1235–1310), Rabbi Yom Tov ben Avraham of Seville (*Ritva*, 1260–1320), and Rabbi Nissim of Gerona (*Ran*, 1320–1376).
30. See Elchanan Reiner, "Transformations in the Polish and Ashkenazi *Yeshivot* during the Sixteenth and Seventeenth Centuries and the Dispute over *Pilpul*," in *ke-Minhag Ashkenaz u-Folin: Sefer Yovel le-Khone Shmeruk* (Jerusalem: Zalman Shazar, 1989), 11 n. 3 [Hebrew], gathers the secondary literature on the nature and development of *pilpul.*
31. For detailed analysis of the pilpulistic methods as well as the objections to these methods by the *Maharal*, Rabbi Ephraim Lunschitz, and Rabbi Isaiah Horowitz, see Haim Zalman Dimitrovsky, "On the Pilpulistic Method," in *Salo Wittmayer Baron Jubilee Volume on the Occasion of his Eightieth Birthday*, ed. Saul Lieberman and Arthur Hyman (Jerusalem: American Academy of Research, 1974), 3:111–82.
32. Rabbi Shmuel ben Eliezer, *Darkhei Noam*, 60b–61a.
33. For Maharal's views on education, see Simḥa Assaf, *Mekorot le-Toldot ha-ḥinukh be-Yisrael*, ed. Shmuel Glick (New York: Jewish Theological Seminary of America, 2001), 2:17–22.
34. Eliyahu Stern, *The Genius: Elijah of Vilna and the Making of Modern Judaism* (New Haven, CT: Yale University Press, 2013), 124–27.
35. See Lamm, *Torah Lishmah.*
36. Ḥayyim of Volozhin, *Nefesh Ha-ḥayyim* 1:16.
37. *Nefesh Ha-ḥayyim* 4:10, see Lamm, *Torah Lishmah*, 114–16.
38. See ibid., 117.
39. See ibid., 155.
40. For more on the debates between the Hasidim and their opponents, known as the Mitnaggedim, see Mordechai Wilensky, *Ḥasidim u-Mitnaggedim*, 2 vols. (Jerusalem: Mossad Bialik, 1970) [Hebrew].
41. Lamm, *Torah Lishmah*, 145.
42. See Normon Solomon, The *Analytic Movement: Hayyim Soloveitchik and his Circle* (Atlanta, GA: Scholars Press, 1993); Chaim Saiman, "Legal Theology: The Turn to Conceptualism in Nineteenth-Century Jewish Law," *Journal of Law and Religion* 21, no. 1 (2006): 39–100; Paul Nahme "Wissen und Lomdus: Idealism, Modernity, and History in some Nineteenth Century Rabbinic and Philosophical Responses to the Wissenschaft des Judentums," *Harvard Theological Review* 110, no. 3 (2017): 393–420.
43. Ḥayyim Soloveitchik, *Ḥiddushei Rabbeinu Ḥayyim Ha-Levi*, Laws of Prayer 4:1.
44. For more on the school of Brisk and its relationship to contemporary intellectual trends, both Jewish and secular, see Aharon Lichtenstein, "The Conceptual Approach to Torah Learning: The Method and Its Prospects," in *Lomdut: The Conceptual Approach to Jewish Learning*, ed. Yosef Blau, New York: Ktav, 2006); Marc Shapiro, "The Brisker Method Reconsidered," *Tradition* 31, no. 3 (1997): 78–102.
45. mAvot 1:1.
46. See Ishay Rosen Zvi, "The Protocol of the Court at Yavne? A new Reading of Tosefta Sanhedrin 7," *Tarbiz* 78 (2009): esp. 470 n. 130.
47. See Haim Shapira, "The Beit Midrash in the Land of Israel in the Period of the Mishnah and the Talmud" (PhD diss., Bar Ilan University, 2001).
48. Shaye J. D. Cohen, "The Place of the Rabbi in Jewish Society of the Second Century," in *The Galilee in Late Antiquity*, ed. Lee Levine (New York: Jewish Theological Seminary of America, 1992), 157–74.

49. Isaiah Gafni, *The Jews of Babylonia in the Talmudic Era: A Social and Cultural History* (New Haven, CT: Yale University Press, 2016), 204–5.
50. Isaiah Gafni, "*Ma'asei beit din ba-talmud ha-bavli: tsurot sifrutiyot ve-hashlakhot historiot*," *Proceedings of the American Academy for Jewish Research* 49 (1982): 23–40.
51. For further analysis, see ibid.
52. On the distinction between the two roles, see Gerson D. Cohen, "The Hebrew Crusade Chronicles and the Ashkenazic Tradition," in *Minha le-Nahum: Biblical And Other Studies Presented to Nahum M. Sarna in Honour of His 70th Birthday*, eds. Marc Brettler and Michael Fishbane, Sheffield, 1993, 44–45.
53. Israel Ta-Shma, "Jewish Judiciary and Law in the Eleventh and Twelfth Centuries in Spain (as Reflected in the Responsa of Alfasi)," *Shnaton Ha-Mishpat Ha-Ivri* Shiput Ivri 1 (1974), 353; Abraham Gross, "Centers of Study and Yeshivot in Spain," in *Moreshet Sepharad: The Sephardi Legacy*, ed. Haim Beinart (Jerusalem: Magnes Press, 1992), 399–410.
54. Ephraim Kanarfogel, "Religious Leadership during the Tosafist Period: Between the Academy and the Rabbinic Court," in *Jewish Religious Leadership: Images and Reality*, ed. Jack Wertheimer (New York: Jewish Theological Seminary of America, 2014), esp. 1:266.
55. For further exploration of this subject, see also Avraham (Rami) Reiner, "Rabbinical Courts in France in the Twelfth Century: Centralisation and Dispersion," *Journal of Jewish Studies* 60, no. 2 (2009): 298–318.
56. For a recent discussion, see Tirzah Kelman, "What Makes a Text Responsa? R. Israel Isserlein's *Terumat haDeshen* as a Test Case," *Jewish Law Association Studies* 30 (2022): 99–110.
57. *Rashbam* on b.Bava Batra 130b, s.v. *u-mar savar*.
58. See Yizhak Ze'ev Kahana, "Ha-pesaq ve-teshuvah," in *Meḥqarim be-sifrut ha-teshuvot* (Jerusalem: Mossad Harav Kook, 1963), 97–107.
59. Moshe Halbertal, *People of the Book: Canon, Meaning, and Authority* (Cambridge, MA: Harvard University Press, 1997), 1.
60. See Marc Hirshman, "Torah in Rabbinic Thought: The Theology of Learning," in *Cambridge History of Judaism*, vol. 4, ed. Steven T. Katz (Cambridge: Cambridge University Press, 2006), esp. 908.
61. For an elaboration on this point, see Saiman, *Halakhah*.

CHAPTER 12

FORMAL LAW AND ITS RELATIONSHIP TO *MINHAG/TAKKANOT*

MARCUS MORDECAI SCHWARTZ

Introduction: The Dynamics of Jewish Custom

JEWISH custom is a difficult subject.[1] As we study the role of custom in Jewish practice and law, we find ourselves overwhelmed by its complexity. Sometimes we hear Jewish customs identified with binding Jewish law, and at other times, just the opposite. One rabbi or Sage may describe one custom as binding and another as not with apparently little reason. We may come across a writer describing custom as silly piety. And yet, the same author might also refer to custom as the sublime work of the children of prophets. Barriers to understanding are high, fortified by inconsistencies in language that have been used to discuss that practices and regulations are not quite law.

Here is the main problem: fine and yet blurred distinctions between practices and observances exist at the margins of Jewish law. Categories often bleed into each other: popular practice becomes standard over time and becomes formal law. To cut through this knot, I apply the term "marginal norm" to any ritual, observance, regulation, or rule that resides outside the formal body of Jewish law but is compelling to observant Jews. This is an attempt to avoid linguistic confusion. I use this phrase throughout this chapter for the sake of consistency and brevity. This term presumes that formal Jewish law lies at the center of traditional conceptions of Jewish religious practice.

Whatever Jewish practice any entity adopts, whether an individual, a family, or an entire community, I claim that they are acting in relationship to an imagined central body of law: a *corpus legibus*. My assumption is that the dynamics of Jewish practice demand the existence of a compelling body of authoritative formal law distinct from folk practices and communal enactments—at least in the minds of its practitioners and decisors. I hope most will find this simplification as helpful as I do. I am worried that it could also be misleading. Many terms are used to refer to these marginal norms. This is an indicator of the variety of religious, popular, and ethical expressions they embody. I claim that for many Jews who observe traditional religious practice, the disembodied nature of the rabbinic oral tradition gives rise to a notional center of Torah (in its largest sense) where the main body of idealized formal law abides. This imagined structure has great symbolic power. This is the *corpus legibus*.

The truth is that most Jews across the scope of history and geography have had a stronger grasp on the symbolic power of Jewish law than its actual content; most have had a more secure understanding of the transcendent character of *halakhah* than the close details of its regulations. Yet, it is precisely the power of this symbolic meaning that has imparted the rabbinic tradition's commanding voice. The transcendent symbolism of Torah and mitzvot shines through to Jewish customs and other bordering practices. This dynamic is gradual and evolutionary: over time the community comes to view practices that began as marginal norms as formal law, reflecting Torah's light.

The Chapter's Design

The confusing diversity of authority we encounter in marginal norms stood at the forefront of my mind as I designed this chapter. I have tried to present the topic in an order that mitigates bewilderment. After this brief preface, I locate the origin of the difficulty in opposing conceptual trends present in classical rabbinic sources. Some rabbis in the Talmud saw the force of custom as absolutely binding on a community. Others viewed it neutrally; for this group the only imperative in operation was that a judge should avoid showing either approval or disfavor. A third group held that popular customs were subject to a decisor's discretion: if the custom was good, it should be upheld; if bad, it should be rejected. I show that there was a great deal of debate in early rabbinic texts about the nature of custom and practice. Knowing this helps us understand why there appears to be so much blurring of the lines around marginal norms in later rabbinic writings. This is the first major section of this chapter.

The next sections explore two major categories that the many literary sources of Jewish law tend to use when speaking of marginal norms. The second section of this chapter examines *minhag* (custom). The third offers an interrogation of the quasi-legislative *takkanah* and *gezeirah* (communal enactment/prohibition) categories. While other categories do exist, these two (customs and communal enactment/prohibition) are the most representative of the sorts of marginal norms I am attempting to explain. In each of these two discussions, I also provide some examples to illustrate these categories of marginal norms. My examples are in no way comprehensive, but I have chosen them because I see them as relevant and enlightening on differences between the categories.

I encourage caution, however, because in all cases, my definition of each category is only correct some large percentage of the time. There is a tendency among a nontrivial number of authorities and sources of Jewish law to blur the distinction between categories for a range of reasons, including organic shifts in meaning and culture, a desire for flexibility, pressing economic or ethical needs, the desire to win an argument, scholarly reflexive contrarianism, and so on. Real-world Jewish legal practice is often resistant to systemization, and frequently confounds even the broadest attempts to define its categories. Despite this limitation, a set of definitions remains helpful.

The Origin of the Puzzle

As students of Jewish law and practice, we often find ourselves confused by a very basic question. Is custom separate from Jewish law or a part of it? Some authorities of Jewish law have at times used the term *halakhah* oppositionally, juxtaposing it with *minhag* or another of the terms for less formal Jewish practice, to distinguish what they see as the more formal *corpus legibus* from more marginal norms. In doing this, they have attempted to impart a limited or restricted meaning to the word *halakhah*. In this usage, *halakhah* refers only to formal Jewish law and its requirements as distinct from the more marginal stipulations of Jewish practice. This can confuse the reader, because marginal norms are also a subcategory of *halakhah* writ large, and observant Jews often understand them as representing constituted requirements of *halakhah* in its more expansive sense.

It often happens that the same author may use the word *halakhah* in each of these two distinct senses, sometimes in rapid succession, without informing the reader. It is only by reading their texts closely and carefully that we may determine when traditional scholars who employ the word *halakhah* intend (in a particular passage) to refer to its narrow sense as the restricted body of formal, official law, or if they mean to use the word to refer to the larger meaning of *halakhah* encompassing custom and convention as well as law.

A fine example of this usage and the careful reading it requires is a passage that Nachmanides (1194–1270) wrote. We find this passage in the *Milkhamot Ha-Shem*, his work defending Isaac Alfasi (1013–1103) from the refutations of Zerahiah Ha-Levi of Girona (1115–*c.* 1186):

> As regards what the author of the Maor[2] (may his memory be a blessing) wrote, about the counting of the *Omer*: ". . . and we also conclude in [the Talmud . . .],[3] Ameimar[4] counts days, but does not count weeks. For he said it was a [mere] remembrance of Temple Times. But even so, we count days and weeks—this is a custom in our hands." But it is nothing other than an essential part of *halakhah!* And we hold [this position] in accordance with the rabbis of the academy of Rav Ashi who counted days and

weeks. And so have ruled all of the *Geonim*, our masters (may their memories be a blessing).[5]

In this passage, a surface reading seems to indicate that Nachmanides is issuing a ruling in agreement with Zerahia Ha-Levi since both rule that the correct practice is to count both days *and* weeks in the daily *Omer*-count marking off the days between Passover and Shavuot. If we read the passage too quickly, we may conclude that he is simply saying that the Maor's ruling is the correct practice. This is, after all, the most common meaning of *halakhah*. It usually indicates the correct *practice* among alternatives. However, the careful reader will discover that this is not his meaning at all, and instead of its more common meaning, he is using the word *halakhah* in opposition to *minhag*. If we take careful note of his presentation of Rabbi Zerahia's position, we see Nachmanides's emphasis more clearly: he is attempting to reject the notion that only counting the *days* of the *Omer* is formally required between Passover and Shavuot, and that counting weeks is a mere custom enacted to recall the fuller required practice of Temple times. Instead of this, he contends that the formal requirement is to count weeks as well as days—even in his time when the Temple does not stand. Therefore, for Nachmanides, counting both weeks and days represents more than just a custom that the people of Israel have adopted to recall the practice of Temple times.

Attempts to Mitigate the Confusion

Some more precise and systematic writers have used the term *din* (lit.: "judgment/reasoning," "ruling," or "legal status") to refer to the formal elements of *halakhah*, and use *minhag* to refer to the less formal ones. This can also be confusing because it alters the usual sense of the word *din*, making of its usually narrowly tailored cloth a broad jurisprudential category. In contrast to the literal meaning of *din*, these authors use the word to instead refer to more authoritatively instituted portions of Jewish law. Some Sages have attempted to further mitigate confusion by applying the word *ikar* (lit.: "root," but connotatively, "essence," or "core" in rabbinic thought) adjectivally to the word *din*. The resulting image is a version of Jewish law and practice split into two major categories: a theoretical "root law" (*ikar ha-din*—an "essential law" or "core law") and a much larger body of practices and conventions based on merely contingent authority.[6]

Understanding the Deceptive Authority of Marginal Norms

Texts referring to marginal norms of Jewish practice may also speak of them using the terms "*minhag shel shetut*" (foolish custom), "*gezeirot be-alma*" (mere proscriptions), "*nahagu bo/bah issur*" (a prohibition arising from popular practice), or "*lo pashta takkanah*" (an enactment with only limited acceptance). While at first, these epithets seem aimed at minimizing the authority of such practices, readers will often find themselves surprised when the authors who employ them will then go on to accept their binding nature. A new reader of *halakhic* texts may find themselves confounded by both the disorder of language and conceptual difficulty they encounter.

Because many of these customs and proscriptions have organic origins, having evolved from popular practices rather than well-considered policy and legislation, dealing with Jewish custom can sometime feel like living in an old house that has had many renovations: there are two sets of doors that go to the same location, needless hallways, superfluous staircases, and so on. Of course, this is also what adds to the house's charm, and in those very "pointless" details we can also feel the grounding of history and the past's gravity, granting meaningful weight to the lightness of lived experience. We can sense the lives that those long gone lived in the house before we were born—just out of our grasp—and even attempt to search again for their now-lost experiences. It is no different with the "marginalia" of Jewish practice. The study of these customs, proscriptions, and enactments frequently allows us to construct a plausible account of quotidian Jewish experiences in places and times that would otherwise be lost to us.

Additional Stumbling Blocks

However, as we embark on our study, we must begin by righting ourselves. It is all too easy to stumble over the block placed before us by the challenging language and theory we find in the sources. A relevant passage in the Babylonian Talmud, tractate Ta'anit:

> It has been taught [in a *baraita*.[7]]: . . . at the *shaharit* [the service in the early morning], at the *musaf* [the service later in the morning], at *minhah* [in the afternoon] and at *ne'ilah* [at sunset] there is [the ceremony of] "lifting up of hands" [performed by the *kohanim* as they deliver the priestly blessing of Numbers 6:24–27]. This is the opinion of Rabbi Meir. Rabbi Yehudah says: At *shaharit* and at *musaf* there is "lifting up of hands," but at *minhah* and *ne'ilah* there is no "lifting up of hands."[8]

Here we find a dispute in practice about a ritual performed during the prayer service on fast days.[9] The practice in the time of the Talmud (and in some communities to this day) was to call the Aaronide priests (the *kohanim*) to bless the congregation near the end of prayer services each morning. Later in the same passage, the Talmud tells us that the Sages of early times prohibited the *kohanim* from performing the blessing in the afternoon service because it was common for people to drink wine later in the day (the blessing is invalid if given while drunk). However, people do not drink on fast days. The dispute is about whether the prohibition on giving the blessing from the afternoon on is still in effect even though the reason for it no longer holds relevance. In other words, is it still prohibited to give the blessing in the afternoon even if people will not be drunk, but there is no recorded legislated exception? Or may we assume that an exemption for fast days was intended by the Sages?

The Talmud continues:

> Rabbi Yehudah said in the name of Rav: The law (*halakhah*) is in accordance with Rabbi Meir. Rabbi Yohanan said: The people follow (*nahagu*) Rabbi Meir. And Rava said: The custom (*minhag*) is in accordance with Rabbi Meir.[10]

Commenting on this more than a century later, the later Talmudic Sages agree that the view of Rabbi Meir is followed, but they disagree about the level of authority that this norm takes. Rav says that it has the weight of formal law; Rabbi Yohanan says that we resolve the dispute by observing the practice of the people; and Rava says that a binding custom exists that accords with Rabbi Meir's position. What is the practical relevance of these seemingly largely theoretical disputes? The Talmud goes on:

> If the *halakhah* is according to Rabbi Meir we teach it in public. But if we say that the custom is according to Rabbi Meir, then we should not teach it publicly, but we may make our decisions in accordance with it. But if we say that the people followed the view of Rabbi Meir, then we do not definitely give a decision in accordance with it, but if they acted on it, we don't make them change.[11]

In sum, the paradigm is that rabbis should propagate formal law, and issue rulings in accord with *established* custom. However, in the case of less formal folk practices, rabbis should not issue a formal ruling, but instead strive for a neutral stance. The Talmud suggests they simultaneously refrain from advocating such a folk practice while also avoiding any attempt to nullify it. As we can see, in a disputed case of formal law judges sometimes ruled in accordance with conventional practice, while simultaneously declining to promote it.

Nahagu is a term contained in the above quote from the Talmud that is distinct from *minhag* since it is a case of indeterminacy in law that is resolved by examination of existing practice, rather than an extra-legal practice that legal authorities treat as compelling out of convention.[12] In other words, *nahagu* represents widespread practice. The *nahagu*-principle posits that areas of controversy can be smoothed by attending to existing practice. We could put the principle in these terms: if there are multiple possible reasonable (but opposed) rulings in cases of religious practice, a decisor of Jewish law should rule in accordance with the extant general practice. For instance, the Mishnah in Berakhot records a dispute about the phrasing of the blessing over water.[13] The Babylonian Talmud's comment on that Mishnah text states that a Babylonian Sage[14] rules that it is proper to follow widespread folk practice.[15] This passage and another like it[16] establish the paradigm of resolving disputes by examining customary practice. This model would be used again and again by judges of Jewish law throughout the Middle Ages and into the modern period.[17]

The Confusion in Summary

To summarize: at the edges of Jewish law, we find subtle distinctions in authority between different practices. But we also find an ongoing dynamic transformation of these categories. We see folk practices donning the fabric of formal law. As discussed, I apply the term "marginal norm" to any practice that resides outside the central formal body of Jewish law (i.e., anything not included in the *corpus legibus/ikar ha-din*), that remains compelling to the traditionally observant Jew. In short, those who observe Jewish law and tradition have found the marginal norms of rabbinic practice to be compelling at a diversity of levels of authority in various times and places.

Minhag

A *minhag* is a custom arising from popular practice and acceptance. While such a custom can simply derive from a pious or ethical impulse as a community goes about daily life, it can also have significant legal implications, setting a compelling precedent in courts. An example from The Babylonian Talmud:

> The people of Hozai had a custom to take the *hallah* [the dough offering of Numbers 15:17-21] offering from rice [flour]. [Some people who objected] came and told Rav Yosef. He said to them, "Let an outsider [a non-*kohen*] eat it in front of them." Abaye raised an objection against him [from a *baraita*]: "As to permitted things that other people are accustomed to prohibit, you may not issue a ruling lifting the prohibition (*i-ata rashai le-hatir*) in front of them." (b.Pesahim 50b–51a)[18]

Though the Mishnah[19] clearly restricts the dough-offering (challah) of Numbers to just five grains (wheat, oats, barley, spelt, and rye), the people of Hozai have the practice of separating the offering from rice flour. Given the contradiction with the Mishnah, some of the residents of the town object to the practice of separating challah from rice flour.[20]

Rav Yosef[21] agrees with the objections. He rules that the custom of taking the challah from rice should be nullified; from now on, he rules, the offering should be taken only from the five grains listed above. To do this, he sets up a counter practice: Only the *kohanim*, descendants of Aaron the High Priest are permitted to eat from the dough offering. If an "outsider" (not one of the *kohanim*) eats from the separated rice-dough challah in front of the residents of the town this will set a precedent that will nullify the objectionable practice. Such an act publicly demonstrates that no such prohibition exists. However, Rav Yosef's younger colleague Abayye objects to his ruling, and presents a source that has higher authority than Rav Yosef commands—a *baraita*. The force of this is important. A *baraita* has more authority than the statement of an *amora* (Rav Yosef in this case). Most later sources of Jewish law have understood this to mean that Abayye wins the argument, and the principle in his *baraita* becomes the jurisprudential standard: judges may not lift prohibitions even when they derive solely from popular practice when there is no pressing need to do so.[22]

Stare Decisis in Jewish Custom?

The above-cited *baraita* ("you may not issue a ruling lifting the prohibition") binds *judges*. This statement may be one of the few cases of a true *stare decisis* principle in Jewish Law. *Stare decisis* is the doctrine in common-law legal systems that binds courts to precedent. The implication is significant: If judges are bound from altering custom, we can understand the tendency among some medieval rabbis to claim that the Talmud views custom and practice as binding on judges, even though no such claim exists regarding *actual case law*![23] But how could they have claimed that precedent isn't binding in decisions of formal law but is binding for mere customs!?

Menachem Elon—a scholar of Jewish law who served as a justice of the Israeli Supreme Court as well as its Deputy President in the late twentieth century—points out that unlike common law, authorities of Jewish law have usually seen precedents in formal law as contingent rather than *strictly* binding. Therefore, they have commonly moved to overturn them by undermining an earlier ruling's legal reasoning and/or by pulling down its interpretation of the relevant passages in the Talmud. Elon argues that the Babylonian Talmud represents a binding *corpus legibus* for rabbinic legal authorities, and that it constrains *halakhists* just as statutes (at least theoretically) constrain judges in continental civil law systems such as Quebec and Louisiana. In other words, formal Jewish law is primarily based on interpretation of literary sources (primarily the Mishnah and the two Talmuds, but the classical collections of *Midrash halakhah* as well), rather than either case law or legislation. The meaning of the Talmud and other classical rabbinic sources is contested in many passages, which is why nearly every responsum must go through the work of establishing just what the relevant sources mean.

Jewish law gets its authority primarily from its literary sources (mostly the Talmud). It derives less authority from either legislation or case law. This is true except for custom. Custom is based in the lived life of a community, not on a text. There is little room to overturn popular practice based on reasoning and interpretation. For this reason, marginal norms are binding, and judges may not overturn custom and practice without great reason. The way that medieval rabbinic sources usually phrase this principle is remarkably direct: "The custom of our ancestors *is* Torah."[24]

Until about the end of the fifteenth century, binding customs seem to have been limited to geographic regions. In other words, Spanish custom was binding in Spain, as was Provençal custom in Provence, and Roman custom in Rome. However, expulsions of Jews from their home countries from the thirteenth to the end of the fifteenth centuries (the last was the expulsion from Spain) changed this. At the end of this period, communities adopted ethnic definitions deriving from the lands of their ancestors. This is the origin of the Ashkenazi/Sephardic difference that we shall see later in the chapter. From this point on, differing customs existed among the Jews along ethnic lines within the same regions, the same cities, and even the same neighborhoods. In many places, the different Jewish ethnic groups had differing customs, many of which were conceptualized as binding upon the members of that particular community within the same neighborhood, city, or region. Sometimes these customs were contradictory on their face, and yet there were many cities in Europe where such groups lived side by side.

Does Custom Overturn Law?

Thus far we have been discussing the question of whether Jewish custom is binding on Jews as if it were law. However, we will now turn to a discussion of whether Jewish custom can ever nullify formal law. We find a surprising principle recorded in the Jerusalem Talmud: "custom overturns law." This seems to mean that when custom conflicts with formal law, judges should rule with the custom and vacate the law. This phrase ("custom overturns law") appears twice in the Jerusalem Talmud, once in the context of employment law[25] and once in the context of levirate marriage.[26] Despite its application to *both* the monetary and the ritual spheres in its original context in the Jerusalem Talmud, medieval authorities usually restricted this principle to disputes over money.[27] In such cases, judges were prone to rule in accordance with the prevailing custom of the time and place they were living, rather than the practice laid before them in the Talmud. This is perhaps similar to the codification of the Uniform Commercial Code in the United States along customary American (and even state) lines, rather than resorting to English common-law precedent.[28] The restriction to money may have taken hold because the principle does not appear in the Babylonian Talmud, the literary source of Jewish law that held the most significance for rabbinic Judges. The Babylonian Talmud does contain the principle that parties may agree to a stipulation in a monetary transaction or contract that differs from the Torah's rules, as long as both parties willingly consent.[29] Later authorities have generally accepted this view.

Customs Arising from Folklore, Superstition, Style, and Aesthetics

Minhag can also be conventionally performative and folkloric, and even have superstitious origins. It may determine the food Jews eat at a festival, such as Hanukkah potato pancakes or donuts, or reveal itself in small pious and devotional acts, such as contemplating the light cast by the havdalah flame on one's fingernails, or reciting Psalms for an ill loved-one's recovery. In thirteenth-century Germany, we encounter an early tendency that sets a long rabbinic paradigm. Rather than object to superstitious and simple folk customs, rabbis ratify them and imbue them with traditional religious meaning, identifying these practices with biblical and Talmudic precedents. In this vein, multiple authorities record an influential responsum that reads:[30]

> Regarding your claim that we are working omens when we take the heads of sheep on Rosh Hashanah, and eat honey and all sorts of sweets, and barley groats with

> fatty meat. . . . Behold, these are good omens, and have a basis in biblical verse and rabbinic lore. The head of sheep that we eat on Rosh Hashanah is so that the Holy Blessed One will place us at the head of all heads, and that we will not be the tail. And regarding the eating of barley groats with meat, and drinking honey and all sorts of sweet things, this is so that the coming year will be upon us fat and sweet, as it says in the book of Ezra (Neh. 8:10), "Go, eat fat foods and drink sweet drinks and send portions to whoever has nothing prepared, for the day is holy to our Lord."[31]

These explanations for customs wind their way through the major codes of the Middle Ages, eventually finding a home even in the great early-modern code of Jewish law, the *Shulhan Arukh*.[32]

Custom may set the clothes and hairstyles Jews wear in their daily lives, such as the widespread donning of the *Judenhut*, an inverted-funnel hat worn almost universally by Jewish men in medieval Germany and northern Italy.[33] It is worth noting that Yitzhak (Eric) Zimmer's 2006 Hebrew-language book, *Olam Ke-Minhago Noheg*, which has several studies on just these sorts of clothing customs, including an extended piece on Men's head coverings.[34] Zimmer also extensively treated women's head coverings in a separate study.[35] The discussion of such head coverings is too complex to treat with the level of inquiry it deserves in this brief survey. Suffice it to say that women's head coverings (or perhaps more correctly, "hair coverings") began in the realm of formal Jewish law in the time of the Mishnah,[36] while men's head coverings were a largely informal and sporadically observed practice that developed largely after the time of the Talmud. However, over the course of history, men's head coverings have come to take on the connotation of formal law, while women's head coverings were perceived as a custom, until their recent restoration to the realm of formal law in the mid-twentieth century. Custom (rather than official rabbinic ruling) can also set ritual practice, determining the language of prayer in the synagogue,[37] the manner of the sounding of the shofar,[38] or the number of Hanukkah lamps in a household, and so on.

Local and Global Customs

There are at least two types of custom: *minhag ha-makom* (local/regional practice) and *Minhag Yisrael* (global Jewish practice). *Minhag Yisrael* is relatively easy to explain. Sometimes so high a percentage of Jews have adopted a practice that it becomes universal, and no community can demur from it without controversy. Such practices include Jewish men wearing head coverings and the recitation of the daily evening prayer in synagogues.[39] On the other hand, *minhag ha-makom* is a bit more complex.

Until roughly the end of the fifteenth century in Europe *minhag ha-makom* (local/regional practice) referred mostly to the customs followed by the Jews in particular geographic areas, such as countries, regions, cities, or towns.[40] As mentioned, expulsion changed this. Here is a minor but illuminating example. During the Middle Ages, a small question arose regarding whether each individual in the household should have their own set of lights for the Festival of Hanukkah, or whether one set of lights was sufficient for all. The "solution" expressed itself here as a difference in practice between Ashkenazic and Sephardic communities: multiple sets of lights became a marker of Ashkenazic identity, while a single set of lights marked Sephardic households. The controversy continued but with the official approval of the different communities, each descending from different geographical regions but now living perhaps in the same neighborhood in northern Europe (see Davis, this volume).[41] This is just one among very many differences in practice between ethnic groups within the body of the Jewish people—groups that mostly formed themselves in response to a whole range of major geopolitical disruptions in late medieval and early modern Europe and North Africa (see Davis, this volume. See also Teplitsky, Bodian, and Ray, all in *The Oxford Handbook of the Jewish Diaspora*).[42]

With the rise of modernity *minhag ha-makom* came to mean the practices retained by transplanted communities living in new areas alongside other Jewish communities, such as the Spanish-Portuguese congregation in Amsterdam.[43] By the eighteenth century, this was true even throughout the Middle East, including Yemen.[44] Differences in distinctions in religious practice, style and method of traditional learning, liturgy, foods, spoken language, and a range of other similar sorts of differences represent a deeply challenging set of questions for study.

For instance, here is but one basic question that few have asked: which of these divergences had their roots in lived mimetic practices and which in differing textual traditions the communities studied in their rabbinic texts? We have not yet established which distinct versions of the Mishnah and the Talmud these various communities had access to. For some reason, this basic work has not caught the attention of Jewish studies. Academic scholars of Rabbinics have been aware—for more than one hundred years—that there were at least three different versions of the Mishnah extant in the Middle Ages. The family lines of these versions split based on geographic settlement.[45] In other words, the Jews took a different version of the Mishnah and the Talmud with them when they left Spain than the Jews in Italy, for example, had been studying. When Spanish Jews arrived on Italian shores they brought their version of the Talmud. Sometimes the differences in the versions were small, only a turn of phrase with no content divergences. However, sometimes the differences could be quite large and have an impact on practice. Since the literary sources of Jewish law are so deeply important, it is sometimes very hard to know why a divergence in custom and practice developed. Are we witness to differences in organic changes in culture that originated from isolation? Or do we see differences in practice because of differing textual traditions? In terms of method, to me this seems like basic work that must precede any investigation of *halakhic* divergence among the communities, because, as things stand now, we cannot know the extent to which the difference we see is the result of variation in text, interpretation, or organically arising praxis.

Having come to the end of our survey of *minhag* (custom), we now turn to the third section of the chapter: an interrogation of *gezaeirah/takkanah*, enactments or popularly accepted promulgated proscriptions.

Two Other Marginal Norms

Thus far we have been discussing custom as organically developing practice. These sorts of customary marginal norms all generally fit under the category of *minhag*. They are "bottom-up" categories. The community enacts practices by simply doing them. It then falls to rabbinic authorities to notice; to approve or to disapprove; to reject those practices or justify them; or to hold their peace. On the other hand, the two sorts of marginal norms that we discuss in this section (*takkanot* and *gezeirot*) are, at least in theory, "top-down." They have a far more legislative quality.

Takkanot[46] are changes in Jewish law made by an authority or court which feels that the current system of formal law fails to fully express the moral and religious values present in the Torah (in its largest sense). This leads an individual or court with sway to proclaim a change in practice. The success of such a proclamation is dependent on the community dynamics. The Jews, as always, vote with their bodies. If they do as the *takkanah* states, then it is a successful change in Jewish law. If they ignore it, and continue to follow the older practice, it has failed.

Gezeirot, on the other hand, are legislated prohibitions. Again, an authoritative body or individual simply declares a new prohibition. They may do so for a number of reasons, including moral delicacy, to assert authority, to protect a precept of the Torah which they see as having been neglected, and so on.

Both sorts of enactments are marginal norms because they rely on the approval of the community for success. Rabbis in other locations will not enforce them if a sizable community of Jews somewhere has not adopted them.

Takkanot

We may divide *takkanot* into two major categories. Early *Takkanot* have a legendary quality and are attributed to great figures from the past. A second grouping of *takkanot* have strong historical credibility and are associated with real authorities. As we shall see, this second category of *takkanah* became a paradigm for increasing Jewish political power during early modernity.

Takkanah usually refers to an enactment initiated by an authority. This authority may be a highly esteemed individual, or a recognized body of Sages constituted for the purpose. This category is as close to legislation as Jewish law gets; however, there is no regular, set process for propagation or acceptance as binding law. Instead, a self-appointed or entrepreneurial entity or individual simply stands up and declares a new requirement of Jewish law based on personal, political, and/or popular authority. There is no enforcement mechanism, and it is binding only to the extent that Jews begin to follow and rabbis start to enforce.

Over time, such enactments can come to have many fates. The community may abandon it. Or a *takkanah* may gradually don the garb of customary practice transforming into a *minhag* before our eyes. Or it may take on the full force and character of formal Jewish law, becoming part of the *corpus legibus* in the minds of the observant. In the former cases, it remains a marginal norm; in the latter, it matures and habilitates, earning its tenure in the body of formal Jewish Law.

Pseudepigraphically Attributed Takkanot

Early *takkanot* (prior to the late twelfth century) are traditionally attributed to authorities as diverse as biblical characters, legendary rabbinic figures, *tannaitic* and Amoraic rabbis, *Geonim*, and early *rishonim*. Many of these attributions may be pseudepigraphic retrojections. The historical origins of these early enactments are lost in the shadowy past. Their first literary appearance in a text can only establish a *terminus a quo* (an early limit) after which we can speak of their historical acceptance within the rabbinic community. That *terminus* should be based on the dating of the literary source in question, though source critical methods can be employed (with great care) in redacted texts to arrive at an earlier date.

Table 12.1 lists examples of such early enactments. The reader may find it surprising that so many basic elements of rabbinic religion are marginal norms rather than formal law. I suspect that this bothered the rabbis of the Mishnah and the Talmud as well. It is perhaps for this reason that they attributed so many of these *takkanot* to biblical and rabbinic founding figures. They knew that these practices were not required by either the Biblical or the old rabbinic tradition. For this reason, they needed to ground the authority of these practices in the personal authority of ancient figures of renown. Note in table 12.1 the centrality of the areas of Jewish religious life that these *takkanot* belong to.

The table is not exhaustive in the least, but the reader can see from the core nature of the areas of these "legendary" *takkanot* that the goal may be to bolster their authority by attributing them to great figures. The motivation may be to avoid a sense of lightness or insecurity that could result from the enactments' informal/marginal nature. Grounding their authority in the reputation of a figure from the past just makes sense.

Takkanot *Associated with Historical Authorities*

We are on firmer historical ground when we discuss the *takkanot* of ad hoc rabbinical assemblies beginning in the twelfth century. A number of late twelfth- and early thirteenth-century rabbis record in their responsa and rulings that in the previous generation or two there were a series of assemblies in France and Germany in which the constituted body voted and passed enactments for their communities.[47] The famous

Table 12.1 ***Takkanot*** **and Areas of Life**

Takkanah	Area of Life
Reading from the Torah on Shabbat, festivals, and the New Moon (b.Megillah 28a)	Communal life in the synagogue
The fixed liturgy of the grace after meals (b.Berakhot 48b)	Torah-required food blessings
The seven days of mourning for the dead (b.Ketubot 3a-b)	Death and mourning
The *eruv* (b.Shabbat 14b, b.Eruvin 21a)	Shabbat observance (!)
The recitation of Hallel (b.Pesahim 117a)	Festival prayer
The Prosbul[a] (M.Sheviit 10:3-4)	Money
The requirement to write the names of the husband and the wife in a bill of divorce, along with the date and signatures of witnesses (b.Gittin 34b) Requiring the presence of the wife or assigned agent before a bill of divorce can be declared invalid (M.Gittin 1:4).	Family law

[a] Requirement that loans be assigned to the court before the Sabbatical year to avoid debt release and its associated credit crunch.

Tosafist Rabbi Jacob Tam (1100–1171) is universally associated with these assemblies. He even seems to have held an organizing and leadership role. At least two generations later, between 1220 and 1223, a group of rabbis from the most prominent German communities of Speyer, Mayence, and Worms continued this trend. They convened in Mayence, to discuss the logistics of collecting taxes and impositions from the Holy Roman Empire on the Jews. During this conclave they promulgated a series of ordinances that received widespread acceptance throughout the French and German Jewish communities. These became known as the Enactments of *Shum* ("*Shum*" is Hebrew acronym for Speyer, Worms, and Mayence). According to later accounts, a number of prohibitions were enacted at the "Great Synod of *Shum*." Some examples: Jews were forbidden from cheating Christians in business or counterfeiting coin; Jewish informers had to make restitution for the harm they caused to other Jews; Jews with positions at court had to pay communal taxes despite their prominence; talking and boisterous behavior were prohibited during prayer; and the Rabbinic courts of Mayence, Speyer, and Worms were given official jurisdiction over all lawsuits between Jews. Over the next thirty years similar conclaves and rabbinic synods met and promulgated more legislation. No general theme pervades these decrees. Instead, they read like the diverse legislative agendas of a community with many needs, on the one hand, and like a group of communal leaders trying to ensure a smoothly functioning community on the other. Ethical behavior and social consideration are emphasized, but so is the authority of the rabbinic judge to enforce communal standards.

These meetings set a paradigm that would be followed by many Jewish communities during the high Middle Ages and early modernity. They resulted in a number of quasi-governmental Jewish associations forming in Central and Eastern Europe. Two of the most prominent of these were the Council of Four Lands (*Va'ad Arba' Aratzot*) which held its seat in Lublin in the second half of the sixteenth century to 1764, and the *Kehilot AHU* or the Union of the Three Communities in Hamburg, Altona, and Wandsbeck from 1674 to 1811. The Polish Council of Four Lands held real political and legal power over the Jews of the then-divided lands of Poland: it passed legislation on a variety of issues, oversaw the regulation and collection of taxes among the Jews, and oversaw civil courts and even minor criminal cases in Greater Poland, Little Poland, Galicia (with Podolia), and Volhynia (see Batnitzky, this volume). The Union of the Three Communities supervised the political and legal life of Jews who were split across three metropolitan areas, which were themselves divided between the Empire of Denmark and the free city of Hamburg. They had a joint court at Altona. The executive of the court was the Chief Rabbi and he exercised jurisdiction over the whole German-Jewish population of the three cities and the duchy of Holstein.

This end of Jewish autonomy in Hamburg/Altona/Wandsbeck came with the Napoleonic conquest of the city of Hamburg on November 19, 1806. By 1811, the French hade made the city the capital of the Département des Bouches de l'Elbe—a prominent city of the French Empire—effectively dissolving the quasi-governmental union of the three urban Jewish communities. Meanwhile in Poland, the Council of Four Lands lost its power under Catherine the Great's puppet King Stanisław August, when the Jews were increasingly tolerated and incorporated more into the body politic of Poland. The emancipations of the Jews and their acquisition of citizenship in the new secular nation-states of the late eighteenth and early nineteenth centuries put paid to rabbinic political or (enforceable) legal power in Europe. From this point on, Jews generally used the courts of the nations that they lived in to resolve monetary disputes (see Resnicoff, this volume). The marginal norms of rabbinic law increasingly became a matter of personal conscience and voluntary religious practice, as they remain to this very day. Of course, the emancipation of the Jews and their incorporation into the citizenry of the modern nation-state also put an end to coercive rabbinic authority to enforce Jewish law, at least without resort to the instruments of the modern state. Most rabbis in most places since the nineteenth century have not had access to such instruments. Whether law is still law if it has no mechanism for enforcement is a matter that rests beyond the scope of this chapter.

Gezeira

Prohibitions that fall under the category of *gezeirah* often have ambiguous historical origins. When such prohibitions are attributed to authorities who flourished prior to the close of the Talmud, they are usually considered as *de-rabbanan* law (of rabbinic authority). However, from the Middle Ages on, rabbis and Sages also referred to their post-Talmudic prohibitions with the term *gezeirah,* often without making a distinction between earlier, Talmudically instituted law, on the one hand, and later enacted prohibitions that should theoretically have a more marginal authority, on the other. Regardless, we should remind ourselves that a *gezeirah* can be a formal Talmudic law (*gezeirah de-rabbanan*), but it can also be a marginal norm, depending on the time of its enactment: whether instituted before or after the Talmud closed.[48] The Talmudic "*gezeirah*" is often translated as "decree," but "barrier" is closer to the sense. As discussed, "*gezeirot*" (plural) are prohibitions enacted by a rabbinic authority against a practice or act despite its permissibility in an earlier framing of formal Jewish law. Later sources of Jewish law refer to these Talmudic rabbinic barriers exclusively with the term *gezeirah.* (On the rabbinic excommunication of individuals see Davis, this volume.)[49]

As mentioned, we may find the term *gezeirah* confusing since it can also refer to later (post-Talmudic) marginal norms. An example of this is the Ashkenazic ban on multiple wives traditionally (and probably erroneously) attributed to Gershom ben Judah (*c.* 960–1040). Throughout the early part of the Middle Ages, the Ashkenazic tendency to only take a single wife was seen as a custom. It was usually not thought of as part of the formal body of Jewish law. But in the thirteenth century, rabbis began to refer to the practice as a prohibition that had been enacted by the Gershom ben Judah.[50] It is worth noting that the notion of a Jewish prohibition on multiple-wife marriage remained largely within the realm of Ashkenazic and western Spanish-Portuguese Jews until the nineteenth century. In Morocco, for example, this remained a matter of negotiation prior to the wedding and high-status women often required that a "single wife" condition be written in the wedding contract into the seventeenth century.[51] After that, it was seen as the *custom* of Jewish Moroccan men to take only one wife. Single-wife marriage did not become a universal Jewish custom until after World War II. Notably, the ban's authority remains contingent in the eyes of some authorities to this very day.[52] It is also unclear whether proponents of the ban saw it as a formal part of Jewish law, or simply frowned upon: later sources of Jewish law refer to the ban as Rabbenu Gershom's *gezeirah*or as his *herem* without distinction, sometimes within the same sentence.

And this brings us full circle: marginal norms are often ambiguously defined. Much of the difficulty is, again, that authors of *halakhic* texts have often used the terms with little precision, making it difficult to understand the quality and force of the norms. That said, trained readers of rabbinic texts are often able to tell from context. In the end, the lesson is that most *halakhic* texts are complex and ambiguous by their nature. Understanding them requires close and careful reading.

Conclusion

The definition and scope of marginal norms in Jewish law defy easy categorization and therefore, present daunting and intimidating challenges. As we have seen, the language is confusing and sometimes incoherent, and the meaning that each category has taken on changes from place to place and time to time. Nonetheless, our examination of the subject has revealed an underlying consistency: authorities of Jewish law often look to folk practice for guidance and confirmation of the rightness of their rulings. The power structures that we discover when looking at these marginal norms are continually shifting. Power moves from the margin to the center, from the folk to the elite, and back again. As we have said, there is a bleeding through of authority across a permeable layer—a type of open border—in which popular practices become law and law becomes popular practice. We have also seen that these shifts come with challenges to rabbinic authority and political independence, particularly in the age of the modern nation-state. Undoubtedly, customs, practices, and communal enactments will remain a fundamental element in the life of the Jewish people. But how this reality will express itself is unpredictable, especially as we now live in an increasingly unstable age, when the solidity and sustainability of the modern nation-state and the twin ideas of the rule of law and judicial supremacy are no longer as firm as they once were, and many feel an increasing sense of vulnerability. Customs have the warmth and power to make us feel safe in the midst of uncertainty. This may have been the original point in any case. Such practices are sustaining in the midst of fear and provide stability and structure when everything is collapsing. The fate of Jewish practice is inextricably linked with the fate of the House of Israel. But, for now, that fate is hidden from our view. So, I leave you with the following question: Without the formal authority of an enforcement body behind them, are not all the norms of Jewish religious practice marginal norms now?

Notes

1. The standard scholarly resources in English are Menachem Elon, *Jewish Law: History, Sources, Principles*, vol. 2 (Philadelphia: Jewish Publication Society, 1994); Joel Roth, *The Halakhic Process: A Systemic Analysis* (New York: Jewish Theological Seminary of America, Moreshet Ser. v. 13, 1986), 205–30; Elliott Dorff and Arthur Rosett, *A Living Tree: The Roots and Growth of Jewish Law* (New York: State University of New York, 1988), 403–34; Daniel Sperber, *Why Jews Do What They Do: The History of Jewish Customs throughout the Cycle of the Jewish Year* (Hoboken, NJ: KTAV, 1999); Daniel Sperber, *The Jewish Life Cycle Custom, Lore and Iconography: Jewish Customs from the Cradle to the Grave* (Ramat Gan: Bar-Ilan University Press and Oxford University Press, 2008).
2. The title of Zerahiah Ha-Levi's work means "the luminary."
3. B.Menahot 66a.
4. A Babylonian rabbi who appears in the Talmud; traditionally considered a fifth- or sixth-generation *amora*.
5. *Milhamot, Pesahim, Dapei Ha-Rif* 26.b, s.v. *Havei yodea*. The translation is my own.
6. For instance, Yosef Ibn Migash (1077–*c*. 1141) wrote that though work on the intermediate days of a festival is prohibited formally on a rabbinic level, all such work is nonetheless permitted from "root law." *Responsa of Ri Migash* (Warsaw: Schriftgeisser, 1870), #145 [Hebrew].
7. A tradition from the *Tannaim* not incorporated in the Mishnah; in other words, an apocryphal Mishnah passage. The *Tannaim* are the rabbis of the Mishnah and coeval works. They have more authority than the *Amoraim*.

8. B.Ta'anit 26.b. Brackets are my clarifying comments.
9. Neilah was recited at every fast day at the time of the Talmud's composition.
10. b.Ta'anit 26.b.
11. b.Ta'anit 26.b.
12. b.Pesahim 103.a, b; Rosh Ha-Shanah 15.b, b.Taanit 26.a; Tosafot to Rosh Ha-Shanah, b.Taanit 26.a.
13. 6:8.
14. Either Abbayye or Rav Yosef. The Talmud is unsure which.
15. b.Berakhot 54.b.
16. b.Eruvin 14.b.
17. See, e.g., *Responsa of Rashba VII*, 350:1, *Sefer Terumat HaDeshen I*, 297:2, *Responsa of Rosh* 55:9. The story of Hillel the Elder using the practice of the people to determine the rule for the Pascal sacrifice on Shabbat (b.Pesahim 66a) has been used by scholars to demonstrate this model. However, it is a poor example. In 1996, Henry Fischel showed that the story closely adheres to the Hellenistic narrative chria form. "Studies in Cynicism and the Ancient Near East: The Transformation of a Chria," in *Religions in Antiquity: Essays in Memory of Erwin Ramsdell Goodenough*, vol. 14, ed. Jacob Neusner (Numen Book Series, 1968), 372–411. Its elements are subordinate to the political moral of the form. This makes it problematic as an example of actual practice.
18. See also b.Nedarim 15.a and 81.b. The translation is mine, but based on Isidore Epstein, *The Babylonian Talmud* (London: Soncino, 1908).
19. m.Hallah 1:1.
20. It is possible that those who objected have only recently developed into rabbinic Jews, while those who follow the practice of separating *hallah* from rice are continuing a pre-rabbinic tradition.
21. A third-generation Babylonian *amora*. We apply the term *amora* to rabbis who lived and taught from roughly 210–540 CE.
22. *Tur/Shulhan Arukh*, YD 214; *Piskei Ha-Rosh* to Nedarim 15a; *Sefer Ha-Mordokhai* to Nedarim 81b; *Hehagot Maimoniot*, *Hilkot Shevuot* 12:12, #3, Responsa of R. Asher b. Yehiel 54:10.
23. Elon, *Jewish Law*, 978–86.
24. *Minhag avoteinu Torah hi.* The use of the feminine pronoun as a copula is emphatic. My use of italics is an attempt to translate this. See Tosafot, *Menahot* 20b s.v. "*Nifsal bi-shekiat ha-hamah kemotah.*" Ritba, *Sukkah 43a*. *Sefer Terumat Ha-Deshen*, Responsum #237. *Tur, OH* 297:1, 591:1, 619:1.
25. Bava Metzia 7:1, 11b.
26. Yevamot 12:1, 12c.
27. *Responsa of Maharik* 9:1, *Responsa of Radbaz* 1, 67:2, *Responsa of Rashba* IV 260:2, V 83:3, *Sefer Terumat HaDeshen*, I 332:2, *Responsa of R. Asher b. Yehiel* 97:1:3, *Responsa of Maharam ben Barukh*, Ed. Prague 537:1,
28. Walter D. Malcolm, "The Uniform Commercial Code in the United States," *International and Comparative Law Quarterly* 12, no. 1 (January 1963): 226–46.
29. B.Bava Metzia 51a. See also B.Kiddushin 19b and the Tosafot there, s.v. *Le-Rabbi Meir.*
30. Attributed to either Nisim Gaon (990–1062) or Netronai Gaon (853–858). *Sefer Ma'aseh Ha-Rokeah*, ed. Sanick, 1912. #139. *Sefer Ra'avia*, ed. Aptowitzer, 1935. 2:547. For the attribution, see Aptowitzer's notes ad locum. Shraga Abramson writes that the words of Nisim Gaon have gotten mixed with those of Maimon Ha-Dayyan, Maimonides's father. See *Rav Nisim Gaon, Hamishah Sefarim: Seridim mi-Hibburav Yotsim la-or al pi Kitvei Yad, Part 3:*

Halakhic Ruling (Jerusalem: Mekitzei Nirdamim, 1965), 328. I have shortened the passage. It contains other customs that I have elided.

31. B.Sukkah 38a.
32. OH 298:3; 299:10 583:1–2; 605. Note that Moses Iserles in his gloss to 299:10 is drawing on the *Kol Bo* when he mentions a version of the custom of drawing water immediately after the conclusion of Shabbat mentioned in a later part of this responsum: "and there are those who say to draw water from wells or natural springs every Saturday night, because the well of Miriam passes through all the wells and natural springs every Saturday night. And one who touches it and drinks from it will be healed from all his afflictions."
33. See the visual evidence from Hebrew Illuminated manuscripts collected by Thérèse Metzger and Mendel Metzger, *Jewish Life in the Middle Ages: Illuminated Hebrew Manuscripts of the Thirteenth to the Sixteenth Centuries* (New York: Alpine Fine Arts Collection, 1982), 145–46. Sara Lipton identifies the hat as an anti-Judaic symbol in Christian manuscripts in *Dark Mirror: The Medieval Origins of Anti-Jewish Iconography* (New York: Metropolitan Books/Henry Holt, 2014), 16–39. But she argues for its origins as a neutral or even positive symbol of ancient wisdom. The Jews reclaimed the symbol as their own. A heraldic shield depicted in a thirteenth century *Mahzor* even uses a grouping of three such hats as a sort of Jewish coat of arms! Ms. Milan Ambrosiana Frag. S.P. II.
34. *Olam Ke-Minhago Noheg* (Jerusalem: Zalman Shazar Center, 2006). See Lawrence Grossman, "The Kipah comes to America," in *Continuity and Change: A Festschrift in Honor of Irving Greenberg's 75th Birthday*, ed. Steven Katz and Steven Bayme (Lanham, MD: University Press of America, 2010), 129–31. And Elisheva Baumgarten, *Practicing Piety in Medieval Ashkenaz: Men, Women, and Everyday Religious Observance* (College Park: University of Pennsylvania Press, 2014), 227.
35. "Head Covering of Jewish Women: Characteristics and Historical Development," in *Ta-Shma: Studies in Judaica in Memory of Israel M. Ta-Shma*, ed. Rami Reiner et al. (Alon Shvut: Tevunot, Mikhlelet Herzog, 2011), 1:404–14 [Hebrew].
36. M.Ketubbot 7:6. Note, however, that the term "*dat yehudit*" has an ambiguous and controversial meaning and may also have originally referred to custom in hoary antiquity. Zimmer, *Olam*, discusses this as well.
37. This has a long and complex scholarly history and there is a large literature. The best places for the reader to start are still Ismar Elbogen, *Jewish Liturgy: A Comprehensive History*, trans. Raymond Scheindlin (New York: Jewish Theological Seminary of America, 1993), 8–9, 273–74, 277–83, 367; and Stefan Reif, *Judaism and Hebrew Prayer: New Perspectives on Jewish Liturgical History* (Cambridge: Cambridge University Press, 1993), 153–206.
38. *Shulhan Arukh*, OH 590:4; *Shulhan Arukh*, OH 671:2.
39. *Hilkhot Ha-Rif Berakhot* 18b.
40. M.Pesahim 4:1–5, B.Pesahim 51b, *Ha-Maor Ha-Katan* ad locum.
41. Hirsch Jakob Zimmels, *Ashkenazim and Sephardim: Their Relations, Differences, and Problems as Reflected in the Rabbinical Responsa. United States* (Brooklyn, NY: KTAV, 1996), 205–7. Tosafot Shabbat, 21b, s.v. "*Ve-ha-mehadrin.*" This continues to express itself as a disagreement between Ashkenazic and Sefardic Jews.
42. A thorough account of intra-ethnic distinctions among Jews is beyond the scope of this chapter. See Joshua Teplitsky, "The Ashkenazic Diaspora of Early Modern Central Europe"; Miriam Bodian, "The Western Sephardic Diaspora"; and Ray, Jonathan, "The Mediterranean Sephardim between the 15th and 20th Centuries," in *The Oxford Handbook of the Jewish Diaspora*, ed. Hasia Diner (Oxford: Oxford University Press, 2021), 344–408. On the often-neglected Italian context, see David Ruderman, "At the Intersection

of Cultures: The Historical legacy of Italian Jewry," in *Gardens and Ghettos: The Art of Jewish Life in Italy*, ed. Vivian B. Mann (Berkeley: University of California Press, 1989–1990), 1–25. On the traditions of Jewish life in Morocco, see Haïm Zafrani, *Two Thousand Years of Jewish life in Morocco* (New York: Sephardic House, 2005). On the Jews of Yemen, see Joseph Tobi, *The Jews of Yemen: Studies in Their History and Culture* (Leiden, The Netherlands: Brill, 1999). The historical survey (3–85) is comprehensive without being tedious. On the Greek context, see the excellent but obscure book by Rena Molho, *Salonica and Istanbul: Social, Political and Cultural Aspects of Jewish Life* (Türkiye: Isis Press, 2005).

43. Jacob Katz, *Tradition and Crisis: Jewish Society at the End of the Middle Ages*, trans. Bernard Cooperman (New York: New York University Press, 1993), 147–51; and Jacob Katz, *Divine Law in Human Hands: Case Studies in Halakhic Flexibility* (Jerusalem: Magnes, 1998), 123–25.
44. Yosef Tobi, "Caro's Shulhan Arukh Versus Maimonides' Mishne Torah in Yemen" (electronic version), in *The Jewish Law Annual*, vol. 15, ed. Berachyahu Lifshitz (2004).
45. See, for instance, Abraham Goldberg, *Commentary to the Mishna Shabbat* (New York: Jewish Theological Seminary of America, 1976), 34–56 [Hebrew]; and David Rosenthal, "Mishna Aboda Zara: A Critical Edition with Introduction" (PhD diss., Hebrew University, 1980), 139. The same is true for the text of the Babylonian Talmud itself. See Yaakov Sussmann (ed.), *Thesaurus of Talmudic Manuscripts*, vol. 3 (Jerusalem: Yad Ben Zvi and Friedberg Genizah Project, 2012), 286 n. 72.
46. The broad semantic range the word *takkanah* possesses makes it difficult to translate. The word includes tones of "adjustment," "correction," "decree," "declaration," and "repair." However, none of these is right.
47. Meir of Rothenburg, *Responsa of Rabbi Meir b. Barukh* (ed. Prague, #1022); Judah Mintz, *Rulings and Responsa of Rabbi Yehudah Mintz and Rabbi Meir of Padua* (ed. Venice, 1553), #10; Israel Isserlin, *Sefer Terumat Ha-Deshen* (ed. Walden. §Responsum #220, §Writings and Rulings # 262), 58. The most comprehensive account remains I. Schipansky, *Ha-Takkanot Bi-srael* (Jerusalem: Mossad Ha-Rav Kook, 1993), 129–54.
48. Recall that the Babylonian Talmud represents a singular binding *corpus legibus* for rabbinic legal authorities. Elon, *Jewish Law*, 978–86.
49. Not as "*herem*." The threat of excommunication was (ironically) an indication that an individual had violated community standards, rather than violated Jewish law. On some other uses of the term "herem" see Marc B. Shapiro, "The Herem on Spain: History and Halaka," *Sefarad* 49 (1989): 381–94.
50. See *Shulhan Arukh* EH 1:10 and *Beit Yosef* to *Tur* EH 1. I think it reasonable to conclude that the attribution to Rabbenu Gershom is pseudepigraphic. One author of the ban may have been the later Rabbeinu Shimshon of Senz (1150–1214). See *Nimukei Yosef*, Yevamot 12b. See also Roberta Kwall, *The Myth of the Cultural Jew: Culture and Law in Jewish Tradition* (Oxford: Oxford University Press, 2015), 60. She notes how the surrounding non-Jewish cultures impact this issue and claims that the ban was not accepted by those Jews living in Islamic cultures where many men had more than one wife but was accepted in Christian Europe. Though this is reasonable sounding to me, clearly more work needs to be done to tease out contraindicating data since Shlomo ibn Aderet (1235–1310) of Christian Spain was a prominent opponent of the ban, and also claimed that the ban was not enforced in Christian Provence. See *Beit Yosef* ibid. s.v. *Katav ha-Rashba*.
51. Zafrani, *Two Thousand Years of Jewish life in Morocco*, 76–78.
52. A. Radzyner, "Halakhah, Law, and Worldview: Chief Rabbis Goren and Yosef and the Permission to Marry a Second Wife in Israeli Law," *Israel* 32 (2018): 261–304.

CHAPTER 13

CODIFICATION AND OTHER STRATEGIES OF CONSENSUS-BUILDING IN JEWISH LAW

JOSEPH M. DAVIS

INTRODUCTION

ONCE a year, on the night of the full moon in March or April, Jewish families around the world celebrate the Passover Seder. They eat unleavened bread (*matzoh*); they list the Ten Plagues; they drink wine—traditional Jews drink specifically four cups of wine—and many Jewish households end their celebration by singing a folksong about a goat.[1] How does this coordinated activity take place? How have Jews in the past and present achieved consensus over questions of Jewish law and practice?

This chapter looks at Jewish consensus-seeking strategies in two different historical eras. It begins by discussing strategies of Jewish consensus during the Middle Ages and the early modern period, between *c.* 1000 and 1800 CE. It then turns to the present day and the recent past, roughly since 1950. There was a period of transition during the nineteenth and early twentieth centuries, during which the pre-modern patterns gradually disappeared, while new patterns emerged. The chapter does not focus on this transitional period but instead furnishes a before-and-after depiction, before the major Jewish crises of modernity and then after.[2]

The chapter initially examines the major strategies by which Jews reached consensus concerning Jewish law and practice during the late Middle Ages and the early modern periods.[3] In pre-modern Judaism, Jewish customs and interpretations of Jewish law were often local or regional. At the same time, international circulation of Jewish texts and international ties among the rabbinate helped standardize the practices of Jewish communities that were geographically distant. This part of the chapter also focuses on two major changes during the 1400s and 1500s: the development of Hebrew printing and the expulsions of Jews from Western Europe, which led to the emergence of "Sephardic" and "Ashkenazic" Jews as transnational ethnic groups of Jews, each one with its own interpretation of Jewish law.

This medieval system of Jewish law was overthrown by the crises of Judaism in the modern world: the rise of modern Jewish ideologies and denominations, the disempowering of local Jewish rabbis and communities, the Holocaust, and the emergence of the modern secular state of Israel. In today's world of international travel and the internet, Jewish consensus takes new forms.

The second part of this chapter discusses strategies of consensus in today's globalized but ideologically fractured Jewish world. It begins by looking at some strategies of consensus and unanimity that are shared by contemporary and pre-modern Jews, such as the use of law codes, the use of rabbinic synods, and the persistence of pre-modern Jewish ethnic divisions. It then focuses on three new strategies, opposing but complementary, for establishing consensus within Jewish subgroups. These three strategies are "strictism," "laxism," and "centrism." Strictism is the defining strategy of ultra-Orthodox Judaism; it achieves consensus by insisting that the community conform to the practices demanded by its strictest members. "Laxism" is the opposite: it achieves a live-and-let-live consensus by allowing people to do as they wish. It is the dominant approach within Reform Judaism. Between them is centrism, a defining strategy for movements such as Modern Orthodoxy and Conservative Judaism. However, elements of all three strategies can be found in each of these contemporary movements, and so the chapter concludes by looking at counterideological instances in which strict Orthodox groups achieve consensus by way of laxity, and progressive groups by way of strictness. The chapter argues that whether Jews are divided geographically, as in the Middle Ages, or ideologically, as in the present day, the strategies for establishing consensus within a small group are often identical to strategies for differentiation and division.

Consensus-Building Strategies in the Late Middle Ages and Early Modern Period

Local Judaism: Formal and Informal Jewish Consensus in the Middle Ages

Medieval Jewish life, even as late as 1800 and beyond, was lived on a local level. The Jews who lived together in one town would interact with one another on a daily basis. They would interact with Jews of other towns or regions much more rarely. In all but the largest cities, there was usually only one synagogue and one pattern of communal prayer.

Jewish life in town was directed by a board or council of Jews, called in Hebrew the *kehilah* or *kahal kadosh* (literally "sacred community").[4] The local community and its governing board often had considerable power over local Jews. Often they could levy fines and sometimes they could even inflict corporal punishment. For instance, some Jewish communities in Poland in the eighteenth century could imprison their members or chain them to a pillory in the synagogue.[5] The leadership of medieval Jewish communities could also excommunicate recalcitrant members. Similar to excommunication in the medieval church, *ḥerem*, as it was called in Hebrew, cast the sinner outside the community. The sinner was not allowed to receive customary honors and members of the community were not allowed to maintain normal social contact with those who were excommunicated. A notable example is the 1656 excommunication of the young heretical philosopher Benedict Spinoza by the Amsterdam Jewish community.[6]

In addition to these formal processes of control by Jewish community leaders, there were also informal processes of consensus-building within Jewish communities.[7] A collection of letters from the Jews of Prague to their relatives in Vienna from 1619 offers a glimpse into these processes of informal social pressure. The Prague Jews encouraged their relatives, sometimes explicitly, sometimes only implicitly or by their own example, to study Torah diligently, to follow proper etiquette in arranging marriages, and to observe pious customs (*minhagim*), such as inviting many guests to a circumcision celebration, including the local rabbi and a godfather.[8]

Some customs, such as designating godparents at a circumcision, began among the laity or within circles of pious Jews, and were later approved by the rabbis.[9] In other cases, rabbis would criticize their communities' customary practices. Issachar Baer Eulenburg (*c.* 1570–1623), a rabbi in seventeenth-century Italy, took his flock to task for putting up only a single mezuzah per house, instead of one in every room, and for allowing men and women to sing Sabbath hymns together. Although these were pious and observant Jews, the sort who sing hymns over Sabbath meals, their customs violated Jewish law as Eulenburg saw it.[10]

The authority of local Jewish ordinances was also sometimes conceived of as stemming from the sacredness of communal oaths. For example, sometime during the late 1600s, in the town of Kastoria (Greece), the local Jews pledged a communal oath that men and women would not dance together at weddings. Even without an oath, customs were often given the force of law, and there was also considerable overlap between local "ordinances" and local "customs." With regard to customs, the medieval tendency toward localism is striking: medieval Jewish customs were typically limited to one town or region.[11]

Forging Consensus among Distant Communities through Travel and the Circulation of Texts

During this period, the Jews, famously, had no king. Jewish people who lived in different regions were generally independent of one another and it was rare for Jewish leaders to exercise power over Jews outside their own towns and perhaps some neighboring villages. The main exception were the Jewish religious leaders (the *Gaonim*, "excellencies") and lay leader (*Resh Galuta*, "exilarch") of Iraq during early Middle Ages, from about 700 CE until about 1000 CE. These leaders exercised considerable power throughout the entire Abbasid Empire, which stretched from Iran to Spain.[12] In an alternative history, one could imagine the *Gaonate* remaining, as the Papacy did, a powerful international religious force. But that did not happen; as the Abbasid Empire declined, so did the power of the *Gaonim*, and no comparable Jewish institution of centralized authority arose in the later Middle Ages to succeed them.

In spite of the absence of centralized institutions, pre-modern Jews in distant lands maintained an impressive level of unanimity on questions of Jewish law and practice. This cohesiveness was achieved through the circulation of sacred and authoritative texts, as well as by transregional communication and travel among rabbis and Jewish religious elites.

During their heyday, the *Gaonim* succeeded in establishing the Babylonian Talmud as an authoritative exposition of Jewish law. Although, after the decline of the *Gaonim*, the rabbinate had no centralized leader, they continued to agree unanimously that Jewish law should be based on some combination of communal tradition and the rulings of the Babylonian Talmud. Thus, the rabbinization of the Jewish Diaspora went hand in hand with the circulation of the Talmud.[13]

However, there also remained (and still remain today) groups of Jews, such as Karaites, Samaritans, and Ethiopian Jews, who did not accept the Talmud.[14] These groups each developed their distinctive Jewish practices, although they all shared a commitment to Biblical law. The Karaites took particular pride in the close adherence of their customs to the exact words of the Bible.

Significantly, even among rabbis, shared reverence for the Talmud did not prevent disputes over Jewish law. Difficult questions of Jewish law and disputes concerning the interpretation and application of Talmudic laws were often resolved by letters known as *responsa*. *Responsa* were decisions regarding specific cases and disputes over Jewish law that were sent by major rabbis to distant communities. The practice of sending *responsa* was begun by the *Gaonim* and continued by later rabbis until the present day. After the decline of the *Gaonim*, the authors of *responsa* generally had no formal authority over local rabbis. In the thirteenth and fourteenth centuries, for example, certain rabbis tried to use *responsa* to coordinate their efforts to restrict Jewish study of the works of Aristotle, a major point of controversy in the Jewish communities of the time. The anti-Aristotelian rabbis scored some notable successes, but overall their efforts underscored the autonomy of the Jews of different regions and towns in Europe and the Middle East (see Morsel-Eisenberg, this volume).[15]

The Talmud was supplemented over the course of the Middle Ages not only by *responsa* but also by commentaries on the Talmud as well as codes of Jewish law. These materials circulated slowly by modern standards, but often they eventually reached the Jews of distant lands, helping to create unified interpretations of Talmudic law. The Talmud commentary of Rashi (*c.* 1040–1105), who lived in France, was being copied in Iraq less than a century after it was written. Moses Maimonides's (1135–1204) *Mishneh*

Torah, which he wrote in Egypt in the mid-twelfth century, had reached nearly all parts of the Jewish world by the end of the thirteenth century.[16]

Some provisions of medieval Jewish law did not follow the Talmud at all. The Talmudic regulations of ritual purity and the Jewish calendar gradually became dead letters. However, despite their hazy non-Talmudic origins, and despite their complexity, the new medieval rules governing the Hebrew calendar were another very striking example of Jewish consensus. During the ancient period, the Jewish calendar had frequently been a matter of dispute, but beginning in the early Middle Ages, it was maintained with great uniformity by geographically dispersed communities of Jews.[17]

How was this uniformity possible before modern communications? The answer must be that pre-modern travel and communications, whether by ship or donkey or camel, were sufficient to maintain a certain level of uniformity.[18] Local Jewish communities were informed about the Jewish practices of other places through various means such as *responsa* and other letters, imported books, shared legal codes, and also by Jewish travelers. In this way, the Jews of distant regions maintained their consensus about Jewish laws and practices, over long periods, in spite of the natural centrifugal drift of distant populations.

Regional Structures and Customs

In addition to the town-centered localism of Jewish self-government, and the international circulation of authoritative texts such as the Talmud and Maimonides's *Mishneh Torah*, regional patterns of consensus concerning Jewish practices also emerged during the pre-modern period. Jews in medieval Spain, for example, were more likely to be in contact with the Jews from other towns in Spain than with Jews in far-off Syria or Germany. Moreover, they were conscious of being "Spanish" Jews, and this regional self-consciousness, along with this pattern of regional contacts, promoted the growth of distinctive, shared Spanish Jewish customs.[19]

In certain places, formal structures of Jewish self-government united the Jews of a region or a kingdom. From about 1050 and into the modern period, the Jews of Egypt were ruled by a single Chief Rabbi.[20] During the seventeenth and eighteenth centuries, the Jews of Poland-Lithuania were governed by a sort of Jewish parliament called the Council of Four Lands, which included both lay leaders and a rabbinic synod, and which united the local communities. However, even among a group of Jews as well organized as the Polish Jews of the 1600s, the power of centralized institutions was limited. For example, the Council tried but failed to produce an authorized edition of the prayer book. Conflicting liturgical traditions stubbornly persisted.[21]

Some Jewish communities in the seventeenth century were highly isolated, and their Jewish practices differed markedly from the others. That was true of the Jews of Ethiopia as well as the Jews of Kaifeng (China).[22] Outside such isolated communities, *responsa*, travel, and the circulation of books connected the local Jews of the European Jewish communities, as well as Jews in the Middle East, and later the Jews of the American colonies.

Printing and Expulsions: The Growth of Transnational Jewish Ethnic Groups

Two events in the late 1400s brought about significant changes in these pre-modern patterns of Jewish consensus. The first, beginning in 1476, was the development of Hebrew printing. The second was the 1492 expulsion of the Jews from Spain, and in parallel, the expulsions of Jews from much of Germany.

The development of Hebrew printing greatly increased the circulation of Jewish law books, strengthening the translocal aspects of Jewish law and the process of *halakhic* consensus, but weakening the purely local aspects. The Venice publishers of Hebrew books, beginning with Daniel Bomberg, were especially successful in establishing an international market. The Jewish printers often played a major role in the spread of Jewish customs. One example is the Passover goat song, "Ḥad Gadya," which the printers of Passover Haggadot made into a customary part of the Passover Seder, despite the lack of any grounding in Talmudic law.[23] The development of printing also diminished local differences in another way. Printed books are identical, word for word. By contrast, medieval manuscripts of the "same" law code or Talmud commentary sometimes codified local or regional understandings of the law and could differ from one another substantially.[24]

The changes brought about by the development of printing went hand in hand with another major change, the emergence of two large transregional Jewish ethnic groups, namely, Ashkenazic Jews and Sephardic Jews. During the late Middle Ages, two European regions, one in Germany and the other in Spain, had developed uniquely rich traditions of written Talmudic interpretation.[25] These two groups of Jews also adopted competing legal codes. The Jews of Germany and northern Europe regarded codes such as the *Sefer Mitsvot Gadol* by Moses of Coucy (fl. 1250) and *Sefer Mitsvot Katan* by Isaac of Corbeil (d. 1280) as highly authoritative.[26] Spanish Jews preferred the legal code of Moses Maimonides, the *Mishneh Torah*.[27]

During the fifteenth and sixteenth centuries, the nature of these two groups of Jews changed fundamentally, and "German" Jews and "Spanish" Jews both became transregional ethnic diasporas.[28] After about 1350, many towns and regions in Germany expelled the Jews, and German Jews emigrated and established new communities in eastern Europe and elsewhere. Similarly, when Spain expelled the Jews in 1492, the Spanish Jews found new homes in the Mediterranean region and beyond.

Two Hebrew names, *Sepharad* and *Ashkenaz*, and the corresponding terms "Sephardic" and "Ashkenazic," require a brief explanation. *Sepharad* and *Ashkenaz* are two lands mentioned in the Bible (Obadiah 1:20, Genesis 10:3) whose names were used in medieval Hebrew as translations for "Spain" (*Sepharad*) and "Germany"

(*Ashkenaz*, related to "Saxony"), respectively. After the 1492 expulsion, there were now "Spanish" Jews who spoke Judeo-Spanish (Ladino) and observed Spanish Jewish customs but no longer lived in Spain: they called themselves "*Sephardim*" and are often called Sephardic Jews in English. Similarly, the descendants of Jews who had lived in Germany but emigrated elsewhere, who spoke Judeo-German or Yiddish, and observed German Jewish customs, called themselves "*Ashkenazim*"—though no longer living within the borders of Germany. Through demographic growth, Ashkenazic Jews from eastern Europe eventually became the majority of all the Jews in the world.

In certain large cities such as Venice, Istanbul, and Jerusalem, Sephardic and Ashkenazic Jews now lived side by side as separate subcommunities of Jews, each with their own synagogues. The differences between the customs of Spanish Jews and German Jews were mostly quite small. For instance, at the end of the fast day of Yom Kippur, Sephardic Jews blow a series of notes on the *shofar* (ram's horn), but Ashkenazic Jews just blow one note. Also, Sephardic Jews eat rice and beans (*kitniyot*) on Passover, whereas Ashkenazic Jews do not. However, because there are so many small differences of this sort, the cumulative difference in Jewish ritual is large.[29]

The means of consensus-building that were available to transnational Jewish groups in early modern Europe are clearly visible in the case of certain communities of Sephardic Jews in the aftermath of the 1492 expulsion of the Jews from Spain. The Jews of Spain and Portugal who remained in Iberia after the expulsion and did not emigrate were not permitted to live as Jews in Spain and Portugal and instead lived as Christians. Some of their descendants, however, left Spain and Portugal, and established new Jewish communities in Western European cities, especially Amsterdam. Growing up as Christians in Spain and Portugal, these new Jews had never observed the laws and customs of rabbinic Judaism, and the religious observances of these returnees were sometimes at odds with rabbinic norms. Gradually, however, over the course of generations, as these new communities of returning Jews learned from the rabbis, the teachers, and the books that they imported from older Sephardic Jewish communities, their interpretation of Jewish law and ritual practices moved into closer conformity with their brethren of the Sephardic Diaspora.[30]

The *Shulchan Arukh*: Consensus and Differentiation through Codification

Since its publication in Venice in 1565, the most authoritative law book in the Jewish world has been the *Shulchan Arukh* (on commentaries to the *Shulchan Arukh*, see Samet, this volume).[31] On account of its widespread acceptance, the *Shulchan Arukh* is the central example of how the printing press helped create consensus on questions of Jewish law. Its history also shows, however, how the publication of legal codes could also crystallize legal disputes between different groups of Jews.

The author of the *Shulchan Arukh*, Joseph Caro (1488–1575), was born in Spain shortly before the 1492 expulsion of the Jews. He lived for many years in the Balkans and moved in 1535 to the Galilee town of Safed. Caro's law code favored the traditions of the Sephardic Jews at the expense of the traditions of the Ashkenazic Jews. Therefore, in 1572, Moses Isserles, the rabbi of Kraków (*c.* 1525–1572), wrote a commentary to Caro's rulings, noting all the places where Ashkenazic customs differed from the Sephardic traditions that Caro had codified. The new Kraków edition of the *Shulchan Arukh* thus included two competing law texts, namely, Caro's original text that codified the law as practiced by Sephardic Jews, and Isserles's commentary codifying Ashkenazic customs. As a result, Jewish law is presented within the same volume as having two authoritative interpretations, one for Sephardic Jews and one for Ashkenazic Jews.

The printed *Shulchan Arukh* does not mention the existence, or even admit the potential existence, of any third group of Jews. The very typography of the book hints at a binary division of Jews into Sephardic and Ashkenazic Jews. In some editions, Caro's rulings are in square Hebrew letters; next to them, Isserles's comments are printed in cursive. Indeed, during the seventeenth century and subsequently, in certain places such as Amsterdam and England, the Jews were divided into exactly these two groups, Sephardim and Ashkenazim.

Many Jews in other places, such as the Jews of Yemen and Iran, did not regard themselves as either Ashkenazic or Sephardic and continued to practice distinctive sets of Jewish customs. However, Caro's rulings without any commentary became widely accepted by Sephardic Jews in their far-flung communities, while Isserles's commentary was accepted by Ashkenazic Jews. Moreover, fortified by the codification of their customs in the *Shulchan Arukh*, Ashkenazic or Sephardic customs sometimes displaced local and regional Jewish customs. Although local Jewish communities remained independent of one another, and local Jewish courts sometimes accorded themselves a high degree of judicial discretion to deal with particular cases, much standardization of Jewish law was achieved over the seventeenth and eighteenth centuries. The authority of the *Shulchan Arukh* as codified by Caro and Isserles was established as a baseline for many Jewish communities, resulting in the marginalization of competing views.[32]

Strategies of Consensus in Jewish Law and Practice in the Contemporary Period

Globally Connected Judaism: From Local to Translocal Differences

It is impossible to exaggerate the sweeping changes in Jewish life between the early modern period and the present. The continuity of local Jewish life was utterly broken by mass migration and the Holocaust. As a result, almost no Jews today live in the same town, and few even in the same country, that their ancestors lived in two centuries ago. In addition, new technologies have revolutionized daily life. In the Diaspora, freedom of religion made the observance of Jewish law voluntary, and Jewish communities today have very limited powers. Particularly in the United States, new Jewish ideologies and denominations, such as Reform Judaism, Conservative Judaism, various types of Orthodox Judaism, Jewish Renewal, and others, vie for the allegiance of modern Jews. The situation of Judaism and Jewish law in the modern state of Israel is equally unprecedented, and Jewish law is now entangled with Israeli secular law in complex ways (on Jewish law in modern Israel, see Edrei, this volume).[33] At the same time, improvements in travel and communication, and most recently the internet, have put Jews in different ends of the globe into easy contact with one another.[34] In the present day, questions such as whether women may read Torah in synagogues, how to celebrate Israeli Independence Day, and who is a Jew are all debated on the basis of transnational Jewish religious ideologies.

As a result of all these changes, Jewish localism, which was so marked an aspect of Jewish law throughout the pre-modern period, and even as late as World War I, has all but disappeared. Even the different sects of Hasidic Jews are now transnational. The groups' names bear proud witness to the localism of the Hasidim in the nineteenth and early twentieth centuries and to the eastern European towns where they originated: Satmar (Satu Mare, Romania), Slonim (in Belarus), Gur (Góra Kalwaria, Poland), and many others. Today, however, each of these groups and many others have followers in America, Israel, Europe, and even Australia.[35]

The Persistence of Pre-Modern Strategies: Law Codes and Responsa, Synods, and Ethnic Divisions

Even in the globally connected Judaism of 2023, many pre-modern methods for creating consensus remain important. As a legal code, the *Shulchan Arukh* still reigns supreme in Orthodox Judaism. It is now flanked by newer Orthodox codes such as Yehoshua Neuwirth's 1965 *Shemirat Shabbat ke-Hilkhatah*, which reinterpreted the Sabbath laws for the new era of electricity and household appliances.[36] There are also new online codes such as the Orthodox website Practical Halacha. Rabbis from all the major denominations also still write and circulate *responsa* to render their decisions on difficult legal questions.

Synods or standing committees of rabbis are even more important today than they were in the Middle Ages (see Kwall, this volume; on the CCAR *Responsa* Committee of Reform Judaism, see Washofsky, this volume). Today, *kashrut* certification for commercially produced food is mostly given by rabbinic committees or synods, such as the *kashrut* division of Union of Orthodox Jewish Congregations (OU).[37] In some nations, official "chief rabbis" continue to exercise considerable influence, nowhere more so than in Israel.[38]

The early modern (1492–1800) ethnic divisions of Jews are also still powerful, especially in Israel. A number of Jewish ethnic groups, such as the Syrian Jewish Diaspora, maintain their customs and differences on a transregional basis.[39] Today's Israelis might prefer to call themselves "Mizrachi" (literally, "Eastern") rather than "Sephardi" ("Spanish"), but the Ashkenazic/Mizrachi divide of today's Israel is the lineal descendant of the early modern Ashkenazic/Sephardic distinction. It is maintained in part by the binary (Ashkenazic vs. Sephardic) structure of the Israeli chief rabbinate.[40] The state of Israel has brought neither unity nor uniformity to the practice of Judaism in Israel.

Self-Sorting as a Mechanism of Consensus Formation

Within the contemporary world of global Jewish groups and denominations, a key dynamic that supports *halakhic* consensus within each group is self-sorting. Membership in Jewish denominations and synagogues is voluntary. The major exception are the ultra-Orthodox Hasidic groups, which have developed strategies of coercion which are often effective both in discouraging nonconformity and in preventing members from leaving the group. In these groups, refusal to live in accord with the dictates of the rabbinic leadership can result in social isolation and the loss of friends, family, income, and home.[41] Outside these ultra-Orthodox communities, however, contemporary Jews freely seek out communities that observe Judaism in a way that is congenial to them.

Today it is not uncommon for synagogues to break apart when one group favors a set of *halakhic* changes, while an opposing group favors the status quo. For instance, over the last fifty years, changes in the roles of women in synagogue ritual have prompted divisions within some groups.[42] A spectrum of synagogues and Jewish groups has developed in the modern period, running from those most open to reform and change to those most opposed. Sometimes a single synagogue may include diverse and even opposing groups which pray separately from one another. However, for the most part, contemporary Jews have sorted themselves into like-minded groups over these issues.

Strictism, Laxism, and Centrism as Modes of Achieving Consensus

Jewish groups today differ in their use of three major strategies for achieving consensus. These three strategies are strictism, laxism, and centrism.[43] Strictism is the dominant ideological impulse of "Ultra-Orthodoxy."[44] Laxism is the dominant impulse of progressive Jewish movements, most notably Reform Judaism. Middling movements such as Conservative Judaism and Modern Orthodoxy rely heavily on the strategy of centrism.

The terms "strictism" and "laxism" are not often used to describe Jewish groups, and certainly not by these groups themselves, and so they require definition.[45] By "strictism" I mean a strategy that achieves consensus by demanding the strictest interpretation of the law. A "strict" rule is the one that constrains the available options. For example, some Orthodox Jews will not eat baked goods unless they are *pas Yisroel*, that is, not only made of kosher ingredients but also baked by Jews or with the participation of Jews. Other Orthodox Jews are more lenient. "Strictism" achieves consensus on debated questions such as this one by adopting the stricter standard. If one is preparing a meal, and one wants everyone in the group to eat a slice of the cake, then the cake must be *pas Yisroel*; otherwise the stricter members of the group will not eat it. The strict standard wins out because it is only standard that everyone in the group will agree to.[46]

In contrast, "laxism" achieves consensus in the opposite way, by allowing many options, and not insisting on too much piety. In our example of *pas Yisroel* and cake, there are several laxist solutions: one might be to serve more than one cake, some *pas Yisroel*, some not, and allow the guests to choose whichever they prefer. Another would be to serve a cake that is not *pas Yisroel* on the understanding that anyone is then free to eat it or not eat it as they please. "Strictism" in this formal sense places a higher premium on uniform behavior than does "laxism." Principles of pluralism or *halakhic* diversity are laxist. Centrism, as the word suggests, aims for a center between strict and lax options.

Lax and stringent interpretations of Jewish law (respectively known as *kulot* and *ḥumrot*) are classic Talmudic concepts (see Pill, this volume).[47] However, Talmudic and medieval rabbis would typically take strict positions on some issues and lax positions on others.[48] Neither strictism nor laxism became common as general policies in Judaism until the modern period. Today, however, these strategies play a crucial role in creating consensus within Jewish communities.

Strictism, Traditionalism, and Literalism in Ultra-Orthodox Judaism

Ultra-Orthodox groups tend to be strict about all manner of questions of Jewish practice, such as food regulations, sexual behavior, laws of prayer, gender segregation, rules regarding clothing, and many others. As was mentioned, in some cases they have established a social system that rewards conformity and punishes deviance. For example, some ultra-Orthodox communities have "modesty committees" that police the "modest" behavior of women.[49] The laws of "modest" appearance are interpreted by some Orthodox groups to permit married women to have long hair, as long as they keep it strictly covered, but other Orthodox groups require married women to crop or even shave their hair. Similarly, regarding the dietary laws, most Orthodox rabbis in New York City interpret the laws of *kashrut* to permit drinking the local tap water, but some other rabbis hold that New York City water cannot be drunk unfiltered.[50]

Interpretations of Jewish law in ultra-Orthodox Judaism are based on a variety of principles: not only "strictism" in the sense of demanding obedience to an exact rule of conduct, but also traditionalism and close adherence to the *Shulchan Arukh*.[51] It should be noted, however, that these three principles sometimes overlap but sometimes conflict with one another. For example, strictism overlaps with but is not identical to a general preference for tradition over innovation. A century ago, in 1923, the ultra-Orthodox groups which demanded "strict" observance of Jewish law were trying to maintain a highly traditional way of life in the small towns of eastern Europe. The laxer groups of that time were mostly trying to make room for modernization. Today, ultra-Orthodox groups still maintain many eastern European Jewish traditions—for example, ultra-Orthodox women continue to wear long skirts and dresses, and Hasidic men wear fur hats.[52] However, in other respects, the principle of traditionalism, as it applied in the ultra-modern societies where today's ultra-Orthodox Jews live, is in unavoidable tension with a general preference for stringency, and ultra-Orthodoxy often demands religious innovations. Simply put, previous generations did not observe all of the stringencies that are now common in ultra-Orthodoxy.[53] For example, in previous generations, demands for Torah study, especially for women, were incomparably lower than they are in ultra-Orthodox Judaism today.[54] Earlier generations were much less likely to demand rabbinic supervision of the food they ate.[55] They did not observe all the stringencies in regard to how to eat *matzoh* and how to drink four cups of wine at the Passover Seder that present-day ultra-Orthodox Jews do.[56] The effort to maintain the religious norms that were observed in small towns in eastern Europe is frequently not the same as aiming for the strictest possible observance.

Regarding literalism, many ultra-Orthodox rules do indeed adhere very closely to the very words of the *Shulchan Arukh*. Other rules are derived from that text by applying a strictist hermeneutic, that is, a general preference for stringent interpretations.[57] Not infrequently, however, Orthodox groups complain justly that the stringent rulings of some ultra-Orthodox groups or sets of rabbis, including some that have been mentioned (cropped hair and filtered water) go well beyond the letter of what is required by the *Shulchan Arukh* and the Talmud.[58]

Ultra-Orthodox groups are frequently differentiated from one another by their degree of strictness or laxity concerning particular practices. For example, certain Hasidic sects are distinguished, in part, by the strictness and the form of their sexual asceticism. Gur Hasidim are directed to have sex with their spouses exactly twice a month, including once a month on Sabbath, a stringency instituted in that group around 1948. Slonim Hasidim, by contrast, are encouraged to have sex more frequently, should they desire to, but they are urged to refrain from sex on the Sabbath.[59] Regarding kosher slaughter, Chabad Hasidim will not eat certain meat that some other ultra-Orthodox Jews will accept.[60] On the other hand, some ultra-Orthodox Jews, such as Satmar Hasidim, reject some Chabad leniencies, such as using modern Hebrew for daily conversation rather than Yiddish.[61] In general, ultra-Orthodox groups, both Hasidic and non-Hasidic, are often differentiated by alternative interpretations of Jewish law, each one equally "strict," but strict in regard to different laws and traditions.[62]

Strictism is thus a strategy of consensus-building, but it is also a recipe for dissent. It produces meticulously pious, relatively homogeneous groups of ultra-Orthodox Jews, but it also produces communities that quarrel frequently over specific *halakhic* requirements and prohibitions. The tendency toward strictism is responsible in no small measure for the fractured and chaotic situation of ultra-Orthodoxy today. In order to balance this tendency toward divisiveness and religious competition, collections of ultra-Orthodox groups often accept a rule of "live and let live," or diversity. In other words, while each group demands strict adherence from its own members, they often adopt a strategy of laxism in regard to one another. The very origin of the "Ultra-Orthodox" or "Haredi" bloc within Judaism was the decision around 1912 by Hasidic and anti-Hasidic Orthodox leaders to work together, to accept one another as Jewish leaders and to accept the fundamental legitimacy of their very different interpretations of Jewish law.[63]

Laxism and Minimalism in Reform Judaism

Although Reform Judaism embraces diversity of observance rather than unanimity, there is still much consensus-building within this liberal movement.[64] Indeed, the celebration of "diversity" is itself a strategy of consensus-building and a principle of laxism. One achieves unanimity by increasing the range of what is permitted, and by agreeing on the principle of "live and let live."

With respect to observance of Jewish ritual, "laxism" is manifested in many ways within Reform Judaism. Rabbinic *responsa* and guides to Jewish practice are presented as "warm recommendations," while the final choice is left to the individual (see Washofsky, this volume). Often options are presented as being parts of a debate or as "voices."[65] Frequently, the movement offers its members a menu of options. A key example was the pathbreaking Reform prayer book *Gates of Prayer* (1975), which offered ten options for Friday night liturgies.[66]

The concept of "lax observance" has two meanings in Reform Judaism. One meaning is what this chapter has called the formal notion of laxism, namely, acceptance of many possible ways of observing Jewish law and practicing Judaism. This is similar to "pluralism," or even "liberty." But the term "lax observance" is also often used to mean "minimal observance," that is, the specific choice of engaging in very few Jewish ritual practices. Over the last half-century Reform Jews have argued over whether to encourage traditional Jewish rituals such as wearing a *kippah* (skullcap) or whether such rituals are not in keeping with the principles of Reform Judaism.[67] The two approaches to preserving unanimity, namely, pluralism and minimalism, both "laxist" in different senses, here oppose one another. The first preserves unanimity by allowing a diverse range of practices within the movement, and the other by establishing a Reform consensus that rejects these traditional practices.

Reform Judaism, in principle, rejects the idea that Jewish law is binding on Jews in the modern world. Indeed the term "Jewish law" has connotations of coercion and the preemption of all other courses of action that Reform Judaism rejects. Nevertheless, Reform temples do enforce "policies" or "guidelines," often with great uniformity. For much of the twentieth century, Reform synagogues were famous for the stringency of their rules of decorum. Today, the decorum at Reform synagogues is much more relaxed, but in spite of its principled commitment to freedom and individualism, the movement often attends to the concerns of their most politically liberal members. Notably, the movement takes strong stands on many public issues and political issues, such as transgender rights, and it exerts institutional pressure on its members to support those stands and to conduct themselves accordingly.[68] The most progressive view is sometimes the consensus view in Reform Jewish groups today.

Centrism, Compromise, and Triangulation: Modern Orthodoxy and Conservative Judaism

Between the extremes of strictism and laxism, movements such as Conservative Judaism and Modern Orthodoxy pursue strategies of consensus-building based on triangulation and compromise. Triangulation here means the effort to position the group between two other groups, one that is stricter and another that is more lax. Conservative Judaism tries to position itself as stricter than Reform Judaism and not as strict as Modern Orthodoxy (see also Kwall, this volume).[69] Modern Orthodoxy, in turn, takes positions that are stricter than Conservative Judaism, but not as strict as ultra-Orthodox groups. "Compromise" here refers to a strategy that often arrives at the same point as triangulation, but by a mechanism that looks at the different positions within the group rather than outside the group.

Centrist strategies of triangulation and compromise often guide *halakhic* decisions among Modern Orthodox Jews. For instance, Modern Orthodox women often wear hats, such as baseball hats, snoods, or headbands, in ways that distinguish them from ultra-Orthodox Jewish women who cover all of their hair in public, as well as from less observant Jewish women who go bare-headed.[70] Compromise also guides many of the decisions of Modern Orthodox synagogues. An example is the divider (*meḥitzah*) that separates the men's and women's sections of Orthodox synagogues. Typically, some members prefer a higher *meḥitzah*, whereas others prefer one is lower. Therefore a Modern Orthodox synagogue will usually opt for a compromise that is neither too high nor too low.[71]

A recent example of triangulation in Conservative Judaism was the 2015 decision of the Law Committee of the Conservative rabbinate that Ashkenazic Jews may eat rice and legumes (*kitniyot*) on Passover. As was mentioned earlier, Ashkenazic Jews traditionally did not eat these foods on Passover, unlike Sephardic Jews.[72] Until 2015, the Conservative movement adhered to the stricter Ashkenazic norm. The new permissive ruling placed Conservative Judaism in the center between Ashkenazic Orthodox Jews, who refrain from rice and legumes on Passover, and Reform Jews whose movement only "warmly recommends" that Jews refrain from eating "foods that obviously contain leaven, such breads and cakes."[73]

Compromises that are forged within Conservative synagogues are also frequent. The length of the prayer services, particularly on the High Holidays, is often a compromise between those who would are comfortable with a longer service and those who would prefer a shorter one. A more complicated example involves synagogue guidelines for food at weddings where the clergy will be officiating. At Beth Tzedec Congregation in Toronto, Ontario, the clergy would prefer all of the food at the wedding to be prepared under kosher supervision. However, they are still willing to officiate as long as some kosher food is available. The synagogue also recommends a set of compromise options, such as kosher appetizers after the ceremony.[74]

Conclusion: The Use of All Three Modern Strategies of Consensus in All Jewish Movements Today

As this chapter illustrates, a one-dimensional model of Jewish religious denominations today is overly simplistic.[75] Every Jewish group uses strictism, laxism, and centrism in different situations. Ultra-Orthodox groups may resent accusations of "laxism" or even "compromise," which are ideologically repugnant to them, and Reform Jews may reject the concept of "strictism." Without doubt, strictism is the guiding rule of ultra-Orthodoxy, while laxism and free choice are the preferred models of Reform Judaism. Centrism and compromise are the defining features of the centrist movements. Still, it is not hard to find relevant examples of all three strategies within all three camps.

In reality, any one of these principles, taken to its extreme, is incoherent. The endpoint of laxism is atomization rather than consensus. Many Jews do create a personalized bricolage of Jewish practices associated with various different Jewish groups, and some Jews observe Jewish practices that are highly individualized.[76] Still, if the only consensus is "live and let live," then one has not achieved any consensus in practice. A single-minded centrism would also be self-defeating, demanding strict obedience to an imagined center. At the other end of the spectrum, the endpoint of strictism is fragmentation. As smaller and smaller Jewish groups, or even individual Jews, observe more and more self-imposed stringencies, consensus is once again lost.

Thus, in the end, the establishment of a consensus on matters of Jewish law depends on the use of all three of these classic strategies of consensus-building, although not always in the same ways or to the same degree. All Jewish religious movements choose from among the same handful of solutions, when faced with the same contemporary puzzles of how to achieve consensus and union.

Notes

1. Philip Goodman, ed., *The Passover Anthology* (Philadelphia: Jewish Publication Society, 1961).
2. See *The Cambridge History of Judaism* (Cambridge: Cambridge University Press, 1984–2021) (eight volumes) for a detailed history of Judaism since the sixth century BCE.
3. On the practice of Judaism during the Middle Ages and early modern period, see Lawrence Fine, ed., *Judaism in Practice: From the Middle Ages through the Early Modern Period* (Princeton, NJ: Princeton University Press, 2001).

4. There is a large scholarly literature on local Jewish self-government in the premodern world. Classic discussions include Salo Baron, *The Jewish Community*, 3 vols. (Philadelphia: Jewish Publication Society, 1948). Also, Jacob Katz, *Tradition and Crisis*, trans. Bernard Cooperman (Syracuse, NY: Syracuse University Press, 2000), 65–102. See also Simon Schwarfuchs, *Kahal: La communauté juive de l'Europe médiévale* (Paris: Maisonneuve et Larose, 1986). An excellent recent study of three eighteenth-century German Jewish communities and their rules governing support for the indigent: Debra Kaplan, *The Patrons and Their Poor: Jewish Community and Public Charity in Early Modern Germany* (Philadelphia: University of Pennsylvania Press, 2020). For the Middle Ages, an exemplary recent study is Pinchas Roth, *In This Land: Jewish Life and Legal Culture in Late Medieval Provence* (Toronto: Pontifical Institute of Mediaeval Studies, 2021). Cf. Shlomo Pick, "Medieval Provençal Jewish Self-Government," *Trumah* 15 (2005): 105–38. For earlier studies, see the bibliography by Nahum Rakover and Azriel Hildeshimer, *Ha-Kehilah* (Jerusalem: Merkaz Zalman Shazar, 1978).
5. Aaron Kirschenbaum, *Jewish Penology: The Theory and Development of Criminal Punishment among the Jews throughout the Ages* (Jerusalem: Magnes Press, 2013) [Hebrew]; Hanina Ben-Menahem, "Shame Punishment in Jewish Legal Culture," *Jewish Law Annual* 19 (2011): 17–38.
6. Yosef Kaplan, "The Social Functions of the Herem in the Portuguese Jewish Community of Amsterdam in the Seventeenth Century," *Dutch Jewish History* 1 (1984): 111–55; Anne Oravetz Albert, "The Rabbi and the Rebels: A Pamphlet on the *Ḥerem* by Rabbi Isaac Aboab da Fonseca [1680]," *Jewish Quarterly Review* 104 (2014): 171–91; Kenneth Stow, *Alienated Minority: the Jews of Latin Europe* (Cambridge, MA: Harvard University Press, 1992), 182–91; Elke Klein, *Jews, Christian Society, and Royal Power in Medieval Barcelona* (Ann Arbor: University of Michigan Press, 2006), 48 and *passim.*
7. Roberta Rosenthal Kwall, *The Myth of the Cultural Jew: Culture and Law in Jewish Tradition* (Oxford: Oxford University Press, 2015), 55–84.
8. Alfred Landau and Bernhard Wachstein, eds., *Jüdische Privatbriefe aus dem Jahre 1619* (Vienna: Braumüller, 1911). Many of the letters are translated into English in Fritz Kobler, ed. and trans., *Letters of Jews through the Ages*, vol. 2 (Philadelphia: Jewish Publication Society, 1954), 449–79. On the importance of reputation among medieval Jewish elites, see Miriam Frenkel, *"The Compassionate and Benevolent": Jewish Ruling Elites in the Medieval Islamicate World: Alexandria as a Case Study* (Berlin: De Gruyter, 2021).
9. A typical example is in the twin medieval commentaries of Rashi and Tosafot on b.Berakhot 2a, the first page of the Talmud: they construct post facto rabbinic rationales for the custom of reciting evening prayers in synagogue in summer before it is dark. Cf. Edward Fram, *Ideals Face Reality: Jewish Law and Life* (Cincinnati, OH: Hebrew Union College Press, 1997).
10. Issachar Baer Eulenburg (or Eilenburg), *Sefer Be'er Sheva'* (Venice: Giovanni Cajun, 1614), 119a, 121a [Hebrew]. Cf. the analysis of deviance from Jewish law in David Malkiel, *Reconstructing Ashkenaz: The Human Face of Franco-German Jewry 1000-1250* (Stanford, CA: Stanford University Press, 2009), 148–99.
11. Matt Goldish, *Jewish Questions: Responsa on Sephardic Life in the Early Modern Period* (Princeton, NJ: Princeton University Press, 2008), 120–22. On the emergence of local liturgical customs in the late Middle Ages, see Lucia Raspe, "The Migration of German Jews into Italy and the Emergence of Local Rites of *Seliḥot* Recitation," in *The Jews of Europe*

around 1400: Disruption, Crisis, and Resilience, ed. Lukas Clemens and Christoph Cluse (Wiesbaden, Germany: Harrassowitz, 2018), 173–94.

12. Robert Brody, *The Geonim of Babylonia and the Shaping of Medieval Jewish Culture* (New Haven, CT: Yale University Press, 1998).
13. On the early reception of the Talmud, see Talya Fishman, *Becoming the People of the Talmud: Oral Torah as Written Tradition in Medieval Jewish Cultures* (Philadelphia: University of Pennsylvania Press, 2011). On the history of the rabbinate, see Simon Schwarzfuchs, *A Concise History of the Rabbinate* (Oxford: Blackwell, 1993).
14. Meira Polliack, ed., *Karaite Judaism; A Guide to Its History and Literary Sources* (Leiden, The Netherlands: Brill, 2003); Steven Fine, ed., *The Samaritans: A Biblical People* (Leiden, The Netherlands: Brill, 2022); Sharon Shalom, *From Sinai to Ethiopia: The Halachic and Conceptual World of Ethiopian Jewry* (Jerusalem: Gefen, 2016). On communication and consensus-building among Karaite communities, see, e.g., Mordecai L. Wilensky, "Exchange of Letters between the Crimean Karaites and the Constantinople Karaites in the Beginning of the XVIIth Century," *Proceedings of the Sixth World Congress of Jewish Studies*, vol. 2, Division B (1976): 201–11 [Hebrew].
15. On the controversies over the study of Aristotle, see Gregg Stern, "Maimonides and the Maimonidean Controversies," in *The Oxford Handbook of Jewish Philosophy*, ed. Paul Franks and Yitzhak Melamed (Oxford: Oxford University Press, forthcoming); and cf. Pinchas Roth, "Regional Boundaries and Medieval *Halakhah*: Rabbinic *Responsa* from Catalonia to Southern France in the Thirteenth and Fourteenth Centuries," *Jewish Quarterly Review* 105 (2015): 72–98.
16. British Library MS Or. 73 is a copy of Rashi's commentary on tractate Bava Metsi'a of the Babylonian Talmud, copied in Mosul in 1192. There is no published bibliography of the extant manuscripts of the *Mishneh Torah*, but see the online catalogue of the Institute of Microfilmed Hebrew Manuscripts of the National Library of Israel. See also Colette Sirat, *Hebrew Manuscripts of the Middle Ages* (Cambridge: Cambridge University Press, 2002), 71–72. There are extant medieval manuscripts of the *Mishneh Torah* written everywhere from Morocco in the west to Iran in the east, and from Germany in the north to Yemen in the south.
17. On the Jewish calendar in the ancient and early medieval periods, see Sacha Stern, *Calendar and Community: A History of the Jewish Calendar, 2nd Century BCE to 10th Century CE* (Oxford: Oxford University Press, 2001). On the early modern period, see Elisheva Carlebach, *Palaces of Time: Jewish Calendar and Culture in Early Modern Europe* (Cambridge, MA: Harvard University Press), 2011.
18. On Jewish travel and communication during eleventh–twelfth centuries, see S. D. Goitein, *A Mediterranean Society*, vol. 1 (Berkeley: University of California Press, 1967), 42–60. On the increases in Jewish travel during early modern period, see David Ruderman, *Early Modern Jewry: A New Cultural History* (Princeton, NJ: Princeton University Press, 2010). See also Sophia Menache, ed., *Communication in the Jewish Diaspora: The Pre-Modern World* (Leiden, The Netherlands: Brill, 1996); Micha Perry, *Tradition and Transmission: Knowledge Transmission among Western European Jews in the Middle Ages* (Tel Aviv: Ha-Kibbutz ha-Me'uḥad, 2010).
19. Javier Castaño, Tanys Fishman, and Ephraim Kanarfogel, eds., *Regional Identities and Cultures of Medieval Jews* (London: Littman Library of Jewish Civilization, 2018). On the origins of Spanish Jewish group consciousness, see Ross Brann, *Iberian Moorings:*

Al-Andalus, Sefarad, and the Tropes of Exceptionalism (Philadelphia: University of Pennsylvania Press, 2021).

20. Mark R. Cohen, "Communal Self-Government: The Genizah Period," in *The Jews in Medieval Egypt*, ed. Miriam Frenkel (Brookline, MA: Academic Studies Press, 2020), 72–85.
21. Katz, *Tradition and Crisis*, 103–12; Adam Teller, "Rabbis without a Function: The Polish Rabbinate and the Council of Four Lands in the 16th-18th Centuries," in *Jewish Religious Leadership*, vol. 1, ed. Jack Wertheimer (New York: Jewish Theological Seminary Press, 2004), 354–84. On the effort to standardize prayer rites in Poland, see Stefan Reif, *Shabbethai Sofer and His Prayer Book* (Cambridge: Cambridge University Press, 1979).
22. Xu Xin, *The Jews of Kaifeng, China: History, Religion, and Culture* (Jersey City, NJ: Ktav, 2003).
23. Joseph Tabory, *JPS Commentary on the Haggadah: Historical Introduction, Translation, and Commentary* (Philadelphia: Jewish Publication Society, 2008), 67–68. On the early history of Jewish printing, see Emile Schrijver, "Jewish Book Culture since the Invention of Printing (1469–*c.* 1815)," in *Cambridge History of Judaism*, vol. 7, ed. Jonathan Karp and Adam Sutcliffe, 291–315. See also Neil Netanel, *From Maimonides to Microsoft: The Jewish Law of Copyright since the Birth of Print* (Oxford: Oxford University Press, 2016). In addition to the "top down" (rabbis to laity) and "bottom up" (laity to rabbis) processes of the establishment of norms, one should also notice a process that one could call "middle out," in which practices become normative after being encouraged by Jewish professionals such as printers, cantors, or, in contemporary Judaism, caterers. Cf. Jenna Weissman Joselit, *Wonders of America: Reinventing Jewish Culture, 1880–1950* (New York: Henry Holt, 1994), 22–36, 89–105 on the role of caterers in establishing informal norms for American Jewish weddings and Bar Mitzvahs.
24. Elhanan Reiner, "The Ashkenazi Elite at the Beginning of the Modern Era: Manuscript versus Printed Book," *Polin* 10 (1997): 85–98; Debra Glasberg Gail, "The *Agur*: A *Halakhic* Code for Print," *Association for Jewish Studies Review* 45 (2021): 1–23.
25. Ephraim Kanarfogel, "Talmudic Studies," in *Cambridge History of Judaism*, vol. 4, 582–619. On the Provençal tradition of Talmud interpretation, see Roth, *In This Land*. On the surprising failure of Italian Jewry to develop its own distinctive Talmudic tradition, see Isadore Twersky, "The Contribution of Italian Sages to Rabbinic Literature," *Italia Judaica* 1 (1983): 383–400. Rashi and the Tosafists, the great medieval Talmud commentators, lived in fact in France rather than Germany, but they were later claimed as part of the "German" (Ashkenazic) tradition. The notion of a distinctive "French" tradition of Judaism was maintained in the fifteenth and sixteenth centuries, after the expulsion of Jews from France, by descendants of French Jews in Italy. See Jeffrey Woolf, "The Authority of Custom in the *Responsa* of Joseph Colon (Maharik)," *Dine Israel* 19 (1998): 43–93 [Eng. sect.].
26. Another late medieval code, the *Arba'ah Turim*, attempted to codify both German and Spanish practices. The author, Jacob ben Asher, was a German rabbi who lived in Spain. See Judah Galinsky, "Ashkenazim in Sefarad: the Rosh and the Tur on the Codification of Jewish Law," *Jewish Law Annual* 16 (2006): 3–23.
27. Isadore Twersky, *Introduction to the Code of Maimonides (Mishneh Torah)* (New Haven, CT: Yale University Press, 1980).

28. See the articles by Joshua Teplitsky, Miriam Bodian, and Jonathan Ray, in *The Oxford Handbook of the Jewish Diaspora*, ed. Hasia Diner (Oxford: Oxford University Press, 2021), 344–408.
29. *Shulchan Arukh* OH 453:1, 623:6. Hirsch Jacob Zimmels, *Ashkenazim and Sephardim: Their Relations, Differences, and Problems, as Reflected in the Rabbinical Responsa* (London: Oxford University Press, 1958).
30. On the efforts to establish Sephardic rabbinic norms within *converso* communities, see the 1980 essay by Yosef Hayim Yerushalmi, "The Re-education of Marranos in the Seventeenth Century," in *The Faith of Fallen Jews: Yosef Hayim Yerushalmi and the Writing of Jewish History*, ed. David Myers and Alexander Kaye (Waltham, MA: Brandeis University Press, 2014), 157–74. See also Yosef Kaplan, ed., *Religious Changes and Cultural Transformations in Early Modern Western Sephardic Communities* (Leiden, The Netherlands: Brill, 2019). Note especially the essays in part two (157–287). Compare the nineteenth- and twentieth-century contacts of major Jewish communities with the isolated Jews of Bukhara: Alanna Cooper, *Bukharan Jews and the Dynamics of Global Judaism* (Bloomington: Indiana University Press, 2012).
31. On Caro, Isserles, and the *Shulchan Arukh*, see Edward Fram, *The Codification of Jewish Law on the Cusp of Modernity* (Cambridge: Cambridge University Press, 2022). See also Joseph M. Davis, "The Reception of the '*Shulḥan 'Arukh*' and the Formation of Ashkenazic Jewish Identity," *Association for Jewish Studies Review* 26 (2002): 251–75; Isadore Twersky, "The Shulhan 'Aruk: Enduring Code of Jewish Law," *Judaism* 16 (1967): 141–58; Yitzhak Raphael, ed., *Rabbi Joseph Karo: Studies and Essays* (Jerusalem: Mossad ha-Rav Kook, 1969)[Hebrew]; Israel Ta-Shma, "Rabbi Joseph Caro and His 'Beit Yosef': Between Spain and Germany," in *Moreshet Sepharad: The Sephardi Legacy*, vol. 2, ed. Haim Beinart (Jerusalem: Magnes Press, 1992), 192–206; Elad Schlesinger, "Four Editions, Four Faces, One Book: Printing the *Shulḥan Arukh* in Amsterdam, 1661-1708," *Studia Rosenthaliana* 46 (2020): 51–70; Mor Altshuler, *The Life of Rabbi Joseph Caro* (Tel Aviv: Tel Aviv University Press, 2016) [Hebrew]. On the circulation of the *Shulchan Arukh*, see, e.g., Yosef Tobi, "Caro's '*Shulhan Arukh*' versus Maimonides' '*Mishne Torah*' in Yemen," *Jewish Law Annual* 15 (2004): 189–215.
32. Edward Fram, "The Use of Codified Law in the Rabbinic Courts of Frankfurt am Main on the Eve of the Enlightenment," *Jewish History* 31 (2017): 129–47; Maoz Kahana, *From the Noda' bi-Yehudah to the Hatam Sofer* (Jerusalem: Merkaz Zalman Shazar, 2015) [Hebrew].
33. For modern Jewish history, see, e.g., *Cambridge History of Judaism*, vol. 8, ed. Jonathan Karp and Adam Sutcliffe. On American Judaism today, see Jack Wertheimer, *The New American Judaism: How Jews Practice Their Religion Today* (Princeton, NJ: Princeton University Press, 2018). There is no agreement either among scholars or in the Jewish laity as to exactly how many Jewish denominations there are today, or how they are to be listed or categorized. Chaim Saiman, *Halakhah* (Princeton, NJ: Princeton University Press, 2018), 213–41.
34. Oren Steinitz, "*Responsa* 2.0: Are Q&A Websites Creating a New Type of Halachic Discourse?," *Modern Judaism* 31 (2011): 85–102.
35. David Biale et al., eds. *Hasidism: A New History* (Princeton, NJ: Princeton University Press, 2018); Marcin Wodziński, *Historical Atlas of Hasidism* (Princeton, NJ: Princeton University Press, 2018).
36. Noham Blas, "The Publication History and Originality of *Shemirat Shabbat ke-Hilkhatah*" (MA thesis, Ben Gurion University, 2019 [Hebrew]). On the *halakhic* guides published by

ArtScroll, see Jeremy Stolow, *Orthodox by Design: Judaism, Print, Politics, and the ArtScroll Revolution* (Berkeley: University of California Press, 2010).

37. Timothy D. Lytton, *Kosher: Private Regulation in the Age of Industrial Food* (Cambridge, MA: Harvard University Press, 2013).
38. Derek Taylor, *British Chief Rabbis, 1664-2006* (London: Vallentine Mitchell, 2007); Itamar Warhaftig and Shmuel Katz, eds., *The Chief Rabbinate of Israel*, 3 vols. (Jerusalem: Heikhal Shlomo, 2002) [Hebrew].
39. Yitzchak Kerem, "Emerging and Disappearing Sephardic and Mizrachi Diasporas," *Avotaynu: The International Review of Jewish Genealogy* 30 (2014): 30–37; Cooper, *Bukharan Jews*.
40. Ari Ariel, "Ethnic Diversity in Israel," in *The Wiley-Blackwell History of Jews and Judaism*, ed. Alan T. Levenson (Malden, MA: Wiley-Blackwell, 2012), 586–600; Harvey Goldberg, "From Sephardi to Mizrahi and Back Again: Changing Meanings of 'Sephardi' in Its Social Environments," *Jewish Social Studies* 15 (2008): 165–88.
41. Nomi Stolzenberg and David Myers, *American Shtetl: The Making of Kiryas Yoel, a Hasidic Village in Upstate New York* (Princeton, NJ: Princeton University Press, 2022). On the limits of coercion within ultra-Orthodox communities today, see Ayala Fader, *Hidden Heretics: Jewish Doubt in the Digital Age* (Princeton, NJ: Princeton University Press, 2022); Lynn Davidman, *Becoming Un-Orthodox: Stories of Ex-Hasidic Jews* (Oxford: Oxford University Press, 2015).
42. Elana Sztokman, *The Men's Section: Orthodox Jewish Men in an Egalitarian World* (Waltham, MA: Brandeis University Press, 2011).
43. Religious strictism is often referred to, both in academic writing and in popular language, as "movement to the right" and religious laxism as the "movement to the left."
44. On American Orthodox Judaism, see Zev Eleff, *Authentically Orthodox: A Tradition-Bound Faith in American Life* (Detroit, MI: Wayne State University Press, 2020); Samuel Heilman, *Sliding to the Right: The Contest for the Future of American Jewish Orthodoxy* (Berkeley: University of California Press, 2006). For critical surveys of recent scholarship on Orthodox Judaism, see Menachem Keren-Kratz, "The Contemporary Study of Orthodoxy: Challenging the One-Dimensional Paradigm," *Tradition* 49 (2016): 24–52; Ayala Fader and Orit Avishai, "Introduction" to special issue, *AJS Review* 46, no. 1 (Spring 2022): 1–10.
45. These terms were coined by Catholic scholars in seventeenth-century France. Blaise Pascal's *Provincial Letters* (1656–1657) is a classic text mocking the "laxist" position taken by some Jesuit scholars of his day. Pascal (1623–1662) and his fellow "strictist" Catholics are sometimes called "Jansenist," after their leader, Cornelius Jansen (1585–1638).
46. Lytton, *Kosher*; Sue Fishkoff, *Kosher Nation: Why More and More of America's Food Answers to a Higher Authority* (New York: Schocken Books, 2010).
47. See also Aviad Hakohen, "*Kulot* and *ḥumrot* in *halakhah*," *Maḥanayim* 5 (1993): 90–103 [Hebrew].
48. As a conscious general principle of Jewish observance, strictism first appears in a kabbalistic/*halakhic*/ethical work entitled *Shenei Luḥot ha-Berit* of Isaiah Horowitz (*c.* 1555–1630), published in 1648. See Joseph Citron, *Isaiah Horowitz's Shnei Luhot Ha-Berit: The Pietistic Transformation of Jewish Theology* (Leiden, The Netherlands: Brill, 2021).
49. Stolzenberg and Myers, *American Shtetl*, 36–42.
50. Amy Milligan, *Hair, Headwear, and Orthodox Jewish Women: Kallah's Choice* (London: Rowman and Littlefield, 2014). Some Orthodox Jews regard New York City tap water as

unkosher unless filtered, because of the presence of tiny crustaceans. See J. David Bleich, "New York City Water," *Tradition* 38 (2004): 70–111.

51. Some scholars also stress the principle of opposition to majority culture in the development of the norms of ultra-Orthodox Jews, like those of other fundamentalist religious groups. See Martin Marty and Scott Appleby, *The Glory and the Power: The Fundamentalist Challenge to the Modern World* (Boston: Beacon Press, 1992); Samuel Heilman and Menachem Friedman, "Religious Fundamentalism and Religious Jews: the Case of the Haredim," in *Fundamentalisms Observed*, ed. Martin Marty and Scott Appleby (Chicago: University of Chicago Press, 1991), 197–264.
52. Barbara Goldman Carrel, "Hasidic Women's Fashion Aesthetic and Practice: The Long and Short of Tzniuth," in *Modest Fashion: Styling Bodies, Mediating Faith*, ed. Reina Lewis (London, I. B. Tauris, 2013), 91–117; Levi Cooper, "Shtreimel Variations: The History of a Hat," *Segula: The Jewish Journey through History* 44 (2018): 32–43.
53. The abandonment of traditions on the basis of new stringent interpretations of Jewish law has been discussed by several scholars. See Lawrence Kaplan, "The Hazon Ish: Haredi Critic of Traditional Orthodoxy," in *The Uses of Tradition*, ed. Jack Wertheimer (New York: Jewish Theological Seminary of America, 1992), 145–74; Haim Waxman, "The Iron Law of *Ḥumrot* and the Haredization of Orthodoxy," in *Religious Zealotry*, ed. Meir Litvak and Ora Limor (Jerusalem: Merkaz Zalman Shazar, 2008), 181–98 [Hebrew].
54. Shaul Stampfer, "Heder Study, Knowledge of Torah and the Maintenance of Social Stratification in Traditional East European Jewish Society," *Studies in Jewish Education* 3 (1988): 271–89.
55. Fishkoff, *Kosher Nation*.
56. This issue is called "Talmudic measures" (*shi'urim*), because it involves measured amounts of *matzah* and wine and measured amounts of time within which the food must be eaten. See Menachem Friedman, "The Lost Kiddush Cup: Changes in Ashkenazic Haredi Culture—A Tradition in Crisis," in *Uses of Tradition*, ed. Wertheimer, 175–86.
57. The major strictist twentieth-century commentary on the *Shulchan Arukh* was the *Mishnah Berurah* by Israel Meir ha-Kohen (or Kagan; 1838–1933); see Simcha Fishbane, *The Method and Meaning of the Mishnah Berurah* (Hoboken, NJ: Ktav, 1991). Many prohibitions that are widely observed today in Orthodox Judaism are based on loose interpretations of the Talmud and the *Shulchan Arukh*. One example is the general prohibition on the use of electric devices on the Sabbath. For a survey of the development of this prohibition, see Daniel Nevin's 2012 *responsum*, "The Use of Electrical and Electronic Devices on Shabbat" (2012), https://www.rabbinicalassembly.org/sites/default/files/public/halakhah/teshuvot/2011-2020/electrical-electronic-devices-shabbat.pdf. See also Michael Broyde and Howard Jachter, "The Use of Electricity on Shabbat and Yom Tov," *Journal of Halakhah and Contemporary Society* 21 (Spring 1991): 4–47.
58. As a matter of principle, ultra-Orthodox Judaism accords its religious leaders wide discretionary authority in deciding Jewish law, and in directing all aspects of the lives and beliefs of their followers, and regards obedience to the *Shulchan Arukh* as a baseline minimum of observance, but not as a bar to additional stringencies. See Lawrence Kaplan, "Daas Torah: A Modern Conception of Rabbinic Authority," in *Rabbinic Authority and Personal Autonomy*, ed. Moshe Sokol (Northvale NJ: Jason Aronson, 1992), 1–60.
59. Benjamin Brown, "Kedushah: The Sexual Abstinence of Married Men in Gur, Slonim, and Toledot Aharon," *Jewish History* 27 (2013): 475–522.

60. Henry Goldschmidt, *Race and Religion among the Chosen Peoples of Crown Heights* (Piscataway, NJ: Rutgers University Press, 2006), 156.
61. Simeon Baumel, *Sacred Speakers: Language and Culture among the Haredim in Israel* (New York: Berghahn Books, 2006). On the other hand, the Modern Orthodox scholar David Berger has expressed his dismay at the tolerance (or as he says, "indifference") that ultra-Orthodox groups show for the distinctive (or as he says, "prohibited") Messianic beliefs of Chabad Hasidim. David Berger, *The Rebbe, the Messiah, and the Scandal of Orthodox Indifference* (Oxford: Littmann Library of Jewish Civilization, 2001).
62. On the differences between Hasidic and non-Hasidic practice of Judaism: Aaron Wertheim, *Law and Custom in Hasidism*, trans. S. Himelstein (Hoboken, NJ: Ktav, 1992).
63. Gershon Bacon, *The Politics of Tradition: Agudat Yisrael in Poland 1916-1939* (Jerusalem: Magnes Press, 1996).
64. Michael Meyer, *Response to Modernity: The History of the Reform Movement in Judaism* (Oxford: Oxford University Press, 1988); Dana Evan Kaplan, *The New Reform Judaism: Challenges and Reflections* (Philadelphia: Jewish Publication Society, 2013).
65. E.g., note the titles of two recent Reform Jewish volumes: Lisa Grushcow, ed., *The Sacred Encounter: Jewish Perspectives on Sexuality* (New York: CCAR Press, 2014); Hara Person and Sonja Pilz, *Voices of Torah*, 2 vols. (New York: CCAR Press, 2011).
66. David Ellenson, "Reform Judaism in Present-Day America: The Evidence of the 'Gates of Prayer,'" in *Threescore and Ten: Essays in Honor of Rabbi Seymour J. Cohen*, ed. Abraham J. Karp (Hoboken, NJ: Ktav, 1991), 377–85.
67. Dana Evan Kaplan, ed., *Contemporary Debates in American Reform Judaism: Conflicting Visions* (New York: Routledge, 2001); Dana Kaplan, *The New Reform Judaism: Challenges and Reflections* (Philadelphia: Jewish Publication Society, 2013), 131–64.
68. See the 2015 "Resolution on the Rights of Transgender and Gender Non-Conforming People" of the Union for Reform Judaism," online, https://urj.org/what-we-believe/resolutions.
69. Neil Gillman, *Conservative Judaism: The New Century* (West Orange, NJ: Behrman House, 1993); Martin S. Cohen and Michael Katz, eds., *The Observant Life: The Wisdom of Conservative Judaism for Contemporary Jews* (New York: Aviv Press, 2012). Just as pluralism is different from minimalism, so is pluralism different from a rigorous centrism, that is, insistence on specific "centrist" norms or compromises. On opposing impulses toward diversity and centrism in the early years of Conservative Judaism, see Michael R. Cohen, *The Birth of Conservative Judaism: Solomon Schechter's Disciples and the Creation of an American Religious Movement* (New York: Columbia University Press, 2012).
70. See Milligan, *Hair, Headwear, and Orthodox Jewish Women*.
71. Etan Diamond, *And I Will Dwell in Their Midst: Orthodox Jews in Suburbia* (Chapel Hill: University of North Carolina Press, 2000), 72–74; Zev Eleff, ed., *Modern Orthodox Judaism: A Documentary History* (Philadelphia: Jewish Publication Society, 2016).
72. Amy Levin and Avram Israel Reisner, "A Teshuvah Permitting *Ashkenazim* to Eat Kitniyot on Pesah," online, https://www.rabbinicalassembly.org/sites/default/files/public/halakhah/teshuvot/2011-2020/Levin-Reisner-Kitniyot.pdf. The responsum is dated November 2015. Compare the responsum of the Reform CCAR 5756.9 from 1996, "Pesah Kashrut and Reform Judaism," online, https://www.ccarnet.org/ccar-responsa/rr21-no-5756-9/. On achieving consensus in pluralist settings, see Ellen Lippmann and Trisha Arlin, "Pluralism in Action: Choosing a New Siddur in an Unaffiliated Synagogue," in *Judaism and*

Pluralism: Honoring the 60th Anniversary of the Academy for Jewish Religion, ed. Leonard Levin (Teaneck, NJ: Ben Yehuda Press, 2016), 123–34.

73. Peter Knobel, ed., *Gates of the Seasons: A Guide to the Jewish Year* (New York: Central Conference of American Rabbis, 1983), 68. Reform Judaism, here and frequently, triangulates as well, placing itself between a minimalist Judaism (see above), which would dispense altogether with the tradition of refraining from eating bread and cake on Passover, and the stricter rules of both Conservative and Orthodox Judaism.

74. "Weddings," https://www.beth-tzedec.org/page/weddings. Consider also the *kashrut* policy at Congregation Or Tzion in Scottsdale, Arizona: "It is our goal to make sure that everyone who enters Congregation Or Tzion, be they members [or] guests of our community, are comfortable in both participating in and eating at all events and programs." https://www.congregationortzion.org/celebrate/kashrut-policy/. For everyone to be comfortable eating, *kashrut* must be observed; for everyone to be comfortable participating, the rules must not be too strict. Congregation Or Tzion's guidelines for the synagogue kitchen are much stricter than those for synagogue events taking place in "non-kosher homes."

75. Menahem Keren-Kratz, "The Contemporary Study of Orthodoxy: Challenging the One-Dimensional Paradigm," *Tradition* 49 (2016): 24–52.

76. Roberta Rosenthal Kwall, *Remix Judaism: Preserving Tradition in a Diverse World*, 2nd ed. (London: Rowman and Littlefield, 2022); Steven Cohen and Arnold Eisen, *The Jew Within: Self, Family, and Community in America* (Bloomington: Indiana University Press, 2000).

CHAPTER 14

DOUBT, STRINGENCY, AND LENIENCY IN JEWISH LAW

SHLOMO C. PILL

Introduction

Doubt is a salient characteristic of legal systems,[1] and Jewish law is no exception.[2] This chapter explores Jewish law perspectives on *safek*, or legal doubt, defined here as uncertainty about the correct legal standard or the right legal outcome or course of conduct in a particular case.[3] After introducing the concept, causes, consequences, and correctives of legal doubt in Anglo-American jurisprudence, we consider legal doubt as an endemic feature of Jewish law by exploring rabbinic ideas on the origins of legal uncertainty and the challenges that *safek* poses for Jewish law and practice. Next, this chapter explores how rabbinic jurisprudence works to resolve legal doubts. We first discuss *who* is authorized to determine legal uncertainties within the *halakhic* system, and next consider two distinct schools of rabbinic thought about *how* to resolve such doubts. One school of thought seeks to resolve legal doubts analytically by achieving clarity through scholarly analysis supported by the jurisprudential validation of individual's legal opinions. A second model aims to resolve doubts by resorting to secondary rules of decision designed to reach *a* determinate legal conclusion rather than necessarily the *right* legal conclusion. From this latter approach—which even adherents of the analytic method of resolving doubts must rely on in cases where despite their best efforts they remain uncertain about the right outcome—emerges what is perhaps the most salient doubt-resolving rule in rabbinic jurisprudence: doubts in matters of biblical law are resolved strictly, and doubts in matters of rabbinic law are resolved leniently. We explore some of the contours, applicability, and practical and legal implications of this central principle, as well as rabbinic conceptualizations of legal leniency and stringency beyond their role in resolving doubts. The chapter concludes by contrasting Western law's generally negative attitude toward legal doubt with rabbinic tendencies to view legal uncertainty as a positive jurisprudential and religious phenomenon, which offers important perspectives on the place of doubt in law more broadly.

Doubt in Western Jurisprudence

In Western jurisprudence, doubt is often described as originating in several related causes.[4] Legal doubt—uncertainty about the content, meaning, or practical import of the law itself—has been variously attributed to the paucity and proliferation of legal norms;[5] the inherent ambiguities of language generally,[6] and of the "open-texture" of legal rules and standards in particular;[7] the subjective nature of interpreting legal texts, traditions, and practices;[8] and to the speculative quality of predictions of judicial behavior.[9] Factual doubt—uncertainty about the real-word contexts in which the law operates and to which abstract legal norms must be applied to determine legal outcomes—results from the limits of eyewitness recollections;[10] the ambiguous nature of many forms of evidence that can be interpreted as reasonably supporting different narratives of past events;[11] and the embedded human biases that color perceptions and recollections of events.[12] Within this Western legal tradition, such doubts are often characterized as jurisprudential vices that carry substantial legal costs.[13] Legal uncertainty undermines the rule of law to the extent that it detracts from peoples' ability to predict and plan for the consequences of various courses of conduct and makes legal outcomes more dependent on the subjective characteristics of individual legal decision makers.[14] Doubt also increases the costs of operating in and utilizing the legal system, as legal actors must continuously hedge against uncertain and unpredictable legal outcomes.[15] Moreover, doubt in law contributes to injustice by shifting costs to more risk-averse parties, such as by incentivizing even innocent criminal defendants to accept plea bargains rather than face the uncertainty of a trial or by allowing wealthy or powerful parties to leverage legal risks to extract favorable settlements from poor, minority, or otherwise disadvantaged opponents in civil cases.[16]

Western legal systems have developed many ways of mitigating the negative consequences of doubt in law.[17] Factual doubt, for instance, is reduced by legally prescribed factual presumptions that set burdens and standards of proof.[18] Since reasonable people can and routinely do disagree in their conclusions about past events based on evidentiary indicators, the law establishes that the facts of a case to which legal standards will be applied to produce legal outcomes shall be determined by a particular trier of fact, usually a judge or jury.[19] As it is often hard to dispositively determine what happened in the past, the law instructs that triers of fact shall resolve reasonable doubts as to the facts of a criminal case in favor of the defendant.[20] In civil cases, where the stakes are lower and the consequences of mistaken factual conclusions are generally less dire, the trier of fact is again expected to resolve doubts in favor of the defendant as long as they determine that an alternative narrative is not more likely to be true.[21] Legal systems further establish how, where, and when factual determinations can and cannot be reached—typically, through the introduction of evidence during an adversarial trial in court, rather than in media reporting or on appeal. Evidentiary rules further enhance factual certainty (at least from the perspective of the law) by prescribing the kinds of evidence that can and cannot be relied on to establish the reality of past events, and by determining valid and invalid ways of impugning the credibility of presented evidence to cast doubt on the veracity of facts that evidence purports to establish.[22] In part, such limitations on the law's cognizance of facts enhance the administrability of justice and the reliability and finality of legal rulings.[23] But beyond this, rules governing the determination of facts help reduce the amount, acuity, and longevity of factual doubts within the legal system.[24]

Anglo-American systems also use a variety of procedural and institutional means to reduce the incidence and severity of legal doubt, and negative impacts of legal doubt, and to lessen the negative impact of such uncertainty when it does manifest. Institutional hierarchies of courts within particular jurisdictions permit high courts to resolve cases with finality, foreclosing the uncertainty engendered by the possibility of further appeals.[25] Such judicial hierarchies also allow for the resolution of differences of opinion among lower tribunals and for the clarification of ambiguities in existing statutes and precedents by courts of final authority.[26] The doctrine of *stare decisis* and the generally binding nature of precedent helps dispel doubts about how courts are likely to resolve cases and increases the degree of certainty people have in the likely legal consequences of their actions.[27] Rules and principles of statutory interpretation attempt to limit the range of acceptable constructions that might be given to legal materials, thus controlling the size of the solution set of possible legal outcomes that contributes to uncertainty about the correct legal rule or likely legal result in a given scenario.[28] Furthermore, attempts to systematize common-law decisions and traditions into carefully crafted statutory codes, as well as efforts to distill complex, multivocal bodies of legal doctrine and theory into authoritative restatements of law help reduce ambiguities and inconsistencies in the law that often leave the correct legal rule in doubt.[29]

Despite these efforts, doubt in the law and its negative impacts persist. As some scholars have noted, attempts to reduce legal and factual uncertainty always entail costs; and many of the strategies for mitigating some of the causes and effects of doubt tend to produce other kinds of uncertainty within the law. Ultimately, in Western jurisprudence, doubt is generally viewed as a vice to be carefully controlled, accounted for, and mitigated where possible.

Origins of Legal Uncertainty

Jewish law, too, views doubt as an expected and inherent characteristic of law. Indeed, in traditional Jewish jurisprudence, the prominence of *safek* is revealed not only in the legislative, interpretative, and judicial activities of rabbinic scholars, but also in the divinely formulated and revealed rules and principles of biblical law. Thus, even those aspects of Jewish law that the rabbis have traditionally attributed to God are characterized by the presence of jurisprudential doubt. Thus, the Torah anticipates uncertainty about the correct rule of law of legally proper course of conduct, and further prescribes a secondary rule of decision for resolving such doubts:

> If a case is too baffling for you to decide, whether in matters of blood or money or ritual impurity—matters of dispute in your gates—and you arise and ascend to the place the Lord your God will have chosen and appear before the priests or the judge that will be in those days and inquire from them and they tell you the law, you shall do as they instruct you from that place that God will have chosen, and you shall be careful to do all that they instruct you. You shall act in accordance with the instructions given you and the law told to you; you shall not turn from that which they instruct you either to the right or to the left.[30]

From this biblical genesis, legal doubt remained a prominent feature in rabbinic legal and religious discourses—from the *Midrash* to the Talmud and post-Talmudic law codes and commentaries, and in homiletic and kabbalistic texts and traditions as well—where it is explained and addressed in ways that should be familiar to students of uncertainty discourses in Western jurisprudence.[31]

Halakhic sources suggest several sources of legal uncertainty. First, legal doubt is a product of the paucity of available legal rules and sources. Sometimes a settled norm that determinately covers a given situation does not exist simply because the law did not address that issue. The Torah, for example, recounts that Moses was initially unsure about how to adjudicate the case of a man proven to have committed blasphemy because God had not yet revealed a rule prescribing a penalty for this sin.[32] In other cases, uncertainty arises because the normative questions raised is genuinely novel due to changes in human experiences. No set of legal materials can fully and adequately address all future contingencies. As Rabbi Jacob Albo explained, "it would be impossible for the text of the Torah to be legally sufficient for all future times, for the details of human existence are constantly changing and are too numerous and varied to be encompassed in a book."[33] Thus, we find numerous *halakhic* doubts have arisen regarding legal questions produced by advancing technologies. Rabbinic scholars have debated the legal implications of mechanical printing for the production of previously handwritten Torah scrolls;[34] the consequences of crossing the international date line—made possible only by the advent of rapid transportation—for the observance of Jewish holiday's tied to calendar dates;[35] the implications of reproductive technologies like in vitro fertilization and surrogacy for the *halakhic* lineage of children born of such methods;[36] and the legal status of the use of electricity, and more recently of digital computing, on the Sabbath.[37] In these and countless other examples, the absence of a previously settled and clear legal standard could be taken to mean that the matter has been left unregulated and subject to personal discretion. Alternatively, the lack of a prescribed rule may require that the right standard be identified by analogy to other areas of the law or by inductive or deductive reasoning. If so, there will be substantial doubts as to which lines of legal reasoning offer the most compelling conclusions, which understandings of the rationales and policies underlying various laws are correct, and which distinctions between analogized rules are legally relevant. Such uncertainties tend to produce a range of alternative legal conclusions, which multiplies the degree to which the "right" *halakhic* rule remains in doubt.

Uncertainties owing to the paucity of legal directives within Jewish law sources can be mitigated by the addition of additional legal materials that provide more standards that cover more cases. Thus, in response to Moses's uncertainty about how to proceed in the case of the blasphemer, God spoke to Moses and legislated the appropriate punishment, clarifying this doubt.[38] However, the recognition of additional legal standards can also produce uncertainties that arise from contradictions or tensions between those rules. Such apparent conflicts exist between numerous biblical commands,[39] and Talmudic discussions are replete with queries that pose contradictions between rabbinic legal teachings.[40] Many post-Talmudic commentators, most notably of the Tosafist school likewise pose and seek to resolve conflicts between conflicting Talmudic texts.[41] Such tensions—between biblical verses, mishnaic texts, Talmudic discussions, or other sources of *halakhah*—engender legal uncertainty. Which rule is the right one; which should be applied to determine the correct outcome in this case? Resolving such doubts requires rabbinic scholars to address these legal contradictions, and rabbis have sought to do so in myriad ways. In some cases, conflicts between sources are solved by identifying which sources rank higher or lower in the hierarchy of Jewish law authority. In other instances, rabbinic interpreters distinguish seemingly inconsistent norms by explaining that each speaks to a different factual circumstance. Other times, commentators use the existence of contradictions between legal standards to identify more fundamental, but previously unarticulated legal principles that resolve the tension between sources while also offering a new *halakhic* norm that can be applied to other cases. Attempts to resolve conflicts between Jewish law sources, as well as choices about which approach to resolving such contradictions is most jurisprudentially sound, are rarely clear-cut; if they were, we likely would not have acknowledged the existence of any intralegal tension in the first place. Instead, different *halakhic* authorities resolve doubts arising from conflicts between Jewish law rules and principles in different ways with such disagreement producing further uncertainty about which approach and which rule of law is the right one.[42]

Even where *halakhic* rules governing a topic exist and do not conflict, rabbinic sources also attest to the idea that legal uncertainty follows from the ambiguity of particular legal norms. Sometimes, legal principles are formulated in inherently vague or ambiguous terms that result in significant doubts about how those standards should apply to specific cases. The Torah's command that "these words . . . shall be as *totafot* between your eyes,"[43] its prescription to "take" several agricultural items including "the fruit of a splendid tree" during the holiday of Sukkot,[44] as well as the prohibition against performing "labor" (*melakhah*) on the Sabbath are examples of such ambiguous norms.[45] Talmudic sources clarify these inherently ambiguous terms: "*Totafot*," a biblical Hebrew term without any precise translation or referent, are small, square, black leather boxes containing several passages of the Torah written on parchment scrolls;[46] the "fruit of a splendid tree" is the *etrog*, or citron;[47] and for Sabbath purposes, "labor" includes thirty-nine categories of creative human activity.[48] The fact remains, however, that the precise parameters and details of the things referred to by these vague terms remain shrouded in rabbinic disputes born of doubt. Similar examples of *halakhic* doubt arising from the inherent vagueness of Jewish legal standards abound.

In other instances, even fairly precise and specific legal rules reveal substantial "open texture" that produces uncertainty about the meaning or practical ramifications of the rule. In rabbinic jurisprudence, such open texture is at least partly a consequence of the limits of text and language to communicate clear legal standards. The Talmud notes that biblical texts can often be understood in different ways: "One verse may teach many legal propositions."[49] And Midrashic sources attest to the rabbinic view that texts can be deconstructed into myriad alternative understandings.[50] Thus, Nachmanides explained that the Bible's rule for resolving legal doubts—to seek the decision of the "priests and the judge"—"is very important; for the Torah was given to us as a text, and it is well known that minds will differ over derivative matters."[51] Maimonides similarly observed that uncertainty is inherent to texts, even divinely revealed scripture;[52] and Rabbi Jacob Albo maintained that any attempt to commit law to text would produce interpretative doubts.[53] This was true, Albo argued, of the Torah, as well as of all subsequent attempts by the rabbis to preserve explanations and clarifications of the Torah's uncertainties.[54] Likewise, Rabbi Shlomo Luria argued that that "even if all the heavens were parchment and all the oceans ink, they would not suffice to fully and clearly communicate even a single point of law."[55] Like Albo, Luria maintained that each attempt to provide doubt-resolving explanations for on the uncertainties of *halakhah* produces "even greater need for additional clarifications, and clarifications upon those clarifications. For it is impossible that the initial clarification of the law could be free of all doubts and nuances such that there would be no need for further explanation."[56] The clarification of doubt through language will always result in new and more numerous uncertainties, requiring yet more clarification, which beget even more doubts.

Rabbinic jurisprudence further suggested that the uncertainty precipitated by the ambiguity and inconsistency of Jewish legal sources is exacerbated by the subjective nature of human perception and interpretation. It is axiomatic in rabbinic thought that every individual is unique, and that each person thus perceives things, reasons, and thinks differently.[57] "Just as no two faces are precisely alike, so too, no two minds are exactly alike."[58] These differences in perspective inevitably produce very different interpretative and analytic understandings of Jewish law among rabbinic scholars, as Rabbi Shlomo Luria asserts: "Each person sees [the law] through their own subjective channel and according to their own capacity . . . this one distant from that one."[59] While Maimonides seems to view this differentiation of rabbinic thinking as an unfortunate consequence of the gradual historical decline in scholars deficient legal training and analytic abilities,[60] others take individualized, subjective understandings of *halakhah* to be an essential quality of Jewish law itself. Thus, some rabbis have associated the diversity of legal understandings with Judaism's quintessential revelatory moment, arguing that the classical rabbinic teaching that the soul of every Jew was present at Mount Sinai when God revealed the Torah connotes that every individual person has a unique way of understanding the meaning and implications of the law God communicated.[61]

Subjectivity not only extends to the interpretative construction of legal norms from *halakhic* texts and traditions but manifests in rabbis' modes of legal reasoning and analysis as well. As Rabbi Israel Salanter explained: "The rabbis reach their legal conclusions not only based on the evidence before them, but also and chiefly based on their personal evaluations and impressions of that evidence. . . . Human beings differ from each other in how they weigh objective evidence [of the law]; they therefore exercise discretion in reaching judgments, as we see from the fact that their views vary so widely."[62] Simply put, different scholars with unique perspectives and cognitive frameworks reason about the law in different ways. Rabbi Judah Loew, for instance, offers a detailed account of how uncertainty about Jewish law arises in part due to the subjective quality of legal reasoning and analysis. Echoing earlier scholars who maintained that Jewish law consists not of clear-cut rules but sets of factors and considerations that simultaneously support alternative legal conclusions as to any given question,[63] Loew explained that the *halakhah* reflects the complexity of creation: "The world is not so straightforward that there would not be a multiplicity of conflicting aspects to things . . . God created all those things and created them with their numerous inconsistent qualities."[64] Thus, when it comes to the law,

> [e]ven if a particular thing is adjudged ritually impure according to the law, it is impossible that that thing does not also have some ritually pure aspects and qualities to it. Likewise, if a thing is ritually pure according to the law, it necessarily has ritually impure aspects to it as well. Now, human beings diverge in their cognitive processes, and it is therefore impossible that all people should think the same way. Therefore, when each person reaching a legal conclusion, they are internalizing one aspect of the issue in accordance with their own reasoning . . . Just as one person will conclude that the subject of a legal question is ritually pure and provide legal reasons and analysis to support its purity—and certainly one aspect of its nature will be as they say—so too, another person that adjudges the same object to be ritually impure will also reason to that conclusion based on another of its aspects.[65]

Talmudic and biblical commentator, Rashi, encapsulates the upshot succinctly: "this scholar analogizes one thing to the other in this way, while that scholar analogizes the same things in another way," and there is thus no way to definitively say which view is correct.[66]

Legal Doubt as Problem

The Torah's primary description of the occurrence of uncertainty in Jewish law demonstrates that like Western jurisprudence, Jewish law views legal doubt as a problem to be resolved. Thus, the Talmud relates that immediately before his death, Moses asked his successor Joshua to inquire about his doubts in matters of Jewish law so that Moses could clarify them before he passed.[67] Joshua responded confidently—perhaps even indignantly—that he had been a model student and had no unresolved doubts about the law. Immediately, the Talmud says, Joshua forgot three hundred points of Jewish law and became uncertain about seven hundred other issues. This led the people to rise up and attempt to depose Joshua, who retained power only by distracting the people by commencing the war for the conquest of Canaan. Legal certainty is thus presented as the ideal state and legal doubt is framed as a serious problem.[68] Moses seeks to insure that lingering legal doubts are clarified with the certainty offered by his own prophetic link to the Divine lawgiver; Joshua takes affront at the insinuation that he would have allowed his own doubts about the law to linger; and the people regard Joshua's subsequent loss of certainty in matters of Jewish law as a mortal defect in his ability to lead.

In the Torah's discussion of the judicial resolution of legal doubts, legal uncertainty manifests as a bar to Jews' proper observance of the law.[69] The Torah's legal actor is immobilized by uncertainty about the correct, legal-prescribed course of action. Faced with this inability to do as the law requires, the Jewish legal actor is commanded to seek clarification of their doubts from the priests and judges. Ultimately, that judicial determination that replaces legal doubt with certainty and thereby precipitates an opportunity and duty to act in accordance with the freshly clarified law. In Jewish tradition, following the law by fulfilling legal duties and abstaining from legal prohibitions is a religious good while contravening the demands of the *halakhah* is a religious ill. Either course of conduct is believed to have personal, communal, societal, global, and even cosmic implications. As Maimonides teaches: "If a person's sins exceed their merits, they will immediately die . . . Similarly, a country whose sins are great will be immediately destroyed . . . Likewise, regarding the entire world, if peoples' sins outnumber their proper actions, it would immediately be obliterated."[70] Correctly determining and observing the law matters. Yet, uncertainty about what Jewish law requires makes obeying the *halakhah* difficult, if not impossible. Even the most well-intentioned individuals are prone to regular—albeit perhaps unintended—legal infractions if they do not know and cannot determine with certainty what the law demands of them.

As noted earlier, legal doubt is closely related to legal disagreement. Interpretative and juridical disputes tend to persist where doubts as to the correct legal norm or result create space for a range of reasonably justifiable legal alternatives, and the ongoing recognition of competing legal viewpoints all perceived as legitimate and viable modes of Jewish observance reinforces uncertainty about which position reflects the correct *halakhic* standard.[71] Disagreement, in turn, is associated with at least two jurisprudential problems in classical rabbinic sources. The Talmud expresses disapproval for the persistence of legal disputes, which it characterizes as a violation of a biblical injunction against the Jewish community splitting itself into distinct groups or sects.[72] Upon issuing this reproach, however, the Talmud proceeds to limit this condemnation of legal disagreement. It concludes that the prohibition on sectarianism applies specifically to scenarios in which competing views and modes of legal practice persist contentiously within a single group or community; it does not forbid the creation of distinct communities that each maintain their own unique *halakhic* traditions and practices.[73] The basic idea remains, however: in at least some contexts, the disagreement born of legal doubt, and the *halakhic* uncertainty engendered by juridical disputes pose significant concerns for Jewish law.[74]

Later authorities offer at least two explanations for the rabbis' wariness about sectarianism stemming from alternative understandings of Jewish law. Maimonides suggests that the Talmud seeks to restrict legal disagreement because it is concerned that persistent legal disputes will produce contentiousness and conflict within the Jewish community.[75] Rashi raises a different concern: legal disputes are problematic because they risk the singular "Torah appearing to be two Torahs."[76] Rashi's explanation hearkens to another Talmudic passage that provides a rabbinic narrative of the origins of *halakhic* dispute.[77] There, the Talmud comments with apparent chagrin at how the once integrous system of Jewish law in which collective acceptance of majoritarian methods for resolving *halakhic* disagreement insured the unity of Jewish law ultimately devolved into a fragmented legal universe of persistently contending *halakhic* opinions wherein opposing parties could not even settle on mutually agreeable means for adjudicating their juristic disputes. As the Talmud notes elsewhere, such entrenched *halakhic* disagreement can lead to the delegitimization of Jewish law in the eyes of at least some of its students and practitioners:

> "Those that are composed in collections" [Ecclesiastes 12:11]: This is a reference to the scholars who sit in many groups and engage in Torah study. These rule something ritually impure and those rule that it is pure; these prohibit and those permit it; these hold something invalid and those hold it valid. One might say: "If so, how can I study the Torah?"[78]

Commentators have explained the question anticipated by the Talmud as a challenge to the integrity and legitimacy of Jewish law. Disagreement that both stems from and precipitates further legal uncertainty raises the possibility that "there is no objectivity in the Torah's laws,"[79] that "Jewish law is more a rule of men than a rule of law."[80]

The "Who" of Clarifying Legal Doubts

If legal doubt poses serious practical and jurisprudential problems, how does Jewish law reduce such uncertainty? One method is institutional. As the aforementioned biblical passage addressing the emergence of legal doubts prescribes, uncertainty is rectified by referring perplexing legal questions to official legal decision makers—the "priests and judge." The rabbinic sources have long understood this biblical passage as referring to and authorizing the system of local and regional courts presided over by the Sanhedrin, the high legislative court that met in Jerusalem during the Second Temple period.

Following the Talmud,[81] Maimonides explicated the essential role of the courts in resolving legal uncertainty:

> If a Jew became uncertain about any legal issue, he would consult the local court. If the judges knew, they told him; if not, he and the judges or their agents went up to Jerusalem where they submitted the question to the court situated at the entrance of the Temple Mount. If the judges knew, they told them; if not, they all proceeded to the court at the entrance of the Temple courtyard. If the judges knew, they told them; if not, they all went to the High Court that convened in the Chamber of Hewn Stone and put the question to the judges. If the law about which they were all uncertain was known to the High Court, either through tradition or through principles of biblical interpretation, they stated it immediately. If the judges of the High Court were also uncertain about issue, however, they debated the question until they reached unanimous agreement or passed the measure by vote, following the majority opinion, and told all the questioners: "This is the law."[82]

The Sanhedrin and lower courts' roles in clarifying legal doubts was reinforced by Jewish law rules of judicial procedure.[83] These procedures encouraged vigorous debate between judges on uncertain legal questions, but ultimately each issue was put to a majority vote, and once determined, all members of the court were expected to sign on to the decision.[84] Public dissent from the court's ruling by minority judges was prohibited,[85] and rabbinic scholars who perpetuated dispute and uncertainty about the matter by subsequently issuing contrary rulings on the same question were subject to severe punishment for contempt.[86]

The institutional doubt-clarifying function of the Sanhedrin and the court system it oversaw was undermined when this system collapsed during extended disruption of Jewish political and religious life in the early centuries of the Common Era. The Sanhedrin's jurisdiction—and thus its ability to definitively resolve legal doubts—was substantially constrained in the decades preceding the destruction of the Second Temple in 70 CE, after which the High Court ceased regular functioning altogether. Moreover, by the early Talmudic period, it became impossible to confer *semikha*, the formal rabbinic ordination that authorized rabbinic scholars to assume the role of "the judge that will be in those days." Without a Sanhedrin to decisively clarify *halakhic* uncertainties, and without formally ordained rabbis whose rulings could provide reliable resolutions of legal doubts, one of the more important means of preventing *safek* in Jewish law was compromised. As Maimonides explained: "When, the High Court ceased to exist, legal disputes increased: one scholar would declare a thing impure and give a reason for his conclusion and another scholar would rule it pure and give a reason for his conclusion; one would forbid, while the other would permit."[87]

The demise of the Sanhedrin and formally ordained rabbis did not mean that legal doubts could no longer be clarified. The Talmud construes the Torah's reference to "the judge that will be in those days" as authorizing the competent Jewish law scholars of every generation—even in eras lacking a properly constituted Sanhedrin—to undertake the critical law-clarifying task that in earlier times might have been fulfilled by the High Court.[88] In the absence of a centralized supreme judicial authority, however, the religious and legal power to clarify *halakhic* doubts became diffuse. "Every court is to its city like the High Court was for all Jewry."[89] Rabbinic courts or officially appointed rabbis could thus decisively resolve legal doubts and their decisions were considered authoritative and binding—but only as to their own local jurisdictions. As Maimonides notes, this decentralization of authority to clarify the *halakhah* precipitated legal uncertainty due to the proliferation of entrenched, normatively legitimate, and widely divergent local determinations on matters of Jewish law:

> Each court . . . issued decrees, enacted ordinances, and established customs for the people of that country—or those of several countries. These practices, however, were not accepted throughout the Jewish people . . . Since each court was independent, and since the Sanhedrin had been defunct for many years . . . people in one country could not be compelled to follow the practices of another country, nor is one court required to accept norms decreed by another court in its own locale. . . . Now, we are beset by any difficulties; everyone is pressured, the wisdom of our Sages has been lost, and the understanding of our wise men has been obscured. Therefore, [the law] . . . has become difficult to grasp, and only a select few comprehend these matters correctly.[90]

For Maimonides and others, the confusion and legal doubt engendered by the absence of centralized judicial power to say what the law demanded a different approach to addressing the problem of *halakhic* uncertainty. Thus, Maimonides and many important rabbinic figures that followed him undertook to codify, synthesize, and restate the vast, multivocal, discordant, and often opaque and uncertain texts and traditions of Jewish law. As Maimonides explained, in response to the doubts and confusion that had proliferated about the correct legal understanding of the Talmud and the many divergent views of post-Talmudic scholars "I . . . contemplated all these texts and wrote that which derives from all these texts regarding the forbidden and the permitted, the impure and the pure, and the rest of the Torah's laws, all in clear and concise terms, so that the entire law could be organized in each person's mouth without questions or objections."[91] If the Sanhedrin was no longer available to resolve legal doubts by adjudicating issues about which the law was uncertain or subject to dispute, Maimonides would step into the breech. In writing a legal code of "clear-cut legal statements," Maimonides meant to reduce doubts about the law both by determining and declaring for others the correct rules of law contained within the often-unclear text of the Talmud and by providing a single standard of Jewish legal practice that the many independent courts and rabbinic scholars scattered throughout the Diaspora could endorse and prescribe.

In subsequent centuries, this codification narrative became a recurring theme in Jewish legal sources. Thus, Rabbi Jacob ben Asher introduced his early fourteenth-century restatement of Jewish law, *Arba'ah Turim*, by noting that because of "our lengthy exile . . . the springs of our wisdom have become stopped up, and our reasoning has become confused. Legal disagreement has proliferated, and there the variety of legal viewpoints has multiplied. As a result, there is no longer any clear law."[92] Rabbi Yosef Karo introduced his *Beit Yosef* commentary on the *Arba'ah Turim*, which sought to collect and synthesize Talmudic and later rabbinic sources, in a similar vein:

> Blessed is God . . . who, out of His abundant love . . . bequeathed to us through Moses righteous laws, commandments, and teachings for our benefit so that we might go in His ways and find favor in His eyes. But behold, every long are the days . . . that we have been going through exile. . . . And the hand of Torah and its students has been lost to us; for the Torah has not become like two Torahs, but like Torahs without number due to number of books we find attempting to clarify its laws. And though the authors' intentions were to enlighten our darkness, the light that we have enjoyed from them has precipitated great confusion and doubt, since every person writes their own book and repeats what has been written before, or records the law contrary to what others have written.[93]

Likewise, Rabbi Karo prefaced his more succinct code of Jewish law by noting that its purpose was to distill the sources collected and discussed in his *Beit Yosef* into a set of brief rule-statements so that "God's perfectly whole Torah will be readily fluent in the mouth of every Jew, and so that when one asks a scholar a legal question, he won't be confused."[94] Similar expressions can be found in numerous other works in which rabbinic scholars have bemoaned the confusion and uncertainty that has resulted from a long period of harsh exile without any centralized legal institutions and authority, have noted that this produced myriad alternative legal rulings and texts authored by rabbis in different regions hailing from different intellectual and religious traditions, and affirmed the need to clarify the great doubts about the *halakhah* by providing a compelling and decisive account of the law, once and for all.[95]

Many rabbinic scholars opposed attempts to clarify *safek* by simplifying of Jewish law through codification.[96] In some cases, this opposition to codification was rooted in jurisprudential principle. As explained below, some *halakhic* authorities maintained that doubt and uncertainty in Jewish law served valuable legal and religious purposes.[97] Others, however, merely pointed out that every attempt to clarify Jewish law through codification merely begot further uncertainty, ultimately undermining its own attempt to reduce *halakhic* doubt.[98] The seventeenth-century scholar, Rabbi Shlomo Luria, for example, argued that even if the original text of the Torah had attempted to fully clarify matters about which doubts and disagreements arose, "it is entirely unavoidable that even that initial formulation would be free of doubts . . . such that there would be no need for an additional clarification, and so on without end. . . . [I]t is utterly impossible to explicate and elucidate all doubts surrounding a matter of the law without this producing disagreement [and thereby contributing to even more uncertainty]."[99]

The "How" of Clarifying Legal Doubts: Two Models

While the Torah's central discussion of legal uncertainty clarifies *who* should provide greater certainty by resolving legal doubts, it does not explicate *how* the "priests and the judge" should go about determining the law in the face of such uncertainties. The Sanhedrin, the ordained rabbi, or the author of a *halakhic* code might be the source from which "the law goes out to all of Israel,"[100] but this does not account for how members of the Sanhedrin, ordained rabbis, or code-writers might go about determining for themselves the right legal rules or conclusions in the face of *halakhic* doubt engendered by vague and contradictory sources and widespread interpretive disagreement.

Rabbinic jurisprudence admits of at least two distinct schools of thought on this important question of judicial methodology. According to one approach, instances of legal *safek* are ideally addressed analytically. When faced with uncertainty about the correct answer to a legal question, a rabbinic scholar should research the issue; interpret, analyze, and reconcile primary and secondary sources of Jewish law including Talmudic texts, commentaries, codes, and responsa; reach a clear and confident understanding of the meaning and import of relevant *halakhic* rules and doctrines; and apply finally those standards to the case or question at hand to yield a ruling or legal-religious guidance. Put differently, this school of thought maintains that the proper method for resolving doubt is for a legal decision maker to study the issue until the uncertainty is clarified in their own mind and they become confident in their determination of the correct *halakhic* outcome. This approach is succinctly prescribed by Rabbi Yosef Karo's instructions to rabbinic court judges: "The judge must be deliberative in their rulings so that they do not determine this issue until the analysis ferments in their own mind and they discuss and debate the matter until it becomes as clear as the sun."[101]

This method of resolving doubts in Jewish law is exemplified by the jurisprudence of Rabbi Yechiel Michel Epstein, one of the most prominent and influential rabbinic scholars of the nineteenth and early twentieth centuries. Epstein's primary legacy is the *Arukh Ha-Shulhan*, a monumentally comprehensive and original restatement of Jewish law.[102] Like other authors of *halakhic* codes, Epstein observed that the goal of his work was to clarify the many doubts and resolve the countless disagreements that had persisted and emerged in the law since the last major effort to synthesize the mass of *halakhic* literature in Rabbi Yosef Karo's sixteenth-century code.[103] To achieve this objective, Epstein studied each legal issue from its biblical sources through relevant Talmudic discourses, post-Talmudic codes and commentaries, and responsa literature. In doing so, he sought first and foremost to arrive at his own understanding of the legal implications of Talmudic discussions; to independently assess the persuasiveness of other scholar's own conclusions on the matter; and to apply his determination of the relevant *halakhic* norms balanced against other religious and pragmatic considerations to yield practical legal guidance that based on his own analysis was legally correct.[104] In sum, when faced with uncertainty about the law, whether due to inherent ambiguities in the primary sources or the presentation of entrenched rabbinic disagreement on the issue, Rabbi Epstein's method for clarifying *halakhic* doubts was to first study the matter himself until he reached a satisfactorily clear understanding of the law based on his interpretation and analysis of primary sources of Jewish law. This method was also adopted by Rabbi Moshe Feinstein, the preeminent authority on Jewish law in twentieth-century America. In his view, while the right *halakhic* norm may be in doubt, each rabbinic scholar is obliged to "to toil and investigate in order to clarify the law through the Talmud and other authorities in accordance with his abilities," and once a competent scholar clarified the law in their own mind, "that is how they should rule."[105]

A second school of thought sought to clarify uncertainties by relying on formalistic rules of adjudication that aim to reduce the range of legitimate legal alternatives and ultimately determine a single *halakhic* outcome in each case. Rabbinic jurisprudence contains numerous principles that purport to govern the correct legal interpretation of the Mishnah and Talmud.[106] Such rules prescribe how to resolve contradictory rule-statements in the Mishnah, establish fixed preferences for which Talmudic Sages' opinions should be treated as normative, and guide the derivation of legal norms from meandering and often not explicitly conclusive Talmudic discussions. Similar rules abound for determining the correct *halakhic* import of post-Talmudic texts, such as codes and responsa.[107] Secondary rules also establish hierarchies of authority among rabbinic scholars and texts, thereby resolving doubts about the correct legal standard on issues about which those authorities disagree.[108] The *halakhah* also includes many rules of adjudication that govern the resolution of litigious disputes, such as the principle that doubts in criminal cases must be resolved in favor of defendants,[109] and the rule imposing the burden of legal and factual proof on civil plaintiffs,[110] which affords civil defendants the right to claim the protection of any reasonably justifiable *halakhic* opinion that would absolve them of liability.[111] Perhaps most saliently, the Talmud construes a biblical verse to establish the principle of majority rule in cases of legal doubt in the face of rabbinic disagreement.[112]

This approach is well illustrated by the juristic methods of Rabbi Yosef Karo who relied heavily on secondary rules of decision in reaching the legal determinations he ultimately recorded as the authoritative rule of law in his sixteenth-century code, *Shulhan Arukh*. Karo noted that in his own time, Jewish law had become terribly uncertain due to the myriad of scattered and often indeterminate Talmudic sources and wide range of later rabbinic interpretations and opinions that bore on virtually every issue.[113] He thus set out to "determine the law by selecting from among the many opinions . . . so that there will be one Torah and one law."[114] Karo acknowledged, however, that any attempt on his part to determine the correct rules of law analytically would likely be countered by others who would offer analytic arguments in support of alternative rulings.[115] This would, of course, undermine his effort to reduce *halakhic* uncertainty and provide Jews with clear instructions for proper religious and legal observance. He therefore decided to select three prominent authorities—Maimonides, Rabbi Yitzchak Alfasi, and Rabbi Asher ben Yehiel—and to determine the law on each issue in accordance with the view of the majority of those scholars.[116] In this way, by declining to provide a basis for his rulings in the analytic interpretation of *halakhic* sources, Karo hoped to avoid having his legal reasoning and textual interpretations subjected to analytic critique. As Nachmanides notes centuries earlier, in jurisprudence "there are no absolute proofs nor typically are there any absolute refutations, for this wisdom is not susceptible to dispositive proofs as in the mathematical or physical sciences."[117] By endorsing the view of two of three highly prominent *halakhic* authorities rather than prescribing legal rules determined through his own interpretation and analysis, Rabbi Karo hoped to avoid his rulings becoming mired in ultimately unresolvable legal arguments, which would only add to and not reduce the uncertainty of Jewish law.

Rabbi Karo's approach is notable for its candidly acknowledging that it does not seek to determine the analytically correct rule of law for each case. Instead, it relies on a secondary rule of decision—that the law follows the view of the majority of three select authorities—that provides a clarity in the face of legal ambiguity and disagreement but does not necessarily always settle on the analytically right *halakhic* standard. From an analytic perspective, there is no particular reason to think that the majority view of these three scholars or the *halakhic* norm indicated by any other formal secondary rule is necessarily correct. Rules like this are designed to produce an answer, which may be relied upon for practical application but not necessarily for *the right* answer.[118] Thus, this second school of thought seems to parallel Justice Louis Brandeis's famous dictum: "it is sometimes more important that the applicable rule of law be settles than that it be settled right."[119] By relying on secondary rules of decision, the *halakhic* methodology exemplified by Rabbi Karo focuses less on determining which legal standard is *right* and more on making *a* standard clear and determinate.

This reliance on secondary rules of decision rather than the exhaustive interpretation and analysis of primary sources to resolve *halakhic* doubts was criticized by opponents of Rabbi Karo's project.[120] Rabbi Shlomo Luria, for example, declared that Karo "made arbitrary and subjective compromises in his rulings . . . with regard to his following two out of the three great scholars while paying no attention to other authorities."[121] Contrary to this approach, Luria affirmed: "I will not mechanically follow one authority over others . . . instead, [my understanding of] the Talmud will determine [my resolution of legal questions]."[122] Rabbi Moshe Isserles, while not opposed to the codification of Jewish law in principle,[123] also took issue with Rabbi Karo's approach to determining the law on the basis of the principle of majority rule. Isserles argued that Karo's decision to elevate the status of his three preferred authorities over all others, and his commitment to ruling in accordance with the view of the majority of those authorities was jurisprudentially unsound and would not necessarily produce correct *halakhic* outcomes.[124] Instead, Isserles argued, the correct rules of law must be determined on the basis of each scholar's own analysis and resultant understanding of the breadth and depth of *halakhic* texts and traditions.[125]

Stringency and Leniency: Doubt Resolution and Beyond

Doubt-resolving secondary rules are not the exclusive province of rabbinic authorities, like Rabbi Karo, who preferred a formalistic rather than analytic approach to clarifying *halakhic* uncertainty. While proponents of the first school of thought preferred to resolve legal doubts analytically, not every interpretative question or rabbinic dispute could be settled to the intellectual satisfaction of every scholar. Sometimes alternative legal positions are well entrenched in the dueling rulings of especially prominent authorities, leading even rabbinic scholars inclined toward analytic method of resolving *halakhic* uncertainties to hesitate before, in rabbinic parlance, "inserting their heads between the mighty mountains,"[126] by presuming to decide which view is correct or by offering their own ruling.[127] Other times, the Talmud and other primary sources of Jewish law may be truly and irresolvably indeterminate such that even after one has exhausted all the interpretative and constructive tools in their *halakhic* toolbox, they remain unsure about the right legal standard. This last scenario is not uncommon. The Talmud is a discursive work that only rarely explicitly declares which recorded opinion is correct, and *halakhic* sources characterize large swaths of Jewish law as "inquiries left unanswered" by the Talmud.[128] In such cases, where analytic methods for resolving legal uncertainties run out, rabbinic scholars of all jurisprudential schools of thought fall back on secondary rules to reach singular, practical conclusions about what the *halakhah* requires.

One particularly prominent method of addressing the sort of legal uncertainty that defies analytic resolution is for rabbinic scholars to adjust their *halakhic* guidance in ways that hedge against the risk of committing legal infractions in doubtful cases. When the *halakhic* permissibility of a certain act is uncertain, one might decide to proceed stringently and not engage in the legally doubtful conduct. Similarly, in cases where particular behavior may be legally required, one might hedge against uncertainty by being careful to fulfill the doubtful obligation, at least until it becomes clear that the conduct at issue is indeed merely permissive. *Humrah*, or "stringency"—the tendency to avoid legal uncertainty by avoiding possibly prohibited acts and fulfilling doubtful obligations—is salient feature of rabbinic jurisprudence. The opposite disposition—to treat uncertain prohibitions or duties as permissive acts—is known as *kulah*, or leniency, and is a similarly important aspect of practical *halakhic* decision-making.

At a high level of abstraction, Jewish law's use of *kulah and humrah* to control for legal uncertainty is summed up by one of the most prominent and explicitly doubt-clarifying secondary rules of decision in rabbinic jurisprudence: "Doubts regarding biblical law are resolved stringently, and doubts regarding rabbinic law are resolved leniently."[129] A complete study of the source, applicability, and exceptions to this principle is far beyond the scope of this chapter.[130] However, a brief overview of the doctrine's internal logic and mechanics will be helpful in understanding some of the ways in which rabbinic authorities have utilized jurisprudences of stringency and leniency to manage practical *halakhic* observance, as well as Jewish law's broader religious aspirations in the face of legal uncertainty.

The principle is rooted in Jewish law's basic distinction between biblical and rabbinic laws. Biblical norms—rules and principles legislated in the Torah itself—carry direct Divine authority. Violating biblical duties or restrictions are thus not merely socially contingent or subjective wrongs; they are objectively wrong behaviors that in rabbinic thought harm the sinner, undermine society, and negatively impact the universe on metaphysical, moral, and ethical levels.[131] The stakes are thus high when dealing with legal uncertainties that carry the risk of erroneously transgressing biblical laws. Such serious risk, rabbinic jurisprudence prescribes, must be hedged against by adopting a stringent position in cases of uncertainty as to biblical norms. Rabbinic laws, by contrast, are new legal duties and prohibitions formally legislated by the rabbis of the Sanhedrin. These laws include both entirely new religious observances, such as the celebration of the holiday of Hanukkah;[132] social and economic regulations, such as the rabbinic rule permitting thieves to repay that value of stolen property rather than the property itself in cases were doing the latter would cause them to incur a substantial loss and thereby discourage correcting past wrongs;[133] and a wide array of rules known as "fences around the Torah," which impose many new obligations and prohibitions that go beyond the demands of biblical law, but which the rabbis, based on experience, determined would help Jews avoid inadvertent violations of actual Torah norms.[134] While *halakhic* jurisprudence maintains that Jews are biblically obligated to obey rabbinic laws,[135] it nevertheless acknowledges that in certain respects violations of rabbinic norms are less grave than biblical offenses.[136] Since even if one were to violate a rabbinic rule, they would not thereby transgress God's substantive command, the *halakhah* treats uncertainties regarding rabbinic law leniently.[137]

Notably, the extent to which this principle successfully resolves *halakhic* doubts is itself uncertain. Rabbinic authorities have noted, for instance, that this rule of decision raises yet more legal questions that cannot be answered with absolute clarity and tend to engender further legal disagreement. Prescribing that doubts in biblical law should be resolved strictly and doubts in rabbinic law should be resolved leniently merely begs the question: Which *halakhic* norms are biblical, and which are rabbinic? In some cases, this question is easily answered: the laws of Hannukah, a rabbinically legislated holiday are unambiguously rabbinic,[138] and the consumption of leavened foods during Passover is clearly prohibited by the Torah.[139] In many other instances, however, whether a legal question implicates biblical or rabbinic norms is uncertain. Consider contemporary rabbinic discussions about the use of electronic devices on the Sabbath. Some authorities have concluded that completing an electrical circuit and thereby causing a device to function is a legally analogous to "building," which on the Sabbath is a biblically prohibited activity. Others, however, argue that using electronic devices merely violates rabbinic strictures against engaging in "weekday activities" during the Sabbath. There is no dispositive way of classifying whether the use of electronic devices implicates biblical or rabbinic laws, and thus rabbis disagree about how to address a range of issues related to electricity use on the Sabbath.[140]

Beyond the difficulties in categorizing *halakhic* rules as biblical or rabbinic, rabbinic jurisprudence also admits of substantial disagreement over the precise scope and application of this doubt-resolving decisional principle. First, like all good rules, this one is not absolute. The Talmud adopts stringent legal rules in several cases involving doubts of rabbinic law, typically due to the high stakes of the *halakhic* issues at play.[141] Some later authorities have used these examples to justify a tendency toward *humrah* on various issues they have views as of substantial importance.[142] Whether any particular issue of rabbinic law warrants such stringency, however, is often a subjective assessment about which *halakhic* authorities disagree. Rabbinic authorities also disagree about whether the rule that doubts regarding rabbinic laws should be resolved leniently applies only in cases where a stringent ruling would entail some cost, or if the principle applies even where there is no apparent advantage to adopting a lenient standard.[143]

Halakhic authorities also disagree about how this principle of Jewish law decision-making interacts with other doubt resolving rules. As noted earlier, rabbinic jurisprudence maintains that the law accords with the view of the majority of scholars. But which principle—majority rule or the stringency in biblical law and lenity in rabbinic law—takes precedence? If a majority of rabbinic scholars reach a more stringent conclusion on a matter of rabbinic law, or a more lenient determination on a question of biblical law, how should one proceed? Maimonides maintained that the imperative to rule stringently/leniently in matters of biblical/rabbinic law preempts the relative weight of rabbinic majorities and minorities.[144] Others disagreed, however, and limited reliance of *kulah* and *humrah* to resolve doubts about biblical and rabbinic law to cases in which there is no majoritarian consensus among *halakhic* authorities about the right legal standard.[145]

Stringency and Leniency beyond Uncertainty

In practice, the adoption of more strict or more lenient constructions of Jewish law has much broader applications beyond the practical hedging against legal uncertainty. *Humrah* is also viewed as an expression of religious piety and legal punctiliousness that may operate even where the correct *halakhic* standard is relatively certain. The rabbis' legislation of protective "fences" around biblical norms is one form of such supererogatory religious observance. Thus, for example, while the Torah prohibits only the consumption of mixtures of livestock meat and dairy, the Talmudic rabbis prescribed that mixtures of poultry meat and dairy would be similarly forbidden because people may otherwise fail to draw the distinction between these two kinds of meat and treat both as permitted owing to the similarities in how Jewish law treats poultry and livestock meat, and the association of the two in general culinary ideation.[146] Similarly, the rabbis forbade moving certain kinds of objects on the Sabbath—for example, a pen—to help Jews avoid inadvertently performing biblically proscribed acts—in this case, writing—while handling such items on the Sabbath.[147]

A related use of *humrah* in Jewish law decision-making emphasizes legal stringency as a means of preserving the integrity of *halakhic* observance and religious commitment in general.[148] For instance, the rulings of Rabbi Yisrael Meir Kagan's *Mishnah Berurah*, published at the turn of the twentieth century when Eastern European Jews were abandoning traditional observance in large numbers, have been characterized as exhibiting a tendency toward *humrah* because the author "sought to strengthen and regulate the spiritual boundaries of the Orthodox Jew."[149] Perhaps the most famous proponent of this use of *humrah* was Rabbi Moses Sofer, who noted that in his own time, in order to shore up the many breeches of religious observance then prevalent, "it is proper to build up the wall and create fences around the Torah—to be more stringent and not to add leniencies."[150] On this view, strict rulings—even in cases where the law unambiguously allows for more permissive determinations—can help solidify commitments to *halakhic* observance by imposing bright-line rules that reduce Jews' exposure to experiences that while technically permitted may be viewed as a slippery-slope to genuine religious offenses. Indeed, as some observers have critically noted, the "slippery-slope argument" is a commonly invoked justification for stringent rulings in contemporary rabbinic jurisprudence.[151] Thus, Rabbi Moshe Feinstein, a preeminent *halakhic* authority of the second half of the twentieth century ruled that women should not wear *tzitzit*, a fringed ritual garment traditionally worn only by men. While Jewish law had long maintained that women are not obligated to wear *tzitzit*, there is unambiguously no real *halakhic* bar on their doing so. Nevertheless, Rabbi Feinstein ruled against the practice because he perceived it as a manifestation of an egalitarian impulse that would eventually produce actual violations of some of Judaism's gendered laws.[152]

Humrah can also express an awareness and sensitivity to the broader moral and ethical values that undergird the specific rules of *halakhah*—a means of helping one not miss the forest for the trees. As Nachmanides explained, the Torah's command, "You shall be sanctified,"[153] instructs against the possibility that "a hedonistic person will find space within the law to be steeped [in sensuous pleasures] . . . and thereby become a degenerate with the 'permission' of the Torah. Therefore, this verse . . . commands in a general way that we should avoid excesses of even those things that are technically permissible."[154] Here, Nachmanides refers to the value of embracing behavioral norms that are more stringent than required by the *halakhah* even—and perhaps especially—when the legal standard is quite clear.[155] For Nachmanides and others, this is one way in which Jews might cultivate a religious ethic and spiritual life that by definition exists only beyond the letter of the law. The Talmud criticizes those that "establish their normative conduct on the law of the Torah and do not go beyond the strict line of the law."[156] *Humrah*—doing that which the law does not require, but which the broader ethos of the law suggest is proper, and avoiding even that which the law does not prohibit, but of which values embedded in the law seem to disapprove—is one way of avoiding that overly legalistic pitfall.

In a similar vein, some scholars have viewed *humrah*—specifically in cases where questions about the right rule of law have been raised, and even where those questions have been resolved through ordinary decision-making processes—as illustrative of one's pious respect for law. Thus, Rabbi Asher ben Yehiel explained that the Talmud records several male rabbis adopting a stricter standard of behavior when interacting with women than the normative *halakhah* required simply as a matter of personal religious stricture. "They were stringent with themselves; one that is stringent shall merit to receive blessings."[157] This idea is elaborated on by Rabbi Eliyahu de Vidas:

> [W]ith respect to food, the Torah . . . discussed that which is permitted and prohibited, and it concludes: "You shall be holy; do not defile your souls" [Leviticus 11:420. The *Zohar* explains that [according to the mystical tradition] . . . one that eats forbidden foods demonstrates thereby that they have no interest is attaining sanctity . . . Therefore, it is proper for a person to be strict with themselves in matters of food, and to eat only that which has no aspect of being forbidden in it at all. The prophet Ezekiel lauded himself for not eating the meat of an animal about which any questions about its legal permissibility were raised—even if a scholar ultimately ruled the meat was permitted—because a doubt about the matter had already been raised . . . There are very many things that are subject to debate among the scholars of Jewish law; this oner prohibits and that one permits. Ezekiel surely would not have eaten such food; he would have considered it absolutely prohibited.[158]

This sort of *humrah* does not attempt to hedge against legal doubt or prevent any actual legal violations. Instead, it serves a personal spiritual function. "The *mahamir* [one that adopts a legally stringent mode of behavior] . . . feels a stronger sense of personal religious identity as a result of his observances. He has gone beyond the call of duty . . . and therefore feels a true and sincere sense of religious accomplishment."[159]

Humrah is not without its drawbacks, however. While the principle that doubts about matters of biblical law should be resolved strictly is broadly accepted, Jewish law sources advise that other uses of *humrah* should be approached judiciously. The Talmud condemns the adoption of unwarranted *halakhic* stringencies as a sort of religious hubris ("*yuharah*"),[160] which later authorities have applied to myriad supererogatory observances.[161] The tendency to rule strictly in matters of Jewish law has also been criticized as imposing unnecessary religious burdens where even the basic demands of the law are not fully observed.[162] Thus, Rabbi Dovid ibn Zimra affirmed that he did "not consider it necessary to impose legal stringencies upon the Jews . . . If only Israel would properly observe the laws that have already been imposed upon them; for when you try to grab too much, you may indeed grab nothing, and the result is that nothing is left in your hand."[163] According to Rabbi Yaakov Emden, moreover, *humrah* leads people to confuse the lines between the law and extralegal stringencies. This results in their making serious errors in their *halakhic* practices and their emphasizing the maintenance of stringencies at the expense of genuine legal duties and prohibitions.[164] Indeed, some rabbis have noted that every legal stringency entails a trade-off that can ultimately undermine other important *halakhic* imperatives. In Talmudic parlance, this is referred to as "*humrah* that is bound to bring one to *kulah*."[165] For example, the decision to observe stringencies with respect to Jewish dietary laws results in the waste of food that may indeed be legally permitted—a potential violation of the biblical injunction against waste.[166]

Like stringency, the idea of *kulah* in Jewish law remains an important jurisprudential concept even beyond its function as a mechanism for resolving legal doubts. The Talmud notes that "the power of [legal] permissiveness is greater" than that of legal restriction.[167] Some commentators have taken this dictum to mean that it generally requires more juristic gravitas and credibility to issue lenient rather than strict rulings. More commonly, however, the Talmudic teaching is understood to indicate that *halakhic* leniency offers several important benefits that make it generally preferable to reach permissive legal decisions rather than to embrace *humrah* as a guide to legal decision-making. Thus, unlike rabbis Sofer and Kagan, some Jewish law authorities have argued that legal leniency is the more appropriate and effective response to Jews' disregard for religious observance. Early twentieth-century American rabbi Chaim Hirschenson exemplified this approach. He regularly adopted lenient *halakhic* positions in order to, as he saw it, "ensure that the Torah and religion may be fortified and the hearts of Jews united with their Father in heaven."[168] In Hirschenson's time, American Jews were widely abandoning traditional observance, and in his mind this was best addressed not by rendering Jewish law more restrictive through *humrah*, but by using the force of *kulah* to adopt greater leniency wherever possible and thereby permit religiously uncommitted Jews to view *halakhah* as something they could realistically embrace.[169]

Many of Rabbi Hirschenson's colleagues took strong exception to his approach. However, less controversially, Jewish law broadly recognizes that *kulah* is an important jurisprudential value for helping ensure that *halakhic* observance does not become unreasonably difficult or impracticable through the unpredictable ups and downs of real-world living. For example, secondary principles that are used to guide *halakhic* decision-making urge the adoption of more permissive, *kulah*-oriented standards of religious conduct in "extenuating circumstances,"[170] in cases where legal questions implicate "great needs,"[171] involve "substantial losses" of property,[172] and where more lenient rulings would better respond to "the needs of the community."[173] In short, while *humrah* in the absence of legal uncertainty may at times be used to give expression to Jews' extra-*halakhic* spiritual strivings, legitimating legal leniency reflects Jewish law's competing tendency to make *halakhah* practical and not overly burdensome as it is observed through the challenges and pressures of life here on earth.

Conclusion: Legal Doubt as Solution

A discussion of legal doubt in Jewish jurisprudence would not be complete without noting an important rabbinic perspective on legal uncertainty that contrasts sharply with conventional Western legal thought. While Western jurisprudence almost invariably sees legal doubt as a substantial problem for legal predictability, consistency, and other rule of law values, important streams of rabbinic jurisprudence and Jewish thought more generally have endorsed a more doubt-positive perspective.

Jurisprudentially speaking, the pervasiveness of *safek* in Jewish law has been seen as a necessary predicate for legal process and decision-making. The *Midrash* teaches that *halakhic* uncertainty is a positive value and that absolute *halakhic* determinacy would have dire consequences: "Had the Torah been given as clear-cut norms, the world would not have a leg to stand on."[174] The Mishnah suggests that this means that uncertainty and doubt about the correct rule of law in any given case is what makes it possible "for any decision maker to stand upon their feet and rule."[175] If the *halakhah* was not always at least somewhat in doubt, rabbinic jurists would find themselves incapacitated by the debilitating worry that their rulings would incorrectly determine the true, "clear-cut" norms of Jewish law. Thus, Rabbi Shmuel ben Meir affirmed that *halakhic* scholars need not feel incapable of making legal determinations due to their uncertainty about the law and facts. Instead, Jewish law affirms that uncertainty is endemic to the system and thereby validates the notion that "a judge has only what their own eyes see and only what their own heart understands."[176] On this view, legal doubt is part of what makes legal process possible.[177]

Legal doubt is also seen as an important mechanism for insuring that Jewish law remains applicable and workable in diverse times, places, and circumstances.[178] Rabbi Moshe Shmuel Glassner observed that when it comes to the actualization of *halakhic* principles, "the changing generations—their views, circumstances, material conditions, and moral outlooks—require changes in the law."[179] Glassner's position was consistent with earlier views that Jewish law cannot be applied mechanically, but has to be understood and applied "in accordance with the needs of the time and place and issue."[180] For Glassner, flexibility in the law is facilitated in part by the prevalence of normative doubt within *halakhah*. On this view, Jewish law consists of often uncertain propositions in order to leave room for the continuous reevaluation of *halakhic* rules in light of prevailing circumstances and "to prevent specific standards from becoming fixed and permanent," which would produce "inconsistency between Torah and life."[181] In a similar vein, *halakhic* doubt produces rabbinic disagreement over the right way to resolve legal issues; such disagreement would, after all, be impossible if a single, correct standard was unambiguously clear. In *halakhic* jurisprudence, the existence of variant legal opinions serves an important purpose by providing rabbinic authorities with a range of alternative but legitimate legal standards that can be relied on when ruling on complex matters.[182]

Notes

1. *See* H. L. A. Hart, *The Concept of Law*, 2nd ed. (New York: Oxford University Press, 1994), 24–125 (describing how doubt is an inevitable by-product of both prospective rulemaking, or legislation, and retrospective rule-applying, or adjudication).

2. On doubt in American and Jewish law and jurisprudence, see generally Shlomo C. Pill, "Law-as-Engagement: A Judeo-Islamic Indeterminacy Jurisprudence for Twenty-First Century American" (SJD diss., Emory University School of Law, 2016), https://papers.ssrn.com/sol3/papers.cfm?abstract_id=3975482.
3. It is important to highlight at the outset that this chapter focuses on legal doubt in Jewish law and does not engage the ways that Jewish legal thinking has conceptualized and addressed factual doubt. As discussed briefly below, unresolved and underdetermined questions of fact are important aspects of doubt in Western law. The same is true for Jewish law. Indeed, an entire genre of Jewish legal literature is dedicated to explicating the complex details of how *halakhah* resolves factual uncertainties about the realia to which legal norms must be applied. The topic of factual doubt in Jewish law has been recently and exhaustively treated in Moshe Halbertal, *The Birth of Doubt: Confronting Uncertainty in Early Rabbinic Litera* (Providence, RI: Brown Judaic Studies, 2020). Halbertal candidly notes, however, that his work "focuses on . . . factual uncertainty" and does not explore how Jewish law addresses legal doubt. Ibid., 4. This chapter attempts to fill that gap, focusing on legal uncertainty in Jewish jurisprudence, and referring the curious reader to Halbertal's excellent work for a thorough discussion of factual doubt in *halakhah*.
4. See generally Jules L. Coleman and Brian Leiter, "Determinacy, Objectivity, and Authority," *University of Pennsylvania Law Review* 142 (December 1993): 549–637.
5. See ibid., 567.
6. See Kent Greenwalt, *Law of Objectivity* (New York: Oxford University Press, 1992), 71–73; Ludwig Wittgenstein, *Philosophical Investigations*, trans. G. E. M. Anscomb, 3rd ed. (New York: Macmillan, 1953), §203; Saul A. Kripke, *Wittgenstein on Rules and Private Language* (Cambridge, MA: Harvard University Press, 1982), 55–113; Christopher L. Kutz, "Just Disagreement: Indeterminacy and Rationality in the Rule of Law," *Yale Law Journal* 103 (January 1994): 1007–14; Coleman and Leiter, "Determinacy, Objectivity, and Authority," 567–72.
7. See Hart, *Concept of Law*, 124–36.
8. See Jan Engberg, "Statutory Texts as Instances of Language(s): Consequences and Limitations on Interpretation," *Brooklyn Journal of International Law* 29 (April 2004): 1141–43.
9. *See* Hart, *Concept of Law*, 124–25; Karl N. Llewellyn, *The Common Law Tradition: Deciding Appeals* (Boston, MA: Little, Brown, 1960), 17–18, 223, 335–36. On the challenges and possibilities of predicting judges' decisions, see generally Theodore W. Ruger et al., "The Supreme Court Forecasting Project: Legal and Political Science Approaches to predicting Supreme Court Decision-making," *Columbia Law Review* 104 (May 2004): 1155–60.
10. See United States v. Wade, 388 U.S. 218, 228 (1967); Russell D. Covey, "Suspect Evidence and Coalmine Canaries," *American Criminal Law Review* 55 (July 2018): 546–48, 547, table 2.
11. See Kutz, "Just Disagreement," 1015–17.
12. See generally Roger J. Traynor, "Fact Skepticism and the Judicial Process," *University of Pennsylvania Law Review* 106 (March 1958): 635.
13. See, e.g., James R. Maxeiner, "Legal Indeterminacy Made in America: U.S. Legal Methods and the Rule of Law," *Valparaíso University Law Review* 41 (December 2006): 519.
14. *See* Coleman and Leiter, "Determinacy, Objectivity, and Authority," 581–83.
15. *See* Peter H. Schuck, "Legal Complexity: Some Causes, Consequences, and Cures," *Duke Law Journal* 42 (October 1992): 18–20.

16. See Uri Weiss, "The Regressive Effect of Legal Uncertainty," *Journal of Dispute Resolution* 2019 (2019): 164–69.
17. *See* Anthony D'Amato, "Legal Uncertainty," *California Law Review* 71 (January 1983): 35–45 (detailing methods historically employed by Western legal systems to reduce legal uncertainty).
18. See William S. Laufer, "The Rhetoric of Innocence," *Washington Law Review* 70 (April 1995): 333–35 (describing procedural and substantive safeguards the law provides in cases involving factual doubt).
19. See generally Ronald J. Allen, "Factual Ambiguity and a Theory of Evidence," *Northwestern University Law Review* 88 (1994): 604–40.
20. See James Q. Whitman, *The Origins of Reasonable Doubt: Theological Roots of the Criminal Trial*, 2nd ed. (New Haven, CT: Yale University Press, 2016), 197–99 (outlining the reasonable doubt standard and how its purpose changed over time).
21. See In re Winship, 397 U.S. 358, 371–72 (1970) (showing something by the preponderance of the evidence requires the trier of fact "to believe that the existence of a fact is more probable than its nonexistence before [he] may find in favor of the party who has the burden to persuade the [judge] of the fact's existence") (J. Harlan, concurring).
22. See Lisa Dufraimont, "Limited Admissibility and Its Limitations," *University of British Columbia Law Review* 46 (June 2013): 244–46 (stating that "limited admissibility represents an inherent structural feature of evidence law").
23. See generally Daniel D. Blinka, "Ethical Firewalls, Limited Admissibility and Rule 703," *Fordham Law Review* 76, no. 3 (January 2007): 1239 (describing the benefits commonly ascribed to admissibility limitations).
24. See ibid.
25. See Robert N. Clinton, "A Mandatory Review of Federal Court Jurisdiction: A Guided Quest for the Original Understanding of Article III," *University of Pennsylvania Law Review* 132 (December 1983): 753–54 (describing Article III and the judicial hierarchy in American jurisprudence).
26. See ibid., 767 (outlining that several delegates at the Constitutional Convention believed that inferior federal courts would serve as a necessary check on state courts and state interference with federal authority).
27. See Frederick Schauer, "Precedent," *Stanford Law Review* 39 (February 1987): 597–98.
28. See Abner J. Mikva and Eric Lane, *Legislative Process*, 2nd ed. (Boston: Aspen, 2002), 114. But see Karl N. Llewellyn, "Remarks on the Theory of Appellate Decision and the Rules or Canons about How Statutes Are to Be Construed," *Vanderbilt Law Review* 3 (April 1950): 395–406.
29. See Herbert Wechsler, "Restatements and Legal Change: Problems of Policy in the Restatement Work of the American Law Institute," *St. Louis University Law Journal* 13 (1968): 190 (describing the purpose of the restatements of law).
30. Deut. 17:8–11.
31. For a broad overview of the causes, varieties, and responses to legal uncertainty in Jewish law, see generally Pill, "Law-as-Engagement," 128–233.
32. See Lev. 24:11–16.
33. Yaakov Albo, *Sefer Ha-Ikarim* 3:23.
34. See Dovid HaLevi Segal, *Turei Zahav* to *Shulhan Arukh* YD, 271:8; Tzvi Hirsh Eisenstadt, *Pithei Teshuvah* to *Shulhan Arukh* YD, 271:7 (s.v. *shel keinah*).

35. See Mordechai Kuber, *Crossing the Dateline*, vol. 1 (Beit Shemesh, Israel: Mosaica Press, 2020), 1–39.
36. See, e.g., John D. Loike and Moshe D. Tendler, "Gestational Surrogacy," *Hakirah* 16 (November 2013): 113–32; J. David Bleich, "Survey of Recent Halakhic Periodical Literature: Surrogate Motherhood," *Tradition* 32, no. 2 (Winter 1998): 146–67.
37. See Michael J. Broyde and Howard Jachter, "The Use of Electricity on Shabbat and Yom Tov," *Journal of Halacha and Contemporary Society* 21 (1990): 4.
38. See Lev. 24:11–16.
39. See, e.g., *Sifri*, Deut. no. 233 (providing a list of five pairs of contradictory biblical verses).
40. *See* Barry W. Holtz, *Back to the Sources: Reading Classic Jewish Texts* (New York: Summit Books, 1984), 135–36.
41. See Aryeh Liebowitz, "The Emergence and Development of Tosafot on the Talmud," *Hakirah* 15 (2013): 147 ("[T]he early Tosafists pored over the Talmud, seeking to identify . . . seeming contradictions that demanded resolution. Sometimes the contradictions between passages related to issues of a technical nature, but more often the contradictions related to fundamental Talmudic principles and placed key passages at loggerheads with one another").
42. For example, rabbinic scholars have long disagreed about the relative weights of the Babylonian and Jerusalem Talmuds. Some authorities preferring the ruling of the Babylonian Talmud in cases where they conflict with the Jerusalem Talmud. See, e.g., Simchah Assaf, *Gaonica: Gaonic Responsa and Fragments of Halachic Literature from the Geniza and Other Sources* (Jerusalem: Darom, 1933), 235; *Tosafot* to b.Berakhot 39.a (s.v. *batzar lei shi'ura*); *Tosafot* to b.Sukkah 26.b (s.v. *velo birech acharav*). Other rabbinic scholars, however, take greater cognizance of the rulings of the Jerusalem Talmud, see, e.g., Yosef Karo, *Kesef Mishneh* to *Mishneh Torah*, Hilkhot Gerushin 13:18, and some prefer it to its Babylonian counterpart, see Eliyahu ben Shlomo Zalman, *Be'ur Ha-Gra to Shulkhan Aruch* OH 546:5 (attributing this position to Maimonides). See generally Michael J. Broyde and Shlomo C. Pill, *Setting the Table: An Introduction to the Jurisprudence of Rabbi Yechiel Mikhel Epstein's Arukh Hashulhan* (Brookline, MA: Academic Studies Press, 2021), 93–95.
43. Exod. 13:16.
44. Lev. 23:40.
45. Exod. 31:13.
46. *See* b.Menahot 34.b.
47. See b.Sukkah 25.a.
48. See b.Shabbat 49.b, 70.a.
49. See, e.g., b.Sanhedrin 34.a.
50. See, e.g., b.Shabbat 88.b ("Each and every statement uttered by God can be broken down into seventy languages . . . like a hammer striking metal splits into many sparks, every statement that went forth from the mouth of God divides into seventy different senses"); *Midrash Rabbah*, Numbers 13:15 ("There are seventy facets to the Torah").
51. Nachmanides, *Perush Ha-Ramban al Ha-Torah*, Deuteronomy 17:11.
52. See Maimonides, *Moreh Nevukhim* 1:71.
53. See Yaakov Albo, *Sefer Ha-Ikarim* 3:23.
54. See ibid.
55. Shlomo Luria, *Yam Shel Shlomo* to b.Bava Kamma, introduction.
56. Ibid.

57. See, e.g., m.Sanhedrin 4:5 ("The Holy One, Blessed be He, created each person in the mold of Adam, yet no person is like their fellow").
58. b.Berakhot 58.a.
59. Luria, *Yam Shel Shlomo.* See also Shlomo Yitzhaki, *Rashi* to b.Ketubot 57.a (s.v. *ha kamashma lan*).
60. *See* Maimonides, *Mishnah Torah*, introduction.
61. See Moshe Hayyim Luzatto, *Derehk Etz Hayyim*, quoted in Hanina Ben-Menahem, Neil Hecht, and Shai Wosner, "Controversy and Dialogue in the Halakhic Sources," *Boston: Institute of Jewish Law, Boston University School of Law* 1 (1991): 100 [Hebrew]. See also Avraham Azulai, *Ba'alei Brit Avraham*, introduction, quoted in Ben-Menahem et al., "Controversy and Dialogue in the Halakhic Sources," 96–99.
62. Yisrael Salanter, *Ohr Yisrael*, no. 30.
63. See Yom Tov Isbilli, *Hiddushei Ha-Ritva* to b.Eruvin, 13.b (*s.v. eilu v'eilu*).
64. Yehudah Loew, *Be'er HaGolah*, quoted in Ben-Menahem et al., "Controversy and Dialogue in the Halakhic Sources," 69.
65. Ibid.
66. Yitzhaki, *Rashi* to b.Ketubot 57.a.
67. b.Temurah 16.a.
68. See Maimonides, *Mishnah Torah*, introduction. See generally Pill, "Law-as-Engagement," 198–202.
69. See Deut. 17:8–11.
70. Maimonides, *Mishneh Torah*, Hilkhot Teshuvah 3:2.
71. See Broyde and Pill, *Setting the Table*, 21–32.
72. See b.Yevamot 13.b.
73. See ibid., 13.b–14.a.
74. See also b.Hagigah 3b.
75. See Maimonides, *Mishnah Torah*, Hilkhot Avodat Kokhavim 12:14.
76. Shlomo Yitzhaki, *Rashi* to b.Yevamot 13.b (s.v. *lo ta'asu agudot audot*).
77. See b.Sanhedrin 88b.
78. See b.Yevamot 13.b–14.a.
79. Nissim Gerondi, *Derashot Ha-Ran*, no. 11.
80. Steven H. Resnicoff, "Autonomy in Jewish Law—In Theory and in Practice," *Journal of Law and Religion* 24, no. 2 (January 2008): 534.
81. See b.Sanhedrin 88.b.
82. Maimonides, *Mishnah Torah*, Hilkhot Maamrim 1:4.
83. See generally b.Sanhedrin 29a–32a.
84. See Yaakov Ben-Asher, *Arba'ah Turim* HM 19:1; Yechiel Michel Epstein, *Arukh Ha-Shulhan* HM 19:2 ("All the judges must sign on to the court's ruling, even a judge that dissented is obligated to sign, for the Torah commands that he nullify his view in the face of the majority's decision").
85. See b.Sanhedrin 29.a ("When the judges leave the court, a judge may not say, 'I voted to exonerate and my colleagues voted to convict, but what can I do, for my colleagues are more numerous than me'").
86. See b.Sanhedrin 86.b–87.a.
87. Maimonides, *Mishnah Torah*, Hilkhot Maamrim, 1:4.
88. See b.Rosh Hashanah 25.b.
89. See, e.g., Shlomo Ben-Aderet, Responsa *Rashbah*, 3:417; Eliyahu Mizrachi, Responsa *Mizrachi*, no. 53.

90. Maimonides, *Mishnah Torah*, introduction.
91. Ibid.
92. Yaakov Ben-Asher, *Arba'ah Turim* OH, introduction.
93. Yosef Karo, *Beit Yosef* to *Arba'ah Turim*, introduction.
94. Yosef Karo, *Shulhan Arukh* OH, introduction.
95. Broyde and Pill, *Setting the Table*, 21–32.
96. See generally Leon Wiener Dow, "Opposition to the 'Shulhan Aruch': Articulating a Common Law Conception of Halakha," *Hebraic Political Studies* 3, no.4 (Fall 2008): 352–76.
97. See *infra*.
98. See, e.g., Albo, *Sefer Ha-Ikarim*. See Pill, "Law-as-Engagement," 155–57.
99. Shlomo Luria, *Yam Shel Shlomo* to b.Bava Kamma, introduction.
100. Maimonides, *Mishnah Torah*, Hilkhot Maamrim 1:1.
101. Yosef Karo, *Shulhan Arukh* HM 10:1
102. See generally Broyde and Pill, *Setting the Table*, 33–44.
103. See Yechiel Michel Epstein, *Arukh Ha-Shulhan* HM, introduction.
104. See generally Broyde and Pill, *Setting the Table.*
105. Moshe Feinstein, Responsa *Igrot Moshe* OC, vol. 1, introduction.
106. See, e.g., Shmuel Hanagid, "Introduction to the Talmud," in *Aiding Talmud Study*, trans. Aryeh Carmel, 4th ed. (New York: Feldheim, 1980), 275–97.
107. See Pill, "Law-as-Engagement," 187–91.
108. See ibid., 186–87.
109. See generally Irene M. Rosenberg, and Yale L. Rosenberg, "Comparative American and Talmudic Criminal Law," *University of Houston Law Center* (February 2016): 11–12, https://www.law.uh.edu/rosenberg/Comparative-American-and-Talmudic-Criminal-Law.pdf.
110. See b.Bava Kamma 46.b.
111. See Loberbaum, *Netivot Ha-Mimishpat, Bi'urim* 4:3. See generally Hanina Ben-Menahem, "Doubt, Choice and Conviction: A Comparison of the Kim Li Doctrine and Probabilism," *Jewish Law Annual at Boston University, The Institute of Jewish Law* 14 (2003): 4–18.
112. See b.Sanhedrin 3.b; Maimonides, *Mishnah Torah*, Hilkhot Sanhedrin 8:1.
113. See Yosef Karo, *Beit Yosef* to *Shulhan Arukh* OC, introduction.
114. Ibid.
115. Ibid.
116. Ibid.
117. Nachmanides, *Milhemet Hashem*, Introduction.
118. See Broyde and Pill, *Setting the Table*, 126.
119. Burnet v. Coronado Oil & Gas Co., 285 U.S. 393, 406 (1932) (Brandeis, J., dissenting).
120. See Menahem Elon, *Jewish Law: History, Sources, Principles*, trans. Bernard Aurbach and Melvin J. Sykes (Philadelphia, PA: Jewish Publication Society of America, 1994), 1369–70.
121. Shlomo Luria, *Yam Shel Shlomo* to b.Hullin, second introduction.
122. Ibid.
123. See Elon, *Jewish Law*, 1349.
124. See Moshe Isserles, *Darkhei Moshe* to *Arba'ah Turim* OC, introduction.
125. See Elon, *Jewish Law*, 1360–65.
126. See, e.g., Shlomo Ben-Aderet, Responsa *Rashbah*, 4:152; Yaakov Ben-Asher, *Arba'ah Turim* EH 154:1; Shabtai Ha-Kohen, *Siftei Kohen* to *Shulhan Arukh* HM 70:16; Yair

Bachrach, Responsa *Havot Ya'ir*, no. 210; Yaakov Chaim Sofer, *Kaf HaHayyim* to *Shulhan Arukh* OC 462:1.

127. This was indeed part of the reason Rabbi Karo resorted to determining the law based on secondary rules of decision. In the *Introduction* to his *Beit Yosef*, he reflects on his initial intent to reach independent analytic conclusions about disputed or uncertain legal issues on the basis of his own understandings of the Talmud. He abandoned this plan, however, and explained that he was ultimately unwilling to presume to claim the right to an opinion in matters of dispute between the great rabbinic jurists: "Who has the courage to lift their head between the mountains—the heights of God?" Yosef Karo, *Beit Yosef* to *Arba'ah Turim* OC, Introduction.
128. Cf. Yaakov Ben-Asher, *Arba'ah Turim* HM 25:1.
129. b.Avodah Zara 7.a; Moshe Isserles, *Remah* to *Shulhan Arukh* HM, introduction.
130. See generally Yitzchak Yosef, *Ein Yitzhak*, vol. 2, 7–280.
131. See, e.g., Gerondi, *Derashot Ha-Ran* (analogizing Torah law to medicine, and noting that violations of Torah law harm the soul just as taking the wrong medicine harms the body).
132. See b.Shabbat 21b–22a.
133. See Maimonides, *Mishnah Torah*, Hilkhot Geneivah 1:13.
134. See b.Yevamot 21b.
135. See *Sefer Hahinukh*, nos. 495–96.
136. For example, Maimonides suggests that one need not repent for accidental violations of rabbinic law, though one must do so for accidental violations of biblical law. Cf. Maimonides, *Mishnah Torah*, Hilkhot Teshuvah, 1:1.
137. See, e.g., Meir Simcha of Dvinsk, *Meshech Chokhma*, Numbers, 17:11.
138. See b.Shabbat 21.b–22.a.
139. See Exodus 12:15, 12:19, 13:3.
140. See generally Broyde and Jachter, "Use of Electricity on Shabbat and Yom Tov," 1.
141. See, e.g., b.Eruvin 35a–b.
142. See, e.g., Yaakov Yehoshua Falk, *Pinei Yehoshua* to b.Pesakhim 9.b; Landau, Yaakov ben Yehudah, *Sefer Ha-Agur*, Hilkhot Helev, §1175.
143. See Yitzchak Yosef, *Ein Yitzhak*, vol. 2, 259–60.
144. See Maimonides *Mishnah Torah*, Hilkhot Maamrim 1:5.
145. See Avraham de Boton, *Lehem Mishnah* to *Mishnah Torah*, Hilkhot Maamrim 1:5 (s.v. *oh ad shelo ha-yah ha-davar barur lahen*).
146. See b.Hullin 116.a.
147. See b.Shabbat 124a; Maimonides, *Mishnah Torah*, Hilkhot Shabbat 21:1, 24:12.
148. See Yeshayah Horowitz, *Shnei Luhot Ha-Brit*, vol. 2, "Beit Dovid, Beit Hokhmah" (arguing that additional legal stringencies become necessary over time because the world continuously provides ever more temptations that pose spiritual dangers and tend to lead Jews away from proper *halakhic* observance).
149. Simcha Fishbane, *The Method and Meaning of the Mishnah Berura* (Hoboken, NJ: KTAV, 1991), 8. But see Michael J. Broyde and Ira Bedzow, *The Codification of Jewish Law and an Introduction to the Jurisprudence of the Mishna Berura* (Boston: Academic Studies Press, 2014), 104–6 (disagreeing with Fishbane's characterization); Benjamin Brown, "Soft Stringency in the Mishnah Berurah: The Jurisprudential, Sociological and Ideological Aspects of Halakhic Formulation," *Contemporary Jewry* 27 (October 2007): 1–41 (offering a different account of the reasons for Rabbi Kagan's tendency toward *humrah*).
150. Moshe Sofer, *Hattam Sofer* OC, 1:60.

151. See, e.g., Rabbi Aharon Lichtenstein, *The Varieties of Jewish Experience* (Hoboken, NJ: KTAV, 2011), 251–52.
152. See Moshe Feinstein, Responsa *Igrot Moshe* OC 4:49.
153. Lev. 19:2.
154. Nachmanides, *Peirush Ha-Ramban al Ha-Torah,* Leviticus 19:2 (s.v. *kedoshim tihyu*).
155. Nachmanides expresses a similar view in his explanation of another of the Torah's big-principle commands, "You shall do what is good and proper in the eyes of God" (Deut. 6:18):

   This is a great principle, for it is impossible for the Torah to have prescribed what is correct in all the many interactions that people have with friends and neighbors, in all the details of peoples' business dealings, and in all the regulations that might be made for the betterment of societies and polities. Thus, after mentioning many of them . . . it goes on to say in a general manner that you should do what is good and right in each situation to the point that one even makes compromises [on their legal rights and due] and goes beyond the strict letter of the la.

   Nachmanides, *Peirush Ha-Ramban al Ha-Torah*, Deuter*onomy* 6:18 (s.v. *ve-asitah et hatov*).
156. See b.Bava Metziah 30.b.
157. Asher Ben-Yechiel, *Piskei Ha-Rosh* to b.Kiddushin 4:24.
158. Eliyahu de Vidas, *Reishit Hakhmah*, Shaar Ha-Kedushah, ch. 15.
159. Shlomo Zuckier, "Ha-Mahamir, Mah Tavo Alav?: Religious Stringencies and Their Psychological Considerations," *Kol Hamevaser* 3, no. 7 (July 2010): 11.
160. See b.Berakhot 17.b; b.Sukkah 26.b.
161. See, e.g., *Tosafot* to b.Berakhot 34.a (s.v. *melamdin*) (bowing during every blessing of the *amidah* prayer).
162. See *Avot De-Rabbi Nattan* 1:5–6 (criticizing Adam for stringently telling Eve not to touch or eat from the Tree of Knowledge, though God had only commanded that they not eat from the Tree, noting that this led Eve to assume Adam lied on both counts and to therefore eat from the Tree after seeing that no consequences followed from touching it).
163. Dovid ibn Zimra, Responsa *Radbaz* 1:163.
164. See Yaakov Emden, Responsa *Sheilat Yaavetz* 2:150.
165. b.Yevamot 30.b; b.Bava Kamma 11.a; b.Niddah 24b.
166. See Hershey H. Friedman, *The Risks and Dangers of Chumras: A Guide to the Sources* (December 2017), 27, https://ssrn.com/abstract=3092766.
167. See b.Berakhot 60.a.
168. Chaim Hirschenson, Responsa *Malki Ba-Kodesh*, vol. 4, 202.
169. See generally Ari Ackerman, "'Judging the Sinner Favorably': R. Hayyim Hirschenson on the Need for Leniency in Halakhic Decision-Making," *Modern Judaism* 22 (October 2002): 261.
170. See Shabtai Ha-Kohen, *Kitzur Be-Hanhagat Issur Ve-Hetter*, §3; Yechiel Michel Epstein, *Arukh Ha-Shulhan* YD 246:66.
171. See, e.g., Moshe Feinstein, Responsa *Igrot Moshe* OC 5:29.
172. See Moshe Walter, *The Making of a Halachic Decision* (Brooklyn, NY: Menucha, 2013), 157–59.
173. See, e.g., Landau, Yehezkel. Responsa *Noda Be-Yehuda (Kama)* OC, no. 33.
174. j.Sanhedrin 4:2.

175. m.Soferim 16:5–6.
176. Shmuel Ben-Meir, *Rashbam* to b.Bava Basra 131.a (s.v. *v'al tigmeru*).
177. Beyond *halakhic* jurisprudence, moreover, doubt—including legal doubt—plays an important positive role in some streams of Jewish religious thought. In the mystical and spiritual systems of Kabbalah and Hasidism in particular, the uncertainty and inability to fully and confidently know with which human beings apprehend and encounter the world is often viewed as the locus of religious growth and spiritual refinement. See, e.g., Shimon Gershon Rosenberg, *Shinrim al Likkutei Moharan*, vol. 1, ed. Natanel Lederberg (Jerusalem, 2012), 270–71 [Hebrew].
178. See Avi Sagi, *The Open Canon: On the Meaning of Halakhic Discourse* (New York: Bloomsbury, 2007), 153–55.
179. Moshe Shmuel Glassner, *Dor Revi'i*, 3.
180. Yehoshua Falk, *Drishah* to *Arba'ah Turim* HM 1:2 (s.v. *kol ha-dan din emet la-amito*).
181. Glassner, *Dor Revi'i*.
182. See Jeffrey I. Roth, "The Justification for Controversy Under Jewish Law," *California Law Review* 76 (March 1988): 381–83.

CHAPTER 15

FORMALISM IN JEWISH LAW

CHAIM SAIMAN

INTRODUCTION

FORMALISM has been described as "the separation of law from life."[1] Critiques that *halakhah* (Jewish law) is overly formalistic predate even the earliest of its formulations in the Mishnah. Jesus admonished the Pharisees for focusing on legal minutia while disregarding what he thought were the "weightier matters of the law, justice, and mercy, and faith."[2] His apostle Paul drew unfavorable comparisons between the dead letter of the old covenant and Jesus's ministry of Spirit.[3] Similar themes are found in the early church fathers who castigated Jews for focusing on concrete particulars rather than loftier spiritual purposes. These claims continue in the medieval period—where the tension between letter and spirit became woven into the Christian antisemitic canon—and proceed apace through the Enlightenment and into modernity.[4] These critiques are also voiced by insiders: the biblical prophets,[5] statements of the Talmudic rabbis and moralists,[6] and obtain more pointed form in the writings of Hassidic masters, Reformers, *maskilim*, and Zionists.[7]

This theological framing has parallels to the oft-discussed tension between formalism and its alternatives developed in general jurisprudence. In recent decades, scholars of Jewish law have reframed and responded to these older polemical debates in the language of modern legal theory.[8]

Results have been sharply divided. Some embrace the premise that Jewish law is highly formalistic yet reject any implication that this is problematic. These scholars cast *halakhah* as a "closed immutable system" which responds primarily to internal legal dynamics rather than to sociocultural forces.[9] The charge of *halakhic* formalism becomes a badge of honor testifying to the system's authenticity.[10] Especially as contrasted to Western or American law, these writers emphasize that while the latter is based on functional and pragmatic responses to shifting societal conventions, as God's law *halakhah* is inherently formalistic.[11] This position is intuitively maintained by many in the Orthodox community, and in legal scholarship, it obtains its most full-throated articulation in the work of Professor Rabbi J. David Bleich.[12] Yet even more moderate observers, such as Professor Benjamin Brown, affirm, "our basic intuitions [sic] is that halakhah is a particularly formalistic system, certainly as compared to modern legal approaches."[13]

An opposing group of scholars work to demonstrate that *halakhic* analysis is often functionalist and driven by substantive values and/or social considerations.[14] They maintain its reputation for formalism is predicated either on antisemitic misreading by outsiders or on pious myths told by insiders—both of which distort how *halakhah* functions in practice and prejudice its ongoing development. The most consistent expositor of this approach in the legal academy is Professor Hanina Ben-Menahem and, in a more historical register, Professor Adiel Schremer.[15] These scholars draw on the legacy of American legal realism, calling on observers to pay less attention to what rabbis *say* about *halakhah* and more to what they *do* when implementing it. Ben-Menachem rejects the claim that Talmudic law's religious orientation necessarily leads to formalism, and argues that, viewed comparatively, Talmudic law is best understood as *less* formalistic than its Western legal counterparts. Schremer draws on the analysis of American realism to argue that at least as much as *halakhic* doctrine, socioreligious values shape the contours of *halakhic* decision-making.

The gulf between these scholarly accounts carries political valence that is often replicated in popular and online discourse between conservative and liberal elements of contemporary Jewish communities. Each side claims to present a more historically and normatively accurate account of Jewish law. Moreover, as American religious and political identities become increasingly entwined, Jewish communities are connecting their *halakhic* hermeneutics with the interpretative methodologies prevailing in American law. Thus, as American Orthodoxy becomes more identified with conservative politics,[16] it began to see formalism, especially as championed by the late US Supreme Court Justice Antonin Scalia, as embodying the correct approach for both American law and *halakhah*. Scalia in turn dubbed himself the "Jewish Justice" and was a celebrated speaker at events sponsored by Agudath Israel, Chabad, and Yeshiva University. The late Justice's former classmate and frequent Supreme Court advocate Nathan Lewin wrote, "Scalia's admiration for Jews and Jewish learning explains the frequent references in his opinions to the Talmud and other Jewish sources, and the significant number of Orthodox Jewish law clerks he hired."[17]

Formalism is a protean concept that takes on different meanings based on the context of usage. This chapter aims to make sense of the diverging opinions by distinguishing between three varieties of legal formalism that are either explicitly or implicitly in play.[18] Contemporary American legal theory generally identifies two central strands of formalism. While both aim to limit the scope of the law by drawing clear lines between legal and social-political reasoning, they adopt different methods. *Modern formalism* is anchored in constraining end-line legal decision makers by allocating interpretative responsibility to other branches or institutions that are better suited to make difficult political and policy choices. Despite exceptions, comparing Jewish and American law along this axis affords the best argument to the scholars who find Jewish law *less* formalistic than its American or modern counterpart. By contrast, an older variant of *classical formalism* strives to produce a conceptually coherent legal structure that presents legal doctrines in a relational and rationalized form which can dictate the outcomes in concrete cases. This flavor of formalism is somewhat more congenial to schools of Jewish law that stressed its conceptual architecture, the Brisker school in particular. Nevertheless, it is not particularly resonant with the broad run of the rabbinic tradition, nor is it the most descriptive expression of Jewish legal formalism.

In contrast to these variants of legal formalism, this chapter introduces what I describe here as *detail-following formalism*, a variant more pervasive in Jewish law. This harkens back to Jesus's critiques of the pre-rabbinic Pharisees and is typified by a religiosity that stresses strict adherence to the multiplicity of legal forms that constitute *halakhah*. It flows from *halakhah*'s penchant for granular regulation twinned with a lingering reticence toward interpreting *halakhah* in purpose-driven terms. This formalism is backed by ritualistic, theological, and mystical concepts generally absent from modern law.[19]

As a final point of introduction, though scholarly debates over formalism and the role of values in Jewish law have gone on for many years, some have argued that it is pitched at too high a level of abstraction to yield useful insights.[20] The sheer vastness of each system makes it easy to locate examples of either highly formalistic or counterformalist reasoning. Moreover, historians of various eras have demonstrated how there are more and less formalist parts of the Mishnah; that different layers of the Talmud may express different approaches on these matters; that the center of gravity might be located differently in the Babylonian versus Jerusalem Talmuds; or even that famous pairs of *Tannaim* and *Amoraim* diverge on precisely these grounds.[21] It is even possible for the same *posek* (*halakhic* authority) to approach different areas of the law through varied jurisprudential methods. To the extent this is true of a single authority, how much more so of individuals separated by cultures and centuries.

This chapter therefore focuses less on specific decisions of *poskim* and more on the structural features and ideological commitments that—though certainly not universal—extend across a wide enough range of eras and personalities to reflect more generalizable characteristics of *halakhic* formalism.

American Legal Formalisms

The Modern Formalism of Constraining Decision Makers

Modern American formalism is a response to the somewhat anomalous role of the judiciary in the American system. Under the US Constitution, lawmaking authority lies with the political branches—Congress and the President—who draw their authority from popular elections. The judiciary stands outside this system because it is appointed rather than elected. It is further insulated from political accountability through lifetime judicial tenure. These structural features lead formalists to conclude that the judicial power should be limited and subservient to the political branches.

The impact of this strand of formalism can be seen across the American legal landscape, and arguments over the scope of the Americans with Disabilities Act (ADA) offer a straightforward example. Enacted in the pre-internet era, the statute prohibits discrimination based on physical disabilities in "places of public accommodation."[22] In early phases of the internet age, courts had to determine whether commercial websites were "public accommodations" and thus required to enable software making them accessible to blind persons.[23]

Formalists cast in the Scalian mold refused to extend the ADA mandates to the online realm, arguing that courts should limit themselves to applying the "plain meaning" of the statutory text Congress enacted. Since the text does not include websites, extending their mandate to the online space is a policy decision that should be left to the Congress rather than read into the law by the courts.

Functionalists who oppose Scalia (often called purposivists) argue that websites are a natural extension of the statute's central aims,[24] and indeed cheaper and less intrusive than many of the statute's other binding mandates.[25] They hold that legal meaning should be developed gradually by judges who carry the responsibility of situating laws into their contemporary legal and social context.[26]

Though Scalia mainly addressed public law, the rhetorical structure of this argument stretches across fields. Classical law and economics scholars maintain that contract law should be formal and limited to enforcing the plain words of the parties' agreement.[27] This contrasts with contextual regimes that encourage courts to interpret the contract via open-ended considerations of justice or fairness. Formalists find this puts too much power in the hands of judges, making the law less predictable, impeding settlement, and dampening a party's desire to engage in long-term contracting. These inefficiencies make society collectively worse off; hence these theorists argue that the best law is one that governs least.

Two important features stand out. First, as legal theorist Fred Schauer notes, this branch of formalism is concerned with the allocation of decision-making power: shifting it away from the end-line interpreter and moving it upstream toward the legislature or parties who drafted the agreement. Questions of justice, policy, or fairness are properly directed to the rule-creator rather than the rule-interpreter.[28] Second, formalism is not an inherent good in and of itself but is justified via other values. For Scalia, these are democratic legitimacy and accountability; for contract law formalists, they are predictability, efficiency, and growing the economic pie. Other writers emphasize how the logic of bureaucracy, standardization, and norm settlement are necessary to run complex societies, or that formalism is the most effective guarantor of fairness and equality under the law.[29] Though formalism sometimes produces results that are hard to swallow, modern legal formalists posit these costs are outweighed by the systemic values formalism promotes and sustains.

Classical Formalism: Building a Conceptual Legal Structure

Before American formalism became fixated on limiting judicial discretion, an older strand, now known as "classical formalism," was concerned that the growing number of common law precedents were contradictory, hard to organize and underreasoned, such that legal authority could be cited to support divergent results.[30] Their goal was to restructure the law along tight conceptual legal principles that would establish a coherent basis for the law while cabining political or social considerations exogenous to concept-driven legal analysis. This type of formalism reached its heyday in America in the late nineteenth century and into the twentieth, and then largely fell out of favor. In other common law countries, it remains strong to this day.[31]

Formalists sought to classify the legal terrain by producing a taxonomy or map of how higher-order abstractions unfolded into the more concrete rules used to decide cases. Ideally, legal analysis proceeds deductively from the realm of legal principle down toward the specific rules used to resolve cases. Upper-level principles were to be general and few, while reasoning downward from them relies on legal logic that is demonstrably separate from policymaking and political considerations.

Modern contract law offers an example of the logic at work. Much like the organizational structure found in *Shulchan Arukh*, preclassical common law did not have the law of contracts as we know it today, but scores of legal rules that governed specific transaction types such as real estate, sale of goods, debt, insurance, apprenticeships, innkeepers, marine carriage, bailments, and so on. Each area contained discrete rules regarding how the relationship was initiated, which terms were mandated, and which were assumed as defaults or subject to negotiation.

Classical formalism structured these rules into principles of greater abstraction that govern all transaction types. The parties' intent and will was promoted as the conceptual core of contract law, and this impacted how rules of formation, breach, duress, and interpretation were reworked and formulated. Outlier cases that could not be made to fit were mitigated, and contracts that functioned under different assumptions, were deemed specialty areas that stood outside the general theory and conceptual structure of the law of contracts.[32]

Classical formalists were attracted to the idea that law was a science.[33] One of the most famous practitioners of this method, Christopher Columbus Langdell, dean of the then newly reconstituted Harvard Law School, offered the analogy of geometry. Judging ideally started atop the conceptual pyramid where impartial logic drew on a few basic postulates to deduce increasingly specific theorems needed to resolve a case. This method left little room for discussions of legal policy or the morality, purpose, or impact of the law, which is why it typically excludes considering issues such as the relative bargaining power of the parties, the substantive fairness of the agreement, or the meaningfulness of the party's assent. Likewise, the broader social and economic impact of how contracts constructed and impacted the rapidly industrializing economy were also deemed exogenous to the internal logic of the legal enterprise.

Both variants of American formalism stem from traditions of limited government that aim to reduce the law's regulatory footprint and create zones of autonomy beyond the reach of law. They also work to constrain legal decision makers by excluding ideas or sources that we may otherwise find relevant.[34]

But important differences remain. Modern formalism is framed in terms of institutional competence: it asks which persons or institutions are best positioned to interpret and adjust legal texts to new or unexpected facts. The primacy of congressionally authorized texts leads modern formalism to follow its literal dictates even if the result is conceptually incoherent or borders on the absurd.[35] Classical formalists, by contrast were more animated by the structure of legal ideas and more likely to interpret legislation as fitting within the broader legal and conceptual rubric.[36] Finally, the two differ on the role of the judge. The rhetorical posture of contemporary formalism is designed to drive a wedge between the judiciary—typically represented as cultural elites—and the general populace—whose interests are said to be undermined by elite judges.[37] Classical formalists were more likely to extoll elite judges and lawyers as expert practitioners of the judicial craft entrusted to articulate the law's abstract principles and apply to them concrete cases.

Functionalism, Realism, and Why It Matters

Both flavors of formalism contrast with functionalism, which calls on judges to apply rules in light of the rationales that legitimize the rule itself. Functionalists both look back to the history and purpose of the rule and forward to how a given application will play out in the world. Legal rules do not decide cases themselves, but establish "rules of thumb" to guide a judge toward enacting the underlying policies. Weighing and balancing are central tasks of the judicial office.

The debate carries both descriptive and normative implications. Descriptively, formalists note that most legal rules present themselves as fairly rigid, and that most judicial opinions demonstrate courts applying the rules with the neutrality that formalism demands. The rival approach has little trouble acknowledging that the law's default instinct is to *appear* formal, and admits that legal actors are incentivized to loudly declare their formalist bona fides. The core realist insight, however, is to pay less attention to what legal actors *say* when constructing doctrinal arguments and more to what they *do*. Realists are skeptical of a sharp divide between internal and external considerations or of the claim that decisions are reached purely through doctrinal logic. They claim that while judges often employ formalist reasoning, these results better explained and motivated by a broader array of factors than expressed in legal writing and argument. In recent years, a voluminous corpus of scholarship has arisen to test the empirical dimensions of these claims.[38]

Whether for American or Jewish law, the debate between these camps carries normative implications for the structural and rhetorical posture of the law. Formalists hold that because judicial legitimacy rests on formally applying the law, legal analysis should be structured to highlight this feature. Realists argue that because extradoctrinal considerations are invariably in play, the complex factors that undergird judicial decisions should be made explicit rather than obscured by formalist rhetoric. Formalists thus prefer tight conceptual categories, bright-line rules, and legal syllogisms, whereas realists are attracted to standards over rules and multifactor balancing tests over categorical thinking. Formalists find these methods too subjective, while realists respond that they draw the true factors guiding the decision to the forefront of legal analysis.[39]

Halakhah and Modern Legal Formalism

Notwithstanding the current affinity between many *halakhically* observant Jews and conservative legal thought, the concerns of modern formalism do not generally motivate *halakhic* reasoning, nor are they typical of its approach to formalism.

The Amalgamation of Powers

The Talmudic tractate Sanhedrin presents a complex governance structure based on kings, priests, prophets, and legislature/courts. It includes highly restrictive rules of evidence, criminal procedure, and civil fines, which are all extraordinarily protective of accused defendants.

Practiced *halakhah*, however, has not generally operated in accord with these restrictive formalities. Instead, it places broad discretion in the hands of the community's leading judges, rabbis, and *poskim* who exert various aspects of legislative, judicial, and executive authority.

Section two of the *Laws of Judges* from the sixteenth-century restatement of *halakhah*, *Shulhan Arukh*, canonize this practice (the glosses of the R. Moses Isserles are presented in italics).

> [If a court] . . . sees that the people are unrestrained in committing sins, *and the exigencies of the hour demand it*, it may pass judgment both with respect to death and monetary penalties as well as to administer all laws of punishment, even if no fully valid evidence is available.
>
> And if he [the sinner] is an intransigent individual, they may flog him by means of the non-Jewish authorities. *And they have authority to expropriate his property and to forfeit it according to whatever they see fit in order to fence in the lawlessness of the generation.* All their acts, however, should be done for the sake of Heaven.[40]

Few ideas run more contrary to contemporary rule-of-law concerns than granting a court near-limitless discretion to act beyond formal legalities and expropriate property or even administer the death penalty. Yet beyond the admonition that the court must "act for the sake of Heaven," and generalized notions of communal consent, a *halakhic* court maintains unchecked and broad discretion to act beyond the law as long as it determines that the exigencies of the hour demand it.

In the modern era, Jewish communities no longer administer the death penalty or expropriate assets. But the absence of a legislative or policymaking body means responses to the vast social changes of the last two centuries generally occur through interpretation. Rabbis and *poskim* decide when to extend, reframe, or curtail laws—when to limit themselves to the plain meaning of the text, and when to attend to its foundational purposes.

Take the case of electricity and Shabbat. No formal source of Jewish law prohibits its use on Shabbat, and determining whether electricity fits within the preexisting categories of Shabbat prohibition has proven difficult.[41] Yet unlike the formalist reading of the Americans with Disabilities Act, no one expects a *posek* to simply note the gap and stay their hand from extending Shabbat prohibitions because it stands beyond rabbinic interpretative capacity. To the contrary, *poskim* establish their authority because the underlying community trusts their understanding of how the law, facts, and technology coalesce into policy.

Beyond specific cases, and even beyond the discretion afforded in *Shulhan Arukh's Laws of Judges*, Jewish legal lore exalts the hypothetical "fifth volume" of the four-volume *Shulhan Arukh*. This nonexistent section is said to contain the *halakhic* rules of intuition, equity, and common sense that apply when the rules stated in the four extant sections do not fully address the question or fit the facts or situational logic of the case.[42]

From the perspective of modern formalism, extending Shabbat laws—and *a fortiori* allowing the ad hoc expropriation of property—is exactly the type of policy issue that stands beyond the judicial role. Few ideas are more contrary to modern formalism than a source of unwritten law accessible to all but the most expert judges. Yet the *halakhic* community relies on the interpretative capacity of *poskim* to draw out the meaning of these texts and apply them to novel or difficult settings. Modern formalism casts the judge as the "other" who must be guarded from usurping policymaking from Congress and subjecting the law to their own agenda. But as Hanina Ben Menahem points out, a *halakhists*' standing does not usually emerge bureaucratically via formal appointment (perhaps by a rival political party). Instead, "[a] judge is accepted because his virtues and personal qualities endow him with the status of guide and mentor."[43] The rabbi/*posek* is commonly presented as the communal tribune of Torah and its values and who inherently operates "for the sake of Heaven."[44]

While modern judges sit within a highly structured system of judicial and state agencies that constitute and limit their power, contemporary rabbis and *poskim* operate in more diffuse institutional settings. Rabbinic authority emerges through a socially contingent and fluid process that is based on the interplay of exertions of rabbinic authority and communal acceptance. This mode surely carries its own constraints, but they are considerably more context-sensitive than the procedural and bureaucratic rules that typify modern formalism.[45]

The Oracles of the Law

Halakhic thought venerates rabbinic interpreters and grants them considerable authority in policymaking. In recent decades, this idea has, in some circles, coalesced into the concept of *da'as Torah*, which posits that certain *halakhic* authorities (*gedolim*) have internalized the structure of the *halakhic* system to such a degree that they assume quasi-legislative functions within it.[46] This concept is the opposite of modern formalism which aims to mitigate the judge's personal qualities and denigrates the judiciary for infiltrating the law with their personal perspectives. The *gadol* or *posek* by contrast is someone who knows how to consult the "fifth section" of *Shulhan Arukh* and is vaunted for having unique, and in some cases extra-human, insights into the law even—or especially—when it cuts against the otherwise plain meaning of canonical texts.[47]

These differences come to light when comparing how a judge and *posek* approach the moral content of the law. Separation-of-powers rhetoric enables judges to cavalierly admit that laws may be silly, misguided, outdated, amoral, and possibly even immoral, or lacking any sense at all.[48] Scalia quipped that laws could be "really stupid but constitutional."[49] This is one of modern formalism's most powerful rhetorical tools: it simultaneously legitimates a deep social dissatisfaction with the law while emphasizing that the court is not the proper address for these complaints.[50]

Halakhists by contrast, tend to be religiously invested in affirming *halakhah*'s wisdom, divinity, and morality and are loathe to declare *halakhic* provisions immoral, outdated, or bad policy. While at some level *halakhah* is understood as God's will whose morality speaks for itself (more on this below), this position does not preclude—and to some degree inspires—rabbinic attempts to reinterpret the law in order to blunt its potential negative social or moral consequences.[51] Rather than label laws "dumb but legal," rabbis are prone to creative interpretations that present *halakhah* as "Godly and wise."

Plain Meaning

These structural differences also highlight why the idea of plain meaning—central to the practice of contemporary formalism—is an imperfect fit for Jewish law. Many *halakhic* texts do not have a plain meaning in the Scalian sense of the term. *Halakhic* interpretation commonly draws out principles, novel inferences, applications, and rules from the existing canon of text. Moreover, it is not even clear which text should be read in a plain meaning fashion. This is certainly not how the Talmudic rabbis read the Torah, nor does it describe Talmudic interpretation of the Mishnah or subsequent rabbinic interpretations of the Talmud.[52]

Indeed, important strands of Jewish legal thought understand that because *halakhah* is sourced in God's limitless wisdom, it defies a single plain meaning. This is reflected in the oft-cited idea that the Torah has seventy facets of meaning, or that the Torah sustains numerous registers of interpretation ranging from plain (*pshat*) to the symbolic (*remez*) and mystical (*sod*). Justice Scalia himself recognized a form of this distinction. Referencing the rabbinic maxim "turn it over, and turn it over, for all is found therein," he noted, "[d]ivinely inspired text may contain the answers to all earthly questions, but the Due Process Clause most assuredly does not."[53]

Even netting out some of the most radical *drashot* (creative interpretations) traditionally ascribed to received oral traditions, many commonplace Talmudic readings of the Mishnah frequently go against the plain sense of the text. Tosafot's readings of the Talmud are oriented toward reconciling the entire canon rather than zeroing in on the plain meaning. Indeed, this phenomenon has generated its own litany of second-order rules: one may not rule based on the plain text of a Mishnah;[54] one does not rule from the plain meaning of the Talmud;[55] and finally, one cannot rule based on the plain meaning of the *Shulhan Arukh*.[56]

Each of these canons reflects how *halakhic* analysis generally blends plain meaning with fine-grained textual inferences strides toward intercanonical coherence and harmonization, conceptual analysis, the authority of received traditions, conformity with communal practice, and perhaps even Divine guidance. Further, when *halakhists* employ literalist and narrow readings, it is not out of structural deference to another body more capable of adjudicating the question, but to the religious authority of prior generations. While the process of rabbinic interpretation is too complex and diverse to be modeled here, its overall interpretative ethos does not mimic the flat plain-meaning approach advocated by Scalia and his followers.

Modern Formalism and Structural Social Changes

The process of secularization and emancipation, the sexual revolution and the push for gender equality, Zionism in modernity, have each occasioned calls for more holistic reassessments of traditional *halakhah*.[57] An oft-cited teaching found in Mishna *Eduyot* explains that a latter rabbinic court can revisit the rulings of a prior court so long as the latter is "greater in wisdom and number (influence)." While this idea may offer some theoretical support for rethinking *halakhah* in light of modern conditions,[58] over the past few centuries this power has been rendered inert owing to the theological concept of "declining generations." This doctrine asserts that contemporary *halakhists* are definitionally less attuned to the Divine will than their predecessors such that their authority within the *halakhic* system is correspondingly limited.[59]

As applied to contentious social issues, the theology of diminished status often mimics the arguments of modern formalism. While rabbinic authorities readily recognize the gap between accepted practices and modern realities, they find themselves powerless to recalibrate *halakhic* rulings.[60] Demands for structural-level *halakhic* change are often met with the refrain that humans—especially humans of the present spiritually degraded generation—are not empowered to change God's law.[61]

In the realms of sexuality and gender equality, these agitations spawned arguably the most famous modern reaction to claims of *halakhic* formalism—Blu Greenberg's quip that "when there is a rabbinic will there is a *halakhic* way."[62] This remark—and reactions to it—have become a flashpoint in energized debates about *halakhic* formalism, realism, feminism, and patriarchy.[63]

If we follow Schauer's understanding of formalism as the gap between decisions made "all things are considered" and decisions constrained by legal rule, however, the degree to which *halakhah* in this area is experienced as formalistic depends on the positionality of the observer. To those who support traditional views on gender and sexuality, *halakhic* practice rests on deep substantive agreement with the underlying values rather than on bare rule-following or a sense that rabbis cannot update the law. Some Orthodox communities reflect this substantive agreement by pushing for even *greater degrees* of gender separation than seemingly demanded by baseline *halakhah*.

Conservative and Reform Judaisms by contrast have largely shifted their practice to conform to the contemporary liberal consensus. Here, *halakhic* practice is not particularly formal as it aligns with the underlying social values.

For the subset of Jews who substantively align with liberal cultural views yet remain steadfast to classical strictures, however, *halakhah* in this area is formalist in the modern-Scalian sense of the term. This is because observance hinges on the existence of the rules as rules that stand beyond the interpretative capacity of the community, rather than a deeper appreciation of their substantive truth, justice, or socioreligious vision. Ronit Irshai has gone on to argue that for some in this camp, surrendering moral intuitions in the face of contrary *halakhic* demands is not simply a consequence of rule-following but a central devotional act that defines what it means to be a committed Jew commanded by God in the modern age.[64] Whether in its more moderate or extreme forms, rabbis of this community often mimic the rhetoric of modern formalism: on the one hand, they appreciate the gap between social and *halakhic* values, yet maintain that commitment to God's law requires submitting human moral intuitions to Divine judgment.[65]

Halakhah and Classical Legal Formalism

An alternate basis of *halakhic* formalism is known as *lomdus*—roughly equivalent to *halakhic* analytical jurisprudence. This approach flowered in the eighteenth century and obtained its most distinctive form in the Eastern European yeshivas of the late nineteenth century. It became known as *Brisk* (and its adherents as *Briskers*) and remains broadly influential within the Orthodox sphere to this day.[66] Because the *Brisker* school offers the closest rabbinic analogue to classical formalism, my analysis centers primarily on this movement.

Brisker theology maintains that *halakhic* concepts are abstract truth claims that maintain an independent ontological existence and are not contingent on social, physical, or political realities. *Halakhic* principles emanate from God who hardwired them into the structure of the universe.[67]

The most philosophically astute expositor of *Brisker* ideas was R. Joseph Soloveitchik who explained that the goal of *halakhah* is to "objectify religiosity" and grant *halakhah* "independence" and "full autonomy" from the contextual factors that inflect human society.[68] He argued that "psychologization or sociologization of *halakhah* strangles its soul" because if "*halakhic* thinking depends on personal variables, it loses its objectivity and devolves into a subjectivity lacking all substance.[69]

Depicting *halakhah* as reified reality corresponds to several features of classical formalism. For example, though many legal systems employ technical legal definitions of common terms occasionally,[70] for the *Brisker*, the matter is foundational. *Briskers* held that *halakhic* definitions are truths emanating from the Divine rather than conventions derived from the vicissitudes of human society; the analysis of terms and concepts is thus directed inward toward *halakhic* sources rather than from materials developed in the broader cultural sphere.

Like classical formalism, *Brisk* aims to peer behind the law's factual husk and reconstruct its underlying conceptual underpinnings. These two movements also present the strongest argument within their respective traditions for employing conceptual tools to develop a systematically coherent approach to law.[71] Moreover, both were attracted to the "law as science" metaphor, and to the view that the law's internal architecture is central to its claims of integrity and validity.[72]

The two movements also contrast with modern formalism in their essentialist tendencies. They posit legal principles as *true* in some deeper sense rather than merely efficient, enhancing of democracy or autonomy, or bureaucratically necessary for ensuring equal treatment under the law. Further, while most classical legal thinkers did not consider the abstract principles of common law as Divine in the way the *Briskers* approached *halakhah*,[73] they were seen as immanent within the body of precedents that comprise the common law tradition.[74]

Brisk and classical formalism also agree that formulating the law in terms of well-defined conceptual principles establishes a bulwark against what R. Soloveitchik termed the "psychologization or sociologization of *halakhah*," or in the language of modern legal discourse, it prevents the law from being influenced by political preferences, social ideals, or consequentialist reasoning. Further, both schools hold that legal reasoning should center on concepts whose definitions and properties emerge from the law itself, and advocate for sharp boundaries between internal legal considerations and extrinsic sociopolitical factors.

Yet for all these similarities, important differences remain. Classical formalism is rooted in assumptions of a liberal political order that is not typically shared by *Brisk* or most other approaches to Jewish law. Second, from an analytical perspective,

Brisk—especially in its founding and most influential generations—and classical formalism push in different directions. Classical formalism aims to create a pyramidic hierarchy of legal concepts that move from a multiplicity of local rules to a smaller set of abstract ideas that unite the legal system.[75] This requires determining the conceptual framework for each area of law, aggregating them together, and affirmatively rejecting competing formulations that muddy the analytical scheme.

Brisker thought tends to work the other way. What initially appears as a single *halakhic* rule is analytically divided into subprinciples, each reflecting an opposing conceptual account of the legal rules in play. Further, when encountering a debate between *halakhic* authorities, the *Brisker* reflex is to show how each adhered to a different—yet legitimate—conceptual account of the rules under review, rather than to assimilate them into a unified framework.

Beyond these features, for all the focus on *halakhic* conceptualism, it is striking how few *halakhic* works are explicitly structured around conceptual *halakhic* principles. The latter strata of the Talmud explicate abstract legal concepts that range across the *halakhic* landscape,[76] and this process of coherentization and system building is expanded in the commentaries of the Tosafists and even more clearly in the writings of Nachmanides and his students in pre-expulsion Spain. Yet because these are platformed as Talmudic commentaries rather than self-standing works on conceptual *halakhic* concepts, they are invariably tied to the Talmud's haphazard structure and intertwined with its process of textual exposition and harmonization. Conceptual ideas emerge, yet a clear conceptual structure of *halakhah* as a whole is harder to decipher.[77]

Notably, the most comprehensive account of *halakhah* to date remains Maimonides's twelfth-century *Mishneh Torah*—the only treatise to assimilate the entirety of Talmudic law into a common framework. But, notably, the treatise is not organized around the types of *halakhic* abstractions favored by the *Briskers*. Beyond that, *Mishneh Torah*'s conceptual structure is tightest at the beginning of each division heading and chapter and it tends to peter out as the divisions and chapters progress.

Even zeroing in on the *Briskers* specifically, few of their works are structured around conceptual *halakhic* principles. Two of the school's most famous exemplars—R. Hayyim Soloveitchik and his son, R. Yiztchak Zev Soloveitchik—wrote works that present relatively brief essays on specific rulings in Maimonides's *Mishneh Torah*. Read cover to cover, however, no "master plan" of *halakhah* or even *Mishneh Torah* emerges. They tend to ignore *Mishneh Torah*'s larger conceptual scheme and target their analysis toward specific *halakhic* rulings.[78] Moreover, each essay stands on its own without any attempt to assimilate the concepts developed in the individual chapters into a more generalizable account of *halakhah*. Much the same holds for other members of the *Brisker* school.[79] Individual essays draw on ideas and sources from across the *halakhic* canon and often bring analytical clarity to confined legal area. But they rarely take the next step of remapping the *halakhic* terrain along the newly elucidated conceptual moorings.[80]

What is true of *Brisk* is even more descriptive of the broader *halakhic* tradition in which it is situated. Even after the so-called *Brisker* revolution, the most common arrangement for practiced *halakhah* remains the decidedly a-conceptual and functional chapter headings of the medieval code, *Tur*, which carry forward into *Shulhan Arukh.*[81] For more theoretical topics, the default generally remains the order of the Talmud itself.[82]

These differences between *Brisk* and classical formalism make the former less suited to one of the central tasks attributed to formalism—creating a legal map that enables a chain of logic to work inexorably from the abstract concept to the bottom-line decision while mitigating the amount of discretionary input available to the decision maker.[83] *Brisker* analysis is highly effective at drawing *halakhic* analysis inward and marking functionalist and historicist arguments legally irrelevant and theologically beyond the pale. But its weaker sense of a unitary structure of *halakhah*, alongside its desire to sustain rather than select between competing conceptual models, makes it less adept at guiding decision makers toward specific outcomes.[84]

Detail-Following Formalism

While *Brisk* has become an influential form of rabbinic scholarship, when focusing on the distinctive features that separate it from other approaches to Jewish law, it is limited to specific geographies and theologies. By contrast, the detail-following formalism outlined below has been a typifying feature of *halakhah* since at least mishnaic times and sustains a wider array of *halakhic* practices and theologies.

To begin with first principles, in contrast to the two variants of American formalism, traditional *halakhic* theology assumes God is the source of *halakhah* and that the Divine source of jurisdiction is not limited. As Robert Cover emphasized, the founding mythos of Western law is the hypothetical state of nature that assumes where human autonomy and freedom from legal authority as the baseline. *Halakhah* does not start from classically liberal premises. It assumes a Sinaitic covenant of divinely revealed law defined by human acceptance of Divine obligation.[85] One way to illuminate the distinction is to consider how each tradition employs the metaphor of a "fence." Legal fences in the liberal tradition are used to demarcate private zones of autonomy where the state—or other parties—cannot enter. The Mishnah by contrast uses the idea of "erecting a fence around the law" as a justification for thickening the web of *halakhic* regulation.[86] This mishnaic metaphor is adopted in Rema's comments to the *Laws of Judges* which empowers a rabbinic court to act beyond the law "to fence in lawlessness."

Rather than limited government, much of what is experienced as *halakhic* detail-following formalism stems from the interplay of two features: (1) a reticence toward offering transparently purposive-driven interpretations of the mitzvot, and (2) *detailism*—the near-obsessive predilection for regulating granular aspects of human behavior.[87]

Purposive Analysis in *Halakhah*

The rationalists of the *halakhic* tradition assume that most of *halakhah* should be understood in terms of discernable purposes that are transparent to human reasoning and promote human goods. A strong countertradition, however, disclaims that material benefit is either the reason for or even the consequence of *halakhic* commands. For these non- and anti-rationalists, mitzvot are alternately framed as a matter of Divine fiat which humans are bound to obey, as commands with rationales that are beyond human comprehension, or in mystical, moral, didactic, or symbolic terms whose impact is measured in cosmically rather than through functional registers. These perspectives all join in denying that successful *halakhic* compliance can be evaluated in the exoteric terms of the here and now.[88]

Notwithstanding these opposing views, in the long run of *halakhic* thinking, there has rarely been equanimity with reading rationales off the biblical verse to directly implicate practice, even in the case of *halakhot* identified as "rational." The parade example flows from Deuteronomy 17:17 which abjures a Jewish king from taking too many wives for fear that they may lead him astray. The *Tannaim* debate whether the prohibition applies categorically, or whether a king is permitted to marry numerous righteous women who will not distract him from the Divine path. In the Talmudic rendering, this debate turns on whether the Torah's legal regime should be molded through purposive readings of the biblical text.[89]

The matter is unresolved in the Talmud, but many subsequent *halakhists* tend to disavow the purposive hermeneutic—at least rhetorically.[90] One Talmudic statement goes on to explain that the Torah deliberately hid most of its rationales because the few which were revealed led King Solomon—reputed as the wisest of all men—to attempt to outsmart the rule by marrying many wives. At the end of his life, however, Solomon was led astray.[91]

None of this is to deny that many areas of *halakhah* bear the imprint—possibly even a dominant one—of purpose-based reasoning. To take a simple example, the Talmud rules that one who swallows the tasteless matzah has fulfilled his obligation to eat it on Passover while one who simply swallows the pungent or bitter *marror* has not.[92] The common explanation flows from purpose: one needs to taste the bitterness of *marror* whereas no such requirement attends to bland matzah.[93] Likewise, while the Torah prohibits muzzling an ox while it is working on the threshing floor,[94] the Talmud permits muzzling a sick ox since the act is undertaken for the ox's benefit.[95] Similar examples abound.[96]

Nevertheless, a structural imbalance remains. Advocates of functional and culturally attuned interpretation often need to explain why they *are not* engaged in a full-blown version of purposive *halakhic* analysis. Purposive reasoning also pushes contrary to *halakhic* grammar, while the opposing view rarely demands special justification. Nonpurposive reasoning does not always carry the day—but it is always an option ready on the horizon and frequently impacts *halakhic* discourse, its conceptual imagery, and its practiced outcomes.

A somewhat extreme but telling example emerges from the commandment to shoo away a mother bird nesting on her eggs or chicks—a topic that has featured in debates over rational interpretations of the mitzvot since the mishnaic era.[97] A plain-sense reading of the verse suggests the purpose of this *mitzvah* is to show concern for the bird's maternal instincts by not forcing the bird to watch as her eggs are taken away. The Talmud (on some readings) debates whether this functionalist approach is correct, but Maimonides leveraged it to argue that since the Torah shows great concern for animal welfare, this sensitivity should apply *a fortiori* to humans.[98]

On this account, the *mitzvah* should only apply when one wishes to take the eggs—why else disturb the mother bird? Many adopted this view,[99] but others held the *mitzvah* attaches whenever one sees a roosting bird—*regardless of the need for the eggs*.[100] This turns the *mitzvah* on its head: rather than spare the mother the pain of watching her eggs taken, she is now lodged off her eggs for no reason other than to perform a *mitzvah* seemingly intended to reduce her pain. Kabbalistic texts lean into this non-functional approach, explaining that sending away the mother bird causes it to search in agony for her offspring. This act arouses the Divine mercy in the supernal realm which flows to the Jewish people.[101] The mitzva-act is significant regardless of whether the eggs are taken for human consumption. Some *halakhists* drew on this mystical reading to establish (or to justify preexisting) *halakhic* practice accordingly.[102]

Detailism

The phenomenon of *halakhic* detailism is best understood through examples. The Torah commands the paschal lamb be roasted whole over a fire rather than cooked in water.[103] Rabbinic sources further prohibit using a metal rod as a spit since the rod may "sear" or "scald" the adjacent meat. The spit must also come from a particular species of low-moisture wood, as high-moisture wood may "cook" the lamb as water evaporates.[104]

While sacrificial rites do not directly lend themselves to strict functional analysis, one can assume a basic symbolism or teleology of Torah's roasting requirement and still remain in wonder over the detailed structure of the ensuing regulation. To the common observer, a lamb lodged over an open fire is being roasted regardless of the material used for the spit. Yet in the Mishnah's more technical understanding, the "roasting" will be undermined if even a small section of meat encounters metal or high-moisture wood. The Talmud extends the discussion to whether roasting over coals qualifies as "fire."[105] This setup allows for formalized definitions of "roasting" and "fire" to drive *halakhic* analysis, making it correspondingly more difficult for purposive hermeneutics to register.

While this process can be identified in a variety of *tannatic* works,[106] it likely becomes a more dominant feature over time—particularly in Ashkenazic *halakhah*. Take one of the opening sections of *Shulhan Arukh* which discusses the obligation to wash one's hands upon arising. The Talmud states that pouring water on one's hands three times removes an "evil spirit." Beyond that, only sparse details are found in the Talmud, Rambam's code, or even the fourteenth-century code *Tur*.[107]

The sixteenth-century writers introduced a number of granular specifications, and by the nineteenth century, standard *halakhic* codes encompassed a multitude of specific triggers and requirements. For example, the degree/amount of sleep necessary to initiate the washing obligation;[108] the requirement to keep the water near the bed to wash even before walking to the bathroom; a prohibition of walking more than a few feet before washing;[109] rules about the positioning of the palms, a requirement to wash by pouring from a cup rather than under a faucet, as well as numerous regulations regarding the cup, quantity, and quality of water.[110]

Staying close to the topic of personal hygiene, a recent book bearing the title *Bathing and Showering in Halacha* elaborates and refines rules related to hygiene.[111] Background *halakhah* prohibits thinking Torah thoughts in a bathroom (until recently, an outhouse) but permits it in a bathhouse. The *Bathing and Showering* handbook applies this to modern conditions where the waste is immediately flushed out but there is often a shower in the same room. It rules that Torah thoughts are permitted in the shower as long as it is separated from the toilet by a wall or a glass shower door. If only separated by a shower curtain, however, Torah thoughts are prohibited since a partition that easily blows in the wind is not *halakhically* valid.[112]

Another chapter interrogates whether a modern shower can be used for purposes of an ablution ritual that requires pouring roughly five gallons of water over a man's head following a seminal emission (known as *Takanat Ezra*). As with handwashing, *halakhah* requires the water to be poured from something designated a *vessel*. Existing *halakhah* stipulates that the five gallons should be divided into no more than three vessels (or the same vessel filled three times).[113] With respect to a shower, the handbook considers whether (1) water from the shower is deemed "poured over" even though it is not physically raised and poured via human action, and (2) whether each pinhole in the showerhead constitutes a separate "vessel," thereby running afoul of the three-vessel rule.[114]

Precision and Form

A formalism predicated on detail-following envisions *halakhah* as consisting of thousands of precise scripts or recipes for living the Godly life. As with a high-end pastry chef, each recipe must be precisely followed step-by-step, lest the delicate pastry fail.[115] The mark of an elite chef is one who possesses both awareness of the precise requirements and the technical skills to perfectly execute them. Similarly, the pious *halakhic* practitioner is defined as someone attuned to all its multifarious rules and religiously committed to executing them.

In the case of the chef, however, the demanded precision can be explained on functional grounds—discerning customers will be able to tell if a pastry was executed correctly or not. Similarly, the dense regulatory regimes of modern law can also be accounted for as necessary to achieve their articulated goals (health, safety, consumer protection, efficient markets, etc.), or through second-order arguments stressing the need to sandardization and the logic of bureaucracy and rule-of-law formalism.

The combined effect of detailism and nonpurposive readings of the mitzvot, however, precludes a functional account of the details and puts more emphasis on aspects that are immune to external standards or justifications. To illustrate, rationalists such as Maimonides omit mention of "evil spirit" in the laws of handwashing and frame it as a requirement for cleanliness demanded prior to engaging in religiously significant activities. This approach leaves the door open to functionalist analysis which interprets the regulatory details as necessary to ensure cleanliness. Mystical approaches, by contrast, emphasize that a deathly spirit falls on the body each night as the soul departs during sleep. To remove the deathly residue remaining on the hands each morning, these *halakhists* introduced numerous precise details that serve as a "ritual weapon" to combat the "metaphysically charged agent of evil."[116] Because these criteria are immune to any transparent forms of exoteric reasoning, adhering to their precise contours reinforces *halakhah*'s formal qualities.

The Religiosity of Detailism

While awareness and attention to details is often a mark of *halakhic* piety, detail-following formalism is further propelled by the religious impulse that pushes toward punctilious and error-free performance. For example, while authoritative codes maintain that the postseminal ablution ritual is no longer required, *Mishnah Berurah* notes that it remains the practice of "men of great deeds."[117] Contemporary *halakhic* manuals such as *Bathing and Showering* tend to nudge practitioners toward maximal compliance and thus include this supererogatory practice in the handbook. Religiosity anchored in maximal compliance therefore tends to multiply the number of detail-laden recipes the *halakhic* performer aims to follow.

Even beyond scripting *more* recipes, the pietistic impulse further encourages *greater care* in ensuring each stage of the recipe was followed to perfection. For example, *Bathing and Showering* explains that while most authorities assume a showerhead constitutes a single vessel, since a minority view deems each pin head to be a separate vessel, the showerhead should ideally be removed to quell any doubts whether the ablution ritual was properly performed.[118] This quest for perfection adds a further nonfunctional details into the compliance regimen. Replicated over thousands of *halakhic* discussions, these religious impulses push *halakhic* analysis further inward generating additional recipes and non-functional technical procedures to follow.

Ritualization and Economic Regulation

While this detail-following formalism is anchored in a ritual conception of law, it also impacts areas of commercial *halakhah* that are classically held to contrast with its ritual aspects. For example, the Torah prohibits delaying wage payments to hired workers.[119] The classical functionalist account sees this as a mechanism to aid the wage-laborer.[120] Over the past few centuries, however, a subset of *halakhic* thinkers used categoric and objectivist reasoning to apply the formalistic logic of ritual to this law. The end stage is a recent ruling holding that when engaging a taxi, the passenger should be careful *not to pay* the driver prior to concluding the trip.[121] The ruling ignores moral or intuitional referents and looks solely to the logic of *halakhic* classification as follows: (1) the *mitzvah* obligation does not formally attach until the contracted-for work has been completed; (2) prepayment would absolve the wage debt before it has matured, thereby (3) preventing the *mitzvah* from attaching to the taxi ride. Because (4) would deprive the passenger from the opportunity to perform the *mitzvah*, thus (5) prepayment should be avoided. Other *halakhists* disagree and raise more functionalist arguments, noting that because the purpose of the *mitzvah* is to ensure timely payment, early payment should be at least acceptable if not preferable.[122] Yet the first approach presents a credible *halakhic* hermeneutic offered by leading authorities. It demonstrates how formal parameters can easily overwhelm the *mitzvah*'s substantive or teleological goals.[123]

Another example emerges from Deuteronomy 24:6, which prohibits distraining all or part of a millstone for purposes of securing repayment of a loan obligation. Scripture describes this as akin to "taking a man's life as a pledge," and Talmudic sources expand the prohibition to including all tools of the trade used to produce income.[124] The rationale would appear to be straightforward: in the absence of trade tools the debtor will be unable to generate the funds necessary to pay off the debt.[125]

The accepted *halakhah*, however, limits this rule to cases where the tools in question are used in late-stage food production yet leaves all other instruments of business or commercial activity free from regulatory restriction.[126] From a functional perspective attuned to the apparent purposes of the *mitzvah*, it is hard to see the logic of applying the prohibition exclusively to items of little economic value while excluding from regulation the assets most relevant to securing loan repayment.

This analysis assumes that the goal of the relevant *halakhah* is to effectively regulate the commercial sphere. A ritualistic conception, however, ignores the impact on the market and (perhaps deliberately) simply focuses on the parameters of *mitzvah* performance. Thus latter *halakhic* sources tend to ignore the issue of whether *halakhah* effectively regulates debt markets and focuses instead on more ritualized legal analysis set on determining whether distraining scissors used to trim vegetables constitutes a single prohibition for the item as a whole or two prohibitions—one for each blade.[127]

This ritualistic conception of *halakhah* may underwrite a wide range of areas of *halakhic* commercial law that permit parties to use transactional formalities to evade or avoid the substantive impact of economic regulations.[128] Returning to the wage payment rule, the Talmud maintains that as long as the employer uses a middleman and does not hire the worker directly, the late wage-payment prohibition does not attach.[129] Similarly, the Talmudic rabbis read Deuteronomy 23:25 as granting a worker harvesting in the field the right to partake of the produce.[130] While the Talmud exultantly describes this right as "eating of Heaven's food," parties are permitted to contract around the regulation. This has the effect of leaving the substantive impact of this law to market conditions and the relevant bargaining power between the laborer and landowner.

Inheritance law offers other settings. Per Torah law, daughters are excluded from inheriting their fathers' estate. A workaround practice has developed whereby the father drafts a document confessing judgment for a large sum of money set to be due one moment prior to his death.[131] This structure ensures that the debt is binding on father's estate and sets up the practice where the daughter forgoes any rights to collect her debt in exchange for a proportional share of her father's estate. A similar technique was developed to evade *halakhic* restrictions on the types of contractual terms or penalty clauses a party may agree to undertake in the event it fails to perform or live up to its contractual obligations (*asmakhta*). Here too, a party is permitted to draft a document confessing judgment in the amount of the proposed penalty and then deposit it with a third-party escrow agent. The agent is instructed to keep the document under lock and only release it if the party failed to perform its obligations under the contract.[132] The net effect is to enforce the penalty clause without running afoul of formal *halakhic* restrictions.

Perhaps the most well-known exemplar of this approach is the *iska* agreement which relies on similar concepts to enable parties to engage in interest-bearing loans notwithstanding Torah prohibition to the contrary. The *iska* restates what is in substance a loan with a defined interest rate as an investment partnership. Under the *iska* agreement, the lending party's obligation to pay out "profits" to its partner is surrendered in exchange for a payment stream mimicing a loan repayment per the prevailing rate of interest. Though framed as a partnership, when it comes to the downside risk of potential losses, the documents establish evidentiary burdens on the lending party that effectively place the risk of the purported partnership's failure on the borrower exclusively.

To be sure, every legal system must grapple with the degree to which transactional formalities can be used to evade legal regulations. In *halakhah*, as in other legal systems, some are embraced, some begrudgingly permitted, and others prevented outright—though in the domain of financial regulation, Jewish law tends to accept and even embrace most of these devices.[133]

But what sets Jewish law apart from modern law is how *halakhah* in these areas tends to move from regulation to ritual thereby adopting some of the detail-oriented fastidiousness typical of other areas of *halakhah*. For example, *halakhic* literature displays considerable concern that when an interest-free loan is undertaken without an *iska*, the borrower may feel the impulse to return certain social graces or minimal favors to the lender which may potentially violate aspects of the prohibition against interest.[134] Likewise, in the inheritance settings, some authorities recommend the father leave a nominal amount outside of estate planning devices (say, $1,000), to ensure that Torah law of inheritance formally attaches to the estate, freeing up the lion's share of assets to be distributed on a proportional basis.[135]

The contraposition between the detailism applied to economically insignificant transactions coupled with the wholesale embrace of the transactional formalities to avoid regulation of economically significant deals, underscores how economic *halakhah* is as subject to the process of ritualization as more classically "ritual" areas of the law.

The Theologies of *Halakhic* Formalism

Several examples presented above raise the possibility that counterfunctional readings of *halakhah* may be a feature rather than a bug. Though not stated expressly, the sub rosa idea is that to the degree that a *mitzvah*'s esoteric and/or counterintuitive legal properties are emphasized, *halakhah* becomes more authentic or holy.[136] In a different register, *Brisker* scholars took pride in structuring *halakhah* as objectified legal concepts intelligible primarily to learned and yeshiva-trained scholars while often denigrating laypersons' efforts to understand Jewish law as grounded in social conventions of the here and now.[137]

Beyond that, formalization shifts authority and influence toward the rabbis which may be useful for reinforcing communal cohesion and identity, especially in modernity. In a different vein, ritualized formalism may be especially attractive in areas of *halakhah* that govern commonplace actions such as eating or handwashing, or with respect to mitzvot that reflect general moral sensibilities such as timely wage payment. When presented functionally, these actions do not code as particularly *halakhic*, or even "religious," but as universal ethics. Though attractive to more liberal Jewish theologies, conservative *halakhah* may rely on formalism precisely for its ability to "separate law from life." In buffeting these practices with specialized *halakhic* recipes, the quotidian becomes Godly and the universal morality becomes the unique spiritual patrimony of Israel. These approaches are rarely stated expressly, but on average their appeal likely works in favor of *halakhic* formalization. As applied to the economic sphere, the process of formalized ritualization is a way of updating the law. It allows the structure of *halakhah* to remain extant while freeing the marketplace from a regulatory regime that is unworkable under shifting economic assumptions and contexts.

Theologically, detail-following formalism draws on several different traditions. Some present it simply as a religious call to adhere to Divine commands with unquestioning precision and devotion.[138] Others stress that because God is perfect and precise, obedience to the Divine law requires the same. This view is often twinned to the claim that the commandments are fundamentally beyond the capacity of human reason. Still others focus on how the laws and traditions of the Talmud have become binding on the Jewish people who strive to fulfill its precepts in all their particular detail. The *Briskers*, and especially R. Soloveitchik, buttressed these ideas by developing a specific ontology which holds that *halakhic* concepts are truths structured into the metaphysics of the universe. Other traditions are grounded in more mystical concerns: how attending to the minute *halakhic* details is necessary for the religious act to be efficacious in bringing harmony in the supernal and *sefirotic* realm,[139] or in causing Divine grace to flow from God toward the mitzva performer or the Jewish nation generally.[140] Although these accounts stem from different theological orientations, they are often mixed and interchanged. Specifics aside, when applied to *halakhic* practice, they all work to reinforce the value of detail-following formalism.[141]

Finally, the detail-following formalism extends beyond whether a particular normative *halakhah* accords with more formal or functional readings. From a didactic perspective, it models that ritualistic details are what *halakhic* discussions are about. It underscores that tradition's leading minds invested considerable thought into these questions and that Jews are commanded to spend their days toiling over their study and implementing them in practice. Fervent Jews become habituated in to a discourse founded on the view that granular and nonfunctional *halakhic* details—whether a speckle of the Paschal lamb was "cooked," or whether the shower has a door vs. a curtain—are important. They *matter* to *halakhah*, to religious life, and ultimately to God.[142] Both critics and admirers of *halakhah* note how this precipitates a religiosity of detailism that stands apart from functional purpose and religious *telos*. Though distinct from the formalism of constraining decision makers or conceptual system building, it casts a long shadow on both legal practice and the cultural image of what *halakhah* is about.

Conclusion

Formalism is an interpretative reflex that exists in every legal system. It is often the preferred default of judges and legal actors, and there are countless of examples in the canons of Jewish and American, legal systems of formalist interpretation, as well as examples of non- or anti-formalist readings.

Yet debates around the role of formalism—and its comparison to other religious and legal systems—have accompanied Jewish law since the pre-mishnaic era. This chapter aims to make sense of the comparative role of formalism in Jewish and modern law by distinguishing between three variants of formalism. Viewed in terms of constraining decision makers, there is a good argument that the religious authorities who emerge as *halakhic* adjudicators have greater interpretative latitude than judges functioning in a bureaucratized political system. And, though some influential streams in *halakhah* resemble classical formalism, *halakhic* discourse is not distinguished by developing unified conceptual schemas that proceed from abstract concepts to bottom-line decisions. *Halakhic* formalism is instead typified by attention to the detailed forms of practice propelled by a religious and ritual logic that is typically absent from Western law.

Acknowledgments

I would like to thank Nomi Stolzenberg, Elana Stein Hain, Yonatan Brafman, Shlomo Pill, Benjamin Brown, Benjamin Porat, Nathan Oman, Suzanne Stone, Emmanuel Bloch, and Tamara Morsel-Eisenberg for helpful comments on this draft. Mark Lammey, Sam Kosloff, and Eitan Oberlander provided valuable discussion partners and research assistance.

Notes

1. Omri Ben-Shahar, "The Tentative Case against Flexibility in Commercial Law," *University of Chicago Law Review* 66, no. 3 (Summer 1999): 781–820, esp. 781.
2. Matt. 23:23 (King James).
3. See 2 Cor. 3:1–6.
4. See sources cited in Chaim Saiman, *Halakhah: The Rabbinic Idea of Law* (Princeton, NJ: Princeton University Press, 2018), 253–54 nn. 3–4; Barry Scott Wimpfheimer, *The Talmud: A Biography* (Princeton, NJ: Princeton University Press, 2018), 173–88 nn. 26–54.
5. See, e.g., Isa. 58; Amos 5.
6. b.Yoma 23.a–b.
7. See citations in Wimpfheimer, *The Talmud*, 188–202; Micha Goodman, *The Wondering Jew* (New Haven, CT: Yale University Press, 2020), 21–29.
8. See, e.g., Suzanne Last Stone, "In Pursuit of the Counter-Text: The Turn to the Jewish Legal Model in Contemporary American Legal Theory," *Harvard Law Review* 106 (1993): 813–94 esp. 847.
9. J. David Bleich, *Contemporary Halakhic Problems: Volume IV* (Hoboken, NJ: KTAV, 1995), *Introduction*. Also available at Sefaria, https://www.sefaria.org/Contemporary_Halakhic_Problems%2C_Vol_IV%2C_Introduction.8.
10. See, e.g., Joseph B. Soloveitchik, *Shiurei Ha-Rav: A Conspectus of the Public Lectures of Rabbi Joseph B. Soloveitchik* (Hoboken, NJ: KTAV, 1974), 97–110; Joseph B. Soloveitchik, *Halakhic Man* (Philadelphia, PA: Jewish Publication Society, 1983), 59.
11. See, e.g., Bleich, *Contemporary Halakhic Problems*, 16 ("*Halakhah* differs from other systems of law in that it does not permit policy considerations to adjudicate between competing theories or precedents"); "Brief of Amicus Curie Agudath Israel of America," p. 6, *Master Piece Cakeshop v. Colorado Civil Rights Commission*, 138 S. Ct. 1719 (2018) ("While U.S. constitutional law may have [the flexibility to adopt to social norms] Jewish law, based upon the divinely revealed Written Law and Oral Law, is immutable")
12. Much of this is contained in the introductory comments to Bleich, *Contemporary Halakhic Problems*, vol. 1, vol. 4, and vol. 5, available at https://www.sefaria.org/texts/Halakhah/Modern/Contemporary%20Halakhic%20Problems.
13. See Benjamin Brown, "Formalism and Values: Three Models," in *New Streams in Philosophy of Halakhah*, ed. Aviezer Ravitzky and Avinoam Rosenak (Jerusalem: Magnes Press, 2008), 233–58, esp. 244 [Hebrew].
14. See, e.g., Avinoam Rosenak, *Halakhah as an Agent of Change* (Jerusalem: Magnes Press, 2009) [Hebrew]; Aaron Kirschenbaum, "A Historical Sketch of the Sources of Jewish Law," in *Equity in Jewish Law: Halakhic Perspectives in Law: Formalism and Flexibility in Jewish Civil Law* (Hoboken, NJ: KTAV, 1991), 289–304; Eliezer Berkowitz, *Not In Heaven: The Nature and Function of Halakhah* (Hoboken, NJ: KTAV, 1983); Yair Lorberbaum, and

Haim Shapira, "Maimonides Epistle on Martyrdom in Light of Legal Philosophy," *Dine Israel* 25 (2008): 123–69; Daniel Sperber, "Congregational Dignity and Human Dignity: Women and Public Torah Reading, Appendix I: On Halakhic Methodology," in *Women and Men in Communal Prayer: Halakhic Perspectives*, ed. Chaim Trachtman (Hoboken, NJ: KTAV, 2010), 123–26; Tamar Ross, "Halakha Contextualized: The Halakhic Status of Homosexuals as Test Case," in *The Halakha as Event*, ed. Avinoam Rosenak (Jerusalem: Van Leer, 2016), 375–430 [Hebrew].

15. See Hanina Ben Menahem, *Judicial Deviation in Talmudic Law: Governed by Men Not Rules* (Reading, UK: Harwood Academic, 1991); Hanina Ben Menahem, "Is Talmudic Law a Religious Legal System: A Provisional Analysis," *Journal of Law and Religion* 24, no. 2 (2008): 379–401; Hanina Ben Menahem, "The Myth of Formalism: (Mis)Readings of Jewish Law from Paul to the Present," *Hebrew University of Jerusalem Legal Studies Research Paper Series* no. 17–5; Adiel Schremer, *Ma'ase Rav: Halakhic Decision-Making and the Shaping of Jewish Identity* (Ramat Gan: Bar Ilan University Press, 2019), 24–26 [Hebrew].
16. See the demographic survey prepared by Mark Trencher and David Myers, *A Survey of Orthodox Jewish Political Attitudes and Behaviors: Haredi and Modern Orthodox* Sectors (September 2023), https://www.harediresearchgroup.org/wp-content/uploads/2023/09/REPORT-Orthodox-Jewish-Political-Attitudes-and-Behaviors-September-2023.pdf.
17. Nathan Lewin, "The Supreme Court's Jewish Gentile: My Memories of Justice Scalia," *Jewish Telegraphic Agency* (February 15, 2016), https://www.jta.org/2016/02/15/obituaries/the-supreme-courts-jewish-gentile-my-memories-of-justice-scalia.
18. In an article titled *Formalism and Values: Three Models*, Benjamin Brown struggles to locate *halakhic* thought within what he identifies as the two central strands of juristic formalism. Brown instead defines *halakhic* formalism as applying particular rules over more abstract ones, especially in favor of rules that speak in the language of purpose or policy. There is value to this analysis, but the main drawback is that it can apply equally to many legal systems, and bears resemblance to rules/standards distinction, as well as Ronald Dworkin's rules/principles distinction. Drawing on Brown's other work, this chapter focuses on the features that distinguish *halakhah* and rabbinic culture from Western law. See Brown, "Formalism and Values: Three Models."
19. My analysis here departs somewhat from Hanina Ben Menahem, "Is Talmudic Law a Religious Legal System?," *Interdisciplinary Journal for Religion and Transformation in Contemporary Society* 7, no. 1 (July 2021): 13–41.
20. See, e.g., Daniel Statman, "Halakha and Morality: A Few Methodological Considerations," *Journal of Textual Reasoning* 6, no. 1 (2010): 7–22.
21. See, e.g., Yitzchak D. Gilat, "R. Eliezer's *Halakhot* in Relation to Bet Shammai and to the Teachings of R. Yohanan B. Zakkai," in *R. Eliezer Ben Hyrcanus: A Scholar Outcast* (Ramat Gan, Israel: Bar Ilan University Press, 1984), 462–91; Binyamin Lau, "A Contemporary Perspective: The Successors of Hillel the Elder," in *The Sages: Character, Context and Creativity: Volume I* (Jerusalem: Maggid Books, 2010), 233–39; Azzan Yadin, "Concepts of Scripture in the Schools of Rabbi Akiva and Rabbi Ishmael," in *Jewish Theologies of Scripture*, ed. Benjamin Sommer (New York: New York University Press, 2012), 47–63; see Hanina Ben Menahem, *Judicial Deviation in Talmudic Law: Governed by Men Not Rules* (Reading, UK: Harwood Academic, 1991).
22. See https://www.ada.gov/topics/title-iii/.

23. See Nat'l Ass'n of the Deaf v. Netflix, Inc., 869 F. Supp. 2d 196 (D. Mass. 2012) (Netflix is a place of public accommodation under the ADA); Young v. Facebook, Inc., 790 F. Supp. 2d 1110 (N.D. Cal. 2011) (Facebook is not a place of public accommodation under the ADA); Robles v. Domino's Pizza, LLC, 913 F.3d 898 (9th Cir. 2019) (Domino's website must comply with the ADA because it is a "good" or "service" in connection with a place of public accommodation).
24. See 1990 U.S.C.C.A.N. 303, 391.
25. See *Netflix*, 869 F. Supp. 2d at 201.
26. See *Netflix* (holding that "the legislative history of the ADA makes clear that Congress intended the ADA to adapt to changes in technology"); see also Carparts Distrib. Ctr., Inc. v. Automotive Wholesaler's Ass'n of New England, Inc., 37 F.3d 12, 19 (1st Cir. 1994) (the meaning of public accommodation "considered together with agency regulations and public policy concerns, persuades us that the phrase is not limited to actual physical structures").
27. See, e.g., Robert E. Scott, "The Case for Formalism in Relational Contract," *Northwestern University Law Review* 94, no. 3 (Spring 2000): 847–76; Alan Schwartz and Robert E. Scott, "Contract Theory and the Limits of Contract Law," *Yale Law Journal* 113, no. 3 (December 2003): 541–620.
28. See Frederick Schauer, *Playing by the Rules* (Oxford: Oxford University Press, 1991), 167–96.
29. Richard Pildes, "The Forms of Formalism," *University of Chicago Law Review* 66, no. 3 (Summer 1999): 607–21, esp. 613 ("formalists of all stripes . . . have always defended formalism, surely at the level of ultimate justification, in terms of purported desirable consequences"); Cass Sunstein, "Must Formalism Be Defended Empirically?," *University of Chicago Law Review* 66, no. 3 (Summer 1999): 636–70, esp. 641 ("Formalism should be defended pragmatically, with close reference to the likely performance of various institutions, and in terms of its consequences; it is not easily defended by reference to quasi-theological claims about the nature of law, legitimacy, or democracy").
30. This section draws on Thomas C. Grey, "Langdell's Orthodoxy," *University of Pittsburgh Law Review* 45, no. 1 (Fall 1983): 1–54; Duncan Kennedy, *The Rise and Fall of Classical Legal Thought* (Frederick, MD: Beard Books, 1970); Morton J. Horwitz, "The Rise of Legal Formalism," *The American Journal of Legal History* 19, no. 4 (October 1975): 251–64; Catharine Pierce Wells, "Langdell and the Invention of Legal Doctrine," *Buffalo Law Review* 58, no. 3 (May 2010): 551–618; Roscoe Pound, "The Role of the Will in Law," *Harvard Law Review* 68, no. 1 (November 1954): 1–19; Peter Birks, *An Introduction to English Private Law* (Oxford: Oxford University Press, 2001), introduction.
31. See Chaim Saiman, "The Law Wants to Be Formal," *Notre Dame Law Review* 96, no. 3 (2021): 1067–14.
32. See Pound, "The Role of the Will in Law."
33. See Roger Berkowitz, *The Gift of Science; Leibnitz and the Modern Legal Tradition* (New York: Fordham University Press, 2010).
34. See Schauer, *Playing by the Rules*.
35. See, e.g., John F. Manning, "The Absurdity Doctrine," *Harvard Law Review* 116, no. 8 (June 2003): 2387–2486, esp. 2388–93.
36. See Saiman, "Law Wants to be Formal"; Gerald J. Postema, "Law's System: The Necessity of System in Common Law," *University of North Carolina Legal Studies Research Paper Series*, no. 2324438 (2013): 1–29.

37. See, e.g., Cass Sunstein, "Justice Scalia's Democratic Formalism," *Yale Law Journal* 107, no. 2 (November 1997): 529–68, 530 ("much of [Scalia's] jurisprudence is designed to ensure that judgements are made by those with a superior democratic pedigree . . . [Scalia] seeks to develop rules of interpretation that will limit the policymaking authority and decisional discretion of the judiciary, the least accountable branch of government"); John F. Manning, "Justice Scalia and the Idea of Judicial Restraint," *Michigan Law Review* 115 (2017): 747, 748 ("[Scalia] did not want the federal judiciary to make an end run around the democratic process by exercising common law discretion 'to *make* the law'"); Antonin Scalia, *A Matter of Interpretation: Federal Courts and the Law*, 1st ed. (Princeton, NJ: Princeton University Press, 1997).
38. See, e.g., Lee Epstein, William Landes, and Richard Posner, *The Behavior of Federal Judges: A Theoretical and Empirical Study of Rational Choice* (Cambridge, MA: Harvard University Press, 2013); Keith J. Bybee, "Paying Attention to What Judges Say: New Directions on the Study of Judicial Decisionmaking," *Annual Review of Law and Social Science* 8 (December 2012): 69–84 (reviewing different lines of scholarly inquiry that empirically test and measure judicial decisionmaking); Elizabeth Mertz, Stewart Macaulay, and Thomas Mitchell, *The New Legal Realism*, vols. 1 and 2 (Cambridge: Cambridge University Press, 2016) (Mertz's introduction to the volume *Law and Social Science in the New Millennium* describes the vast literature testing the empirical claim of legal realism). This scholarship contrasts with Haym Soloveitchik's assertion that the central ideas of legal realism have not been subjected to empirical scrutiny. Haym Soloveitchik, *Collected Essays*, Vol. 3 (Liverpool, UK: Littman Library of Jewish Civilization, 2020), 413.
39. See Alexander T. Aleinikoff, "Constitutional Law in the Age of Balancing," *Yale Law Journal* 96, no. 5 (April 1987): 943–1005; Pierre Schlag, "Rules and Standards," *UCLA Law Review* 33, no. 2 (December 1985): 379–430; James G. Wilson, "Surveying the Forms of Doctrine on the Bright Line-Balancing Test Continuum," *Arizona State Law Journal* 27, no. 3 (Fall 1995): 773–844.
40. Hoshen Mishpat 2:1.
41. See *Shut Minhat Shlomo* Vol 1. and especially §9–11.
42. See Benjamin Brown, *Hazon Ish* (Jerusalem: Magnes Press, 2011), 196, 278, and 831 for snapshots of how Hazon Ish deployed this idea. This idea was also manifested by R. Soloveitchik, see Mayer Twersky, "Halakhic Values and Halakhic Decisions: Rav Soloveitchik's Pesak Regarding Women's Prayer Groups," *Tradition* 32, no. 2 (Spring 1998): 5–18, and finds expression in R. Asher Weiss's use of the term "*ratzon Hashem*" (the will of God) or "*ratzon haTorah*" (the will of the Torah) used to reflect uncodified *halakhic* norms and requirements. See Asher Weiss, "*Ratzon HaTorah*," in *Minchat Asher al Sefer Devarim* Essay 51 (Jerusalem: Machon Minhat Asher, 2009), 356–61 [Hebrew].
43. Hanina Ben Menahem, "Postscript: The Judicial Process and the Nature of Jewish Law," in *An Introduction to the Sources of Jewish Law*, ed. N. Hecht et al. (Boston 1996).
44. The primary exception is the role played by the Israeli rabbinate in issues of marriage and personal status. These rabbis are government functionaries imposed on the community rather than authorities who emerge from within communal structures.
45. Notably, the current Israeli government has proposed legislation seeking to bureaucratize *halakhah* into a state-like system by making rabbis of neighborhoods formally inferior to the rabbi of a city, and in turn the city rabbi formally inferior to the centralized rabbinate. See Ariel Finkelstein, "The Bill Regarding Local Rabbis Will Strengthen the Chief

Rabbinate and the Minister at the Expense of the Local Governance," July 9, 2023. https://www.idi.org.il/knesset-committees/49940 [Hebrew].

46. See Lawrence Kaplan, "*Da'as Torah:* A Modern Conception of Rabbinic Authority," in *Rabbinical Authority and Personal Autonomy*, ed. Moshe Sokol (Northvale, NJ: Jason Aaronson, 1992), 1–60.
47. See Ben Menahem, "Postscript: The Judicial Process and the Nature of Jewish Law."
48. See Barnhart v. Sigmon Coal Co., Inc., 534 U.S. 438, 461–62 (2002) (noting in the context of an apparently incoherent statutory regime that that deals brokered between the political branches "are not for us to judge or second-guess. . . . [P]arties should not seek to amend the statute by appeal to the Judicial Branch").
49. See Associated Press, "Scalia: Stupidity Constitutional," *Politico* (October 2, 2013), https://www.politico.com/story/2013/10/antonin-scalia-supreme-court-stupidity-sometimes-legal-097766.
50. See Grupo Mexicano de Desarrollo SA v. Alliance Bond Fund Inc., 527 U.S. 308, 333 (1999) ("The debate concerning [the scope of a remedial power granted to the courts] should be conducted and resolved where such issues belong in our democracy: in the Congress").
51. Indeed, much of the scholarship on the question of "*halakhah* and values" of the past several decades is dedicated to showcasing such examples. See Ben Menahem, *Judicial Deviation in Talmudic Law*; Ben Menahem, "Is Talmudic Law a Religious Legal System"; Ben Menahem, "The Myth of Formalism"; Schremer, *Ma'ase Rav*. Generally, this process is either unconscious, subconscious, or at least not explicit. On occasion, *poskim* may be direct. See, e.g., Jehiel Jacob Weinberg, *Kitvei ha-Gaon Rabbi Yehiel Yaakov Weinberg. Vol. 1*, ed. Marc B. Shapiro (Scranton, PA, 1998), 60, "in a case where there is a debate amongst the *rishonim*, rabbis should decide against the view that runs contrary to societal norms and casts our holy Torah in a negative light."
52. See Stein Hain, this volume.
53. Caperton v. A.T Massey Coal Co., 556 U.S. 868, 903 (2009) (Scalia J., dissenting).
54. See Rashi's commentary to b.Sotah 22.a., *she-Morin halakhah mitokh Mishnah*. The statement may have intended something different in its original context.
55. See, for example, sources cited in the introduction to R. Ovadya Yosef's *Shut Yabia Omer* Volume 1.
56. See, for example, the various rules of interpretation and qualifications for interpreting the *Shulkhan Arukh* collated in *Sefer Yad Malakhi* (1767). Repr. Bnei Brak: Mishor, 2001, 548–56
57. See Tucker, Levmore and Gotlib, Edrei, and Batnisky, all this volume.
58. m.Eduyot 1:5. See also j.Shabbat 1.4 and b.Gittin 36.b.
59. See, e.g., Menachem Kellner, *Maimonides on the Decline of the Generations and the Nature of Rabbinic Authority* (Albany: State University of New York Press, 1996); Brown, *Hazon Ish*.
60. Brown, *Hazon Ish*; Lawrence Kaplan, "The Hazon Ish: Haredi Critique of Traditional Orthodoxy," in *The Uses of Tradition: Jewish Continuity in the Modern Era*, ed. Jack Wertheimer (New York: Jewish Theological Seminary Press, 1998), 145–73.
61. See Soloveitchik, *Shiurei Ha-Rav*; Soloveitchik, *Halakhic Man*; Bleich, *Contemporary Halakhic Problems*; "Brief of Amicus Curie Agudath Israel of America."
62. Blu Greenberg, *On Women and Judaism: A View from Tradition* (Philadelphia, PA: Jewish Publication Society, 1981), 44.

63. See, e.g., Adam S. Ferziger, "Feminism and Heresy: The Construction of a Jewish Metanarrative," *Journal of the American Academy ` of Religion* 77, no. 3 (September 2009): 494–546. Greenberg's critique is largely supported by Ronit Irshai, "Toward a Gender Critical Approach to the Philosophy of Jewish Law (Halakhah)," *Journal of Feminist Studies in Religion* 26, no. 2 (Fall 2010): 55–77. Significant critiques of this view were penned by R. Aharon Lichtenstein, who noted, "the notion that 'where there is a rabbinic will there is a halakhic way' both insults gedolei Torah collectively, and, in its insouciant view of the totality of *halakha*, verges on the blasphemous." Aharon Lichtenstein, "The Human and Social Factor in Halacha," *Tradition* 38, no. 1 (Spring 2002): 1–25, esp. 13. See also Bleich, *Contemporary Halakhic Problems*, introduction ("In recent decades the argument has been made that in the modern era . . . the talmudic vision of women has been rendered obsolete, and [*halakhic* rules that flow from this perspective] must be regarded as nugatory. Years ago, R. Joseph B. Soloveitchik declared that rejection . . . 'borders. . . on the heretical'").
64. Ronit Irshai, "Homosexuality and the 'Aqedah Theology,'" *Journal of Jewish Ethics* 4, no. 1 (2018): 19–46.
65. See, e.g., Efrem Goldberg, "Let My People Go!," https://rabbiefremgoldberg.org/let-my-people-go ("Agunah is an example of what the Rav [Rabbi J. B. Soloveitchik] described as a time that we throw our hands in the air and submit our understanding to the will and laws of the Almighty."); Goldberg, "Our Generation's Sacrifice," https://rabbiefremgoldberg.org/our-generation-s-sacrifice (in discussing gay marriage, "it takes tremendous *mesirus nefesh*, incredible sacrifice, to be willing to subjugate our contemporary values, and even possibly our personal views, to standards established by the Torah and halacha and to defend and maintain the Torah position. . . . Perhaps surrender and submission are our test, our generation's trial").

    In a somewhat different light, Aryeh Klapper has written that the prohibition against gay marriage should go through a process of "chokification" defined as "a declaration that laws that once depended on the now-unintelligible premise should be regarded as either beyond human comprehension or else as arbitrary rules intended to train us to obedience." See Aryeh Klapper, "Chok, Mishpat and Obergefell," *Modern Torah Leadership* (July 3, 2015), https://moderntoraleadership.wordpress.com/2015/07/03/chok-mishpat-and-obergefell/.
66. On the *Brisker* method, see Norman Solomon, *Analytic Movement: Hayyim Soloveitchik and his Circle* (Tampa: University of South Florida, 1993); Marc B. Shapiro, "The Brisker Method Reconsidered," *Tradition* 31, no. 3 (Spring 1997): 78–102; Shlomo Tikochinsky, "Methods of Learning in 19th Century Lithuanian Yeshivas" (PhD. diss., Hebrew University, 2004); Yosef Blau, ed., *Lomdut: The Conceptual Approach to Jewish Learning* (New York: Yeshiva University Press, 2006).
67. See Chaim Saiman, "Legal Theology: The Turn to Conceptualism in Nineteenth-Century Jewish Law," *Journal of Law and Religion* 21, no. 1 (2005–2006): 39–100; Saiman, *Halakhah*, 195–212.
68. Soloveitchik, *Halakhic Man*, 59.
69. Joseph B. Soloveitchik, "Ma Dodekh MiDod," in *Divrei Hagut v'Haaracha* (Jerusalem: World Zionist Organization, 1981), 57–97 [Hebrew].
70. See examples cited in Saiman, *Halakhah*, 206.
71. See Yonatan Y. Brafman, "Systematicity and Its Limits in Lithuanian Talmudism," in *Talmud and Philosophy*, ed. Sergey Dolgopolski and James Redfeld (Indianapolis: Indiana University Press, forthcoming).

72. Ibid.
73. See Wells, "Langdell and the Invention of Legal Doctrine."
74. See Ernest J. Weinrib, "Legal Formalism: On the Immanent Rationality of the Law," *Yale Law Journal*, 97, no. 6 (1988): 951–54.
75. See, for example, G. W. Leibnitz, "One of the Chief Ways of Making Jurisprudence More Manageable, and of Surveying Its Vast Ocean, as though in a Geographical Chart, Is by Tracing a Large Number of Particular Decisions Back to More General Principles," in *Leibniz: New Essays on Human Understanding*, ed. Karl Ameriks and Desmond M. Clarke, trans. Peter Remnant and Jonathan Bennett (Cambridge: Cambridge University Press, 1996), 371.
76. See Leib Moscovitz, *Talmudic Reasoning: From Casuistics to Conceptualization* (Tübingen, Germany: Mohr Siebeck), 2002.
77. See Brown, "Formalism and Values: Three Models," 245–46.
78. Notably, *Briskers* had relatively little to say about the more philosophical sections of *Hilkhot De'ot* or the eschatology of *Hilkhot Melahim*. Moreover the *Brisker* analytical-conceptual categories bear little resemblance to those used by Maimonides to structure *Mishneh Torah*.
79. For example, *Birkhat Shmuel* of R. Baruch Ber Leibovitz, and *Kovetz Shiurim* of R. Elchanan Wasserman.
80. There are some exceptions. Probably the most important pre-*Brisker* example is R. Aryeh Leib ha-Kohen's, *Shev Shmat'ta* (1804) which is devoted to the issue of decision-making in cases of factual or legal doubt. From the *Brisker* orbit, R. Shimon Shkopf's *Sha'arei Yosher* (1928) and his student, R. Moshe Avigdor Amiel's, *Ha-Middot le-Heker ha-Halakhah* (vol. 1, 1939; vol. 2, 1942; vol. 3, 1945), aim to articulate the fundamental principles of significant areas of *halakhah* in the systematic method of principles and particulars. See Yosef Lindell, "A Science Like Any Other? Classical Legal Formalism in the Halakhic Jurisprudence of Rabbis Isaac Jacob Reines and Moses Avigdor Amiel," *Journal of Law and Religion* 28, no. 1 (2013): 179–224; see also Brafman, "Systematicity and Its Limits." These latter works are not simply collations, but books where later chapters build on the analysis developed in earlier ones.

    Beyond that, *halakhic* scholars associated with the *Mishpat Ivri* school frequently recast *halakhic* material using the conceptual categories of modern law. An early entrant to this field is R. Isaac Herzog, *The Main Institutions of Jewish Law* (London: Soncino, 1939). Subsequent scholarship in this tradition continues to assimilate *halakhic* and Western legal categories granting the source material a more conceptual organizational structure.

    Finally, as the *Brisker* method develops among students of R. Joseph Soloveitchik and R. Aharon Lichtenstein who are more open to contemporary philosophical and jurisprudential, it is likely that more wholistic mappings of *halakhic* terrain will continue to emerge.
81. See Isadore Twersky, "'The Shulchan Aruch': Enduring Code of Jewish Law," *Judaism* 16, no. 2 (Spring 1967).
82. For a discussion of the role of how format and organization of *halakhic* materials impacts its normative authority, see Morsel-Eisenberg, this volume.
83. See Grey, "Langdell's Orthodoxy," 5–11; Kennedy, *The Rise and Fall of Classical Legal Thought*, 13–14.
84. On the *Brisker* aversion to concrete *halakhic* decision-making, see Saiman, "Legal Theology," 73–75. For how the *Brisker* method is utilized in *halakhic* decision-making,

see Mordechai Willig, "The *Brisker* Derekh and Pesak Halakhah" (2006); Blau, *Lomdut*, 115–29.

85. Robert M. Cover, "Obligation: A Jewish Jurisprudence of the Social Order," *Journal of Law and Religion* 5, no. 1 (1987): 65–74: p. 66. See also Porat, this volume.
86. See m.Avot 1:1.
87. Moshe Halbertal, "The History of Halakhah and the Emergence of Halakhah," *Dine Israel* 9 (2013): 1–23 [Hebrew].
88. The literature is vast. Some recent work on this topic is found in Jeremy Brown and Marc Herman, eds., *Accounting for the Commandments in Medieval Judaism* (Leiden and Boston: Brill, 2021), and in several studies by Yair Lorberbaum. See Yair Lorberbaum, "The Rise of Halakhic Religiosity of Mystery and Transcendence," *Dine Israel* 34 (2022): 1–49; Yair Lorberbaum, "On Rules and Reason in Law and in Halakhah—A Fresh Conceptual Framework for the Study of the Rationale of the Commandments," *Jerusalem Studies in Jewish Thought* 26 (2021): 1–76 [Hebrew]; Yair Lorberbaum, "Two Concepts of Gezerat Ha-Katuv: A Chapter in Maimonides' Legal and Halakhic Thought," published in three parts in *Dine Israel* 28 (2011): 123–61; *Diné Israel* 29 (2013): 101–37 and *Dine Israel* 31 (2016): 159–210. See also Daniel Matt, "The Mystic and the Mizwot," in *Jewish Spirituality: From the Bible through the Middle Ages*, ed. Arthur Green (New York: Herder & Herder, 1986), 370–72. See also Ariel Evan Mayse, this volume.
89. b.Sanhedrin 21.a; b.Bava Metzia 115.a.
90. See, for example, R. Asher Weiss's reading of the rulings of earlier sources. Asher Weiss, "*Ta'amei De'Kra ve-Ta'amei ha-Mitzvot*," in *Minchat Asher al Sefer Bamidbar*, Essay 42 (Jerusalem: Machon Minchat Asher, 2006), 285–96 [Hebrew].
91. b.Sanhedrin 21.a.
92. b.Psahim 115.b.
93. Rashbam to b.Psahim 115.b. *Shulkhan Arukh* OC 475:3.
94. Deut. 25:4.
95. b.Bava Metzia 90.b. See also Rosh cited in *Shitta Mekubetzet* therein who explains that purposive interpretations are permitted when they accord with the simple reading of the Torah verse.
96. See sources collected by Asher Weiss, "*Ta'amei De'Kra ve-Ta'amei ha-Mitzvot*."
97. b.Berachot 33.b; Rambam *Mishneh Torah*, Tefllia 9:7; *Ramban al ha-Torah* to Deut. 22:6.
98. *Guide to the Perplexed* 3:48.
99. Of the later authorities, see *Shut Hatam Sofer* OH #100; *Hazon Ish* YD 175.
100. *Shut Havot Yair* #67.
101. *Tikkunei Zohar* 23.a; *Zohar Hadash, Midrash Ruth, Ma'amar Kan Tzippor*
102. A detailed discussion of the rationalist and kabbalistic approaches to this *mitzvah* can be found in Natan Slifkin, "Shiluach HaKein: Compassion or Cruelty?" in *Rationalism vs. Mysticism: Schisms in Traditional Jewish Thought* (Jerusalem: Torah and Nature Foundation and Gefen Books, 2020), 432–67.
103. Exod. 12:9.
104. m.Psahim 7:1; b.Psahim 74.a–76.b.
105. b.Psahim 75.a–b.
106. See Moshe Halbertal, "The History of Halakhah and the Emergence of Halakhah," *Dine Israel* 29 (2013): 1–23.
107. Handwashing before morning prayer is discussed in b.Berakhot 15.b. b.Berakhot 60.b discusses various blessings made as part of the morning routine including washing the

hands. b.Shabbat 108.b–109.a discusses an evil spirit which rests on the hands in the morning which can be removed via threefold washing. Rambam codifies the first two sources in Chapters 4 and 7 of *The Laws of Prayer* but does not relate to the third. *Tur*, OH §4 includes the threefold requirement. A fulsome discussion is found in *Arukh ha-Shulkhan* OH 4:2.

108. *Shaarei Teshuva* OH 4:10.
109. *Shulkhan Arukh* OH 4:1 with *Mishnah Berurah* 4:2; *Biur Halakhah* OH 4, "*ve'afilu*."
110. *Shulkhan Arukh* OH 4:7, 159, 160:9,160:14; and *Mishnah Berurah* 159:5–6; 160:39; 160:67.
111. Menachem M. Abramson, *Bathing and Showering in Halacha: Shabbos, Yom Tov, the Nine Days and More* (Lakewood: Israel Bookshop Publications, 2022). Detailed *halakhic* compendia of this genre are a product of the twentieth century, yet the broad outlines of most of what is covered is extant in older writing.
112. Abramson, *Bathing and Showering in Halacha*, 15–18.
113. *Mishnah Berurah* 88:4.
114. Abramson, *Bathing and Showering in Halacha*, 20–23.
115. In her enlightening study of ritual studies and rabbinics, Mira Balberg usefully explains that in the rabbinic context, not much distinguishes between *law* and *ritual* since both ideas are subsumed under the category of *halakhah*. *See* Mira Balberg, "Ritual Studies and the Study of Rabbinic Literature," *Currents in Biblical Research* 16, no. 1 (2017): 71–98. This accords with Shai Lavi's analysis that the law/ritual distinction is not native to Jewish thought but traces to nineteenth-century German Protestant discourse. See Shai Lavi, "Enchanting a Disenchanted Law: On Jewish Ritual and Secular History in Nineteenth Century Germany." *UC Irvine Law Review* 1, no. 3 (2011): 813–43.
116. See Martin L. Gordon, "Netilat Yadayim Shel Shaharit: Ritual of Crisis or Dedication?" *Gesher* 8 (1981): 36–72, esp. 39–41 and nn. 38–52 nn. 57–58.
117. *Mishnah Berurah* 88:4. Benjamin Brown has argued that the work uses "soft stringency" to nudge people to more optimal *halakhic* compliance. See Benjamin Brown, "'Soft Stringency' in the Mishnah Berurah," *Contemporary Jewry* 27, no. 1 (October 2007): 1–41. A contrary analysis is presented by Michael J. Broyde and Ira Bedzow. See Michael J. Broyde and Ira Bedzow, *The Codification of Jewish Law and an Introduction to the Jurisprudence of the Mishna Berura* (Boston: Academic Studies Press, 2014).
118. Abramson, *Bathing and Showering in Halacha*, 20.
119. Lev. 19:13; Deut. 24:14–15.
120. See Chaim Saiman, "Talmud Study, Ethics and Social Policy: A Case Study in the Laws of Wage-Payment as an Argument for Neo-Lamdanut," *Jewish Law Association Studies* 25 (2014): 225–61, esp. 227 nn. 5–6, and 228–32.
121. See R. Asher Weiss, *B'al Talin*, Ke- Teitzei, 5774 citing the position of Hafetz Hayyim and R. S. Y. Elyashiv.
122. R. Asher Weiss disagrees, noting that, "in financial dealings and commandments between persons the logic [used to apply the law in concrete settings] follows the rationale of the mitzva."
123. For discussion of kabbalistic and functional logic of the wage-payment mitzva interact in Hassidic rulings, see Saiman, "Talmud Study," 241–44.
124. t.Bava Metzia 10:11. b.Bava Metiza 116a.
125. Rashi to Bava Metzia 116a; Rama cited in *Shulhan Arukh* Hoshen Mishpat 97.
126. *Shulkhan Arukh* Hoshen Mishpat 97:8 and Rema's gloss.
127. See *Tur* and *Shulhan Arukh* Hoshen Mishpat 97:10 and commentaries therein.

128. Two recent works address the issue of using transactional formalities to evade *halakhic* regulations. See Elana Stein Hain, *Circumventing the Law: Rabbinic Perspectives on Loopholes and Legal Integrity* (University of Pennsylvania Press 2024); and Daniel Z. Feldman, *Letter and Spirit: Evasion, Avoidance and Workarounds in the Halakhic System* (Maggid Press, 2024).
129. See b.Bava Metzia 111a; For further analysis, see the discussion in Saiman, *Talmud Study, Ethics and Social Policy*. Similar issues arise under American law which aims to regulate whether a landowner can use a middleman to avoid various wage-payment obligations under the "joint employment doctrine." See M. Linder, "The Joint Employment Doctrine: Clarifying Joint Legislative-Judicial Confusion," *Hamline J. Pub. L. & Pol'y* 10 (1989): 321–22; M. H. LeRoy, "Farm Labor Contractors and Agricultural Producers as Joint Employers under the Migrant and Seasonal Agricultural Worker Protection Act: An Empirical Public Policy Analysis," *Berkeley J. Emp. & Lab. L.* 19 (1998): 175.
130. b.Bava Metzia 92a; see also Saiman, *Halakhah*, 95–100.
131. See Rema to *Shuhan Arukh* Hoshen Mishpat 281:7 and Even Ha'Ezer 113:2
132. *Shulkhan Arukh* Hoshen Mishpat 207:16, and Rema's gloss and commentaries.
133. Two recent books examine this phenomenon in *halakhah* from different angles. See Elana Stein Hain, *Circumventing the Law: Rabbinic Perspectives on Loopholes and Legal Integrity* (College Park: University of Pennsylvania Press, 2024); and Daniel Feldman, *Letter and Spirit: Evasions, Avoidance and Workarounds in the Halakhic System* (Jerusalem: Maggid Books, 2024).
134. The borrower is generally permitted to socially engage with the lender to the same degree they engaged prior to the loan, but the borrower cannot bestow any additional favors or social graces on the lender owing to the loan. However, if the favor is one that is conducted in public (such as honoring the lender in synagogue), it may be prohibited in all circumstances. See, for example, Shakh to *Shulhan Arukh*, Yoreh De'ah 160:
135. See Chaim Jachter, *Yerushah—Shtar Chatzi Zachar and its Contemporary Variation*, https://www.koltorah.org/halachah/yerushah-shtar-chatzi-zachar-and-its-contemporary-variation-by-rabbi-chaim-jachter.
136. See Lorberbaum, "The Rise of Halakhic Religiosity," citing Rabbi Shneur Zalman of Liady, "with regard to a commandment that one does not comprehend its reasons—that is loftier" This view is affirmatively rejected by Maimonides in *Guide for the Perplexed*, 3:31.
137. This idea is expressed forcefully by Rabbi Joseph B. Soloveitchik. See Abraham R. Besdin, "The 'Common Sense' Rebellion against Torah Authority," in *Reflections of the Rav Volume One* (Hoboken, NJ: KTAV, 1993), 139–49.
138. See the discussion in Ephraim Kanarfogel, "Ta'ame Ha-Mizvot in Medieval Ashkenaz," in Brown and Herman, *Accounting for the Commandments in Medieval Judaism*, 177.
139. See also Zohar 3:105.a ("The action below is always essential in order to arouse Above. Come and see: One who says that the action is not always essential, or pronouncing words or producing sounds, may his spirit deflate").
140. See generally sources in Lorberbaum, "The Rise of Halakhic Religiosity of Mystery and Transcendence," and Lorberbaum, "On Rules and Reason in Law and in Halakhah."
141. See Lorberbaum, "The Rise of Halakhic Religiosity."
142. While *halakhic* theologies differ on the degree to which the particulars of the *mitzvah* observance are important, from God's perspective, they generally accord that the human requirement to obey the Divine command is of primary religious significance.

CHAPTER 16

JEWISH LAW AS A DUTY-BASED SYSTEM AND WHY IT MATTERS

BENJAMIN PORAT

INTRODUCTION

ONE of the features that distinguishes Jewish from modern law is its legal language.[1] While Jewish law often suggests rules that might resemble certain laws in modern legal systems, they are expressed through a different legal dialect. Modern legal discourse predominantly employs the language of rights, whereas Jewish law operates with a language centered on duty, rooted in the significance of commandments (*mitzvot*) and obligations. While cornerstones of contemporary law are basic rights such as "the right to life" and "the right to property," the parallels in Jewish law are commandments such as "you shall not murder" and "you shall not steal." The *Talmud* relates that God granted the Israelites 613 commandments at Sinai, rather than 613 rights, and humans are foremost are conceived as duty bearers, rather than rights holders.[2] Although there are exceptions where Talmudic Sages recognized the existence of interpersonal legal rights,[3] these exceptions do not alter the overall focus in Jewish law on terms of duties.

This difference intrigued many scholars over the course of the past century. Isaac Breuer addressed this issue in a lecture he delivered in Frankfort in 1910.[4] Afterward, Israeli Supreme Court Justice Moshe Silberg, treated this fundamental difference between the two legal traditions,[5] and another Israeli Supreme Court justice, Haim Cohn, discussed this topic in a book entitled *Human Rights in Jewish Law*.[6] Another article was written by Rabbi Aharon Lichtenstein, who argued that the language of the Torah is based on fundamental terms such as *mitzvah* and *hiyuv*—commandment and obligation—rather than individual rights.[7] The most influential article on this topic was written by Robert Cover, a professor of law at Yale Law School, which examined the profound implications that exist between a legal system based on rights and a legal system based on duties, such as Jewish law.[8]

The fact that a particular legal system adopts a rights-based discourse does not mean it fails to acknowledge the existence of corresponding duties. For instance, legal recognition of an individual's right to life or private property entails that others are prohibited from causing harm to their life or damaging their property. Similarly, when a legal system adopts a duty-based discourse, it does not imply a denial of corresponding rights. Duties such as "you shall not murder" and "you shall not steal" inherently give rise to reciprocal rights for individuals not to be murdered or robbed. If someone's property is stolen, they have the right to seek legal action for its return. Hence, the fundamental differentiation between rights-based and duty-based legal systems lies in their starting point and the way they frame their legal rules. According to a well-known maxim, "a difference is a difference only if it makes a difference." This chapter is dedicated to analyzing a variety of legal outcomes that result from the decision of Jewish law to frame its legal dialogue through duties rather than rights.

Opposing Approaches and Their Rejection

Before delving into the intricacies of this subject, it is crucial to address the approaches that challenge the fundamental assertion that Jewish law is solely focused on duties, through evidence showcasing its recognition of rights. Biblical scholar Moshe Greenberg argues that elements of rights-based language can be identified within biblical law.[9] According to his view, the biblical terminologies that serve this function are *mishpat* (law) and *tzedaka* (right), and the verb *tza'ak* (cried out). For example, the verse, "the birthright [*mishpat habekhora*] is his due" (Deut. 21:17) means the first born has the right to receive a double portion in the inheritance of his father. Likewise, when Mephiboshet says to David "What right [*tzedaka*] have I to appeal [*liz'ok*] further Your Majesty?" (2 Sam. 19:29), he means "I no longer hold a right that I can claim from you." Greenberg thus concludes: "The concept of human rights, arising from the very idea of justice, existed among the authors of the Bible."[10]

While Greenberg's argument about the recognition of individual rights in Scripture is correct, these rights are ultimately derived from the primary biblical concept of obligations imposed on the other party, as discussed earlier. An example of this can be seen in the laws of inheritance (Deut. 21:15–17), addressed by Greenberg. These verses impose affirmative and prohibitive obligations on the father, preventing him from discriminating against his first-born son. The Bible states that "the birthright [*mishpat habekhora*] is his due" only as a result of these duties, such that the father's duty generates the right of inheritance for his first-born. Much like the rest of the biblical law, duty forms the cornerstone.

A sharper argument has recently been made by Itamar Rosensweig and Shua Mermelstein, who argue, contrary to Cover and Lichtenstein, that "rights play a central role in Jewish law" because "certain *mitzvot* are best understood as protecting individuals' rights."[11] For instance, Maimonides (twelfth century) defines the *mitzvah* that allows the worker to eat from the food he produces for his employer.[12] According to Rosensweig and Mermelstein, this *mitzvah* "is explicitly formulated by Maimonides as a worker's entitlement."[13] However, a closer examination of Maimonides's wording reveals just the opposite. Not only does Maimonides not mention the term "right," but he actually clearly articulates the permission given to the worker to consume the employer's food as the employer's (prohibitive) obligation:

> Whenever workers are working at anything which grows from the soil and has been completely processed whether severed from the soil or still attached to it, and their work constitutes a final processing *the employer is enjoined* to allow them to eat of that at which they are working.[14]

This example clearly demonstrates how, in Jewish law, obligations generate rights, rather than the other way around. There is no doubt that the purpose of the employer's obligation is to protect the worker's interests. However, this goal is achieved through the vocabulary of duties, rather than the language of rights.

Another example brought up by Rosensweig and Mermelstein is the law of charity (*tzedaka*). While they acknowledge that this law is formulated as a duty, they argue:

> the substantive *halakhic* rules of charity reflect the *halakha*'s emphasis on protecting the rights of the recipient . . . the Jewish law obligation to give charity can be seen as deriving from the right of the poor person to welfare . . . the right of the poor person to welfare is more fundamental than the giver's duty. This is because it is the poor person's right that grounds the giver's duty.[15]

Here, again, this example demonstrates the opposite. According to Jewish law, the duty incumbent on an individual to give charity to a poor person does not grant the poor person a claim right to receive the money. The one who gives charity has the discretion to decide to whom they will give the money. For example, according to *Rashi*: "if a poor person sues him [to receive his money], he can answer: I prefer to give it to a different poor person."[16] There is no clearer expression of the idea that the owner's duty to give charity to the poor does not generate a correlative right for a specific poor person to receive money from that individual.

The question of whether and to what extent the duty of charity generates a corresponding right for the poor is complex and goes beyond the scope of this short chapter.[17] However, it is evident that the formulation of charity laws as duties rather than rights is crucial to understanding the fundamental nature of this *halakhic* institution.

In a broader perspective, the fact that Jewish law is duty-based does not mean that its laws should be understood as obligations owed solely to God (as *mitzvot bein adam la-makom*).[18] Jewish law dedicates many of its laws to protecting the interests of individuals, particularly those who are more vulnerable. However, this protection is achieved by imposing duties on individuals (*mitzvot bein adam la-chaveiro*), which, in some cases, generate correlative rights to the protected party. For instance, the laws of charity determine the amount of charity based on the needs of the poor, and the court can enforce giving charity on those who refuse to fulfill their duty. This highlights the central purpose of safeguarding the welfare of the needy. Yet, while protecting the interests of the needy can be accomplished either through granting them rights or imposing duties on the well-offs, Jewish law clearly opts for the latter approach.

Where Should the Line Be Drawn between the Two Legal Discourses?

Determining where to draw the line between Jewish and modern law on this score proves a challenging task. Is the focus on duties a unique characteristic that sets Jewish law apart from other legal systems? This cannot be the case since there are other legal systems that are also duty-based. Another alternative is that the distinction lies not between Jewish and modern law, but between religious law in general and modern legal systems. For instance, similar claims are made regarding the Christian[19] and Islamic[20] legal traditions, suggesting their emphasis on the language of duties.

However, we should give pause before making simplistic correlation between religious legal systems and duty-based law, and secular legal systems and rights-based law. Socialist law is certainly not a religious legal system, yet it places a strong emphasis on the concept of duty.[21] On the other hand, the American Declaration of Independence is rooted in rights-based discourse despite its clear use of religious language.[22] Although there are not many examples of this kind, we should not readily accept the notion that the language of rights is inherently secular, while the language of duties is strictly religious.

Another possible argument is that a legal language centered around duties is more suitable for a legal system that lacks sovereign authority. This is because a rights-based system relies on a centralized and effective power to enforce those rights, which was absent in communal legal systems like Jewish law during the medieval period. On the other hand, a language of duties is better suited for a communal stateless legal system, as it fosters an internal sense of responsibility that motivates citizens to abide by the law without external enforcement mechanisms. From this perspective, the distinction between duty-based law and rights-based law should be drawn at the emergence of the modern centralized state. However, this argument fails to fully address the issue. As previously demonstrated, there are modern examples of centralized state-based legal systems that operate based on the concept of duty. Additionally, the origin of the duty-based language in Jewish law predates the period following the destruction of the Temple and loss of sovereignty, as it can already be found in biblical law.[23]

Therefore, I consider the language of duty to be a choice that arises from a particular worldview and set of values, as will be explained, rather than being solely influenced by certain historical circumstances.

Why Does the Difference Matter?

At this juncture, we should ask whether the difference between stating legal principles as duties rather than rights is merely semantics or whether it carries legal meaning.

Some maintain the distinction creates two distinct legal universes. According to Silberg, "[M]odern law has no interest in duties; its sole interests are rights, and the debtor's duty to pay is only a short way of indicating the possibility of a payment coerced by the creditor . . . [T]his is not true in Jewish law . . . [T]he payment of a debt is the fulfillment of a precept (*mitzvah*); and the payment of a debt is the prototype of the whole system of legal obligations. If it is no more than a religious precept, a religious-moral obligation of the debtor, then the duty is the primary thing and the right secondary, if not less than that."[24]

In line with this perspective, Cover elaborates that the choice of language in which a law expresses its rules is as significant as the substantive content of those rules.[25] The discourse of rights and the discourse of duties uphold two distinct social ethos. The right-based discourse reinforces the ethos of safeguarding individuals from the authority of the modern state. Consequently, the foundational narrative of this discourse is the social contract, wherein each citizen relinquishes certain liberties and rights in exchange for the benefits provided by the state. According to this ethos, an individual attains her humanity by asserting her rights. On the other hand, the discourse of duties reinforces the ethos of a society established to pursue higher values, such as religious or moral ideals. The formative myth of the duty-based discourse is the giving of the Torah at Sinai, during which the people gathered to willingly accept the responsibility of fulfilling the commandments. In this paradigm, an individual realizes her humanity by fulfilling her obligations.

In the Coverian account, the difference between the two legal societies comes to light in the following example. When does a minor become a full member of the community? In a rights-based discourse, legal maturity is the point at which an individual is an independent bearer of legal rights. For example, the age at which one is eligible to exercise the right to vote.[26] On the other hand, in a duty-based discourse, joining the community happens when a minor becomes independently obligated under the law. In Jewish law, a minor becomes an adult at the age of *bar/bat-mitzvah*, when they assume the same legal obligations as the rest of the community.

Cover explains how this distinction accounts for several intriguing phenomena, such as the uniqueness of the feminist struggle within the religious-*halakhic* world. While feminism generally advocates for equal *rights* for women, such as the rights to vote, hold office, and fair working conditions, religious feminism also strives for equal *obligations* for women, including the opportunity to engage in Torah study, participate in communal prayer, and fulfill obligations such as wearing *tallit* and *tefillin*.[27] The pursuit of equality revolves also around participation in religious commandments and obligations, rather than merely focusing on equal rights.[28]

Not everyone concurs, however, that the distinction between duty-based law and rights-based law is quite as stark. According to Haim Cohn, although Jewish law emphasizes commandments and obligations, it uses these tools to establish an entire world of rights: "Thus, prohibitions such as 'thou shalt not steal' (Exod. 20:15; Deut. 5:19) and 'thou shalt not remove thy neighbor's landmark' (Deut. 19:14) and the injunction to return lost chattels (Deut. 22:1–3), all impose a negative or positive duty: but they may be read to imply a right to property and possession—a right which is nowhere spelled out as such."[29] According to his perspective, it seems that the disparity between duty-based and rights-based laws is no more than a matter of semantics. For instance, the prohibition of defamation establishes the right to reputation, while the obligation to adjudicate justly establishes the right to due process and a fair trial.[30] Consequently, the modern Jewish individual is not expected to grapple with a conflict between her Jewish identity, rooted in an awareness of commandments and obligations, and her Western identity, founded on an awareness of rights. Instead, these two spheres are interconnected and mutually complementary.

This can be elucidated through the Hohfeld's correlative axiom introduced in the early twentieth century by the legal scholar Wesley Newcomb Hohfeld.[31] According to Hohfeld's analysis, a right and a duty represent two facets of the same legal relationship: a right always pertains to a duty bearer, and a duty is invariably directed toward a right holder. Consequently, a reciprocal duty accompanies every right, just as a reciprocal right accompanies every duty.[32] The query of whether a given system contains more rights or more duties is analogous to a door, where one side says "push" and the other side reads "pull." The door can be both pushed and pulled, yet it remains the same door.

Though rights and duties may correlate, this does not mean their boundaries are precisely the same. Consider the scenario where every citizen is endowed with the right to education. Nevertheless, determining whether the state, local authority, or parents bear the duty becomes a complex task.[33] Likewise a duty of the well-off to support the less fortunate (as exemplified by the commandment of *tzedaka*, charity) need not confer upon each impoverished individual a right to sue a property owner for charitable aid, as the right may be actionable against the community instead. (Indeed this is exemplified by the laws of *tzedaka*, charity.)

While the decision to employ the language of rights or duties may lead to ambiguity that occasionally hinders identifying the reciprocal duty bearer or right holder, this does not undermine Hohfeld's assertion that rights and duties are inherently correlated. Later, I set out other reasons for rejecting Cohen's approach that the difference between a rights-based law and a duty-based law is only a matter of semantics; however, the challenge of pinpointing the correlative holder of a right/duty is not among them.

Against this backdrop, I propose a third perspective on this matter which assumes that while rights and duties may correlate there is legal significance to the starting point of the journey. This is because a rule originating from a right, even assuming the ensuing obligation, functions differently from a rule rooted in the concept of duty which gives rise to a corresponding right. The manner in which we frame our legal world profoundly influences its operational dynamics.[34]

Duties toward Nonhumans

Duties are typically imposed upon an individual while being oriented toward another person possessing the corresponding right. The commandment "you shall not steal" signifies the owner's entitlement to private property. This principle extends to duties that apply toward a collective as well. For instance, the duty incumbent upon an individual to pay taxes signifies the state's right to levy taxes from that individual. However, how are duties not directed to other humans analyzed? Take, for example, the prohibition against animal abuse, the duty to safeguard the environment, or the proscription of making defamatory remarks about the deceased. In these scenarios, identifying the duty bearer—the individual commanded not to undertake certain actions—is straightforward. Yet, the question remains: who assumes the role of the right holder? Can animals,[35] trees[36] and rivers,[37] and the deceased[38] be considered right holders?

This question hinges on our understanding of the concept of a right.[39] Some contend that whoever benefits from the fulfillment of an obligation is designated as the right holder. For instance, parents are obligated to provide financial support to their child. Since the child is the beneficiary of this support, they are considered to be the right holders. In the view of legal philosopher Joseph Raz, if X's well-being is a sufficient reason for holding Y to be under a duty, then X is a right holder ("the interest theory").[40] Within this framework, it stands to reason that if the beneficiaries of certain obligations are animals and, potentially, even trees, there is no reason why they could not be deemed right holders. Others argue that being a right holder means something different. A right holder is not necessarily the beneficiary of a certain obligation; rather, it is the one who has the authority to decide whether to enforce the obligee to fulfill his obligation or to waive it; A right holder is considered "a small-scale sovereign" ("the will theory").[41] Here is an example: labor laws often establish stringent regulations concerning minimum wages and maximum daily working hours. These regulations are primarily designed to safeguard the well-being of employees. However, if an employee lacks the option to waive these regulations—he cannot agree to work for a wage lower than the minimum or to exceed the legally permitted working hours—then, according to the "will theory," the employee may not be considered the right holder. He does not have the authority to decide whether to insist on minimum wages and maximum daily working hours or to waive it. Clearly, according to this perspective, exercising rights is an action unique for human beings as intelligent beings, and therefore only humans could qualify as right holders. Advocates of this standpoint may need to complicate their argument to claim that the prohibition against animal abuse engenders the right of other individuals to reside in a world devoid of animal cruelty. Similarly, the proscription against environmental pollution bestows upon others the right to inhabit a pristine environment. And the prohibition against defamatory remarks about the deceased confers upon the deceased's family the right to safeguard their loved one's reputation from harm. The problem with this assertion lies in the fact that if there are no individuals adversely affected by these actions (such as a deceased person with no relatives), there exists no legal rationale for prohibiting these actions.

Right-based discourse must engage in considerable exertion to account for obligations toward nonhumans: either stretching the scope of the concept of rights to encompass nonhumans, or constraining the prohibited action to cases where a distinct individual is unequivocally harmed. Conversely, the duty-based discourse encounters no such quandary since there exists no analytical distinction between the prohibition against inflicting suffering upon animals,[42] the obligation to refrain from making defamatory remarks about the deceased,[43] and the duty not to harm fellow human beings. As articulated by legal scholar Mary Ann Glendon, "[W]here environmental issues are concerned, the biblical language of stewardship may be more appropriate than endowing trees with rights, and more conducive to responsible use of resources than vague promises that everyone has a "right" to a healthy environment."[44]

Affirmative vs. Prohibitive Duties

Hohfeld and his circle contended that it is essentially fruitless to inquire whether there exists a surplus of rights or duties. This is because rights inherently spawn corresponding duties, rendering the count of duties unaffected by the linguistic differentiation between rights talk and duty talk. Nevertheless, it could prove useful to contemplate how the selected legal language impacts the balance between affirmative (to do *x*) and prohibitive (to not do *x*) duties. Rights-based legal systems generally exhibit a paucity of affirmative obligations placed upon citizens, with primary examples comprising obligations to pay taxes and to fulfill civic responsibilities such as responding to a court summons to give testimony, and, depending on the state, the affirmative duty to serve in the army, participate in jury duty, and vote in elections.[45] This narrow list means that in states that emerge out of the common-law tradition, there is no legal duty for a person to rescue another individual in peril.[46] In stark contrast, prohibitive duties, encompassing obligations not to commit acts like murder, theft, rape, or defamation, are exceedingly prevalent within rights-based legal systems.

This phenomenon should not surprise us. Prohibitive duties restrain an individual from engaging in specific actions yet otherwise grant them the freedom to undertake any other action of their choosing. On the other hand, affirmative duties mandate an individual to execute a particular action and simultaneously preclude them from engaging in any other action during that time frame. This point was addressed by Israeli Supreme Court Justice Misha'el Heshin who elucidated why Western democratic states consistently endeavor to minimize the affirmative duties imposed on their citizens:

> there are far fewer positive duties than negative duties . . . negative duties invade an individual's area of freedom less than positive duties . . . In other words, consistent with liberal democracy and individual rights—among other things—it is easier to impose negative duties on the individual than positive duties. We learn from this that before imposing a positive duty on an individual, we must consider and reconsider whether our decision goes too far, whether we have exceeded what is appropriate and permissible under the basic perspective accepted in our society.[47]

As a duty-based system, Jewish law shows minimal hesitation in imposing significant affirmative duties on individuals. A vivid instance of this is the injunction "do not stand by your fellow's blood" (Lev. 19:16), which entails the legal responsibility to rescue someone whose life is endangered.[48] Another compelling illustration lies in how Jewish law has shaped the obligation to return a lost object to its rightful owner.[49] While numerous legal systems stipulate that an individual who finds a lost item must return it to its owner, in a rights-based systems the duty to return a lost item is incumbent only upon the individual who elects to pick up the item.[50] A person who encounters a lost possession may opt to ignore it and proceed without incurring legal consequences. By contrast, following Deuteronomy 22:1, Jewish law imposes a duty to return a lost item extends to anyone who sees it, which is a considerably broader obligation than one grounded in purely voluntary action.[51]

A symbolic expression of this idea is found in the famous homily of Rabbi Simlai:

> Rabbi Simlai taught: 613 *mitzvot* were stated to Moses, [consisting of] 365 prohibitions corresponding to the number of days in the solar year, and 248 positive *mitzvot* corresponding to the number of a person's limbs.[52]

According to Rabbi Simlai, the ratio of affirmative to prohibitive commandments is roughly 60:40. Even if these figures carry mainly symbolic meaning, aiming to illustrate fundamental tendencies, this homily highlights the manner in which a duty-based legal system exhibits considerably less reluctance to impose a multitude of affirmative duties upon its citizens.

Stated more abstractly, within rights-based legal systems, the focal point lies in defining the limits that citizens should refrain from breaching (prohibitive duties). They do not attempt to outline the actions required for realizing the desired way of life citizens should embrace (affirmative duties). In contrast, duty-based legal systems strive not only to elucidate what citizens are prohibited from doing but also to define the appropriate way of life and to imbue an individual's life with affirmative duties.

Is Claiming a Right Necessary?

Another divergence between rights-based and duty-based legal systems lies in the necessity of claiming a right.[53] Comparative analysis demonstrates that in rights-based legal systems, if a right holder refrains from claiming their right, for example, because they are not aware of it, no corresponding obligation is imposed upon the opposing party. Conversely, duty-based legal systems tend to assign diminished significance to the act of claiming the right and obligate the counterparty to fulfill their duty even if the right holder is unaware of their right and did not claim it.[54]

Two examples vividly illustrate this point. Consider a scenario where an individual causes damage to another party's property who remains unaware of the incurred damage. Does a duty arise for the tortfeasor to provide compensation, or, at the very least, to inform the owner? Or does no obligation materialize as long as the owner refrains from asserting her right? The crux of the matter is not whether a moral duty exists to notify the plaintiff and provide compensation but rather whether legal repercussions ensue for the defendant who neglected to apprise the plaintiff and thus eludes their liability (i.e., must specific legal sanctions be imposed upon him for failing to inform the other party about the damage he caused?). Advocates of the "civil recourse" theory argue that while the plaintiff indeed possesses the right to receive compensation, this entitlement hinges on her initiation of a legal claim for her rightful due. Hence, there is no inherent obligation for the defendant to take proactive measures in informing or compensating the plaintiff.[55] Conversely, proponents of the "corrective justice" theory contend that the defendant's duty to provide compensation to the plaintiff operates independently of whether the plaintiff has filed a lawsuit against the defendant.[56]

It's not surprising to discover that the perspective gleaned from *halakhic* sources aligns with the notion that a defendant's duty to provide compensation is separate from the plaintiff's claiming of her right. The argument follows this line: Compensating a plaintiff constitutes an affirmative obligation imposed upon the defendant.[57]The defendant's obligation to provide compensation doesn't stem from a court judgment; rather, it arises from the very occurrence of the damage. Hence, this obligation exists even when a court decision is pending.[58] The amalgamation of these assumptions implies that the defendant's obligation to compensate the plaintiff does not depend on the plaintiff's claim of her right.[59]

A second example arises from the laws of evidence. When an individual is summoned by the court to provide testimony, they undeniably hold the obligation to comply. Yet, what if the pertinent parties remain entirely unaware that this individual witnessed the event in question? Does an obligation exist to inform the court and voluntarily provide testimony? The prevailing consensus within modern rights-based legal systems is that this duty is contingent upon receiving a summons to appear in court and testify.

Jewish law takes a different approach. While in matters of monetary cases the obligation to provide witness is triggered by a claim from one of the parties; in cases involving capital punishment, a witness must come forward of their own volition. In capital cases, this duty emerges even if both parties and the court are unaware that this individual was a witness to the event. This distinction is captured by Sefer ha'Hinukh who explains:

> However, there is a difference between monetary laws, and capital and other laws in the Torah. As with monetary laws, a man is not obligated to testify about them on his own, unless a party in the case or the court solicits him. But with capital laws and other prohibitions in the Torah . . . a person is obligated to come on his own and say the testimony in front of a court, so as to destroy the evil and to separate a man from a prohibition.[60]

Regarding criminal cases, Jewish law perceives the obligation of a witness to testify as being directed toward the legal system itself. Consequently, the witness bears the duty to provide testimony that is not contingent upon receiving a court summons.[61]

These examples illustrate that while the relationship between rights and duties is reciprocal, the point of initiation can prove decisive. When right is regarded as the law's organizing concept, the act of claiming a right assumes heightened centrality. A human being is someone who asserts their rights. Conversely, within a framework dominated by the concept of duty, the realization of one's humanity unfolds through the fulfillment of their obligations. These duties tend to stand independently, not contingent upon the opposing party's claiming of a right.

Deciding between Conflicting Norms

Another facet through which the difference between rights-based and duty-based laws becomes evident is in resolving conflicts between norms. When the conflicting norms are distinct from each other—such as a clash between saving one person's life at the cost of damaging another's property—the resolution can be based on the content of the conflicting norms. For example, protecting human life is more important than protecting the owner's property and therefore takes precedence. Alternatively, the resolution can be based on the different legal status of each of the conflicting norms. For example, if one of the conflicting norms is a constitutional norm while the other is a standard legal norm, then the former overrides the latter. Nevertheless, when addressing conflicts between identical norms, the approach varies based on whether the dilemma is framed as a confrontation between conflicting rights or as a contest between conflicting duties.[62]

I will illustrate this using the classic dilemma described by Cicero, which involves two individuals drowning in a river while grasping onto a plank that can only save one of them.[63] Does an individual have the right to forcefully take the plank for themselves, resulting in the death of the other person, or are they obliged to relinquish the plank in order to save the other, even at the risk of their own life? This predicament can be cast as a clash between rights or as a confrontation between duties.

Through the lens of a rights-based law, this dilemma introduces a clash between two equivalent rights: the right to life held by each individual clutching the plank. In this perspective, it's untenable to argue that A's right to life outweighs B's right to life.[64] Consequently, a potential resolution could be to draw lots, ensuring both individuals possess an equal chance at rescue. Alternatively, another conclusion is that, as their rights are on par, each person possesses the entitlement to strive to secure the plank for themselves, ultimately allowing the stronger of the two to survive. Indeed, these are the conclusions reached by an American court when deliberating a comparable case involving too many individuals attempting to board a rescue boat meant for only a few.[65]

From a duty-oriented perspective, the scenario unfolds quite differently. Here, a collision arises between two distinct duties. On one hand, if the individual seizes the plank for himself, he will be responsible for the death of the other person and transgress the prohibition against murder. On the other hand, should he relinquish the plank, he may only be in danger of contravening the prohibition against taking one's own life. When the prohibition against murder and the prohibition against suicide stand opposed, the resolution becomes apparent: the prohibition against murder holds greater gravity.[66] Consequently, a person is not justified in preserving his own life if it requires taking another's.

Certainly, this is the conclusion that Rabbinic authorities arrived at as reflected in several *Talmudic* passages. Although the Talmudic sources do not address Cicero's exact case, the rabbis deliberate on cases that are close enough from which to infer and draw comparisons.[67] For instance, the mishnaic Sages discussed the scenario of two individuals wandering in the desert, one of whom possesses a pitcher of water capable of saving just one person. This case doesn't directly mirror Cicero's specific dilemma, as the one who owns the water is not in immediate endangerment of his life. Nonetheless, subsequent commentators employed the following passage to discern the Jewish legal perspective on Cicero's predicament:

> If two people were walking on a [desolate] path and there was a jug of water in the possession of one of them, if both drink, [both will] die, but if one of them drinks, he will reach a settled area. Ben Petora taught: It is preferable that both of them drink and die, and let neither one of them see the death of the other. Until Rabbi Akiva came and taught that the verse states: "And your brother shall live with you" (Leviticus 25:36) [indicating that] your life takes precedence over the life of the other.[68]

According to Rabbi Akiva, a person who is not in immediate peril (as he has sufficient water) is not obliged to imperil himself to rescue another whose life is at stake. Guided by this interpretation, the authorities inferred that when two individuals jointly possess the water, placing both their lives in jeopardy, it becomes impermissible for one to appropriate the water for himself, thereby causing the other's demise.[69] In such a situation, an individual facing danger cannot safeguard himself by sacrificing the life of his companion.[70] The prevailing consensus among the authorities is that even resorting to casting lots is prohibited if it entails one person saving himself while putting the other's life in jeopardy.[71]

This analysis underscores that the way in which conflicting norms are framed—either as a clash of rights or as a clash of duties—is prone to influence the method of deciding. A conclusion drawn from a rights-based analysis is likely to prioritize solutions that lean toward self-interest, whereas a decision stemming from a duty-based analysis will tend to highlight the duty to rescue the other, or at the very least, abstain from causing harm to them.[72]

The Source of the Differences between the Two Types of Legal Discourses

A synthesis of the aforementioned points reveals that the decision to frame a legal system through the lens of rights or duties holds significant legal implications concerning the operation of legal rules. Jewish law serves as an exemplar of a legal system founded upon the centrality of the concept of duty, diverging from contemporary legal systems that pivot on the concept of right: Jewish law readily acknowledges obligations toward entities beyond humans, even when the associated correlative rights are uncertain; Jewish law encompasses a multitude of affirmative duties; the majority of duties within Jewish law are not contingent on the counterparty's assertion of rights; and when faced with conflicting norms, Jewish law interprets them as clashes between duties, ultimately resolving them through a more altruistic approach than rights-based legal systems.

These differences between the two types of legal discourses are not logically derived by the decision to choose the language of rights or of duties. For instance, it's conceivable to envisage a legal world that employs the language of rights and simultaneously acknowledges rights that entail affirmative duties (in this world, an individual facing a life-threatening situation holds a right that another will act to rescue him). Similarly, it's plausible to conceive of a legal world that employs the language of duties, yet primarily recognizes prohibitive duties and not affirmative duties (in such a scenario, a prohibition against murder will exist, but there might not be an obligation to rescue someone in jeopardy). In theory, a rights-based legal system could recognize the validity of rights even in the absence of their assertion (an individual's entitlement to receive compensation following an accident wouldn't be contingent upon the plaintiff's claim for damages), much like it's conceivable to imagine a duty-based legal system where duties hinge on the right holder's assertion of what they deserve (the defendant would be obligated to compensate the plaintiff only if the latter initiates legal proceedings for compensation).[73]

Hence, as a matter of formal logic the adoption of a particular linguistic framework does not necessitate specific outcomes, but in practice it does undoubtedly help to predict them. Experience shows that opting for a rights-based discourse tends to favor prohibitive over affirmative duties. This underscores the significance of asserting rights, and pushes toward self-centered decisions in scenarios such as lifeboat ethics where norms are in direct conflict. Conversely, selecting a duty-based discourse is likely to allocate a broader scope to affirmative duties, diminishing the emphasis on asserting rights, and endorsing more altruistic decisions in resolving conflicts between norms.

The reason for this lies in the fact that the choice between a rights-based language and a duty-based language arises from differing sets of values. Opting for a rights discourse aligns with a preference for values like individualism, personal autonomy, self-responsibility, and negative freedom. Conversely, opting for a duty discourse aligns with a preference for values like community, social responsibility toward others, and positive freedom. While the adoption of a specific legal language does not necessarily mandate particular outcomes, it mirrors a choice of specific values, thereby foreshadowing the nature of the legal outlines.

Legal Language and Social Interests

Another perspective to view the distinction between a rights-based law and a duty-based law is to analyze which social groups each type of discourse benefits. Which groups would lean toward a rights discourse, and which towards a duty discourse? The picture that emerges is intricate.

On one hand, it seems that marginalized groups within society might favor a duty-based discourse. Individuals living in poverty, minority groups, people with disabilities, and the elderly are examples of those who encounter difficulties in asserting their rights and claiming the assistance that the State owes them. This highlights a challenge faced by rights-based legal systems, often termed as "non-exercise of rights," where certain populations fail to assert their rightful claims.[74] Duty-based legal systems address this issue by establishing that the responsibility of the community to support vulnerable groups is not contingent upon those groups initiating legal action to seek the assistance they rightfully deserve.

Rabbi Yaakov Ba'al Ha'Turim (thirteenth–fourteenth centuries) formulated the following rule in this manner:

> whoever is in need to receive [money] from the charity fund, and does not wish to ask for assistance, they [the charitable fund managers] deceive and give him gifts through respect, as though it is not charity, and if he does not want [to accept these] we provide for him in the form of a loan, and if he does not want [to accept this] we say to him give us a collateral so he will not be embarrassed, and we do not collect from him afterwards.[75]

In a broader context, some argue that the paramount right safeguarded by the rights-based discourse is the right to private property, a protection that predominantly benefits the more affluent segments of society. According to this view, the discourse centered on rights reinforces the positions of the most powerful, thereby serving a capitalist viewpoint.[76] Therefore, it is anticipated that marginalized groups would be inclined to inhabit a legal environment framed in the language of duties.[77]

The alternative argument is that silenced populations tend to favor the rights-based discourse. These groups seek not preferential treatment but rather the chance to voice their opinions and assert their rightful claims. For instance, advocates of feminist movements often stress that their goal extends beyond improving the well-being of women, such as securing higher salaries and workplace integration. Instead, they aim to empower women to express their perspectives autonomously, without depending on men to speak on their behalf. Women should be recognized as legal subjects rather than mere legal objects. From this vantage point, women are inclined to favor a world that employs the language of rights. The same holds true for other silenced groups which are motivated not solely by achieving material improvement but also by the desire to have a platform to express themselves in the public sphere as legal subjects.

Considering the pros and cons associated with each type of legal discourse leads to the conclusion that rather than adopting a binary approach, there is merit in aiming to integrate both types of discourse. This would involve crafting a comprehensive legal vocabulary that draws equally from the tradition of duty-based discourse, like that found in Jewish law, and the tradition of rights-based discourse embraced by modern Western societies.[78]

Here is an example of a potential integration of both types of legal discourse. Within the realm of human rights, it is common to distinguish between negative rights, known as first-generation human rights, and positive rights, known as second-generation human rights.[79] The former category encompasses a person's entitlement not to suffer harm (such as the rights to life, to property, and to freedom of speech), along with the right to elect and to stand for election. While the latter category pertains to a person's entitlement to receive from the State what's essential for their well-being (such as the rights to access to healthcare, to education, and to a basic standard of living).

In light of this distinction, I argue that while it is important that the first category should be articulated in the language of rights, it is essential that the second category be formulated through the dialect of duties. This is due to the different legal purpose of each category. As for the first category, especially with regard to the rights to vote and to stand for election, it is important for the law to unambiguously establish that every citizen possesses the opportunity to voice their preferences within the political arena. It is not enough that the state will fulfill its duty and take care of the interests of silenced groups; rather, it's imperative that these groups have the platform to independently amplify their voices and pursue what they deserve as legal subjects.

Conversely, the second category would find better alignment when expressed through the language of duties. This classification mandates well-to-do citizens' involvement in funding support for marginalized groups (via the tax system). This is best facilitated through a legal lexicon inherently rooted in altruism. In this regard, the language of duties proves more fitting compared to the more self-centric nature of the language of rights.

This integrative approach has the potential to generate a rich constitutional language that leverages the advantages of both rights-based and duty-based terminology, resulting in the formation of a multidimensional legal discourse.

Conclusion

Jewish law shapes its legal principles using the language of duties. Although establishing duties implies the recognition of correlated rights, the formulation of legal rules in Jewish law highlights the obligation imposed on one party rather than the right bestowed on the other.

Legal rules framed as duties exhibit distinct behavior from those framed as rights. Throughout this chapter, I have explored various implications of this distinction. For instance, Jewish law encounters no difficulty in imposing duties to safeguard the interest of nonhumans that cannot be regarded as right-bearers. Jewish law emphasizes affirmative duties that extend beyond prohibitive ones. Within Jewish law, the act of asserting a right is not as pivotal; consequently, the opposing party must usually fulfill their duty even if not yet prosecuted to do so through the court system. Jewish law resolves conflicting norms in an altruistic manner that diverges from the self-centered nature of rights-based systems.

These disparities between the two forms of legal discourse do not stem logically from the decision to adopt either a language of rights or a language of duties. Rather, the choice between a rights-based language and a duty-based language emerges from differing sets of values that subsequently influence how legal rules behave.

Hence, there is considerable significance in introducing Jewish law and its language of duties to modern Western law. This endeavor has the potential to assist us in cultivating a legal language that carries greater nuance than our current legal articulations.

Notes

1. This chapter presents a comprehensive overview of the tension between rights-based and duty-based law, building upon various articles I have published, as indicated in the footnotes. Those desiring further exploration and depth on these matters are encouraged to look into the referenced articles.
2. In the language of the Sages, to be a "right holder" means to be a worthy person, who assumes good deeds or virtue. For example, "if she had any merit (*zechut*) it would suspend her punishment"; m.Sotah 3:4, Shaye J. D. Cohen, Robert Goldenberg, and Haim Lapin (eds.), *The Oxford Annotated Mishnah: A New Translation of the Mishnah* (New York: Oxford University Press, 2022); "merit (*zechut*) is brought about through the meritorious . . . and liability is brought about through those who are liable" (t.Yoma 4:12 trans.

by Sefaria). In these contexts, the term "right" (*zechut*) does not mean a right held against another person for the performance or nonperformance of an action.

3. "One who disputes the ownership of a field and he is signed as a witness regarding it . . . the Sages say: he has lost his right" (m.Ketubbot 13:6); "When a neighbor comes to displace the purchaser, but before he displaces him he sells him the field he owns that borders on the property, he forfeits his right" (Mishneh Torah, Laws of Neighbors 13:9, trans. Eliyahu Touger [Jerusalem: Moznaim, 1986]).
4. See Yitzhak Breuer, "The Law of the Female, Slave, and Foreigner," *Tziyunei Derech* (1981): 57–86 [Hebrew].
5. Moshe Silberg, "Law and Morals in Jewish Jurisprudence," *Harvard Law Review* 75 (1961): 313; Moshe Silberg, *Method of the Talmud* (Jerusalem: Magnes, 1996), 66 [Hebrew].
6. Haim H. Cohn, *Human Rights in Jewish Law* (New York: KTAV, 1984).
7. Aharon Lichtenstein, "Individual Rights in Halakha," *Congress Monthly* 45 (1978): 4–8.
8. Robert M. Cover, "Obligation: A Jewish Jurisprudence of the Social Order," *Journal of Law and Religion* 5 (1987): 65–74.
9. Greenberg, Moshe, "The Term "Right" in Scripture," *A Light for Jacob: Studies in the Bible and the Dead Sea Scrolls*, ed. Y. Hoffman and F. H. Polak (Jerusalem: Bialik, 1997), 68–77 [Hebrew].
10. Ibid., 76.
11. Itamar Rosensweig and Shua Mermelstein, "Rights and Duties in Jewish Law," *Touro Law Review* 37 (2022): 2179–2209.
12. *Sefer ha-Mitzvot*, Positive Commandments, no. 201.
13. Rosensweig and Mermelstein, "Rights and Duties in Jewish Law," 2193.
14. Mishneh Torah, Laws of Hiring 12:1, trans. Jacob J. Rabinowitz (Yale University Press, 1949).
15. Rosensweig and Mermelstein, "Rights and Duties in Jewish Law," 2195–96.
16. *Rashi*, Bava Kama 39a, s.v. "*mishum.*" An exception to this is the case where there is a special relationship between the rich and the poor, as for example when they are relatives. See *Mahaneh Ephraim*, Zekhiyah u-Matanah 8.
17. On that, see Benjamin Porat, "The Right to a Dignified Living in Light of Jewish Law: Its Constitutional Status," *Mishpatim* 51 (2022): 383–486 [Hebrew].
18. Contra Rosensweig and Mermelstein, "Rights and Duties in Jewish Law," 2204.
19. See, for example, Mary Ann Glendon, *Rights Talk: The Impoverishment of Political Discourse* (New York: Free Press, 1993).
20. Zulfiqar Adnan, "Jurisdiction over Jihad: Islamic Law and the Duty to Fight," *West Virginia Law Review* 120 (2017): 427–68.
21. See *Constitution (Fundamental law) of the Union of Soviet Socialist Republics* (1936), Article 131: "It is the duty of every citizen of the U.S.S.R. to safeguard and strengthen public, socialist property"; Article 133: "To defend the fatherland is the sacred duty of every citizen of the U.S.S.R." On that, see George L. Kline, "Socialist Legality and Communist Ethics," *The American Journal of Jurisprudence* 8 (1963): 21–34.
22. Regarding the debate surrounding the religious nature of the American Declaration of Independence, see Alan Dershowitz, *America Declares Independence* (Hoboken, NJ: John Wiley & Sons, 2003).
23. However, one can argue that even in the case of biblical law, it was not intended to be enforced by courts, but rather as self-executing rules. See, for example, Bernard S. Jackson, *Wisdom-Laws: A Study of the Mishpatim of Exodus 21:1-22:16* (Oxford: Oxford University Press, 2006).

24. Silberg, "Law and Morals in Jewish Jurisprudence," 313. Silberg alludes to the Talmudic passage of Bava Batra 174a (and Ketubbot 86a; Arakhin 22a). For a critical analysis of this reading, and for more sources on this subject, see Arye Edrei, "An Orphan's Obligation to Pay His Father Debt's: A Legal or Moral Duty," in *Studies in Jewish Law*, ed. Aharon Enkar and Duetch Sinai (Ramat-Gan: Bar-Ilan University, 1998), 31 [Hebrew].
25. Cover, "Obligation."
26. Certainly, there might exist additional rights conferred at various stages of life, such as the legal capacity to sign a contract. It is also essential to keep in mind that an integral facet of the transition to the status of legal maturity in modern law involves the ability to bear criminal liability for one's crimes.
27. This is not to diminish the significance of the endeavor by religious Jewish women to secure equal rights, including the right of chained wives (*agunot*) to extricate themselves from the constraints of unsuccessful marriages.
28. Cf. Daphne Barak-Erez, "The Feminist Battle for Citizenship: Between Combat Duties and Conscientious Objection," *Cardozo Journal of Law & Gender* 13 (2007): 531–60.
29. Cohn, *Human Rights in Jewish Law*, 18.
30. See also Yehuda Brandes, *Judaism and Human Rights: The Dialectic between "Image of God" and "Holy Nation"* (Jerusalem: The Israel Democracy Institute, 2013) [Hebrew]; Yehuda Brandes, *Judaism and Civil Rights: Israel's Civic Tradition* (Jerusalem: The Israel Democracy Institute, 2019) [Hebrew].
31. Wesley Newcomb Hohfeld, *Fundamental Legal Conceptions as Applied in Judicial Reasoning* (New Haven, CT: Yale University Press (1919), 38. See Matthew H. Kramer, "Rights without Trimmings," in *A Debate over Rights: Philosophical Enquiries*, ed. Matthew H. Kramer, N. E. Simmonds, and Hillel Steiner (Oxford: Clarendon Press, 1998), 24.
32. Cf. Glanville Williams, *Salmond on Jurisprudence*, 11th ed. (London: Sweet & Maxwell, 1957), 264: "There can be no right without a corresponding duty, or duty without a corresponding right, any more than there can be a husband without a wife, or a father without a child."
33. See Cover, "Obligation."
34. It is conceivable that Cover may not object to the refined perspective presented here. However, in this chapter, I place more emphasis on the correlation between rights and duties, while still highlighting the distinctions between the two legal traditions based on how they choose to frame their legal rules.
35. Matthew H. Kramer, "Do Animals and Dead People Have Legal Rights?," *Canadian Journal of Law & Jurisprudence* 14 (2001): 29–54.
36. See, e.g., Christopher D. Stone, *Should Trees Have Standing? Law, Morality, and the Environment*, 3rd ed. (New York: Oxford University Press, 2010).
37. See Erin O'Donnell, *Legal Rights for Rivers: Competition, Collaboration and Water Governance* (Abingdon, UK: Routledge, 2019).
38. See Kirsten Rabe Smolensky, "Rights of the Dead," *Hofstra Law Review* 37 (2009): 763–803.
39. See Alon Harel "Theories of Rights," in *The Blackwell Guide to the Philosophy of Law and Legal Theory*, ed. Martin P. Golding and William A. Edmundson (Malden, MA: Blackwell, 2006), 191–206.
40. Joseph Raz, *The Morality of Freedom* (Oxford: Oxford University Press, 1986), 166.
41. H. L. A. Hart, *Essays on Bentham: Studies in Jurisprudence and Political Theory* (Oxford: Clarendon Press, 1982), 183.
42. For example, "the matter of [causing] pain to animals, which is a prohibition of the Torah" (*Sefer Ha'hinukh*, Command 550).

43. *Shulhan Arukh*, OH 606:3 (trans. by Sefaria), "Early rabbinic authorities decreed, coupled with ban, that the living should not slander the dead."
44. Glendon, *Rights Talk*, 176.
45. In this context, I am referring to obligations thrust upon a citizen not as a result of their choice. This differs from obligations that arise due to an individual's decisions, like contractual obligations or parental duties toward their children.
46. See, for example, Ernest Weinrib, "The Case for a Duty to Rescue," *Yale Law Journal* 90 (1980): 247–93.
47. HJC 164/97 Contram Ltd. v. Minister of Finance, 52(1), PD 289, 360 (2007) (Isr.), https://versa.cardozo.yu.edu/opinions/conterm-ltd-v-finance-ministry, para. 31 (with minor changes in translation).
48. Ernest Weinrib, "Rescue and Restitution," *Svara: A Journal of Philosophy and Judaism* 2 (1990): 59–65, republished in Martin Golding (ed.), *Jewish Law and Legal Theory* (Aldershot, UK: Dartmouth, 1994). Israeli law adopted this rule of Jewish Law and enacted the You Shall Not Stand Idly By Your Brother's Blood Law, 5758–1998. The differences between the rule in Jewish law and its counterpart in Israeli law are discussed in Yuval Sinai and Benjamin Shmueli, *Maimonides and Contemporary Tort Theory: Law, Religion, Economics, and Morality* (New York: Cambridge University Press, 2020), 184.
49. See Michael J. Broyde and Michael Hecht, "The Return of Lost Property According to Jewish & Common Law: A Comparison," *Journal of Law and Religion* 12 (1995): 225–53.
50. See, for example, 2006 New York Code—Lost and Found Property (§251): "The term "finder" as used in this article means the person who first takes possession of lost property."
51. In the language of Maimonides "The return of lost property to an Israelite is a positive commandment, for Scripture says: 'Ye shall surely return them to your brother' (Deut. 22:1). Moreover, if one sees the lost property of Israelite and ignores it and leaves it, he transgresses a negative commandment in addition to disregarding a positive commandment, for Scripture says: 'Thou shalt not see thy brother's ox (or his sheep go astray) and hide yourself from them' (ibid). If he returns it, however, he has fulfilled a positive commandment" (Mishneh Torah, Laws of Robbery and Lost Property 11:1, trans. Hyman Klein [Yale University Press, 1982]).
52. b.Makkoth 23b (The William Davidson Talmud, Koren—Steinsaltz). On that, see Arthur Hyman, "Rabbi Simlai's Saying and Beliefs Concerning God," in *Perspectives on Jewish Thought and Mysticism*, ed. Alfred L. Ivry, Elliot R. Wolfson, and Allan Arkush (Amsterdam: Harwood Academic, 1998), 49–62.
53. For an extensive discussion, see Benjamin Porat, "Is Claiming a Right Necessary: Between a Rights-based Discourse and a Duties-based Discourse," *Dine Israel* 35–36 (2022): 327–64.
54. Clearly, this analysis will change if it turns out that the right holder refrained from filing a lawsuit due to her waiver of the right. Typically, Jewish law refrains from compelling the plaintiff to accept compensation against her volition. Consequently, if the plaintiff was cognizant of the inflicted damage and consciously opted to relinquish her right while abstaining from suing the defendant, the latter will be absolved from the obligation to provide compensation.
55. In the view of Zipursky, "There is no statute in tort law imposing a duty to pay . . . liability is required, but the failure to pay is not prohibited by tort law." Benjamin C. Zipursky, "Civil Recourse, Not Corrective Justice," *Georgetown Law Journal* 91 (2002–2003): 720. See also Benjamin C. Zipursky, "Substantive Standing, Civil Recourse, and Corrective Justice," *Florida State University Law Review* 39 (2011–2012): 309; Nathan B. Oman, "Why There Is No Duty to Pay Damages: Powers, Duties, and Private Law," *Florida State University Law Review* 39 (2011–2012): 137–61.

56. According to Coleman, "Corrective justice imposes the duty to repair the wrongs one does." Jules L. Coleman, *Risks and Wrongs* (Oxford: Oxford University Press, 2002), 321. See also Ernest J. Weinrib, *Corrective Justice* (Oxford: Oxford University Press, 2012), 81; Ernest J. Weinrib, "Civil Recourse and Corrective Justice," *Florida State University Law Review* 39 (2011–2012): 273–97; Stephen R. Perry, "The Moral Foundations of Tort Law," *Iowa Law Review* 77 (1992): 503; John Gardner, "Torts and Other Wrongs," *Florida State University Law Review* 39 (2011): 57.
57. "Since repayment of debt by the debtor is a biblical command, and we compel the fulfillment of positive commands, therefore we access his property and fulfil for him this obligation even against his will . . . since scriptures command him to pay damages" (*Hidushei Ha'Ramban*, Bava Batra 175b).
58. For example, Rabbi Yehiel Mikhel Harlap wrote, "In monetary issues . . . he himself is obligated, and the courts are not imposing any new obligations upon him, only inform him [the plaintiff] his obligation under Torah law." "His Agents in Monetary Law, Bills of Divorce, and Accepting Converts in Contemporary Times" *Or HaMizrah* 10 (1961): 40 [Hebrew], pursuant to *Ketzot ha'Hoshen* 1, 7.
59. This insight found expression in the following words of Rabbi Aryeh Leib Heller (eighteenth century): "It appears that even though the other person did not know that they were damaged [. . .], since he [=the damager] knows that he is liable, it is like any other debt where one knows their legal obligation to pay, such as in cases of theft or robbery or damage, where even though the other party does not know, if one knows oneself that one is liable, one must pay them. And the same applies in this case, and there is no need for [Knowledge] of this on the part of the other person" (*Ketzot HaHoshen* 153, 4). See also Rabbi Israel Wolf, *Sha'ar Mishpat*, 9, 160a) in the context of the law of a thief: "it is obvious he must restore it even if the plaintiff does not sue" "it is obvious he must restore it even if the plaintiff does not sue" (*Sha'ar Mishpat*, 9, 160a).
60. *Sefer Ha'Hinukh*, Command 122 (trans. by Sefaria).
61. In the words of Eliav Shochetman, *Civil Procedure in Rabbinical Courts* (Jerusalem: Sidrei Mishpat, 2011), 762–63 [Hebrew]: "One who is aware of an evidence that concerns the other is obligated to appear and give testimony even if he is not summoned by the interested litigant, as it is quite probable the litigant is not aware of that witness . . . on testimony concerning prohibitions or capital law, which cannot be waived, it is of no consequence whether or not he is summoned, and in either case must appear and give testimony."
62. For an extensive discussion, see Benjamin Porat, "Deciding between Contradicting Norms: Rights-Based Law vs. Duty-Based Law and Their Social Ramifications," *American Journal of Comparative Law* 20 (2022): 1–25.
63. *De Officiis*, Book III, 23.
64. In fact, Cicero posited that we could evaluate the different worth of the two individuals drowning in the river based on distinct criteria. However, this premise has been discredited in the modern era, where the principle of human dignity presupposes equal value for every individual's life.
65. United States v. Holmes, 26 F. Cas. 360 (E.D. Pa. 1842).
66. The prohibition against murder is clearly stated in the Torah, and its corresponding punishment is the most severe among the potential penalties.
67. For a discussion why the rabbis did not address explicitly the particular case of Cicero, see Saul Lieberman, "How Much Greek in Jewish Palestine?," in *Biblical and Other Studies*, ed. Alexander Altman (Cambridge, MA: Harvard University Press, 1973), 124.

68. b.Bava Metsi'a 62a (The William Davidson Talmud, Koren—Steinsaltz). See also Sifra, Behar, Parsha 5.
69. Rabbi Shmuel Eidels, Hiddushei Aggadot, Bava Metsi'a 62b.
70. This principle emerges from additional sources, such as, t.Terumot 7:20; b.Sanhedrin 74a, b.Pesahim 25b; b.Yoma 82b.
71. For a summary of the views of *halakhic* arbiters (*poskim*), see Porat, "Deciding between Contradicting Norms," 18.
72. This is not the only option for analyzing the dilemma from the perspective of rights-based discourse. For an alternate analysis, see ibid., 22.
73. Actually, this example is not all that imaginative. With regard to the prohibition against delaying wage payment, Jewish law determines that the employer only violates this prohibition if the employee sues for the wages. See, for example, m.Bava Metsi'a 9:12, "The law is one and the same for the hire of a person, the hire of an animal. And the hire of utensils: *On his day you shall give him his hire,* applies to each; and *You shall not let the wages of the laborer rest with you overnight until the morning* applies to each. When? When he claimed his hire from him; but if he did not claim from him, the employer does not transgress." On this topic, see Porat, "Is Claiming a Right Necessary," 350.
74. On that, see Andrea Durbach, "The Right to Legal Aid in Social Right Litigation," in *Social Rights Jurisprudence: Emerging Trends in International and Comparative Law*, ed. Malcolm Langford (Cambridge: Cambridge University Press, 2008), 59–72.
75. *Tur* YD 253. Also see *Arukh ha-Shulhan*, YD 253:17: "a poor person who does not wish to accept charity, yet we are aware he needs it, we are under an obligation to make efforts for him to accept it."
76. See, for example, Jennifer Nedelsky, *Private Property and the Limits of American Constitutionalism: The Madisonian Framework and Its Legacy* (Chicago: University of Chicago Press, 1990); Mark Tushnet, "An Essay on Rights," *Texas Law Review* 62 (1984): 1386. See also Glendon, *Rights Talk*; Ronald Beiner, *What's the Matter with Liberalism* (Berkeley: University of California Press, 1992); Paul Kahn, *Putting Liberalism in Its Place* (Princeton, NJ: Princeton University Press, 2008); Samuel Moyn, *Not Enough: Human Rights in an Unequal World* (Cambridge, MA: Harvard University Press, 2019); Thomas Piketty, *Capital and Ideology* (Cambridge, MA: Harvard University Press, 2019).
77. On this see Porat, "'The Right to a Dignified Living in Light of Jewish Law," 419–31.
78. In this context, it is worth examining an intriguing phenomenon that unfolded in *halakhic* literature during the twentieth century. A noticeable shift can be observed in the realm of rabbinic writings over the past century, particularly among scholars and yeshiva leaders within the Lithuanian Jewish world. This shift involves a growing emphasis not solely on comprehending the obligations prescribed by *halakha* but also on tracing the corresponding rights that *halakha* establishes. For example, see Aaron Soloveichik, *Logic of the Heart, Logic of the Mind: Wisdom and Reflections on Topics of Our Times* (Jerusalem: Genesis Jerusalem, 1991), 63: "This key concept of k'vod habrihyos, the dignity of all human beings, constitutes the basis of human rights."
79. See Karel Vasak, "Human Rights: A Thirty-Year Struggle: The Sustained Effort to Give Force of Law to the Universal Declaration of Human Rights," *Unesco Courier 30* (1977): 29–32.

PART III

JEWISH LAW AND PRACTICE IN MODERNITY

A

Movements and Denominations

CHAPTER 17

MODERNITY, SECULARISM, AND THE TRANSFORMATION OF JEWISH LAW

LEORA BATNITZKY

Introduction

In academic and nonacademic circles alike, many believe that Jewish law uncomplicatedly bridges the Jewish past, at least from the Talmud forward, to the Jewish present. According to this view, while Jewish law may change, or appear to change, the category, or concept, of Jewish law marks the continuity between Jewish life and practice over time. As some of the chapters in this volume show, the modern development of different Jewish denominations reflects internal Jewish disagreements about numerous questions, such as whether Jewish law does in fact change or only appears to change; how Jewish law changes if it does indeed change; how to balance concerns and needs of the present with past precedent; whether Jewish law is in fact authoritative in the modern period, and if so, who has the authority to decide on the answers to these questions. These are, of course, questions with which all legal systems grapple. Yet there is a stark contrast between asking these questions about Jewish law in the modern context and asking these questions about other modern legal systems. Most modern legal systems are tied to and gain their authority by virtue of their connection to sovereign states, which enforce their respective systems of law. Following the laws of a sovereign state is not voluntary. With some complicated exceptions within the state of Israel (Edrei, this volume). adherence to Jewish law is, theology aside, wholly voluntary. For this reason, conceptions of Jewish law in the modern period have come to resemble modern conceptions of religion, which sovereign states also define in terms of voluntary association.

This chapter argues that modernity converted Jewish law, both practically and conceptually, into a solely *religious* enterprise. This is not to deny that historically Jewish law was religious but rather to point out that in pre-modern contexts, Jewish law also had a political dimension that has been greatly diminished, if not eradicated, by modernity. Here I follow the eminent historian of the Jews, Jacob Katz, in defining modernity in terms of *the disintegration of pre-modern corporate Jewish communities*.[1] This means that the analysis offered in this chapter focuses largely on transformations to the category of Jewish law beginning in the eighteenth century in western and eastern Europe.

Understanding modern debates about Jewish law in this way allows us to appreciate two significant points. First, modern conceptions of Jewish law signal not continuity but a break with the past. Second, despite their profound differences, the views of Jewish law advanced by divergent Jewish communities, both within and outside denominational streams of Judaism, have more in common with each other than their self-presentations might suggest. The chapter makes these arguments in four sections. The first section considers the modern development of "law" and "religion" as distinct categories. Next, the chapter focuses on the different sorts of modern privatization of Jewish law that occurred in western and eastern European Jewish contexts, respectively. The third part turns to overlaps between modern Jewish conceptions of law and modern legal theory. The fourth part considers the role of democracy and egalitarianism as they play out in feminist approaches to Jewish law in shaping these different conceptions. Finally, the conclusion draws out some of the implications of this analysis for thinking about what secularism might mean as well as recognizing the plural nature of the modern transformation of Jewish law.

Law and Religion as Distinct Categories

There are multiple markers of modernity, including new ways of thinking brought about by scientific revolution; new political and economic structures, be they the Spanish conquest of the Americas, the development of modern nation-state and capitalism, or the spread of European colonialism; and new kinds of hatred and mass violence. Although these are all plausible interpretations of modernity, for the purposes of understanding the modern transformation of Jewish law as well as the development of modern legal theory more generally, it may be most helpful to understand modernity in terms of the development of an absolute distinction between the category of law and the category of religion. This distinction is directly tied to the development of sovereign nation-states. With the rise of the modern nation-state, law and modern legal institutions became the key vehicles through which sovereignty would be exercised.[2]

Early modern political jurisprudence, and in particular the philosophies of law articulated by Hugo Grotius (1584–1654), Samuel Pufendorf (1632–1694), and Christian Thomasius (1655–1728), attempted to provide theoretical frameworks for thinking about and implementing state and international law as distinct from church, empire, and estates.[3] A fully adequate account of these early modern jurists is far beyond the scope of this chapter, but for our purposes two general points are important. First, Grotius, Pufendorf, and Thomasius each attempted to defend a particularly modern (as distinct from a medieval Catholic) conception of natural law rooted in the individual's, and analogously the sovereign state's, right to self-preservation. Each emphasized a natural right of sovereign states to govern their citizens and to defend themselves as well as a kind of natural justice that governed the relations between sovereign states. Second, while each of these jurists wrote from within a Christian context, a cornerstone of each of their arguments was what we might call, somewhat anachronistically, a distinction between the private and public spheres, with religion belonging to the former and the pursuit of social harmony and political security guaranteed by law to the latter. This division between, on the one hand, law defined *only* in terms of state law and, on the other hand, religion defined in terms of a private sphere, came to characterize not only early modern political and legal theory but also how Jews, in both western and eastern Europe, began to redescribe and transform Jewish law.

To recognize the modern reorientation of Jewish law, we need to appreciate the pre-modern political condition of Jews. Prior to the rise of the modern nation-state, Jews, like all other people, were not considered individuals with individual rights. Rather, Jewish individuals were legally defined as members of particular Jewish communities, *kehilot,* or corporate bodies that were granted rights of residence by an external authority, such as kings, emperors, or lords of large estates. These authorities could expel Jewish communities, collect taxes from Jewish communities, regulate which professions Jews were allowed to occupy and which not, as well as punish Jews collectively. But Jewish communities were also self-governing and Jewish law was extensive in its scope and reach. "Jewish law" broadly conceived consisted of laws based on the interpretation of traditional sources, such as the Talmud and its medieval commentators, formal *halakhic* codes derived from these traditional sources, *takanot* (local ordinances or bylaws of particular communities enacted by lay leadership), as well as local customs not formally encoded. Historically, *halakhah* was intertwined with and even lent authority to, other forms of Jewish law that today would not be considered strictly *halakhic*, such as takanot and local customs. As we will seelater, in the modern period "Jewish law," or *halakhah*, is detached from governance and is confined to either formal codes or the rules and principles derived from the interpretation of traditional sources.[4]

Within classical Jewish sources, Jewish law largely falls under the category of what we call today private law—that is, law pertaining to the relations between individuals and small groups, such as contracts and torts. Nevertheless, as we see even from our very brief consideration, the political and legal framework of Jewish law in pre-modern contexts also affected Jewish society as a whole. For this reason, in the pre-modern context, Jewish law was also arguably what we call today public law (i.e., law pertaining to society as a whole). Individual Jews simply had no choice about whether or not to follow Jewish law which, understood in the capacious terms previously described, governed Jewish communities far more analogously to the modern state than Jewish law governs any Jewish community today. In the concise formulation of the renowned historian of the Jews Salo Baron, pre-modern corporate Jewish communities "had more competence over its members than the modern Federal, State, and Municipal governments combined. Education, administration of justice between Jew and Jew, taxation for communal and State purposes, health, markets, public order, were all within the jurisdiction of the community-corporation."[5] When Jews were admitted to various nation-states as individual citizens, a complex and largely incomplete process that began in the late eighteenth century and did not end until the twentieth century, they were legally defined as individuals.[6] That this process of becoming individual citizens of modern nation-states is usually referred to as "emancipation" is telling. Jews were freed not just in terms of their release from prohibitions on activities and professions formerly forbidden to them, but they were also freed from the collective authority of corporate Jewish communities to become free individuals.

Arguments put forth by Benedict de Spinoza (1632–1677) in his *Theological-Political Treatise*, published anonymously in 1670, help us understand the conceptual and practical challenges that modern Jews who reformulated Jewish law in the face of the dissolution of traditional corporate communities would have to face. Spinoza is significant for our topic for two reasons. First, Spinoza lived just as the modern nation-state was beginning to be conceptualized and his biography offers an entryway to understanding what would become the modern Jewish experience and predicament. As is well known, Spinoza was excommunicated from the Amsterdam Jewish community in 1656.[7] His excommunication demonstrates the political power of the pre-modern Jewish community as described above, but his ability to live an independent life free of any religious community also anticipates later developments in which the Jewish communities would no longer exercise political or legal power over individual Jews. Second, and perhaps more importantly, Spinoza's account of Jewish law also set the conceptual challenge for modern theories of Jewish law. As we will see, this is Spinoza offers an account of law that denies post-biblical Jewish law the status of law. For Spinoza, "law" is the purview only of a sovereign state.

As should be evident by many essays in this volume, what is called "Judaism" and "Jewish law" today developed post-biblically. Nevertheless, in his *Theological-Political Treatise*, written for a largely Christian audience, Spinoza equates Jewish law with what he calls the laws of the Hebrews, that is, with the laws of the Old Testament. Spinoza argues that the laws of the Hebrews were only pertinent in the context of their original, political meaning: "ceremonial observances . . . formed no part of the Divine law, and had nothing to do with blessedness and virtue, but had reference only to the elections of the Hebrews, that is . . . to their temporal bodily happiness and the tranquility of their kingdom, and . . . therefore they were only valid while that kingdom last."[8] Despite the fact that his excommunication suggests otherwise, Spinoza contends that because the ceremonial law no longer corresponds to a political kingdom, it no longer can be meaningfully conceived as law.[9] Spinoza distinguishes law that is by definition tied to the sovereign state from true religion that demands only knowledge and love of God. For Spinoza, Jewish law, and Judaism more broadly, therefore qualifies neither as law, since it is not tied to a sovereign political order, nor as religion, which he defines in terms of internal states of mind as opposed to particular actions or rituals.

Spinoza's formulations are instructive because Jewish law fits uneasily into the distinctly modern categories of either law or religion. This led Jewish thinkers to theorize a concept of Jewish law as something religious and not political. It is important to underscore that while there are conceptual problems at play here, modern Jewish accounts of law had to grapple not just with theoretical questions of how to conceive of Jewish law but also with a fundamental challenge to the authoritative status of Jewish law for Jews. As Jacob Katz has put it, with the eventual disintegration of corporate Jewish communities, the political predicament for Jewish traditionalists was stark: "the observance of the Jewish tradition could and would be enforced by the organs of the Jewish community. The authority to do so was conferred on the Jewish community by the state, and constituted a part of communal autonomy. There was also a measure of control over the ideas. . . . The post-traditional Jewish community was denied the right to impose its will concerning thought and action on the individual."[10]

With the waning power of pre-modern Jewish communities, some communal leaders, rabbis and thinkers, like early modern jurists, constructed accounts of Jewish law in order to change Jewish law for the modern age.[11] In contrast, other communal leaders, rabbis, and thinkers constructed theories of Jewish law to preserve Jewish laws in the modern age.[12] As we will see in the next two sections, "Jewish Law as Religion" and "Legal Theory," the modern constructions of "ceremonial law" and *halakhah* as distinct modern categories reflect the circumscribed scope of what could be considered Jewish law in the modern period, in which *halakhah*, is considered akin only to "ceremonial law" and entirely distinct from governance. In short, *halakhah* in the modern period is stripped of any political dimension and comes to be understood as fundamentally "religious" as opposed to "political."

A point of terminology helps us appreciate the modern transformation of Jewish law. Today the Hebrew word "*dat*" is most often translated as religion, but historically the term referred to law. The word is biblical and appears in the book of Esther. There it means law, both the Jewish people's and the king's: "And Haman said unto king Ahasuerus: 'here is a certain people scattered abroad and dispersed among the peoples in all the provinces of your kingdom; and their laws [*dateihem*] are different from those of every people; they neither keep the king's laws [*datei hamelekh*]; therefore it does not profit the king to suffer them.'" Here "dat" is generic and implicitly political. As the Israeli scholar Avraham Melamed has shown, up until the early modern period, Jewish thinkers such as Saadia Gaon, Moses Maimonides, Joseph Albo, Judah Messer Leon, and Nissim of Marseilles used the term "*dat*" in a variety of ways, but all these usages referred to law, whether human or Divine, and not to particular beliefs, Jewish or otherwise.[13] Simone Luzzatto's 1638 *Discorso circa il stato degl' hebrei et in particolar dimoranti nell'inclita città di Venetia* marks a change in the meaning of *dat*. Luzzatto describes Judaism as a religious faith like Christianity by translating "*dat*" as "religio" and "religione." Spinoza would follow Luzzatto in distinguishing between law (*lex*) and religion in his *Theological-Political Treatise*. This brings us full circle to the conceptual challenge Spinoza presented to any modern conception of Jewish law. If law and religion are mutually incompatible categories, can Jewish law ultimately fit easily into either category?

Jewish Law as Religion

The narrowing, or privatization, of Jewish law is clearest in the western European context, though we will also consider below a parallel narrowing and privatization of Jewish law in the eastern European context. Moses Mendelssohn (1729–1786) followed Spinoza in strictly differentiating the ceremonial law from the laws of the modern state. But whereas Spinoza argues that Jewish law could only be valid if Jews were a sovereign people, Mendelssohn claims that Jewish law is simply *not* political in nature. Instead, according to Mendelssohn, Jewish law, or the ceremonial law, is *only* religious. Mendelssohn made his argument about the fundamentally religious nature of Jewish law in the context of the German Enlightenment and the corresponding Jewish intellectual enlightenment (the *Haskalah*). Mendelssohn lived before the beginning of Jewish emancipation in Prussia (which followed Napoleon's defeat in 1806), but he nevertheless imagined a political reality in which Jews would no longer be legally and politically defined as members of the corporate Jewish community but rather as individual citizens. As such, Mendelssohn's conception of Jewish law mirrors more closely a modern conception of religion advocated by his Protestant contemporaries far more than it resembles conceptions of what would become state law.

In his 1783 *Jerusalem: or on Religious Power and Judaism*, Mendelssohn, a contemporary of Thomas Jefferson's, defines the state in terms of its sovereign power and right to coercion. Religion, in contrast, "knows of no punishment, no other penalty than the one the remorseful sinner voluntarily imposes on himself. It knows of no coercion, uses only the staff [called] gentleness, and affects only mind and heart."[14] Mendelssohn contrasts the Jewish religion with Christianity. Judaism is a religion of law, argues Mendelssohn, but it is not a religion of dogma as is Christianity. For this reason, argues Mendelssohn, adherence to the Jewish religion would not compete with the laws of the state but instead would continue to be a source of spiritual edification for individual Jews. Here Mendelssohn defines Jewish law in terms of what he calls the ceremonial law: "The ceremonial law itself is a kind of living script, rousing the mind and heart, full of meaning, never ceasing to inspire contemplation and to provide the occasion and opportunity for oral instruction."[15]

Given that he lived at a time in which Jewish law played a public role in disciplining individual Jews within Jewish communities, Mendelssohn, like Spinoza, knew that his description of Jewish law was not historically accurate. Unlike Spinoza, Mendelssohn was dedicated to preserving the vitality of Judaism for modern Jews. While Jews did not yet possess civil rights when Mendelssohn wrote, he anticipated the time when individual Jews would possess political rights. Therefore, he felt compelled to justify the continued survival of Jewish law for this future time to both non-Jews (who would demand that the Jewish people not constitute a nation within a nation) and to Jews (who would not be compelled politically to follow Jewish law). Further, Mendelssohn denied that, from a strictly theological point of view, Jewish law was voluntary for Jews: "He who is not born into the law need not bind himself to the law; but he who is born into the law must live according to the law; and die according to the law."[16] Nonetheless, he divorced theology, or religion, from politics in sharply distinguishing the political rights of Jewish individuals from any collective rights of the Jewish community which, he argued, should be abolished.

Mendelssohn's characterization of Jewish law as wholly religious, and therefore not at all political, became the basis of modern Jewish depictions of Jewish law for both those who self-consciously reformed Judaism in accord with modernity as well as for those who claimed that the nature of Jewish law (even if not also the details) was not subject to change. Most notably in the context of western Europe, the concept of Jewish law put forward by the founder of what came to be known as Orthodoxy, Samson Raphael Hirsch (1808–1888), was predicated not on a rejection but rather on an intensification, of Mendelssohn's premises. The same is true for those who would become proponents of Reform Judaism. Both camps strictly separated Jewish "religion" from "politics" by denying any political significance or function to Jewish law.[17]

Hirsch, living after Jews had received some though not all political rights as individuals, recognized and accepted the grave implications of emancipation for Jewish communal authority. He quickly "dropped all demands for judicial autonomy and continuance of Jewish civil law," and when the Berlin Orthodox Seminary was founded in 1873, there were no courses on Jewish civil law included in the curriculum.[18] Drawing on the very modern concepts that usurped traditional Jewish identity and authority, Hirsch agreed with Mendelssohn in arguing that the Jewish religion is not coercive but concerns only heart and mind. In making this claim, however, Mendelssohn recognized that historically the Jewish community had used coercion but, he contended, this betrayed the true meaning not only of Judaism but also of the religion more broadly defined. Hirsch went further than Mendelssohn, claiming not only that coercion had never existed within the Jewish community but also that the traditional community only existed by virtue of "those loyal to the divine law and the obligation to belong and to support the local congregation."[19] He contended it was this "unity of religious outlook," and not political life, that linked Jewish communal life throughout the ages.[20]

Hirsch welcomed the separation between church and state in which the traditional Jewish community's "timeless principles . . . will move and guide the genuine Jew, without compulsion . . . in every fiber of his heart and every stirring of his will."[21] In his affirmation of Orthodox Judaism's relation to civil society, Hirsch reiterated Mendelssohn's insistence that Judaism concerned spiritual and not political matters: "It is certainly possible for us to attach ourselves to the State, wherever we may find ourselves, without harm to the spirit of Judaism. . . . It is precisely the purely spiritual nature of Israel's nationhood that makes it possible for Jews everywhere to tie themselves fully to the various states in which they live."[22] Here Hirsch was in complete agreement with Abraham Geiger (1810–1874), the Reform Movement's spiritual founding father, who argued that the study of Judaism can only be a history of "spiritual achievements" because "it is precisely to its independence from political status that Judaism owes its survival."[23]

The experience of eastern European Jews differed significantly from their western counterparts, and the details of their conceptions of Jewish law varied greatly as well. But the sphere of Jewish law in eastern Europe was also privatized, albeit in different ways than in western Europe. At the end of the eighteenth century, as western Europe moved away from the feudal and corporate structure of medieval Europe toward unified and sovereign states, the Habsburg, Ottoman, and Russian Empires had at the same time absorbed all of the previously independent countries of eastern and central Europe. Eastern and central Europe reinstated feudal institutions. The eastern European Jewish individual, like their pre-modern ancestors, was still defined legally, politically, and theologically as a member of the Jewish community. But as a result of the economic and political turmoil of Eastern Europe generally, the Jewish community changed dramatically from within. In 1764, the Polish government dissolved the Council of the Four Lands, a centralized body that had governed Polish Jewry for two centuries.[24] While, for all intents and purposes, Jewish communities remained self-governing, they no longer could count on institutional support from one another. Devasting financial pressures no longer allowed communities to support the social and educational infrastructure they had previously provided.

As the structure of Jewish autonomy continued to fall apart over the next century, rabbinic scholars reconceptualized Jewish law in terms of what might best be described as the spiritual formation of individual Jewish men. These privatized notions of Jewish law found expression either in the form of study and direct engagement with early rabbinic sources or in the understanding of law as a spiritual and ethical exercise. Both of these new conceptions of Jewish law stood in opposition to the two monumental medieval legal codes, developed by Yosef Karo (1488–1575) and Moshe Isserles (1525–1572). These codes, known, respectively, as the *Shulhan Arukh* ("the prepared table") and the *Mapah* ("the table cloth"), present Jewish law as mainly concerned with the practicalities of everyday life. Both the intellectual and ethical interpretations of Jewish law can be understood as responses to the collapse of what had been the political function of Jewish law. This reconceptualization of Jewish law marked a paradigm shift that continues to shape observant Jewish life today.

We can see this modern transformation clearly with the advent of modern Lithuanian Yeshivot. Prior to the eighteenth century, yeshivot had been supported by local communities. But largely due to economic reasons, continued local support was no longer possible. The intellectual standards for rabbis also deteriorated significantly. For instance, in 1720, rabbis were required to study for twelve years before they were ordained. By 1761, ordination only required that the rabbi be older than twenty. The erosion of the *kehillah* went hand in hand with the loss of rabbinic authority in governing everyday life. This erosion also made room for the development of a new kind of rabbinic figure, one whose focus was not the governance of everyday life but rather intellectual gravitas.

One of the most vibrant intellectual expressions of Jewish civilization emerged from this communal morass, which led to a new kind of Jewish elite and a new conception of Jewish law. Here we meet a towering figure of modern Judaism, Rabbi Elijah ben Solomon (1720–1797), known as the Vilna Gaon, who was a contemporary of Mendelssohn's. As the Israeli scholar Immanuel Etkes explains:

> [The Vilna Gaon] established a model of excellence in Torah study. His extraordinary achievements were the result not only of his talents but also of his way of life, mainly his withdrawal from all worldly matters and his unbounded devotion to Torah study.... Torah study was also the most promising means for spiritual elevation and for bringing the individual close to God.[25]

Consequently, in 1803, Rabbi Hayyim of Volozhin (1749–1821) created a new model of a yeshiva, which was no longer a community endeavor but rather an elite institution not for local students but for the very best students throughout the Russian empire. This institution, and others like it, were supported by voluntary, individual donations from Jews in the Pale of Settlement, in western Europe as well as the United States.

The transformation of a conception of Jewish law from, at the very least, part of a system of political order into an intellectual and spiritual exercise for individual Jewish men is evident in at least two ways. First, the Volozhin Yeshiva (like other nineteenth-century Lithuanian yeshivot) severed the institutional connection between yeshivot and their communities. Second, the study of Jewish law became entirely detached from the practical application of Jewish law. Preparing for rabbinic ordination was viewed as a less pristine form of Torah study, one that ignored the most substantive (i.e., analytically rigorous) areas of law. Yet there was also an explicitly theological dimension to study in the Volozhin Yeshiva. Study for its own sake (*Torah l'shma*) was accompanied by a theology whose aim was both to understand conceptually the contours of God's law as well as to discipline the evil impulse in each individual's soul. Studying with a partner within the yeshiva (what is known as a *hevruta*, from the Hebrew word for friend, *haver*) was intimately tied to the disciplining of the individual's soul.[26]

Notably, the conception of law developed in Volozhin was even more divorced from politics and even more focused on the individual than was Hirsch's orthodoxy. Hirsch distinguished orthodoxy, what he called "*gesetzestreues Judentum*" (something like "faithful to the law Judaism") from other forms of Judaism. But all Jews could be, and should be, from Hirsch's perspective, equally faithful to the law because the law is intimately tied to ordinary life, even if its scope had been significantly diminished after emancipation. The Lithuanian yeshiva, in contrast, distinguished, to a far greater extent than had been the case throughout Jewish history, the Jewish elite from the non-elite, the study of law from the practice of law, as well as the significance of individual intellectual innovation and creativity as marks of religiosity. Put somewhat differently, the concept of law developed in the Lithuanian yeshivot was decisively modern in its individualist, intellectualist, and spiritualist orientation despite being a defense of traditionalism and a rejection of certain modern currents of thought.[27]

The individualism imbibed by Lithuanian yeshivot was already criticized in its own day by what we would call today "Ultra-Orthodoxy." For the ultra-Orthodox critics of the Lithuanian yeshivot, the emphasis on intellectual innovation, coupled with some of the outer trappings of modernity (short jackets, shaving, and marrying late), reflected an ultimate concession to modernity and its ideal of a free individual who has it in his power to create himself. Born in Lithuanian, Avraham Yeshayahu Karelitz (1878–1953) immigrated to Mandatory Palestine in 1933 and became the major Jewish legal authority for ultra-Orthodoxy in mandate Palestine and then in the State of Israel. Karelitz is known through his *responsa* and scholarship, which were printed under the title, *HazonIsh* (Vision of Man), his commonly used appellation. Lawrence Kaplan concisely captures Karelitz's criticism of the method of the Lithuanian yeshiva as follows: "For the *Hazon Ish*, the analytic approach allows too much room for self-expression, for the play of the individual's own intellectual powers unconstrained by the discipline of the text . . . it concedes too much to the modern temper, to the modern emphasis on the self and its intellectual autonomy, even if it is self-engaged in exercising its intellectual autonomy in the realm of traditional Talmudic scholarship."[28]

Affinities between Modern Jewish Conceptions of Law and Modern Legal Theory

Modern transformations of Jewish law find some striking parallels in modern legal theory. This should not be surprising for two interrelated reasons. First, much of modern and contemporary legal theory attempts to provide a theoretical justification for the moral and political practices of law in post-Christian societies, and therefore functions as theology once did. Second, as the American Jewish legal scholar Robert Cover argued in his seminal essay "Nomos and Narrative," law (or *nomos*) cannot adequately be understood apart from the stories that communities governed by law tell about themselves ("narrative").[29] Given that modern Jewish accounts of law are indeed modern, it follows that their narratives would overlap with other modern narratives. This section considers some crossovers between modern accounts of Jewish law, modern legal theory, and different modern narratives about the nation-state shared by Jewish thinkers and legal theorists alike.

The argument, usually associated with the Modern Orthodox movement,[30] that *halakhah* is an autonomous realm whose dynamic structure can only be understood from an internal perspective shares much with strands of legal positivism and formalism. While the terms "positivism" and "formalism" remain hotly debated in contemporary legal theory, I use the term "positivism" here to refer to the claim that law is autonomous from politics, and "formalism" to refer to the added claim that the law is internally coherent and self-generating.[31] Affinities between Mendelssohn, Hirsch, and some positivists and formalists stem from a shared endorsement of the modern nation-state. As the American legal philosopher Liam Murphy has suggested, "We must approach the traditional question about the concept of law as a practical aspect of political theory."[32] Indeed, positivist claims that law is its own sphere and not subject to the claims of politics defend not just the rule of law but also modern liberal states. Similarly, Mendelssohn's and Hirsch's shared claim that Jewish law is not political is in the service of conserving Jewish law within political contexts in which Jews have individual rights and Jewish law has no political authority.

A note on terminology is helpful here. For pre-modern Jews, *halakhah* was not an autonomous category but was subordinate to *Torah*. As such, it was considered a comprehensive category, which referred not only to politics and law but also to any and all Jewish teachings as well as to human knowledge broadly conceived, including what we would call today "culture" and "science." For this reason, in his *Mishneh Torah*, Maimonides does not use the term "*halakhah*" as a free-standing category; instead he uses the term "*hilkhot*," meaning laws of, as in "laws of divorce." So too, throughout the *Guide of the Perplexed*, Maimonides does not use the term "*halakhah*" to refer to what is often translated into English as "the law of Moses," but rather refers to "the *Torah* of Moses." In the original Judeo-Arabic, Maimonides uses the term "*sharia*," as opposed to "*fiqh*," the former corresponding to *Torah*, the latter to *halakhah*.[33]

In contrast, Mendelssohn and Hirsch, who both argue that Jewish law can mesh easily with the modern nation-state, use the term "*Gesetz*" to insist that Jewish law is an autonomous category from politics. Whereas Mendelssohn uses the term "*göttliche Gesetzgebung*," Hirsch prefers "*mosaïche Gesetzgebung*." In narrowing *Torah* to law (*halakhah/Gesetz*), Mendelssohn and Hirsch insist that Jewish law is fundamentally apolitical. Once again, this terminology goes hand in hand with Mendelssohn's and Hirsch's affirmative narrative about the coherence between Jewish *religious* law and the modern state (for the interrelationships between Jewish and secular legal systems, see Resnicoff, this volume).[34]

Notably, neither Mendelssohn nor Hirsch attempts to understand the relation between *halakhah* and the laws of the modern state in terms of *Issur Arkaot* or *Dina DeMalkhuta Dina*, both of which understand Jewish and "secular" law as two types of political authority. Instead, both Mendelssohn and Hirsch claim that Jewish law is not a type of law like state law but rather that Jewish law is different *in kind* from state law. For Mendelssohn and Hirsch, viewing Jewish law and "secular" law under the common rubric of "law" is a category error. In contrast, *Issur Arkaot* and *Dina DeMalkhuta Dina* both suggest that Jewish law and "secular" law, while different in a variety of significant ways, are similarly concerned with governance.

Just as positivists distinguish between law and politics, so too they separate law from custom. Mendelssohn, in his correspondence with the leading Jewish authority Jacob Emden (1697–1776), insists on the separation of Jewish law from custom. The impetus for this correspondence came from a 1772 law, enacted by Duke Friedrich of Mecklenburg-Schwerin, mandating delayed burial in order to make sure that no one was accidently buried alive. This law directly opposed Jewish law, which demands a quick burial. In his letter to Emden, Mendelssohn argues that by sharply distinguishing between law and custom, it is possible to reform modern Jewish law by looking to a particular Jewish law's original meaning and intention.[35] In this context, Mendelssohn suggests that the Jewish practice of immediate burial actually reflects Jewish custom and not law. Therefore, from Mendelssohn's point of view, there is not an inherent conflict between the Duke's demand that burial be delayed and actual Jewish law when separated from what was only a custom.

Hirsch's conception of Jewish law is summed up in his assertion that "The beginning of the Revelation of the law at Sinai is the guarantee of the completeness of the law through Moses . . . for the law, both written and oral, was closed with Moses at Sinai."[36] Once again, the Hebrew terms for what are translated as "written law" and "oral law" are "written *Torah*" and "oral *Torah*," and not "law" or *halakhah*. In claiming that the law (and not *Torah*) was closed with Moses at Sinai, Hirsch not only narrows the scope of *Torah* but goes farther than Mendelssohn in arguing that the Bible and the Talmud were given at once, and were and are not subject to historical change. For Hirsch, this means that there is an internal and formal coherence between the written and oral law.

In arguing for the internal coherence of law, Hirsch's concept of law bears a remarkable similarity to Ernst Weinrib's affirmative statement that "In the formalist conception, law has a content that is not imported from without, but elaborated from within. . . . Legal creativity here is essentially cognitive, and it is most naturally expressed in adjudication conceived more as the discovery than as the making of law."[37] Hirsch and Weinrib both insist that law is a self-generating, internally coherent, autonomous system. In his commentary on Exodus 21:1–24:18, the weekly portion that contains the first body of civil legislation in the Hebrew Bible, Hirsch offers an analogy for understanding the relation between the written and oral law:

> The Written Law is to the Oral Law in the relation of short notes on a full and extensive lecture on any scientific subject. For the student who has heard the whole lecture, short notes are quite sufficient to bring back afresh to his mind at any time the whole subject of the lecture. . . . For those who had not heard the lecture from the Master, such notes would be completely useless. . . . Words, marks, etc., which serve those scholars who had heard the lecture as instructive guiding stars to the wisdom that had been taught and learnt, stare at the uninitiated as unmeaning sphinxes.[38]

This analogy suggesting that the written law is shorthand for the oral law explains how rabbinic law does not differ from, but is internally consistent with, biblical law. In his commentary to the weekly Torah portion from the book of Exodus to which this quotation is the preface, Hirsch seeks to explain among other things how rabbinic law that interpreted "an eye for an eye" in terms of monetary damages is not a break with the apparent literal meaning of the Bible, but rather is the true meaning of "an eye for an eye."

Hirsch is especially at pains to distance Judaism from the laws of slavery with which this portion begins, claiming that freedom in the law, and not slavery, is the meaning of these laws.

The approach to studying the Talmud developed by the Lithuanian yeshivot provides another parallel with legal positivism and formalism's insistence that law is a self-contained sphere wholly separate from politics. As we saw beforethe Lithuanian yeshiva was a distinctly modern, elite institution which transformed Jewish law. Called alternatively "Conceptualism," "the Analytic movement," or simply "the Brisker method," the unique legal method developed by the Lithuanian yeshiva is characterized by the construction of general, abstract categories for the sake of understanding particular legal rules or positions. From this perspective, legal disputes are analyzed as reflecting disagreements about abstract categories as opposed to deriving from differences of historical context, policy aim, or even textual interpretation. As Chaim Saiman has argued, the Brisker method, developed by Rabbi Hayyim Soloveitchik (1853–1918), has striking parallels to classical legal thought in the United States that made its home at Harvard law school in the nineteenth century. The commonality between the two is found in "the assumption that law is comprised of analytic concepts which can be apolitically applied through a series of deductions made from the core legal principles."[39] In its focus on conceptual analysis, as opposed to practical rulings or matters of public policy, the understanding of law offered by the Lithuanian yeshiva is more analogous to Harvard Law School than to the traditional yeshivot supported by local Jewish communities prior to the eighteenth century. Whereas the resemblances between Mendelssohn, Hirsch, positivism, and formalism reflect a shared commitment to the sovereignty of the modern nation-state, the similarity between the Brisker method and Classical Legal Thought reflects a particularly modern devotion to the intellectual study of law for its own sake.

In contrast to the positions described above, ultra-Orthodox Judaism offers a different narrative about Jewish law which is rooted in the rejection of the modern nation-state and affirmation of an inextricable tie between theology, law, and politics. As ultra-Orthodox Judaism criticized and rejected a variety of other formulations of orthodoxy that strictly separate religious law from any kind of politics,[40] as well as Zionism and of course Liberal Judaism, the concept of *Da'at Torah* (literally "knowledge of Torah") developed as a theological, legal, and political ideology. One of its earliest proponents was Yisrael Meir Kagan (1838–1933), often referred to as *Hafetz Ḥayyim* (Desirer of Life, the title of one of his famous works) who described *Da'at Torah* in the following terms: "He whose knowledge is the knowledge of the Torah (*Da'at Torah*) can solve all the problems in the world, for the individual and for the collective."[41] For Kagan, and many others following him, the Torah scholar who embodies this ideal becomes one with Jewish law. His opinion, even on issues that are not narrowly "legal," is authoritative. Put into more mundane terms, this means that within isolated, ultra-Orthodox communities, it is Torah scholars, and not recourse to *halakhah* understood as an internal realm in and of itself, who authorize the behaviors of their communities.

The doctrine of *Da'at Torah* finds parallels not in legal positivism, formalism, or conceptualism but rather in twentieth-century political theology, which emerged as a criticism of all modern legal theory as well as the modern nation-state. In the context of modern legal theory, "political theology" is a term made famous by the Nazi jurist Carl Schmitt (1888–1985), who argued that the modern state, and especially the modern ideas of sovereignty and law that define the modern nation-state, had its unacknowledged origins in theology: "all significant concepts of the modern theory of the state are secularized theological concepts."[42] For Schmitt, recognition of the modern state's theological origins points to the weakness and ultimate unsustainability of the modern state, which, in its commitment to the rule of law, conceives of law as its own distinct realm. It goes without saying that there are enormous differences in the worldviews of Schmitt and proponents of *Da'at Torah*. Nevertheless, Schmitt allows us to understand important features of *Da'at Torah*. According to Schmitt, "every legal order is based on a decision . . . and not on a norm,"[43] which means that law is not ultimately constitutionally or even rule bound but instead always depends upon extralegal political authority. In the case of Schmitt, following Hobbes, this extralegal authority is a sovereign of a particular nation-state. In the case of ultra-Orthodoxy, this extralegal authority is a Torah scholar revered by a particular Jewish community. Strikingly, proponents of *Da'at Torah* do not contend that all legal rulings require a textual basis (such as traditional sources or legal codes). Instead, the authority of law derives from the authority of a given rabbinic figure who embodies *Da'at Torah*. As a number of scholars have suggested, the institutionalization of *Da'at Torah* in ultra-Orthodox communities lends itself to notions of rabbinic infallibility and as such may be more analogous to papal institutions than to historical rabbinic models of authority.[44]

Although *Da'at Torah* arguably returns Jewish law to the realm of the political, it also differs from pre-modern Jewish law which, we have seen, rested not on the authority of one (or even more than one) rabbi but instead on lay leaders as well. So too, *Da'at Torah* is also distinctively modern because in Israel, North America, and Europe today, ultra-Orthodox life is made possible by the benefits of modern democratic societies and their commitment to religious freedom, which allow for, and in some cases support, the rights of private communities to separate themselves from the dominant public order of the sovereign state (For more on Jewish Orthodoxy and ultra-Orthodoxy, see Ferziger, this volume).[45]

Despite the significant differences in the narratives about law that various modern Jewish communities offer, they all remain, in one way or another, dependent on the modern nation-state. As we have seen, the characterization of Jewish law as strictly religious, as opposed to political, stems from the modern assumption that the modern state has a monopoly on politics and any law attached to politics. At the same time, the kinds of legal theories offered by a variety of modern Jewish thinkers to describe the inner workings of Jewish law as a realm unto itself resemble a number of different strands in modern legal theory. Since the modern legal theories discussed above themselves emerged together with the modern nation-state, this likeness is not surprising. So too, it is not surprising that the rejection of the notion that Jewish law is a self-contained, separate sphere of law in favor of a more comprehensive political and theological vision captured by *Da'at Torah* shares features with claims about "political theology." *Da'at*

Torah and political theology are premised on an opposition to modern claims about the nation-state and the separate spheres of politics, morality, and law. To state the obvious, such opposition is rooted in responding to the political reality of the modern nation-state. Moreover, it is through the mechanisms of the modern nation, and especially its commitment to religious freedom, that many ultra-Orthodox communities are able to secure their isolationist communities.

Democracy, Egalitarianism, and Feminism

The modern nation-state's allegiance to the rule of law brings with it, in theory at least, commitments to democracy and egalitarianism. The influence of modern democracy and its egalitarian ideals on modern arguments about Jewish law are especially evident in a number of Jewish feminist conceptions of Jewish law that attempt to reconcile gender egalitarianism with large parts of Jewish law that are at the very least inegalitarian, if not patriarchal. As we have seen with modern arguments about Jewish law generally, feminist arguments about Jewish law are made across a broad ideological spectrum. In this section, we will consider four Jewish feminist arguments about law. While they differ from one another, all emphasize the necessity and significance of the stories or narratives that underlie and constitute legal systems. As a general matter, Robert Cover's seminal essay, "*Nomos* and Narrative," referenced earlier, provides an important conceptual framework for thinking about gender in Jewish law.

Rachel Adler, who has long been associated with the Reform movement's Los Angeles campus of Hebrew Union College-Jewish Institute of Religion, turned directly to Cover in order to extend a conception of *halakhah* to liberal Judaism. In *Engendering Judaism*, Adler, following Cover, seeks to reinstitute *halakhah* as a holistic and pedagogic *nomos* for liberal Jews. As she puts it: "*Halakhah* is the act of going forward, of making one's way. A *halakhah*, a path making, translates the stories, and values of Judaism into ongoing action. That makes it an integral component of Judaism . . . not merely of orthodoxy, but of any kind of Judaism. Such a definition of *halakhah* breaks the traditionalist monopoly on the word *halakhah*."[46] Drawing on Cover, Adler stresses that new narratives create new norms. As such, liberal communities, which imagine new Jewish worlds in keeping with modern egalitarian commitments, can and should be *halakhic* communities. Understood in this way, Adler suggests, liberal *halakhic* communities might even provide an impetus for traditionalist Jews to reimagine their communal narratives and legal norms.

Tamar Ross, an Orthodox feminist philosopher who retired from a distinguished career at Bar Ilan University, is sympathetic to, but ultimately critical of, Adler. She commends Adler for her "richly imaginative" approach to Jewish texts and law. However, building upon Hans-Georg Gadamer's arguments about legal hermeneutics in *Truth and Method*,[47] Ross maintains that "Any interpretation must contend with certain existing frames of reference in order to qualify as relevant and worthy of consideration in the eyes of the traditionalist. Irrespective of more specific and substantive considerations of content, three elements are indispensable: appeal to the consensus of experts, solidarity with the larger community in which the transformative narrative is played out, and acknowledgment of the law's claims to transcendence."[48]

The difference between Adler and Ross reflects their opposing ideological commitments (Adler to liberal Judaism and Ross to orthodox Judaism), but it is important to recognize that their divergence is also an expression of different theories of law. We can appreciate this looking at a central point in Cover's *Nomos and Narrative.* Cover argues that law functions in two basic modes, what he calls the *paideic* and the "imperial." The term "*paideic*" suggests "(1) a common body of precept and narrative, (2) a common and personal way of being educated into this corpus, and (3) a sense of direction or growth that is constituted as the individual and his community work out the implications of their law."[49] In contrast, Cover suggest that under the imperial mode, legal norms are institutional and considered universal. In other words, the imperial mode of law is "world maintaining." Despite the distinction between the paideic and the imperial, Cover stresses that that "no normative world has ever been created or maintained wholly in either the paideic or the imperial mode."[50] Applying these two modes to Adler and Ross, it is clear that Adler mainly focuses on the paideic mode of law in her reimagining *halakhic* narratives through a liberal lens, whereas Ross, in stressing the roles of experts and the law's claim to transcendence, emphasizes that there are not just paideic but also imperial dimensions to *halakhah*.

Another significant orthodox feminist thinker, Tova Hartman, also pays attention to the stories communities tell about themselves and law. But whereas Adler and Ross, despite their differences, both criticize positivist and formalist accounts of Jewish law, Hartman offers a feminist account of Jewish law within the context of positivism. In reasoning similar to that of Mendelssohn, Hirsch, and contemporary legal positivists, Hartman insists that it is necessary to distinguish between true *halakhah*, which contains resources for egalitarian ideals, and patriarchal ideology, which is not actually *halakhic*. Orthodox arguments against more inclusive roles for women, Hartman contends, are often made not on the basis of *halakhah* but instead by offering narratives that invoke the possibility of feminist threats to Jewish religious and cultural stability. As Hartman puts it, "Collectively, the array of rhetorical strategies these rabbis employ—defining the desire for anything beyond the status quo as foreign and dangerous to tradition, attacking the motivations of those petitioning for such change, associating them with classic cultural villains, and defining them as enemies of Jewish stability and continuity—all point to one cultural fact: the only way for the community to survive is for women's roles not to change."[51] But this antifeminist narrative, Hartman points out, is simply an articulation of fear of change that does not admit that on *orthodox*, that is on *halakhic*, grounds, there are resources for more inclusive practices, such as permitting all women prayer groups and publicly reading the wedding contract (*ketubah*) at Jewish weddings (see Kwall, this volume, for further discussion of these points).

Ronit Irshai, a student of Ross, builds upon Adler, Ross, and Cover in rejecting the notion that Jewish law is a closed system that must rely upon its internal rules and processes. But Irshai also goes further in suggesting that instead of moving only from the direction of narrative to nomos, Jewish feminists also must move from nomos to narrative. For Irshai, this means that what is needed is not only new theological narratives but also an "alternative *halakhic* story." Irshai offers the following example:

> [I]n all matters related to abortion and contraception, the signal tendency is one of stringency, while in matters related to modern artificial fertility, the decisions tend to be extremely lenient. In other words, sex without procreation is treated strictly; procreation without sex is treated leniently, on the premise that reproduction at almost any cost is the preferred value. What can account for this pronatalist tendency? Multiple explanations have been offered, but I believe they must be supplemented by an understanding of the gender-related issues that underlie the ideology reflected in the decisions. In my judgment, a latent concept of gender that defines women and femininity with reference to women's biological functions constitutes a necessary (though not sufficient) condition for this trend. This concept does not regard woman as an "end in itself" (in the Kantian sense); rather, it sees her primarily in her reproductive role—as a means.[52]

In looking for the concepts that underlie specific *halakhic* decisions, Irshai argues that feminists can and must replace problematic concepts (such as seeing women only as a means for reproduction) with more egalitarian ones already found in *halalakhic* discourse (see also Fischer, this volume). In suggesting that *halakhah* includes implicit concepts that must be made explicit, Irshai's argument is broadly reminiscent of the American philosopher, lawyer, and constitutional scholar, Ronald Dworkin, who insisted, against positivism, that law is made up of not only rules but also what he called principles, which are standards "to be observed."[53]

As we have seen in the last two sections, the overlaps between modern Jewish conceptions of Jewish law and modern legal theories are considerable, and they are also not ideologically predictable. Positivist conceptions of law can be put to conservative use, such as in Hirsch's case, but they can also allow for the possibility of moving beyond ideology to a more expansive consideration of what is possible within the bounds of Jewish law, such as in Hartman's case. At the same time, the embrace of the intimate tie between law and narrative as reflected particularly in Robert Cover's work, can bolster orthodox, liberal, and feminist understandings of Jewish law. Finally, despite the religious obligation that many Jews believe defines their relationship to Jewish law, all of the legal theories considered in the last two sections operate within the context of modern societies. As such, adherence to Jewish law, however it is understood theologically, is legally and politically voluntary. These modern societies include Jewish communities committed to egalitarianism and religious pluralism as well as Jewish communities supportive of antidemocratic religious communities, such as various ultra-Orthodox communities that do not identify with their surrounding democratic environments that sustain their legal existence.

Conclusion

We have seen in this chapter that conceptions of Jewish law have been transformed in the modern period by a large variety of Jewish points of view. The effect of these transformations was to transform law into a sphere that more resembles religion than it does law as it is understood in the modern world. These varying conceptions reflect the modern disintegration of semiautonomous, pre-modern Jewish communities. They also reflect the general fragmentation of modernity, in which we tend to think that there are separate spheres of life such as law, religion, morality, economics, and politics, among others. With this general fragmentation of modernity, conceptions of Jewish law, like conceptions of religion, morality, economics, and politics, have narrowed as well. As we have seen, with the eventual establishment of modern nation-states, the modern notions of "Jewish law," "ceremonial law," and even *halakhah* came to reflect smaller and more fixed dimensions of Jewish life.

By way of conclusion, let us return to this chapter's title: "Modernity, Secularism and the Transformation of Jewish Law" and ask about the meaning of "secularism." Since the early twentieth century, a number of scholars have made various arguments for what can generally be described as a "secularization thesis," which links modernity, in opposition to prior historical periods, to increased rationality and the eradication of religion. Perhaps most famously, Max Weber described the modern world as a "ghost of dead religious belief," which produces "specialists without spirit, sensualists without heart."[54] For Weber and other proponents of the secularization thesis, secularism and secularization are simply sociological facts, which reflect the absence of religion and more specifically the lack of religious *belief*. But this understanding of secularism is problematic for two main reasons. First, Weber and others believed on empirical grounds that as the world became ever more modern, religion would go away. However, as should be clear to anyone who reads the newspaper, this did not happen. Indeed, it is arguable that large parts of the modern world seem to have become ever more religious. Second, and more important for the purposes of this chapter, the ideas of secularism and secularization imply that secularism replaces religion. This is in keeping with the notion that religion is primarily about belief which, according to the secularization thesis, melts away as it is replaced by disenchanted rationalism, by which Weber and others mean instrumentalized reasoning that is geared only toward practical ends. But once we understand modernity more in terms of the rise of the power of the nation-state, and religion as not just about belief but about practice, it is more accurate to say that what we call today "religion" was born together with what we call the "secular." Both religion and the secular are products of the modern nation-state's reduction of religion to individual belief, and relegation of all other realms of life to the "secular."[55]

The modern transformation of Jewish law into something wholly religious is an important, though often neglected, case study for thinking about the limits of modern conceptions of the "secular," "religion," "law," and "politics." Although the modern makeover of Jewish law is best described in terms of religion, individual belief is not a primary, or in some cases even a necessary, feature of Jewish law. As many of the essays in this volume show, traditionally and historically understood, Jewish law is comprehensive and affects all aspects of an observant Jew's life. To take but one basic example, the laws of *kashrut* (keeping kosher) are not easily relegated to religious, as opposed to secular, commitments or experiences.[56]

Jews will continue to negotiate both the limits and the transformative possibilities of understanding Jewish law within the contours of the nation-state. Plus, Jews will continue to argue among themselves about the scope and meaning of Jewish law. Other chapters in this volume offer some understanding of the shape and criteria of such arguments. What this chapter has shown, however, is that despite enormous differences among different Jewish communities about what Jewish law is, and what it should be, any conception or implementation of Jewish law must grapple with the ways in which nation-states have usurped not just the concept of law, but also the governance by law for themselves. As we have seen, this is not just a conceptual problem but also a practical one because since beginning of the modern period, adherence to Jewish law, like adherence to any religion, is voluntary. This voluntary reality not only breaks with the legal realities of pre-modern Judaism but also has brought about a plurality of conceptions of Jewish law that must, inevitably, compete with each other in the marketplace of ideas.

Notes

1. Jacob Katz, *Tradition and Crisis: Jewish Society at the End of the Middle Age* (1961), trans. Bernard Dov Cooperman (Repr., New York: Syracuse University Press, 2000).
2. The Treaty of Westphalia of 1648 began the process of institutionalizing the secularization of politics through modern systems of law.
3. For an overview, see Richard Tuck, *The Rights of War and Peace: Political Thought and the International Order from Grotius to Kant* (New York: Oxford University Press, 2001).
4. Once again, see Edrei for how religious Zionists have tried to expand this modern conception of *halakhah* in the State of Israel.
5. Salo Baron, "Ghetto and Emancipation," *The Menorah Journal* 14 (1928): 515–26.
6. For a discussion of the uneven process of emancipation, see David Sorkin, *Jewish Emancipation: A History Across Five Centuries* (Princeton, NJ: Princeton University Press, 2019).
7. On Spinoza's life and beliefs, see Steven Nadler, *Spinoza: A Life* (Cambridge: Cambridge University Press, 1999), as well as Steven Nadler, *A Book Forged in Hell: Spinoza's Scandalous Treatise and the Birth of the Secular Age* (Princeton, NJ: Princeton University Press, 2011).
8. Benedict Spinoza, *Theologico-Political Treatise*, trans. R. H. M. Elwes (New York: Dover, 1951), 69.
9. Spinoza famously suggests that if Jews reestablished a state, Jewish law could come back to life. This is theme picked up by a variety of Zionist thinkers beginning in the nineteenth century. For a helpful analysis, see Warren Zev Harvey, "Spinoza's Counterfactual Zionism," *Iyyun* 62 (July 2013): 235–44.

10. Jacob Katz, *Toward Modernity: The European Jewish Model* (New Brunswick, NJ: Transaction Books, 1987), 1.
11. See sections "Jewish Law as Religion" for discussion of Mendelssohn and "Democracy, Egalitarianism, and Feminism" for discussion of feminist approaches to Jewish law.
12. See section "Affinities between Modern Jewish Conceptions of Law and Modern Legal Theory" on Hirsch and ultra-Orthodoxy.
13. Avraham Melamed, *Dat: mi-ḥoḳ le emunah* [*Dat: From Law to Religion*] (Tel Aviv: Hotsa'at ha-Ḳibuts ha-me'uḥad, 2014).
14. Moses Mendelssohn, *Jerusalem or On Judaism and Power*, trans. Allan Arkush (Brandeis University Press, 1983), 130.
15. Ibid., 102–3.
16. Ibid., 134.
17. Some proponents of "positive historical" Judaism, what came to be known in the United States as Conservative Judaism, insisted on viewing Jewish law in more capacious terms. See the discussion of the political fallout of Heinrich Graetz's claim that Judaism is always simultaneously religious and political in Leora Batnitzky, *How Judaism Became a Religion* (Princeton, NJ: Princeton University Press, 2011), 43–48.
18. Ismar Schorsch, *Jewish Reactions to German Anti-Semitism* (Philadelphia: Jewish Publication Society, 1972), 10.
19. Samson Raphael Hirsch, "Die Trennungsfrage in Carlsruhe," *Jeschurun* 25 (1870): 128. See Katz's discussion of this publication in Jacob Katz, *A House Divided: Orthodoxy and Schism in Nineteenth Century European Jewry*, trans. Ziporah Brody (Hanover, NH: University Press of New England, 1998), 239.
20. Samson Raphael Hirsch, "Jewish Communal Life," in *Judaism Eternal*, trans. and ed. Isadore Grunfeld (London: Soncino Press, 1965), 100.
21. Samson Raphael Hirsch, *Collected Writings*, vol. 6 (New York: Feldheim, 1996), 75.
22. Samson Raphael Hirsch, *Nineteen Letters* (Jerusalem: Feldheim, 1995), 224.
23. Abraham Geiger, "A General Introduction to the Science of Judaism," in *Abraham Geiger and Liberal Judaism: The Challenge of the Nineteenth Century*, ed. Max Weiner (Philadelphia: Jewish Publication Society, 1962), 155.
24. For an overview of the transformation of eastern European Jewry, see Israel Bartal, *The Jews of Eastern Europe, 1772-1881*, trans. Chaya Naor (Philadelphia: University of Pennsylvania Press, 2006).
25. Immanuel Etkes, "A Shtetl with a Yeshiva: The Case of Volozhin," in *The Shtetl: New Evaluations*, ed. Steven T. Katz (New York: New York University Press, 2007), 41.
26. In Hayyim of Volozhin's words: "'Acquire a friend' [Sayings of the Fathers, 1:6] . . . with whom one can take counsel also concerning matters of Divine service. For if you are wise in your own eyes, the Evil Impulse can blind your eyes and make the crooked and the hilly [to appear] straight. Therefore, you must take counsel with a friend, for your own evil impulse is not so close to him, as to be misleading." As cited in Immanuel Etkes, *Rabbi Israel Salanter and the Mussar Movement*, trans. Jonathan Chipman (Philadelphia: Jewish Publication Society, 1993), 52
27. See Chaim Saiman, *Halakhah: The Rabbinic Idea of Law* (Princeton, NJ: Princeton University Press, 2020), for further discussion of the Lithuanian yeshivot and their conception of *halakhah*.
28. Lawrence Kaplan, "The Ḥazon Ish: Ḥaredi Critic of Traditional Orthodoxy," in *The Uses of Tradition: Jewish Continuity in the Modern Era*, ed. Jack Wertheimer (New York: Jewish Theological Seminary Press, 1992), 145–73.

29. Robert Cover, "The Supreme Court. 1982 Term—Foreword: Nomos and Narrative," 97 *Harvard Law Review* 4, no. 4 (1983): 34.
30. But which also has roots in Mendelssohn, as discussed above.
31. There are positivists who deny they are formalists (see H. L. A. Hart, *The Concept of Law* [Oxford: Oxford University Press, 1961], 124–54), formalists who deny they are positivists (Ernst Weinrib, "Legal Formalism: On the Immanent Rationality of the Law," *Yale Law Journal* 97 [1988]: 949–1016); and positivists who claim they are also formalists (Frederick Schauer, "Formalism," *Yale Law Journal* 97 [1988]: 509–48).
32. Liam Murphy, "The Political Question of the Concept of Law," in *Hart's Postscript: Essays on the Postscript to 'The Concept of Law*, ed. Jules Coleman (Oxford: Oxford University Press, 2001), 373.
33. Moses Maimonides, *Dalālat al-hāirīn*, ed. Solomon Munk (Jerusalem: Y. Yunovits, 1929), 3:27.
34. Notably, neither Mendelssohn nor Hirsch attempts to understand the relation between *halakhah* and the laws of the modern state in terms of *Issur Arkaot* or *Dina DeMalkhuta Dina* (discussed in Resnicoff, this volume), both of which understand Jewish and "secular" law as two types of political authority. Instead, both Mendelssohn and Hirsch claim that Jewish law is not a type of law like state law but rather that Jewish law is different *in kind* from state law. For Mendelssohn and Hirsch, viewing Jewish law and "secular" law under the common rubric of "law" is a category error. In contrast, *Issur Arkaot* and *Dina DeMalkhuta Dina* both suggest that Jewish law and "secular" law, while different in a variety of significant ways, are similarly concerned with governance.
35. For a translation of this correspondence, see Leora Batnitzky and Yonatan Brafman, eds., *Jewish Legal Theories* (Chicago: Brandeis University Press, 2018), 7–14.
36. Samson Raphael Hirsch, *Horeb*, trans. I. Grunfeld (New York: Soncino, 1962), 20.
37. Weinrib, "Legal Formalism," 956.
38. Samson Raphael Hirsch, *Pentateuch: Translation and Commentary*, trans. Isaac Levy (Gateshead, UK: Judaica Press, 1973), 288.
39. Chaim Saiman, "Legal Theology: The Turn to Conceptualism in Nineteenth-Century Jewish Law," *Working Paper Series* 81 (2007): 39, https://digitalcommons.law.villanova.edu/wps/art81.
40. Proponents of various forms of this kind of orthodoxy would include not only Hirsch but also, in the American context, Joseph Soloveitchik and, in the Israeli context, Yeshayahu Leibowitz. For more on the overlaps between these different orthodox figures and their varied contexts, see Batnitzky, *How Judaism Became a Religion*, chs. 2 and 3.
41. As quoted in Benjamin Brown, "Jewish Political Theology: The Doctrine of 'Da'at Torah' as a Case Study," *The Harvard Theological Review* 107, no. 3 (July 2014): 259.
42. Carl Schmitt, *Political Theology: Four Chapters on the Concept of Sovereignty*, trans. George Schwab (Chicago: University of Chicago Press, 1982), 36.
43. Carl Schmitt, *The Crisis of Parliamentary Democracy*, trans. Ellen Kennedy (Boston: MIT Press, 1988), 10.
44. Jacob Katz, "The Unqualified Authority Claimed for Halakhists," *Jewish History* 11, no. 1 (Spring 1997): 41–50.
45. As Benjamin Brown has remarked: "The fact that Da'at Torah functions within a non-sovereign framework makes it, somewhat ironically, more democratic than it appears. For instance, Haredi authorities never sought to establish enforcement mechanisms, preferring instead that their political power derive from their ethical-religious authority. Yet

without enforcement mechanisms, the Torah sages cannot function as a truly authoritative governing body. Furthermore, participation in Haredi society is essentially voluntary: in principle, anyone who does not trust its leadership is free to leave . . . while on the theoretical level Da'at Torah embodies an almost belligerently antidemocratic approach, one that is exceptional among other Jewish and Christian political theologies of the twentieth century, it paradoxically features an *implied* democratic spirit, in that it cannot impose leadership on anyone who does not voluntarily choose to subordinate himself to it" (Benjamin Brown, "Jewish Political Theology: The Doctrine of 'Da'at Torah' as a Case Study," *Harvard Theological Review* 107, no. 3 [2014]: 227). The lines between Orthodoxy and ultra-Orthodoxy are often blurred in today's world but they nevertheless remain broadly distinguished by the degree to which different communities isolate themselves from other Jews and broader society.

46. Rachel Adler, *Engendering Judaism: An Inclusive Theology and Ethics* (Boston: Beacon, 1999), 21–22.
47. Hans-Georg Gadamer, *Truth and Method*, 2nd ed. (London: Bloomsbury, 1994).
48. Tamar Ross, *Expanding the Palace of Torah: Orthodoxy and Feminism* (Waltham, MA: Brandeis University Press, 2004), 156
49. Cover, "The Supreme Court. 1982 Term—Foreword," 12–13.
50. Ibid., 114.
51. Tova Hartman, *Feminism Encounters Traditional Judaism: Resistance and Accommodation* (Waltham, MA: Brandeis University Press, 2007), 118.
52. Ronit Irshai, "Towards a Gender Critical Approach to the Philosophy of Jewish Law (Halakhah)," *Feminist Studies in Religion* 26, no. 2 (2010): 67
53. Ronald Dworkin, *Taking Rights Seriously* (Cambridge, MA: Harvard University Press, 1977), 75.
54. Max Weber, *The Protestant Ethic and Spirit of Capitalism* (New York: Penguin Classics, 2002). Notably, Weber, who was trained in law, tied modernity's cage not just to the rise of global capitalism and increased bureaucracy but also to ever increasing formal rationality in law for which he found a precedent in ancient Judaism. See Max Weber, *Ancient Judaism* (New York: Free Press, 1967), 181–82.
55. Individual belief is often presented as an apolitical notion. Yet the relegation of religion to individual belief by the nation-state is based on state power which insists that "religion" and "politics" are wholly separable realms of life. The histories of Judaism, Christianity, and Islam suggest otherwise. More importantly, the present-day realities of many religious communities, both in the United States and around world, indicates that religion has not and perhaps cannot be confined to the so-called private sphere. As Talal Asad has put it: "If the secularization thesis no longer carries the weight it once did, this is because the categories of 'politics' and 'religion' turn out to implicate one another more profoundly than we thought, a discovery that has accompanied our growing understanding of the powers of the modern nation-state. The concept of the secular cannot do without the idea of religion." Talal Asad, *Formations of the Secular* (Redwood City, CA: Stanford University Press, 2003), 200.
56. For more on this point, see Roberta Rosenthal Kwall, *Remix Judaism: Preserving Tradition in a Diverse World* (Lanham, MD: Rowman & Littlefield, 2020), esp. 45–76.

CHAPTER 18

JEWISH LAW AND ORTHODOX LAW

ADAM S. FERZIGER

INTRODUCTION

FROM Biblical accounts until the past three centuries, Jews/Israelites distinguished themselves from other groups through the legal groundwork and requirements of their religion. With the adoption by many modern Jews of secular lifestyles, this axiomatic dynamic came to an end. This chapter focuses on one striking aspect of how Jewish law, as expressed by its Orthodox proponents, responded and in the process transformed under the new circumstances.

The normative legal foundation of Judaism received its most prolific expression in the literature that arose from around the end of the Second Temple period (70 CE) onward.[1] As to multiple types of Jewish individuals that swayed from the law, the Talmud and medieval codes, novellae and responsa deliberate their status and the sanctions to be placed upon them. Yet the pre-modern standards that were established arose out of an assumption that the same basic Jewish identity encompassed all, and that those who deviated needed to be disciplined with the aim of their return to the standard path. Thus, Jewish law was, in principle, directed toward all Jews but not to non-Jews.[2]

No doubt the Talmud also discusses various Jewish sects that did not accept rabbinic authority. However, even in these instances, the vast majority of the cases focus on discrepancies connected to the specifics of the law. Rarely does one find internal debate concerning the fundamental legal underpinnings of Judaism itself.[3] Recalling Paul of Tarsus's proclamation that Jesus was the "end of the Law,"[4] those born Jews who rejected the axiom of law paved a path toward an alternative religious construct.

Approximately three hundred years ago, the situation within Judaism began to change. The adjustment of large segments of European Jews to new societal realties was often accompanied by permanent abandonment of religious compliance. Sometimes, this was a reflection of their adoption of new philosophical approaches or theologies—like

Reform—that claimed legitimacy on the basis of original, nonlegal understandings of Judaism. Often, though, it simply showed that individuals were embracing the norms of the broader society that had opened its welcoming doors.[5] Regardless of the motivations, the net result was that rather than commitment to Jewish law serving primarily as a dividing line between Jews and Gentiles—or those gravitating toward apostasy, it transformed into a vehicle for determining internal boundaries between types of positively identifying Jews as well. In Western societies, where diverse formulations of Judaism arose, those who remained steadfast in their conformity to *halakhah* came to be known as the Orthodox.[6]

The manner through which the rabbinical authorities articulated Jewish legal decisions under modern conditions highlights differences between Orthodox Jews and other Jews. The internal divisions certainly come across boldly in patently polemical rulings or those related to interdenominational struggles. The queries explored here, moreover, are ones that are not directed specifically to such conflicts (indirect contextual factors can never be fully dismissed). Nonetheless, the more nuanced dichotomies uncovered below demonstrate a clear, self-conscious emphasis by the authors on disparities between their core constituencies—the Orthodox, as opposed to non-Orthodox or nonobservant Jews.

Attention to such divergences, I maintain, is not simply a cosmetic or technical matter. When evidenced broadly, it reflects a more foundational characteristic of the transition of Jewish law from its pre-modern to "Orthodox" articulation. A system that celebrated divisions between Jews and non-Jews shifted to one that did not abandon prior principles regarding non-Jews—although many authorities sought to neutralize them[7]—but brought to the fore that which differentiated between Orthodox Jews and their Jewish counterparts.

Orthodoxy, Modernity, and Jewish Law

The term "Orthodoxy" was introduced to internal Jewish discourse during the late eighteenth century, when "enlightened" *maskilim* applied it pejoratively to a traditionalist Judaism that in their eyes was fast becoming obsolete.[8] From the mid-nineteenth century onward, more conservative elements of Central European Jewish society began to wear the name "Orthodox" with pride,[9] as they claimed that its adherents were the exclusive bearers of authentic Judaism.[10] Their basic message was that while external social and political realities had changed dramatically, and alternative forms of Judaism had begun to be expressed, only the Orthodox had succeeded in insulating the true Judaism from these powerful influences. Any evident outward changes were in appearance only and were not to be interpreted as a dilution of, or deviation from, the religious values and lifestyle of their forefathers.[11]

The academic investigation of Orthodoxy, which emerged as a prominent subfield of Jewish studies from the 1980s, challenged partisan assumptions regarding its immunity to change.[12] Attention was directed toward the ability to choose one's form of religious expression or the lack thereof, as a fundamental characteristic that distinguishes modern Jewish life from the "taken for grantedness" of pre-modern society.[13] Within such a conceptual outlook, all religions practiced in modern society, including the seemingly "ultra-conservative" approaches, are innovative/reactionary formulations, chosen by their adherents, rather than simply inherited. This choice may lead to some type of accommodation or compromise to new circumstances. Alternatively, it may engender dramatic efforts to reject the surrounding culture.

While emphasis on the relative novelty of Orthodoxy has not been without its critics,[14] it has established itself as a dominant approach among leading scholars in the field. Thus, the past half century has witnessed a proliferation of articles and monographs that analyze different aspects of Orthodoxy in light of its identification as a modern movement. Central to many discussions of Orthodoxy has been its oft-times polemical relationship toward Jewish groups that espoused ideologies judged to represent a more radical departure from pre-modern tradition.

The predominant academic perception of Orthodoxy as a modern Jewish movement does not contradict the fact that its adherents stand out in comparison to those identified with other contemporary Jewish movements in levels of continuity of deeply entrenched practices and beliefs. While American Conservative Judaism also historically mandated observance of the *halakhah* as proper religious behavior—although based on a far more expansive understanding of what constituted legitimate change in law, the level of lay Conservative adherence has not followed suit. In fact, twenty-first-century American Conservative congregations draw on almost identical constituencies to those of the Reform.[15] Notwithstanding, the rise of another modern Jewish movement that predicates its worldview on Jewish law pushed American Orthodox advocates in particular to clarify that which distinguishes between their self-understood "authentic" approach to *halakhah*, and that of their contrary competitors.[16]

Relatedly, one of the outgrowths of the development of the academic subdiscipline of Orthodoxy has been concerted efforts to analyze modern and contemporary Jewish law with an eye to that which reflects its "Orthodox" character in comparison to pre-modern approaches. Much work has examined the inclinations of individual major adjudicators, while thematic investigations focus on strictness,[17] leniency,[18] ideological motivations,[19] and theoretical approaches to adjudication.[20] Other expositions have sought to connect certain legal approaches with the origins of specific Orthodox subgroups: Lithuanians,[21] Hasidim,[22] Mizrahi (Eastern/Sephardic),[23] German Neo-Orthodoxy,[24] Hungarian ultra-Orthodoxy,[25] American Modern Orthodoxy,[26] American Haredim,[27] and Israeli Haredim,[28] among others. Increasingly, contemporary scholars have inspected Orthodox law through the lens of gender.[29] Israeli researchers, in particular but not exclusively, have also questioned whether a uniquely Religious-Zionist (Orthodox) *halakhah* has arisen since the establishment of the State of Israel in 1948.[30]

All these issues manifest legal innovations that fit under the rubric of Orthodox navigations of societies rooted on choice and the variety of responses that this predicament engenders. Yet other than the chronology and the overall environment of secularization, the different instances or trends do not add up to a shared unique element that points to Orthodox *halakhah*'s departure from its pre-modern precursor. My argument, to reiterate, is that one fundamental dissimilarity from the precursors to Orthodoxy is to be found in the fact that the earlier approach is rooted in the core division between Jews and Gentiles, while the latter one manifests more clearly how Orthodox Jews differ from their non-Orthodox and nonobservant Jewish brethren. In practical terms, the latter orientation more readily produces two levels of Jewish legal rulings, one directed toward the Orthodox and one for everyone else.

This chapter engages a range of cases from the late nineteenth through the twenty-first centuries—not directly related to interdenominational conflicts—that illustrate critical aspects of this foundational understanding. The instances presented here cover a relatively broad Orthodox gamut from ideological, chronological, as well as geographical perspectives. To be sure, the examples are by no means exhaustive, but they offer effective portals of entry into a uniquely Orthodox Jewish legal discourse and its core tropes.

Kosher Food and Kosher Jews

From the mid-1890s until his own passing in 1921, Rabbi Dr. David Zvi Hoffmann was the most prominent *halakhic* authority in Germany.[31] He served as rector of the Orthodox rabbinical seminary established by Rabbi Dr. Esriel Hildesheimer in Berlin and head of the religious court attached to the independent Orthodox *Adass Jisroel* community.[32]

One can identify within Hoffmann's viewpoint the integration of elements that had emerged as part of the development of Orthodoxy over the previous century. In fact, his educational background attests to his intensive exposure to five of the most influential figures in nineteenth-century Orthodoxy. Born in Verbó, Hungary (currently Slovakia), he studied in the yeshivah of Rabbi Moses Schick (Maharam Schick), the foremost student of the famed Hatam Sofer,[33] and who was destined to become the most authoritative spokesman for Orthodox communal separation from other Jews in Hungary after the Congress of 1868–1869.[34] Hoffmann then went to Eisenstadt, where he began his lifelong path as a protegé of Hildesheimer. Before leaving Hungary, he also spent time under the tutelage of the "Ketav Sofer," Rabbi Abraham Samuel Benjamin Sofer,[35] who headed the Pressburg yeshivah that his father, the Hatam Sofer, had founded. While completing his academic degree, he moved to Germany. His first position was as a teacher in the town of Hochberg, near Würzburg. There, he forged a close connection with Rabbi Seligmann Baer Bamberger, and also married the daughter of one of the leading members of the Würzburg community.[36] Finally, before accepting an appointment as a lecturer in Hildesheimer's newly founded rabbinical seminary in 1873, Hoffmann taught for two years at Rabbi Samson Raphael Hirsch's *IRG* school in Frankfurt am Main. Hoffmann, like Hirsch, saw the synthesis of Judaism and secular culture as a positive phenomenon.[37] He also followed Hildesheimer's and Bamberger's examples in his devotion to the training of modern Orthodox Jewish educators and rabbis. Moreover, he inherited Hildesheimer's role as an Orthodox proponent of *Wissenschaft des Judenthums*.[38] Yet, Hoffmann also maintained his connections to his Hungarian roots. This is particularly apparent in his responsa, in which he displayed great reverence for the opinions of the Hungarian rabbinic authorities. Like his synthesis of numerous Orthodox trends within his background, Hoffmann's involvement with developing tolerant ways for dealing with Jews from a variety of backgrounds can be seen as a climax in the evolution of nineteenth-century Orthodox approaches to the issue. The following example highlights his two-tier approach to application of Jewish law.

A certain restaurant/public cafeteria that clearly catered to Jewish clientele had been using meat that was said to be kosher but had been slaughtered by a public Sabbath desecrator—who according to many authorities is disqualified to serve in this capacity. The proprietor had subsequently turned to an Orthodox rabbi in order to receive kosher certification for the restaurant. The owner offered to purchase meat from an observant slaughterer. He was unwilling, however, to replace the restaurant's pots and tableware with new sets. This raised *halakhic* questions, since, if it was assumed that the meat previously served in the restaurant was non-kosher—having been slaughtered by a Sabbath desecrator—then the pots in which food was prepared and possibly the earthen tableware as well would have been forbidden for use for at least twelve months.[39]

In ruling on this question, Hoffman considered two issues. First, whether, in fact, meat slaughtered by a Sabbath desecrator was prohibited. Second, even if the meat was forbidden, was it possible that the pots and tableware did not need to be replaced? On both counts, he found room for ruling leniently. After citing all the various sources that led him to his conclusion, however, Hoffman instructed his correspondent to act as follows:

> Your eyes shall be trained, so that if a God-fearing man asks [about the restaurant], tell him secretly that a *ba'al nefesh* (an observant person)[40] should be strict with himself and abjure from eating in this restaurant and that you only took responsibility for supervision in order to save the masses from a grave prohibition.[41]

Even if the food in the restaurant was formally kosher, it was not a legitimate choice for Orthodox consumption.

On the one hand, this responsum testifies to Hoffmann's appreciation for the Jewish connection of the nonobservant majority. Had he been looking out only for his natural constituency, the Orthodox, he could have ruled strictly and prevented the possibility of any misunderstandings taking place. Yet a sense of "collusion" among the faithful arises from his remarks; Orthodox Jews operate according to a separate legal standard from other Jews.[42] This was to be accomplished by sharing the "secret" that this restaurant was only acceptable for those on a lower level of the Jewish totem pole. Hoffmann was willing to sanction one legal standard for the masses, while he demanded that the Orthodox strive for a distinct level of law abidance.

This two-tier ruling adumbrated an observation that Hoffmann shared in another responsum regarding whether nonobservant Jewish men could be counted for a prayer quorum of ten. There he gave sharp expression to his overall perception that Jewish law, like modern Jewish society, needed to recognize that it no longer could speak in one voice to a core Jewish populace. At least in turn-of-twentieth-century Germany, the Orthodox *halakhah* must account for two distinct groups—its loyal minority and nonobservant majority: "the God-fearing in our times are the ones who are called 'separate' and 'distinct,' while the sinners are the ones who follow the ways of the land."[43] Indeed, in that source he actually referenced terminology generally utilized within the dietary realm, when he distinguished between "Kosher people" and other Jews.[44] Notably, a similar division is identifiable in the rulings of an older Hungarian rabbinical colleague who, unlike the moderate Hoffmann, was known as a leading ultra-Orthodox activist.

Legal Behavior and Orthodox Behavior

In the course of a thirty-five year rabbinical career, Rabbi Hayyim Sofer's (1821–1886) reputation grew as one of the most conspicuous zealots within the Hungarian Orthodox rabbinate. In 1867, Sofer was appointed rabbi of Munkács, a Hasidic center that was among the largest and most prestigious communities in northeastern Hungary (current-day Ukraine). In 1879, as the rabbi of the newly constituted independent Orthodox community in Budapest, he conditioned his acceptance of the position on the prerequisite that all members be fully observant of Sabbath and dietary laws. In addition, he would make surprise visits to homes of congregants whom he suspected of violating the Sabbath. After he became too ill to go personally, he appointed official supervisors to continue this task.[45]

Sofer's personal fame, however, was also the result of his vast erudition in the intricacies of Jewish law and in his ability to apply this knowledge to issues confronted by his contemporaries. Other rabbis throughout Hungary continuously sought his opinions. In fact, his polemical writing is only a fraction of his entire literary corpus. The majority of his compositions are exegetical or legal in nature. Even when addressing legal issues, Sofer did not hide his ideological positions. Yet his *halakhic* writing is indicative, primarily, of a knowledgeable and authoritative adjudicator plying his trade. Indeed, in numerous cases he points to apparent conflicts between his legalistic conclusions and his ideological proclivities. Most illuminating for the current discussion, is his sharp articulation of the fact that normative Jewish law and Orthodox Jewish practice are not the same thing, as the case at hand illustrates.[46]

Talmudic regulations render Gentile libational wine forbidden. Medieval rabbinical authorities added a Jew who is a public Sabbath desecrater to the list of those whose wine should not be drunk—possibly as a threat against those moving toward apostasy who might be hesitant to cut off their social ties with family and friends. Other more moderate contemporary rabbinic authorities had argued that for a variety of reasons these prohibitions did not apply to the modern Sabbath desecrater.[47] In principle, Sofer and many of his Hungarian cohorts disagreed vehemently with this position.

The legal basis for the following question stems from the fact that punishment for contravening rabbinically mandated restrictions is generally less strict than if one violates a biblical proscription.[48] Can an Orthodox Jew, R. Sofer was asked, drink the wine of another Jew who regularly desecrates the Sabbath regarding rabbinical prohibitions (such as carrying money and leading his animals to his fields), although no witnesses can testify that he openly committed biblical offenses (lighting a fire, actually laboring in his field)? The specific issue that must be analyzed in weighing the need for a sanction on the wine, revolves around whether rabbinically proscribed acts render the person an "apostate regarding the entire Torah" whose wine is forbidden?[49]

Initially, Sofer argued that there was precedent for a prohibition of such an individual's wine. His thorough review of the relevant legal literature, nonetheless, elicited a different conclusion. The local religious judges could not, from a formal legal standpoint, forbid the wine of one who had only transgressed rabbinically mandated Sabbath prohibitions.[50]

Rather than conclude on this note, he said that even if the judges cannot forbid the wine, this does not mean that the formal law should be the basis for the behavior of the rest of the community:

> I say . . . that which our Sages of blessed memory told us, 'Jerusalem was destroyed because they based their rulings on pure Torah [*halakhic*] law,' [indeed] the religious judge can only rule based on what he sees, he must act according to the fundamentals of the Torah and not according to his logical understanding . . . But lay people who have been blessed by God with wealth and honor, what business do they have examining whether the ruling is clearly consistent with Torah [*halakhic*] law. They should make a decision, rather, based on their intellect and the fear of the Lord within them, to distance themselves from people who have the gall to throw off the burden and desecrate the Sabbath, whether this be regarding fences built to defend the law, rabbinical prohibitions or positive [biblical] commandments, it behooves them to disassociate from these evildoers in every way possible. . . The Temple was destroyed because people acted according to the letter of the law and asked if the wine of such a Sabbath desecrater is permitted or whether he can be included in a prayer quorum."[51]

Despite being expressed by an authority who sat on the opposite side of the late nineteenth-century Central European Orthodox spectrum, this "Ultra-Orthodox" ruling shares a common trope with that of Hoffmann. According to Sofer's statement, there are two levels at which one can evaluate the permissibility of wine touched by a perpetrator of rabbinically proscribed Sabbath violations. The first is for religious judges. They must operate according to the guidelines of legal jurisprudence. On this basis, there was insufficient grounds for forbidding the wine. Normally this would be the exclusive basis for rendering a *halakhic* decision. Beyond the formal, legal perspective, however, Sofer argues that there is an additional stage from which to address such cases. God-fearing Jews have to be guided by their own religious instinct and act accordingly. In this case, he believed that this would inevitably lead to the conclusion that the wine must be forbidden, and that people should refrain from social contact with an individual whose touch can cause the wine to achieve a forbidden status. The inability to rise above the formal strata, he claimed, was so theologically offensive, that it paved the way in the past to the destruction of the Temple.[52] A repetition of the same offense in modern times, then, would have similarly deleterious effects upon Jewish life.

Sofer's articulation of a legal recommendation here is quite innovative. In the end, the acceptable standard for judging a person and his actions is not the formal *halakhah*—which permits the wine—but rather personal religious sensitivity or reasoning, which finds a compelling basis for forbidding it. Moreover, the ability to decide has been removed from the official religious authority, who must remain allegiant to traditional legal procedure, and granted, instead, to the "God-fearing" wisdom of the laypeople.

Strikingly, Sofer's two-tier method is quite similar to that of Hoffmann. No longer is Jewish law characterized by that which is formally permitted or forbidden. Rather, two strands emerge, with the higher one not relegated purely to exceptional "pietists." In Hoffmann's case he permitted the non-Orthodox to follow the formal standard, while instructing those in charge of kosher supervision at the restaurant to indicate to potential Orthodox clientele to refrain from eating there. In practice, Sofer does not offer a permissible option—presumably because his target audience was purely the Orthodox. Notwithstanding, like Hoffmann he formulates a policy that highlights an Orthodox level of performance that is distinct from the formal standard.

Suspension of the Sabbatical Year Laws—For Whom?

According to Biblical and rabbinical sources, it is forbidden to work the Land of Israel every seventh year of a set sabbatical cycle. While there are opinions that indicate that already in ancient times the precise count was lost and therefore the laws suspended, most authorities considered them to remain valid at least on a rabbinical level. The issue became especially pressing during the late nineteenth century when Zionist pioneers began to establish agricultural settlements in Turkish Palestine. Ceasing production for a year would have decimated the fragile economic foundations that were being laid.[53]

From 1876 onward, Orthodox rabbis debated whether dispensations existed that would permit continuing to work the fields. According to most sources, the prohibition only applied to land owned by Jews. Thus, the more lenient approach claimed that if a technical "sale" of the land to non-Jews was arranged, the Jewish farmers would be permitted to continue their normal activities and not lose their income. Over time, this approach was greeted with swelling levels of negativity and rancor by most of the anti-Zionist local rabbinic establishment, who poked holes in what they saw as a politically motivated "neutering" of the authentic law.

In 1904, Rabbi Abraham Isaac Kook (1865–1935) arrived in Palestine to serve as rabbi of the port town of Jaffa and farming communities in the region. Already in his native Lithuania, Kook stood out among his Orthodox colleagues for expressing support for the early Zionist settlement. After arrival, his reputation grew among the Zionists due to his positive approach toward the young pioneers who were building the land, despite their overall alienation from religious observance.[54] Famously he supported the "selling the land permissive ruling," and penned a 250-page book that set out both the ideological and legal foundations of his approach.[55]

Numerous scholars of Kook, Religious Zionism, and *halakhah* in modern times have addressed aspects of the *Shemittah* controversy. Among the most prolific and piercing studies is that of Jewish law scholar Arye Edrei, which appeared in 2009–2010.[56] In a second article on the topic, Edrei places particular emphasis on the paradigmatic quality of the episode for deciphering the emergence of a novel "Zionist *halakhah*" that emerged from the new realities of a modern Jewish society in Turkish and British Mandate Palestine, and especially the establishment of the State of Israel.[57]

One of Edrei's main points is that Kook's lenient decision arose out of his concern for all Jews, regardless of their personal religious commitment. Thus, he felt compelled to put forward a permissive ruling that would cover the activities of all the Jewish farmers and not just the observant ones. This position stood in contrast to the subsequent decision of the preeminent mid-twentieth-century non-Zionist authority, Rabbi Abraham Yeshayahu Karelitz (*Hazon Ish*).[58] The latter directed his judgments purely toward committed Orthodox farmers, who were willing to accept his strict limitations as to which agricultural activities could be allowed even during the sabbatical year. This distinction, asserts Edrei, highlights a quintessential difference between twentieth-century non-Zionist/Haredi *halakhah*, on one hand, and the Zionist approach advanced by Kook and his followers, on the other. Haredi Jewish law is directed purely toward an elite, observant population, while Zionist authorities target a broad and diverse Jewish constituency.

Ostensibly, this argument—regarding both Karelitz and Kook—runs counter to the core thesis in this chapter. Namely, according Edrei's scheme, each figure focuses on one population or tier. For Karelitz, Jewish law must target Orthodox people who observed, a modern novelty unto itself, whereas Kook appeared to follow the spirit of pre-modern traditional Jewish law in that it directed itself equally to the entire Jewish population. My assertion of a two-tier framing—one for the Orthodox and one for others—does not appear to fit with either of these paradigms.

Regarding Kook, at least, the portrayal of a post-traditional all-inclusive legal approach for all Jews may be called into question. Despite his forthright support for the selling the land dispensation, in numerous personal correspondences regarding the sabbatical year—often to conservative rabbinical colleagues that he knew from Lithuania such as Rabbi Chaim Berlin—Kook shared his own deep reservations regarding aspects of the permissive approach.[59] Moreover, he made clear that despite standing behind his lenient decision, he did not personally follow it and was exceptionally fastidious in following all the restrictions on eating produce grown in fields during the Sabbatical year.[60]

Some may dismiss these records as reflecting Kook's overall tendency to be extraordinarily strict in his own religious performance, possibly a manifestation of a form of mystical pietism.[61] Alternatively, his unwillingness to partake stemmed from his deep desire to reassert the biblical commandments that "laid fallow" for so many centuries.[62]

However, notwithstanding clear differences in the circumstances, there are also echoes of Hoffmann's direct instruction to the kosher supervisor to tell observant Jews to avoid the cafeteria. Namely, like Hoffmann's permission to certify the restaurant as kosher but prevent strictly Orthodox Jews from accepting this standard, Kook's hyperlenient Zionism-inspired ruling is essentially geared toward the secular or mildly committed, while the more punctilious were to model themselves after the behavior of their rabbi and teacher. Thus, here too, a two-tier Orthodox *halakhah* that differentiates between Orthodox standards and those for most Jews is manifest.

Kook's son and direct successor, Rabbi Zvi Yehuda Kook, was unequivocal in institutionalizing the shemittah leniency for all Jews in Israel. That said, other prominent Kook followers took a path more similar to the two-tier interpretation that I have rendered here. While they supported the application of the sale of land approach for the broader Israeli Jewish public, they encouraged observant farmers to refrain from work of the land that is in principle forbidden during the sabbatical years. On a personal level, they sought to avoid ingesting produce that emanated from fields sold to Gentiles through the predominant legal "loophole."[63]

Rather than an all-inclusive Zionist *halakhah*, I suggest that Kook's sabbatical leniency may be termed, paradoxically, "secular *halakhah*." Like Hoffmann, his aim was to prevent those distanced from traditional observance, and for that matter a fresh Jewish society founded by this population, from adopting categorically prohibited behaviors whenever possible. Yet insofar as the Orthodox were concerned, he modeled a completely different standard that some of his closest followers perceived as the ideal "Orthodox" behavior.

The Shomer Shabbat Burial Section

A far less known, contemporary Israel-based example of the two-tier character of Orthodox *halakhah*, is the existence of separate burial areas reserved for observant Jews in many Israeli municipal cemeteries.

The Talmud declares that "a wicked person should not be buried alongside a righteous one."[64] Yet numerous rulings have appeared over the centuries that question who may be considered "wicked" (*rasha*) in regard to this principle, including some who apply this term exclusively to Gentiles or to apostates. There is, nonetheless, a long history of rabbis and community elders being interred in a special area of the cemetery. On the other side of the coin, various known deviants were sometimes relegated to less honorable sections. Yet this was generally applied on an individual basis and not to defined subcollectives within Jewish society.[65]

That said, the communal schisms between Orthodox and Reform or Neologue communities that transpired in Central Europe from the mid-nineteenth century led to the creation of distinct denominational burial grounds or sections of Jewish cemeteries in some locales—although these remained a minority.[66] Particularly in twentieth-century America, where Jewish religious life was dominated by denominational divides, those who were members of individual synagogues (rather than the European communal membership model) generally acquired plots in sections of cemeteries that were purchased by the congregation for its dues-paying constituency. Thus interment according to denominational identity achieved seminormative status.[67]

In Israel, by contrast, burial is a right provided to all citizens through National Insurance (social security). Like most religious services under the auspices of the state, except for a few recently established exceptions, all cemeteries and burial societies function according to Orthodox legal standards and under the supervision of Orthodox authorities. Therefore, almost all Jewish burials that take place in Israel may be defined in principle as Orthodox.[68] All the same, in many municipal and regional cemeteries that service both observant and nonobservant populations, burial societies set aside areas for observant Jews, who generally must reserve plots in advance. This option was little known outside closed Orthodox circles, but in recent decades it has come to the attention of various publics, and a wide spectrum of Orthodox rabbis have addressed the issue—often on websites dedicated to engaging questions of practical *halakhah* (see Figure 18.1).

One such site, din.org.il, is run by a consortium of Haredi rabbis—from Lithuanian-mitnagedic, Hasidic, and Sephardic/Mizrahi backgrounds. The main figures who field queries are listed, but the names of the respondents do not necessarily appear on the specific ruling—which heightens the sense that it is the accepted position, rather than the opinion of an individual authority.

In August 2015, a correspondent asked a series of questions regarding burial, including whether it was required to bury the Sabbath observant separately from nonobservant Jews, even when the latter grew up among non-Jews and therefore had minimal exposure to religious education. According to a large number of authorities, such an individual would be not be subject to traditional sanctions, since they would be deemed an "infant taken captive" who—due to their ignorance—was not responsible for their actions.[69] Despite this avenue for leniency, the answer given was quite unequivocal: "A person who does not observe the Sabbath should not be buried with one who does, in larger communities it is the custom to dedicate distinct sections for Sabbath observers and for those who do not observe—including infants taken captive."[70] In other words, despite the existence of a formal basis for permitting burial of almost all Jews together,

FIGURE 18.1 Netanya, Israel—New Cemetery—"Mehadrin—More Punctilious" Burial Section.
Photo credit: the author.

an ostensibly voluntary two-tier framing was asserted that essentially codifies an Orthodox *halakhah* that differentiates between different types of Jews.

A well-informed anonymous inquirer turned to Rabbi Avraham Yosef and delineated a list of four reasons given by authorities to refrain from applying the principle of "a wicked person should not be buried alongside a righteous one." Yosef was quite absolute in his response, and even offered an explanation that expresses his deep sympathy for his Orthodox constituents, along with practical instructions: "Today as well one must make great efforts to bury in separate sections, for it causes great pain to the deceased to be interred next to a wicked person. In all such requests, the burial society asks for a letter from one's local rabbi (affirming that this person is Sabbath observant)."[71]

Yosef is a well-regarded authority—especially among Sephardic/Mizrahi Jews—although he has recently been embroiled in serious legal troubles—who is the former Chief Rabbi of the city of Holon (just south of Tel Aviv) and brother of the current Sephardic Chief Rabbi of Israel.[72] Their father, Rav Ovadiah Yosef, was the Sephardic Chief Rabbi as well as one of the most influential *halakhists* of the twentieth century. He was known, among others, for his exceptional leniencies regarding nonobservant Jews, especially those whom despite their personal behavior he believed to maintain sincere connections to Jewish tradition.[73] Notwithstanding, his son emphasized the "grave" importance of separate Orthodox burial.

Perhaps even more intriguing is an earlier ruling of Rabbi Yaakov Ariel, a leading contemporary follower of the Kook school of Religious Zionism, who served for twenty-seven years as the Ashkenazi Chief Rabbi of Ramat Gan, another large Central Israel municipality that is part of the Greater Tel Aviv area. Ariel, who won the Israel Prize for his rabbinic scholarship, has dedicated considerable efforts to drawing secular and observant Jews closer, including serving as the founding chairman and head *halakhic* authority of the Tzohar rabbinic organization that was created just for that purpose. At the same time, Ariel has been criticized at times for intolerance, especially regarding gender-related issues.[74]

In September 2004, Ariel responded to an emotional letter from the son of a woman who had recently passed away and was buried in a cemetery that had just been established. The night before the funeral, the husband of the deceased—who had great difficulty walking, requested a plot close to the entrance. Despite the nearly virgin burial ground, to his surprise, the response of the burial society was "no, you can't be here, this is the Sabbath observers' section." When the father noted his disability, the person in charge retorted, "how often will you come here, once or twice a year?" After learning the source for the separate sections, the son demanded to know from Ariel, "Who licensed these employees of the local religious council to distinguish between who is wicked and who is righteous? Are all Sabbath observers righteous? . . . How can the *Shulhan Arukh* (Code of Jewish Law) be followed without offending [the memory] of my mother?"[75]

Ariel replied with apologies for the insensitivity of the burial society clerks, suggesting that these must have been substitutes for the usual figures, or perhaps it was simply an especially stressful day. However, he then went on to justify the continued separation of observant and nonobservant sections. Aware as he was of the difficulty in providing a compelling formal reason, he explained that inasmuch as the questioner found the prevailing approach offensive, so were those who keep the Sabbath repelled by the thought of being buried next to the nonobservant. So much so that if the policy were to be changed they would refuse to be buried in that cemetery, and might even disinter their deceased relatives. According to Ariel, forcing the Orthodox to act otherwise was an equivalent act of coercion, especially when "the issue of Sabbath observance is so foundational to Judaism, but this is not the place to explain in detail."[76]

Ariel's answer acknowledges the anguish of the nonobservant, but in the end he refused to renege upon what had become an accepted practice that, once again, sustained the differences between observant and nonobservant Jews. Coming as it does from a relatively moderate disciple of the Kook school, it further emphasizes the degree to which such legal strategies reflect a genuine characteristic of Orthodox *halakhah*.

Indeed, another query directed toward a far lesser-known figure bears out further the apparent "normativization" of the separate burial standard. In February 2010, Rabbi Uziel Eliyahu of the Misgav Regional Council, northeast of Haifa, was put on the defensive by a correspondent who was taken aback by the fact that in the Misgav cemetery, there was no dedicated area for Sabbath observers. The writer acknowledged that he personally lived in Rehovot (south of Tel Aviv), but he had observant relatives who lived under Eliyahu's jurisdiction who would be forced to be buried next to nonobservant Jews.

Like Ariel, Eliyahu identifies with the Religious Zionist sector, yet he was far less supportive of separate burial and produced a rich array of references to prove that this was not a religiolegal requirement. In parallel, he drew on multiple sources including Kook to emphasize the fact that all Jews are God's chosen children. After these extended forays, however, he concluded by sharing the compromise solution that he had achieved in consultation with more distinguished authorities. In order to fulfill even the most literal and strict understanding of the Talmud's mandate against burial of the wicked with the righteous, each burial plot was isolated from its neighbors by at least six cubits. Thus, from a formal perspective, they were each considered independent personal cemeteries. Under such conditions, even if they appeared to be in consecutive rows, officially there was no legal relationship between one grave and the next.

Through this solution, Eliyahu demonstrated his discomfort with the position taken by the previous figures cited above. At the same time, the complex alternative that he produced reinforces the degree to which separating the burial of Orthodox and nonobservant Jews has achieved a level standardization. Only through a loophole that avoided the situation completely could he make the claim that the cemetery under his supervision fulfilled the fundamental requirements of the law as interpreted by contemporary authorities. No doubt, this did not fully satisfy his "interrogator" who would have perceived—like Sofer above—that sometimes formally acceptable decisions could nonetheless undermine a foundational aspect of Orthodox law—the distinction between observant and nonobservant Jews.[77]

Between Orthodox and Conservative Jewish Law

All four cases expanded upon above illustrate variations on the way the two-tier approach to religious adjudication has gained currency within Orthodox *halakhah* over the past two hundred years. They all share a common theme of articulating clear differences between how Jewish law should be applied to observant Jews as opposed to nonobservant ones. In order to sharpen my claim that this two-tier approach characterizes "Orthodox" legal rulings, I will conclude with a brief expedition into the worldview of Orthodoxy's closest denominational "cousin," American Conservative Judaism as articulated by one of its founding figures.

Rabbi Solomon Schechter (1847–1915) was brought to New York from England in 1902 to serve as the president of the faculty of the Jewish Theological Seminary (JTS), the fledgling institution that under his guidance would seed the emergence of Conservative Judaism as a novel religious denomination. Born to a Hasidic family in Focsani, Rumania, he attended traditional yeshivot before receiving rabbinical ordination at the more modern-oriented Vienna Rabbinical Seminary in 1879. There he also gained exposure to critical methods of scholarship which he developed further during his subsequent years as a student at the University of Berlin. In England he received an appointment at London's Jews' College (1882–1890) and in 1890 he moved to the University of Cambridge where he rose to the rank of reader in Talmudics and gained world renown for his groundbreaking work on the Cairo Genizah documents (synagogue vault).[78]

Soon after his arrival in New York, Schechter's more liberal ideological opponents recognized that his positions differed from that of the Orthodox establishment. In 1905, Rabbi Judah Magnes of Manhattan's Reform Temple Emanuel contrasted two camps among the traditionalists: "There is an orthodoxy that is in principle fixed and immovable . . . there is another kind of Orthodoxy which, holding fast to Jewish tradition, admits the possibility of change and development, of accommodation to new surroundings. Such an Orthodoxy is that of a . . . Solomon Schechter."[79]

Schechter introduced the term "Catholic Israel" (literally "the whole of Israel"/*Klal Yisrael*) to describe Judaism's key character, which he defined as "the religious consciousness of the bulk of the nation."[80] The core spirit of historical Judaism is embedded in the people and the traditions that they inherited from previous generations. Through their collective lives they bear witness to its ideals. This body, as such, is vested with the authority to dictate ongoing normative religious behavior and initiate changes as deemed necessary.

With this commitment to the collective voice of the people, Schechter hoped that the majority of America's rapidly expanding Jewish population would coalesce around a path that—unlike Classical Reform Judaism—was grounded in traditional practice but less dogmatic and more responsive to modern life than the immigrant Orthodox rabbis. This ideal of a religious movement that spoke through the traditional language of Jewish law and liturgy, while advocating interpretations and policies that highlighted sensitivity to the nature of its broad constituency, became one of the hallmarks of the Conservative movement.

Yet inasmuch as Schechter's formulation inspired a deep appreciation for the voice of the people, the practical challenges of creating a religious stream rooted in the collective will was a daunting task. Did every Conservative Jew, regardless of their personal beliefs and behaviors, constitute a legitimate voice within Catholic Israel? What if the majority no longer demonstrated fealty to even the most lenient understandings of the basic principles of Jewish law?

Conclusion

Among those who inherited Schechter's legacy there were debates. Some, like the future Zionist leader Henrietta Szold,[81] deemphasized standards of observance for the sake of unity.[82] While others, such as Conservative religious authority and scholar Robert Gordis,[83] put forward a more narrowly defined version of Schechter's concept that acknowledged differences between observant and nonobservant Jews, but limited the relevance of these distinctions to whether one was qualified to be an arbiter of practical Jewish law, "It need hardly be emphasized that that this conception does not read any Jew out of the Jewish fold. It merely declares . . . that only those should have a voice in determining the character of Jewish law who recognize its authority."[84]

Despite their clear differences in practical application, both Szold and Gordis celebrated Schechter's vision that was predicated on a unified perception of the Jewish people. The collective voice of the entire Jewish people was the source for Jewish law's ongoing development and vibrance. Thus, the very idea of cultivating two separate paths of Jewish law, a lenient one that might enable the nonobservant to maintain some level of conformity in parallel to another stricter version that was the nearly exclusive domain of the Orthodox, was completely foreign to Schechter and his movement. For it undermined his basic belief in the validity of the totality of the Jewish people as the source of best practice.

According to this understanding, it is not merely their respective approaches to the evolution of Jewish law that distinguishes Orthodox Judaism from its Conservative counterpart. Rather, an equally fundamental question that sits at the root of the divide is whether in a modern, secularizing society, one strand of Jewish law can still address the realities of the diverse Jewish collective.

Unlike Schechter's vision of a singular identifiable collective voice, as I have attested throughout this discussion, Orthodox legal adjudication indicated that such a conceptual outlook was the precinct of the premodern condition of relative homogeneity. By contrast, the heterogeneous reality of post-emancipatory Judaism necessitated that two related but distinct planes or levels of Jewish law operate simultaneously, one that accounts for the nonobservant majority, and one geared toward the punctilious religious lifestyles of the categorically observant.

Notes

1. Chaim N. Saiman, *Halakhah: The Rabbinic Idea of Law* (Princeton, NJ: Princeton University Press, 2018). To be sure, Priests and Levites had special legal requirements.
2. Sacha Stern, *Jewish Identity in Early Rabbinic Writing* (Leiden, The Netherlands: Brill, 1994).
3. For alternative renderings of the development of ancient Judaism, see, e.g., Seth Schwartz, *The Ancient Jews from Alexander to Muhammad* (Cambridge: Cambridge University Press, 2014).
4. Rom. 10: 4.
5. Shmuel Feiner, *The Origins of Jewish Secularization in Eighteenth-Century Europe* (Philadelphia: University of Pennsylvania Press, 2010).
6. Adam S. Ferziger, *Exclusion and Hierarchy: Orthodoxy, Nonobservance, and the Emergence of Modern Jewish Identity* (Philadelphia: University of Pennsylvania Press, 2005).
7. Moshe Halbertal, "Ones Possessed of Religion: Religious Tolerance in the Teachings of the Me'iri," *Edah Journal* 1, no. 1 (2000): 2–25; Ruth Langer, "Jewish Understandings of the Religious Other," *Theological Studies* 64, no. 2 (2003): 255–77.

8. Regarding early uses of the term "Orthodox" in reference to Jews, see, e.g., Alexander Altmann, *Moses Mendelssohn* (Birmingham: University of Alabama Press, 1973), 241; Ya'akov Zur, *Bein Orthodoksiah le-Zionut* (Ramat Gan: Bar-Ilan University Press, 2001), 27–30.
9. Samson Raphael Hirsch, "Die Religion im Bunde mit dem Fortschritt" ["Religion Allied to Progress"], trans. Isidor Grunfeld, in *Judaism Eternal: Selected Essays from the Writings of Rabbi Samson Raphael Hirsch*, trans. Isidor Grunfeld (London: Soncino Press, 1956), 224–38.
10. Mordechai Breuer, *Modernity within Tradition*, trans. Elizabeth Petuchowski (New York: Columbia University Press, 1992), 9.
11. On a larger scale, Peter Berger has offered this attitude within Orthodox Judaism as a characteristic trait of religious orthodoxies. See Peter Berger, *The Heretical Imperative* (New York: Free Press, 1979), 29; Similarly, see R. J. Zwi Werblowsky, *Beyond Tradition and Modernity* (London: n.p., 1976), 4.
12. Charles Liebman "Orthodox Judaism," in *The Encyclopedia of Religion*, vol. 11, ed. Mircea Eliade (Chicago: University of Chicago Press, 1987), 123. The author still felt comfortable at that time writing: "There is little scholarly material in any language on most aspects of the social and religious history of Orthodox Judaism." The works of historian Jacob Katz and Liebman were the first to fully articulate this approach. See, e.g., Jacob Katz, "Orthodoxy in Historical Perspective," in *Studies in Contemporary Jewry*, ed. Peter Y. Medding (Bloomington: Indiana University Press, 1986), 2:3–17; Charles S. Liebman, "Religion and the Chaos of Modernity," in *Take Judaism for Example*, ed. Jacob Neusner (Chicago: Chico Press, 1983), 148.
13. Liebman, "Religion and the Chaos of Modernity," 147–48.
14. See, for example, Julius Carlebach, "The Foundations of German-Jewish Orthodoxy: An Interpretation," *LBIYB* 33 (1988): 88–91; Menachem Keren-Kratz, "The Contemporary Study of Orthodoxy: Challenging the One-Dimensional Paradigm," *Tradition* 49, no. 4 (2016): 29–52; Avi Sagi, "Ha-Orthodoksiah ke-Ba'ayah," in *Ortodoksiah Yehudit: Hebetim Hadashim*, ed. Aviezer Ravitsky, Yoseph Salmon, and Adam S. Ferziger (Jerusalem: Magnes Press, 2006), 21–54.
15. Adam S. Ferziger, "Between Catholic Israel and the K'rov Yisrael: Non-Jews in Conservative Synagogues (1982–2008)," *Journal of Jewish Studies* 61, no. 1 (Spring 2010): 88–116.
16. Seth Farber, "Reproach, Recognition and Respect: Rabbi Joseph B. Soloveitchik and Orthodoxy's Mid-century Attitude toward Non-Orthodox Denominations," *American Jewish History* 89, no. 2 (2001): 193–214; Jonathan D. Sarna, "The Debate over Mixed Seating in the American Synagogue," in *The American Synagogue*, ed. Jack Wertheimer (Cambridge: Cambridge University Press, 1987), 273–90.
17. Benjamin Brown, "Hahmarah: Hamishah Tipusim min ha-Et ha-Hadashah," *Dinei Yisrael* 20–21 (2001): 133–50.
18. Ari Ackerman, "'Judging the Sinner Favorably': R. Hayyim Hirschensohn on the Need for Leniency in Halakhic Decision-Making," *Modern Judaism* 22, no. 3 (October 2002): 261–80.
19. Jacob Katz, *Divine Law in Human Hands: Case Studies in Halakhic Flexibility* (Jerusalem: Magnes Press, 1998).
20. Alan Jotkowitz, "Nomos and Narrative in Jewish Law: The Care of the Dying Patient and the Prayer of the Handmaid," *Modern Judaism* 33, no. 1 (2013): 56–74.

21. Alan Nadler, "Soloveitchik's Halakhic Man: Not a 'Mithnagged,'" *Modern Judaism* 13, no. 2 (May 1993): 119–47.
22. Maoz Kahana and Ariel Evan Mayse, "Hasidic Halakhah: Reappraising the Interface of Spirit and Law," *AJS Review* 41, no. 2 (2017): 375–408.
23. Zvi Zohar, *Rabbinic Creativity in the Modern Middle East* (London: Bloomsbury, 2013).
24. David H. Ellenson, *Tradition in Transition: Orthodoxy, Halakhah and the Boundaries of Modern Jewish Identity* (Lanham, MD: University Press of America, 1989).
25. Michael K. Silber, "The Emergence of Ultra-Orthodoxy: The Invention of Tradition," in *The Uses of Tradition*, ed. Jack Wertheimer (New York: Jewish Theological Seminary, 1993), 23–84.
26. Chaim I. Waxman, *Change and Halakhic Evolution in American Orthodoxy* (Liverpool: The Littman Library of Jewish Civilization, 2017).
27. Haym Soloveitchik, "Rupture and Reconstruction: The Transformation of Contemporary Orthodoxy," *Tradition* 28 (Summer 1994): 64–130.
28. Alan J. Yuter, "The Haredi Reading of Jewish Law: A Review Essay of Steven H. Resnicoff, Understanding Jewish Law," *Review of Rabbinic Judaism* 17, no. 1 (2014): 57–111.
29. David H. Ellenson, "To Reshape the World: Interpretation, Renewal, and Feminist Approaches to Jewish Law and Legal Ruling in America and Israel," *Journal of Jewish Ethics* 2, no. 2 (2016): 38–63; Ronit Irshai, *Fertility and Jewish Law: Feminist Perspectives on Orthodox Responsa Literature* (Waltham, MA: Brandeis University Press, 2012).
30. Arye Edrei, "Judaism, Jewish Law, and the Jewish State in Israel," in *The Cambridge Companion to Judaism and Law*, ed. Christine Hayes (Cambridge: Cambridge University Press), 337–64; Alexander Kaye, *The Invention of Jewish Theocracy* (Oxford: Oxford University Press, 2020); Suzanne Last Stone, "Law in Light of Zionism: A Comparative View," *Israel Studies* 19, no. 2 (Summer 2014): 111–32.
31. Breuer, *Modernity within Tradition*, 251.
32. David H. Ellenson, *Rabbi Esriel Hildesheimer and the Creation of a Modern Jewish Orthodoxy* (Birmingham: University of Alabama Press, 1990).
33. Maoz Kahana, *Mi-ha-Noda Be-Yehuda la-Hatam Sofer* (Jerusalem: Merkaz Shazar, 2015).
34. On Schick, see, e.g., Adam S. Ferziger, "Schick, Mosheh Ben Yosef," in *Oxford Dictionary of the Jewish Religion*, ed. R. J. Zwi Werblowsky and Geoffrey Wigoder (Oxford: Oxford University Press, 1997), 611; Yekutiel Yehudah Greenwald, *Le-Toldot ha-Reformazion be-Germanyah u-ve Hungaryah* (Jerusalem: Hod, 1972); Shanyer Z. Leiman, "R. Moses Schick: The Hatam Sofer's Attitude toward Mendelssohn's Biur," *Tradition* 24, no. 3 (1989): 83–86; Alex Schick, "Moses Schick," in *Men of the Spirit*, ed. Leo Jung (New York: Kymson, 1964), 301–26.
35. David Zvi Levinger, "Yeshivat Pressburg be-yemei ha-Ketav Sofer," *Yerushateinu* 11 (2020–2021): 240–70.
36. Binyamin Shlomo Hamburger, *Nesi ha-Levi'im—Toldot Rabeinu Y'D ha-Levi Bamberger mi-Wurzburg* (Bnei Brak: Z. Bamberger, 1991); Shnayer Z. Leiman, "Rabbi Joseph Carlebach, Wuerzburg and Jerusalem: A Conversation between Rabbi Seligmann Baer Bamberger and Rabbi Shumuel Salant," *Tradition* 28, no. 2 (1994): 58–63.
37. Ephraim Chamiel, *The Dual Truth: Studies on Nineteenth-Century Modern Religious Thought and Its Influence on Twentieth-Century Jewish Philosophy*, vol. 1 (Boston: Academic Studies Press, 2019), 1–26.
38. Tova Ganzel and Elli Fischer, "Eshnav le-Darkei Avodato shel Ha-Rav David Zvi Hoffmann be-Pesikat Halakhah," *JSIJ* 22 (2022), https://jewish-faculty.biu.ac.il/files/jewish-faculty/shared/JSIJ22/ganzel_fischer.pdf; Me'ir Seidler and Alexander A. Dubrau, "David Zvi

Hoffmann's (1843–1921) Commentary on the Pentateuch in the Context of German-Jewish Orthodoxy's Struggle over the Dogmatic Principles of Torah," *Journal of Jewish Studies* 72, no. 2 (2021): 397–417; Marc Shapiro, "Rabbi David Zvi Hoffmann on Torah u-Madda," *Torah u-Madda Journal* 6 (1995–1996): 129–37; Marc Shapiro, "Rabbi David Zvi Hoffmann on Orthodox Involvement with the Hebrew University," *Tradition* 33, no. 3 (1999): 88–93.

39. David Zvi Hoffmann, *Shu't Melammed le-Hoil* II (Frankfurt: Hermon, 1926), 52.
40. See Prov. 23:2; The *Rashi* commentary to *B. Pesahim* 40a and to *B. Nidah* 16b defines *ba'al nefesh* as a "*hasid*" (righteous person). While in *B. Hullin* 6a, *Rashi* invoked the term "*adam kasher*"—a "kosher" or *halakhically* proper person in his definition. In the current context, it appears that the latter definition was the one that Hoffman had in mind.
41. Hoffmann, *Shu't Melammed le-Hoil* II, 52.
42. See the discussion of modern and ancient examples of Jews using dietary behavior as a vehicle for identifying each other and creating boundaries in Albert I. Baumgarten, "He Knew that He Knew That He Knew That He Was an Essene," *Journal of Jewish Studies* 48, no. 1 (Spring 1997): 53–61.
43. *Shu't Melammed le-Hoil* I, 29.
44. Ibid.
45. For biographical background, see Y. Yosef Cohen, *Hakhmei Hungaryah* (Jerusalem: Machon Yerushalayim, 1997), 26–157, 354–56; Jacob Katz, *A House Divided* (Waltham, MA: Brandeis University Press, 2005), 64–68, 226–28; Yosef Zvi Sofer, *Toldot Soferim* (London: Hoenig Press, 1963); Yosef Zvi Sofer, ed., *K'N Sofer* (London: Hoenig Press, 1963); "Kunteres Darkhei Hayyim," in R. Hayyim Sofer, *Responsa Mahane Hayyim* 8 [*Even ha-Ezer*] (Jerusalem: Divrei Soferim, 1971), 1–14; Kinga Frojimovics, Géza Komoróczy, Viktória Pusztai, and Andrea Strbik, *Jewish Budapest* (Budapest: Central European University Press, 1999), 438.
46. Adam S. Ferziger, "Religious Zealotry and Religious Law: Rethinking Conflict and Coexistence," *Journal of Religion* 84, no. 1 (2004): 48–77.
47. Zvi Zohar and Avi Sagi, *Ma'agalei Zehut Yehudit ba-Sifrut ha-Hilkhatit* (Tel Aviv: Ha-Kibbutz ha-Me'uhad, 2000).
48. On the distinction between biblical and rabbinical prohibitions, see Menachem Elon, *Jewish Law*, vol. 1 (Philadelphia, PA: Jewish Publication Society, 2003), 208–23.
49. Hayyim Sofer, *Shu't Mahane Hayyim* 2 [Yoreh Deah] (Jerusalem: Divrei Soferim, 1971), 1.
50. Ibid.
51. Ibid.
52. Notably, the case cited in the Talmud to demonstrate that acting according to the letter of law precipitated the destruction relates to a Sage, Rabbi Zekhariah ben Avkilus, who insisted on enforcing a strict ruling rather than adopt an expansive understanding of the situation that could have prevented catastrophe. See B. Gittin 56a.
53. See Arye Edrei, "From Orthodoxy to Religious Zionism: Rabbi Kook and the Sabbatical Year Polemic," *Dine Israel* 26–27 (2009–2010): 45–145, and the rich notes there.
54. Yehudah Mirsky, *Rav Kook: Mystic in a Time of Revolution* (New Haven, CT: Yale University Press, 2014).
55. Abraham Isaac Kook, *Shabbat ha-Arez*, 2nd ed. (Jerusalem: Hayyim, 1909).
56. Edrei, "From Orthodoxy to Religious Zionism."
57. Arye Edrei, "Shorshei ha-Pesikah ha-Zionit: Ha-Rav Kook ve-Pulmus ha-Shemitah," in *Al Da'at Ha-kahal* [Festschrift in Honor of Aviezer Ravitzky], ed. B. Brown et al. (Jerusalem: Zalman Shazar Center and the Israeli Democratic Institute, 2012), 833–96.

58. Binyamin Brown, *Hazon Ish* (Jerusalem: Magnes Press and Yeshiva University, 2011).
59. Eliezer Brodt, "Corrections and Clarifications on Two Editions of R. Chaim Berlin's Responsa: An Egregious Example of Censorship," *The Seforim Blog* (October 12, 2009), https://seforimblog.com/2009/10/eliezer-brodt-corrections-and/.
60. Sources and references can be found in Yehudah ha-Levi Amihai, "Ha-Rav Kook ve-Heter ha-Mekhirah," *L-Ma'aseah–Actualia Hilkhatit* [Makhon ha-Torah ve-ha-Arez], https://tinyurl.com/4hh77adr.
61. Benjamin Ish-Shalom, *Rav Avraham Itzhak HaCohen Kook: Between Rationalism and Mysticism* (Albany: State University of New York Press, 2012); Elliot Wolfson, "Secrecy, Apophasis and Atheistic Faith in the Teachings of Rav Kook," in *Negative Theology as Jewish Modernity*, ed. Michael Fagenblat (Bloomington: Indiana State University Press, 2017), 131–60.
62. Jeffrey Saks, "A Portrait of Two Artists at the Crossroads: Between Rav Kook and SY Agnon," *Tradition* 49, no. 2 (2016): 32–52.
63. See, e.g., Kobi Nahshoni, "Ha-Rav Ariel: Heter Mekhirah–Gishah lo Yehudit," *YNET* (August 28, 2007), https://www.ynet.co.il/articles/0,7340,L-3441915,00.html; Arye Yoeli, "Ziknei ha-Rabbanim ha-Serugim Danu: Ozar Beit Din o Heter Mekhirah," *Srugim* (February 9, 2021), https://tinyurl.com/27xuv3s4.
64. *B. Sanhedrin* 47A.
65. Yekutiel Yehuda Greenwald, *Kol Bo al Aveilut* (Columbus, OH: n.p., 1947), 179–80, esp. 191–93.
66. Ferziger, *Exclusion and Hierarchy*, 127–30.
67. Alan Amanek, *Dust to Dust—A History of Jewish Death and Burial in New York* (New York: New York University Press, 2019).
68. Guy Ben-Porat, *Between State and Synagogue: The Secularization of Contemporary Israel* (Cambridge: Cambridge University Press, 2013), 129–54.
69. Ferziger, *Exclusion and Hierarchy*, 90–112.
70. NA, "Kevurat Anashim she-einam Shomrei Shabbat" (August 2, 2015), hhttps://din.org.il/2015/08/02/%D7%A7%D7%91%D7%95%D7%A8%D7%AA-%D7%90%D7%A0%D7%A9%D7%99%D7%9D-%D7%A9%D7%90%D7%99%D7%A0%D7%9D-%D7%A9%D7%95%D7%9E%D7%A8%D7%99-%D7%A9%D7%91%D7%AA/.
71. Avraham Yosef, "Helkat Shomrei Shabbat," *Moreshet* (July 10, 2020), shut.moreshet.co.il/shut2.asp?id=194035.
72. TOI Staff, "Son of Shas Former Spiritual Leader: Lapid Should Go to Hell, with His Dad," *Times of Israel* (September 12, 2019), https://www.timesofisrael.com/son-of-shas-former-spiritual-leader-lapid-should-go-to-hell-with-his-dad/.
73. Nissim Leon, "Zikui Harabim: Ovadia Yosef's Approach toward Religious Activism and His Place in the Haredi Teshuvah Movement within Mizrachi Jewry," *Studies in Contemporary Jewry* 22 (2008): 150–68.
74. Eliyahu Galil, "Hitbatuyot Shenuyot be-Mahloket ve-Gadlut be-Torah—Mi-Hu Rav Ya'akov Ariel?" *Yisrael ha-Yom* (February 5, 2020), https://www.israelhayom.co.il/article/730941.
75. Ya'akov Ariel, "Kevurat Hiloni le-yad Dati," *Yeshiva* (September 28, 2004), https://www.yeshiva.org.il/ask/8153.
76. Ibid.
77. Uziel Eliyahu, "La'mah ein Helkat Shomrei Shabbat be-veit ha-Almin," *Kipa* (February 15, 2010), https://tinyurl.com/a754ruwh.

78. Michael R. Cohen, *The Birth of Conservative Judaism: Solomon Schechter's Disciples and the Creation of an American Religious Movement* (New York: Columbia University Press, 2012).
79. Cited in Jonathan Sarna, *American Judaism* (New Haven, CT: Yale University Press), 189.
80. Solomon Schechter, *Aspects of Rabbinic Theology* (New York: Schocken Books, 1961), xxi. See an expanded text in Solomon Schechter, *Studies in Judaism* (New York: Meridian Books, 1958), 15–17.
81. Gail Twersky Reimer, "Henriette Szold: A 'Pretty Certain Miriam,'" in *Gender and Religious Leadership: Women Rabbis, Pastors, and Ministers*, ed. Kathy Ehrensperger et al. (Lanham, MD: Lexington Books, 2019), 113–26.
82. Henrietta Szold, "Catholic Israel," *The American Hebrew* (1913). Repr., Mordecai Waxman, ed., *Tradition and Change: The Rise of the Conservative Movement* (New York: Burning Bush Press, 1958), 125.
83. Robert Gordis, "Process and Pluralism in Conservative Judaism," *Judaism* 37, no. 1 (1988): 48–58.
84. Robert Gordis, "Authority in Jewish Law," in *Conservative Judaism and Jewish Law*, ed. Seymour Siegel (New York: Rabbinical Assembly, 1977), 64.

CHAPTER 19

LAWMAKING IN THE CONSERVATIVE MOVEMENT

A Balance of Law and Norms

ROBERTA ROSENTHAL KWALL

Introduction

The movement of Judaism commonly known as the Conservative Movement, or Conservative Judaism, is an American phenomenon whose roots can be traced to the founding of its flagship institution, the Jewish Theological Seminary (JTS), in 1886. About a hundred years later, the five main organizational arms of Conservative Judaism issued the Statement of Principles of Conservative Judaism, the first document produced by the entire movement detailing its guiding principles, beliefs, and practices.[1] In this chapter's discussion of *halakhah*, Jewish law, "*halakhah* consists of the norms taught by the Jewish tradition; how one is to live as a Jew." The use of the term "norms" suggests a departure from the prevailing Orthodox view that *halakhah* emphasizes Divine command rather than normative practice.

The embrace of a norms-driven approach can be understood as driven by Conservative Judaism's adoption of a theological predicate that differs from Judaism's traditional theology, positing *halakhah* as the embodiment of God's direct communication to the Jews in the form of the Revealed Written Law, the Torah, as well as the accompanying Oral Law.[2] In contrast to Orthodoxy, Conservative Judaism embodies an historical approach that maintains that the Torah should not be understood as emanating from God directly but rather as the written product of human beings produced in specific times and places.[3]

By rejecting the idea that the Torah was literally transmitted by God to Moses, the historical approach's view of the Written Law introduced a new dynamic regarding the origin and consequent application of the law. Specifically, Revelation is seen as the product of both Divine and human elements.[4] Those who maintain an historical approach to *halakhah* believe that the Five Books of Moses were "produced by a series of . . . inspired [human] authors who were influenced in their work by the conditions which obtained in their day."[5] In other words, this perspective understands Revelation by defining it "as a complicated and complex process of divine-human encounter and interaction" rather than as God's direct communication to mankind.[6]

Conservative Judaism's historical approach also sees the content of the rabbinic literature produced during the Talmudic era largely as a function of human output rather than as the result of direct Divine Revelation. This perspective reflects the view that Jewish law is binding because it is a system that maintains the importance of keeping God's commandments, but that the essence of those commandments "can only claim to be true within the confines of the human condition and within the parameters of specific historical conditions."[7]

In light of this philosophy, the historical approach also embraces a legal process that incorporates secular as well as Jewish sources. Originally, Jewish law was studied and interpreted only through the Talmud, the legal codes, and the responsa literature. The historical approach relies upon these primary sources, but it additionally incorporates "the same methods used to study other ancient civilizations such as cross-cultural studies, linguistic comparisons and analysis, and in the twentieth century, archeology."[8] In this regard, the historical method adopts a methodology that situates Jewish law in the overall cultural context in which it develops, rather than as an autonomous entity.

Thus, the historical approach characteristic of Conservative Judaism reflects not only a substantial theological shift from the conventional Orthodox perspective, but also a shift with respect to the process of lawmaking. These changes impact both the legal process of Conservative Judaism as well as the actual decisions that emanate from the movement's rabbinic leadership. As a result, the law resulting from Conservative Judaism often, but not always, produces more lenient interpretations.

This chapter initially outlines the lawmaking structure of Conservative Judaism with a focus on the movement's Committee on Jewish Law and Standards, the primary body providing lawmaking guidance for Jews worldwide.[9] It then illustrates more specifically how Conservative Judaism's distinct theological and lawmaking approach can impact legal rulings by examining two representative decisions, both responding to significant changes in the lived reality of Jews. The first decision, issued in 1950, permitted driving to synagogue and a limited use of electricity on Shabbat. The second decision, written in 2020 during the onset of COVID-19 pandemic, concluded that it is permissible to stream services on Shabbat and other holy days subject to certain parameters. The chapter concludes with some observations about a possible future direction for Conservative Judaism in light of its norms-oriented lawmaking process.

Lawmaking under the Conservative Movement

According to Conservative authorities, the rabbis of the Talmud may not be the final arbiters of Jewish law because the law, as a human system, must be allowed to develop in response to changing human conditions.[10] Conservative Judaism's perspective on lawmaking also opposes the claim that the codifications of Jewish law are "authoritative and binding," but instead sees these texts as furnishing guidance.[11] This viewpoint clearly allows "for the possibility of a subjective and a social element in *halakhic* decision."[12] In other words, the Conservative movement's approach to lawmaking embraces the idea that what is considered *halakhic* is largely a human decision and interpreted through a cultural lens. These points are a major source of disagreement between the mainstream Orthodox and Conservative legal perspectives.

The Rabbinical Assembly, the international association of Conservative rabbis, established in 1927 the Committee on Jewish Law (CJL), the body charged with the responsibility for determining legal positions considered *halakhically* acceptable by the movement.[13] In 1949, the name of the committee was changed to the Committee on Jewish Law and Standards (CJLS), reflecting the Committee's purpose of "raising of the standards of piety, understanding and participation in Jewish life."[14]

The proceedings of the CJL/CJLS from 1927–1970 were published in 1997 on the seventieth anniversary of the committee's founding. In the introduction to this volume, Rabbi David Golinkin observed that from its inception, the purpose of this committee was not "clearly defined." Specifically, there was a lack of clarity and consensus as to whether it should set behavioral standards for the entire movement or formulate a philosophy of *halakhah*, and whether it should only write responsa or also enact *takkanot* (changes to the law). Golinkin noted that the committee grappled with these issues continually, and even though these open issues led to the reconstitution of the committee in 1949, "they were never fully resolved."[15]

A close reading of the published deliberations in connection with this change reveals that the committee understood change to be a significant component of Jewish law, but that any proposed changes in the law should be designed to increase its relevance to the Jewish people to make life more meaningful.[16] Yet, the deliberations also clarify that the committee's conception of *halakhah* "introduces possibilities of amendment beyond the strict and formal procedures traditionally followed in effecting change." The Committee was prepared to liberalize but only where "change will deepen the people's connection to Judaism."[17] The deliberations also emphasized the vast changes that have occurred in the lives of Jews over the past century, noting: "Our task is . . . to forge a relationship between a law that has remained virtually unchanged and a life that has been marked by immense and radical change."[18]

According to Elliot Dorff, the former chair of the CJLS, Jewish law "requires rabbis first to study those precedents within their historical contexts and then to weigh them together with contemporary circumstances (economics, demographics, etc.) and a host of other Jewish forms of expression (stories, theology, history, morals, etc.) to make a considered, wise and clearly Jewish judgment about what they think God wants of us now."[19] In addition, Jewish law "mixes things up further by taking into account past and current Jewish customs."[20] Moreover, this historical approach to *halakhah* is inclined to call for changes in the law when the status quo "results in the kind of injustice that reasonable persons would see as detrimental to Judaism itself."[21]

From a process standpoint, the CJLS currently is composed of twenty-five voting members[22] and represents a range of viewpoints. It often issues diverse, and sometimes even contradictory, opinions. The CJLS members even have the option of voting affirmatively for contradictory opinions, presumably to give congregational rabbis a choice of perspectives. Six votes are needed in order for a given opinion to be considered official by the CJLS. This approach underscores how, in practice, Conservative Judaism embraces a multiplicity of values and approaches. Further, according to the internal dynamics of the Conservative movement, individual congregational rabbis act as the *mara d'atra*, the teacher of the local community, and they have the responsibility for determining how the law can best be applied in particular synagogue communities.[23] In exercising this role, Conservative rabbis consider the decisions of the CJLS, but individual rabbis have the authority to rule otherwise on most matters.[24]

Still, despite the fact that the Conservative movement sees itself as a "big tent" with room for differing viewpoints, there are certain *halakhic* standards for the movement that cannot be abdicated by individual rabbis. Specifically, the Rabbinical Assembly has adopted three Standards of Rabbinic Practice to which all Conservative rabbis must adhere. These standards prohibit a Conservative rabbi from officiating at an intermarriage, require a Jewish writ of divorce, known as a *get*, before remarriage pursuant to Jewish law, and define Jewish membership according to the mother's religion or a *halakhic* conversion (see Levmore and Gotlib, this volume).[25] Conservative rabbis who violate any of these standards are no longer eligible for membership in the Rabbinical Assembly.[26]

The Sabbath *Responsum*

In 1950, the CJLS issued its controversial opinion entitled *Responsum on the Sabbath* ("Sabbath *Responsum*"). This opinion, written in the context of an attempt to encourage greater observance of the Sabbath among Conservative Jews, allowed driving to the synagogue on Shabbat in order to attend services as well as the use of electricity to enhance the Sabbath's enjoyment.[27]

Regarding use of an automobile on Shabbat, Orthodox Jewish law holds that starting the engine entails combustion of gasoline to produce power, thereby constituting a prohibited derivative of the biblical prohibition of creating fire.[28] Similarly, Orthodox *halakhah* holds that turning lights on and off on Shabbat is biblically prohibited as creating and extinguishing a fire.[29]

In contrast, the Sabbath *Responsum* states that burning for the sake of producing power is not a violation of the biblical prohibition of burning because it does not involve burning for the sake of a specifically proscribed purpose.[30] For this reason, the Sabbath *Responsum* argues that igniting the engine involves the violation of a rabbinically prohibited activity, and therefore, can be excused for the purpose of observing Shabbat.[31]

Similarly, with respect to the use of electric lights on Shabbat, the Sabbath *Responsum* asserts that this activity does not constitute a violation of a biblical law but rather involves a *sh'vut*, a prohibition enacted by the Sages designed to protect the special atmosphere of Shabbat and prevent the commission of inadvertent violations. Therefore, this prohibition can be set aside for the sake of observing Shabbat, based on the rationale that *halakhah* is designed to be "an instrument of the people."[32]

Significantly, however, the CJLS did not view its leniencies as part of a program of Shabbat observance destined to be "the full and complete regimen of Sabbath observance, valid for all Jews for all times and for all places." In language that strikes a chord with contemporary Conservative Jews who lived through the COVID-19 pandemic seventy years later, the CJLS observed that it acted "to meet the particular situation that confronts us, a situation without parallel in the long annals of Judaism."[33] An important part of the social reality confronting the CJLS in mid-twentieth-century America[34] was that most Jews in the United States no longer lived in walking distance to a synagogue. The Sabbath *Responsum* embodies the value judgment that "the positive values involved in the participation in public worship on the Sabbath outweigh the negative values of refraining from riding in an automobile."[35]

Equally significant, the articulated theory of the Sabbath *Responsum* emphasizes that, although it considers current social realities, it also attempts to derive its conclusions from the received Talmudic and subsequent Jewish legal tradition.[36] It justifies its rulings on both driving and the use of electricity "by applying *halakhic* precedents to the scientific processes by which electricity is produced and automobiles operate."[37] This balancing of current realities with conclusions alleged to be derived from the tradition is characteristic of many of the opinions issued by the CJLS.[38]

A minority opinion authored by Rabbi Ben Zion Bokser repudiates the Sabbath *Responsum* and urges a continuation of the movement's long-standing position on these issues.[39] Bokser emphasizes the importance of a Shabbat experience grounded in the home and quality family time: "There can be no Sabbath atmosphere, none of its sanctifying or relaxing elements, without the rejection of the things that undermine the home's fixity, and threaten the stability of the family as an integrated unit of human life."[40] He also speaks of the nervous tension that travel imposes and the value of Shabbat as "an emancipation from the machines and the complexities" of modern life.[41]

Although Bokser disagrees with the *halakhic* changes accepted by some of his colleagues, his rationale generally manifests an historical (rather than normative Orthodox) orientation given its focus on sociological and psychological arguments. Moreover, toward the end of his opinion, he expressly recognizes that if "[g]iven a choice between travel on the Sabbath or the total denial of the opportunities of worship on Sabbaths and festivals, we would regard traveling as the less objectionable alternative."[42]

Between 1950 and the 2020 CJLS decision concerning streaming of services on Shabbat and other holy days, the CJLS issued some other opinions building on the Sabbath *Responsum*. In 1961, a question was raised concerning the Sabbath *Responsum* that underscored the difficulty of its practical application in the real world. The question was whether the Sabbath *Responsum* could be extended to permit riding on Shabbat to a synagogue other than a person's regular place of worship, in order to attend a Bar *Mitzvah*. In response, the CJLS issued a statement stipulating that its ruling permitting travel on Shabbat is limited just to travel for attendance at a synagogue for purposes of worship. Therefore, the statement explained that the reach of its ruling does not extend to "travel for social purposes or . . . travel to the synagogue in order to attend a Bar Mitzvah ceremony or reception, for the motivation here is not the service of God but the honor of man."[43] Although perhaps well-intentioned, this official limitation underscores a significant difference between the limits endorsed by the CJLS and the real-world habits of most Conservative Jews.

In 2012, Daniel Nevins, the former dean of the rabbinical school at JTS, grappled in greater detail with the legal technicalities as well as the extralegal issues involved in the use of electricity.[44] Although his analysis and conclusion with respect to the permissibility of turning on incandescent light bulbs draws from the 1950 Sabbath *Responsum*,[45] the responsum by Nevins is far more extensive and addresses newer forms of technology.[46] Nevins does not believe the use of electricity per se is a violation of the biblical prohibition of burning, but he reasons that the use of many electrical appliances is still forbidden on the ground that they violate other prohibited labors on Shabbat.[47] For example, the use of cell or smart phones that record information is prohibited as a functional equivalent of conventional writing and therefore constitutes a derivative of the biblically prohibited labor of writing.[48] Similarly, he would prohibit the use of electrical microwave ovens as well as dishwashers (absent a delay timing function) on the basis that they constitute a derivative of the biblically prohibited labor of cooking because they heat food and water.[49] On the other hand, his *responsum* reveals an interesting sensitivity to modern environmental concerns. Nevins asserts that because he does not understand turning electrical appliances off to involve prohibited labor, the principal of "conserving natural resources indicates that we should turn off unneeded appliances on Shabbat."[50]

Within the ranks of the Conservative movement's CJLS, it seems as though the views of Nevins are widely accepted, as his *responsum* generated a vote of seventeen acceptances, two rejections, and two abstentions. This vote suggests that at least with respect to Conservative Judaism's lawmaking body, a consensus has developed over the past sixty years concerning the permissibility of using electricity on a limited basis on Shabbat. With respect to the driving issue, however, the existence of a consensus seems more difficult to determine.[51] Interestingly, JTS prohibits its rabbinical and cantorial students from traveling on Shabbat but allows more latitude with respect to electricity in accordance with the 1950 *responsum* and the more recent one authored by Nevins.[52]

At the time the Sabbath *Responsum* was issued, and for decades afterward, it produced a firestorm of protest.[53] One opponent claimed that the *responsum* was indeed revolutionary in that the Rabbinical Assembly "decided that it was a competent authority to challenge the decisions of other groups in the American rabbinate" and affirm that it has the right to choose leniency in this regard.[54] Over fifty years after the Sabbath *Responsum* appeared, it was still spurring commentary and controversy.[55]

The Sabbath *Responsum* has also been criticized from a theological perspective. Specifically, the Sabbath *Responsum* and the subsequent written discussions do not explicitly acknowledge that traveling on Shabbat is a sin.[56] Perhaps this omission reflects the more fluid nature of legal interpretation characteristic of the Conservative movement, a quality that arguably stems from its emphasis on the human element of the legal sources. In criticizing the traveling aspect of the Sabbath *Responsum*, David Novak (an ordained Conservative rabbi) states that allowing riding to the synagogue presents a "fundamental spiritual problem": "The assumption underlying this dispensation ignores the possibility of repentance (*teshuvah*). To tell people who are not living according to the law of the Torah that what they are doing is correct is to close the door of return in their faces. It places a 'stumbling block before the blind.'"[57]

As this discussion illustrates, the legal process adopted by the CJLS manifests an explicit acknowledgment of the role of culture and sociology in lawmaking. The approach of the CJLS's Sabbath *Responsum*, including the opinions of those rabbis who opposed change, is consistent with an overall focus on law as a product of historical context. When the law is seen in this manner, it inevitably becomes more malleable in both theory and practice. Still, the tradition always is given a vote according to this perspective, and there are boundaries that cannot be crossed despite the law's purported flexibility. For example, although Conservative authorities disagree as to whether driving to the synagogue on Shabbat for purposes of attending a prayer service should be permissible, there is unanimity that driving to the dry cleaner after the service clearly is beyond the boundaries of the tradition. Admittedly, this approach is messier than one that draws more hard and fast lines, but the same can be said for real-life situations in practice.

Streaming of Services on Shabbat and Yom Tov

As the COVID-19 pandemic swept the globe during the spring of 2020, the CJLS tackled the issue of "whether it is permitted for a synagogue or other prayer community to offer a stream of its services on Shabbat or Yom Tov" and "if so, what are the concerns that must be addressed when this is done?"[58] Early on in the CJLS's *teshuva* (opinion) on the use of streaming of services on Shabbat and other holy days, it was suggested that the pandemic can be seen "as a time for *hora'at sha'ah,* unusual steps not consonant with traditional practice."[59] The *teshuva* opens with both an expression of hope but also a frank acknowledgment of the lived reality of many Conservative Jews:

> We hope that rabbis and communities will remain within the bounds of this guidance in full. We are realistic that some may see this as a time for *hora'at sha'ah*, unusual steps not consonant with traditional practice. . . .
>
> While this paper spends significant time addressing the acute needs of the current situation, we also understand that eventually a "new normal" will emerge. By that time, societal norms and expectations, as well as the range of available technical solutions, may have evolved significantly. The paper's conclusions must therefore be reassessed [as] we approach that time.[60]

The *teshuvah* was approved by nineteen of the twenty-five members of the CJLS because three members of the committee abstained and three others dissented. Each dissenter wrote a separate opinion taking issue with the *teshuvah's* result and reasoning.[61] The *teshuvah* builds upon prior directives issued during the COVID-19 pandemic discussing the *halakhah* involved in assembling a virtual *minyan* (prayer quorum of ten individuals) and permitting Seders on Zoom on the first two nights of Passover.[62] Despite the clear limitations embraced by both of these prior directives as well as the subsequent *teshuvah* concerning Shabbat and Yom Tov, the CJLS was realistic about the probability of "opening the floodgates" given the leniencies of these opinions. Also, although the *teshuvah* commanded a strong majority of support from the members of the CJLS, and later from the rabbis in the field, support for its leniencies is not universal among pulpit rabbis.[63]

A central predicate of the *teshuvah* is that for most Jews (including most Conservative Jews), community prayer is a central part of the prayer experience for Shabbat and holidays.[64] Early on, the *teshuvah* raises, but does not explicitly answer, the following question: "is it necessary to risk serious violations of the letter and spirit of Shabbat in order to enable participation in religious practices which are laudatory, but ordinarily would not supersede a Biblical prohibition?"[65] The general tenor of the opinion is that despite the arguable violations of Jewish law triggered by certain uses of technology for purposes of prayer on Shabbat and other holy days, leniencies may well be necessary as a practical matter for certain communities. Therefore, although the *teshuvah* encourages minimizing the type and extent of *halakhic* violations by virtue of its specific recommendations, it also reflects a practical rather than absolutist approach to the issue of using technology for prayer on days during which such use is traditionally forbidden.

The *teshuvah* contains a protracted discussion about potential violations in connection with streaming on Shabbat, and how to mitigate such violations. It also probes the permissibility of viewing a stream that has been allowed to remain on or is activated automatically. These discussions entail a considerable degree of mental gymnastics given the variable types of technological options available. For example, the *teshuvah* notes that it is easier to address concerns when a service is being streamed from a synagogue given the likelihood of the presence of a non-Jew who can monitor the equipment. It also notes, however, that on the receiving side, this well-known workaround is not as viable and members are likely to interact with the equipment in a way that is prohibited.[66] For this reason, the *teshuvah* frankly acknowledges that "we must be realistic that some users will violate Shabbat in more serious ways."[67] Also, as the pandemic raged on during the summer of 2020, it became palpably clear that even the option of streaming from within a synagogue was not especially feasible.

The *teshuvah* attempts to strike a balance between the finer points of *halakhah* and the larger extralegal factors, an approach representing the hallmark of lawmaking in the Conservative movement. The essence of the ruling is that because the pandemic represents *she'at hadehak* (pressing or unusual circumstances), it can be appropriate "to rely on loopholes to skirt prohibitions that are only *shv'ut*" (not biblical in nature).[68] Therefore, although "under normal circumstances, one should not activate a stream or interact directly with a device in other ways on Shabbat, . . . there are a number of leniencies that may be called upon that may apply in unusual circumstances to minimize violations."[69]

After a detailed analysis, the *teshuvah* reaches several conclusions about the permissibility of Conservative synagogues offering streaming or interactive videoconferences of services on Shabbat and Yom Tov, including the following:

> The equipment must be set up to be running before the holy day, or operate on a timer.
>
> While a non-Jewish employee may (and probably should) be assigned to handle potential technical glitches, it is strongly preferable to choose a streaming solution which is always on, or which activates automatically at a set time, over one which must be activated manually, even if a non-Jew is designated in advance to do so.
>
> . . . .
>
> Initiating a recording on Shabbat is a violation of Shabbat. Individual rabbis must use discretion in determining whether it would be appropriate to configure a device before Shabbat to record on Shabbat for download after Shabbat.[70]

In addition, the *teshuvah* emphasizes that with respect to viewers of the video feed, they should participate in a way that "does not involve their direct interaction with an electronic device." Suggestions include "leaving the stream on from before the holy day, . . . using the equivalent of a timer, or by arranging in advance for a non-Jewish person to activate the stream."[71] Still, the *teshuvah* is realistic to the extent that it acknowledges that "many home users will also not appreciate the nuances of Shabbat observance" and "may not think twice about adjusting home equipment."[72] In an attempt to establish some guidance for adopting a more mindful perspective regarding the use of electronic equipment for prayer on Shabbat and holy days, the author of the *teshuvah*, Rabbi Joshua Heller, writes:

> I recognize that this suggestion might not be widely adopted, but it would be preferable for users to do something that makes it clear that they are using their device in an unusual way, and discourages them from interacting with it (for example, on a

> computer, covering the keyboard or unplugging an external mouse or on any device, setting do not disturb or "parental controls"). Furthermore, the act of designating the use of the device before Shabbat should be done in an explicit way. A formula could be created or recited that would remind the user and other members of the household of the limitations.[73]

In addition, the *teshuvah* clarifies that although the video links providing access to the services are likely to be accessed by some who will not choose to be respectful of the letter or spirit of the laws of Shabbat, synagogues are mandated to offer the stream "in a way that minimizes the types of violations that might be committed by users accessing it, in particular by eliminating the need for any typing." The *teshuvah* suggests this can be accomplished by "allowing access through a simple link, or allowing a password to be typed before Shabbat."[74]

The *teshuvah* provides additional types of guidance to reduce the potential for violations on the part of congregants who avail themselves of services on Zoom during Shabbat and holy days. For example, it cautions that "effort must be made to provide those participating via video with a copy of the siddur/humash in a physical format, or to encourage them to download and print out before Shabbat so that they do not have to make further use of a device on Shabbat or Yom Tov."[75]

An especially interesting aspect of the *teshuvah* focuses on whether this CJLS decision will tempt congregants to violate Shabbat and Yom Tov. The *halakhic* principle here is called *Lifnei iver lo titein mikhshol*, which draws directly from the Torah and prohibits putting something before a blind person that might cause them to stumble. The *teshuvah* notes that in the rabbinic literature, "the verse is adapted figuratively to refer to many types of behavior that might encourage another to violate a prohibition."[76] Interestingly, the *teshuvah* explains that "the most useful parallel cases revolve around views of driving to synagogue in the mid-twentieth century," a topic covered earlier in this chapter. The *teshuvah* observes that even though operating a motor vehicle constitutes a violation of biblical law, most Conservative synagogues "provide parking facilities for those who choose to use them."[77]

A critical step in the reasoning on this score emphasizes that although some will violate *halakhah* with respect to how the stream is accessed and used, the option of setting up the stream prior to Shabbat represents a legally valid option. In the same way, although driving to synagogue entails a violation of traditional *halakhah*, the availability of legally permissible options such as walking or staying over with friends who live in walking distance seemingly justifies providing additional options. Thus, the *teshuvah* states: "We make an option available because we can rely on the fact that there is a permitted way to participate, even though we know that some (or even many) may choose to participate in a way that is not permitted."[78] The following language from the *teshuvah* provides an important capsulation of the CJLS approach on this point:

> Based on this reasoning, it is important that any video option is offered in a way that minimizes, rather than increases, violations of *hilkhot Shabbat,* and that there

> be at least some way, even if it is less convenient, to participate without such a violation. The stream should be made available with the fewest number of actions (opening an app, or clicking an easy bookmark), and no typing. If the service is protected by a password, the link should be in a password protected part of a website that could be logged into before Shabbat, or accessed with a unique personal link that incorporates the password. In contrast, requiring a user to type a password on Shabbat immediately before accessing a stream might fall into the category of "*lifnei iver*" because we are actually encouraging typing that the user would not otherwise have done.
>
> To summarize this portion of the analysis, we must acknowledge that if streaming services are made available, people will access them in ways that are not in the spirit or the letter of the *hilkhot Shabbat*. However, we can understand that if one makes it possible for the stream to be accessed in ways which are not a violation of Shabbat, one is not responsible for the actions of those who choose to access it in other ways. Nevertheless, we must take every opportunity to minimize these violations.[79]

The *teshuvah* walks a fine line between sensitivity to the legalities of Jewish tradition on the one hand, and appreciation for the realities brought about by needs of many Conservative Jews during an unprecedented time of crisis. It also displays a sense of realism both with respect to the potential difficulty of eventually pulling back from electronic measures on Shabbat and Yom Tov once this precedent has been established, as well as the norms of observance among Conservative Jews, many of whom were using electronics in varying degrees even prior to the pandemic.[80] The following candid observation draws an apt comparison with the part of the Sabbath *Responsum* dealing with driving to synagogue discussed earlier:

> Even if every effort is made to remain within the letter of the law, it is clear that encouraging large numbers of Jews to spend more time in front of a screen on Shabbat can have a deleterious effect on the atmosphere of Shabbat. In the mid-20th century, the Conservative movement encouraged driving "to synagogue only" on Shabbat. One could debate whether this had the intended effect. While encouraging Jews to drive to synagogue on Shabbat may have helped create major congregations in the suburbs, but it also led to Jews taking their wallets with them and travelling to many other places as well.[81]

Given the prominent role the Conservative movement attributes to extralegal factors in fashioning *halakhah*, it is certainly logical to consider the prevailing norms of Conservative Jews in fashioning rulings, particularly rulings involving matters that are highly relevant to the majority of practicing Conservative Jews. Still, when contemplating the appropriate role of social norms in rendering *halakhic* decisions, it is worth asking whether Conservative Judaism wishes to *create* the appropriate religious norms or *respond* to already existing norms. Although the *teshuvah* does not explicitly position itself as a response to existing norms among adherents to the movement, it clearly evidences an awareness of the need for its leadership to affirmatively create appropriate religious norms. This recognition exists throughout the *teshuvah* but especially in the final paragraph:

> The wider intrusion of technology into Shabbat and Yom Tov worship will require greater fences to preserve the sanctity of the day. It is a short step from watching services to emailing, online shopping, and other activities which violate the letter and spirit of the law. Simple solutions, like covering one's keyboard or setting "do not disturb," will be valuable, but will not suffice. Serious communal efforts, perhaps including newly created rituals carried out on the eve of Shabbat that demarcate tolerated from unwelcome technology, will be required to maintain the sanctity of holy time in the face of unprecedented pressures.[82]

The Challenge of Creating a Culture of Thicker Religious Norms in Non-*Halakhic* Communities

The lawmakers of the Conservative movement confront a difficult task. Specifically, they seek to prescribe religious practices that place a premium on Jewish tradition but that also are in tune with the larger American culture and the norms of most Conservative Jews. The foregoing discussion highlights how difficult this process can be in the context of topics that relate primarily to Jewish ritual but do not pose barriers for distinct groups of individuals. With increasing frequency, however, the CJLS specifically and the Conservative movement as a whole have had to grapple with how Jewish tradition should be applied when the norms of the tradition are out of step with larger social changes.

One set of issues representative of this struggle involves various restrictions traditional Judaism imposes on women. Traditionally, women cannot serve as rabbis but in 1983, the faculty of the JTS made the groundbreaking decision to ordain women. Rabbi Joel Roth, a professor at JTS, wrote a responsum that was widely seen as providing the *halakhic* justification for this decision. Roth argued that the *halakhic* sources can support the conclusion that women can choose to obligate themselves to perform certain mitzvot from which they are exempted, and that such women who take on this obligation are equally obligated with men, and therefore can execute the same functions, including those associated with public prayer.[83]

In 2002, Rabbi David Fine wrote a responsum specifically affirming that women are eligible to count in a prayer quorum (*minyan*) and lead services.[84] In this responsum, he offers interesting commentary on the impact of Rabbi Roth's rationale concerning ordination of women. Fine observes that the decision to ordain women substantially bolstered the egalitarian nature of many Conservative synagogues, and as a result, few synagogues actually followed Rabbi Roth's more qualified position concerning the ability of women to count in a minyan and lead services. Fine observed that "the sociological trend towards greater egalitarianism far outweighed the *halakhic* concerns of certain rabbis and other educated laypeople."[85]

The CJLS's opinions on homosexuality provide another recent example of this struggle between Jewish tradition and changing social norms. By the early years of the twenty-first century, the issue of social acceptance of homosexuality became a hot topic of public discourse both in the nation as a whole as well as within the Conservative movement. On the secular level, Massachusetts became the first state to recognize same-sex marriage in 2003,[86] but by the time the US Supreme Court legalized gay marriage in 2015, many states had already done so.[87] During this period, the CJLS was engaged in numerous deliberations on the topic of whether homosexuality is a *halakhically* valid lifestyle choice. Although a detailed discussion of this issue is beyond the scope of this chapter, a few comments about the history of the CJLS's discussions on this topic are important for understanding the delicate dynamics between lawmaking in the Conservative movement and the practical concerns of Conservative Jews.

The CJLS initially took up the issues of rabbis officiating at same-sex commitment ceremonies and admission to the movement's schools in 1992, disallowing both.[88] The CJLS was asked to revisit these issues again in 2003, and in 2006, it issued numerous opinions, reflecting different points of view.[89] Moreover, the two opinions that passed with a majority vote reached opposite conclusions. One of these opinions concluded that it is permissible to ordain openly gay rabbis and for Conservative clergy to perform commitment ceremonies for homosexuals if they are so inclined. This opinion also instructed gay men to avoid anal sex given the biblical prohibition.[90] Another argued that the tradition's view of same-sex sexual relations should be maintained (see Eleff, this volume).[91]

In 2012, the authors of the 2006 CJLS opinion permitting rabbinic officiation of same-sex ceremonies issued an appendix to the earlier opinion titled *Rituals and Documents of Marriage and Divorce for Same-Sex Couples*. This opinion was passed by the CJLS with fifteen affirmative votes and one abstention, compared to the 2006 opinion that garnered thirteen favorable votes with twelve opposed.[92] In his book *The New American Judaism*, JTS professor Jack Wertheimer comments in a footnote that "with openly LGBTQ students enrolled in the Conservative rabbinical seminaries, that position is now the only tenable one, and the more restrictive opinions by the Law Committee are dead letters."[93] Further, although the issue of gender identity is distinct from sexual orientation, it is worth noting that in 2017, the CJLS issued a *teshuvah* titled "Transgender Jews and *Halakhah*" with eleven affirmative votes and eight abstentions. This opinion held that transgender Jews are "to be recognized as their publicly declared gender" regardless of whether their process of transition includes medical procedures or treatments.[94]

These decisions by the CJLS are completely understandable in light of the reality that most Conservative Jews are politically and socially liberal, and thus mirror liberal Americans more generally. Moreover, from a political and social standpoint, most Conservative Jews also mirror the majority of Reform Jews.[95] Both the 2013 and the 2020 Pew Reports studying the American Jewish community revealed that a high percentage of both Reform and Conservative Jews favor acceptance of homosexuality.[96]

More generally, both Pew Reports furnished ample evidence for the proposition that American Jews tend to be disproportionately politically liberal, although as one moves toward the traditionally religious end of the spectrum, there is an increased tendency toward more conservative social opinions.[97]

Given these realities, the CJLS is faced with striking a delicate balance between looking outside Jewish tradition to ensure the relevance of its rulings for the majority of its constituents, on the one hand, and embracing a version of Judaism that emphasizes the importance of *halakhic* religious ritual on the other. Going forward, maintaining this balance is likely to become even more challenging given the pressure Conservative Judaism faces to become increasingly more liberal to draw younger members.[98]

Still, there is evidence suggesting that despite their liberal tendencies both religiously and politically, Conservative Jews continue to embody a rather unique ability to appreciate, and gravitate toward, thicker religious-cultural norms than most religiously liberal Jews. Arnold Eisen, the former Chancellor of the JTS, confirmed this perspective in his 2019 Sklare lecture published in the journal *Contemporary Jewry*. Drawing from his substantial anecdotal experience, Eisen observed that although no more than one-third of Conservative Jews are likely to say that religion is the most important part of their Jewish identity,[99] "Kaplanian or Heschelian Judaism" resonates more than one would suppose with Jews who are exposed to appropriate educational tools and rich ritual experiences.[100]

The most recent installment of the *Longitudinal Study of Young Jews Raised in Conservative Synagogues* also appears to support Eisen's observations by suggesting that Jews who remain affiliated with Conservative Judaism do indeed maintain thicker norms of Jewish observance than many other religiously liberal Jews. This study initially interviewed more than 1,400 thirteen- and fourteen-year-old boys and girls living in the United States and Canada, and their parents. The study followed this group for twenty-three years, with the most recent set of interviews conducted in 2018–2019, consisting of more than four hundred participants. This recent set of findings revealed that although the group taken as a whole showed a decline in religious observance, among the 43 percent who maintained their original Conservative identity there was still a higher level of observance as measured by synagogue affiliation, attendance, fasting on Yom Kippur and feeling that being Jewish is "very important in their life."[101]

The results of both the *2013* and *2020 Pew Reports* also reveal higher levels of ritual observance among Conservative Jews compared to Reform regarding behavior such as synagogue membership and attendance, fasting on Yom Kippur, lighting Shabbat candles, and keeping a kosher home. For example, according to the *2020 Pew Report*, whereas 24 percent of Conservative Jews reported keeping a kosher home, this was true of only 5 percent of Reform Jews.[102]

Although the statistical and anecdotal data suggest that Jews who identify with the Conservative movement still exhibit stronger norms of observance than other religiously liberal Jewish groups, these sources also demonstrate that the technicalities of Jewish law are not especially significant in their lives. These realities point toward to probability that the future survival of Conservative Judaism will depend on the creation and maintenance of cohesive communities that are characterized by a rich set of consistently observed religious-cultural norms more so than by compliance with the details of Jewish law.

In his dissenting opinion to *Streaming Services on Shabbat and Yom Tov*, Rabbi David Schuck[103] makes the case for the importance of Conservative rabbis empowering their congregants to observe more Judaism at home, specifically with respect to the *Shabbat* experience. Rabbi Schuck's dissent furnishes an important reminder of the need for more attention to the development and implementation of thicker and more consistently observed religious-cultural norms among Conservative communities such as synagogues, camps, and youth groups. For example, busy, young families need to be educated about the importance of developing a greater appreciation for the benefits of consistently observing home-based Shabbat rituals. These discussions should emphasize the importance of contemporary meaning-making in connection with ancient Shabbat traditions and consider how best to teach and persuade Conservative Jews regarding the personal benefits of celebrating Shabbat with more regularity and intentionality, on both communal *and* personal levels.

In 1994, Rabbi Haym Soloveitchik published a groundbreaking article arguing that transmission of Judaism is best accomplished through a mimetic tradition rather than intellectual enterprises.[104] Soloveitchik was speaking to Orthodox communities, but his focus on the importance of lived experience also is relevant to religiously liberally Jews, especially Jews for whom ritual has some degree of appeal. Although Conservative Judaism has not been particularly successful in persuading the majority of its constituents that compliance with Jewish law is essential, it has demonstrated that Jews who may not be living within the *halakhic* system still can be attracted to a thick religious-cultural practice.[105] Conservative Judaism's historical focus on the extralegal dynamics of Jewish tradition has the potential to facilitate the development of communities with sufficiently thick religious-cultural norms to support a distinct type of religiously liberal Judaism to thrive.

Acknowledgments

I would like to thank the following individuals for their assistance, including reviews of earlier versions of this chapter: Reni Dickman; David Fine; Alex Freedman; Joshua Heller; Vernon Kurtz; Michael Schwab; and Benjamin Steiner. I am also grateful for the capable research assistance of Catherine Fabiano, who was my student at DePaul University College of Law at the time of her work on this project.

Notes

1. Emet Ve-emunah, *Statement of Principles of Conservative Judaism* (New York: Jewish Theological Seminary of America, 1988). The five organizational arms were the Jewish Theological Seminary of America; the Rabbinical Assembly; United Synagogue of America; Women's League for Conservative Judaism; and Federation of Jewish Men's Clubs. For a detailed discussion of the history of the development and growth of the

Conservative Movement in the United States, see Jonathan D. Sarna, *American Judaism: A History*, 2nd ed. (New Haven, CT: Yale University Press, 2019).

2. See, e.g., Steven H. Resnicoff, "Autonomy in Jewish Law—In Theory and in Practice," *Journal of Law and Religion* 24, no. 2 (2009): esp. 510; Elliot Dorff, "Judaism as a Religious Legal System," *Hastings Law Journal* 29, no. 6 (1978): esp. 1330 n. 70. Lifshitz, this volume.
3. Elliot N. Dorff, *The Unfolding Tradition* (New York: Aviv Press, 2005), 50 (discussing the views of Zacharias Frankel, who is regarded as "the ideological founder" of the Conservative Movement).
4. For a description of the various theories of Revelation within the Conservative movement and their implications for how the formation of the text of the Torah is understood, see Elliot N. Dorff, *Conservative Judaism: Our Ancestors to Our Descendants* (New York: Youth Commission, United Synagogue of America, 1996), 96–150. See also Joel Roth, "Musings Toward a Personal Theology of Revelation," *Conservative Judaism* 64, no. 1 (2012): 31 (arguing that the Torah's "sanctity is entirely based on God's providence working through natural processes").
5. Louis Jacobs, *A Tree of Life: Diversity, Flexibility and Creativity in Jewish Law*, 2nd ed. (Liverpool: Littman Library of Jewish Civilization in association with Liverpool University Press, 2000), 224.
6. Ibid., 224.
7. Byron L. Sherwin, "Philosophies of Law," in *In Partnership with God: Contemporary Jewish Law and Ethics* (Syracuse, NY: Syracuse University Press, 1990), 29.
8. Dorff, *Unfolding Tradition*, 48.
9. It should be noted that the Conservative movement has a distinct lawmaking body governing matters for Conservative Jews in Israel, known as *Masorti* (traditional).
10. *See* Jacobs, *Tree of Life*, 222.
11. Sherwin, "Philosophies of Law," 32, 45, 225 n. 115 (noting the Conservative movement's position on this issue).
12. Ibid., 32.
13. See David Golinkin, "Introduction," in *Proceedings of the Committee on Jewish Law and Standards of the Conservative Movement, 1927–1970*, ed. David Golinkin (New York: Rabbinical Assembly, 1997), iii–xiii (hereinafter 1 Proceedings). See also Zev Eleff, "The Parting of the Way? Open Orthodox Judaism in Historical Perspective, Symposium on Open Orthodoxy II," *Torah Musings*, August 18, 2015, https://www.torahmusings.com/2015/08/symposium-on-open-orthodoxy-ii/ (last visited August 1, 2023) (discussing the 1927 founding of the Committee on Jewish Law and some of its early struggles).
14. Morris Alder, "Report of Committee on Jewish Law and Standards," in Golinkin, ed., 1 *Proceedings*, 309.
15. Golinkin, "Introduction," vii (discussing the achievements and difficulties of the Committee).
16. Adler, "Report," 307–8.
17. Ibid., 309–10.
18. Ibid., 307.
19. Dorff, *Unfolding Tradition*, 332.
20. Ibid., 332. It is important to underscore that this view of Jewish law is one of many variations embraced by the Conservative movement. See generally Dorff, *Unfolding Tradition*, for a comprehensive treatment of theories of law within the Conservative movement. For an account of the propriety of extralegal considerations in *halakhah* by a Modern Orthodox

authority, see Nathaniel Helfgot, "Decision-Making on Matters of *Halakhic* Public Policy of *Meta-Halakhic* Issues: Some Tentative Thoughts," *The Lehrhaus*, April 1, 2012, https://thelehrhaus.com/scholarship/decision-making-on-matters-of-halakhic-public-policy-or-meta-halakhic-issues-some-tentative-thoughts (last visited August 1, 2023).

21. Jacobs, *Tree of Life*, 221. In this regard, the views of Conservative thinkers in the United States were very influenced by Justice Benjamin Cardozo, who called for the consideration of socioeconomic factors into the lawmaking process. See, e.g., Isaac Klein, "Towards a Philosophy of Conservative Judaism," in Golinkin, ed., 1 *Proceedings*, 234, 253 (commentary by Morris Adler). See also Benjamin N. Cardozo, *The Nature of the Judicial Process* (New Haven, CT: Yale University Press, 1921).
22. In addition to the twenty-five voting members, the CJLS has five nonvoting lay or cantorial members.
23. *See* Dorff, *Unfolding Tradition*, 484.
24. This path has been embodied in the structure of the CJLS since 1985. See ibid., 405 (discussing Rabbi Gordon Tucker's paper concerning individual rabbinic autonomy).
25. Ibid., 405.
26. Ibid., 405.
27. Morris Adler et al., "*Responsum* on the Sabbath" [hereinafter Sabbath *Responsum*]. In 3 *Proceedings Committee on Jewish Law and Standards of the Conservative Movement, 1927–1970*, ed. David Golinkin (New York: Rabbinical Assembly, 1997), 1109–34. See also Jenna Weissman-Joselit, "In the Driver's Seat: Rabbinic Authority in Postwar America," in *Jewish Religious Leadership: Image and Reality*, vol. 2, ed. Jack Wertheimer (New York: Jewish Theological Seminary Press, 2014), 659–70.
28. The Torah explicitly prohibits burning wood, or any other combustible material on Shabbat. Exodus 35:3. Still, from a *halakhic* standpoint, the rabbinic tradition rather than the Written Torah determines the particulars of how Shabbat is to be observed. Although the Torah generally prohibits performing labor on Shabbat and even specifies certain prohibited activities, the Mishnah enumerates "forty less one" specific labors that are proscribed on Shabbat. The Sages derived these thirty-nine prohibited tasks, known in Hebrew as *avot m'lakhah*, from the principal categories of work necessary to construct the Tabernacle. See m.Shabbat 7:2. For a discussion of the normative position of Jewish law concerning use of an automobile on Shabbat, see David Novak, "Riding on the Sabbath," in *Law and Theology in Judaism* (Brooklyn, NY: KTAV, 1974), 29.
29. See Michael Broyde and Howard Jachter, "The Use of Electricity on Shabbat and Yom Tov," *Journal of Halacha and Contemporary Society*, no. 21 (Spring 1991): 5, 8.
30. Sabbath *Responsum*, in 3 Proceedings, ed. Golinkin, 1127.
31. Sabbath *Responsum*, in 3 *Proceedings*, ed. Golinkin, 1128.
32. Sabbath *Responsum*, in 3 *Proceedings*, ed. Golinkin, 1127. A minority opinion issued by Rabbi Neulander extended permission to use electricity to all activities that do not involve *avot m'lakhah* even if such activities are not necessarily connected with the performance of a commandment. See Arthur Neulander, "The Use of Electricity on the Sabbath," in 3 *Proceedings*, ed. Golinkin, 1162–68 (Section C of the 1950 Sabbath *Responsum*).
33. Sabbath *Responsum*, in 3 *Proceedings*, ed. Golinkin, 1118.
34. The Sabbath *Responsum's* position on driving to synagogue on Shabbat has been rejected by the *Masorti* movement in Israel. See David Golinkin, "Riding to the Synagogue on Shabbat," Responsa for Today, http://www.responsafortoday.com/engsums/4_3.htm (last visited August 1, 2023).

35. Sabbath *Responsum*, in 3 *Proceedings*, ed. Golinkin, 1118, 1120, 1129.
36. Ibid., 1126–29 (discussing these aspects of the tradition).
37. Dorff, *Unfolding Tradition*, 486 (commenting on Sabbath *Responsum*).
38. See ibid., 486 (commenting on Sabbath *Responsum*).
39. Ben Zion Bokser, "The Sabbath Halakhah—Travel, and the Use of Electricity," in 3 *Proceedings*, ed. Golinkin, 1153 (Section B of Sabbath *Responsum*).
40. Ibid., 1157 ("If we want to preserve the Sabbath, then we must create fixed home experience and limit movement away from home, in order that the family be kept together").
41. Ibid., 1158.
42. Ibid., 1160.
43. A Statement Adopted by the Committee on Jewish Law and Standards, *Travel on the Sabbath*, in 3 *Proceedings*, ed. Golinkin, 1188.
44. Daniel S. Nevins, "The Use of Electrical and Electronic Devices on Shabbat," in *Rabbinical Assembly* (2012), 7, https://www.rabbinicalassembly.org/sites/default/files/public/halakhah/teshuvot/2011-2020/electrical-electronic-devices-shabbat.pdf (last visited August 1, 2023).
45. Specifically, Nevins reaffirms Section C of the 1950 *Responsum* entitled *The Use of Electricity on the Sabbath*, authored by Rabbi Arthur Neulander. See Neulander, "Use of Electricity on Sabbath." Section C rejects the argument that the use of electric lights on Shabbat constitutes a violation of the biblical prohibition of burning. For a detailed discussion of the differences between the 1950 *Responsum* and Rabbi Neulander's position, *see* David J. Fine, "Reflections on the Driving Teshuvah," *Conservative Judaism* 56 (2004): 33, 37.
46. Nevins argues that electric lights are not considered fire, and therefore their use should not be considered biblically prohibited as burning. Nevins, "Use of Electrical and Electronic Devices," 22. He maintains that "the process, the purpose and the result of using an electrical lighting fixture are all dissimilar to the process, purpose and result of burning wood, gas or any other fuel." Nevins, "Use of Electrical and Electronic Devices on Shabbat," 28. In supporting his argument, Nevins further emphasizes that the thirty-nine categories of labor the Talmudic Sages prohibited "were concerned with making permanent, or at least durable, changes to one's physical environment." Ibid., 38.
47. See ibid., 54–55.
48. Ibid., 34.
49. Ibid., 21. "Any device which directly heats food or water to a scalding temperature may not be operated on Shabbat." Ibid., 55. The Sages considered "cooking" to be prohibited regardless of the substance in question and regardless of whether the substance came into direct contact with fire. Ibid., 20. Under this line of reasoning, the use of an electric flat iron to straighten one's hair on Shabbat would be considered "cooking" the hair, and thus prohibited as a derivative of cooking.
50. Ibid., 50. Nevins argues, "If we are commanded to remember the majesty of God's creation on Shabbat, then surely we should not observe it in a way which wastes the resources which God has so graciously provided." Ibid., 49. It is important to understand, however, that Nevins reaches this conclusion only as a corollary to his conclusion that turning off an electrical appliance is not prohibited labor because were his conclusion otherwise, he acknowledges that "the principle of not wasting resources does not supersede the prohibition" of labor. Nevins, see note 44, at p. 49.
51. Ibid., 77 n. 191 (expressing concerns about driving to synagogue in an electric car but indicating that those who accept the 1950 CJLS opinion permitting driving "in a gas

powered car would be justified extending this permission to electric cars"). But for this note, Nevins does not discuss the issue of driving. In 2023, the CJLS passed two opposite rulings regarding the permissibility of driving to synagogue on Shabbat using an electric car. Marcus Mordecai Schwartz and Chaim Weiner, "A New Responsum on the Sabbath," *Rabbinical Assembly* (2023), 1–37, https://www.rabbinicalassembly.org/sites/default/files/2023-07/schwartz-weiner-sabbath-final.pdf (last visited August 1, 2023); David J. Fine and Barry J. Leff, "A Renewed Responsum on the Sabbath," *Rabbinical Assembly* (2023): 1–13, https://www.rabbinicalassembly.org/sites/default/files/2023-07/fine_leff_shabbat-final.pdf (last visited August 1, 2023).

52. E-mail from Rabbi Daniel S. Nevins to author (March 8, 2021, 1:14 p.m. CST).
53. See, e.g., Sabbath *Responsum*, in 3 *Proceedings*, ed. Golinkin, 1169–85 (discussion); Novak, "Riding on the Sabbath."
54. See Sabbath *Responsum*, in 3 *Proceedings*, ed. Golinkin, 1173–74 (discussion, comments by Rabbi William Greenfield).
55. See Fine, "Reflections on the Driving Teshuvah," 21–50.
56. See Sabbath *Responsum*, in 3 *Proceedings*, ed. Golinkin, 1182 (discussion, comments by Rabbi Gordis on the Sabbath *Responsum* pertaining to the issue of travel).
57. Novak, "Riding on the Sabbath," 29 (quoting *Pesahim* 22b [Babylonian Talmud], interpreting Leviticus 19:14).
58. See Joshua Heller, "Streaming Services on Shabbat and Yom Tov," *Rabbinical Assembly* (2020), https://www.rabbinicalassembly.org/sites/default/files/2020-05/Streaming%20on%20Shabbat%20and%20Yom%20Tov%20Heller.pdf (last visited August 1, 2023).
59. Ibid., 1.
60. Ibid., 1.
61. Amy Levin, "A Dissent and a Challenge," *Rabbinical Assembly* (2020): 1–5, https://www.rabbinicalassembly.org/sites/default/files/2020-05/Streaming%20Services%20on%20Shabbat%20and%20Yom%20Tov%20Dissent-%20Levin.pdf (last visited August 1, 2023); Avram Israel Reisner, "Zoom Is Not the Way: A Dissent," *Rabbinical Assembly* (2020): 1–2, https://www.rabbinicalassembly.org/sites/default/files/2020-06/cjls%20Lo%20Zoom%20HaDerekh%20streaming%20dissent.pdf (last visited August 1, 2023); David A. Schuck, "A Dissent," *Rabbinical Assembly* (2020): 1–9, https://www.rabbinicalassembly.org/sites/default/files/2020-06/Streaming%20Services%20on%20Shabbat%20and%20Yom%20Tov-%20A%20Dissent-%20Final%20Copy%20%281%29.pdf (last visited August 1, 2023). See also David J. Fine, "Streaming Services on Shabbat and Yom Tov: A Concurring Opinion with a Note on Dukhening," *Rabbinical Assembly* (2020): 1–7, https://www.rabbinicalassembly.org/sites/default/files/2020-05/StreamingConcurrenceDavidFine.pdf (last visited August 1, 2023).
62. See "CJLS Guidance for Remote Minyanim in a Time of COVID-19," *Rabbinical Assembly* (March 17 2020): https://www.rabbinicalassembly.org/story/cjls-guidance-remote-minyanim-time-covid-19 (last visited August 1, 2023) (allowing latitude in the COVID environment to constitute a virtual minyan especially for the purpose of saying the Mourner's Kaddish); "Streaming Seder," *Rabbinical Assembly* (March 25, 2020), https://www.rabbinicalassembly.org/story/streaming-seder (last visited August 1, 2023) (recommending refraining from recording or typing as well as other safeguards for Seders conducted on Zoom during the COVID pandemic to minimize violation of *halakhah*).
63. *See* Stewart Ain and Johanna Ginsberg, "Livestream Ruling Testing Conservative Movement," *New York Jewish Week*, May 20, 2020, https://jewishweek.timesofisrael.com/

livestream-ruling-testing-conservative-movement (last visited August 1, 2023) (discussing views of rabbis who have not embraced the ruling and are feeling isolated).

64. Heller, "Streaming Services on Shabbat and Yom Tov," 3.
65. Ibid., 4.
66. Ibid., 16.
67. Ibid., 16.
68. Ibid., 12.
69. Ibid., 14.
70. Ibid., 28.
71. Ibid., 28.
72. Ibid., 16.
73. Ibid., 17.
74. Ibid., 28.
75. Ibid., 28.
76. Ibid., 18. The source of this phrase is Leviticus 19:14.
77. Ibid., 19. Heller notes that the Sabbath *Responsum* suggested that operating a motor vehicle is a rabbinic violation, see Sabbath *Responsum*, in 3 *Proceedings*, ed. Golinkin, but he states that "it seems more likely to me that operating a vehicle that operates by burning fuel is a violation on a Biblical level." Heller, "Riding on Shabbat," 19.
78. Ibid., 20.
79. Ibid., 20–21.
80. During the summer of 2021, the CJLS approved an opinion by Joshua Heller, "Are We There Yet? The Pandemic's End, and What Happens Then," *Rabbinical Assembly* (June 2021): 1–5, https://www.rabbinicalassembly.org/sites/default/files/2021-07/Pandemic%27s%20End%20Sources.pdf (last visited August 1, 2023). This opinion dealt with how to assess new practices in a post-COVID world when the urgent need for innovative measures is not as pressing. That opinion mentioned that there will be an update to the original *teshuvah* discussed in this chapter but as of this writing, no further opinions have been published. Around the same time, two oppositional opinions were passed addressing the permissibility of constituting a minyan electronically. *See* Joshua Heller, "Counting a Minyan via Video Conference," *Rabbinical Assembly* (July 10, 2021): 1–50, https://www.rabbinicalassembly.org/sites/default/files/2021-07/heller%20-%20zoom%20minyan.pdf (last visited August 1, 2023) (arguing for ways to use technology on an ongoing basis to constitute a *minyan*) and David Fine, "A Minyan Is Constituted in Person," *Rabbinical Assembly* (July 2021): 1–18, https://www.rabbinicalassembly.org/sites/default/files/2021-07/fine%20-%20minyan%20in%20person.pdf (last visited August 1, 2023) (reaffirming that under "normal" circumstances, a *minyan* requires ten people in person, although others can join remotely).
81. Heller, "Streaming Services on Shabbat and Yom Tov," 27.
82. Ibid., 28.
83. Joel Roth, "On the Ordination of Women as Rabbis," *Rabbinical Assembly* (1984): 1–51, https://www.rabbinicalassembly.org/sites/default/files/public/halakhah/teshuvot/19861990/ordinationofwomen2.pdf (last visited August 1, 2023). Interestingly, the CJLS never officially approved Roth's responsum or any other one on this topic. Dorff, *Unfolding Tradition*, 494.
84. Fine's responsum actually affirmed a 1973 ruling that "men and women should be counted equally for a minyan." He notes, however, that although the above wording was approved, there was no agreement on the rationale among those who voted in favor. David J. Fine,

"Women and the Minyan," *Rabbinical Assembly* (2002): 1–29, https://www.rabbinicalassembly.org/sites/default/files/assets/public/halakhah/teshuvot/19912000/oh_55_1_2002.pdf (last visited August 1, 2023).

85. Ibid. Another important set of responsa permitted women to serve as witnesses, overturning Jewish law's normative prohibition of women acting in this capacity. Rabbi Roth's responsum on ordaining women also dealt with this issue, but in 2001, the CJLS approved two responsa allowing women to act as witnesses. Myron S. Geller, "Woman Is Eligible to Testify," *Rabbinical Assembly* (2001): 1–31, https://www.rabbinicalassembly.org/sites/default/files/assets/public/halakhah/teshuvot/19912000/geller_womenedut.pdf (last visited August 1, 2023); Susan Grossman, "*Edut Nashim K'edut Anashim* (The Testimony of Women is like the Testimony of Men)," *Rabbinical Assembly* (2001): 1–31, https://www.rabbinicalassembly.org/sites/default/files/assets/public/halakhah/teshuvot/19912000/geller_womenedut.pdf (last visited August 1, 2023).
86. Goodridge v. Dep't of Pub. Health, 798 N.E.2d 941 (Mass. 2003).
87. In Obergefell v. Hodges, 576 U.S. 644 (2015), the Supreme Court ruled that all states must authorize same-sex marriage and recognize such marriages performed in other states. For a breakdown of the chronology of same-sex marriage in the United States, see "Same Sex Marriage, State by State," Pew Research Center, June 26, 2015, https://www.pewforum.org/2015/06/26/same-sex-marriage-state-by-state/ (last visited August 1, 2023).
88. See "Consensus Statement on Homosexuality," *Rabbinical Assembly* (March 25, 1992), https://www.rabbinicalassembly.org/sites/default/files/public/halakhah/teshuvot/19912000/consensus_homosexual.pdf (last visited August 1, 2023).
89. The two majority opinions are Joel Roth, "Homosexuality Revisited," *Rabbinical Assembly* (2006): 1–34, https://www.rabbinicalassembly.org/sites/default/files/public/halakhah/teshuvot/20052010/roth_revisited.pdf (last visited August 1, 2023); and Elliot N. Dorff et al., "Homosexuality, Human Dignity & *Halakhah*: A Combined Responsum for the Committee on Jewish Law and Standards," *Rabbinical Assembly* (2006): 1–36, http://www.rabbinicalassembly.org/sites/default/files/public/halakhah/teshuvot/20052010/dorff_nevins_reisner_dignity.pdf (last visited August 1, 2023). A third opinion also passed the committee but not with a majority vote: Leonard Levy, "Same-Sex Attraction and *Halakhah*," *Rabbinical Assembly* (2006): 1–84, http://www.rabbinicalassembly.org/sites/default/files/public/halakhah/teshuvot/20052010/levy_ssa.pdf (last visited August 1, 2023). In addition, there were two dissenting opinions: Myron S. Geller et al., "The *Halakhah* of Same-Sex Relations in a New Context," *Rabbinical Assembly* (2006): 1–23, https://www.rabbinicalassembly.org/sites/default/files/public/halakhah/teshuvot/20052010/geller_fine_fine_dissent.pdf (last visited August 1, 2023); Gordon Tucker, "*Halakhic* and *Metahalakhic* Arguments concerning Judaism and Homosexuality," *Rabbinical Assembly* (2006): 1–31, http://www.rabbinicalassembly.org/sites/default/files/public/halakhah/teshuvot/20052010/tucker_homosexuality.pdf (last visited August 1, 2023).
90. Dorff et al., "Homosexuality, Human Dignity & *Halakhah*," 19.
91. Roth, "Homosexuality Revisited." For a detailed account and analysis of all of the opinions issued in 2006, see Roberta Kwall, *The Myth of the Cultural Jew* (Oxford: Oxford University Press, 2015), 69–178.
92. Elliot N. Dorff et al., "Rituals and Documents of Marriage and Divorce for Same-Sex Couples," *Rabbinical Assembly* (2012): 1–20, http://www.rabbinicalassembly.org/sites/default/files/public/halakhah/teshuvot/2011-2020/same-sex-marriage-and-divorce-appendix.pdf (last visited August 1, 2023).

93. Jack Wertheimer, *The New American Judaism: How Jews Practice Their Religion Today* (Princeton, NJ: Princeton University Press, 2018), 302 n. 11. In 2006, the CJLS passed a second opinion arguing that the tradition's view on same-sex relationships should be maintained, but this opinion did not receive a majority vote. See Levy, "Same-Sex Attraction and *Halakhah*."
94. Leonard A. Sharzer, "Transgender Jews and *Halakhah*," *Rabbinical Assembly* (2017): 1–30, https://www.rabbinicalassembly.org/sites/default/files/public/halakhah/teshuvot/2011-2020/transgender-halakhah.pdf (last visited August 1, 2023).
95. In 2000, the Reform movement voted by a large majority to support the decision of individual rabbis to officiate at same-sex ceremonies. "Resolution of Same Gender Officiation." Central Conference of American Rabbis, 2000, http://ccarnet.org/rabbis-speak/resolutions/all/same-gender-officiation/ (last visited August 1, 2023).
96. See "Social and Political Views," in "A Portrait of Jewish Americans," 96–106. Pew Research Religion and Public Life Project, October 1, 2013, https://www.pewforum.org/2013/10/01/jewish-american-beliefs-attitudes-culture-survey/ (last visited August 1, 2023) [hereinafter *2013 Pew Report*] (80 percent Conservative; 92 percent Reform compared to 32 percent of Orthodox Jews as a whole). See also "Marriage, Families and Children," in "Jewish Americans in 2020," 93–109, Pew Research Center, May 11, 2021, https://www.pewforum.org/2021/05/11/jewish-americans-in-2020/ (last visited August 1, 2023) [hereinafter *2020 Pew Report*] (63 percent of Conservative Jews say rabbis should perform same-sex marriage ceremonies compared to 84 percent of Reform and 9 percent of Orthodox). Among Modern Orthodox Jews specifically, there is evidence of considerably more acceptance of homosexuality. In a 2017 study of just the American Modern Orthodox community, 58 percent of all American Modern Orthodox Jews indicated support for accepting gays as synagogue members, with 85 percent support among those who identify as being in the liberal end of the spectrum of Modern Orthodox observance. "The Nishma Research Profile of American Orthodox Jews," Nishma Research (September 28, 2017), 1–96, https://nishmaresearch.com/assets/pdf/Report%20-%20Nishma%20Research%20Profile%20of%20American%20Modern%20Orthodox%20Jews%2009-27-17.pdf (last visited August 1, 2023). For a discussion of developments on this topic in the Modern Orthodox communities in the United States and Israel, see Chaim I. Waxman, *Social Change and Halakhic Evolution in American Orthodoxy* (Liverpool: The Littman Library of Jewish Civilization in association with Liverpool University Press, 2017).
97. From a political standpoint, Pew revealed a marked difference between Orthodox Jews as a whole and religiously liberal Jews. Pew also revealed that American Jews are among the most Democratic groups in the population, although among Orthodox Jews there is more of a tendency to identify with or lean toward the Republican Party. See *2013 Pew Report*, 95–106; *2020 Pew Report*, 159–69. See also Herbert F. Weisberg, *The Politics of American Jews* (Ann Arbor, MI: University of Michigan Press, 2019), 9–10, 51–54 (noting that most American Jews have incorporated being Democratic as part of their Jewish identity, with the vast majority disfavoring regulation in the realm of cultural or moral areas). That said, among Modern Orthodox Jews, there may be less of a tendency to vote Republican. See "Nishma Research: A Political Survey of the American Orthodox Jewish Community" (January 2020), 1–20, http://nishmaresearch.com/assets/pdf/Nishma%20Research%20Political%20Survey%20of%20the%20Orthodox%20Community%20Jan.%202020.pdf (last visited August 1, 2023).

98. According to scholars who study more broadly Gen Z, those born between 1995 and 2010, religion and spirituality are important, but the same cannot be said for formal affiliation and participation. They have noted a decline of affiliation in general from Boomers to Gen X, with a plateau among Millennials and Gen Z. See Corey Seemiller and Meghan Grace, "Religion and Spirituality," in *Generation Z: A Century in the Making* (Oxfordshire: Routledge, 2018). It is also worth noting that in November 2020, the United Synagogue of Conservative Judaism (USCJ) hired Dr. Keren R. McGinity as the Interfaith Specialist charged with serving congregations and helping to determine the direction of the USCJ in the coming years. Such a position arguably would have been unthinkable even earlier in the twenty-first century, as there is no question that the public discourse of the USCJ regarding intermarriage has become far more inclusive over the past twenty years.
99. Arnold M. Eisen, "Boomers, Millennials and the Shape of American Judaism," *Contemporary Jewry* 39, no. 2 (June 2019): 348.
100. Ibid., 349. Eisen's comments refer to the strong influence of Mordecai Kaplan and Abraham Joshua Heschel upon Conservative Judaism.
101. Ariela Keysar and Barry A. Kosmin, "The Bar/Bat Mitzvah Class of 5755," *Jewish Theological Seminary of America* (June 2020): 1–42, https://live-jts.pantheonsite.io/wp-content/uploads/2021/09/jts_20up_report_june_2020.pdf (last visited August 1, 2023). (For example, this report showed that 65 percent of those remaining Conservative said being Jewish was "very important" in their lives compared to 35 percent of others; 51 percent of Conservatives were affiliated compared to 29 percent of others; 12 percent of Conservatives never attend services compared to 33 percent others; and 74 percent Conservatives fast on Yom Kippur compared to 49 percent of others). The *2020 Pew Report* showed a similar retention rate for Conservative Jews as the longitudinal study discussed in the text, specifically 41 percent. See *2020 Pew Report*, 44.
102. See *2020 Pew Report*, 70–92.
103. See Schuck, "Dissent."
104. Haym Soloveitchik, "Rupture and Reconstruction: The Transformation of Contemporary Orthodoxy," *Tradition* 28, no. 4 (Summer 1994): 64–130.
105. For an interesting take on a future for Conservative Judaism that is less focused on *halakhahic* details and more on a culture of richer Jewish observance, see Elliot Cosgrove, "A Choosing People," *Sources Journal: A Journal of Jewish Ideas* (Spring 2023), https://www.sourcesjournal.org/articles/a-choosing-people (last visited August 1, 2023).

CHAPTER 20

NORTH AMERICAN REFORM JUDAISM AND THE *HALAKHAH*

Guidance versus Governance

MARK WASHOFSKY

Introduction

The Reform movement in Judaism took institutional form in early nineteenth-century Germany, though its intellectual roots lie in the European Enlightenment or Haskalah of the eighteenth century and, according to some, even earlier.[1] That movement, whose members call themselves "Reform," "Liberal," or "Progressive," exists today in many countries, but this chapter focuses primarily upon the situation in North America, where Reform Judaism claims to represent the largest "denomination" of religious Jewry.[2] Yet to the extent that a "Reform" version of "Judaism" necessarily involves certain identifiable tendencies, this chapter's observations have relevance beyond its self-imposed geographical limits.

The explicit project of Reform Judaism in all periods and places of its existence has been to adapt traditional Jewish religion to the demands of modernity, by which it means the culture and civilization of the liberal West. Reform has from its beginnings asserted its authority to alter, modify, or eliminate forms of observance that conflict with the modern temperament. This claim has obvious implications for Reform's relationship with *halakhah*, the Jewish legal tradition. While the term "*halakhah*" is not perfectly synonymous with "Jewish law,"[3] it does partake of law's binding or obligatory nature. As Maimonides puts it in the Introduction to his *Mishneh Torah*, "all Jews are obligated (*chayavin*) to follow the decisions conveyed in the Babylonian Talmud, inasmuch as the entire people of Israel ratified (*hiskimu*) them." This idea of obligation (*chiyuv*) entails that decisions regarding religious practice be arrived at in accordance with the accepted *halakhic* process, the quasi-judicial method of interpretation and application of the traditionally recognized authoritative literary sources to the question at hand. By contrast, Reform Judaism rejects the binding authority of the Talmud and *halakhah*. According to this view, communities and individuals may introduce changes they deem necessary and desirable to the structure of traditional Jewish observance, irrespective of whether those changes can be justified by recourse to the authoritative sources and the accepted *halakhic* process.

Given the absence of binding authority, it might seem as though Reform Judaism is essentially "non-*halakhic*" and that the Jewish legal tradition plays no significant role in Reform Jewish life. This conclusion, however, would be a hasty one. The proper function of *halakhah* has long been a subject of controversy within North American Reform circles and is vigorously debated to this day.[4] This chapter surveys the controversy with respect to doctrine and practice. The initial section, "Doctrine," considers the more or less official stance of Reform Judaism on the nonbinding and therefore nonauthoritative nature of *halakhah* as expressed in the writings of its leading contemporary religious thinkers and the formal pronouncements of Reform rabbinical bodies. The subsequent section, "Practice," discusses the rather substantial *halakhic* literature produced by this supposedly non-*halakhic* movement. The final section, "Toward a Theory of Reform *Halakhah*," accounts for the existence of this literature in a movement that officially rejects the binding authority of *halakhah*.

DOCTRINE

Rabbi Eugene Borowitz (1924–2016), widely regarded as the leading religious thinker of twentieth-century North American Reform Judaism, summarized mainstream Reform's objection to traditional *halakhah* with the following observations:

> As long as Jews continue to believe that a God-given dignity adheres in each single self, a *halakhah* that requires the significant surrender of "conscience" will be unacceptable. The issue can perhaps be put most clearly in terms of the immediate implication of the term *halakhah*: discipline. . . . The *halakhah* is not just something that the *rav* "says" but a ruling that, once he has specified it, the people are *required* to do, classically, by God's own authority. Any concept of *halakhah* that foregoes this notion of requirement should not call itself "*halakhah*."[5]

For the non-Orthodox Jews Borowitz describes, the moral autonomy ("conscience") of the individual Jew occupies the summit of religious value. The sense of obligation ("discipline," "requirement") that is endemic to traditional Jewish law is therefore inimical to the commitment to individual autonomy. There is no room for traditional *halakhah* in the religious lives of these Jews. And while Borowitz leaves room for these Jews to consult the *halakhic* tradition as a source of nonobligatory "guidance," he insists that such a "*halakhah*" in the absence of obligation is not truly *halakhah*.

Borowitz's position is hardly unique to him. The rejection of the authority of traditional *halakhah* over the religious decisions of individuals and communities is a common theme running explicitly or implicitly through the major doctrinal statements of the American Reform rabbinate from the nineteenth century to the present. The first of these statements is the Pittsburgh Platform of 1885.[6] Although the platform was the creation of an ad hoc meeting of rabbis assembled for this purpose rather than of a rabbinic body enjoying official status,[7] it became widely accepted as *the* statement of American Reform Judaism, the standard by which Reform distinguished itself both from Orthodoxy and from other approaches to non-Orthodox Judaism. While it sketches the outlines of a systematic Reform theology, for our purposes its most important statements are found in its third and fourth paragraphs:

> We recognize in the Mosaic legislation a system of training the Jewish people for its mission during its national life in Palestine, and today we accept as binding only its moral laws, and maintain only such ceremonies as elevate and sanctify our lives, but reject all such as are not adapted to the views and habits of modern civilization.
>
> We hold that all such Mosaic and rabbinical laws as regulate diet, priestly purity, and dress originated in ages and under the influence of ideas entirely foreign to our present mental and spiritual state. They fail to impress the modern Jew with a spirit of priestly holiness; their observance in our days is apt rather to obstruct than to further modern spiritual elevation.

These passages are justly famous (or, depending upon one's religious stance, notorious) for their explicit rejection of several substantive areas of *halakhic* observance. More importantly in the present context, they do away entirely with the notion of legal discipline, the idea that the Jew's religious behavior should be defined and determined by *halakhah*. The culture of modernity[8] replaces the traditional *halakhic* texts and process as the standard by which every traditional ritual observance is to be evaluated. While the language in which this idea is expressed has changed over the years,[9] the doctrinal point has been set in stone. To the extent that Reform Judaism can be defined as "non-*halakhic*," that definition rests upon the assumption that some source of authority other than traditional Jewish law is the chief factor that determines contemporary practice. That assumption finds its roots and its justification in the language of the Pittsburgh Platform.

All doctrinal statements, of course, should be read in the context of their time. The Pittsburgh Platform, for example, is a product of the rationalist "classical" period of North American Reform Judaism, a time when Reform rabbis preached the primacy of ethical conduct and minimized the importance of ritual observance. In subsequent years, perceived changes in the cultural and intellectual environment of Reform Judaism have led the Reform movement's rabbinical association, the Central Conference of American Rabbis (CCAR), to adopt three other platforms, each of which departs in significant ways from the 1885 document's negative stance on "ceremonies." During the initial decades of the twentieth century, Reform experienced a religious "reorientation"[10] that sought to balance the dominant rationalism of classical Reform with the perception that Jewish life requires an emphasis upon ritual as well as ethical practice. Thus, the Columbus Platform of 1937, the second major doctrinal statement of the Reform movement, declares:

> Judaism as a way of life requires in addition to its moral and spiritual demands, the preservation of the Sabbath, festivals and Holy Days, the retention and development of such customs, symbols and ceremonies as possess inspirational value, the cultivation of distinctive forms of religious art and music and the use of Hebrew, together with the vernacular, in our worship and instruction.

In 1976 the CCAR's Centenary Perspective, also known as the San Francisco Platform,[11] explicitly responded to "the extraordinary events of the past generation" such as the Holocaust, the establishment of the State of Israel, and "the explosion of new knowledge and of ever more powerful technologies, and the spiritual emptiness of much of Western culture." It asserted that Reform Judaism prizes "diversity within unity" and that "Reform Jews respond to change in various ways according to the Reform principle of the autonomy of the individual." Regarding religious observance, it declares that "Reform Jews are called upon to confront the claims of Jewish tradition, however differently perceived, and to exercise their individual autonomy, choosing and creating on the basis of commitment and knowledge."[12]

Obviously, this claim of autonomy cuts both ways. Based on the principle of informed choice, Reform Jews are entitled to reject particular traditional practices or even entire departments of observance, as the 1885 Pittsburgh Platform rejects *kashrut.* But this same principle allows Reform Jews to adopt for themselves any number of ritual observances that previous generations rejected.[13] This is precisely what a significant number of Reform Jews did, to the point that some observers speak of a "return to tradition"[14] within the movement. At the end of the twentieth century the CCAR seemed to endorse this trend[15] in its "Statement of Principles" (Pittsburgh, 1999):[16]

> We are committed to the ongoing study of the whole array of *mitzvot* and to the fulfillment of those that address us as individuals and as a community. Some of these *mitzvot*, sacred obligations, have long been observed by Reform Jews; others, both ancient and modern, demand renewed attention as the result of the unique context of our own times.

The endorsement, to be sure, is carefully phrased and less than full-throated, but the difference between the two Pittsburgh statements, of 1885 and of 1999, on the subject of traditional ritual observance is significant.

This difference should also not be overstated. Contemporary North American Reform may have developed an affinity for "tradition," but it certainly has not reestablished a system of legal discipline: voluntary adoption of traditional practices is not the same thing as a sense of *halakhic* obligation. Further, none of the post-1885 CCAR platforms even hints at the restoration of a decision-making process based upon binding rabbinical rulings (*pesak halakhah*). Not a single one of these platforms mentions the word "*halakhah*." All of them acknowledge, at least by implication, what Borowitz calls the "stumbling block" on the path to a restoration of *halakhah*, namely, "the authority we have invested in selfhood."[17] Borowitz is referring to the Kantian proclamation of the autonomy of the individual that negates obligation to a source of authority lying outside individual conscience and informed choice. Effectively, all the platforms assume that *halakhah* is "unacceptable" in a Reform context if it is understood as a set of requirements and a legal process to which individuals and communities must adhere against their autonomous will.

Practice

For Borowitz, *halakhah* means "discipline," the exertion of obligatory authority upon the Jew. Thus, "(w)ith so many Jews only willing to accept *halakhah* as *guidance*, I am convinced that we have come to the end of the period when Jewish living could still be disciplined by rabbinic *halakhah*."[18] That he italicizes "guidance" suggests that he has in mind an oft-quoted statement by Rabbi Solomon B. Freehof (1892–1990),[19] the preeminent Reform *halakhic* scholar of the twentieth century:[20] "the law is authoritative enough to influence us, but no so completely so as to control us. The rabbinic law is our guidance but not our governance."[21] The idea that "authority" can exist in the absence of obligatory force is the foundation of Reform's concept of *halakhah*, a point I will return to at the end of the chapter. For the moment, it is enough to note that the story of *halakhah* in Reform Judaism can be sketched as a dichotomy between doctrine and practice: however problematic the concept of *halakhah* might be as a matter of doctrine or theory in Reform Judaism, Reform writers have produced a sizable *halakhic* literature, that is, writing that involves the interpretation and application of traditional Jewish legal sources.

This literature begins with the inception of Reform Judaism in early nineteenth-century Europe, and it was being produced even during American Reform's "classical" period, when the movement tended to locate its roots in the Bible, especially the prophetic literature, and to reject the Rabbinic/*halakhic* literature as largely irrelevant to its concerns. Addressing this apparent irony, Freehof writes:

> The weakness of the position was primarily that the self-description of Reform as being solely Biblical was simply not true. All of Reform Jewish life in all its observances was actually post-Biblical in origin. None of the arrangements of worship, the hours of service, the text of the prayers, no matter how rewritten, was primarily Biblical. The whole of Jewish liturgy is an achievement of post-Biblical times. The religious calendar, based indeed upon Scripture, was elaborated and defined in

> post-Biblical times. Marriage ceremonies and burial rites were all post-Biblical. The Bible, of course, was the source of ethical ideas, but the actual religious life was rabbinic. Early Reform may have rejected rabbinic authority, but it could not avoid the historical rabbinic constructs that lived in the pageantry of the Jewish mode of life.[22]

The word "*halakhic*" can properly be substituted for "rabbinic" in this passage. Although the Talmud may not be "binding" upon Reform Jews, the foundation of Reform observance is nonetheless located in the Talmud and the *halakhah.* To speak and argue intelligibly about Jewish practice, including *Reform* Jewish practice, Reform rabbis have no choice but to engage with those texts. As Freehof observes: "since the religious observances were all rabbinical in source, the various questions that from time to time needed to be answered all involved the Halachic literature."[23] Those answers constitute the explicitly *Reform halakhic* literature.

In its earliest iterations, this literature resembled traditional *halakhic* writing in all formal respects, composed "in Hebrew, in the style of the *She'elot u-teshuvot* [responsa], which for centuries had been used by rabbinic authorities."[24] What makes it "Reform" is that it sought to defend the innovations that the European reformers introduced into synagogue worship, the language and text of the prayers, and other areas of observance. Perhaps the first "Reform" *halakhic* responsum is an opinion by Rabbi Menachem Mendel Steinhardt (1812) in support of a ruling by the Royal Westphalian Consistory of the Israelites (the governing body of the Jewish community in the Westphalia region of Germany) permitting the consumption of legumes (*kitniyot*) during Pesach.[25] In 1818, Eliezer Lieberman published *Nogah Hatzedek*, a collection of responsa by four rabbis defending various liturgical innovations established by the Reform community of Berlin. These included the use of the organ during synagogue worship, the institution of vernacular prayer, the adoption of the Sefardic pronunciation of Hebrew, and the elimination of the silent *Amidah.* Opponents of these changes, a group eventually to be called "Orthodox," responded in 1819 with *Eleh Divrei Hab'rit*, a collection of forty rabbinical opinions attacking the ritual innovations of the Berlin and Hamburg Reform congregations. The Reformers answered those criticisms in pamphlets entitled *Cherev Nokemet N'kam B'rit* and *B'rit Emet.* These exchanges, described by one observer as "the battle of the proof texts,"[26] included a great deal of heated rhetoric, in part because opponents sensed that any intentional, directed effort toward religious reform threatened the survival of traditional Judaism.[27]

The fact remains, though, that these exchanges read like traditional *halakhic* disputes. The early Reform rabbis are not yet operating out of a self-consciously "denominational" framework; rather, they speak to their non-Reform rabbinic counterparts in the language of traditional *halakhic* argumentation that would be familiar and theoretically persuasive to them The opponents did take the Reformers' *halakhic* reasoning seriously enough to refute it directly and at times forged creative new *halakhic* theories of their own, particularly when the Reformers seem to have the better of the argument.[28]

By the 1820s, this literary activity declined steeply, as European Reform rabbis by and large ceased writing *halakhic* responsa in the traditional style. Several explanations are commonly advanced for this phenomenon.[29] First, the scope and pace of change had quickened, and the Reformers were now discussing innovations that were more difficult to justify by recourse to the traditional legal sources.[30] Second, the audience for their work had also changed. Reform rabbis were now writing for each other and for their own communities rather than for an imagined universal Jewish readership. This change is most notable in the Reformers' rhetoric of justification. Their essays, articles, and speeches tended to support their innovations in the discourse of theology, rationalism, and the methods of critical historical inquiry known as *Wissenschaft des Juedentums*—"the needs of the time, the needs of reason, and the needs of nature"[31]—rather than that of traditional *halakhic* precedent and analysis. While Reform rabbis delivered addresses and lectures on matters of religious observance, particularly at the rabbinical conferences,[32] and wrote learned opinions (*Gutachten*, as they were generally called), these generally do not qualify as *halakhic shi'urim* (lectures) or responsa in the traditional sense of those terms.

But in the United States, the Reform movement recovered its foothold in the Jewish legal tradition, developing a *halakhic* discourse of its own. *Halakhic* literature played a role in the discussions and debates among American Reform rabbis during the late nineteenth century, although the significance of that role can be questioned. For example, attendees at the 1869 Philadelphia conference of reform-leaning rabbis voted to accept civil divorce as sufficient for remarriage in the absence of a *get*, the traditional Jewish document of divorce. They justified this on the basis of a novel *halakhic* theory advanced by the German Reform Rabbi Samuel Holdheim that Jewish law regards divorce not as a matter of ritual prohibition (*isur veheter*) but instead as an example of civil or monetary law (*dinei mamonot*) in which the law of the State is accepted as valid under *halakhah* (The principle here is *dina d'malkhuta dina*. See Resnicoff, this volume, and Levmore and Gotlib, this volume). The theory is, to say the least, contestable,[33] and it was far from the only justification the attendees cited for their decision.[34] Similarly, in the discussions of ritual practices at the earliest meetings of the CCAR, "American Reform rabbis, like their European counterparts, read the traditional texts more or less critically, or felt free to ignore them altogether."[35] Jewish law, in other words, was present in these rabbinical discussions, but it was neither the determining factor in the ultimate decisions nor the predominant language in which those decisions were framed and argued.

Matters begin to change, although gradually, with the establishment of the CCAR Committee on Responsa in 1906. The Committee was created in the wake of a dispute among members of the CCAR over the best way to aid members seeking guidance as to the correct practice on questions relating to life cycle rituals. While some of the rabbis wanted a set of fixed rules, others strenuously opposed anything resembling a code of law. The Committee on Responsa was therefore a compromise between these positions. Its task was to issue "appropriate answers" to questions involving "Jewish customs and traditions," with those answers appearing in the CCAR *Yearbook*. Its responsa were not to be regarded as binding upon CCAR members, nor did they represent official CCAR policy unless adopted by a vote of the CCAR as a whole.[36] By "appropriate answers" the CCAR may have meant that the responsa should meet the criteria of contemporary academic scholarship. Perhaps this is why the Committee was invariably chaired during the initial decades of its existence by a member of the faculty of the Hebrew Union College (HUC), the North American Reform movement's rabbinical seminary. Not all of these chairpersons specialized in *halakhic* literature, and their decisions do not, in the main, read like traditional *halakhic t'shuvot* (responsa). The first chair, Kaufmann Kohler (who served from 1906–1921), was known primarily as a Bible scholar and theologian;[37] Jacob Mann (1934–1939) was a historian; and Israel Bettan (1940–1954) was a professor of *Midrash* and homiletics.

The responsa issued during these years tended to be brief, with citations from the Bible and Talmud as well as academic scholarship but rarely from any post-Talmudic *halakhic* authorities. The principal exception to this rule is Jacob Z. Lauterbach, a professor of Talmud at HUC, who chaired the Committee from 1923 to 1933 and whose work in this field combined deep erudition in the *halakhic* sources and in academic scholarship. Still, Lauterbach's "responsa," particularly such longer efforts as "Worshiping with Covered Heads"[38] and "Naming of Children"[39] resemble academic historical studies more than traditional *halakhic pesak* (decision-making).

The work of Solomon B. Freehof, chair of the Responsa Committee from 1955 to 1976, marks a decisive change in this trend. Like his predecessors, Freehof served for a time as a faculty member at Hebrew Union College, but unlike them he spent most of his professional career as a congregational rabbi.[40] He differed from his predecessors in his scholarly concentration, which is evident in two ways. First, the preponderance of his published work consists of responsa and other explicitly *halakhic* texts. Second, though he was familiar with the major works and trends in academic Jewish studies, Freehof wrote his *halakhic* texts as a *halakhist* rather than from the perspective of an academic scholar. Accordingly, his literary style more closely resembles that of traditional rabbinic-legal discourse than that of a university professor. To use a legal metaphor, the difference between the responsa of Freehof and those of Lauterbach is analogous to the difference between a judicial opinion and a legal historian's essay on the same issue.

Freehof's reputation as "the first genuine Reform *posek*"[41]—that is, authoritative *halakhic* decisor—rests upon these responsa, published either in volumes of the *CCAR Yearbook* or in his own collections. Indeed, the term "Reform responsa," signifying a unique genre of *halakhic* writing, originates with him; none of his predecessors used it to describe their work. In these writings he displays his deep knowledge of the *halakhic* literature as well as his experience as a decisor, which he first acquired during World War II as chairman of the Responsa Committee of the Jewish Welfare Board's Committee on Army and Navy Religious Activities.[42] Freehof's tenure as head of the CCAR Responsa Committee coincides with a growing interest in responsa among Reform rabbis and laity, as evidenced by the much larger number of *she'elot* (inquiries) he received compared to those of his predecessors. That interest, in turn, appears to reflect the changing religious climate within Reform Judaism, as witnessed by the new openness to ritual observance expressed in the 1937 Columbus Platform and by the recurring calls among Reform rabbis at the time for the CCAR to establish a "code"—or at least a set of clear standards—of religious practice for the movement.

Freehof's lasting achievement, above and beyond the decisions he reached on specific issues, was to make traditional *halakhic* discourse a legitimate (though by no means the exclusive) language of debate over questions of religious practice in the North American Reform movement. Following his term as chair, the Responsa Committee under the leadership of his successors[43] has continued issuing responsa in his style,[44] in two important respects. First, the Committee continues to regard its opinions as advisory rather than obligatory, as "guidance, not governance," for the individuals and communities who submit the *she'elot* (inquiries) as well as for the wider Reform movement. Second, the responsa continue to speak the language of *halakhah*. While they at times step outside the boundaries of *halakhic* debate to draw upon other forms of scholarship (primarily history and legal theory), their predominant voice is the internal perspective of a participant of the Jewish legal process as opposed to the external perspective of an academic scholar.[45] If bulk is any indication, the role of these texts within Reform Judaism is significant. At this writing, there exist well over 1,300 "official"[46] Reform responsa, which makes this literature by far the largest genre of Reform Jewish writing on questions of religious observance.

The North American Reform movement has also produced numerous monographs on religious practice that are rooted to varying degrees in the traditional *halakhic* sources. Their publication began during the first decades of the twentieth century, the years leading up to and following the adoption of the CCAR's Columbus Platform. This was the period during which the movement reevaluated its stance toward ritual observance and began moving away from what some considered the excessively anti-*halakhic* stance of "classical" Reform Judaism.[47] Some members of the CCAR went as far as to call for the creation of a code of religious practice for Reform Jews, though the majority of the membership opposed the idea. In a paper delivered at the 1941 convention of the CCAR, Solomon B. Freehof forged a compromise between these two streams of thought that persists to this day. On the one hand, Freehof rejected the idea of an authoritative code of practice, both because Reform Jews did not think of ritual matters as "law" and because the Reform rabbinate lacked the authority to make pronouncements concerning large swaths of Jewish observance that most Reform Jews had long since abandoned, particularly the observance of Shabbat and *kashrut* (the dietary laws). On the other hand, he endorsed the idea of a non-authoritative "guide" to Reform religious practice that would rely heavily upon existing statements and decisions of the movement such as responsa, resolutions of the CCAR, and other materials.[48] Such a guidebook would stay away from those "rituals and ceremonies" that Freehof felt were beyond the authority of Reform rabbinical pronouncement.[49] It would, however, identify the already-existing consensus position of Reform Judaism in other areas of practice.

Freehof followed this proposal with the publication of *Reform Jewish Practice and Its Rabbinic Background* in 1944.[50] In the Introduction,[51] he summarizes his approach to the "codification" of Reform observance:

> It is not the purpose of this book to be, even in the humblest way, a Shulhan Aruk. It does not attempt to lay down the norm of practice, except in two or three disputed

> situations where some preference must be made. Its chief purpose is to describe present-day Reform Jewish practices and the traditional rabbinic laws from which they are derived.

These words advance two specific claims. The first claim, repeating the thrust of his 1941 CCAR paper, is that the goal of a work such as this is descriptive rather than prescriptive, thus seeking to allay the objections of those Reform Jews who would question the authority of any Reform rabbinic personage or collective body to make binding declarations of law. Indeed, it is on this point that Freehof lays out his theory that what is traditionally called *halakhah* developed from the historically conditioned, ever-changing *minhag*, "the custom of the people," which in his view retains superiority over *halakhah* itself: "The Minhag created by the masses was the raw material which the law took up and shifted, rearranged, justified and embodied as the legal practice. The law itself did not create. The people created and the law organized."[52] In other words, *minhag*, the creative power of popular practice, exerts a superiority over *halakhah*, or formal law. However debatable this theory might be as a matter of legal history,[53] by formalizing the status of existing practices as *minhag* Freehof transforms them into a source of authority to which a Reform *posek* might appeal as justification for their decisions.

The second claim is that these Reform practices are "derived" from the Jewish legal tradition. He thus portrays Reform Jewish practice not as the product of a radical, rationalistic break with that tradition but as an authentic, organic development of the Rabbinic heritage that is the foundation of all Jewish religious life. His explanations for these practices situate them within traditional *halakhic* discourse. This is especially true of the 1976 "augmented" edition, his latest one, which includes a number of Freehof's responsa that, with some exceptions,[54] deal with subjects covered in the earlier editions and aim to provide *halakhic* justification for the existing Reform *minhag*.

By the 1970s, the Reform movement was experiencing what its leading historian has called "a period of renewal" that intensified this trend toward "greater traditionalism" in "nearly every Reform congregation."[55] Coincidentally or not, the CCAR was ready for a more prescriptive approach toward ritual observance. This is evident in W. Gunther Plaut's *A Shabbat Manual* (1972), which opens with a consideration of what "*mitzvah*" might mean in a movement that grants first priority to personal autonomy.

> Mitzvah . . . is what a Jew ought to do in response to his God and to the traditions of his people. This response comes from personal commitment rather than from unquestioning obedience to a set of commandments which past tradition thought to be the direct will of God. By making choice and commitment part of our plan of life, we willingly and purposefully strengthen our bonds with the God of Israel and with our people.[56]

Ritual observance is no longer justified simply by a description of, or an appeal to, the existing consensus. It is now presented as an "ought." Though the traditional *halakhah* still does not exercise binding authority over Reform Jews—Plaut describes the details of his guidebook to Shabbat observance as "options and opportunities"[57]—the Reform rabbinate was now openly endorsing religious discipline[58] to its people. This new trend became more pronounced with the publication of several other guidebooks, "code"-like volumes setting forth standards for observance, again not as obligatory rules but as warm recommendations.[59] As Simeon Maslin, the editor of the first of these, put it: "Some may read this book and decide that the mitzvot suggested are too many or too demanding. But a few mitzvot observed with *kavvanah* [intention] will lead to an enlargement of commitment as time goes on. The secret of observing mitzvot is to begin."[60] These works include extensive reference notes, mostly drawn from the Rabbinic and *halakhic* literature. As with Freehof's *Reform Jewish Practice*, these notes serve as both a scholarly apparatus and as framing device: by locating the roots of Reform observance in the *halakhic* tradition, they argue for the Judaic authenticity of that observance.

To complete our catalogue of the Reform *halakhic* bookshelf, we should mention several other movement publications. *Gates of Understanding* and *Divrei Mishkan T'filah*,[61] commentaries to the CCAR's two most recent *siddurim* (prayerbooks), trace the historical and *halakhic* background to the movement's official liturgy. The various "Rabbi's Manuals" published by the CCAR, handbooks containing life cycle liturgies, also offer sections of "Historical and Halachic Notes." These sections, following in Freehof's "guidance, not governance" footsteps, "do not establish or create a new Reform Halacha; rather, they aim to inform the rabbi of prevailing practice based on the historic continuities and discontinuities of Reform" by drawing upon traditional *halakhic* sources, resolutions of the European rabbinical conferences, and CCAR resolutions and responsa.[62] *Jewish Living: A Guide to Contemporary Reform Practice*[63] attempts a summary of all Reform *halakhic* writing that appeared to the date of its publication (2010). Resembling Freehof's *Reform Jewish Practice* in that it offers the Rabbinic-*halakhic* and the Reform-*halakhic* sources for Reform observance, it updates him as well, reflecting the realities of Reform practice at the beginning of the twenty-first century.[64]

Toward a Theory of Reform *Halakhah*

The foregoing part illustrates a paradoxical situation: namely, the existence of a substantial corpus of *halakhic* literature within a Jewish movement that officially renounces the concept of legal discipline and the obligatory authority of *halakhah*. This situation prompts the questions of how this nonbinding *halakhic* literature functions in Reform Judaism and what role it serves. Given that no definitive response to these questions has ever been embraced by Reform Judaism's official institutions, I cannot pretend that I have anything that amounts to a comprehensive answer. Nonetheless, I think that the following four suggestions are helpful in pointing the way toward the explanation we seek.

First, in Reform Judaism *halakhah* functions as a discourse, a language for making meaning, in which the emphasis is less upon the rule or decision than upon the process of argument by which the decision is reached. This stands in contrast to Borowitz's assertion in the section "Doctrine," that a *halakhah* that serves merely as guidance and "that foregoes this notion of requirement should not call itself '*halakhah*.'"[65] His point is arguable, but it is also a trap. It is an example of a stipulative definition, one that "proposes ('stipulates') that language shall be used in a given way" rather than a *lexical definition*, "a kind of report on how language is used."[66] Once one has accepted an author's stipulative definition, one may well have no choice but to accept that author's conclusions.[67] In this case, if we use the lexical definition rather than the stipulative definition proposed by Borowitz, we would conclude that, if a community of practice uses the term "*halakhah*" to describe a discourse that exerts persuasive (as opposed to binding) authority, then there are no a priori grounds upon which to reject that usage.[68] Such a discourse can still qualify as "*halakhah*,"[69] even though there is a significant difference between a *halakhah* that presents itself as "obligatory" and one that serves as "guidance, not governance." Given that this Reform genre of writing deals with the interpretation and application of texts that are universally recognized as *halakhic*, the only reason to deny it the label "*halakhah*" is to confine that term to its Orthodox usage and conception.

Second, although the movement proclaims its allegiance to personal religious autonomy, its rabbinate is not neutral or indifferent toward the decisions the people make. Not all creative choices are created equal; decisions ought to be justified, and it matters *how* they are justified. They key word here is "authenticity": Reform *halakhic* literature is aimed at an audience concerned that its religious practice, though freely chosen, is founded upon a solid interpretation of Jewish tradition and that the best way to reach such an interpretation is to engage with *halakhah*, the discourse with which Jews have historically justified their religious decisions. Each Reform *halakhic* writing, but particularly the responsa in which the authors display their reasoning step by step, is best read as an argument of authenticity to its intended audience, a claim that *this* answer, rather than other possible answers, represents for Reform Jews the best interpretation of the tradition on the question at hand.

At times, this claim of authenticity comes to defend an existing Reform practice that departs from the traditional norm. One interesting example is a responsum by Freehof to the following *she'elah*, submitted by Reform Rabbi Stanley Brav of Cincinnati, Ohio:[70]

> At one of the smaller American colleges, because of the heavy student schedule it seems impossible to have services other than on Friday night. The students, therefore, have services at that time and also read the Torah. The local rabbi prohibits the reading of the Torah on Friday night (which is not a traditional Torah-reading time) and declares that reading the Torah at this traditionally unauthorized time would make the Torah unfit for proper use at regular services. Is this judgment of the rabbi justified by the legal tradition?

While the college student group is apparently not affiliated with the Reform movement, their practice of reading Torah on Friday night mirrors a Reform custom of long standing. During the late nineteenth and early twentieth centuries, when many Jews were employed in occupations that required work on Shabbat, attendance at *tefilat shaharit,* morning services on Saturday, declined to anemic levels. The Reform movement responded by instituting a "late" (after dinner) Friday evening service so that its members could attend in larger numbers. This service usually featured a Torah reading, a practice that continues in some Reform congregations.[71] Thus, when Freehof is asked to evaluate the local rabbi's prohibition of Friday night Torah readings on the basis of "the legal tradition," he is also being asked whether this Reform custom is justified according to the *halakhah.*

Lacking any *halakhic* source that expressly permits the reading of Torah at nontraditional times, Freehof approaches the question from the reverse angle, asking whether there exists an explicit *halakhic* prohibition against the practice. Drawing upon his extensive knowledge of the responsa literature, he writes that a similar question was posed in the nineteenth century to Rabbi Naftali Zvi Yehuda Berlin ("Netziv," d. 1893), the *rosh yeshiva* (head) of the storied Lithuanian academy of Volozhyn and the author of several well-regarded works of Talmudic scholarship.[72] The *she'elah* came from a rabbi in America who, much like the local rabbi in the question addressed to Freehof, objected when a congregation in his city proposed to read from the Torah on a Sunday morning as part of its dedication ceremony for a new ark (*aron kodesh*) in its sanctuary. The American rabbi based his objection upon the principle of *bal tosif,* the prohibition against adding to the system of obligatory observances,[73] and he asked Berlin for a supporting opinion. Berlin rejects that argument: the *bal tosif* prohibition applies only to commandments that are derived from the Torah itself (*mid'oraita*) and not to *mitzvot* such as the public reading of the Torah which are based on Rabbinic enactment (*miderabanan*). He endorses the rabbi's objection, however, on other grounds, namely, that the Talmud Yerushalmi requires that any reading from a Torah scroll in public must be accompanied by the appropriate *b'rakhot* (benedictions), which leads him to conclude that to read from the Torah at a time that is not prescribed by *halakhah* would violate the prohibition against reciting *berakhah levatalah,* unnecessary benedictions. Freehof suggests that Berlin is "uncertain" as to the correctness of his ruling, which in Freehof's view has less to do with *halakhah* than with "the general Orthodox mood" that "objects to any unauthorized novelty (i.e., if it really is unauthorized)."[74] The implication: if the Sage of Volozhyn is not sure that he has found a solid *halakhic* impediment to public reading of the Torah at a nontraditional time, it is likely that no such impediment exists.

As for the pronouncement of the college town rabbi that reading from the Torah scroll on nontraditional occasions would render it ritually defective (*pasul*), Freehof retorts that there is no evidence in the *halakhah* to support this contention. This enables him to dismiss the pronouncement as an example of rabbinic overreach that the student group can safely ignore. In this *teshuvah,* then, Freehof uses the words of two Orthodox rabbis to demonstrate that the "*halakhic*" opposition to this Reform practice stems from purely sectarian motives—an anti-Reformist mood rather from any substantive consideration of Jewish law. His Reform readers can therefore claim that *halakhah* supports (because it doesn't clearly deny) the Jewish authenticity of their custom.

In other cases, the argument will critique an existing practice and advocate that Reform Jews frame the issue and think about it in a different way. Consider the *teshuvah* by the CCAR Responsa Committee entitled "A Defective 'Holocaust' Torah Scroll."[75] A Reform congregation possesses one of the Czech Torah scrolls that were taken by the Nazis and then rescued and cared for by London's Westminster Synagogue Memorial Trust. The scroll is a complete *sefer torah*, but sections of its script have flaked away. A qualified scribe (*sofer*) has told the congregation that, because the parchment will not hold new ink, the scroll cannot be repaired. It is therefore *pasul*, ritually defective and therefore unfit for public Torah reading.[76] Nonetheless, due to the special history and provenance of this *sefer torah*, the congregation has determined to use it for public reading in sections where the script is legible, especially at Shabbat services when young people become Bar or Bat *Mitzvah*. But now "a question has been raised" against this practice. Is it proper for a Reform congregation, which is not "bound" by the traditional *halakhah*, to read from a *pasul* Torah scroll during its public worship, especially one that has become "a significant part of our congregation's life"? The *teshuvah* begins by framing the question as "a conflict between two profoundly important Jewish religious values": the honor due to a Torah scroll (*k'vod sefer torah*) which is defined by *halakhic* rules such as the one that prohibits public reading from a ritually defective scroll, versus the act of remembering the events of the Shoah, which "has taken on for us the character of a religious duty."[77] This "conflict" signals to the reader that the question is a difficult one, that it cannot be resolved simply by dismissing the rules defining a ritually fit Torah scroll (*sefer torah kasher*) as mere technicalities of no importance to a Reform community. Rather, the correct answer to this question requires that a balance be drawn between these values, "both of which make powerful claims upon our attention." The responsum thus seeks to provide a model for such "balanced" thinking to a Reform Jewish audience.

The opinion initially analyzes the *halakhic* rules, codified by Maimonides (*Rambam*),[78] which indeed define a Torah scroll such as this one to be *pasul*. It turns out, though that "the very same Maimonides is the author of a responsum that rules to the opposite effect," namely, that a community may fulfill the obligation of public Torah reading by reading from an incomplete Torah scroll and may even recite the appropriate benedictions before and after the reading.[79] The CCAR responsum describes the theory that *Rambam* develops in this *teshuvah*, which contradicts the Talmudic law behind the ruling in his *Mishneh Torah*, and traces the debate over that *teshuvah* among the medieval authorities (*rishonim*). The history of that debate demonstrates that although *Rambam*'s responsum is a minority opinion (*da`at yachid*) the traditional *halakhah* "does not clearly forbid the reading from a *pasul* scroll."[80]

From this history, the CCAR responsum moves to a discussion of "The Issue from a Reform Jewish Perspective," where it sets out two plausible and conflicting answers to the congregation's question. The first answer, which allows reading from the ritually defective Czech scroll, rests upon the following two foundations: (1) the *halakhic* impediment to reading from a *pasul* scroll is not absolute and, at any rate, Reform *halakhic* thinking is quite willing to rely upon a minority opinion when that opinion represents "an uplifting and 'liberally affirmative'[81] interpretation of Jewish tradition"; and (2) given the vital importance of remembering the Shoah, "there is no reason to forbid the use of this scroll." The second answer, which prohibits the reading, is also based upon two justifications: (1) the *halakhic* rules that define the *kashrut* of a *sefer torah* are no mere technicalities but rather the constitutive elements of a ritual act we Reform Jews regard as a *mitzvah*; (2) since we can and do "remember the Shoah" in numerous ways, it is unnecessary and indeed inappropriate to "alter the contours and content of our religious practice" by reading from a ritually defective scroll in order to achieve that goal. The responsum seeks to persuade the congregation that this second answer is the better one, the one that most closely corresponds to our sense of Jewish authenticity.

We should insist, instead, that our regular weekly, Shabbat, and holiday Torah portions be read from a *sefer torah kasher*. This is the standard bequeathed to us from Jewish tradition. This was the standard observed by the Czech community from which the scroll in question originated. And it remains the standard which informs Reform Jewish life, the standard to which we educate our children and to which we ought to aspire.

The responsum thus concludes with a critique of the congregation's practice rather than, as in the previous responsum to the college group, a defense of it. Even so, the responsum goes on to suggest some ways in which the congregation might properly read from the Czech scroll during its worship services. As in the previous responsum, we see here an effort to persuade a Reform Jewish audience with arguments that are rooted in, and speak from, both the *halakhic* tradition and a particular conception of Jewish authenticity.

The theme of "persuasion" leads to my third suggestion: if Reform *halakhic* literature is about persuasion and authenticity, it follows that there exists a community of argument, an intended readership that the literature engages and that it hopes to persuade. Each Reform *halakhic* writing invokes the audience it wishes to persuade,[82] namely, an audience of readers who take both the Jewish legal tradition and the specifically Reform Jewish tradition with all seriousness. Thus, Reform *halakhic* literature will tend to be recognizably "Reform," that is, motivated by the movement's fundamental values and affirmations, committed to the proposition that Torah "cannot exist in the absence of certain essential moral and ethical commitments."[83] These include, but are not restricted to, the principle of equality of participation in ritual life without reference to gender identification; the moral and ethical equality of all humankind;[84] and openness to the permissibility and desirability of religious innovation and creativity. Reform *poskim* are unlikely to reach decisions that run afoul of any of these principles. This literature is also recognizably "Reform" in that it draws upon prior Reform responsa as persuasive (i.e., nonbinding) precedent. On the other hand, as an arm of the CCAR, the Responsa Committee considers itself bound to resolutions adopted by the CCAR as a whole. Reform responsa dealing with such subjects as cremation,[85] the validation of same-gender marriage,[86] and the requirement of circumcision for male converts[87] are representative of these tendencies.

Fourth, the fact that this *halakhic* literature is written by Reform rabbis and aimed at a Reform audience potentially opens the way for insights and innovative interpretations (*chidushim*) that might not occur or that might gain traction much more slowly in *halakhic* writing for other audiences. One example is R. Solomon Freehof's permission for the burial of non-Jewish spouses and other relatives in a Jewish cemetery. He based this permission on a two-part *halakhic* theory: first, that the "sacred" status of the Jewish cemetery, though deeply entrenched in popular custom, is not well-founded in *halakhah*; and second, that the Jewish owner of a burial plot may bury anyone he wishes within his own property (*betokh shelo*).[88] Another example is the Responsa Committee's decision "Treatment of the Terminally Ill."[89] While most *halakhic* treatments of the question work within the constraints of the rules concerning the person whose death is imminent,[90] the responsum develops a different theory based upon the obligations flowing from the *mitzvah* of healing and medical practice (*refu'ah*). Hence, any medical treatment may be discontinued once it has been determined to have lost its therapeutic efficacy, a judgment as to just what would count as effective or successful treatment in any individual case.[91] The suggestion here is that *chidushim* such as these are more likely to occur in a Reform *halakhic* setting than in others, not only because Reform *halakhists* are more likely to derive them but also because a Reform *halakhic* audience is more likely to find them persuasive.

Conclusion

This chapter has described what I have called a paradox (other non-Orthodox Jewish movements might be said to confront a similar, if not identical, paradox, see Kwall, this volume), namely, that Reform Judaism has produced a significant *halakhic* literature even though its doctrine rejects the binding authority of the *halakhah*. The question naturally arises: what purpose does "Reform *halakhah*" serve if it exercises no obligatory power upon the religious life of Reform Jewish individuals and communities? Additionally, what influence can it wield if the preponderant majority of Reform Jews, who do not shape their lives in accordance with *halakhic* guidelines or directives, are not truly part of the "intended audience" I have just described? In short: why *do* the rabbis of a non-*halakhic* movement write *halakhic* literature?

It is possible, of course, that the rabbis are simply talking to each other against the backdrop of massive indifference on the part of their laity. Another answer, one that those rabbis presumably would prefer, is that they produce these works in order to *teach* their laity. If Reform Judaism privileges personal autonomy, we have seen that it also advocates that individual choices be made "on the basis of commitment and knowledge." Given that, as Solomon Freehof and other Reform *halakhists* have emphasized, the necessary information for these "informed" choices is to be found in the *halakhic* literature, Reform responsa and other *halakhic* writings can be said to serve the educational function of supplying that information to Reform Jews. By nurturing the connection between Reform religious practice and the Jewish legal tradition, Reform *halakhic* literature supports the movement's claim for the Judaic authenticity of its religious practice. And by rendering *pesak* (*halakhic* rulings), Reform *halakhic* literature suggests to its readers that not all autonomous choices are equally good. Some are better, some are worse, and the Reform *halakhic* process is the arena in which these evaluations are argued. That such argument can take place in the absence of obligatory authority is a cornerstone of Reform *halakhic* doctrine. As I have written elsewhere:

> It has therefore never been our intention to put an end to all debate by writing our responsa, even though we believe that the answers we have reached are the best ones available. We see our *t'shuvot* rather as invitations to learning and debate. In each one, we offer a carefully considered response to a question of Jewish religious practice, a response that consciously bases itself within the tradition of the halachah, the literary and intellectual home of Jewish religious practice and the language in which Jews in every generation have argued their practice. In so doing, we hope that we have contributed in some way to the age-old process of *talmud Torah*, the study of Torah. And we hope that our readers, whether they agree or disagree with any of our conclusions, will follow in our footsteps.[92]

That, perhaps, is what "guidance, not governance" ultimately means: the existence of a Reform *halakhic* literature is evidence that, in the Reform movement, autonomy coexists with authenticity. If Reform doctrine posits a commitment to personal religious choice, it also recognizes that some choices are better than others. The determination that any particular choice is the better or best one requires argument. And that argument, precisely because it is a *Jewish* one about *Jewish* religious practice, will necessarily be rooted in, and informed by, the Jewish legal tradition.

Notes

1. The authoritative history of the Reform movement is Michael Meyer, *Response to Modernity: A History of the Reform Movement in Judaism* (New York: Oxford University Press, 1988). Gershom Scholem suggests that the antinomian tendencies of the seventeenth-century Sabbatian movement prepared the ground for Reform Judaism; see Gershom Scolem, *Major Trends in Jewish Mysticism* (7th printing) (New York: Schocken Books, 1973), 304. For critiques of Scholem's theory, see David Biale, *Gershom Scholem: Kabbalah and Counter-History* (Cambridge, MA: Harvard University Press, 1982), 84–88; and Jacob Katz, *Divine Law in Human Hands: Case Studies in Halakhic Flexibility* (Jerusalem: Magnes, 1998), 504–30.
2. "The Reform Movement in North America," The Reform Jewish Community of Canada, https://www.therjcc.ca/reform-movement. This chapter does not discuss the experience of Reform communities in Israel, but it is worth noting that the leading figure in Reform *halakhah* in Israel is Rabbi Moshe Zemer (1932–2011). Many of his writings are collected in Moshe Zemer, *Halakhah Sh'fuyah* (Tel Aviv: Dvir, 1993); and Moshe Zemer, *Evolving Halakhah: A Progressive Approach to Traditional Jewish Law* (Woodstock, VT: Jewish Lights, 1999). For an analysis of his work, see Shai Akiva Wozner, "*Hahalakhah hareformit*

b'ikvot hasefer Halakhah Sh'fuyah," in *Hayahadut Hareformit: Hagut, Tarbut, v'Chevrah*, Avinoam Rozenak, ed. (Jerusalem: Van Leer/Hakibbutz Hameuchad, 2014), 261–86.

3. See Chaim Saiman, *Halakhah: The Rabbinic Idea of Law* (Princeton, NJ: Princeton University Press, 2018), 13–14: "the term 'Jewish law' fails to do justice to halakhah . . . while halakhah is undoubtedly law, it is also something else . . . not only a body of regulations, but a way, a path of thinking, being, and knowing." "Jewish law" is the usual translation of *mishpat ivri*, which denotes the modern academic movement devoted to the application of contemporary methodologies of legal research to the study of the texts and history of the *halakhah*. Whether such methodologies are appropriate to the study of the *halakhah*, a normative system based upon religious grounds, has long been a source of debate among academic scholars; see Yitzhak Englard, "*Mehkar hamishpat ha'ivri: mahuto umatarotav*," *Mishpatim* 7 (1976): 34–65; and Menachem Elon, "*Od l'inyan mehkaro shel hamishpat ha'ivri*," *Mishpatim* 8 (1977): 99–137.
4. As witnessed by the special issue, "Halachah and Reform Judaism," *CCAR Journal* (Spring 2020), the quarterly publication of the North American Reform rabbinate.
5. Eugene Borowitz, *Renewing the Covenant: A Theology for the Postmodern Jew* (Philadelphia: Jewish Publication Society, 1991), 282.
6. See Meyer, *Response to Modernity*, 265–70. The texts of the platforms discussed can be found at https://www.ccarnet.org/rabbinic-voice/platforms.
7. The subsequent platforms were adopted by the Central Conference of American Rabbis (CCAR), the professional association of Reform Rabbis in North America. The CCAR, however, was not founded until 1889.
8. As the platform phrases it in the passages quoted above: "the views and habits of modern civilization" and "our present mental and spiritual state."
9. For example, the term "autonomy," cited frequently by Borowitz, *Renewing the Covenant*, does not appear in is the Pittsburgh Platform.
10. Meyer, *Response to Modernity*, 296ff.
11. The document was written under the guidance of Eugene Borowitz.
12. "Reform Judaism: A Centenary Perspective," https://www.ccarnet.org/rabbinic-voice/platforms/article-reform-judaism-centenary-perspective.
13. See the Reform responsum no. 5759.7, "The Second Festival Day and Reform Judaism," in Mark Washofsky, *Reform Responsa for the Twenty-First Century*, 2 vols. (New York: Central Conference of American Rabbis, 2010), 1:49–51, as well as https://www.ccarnet.org/ccar-responsa/nyp-no-5759-7 at notes 1–10.
14. Marc Lee Rafael "The Emergence and Development of Tradition in Reform Jewish Worship, 1970-1999," *Jewish History* 15, no. 2 (2001): 119–30.
15. This raises the question of the relationship between the elites (the rabbis) and the laity in the generation of religious change in contemporary American Judaism. See Roberta R. Kwall, *The Myth of the Cultural Jew: Culture and Law in Jewish Tradition* (New York: Oxford University Press, 2015).
16. https://www.ccarnet.org/rabbinic-voice/platforms/article-statement-principles-reform-judaism.
17. Borowitz, *Renewing the Covenant*, 281.
18. Ibid., 282.
19. "Suggests," because he does not cite Freehof at all in his book.
20. On Freehof's influence as a Reform *halakhist*, see *Reform Responsa*. For a comprehensive survey see Joan S. Friedman, *"Guidance, Not Governance": Rabbi Solomon B. Freehof and*

Reform Responsa (Cincinnati, OH: Hebrew Union College Press, 2013). And note the title of her book.

21. Solomon B. Freehof, *Reform Responsa* (Cincinnati, OH: Hebrew Union College Press, 1960), 22.
22. Ibid., 16.
23. Ibid., 18.
24. W. Gunther Plaut, *The Rise of Reform Judaism: A Sourcebook of Its European Origins* (Philadelphia: Jewish Publication Society, 2015), 33. And see the following note.
25. Meyer, *Response to Modernity*, 37, describes the responsum as "Reform." By contrast, Jacob Katz distinguishes between Steinhardt's "traditional" responsum and the reformist rhetoric of the Consistory's proclamation of the permit (*heter*). See Jacob Katz, "Towards a Biography of the Hatam Sofer," trans. David Ellenson, in *From East and West: Jews in a Changing Europe 1750-1870*, ed. Frances Malino and David Sorkin (Oxford: Basil Blackwell, 1991), 252.
26. Jakob Petuchowski, *Prayerbook Reform in Europe: The Liturgy of European Liberal and Reform Judaism* (New York: World Union for Progressive Judaism, 1968), 84–104.
27. Gerald Blidstein, "Early Reform and Its Approach," *Tradition* 11, no. 3 (1970): 80–89.
28. See Mark Washofsky, "Halakhah in Translation: The Chatam Sofer on Prayer in the Vernacular," *CCAR Journal* 51, no. 3 (2004): 127–48, on the Hatam Sofer's innovative argument prohibiting the recitation of the *tefilah* in the vernacular. While the plain meaning of the *halakhic* texts permits the recitation in languages other than Hebrew, Sofer argues—with little or no direct precedent—that those texts do not refer to the formal synagogue *tefilah*.
29. For detail on what follows in this paragraph: Meyer, *Response to Modernity*, 100–42; Friedman, *"Guidance, Not Governance"*, 3–4; Plaut, *Rise of Reform Judaism*, 185–259; Walter Jacob, *American Reform Responsa: Collected Responsa of the Central Conference of American Rabbis 1889-1983* (New York: CCAR Press, 1983), xv–xvi; Solomon B. Freehof, *The Responsa Literature* (Philadelphia: Jewish Publication Society, 1959), 172–73; Peter J. Haas, "Reform Responsa: Developing a Theory of Liberal *Halakhah*," in *Liberal Judaism and Halakhah*, ed. Walter Jacob (Pittsburgh: Rodef Shalom Press, 1988), 43–46; David Ellenson, "A Disputed Precedent: The Prague Organ in 19th Century Central European Legal Literature and Polemics," *Leo Baeck Institute Yearbook* 40 (1995): 251–64.
30. Jacob, *American Reform Responsa*, xv: "The writing of responsa was halted because of the pace of the Reform revolution. The life of our people was changing rapidly, and it became impossible to argue about each detail. When thousands were using streetcars on Shabbat, an essay justifying the practice was hardly necessary."
31. Plaut, *Rise of Reform Judaism*, 261, in his translation from *Torath-Chajim*, a "code" of practice by Rabbi Leopold Stein (Strassburg: J. Schneider, 1877).
32. At Brunswick (1844), Frankfurt-am-Main (1845), and Breslau (1846). On the conferences see Meyer, *Response to Modernity*, 8 and 132ff. Plaut, *Rise of Reform Judaism*, offers English translations of a number of these addresses.
33. While divorce in Jewish law certainly involves the settlement of property issues between the divorcing spouses, the creation and undoing of marital status and the concomitant prohibitions of *arayot* (incest and adultery) are very much matters of *isur veheter*.
34. *Protokolle der Rabbiner-Conferenz, abgehalten zu Philadelphia* (New York: S. Hecht, 1870). See Solomon B. Freehof, *Reform Jewish Practice and Its Rabbinic Background* (Augmented ed.), vol. 1 (New York: KTAV, 1976), 99–110. The primary grounds for the decision was a

"theological" argument, also contestable, that while marriage is a "religious" act deserving of "consecration," divorce, which marks the opposite of consecration, is not to be regarded as a matter for religious jurisdiction. See Mark Washofsky, "Getting Our *Get* Back: On Restoring the Ritual of Divorce in American Reform Judaism," in *The Sacred Encounter: Jewish Perspectives on Sexuality*, ed. Lisa Grushcow (New York: CCAR Press, 2014), 407–16.

35. Friedman, *"Guidance, Not Governance"*, 6.
36. On this history, see ibid., 7–9.
37. Author of *Jewish Theology, Systematically and Historically Considered* (New York: Macmillan Co., 1918).
38. In Jacob, *American Reform Responsa*, 8–20, https://www.ccarnet.org/ccar-responsa/arr-8-21. The responsum was issued in 1928.
39. In Jacob, *American Reform Responsa*, 151–92, https://www.ccarnet.org/ccar-responsa/arr-151-193. The *responsum* was issued in 1930.
40. Freehof served as the rabbi of Congregation Rodef Shalom in Pittsburgh, Pennsylvania, from 1934 to 1966.
41. Friedman, *"Guidance, Not Governance"*, 24.
42. Ibid., 42–43. The Committee consisted of Freehof, Orthodox Rabbi Leo Jung, and Conservative Rabbi Milton Steinberg.
43. Walter Jacob (1976–1990), W. Gunther Plaut (1990–1996), Mark Washofsky (1996–2017), and Joan S. Friedman (2017–present).
44. The practice has been for the Committee to issue its decisions as it were *per curiam*, in the name of the Committee as a whole. Members who disagree with the majority opinion may write individual dissents.
45. On the distinction between the "internal perspective" (that of a lawyer or a judge) and "external perspective" (that of an academic scholar) on law and legal practice, see H. L. A. Hart, *The Concept of Law*, 2nd ed. (Oxford: Clarendon Press, 1994), 89; and Ronald Dworkin, *Law's Empire* (Cambridge, MA: Belknap Press/Harvard University Press, 1986), g14.
46. I.e., those published either by the CCAR Press or the Hebrew Union College Press and available at the Responsa Committee website (https://www.ccarnet.org/rabbinic-voice/reform-responsa).
47. Friedman, *"Guidance, Not Governance"*, 24–41, offers a detailed account of the events described in this paragraph.
48. These included the records of the earlier German rabbinical conferences and synods, rabbis' manuals, and CCAR liturgical publications.
49. Friedman, *"Guidance, Not Governance"*, 33–34.
50. Freehof, *Reform Jewish Practice and Its Rabbinic Background*. The "augmented" edition includes this original volume and a second volume published in 1952.
51. Ibid., 15.
52. Ibid., 7.
53. Friedman, *"Guidance, Not Governance"*, 56–59, offers a critique. We might add that traditional rabbinical authorities would certainly not define *minhag* as determinative of or superior to *halakhah* as Freehof does. Then again, Freehof is writing here from the "external" viewpoint of the historian rather than from the "internal" viewpoint of a practitioner of the traditional *halakhic* system.
54. The most obvious "exceptions" are contained in the book's final chapter, a collection of Freehof *responsa* on "Medical Ethics" that, as far as I am aware, is the earliest "official" Reform publication on that subject.

55. Meyer, *Response to Modernity*, 373.
56. W. Gunther Plaut, *A Shabbat Manual* (New York: CCAR Press, 1972), 7.
57. Ibid.
58. See H. Leonard Poller's forward to Mark Dov Shapiro, *Sha-a-rei Shabbat/Gates of Shabbat: A Guide for Observing Shabbat* (New York: CCAR Press, 1991), vii: "A generation ago Reform Judaism entered into a new age of religious discipline. With the publication of *A Shabbat Manual* by Rabbi W. Gunther Plaut, an authoritative guide for Sabbath observance was welcomed into the lives of Reform Jews."
59. Shimeon J. Maslin, *Shaarei Mitzvah* [Gates of Mitzvah] (New York: CCAR Press, 1979), dealing with life cycle observance; Peter S. Knobel, *Shaarei Mo-eid* [Gates of the Seasons] (New York: CCAR Press, 1983), covering Shabbat and the festivals; and Mark Dov Shapiro, *Sha-a-rei Shabbat* [Gates of Shabbat: A Guide for Observing Shabbat] (New York: CCAR Press, 1991). The latter is a substantial reworking and expansion of Plaut's *Shabbat Manual*, although Knobel, *Shaarei Mo-eid*, 21, already describes his section on Shabbat observance as a "revision" of Plaut's "Catalogue of Shabbat Opportunities."
60. Maslin, *Shaarei Mitzvah*, 5, p. 5.
61. Lawrence A. Hoffman, *Gates of Understanding*, 2 vols. (New York: CCAR/UAHC Press, 1977–1984); Richard Sarason, *Divrei Mishkan T'filah* (New York: CCAR Press, 2017).
62. W. Gunther Plaut, "Historic and Halachic Notes," in *Maag'lei Tzedek* [A Rabbi's Manual] (New York: CCAR Press, 1988); Mark Washofsky, "Historical and Halachic Notes," in *L'chol Z'man V'eit* [For Sacred Moments: The CCAR Life-Cycle Guide] (New York: CCAR Press, 2015). The quotation is from Plaut, *Shabbat Manual*, 220.
63. Mark Washofsky, *Jewish Living: A Guide to Contemporary Reform Practice*, rev. ed. (New York: URJ Press/Behrman House, 2010).
64. E.g., Washofsky, *Jewish Living*, 6–15 ("*Kippah, Tallit, T'fillin*"), 131 ("Yom HaAtzma-ut"), 132–39 ("Jewish Status and 'Patrilineal Descent'"), and 291–316 ("Judaism and Society").
65. See Borowitz, *Renewing the Covenant*.
66. See Michael T. Ghiselin, *Metaphysics and the Origin of Species* (Albany: State University of New York Press, 1997); and E. D. Hirsch, Jr., "Some Aims of Criticism," in *What Is Literature?*, ed. Paul Hernadi (Bloomington: Indiana University Press, 1978), 24–34.
67. An example: to the extent that one chooses a narrower rather than a wider definition for the term "literature"—say, restricting it to imaginative or belletristic writing—one can exclude from its circumference any number of works that others would plausibly recognize as "literary." See Hirsch, "Some Aims of Criticism": the "aesthetic" definition, which restricts the label "literature" to the imaginative genres, is a "stipulative" one, an attempt to determine how a word *ought* to be used, as opposed to a "descriptive definition" that focuses upon the ways in which the term is actually used by knowledgeable and competent persons.
68. In the same way that a "persuasive" precedent, though not "binding," is still a precedent; see Richard Bronaugh, "Persuasive Precedent," in *Precedent in Law*, ed. Laurence Goldstein (Oxford: Clarendon Press, 1987), 217–47. On "persuasive" precedent as opposed to "binding" precedent in Jewish law, see Zerah Warhaftig, "Precedent in Jewish Law," *Shenaton Hamishpat Ha'ivri* 6–7 (1979–1980): 105–32 [Hebrew], and Menachem Elon, *Jewish Law: History, Sources, and Principles*, trans. Bernard Auerbach (Philadelphia: Jewish Publication Society, 1994), 1729–30.
69. Compare James Boyd White, *Heracles' Bow: Essays on the Rhetoric and the Poetics of the Law* (Madison: University of Wisconsin Press, 1985), x–xi, who describes his sense of "law"

as "a social and cultural activity, something we do with our minds, with language, and with each other. This is a way of looking at the law, not as a set of rules or institutions or structures . . . but as a kind rhetorical and literary activity. . . . By (rhetorical) I mean not merely the art of persuasion—of making the weaker case the stronger, as the Sophists were said to do—but that art by which culture and community and character are constituted and transformed."

70. Solomon B. Freehof, *Modern Reform Responsa* (Cincinnati, OH: Hebrew Union College Press, 1971), 14–17, https://www.ccarnet.org/ccar-responsa/mrr-14-17.
71. On the creation of the "late" Friday evening service, an initiative led by Rabbi Isaac Mayer Wise in response to agitation to move the main worship service of the week to Sunday morning, see Meyer, *Response to Modernity*, 290–92. The practice of reading Torah on Friday night is noted in the prayerbooks published by the CCAR
72. The responsum is *Resp. Meshiv Davar* 1:16.
73. *Sifre* to Deuteronomy 13:1; b. Rosh Hashanah 28b.
74. Freehof's remark "if it really is unauthorized" suggest that Berlin's proof is a weak one. And Berlin himself concedes that the Babylonian Talmud, b.B'rakhot 21a, does not require a *berakhah* any and every time the Torah is read. He could legitimately have ruled according to the Bavli, as the more authoritative source, over the Yerushalmi, in which case the concern over *berakhah l'vatalah* disappears. Instead, he follows the Yerushalmi out of stringency. That's his choice, but it *is* a choice, and another *posek* might choose differently.
75. In Washofsky, *Reform Responsa for the Twenty-First Century*, 2:59–70; https://www.ccarnet.org/ccar-responsa/nyp-no-5760-3.
76. That is, it cannot be used to fulfill the *mitzvah* of public Torah reading (*keri'at hatorah berabim*).
77. In its note #2 the responsum points to the declaration to this effect in Knobel, *Shaarei Moeid*, 103: "It is a *mitzvah* to remember the six million Jews who were murdered in the *Sho-ah* by attending special memorial services." On the meaning of *mitzvah* in a Reform context "not as obligatory rules but as warm recommendations"; see Maslin, *Shaarei Mitzvah*, p. 5. See also this chapter's discussion of Plaut's *A Shabbat Manual* and the other guidebooks to Reform observance published during the 1980s and 1990s.
78. *Mishneh Torah, Hilkhot Talmud Torah* 10:1.
79. The responsum exists in all the editions of *Rambam*'s responsa: *Resp. P'er Hador*, 9; *Kovetz T'shuvot HaRambam*, no. 15; *T'shuvot HaRambam*, ed. A Freiman (Jerusalem: M'kitzei Nirdamim, 1934), no. 43; and *T'shuvot HaRambam*, ed. Y. Blau, vol. 2 (Jerusalem: M'kitzei Nirdamim, 1960), no. 294.
80. Indeed, on the basis of that responsum the tradition regards the reading from a *pasul* scroll acceptable *b'di`avad;* see *Shulchan Arukh* YD 279:2 and in *Beit Yosef ad loc.*
81. The term, the responsum notes, is drawn from Freehof, *Reform Responsa*, 23.
82. See Chaim Perelman and Lucie Olbrechts-Tyteca, *The New Rhetoric: A Treatise on Argumentation* (Notre Dame, IN: Notre Dame University Press, 1969), 19: "Argumentation aims at securing the adherence of those to whom it is addressed, it is, in its entirety, relative to the audience to be influenced."
83. Washofsky, *Jewish Living*, xxvii.
84. I.e., one's obligation toward the other in the category of "ethical *mitzvot*" (*mitzvot shebein adam lechavero*) will be the same whether the other is a Jew or a non-Jew. In matters of ritual (*mitzvot shebein adam lamakom*), however, the distinction between Jews and non-Jews retains its relevance.

85. CCAR responsum 5766.2, "When a Parent Requests Cremation," in Washofsky, *Reform Responsa for the Twenty-First Century*, 2:193–207, https://www.ccarnet.org/ccar-responsa/rr21-no-5766-2.
86. CCAR responsum 5774.4, "Same-Sex Marriage as *Kiddushin*," https://www.ccarnet.org/ccar-responsa/same-sex-marriage-kiddushin.
87. See the responsum "Circumcision for an Eight-Year-Old Convert," in Washofsky, *Reform Responsa for the Twenty-First Century*, 1:99–120, https://www.ccarnet.org/ccar-responsa/rr21-no-5756-13, which sharply criticizes the reasoning behind a resolution of the CCAR but does not suggest that the resolution is null and void.
88. "Non-Jewish Burial in a Jewish Cemetery," Jacob, *American Reform Responsa*, 335–41, https://www.ccarnet.org/ccar-responsa/arr-335-341.
89. CCAR Responsum no. 5754.14, in W. Gunther Plaut and Mark Washofsky, eds., *Teshuvot for the Nineties* (New York: CCAR Press, 1997), 337–64, https://www.ccarnet.org/ccar-responsa/tfn-no-5754-14-337-364.
90. *Tur*, *Beit Yosef*, and *Shulchan Arukh Yoreh De'ah* 336:1.
91. See Mark Washofsky, "A Time to Heal and a Time to Cease from Healing: Reform Halakhah on End-Stage Medical Care," in *U-vacharta Ba-chayim*, ed. David Birnbaum and Martin S. Cohen (New York: New Paradigm Matrix, 2018), 215–28, http://www.mesorahmatrix.com/u-vacharta.
92. Washofsky, *Reform Responsa for the Twenty-First Century*, xxii–xxiii.

CHAPTER 21

THE IMPACT OF ZIONISM ON JEWISH LAW

ARYE EDREI

INTRODUCTION: *HALAKHIC* CHALLENGES INHERENT IN THE ZIONIST ENTERPRISE

WITH the establishment of the State of Israel in the first half of the twentieth century, the nature of Jewish collective life was transformed from diasporic communal life to a sovereign state. Assuming that such radical change demands a rethinking of many areas of the law, we will examine the discourse and various aspects of Jewish legal culture in response to the new reality.

Jewish law perceives itself as a comprehensive, all-encompassing normative system that directs its recipients as to how to conduct their lives in every time, place, and realm. Nevertheless, aspects of law that were not relevant to diasporic Jewish life until the ingathering of Jews in the Land of Israel were not discussed in the classic Jewish legal literature. Other areas of law have consisted of theoretical rather than practical discussion for over fifteen hundred years and have not benefited from continuity of legal interpretation and practice. Finally, despite having been the subject of *halakhic* analysis over the ages, the new demographic reality has demanded change and rethinking of other aspects of *halakha* and life.

Prior to the emergence of the State of Israel, Jewish life in the nineteenth century underwent further upheavals that are relevant to our topic. First, Jews attained citizenship in several European countries, leading to the abrogation of communal autonomy. The result was that for the first time in its history, Jewish law was focused exclusively on the personal sphere and ritual life, while the public arena, which had always been the center of *halakhic* interest, was removed from its authority. This shift was also considerably impacted by Christian liberal thought, which, following the Enlightenment, secularization, and the European religious wars, unseated religion from the public sphere and raised obstacles to returning Jewish law to the public realm. Second, deep divisions about the essential nature of Jewish law split the Jewish community itself. On the one hand, Reform Judaism called for a thorough overhaul of Jewish law and a reassessment of its centrality in the Jewish experience; on the other, Orthodoxy withdrew inward, resisted any change, and opposed cooperation with those who had abandoned Jewish law.

These rifts profoundly influenced the attitude to Zionism and the *halakhic* discussion regarding the State of Israel. It also led to a split within Orthodoxy between supporters and opponents of the new Zionist movement. Many in the latter camp objected to cooperating with a secular movement, advocating that Orthodoxy should maintain an unbending separatist stance. In addition, they viewed the Zionist Idea as a sacrilegious rebellion against the messianic idea and thus bitterly opposed taking human initiative that would change the standing of the Jews as an exilic people. They refused to conceive of a non-utopian Jewish state and regarded Israel as a continuation of the exile, or, at best, a Jewish community in the holy land.

The religious-Zionist rabbis discussed below all identified with the Zionist idea and the establishment of the State of Israel. They regarded the State of Israel as a meaningful and primary expression of Jewish nationalism and contemporary Judaism, which was afforded religious import. This found expression, inter alia, in imparting some aspect of religious meaning to the State's national holidays and symbols, advocating army service, and ideologically supporting the establishment of *yeshivot* (Talmudic academies) that combined Torah study and military service. From a philosophical perspective, the substantive innovation of religious Zionism was to separate between the utopian and concrete, and to envision a Jewish state that is not the eschatological redemptive state discussed in medieval Jewish literature, but that nevertheless possesses religious significance.[1]

Since the State of Israel was deemed meaningful, religious Zionism aimed to foster its Jewish identity and retain its connection to the world of Jewish values. Above all, religious-Zionist ambition was to both reshape *halakha* while maintaining the state and its institutions in accordance with *halakhic* mandates. They advocated for working together with secular Zionists, and at the same time felt obligated to buttress and enhance the state's religious significance and identity. While modern Jewish nationalism aimed to replace religion with political nationalism as the organizing principle of the Jewish collective identity, its religious counterpart aspired to fuse religion and nationalism, arguing that unification between religion and nationalism characterized Jewish thought from its inception. Most religious Zionists rejected the idea of limiting religion to the private sphere and aspired for the arena of politics and "building the land" to be guided by *halakhic* vision and principles. This desire patently clashed with the mainstream Zionist understanding that the State is a secular entity.

It was inconceivable to the religious Zionist rabbis that *halakha*, which delves into every stratum of life, would retreat on an issue as central as public life. But they also realized that *halakha* would have to undergo significant updates in order for it to be relevant in the new reality. They felt obligated to articulate a normative system that could regulate the state's existence. The main concern of this article is not the debate within Zionism or the state about the status of religion and *halakha*, but on the internal discourse of religious Zionist rabbis on the question of how *halakha* can be relevant and meaningful, a discourse that in many cases is innovative and revolutionary. A few individual rabbis—those that will be at the center of our discussion—produced an impressive literary corpus on *halakha* and state.[2] These leading religious Zionist rabbis were a minority in the broader rabbinic milieu. While on the whole, the political and social Zionist revolution did not trigger a matching *halakhic* upheaval, after more than seventy years, religious Zionist *halakhic* rulings have been gradually formulated and eventually accepted and entrenched.

While the *halakhic* proposals discussed below did not attain full consensus, they emerge from influential decisors. They all identified with the Jewish state and sought to bridge between *halakhic* axioms and a sovereign democracy. The primary decisors we will discuss are R. Abraham Isaac Kook (1865–1935), R. Isaac Herzog (1888–1959), R. Ben-Zion Meir Uziel (1880–1954), R. Shaul Israeli (1909–1995), and R. Shlomo Goren (1917–1994), as well as additional rabbis mentioned in the course of the discussion. This is not an exhaustive synopsis, but we rather offer a broad overview which indicates the fundamental questions and prime innovations developed by these authorities.

In our discussion, we will focus on two significant changes in Jewish existence tied to the establishment of the State of Israel—the nature of the Jewish collective and Jewish sovereignty.

The second section that follows this introduction focuses on the issue of Jewish identity. Zionists argued that the organizing principle of the new Jewish collective was no longer religious commitment, as it was in the past, but rather national identity. The internalization of this fact within *halakhic* thought was one of the most significant and important revolutions in the *halakhic* discourse in the twentieth century.

The third and fourth sections focus on the implications of the new Jewish sovereignty on the *halakhic* discourse. The third section deals with the transition from being a minority community in the Diaspora to becoming a majority society in a Jewish sovereign state. Responsibility for the entire population was an unprecedented phenomenon in the history of *halakha*, and required a fundamental change in *halakhic* thought. The fourth section deals with the state itself, including its structure and governing institutions. It attempts to uncover the *halakhic* discourse on how to bridge between the two primary foundations of the Jewish state—the Jewish tradition and liberal democracy.

The fifth and final section takes an integrated look at these two foci—Jewish identity and sovereignty—by analyzing one of the deepest and fascinating *halakhic* discussions relating to the Jewish state, the relationship between Jewish law and the state law. Particularistic Jewish law was one of the main components of Jewish identity throughout the long period of exile. What then is its contemporary status when the state judiciary and legislation body are primary symbols of any sovereign state, including the Jewish state? Prominent personalities in the world of *halakha* and the world of Israeli law held that a controlled internalization of Jewish law into Israeli law would not affect the sovereignty of the state because it would come from a sovereign decision of the state.

On the other hand, it would add to the state law a significant identity dimension that could serve as the bridge between the two foci of the Jewish state. They believed that the law could turn the state into a catalyst for Jewish cultural development and progress by integrating democratic values in the *halakha*, and conversely integrating Jewish values in Israeli law.

Jewish Identity in an Era of Nationalism: New Parameters

The Covenant of Fate and the Covenant of Destiny: The Status of the Secular Jew

Classical *halakha* understood the acceptance of the burden of the *mitzvot* as a boundary marker, and those who refused to abide were labeled as "deviant." The *halakhic* discourse, therefore, has long examined the status of "transgressors"—those who do not observe the commandments—in the Jewish collective. Can they participate in various rituals? Is it obligatory to aid them, or perhaps, on the contrary, is one required to punish them?

In the nineteenth century, many Jews abandoned the traditional halakhic lifestyle, and so it was unclear whether a *halakhic* perspective defining the majority as "deviant" remained relevant. R. Jacob Ettlinger (1798–1871) adopted a moderate view and recruited the Talmudic category of *tinok shenishbah* (a Jewish child or minor who was taken captive, and therefore ignorant and not liable), to describe the contemporary transgressor. At the other end of the scale was the "founding father of Orthodoxy," the *Hatam Sofer* (R. Moses Sofer, 1762–1839), who viewed the Sabbath desecrator "as if his name has been expunged from Israel, until he returns to the Lord and He will have mercy on him."[3] R. Samson Raphael Hirsch of Frankfurt (1808–88) went as far as insisting that the Orthodox community formally split from the Reform community. While all agreed that Talmudic laws regarding sinners could no longer apply as they are, they disagreed about whether the community could include those who left faithful observance.

This question took a fascinating turn in the context of Jewish nationalism. The Zionist national aspirations and the efforts to realize them, emphasized the consciousness of the secular Zionists as belonging to the Jewish community and dedicating their lives to its future. To some of the Orthodox rabbis, the ideology of orthodox separatism now seemed impossible.

Advocates of cooperation had to set forth a *halakhic* theory to justify cooperation with the Zionists while setting its scope and limits. The dominant approach proposed a priori cooperation in the practical sphere of life, while erecting distinct walls in the realm of religious lifestyle and belief. This view was held by R. Samuel Mohilewer (1824–98), one of the leaders of the Hibbat Zion movement, and R. Isaac Jacob Reines (1839–1915), the founder of the Mizrachi movement. Following the establishment of the State, R. Joseph Soloveitchik (1903–93), the leader of American modern Orthodoxy theologized and conceptualized this position by distinguishing between the "covenant of fate" and the "covenant of destiny."[4] This allowed acknowledgment of an authentic Jewish identity based on communal and national affiliation, solidarity, and responsibility. In this approach we find, for the first time in Jewish thought, a religious-philosophical position that accepts a definition of Jewish identity in purely national terms, rather than based on fidelity to an observant lifestyle.

This definition promoted an ideology that saw cooperation with the secular national movement as a positive Jewish value. It stands in contrast even to R. Ettlinger's moderate stance in the nineteenth century, which did not envision imparting Jewish significance to non-*halakhic*—and certainly not to anti-*halakhic*—ideas, groups, or ideologies. For Ettlinger, secular Jews were at best tolerated, but there was no place for Jewish values or identity divorced from religion and *halakha*. In contrast, religious Zionist rabbis put forth a model that considered religious and secular Jews as working together to promote a Jewish enterprise.

Despite the dual-track model, early religious Zionist decisors already understood that maintaining the boundaries between the two layers of identity was difficult. The consciousness of the covenant and partnership of fate burst into *halakhic* reasoning and required *halakhic* innovations. I will cite one example from deliberations by the Chief Rabbis—Herzog and Uziel—during the transition from the British Mandate to the state.

The rabbis understood well that Talmudic law that disqualifies the testimony of transgressors could not be applied in a democratic country. In addition, religious Zionist rabbis considered it inappropriate for the law to apply because it would contradict the spirit of social cooperation that they advocated. Their resolution, issued on the eve of the establishment of the state, suggested an innovative approach to allow such testimony.

The Talmud distinguishes between a "defiant" sinner, who disavows *halakhic* commitment, and one who does so by giving in to his urges and desires. While the Talmudic Sages are unanimous in invalidating the latter's testimony, they differ regarding the defiant sinner. The seemingly counterintuitive opinion was that the "defiant" sinner is fit to testify, while the one who sins "to satisfy his appetite" is not. The Talmud explains that the concern that one would give false testimony is greater in the case of a person who surrenders to his desires. Nevertheless, the conclusion of the Talmudic discussion was that the act of sinning is the invalidating factor, and not the concern of giving false testimony. Therefore the law should be to follow the opinion that disqualified every sinner.

Despite the Talmud's conclusion, Chief Rabbis Herzog and Uziel suggested to adhere to the rejected opinion. Unlike in the past, in modern secular reality, "secularity" does not attest to a lack of morals, wrote the Chief Rabbis. In their mind's eye, they saw the nonobservant socialist pioneer who struggled for the establishment of the state as member of the Jewish community, and they were not prepared to declare him immoral.[5] Underlying this approach was the desire to conceptually organize the Jews in the Land of Israel as a community of inner Jewish meaning that could be defined as such with *halakhic* tools and concepts.

R. Yehuda Amital (1924–2009), a prominent religious Zionist rabbi in the second half of the twentieth century, took a sober look at the Jewish community in Israel and argued that the Talmud's stance regarding transgressors does not currently pertain. The Torah could not demand a rigid attitude toward the majority of the people, especially since they are honest and moral, and loyal to the Jewish people and the Land of Israel. Deeply embedded in his thought is the profound religious sentiment regarding the essence and destiny of the State of Israel as a manifestation of the sanctification of the Name of God. Israeli society is the current Jewish collective. Since a majority of its Jewish citizens are not observant, ritual observance cannot be the defining characteristic of the collective, such that the majority would be characterized as the excluded "other."[6]

R. Kook and the Status of the Secular Jew: Shemittah (Sabbatical Year) as a Test Case

R. Abraham Isaac Kook—one of the leading thinkers and decisors of the twentieth century—advocated from a philosophical and theological perspective that all Jewish settlers should be seen as one community. He came to the Land of Israel in 1904, out of identification with the Zionist idea, and was appointed rabbi of Jaffa and the new settlements. R. Ettlinger's dualistic worldview that distinguishes between different circles of identity, the religious and the national, essentially contradicted R. Kook's worldview. The fact that religion and nationalism are represented by different social groups is destructive. According to R. Kook, nationality and religion are two complementary forces, and *Knesset Israel* [the collective of Israel] is not whole without each. Each of these group possesses a part of the truth. Each must acknowledge this partiality and understand that perfection will be attained only through the unity of these complementary forces. R. Kook believed that the rebellion of the secular nationalists embodied important positive values that had been abandoned by Orthodoxy and should be reclaimed.[7]

This philosophical and theological position clearly influenced Rabbi Kook's *halakhic* decisions that laid the foundations for Zionist *halakhah*. In 1910, R. Kook published his book *Sabbat ha-Aretz* (lit. the Sabbath of the Land) that provided a legal and philosophical-ideological basis for a sweeping *halakhic* approach that permitted working the fields during *shemittah* (the Sabbatical year, as explained below). This laid the cornerstone for a "Zionist *halakhah*" that deviated from principles of Orthodox legal decision-making developed in nineteenth-century Europe.

The biblical law of *shemittah* requires that the land lie fallow in the seventh year. Certain agricultural labors are forbidden by Torah law, and others by rabbinical law; likewise, fruits are declared ownerless on behalf of the poor. Because these agricultural laws are applicable only within the bounds of the Land of Israel, they had not been practiced for many centuries when Jewish agriculture was absent from the land. The return to an "abandoned" law is always a complicated matter, lacking a tradition of the way in which it is to be observed and a continuity of ongoing interpretation.

Agriculture was the almost exclusive basis for sustaining the new settlements in the Land of Israel in that era, and its abandonment for a year was liable to threaten its very existence. We know that in the distant past, during the Second Temple period and following centuries, the observance of this law posed an extremely daunting challenge. There are extant testimonies to tax exemption during the Sabbatical year, but as relations between the Jews and the Romans deteriorated, this exemption was canceled, and in the second century CE the rabbis grappled with the question of whether and how to be lenient regarding the *shemittah* laws. Nonetheless, the Sabbatical year was preserved in the collective Jewish memory as a vision for the messianic era when a person could rest from his toil and engage in spiritual matters, leave aside his property, and let the poor partake of the fruits. However, this vision could not be put into practice currently because it would inevitably lead to the collapse of the Jewish settlements in the Land of Israel.

At the beginning of the First Aliyah, a group of Lithuanian rabbis, among them Rabbi Isaac Elhanan Spector, the Rabbi of Kaunas—considered one of the greatest decisors of the generation and who supported Jewish settlement activity—instituted a leniency to work the land under certain restrictions. The leniency was based on the sale of the agricultural lands to a non-Jew for the duration of the *shemittah* year ("the permit of sale") This type of legal maneuver—a fictitious sale for a limited time designed to circumvent observance—had already been invented in other contexts, such as the sale of leavened matter to a non-Jew for Passover. While the practical significance of such permission is the abrogation of the commandment, its ideological import is a declaration of loyalty to the *halakha*. During the Second Aliyah period, when R. Kook was in the Land of Israel, the controversy surrounding this permit was rekindled in full force. R. Kook's support for the permissive sale also relied on ideological arguments concerning the essential nature of the new *Yishuv* (Jewish settlement), despite the fact that most of the settlers were not observant and for whom the Sabbatical year held no significance. For these settlers, agriculture and labor were a principled ideal aimed at restoring a "normal," "productive" Jewish existence coupled with tilling the soil of the Land of Israel. R. Kook's support for the permit of sale aroused a controversy of rare intensity in the *halakhic* community. It was universally understood that not only *shemittah* was at stake as R. Kook's ruling represented the cornerstone of a new *halakhic* approach toward the Zionist settlement in the Land of Israel. We will devote a short discussion to appreciate the importance of the permit of sale and its foundational role in fashioning Zionist *halakha*.

R. Jacob Wilovsky, the rabbi of Safed and the most vocal opponent of R. Kook and the permit of sale, proposed that the two travel to Europe to raise funds so that the settlers could let their fields lie fallow. In response, R. Kook noted the limitations of this sort of aid:

> We might be able to find succor for those owning fields and vegetable gardens, and for those with olives, and for a few among the owners of vineyards and orchards,

> those for whom the fear of the Lord is strong in their hearts and who are desirous of observing the seventh year devotedly, but for the public as a whole, this is not possible at present.[8]

The *halakha* must provide a feasible solution for the entire community. R. Kook's refusal to see the observant—"whom the fear of the Lord is strong in their hearts"—as his target community as a legal decisor, marks a significant divergence from the principles of nineteenth century Orthodoxy. R. Kook viewed all Jews who considered themselves part of the Jewish people and who came to build its land and future, as the addressees of his ruling. Rabbi Kook's position was that *halakha* that is incapable of directing the entire Jewish community, regardless of whether they consider themselves bound to it, is flawed as a normative system. Accordingly, he forcefully opposed solutions which were good for a minority (i.e., the observant)—such as fundraising—as had been proposed by R. Wilovsky, and afterward by the *Hazon Ish* (R. Abraham Isaiah Karelitz), the leader of ultra-Orthodoxy in Israel. For this reason, R. Kook raised the question of exports and explained the broader need to take into account the fear of losing international markets during the *shemittah* year. For him, any solution that the entire Jewish community could not follow was not acceptable.

As we have seen, Orthodoxy was already split regarding its attitude to the Zionist idea. The Sabbatical year polemic was a turning point in the *halakhic* world: no longer was there only a rift on the ideological question; now there was also a division between two fundamental *halakhic* conceptions. R. Kook in effect laid the groundwork for a school of religious Zionist rulings. He argued that the new reality required changes in the *halakha*, and distinguished his proposals from the changes set forth by the Reform movement in the preceding century, which he categorically rejected. His most important innovation was the very redefinition of the intended community, asserting that the secular settlers are part of the community to whom the *halakhic* rulings are addressed, regardless of whether or not they actually observe the *halakha*. Jewish law in the Zionist era must be cognizant of the society as a whole, and only *halakhic* rulings capable of addressing the entire society are valid.

"Who Is a Jew?": Israel as the New Jewish Collective

A tempestuous halakhic controversy on the question of "Who is a Jew"—a status that entitles one to immigrate to Israel by virtue of the Law of Return—has accompanied Israel throughout its existence. What should the requirements for joining the Jewish people be in a country that defines itself as a secular Jewish nation-state? Will it subscribe to halakhic requirements or to new ones that suit its conception of the novel secular national and cultural Israeli identity? After a number of struggles (a review of which would exceed the purview of the current article), the legislature added to "the Law of Return" a definition that adopted categories close to the *halakhic* definition. It established that the right of "return" is granted to a person who "was born to a Jewish mother or has converted to Judaism." The law rejected including those who self- defined as Jews which was preferred by liberal thinkers and by the Supreme Court prior to the amendment of the law. However, the question as to what qualifies as conversion, and who is authorized to perform it, was left undecided, and a secondary debate, no less poignant, ensued. The problem became acute after the large waves of immigration from the USSR came to Israel in the 1970s and the 1990s. The legislature also added to the Law of Return the right of return to a **non-Jew** who is "a child and grandchild of a Jew, the spouse of a Jew, the spouse of a child of a Jew, and the spouse of a grandchild of a Jew." The immigration waves included many who were not Jews, but were family members or descendants of Jews, and who became Israeli citizens by force of the Law of Return, a reality that reignited the conversion controversy.

The rabbinic world was left to confront the question: given the new realities of Israeli sovereignty and the complexities of modern Jewish identity, should a new approach to conversion be developed? The concepts we discussed above were at the center of the halachic discussion.

The question of conversion had already erupted in Europe in the nineteenth century, with growing secularization, the collapse of the walls separating the Jewish community and its surroundings, and especially with the acceptance of civil marriage. The situation in which the Jewish spouse of a non-Jew sought to convert the spouse and join the Jewish community was contentious. The dilemma facing the rabbis of the time is that because the lifestyle of these potential converts had not essentially changed, they would be precluded from traditional conversion which is premised on joining the Jewish community through the full acceptance of religious practices. On the other hand, the very request to convert indicates that the couple wishes to belong to the community and adopt some sort of Jewish identity. The real question that had to be decided was not only the acceptance of the convert, but whether to accept or reject the parts of his family that were born Jewish; rejection of the convert patently meant the rejection of his Jewish family, effectively expelling these born Jews from the community.

Some decisors maintained that those on the borderline were not to be rejected. Instead, the situation required a degree of mutual responsibility toward the potential convert and their family, leading to greater leniency in the demands of conversion. This was a sort of "price" that the decisor was willing to pay for keeping the convert's Jewish spouse and children within the community. Although they did not say so outright, these decisors understood that a policy of inclusion meant the recognition of a communal Jewish identity that was not based on fully joining a *halakhically* observant community. In contrast, other decisors strenuously opposed this view, and were willing to suffer the loss of many members of the community. They steadfastly maintained that there can be no Jewish identity other than the religious identity of observance.

This controversy came to the fore once again in Israel in the 1970s, and gained greater force in the 1990s. The debate centered on the degree to which nationality could serve as a criterion of Jewish identity. The legal considerations of the decisors were divided along similar lines to those of the nineteenth century. It was fairly evident that the convert would not embrace a full religious lifestyle, but it was also clear that he deemed himself to be part of the Jewish community in Israel. The fact that the dispute was conducted within the State of Israel heavily influenced the discussion. One argument was that anyone who immigrated to Israel is to be viewed as seeking to bond his fate with the Jewish people. Another proposition was the responsibility of the decisor to preserve Israel as a Jewish community, and to prevent the mixed marriages that would take place in the country if conversion were not an option. Both facets of the covenant of fate were clearly at work here: the conversion candidate demonstrated his being a participant in the covenant, and the decisor was responsible for the fate of the community. Both considerations were linked to the recognition of Israel as a Jewish community and the consequences of this reality for Jewish identity. The deep meaning of the controversy that has been ongoing in Israel for three decades is whether conversion to the covenant of fate is to be recognized.[9]

Soon after the establishment of the state, R. Herzog suggested that the choice of a mixed couple to immigrate to Israel should be regarded as proof that their intent was "for the sake of heaven," using the Talmudic term for legitimate conversion: "For their intent is clearly to adhere to the Jewish people, in its land."[10] This dramatic idea, that immigration to Israel, becoming a citizen there, and requesting to join the Jewish people meets the criteria of Jewish identity, was reinforced by the succeeding Chief Rabbis. The question arose during the immigration wave of the 1970s, when the second Ashkenazic Chief Rabbi, Isser Yehuda Unterman (1886–1976), expressed explicit support for leniency in the conversion of the new immigrants from the Soviet Union. He stated that when he served as a rabbi in England, he ruled stringently, but in Israel, "those who came to the Land of Israel, removed themselves from their entire former surroundings, are known in all their documents as Jews, and clearly have no intent to continue adhering to any foreign belief."[11] Rabbi Unterman obscures the difference between the religious and the national identities and views national affiliation in religious terms. Immigration and identification as a Jew within the setting of the State of Israel should be seen as cleaving to the Jewish people and an abandonment of any other faith. R. Unterman held that the covenant of fate between all the Jewish inhabitants imposes on the decisor the responsibility of imparting religious significance to this covenant and to those who wish to join it.

In a similar vein, the third Chief Rabbi, R. Shlomo Goren (1918–1994), asserted that the essence of conversion is joining the Jewish people, while the obligation to observe the commandments is a consequence of this joining:

> It is written explicitly regarding Ruth: "Your people shall be my people, and your God my God" (Ruth 1:16). In order to convert, one must also join the Jewish people, and not only the God of Israel [. . .] the obligation of the commandments of each Jew is a consequence of his affiliation to the Jewish people.[12]

Leading rabbis made even more explicit statements in the 1990s by recognizing a national Jewish identity. R. Haim Amsalem, a leading advocate for converting the immigrants in Israel, believes that it is obligatory to be lenient in a conversion of any descendant of a Jew. Regarding IDF soldiers who wish to convert, he stated:

> He [the convert] sees his self-sacrifice, identification, and willingness to sacrifice himself for the Jewish people, as the main element of Judaism. In our time this might be a sufficient reason to accept him.[13]

The covenant of fate is unequivocally suggested here as a criterion of identity and affiliation.

This opinion is also implicitly held by a considerable number of leading Zionist rabbis who encourage leniency in the conversion of immigrants. Many of them speak of the need to prevent marriages between Jews and non-Jews in Israel. Their responsibility to Israeli society impels them to aid it in remaining a Jewish society and averting assimilation. The covenant of fate obliges them to provide secular Israeli society with a *halakhic* conversion system and to extend to them the greatest possible degree of leniency.

This notion of responsibility to Israeli society and to the State of Israel recurs in the writings of many of these rabbis. Thus, for instance, R. Yisrael Rosen, who headed the project to establish a special network of conversion courts to convert the members of the families of immigrants from the Soviet Union, writes:

> I lovingly and willingly accept the accusation [. . .] of national motives. I am of the opinion that these aspects have a broad legitimacy in the halakhah, and certainly on pan-Israeli social issues.[14]

Some rabbis emphasize the prevention of intermarriages, and others, their responsibility to the community for the preservation of the State of Israel as a Jewish state. Consistent with their conflicting ideological commitments, the ultra-Orthodox decisors forcefully oppose this manner of *halakhic* ruling and all that it implies.

The change in the focal points of Jewish identity, with secularization, on the one hand, and the establishment of a Jewish nation-state on the other, highlighted the fundamental question of the essential nature of conversion. For many of the Zionist decisors, the covenant of fate demanded an inclusive and expansive approach to converts. The notion that immigration and the acquisition of Israeli citizenship could be seen as a significant fact in the conversion process was revolutionary. While these decisors were not prepared to formally waive the demand for acceptance of the "yoke" of the Jewish religion's commandments, they plainly understood that the convert's acceptance of the commandments functioned on the normative and declarative level, rather than in the practical realm.

In recent years, the Chief Rabbis have come to identify less with the ideas of religious Zionism, and are less sympathetic to the lenient approach to conversion. As a result, prominent rabbis in religious Zionism have established private conversion courts that are more inclusive, and, as discussed above, that consider the needs of society as a whole. Their conversions have been recognized by the Israeli courts.

Sovereignty and Majority: The Responsibility of Jewish Law for the Entire Populace

From Community to State: Are the Diaspora Laws Valid?

The typical condition of a Jewish community as a minority created a pattern of *halakhic* Jewish life in which reliance on non-Jews was an important component in enabling Jewish life to function within a *halakhic* framework. The paradigmatic example is reliance on a non-Jew known as the "Sabbath non-Jew," who was available to perform certain actions on behalf of Jews who were restricted from laboring on Shabbat. This idea was extended to other realms, such as modern medicine, and reliance greatly intensified in the wake of the industrial and technological revolutions.

Halakha, as formulated at the end of the nineteenth century, could not guide Jews how to manage their home or business on the Sabbath without the aid of a non-Jew. In the Zionist rural settlements, this question arose in the early 1920s concerning the milking of cows. When Jews living in the Diaspora owned livestock, it was understood that a non-Jew would do the milking on the Sabbath. Some rabbis, R. Kook prominently among them, believed that unlike the case of the sabbatical year, which had no precedent, there was no reason why the established practice of engaging a non-Jew could not continue in the Land of Israel, with the native Arabs performing the actions forbidden to Jews, such as milking. Many fundamentally opposed this approach claiming that the forced *halakhic* reliance on a non-Jew was part of the ills of the Diaspora. For this group, part of the Zionist revolution included promoting Jewish self- sufficiency in work and productivity.

After the establishment of the state and the demographic shift in which the Jews had become the decisive majority, it became clear that a reliance on non-Jews could not offer a comprehensive solution. Being responsible only for a minority group, Jewish law in the Diaspora could afford to be a normative system relevant only to a small minority that adopted it, while an entire society could not live by it. Thus, for example, a decisor in the Diaspora could ignore questions related to generating electricity or deploying the police on the Sabbath. He could forbid medical school autopsies, knowing that the school would continue to function regardless of the *halakhic* position. In a Jewish-majority society, however, it was vital to develop *halakhic* answers for the maintenance of essential services.

Many Zionist rabbis viewed it as their cardinal *halakhic* responsibility to set forth a *halakhic* corpus by which a state with all its institutions could exist. These writings indicate that this domain required creative ways of thinking, different from what had been accepted in diasporic *halakha*. In this context, a well-known religious Zionist thinker, Yeshayahu Leibowitz, famously called upon the rabbinical establishment to enact a new *halakha*. He argued that ignoring the problem meant acknowledgment of the irrelevance of the *halakha* in the new Jewish reality, and a de facto recognition of the secular Jew as the new "non-Jew." Non-Zionist rabbis firmly rejected this call. Even some Zionist decisors hesitated, maintaining that groundbreaking innovations were appropriate only where their acceptance was probable. Since the state would not heed the directives of the *halakha* in any event, such innovations were not to be formulated.

We turn our attention to two examples of innovative rulings stressing the importance of responsibility for an entire society.

Autopsies and the Health System

Autopsies conducted for medical research and teaching challenged European Jewry from the end of the nineteenth century onward. Based on various *halakhic* values relating to the obligation of respect for the dead, most rabbis categorically refused to allow them. Yet, since the value of the saving of life unquestionably overrides those values, the question revolves around the degree of immediate linkage between this normally forbidden activity—autopsies—and the possibility of saving lives as a result in the future. At the end of the eighteenth century, R. Ezekiel Landau (1713–93), the Rabbi of Prague and the author of the *responsa Noda be-Yehudah*, permitted an autopsy only when the "saving of life" could be precisely defined, namely, it would aid in curing another specific patient suffering from the same disease as the deceased. R. Landau's position requiring an "immediate" causal connection between the autopsy and lifesaving, which obviously prevents the opening of medical schools, was widely adopted in the *halakhic* literature and prevailed in the Diaspora, in which the existence of medical schools was not dependent upon the Jews. This position caused problems and spurred attacks against Jews, especially in Polish universities in the early twentieth century, which in some cases went so far as to call for the expulsion of Jews from medical school until Jewish corpses were made available for autopsy.

But how would medical studies be conducted in Israel? This example finely illustrates the need for *halakhic* preparedness for a situation in which Jewish law bears responsibility for all realms of life and for society as a whole, and can no longer rely on the surrounding non-Jewish majority society to solve such problems. This issue delayed the opening of the country's first medical school at Hebrew University until R. Herzog and R. Frank (1873–1960), the rabbi of Jerusalem, reached an agreement with Hadassah Hospital allowing autopsies in cases in which explicit consent for this had been given during the deceased's lifetime. They also stipulated that the autopsies would be conducted with proper respect for the dead and with burial of all the body parts at the conclusion of the process.

R. Ovadia Hadaya (1889, Aleppo–1969, Jerusalem), a member of the Chief Rabbinate Council and the Rabbinical Appeals Court, was a Sephardic rabbi and Kabbalist who greatly identified with the State of Israel. In 1963, he published an article on autopsies calling for reconsideration of this prohibition in modern Israel. Professional training of a surgeon who will save many lives throughout his professional life, he claimed, requires long-term preparation and study, and therefore the demand for "immediate" lifesaving should be abandoned, and autopsies should be permitted also for generally "saving lives in the future." He added that this was especially so at present:

> For the State of Israel has been established [. . .] and no physician can learn without this [i.e., autopsies]. If no form of permission will be found, there will not be any physician in the country who will be capable of being a surgeon, and, Heaven forbid, there will be great danger for the patient who needs surgery, but with no succor. If we were to require the physicians to travel abroad to learn in other countries, the enmity and hatred of the Jewish people as a whole, and especially of the State of Israel, would increase.[15]

R. Goren conceptualized these arguments and drew them into sharper focus. He stated that in the reality in which the country is responsible for the populace as a whole, there is no room for considerations of solely saving the life of an individual. Relating to the society as a whole, there is always direct linkage to a life-saving situation:

> It is clear to us that without autopsies in medical schools, they will not produce appropriate physicians. This is called "a patient before us," since the Jewish state is responsible for the health of the population and must engage in long-range planning of these services.[16]

This principle was applied by R. Goren and other rabbis in a variety of topics related to the public health system. R. Goren discussed the question of establishing a skin bank for transplants, especially for burn victims. The issue of organ transplants triggered a *halakhic* discussion, mainly concerning the determination of the time of death, since some organs can be harvested only as long as there still is a heartbeat. In 1987, the Chief Rabbinate adopted a protocol of Harvard University that defined brain death as "death." The question of organ banks came up in reference to organs that could be harvested after death and stored until needed. R. Goren wrote that R. Landau's position was correct "only regarding Jewish physicians in the Diaspora, who are not responsible for the public's health in any country." When, however, the health system is responsible for the entire populace and is required to engage in long-term planning, those who will fall sick in coming years should be considered as if they are already before us: "the state is permitted to employ the criteria of saving life in regard to those who will become ill in the future."

Rabbi Goren argued that the "statistical patient" who will certainly come is actually "before us." Going beyond the logical argument that distinguishes between the diasporic condition and that of a state, R. Goren added an important Talmudic source that draws a distinction between saving the life of an individual and that of the public, and regarded the governmental responsibility for health as saving the life of the public.[17]

R. Yuval Cherlow, a leading Zionist rabbi of more recent decades, is an expert and prolific writer on problems of public health and medical ethics, and his rulings relating to the state's medical system reflect the considerations developed above. First, he has adopted the *halakhic* applications regarding the statistical patient. Second, as a member of the public committee that prioritizes medicines to be covered by the public health insurance system, he adopted R. Goren's distinction between saving the life of an individual and that of the public. Decisions during wartime must prioritize the life and needs of the public over the life of an individual, and the same holds for guidelines regarding the health system. Thus, sometimes a medicine that will benefit many should be prioritized over saving the lives of a few. Third, the application of the rule: "Your life comes before that of your fellow" requires also considering the prevention of severe pain and suffering of an individual, even if it is not a matter of life and death. Suffering harms human dignity, which is a *halakhic* value, and at times even has the same weight as the saving of life.[18] All of these are decisions on questions that *halakha* did not address prior to the rebirth of Jewish sovereignty.

Police and Security

The challenge of police operations on Sabbath was subject to an innovative analysis by Rabbi Shaul Israeli, a creative and original adjudicator, and one of the most prolific religious Zionist rabbis. His discussion relates directly to two of the focal points of this chapter, namely, *halakhic* responsibility for society as a whole, and the *halakhic* attitude to and responsibility for nonobservant Jews.

Police activity saves lives and saving of life overrides Sabbath observance. However, defining the boundaries and identification of an event as life threatening is a complicated task. How, for example, shall we relate to regular police activity to maintain order and peace in society? After all, we never know when an incident might turn life threatening. An additional, and crucial, question is whether police officers going to an event involving the saving of life are permitted to return on the Sabbath at the end of their activity.

These questions closely resemble the "statistical patient" issue of the health system discussed above. Rabbi Israeli employed the same considerations, and permitted violating the Sabbath even for life saving that can only be anticipated statistically. Accordingly, he permitted routine police patrols and allowed police officers to return, despite not knowing of a specific danger: "Saving a life that is not yet before us [. . .] but we clearly know will come at some time, even though we do not know when or how—we regard this as if it were already before us."[19]

More important is his assertion that *halakhic* rulings in the State of Israel must take into account the public as a whole and be applicable to that broader public. This position has many implications. First, Rabbi Israeli applied the *halakhic* category of saving the life of the public, which, as shown above, provides a great deal of flexibility. Second, in his opinion, even if there were a *halakhic* directive for the police not to take action in certain situations, or to not return to the station after the activity, only religious police officers would heed this directive. This would result in the public consciousness that the *halakha* is only capable of answering the country's needs by utilizing a secular Jew acting as a "Sabbath non-Jew." The conception that the *halakha* is responsible for providing a norm applicable to the entire public follows the direction charted by R. Kook in the *shemittah* controversy. R. Israeli, however, goes even further and explicitly takes into account the public consciousness on the issue and the fact that the secular police officer would not heed the *halakhic* injunctions.

Another important reason for his lenient ruling is the fear of a ruling that would lead to observant individuals refraining from enlisting in essential services, such as the police. He encouraged the observant to join the police, despite the need to conduct nonessential activities on Sabbath. He did so out of the belief that the presence of an observant officer would promote the values of the police in the spirit of Judaism, not only in the context of Sabbath observance, but also in other contexts as well. Here, too, we have a sweeping approach that bears in mind the state institution and that simultaneously seeks to limit its total amount of Sabbath violations by encouraging religious people to enlist, even at the cost of permitting otherwise prohibited actions for individual police officers.

Sovereignty and Democracy: Israel as a Jewish and Democratic State

Democracy and Jewish Law

The definition of Israel as a "Jewish and democratic" state in the Basic Laws that were enacted in 1993 reflects the essential tension in Israel between its being a Jewish nation-state and a democracy. This tension began with the first Zionist settlement activity and continued in the construction of the country's Declaration of Independence. The rabbis discussed in this chapter were all aware of this tension and employed this dialectic in their reasoning. None sought to fashion the state and its institutions as a religious state, in the strict image of the messianic state imagined by Maimonides, in which the political body—the king and the state—also functioned as a source of spiritual and religious leadership.

Instead, most Zionist rabbis wished to bridge between the state's two sources of meaning: Western democracy and the Jewish tradition. Such a framework would support a Western democratic state, while at the same time imparting to the state a Jewish character and meaning grounded in Jewish concepts and values. They wished to enhance the state's Jewishness while accepting its democratic principles.

The decision in favor of democracy taken by a majority of religious Zionist thinkers and decisors was not merely pragmatic, but a substantive and ideological discourse that searched for *halakhic* models to formulate a Jewish democracy. This significant approach to defining the state's institutions through *halakhic* definitions was a clear sign of religious thought embracing the state and a reflection of its view of the State of Israel as a Jewish polity.[20]

Some based their models on "community laws," formulated under medieval *halakha*. These laws authorized the community to enact legislation and adjudicate according to the needs of the time and place, while distinguishing between the ideal vision of classical *halakha* and the temporal needs of the hour. These *halakhic* powers given to the community allowed it to exercise the autonomy given by the non-Jewish state. Others based themselves on the *halakhic* concept of the "Biblical Laws of Kingship" (*mishpat ha-melekh*), which grants broad powers to the executive/king, arguing that this model should apply to the modern democratic government in Israel.

Already in 1915, R. Kook wrote that the Israelite king receives his authority from the nation and that without its consent, his appointment is not valid. Consequently, in the absence of a king, his "legal powers return to the nation as a whole."[21] R. Kook's intuitive statement was given a firm basis and was subject to a thorough analysis by his successors. R. Israeli concluded that any form of government chosen by the people receives the classic powers of the Israelite king and that the country's leader need not be a spiritual or rabbinic figure. R. Israeli added a far-reaching argument, concluding that direct election by the people is *halakhically* preferable to the Talmudic rule that the prophet and Sanhedrin (High Court) select the king. This direction, taken by R. Kook and his successors, not only brings Judaism closer to democracy but also bring democracy closer to Judaism in that a democratic State of Israel could now be regarded as an embodiment of the utopian Jewish state.

The biblical idea of "covenant" was another concept enlisted by several scholars to bridge between Jewish tradition and democracy. According to this radical theory, the Divine command had no validity unless it was freely accepted by the community. On this view, the prerequisite of autonomous national acceptance of the law was unparalleled in antiquity, including in Greece and the East, yet it lies at the heart of religious and political thought in the Bible and the rabbinic tradition. A few religious Zionist rabbis—mainly from North America, such as R. Chaim Hirschensohn (1857–1935), R. Simon Federbusch (1892–1969), and R. Samuel Mirsky (1899–1967)—argued that the biblical concept of covenant long preceded the social contract of Hobbes and Rousseau, leading them to conclude that the democratic form of government is the will of the Torah.[22]

Equality and the Attitude to the Non-Jew

Although it was relatively easy for a democratic regime to win *halakhic* backing, bridging between the *halakha* and democratic culture as expressed in other liberal and modern values—such as attitudes toward non-Jews and the principle of human equality—were among the most significant challenges that sovereignty posed to Jewish law. Among other causes of this difficulty are biblical laws demanded the exclusion of idolaters from the land of Israel, and even more importantly, the medieval Jewish political tradition that considered separation necessary in order to retain Jewish survival and uniqueness.

Israel's Declaration of Independence states that the state "will ensure complete equality of social and political rights to all its inhabitants irrespective of religion, race or sex." It seems to me that most Zionist rabbis willingly adopted these egalitarian values, and not simply because they lacked an alternative. Nevertheless, they usually refrained from explicitly developing a *halakhic* framework that would redefine the relationship between Jews and non-Jews, preferring to deal creatively with any specific *halakha* that was unacceptable from a democratic point of view. The rabbis preferred the traditional *halakhic* reasoning and interpretive method used to effect a change, over ideological and principled statements. Despite the similarity in the results, the rabbinic formalistic discourse was not always music to the ears of human rights advocates who desired an explicit statement on the principle of equality.

R. Unterman, who succeeded R. Herzog as Chief Rabbi, authored an important article on saving the life of a non-Jew on the Sabbath.[23] Admittedly, rabbis in the Diaspora found a way to circumvent the Talmudic norm that prohibited a Jew from violating the Sabbath to save a non-Jew. Notwithstanding this, R. Unterman's argument is a prime example of the existence of a renewed discussion that recognizes the new reality in which Jews are the majority, and are responsible for health and rescue systems for all the citizenry. On the path to leniency, R. Unterman used the *halakhic* concepts of *mipnei shalom* ("on account of the ways of peace") and *mishum eivah* ("on account of preventing enmity"), which are usually understood not as values-based arguments, but as mere utilitarian arguments intended to protect Jews from harm inflicted by non-Jews. R. Unterman was attacked for the absence of a principled, moral underpinning for his ruling, which reflects the lack of public satisfaction with this sort of formalistic, utilitarian reasoning. R. Unterman responded in an important article in which he interpreted these concepts not in a utilitarian fashion, but as "ensuing from the very morals of the Torah," as based on the verse (Prov. 3:17) "Her [i.e., the Torah's] ways are pleasant ways, and all her paths, peaceful." His premise was that the attitude to the non-Jew must be fashioned following this interpretative rule and its aim, and to prefer interpretation that leads to peace. This interpretation is an excellent example of both the innovative approach and the traditional discussion method of the religious Zionist rabbis.

Some of Rabbi Herzog's rulings can serve as an example of a more direct and clear approach to the problem of equality. Thus, for example, in the *halakhic* code for civil law that he initiated for the purpose of advancing his idea of Jewish Law in the Jewish State, he proposed writing "it is forbidden to deceive any person" instead of "it is forbidden to deceive one's fellow" that appears in the *Shulhan Arukh*. He also added general guidance to his rabbinic colleagues: "You would do well to delete all discrimination."[24] The main section of another book he began writing on constitutional law was devoted to attaining equality for all the citizens of the Jewish state: non-Jews and Jews, men and women, the observant and the non-observant.[25] Concerning inheritance law, R. Herzog proposed enacting a rabbinical ordinance that would equate sons and daughters, which would have the effect of overriding the biblical rule favoring sons. He expended a tremendous amount of energy defending and explaining the proposed ordinance, and maintained that it was incumbent upon the rabbinic leadership to be attentive to the female public that longed for equal status.[26] Rabbis Herzog and Goren's discussion of the judicial system (discussed below) offers another example of the rabbis' vigilance regarding the problem of equality in *halakha*.

Developments in two opposing directions began in the 1980s. On the one hand, regressive voices advocating intolerance toward the Arab population were heard, fueled largely by terror attacks as well as extremist opinions, such as those of Meir Kahana and his followers. On the other hand, many rabbis responded to the public's dissatisfaction with the pragmatic *halakhic* discourse that did not produce fundamental ideal texts on these weighty issues such as equality for the entire population. The latter included several prominent Zionist rabbis, including R. Aharon Lichtenstein, R. Yehuda Amital, R. Nachum Rabinowitz, and R. Yuval Cherlow, all heads of leading *yeshivot*. They all searched for ways to impose a *halakhic* obligation for equality among all the country's citizens, and a similar mandatory obligation for the life and physical well-being of every individual. Thus, R. Amital wrote to his students that the Declaration of Independence had binding *halakhic* standing and must be seen as a covenant forged between all the Israeli leaders who were signatories and all the inhabitants of the country. Such a covenant is *halakhically* binding, and it is forbidden to deviate from it.[27]

Israel and International Law

Special attention should be given to an intriguing discussion, conducted mainly during the first decades of the State, regarding the state's commitment to international law, including the granting of civil equality to all citizens.

On the eve of the establishment of the state, R. Herzog, who devoted much thought to the question of *halakha* and state, began writing the above-mentioned book on constitutional law. The uncompleted book was published after his death, in the late 1980s. The book is concerned with the encounter between the *halakha* and democratic values, including the attitude toward minorities. R. Herzog declared that the *halakhot* imposing limitations on idolaters and other non-Jews in the Land of Israel were no longer in force. In his opinion, those laws had been instituted for a situation in which the Jewish people acquired sovereignty by itself. However, the State of Israel, he argued, was given to the Jewish people with the consent of the nations of the world and on condition that it be a democracy and impart full equal rights to all citizens, regardless of religion. The essence of his argument is that he did not envision the State of Israel as the Jewish state of the redemptive era, but rather as a country within the framework of international law, and thus subject to it. This is a powerful *halakhic* step. R. Herzog determined that, in terms of the *halakha*, the state is subject to international law, and for that reason, he revoked the validity of the halakhic laws discriminating against non-Jews.

In the early 1950s, R. Israeli took this claim a step further claiming that the State of Israel is *halakhically* bound by international law. The Jewish people in the Diaspora were subject to the law of the land, by force of the Talmudic rule that "the law of the land is law [binding for Jews]."[28] In the era of a sovereign Jewish state, R. Israeli claimed, this rule applies to the State, and it, therefore, bound by "the law in force between the states." A "state" is a concept that exists by force of international law and the consent of the nations of the world, and consequently, a Jewish state is subject to the laws incumbent upon states. R. Israeli gave concrete *halakhic* significance to this theory, ruling that Israel may wage wars, since international law permits this, not because the *halakha* permits it. War is not an internal Jewish matter but an external interaction with other nations, and in such a case, the *halakha* determines that the law in force is that which is agreed upon by the nations. As long as the war "is waged in accordance with what is practiced among the peoples [of the world], it is permitted by the Torah." Since it is international law that permits the Jew to go to war:

> if all the nations were to reach an agreement prohibiting war, in such a manner that it would cease to be what is practiced among the peoples, war would no longer be [*halakhically*] legal, nor would conquest, and a people that went forth to war would be judged by the law of murder and bloodshed.[29]

Maimonides's laws of war are not valid in the State of Israel because the state was created by international law and is not a messianic *halakhic* state. This position aroused criticism, with some arguing that R. Israeli effectively subordinated Jewish morality to that of the non-Jewish peoples. His critics, however, were not cognizant of the power of his innovation in establishing a normative hierarchy in which international law stands above the *halakha*.

R. Haim D. Halevy (1924–88), rabbi of Tel Aviv, a student of R. Uziel and one of the eminent Zionist rabbis, continued in this direction and amplified it:

> In the democratic Western world of which we are part, equal rights for every person is the basis of social life, and there is no room for discrimination on the background of religion. And even if we were a tremendous world power, we could not act in this way.[30]

Not only is the state subject to the international law that afforded it recognition, international law gave it its very identity, since its essential nature is that of a democracy. "Our hands are not strong" is a Maimonidean category describing a situation in which the *halakhot* regarding non-Jews are not in force because the Jews do not rule. Now, R. Halevy writes, this is the valid halakhic situation, not because the Jews are weak, but because they received their sovereignty from the nations on condition that the state be democratic, a condition to which they must adhere. Furthermore, R. Halevy advanced a far-reaching argument pertaining to the altered mutual relations between Jews and non-Jews. The nations' recognition of Israel also obligates the state to recognize the conditions stipulated by the nations. These Zionist rabbis who regarded the creation of the State of Israel as a miracle effected through the agency of non-Jews, assert that this fact changes the balance of power and mutual relations and commitments between *halakha* and international law and between Jews and non-Jews.

Sovereignty and Identity Meet: Interaction between Jewish Law and Israeli Law

Retaining particularistic Jewish law and its associated judicial system was extremely important to the medieval Jewish community. The surrounding regime and society usually respected this aspiration, and the Jews were granted legal autonomy, which was a key enabler of Jewish existence as a separate community. The Talmud also required maintaining a Jewish legal system, and forbade Jews form turning to "*erkhaòt shel nokhrim*" (non-Jewish judiciaries). Law enjoyed a central place in the Jewish canonical literature and in the traditional course of religious studies, reflecting a conception of law as not merely an instrumental tool for organizing life in a society but also an expression of a world of values.

Indeed, even the circles of cultural Zionism, who saw the development, prosperity, and spread of Jewish culture and the Jewish world of values, turned to law as an important field of activity. Back in 1918, they founded the Jewish Law Society whose purpose was:

> To investigate in particular the law in its Hebrew national form, as it has developed over thousands of years of existence with our people in Israel and in the Diaspora, and to collect the necessary material for the continuation of the development and for a new creation in our country.[31]

This is not the place to discuss the rise and fall of the movement for Jewish law. We will only look at the lively discourse of the religious Zionist rabbis on the subject around the time of the establishment of the State and shortly thereafter. The application of *halakha* in state law and judiciary seemed like the realization of the long-standing dream of "I will restore your magistrates as of old" (Isa. 1:26). Yet everyone was aware of the chasm between the *halakha* as it had been formulated in the medieval period, and what would be required in the current situation. Thus, for instance, *halakhic* legal procedure discriminates against non-Jews, women, and the nonobservant, all of whom were unfit to give testimony or to serve as judges. Beyond that, *halakhic* criminal law has extremely restrictive evidentiary rules. In practice it does not enable conviction and therefore cannot ensure the well-being of the public. The adoption of *halakha* as state law would obviously require a groundbreaking discourse that would generate *halakha* suitable for the needs of the society, and that would be accepted in a democratic society. While public law was foremost in the consciousness of those engaging in this discourse, they also considered private law, which would be highly significant in fashioning of the society's values, culture, and identity. Private law is highly developed in the Talmudic literature, and neglecting it could be viewed as the opposition and detachment of the state from the sources of Jewish culture.

Religious Zionist rabbis who identified with the state in every sense sought to influence its law in the spirit of Jewish legal culture. This in itself is a fascinating innovation, because in the Diaspora, *halakhic* decisors did not wish to influence state law. Zionist decisors, however, sought to create linkage between the state and its institutions and the continuum of Jewish culture. Applying the diasporic model, that differentiates between state law and *halakha* and forgoes the dream of renewing and applying the Jewish Law, stands in contradiction to the Zionist-religious idea.

Speaking generally, the Zionist decisors exhibit three approaches. A majority of the decisors, at least in the state's early years, refused to relinquish either *halakhic* law and its values or the *halakhic* aspiration for influence in the public sphere; however, they agreed that significant changes had to be instituted in the *halakha*. The second approach called for the adoption of state law as Jewish law, dispensing with any *halakhic* content. The third approach proposed *halakhic* courts parallel to the state judicial system, with the choice of the place to litigate open to the will of the parties. This model, a reconstruction of the diasporic one, was put forth mainly after the failure of incorporating *halakha* into state law.

R. Goren led the approach that preferred state law. Based on the principle of freedom of stipulation in Talmudic law, and on communal law—which was developed in medieval Europe and was based on communal consensus—he believed that an individual or the public can accept different laws upon themselves.[32] He thereby ruled that Israeli law obtains *halakhic* validity by force of the citizenry's acceptance. Furthermore, the State of Israel is a Jewish political body, and as such is afforded the legislative and judicial powers of the Israelite king or the medieval Jewish community. The obvious conclusion is twofold. First, the state is authorized to legislate whatever is for the public good, and such laws have *halakhic* force. Second, the prohibition of turning to a "non-Jewish judiciary" does not apply to Israeli courts. R. Goren went so far as to declare that one who violates Israeli law is obligated to repent in the religious sense.

R. Goren assumed a positivist approach to law: the content of the law reflects social agreement, not an immanent value. All law, including *halakha*, intrinsically comprises agreement on the arrangements that successfully direct society, but does not necessarily bear values-based content. The law's validity ensues from its enactment via the proper legislative process—communal acceptance—rather than by merit of its morality or truthfulness. His positivist conception of law, together with his perception of the state institutions as authentically Jewish, led him to give a broad interpretation to the Talmudic sources that discuss the law's freedom of stipulation, and offer the legitimacy granted to the Jewish community, or even that of the Israelite monarchy, to the state's legislation and institutions.

R. Goren wrote extensively on questions of *halakha* and state with the aim of applying *halakha* in the public sphere by revitalizing dormant *halakhic* realms—such as laws of war and public health. But surprisingly, he was ready to forgo the law that characterized the Jewish community through the centuries, and to which fidelity was required by Talmudic norms. I believe that, beyond the jurisprudential perception set forth above, his view deeply resonated with the Zionist discourse of the time, which sought to return to Biblical Judaism. He imagined a pre-rabbinic reality in which the collective Jewish identity was not primarily shaped and identified by law. It was only later, after the destruction of the Temple, and in the absence of a political framework, that the Sages of the Mishnah and Talmud emphasized the centrality of a particular legal system in molding the collective Jewish identity.

The second approach was spearheaded by R. Herzog, who perceived law as part of the spiritual renaissance necessary for the Zionist enterprise. This stance forms the basis for the "*mishpat ivri*" (Hebrew law) movement that was supported by the adherents of cultural Zionism, and which produced a respectable list of legal scholars and judges. R. Herzog held that forgoing Torah law in the Jewish state constituted "raising a hand against the Torah of Moses," an expression drawn from Maimonides's discussion of the prohibition to reject Torah law in favor of adjudication in a non-Jewish judiciary.[33] Using this expression, R. Herzog amplified the ban on resorting to a non-Jewish legal system arguing that by abandoning Torah law, the state raises its hand against the Mosaic code. For him, the obligation of a sovereign Jewish collective to maintain a legal system exceeds that of a Diaspora community, and unquestionably that of the individual. Faithful to his opinion, he searched for a way to introduce *halakhic* content into Israeli law and courts. Contrary to R. Goren, R. Herzog maintained that the contents of the law are more important than the institutions, and therefore, when appealing to the state courts, the ban on involving a non-Jewish legal system would apply unless the courts adopted Jewish law content.

R. Herzog was faithful to Talmudic literature and to the model of medieval Jewish life in which law played a key role in formulating the collective Jewish identity. He wondered why the Talmudic tractates dealing with civil law were written? Why was *Hoshen Mishpat*, the civil law section of *Shulhan Arukh*, written? What was their meaning and importance, if they could easily be abandoned, as R. Goren maintained? For R. Herzog, law was the cardinal constitutive element of Jewish identity, and was at the core of Jewish culture. Accordingly, the Jewish state could not waive it and detach itself from the heart of Jewish culture and identity.

At the same time, he also believed that there could be no renaissance without innovation; it was evident that the *halakha* was not suitable to be the law in practice in a modern democratic state. This accounts for his dual battle: an external battle seeking to base state law on Jewish law, and an internal battle within the rabbinic world to adapt the *halakha* toward statehood. In this spirit, he proposed changes and took many initiatives—including establishing an institute for the research of *halakhic* law—meant to overcome the main obstacles and adjust the *halakha* to suit contemporary needs and the fundamental principles of democracy. For R. Herzog, resolving contradictions between society's needs and the *halakha* was an obligation of the *halakhic* leader. He viewed the necessary changes as an opportunity for the *halakha*, not a price.

The changes he suggested were in content and in form. He believed that *halakhic* leadership must offer an accessible, organized, and orderly book of *halakha*, so that it could fulfill its calling. To this end, he initiated the writing of a new *halakhic* code, and within this context, he even sought to introduce significant changes in content. Additionally, he sought to renew the tradition of legislation—enactment of ordinances—which he regarded as essential for the functioning of *halakha*. He viewed the new ordinances that he proposed as legislation based on existing *halakhic* principles, arguing that *halakha* had always acted in this manner: extracting, ordering, and conceptualizing rules from existing principles, although this transition was usually effected through interpretation. His opponents in the rabbinic world deemed the enactment of regulations a radical move that ran counter to the *halakhic* tradition of developing new laws only through interpretation following the demise of the Sanhedrin. During his term as Chief Rabbi, the Chief Rabbinate enacted ordinances on various aspects of family law. Some introduced extremely significant innovations, including child support until the age of fifteen and the prohibition of levirate marriage. The Chief Rabbinate Council has not enacted new regulations since the time of R. Herzog.

As regards the state court system, R. Herzog did not suggest setting aside the separate *halakhic* courts, but rather making use of *halakhic* content in the state courts. In his vision, the judges—nonobservant men and women, or even non-Jews—would study *Hoshen Mishpat* and be partially trained in Jewish law. Using Jewish law when sitting in judgment would remove the ban on utilizing a "non-Jewish judiciary" from the state judicial system despite the courts not otherwise conducting themselves according to *halakha*.

R. Herzog clearly understood that this solution would not make the state system "*halakhic*," but it would embed the spiritual treasures and world of values of Jewish law within the state legal system. This hybrid mixture that R. Herzog envisioned was not (only) a compromise. He was aware of the substantive disparity between Jewish law and the needs of the contemporary reality, and he wanted to resolve these difficulties by incorporating *halakha* into state law. He argued that the necessary changes—such as the inclusion of women and non-Jews—are a *halakhic* need, and that the inclusion of the *halakha* in state law would advance these goals.

R. Herzog applied a historical-cultural approach to law, and accordingly perceived of *Hoshen Mishpat* as a cultural asset that reflects the Jewish world of values. He predicated that on the view that although the majority of Israeli Jews are not observant, they have a deep Jewish consciousness and identity, and seek a basis for a common Jewish culture. The law can play a central role in filling this need by bridging all Jews in Israel. *Halakhic* sources would fulfill their value-based and cultural identity function when placed at the heart of the Israeli legal discourse.

R. Herzog did not naively imagine that the judicial process involves the simplistic application of law to the case at hand. As a *halakhist* and a common law jurist, he knew that the judicial process requires discretion in interpretation, selection among sources, and decision-making. It was clear to him that state courts would interpret the *halakha* within the context of Israeli identity and culture. He nonetheless viewed the very use of the *halakha* as a significant value that lifts the ban on "non-Jewish courts." He removed the ban from courts established by Israeli law which drew their authority from the state and most of whose judges were categorically disqualified under *halakha*. All this, however, was conditional on judges maintaining an ongoing discourse with the Jewish law sources. He envisioned Israeli law being built on a continuum with the centuries-long legal discourse; it would interpret the *halakha* and erect an additional floor in the edifice of the *halakhic* discourse itself. This expressed his profound aspiration, and main goal, of bridging and merging horizons between the sovereign State of Israel and the time-honored Jewish tradition. This bridge was two-directional, not only positioning the values of Jewish culture within the State of Israel, but also empowering the state institutions by giving them a role in fashioning Jewish culture and its world of content. R. Herzog understood that like every interpreter, Israeli judges would impose their ideas and opinions on the interpreted text. He thus wished to integrate the *Shulhan Arukh* into the secular Israeli court, while at the same time giving *halakha* a platform for responding to the contemporary reality.[34]

Despite the difference between the positions held by R. Goren and R. Herzog, there is a significant resemblance between them. Both granted state institutions halakhic standing, and a role in fashioning the *halakha* itself. R. Goren perceived Israeli legislation as that of a Jewish community which is *halakhically* binding, while R. Herzog proposed viewing the Israeli court as a Jewish judicial institution. There was no political follow-up to their proposals, and it is too early to thoroughly examine the degree of their influence. Their ideas, however, are without a doubt the most fascinating and radical to be advanced within religious Zionist thought.

A considerable number of judicial decisions delivered over the years reflect a proximate conception to that of R. Herzog. They were based on *halakhic* literature and suggested new interpretations and ideas that were transmitted from the Israeli court to the *halakhic* world. The work of Justice Menachem Elon, who was a professor of Jewish Law at the Hebrew University, and then served for sixteen years as a Supreme Court justice, is an outstanding example of this position. In a number of judgments, Elon contended with the Chief Rabbinate regarding its *halakhic* position, thereby seeking to influence *halakha* itself. In other judgments, mainly on constitutional and administrative matters, he offered a new and adapted interpretations of the medieval Jewish sources to create "state *halakhot*." Internally, within the Supreme Court, he attempted to renew the medieval tradition of communal Jewish law. He wished to bring it up to date and elevate it from communal to state law. Elon believed that the absorption of Jewish law by the Israeli court would aid in its renaissance.[35]

Conclusion

At the heart of the scholarly study of *halakha* is the affinity between Jewish law and the social and cultural reality; the development of the *halakha*, and the changes it has undergone due to historical, social, and ideational processes; the manner in which these changes take shape; the way in which they are presented and justified in the *halakhic* literature; and their relation to the ideological worldview of the decisor. The intensity of the Jewish drama in the second half of the twentieth century offers an excellent opportunity to examine the ways in which *halakhic* decisors thought about these issues. Moreover, much light has been cast on the "Zionist century" and the State of Israel from different directions and in varied scholarly disciplines that explore history, society, thought, literature, law, and more. *Halakha* in the Israeli context provides another important aspect for our understanding of Israel.

Notes

1. Despite the agreement on the practical level, opinions differed on the theological significance of the enterprise. Some rabbis and religious Zionist ideologues saw in the Zionist enterprise an improvement of the status of the Jewish people but separated this from Redemptive theology. Others, most prominently R. Abraham Isaac Kook, viewed the Zionist endeavor as an active advancement of the Redemption. For a discussion of the main religious approaches regarding Zionism, see Aviezer Ravitzky, *Messianism, Zionism, and Jewish Religious Radicalism* (Chicago: University of Chicago Press, 1996); for a discussion from historical and social point of view, see Yosef Salmon, *Religion and Zionism: First Encounters* (Jerusalem: Hebrew University Magnes Press, 2002); for a comprehensive systematic analysis, see Menachem Freidman, "The State of Israel as a Theological Dilemma," in *The Israeli State and Society: Boundaries and Frontiers*, ed. Baruch Kimmerling (Albany: University of New York Press, 1989), 165–215.
2. The establishment of the Chief Rabbinate by R. Kook in 1921 had only minor influence, as controversies between conservative and innovating rabbis paralyzed its ability to issue groundbreaking *halakhic* rulings.
3. Responsa *Hatam Sofer*, vol.5, Choshen Mishpat, 195 [Hebrew].
4. See Joseph B. Soloveitchik, *Kol Dodi Dofek: Listen—My Beloved Knocks*, ed. Jeffrey R. Woolf, trans. David Z. Gordon (New York: Yeshiva University Press, 2006). Based on festive sermon delivered on the eighth Israel's Independence Day (1956). First published in Hebrew in 1964.
5. See Arye Edrei, "Secularism and Nationalism: The Modern Halakhic Discourse on the Identity and Boundaries of the Jewish Community," in *Secularism in Question: Jews and Judaism in Modern Times*, ed. Ari Joskowitcz and Ethan Katz (University of Pennsylvania Press, 2015), 232–58.
6. Yehuda Amital, *Jewish Values in a Changing World*, ed. Amnon Bazak, trans. David Strauss, trans. and ed. Reuven Ziegler (Jersey City, NJ: KTAV, 2005), 186.
7. Abraham Isaac Kook, *Orot*, 2nd ed. (Jerusalem: Mossad Harav Kook, 1961), 70–72 [Hebrew]. For English translation, see Abraham Isaac Hakohen Kook, *Orot*, trans. Bezalel

Naor (Northvale, NJ: Jason Aronson, 1993), 176; see Yehudah Mirski, *Rav Kook: Mystic in a Time of Revolution* (New Haven, CT: Yale University Press, 2013), 110–13.

8. Abraham Isaac Kook, *Igrot hareaya* (Jerusalem: Mossad Harav Kook, 1962), 1, 247 [A letter to Rabbi Y. D. Wilovsky of Zfat, from March 26, 1909] [Hebrew].
9. See Arye Edrei, "From 'Who Is a Jew', To 'Who Should Be a Jew': The Current Debates on *Giyur* in Israel," in *Conversion, Intermarriage, and Jewish Identity*, ed. Adam Mintz, Marc D. Stern, and Robert S. Hirt (New York: The Michael Scharf Publication Trust of the Yeshivah University Press, 2015).
10. Isaac Herzog, *She'elot u-teshuvot hekhal Yitsḥaḳ*, vol. 1, Even ha-'ezer (Jerusalem: Agudah le-Hotsa'at Kitve Rosh ha-Rabanim ha-GeRI'AH Hertsog Z.tS.l., 1960), 21 [A responsum given on December 23, 1948] [Hebrew].
11. Isser Yehudah Unterman, "The Laws of Conversion and their Implementation," in *Torah SheBe-'al peh* (Jerusalem: Mossad Harav Kook, 1974), 13 [Hebrew].
12. Rabbi Shlomo Goren, "Kefirah be-'am Yiśra'el le'inyene giyur [Hebrew]" [Denouncing the People of Israel in Matters of Conversion], *Shanah be-shanah* (1983): 149.
13. Hayim Amsalem, *Ve-hayalim ygaber: Be-'inyene giyuram shel hayalim mezera Yiśra'el ha-meshartim be-tsahal* [On the Issue of the Conversion of Soldiers of a Jewish Seed Who Serve in the I. D. F.] (Jerusalem, 2010), 6–7 [Hebrew].
14. Rabbi Yisrael Rosen, *Ve-ohev ger: Or 'al ha-giyur be-Yiśra'el* [Love the Convert: Light on Conversion in Israel] (Alon Shevut: Mekhon Tsomet, 2010) [Hebrew].
15. Ovadia Hedaya, "Nituah metim le-tsorkhe limud refu'ah" [Autopsies for the purpose of studying medicine], *ha-Torah ṿeha-medinah: Bamah leverure Halakhah be-'inyene ha-medinah be-Yiśra'el* 6-7 (1953–1954): 194–95 [Hebrew].
16. Rabbi Shlomo Goren, "Limud anatomyah be-vet ha-sefer le-refuah kefi ha-halakhah" [Studying anatomy in medical school according to Halacha], in *Torat ha-refuah* (Jerusalem: Ha'idra rama u-masora la-'am, 2001), 225, 235 [Hebrew].
17. Rabbi Shlomo Goren, "Mavo le-hashtalat evarim le'or ha-halakhah" [Introduction to organ transplantation in the light of Halacha], in *Torat ha-refuah* (Jerusalem: Ha'idra rama u-masora la-'am, 2001), 79 [Hebrew]
18. Rabbi Yuval Cherlow, "Hakhlalat terufot le-eikhut hayim be-sal haberi'ut" [Including medicines for quality of life in the health services], *Tehumin* 28 (2008): 383 [Hebrew].
19. Shaul Israeli, *'Amud ha-yemini: berure halakhah be-'inyene medinah* (Tel Aviv: Moreshet, 1966), ch. 17 [Hebrew].
20. See Benny Port, ed., *Mahshavot 'al demokratyah Yehudit* [Reflections on Jewish Democracy] (Jerusalem: Israel Democracy Institute, 2010), 17–58 [Hebrew].
21. Abraham Isaac Kook, *Mishpaṭ kohen: Teshuvot be-mitsṿot ha-teluyot ba-Arets* (Jerusalem, 1937), 337, 144 [A letter to Rabbi S. Z. Pines from Switzerland dated December 26, 1915] [Hebrew].
22. See Ḥayim Hirshenzon, *Eleh divre ha-berit*, vols. 1–3 (Jerusalem: Defus 'ivri, 1926–1928) [Hebrew]; Simon Federbusch, *Mishpaṭ ha-melukhah be-Yiśra'el* (Jerusalem: Mossad Harav kook, 1952), 33 [Hebrew]; The affinity between these two principles and the foundations of American constitutional law is evident. Hirschenzon often draws comparisons between the Torah regime and the American Constitution. See David Zohar, *Mehuyavut yehudim ba-'olam ha-moderni: ha-rav Hayim Hirshenzon ve-yahaso el ha-moderna* [Jewish Commitment in a moder World: Rabbi Hayyim Hirschensohn and His Attitude Towards the Moderna] (Jerusalem: Shalom Hartman institution, 2003), 163 [Hebrew]; Daniel J. Elazar, "Ra'ayon ha-berit ve-yisudah shel amerikah" [Covenant and the American

Founding], in *Be'ikvot kolombus: Amerika 1492–1992* [Following Columbus: America], ed. Miriam Eliav-Feldon (Jerusalem: The Zalman Shazar Center, 1997), 255 [Hebrew]; E. Brooks Holifield, *The Covenant Sealed: The Development of Puritan Sacramental Theology in Old and New England (1570–1720)* (New Haven, CT: Yale University Press, 1974).

23. Isar Y. Unterman, "Hatsalst goi be-shabat" [Saving life of non-jew on Sabbat], *Ha'aretz*, April 4, 1966 [Hebrew]; Isar.Y. Unterman, "Darkhe shalom ve-hagdaratam" [The definition of the *halakhic* concept of 'ways of peace'], *Or Hamizrach* 15, no. 4 (July 1966): 277 [Hebrew].
24. Isaac Herzog, *Tehuqah le-Yiśra'el*, vol. 3, ed. Itamar Warhaftig (Jerusalem: Mossad Harav Kook, 1989), 278 [Chief Rabbi Herzog's letter from July 25, 1952] [Hebrew].
25. Isaac Herzog, "Zekhuyot ha-mi'utim lefi ha-halakhah" [Minority right according to Jewish Law], in *Tehuqah le-Yiśra'el al-pi ha-tora*, vol. 1, ed. Itamar Warhaftig (Jerusalem: Mossad Harav kook, 1989), 12–21 [Hebrew].
26. See Herzog, *Tehuqah le-Yiśra'el*, 2:1–170.
27. Yehudah Amital, "Ha-yahas le-mi'utim 'al-pi ha-torah bemedinat Yisra'el" [The attitude towards minorities in the State of Israel according to Jewish Law], Daf kesher, accessed Oct. 30, 2023 [Hebrew], http://gush.net/dk/1to899/200daf.htm.
28. See Resnicoff, this Volume
29. Shaul Israeli, "*Takrit Kibiyeh le-Or ha-Halakha*" [The Kibiyah Incident in Light of Jewish Law], *Torah u-medinah* 6–7 (1953–54): 71–113 [Hebrew]. The first step toward this idea R. Israeli made shortly after the establishment of the state. In his article "Halakhic Content of The Establishment of The State," in *Sefer Erets ḥemdah be-hilkhot Erets-Yiśra'el* (Tel Aviv: Moreshet, 1957), 30 [Hebrew]. He claimed that the United Nations' resolution on the establishment of a Jewish state invalidated the Talmudic prohibition (known as the "three vows) on rebelling against the non-Jewish nations and "rising up as a wall" (usually interpreted to mean organized or armed immigration to the Land of Israel without the prior approval of the non-Jewish nations).
30. Ḥayyim David Halevi, "Darkhe shalom ba-yaḥasim she-ben yehudim le-she-enam yehudim" [Ways of peace' in the relationship between Jews and non-Jews], *Teḥumin* 9 (1988): 71–81 [Hebrew]. See also Suzanne L. Stone, "Sovereignty and Ethics in the Thought of Rabbi Ḥayyim David Halevi," in *Swimming against the Current: Reimagining Jewish Tradition in the Twenty-First Century Essays in Honor of Chaim Seidler-Feller*, ed. Shaul Seidler-Feller and David N. Myers (Boston, MA: Academic Studies Press, 2020).
31. Shmuel N. Eisenstadt and P. Daykan, "Teudatenu," *Hamishpat ha-ivri: riv'on mada'i* (1918) [Hebrew]. See Asaf Likhovski, *Law and Identity in Mandate Palestine* (Chapel Hill: University of North Carolina Press, 2006).
32. See Rosensweig, this volume.
33. See Maimonides, *Mishneh Torah*, vol. 14, *Sefer shoftim: Halakhot sanedrin* [Laws of Sanhedrin], chap.26:7; Herzog, *Tehuqah le-Yiśra'el*, 1:164.
34. See Arie Edrei, "A Religious Zionist Dream: Rabbi Herzog's Vision of Israel Law," *The Jewish Quarterly Review* 112, no. 4 (Fall 2022).
35. See Arye Edrei "*Halakhah* from the Bench? A New Perspective on the Use of Jewish Law in Israel's Supreme Court," in *The King Is in the Field: Essays in Modern Jewish Political Thought*, ed. J. Cooper and S. H. Brody (Philadelphia: University of Pennsylvania Press, 2023), 54–76.

B

Halakhic *Responses to Modernity*

CHAPTER 22

HALAKHIC RESPONSES TO MODERNITY

Attitudes toward Non-Jews in Liberal Societies

ETHAN M. TUCKER

Introduction and Framing

THE Torah tells a grand narrative of humanity, woven of two parts. It is, on the one hand, a universal story, beginning with the creation of the first human beings, who are the ancestors of all. On the other hand, there emerges from that story a more particular narrative, that of Abraham, Isaac, Jacob, and their descendants. The Torah proceeds to relate how this people, in turn, is transformed by a revelatory encounter with God, who endows them with a code of conduct and responsibilities that set them apart from the rest of the world. A basic tension endures as one reads this narrative. To what extent has the universal been replaced by the particular? In which ways are the Gentiles of the Bible fundamentally outside its narrative and scope of concern, at least until some messianic future? Does God's role as creator of all persist in ways that are meant to affect governance and behavior in the here and now? Do Gentiles remain a central piece of the law's concern, only finding themselves treated differently when their practices are at odds with Divine desires and priorities?

These questions have potentially extensive answers on the exegetical, philosophical, and theological planes. In this chapter, the focus will be on how *halakhah* (Jewish law) has tackled these questions and how modern voices have reassessed some earlier answers when under the pressures of Jewish integration into society. Our analysis will both categorize some of the specific modern responses to Jewish-Gentile difference in *halakhah*, but will also serve as a window into *halakhah*'s capacity more broadly to respond to modernity.

Background

Biblical Law

Differences in the treatment of Israelites and non-Israelites are already encoded into biblical law.[1] Three prominent examples stand out: first, Leviticus[2] allows Israelites to purchase non-Israelites as slaves and to pass them on to their heirs. By contrast, any enslavement of Israelites by Israelites in perpetuity is forbidden. Second, a passage in Deuteronomy[3] forbids intermarrying with the indigenous nations of Canaan, warning that intermarriage will lead to an infiltration of idolatry into Israelite culture and practice. Third, a distinct passage in Deuteronomy[4] forbids Israelites from lending money on interest to Israelites, while permitting the same when lending to non-Israelites.[5]

These examples seem to indicate clear border lines between Israelites and non-Israelites, setting up two categories of people who are classified differently under the law. A closer look, however, suggests that this seemingly clear record may be considerably more complex. Yes, the passage in Leviticus distinguishes between Israelites and non-Israelites when it comes to slavery. But this chapter as a whole takes for granted that, barring Israelite intervention to redeem their brethren, non-Israelites routinely enslaved Israelites and passed them on as property.[6] As an extension, we can also presume that non-Israelites would have loaned Israelites money on interest. Does the Torah mean to enshrine a difference between Israelites and non-Israelites with regard to these matters, or does it merely license playing by conventional economic rules and demanding a higher standard within the Israelite family? The Bible itself does not necessarily suggest that it is reasonable to own non-Israelites as slaves or to lend them money on interest *because* they are non-Israelites. If confronted with a world in which non-Israelites refrained from enslaving and charging Israelites interest, would the Bible endorse distinctions based on national origin alone?

Furthermore, with respect to intermarriage, one can ask: Is the prohibition here generalized to all non-Israelites, or does it only apply to the seven indigenous nations that pose a particular threat to Israelite identity and culture? Is the concern even about intermarriage per se, or is the ban a secondary tool for warding off the religious threat of the worship of foreign gods?[7]

However philosophically and anthropologically broad these laws and regulations may have been, the definitional lines between Israelites and others remained reasonably clear and fixed during the First Temple period. Biblical sources do not lay out any clear pathway for non-Israelites to become Israelites. A number of sources—most notably the book of Ruth—show how a non-Israelite *woman* might marry into a patriarchal Israelite clan and have offspring that are part of the Israelite nation. Non-Israelite men, by contrast, seem to remain inexorable outsiders, at least on the ethnonational plane, even if they can become Israelite allies and/or devotees of the God of Israel.[8] Differential treatment of Israelites and non-Israelites under the previously stated laws would thus have reflected, more than created, any boundary lines between the groups. Nonetheless, the background provided by the Torah's legislation forces us to confront various categories of difference and to begin to ponder what their purpose is and how these potential purposes might shape Jewish-Gentile boundaries in later times and places.

Classical Rabbinic Sources

Rabbinic sources witness an expansion of the various laws that reinforce distinctions between Gentiles and Jews. In certain ways, the rabbinic system of thought and practice hardens the boundary between these two populations, even as it renders that boundary more permeable. To wit, rabbinic sources all take for granted that a Gentile can convert to Judaism and become a Jew. In biblical literature, the term *ger* primarily refers to non-Israelites who live on Israelite territory and enjoy certain equal rights and privileges. But rabbinic sources generally understand the word *ger* to encompass the proselyte, someone who, by going through an embodied ritual and willingly entering into the covenant between God and Israel, becomes a Jew, essentially indistinguishable from the native born.[9] Nonetheless, the possibility of conversion raises the possibility that Jewish-Gentile differences are meant to remain clear and without nuance until such point as conversion takes place. If Gentility is no longer immutable for any given person, its very contingency as a state may encourage uncompromising standards for as long as it is in place.

Rabbinic sources indeed preserve a more expansive record of regulated differences between Jews and Gentiles. Here too, it is helpful to focus on six of the most prominent examples. First, Mishnah *Avodah Zarah* forbids going into a private space to get a haircut from a Gentile barber, seemingly for fear that the Gentile will use the barber's tool to do harm to the Jew.[10] This is one of a number of regulations that are focused on Jewish safety, treating the average and paradigmatic Gentile as a violent threat to Jewish life and limb. Second, Mishnah *Avodah Zarah* also limits or forbids commerce on the days prior to and following a range of Gentile festival days.[11] This and other regulations in that tractate seem focused on putting meaningful distance between Jews and any sort of idolatrous practice, including any sort of condoning or secondary engagement with Gentile/idolatrous culture. Third, during the time of Beit Shammai and Beit Hillel, eighteen decrees are passed to shore up Jewish-Gentile boundaries, including on many matters related to food, such as the consumption of wine owned or touched by Gentiles, as well as a broader ban on intimacy and intermarriage.[12] These and other decrees fall in the category of social legislation and are meant to keep the Jewish and Gentile populations separate to greater or lesser degrees. Fourth, Tosefta Bava Metzia states that when it comes to Gentiles, one neither "helps them out of a pit nor lowers them into one."[13] This seems to indicate a general paradigm of indifference when it comes to Gentile well-being and is intended to legitimate and even strengthen a notion that Jews should be generally more concerned with the welfare of Jews than of Gentiles. Fifth, as a more extreme extension of this general idea, Mishnah Yoma implies that one would not violate Shabbat in order to save the life of a Gentile.[14] This is further confirmed by b.Avodah Zarah, which states that one may not violate Shabbat to help a Gentile woman give birth, even for pay.[15] Here, we have the notion that concern for Gentile life is simply not as serious as a concern for Jewish life, particularly when it comes to the overriding of significant religious prohibitions. Finally, in addition to the biblical hierarchies pertaining to loaning on interest, other sources prioritize Jewish assets over Gentile ones. For instance, Mishnah Bava Kama rules that when a Jew's ox gores a Gentile's ox, no damages need be paid, even though Gentiles are fully responsible (under Jewish law) for any damage they cause to a Jew's property.[16] This and other sources suggest that Jews and Gentiles can be treated differently when it comes to monetary matters and basic fairness and equality under the law.

Already in the classical rabbinic canon, we find that each of these categories is treated by at least one voice with some degree of complexity, opening up, in theory or in practice, the possibility of applying the law regarding these six examples differently in different contexts. Each of these nuanced additions creates room for treating the legislation around Gentiles as second order, based on behavior, as opposed to first order, based on identity or status.

Certain sources simply assess whether the concern in play is present in a given context and assume that with a shifting context, the law's application surely shifts as well. For instance, b.Avodah Zarah[17] permits getting a haircut from a Gentile if the Jew is able to look in a mirror while the haircut is taking place. This seems to affirm the problem as being solely about safety; as soon as the Jew can ensure that nothing dangerous is happening, the action becomes permitted.

Other sources focus on driving a wedge between the more narrow, ideological/religious category of idolater, and the broader, potentially more neutral category of Gentile. We noted previously that the Mishnah forbids any kind of commerce around non-Jewish holidays. Nonetheless, b.Avodah Zarah[18] reports that Rav Yehudah would send his Gentile friend Avidarna gifts on *the actual day* of a Gentile festival. Rava did the same for his Gentile acquaintance. Both justify their behavior by saying that they happened to have concrete and clear knowledge that their colleagues were not idolaters. This suggests that the entire concern in this area of law is idolatry; once that concern has been removed, a person's Gentile status is no longer relevant and the prohibition can be lifted. We find a similar approach there to addressing the restrictions set up around Gentile wine. One view, attributed to R. Shimon b. Gamliel, says that the wine of a *ger toshav* (someone who acknowledges the Jewish God, observes the basic Noahide laws, yet is a Gentile) is not subject to the normal rules on Gentile wine, and one may even drink it![19] There are other opposing views there, including an earlier, anonymous view that seems to permit benefiting from the wine of a *ger toshav* while still forbidding its consumption. Nonetheless, we have here another example of a prohibition relating to Gentiles being constructed as truly being about idolaters.

Sometimes, rabbinic sources seem to partially neutralize statements of indifference to Gentile welfare by invoking a broader principle of promoting general welfare. A series of rabbinic statements authorize behaviors that display concern for the Gentile poor and dead under the rubric of *darkhei shalom* (the "ways of peace").[20] This may be a defensive formulation to avoid friction. Alternatively, it may be a more proactive stance of encouraging comity in pursuit of an environment where mutual assistance will be reliably present. Either way, these rulings usher in a more active Jewish code of care when it comes to Gentile needs.

A few sources suggest that certain distinctions between Jews and Gentiles can be erased when maintaining them would lead to enmity and, possibly, a presumptive danger for Jews. Tosefta Avodah Zarah explicitly permits greeting Gentiles on their holidays for this purpose.[21] This turns a concern for Jewish safety on its head, invoking this concern as a basis for *blurring* certain boundaries with Gentiles.

Finally, a few Talmudic passages offer rationalizations for various laws in ways that potentially deessentialize them and open the door to minimizing or shifting their application. Elsewhere in b.Avodah Zarah, R. Yosef suggests that if a professional Jewish nurse or midwife were to refuse to deliver a Gentile baby on Shabbat, even for pay, this would spark enmity among Gentiles.[22] He proposes that perhaps the fear of this enmity should allow the Jew to violate Shabbat on behalf of the Gentile in this sort of case. Abaye rejects this, saying that Gentiles can be pacified by being told that Jews can only violate Shabbat for those who observe Shabbat. While this holds the earlier legal line, it opens up the possibility that where Gentiles will not buy this rationalization and, as a consequence, enmity will result, violation of Shabbat may indeed be permissible to save a Gentile's life. Another example of this dynamic can be found in b.Bava Kama, where R. Abahu explains the discrepancy between payments around Jewish and Gentile oxen in the following manner: Originally, Gentiles were to be treated the same as Jews. Once God saw that the Gentiles did not observe the Noahide laws—which include a prohibition on theft and a responsibility to set up a fair court system—God permitted the Jews not to reimburse Gentiles for damages to the latter's property.[23] Again, this holds an earlier legal line, but it opens up the possibility of arguing that Gentile who *do* behave fairly and who *do* observe the Noahide laws, ought to be treated equally to Jews.

These interpretative moves and expansions form the legal lexicon for all later rabbinic rulings that seek to open up daylight between the black-letter rabbinic laws concerning Gentiles and contemporary cases that they seek to address with a different orientation. The same core questions course through this entire topic. Specifically, when are laws that treat Jewish-Gentile difference essentially conditioned on offending elements of Gentile practice and culture? When such is the case, can we presume differences in how Jews and Gentiles were treated under rabbinic law would largely dissolve when such behavior is not at issue? When are the rulings more fundamentally grounded in the Gentile's non-Jewishness? When the rulings are based around that identifying feature, would we expect the differences and boundaries to be persistent until the a person's status were to change, as when a Gentile converts to Judaism?

Medieval Approaches

Our final port of call before we reach the modern period is the Middle Ages. It is in medieval times that we find the first attempts to deal broadly with entire Gentile societies, as opposed to the individual anomalies and acquaintances that are the focus of rabbinic sources. As Jews confront a fixed existence under Muslim and Christian regimes, there are meaningful efforts to arrive at more comprehensive approaches that will allow for at least commercial, if not broader interactions between Jews and Gentiles. These interactions, facially opposed to Talmudic law, required creative hermeneutic application of some of the nuance we have already seen in the classical canon.

Maimonides and Muslims

Maimonides is the most prominent of many authorities who argued that Muslims are not idolaters, and therefore various laws should not apply to them.[24] In one concrete case, Maimonides is lenient with wine owned or touched by Muslims. Muslims are certainly Gentiles, and Gentile wine is forbidden by the Talmud, both for consumption and for monetary benefit. Nonetheless, Maimonides builds off of a Talmudic position that holds that it is permissible to benefit from (but not to consume) a *ger toshav*'s wine. He expands that ruling to say the following:

> A *ger toshav* is a person who has accepted upon himself the seven Noahide *mitzvot*, as we have explained—it is prohibited to drink his wine, but it is permitted to derive benefit from it. **And so too any Gentile who does not worship idols, such as the Muslims, their wine may not be drunk, but one may derive benefit from it . . .** But those who worship idols, one may not derive benefit from their wine.[25]

Maimonides's ruling here essentially eliminates the ban on benefiting from Gentile wine for anyone who lives in Muslim lands.[26] It does so by emphasizing that, for the purposes of the ban on benefiting from Gentile wine—which centers around idolatry—Muslims are legally distinct from Talmudic Gentiles, on account of their behavior and their faith.

Tosafists and Christians

The Tosafists of France made a similar move with respect to Christian wine. They were confronted with a reality wherein Jews always did business with Christians on their holidays, especially the weekly holiday of Sunday. How could this be justified in light of Talmudic precedent, which forbids not only transactions on festivals but also transactions several days prior to the festival? Here is one conceptual/textual defense they offer:

> It seems the reason people are lenient is because we know that the Gentiles in our midst do not worship idols, and therefore it is permitted just as it was for Rav Yehudah to send a gift to Avidarna on the day of his holiday, saying, "I know that he does not worship idols."[27]

The argument here is a practical one, claiming that Christians simply don't engage in the kinds of idolatrous practices that offended Talmudic authorities regarding the Gentiles of their day. In other places, Tosafot argue for the monotheism of Christianity itself on doctrinal/theological grounds.[28] Similar to Maimonides, Tosafot take Talmudic precedents about individuals and expand them into strategies for an entire society. In the process, the ban on commerce on Gentile holidays effectively disappears.

Meiri's Comprehensive Approach

A more discerning reader of Maimonides and Tosafot will perceive that their recategorizations of Muslims and Christians, respectively, are limited to specific cases. Maimonides is lenient with Muslim wine and elsewhere implies that it is perfectly permissible to enter a mosque. However, he never suggests that the other aspects of Jewish-Gentile law do not apply to them, implying that other aspects of social legislation meant to separate the groups still hold, including inequities in civil law and the prohibition on Jews violating Shabbat to save Gentiles.[29] This is true for Tosafot as well, who seem almost exclusively focused on matters of commerce and allowing Jews to function in a Christian-dominated economy.

The first and, in many ways, only attempt to address the fuller range of Talmudic laws that differentiate between Jews and Gentiles was offered by R. Menahem HaMeiri, a Provencal scholar active in the thirteenth and fourteenth centuries. Meiri's work was not printed until the late nineteenth and early twentieth centuries and thus had little influence on interpretations and policy in the centuries immediately after his death. Nonetheless, his influence on later modern thinking in this arena is profound.

Essentially, Meiri argued that every time the term "Gentile" appears in rabbinic literature, one cannot understand its scope without intuiting, investigating, and debating the purpose of the laws in which the reference to Gentiles is embedded. Meiri argues that the sociological scope of the Gentile always corresponds with the goals that a given law is aiming to accomplish. Sometimes this interpretative move is virtually compelled by the texts themselves. It stands to reason that the Talmudic regulations meant to protect Jews from vicious and vengeful barbers simply wouldn't apply to neighbors one experiences as kind and concerned for one's welfare. But Meiri goes much further, arguing that certain laws—delivered without exceptions in the Talmud—are intrinsically bound by their sociological context. So, for instance, he has the following to say about inequities between Jew and Gentile with respect to civil law in the Talmud:

> If a Jew's ox gores a Gentile's ox, the Jew is exempt . . . and if a Gentile's ox gores the ox of a Jew . . . the Gentile pays full damages, because [Gentiles] have no regard for other people's possessions, so we penalize them so that they will not become accustomed to destroying things. According to what it says in the Talmud, this would only apply to nations who are not bounded by the ways of religion and norms, as it says about them in the Talmud: "God saw that the Gentiles were not keeping the seven Noahide laws that they had accepted upon themselves, arose and permitted their possessions," provided they deserve this. If they *do* follow the seven Noahide laws, our dealings

> with them should be as their dealings with us. We should show ourselves no favors in cases with them. It is thus obvious that the same is true of nations bound in the ways of religion and norms.[30]

Meiri here leans into the Talmud's justification for not compensating Gentiles for Jewish-caused damage to their property. If the basis for this discrepancy is Gentile indecency and immorality, then the legal category must be *about* basic decency and morality. Once the Gentiles in question are "bound in the ways of religion and norms," they should have the same legal status as Jews. He similarly reevaluates passages that seem indifferent to the well-being of Gentiles:

> When harm comes to Gentiles we are not commanded to try to save them. But in this case of Gentiles as well, you need to apply the distinction we mentioned earlier with regard to the type of Gentile we are speaking about. This refers to idolaters who are not bound by the ways of religion—indeed, all transgressions and disgraceful things are pleasing to them . . .
>
> Therefore, anyone who worships God, even if he is not part of the religion [i.e. Judaism] is not included in this law God forbid![31]

Even regarding as weighty a matter as Shabbat violation, Meiri says that the refusal to allow violating Shabbat to save Gentile life only applies to idolaters, "for whom we are not commanded to violate Shabbat since they have no religion/boundaries."[32] Meiri thus radically shrinks and shifts the Talmudic law, applying it only to "unbounded" Gentiles who have no faith community analogous to Judaism and no sense of social responsibility.

Nonetheless, Meiri does not dissolve the category of Gentile entirely. When it comes to laws that he determines to be about maintaining Jewish distinctiveness—a goal separate from avoiding idolatry—Meiri asserts that the Talmudic Gentile of old and the Provencal Christian of his own day are identically positioned with respect to the law. Regulations around drinking wine and other food boundaries remain in effect, because the *purpose* of those laws is separation and is not a function of the (in)decency of the Gentile in question.[33] Still, the analysis here is sweeping and comprehensive, essentially breaking down the category of Gentile into different components, divergent elements of which rise to the fore depending on the religious and social context of the laws under discussion. This creative, deconstructive approach foreshadows pathways taken, and not taken, in the modern period.[34]

Modern Approaches

With these anchor texts and approaches in the background, we are poised to explore the modern engagement with this topic. As Jews attained Emancipation in Europe, perhaps the most vexing and embarrassing issues were matters of Jewish-Gentile distinction as laid out in Talmudic law. While these points had been the foci of various medieval disputations and incriminations in the Middle Ages, in modernity these points of law served as potential obstacles to Jewish integration into the broader society. In particular, modern discourse around these issues is not *only* focused on practical problem solving but also on defending the sort of Jewish particularism they represented to a more universalist world in which Jews were and desired to be a part. Jewish responses to these matters of law and practice reflect a simultaneous dialogue with the external and internal worlds that Jews increasingly inhabited simultaneously.

One central pivotal point of conflict in modernity, useful for understanding the core dilemma here, was Napoleon's convening of a Jewish Sanhedrin in Paris in 1806. This council of elders was assembled to answer twelve questions that pertained directly to the possibility of Jews treating their fellow Gentiles as equals. A number of the questions were inquiries regarding the potential conflict between Jewish laws of marriage and divorce and those of the French state. But others were essentially versions of the following: "If we extend the Jews equal rights as citizens, do we have a guarantee that you will act with loyalty and fairness to your fellow French citizens?" Is this even possible given the legacy of Talmudic law? Here are a few queries put to the great French rabbis of the day:[35]

- May a Jewess marry a Christian, or a Jew a Christian woman? Or does Jewish law order that the Jews should only intermarry among themselves?
- In the eyes of Jews, are Frenchmen not of the Jewish religion considered as brethren or as strangers?
- What conduct does Jewish law prescribe toward Frenchmen not of the Jewish religion?
- Does Jewish law forbid the Jews to take usury from their brethren?
- Does Jewish law forbid, or permit, usury in dealings with strangers?

These questions—leading to be sure, and inviting only one viable set of answers—set the tone for any efforts to ground more parochial practice in the context of a universalist ethos. Broadly speaking, Jewish responses in modernity to laws concerning Gentiles can be grouped into four categories: First, some responses functioned as apologetics meant to constitute efforts to justify the laws and fundamentally defend them. Second, some authorities argued for a change in the earlier law based on Jewish safety. These are claims that, if the law were to be applied as it always had, it would endanger Jewish life, thus warranting a new approach. Third, some positions relied on the idea that the move to change a law is not based on an imminent fear for Jewish safety, but rather is grounded in a fear of defaming Jews and the Jewish religion. This approach is concerned with Judaism's broader reputation. Finally, certain authorities argued for a broader redefinition of the category of Gentiles, as part of a more comprehensive, principled effort to think about Jewish-Gentile difference on a more definitional level. In this final approach, by reevaluating who fits into the definition of Gentile, new possibilities emerge for how the relevant laws concerning Jews and Gentiles may or may not be applied. We will examine each of these categories in turn.

Apologetics

This term is not meant here to be derogatory. An apologetic simply seeks to explain and justify the law and to persuade others to believe in its justness and reasonableness as well. As such, it can be an important tool for defending traditions against external charges. It can also lay the groundwork for later changes in the law, should the apologia both be taken seriously and no longer apply convincingly in other circumstances.[36]

A number of laws about Gentiles were treated this way by modern authorities. The Jewish Notables of the Paris Sanhedrin responded to Napoleon's question of intermarriage by saying, in part: "Such is the opinion of the Rabbis, members of this assembly. In general, they would be no more inclined to bless the union of a Jewess with a Christian, or of a Jew with a Christian woman, than Catholic priests themselves would be disposed to sanction unions of this kind."[37] In other words, there is nothing unusual about Jewish particularity when it comes to marriage law—the Catholic Church, too, insists both partners be baptized if the marriage is to be considered a sacrament.

Another modern authority, R. Baruch Halevi Epstein, similarly tries to defend the gap between Jews and Gentiles around the laws of interest:

> Don't be shocked by the Torah's command to lend money on interest to Gentiles, in the fashion of the enemies of the Jewish people and its Talmud who have inveighed against it. When Israel left Egypt and received the Torah, they were a nation dwelling apart, and they agreed that each of them would show special kindness to one another, in matters of finance and commerce. This is the meaning of the command, "Do not lend money on interest to your brother": Just as he will not charge you interest, so too, you may not charge him interest. However, the other nations, since when they would lend to Israel they would charge interest, it is then only fair that Israel was permitted to charge them interest.[38]

Here, too, the argument is that Jewish "discrimination" against Gentiles is nothing more than the common practice of the market. If Jews extend certain privileges to one another, they are no different than unions and guilds that extend such benefits to their own members but not outsiders. It is these benefits that are unusual, not their absence.

Even the stickiest of differences—the ban on violating Shabbat to save Gentile life—is open to apologetic defense. A number of authorities emphasize that one of the fundamental justifications for violating Shabbat is that the person saved will be able to observe Shabbat many more times in the future, making the trade-off worth it in terms of aggregate Shabbat observance.[39] And on this logic, one indeed may not violate Shabbat to save the life of a Jewish Shabbat violator.[40] More broadly, Jews who violated Shabbat in public were often given the status of Gentiles in *halakhah*, allowing this analysis to affect all the categories we have already noted, and rendering the entire Jewish-Gentile discourse as nothing more than a proxy for the axis of basic commitment to Jewish observance. This logic creates its own problems, but completely redirects the law from being about some difference between Jews and Gentiles to being a law about Shabbat observance, with no specific privilege given to Jews. And this line of argument has some backing in Talmudic precedent: the same Talmudic text that seems to express indifference when it comes to Gentile life—one neither lowers them into nor raises them out of a pit—expresses outright hostility to Jewish heretics—one is meant to lower them into the pit![41]

In short, the strategy of apologetic has been one significant modern Jewish strategy for dealing with Jewish legal rulings that seem to discriminate against Gentiles. It is a limited approach that effects no change on the practical plane. But it has at times provided an effective talking point for Jews who wanted to adhere to traditional standards while still seeming to be decent members of a broader society.

Changing the Law to Avoid Danger and Enmity

It is a cardinal principle of Jewish law that nearly all prohibitions can be suspended when their violation will prevent a death. This is neatly summarized in the following text: "The mitzvot were only given to Israel so that they might live through them . . . nothing stands in the face of preserving a life."[42] This principle was ready at hand for many rabbis throughout the centuries who wished to permit something that would otherwise have been forbidden. One short example will bear this out. Classical Jewish law forbids extinguishing a fire on Shabbat—there is no justification for violating the sacred day in this way just in order to save loss of property. With the exception of some indirect forms of extinguishing that were permitted, Jews were expected, in theory, to allow their homes and possessions to burn to the ground in the name of Shabbat observance. (The general assumption was that people would be able to safely evacuate such that the blaze itself would not put any Jewish lives at risk.) One can imagine this was often a difficult precept to which to adhere, but in the Middle Ages we get the following broader dispensation: "Our teachers permitted extinguishing a blaze on Shabbat because we now dwell amidst the Gentiles, and when there is a blaze, they loot and kill."[43] Here, we get a blanket permission to do what the Talmud had forbidden. But it is done under the rubric of saving Jewish lives. True, you may not violate Shabbat to save your house, but you may violate Shabbat to save your life. To the extent that allowing a fire to grow will create general disorder and put lives at risk, one is permitted—even required—to douse the fire before it can grow to dangerous proportions.

This basic approach inspired a number of other solutions to the problems of Jewish/Gentile inequity before the law. As we have seen, the question of Shabbat violation in order to preserve and sustain Gentile life was particularly contentious. In particular, as Jews entered into the field of medicine, which was increasingly regulated and professionalized over time, the notion that a Jewish doctor would not treat Gentile patients on Shabbat became increasingly untenable. We get one picture of a widening gulf between the instinctive behavior of Jewish doctors and the jurisprudence that emerged naturally from the canonical sources in the following text:

> One may not assist a Gentile woman to give birth—even for pay, which is permitted during the week for fear of enmity. . . . this is forbidden on Shabbat because she can evade by saying that Jews do not violate Shabbat except for one who observes Shabbat. . . . Know that the doctors in our day—even the most observant among them—are not careful about this at all. Each and every Shabbat they travel long distances to heal Gentiles and they write and grind medicines. They have no basis for this. . . . These doctors are bona fide intentional Shabbat violators, may God help us![44]

This text, building off of the Talmud in Avodah Zarah 26a,[45] notes that there is no justification in the Talmud for violating Shabbat for the sake of a Gentile. Even though this might cause enmity, there is a ready excuse—Jews only violate Shabbat for those who observe Shabbat. Nonetheless, Jewish doctors are treating all their patients, even when numerous biblical violations of Shabbat are involved.

One major strategy for squaring this circle was to cast the act of violating Shabbat to save and preserve Gentile life as an act of self-defense. Yes, the Talmud seems to say that we don't have to worry about the enmity that might arise from a Jewish refusal to treat a Gentile patient. But if the concern is not merely enmity but fear for deadly reprisals on Jews, then this transforms into a case of preserving *Jewish* life, the pursuit of which justifies violating Shabbat. The first to articulate this approach was R. Moses Sofer (Hungary, nineteenth century). He writes that if it were to be *dangerous* for Jews not to treat Gentiles on Shabbat, then even Biblical violations are permitted.[46] R. Moshe Feinstein (United States, twentieth century), argues that this approach is virtually implicit in the Talmudic text itself:

> I will answer regarding your question about a Gentile. It is clear and simple that the excuse offered by Abaye in the Talmud [i.e. that Jews can only violate Shabbat to save the lives of those who observe Shabbat] will not be accepted in [the United States], neither by the patients and their families, nor by the authorities. Therefore, if he offers this excuse in the hospital, not only if there is no other doctor available, in which case they will certainly not listen to him, but even if there is another doctor, they will consider him to be a criminal and a murderer . . .
>
> When a case arises where the doctor must be in the hospital on Shabbat or where a Gentile patient in mortal danger comes to see him . . . the doctor must treat him, even if Biblical violations of Shabbat are involved . . . given that in [the United States] Abaye's excuses will not be accepted and it will be a bona fide danger to himself and his relatives. And even if he does not worry for his own life, we should be worried for the enormous enmity from the state and the government and the dangerous consequences that could result. . . . In our time, it seems to me that we should worry for this danger in all places, also on account of the fact that news from all over the world is now published in newspapers, such that this would quickly become a global problem that would spread incitement until a significant number of Jews could be

> killed. Therefore, it seems obvious that in our time we treat this as a real danger and one should permit when such cases come up.[47]

Another formulation of the ways in which Jewish care and safety is wrapped up in a more universal ethic is articulated by R. Eliezer Melamed He writes that the basis for violating Shabbat to save the life of a Gentile is grounded in "a de facto mutual agreement among the nations of the world to come to each other's mutual aid. If we want Gentiles to save Jews, we too need to commit to saving them. Thereby, saving the life of a Gentile is for the purpose of saving the life of a Jew and therefore supersedes Shabbat."[48] Rav Melamed grounds this way of thinking in part in the notion of there being an effective, scientifically grounded field of medicine with universally recognized rules and principles, thus making the idea that the member of one group would not heal the member of another being incoherent and therefore repellent. In earlier times, he argues, when healing was more closely linked to religion, it was potentially a more plausible claim that someone's faith would preclude them from healing on Shabbat and that perhaps their healing powers in fact would not work and might even redound to the detriment of the person seeking healing. But today, anyone who is a partner in the ecosystem of medicine is expected to be in as a full partner, and that requires healing anyone and everyone who needs that help, even on Shabbat. To opt out of that system, even in part, is ultimately to make Jews vulnerable.

This approach, while advocating for a major shift in the law, has the jurisprudential benefit of its conservatism. No real changes to prior discourse are proffered. As in the case of extinguishing a blaze on Shabbat, the age-old exception of violating Shabbat to save (Jewish) lives is invoked in order to allow for an even greater degree of flexibility than would have been possible in the past. Its limitations—both theoretical and practical—are also evident. First, there is no shift in the balance of Gentile lives and Jewish Shabbat observance, and to the extent that it is precisely this gap that is bothersome to many modern Jews, this approach is an evasion. Second, if the only concern is a threat to Jewish lives, there may still remain a preference to assign a Gentile to these care tasks on Shabbat, as long as doing so will not provoke outrage. Anyone looking for a more comprehensive shift will find this limited. Third, one might dispute whether Jewish lives will actually be in danger if the Talmudic policy was adhered to. More specifically, might the risks involve simply social ostracism and/or fines and imprisonment? If so, are these concerns sufficient to warrant an unjustified violation of Shabbat?

Unsurprisingly, a tweak on this view emerges to address this last concern. Some tried to argue for leeway here not based on actual danger to Jewish lives, but by arguing for the violation of Shabbat to be an almost incidental part of the activity. The Jewish doctor can claim that her only goal is to avoid losing her license or being fined or imprisoned. If so, the activity becomes similar to the Talmudic case of a person who digs a hole in the ground on Shabbat but does not need the dirt. This sort of case is one where the physical action is forbidden, but one is not performing it for its main functional purpose—in this case, to use the dirt that one has excavated. There is a tradition that these sorts of nonfunctional actions are only rabbinically forbidden and can therefore be suspended in cases of need, even short of risk to life, such as general Gentile enmity toward Jews. Some modern authorities try to deploy this sort of argument to justify flexibility with regard to Shabbat violation for Gentile life:

> According to this logic, our case is one where the entire intention of the doctor when treating the Gentile patient on Shabbat is to avoid punishment by the government. This sort of treatment is considered under compulsion, and moreover, the doctor's motivation is also so that Jewish patients under the care of Gentile doctors not be put in danger. This is therefore defensibly categorized as a forbidden action not being done for its normal functional purpose, and there is thus no Biblical violation at stake.[49]

Essentially, conceiving of the medical treatment as not truly being directed toward the patient but rather toward concerns of other terrible outcomes renders the actions sufficiently indirect for Shabbat purposes to allow for leniency without revisiting the fundamental elements of this area of law. This approach also doesn't really require a direct claim that Jewish lives will be put in danger; it can rely solely on the intentions and focus of the practitioner.

More broadly, the category of *eivah*, the fear of causing enmity, has been invoked by modern authorities to permit a range of rules that would otherwise be in place. As noted, the Talmud already permits interaction with a Gentile on the day of his festival in order to avoid enmity.[50] Can this rubric also be allowed to break down other social barriers? R. Yehoshua Falk Katz (Poland, sixteenth–seventeenth centuries) argued that, though the Talmud forbids a Jew from attending a family wedding of an idolatrous friend, this is permitted if not attending will generate enmity. Later authorities quote this view to permit Jews to attend parties with non-Jewish colleagues and friends to avoid offense.[51]

In sum, this view allows Jews wiggle room on various laws in the name of concerns for Jewish self-preservation and to avoid unnecessary Gentile antagonism. The consequences are significant in terms of leniency, but the underlying structure of the law and its assumptions remain intact.

Fear of Defaming Jews and the Jewish Religion

This third approach is slightly different than the prior one. Even if there is no danger to Jewish lives, and even if something like enmity will not really be in evidence, Jewish behaviors toward Gentiles might evoke scorn for Jews and Judaism. In internal Jewish language, this is the fear of the desecration of God's name (*hilul hashem*), whereby his putative ambassadors on earth become, to the Gentiles, exemplars of all that is wrong and backward.

Fear that adherence to Jewish law might lead to this outcome is again as old as the Talmud. While the strict letter of the law declares that Jews are exempt from returning the lost objects of Gentiles, the Talmud quotes R. Pinhas ben Yair as saying that if failing to return a Gentile's lost object will lead to a desecration of God's name, then it is forbidden to hold on to it.[52] A story in the Talmud Yerushalmi recalls how one rabbinic Sage returned an expensive jewel that a Gentile left on the neck of a donkey that he had purchased, just so he could hear the Gentile say, "Blessed is the God of the Jews."[53]

These impulses, both positive and negative, have been another driver of *halakhic* thinking in modernity. R. Mordechai Shmuel Ghirondi (Italy, nineteenth century) also took up the question of Jews serving as doctors for Gentiles on Shabbat. While he sought a similar set of practical solutions to the authorities we explored, the tone and orientation are quite different. Instead of a concern for the safety of individual Jews, we find a concern for Judaism itself:[54]

> The times have changed, the Gentiles in our day are our brethren and allies, they are monotheists like us. . . . We must violate Shabbat on their account . . . traveling even by coach in order to heal them, and we must perform forbidden labors in order to save their lives and to tend to the production of drugs prepared in Jewish apothecaries, even when their lives are not in danger, for the matter is one of sanctifying God's Name. If we do not, we will give the Gentiles a weapon with which to attack us, and they will forbid us to serve as doctors even during the week. We have found the basis for permitting anything that will cause enmity . . . [the Talmud implies that] wherever enmity will unavoidably result, and no effective excuse can be offered, we violate Shabbat even for Gentiles.

In another letter, he gives voice to the Jewish doctors of the day, who inveigh against their rabbinic leadership: "Why do you do this to your servants, making us repulsive in the eyes of the Gentiles, by forbidding us to go outside of the city by coach so that we could heal the sick from their illnesses and save them from death? The matter is one of desecrating God's Name! Why should this be any different from the case of putting out a fire on Shabbat?" Note that the language here is *not* focused on the equality of Gentile life per se; R. Ghirondi and the doctors in his community are arguing for the violation of Shabbat even when Gentile life is not at risk! The Talmudic discourse of enmity is redirected here not to focus on a threat to the life of the Jews but to the larger question of whether Jews will be respected, allowed to function in socially critical professions like medicine, and whether, as a result, God's Name—assumed to be uniquely associated with the Jews—will be profaned or sanctified. The precedent of extinguishing a blaze on Shabbat is understood to point the way to any action that will prevent the Jews from being seen as social pariahs. In yet another letter, R. Ghirondi makes clear that his concern is also for the viability of Judaism in the modern world if this course is not taken: "If we do not find a way to permit some of these things, the Gentiles will place a heavy yoke upon us, as they did in former times. And this will lead to many Jews turning their backs on the divine religion [=Judaism] entirely, and they will, God forbid, leave the holy community."

His colleague and teacher, R. Avraham Reggio, rejected this line of reasoning, insisting that Shabbat violation for Gentiles be more tightly tied to situations where

Jewish life would actually be in danger. Nonetheless, others have argued in the style of R. Ghirondi for other sorts of permissions. R. David Zvi Hoffman (Germany, nineteenth–twentieth centuries) addresses the question of draft dodging by Jews who do not want to be compelled to serve in the German army for fear of routine Shabbat violation. He says the following:

> There is no doubt that it is even more than a standard-level *mitzvah* to avoid draft dodging, because one who does so causes the desecration of God's Name if it comes to light. And this redounds to the detriment of Jews, for the anti-Semites will say that the Jews do not follow the laws of the land . . .
>
> Even if we were to say that every Jew should attempt to dodge the draft so as to avoid the desecration of Shabbat . . . most would not succeed, and this would cause a great desecration of God's Name to no avail. Therefore, the best course is to trust in God and maybe he will find favor in the eyes of his commanders and they will let him observe Shabbat and he will thereby do what is right both in the eyes of God and men.[55]

Here, we see R. Hoffman licensing a path of behavior that will almost certainly result in major Shabbat violations for the Jew, without a tight claim that said violations are directly in service of saving lives. The basis is ultimately the defaming of Jews and Judaism, and a sense of responsibility for how the Jewish collective will bear the consequences of certain modes of behavior that don't take this consideration into account.

Redefining the Category of Gentiles

Finally, a more dramatic approach simply revisits the question of who is a Gentile for the purposes of these laws. The Paris Sanhedrin already offered this approach when pressed on its list of questions, even including the question of intermarriage. Siding with one line of Talmudic and medieval precedent,[56] they asserted that the Torah's ban on intermarriage only applied to the seven indigenous nations of Canaan. This dodge allowed them to cast the remaining opposition to intermarriage in Jewish tradition as nothing more than rabbinic preference and procedure, but allowing Jews to recognize civil marriages with contemporary French Gentiles as perfectly legitimate under Torah law.

This was not a full *halakhic* argument to be sure, and it comes off and functions as a very technical evasion. But playing with who is and who is not a Gentile indeed became a meaningful mode of *halakhic* analysis attractive to a number of modern voices. We already saw in the Meiri that earlier thinkers had questioned whether the category of "Gentile" in the Talmud was perhaps, in fact, shorthand for "idolater," or even for a type of uncivilized barbarian whose heart would show the Jew no kindness and thus warranting an indifferent cold-heartedness in return. Some outlier rabbinic views suggested extending the Maimonidean claim regarding wine, arguing that other forms of rabbinic social legislation should not apply to non-idolatrous Gentiles, such as

Muslims. R. Israel Jacob Hagiz (Morocco/Italy/Land of Israel, seventeenth century) and R. Rafael Berdugo (Morocco, seventeenth–eighteenth centuries) suggested that a good argument could be made for saying that the Talmudic prohibitions on Gentile bread and cooked food should not apply to monotheistic Muslims.[57] While even they did not recommend adopting this in practice, their creative thinking reflects a reexamination of Jewish-Gentile (in these cases, Muslim) relationships in a shared society.

R. Hayyim David Halevi (Israel, twentieth century) argued for this sort of broader reassessment of the status of non-Jews when thinking about the Talmudic sources that regulated Jewish treatment of Gentiles in matters of civil and criminal law. R. Halevi seeks to cut the Gordian knot here, giving strong voice to the notion that the Gentiles of old and of today are completely nonanalogous:

> We should understand all the laws pertaining to Gentiles as being under the grand, historic rubric of purging the world of idolatry in order to establish the Kingdom of God. And therefore, a number of things were only grudgingly permitted for the purpose of promoting the "ways of peace" [such as burying the Gentile dead]. We should be proud of the fact that Jews were at the vanguard of human and moral culture as we fought this war [against idolatry] and won it. But in our own times, when there are no real idolaters—there at most ancestral cultures and traditions . . . there is no reason whatsoever, in my opinion, to relate to the Gentiles of our own day as having the status of Talmudic Gentiles. . . . These relationships should not be maintained merely under the rubric of "ways of peace" but as human and ethical obligations.[58]

In his quest for a basis for greater equity in Jewish law, R. Halevi interestingly rejects the clearest Talmudic precedent for treating Gentiles and Jews equally in a whole host of areas. The license or imperative to bury, clothe, and feed Gentiles "on account of peace" reads to him like a secondary justification that itself reifies the basic inequality at play. This made perfect sense when Gentiles were understood by Jews to be agents of civilizational destruction, religious corrosion, and moral corruption, even as the Jews' shared place in society with them nonetheless required some concrete actions to promote a functional comity. Today, however, the Gentiles can and must be engaged with solely on the basis of their humanity.

In another similar move, but with some interesting nuance, R. Nahum Rabinovitch issues a two-tiered ruling, as he contemplates the role of a religious paramedic at the scene of a terror attack on Shabbat.[59] First, the Gentile perpetrator of the murder should be given medical attention on Shabbat, even if such treatment requires Shabbat violation, but this should only be done under the more limited theory of avoiding enmity. Second, contemporary, decent, law-abiding Gentiles are in the category of *ger toshav* and such Gentiles *do* trigger the requirement to violate Shabbat just like Jews.[60]

This fourth, reevaluative approach, whether in its broader or more nuanced forms, is clear and elegant, and enjoys some meaningful precedent. It is reasonable to ask why it is not more dominant, at least among many major modern authorities of *halakhah*.

A number of factors seem to be at play here, all of which teach us interesting dynamics about *halakhic* discourse, at least as engaged by many of its most prominent expositors.

Initially, there are doubts regarding the normative force of the medieval views from which this approach can draw strength. R. Rabinovitch's ruling relies on a medieval opinion that is in fact a stray comment that seems to have escaped the attention of most and it leaves few footprints in the *halakhic* record until its redemption by a few moderns. Moreover, there is some indication that other medieval authorities, like Maimonides, may have thought differently about the *ger toshav* when it comes to Shabbat violation.[61] With regard to Meiri, his entire Talmudic commentary was largely lost and not printed in full until the early twentieth century. Given that one of the most powerful aspects of *halakhic* discourse lies in its ability to work with precedent to make the present continuous with the past, working with an approach like that of the Meiri can feel like an archaeological discovery that is unmoored from living, Jewish tradition.

There are other potential limitations. The category of *ger toshav* is, on the one hand, a strong Talmudic precedent for treating a certain type of Gentile differently from others. But, on the other hand, there are a number of Talmudic and medieval statements that the category of *ger toshav* is only fully operative when the Jubilee year is in legal force.[62] This questions whether the category of *ger toshav* can be a useful legal rubric in the contemporary world. Even past uses of the category in Talmudic and medieval times generally allowed for *ignoring* prohibitions—like benefiting from wine that someone touched, or bringing a Gentile a gift on their holiday. Practical precedent for *active* violation of Shabbat on a Gentile's behalf, or other clear expressions of a Gentile's full equality to a Jew under the law, are harder to come by.

Finally, and perhaps most significant, this approach of redefinition is atypical in its scale for the usual aesthetics of *halakhah*. Usually, *halakhic* discussions hold various categories and identities constant and explore how the law might be applied differently in boundary cases. Playing with the definition of legal categories and identities themselves—as Meiri does—is potentially destabilizing. Nonetheless, the directness, elegance, and honesty of this approach will be compelling to those seeking a clean, direct path to treating Gentiles and Jews equally under the law.

Conclusion: What Remains Unsaid

For all that modern *halakhah* has offered on this topic, it is interesting to note a number of directions that have not generally been taken. The core material here unavoidably *does* distinguish between Jews and at least *some* Gentiles, and indeed accepts and embraces the notion that there are some people who are meant to be left in a pit and do not warrant the violation of Shabbat. Thus, it should not be surprising that even the broadening approach of people like R. Hayyim David Halevi—emerging from the Talmudic category of *ger toshav* and from the Meiri's pioneering dissection of the category of Gentile—does not reject the earlier law wholesale. That is, R. Halevi does not argue that even Gentiles of old should never have been left to languish in a pit. For a statement to be within the bounds of *halakhic* discourse, it must be in continuous relationship with prior precedents. The category of Gentile can be maintained, expanded, or de facto eliminated. But it cannot *de jure* be removed from the map without triggering a sense of larger rupture to the system.

Similarly, even the Paris Sanhedrin did not argue for the complete dissolution of distinctions between Gentiles and Jews. Whether intermarriage was a matter of biblical or rabbinic concern, whether it was a moral wrong or an impossibility due to rabbinic procedure, it was hardly an option to dissolve the boundary between Jew and Gentile altogether. Some distinctions clearly remained necessary as long as Jews were to remain a distinct people and religious group defined, at least in part, through descent.

For those grappling with the status of Gentiles in Jewish law in modernity, the essential questions are where, when, and why Jewish-Gentile *difference*, a given in the *halakhic* system, is meant to generate any form of Jewish *privilege*. For some voices, the sort of hierarchy presumed by earlier texts is meant to live on, if only in more limited contexts, as an essential feature of these divergent identities and statuses. For others, any sense of hierarchy between Jew and Gentile is nothing more than a proxy for the religious, moral and social judgments of another age.

More broadly, a close tracking of this topic reveals many of the features of *halakhic* discourse that have made it so historically durable: its ability to redirect exceptional cases to serve as new norms, to probe the reasons behind case law with an eye to reapplication, and even the possibility of reevaluating legal categories as ultimately representing values that may require recategorization in a new age and in new contexts, all while speaking the language of the past to address the needs and challenges of the present.

Notes

1. It is worth noting here that different passages in the Torah refer to the *nokhri*, a foreigner who is not a permanent resident of the land, and the *ger*, a non-Israelite who resides permanently on the land with Israelites. The *ger* is subject to more requirements and enjoys more protections, including a promise of procedural equality under the law. See Numbers 15:15–16 for one such example. Nonetheless, it seems that the *ger* is not treated as a full equal to Israelites in some respects, including the prohibition on owning Israelite slaves as property, a prohibition that Leviticus 25:45 does not seem to apply to the *ger*. For the purposes of this discussion, meant to highlight modern approaches to this question, these finer distinctions—highly relevant to a deeper understanding of the biblical text—will be elided.

   In addition, for more on the critical questions surrounding the construction of the biblical category of Israelite and its respective others, as opposed to the rabbinic dichotomy of Jew versus *goy*, or generic Gentile, see Adi Ophir and Ishay Rosen-Zvi, *Goy: Israel's Multiple Others and the Birth of the Gentile* (Oxford: Oxford University Press, 2018). Again, this important shift is less central for the focus of this chapter, which is centered on modern approaches to a Jewish-Gentile dichotomy already firmly in place by modernity for almost two millennia.
2. Lev. 25:44–46.

3. Deut. 7:3–4.
4. Deut. 23:21.
5. Per the previous note, this specific permission to lend money on interest seems like it did not apply to the *ger*, at least according to the plain meaning of Leviticus 25:36.
6. See Lev. 25:47.
7. Note that the language of Deuteronomy 7:3–4 quite plausibly trends in this second direction. The more specific formulation also sits well with the differing treatment of various nations throughout the Bible, as in Deuteronomy 23:4–9. See also I Kgs. 11:1–2.
8. For one example, see the Aramean general Na'aman, as described in II Kings 5.
9. While there are a number of details in *halakhah* that continue to preserve a special status for *ger*/proselyte, including certain disabilities such as serving as a judge over native-born Jews in capital cases, the distinctions are relatively few. Most important, the dominant strand in *halakhah* sees any such limitations or legal disabilities as limited to the first generation. As Shemot Rabbah 27:5 puts it: A male convert can have a grandson who is the high priest. When this convert marries a native-born Jew, his daughter is then eligible to marry a priest, and the convert's grandson from that union, a priest himself, could then be appointed high priest. And thus the most privileged lineal position in Judaism can descend from someone with no ancestral Jewish lineage whatsoever.
10. Mishnah Avodah Zarah 2:2.
11. Ibid. 1:1–3.
12. These decrees are referenced in a number of places and are most clearly enumerated in Yerushalmi Shabbat 1:4. While the Torah seems to forbid intermarriage, Beit Shammai and Beit Hillel seem to have understood that passage as limited to the seven indigenous nations of Canaan, a point we will return to. The Talmud Bavli takes up the question of the interaction of the biblical verses and these later ordinances on Avodah Zarah 36b.
13. Tosefta Bava Metzia 2:33.
14. Mishnah Yoma 8:7.
15. Talmud Bavli Avodah Zarah 26a.
16. Mishnah Bava Kama 4:3.
17. Talmud Bavli Avodah Zarah 29a.
18. Ibid. 64b–65a.
19. Ibid. 64b. This discussion is, of course, only focused on the status of the wine as affected by Gentile contact. There can be other issues with wine that might affect its consumption under Jewish law, including concerns about fining agents that come from non-kosher animals. That is beyond the scope of our discussion here.
20. See Tosefta Gittin 3:13–14; Yerushalmi Gittin 5:9; and Bavli Gittin 61a.
21. Tosefta Avodah Zarah 1:3.
22. Talmud Bavli Avodah Zarah 26a.
23. Talmud Bavli Bava Kama 38a.
24. See his *Responsa* #448.
25. Maimonides, Laws of Forbidden Foods, 11:7.
26. Maimonides was emphatic that Christians were idolaters and that all restrictions around Gentile wine applied to them in full force. See his commentary to Mishnah Avodah Zarah 1:3–4. But this would have been more of an occasional concern for someone living outside of Christendom.
27. Tosafot Avodah Zarah 2a s.v. *asur*.

28. See Tosafot Sanhedrin 63b s.v. *asur*. The goal there is to justify permitting accepting an oath from a Christian, even though the name of a Christian saint may be invoked in the process.
29. With respect to the one legal disadvantage of Gentiles in Jewish civil law, see Maimonides, Laws of Monetary Damages 8:5, where the language *does* seem to ground this in assumptions of Gentile legal systems rather than in their essential status. Still, no carve-out for Muslims is offered, as in the case of wine.
30. Beit Habehirah Bava Kama 37b.
31. Beit Habehirah Avodah Zarah 26a.
32. Beit Habehirah Yoma 84b. For another medieval example of removing specific sets of Gentiles from their normal category for the purposes of Shabbat violation, see Nachmanides (Ramban), glosses on Maimonides's Sefer Hamitzvot, Forgotten Positive *Mitzvah* #16. He says there that anyone with the status of a *ger toshav* triggers an obligation to violate Shabbat.
33. See Meiri Avodah Zarah 38b for one example of his thinking on this topic.
34. For a fuller account of Meiri's approach on this issue, see Moshe Halbertal, *Between Torah and Wisdom: Rabbi Menaḥem ha-Meiri and the Maimonidean Halakhists of Provence* (Jerusalem: Magnes Press, 2000), 80–108 [Hebrew].
35. Paul Mendes-Flohr and Jehuda Reinharz, "Napoleon's Instructions to the Assembly of Jewish Notables," in *The Jew in the Modern World: A Documentary History*, 2nd ed., ed. Paul Mendes-Flohr and Jehuda Reinharz (Oxford: Oxford University Press, 1995), 125–26.
36. See Tamar Ross, *Expanding the Palace of Torah Expanding the Palace of Torah: Orthodoxy and Feminism* (HBI Series on Jewish Women) (Waltham, MA: Brandeis University Press, 2004), for a further analysis of the role of apologetics in the historical development of *halakhah*.
37. Paul Mendes-Flohr and Jehuda Reinharz, "The Assembly of Jewish Notables: Answers to Napoleon," in *Jew in the Modern World*, ed. Mendes-Flohr and Reinharz, 129.
38. Torah Temimah, Notes to Deuteronomy 23:108.
39. See Talmud Bavli Yoma 85b for one instance of this justification.
40. See R. Joseph b. Meir Teomim, Peri Megadim Orah Hayyim Mishbetzot Zahav 328:6.
41. See Tosefta Bava Metzia 2:33, cited previously.
42. Tosefta Shabbat 15:17. The text, naturally, goes on to provide exceptions to this rule, exceptions that include idolatry, sexual offenses, and murder. Furthermore, in a time of religious persecution, one may be expected to give one's life on principle rather than succumb to pressure. Still, the exceptions here are the exceptions to a broad principle, one that notably warrants Shabbat violation.
43. R. Isaac b. Moshe of Vienna, Or Zarua II:149.
44. Mishnah Berurah 330:8., R. Israel Meir Kagan, nineteenth–twentieth centuries.
45. See the discussion of this text in the section on Background, Classical Rabbinic Sources.
46. *Repsonsa Hatam Sofer* II:131.
47. *Responsa Iggerot Moshe Orah Hayyim* IV:79.
48. Peninei Halachah, Elaborations on Shabbat 27:3.
49. R. Ovadiah Yosef, Yabia Omer VIII, Orah Hayyim #38. Israel, twentieth–twenty-first centuries.
50. See the discussion in the section on Background, Classical Rabbinic Sources.
51. See R. Moshe Feinstein, and Iggerot Moshe, Yoreh Deah II:117. By contrast, R. David Halevi Segal, in Taz Yoreh Deah 152:1, held that fear of enmity could never be a basis to be

lenient with prohibitions that are entirely *about* creating distance between Gentiles and Jews. If the ban on attending an idolater's wedding is actually the desire to harden a social boundary, then it is incoherent to invoke the fear of enmity as a mitigating factor. R. Menashe Klein, Mishneh Halakhot VII:118, takes this tack.

52. Talmud Bavli Bava Metzia 113b.
53. Talmud Yerushalmi Bava Metzia 2:5.
54. The passages here are cited in M. Benayahu, "An Exchange of Letters between Italian Sages with Regard to Questions of the Practice of Medicine on Shabbat from the Beginning of the Age of Religious Reform," *Asufot* 14 (2002): 299–313.
55. *Responsa Melamed Lehoil* I:42, R. David Zvi Hoffman, Germany, nineteenth–twentieth centuries.
56. See Talmud Bavli Kiddushin 68b and *Tur* Even Haezer 16.
57. See R. Hagiz, quoted in R. Jacob Faraji, *Responsum* #39, and Torot Emet on Yoreh Deah 112.
58. *Responsa Aseih Lekha Rav* 9:33, R. Hayyim David Halevi, Israel, twentieth century.
59. *Responsa Melumdei Milhamah* #43. R. Rabinovitch passed away in 2020.
60. R. Rabinovitch here is following the ruling of Ramban in his glosses on Maimonides's Sefer Hamitzvot, Forgotten Positive *Mitzvah* #16, referred to above.
61. See Maimonides, *Laws of Shabbat* 2:12, where he seems to say that one *is* concerned with the welfare of a *ger toshav*, but one nonetheless does *not* violate Shabbat for such a person.
62. See Talmud Bavli Arakhin 29a and Maimonides, *Laws of Idolatry* 10:6.

CHAPTER 23

THE ROLE OF SCIENTIFIC FINDINGS IN CONTEMPORARY JEWISH LAW

DANIEL REIFMAN, ISRAEL BELFER,
AND RACHEL S. A. PEAR

Introduction

The role of science within *halakhic* discourse has become an increasingly pressing issue during the modern era. Science is one of the most distinctive elements of modern culture and consciousness, and the scientific advances of the past half millennium have posed unprecedented questions and challenges for *halakhic* authorities to address. Following a brief consideration of the role of science in pre-modern *halakhic* discourse, this chapter will analyze the role of science in *halakhah* through the lens of key *halakhic* controversies that have developed since the Scientific Revolution.

Science in Pre-Modern *Halakhic* Literature

If we wish to trace the relationship between science and *halakhah* back into earlier periods of *halakhic* history, we should acknowledge we are not presuming to unearth a full-fledged ancient equivalent of modern scientific discourse. Many of the features that we associate with science, including controlled experimentation, did not fully develop in Europe as a way of relating to the world until the High Middle Ages at the earliest.[1] Indeed, the very notion of there being a distinct discourse called "science" whose influence on *halakhah* needs to be addressed is, to some degree, a distinctly modern concern.[2]

Nonetheless, rabbinic literature contains many examples of statements that we would consider scientific based on one essential criterion: they posit an account of the functioning of some aspect of the natural world. Most of these statements are simply descriptions of nature or the cosmos with no direct prescriptive implications. Moreover, even among those statements that do have prescriptive implications, the large majority of those have traditionally been classified as belonging to nonlegal codes of behavior (e.g., concerning personal health or medical care) that are distinct from the legal corpus of *halakhah*.[3] There are relatively few areas of rabbinic law in which a postulate about the natural world has direct implications for a *halakhic* ruling.

One particularly clear example concerns the types of grain that may be used to make matzah for the Passover seder. The Mishnah states:

> These are the substances with which one may fulfill one's obligation [of eating matzah] on Passover: wheat, barley, spelt, oats and rye.[4]

The Talmud *Bavli* comments as follows:

> . . . These [grains are valid for matzah], but not rice or millet. What is the source of [this distinction]? R. Shimon ben Lakish said, and thus was taught from the house of R. Yishmael, and thus was taught from the house of R. Eliezer ben Yaakov: The verse states, "You shall not eat anything leavened with [the Passover sacrifice]; for seven days thereafter you shall eat unleavened bread"—**that which becomes leaven, one may use to fulfill one's obligation of matzah, thus excluding those [grains] that do not become leaven but rather decay.**[5]

The *Bavli* correlates the *halakhic* distinction between different types of grain with a distinction between leavening (*himutz*) and decaying (*sirhon*), which would seem to be observable physical processes distinct from the legal categories to which they correspond. This understanding is bolstered by the parallel passage in the Talmud *Yerushalmi*:

> The sages inspected and found that no [grain] becomes matzah or leaven except these five species, **while all other species do not become matzah or leaven but rather decay.**[6]

This passage is an unusually explicit account of the rabbis justifying a *halakhic* ruling with what could be considered a scientific study. Whether the *Yerushalmi* means to say that the rabbis performed a controlled test or simply observed a series of cases, it is clear that they are making an empirical observation that leads them to postulate a principle regarding the development of dough with different types of grains.

This example is also noteworthy for the fact that the correlation between the scientific postulate and the *halakhic* ruling that it comes to explain is strictly positive. Neither in the Talmud nor in later *halakhic* literature do we find an instance of a grain that becomes leaven that is not fit for making matzah, or conversely a grain that does not become leaven that is fit for making matzah. Generalizing from this specific example, we might formulate a *deductive model* of the role of scientific postulates in *halakhah*: scientific statements serve as the logical predicates upon which *halakhic* rulings are based. There is a certain intuitive logic to this approach: one would assume that in order to properly apply *halakhic* principles to a set of circumstances, a *halakhic* authority requires a correct understanding of those circumstances, and this is what scientific postulates often seem to provide.[7]

However, even a cursory survey of *halakhic* literature indicates that a strictly deductive model cannot account for the way scientific postulates and technological circumstances function within *halakhah*. Simply put, there are too many instances of imperfect correlation between *halakhic* rulings and the scientific postulates invoked to explain them. A prominent example is the explanation for which physiological defects render an animal non-kosher as a *terefah*. The Mishnah[8] lists eighteen such defects (these conditions themselves are in turn referred to as *terefot*), and then concludes: "This is the general rule: If no animal in a similar condition can survive, it is a *terefah*." The clause, "no animal in a similar condition can survive," suggests a scientific assessment of the animal's physical state, such that the fundamental definition of a *terefah* is predicated on a scientific proposition: an animal is a *terefah* because it has a terminal medical condition.

Yet from the discussion of this Mishnah in the Talmud, it is clear that the relationship between the scientific proposition and the classification of animals as *terefot* is not as straightforward as the mishnah's language suggests. The Talmud cites several challenges to the Mishnah based on instances in which the conditions listed in the Mishnah prove not to be fatal, including several passages that, like the *Yerushalmi* cited above, reflect a measure of experimentation on the part of the rabbis. For example:

> It was said of Rabbi Shimon ben Halafta that he was a researcher of things, and he would do things to disprove Rabbi Yehudah's view. As Rabbi Yehudah says: If [a bird's] feathers are gone, it is invalid [as a *terefah*]. Rabbi Shimon ben Halafta once had a hen whose feathers were gone, and he placed it in an oven and wrapped it in a bronzeworkers' apron, and it grew wings even larger than the original ones.[9]

The Talmud cites a range of approaches to address such disparities between scientific evidence and *halakhic* rulings, but owing to the discursive and multivocal nature of the Talmud text, it does not do so systematically. However, this issue continues to occupy the medieval *halakhic* authorities, and their assessments of the role of veterinary medicine in the laws of *terefot* represent some of the earliest explicit analysis of the broader relationship between science and *halakhah*. Yet in point of fact, none of the medieval authorities articulates a single, consistent approach on this issue. For example, in a responsum[10] regarding an animal with an extra limb—a defect considered to be a *terefah* despite empirical evidence suggesting that it is not always fatal, the thirteenth-century authority R. Shlomo b. Aderet (Rashba) makes sweeping assertions about the primacy of *halakhah* over science, insisting that any scientific evidence that contradicts an established *halakhic* ruling must be assumed to be false.[11] Yet toward the conclusion of his responsum, he concedes that perhaps this and other defects are not necessarily fatal, and are considered *terefot* only due to analogies with other, invariably fatal conditions.

Maimonides offers a similarly divided approach. Regarding a defect that is *not* deemed to be a *terefah* even though science considers it to be fatal, Maimonides insists on the primacy of *halakhah* and states that the scientific evidence is assumed to be incorrect. However, in the converse situation—a condition that *is* considered a *terefah* even though science determines it not to be fatal—Maimonides states only that the *halakhah* does not change in response to the scientific evidence, not that the evidence is assumed to be faulty.[12]

This latter approach—that the classification of a defect as a *terefah* does not necessarily correlate with a scientific assessment of its consequences—points to what we might call an *independence* or *positivist model*[13] of the relationship between science and *halakhah*. Legal positivism reflects the notion that law constitutes a self-contained system of meaning, such that legal adjudication is not dependent on moral or other external considerations. Likewise, a positivist model of *halakhah* would reflect the idea that *halakhic* adjudication is not dependent on scientific categories or distinctions.[14] Yet from the fact that Maimonides relates differently to different types of tension between veterinary science and the laws of *terefot*, it is clear that he does not endorse an exclusively positivist model of *halakhah*.

To summarize thus far, even though pre-modern *halakhic* literature contains relatively few examples of explicit scientific reasoning, these examples are sufficient to demonstrate the difficulty of finding an overarching theoretical model that satisfactorily accounts for the way science functions within *halakhic* discourse. In most areas of *halakhah* where scientific postulates figure prominently, the correlation between those postulates and *halakhic* rulings seems almost haphazard—less consistent than the logical deduction model would predict, yet more substantial than the positivist model would predict. To the extent that these models have been articulated within *halakhic* literature, they function as modes of argumentation, ways for a *halakhic* authority to justify their ruling in a specific case involving a scientific consideration, rather than principles that can be applied across the board. Indeed, a more extensive survey of *halakhic* literature might lead us to further divide these models into a more nuanced typology of claims that *halakhic* authorities make about the impact of science on *halakhic* adjudication. However, all these models are fundamentally *prescriptively* oriented—assertions as to what degree *halakhah should* correlate positively with science. One who attempts to understand any one of these models as *descriptive*—articulating a comprehensive theory of the role science *actually* has played within *halakhic* discourse—will quickly find themselves beset with a bevy of counterexamples.

Toward an Alternate Conception of the Relationship between Science and *Halakhah*

Until this point, we have treated the interplay between science and *halakhah* as a distinct phenomenon, separate from the broader academic discussion of the interface of science and religion, a field that has developed over the past half century. While much scholarship on science and religion has been focused on religious belief systems due to the prevalence of issues relevant to Christianity, recent research has brought more attention to systems of religious practice, such as *halakhah*. Hence as we shift our focus to the modern era, we would like to offer an alternate model for describing the interplay between science and *halakhah* by considering approaches to the interface of science and religion. Later in the chapter we will consider how various distinctive elements of *halakhic* practice affect *halakhah*'s particular relationship with science.

One motif in the study of the interface of science and religion has been the creation of models or typologies.[15] For example, paleontologist Stephen Jay Gould offered the description of science and religion as necessarily separate, independent discourses, or as he phrased it, "non-overlapping magisteria."[16] The Israeli public intellectual Yeshayahu Leibowitz also posited an analogous 'separation' approach.[17] Other scholars have emphasized the harmony between the realms of science and religion. These separation and harmony approaches bear resemblance to the models of the relationship between science and *halakhah* that we outlined above—the deductive model and the positivist model. The assumption that science and religion are fundamentally in harmony dovetails with the deductive model, which assumes a high degree of correlation between the two discourses, while the positivist model reflects the assumption that each discourse operates in isolation.

Just as we have found both the deduction and positivist models wanting as comprehensive accounts of the role science plays in *halakhic* discourse, so, too, scholars in the field of science and religion have critiqued the separation and harmony approaches as inadequate to describe the complex interplay between science and religion. Approaches focused on harmonizing science and religion have been described as apologetic, while the idea that science and religion are wholly separate has been challenged as ignoring the many areas in which scientific and religious perspectives are thoroughly intertwined.

Perhaps the only model to survive critique is the broad *dialogue* model, which emphasizes the significant vectors of influence between the two fields of science and religion without the expectation that they will always be homologous or even commensurable. More than simply a compromise position between harmonization and complete separation, a dialogue model fundamentally changes the significance of patterns of similarity and difference between science and religion: it is specifically those features that make each one a distinct, independently meaningful discourse that enable it to contribute to a fruitful dialogue with the other. Applying a dialogue model to the relationship between *halakhah* and science requires us to identify the elements of each discourse that differentiate it from the other, since it is those elements that lead to the most significant "conversations" even as they also have the potential to generate tension. As with any dialogue, the outcome is not always complete agreement between the two; our analysis will focus on the *process* of interaction between science and *halakhah*. In some cases, this interaction leads *halakhic* authorities to reexamine foundational assumptions and develop a richer *halakhic* vocabulary. At other times, the tension between the two discourses leads *halakhic* authorities to close ranks and reject innovative conceptual models.

One of the main features of scientific discourse that has the potential to generate tension with *halakhah* is science's propensity for change, as exemplified by the occurrence of paradigm shifts and emergence of new technologies during the modern period. When a traditional *halakhic* ruling is associated with a particular scientific proposition, to what extent will scientific change impact the application of this ruling? To return to one of the examples cited above: in the aftermath of the chemical revolution, should *halakhic* authorities actively try to analyze the difference between *himutz* and *sirhon* in biochemical terms?[18] What if the biochemical distinction between these processes does not correlate with the *halakhic* distinction between those grains that may be used for matzah and those that may not: should the *halakhah* be amended in response to our new scientific understanding? Based on the logical deduction model, a scientific premise will always precede the corresponding *halakhic* ruling as a factual backdrop; as modern scientific progress changes this backdrop, it would necessarily modify or even undermine *halakhic* rulings that were based on earlier, faulty understandings of the natural world. Yet we have already observed that *halakhah* frequently does not correlate with science in this way.

The examples discussed—cases of interplay between science and *halakhah* in the modern era—are all marked by this sort of tension, where scientific or technological advances threaten to undermine existing *halakhic* practice. These examples attest to the range of possible responses to this tension on the part of *halakhic* authorities, and more broadly, to the diverse and often subtle ways that scientific changes influence *halakhic* adjudication and practice.

Divergence of *Halakhah* and Modern Science: The *Metzitzah* Controversy

One of the earliest and most persistent conflicts between *halakhah* and modern science in the modern period is the controversy over *metzitzah*, suctioning blood from the circumcision wound. In discussing the performance of circumcision on Shabbat, the Mishnah mentions *metzitzah* as one of the components of the ritual that may not be omitted even when circumcision is performed on Shabbat:

> We perform all necessary acts for the circumcision on Shabbat: we circumcise, we expose [the corona by tearing the mucosal membrane], we suction, and we place upon the wound a bandage with cumin.[19]

The Mishnah does not elaborate on the nature and purpose of *metzitzah* or why it is performed even on Shabbat. However, from later in the chapter we may infer that *metzitzah* is external to the primary circumcision ritual. The Mishnah[20] rules that a circumcision is not valid if one did not remove all of the foreskin or if one neglected to tear the mucosal membrane beneath the foreskin, but makes no similar pronouncement about neglecting to suction or bandage the wound. The notion that that *metzitzah* is not necessary for the validity of the circumcision is further supported by the Talmud's discussion of R. Papa's injunction regarding a *mohel* who does not suction the wound:

> R. Papa stated: "A surgeon who does not perform suction [following a circumcision] endangers the baby and is dismissed."
>
> This is obvious—since we desecrate the Shabbat for it, it must be a danger [to omit it]! You might have thought that the [reason one may suction on Shabbat is] that the blood is stored up, [so that drawing it out is not a violation of Shabbat]. Now we have learned [from R. Papa] that the blood is the result of a wound [such that drawing it out is a Shabbat violation, and the reason that one may suction it nonetheless is that it prevents a life-threatening condition].
>
> And [suctioning] is comparable to bandaging and [applying] cumin: just as it is dangerous when bandaging and [applying] cumin are not performed, so, too, it is dangerous when suctioning is not performed.[21]

R. Papa's rationale indicates that *metzitzah* served a medical rather than ritual purpose, like the practice of bandaging and dressing the wound. (The need for R. Papa to invoke—or perhaps impose—a sanction for a *mohel* who does not suction the wound might indicate that there were those who questioned its medical value even in the rabbinic period.) This assumption is further bolstered by the *Bavli*'s analysis of R. Papa's position: it assumes that if the act of *metzitzah* constitutes a *melakhah* (action biblically prohibited on Shabbat), the only reason for the Mishnah to permit its performance on Shabbat is that it prevents a potentially life-threatening condition. The *Bavli* does not consider the possibility that *metzitzah* is integral to the circumcision ritual, which is permitted on Shabbat on its own merit.

The nature of the "danger" R. Papa refers to is not specified, either by the *Bavli* or by almost any of the medieval commentaries.[22] It is not unlikely that this lack of elaboration reflects the fact that pre-modern readers would have been familiar with this danger as a fact of life. It is also not unlikely that this familiarity is rooted in a culture-specific medical paradigm. Modern medicine would then allow us to discount the therapeutic value ascribed to *metzitzah*, to say nothing of its prophylactic necessity.[23] Based on the deductive model described above, the paradigm shift of modern medicine would undermine the requirement of *metzitzah* as part of the circumcision ritual. Indeed, there are indications that in the first half of the nineteenth century, the practice of *metzitzah* was already in decline in some western European communities, even among religious traditionalists.[24]

An illustrative parallel to the decline in the practice of *metzitzah* is the discontinuation of another formerly required practice related to circumcision: *rehitzah be-hammin*—the need to bathe the baby in hot water following the circumcision. Like *metzitzah*, this practice was deemed by the Talmud[25] to be so therapeutically necessary that it justifies violation of Shabbat. Yet by the end of the Middle Ages, the leading codifier R. Yosef Karo acknowledged—with unusual frankness and little explanation—that *rehitzah be-hammin* was no longer being practiced.[26] Unlike the decline in the practice of *metzitzah* in the early nineteenth century, there is no written reference to the decline of *rehitzah be-hammin* during the period when it was occurring, so we do not understand what caused it. This lacuna strongly suggests that the discontinuation of *rehitzah be-hammin* occurred organically within the community of practitioners, rather than by a self-conscious process of adjudication among *halakhic* authorities.

To what extent can we say that the discontinuation of *rehitzah be-hammin* reflected a scientific reassessment of its stated medical rationale? Given the amorphous nature of this decline—the fact that it cannot be traced to a particular individual, event, or even locale, it is difficult to say more than that *something* shifted in the general scientific consciousness of the Jewish community to undermine the perception of this practice as therapeutically beneficial. Nonetheless, the significance of this shift should not be underestimated. The deductive model may suggest a process of self-conscious, rational deliberation among *halakhic* authorities, yet the example of *rehitzah be-hammin* demonstrates how the dynamic between the discourses of science and *halakhah* often plays out in a far less self-conscious and more diffuse manner.

The decline in the practice of *metzitzah* shares important elements with the discontinuation of *rehitzah be-hammin*. It is clear that around the turn of the nineteenth century, something shifted in the perception of *metzitzah* as therapeutically necessary, and this shift seems to have been both amorphous and unself-conscious rather than an intentional reconsideration within the scholarly community. Yet a closer look at how modern circumstances impacted the practice of *metzitzah* yields an even more complex picture. To begin with, it appears that the shift in scientific understanding did not in and of itself cause the practice to wane; rather, it merely laid the groundwork for the discontinuation of *metzitzah* for other reasons, primarily concerns—both hygienic and aesthetic—of the way *metzitzah* was traditionally practiced: *oral* suction of the circumcision wound (*metzitzah be-peh*) by the *mohel*.[27] At its most extreme, this reaction included concern that *metzitzah be-peh* was the cause of disease outbreaks among recently circumcised baby boys.[28]

Moreover, the general disdain for *metzitzah be-peh*, even the concern that it was responsible for disease, did not consistently undermine the notion that *metzitzah* more generally had therapeutic value, a point that continued to be debated for some time.

Some of the earliest published statements calling for abolishing *metzitzah* cited both its lack of therapeutic value and its potential health hazards,[29] whereas others acknowledged only the potential hazard while maintaining the assumption that it still had medical value.[30] The overall picture, then, indicates that developments in scientific knowledge and medical practice played a complex role in the shifting dynamics over *metzitzah*. This complexity fits well with the idea that the relationship between *halakhah* and science is best conceived of as a dialogue: a conversation that happens in multiple registers, and often does not result in complete agreement.

One factor that prevented *metzitzah* from the same organic discontinuation as *rehitzah be-hammin* was the way it became caught up in the broader religious tensions of the time. The first Reform Rabbinical Assembly, in 1844, discussed a proposal to abolish *metzitzah*, amid more general rumblings in Germany to abolish the requirement for circumcision altogether. This generated a swift backlash from traditionalist rabbinic authorities, who defended the necessity not only of *metzitzah* but specifically *metzitzah be-peh*. But in the *halakhic* discourse that ensued, there is virtually no reconsideration of the therapeutic rationale for *metzitzah*. The main point on which traditionalist scholars differ is how much credence to give to medical assertions about the danger of *metzitzah be-peh* rather than its purported benefit; those scholars inclined to give credence to doctors' warnings insisted that the purpose of *metzitzah* could be accomplished through means other than direct oral suction, such as use of a sponge or pipette. But these proposals rarely address that purpose with any depth. For example, in his responsum permitting *metzitzah* to be performed with a sponge rather than by oral suction,[31] R. Moshe Sofer (1762–1839), known as the *Chatam Sofer*, insists that his interlocutor "exhort the expert doctors to testify truthfully whether the sponge has the same effect as oral *metzitzah*," seemingly oblivious to the fact that the doctors would almost certainly claim that *metzitzah* has no therapeutic value at all.

Given the controversy surrounding *metzitzah* from the mid-nineteenth century and on, one might counter that it was only the ideological issues that prevented a genuine scientific assessment of *metzitzah* from guiding the *halakhic* discussion; had *metzitzah* not been such a freighted issue, one might reason, *halakhic* authorities would have engaged in a measured, rational assessment as to whether the Talmud's rationale was still relevant. It is certainly true that within the voluminous writings from the main period of the *metzitzah* controversy—from the mid-nineteenth through the early twentieth centuries, most of the arguments for not giving weight to the Talmud's rationale for *metzitzah* are fairly apologetic: scholars assert the inviolability of all established laws, customs or practices; insist on the wisdom of the Sages' understanding of nature; muse on the possibility of other rationales for *metzitzah*; etc.[32] Nonetheless, the evidence suggests that the contours of the debate were not due to ideology alone. The aforementioned responsum of the *Chatam Sofer* predated any public proposal to abolish *metzitzah* (which occurred only after his death in 1839), so that, unlike later traditionalist authorities, he does not automatically dismiss the significance of the rationale. Yet the *Chatam Sofer* cites the rationale only in rejecting the idea that *metzitzah* had to be performed specifically by oral suction; the basic necessity of *metzitzah* is simply taken for granted. The same can be seen on the opposite side of the ideological spectrum once the controversy over *metzitzah* had waned: despite early opposition to *metzitzah* among non-Orthodox scholars, by the late twentieth century, *metzitzah* was still practiced in some form across the denominational spectrum.[33] Again, there is no attempt among non-Orthodox *halakhic* authorities to explain *why* this is so; the normativity of *metzitzah* is simply, uncritically accepted.

Even more noteworthy is the discussion regarding the performance of *metzitzah* on Shabbat. As noted above, the Talmud makes clear that suctioning the blood from the circumcision wound on Shabbat constitutes a biblical prohibition, such that it is permitted only because it is necessary as a life-saving measure. Hence regardless of whether one considers therapeutic value to be essential to justify the practice of *metzitzah* in general, it would seem to be indispensable for justifying the performance of *metzitzah* on Shabbat. Yet by and large, *halakhic* authorities either refrain from calling for a complete ban on *metzitzah* on Shabbat or make no distinction between Shabbat and weekday at all.

In sum, the trajectory of the *metzitzah* controversy—from the initial decline in the practice of *metzitzah* to the avoidance of discussing the Talmud's medical rationale to the widespread acceptance of alternatives to *metzitzah be-peh*—underscores both the complexity and the limitations of science's role in *halakhic* discourse. To return to our observation that the dialogue model requires us to understand the elements that give each discourse its own internal momentum, the *metzitzah* controversy challenges us to consider what distinctive features of *halakhic* discourse led to the almost universal continuation of this practice even as modern medicine undermines its purported therapeutic value.

Perpetuation of Practice in *Halakhah*: Food Absorption in Cooking Utensils

Alongside the significance of *metzitzah* within ideological debates in the mid-nineteenth century, one of the factors that led to the continuation of *metzitzah* might be called the *perpetuation of practice.* We tend to think of *halakhah* in terms of the arguments and decisions that are articulated in the written record of *halakhic* literature, including the rationale(s) invoked to explain the law. Yet this focus ignores the fact that *halakhah* is also manifest in patterns of practice, which are influenced by factors other than verbally articulated arguments. One such factor is the degree to which a given aspect of *halakhah* has been *embodied* in the patterns of *halakhic* observance, either in a physical object or, as in the case of *metzitzah*, in the form of a ritual. The very nature of the ritual of *brit milah*—a rigid, repeating pattern of behavior, performed by a trained (though not necessarily scholarly) class of practitioners—creates a condition in which *metzitzah* becomes self-perpetuating regardless of the relevance of the rationale for its original inclusion. This condition obviously does not mean that *metzitzah* was immune to change or discontinuation: as we noted above, the practice of *metzitzah* was waning in certain circles in the first half of the nineteenth century. Yet as we mentioned, it seems clear that this was caused by cultural concerns related to the specific method by which *metzitzah* was being performed. As new methods of *metzitzah* were developed that fit better with the cultural sensibilities of nineteenth-century Europe, using a sponge or pipette, *metzitzah* once again became an integral portion of *milah*, such that it endures irrespective of the relevance of theoretical explanations. The practice of *metzitzah* was recast in a new, more medicalized form, one consistent with our modern scientific sensibilities.

This phenomenon of perpetuation of practice is even more evident in another *halakhic* issue whose basis has been challenged by modern science. One of the key principles in the laws of *kashrut* (dietary practices) is that *keilim* (vessels) retain the taste of foods cooked therein, taste which would then be imparted into food subsequently cooked in those vessels. This principle has wide-ranging practical implications, most profoundly the requirements to have a separate set of utensils for kosher use and, within the kosher kitchen, separate utensils for meat and dairy use. In their application to modern industrial *kashrut*, these implications have significant economic consequences, since they require production facilities to be used for only kosher products or to undergo intensive cleaning (a process known as *kashering* or kosherization) before producing food to be certified as kosher.

The scientific assumption behind this principle is consistently explained by the idea that the taste of the food in question is absorbed (*balu'a*) into the walls of the vessel and then subsequently exuded into other food. The extent to which this assumption was true of vessels in pre-modern society (most of which were unglazed ceramic or cast iron, both clearly porous materials) is not clear. However, in the past few decades, scholars have revisited the assumption of *beliyah* (absorption) of food in modern cooking utensils through the lens of material science.[34] The few experimental investigations have yielded somewhat varied results, but it is overwhelmingly clear that whatever the amount of absorption and exudation in most materials, it is far below the threshold of what would render food cooked in those dishes non-kosher.[35]

The issue of *bliyah be-keilim* (absorption of taste in vessels) is an illustrative contrast to *metzitzah* in that there is little practical or ideological pressure to change the *halakhah*; hence the tenor of the *halakhic* discourse about the scientific reality of *beliyah* is entirely different than the debate concerning *metzitzah*. Whereas *metzitzah* was (and intermittently continues to be) the subject of rancorous public controversy, discussion of the question of *beliyah be-keilim* has been mainly academic, limited to a small group of scholars. Another point of contrast is that in the case of *beliyah be-keilim*, the scientific rationale for the need for separate utensils is articulated explicitly in *halakhic* literature. Yet despite these differences, *halakhic* authorities' approaches to this issue are remarkably similar in style and even in substance to the responses to the *metzitzah* controversy. They tend to insist on the inviolability of venerable *halakhic* standards, to disparage the accuracy of modern scientific evidence, or to propose alternate reasons to maintain the requirement for separate utensils (e.g., the concern that dishes might have actual food residue). Virtually no *halakhic* authority has proposed significant changes to current *kashrut* practices.

While the specific arguments that *halakhic* authorities give for the lack of change should not necessarily be dismissed as apologetics (though some of these are more substantive than others), the degree of unanimity among their conclusions, along with the similarities to the discourse around *metzitzah*, suggest that these arguments do not tell the whole story. Rather, as we have suggested, it seems that the dynamic of practice is an un-self-conscious force that affects the way elements of *halakhah* change or remain the same over time. We have suggested that an important factor that leads to the perpetuation of certain *halakhic* practices is their degree of embodiment in Jewish life: the ritualized performance of *metzitzah*; the fundamental way that *beliyah be-keilim* shapes the logistics of kosher food production, both domestic and industrial.

Cognitive Dissonance and Sense Construction: The *Kashrut* of Parasite-Infected Fish

There is obviously much more to consider when we analyze how and why *halakhic* practices change or persist over time; the degree of embodiment is only one factor that affects how well a *halakhic* practice will be preserved in the face of change. The reason this embodiment is especially pertinent to the laws we have analyzed is that, in light of scientific developments, these laws no longer make sense with our understanding of nature. *Metzitzah* no longer coheres with our sense of medical treatment; *beliyah be-keilim* no longer makes sense to us as a realistic concern. The religiolegal framework within which these laws are embedded provides an alternate context in which they can cohere: regardless of their original rationales, these actions have become part of our intuitive sense of "how to circumcise" and "how to keep kosher."

The logical corollary of this idea is that in the absence of an embodied practice, *halakhic* laws would tend to change in concert with scientific developments to prevent cognitive dissonance between *halakhah* and science. An instructive test case for this idea is the current *halakhic* debate regarding the *kashrut* of fish infected with endoparasites (parasites found in the internal organs of the host organism). In the laws of *kashrut*, it is axiomatic that insects, worms, or other vermin—collectively referred to as *sheratzim*—are strictly prohibited for consumption (excepting certain species of locusts).[36] Nonetheless, from the Talmud *Bavli*'s discussion of different types of foods or drinks infested with vermin,[37] it is clear that, in at least some cases, the food or drink may be consumed even though one is also consuming *sheratzim*. The rationale for this leniency is primary based on midrashic exegesis; for example: "[Every swarming thing that swarms] *upon the earth* [Lev. 11:41] [serves] to exclude *zizin* found in lentils, and mosquitoes found in *kelisim*, and worms found in dates and in dried figs."[38] However, the Talmud also explains this leniency in more conceptual terms: "Rav Sheisha son of Rav Idi says: Parasite worms are permitted [to be eaten with meat]. What is the reason? They originate from [the animal's flesh]."[39] This latter explanation seems to invoke the theory of spontaneous generation, a belief common in the pre-modern world and one attested elsewhere in *halakhic* literature.[40] While this explanation functions as an elaboration on the midrashic rationale (creatures that have lived only within food have never "swarmed upon the earth"), it also implies that creatures that generate from food are not considered independent entities: they retain the *halakhic* properties of the food from which they spawned.[41]

The assumption that vermin found in food or drink under certain circumstances may be consumed remains unquestioned by *halakhic* authorities well into the modern period, and both the above talmudic expressions—the midrashic and the conceptual—are cited frequently and generally used interchangeably. However, as the theory of spontaneous generation was challenged and eventually rejected by scientists in the eighteenth and nineteenth centuries, the permissibility of vermin-infested food was called into question. A particular point of contention is a ruling cited in *Shulchan Arukh*[42] that parasitic worms found in the flesh of fish (or between the flesh and the skin) are kosher, as opposed to those found in the intestines of fish, which are prohibited. This distinction implies that worms found in the flesh are assumed to have generated within the fish, whereas those in the intestines are assumed to have been ingested from outside. Yet modern scientists' documentation of the life cycle of fish endoparasites, notably Anisakis worms, has shown that the eggs from which parasites develop are expelled into the water and that the larvae pass through a number of aquatic hosts before being ingested by the fish that are the subject of *halakhic* interest. Based on this, we may assume that *all* endoparasites found in fish have been ingested, and those found in the fish's flesh have simply migrated from the intestines into the muscle tissue. Here again is a divergence between the ruling and its scientific rationale, but unlike in the cases of *metzitzah be-peh* and *beliyah be-keilim*, in this case there is no element of ritualized practice: to the extent that earlier generations consumed parasite-infected fish, they likely did so un-self-consciously. Without a definitive anchor in *halakhic* practice, the permissibility of consuming parasite-infected fish has become the subject of consternation and debate between contemporary *halakhic* authorities.

Several factors raise the stakes of this issue above those of the earlier examples we analyzed. One factor is that the tension between the Talmud's explanation and modern science on this issue is more acute than in either of the previous cases we analyzed. The scientific rationale that Talmud articulates for the *kashrut* of infested food—that vermin generate spontaneously within the food—is a fairly specific proposition (in contrast with the unspecified danger ostensibly prevented by *metzitzah*) that modern science categorically rejects (as opposed to the absorption of food particles in vessels, which modern science merely qualifies). For the modern subject, it is cognitively dissonant to divorce one's *halakhic* conception of parasites—that they are indigenous to the host organism—from one's scientific conception—that parasites are foreign entities. A second set of factors stems from the legal severity of this issue: if the Talmud's reasoning cannot be relied on, then consuming a parasite-infected fish violates a biblical prohibition. This severity cuts both ways. On the one hand, there is a natural religious inclination to be stringent rather than risking such a serious transgression. On the other hand, to overturn the Talmud's ruling is to impugn the behavior of earlier generations as gravely sinful. For all these reasons, this case poses a severe test for the process of sense construction, both in the dialogue between science and *halakhah* and within *halakhic* discourse itself.

A common approach to a conflict of this sort is to reinterpret the Talmud's rationale in a way that it no longer contradicts modern scientific knowledge. In such cases where the Talmud invokes the notion of spontaneous generation,[43] some *halakhic* authorities have proposed reframing the Talmud's statement in terms of the limitations of unaided human perception: when the Talmud speaks of vermin as generating from the flesh of cattle or fish, it is not referring to the properties of vermin themselves but rather to what *seems* to be occurring to the naked eye. (This approach relies on the assumption—articulated by numerous modern authorities—that entities not visible to the naked eye are considered *halakhically* nonexistent; *halakhah* relates to only that which we experience directly.[44]) Of course, this approach resolves the problem of Anisakis worms and other aquatic endoparasites only if one assumes that parasite larvae are not visible to the naked eye at the point that they are first ingested, a matter that is still under debate.[45] A more fundamental problem with this approach is that it feels apologetic: it's hard to convince oneself that this is what the Talmud actually meant to say.[46]

The tenuousness of this reinterpretation, combined with the severity of the potential prohibition, has led many contemporary authorities to prohibit the consumption of parasite-infected fish. In order to square this ruling with the *Shulchan Arukh*'s permissive ruling, they follow a well-trodden path regarding contradictions to scientific propositions found in the Talmud: the claim that *nishtanu ha-teva'im* (lit., "the nature of things has changed").[47] Taken literally, this phrase seems to assert that there has been a fundamental change in the natural order; indeed, a number of scholars have proposed that that the Talmud's discussions of vermin in this and other *halakhic* contexts are referring to different types of creatures than those that are the subject of contemporary scientific observations.[48] It is not clear how implausible the notion of nature undergoing fundamental changes would have seemed to pre-modern *halakhic* authorities, but for a contemporary audience, it strains credulity.

However, it should be emphasized that *nishtanu ha-teva'im* and similar phrases are not always used to indicate a fundamental change in nature. In many cases, *halakhic* authorities use this phrase to suggest that contemporaneous *conditions* (e.g., climatic and technological) are different than the ones in which rabbinic laws were instituted.[49] In this vein, some contemporary authorities who are stringent regarding parasite-infected fish have suggested that circumstantial changes in the modern fishing industry—longer storage times, importation of fish from different climates, etc.—have significantly increased the incidence of fish endoparasites in the kosher fish market.[50]

This explanation does not resolve the difficulty with the Talmud's rationale, but it accomplishes a different goal: to avoid casting aspersion on earlier generations' *halakhic* practices in a way that seems consistent with modern scientific principles.

For those who push back against this stringent ruling and maintain that the traditional leniency on consuming parasite-infected fish is still relevant, a major motivating factor is the internal coherence of *halakhah* as a system. Whether or not it is possible to explain the Talmud's rationale in a way that feels consistent with the perspective of modern science, it is no less important to the consciousness of the modern observant Jew that *halakhah* maintain its own integrity rather than risk being perpetually upended by scientific discoveries. Hence these authorities not only raise the religious problem of impugning earlier generations' practices, they also argue that, from a formal legal perspective, the *Shulchan Arukh*'s ruling is not dependent on any particular rationale once it has been established.[51] In effect, their arguments constitute a version of the positivist model we articulated above, reminiscent of some of the arguments raised by traditionalist authorities during the *metzitzah* controversy to insist on the need to continue performing *metzitzah* (or even *metzitzah be-peh*).

Nonetheless, the cognitive dissonance that this lenient position creates is not insignificant: it requires one to divorce one's *halakhic* consciousness—where there is fundamental distinction between worms found in the intestines and those found in the flesh—from one's scientific consciousness—where this distinction is meaningless. Hence some *halakhic* authorities who insist on the independence of *halakhah* in this area *also* posit the above reinterpretation of the Talmud's rationale. In addition, it is unlikely that this cognitive balancing act would be possible were fish endoparasites a truly pervasive problem; rather, the concern is that parasite infection might be frequent enough to warrant *inspection* of all fish sold as kosher.

Incorporating New Technologies: Electricity Use on Shabbat

If these cases demonstrate the relationship between science and *halakhah* once *halakhic* rulings have already been established, we may gain a different perspective on that relationship by considering the role of science in the way *halakhic* authorities address *halakhic* questions related to new technologies and novel scientific discoveries impacting daily life. A prime example is the use of electric, and later electronic, technology on Shabbat. This is an almost unparalleled challenge for *halakhah*, an entity so different from previous life experience and models of the world that it challenges, and in some cases exhausts, *halakhic* authorities' capacity for finding relevant *halakhic* precedents and conceptual tools. Given the dearth of resources within *halakhic* discourse, authorities are compelled to draw on scientific models, actively bringing science into conversation with *halakhah*. Yet as we will see, science is only one factor in the discussion; other factors are the practical and social implications of this new technology, which are no less novel than its scientific aspects.

The issue of electricity on Shabbat came to the fore at the close of the nineteenth century, even before the full stabilization of widespread electricity use. In some cases, the issue was merely a matter of *halakhic* curiosity, in others the discussion was prompted by rising industrialization and the anticipation of the breadth of electricity's potential applications. By the turn of the last century, there was keen public interest in how *halakhah* would relate to electricity. A *halakhic* consensus quickly emerged regarding what may have been the most prominent manifestation of this new technology: the incandescent light bulb. Scholars agreed that turning on a lightbulb should be prohibited on Shabbat, following Maimonides's ruling that heating metal to the point of incandescence is a *toladah* (corollary) of a *melakhah* (biblically prohibited activity on Shabbat)—either kindling or cooking. Aside from this one application, there was little agreement on how to define electricity in *halakhic* terms, or on what should be the normative approach to its existence and use.

Despite this lack of consensus, there was an important common factor in the early stages of this debate, namely, that an accurate scientific understanding of electricity was deemed essential to any ruling on its use on Shabbat, even if this understanding was not the only decisive factor. In contrast to the *metzitzah be-peh* controversy, where many traditionalist *halakhic* authorities openly challenged the relevance or accuracy of scientific evidence, virtually all *halakhic* authorities who weighed in on the issue of electricity on Shabbat began their analysis with an assessment of electricity in scientific or quasi-scientific terms. *Halakhic* authorities frequently consulted with scientists (though not always with great profundity),[52] and also critiqued others' *halakhic* positions as reflecting inaccurate conceptions of the science of electricity. When authorities deigned to rule mainly on the effects of electric devices, rather than their underlying mechanisms, their responsa were typically not well received.

Within the first few decades of rabbinic discussion of this issue, it became clear that the scientific understanding of electricity did not translate neatly into any one *halakhic* category. This was demonstrated most decisively by Rabbi Shlomo Zalman Auerbach (1910–1995), a young Israeli scholar who would eventually become one of the leading *halakhic* authorities of the twentieth century. In his book, *Me'orei Eish*,[53] Auerbach systematically assesses and debunks all previously formulated theories regarding the *halakhic* classification of electricity, both in *halakhic* terms and on scientific grounds. He argues that apart from electric devices that produce heat, light, or sound, there is no formal argument on which to base a prohibition on manifesting electricity itself on Shabbat. Auerbach himself did not—then or subsequently—provide an alternative definition for the *essence* of electricity, neither in its physical sense nor in a *halakhic* analog to it. This was not for lack of familiarity with the subject; indeed, it is because of his careful analysis of the *halakhah* in light of his lifelong consultations with scientific experts in the field that he came to his non-conclusion. Nevertheless, Auerbach refrained from permitting electricity use except in extenuating circumstances,[54] a point we will revisit below. In the decades since Auerbach's initial publication on this topic, most *halakhic* authorities have accepted his basic premise that there is no overarching formal definition for electricity use on Shabbat. Hence, aside from specific exceptions (such as incandescent lightbulbs), these authorities consider electricity use on Shabbat to be at most rabbinically—rather than biblically—prohibited.

The main contending *halakhic* approach to electricity is represented by Rabbi Abraham Isaiah Karelitz (1878–1953), known as the *Chazon Ish*. He names a specific *halakhic* identity for the completion of a live circuit: the *melakhah* of *boneh* (building) on Shabbat. A key aspect in the *Chazon Ish*'s reasoning is expressed in the Aristotelian terminology for turning an inanimate piece of matter into something "active" and "alive": "fashioning a form [*tzurah*] for matter [*geshem*] such that it serves a function is certainly considered *boneh*."[55] The word *geshem* used here is the medieval philosophical term for "matter" in the Aristotelean sense: substance in need of form to be determined in the hylomorphic paradigm. According to the *Chazon Ish*, this addition of form to matter in a way that makes it functional is fully considered *boneh*, even though it is only a temporary change.[56] In his discussion with Auerbach, who found this analysis problematic, the *Chazon Ish* insists on the particular condition of an electric circuit that distinguishes it from any other instance of form-giving (like heating):

> The connection of the electric wire awakens the electrical power intrinsic to the wire itself, which is from the synthetic fusion at the root of their creation; this usage is always [available], and the establishment of its character by the connection, making the disconnected wire become one with the electrical machine, is possibly *boneh* . . . for transforming the wire itself from death to life is *boneh*.

Notwithstanding the somewhat convoluted use of terms in this passage, it is clear that the *Chazon Ish* is attempting to find a distinct *halakhic* expression for what he sees as the essence of electricity: a synthesis or fusion that the material is primed for, which is instigated by the closing of the circuit. This essentialism makes the *Chazon Ish*'s approach fundamentally different than virtually all other *halakhic* negotiations with electricity, which focus on physical manifestations of electricity with analogues that have already been classified within *halakhic* literature, such as the manipulation of energy (e.g., kindling a fire) or achieving an effect (e.g., perfuming clothing).

In sum, both the *Chazon Ish* and Auerbach insisted on being fully and deeply informed on the scientific and engineering details of electricity function and use. They arrive at opposite ends of the possible *halakhic* spectrum, in part because they take different approaches to the process of translating from the language of science to the language of *halakhah*. The *Chazon Ish* focuses on the single most remarkable feature of electric appliances, namely, the way they seemingly bring inanimate objects to life, and assumes that within the laws of Shabbat—the area of *halakhah* most concerned with the scope of human creative activity—there *must* be *halakhic* language to express the monumental significance of that innovation. Auerbach pointedly does not share this assumption: through a point-by-point comparison of electric technology with all established categories of *melakhah*, he concludes that the scientific language used to describe electrical technology cannot accurately be translated into *halakhic* terms; on this point the two systems are simply incommensurable.

The stark difference between their theoretical approaches belies the fact that there is not much practical difference between their positions. As noted above, Auerbach functionally prohibits using electrical appliances on Shabbat for all but cases of dire need, despite his determination that most of them involve no technical violation of Shabbat. This point is articulated most clearly in his discussion of telephone use on Shabbat:

> I have thus explained why, in my humble opinion, in this case where one has not performed an act of kindling or extinguishing but rather only connected the telephone to the circuit, it is not prohibited on Shabbat or Yom Tov . . . (But it seems to me that the masses don't know enough to distinguish thus, and might come to erroneously conclude that it is permissible also to light or extinguish electric [lights] on Shabbat, and therefore even according to us one should not permit this except in a case of great need . . .) . . . But what can I do, as this elder, Rabbi Yitzhak Yehudah Shmelkes, already ruled on the matter of whether one may speak on the telephone on Shabbat [and prohibited it], and the matter requires adjudication . . . (But see there, for [Shmelkes] also wrote, "In my opinion, one should prohibit making soda water on Shabbat since there one is creating a chemical concoction," but even so, in practice the masses are lenient on this matter).[57]

In explaining his hesitancy to promulgate his lenient ruling, Auerbach cites two factors, both of them instances of a sociological factor outweighing scientific analysis in the context of *halakhic* adjudication. The first factor is the concern that the public will conflate different types of electrical devices, so that a permissive ruling regarding the use of telephones on Shabbat will lead people to conclude that they may also turn on and off lights. The very novelty of electricity—the fact that all these devices entered modern society as a single technological revolution—causes the public to lump all of its applications together, even though from a technical *halakhic* perspective they are utterly dissimilar.

The second factor is the fact that the stringent position of Yitzhak Yehudah Shmelkes (and others) had already become accepted practice; Auerbach feels that his hands are effectively tied. (Note the inverse phenomenon regarding the carbonation of water on Shabbat, where Shmelkes's stringent ruling was undermined by an entrenched lenient practice.) This argument echoes the notion of perpetuation of practice that we described above in the context of *metzitzah* and *beliyah*. Yet in this case, the tradition of refraining from using electric devices on Shabbat in question was only a few decades old by the time Auerbach cited it. Moreover, unlike in the previous cases we analyzed where the practice in question was established based on a now-rejected scientific premise, in the case of electricity there was no scientific paradigm shift that could explain why a previously established practice would now be called into question. Hence, if Auerbach finds himself faced with an established tradition, we need to consider how that tradition was established in the first place.

Here we may appeal to a different element of the dynamic of practice: not the tendency of the *halakhic* community to perpetuate those laws that are deeply ingrained within Jewish life, but the impulse to integrate new cultural and technological phenomena into Jewish life in a way that seems consistent with *halakhah* as a lived religious experience, in this case the character of Shabbat. Jacob Katz refers to this factor as "ritual instinct," and invokes it to explain ways in which Jews' Shabbat observance during the Middle Ages diverged from the formal parameters articulated in *halakhic* literature, toward both stringency[58] and leniency.[59] As applications of electrical and electronic technology have pervaded modern life, Shabbat-observant Jews have processed these innovations not only in terms of technical legal categories, or even in terms of the less technical classifications that Auerbach mentions ("all electrical devices are the same"), but also in terms of how these activities cohere with the overall atmosphere of Shabbat observance. As with the elements of *halakhic* practice we analyzed earlier, this factor is unself-conscious, intuitive, and amorphous, but no less significant for these characteristics.

At this point we should once again ask: What can be said about the role of scientific reasoning in the *halakhic* adjudication of new technologies like electricity? It may seem that, as in the case of *metzitzah*, science plays a fairly limited role, more negative than positive: *halakhic* authorities' consideration of the science of electricity ultimately leads them to conclude that electricity use does not fit any of the formal categories of *melakhah* on Shabbat. This is not to say that the negative classification of electricity does not have certain concrete ramifications: as noted above, it allows for *halakhic* authorities who follow Auerbach's position to be more lenient in extenuating circumstances. But overall, the functional classification of electricity use on Shabbat is determined to a far greater extent by the dynamic of practice, just as in the cases of *metzitzah* and *beliyah be-keilim*.

Where the issue of electricity use on Shabbat differs from these other examples is that the very innovative nature of this technology and its expanding range of applications to our lives has meant that ritual instinct alone is not sufficient to determine the status of electricity use. For example, there are countless applications where electricity is imperceptible to the end user, through large-scale industrialization and automation[60] as well as the embedding of electricity in an ever-widening range of everyday activities: the use of solar panels for hot water tanks, motion sensors and surveillance cameras,[61] LED screens and lighting, etc.[62] In these cases, there is no instinctive reaction to speak of on the part of the user. Rather, it falls to *halakhic* authorities to adjudicate them, and in doing so they continue to consult the relevant scientific definitions of this technology and to apply them to the particular way it is used on Shabbat (e.g., how direct is the relationship between the user's action and the activation of the electric effect). Consequently, the discourses of *halakhah* and science continue to be in prolonged dialogue with one another, as *halakhic* authorities incorporate models and concepts from science and translate them into *halakhic* terminology. For this reason, the ongoing discussion of electricity use on Shabbat exemplifies the dialogue model in contemporary *halakhic* jurisprudence: a generative relationship between parallel discourses without an expectation that the two will be in perfect correlation with one another.

Conclusion

In this chapter, we have sought to highlight the complexity of the relationship between science and *halakhah*. We suggested that the model of dialogue is useful in highlighting those features that make each sphere a distinct, independently meaningful discourse, enabling it to contribute to a fruitful and multidimensional interaction with the other. The specific cases we have analyzed exemplify some of the distinctive aspects of *halakhah*—including the dynamics of *halakhic* practice and the need for cognitive coherence among *halakhic* adherents—that have shaped the way *halakhah* has absorbed scientific discoveries and technological developments in the modern era.

Notes

1. Alistair Cameron Crombie, *Styles of Scientific Thinking in the European Tradition: The History of Argument and Explanation Especially in the Mathematical and Biomedical Sciences and Arts* (London: Duckworth, 1994), 499–550.
2. See, e.g., analyses by historians like Peter Harrison and Noah Efron, *Science and Religion: New Historical Perspectives*, ed. Thomas Dixon, Geoffrey Cantor, and Stephen Pumfrey (Cambridge: Cambridge University Press, 2010), 24–34, 258–59.

   Because the use of terms like "science" in reference to periods before the eighteenth century risks being anachronistic, all such references in this chapter should be taken as shorthand for the sake of readability.
3. In relating to *halakhah* primarily as law, we do not mean to say that it should be treated *solely* as a legal system. Legal elements of *halakhah* are largely inseparable from its religious character, and there are many elements of *halakhah* that are better characterized as ethical or moral rather than legal. Nonetheless, the overwhelmingly legal character of *halakhah* is self-evident. For example, see Moshe Silberg, *Talmudic Law and the Modern State*, trans. Ben Zion Bokser (New York: Burning Book Press, 1973), 1–10.

   Crucially, *halakhah* meets H. L. A. Hart's most basic criterion for a legal system, namely, the rule of recognition (*The Concept of Law* [Oxford: Oxford University Press, 1961], 79–88): subjects of *halakhah* recognize the binding authority of *halakhah* on their behavior. This element also serves as the basis for the distinction we are making here between those prescriptions in rabbinic literature that have traditionally been considered legal and those that have not: only the former are recognized as binding by the community of *halakhic* adherents.
4. mPes 2:5. The identification of the last two grains is somewhat problematic; see Ra'anan, Moshe. "'And the Oats, and the Rye'—Oats," Daf Yomi Portal [Hebrew]. https://www.dafyomi.com/DYItemDetails.aspx?itemId=12371.

5. bPes 35a.
6. jPes 2:5.
7. Of course, this oversimplifies the nature of scientific postulates: like any other discourse, science is a cultural construct whose categories and distinctions are predicated on a particular conceptual structure, what Thomas Kuhn famously referred to as a paradigm. In the context of *halakhic* discourse, this point is best appreciated in cases where a *halakhic* authority's trust in the certainty of science proves misplaced, as when a ruling is based on a regnant scientific assumption that is later called into question.
8. mHul 3:1.
9. bHul 57b.
10. *She'elot u-Teshuvot Rashba* 1:98. For a similar opinion see *She'elot u-Teshuvot ha-Rivash* 1:447.
11. This dismissive attitude toward science reflects one prominent perspective on the Aristotelian rationalist tradition during the Middle Ages. Rashba's resistance to the use of science in *halakhic* adjudication may be attributed to tension between reason and revelation as competing sources of authority and truth. Cf. David B. Ruderman, *Jewish Thought and Scientific Discovery in Early Modern Europe* (Detroit, MI: Wayne State University Press, 2001), 73; and Avraham Weinroth, *Consideration in Halacha-Science Relations* (Tel Aviv: Machshavot, 1991), 10.
12. Maimonides, *Mishneh Torah*, Laws of Ritual Slaughter 10:12–13; see also Maimonides, *Guide to the Perplexed*, III:14. Shlomo Auman ("Between Torah and Science," *Hama'ayan* 23, no. 3 [1983]: 1–7 [Hebrew]) offers the simplest explanation of the discrepancy between the two approaches presented in *Mishneh Torah*: it is impossible to prove the necessary fatality of a defect not mentioned in the Talmud, but it is far easier to demonstrate that a defect mentioned in the Talmud is not always fatal.
13. This is distinct from the term "*halakhic* positivism" as used by Shneur Segal, "The Halakhic Ruling of Rabbi Shlomo Zalman Auerbach on the Subject of Electricity" (MA diss., Bar-Ilan University, 2017), 28–30 [Hebrew]. Segal's term relates more directly to the scientifically optimistic prospect of achieving certainty with regard to the world through scientific means.
14. One might buttress this idea further by suggesting that *halakhah* reflects a metaphysical rather than scientific reality, though this idea is rarely articulated within *halakhic* discourse.
15. For example, see Denis R. Alexander, *Models for Relating Science and Religion* (Cambridge: The Faraday Institute for Science and Religion, St. Edmund's College, 2007).

    A parallel motif has been *critiques* leveled at the attempt to create such models or typologies, due to concerns that they do not capture how people actually approach these subjects, and also that they simplify or reify particular perspectives (e.g., *Science and Religion: Some Historical Perspectives*, ed. John Hedley Brooke [Cambridge: Cambridge University Press, 1991]; and *Rethinking History, Science, and Religion: An Exploration of Conflict and the Complexity Principle*, ed. Bernard Lightman, 1st ed. [Pittsburgh, PA: University of Pittsburgh Press, 2019]). The "model" we describe for the interaction of *halakhah* and science takes these critiques to heart: our focus is to push back against more closed models that belie the complex and dynamic relationship between these discourses. For an example that might be considered parallel in spirit regarding the continued search for "mid-scale patterns" in the face of complexity, see Bernard L. Numbers, "Simplifying

Complexity: Patterns in the History of Science and Religion," in *Science and Religion*, ed. Dixon et al., 263–82.

16. Stephen Jay Gould, *Rocks of Ages: Science and Religion in the Fullness of Life* (New York: Ballantine, 1999).
17. Yeshayahu Leibowitz, *Judaism, the Jewish People and the State of Israel* (Jerusalem: Schocken Books, 1975).
18. For example, see She'ar Yashuv Cohen, "*Chumtzat Limon, Glukoza u-Gluten be-Pesach*," *Techumin* 1 (1980): 68–96.
19. mShab 19:2.
20. mShab 19:6.
21. bShab 133b.
22. The only exception is the obscure *Kelalei ha-Milah* of R. Yaakov ha-Gozer (lit., "the circumciser"; Germany, thirteenth century): "After splitting the membrane, one takes the organ into his mouth and sucks blood out with all one's strength, because blood coagulates within the tip of the penis" (*Zikhron Berit la-Rishonim*, ed. Yitzchak Glassberg [Berlin, 1892], 20). Maimonides (*Mishneh Torah*, Laws of Circumcision 2:2) hints at the purpose of *metzitzah* in saying that, "one sucks the circumcision until blood in the far reaches is extracted," but he doesn't elaborate. However, see the interpretations of Maimonides's wording in Shlomo Sprecher, "Mezizah Be-Peh [Therapeutic Touch or Hippocratic Vestige?]" *Hakira* 3 (2006): esp. 18–22.
23. Mordechai Halperin has proposed an innovative historical-medical explanation of the purpose of *metzitzah*: to prevent hypoxia of the glans penis and with it the possibility of penile necrosis; "*Metzitzah u-Rehchitzah be-Chamin le-Achar Berit Milah—Mashma'ut Refu'it, Mishpatit ve-Hilkhatit shel Pitron ha-Ta'alumah*," *Sefer Assia* 11 (2009): 151–70. To date, the critique offered by Shlomo Sprecher ("Mezizah Be-Peh") is the only scholarly assessment of Halperin's proposal.
24. Jacob Katz, *Divine Law in Human Hands: Case Studies in Halakhic Flexibility* (Jerusalem: Magnes Press, 1998), 370.
25. bShab 134b.
26. *Shulchan Arukh* OH 331:9.
27. "*Katz, Divine Law in Human Hands*," 362–65.
28. The earliest extant reference to this concern is in Rust, Johann Nepomuk, *Helkologie Oder Über Natur, Erkenntniss Und Heilung Der Geschwüre* (Vienna: Luzern, 1811). Rust attributed a syphilis epidemic among newly circumcised infants in Krakow to the performance of *metzitzah be-peh*.
29. See the positions of R. Zecharia Frankel and R. Zvi Hirsch Fassel cited in Katz, *Divine Law in Human Hands*, 369–72.
30. See the responsum of *Chatam Sofer* cited below; also *Tiferet Yisrael*, Shabbat, *Bo'az* 19:2.
31. This responsum was not included in *Chatam Sofer*'s collected responsa. Sprecher ("Mezizah Be-Peh") offers an analysis of the controversy this engendered, along with a full text of the responsum.
32. A few *halakhic* authorities, notably Frankel and Fassel (cited in Katz, *Divine Law in Human Hands*, 369–72), did in fact propose abolishing *metzitzah* based on a frank rejection of its prophylactic value.
33. Isaac Klein, *A Guide to Jewish Religious Practice* (New York: Jewish Theological Seminary of America, 1979), 424; Mark Washofsky, *Jewish Living: A Guide to Contemporary Reform Practice* (New York: UAHC Press, 2001), 145.

34. Yair Frank and Dror Fixler, "*Beliyah u-Peleitah be-Keilim le-Or Totza'ot ha-Mivchan ha-Mada'i*," *Techumin* 34 (2014): 113–29; Chaim M. Finson, "Absorption in Cookware: A Study in Perception: Is There Perceived Taste from Absorption in Modern Cookware?" (MA diss., Bar-Ilan University, 2015) [Hebrew]; Yaakov Ariel, "*Beliya be-Keilim*," *Emunat Itekha* 126 (2020): 71–75.
35. Analysis of this issue using experimentation has some precedent; for example, see *She'elot u-Teshuvot Ridvaz* 3:844.
36. Lev. 11:20–23, 41–42.
37. bHul 66b–67b.
38. Ibid., 67b.
39. Ibid.
40. For treatment of spontaneous generation as a given fact in *halakhic* discourse, see bSanh 91, bHul 126–127a. See also Ahuva Gaziel, "Spontaneous Generation in Medieval Jewish Philosophy and Theology," *History and Philosophy of the Life Sciences* 34, no. 3 (2012): 461–79.
41. "[Regarding] vermin that develop from food and drink, these are not like vermin *but rather like food* . . ." (*She'iltot Shemini* §84). Hence the distinction posited in the Talmud (bHul 67b) between vermin found in the flesh of cattle, which are not kosher since they—like their hosts—require ritual slaughter, and vermin found in the flesh of fish, which are kosher since fish do not require ritual slaughter.
42. YD 84:16.
43. Another instance where the Talmud invokes spontaneous generation as a rationale for a *halakhic* ruling is the law permitting killing lice on Shabbat (bShab 107b; cf. Rashi, bShab 12a s.v. *matirin*).
44. For example, see Israel Lipschütz, *Tiferet Yisrael*, Avodah Zarah, *Bo'az* 2:3; Jehiel Michal Epstein, *Arukh ha-Shulhan*, YD 83:15; Moshe Feinstein, *She'elot u'Teshuvot Iggerot Moshe*, YD 2:174.
45. Moshe Katz, "*Tola'at ha-Anisakis—Asurah mi-De'orayta o Muteret le-Khatchilah*," *Emunat Itekha* 98 (2013): esp. 140–41.
46. Natan Slifkin, "Letter to the Editor," *Tradition* 44, no. 4 (2011): 79–81.
47. This term first appears in the Epistle of Rav Sherira Gaon (*Teshuvot ha-Geonim* §394) regarding medical prescriptions that appear in the Talmud: Sherira insists that these are not to be considered binding *halakhic* rulings since they were based on the common medical knowledge of the day, which was no longer considered correct. For an early medieval use of this phrase, see *Tosafot* bAZ 24b s.v. *parah*. The most comprehensive scholarly treatment of this concept is found in Neriyah Gotel, *Hishtanut ha-Teva'im be-Halakhah* (Mekhon Yahdav, 1995).
48. J. David Bleich suggests this idea regarding the *kashrut* of parasite-infected fish in "Survey of Recent Halakhic Periodical Literature: Spontaneous Generation and Halakhic Inerrancy," *Tradition* 44, no. 4 (2011): 55–75. Other authorities make similar proposals regarding the issue of killing lice on Shabbat; see Moshe Shmuel Leitner, "*Harigat Kinim bi-Zemaneinu*," *Yeshurun* 16 (1995): 592; Avigdor Neventzal, "Imprimatur," in Gotal, *Hishtanut ha-Teva'im be-Halakhah*.
49. A good example of this usage is Israel Lipschütz's proposal that the danger which *mezizah* is supposed to prevent is prevalent in warm climates—the *sitz im leben* of the Talmud's ruling—but far less common in the colder climates of northern Europe (*Tiferet Yisrael*, Shabbat, *Bo'az* 19:2). However, in most instances in which *nishtanu ha-teva'im* is invoked,

it is ambiguous as to whether the change being referred to is systematic or merely circumstantial.

One should also consider the possibility that *nishtanu ha-teva'im* sometimes functions as a euphemistic way of dismissing the rabbis' scientific statements altogether (as is often the case when questionable propositions in *halakhic* discourse are attributed to "scribal errors" or "misguided students"), rather than a genuine attempt to resolve them with current scientific evidence.

50. Katz, "*Tola'at ha-Anisakis,*" 140; J. David Bleich, "Survey of Recent Halakhic Periodical Literature: Piscatorial Parasites," *Tradition* 44, no. 1 (2011): esp. 74–75.
51. Katz, "*Tola'at ha-Anisakis,*" 140–41; Slifkin, "Letter to the Editor" (and sources cited therein).
52. For example, see the earliest published opinion of a scientist on the matter of *halakhah* and electricity. William Crookes, "Sabbath Observance and the Electric Light," *Jewish Chronicle*, January 8, 1892, 12–13.
53. Shlomo Zalman Auerbach, *Me'orei Eish*, 2nd ed. (Jerusalem: Moriya, 1980).
54. *She'elot u-Teshuvot Minchat Shlomo* 1:9, 11.
55. *She'elot u-Teshuvot Chazon Ish*, OC 50:9. Further elucidation of his stance is in his correspondence with Auerbach in published in *She'elot u-Teshuvot Minchat Shlomo* 1:11.
56. On the use of Aristotelian language in the *Chazon Ish*'s ruling on electricity, see Amitay Katz, "The Halachic Decisions of the *Chazon Ish* in the Fields of Electricity on Sabbath and Yom Tov and Its Consequences" (MA diss., Tel Aviv University, 2012), 32–38 [Hebrew]. This sort of use of Aristotelian terms to describe modern scientific concepts in *halakhic* discourse is idiosyncratic but not unprecedented; for a similar example in the rulings of Rabbi Joseph Rosin (the "Rogatchover," 1858–1936), see Israel Belfer and Israel Ori Meitlis, "Rabbi Joseph Rozin's Disagreement with Solomon Maimon and John Locke: Manuscript Completion, Motivation and Meaning," *JSIJ* 20 (2021): esp. 17 [Hebrew].
57. *She'elot u-Teshuvot Minchat Shlomo* 1:9.
58. Jacob Katz, *The "Shabbes Goy": A Study in Halakhic Flexibility* (Philadelphia: Jewish Publication Society, 1989), 25 (regarding the widely observed prohibition against river travel on Shabbat in Babylonia and Egypt).
59. ibid., 231 (regarding reliance on non-Jews' performance of prohibited activities on Shabbat).
60. For example, see Yehuda Brandes, "Unplugging and Automation on Shabbat: Preserving *Halakhic* Ideas," *Akdamut* 22 (2009): 96–118 [Hebrew].
61. Eli Reif, "*Shimush be-Daltot Magneti'ot u-be-Kartis Zihui Digitali,*" *Emunat Itekha* 112 (2016): 113–29.
62. Dror Fixler, "Using Light-Emitting Diodes (LED) on Shabbat," *Hama'ayan* 51, no. 3 (2011): 24–34 [Hebrew].

CHAPTER 24

DIVORCE AND *AGUNAH*

Halakhic Responses to Modernity

RACHEL LEVMORE AND STEVEN GOTLIB

Introduction

JEWISH law dictates that divorce requires the husband's agreement to end the marriage. His refusal to do so gives rise to a situation known as the "chained woman" or *agunah* (pl. *agunot*) in Hebrew. If the husband were to disappear, fall into a permanent vegetative state, or intentionally refuse to grant his wife a bill of divorce (*get*), she would remain "chained" to him indefinitely. Her life would be frozen in time; she would be unable to establish her independence or start a new family. The existential angst of an *agunah* is not hers alone, though; such tragic situations tear at the very fabric of a healthy Jewish society.[1]

Agunot whose husbands have chained them to an unwanted marriage by being unavailable or unwilling to grant a *get* have been a cause of great dissension in the twentieth and twenty-first centuries. This chapter explores the development of Jewish divorce law from the Bible through the present as well as how the *agunah* problem has been addressed across Jewish denominations in the United States and Israel.

Development of Jewish Divorce Law

In traditional Jewish law, the dissolution of a marriage via divorce occurs when the husband willingly places the *get* in his wife's hands. If it is given as the result of coercion rather than his free will, the *get* is considered invalid and the couple remains bound in wedlock. Specific laws pertaining to this situation developed through two thousand years of rabbinic adjudication.[2]

Biblical Law

The foundation for Jewish divorce law is found in the Bible:[3]

> When a man takes-in-marriage a woman and espouses her, and it happens: if she does not find favor in his eyes—for he finds in her something of "nakedness"—he may write for her a Document of Cutoff; he is to place (it) in her hand and (thus) send-her-away from his household.

The various stages of divorce are denoted in the above verse: establishment of grounds for divorce such as inappropriate sexual behavior;[4] transmission of a formal document from the husband to the wife; and separation of homes. The husband is the active agent in the process while the woman is passive. This is the basis of the fundamental Talmudic assumption[5] that a woman may be divorced against her will, but the divorce is valid only when the man freely agrees to it.[6]

A coerced writ of divorce (*get me'usseh*) is only valid under certain conditions.[7] If the husband is compelled by a Jewish court, the divorce is valid[8] and is assumed to have been done in accordance with Jewish law.[9] The Talmud explains this permission as an extension of the commandment to listen to the statement of the Sages.[10] A *get* is also valid even when a secular court compels a man to obey the rabbinical court judges.[11] In all other cases, a coerced *get* is invalid.[12]

The *get* itself has no features that indicate its invalidity, but the ramifications of an invalid coercion are most serious.[13] When a woman receives a valid *get*, she "goes out from his house and becomes another man's."[14] With an invalid *get*, however, it would be forbidden for her to become "another man's" wife since she has not really gone "out from [her husband's] house." Due to the *get*'s invalidity, she is still considered married to the initial husband. If she were to marry[15] or have sexual relations with another man, both she and the new man would be in violation of the biblical prohibition of adultery, and children born of this second "marriage," as well as their descendants, would be branded as *mamzerim* and thus be prohibited from marrying anyone besides others in their situation.[16]

Since coercing the husband to grant a divorce can be catastrophic, the Sages were extremely careful in this matter.[17] This general situation is a result of the foundational Torah ruling discussed earlier that a husband may divorce his wife against her will but a woman demanding divorce from her husband requires his acquiescence.[18]

Rabbinic Law

These concepts were further developed through rabbinic rulings and decrees. One important ordinance regarding divorce was issued by Rabbi Gershom ben Yehudah (*c.* 1960–1028), which sought to equalize, to a limited degree, the wife's status through the following three rulings:

1. Prohibiting polygyny, the practice of a man marrying more than one woman, in order to protect the status of the original wife.
2. Prohibiting the initiation of divorce without the wife's consent.
3. Permitting a man to marry a second wife (in cases where he would otherwise find himself the "chained" spouse) only with permission from a hundred rabbis from "three lands" (i.e., three different provinces).

The *Herem d'Rabbenu Gershom,* as these rulings are collectively known, was adopted by all Eastern European (Ashkenazic) Jewish communities, but it was not adopted by Spanish and Middle Eastern (Sephardic) communities due to different cultural norms. Ashkenazic Jews lived in Christian cultures that already prohibited polygyny whereas Sephardic Jews largely lived in Muslim cultures where polygyny was widely practiced.[19]

The prohibition of divorcing a woman against her will is the logical and unavoidable result of the prohibition of polygyny. If a man wished to marry a second wife, in absence of legal polygyny, he would simply divorce the first wife to make room for the new one. By prohibiting the divorce of a woman against her will, Rabbenu Gershom protected the first wife's rights and status.

Although Rabbenu Gershom enacted his ruling only until the end of the fifth millennium, it is still accepted and applied today[20] with no limitation on time or place.[21] In general, contemporary Jewish divorces must be arranged with the agreement of both parties. As a result of this ordinance, it is no easy matter for a husband to demand divorce from his wife today.

Nevertheless, the difficulty of the husband in getting a divorce cannot be compared with that of the wife for three reasons. First, the prohibition against marrying a second wife is rabbinic. Violating this sort of prohibition is therefore considered significantly more minor than violating a biblical law. Second, transgressing the prohibition against polygyny does not invalidate the second marriage contract (*kiddushin*) since a man is biblically permitted to have more than one wife. Finally, an escape clause is given to the husband through the permission of one hundred rabbis while no such option exists for the wife.[22] These three factors make it possible for a man to choose, albeit with difficulty, to escape a marriage to which he finds himself chained while no such choice is possible for a woman since she is biblically prohibited from remarrying without a *get*.

The *Agunah* Problem in the Modern Era

During the nineteenth century, in reaction to industrial development, rabbinic responsa dealing with the issue of a husband's disappearance multiplied in Europe according to the pace and geographical spread of the railroad.[23] Those who were previously confined to lifelong residence in a particular town could easily travel elsewhere, thus abandoning their spouses and creating *agunot* via their refusal to grant a *get*.

Furthermore, the need for acceptance by the party being sued for divorce rendered it possible for them to issue far-reaching demands in exchange for agreement. Sometimes these demands were financial while in other instances they involved child custody or support.[24] In some cases, the party being sued for divorce simply refuses to arrange a *get*—irrespective of a civil divorce.[25] Discussion of the modern treatment of *agunah* cases in the sections that follow focus on these situations in the United States and Israel, the two largest Jewish populations in the world.[26]

The United States

The Jewish community in the United States is made up of three major denominations, each with unique positions on the nature of Jewish law. As such, they produce distinct approaches to dealing with the *agunah* issue. Reform and Conservative Judaism have largely eliminated *agunot* while Orthodoxy has developed creative ways of mitigating, though not eradicating, the issue.

Non-Orthodox Approaches to Agunot

The Reform and Conservative movements represent a majority of the Jewish population in the United States. Owing to their different positions on the binding nature of Jewish law, Reform and Conservative Judaism have developed very different ways of addressing the challenges facing *agunot*.

Reform Judaism, which does not believe Jewish law to be binding on their adherents, determined civil divorce to be a dissolution of Jewish marriage in legal opinions (*responsa*) from 1869[27] and 1929. The 1929 decision specified that since divorce is purely a civil, legal action, the rabbi has no connection to it, and therefore, it is not his place to act as an officiant as with marriage.[28] Consequently, the *agunah* problem was eliminated within Reform Judaism.

The Conservative movement, which does believe in the binding nature of Jewish law, takes the need for a *get* seriously. The requirement of a *get* for remarriage is one of three standards of practice to which all Conservative rabbis must adhere if they wish to remain members of the movement's Rabbinical Assembly.[29] The Conservative Movement's most commonly used[30] solution is the insertion in the marriage document (*ketubah*) of a statement known as the Lieberman clause, named after Professor Saul Lieberman, who originally proposed the use of this technique. The clause states that it is

> agreed that should either [spouse] contemplate dissolution of the marriage, or following the dissolution of their marriage in the civil courts, each may summon the other to the Bet Din of The Rabbinical Assembly and the Jewish Theological Seminary, or its representative, and that each will abide by its instructions so that throughout life each will be able to live according to the laws of the Torah. This ketubah is not to be regarded as mere rhetoric or as a perfunctory legal form. We have performed the act which in Jewish law makes the obligations of this document

> legally binding on the part of ________________, the groom, to ____________ _____, the bride, and on the part of ________________, the bride, to ________ _________, the groom, with an instrument fit for that purpose, in order to confirm all that is stated and specified above, which shall be valid and immediately effective.[31]

In other words, both spouses agree, in their marriage contract itself, to abide by the ruling of a specific rabbinical court in the event of divorce. Thus, within the Conservative Movement there is full recognition of the *agunah* problem coupled with solutions proposed throughout the twentieth century.

The debate regarding the resolution of the *agunah* problem proved to be a determining factor in the growing division between the Conservative Movement and Orthodoxy, which rejected the Lieberman clause's validity.[32] Discussions were held between Saul Lieberman and a leading Orthodox rabbi, Joseph B. Soloveitchik, to create a joint Rabbinical Court charged with divorce matters and to include a new clause in the *ketubah* to prevent the *agunah* problem. But they did not reach an agreement[33] due to opposition from the broader Orthodox community based on concerns regarding both the competence of the proposed Rabbinical Court and the *halakhic* validity of the clause itself.[34]

From an Orthodox point of view, neither Reform nor Conservative marriages produce *agunot* upon their dissolution due to the rulings of Rabbi Moshe Feinstein, the recognized leading American decisor of Orthodox Jewish law in the twentieth century. He ruled, against the previous leading authority, that marriages performed by Reform and Conservative rabbis are not to be considered valid *halakhic* marriages in the first place.[35] Therefore, women married in Conservative or Reform ceremonies were not in need of a *get* at all. In nullifying Reform, Conservative, and civil marriages, Rabbi Feinstein eliminated the problem of an *agunah* arising from these marriages even according to Orthodoxy.

Orthodox Approaches to Agunot

Rabbi Feinstein demonstrated leadership and flexibility in responding to many difficult cases in the United States within the Orthodox context. For example, he ruled in favor of nullifying marriages on the basis of a mistaken transaction due to, for example, a major blemish basic to marital relations which existed at the time of the wedding but was hidden from the bride at that time.[36] Examples of this situation include a physical or mental health condition or homosexuality. Even in these cases, however, Rabbi Feinstein wrote that an attempt must be made to achieve the *get*, but if that proved impossible, the marriage could be nullified. Such leniency, however, could not be utilized in cases where a *get* could be legitimately acquired.

Classic cases of *agunah* in which the husband disappeared without knowledge of his death were not prevalent in the late twentieth century until the September 11, 2001, terrorist attacks.[37] Married Jewish men and women were among the almost three thousand individuals killed, with no witnesses to their deaths. Wives were left as *agunot*, and one husband as an *agun*, but the Orthodox Beth Din of America (BDA) was ultimately able to permit many of the *agunot* to remarry.[38]

Still, *get*-refusal continues to be a problem. This is especially so in countries (such as the United States and Canada) where rabbinical courts have no legal authority. At best, a rabbinical court may issue a contempt order (*seruv*), declaring the spouse to be subject to public ostracism and condemnation, while simultaneously urging the religious community to take appropriate action.[39] Thus, this lack of jurisdiction spurred a preventative approach as opposed to a curative solution.[40]

In 1979, Rabbi Feinstein stated that it is permissible to include the following condition between spouses in a prenuptial document: "If after they are married they want to separate . . . he will not delay in giving the *get*, nor will she refuse to accept it when the rabbinical court instructs them accordingly."[41] He added that the civil courts could then compel both parties to obey the rabbinical courts, though he did not specify the grounds by which this would be enforced. Rabbi Feinstein clearly stated that the resulting *get* will not be considered coerced since the courts are only enforcing the decision that had already been made by a rabbinical court.

Following Rabbi Feinstein's ruling, the Rabbinical Council of America (RCA) tried to devise a prenuptial agreement that would be acceptable to Modern Orthodox Jews. A commission of the RCA presented its proposal for a prenuptial agreement based on a mechanism of spousal support that would be paid by the recalcitrant spouse until the giving of the *get*, and Rabbi Joseph B. Soloveitchik expressed his acceptance of the agreement.[42] His acceptance was significant because, when taking a step perceived to be bold within Orthodoxy, it is imperative to garner support from the most widely respected rabbis in the United States as well as in Israel.

To garner further support for the prenuptial agreement, the RCA asked for the opinion of the Ashkenazi Chief Rabbi of Jerusalem, Rabbi Yaakov Betzalel Zolty.[43] In 1993, Rabbi Zolty agreed to the idea of obligating a recalcitrant husband legally separated from his wife to pay spousal support based on the fact that his wife was unable to remarry on his account. Rabbi Zolty's responsum provided the foundation for the future gradual acceptance of prenuptial agreements by Orthodox rabbis internationally.[44] Thus, the *halakhic* obligation to support a wife for the duration of a Jewish marriage that was supported by Rabbi Zolty was subsequently employed in prenuptial agreements drawn up in both the United States[45] and Israel.[46]

The RCA's original prenuptial agreement for the prevention of *get*-refusal was drawn up in Hebrew and brought before several leading rabbis in early 1992.[47] In signing the agreement, the husband obligates himself to a daily amount of spousal support, which he is required to pay until granting his wife a *get*. The underlying theory is that when faced with a choice of daily payments to his wife or voiding that support obligation by giving a *get*, a recalcitrant husband would most likely prefer to immediately grant the *get*. Ultimately, the prenuptial agreement was accepted by the RCA, which obligated its members to officiate at weddings only where the couple signed this document.[48]

In 1996, the text of the *halakhic* prenuptial agreement was incorporated into the framework of a legally binding arbitration agreement which designated the BDA as the arbitrating body. This measure was taken to address the lack of the rabbinical court's ability to summon a recalcitrant husband and obligate him to obey its ruling.[49] According to this agreement, the couple would be legally bound to attend arbitration at the assigned rabbinical court (the BDA or any other mutually agreed upon in writing), and abide by its ruling, which would then be enforceable in a civil court. In turn, the rabbinical court would also be bound to rule in accordance with the conditions stipulated in the prenuptial agreement.

The challenge remained, however, of disseminating the prenuptial agreement to all subsets within Orthodoxy, and to strongly encourage all marrying couples to sign it. In order to promote universal use, the RCA resolved that all member rabbis could only officiate at weddings in which the prenuptial agreement was signed.[50] Many rabbinic heads of Yeshiva University also encouraged couples to sign the agreement.[51]

While this encouragement did not come without criticism,[52] the RCA and Yeshiva University now advocate for use of this agreement.[53] By 2005, ten years after the introduction of the RCA's prenuptial agreement, there was evidence that this tool had been effective in preventing the rise of *agunot*.[54] In 2006, the RCA officially resolved to bar all member rabbis from officiating at weddings where no prenuptial agreement had been signed.[55]

Another approach, relating to the problem of the *agunah* whose husband has disappeared or become incapacitated, was offered by Rabbi Professor Michael Broyde's "Tripartite Agreement," named for its combination of three distinct *halakhic* mechanisms into one document.[56] The strengths of Rabbi Broyde's solution are that it need not rely at all on civil enforcement and that the three *halakhic* mechanisms complement and validate each other when connected together. On the other hand, however, individually these halachic mechanisms each remain theoretical and contested within mainstream Orthodoxy. Regardless, many couples in the United States and Israel have signed this document.[57]

Despite the availability of prenuptial agreements and their growing popularity in parts of the Orthodox community, they did not spread easily within the more tightly knit ultra-Orthodox. Several high-profile cases in the twenty-first century that could have been prevented by use of a prenuptial agreement demonstrated this reality. The public exposure, both in Jewish circles[58] and in the general media,[59] caused great distress and embarrassment to the Orthodox community as a whole. As a result, calls to sign prenuptial agreements were targeted specifically toward members of the ultra-Orthodox communities that had been most resistant to the idea.[60]

After a significant number of ultra-Orthodox families suffered drawn-out divorce turmoil, the Yashar Initiative was founded for the purpose of developing a prenuptial agreement for the prevention of *get*-refusal geared to the ultra-Orthodox community. Phrased in traditional language and covering issues beyond *get*-refusal such as child custody, it was published in English, Hebrew, and Yiddish in 2020.[61] Although several ultra-Orthodox rabbinic leaders have issued their endorsement of this agreement,[62] it remains to be seen if its use will spread among their constituents.

Israel—Divorce in the Jewish State

Israel is in a unique situation in responding to the challenge of *get*-refusal.[63] Civil legislation by the Knesset (Israeli Parliament) established the Rabbinical Court System which maintains designated powers and specific areas of jurisdiction. Thus, Israeli law explicitly provides that matters of marriage and divorce involving Jews who are citizens or residents of the State of Israel come under the sole jurisdiction of the Israeli Rabbinical Court System.[64] In other words, there is no civil marriage or divorce in Israel because the various rabbinical courts are empowered by the civil law to rule according to *halakhah* in these matters.[65] Because all Jews in Israel marry and divorce under the auspices of the State, they do so in an Orthodox ceremony regardless of their religious beliefs, or lack thereof. Thus, the problem of *get*-refusal appears across Israeli society and is not limited to only the Orthodox community.[66]

It is impossible to know exact numbers of current or former victims of *get*-refusal in Israel. Israeli women's organizations report numbers ranging from the "thousands" to 100,000.[67] This discrepancy in numbers partially stems from the fact that many women are too frightened of further abuse to turn to the rabbinical courts to file a suit. Since all those applying for formal divorce must use the official Orthodox rabbinical courts, those in a contentious situation are faced with an existential challenge. The party who is suing for divorce is battling on two fronts—to persuade their spouse to agree to the divorce and to persuade the rabbinical court that a divorce is appropriate in their specific case.

While the types of resolutions reached by rabbinical courts vary, cases are known where rabbinical courts have asked the parties to achieve "peace in the home,"[68] despite the demand made by one of the spouses for a divorce. Alternatively, sometimes rabbinical courts simply refrain from ruling in favor of divorce. If, however, the court concludes that there is no chance of reconciliation, then it may simply recommend a divorce, obligate the husband to give the *get*, or even rule for coercion. In the case of the wife refusing the *get*, rabbinical courts may issue a permit for the husband to marry a second wife.[69]

It is important to note that even if a rabbinical court rules in favor of divorce, its judgment is not constitutive. In other words, the court's judgment does not create a new legal reality in which the marriage has come to an end. That can only be done by the granting of a *get* by the husband and its acceptance by the wife. The court can only decide in favor of a divorce or reject the suit for divorce. To date, no Orthodox rabbinic authority has been able to solve a situation in which there was no preventative measure (such as a prenuptial agreement) in place already. Thus, Rabbi She'ar Yashuv Cohen, Chief Justice and Chief Rabbi of Haifa, described the *agunah* problem as "the problem of our generation":[70]

> The judges of Israel often hear the desperate cries of women whose husbands treat them cruelly for purposes of revenge; the wickedness and heartlessness of these

husbands delay these women in getting a divorce, remarrying in accordance with the laws of Moshe and Israel and building a Jewish family in order to rebuild the ruins of their lives. Those husbands brazenly rebel against the judgments requiring them to grant their wives a divorce, appeal them in various courts of law, mock the rabbinical courts, and laugh at the distress of their wives.

The Role of Grassroots Activism

The turn of the twenty-first century witnessed a shift in the discussion and treatment of the *agunah* problem from an intra-rabbinic debate to grassroots activism both in the United States and in Israel. The Jewish Orthodox Feminist Alliance (JOFA) was founded in the United States in 1997 by Blu Greenberg, whose famous motto is "where there is a rabbinic will there is a *halakhic* way."[71] While JOFA was not founded specifically to address *get*-refusal, it was a major issue at the time of its founding. To raise consciousness in the United States, Israeli scholar-activists were repeatedly invited to speak at JOFA conferences about the *agunah* problem.[72] In addition to JOFA's activities, there is a lay group, the Organization for the Resolution of Agunot (ORA; getora.org), which actively works toward convincing recalcitrant husbands to give the *get* in individual cases.

Ties intensified between activists in the United States and Israel who were working to resolve cases of American *agunot*,[73] and who partnered through academic/rabbinic research.[74] Israeli rabbinical court advocates and attorneys continue to make use of Israeli law to free Diaspora *agunot* within the Israeli rabbinical court system.[75] Bonds further intensified with Greenberg's initiative of an invitation-only "*Agunah* Summit,"[76] where a panel of Israelis presented *halakhic* solutions to this problem.[77]

The *Agunah* Summit spurred the creation of the International Beit Din (IBD), headed by Rabbi Simcha Krauss, for the purpose of freeing *agunot*, wherever in the world they may be, who could not be helped by the more traditional Orthodox rabbinical courts.[78] The IBD was, however, publicly criticized by prominent American Orthodox rabbis, including Rabbi Hershel Schachter of Yeshiva University, due to the leniency and novelty of their positions.[79] Despite its controversy, the IBD indicates that "based on its caseload, it is the most active court for *agunot* in the United States."[80] Although recognized mainstream Modern Orthodox bodies do not rely on the IBD, JOFA refers *agunot* to the IBD on their website.[81]

Organizations dealing with *agunah* prevention encouraged marrying couples to sign *halakhic* prenuptial agreements both in the United States[82] and in Israel.[83] An innovative, community-based educational approach began in Israel in 2015 with the first "Postnuptial Signing Party" where married couples sign a *halakhic* postnuptial Agreement for Mutual Respect to serve as an example for their children and the community.[84]

Other lay-led grassroots initiatives with women leading the charge involve the use of social media. Activists have taken to the internet using tactics of shaming and protesting *get*-refusers.[85] This phenomenon was even reported in *Vogue Magazine* where it was noted that "part of the success of this social-media-fueled process has been the pressure it has put on authority figures within the community."[86]

The grassroots efforts discussed in this section demonstrate a powerful means of addressing the challenges faced by *agunot*. The first decades of the twenty-first century demonstrated *halakhic* innovation and self-sufficiency by invoking curative, case-by-case resolutions as well as preventative solutions within Orthodoxy. Acceptance across the board, however, is still lacking in the extended Orthodox community.

Conclusion

In America, each of the three major denominations provided unique treatments to the *agunah* problem. These included regarding divorce as purely a civil matter, utilizing civil law to provide solutions through a hybrid with Jewish legal mechanisms, and entirely relying on *halakhah*. Reform Judaism eliminated the problem by declaring that civil divorce can dissolve a Jewish marriage, and Conservative Judaism developed Jewish law such that the power to dissolve a Jewish marriage was transferred from the husband to the movement's Rabbinic Court. Both of these solutions were uniformly accepted by the membership of these two movements.

Orthodox Judaism, in both America and Israel, is rigid in its legal approach to the sanctity of marriage and divorce. As a result, it is still in the process of developing solutions to the problems faced by *agunot*. Additionally, some of the mechanisms that have been adopted are not yet universally accepted. While the relatively widespread signing of prenuptial agreements has proven enormously helpful in preventing *get*-refusal, Orthodox Judaism has yet to completely resolve the plight of the *agunah*—whether through preventative means or with curative measures. The challenge to employ both methods in a systematic manner remains to this day. May the plight of the *agunah* be eradicated speedily in our days.

Acknowledgments

Dr. Levmore is grateful for the assistance of Young Israel-Israel Region; The Jewish Agency for Israel; The Hadassah-Brandeis Institute Translation Award; Targum Shlishi, a Raquel and Aryeh Rubin Foundation; The Fanya Gottesfeld Heller Center for the Study of Women in Judaism, Bar Ilan University; Sylvia & Albert Milhado.

Notes

1. Rachel Levmore, "Ethics of the *Agunah* Problem," *Conversations* 8 (August 2010): 112–23, https://www.jewishideas.org/article/ethics-agunah-problem.

2. For a thorough examination of rabbinic law through the ages, see Rachel Levmore, *Minee Einayikh MeDim'ah: Heskemei Kedam Nissuin L'Miniyat Seiruv Get* (Jerusalem: Mosdot Ariel and the Council of Young Israel Rabbis, 2009) [Hebrew].
3. Deut. 24:1. Translation: Everett Fox, *The Five Books of Moses: The Schoken Bible: Vol 1* (New York: Schocken Books, 1995).
4. m.*Gittin* 9:10 lays out the acceptable grounds for a man to divorce his wife according to three different schools of thought: *Beit Hillel* states that inappropriate sexual behavior is what constitutes valid grounds; *Beit Shammai* includes a wife who burns her husband's food; while Rabbi Akiva does not search for fault but rather focuses on the husband himself—if he has found a different woman more appealing than his wife.
5. m.*Yevamot* 14:1.
6. Maimonides, *Mishneh Torah Hilkhot Gerushin* 1:1.
7. See m.*Ketubot* 7:10 and b.*Ketubot* 77a for the list that makes up the basis of discussions regarding *get* coercion; Rashi and Tosafot to b.*Ketubot* 70a; Resp. Rosh, 43:3 and *Tur*, EH, 154; *Siftei Kohen* in *Gevurat Anashim*, 29.
8. m.*Gittin* 9:8; *Mekhilta deRabbi Ishmael*, ed. Horowitz-Rabin, Mishpatim, section A.
9. *Korban Ha-Edah* commentary, b.*Gittin* 9.
10. b.*Bava Batra* 48a. Similarly in m.*Arakhin* 5:6; b.*Yevamot* 106a.
11. For example, *The New York Get Law* (State of New York: Domestic Relations Law §236B(5)), §253(6).
12. Menachem Kahana, "*Gillui daat veones begittin*," *Tarbiz* 62 (5753): 225–63. Regarding the question of whether compulsion by means of imprisonment, a method employed in Israel's State Rabbinical Courts, is considered a *get meusseh*—see Ovadia Hadaya, Resp. *Yaskil Avdi* (Jerusalem, 5719), Part 6, EH 96; Zerah Warhaftig, *Mechkariim Bemishpat Ha-Ivri* (Ramat Gan, 5745), 148–208 [Hebrew]; Shlomo Dichovsky, "*K'fiyyat Get*," *Tehumin* 1 (5740): 248–54 [Hebrew]; Hayyi Sha'anan, "Ways to Compel a Divorce," *Tehumin* 6 (5750): 203–13 [Hebrew]; Resp. Tzitz Eli'ezer 4:21 [Hebrew].
13. This forms the basis for increased stringencies throughout rabbinical responsa leading to almost complete limitation of coercion—from the twelfth-century ruling of Rabbenu Tam (*Sefer Hayashar* 77) to the seventeenth-century Shach (*Gevurat Anashim* 29) who both prohibited coercion.
14. Deut. 24:2.
15. The sanctification of the marriage does not take effect, but the woman and her new husband are unaware of this.
16. *Siftei Kohen*, *Gevurat Anashim*, 49; *Igrot Moshe*, EH 3:43, where Rabbi Moshe Feinstein wrote that "Yet there exist today no circumstances justifying compulsion, and in any case the object should be to persuade him to grant the divorce of his own free will."
17. Zerah Warhaftig, *Studies in Jewish Law* (Ramat Gan, 5745), 148–208 [Hebrew]; Ezra Batzri, "*Get Me'usseh*," *The Jewish Law Annual* 16–17 (5750–5751): 535–53; Elimelech Westreich, "The Rise and Erosion of the *moredet* Justification," *Jewish Law Annual* 21 (5758-5760): 123–47 [Hebrew]; Menahem Elon, *Jewish Law: Its History, Its Sources, Its Principles*, 1st ed. (Jerusalem, 5733) [Hebrew]; Avraham Grossman, *Pious Women and Rebellious Women: Jewish Women in Europe in the Middle Ages* (Jerusalem, 5761), ch. 10 [Hebrew],
18. Levmore, *Minee Einayikh MeDim'ah*, 56–57.
19. Resp. Rosh, 43; R. Moshe Isserlis, SA EH 1:10. See Benzion Sharshewsky, *Family Law* (Jerusalem, 1993), 61 [Hebrew]; Rachel Biale, *Women and Jewish Law: The Essential Texts, Their History, and Their Relevance for Today* (New York: Schocken Books, 1995), 50–51.

20. The prohibition of polygyny was adopted as a regulation of the Chief Rabbinate of the State of Israel at the National Rabbinical Convention held in 5710 (February 1950), "in order to maintain the peace in Israel, in public and within the family." See The Chief Rabbinate of Israel, *Takkanot Ketuvot Legidrei Ishut* (Shevat 5710), §2(b); Zerah Warhaftig, "Chief Rabbinate *Takkanot*," *Tehumin* 15 (5755): 81–117 [Hebrew]. In addition, two laws of the State of Israel forbid one to be married simultaneously to two wives: Rabbinical Courts' Jurisdiction Law (Marriage and Divorce), 5713 (1953); Penal Law 5737 (1977), § 176. The prohibition against bigamy is anchored in rulings of the rabbinical court as well. See Case No. 361/37, Rabbinical Court Judgments, ed. Dov Katz (Jerusalem, 5735–5737), 249–60 [Hebrew].
21. Resp. Ran 38:10, and Resp. Rosh 42. See Sharshewsky, *Family Law*, 279. As a result, in the State of Israel at the present time neither the husband nor the wife can divorce the other against their will.
22. Prof. Ariel Rosen-Zvi, describes the "lack of symmetry between husband and wife regarding the justification for agreeing to and enforcing the granting of a divorce, which acts to the detriment of the wife. In many cases, that which suffices to oblige a woman to receive a *get* is not sufficient when a wife sues to have her husband obligated to grant her a *get.*" Ariel Rosen-Zvi, *Jewish Law and a Secular Reality, Freedom of Conscience and Religion* (Association for Civil Rights, 5750), 153–206 [Hebrew].
23. Prof. Mordechai (Motti) Zalkin in Rachel Levmore, "Jews, We Have a Problem," *The Jerusalem Post*, February 21, 2010, p. 14, http://www.jpost.com/Opinion/Editorials/Article.aspx?id=169240#; Zalkin in private conversation, May 7, 2021: "Exactly during the period that the railroad spread, there was an increase in the number of *agunot*. The railroad enabled the young men to disappear. It is connected to the immigration to the U.S."
24. Pinhas Shifman, *Family Law in Israel* (Jerusalem, 5748), 120 [Hebrew]; Ezra Batsri, "*Get Meuseh*," *Jewish Law Annual* 16–17 (5750–5751): 535–53 [Hebrew].
25. Robert Hirt et al., "Pastoral Considerations," in *The Prenuptial Agreement, Halakhic and Pastoral Considerations*, ed. Basil Herring and Kenneth Auman (Lanham, MD: Jason Aronson, 1996), 69–70.
26. For England see Rachel Levmore and Daniel Clarke, "The Prenuptial Agreement of Mutual Respect, Get and English Law," *Jewish Law* (December 2008), http://www.jlaw.com/Articles/getAndEnglishLaw.pdf.
27. "The dissolution of marriage is, on Mosaic and rabbinical grounds, a civil act only which never received religious consecration. It is to be recognized therefore as an act emanating from the judicial authorities of the state. The so-called ritual *get* is in all cases declared null and void." Cited in Yael Levy, "The Agunah and the Missing Husband: An American Solution to a Jewish Problem," *Journal of Law and Religion* 10 (1993–1994): 49–71. See also Report of Recording Secretary, *CCAR Fortieth Annual Convention*, vol. 39, ed. Isaac E. Marcuson (June 1929), 43: the 1929 decision affirmed that It was moved and adopted that the Executive Board felt that it was not within the province of the Conference to sanction a divorce by issuing a *get* or certificate as the Rabbi does in case of a marriage. That when the Rabbi officiates at a marriage, he does so as an officer of the State. But a divorce is purely a legal action with which the Rabbi has no connection.
28. *CCAR Fortieth Annual Convention*, 43.
29. See Elliot Dorff, *The Unfolding Tradition: Jewish Law after Sinai* (New York: Aviv Press, 2005), 405. See also Mayer E. Rabinowitz (Chair, Joint Bet Din Conservative Movement),

Issues in Jewish Ethics: Agunot—Abandoned Wives (Jewish Virtual Library, 1998), www.jewishvirtuallibrary.org/agunot-abandoned-wives.

30. While the Lieberman clause is the most common method used in the Conservative Movement, they also offer their own version of a prenuptial agreement for couples who wish to avoid mentioning the possibility of divorce in their marriage contract.
31. *The Rabbi's Manual of the Rabbinical Assembly*, vol. 1 (The Rabbinical Assembly, New York, 1998), 16; Rabinowitz, ibid. Significantly, the Appeals Court in the State of New York supported the imposing of the Lieberman clause in the case: Avitzur v. Avitzur, 446 N.E. 2d 136, 137 (N.Y. App. Div. 1983); Michelle Greenberg-Kobrin, "Civil Enforceability of Religious Prenuptial Agreements," *Columbia Journal of Law and Social Problems* 32, no. 4 (Summer 1999): 359–99.
32. Jonathan D. Sarna, *American Judaism: A History* (New Haven, CT: Yale University Press, 2004), 240–41; Fabian Schonfeld, "The Conservative Beth-Din," cited in Zev Eleff, *Modern Orthodox Judaism* (Philadelphia: Jewish Publication Society, 2016).
33. Louis Bernstein, *Challenge and Mission* (n.p., 1982); "Saul Lieberman (1898–1983)," Jewish Virtual Library, https://www.jewishvirtuallibrary.org/saul-lieberman, Irving Greenberg, "Two Doors Rabbi Soloveitchik Opened and Did Not Walk Through," in *Rav Ba'olam Hachadash*, ed. Avinoam Rosenak and Naftali Rotenberg (Jerusalem: Magnes Press, 2010), 245–77 [Hebrew], https://www.rabbiirvinggreenberg.com/writing/scholarly-articles/.
34. Norman Lamm, "Recent Additions to the Ketubah: A Halakhic Critique," *Tradition* 2, no. 1 (1959): 93–118; Marc B. Shapiro, *Saul Lieberman and the Orthodox* (Scranton, PA: Scranton University 2006), 15–36.
35. Moshe Feinstein, *Iggrot Moshe* (New York, 1961), Even Haezer III no. 76, 77; no. 75: Civil marriage; Iggrot Moshe, Even Haezer IV, no. 75. Iggrot Moshe, Even ha-Ezer 4:13, 4:46. Similarly: Ahron Soloveitchik, "*Kiddushin* Conducted by a Conservative Rabbi," *Tehumin* 20, no. 297 (5760): 309–10 [Hebrew]; Haim Jachter, "Conservative *Kiddushin*," *Tehumin* 18, no. 84 (5758) [Hebrew].
36. *Igrot Moshe*, EH, regarding mental illness 1:80; regarding impotency 1:69 and 4:52; regarding homosexuality 4:113. See Shlomo Riskin, "*Hafka'at Kiddushin*: Towards Solving the Aguna Problem in Our Time," *Tradition* 36, no. 4 (Winter 2002); David Bass, "*Hatarat Nissuin b'Ta'anat Mekach Ta'ut*," *Tehumin* 24 (2004): 194–218 [Hebrew].
37. https://www.history.com/topics/21st-century/9-11-attacks.
38. Yona Reiss, *Contending with Catastrophe: Jewish Perspectives on September 11th*, ed. Michael J. Bryode (K'hal Publishing and the Beth Din of America, 2011), 17; Chaim Jachter, "The Beth Din of America's Handling of the World Trade Center Agunot—Part One: Methodology of *Agunah* Crisis Management," https://static1.squarespace.com/static/52a75d36e4b06a3e88b21253/t/52eabe6fe4b07b90a848dcc2/1391115887699/The+Beth+Din+of+America+ruling+about+the+World+Trade+Center+agunot.pdf; Chaim Jachter, The Beth Din of America's Handling of the World Trade Center Agunot—Four parts (audio), YUTorah Online, https://www.yutorah.org/search/?teacher=80396&collection=3639.
39. Beth Din of America, https://bethdin.org/wp-content/uploads/2015/07/FAQDivorce.pdf.
40. The earliest community-wide *halakhic* prenuptial agreement adopted for the prevention of *get*-refusal was that of Morocco in the mid-twentieth century. Morocco's *agunah* problem appeared with the advent of civil marriage and divorce. Faced with the situation of young husbands obtaining a civil divorce and not bothering to arrange a *halakhic* one as well, the country's rabbinical leaders convened in a groundbreaking attempt of an official regional

rabbinate to find a global solution. At the fifth annual convocation of the Rabbinical Council of Morocco (December 16, 1953) a resolution was reached determining that every Jewish groom would sign a premarital contract. His contractual obligation clarified that if he were to divorce his wife in a civil divorce, he would continue to provide financial support for her as long as he has not divorced her in accordance with Jewish law—by means of a *get*, giving the husband a financial incentive to give the *get* as soon as possible. Levmore, *Minee Einayikh MeDim'ah*, 66–67.

41. Moshe Feinstein, *Iggrot Moshe*, EH, 4:107 (23 Marheshvan 5740).
42. "The RCA Commission: Solving the Problem of *Gittin*," *Hamevaser* 22, no. 2 (October 27, 1983).
43. The response was in answer to Rabbi Abner Weiss of Riverdale (representing the RCA), New York, dated 27 Tishrei 5747 (1986).
44. Sephardic Chief Rabbi of Israel, Rabbi Shlomo Amar, *Shema Shlomo* (Bnei Brak, 5768), EH, vol. 6, §§19–20.
45. "Beth Din of America-Binding Arbitration Agreement" (theprenup.org), initiated by the Rabbinical Council of America (rabbis.org).
46. "The Agreement for Mutual Respect" (jewishprenup.org/), authored by Rabbi Elyashiv Knohl, Rabbi Dr. David Ben Zazon, and Dr. Rachel Levmore, Rabbinical Court advocate.
47. It was introduced to the public in 1994, https://theprenup.org/origins-of-the-prenup/; the rabbis who gave their approbation were Rabbi Hayyim Cimbalist, Rabbi Zalman Nehemiah Goldberg, Rabbi Ovadia Yosef, Rabbi Yitzhak Liebes, and Rabbi Gedaliah Dov Schwartz.
48. 2016 Resolution: https://rabbis.org/2016-resolution-requiring-the-use-of-prenuptial-agreements-for-the-prevention-of-get-refusal/; 2013 Resolution: https://rabbis.org/2013-resolution-prenuptial-agreements-for-the-prevention-of-get-refusal/.
49. Avraham Weiss, "The Modern Day *Agunah*: In Retrospect and Prospect," in *The Prenuptial Agreement, Halakhic and Pastoral Considerations* Chapter I, ed. Basil Herring and Kenneth Auman (Lanham, MD: Jason Aronson, 1996), https://www.rabbis.org/pdfs/PNA_Booklet.PDF. Marc Stern, "A Legal Guide to the Prenuptial Agreement for Couples about to be Married," in *The Prenuptial Agreement, Halakhic and Pastoral Considerations* Chapter III.
50. www.getora.org/endorsements.
51. "A Message to our Rabbinic Colleagues and Students," *The Jewish Press*, February 25, 2000, p. 28; "Chained Women Could Have Used Prenuptial Pacts," *Forward*, February 25, 2000; https://res.cloudinary.com/orthodox-union/image/upload/v1531912119/Theprenup.org/YU_Roshei_Yeshiva_Prenup_Letter.pdf; Levmore, "Ethics of the Agunah Problem."
52. Yehuda David Bleich, "*A Proposed Solution to the Problem of the Husband Who Refuses to Divorce*" [Hebrew], *or Ha-Mizrah*, 38(a) (Tishre 5750, October 1989), 57–78, criticizes this proposed agreement and concludes: "We find that this document of obligation contains a threat to compel the husband to divorce, in a halachically improper fashion." https://www.broydeblog.net/uploads/8/0/4/0/80408218/broyde_sternbuch_reply.pdf.
53. https://www.rabbis.org/pdfs/RCAIntroForJoinUs.pdf.
54. In February 2005, Rabbi Yona Reiss of the BDA noted that out of thirty such couples (the updated number), they all concluded divorce proceedings in a reasonable period of time after turning to the Beth Din. In cases of a signed agreement followed by a request to divorce, the *get* was given *before* the conclusion of the civil divorce proceedings (Discussion Panel, Yona Reiss and Rachel Levmore, Stern College New York, February 16, 2005). Rabbi Reiss stated: "In 100% of the cases, the *get* was given in a timely fashion." Reiss clarified

that signing the agreement had no effect on the number of couples seeking divorce and does not serve as its cause. This continues to be the case to date. See Heshey Zelcer, "A Prenuptial Agreement by and for the Haredi Community," *Hakirah* 27 (2019), https://hakirah.org/vol27Zelcer.pdf.

55. May 18, 2006, resolution of the Rabbinical Council of America. See "Use of Prenuptial Agreement," https://rabbis.org/use-of-prenuptial-agreement/. In addition to the well-established Rabbinical Council of America, the newer and more liberal International Rabbinic Fellowship mandated the use of "a halachic prenuptial agreement"—referring to the RCA/BDA prenuptial agreement—for its membership officiating at weddings in 2012. https://www.internationalrabbinicfellowship.org/news/international-rabbinic-fellowship-takes-historic-step-to-prevent-future-agunot.
56. These three mechanisms are (1) *kiddushin al tnai*—conditional marriage, (2) *get b'harshaa*—divorce writ by proxy, and (3) *takanat kahal*—communal edict providing for an annulment. In addition the bride employs her own independent condition to accept the marriage.
57. Michael J. Broyde, "An Unsuccessful Defense of the Bet Din of Rabbi Emanuel Rackman," 21–22; "A Proposed Tripartite Prenuptial Agreement to Solve Some of the Agunah Problems: A Solution without Any Innovation," in *Jewish Law Association Studies*, ed. Leib Moscovitz (Deborah Charles Publications, 2010), 20; Matityahu Broyde and Rachel Levmore, "*Hahut Hameshulash Lo B'mehayrah Yinatek*," *Tehumin* 37 (2017) [Hebrew], Machon Tzomet, 228–39, jewishprenup.org/articles/; "The Tripartite Agreement: A *halakhic* Prenuptial Agreement to Solve the *agunah* Problem," www.jewishprenup.org.
58. *The Jewish Press* publishes a weekly column listing the names of get-refusers alongside the call of Rabbi Reiss to sign the prenuptial agreement. Numerous articles educating the mostly ultra-Orthodox readers were published regularly and continuously.
59. The refusal of Jewish men to grant Jewish women a *get* has been reported in the American and Israeli press, both mainstream and on social media. See *The New York Times*, https://www.nytimes.com/2014/03/22/us/a-wedding-amid-cries-of-unfinished-business-from-a-marriage.html; *The Wall Street Journal*, https://www.wsj.com/articles/BL-METROB-18751; *The New York Post*, https://nypost.com/2013/11/04/orthodox-jewish-womans-plea-for-a-divorce/; *The Daily News*, https://www.nydailynews.com/new-york/lost-women-struggle-jewish-divorce-orthodox-husbands-article-1.1085440; *The Jerusalem Post*, http://www.jpost.com/Opinion/Op-EdContributors/Article.aspx?id=203305; YouTube, Facebook, Twitter, etc.
60. Heshey Zelcer, "A Prenuptial Agreement by and for the Haredi Community," *Hakirah* 27 (2019), https://hakirah.org/vol27Zelcer.pdf.; Rachel Levmore, "Getting Serious about *Get*-Refusal," *The Jewish Press*, July 11, 2012. Rachel Levmore, "*Parents: International Agunah Day 5776*," *The Jewish Press*, March 16, 2016.
61. https://yasharinitiative.org/.
62. https://yasharinitiative.org/index.php/haskamos.
63. Amihai Radzyner, "Jewish Law, State, and Social Reality: Prenuptial Agreements for the Prevention of Divorce Refusal in Israel and the United States," *Journal of Law and Religion* 33 (2018): 61–88.
64. The Jurisdiction of Rabbinical Courts (Marriage and Divorce) Law No. 64, 5713–1953, https://main.knesset.gov.il/EN/about/history/documents/kns2_rabbiniccourts_eng.pdf; Broyde, *Marriage, Divorce, and the Abandoned Wife in Jewish Law*, 9.

65. Parallel jurisdiction exists in matters ancillary to divorce with Israel's civil Family Court. See Family Court Law, 5755–1995, § 25b, https://www.nevo.co.il/law_html/law00/98460.htm [Hebrew].
66. There is no civil marriage or divorce in Israel, therefore if there is no *get*, the legal personal status of both partners remains "married" and neither is free to remarry. Rachel Levmore, "*Get*-Refusal and the Agreement for Mutual Respect: Israel Today," *Hakirah* 9 (Winter 2010): 173–90, http://www.hakirah.org/Vol%209%20Levmore.pdf.
67. The country's Director of Rabbinical Courts reported in 2008 that there were only 180 cases of women who were being refused their *get*, and 190 cases of men whose wives were refusing to accept a *get*. Bar-Ilan University's Rackman Center based on a scientific telephone survey. Cited in Rachel Levmore, "The *Aguna*: A Statistical or a Real-Life Problem?," *Jerusalem Post*, August 30, 2009, http://www.jpost.com/Opinion/Op-Ed-Contributors/The-aguna-a-statistic-or-a-real-problem.
68. For example, Case No. 561/36 in Dov Katz (ed.), *Rabbinical Judgments 10*, Jerusalem (5735–5737), 249–60 [Hebrew].
69. The Israeli Rabbinical Courts issue approximately ten such permits per year. See Amihai Radzyner, "Rabbenu Gershom in the State of Israel: Enforcing get on the Woman or Permitting the Husband to Marry a Second Wife?," *Dinei Israel* (2001): n. 19 [Hebrew].
70. Shear Yashuv Cohen, "*K'fiyyat Get* in Our Day," *Tehumin* 11 (5750): 195–202 [Hebrew].
71. Blu Greenberg, *On Women and Judaism* (Philadelphia: Jewish Publication Society, 1998.
72. Beginning in February 1997, https://jwa.org/thisweek/feb/16/1997/conference-on-feminism-and-orthodoxy.
73. Rabbinical Court Advocate Dr. Rachel Levmore, The *Agunah* & *Get* Refusal Prevention Project, Young Israel-Israel Region, and the Jewish Agency, https://www.boneizion.org.il/2016-bonei-zion-prize-recipients/, and the *Yad La'Isha* Legal Aid Center of Ohr Torah Stone, http://yadlaisha.org.il/, both cooperate with US cases with a connection to Israel handled by ORA, https://www.getora.org/. By utilizing Israeli law an American get-refuser present in Israel can be compelled to give a *get* in the Israeli Rabbinical courts—which is recognized as valid the world over.
74. For example, Elyashiv Knohl, "The Ketubah and Prenuptial Agreements," *Tehumin* 21 (2001): 324–39 [Hebrew]; Shlomo Riskin, "*Hafka'at Kiddushin*: Towards Solving the Aguna Problem in Our Time," *Tradition* 36, no. 4 (Winter 2002), https://traditiononline.org/hafkaat-kiddushin-towards-solving-the-aguna-problem-in-our-time/; rebuttal by Jeremy Weider, "*Hafka'at Kiddushin*: A Rebuttal," *Tradition* 36, no. 4 (2002): 37–43, https://traditiononline.org/hafkaat-kiddushin-a-rebuttal/; and Shlomo Riskin, "Responses," ibid.; David Bass, "*Hatarat Nissu'in Beta'anat Mekah Ta'ut*," *Tehumin* 24 (2004): 194–218 [Hebrew]; David Bass, "*Betailut Nissu'in Beta'anat Mekah Ta'ut*," *Tehumin* 31 (2011): 291–302 [Hebrew]; Bernard S. Jackson, Agunah: *The Manchester Analysis* (*Agunah* Research Unit, vol. 1–5) (2011), http://static1.1.sqspcdn.com/static/f/784513/25919455/1422985191143/Jackson+Agunah.pdf?token=S5rwtHv2yKCi2hJfaFHOzolePu8%3D; Avishalom Westreich, *Talmud-Based Solutions to the Problem of the* Agunah (Deborah Charles Publications, 2012); publications and conferences of The Rackman Center for the Advancement of Women, such as "Prenuptial Agreements," ed. Ruth Halperin-Kedari (Bar Ilan University, 2003) [Hebrew], https://rackmancenter.com/wp-content/uploads/2013/08/%C3%97%E2%80%BA%C3%97%C2%A4%C3%97%E2%84%A2-%C3%97%C2%A9%C3%97%E2%80%9D%C3%97%E2%80%A2%C3%97%E2%80%9C%C3%97%C2%A4%C3%97%C2%A1

%C3%97%E2%80%9D.pdf; Shay Zilberberg and Amihai Radzyner, "*Tehiyata Shel Ilat Mot Hanissu'in*," *Mishpatim* 49 (2019): 113–68 [Hebrew]; Matityahu Broyde and Rachel Levmore, "*Hahut Hameshulash Lo B'mehayrah Yinatek*," *Tehumin* 37 (2017)[Hebrew], Machon Tzomet, 228–39, jewishprenup.org/articles/.

75. Rachel Levmore, "Saviors of Diaspora 'Agunot,'" *Jerusalem Post*, September 10, 2020, https://www.jpost.com/opinion/how-israels-rabbinical-court-saves-agunot-in-the-diaspora-opinion-641690; Rachel Levmore, "US Agunot Have Reason to Celebrate," *The Jewish Press*, February 19, 2021, https://www.jewishpress.com/indepth/opinions/u-s-agunot-have-reason-to-celebrate/2021/02/18/; 1. Rachel Levmore, "*Agunot*: Follow These Instructions," *The Jewish Press*, March 10, 2022, p. 11, https://www.jewishpress.com/indepth/opinions/agunot-follow-these-instructions/2022/03/09/; Rachel Levmore, "International *Agunah* Day for Those in the Diaspora," *Times of Israel*, March 15, 2022, https://blogs.timesofisrael.com/international-agunah-day-for-those-in-the-diaspora/.
76. The Tikvah Center for Law & Jewish Civilization and JOFA, NYU, June 24, 2013, https://www.law.nyu.edu/news/Tikvah-Center-holds-2013-Agunah-Summit. The Second *Agunah* Summit was held in Bar Ilan University's Law School, March 3, 2014, https://law.biu.ac.il/sites/law/files/shared/program_3.3.2014_0.pdf, https://www.youtube.com/watch?v=S2Xxc3vtiao&persist_app=1&app=desktop&client=mv-google&gl=US&hl=en, https://www.youtube.com/watch?v=Q3EmuduTPX8 and https://www.youtube.com/playlist?list=PLXF_IJaFk-9CT6AUlefU-EmO1wtGUs3lW.
77. Rabbi David Bigman, Dr. Rachel Levmore, Professor Berachyahu Lifshitz, Rabbi Shlomo Riskin, and Professor Moshe Halbertal, https://vimeo.com/69336476.
78. https://www.internationalbeitdin.org/, "*Beit Din to Relieve Agony of Agunot*", Jewish Link, December 13, 2013, https://jewishlink.news/world-us/2160-beit-din-to-alleviate-agony-of-agunot.
79. Dean at Rabbi Isaac Elchanan Theological Seminary (RIETS), part of Yeshiva University, and *halakhic* advisor for the Orthodox Union. See Rabbi Hershel Schachter and others, "Protest Letter," July 2015 [Hebrew], http://www.torahweb.org/torah/docs/ibd-machaa.pdf; https://www.torahmusings.com/2015/09/a-review-of-international-beit-din-case-105/. The IBD response: Simcha Krauss and Yehudah Warburg, "Response to Rav Schachter's Criticism of the International Beit Din on Torahweb.org," Jewish Link, September 3, 2015, https://jewishlink.news/index.php?option=com_content&view=article&id=9424:response-to-rav-schachters-criticism-of-the-international-beit-din-on-torahweborg&catid=156:features&Itemid=585. Particular solutions offered by the IBD have also been challenged by the more progressive Rabbi Jeremy Wieder, also of Yeshiva University: Get Zikkuy and Yihud ha-Edim: A Response to the IBD Controversy (yutorah.org).
80. https://www.internationalbeitdin.org/.
81. JOFA Resources for Agunot | Jewish Orthodox Feminist Alliance.
82. ORA-Organization for the Resolution of Agunot, getora.org.
83. Young Israel-Israel Region, https://yiisrael.com/programs/get-refusal-prevention/#agree.
84. Beit Hillel, "International Agunah Day 5776," https://eng.beithillel.org.il/taanit-esther-international-agunah-day-5776/, reported on Dr. Levmore's initiative which became popular over the years. For one example out of many, unique in that it was held in English, see Postnup Agreement for Mutual Respect signing event in Tzfat: R' Yacov Drori and Dr. Rachel Levmore, https://www.youtube.com/@internationalyoungisraelm0903.

85. Jackie Hajdenberg, "NJ Court Rules in Favor of Woman Who Used Social Media to Lobby for Jewish divorce," September 8, 2023, https://www.jta.org/2023/09/08/united-states/nj-court-rules-in-favor-of-woman-who-used-social-media-to-lobby-for-jewish-divorce?utm_source=JTA_Maropost&utm_campaign=JTA_DB&utm_medium=email&mpweb=1161-61917-17886.
86. Liana Satenstein, "How Orthodox Women Are Using Social Media to Liberate Each Other from Dead Marriages," https://www.vogue.com/article/agunah-get-refusal-social-media-campaign-orthodox-women.

CHAPTER 25

JEWISH COMMERCIAL LAW AND MODERN POLITICAL ECONOMY

ITAMAR ROSENSWEIG

Introduction

JEWISH law offers a comprehensive system of commercial law. It delineates laws of property, contracts, torts, employment, partnerships, agency, bailments, debts, tenancy, economic competition, and inheritance. It also articulates rules to regulate society, such as laws of taxation, public service, elections, governance, zoning, privacy, and distributive justice. This chapter considers how Judaism's ancient system of law keeps pace with changing commercial practices and evolving socioeconomic norms.

Commercial practices evolve with time and differ from society to society. New York and London's economy in the twenty-first century radically differs from the marketplace contemplated by the Mishnah and Talmud. The engines and instruments of modern commerce—stocks, bilateral executory contracts, wire transfers, corporations, futures, derivatives, buy-with-one-click, patents, and artificial intelligence—have little or no precedent in classical *halakhah*. Under the internal rules of Jewish law, transactions executed via these modern instruments would either be voided *ab initio* or reconceptualized into relationships that entail obligations and liabilities vastly different from the parties' intentions.

An example illustrates the point. It is settled Jewish law that a person cannot purchase an item or an asset that the seller does not possess, all the more so one that does not yet exist.[1] But in today's real estate market, buyers routinely purchase not-yet-constructed units in residential skyscrapers, even before cement has been poured into the building's foundation. The same is true regarding contemporary retail markets that rely on drop-shipping. Retail giants like Walmart and Amazon sell merchandise online that they do not yet possess in their warehouses and have not yet even ordered from their supplier.

When modern commercial practices diverge from the internal rules of Jewish law, we might expect *halakhah* to invalidate the commercial practice. This would require Jews either to forbear from transacting via such instruments or to execute all transactions in duplicate via a valid Jewish law mechanism. This is *halakhah*'s stance regarding family law, where a marriage can be effectuated only through *kiddushin* and dissolved exclusively through *gerushin*, which must be done parallel to whatever process is required by state law. Yet, with respect to commercial practices, rather than rejecting the prevailing commercial norms, decisors of Jewish law across generations have consistently sought to recognize these commercial practices and to validate them within Jewish law.

This chapter surveys three mechanisms of Jewish law that *halakhic* jurists have employed to validate commercial practice: rabbinic legislation, the political authority of the state or sovereign, and custom. These mechanisms serve as principles of incorporation through which Jewish law can recognize and incorporate external commercial and political-economic norms. These principles of incorporation are internal to Jewish law, but their legal effect is to give *halakhic* recognition to practices and instruments outside of Jewish law.

In this chapter, I argue that Jewish commercial law comprises two types of rules. Some rules are native and internal to Jewish law and intrinsically valid. Other rules are external to Jewish law but become *halakhically* valid through incorporation. A different way of formulating this idea is that Jewish commercial law is constituted by (i) a set of native, internal rules and (ii) principles that incorporate and validate external practices.[2]

Further, I argue that Jewish commercial law contains these principles of incorporation to keep pace with changing commercial practices and instruments that evolve with time and vary across societies. *Halakhah* provides recognition of productive and beneficial commercial practices to regulate commerce while also facilitating economic growth and efficiency. Were *halakhah* to constrain business to the internal rules native to Jewish law, it would choke economic growth and significantly inhibit market efficiency. I contend that these economic virtues—efficiency and growth—are values within Jewish commercial law and that they ground and partially explain the principles of incorporation examined in this chapter. In other words, Jewish law is designed with principles of incorporation to enable efficient interaction with the marketplace as it evolves over time and across societies.

The chapter unfolds as follows. The first three sections introduce and explain the three principles of incorporation. The first section discusses rabbinic legislation (*takanah*) as a method of incorporating beneficial commercial practices. The second section examines the authority of the political sovereign (*mishpat hamelekh* and *dina de-malkhuta dina*) to enact *halakhically* binding laws and regulations for the economy. The third section analyzes the *halakhic* power of commercial custom and practice (*minhag ha-sochrim*). The fourth section argues that the principles of incorporation are designed to enable

Jewish law to engage with a dynamic marketplace and an evolving society at different levels of granularity and permanence. The fifth section explains the significance of the native provisions of Jewish commercial law (*Hoshen Mishpat*) in light of Judaism's willingness to incorporate external economic norms that temporarily displace them.

Rabbinic Legislation

One mechanism for incorporating marketplace practices is rabbinic legislation (*takanah*). Jewish law confers upon the rabbinic council (*Sanhedrin*) broad powers to legislate and enact ordinances.[3] The Talmud contains hundreds of examples of rabbinic legislation across all areas of *halakhah*, including numerous examples of legislation enacted to improve the economy and the marketplace.[4] Sometimes, the Sages used their legislative power to validate prevailing commercial practices.

Consider the example of debt transfer. Under the internal rules of Jewish law, it is either impossible or exceedingly cumbersome to transfer debts.[5] According to some authorities, this is because a debt is a personal relationship between a creditor and a debtor. It, therefore, cannot be sold to a third party. According to other authorities, debts are intangible, and the Talmud is quite strict on transactions involving "thingless" things.[6]

In a commercial society, the sale and mobility of debt power the engine that drives the economy. Unsurprisingly, the dominant (Gentile) commercial practice in Talmudic times permitted the sale of debts. The prevailing custom was to assign the debt through "triple presence" (*ma'amad shelashtan*)—a face-to-face meeting between the debtor, the creditor, and the purchaser.

To facilitate the transfer of debt, the Sages of the Talmud incorporated the dominant practice of triple presence into Jewish law through rabbinic legislation (*takanah*).[7] One historian of *halakhah* describes it this way:

> The non-transferability of debts had long hung around the neck of Jewish merchants like an albatross. According to many views, the very assignment of debts is of rabbinic origin. By pentateuchal law (*mi-de-oraita*) debts cannot be sold or transferred. The sages had realized that business demanded assignment, and they instituted it by means of transfer of the bill of indebtedness with or without an accompanying note (*mesirah* or *ketivah u-mesirah*).... This rapidly proved too cumbersome, and so the Sages then instituted transfer by triple presence because this was the custom of merchants at the time.[8]

The Talmud contains other examples of rabbinic legislation (*takanot*) designed to keep pace with a changing commercial world. For instance, when the Sages noticed that lenders had become less willing to extend capital, they enacted several reforms to incentivize creditors to lend. They abolished burdensome biblical court procedures, such as the rigorous cross-examination of witnesses, which had made it difficult to collect outstanding debts.[9] They instituted the *pruzbul* to circumvent the biblical cancelation of debts on the sabbatical year.[10] They also improved the type of real property a lender could garnish to satisfy an unpaid debt.[11] The Sages enacted these regulations to respond to changing social conditions that had made creditors less willing to extend capital.

The Sages also instituted other market reforms to make commerce more efficient. Under biblical law, for example, if stolen property surfaces in the market—such as when a merchant unwittingly buys it from a thief and sells it to a customer—the owner of the item (the victim from whom it was stolen) is entitled to reclaim it from the customer, at no cost.[12] The customer is saddled with the loss, and if he seeks to be made whole, his only recourse is to track down the thief and sue him. The Sages realized that the biblical law had a chilling effect on the marketplace. Customers ran the risk of forfeiting the goods they purchased and would have to absorb the financial loss. This deterred customers from shopping at the marketplace.[13]

The Sages, therefore, passed legislation "to improve the marketplace" (*takanat hashuk*). They shifted the risk of loss from the consumer to the owner (the person from whom the item was stolen). The new legislation provided that the owner must reimburse the customer before he can reclaim the item from him. In other words, the owner now had to absorb the financial loss, and if he wanted to be made whole, *he* must track down the thief and sue him. This rabbinic market reform allowed buyers to purchase goods from the marketplace without the risk of loss, restoring confidence in markets.

In the examples just described, the Sages enacted legislation in response to changing commercial realities. They incorporated commercial practices of debt assignment via triple presence to facilitate credit mobility even though the internal rules of Jewish law do not permit it. They relaxed the biblical court procedure of cross-examination, strengthened creditors' collection rights, and created a legal mechanism to circumvent the sabbatical cancelation of debts—all to incentivize lenders to extend capital. They also shifted the legal risk of loss away from merchants and consumers to restore confidence in the marketplace. These examples illustrate how rabbinic legislation has allowed *halakhah* to engage dynamically with evolving commercial life.

Some authorities explain that the Torah envisions a world of evolving markets and changing commercial circumstances. According to this view, it is impossible to legislate immutable, fixed rules to govern commerce and trade for all time and eternity. Therefore, the Torah articulates general principles of commercial fairness and efficiency, and it tasks the Sages of each generation to craft rules and regulations that reify these principles in a manner tailored to each society's unique features.

Ramban, for example, explains that because social and economic arrangements are so complex, dynamic, and varied, "it is impossible for the Torah to mention all of man's conduct with his neighbors and fellows, all of his business dealings, and all of the regulations that improve society and civilization."[14] Therefore, rather than attempting to prescribe fixed rules of commerce for all time and eternity, the Torah commands the general principle that commerce and trade should be governed by rules that are "right and good," and it provides several exemplifications of such conduct.[15]

R. Vidal of Toulouse, a disciple of Ramban's academy, develops this idea further. Commenting on the Sages' enactment assigning the right of first refusal on a sale of real estate to the owner of the abutting lot, which the Sages legislated as a concretization of "you shall do the right and good,"[16] R. Vidal explains:

> Our perfect Torah issued general principles to guide the conduct of men . . . as it says "you shall do the right and the good." The intention [of this verse] is that one should act always in a proper and righteous manner towards others. Now, it would have been inappropriate for the Torah to command particular rules on these matters, for the commands of the Torah must apply across all time and in each generation and in every context. Therefore, the Torah could only command these as general principles, for human behavior and conduct is always changing in accordance with the times and the people. The sages therefore legislated specific rules to benefit society which they subsumed under these general principles, some of which they enacted as enforceable law. . . . It is in this sense that they say, "the words of the sages are more beloved than the words of the Torah."[17]

And so argues R. Yosef Albo:

> It is impossible for the Torah to be complete in the sense that it provides [detailed rules] for all time—for the specific commercial affairs of men are always changing, and no book could detail all the possible circumstances. Therefore, Moshe was given at Sinai general principles . . . so that the sages of every generation can enact laws as the specific circumstances change.[18]

In summary, Jewish law, from its inception, recognized that commercial practices evolve with time and across societies. Judaism therefore delegated to the Sages of each generation the responsibility of administration and legislation. The Sages are charged with enacting proper legislation and rules to regulate commerce in a manner that achieves the underlying goals of the political-economic principles set forth in the Torah.[19]

Although rabbinic legislation is an integral part of the *halakhic* system—and a crucial tool for interfacing with evolving commercial and economic norms—it is not always practicable. Rabbinic legislation requires a centralized rabbinic council authorized to bind the Jewish people. In its purest form, it is limited to the *Sanhedrin*, the rabbinic council recognized as the supreme legal authority for all of Israel that convened daily in the Temple in Jerusalem. Such a centralized rabbinic council existed through the period of the Tanaim, but it was disbanded in the early centuries of the Common Era. The later Sages of the Talmud also enjoyed widespread support such that their enactments were deemed binding on all of Jewry, but they were the last rabbinic body to wield that legislative authority.[20] The *Geonim* of Babylonia were the institutional successors to the Talmudic Sages, but their yeshivot did not achieve the universal support of Jewry. They legislated scores of *takanot*, including commercial ones, but their enactments were not considered universally binding.[21]

Some scholars believe that contemporary local rabbinic councils wield legitimate *halakhic* legislative authority and are authorized to enact *takanot* within their jurisdiction.[22] Yet even if they possess this authority de jure, they do not exercise it de facto. They certainly do not exercise it with any consistency or regularity, especially not in commercial matters.

Thus, after the dissolution of the Sanhedrin—and certainly after the sealing of the Talmud and the demise of the *geonic* academies—Judaism lacked a central, authoritative legislative body that would regulate commerce through rabbinic *takanot*. For contemporary jurisprudence, rabbinic legislation is not a live or viable mechanism for incorporating commercial norms.

The Law of the Sovereign

The second principle through which Jewish law incorporates marketplace practices is *dina de-malkhuta dina* ("the law of the kingdom is the law"). This principle gives *halakhic* force to laws passed by sovereigns and governments, particularly laws that pertain to political economy, commerce, and governance.[23] Through *dina de-malkhuta dina*, Jewish law recognizes the sovereign's authority to collect taxes, reassign property rights, and enact laws regulating commerce and trade.[24]

For generations, *dina de-malkhuta* has enabled Jewish law's interaction with the contemporary marketplace. *Halakhic* decisors consistently appealed to *dina de-malkhuta* to incorporate mercantile practices into Jewish law. The Mishnah and Talmud appeal to *dina de-malkhuta* to validate financial contracts and documents executed in non-Jewish courts—documents and contracts that would otherwise be invalid under the internal rules of Jewish law.[25] Later authorities applied *dina de-malkhuta* to incorporate sweeping commercial rules that have no internal basis within *halakhah*, such as bankruptcy statutes,[26] copyright and intellectual property,[27] rent control,[28] conveyances in futures and intangibles,[29] novel methods of conveyance,[30] and corporations.[31]

It is no trivial matter that *halakhah* should recognize the law of the political sovereign. Just as there is no obligation for the United States to recognize the laws passed by the Parliament of Great Britain, it should not be taken for granted that *halakhah* would incorporate the law of the kingdom. We could readily imagine a world where Judaism remains indifferent to the law of the surrounding polity. In this world, Judaism legislates for itself and conducts its legal and political affairs exclusively from within. Why does Judaism recognize the law of the sovereign?

The most compelling explanation of *dina de-malkhuta dina* is that Judaism envisions a separation of powers between rabbinic-religious governance and political-economic governance. The political sovereign—ideally the Judean monarch—oversees the political economy. The rabbinic leadership—ideally the Sanhedrin—oversees Jewish ritual law and *halakhic* justice.[32]

The sovereign's mandate to preside over the political economy is enshrined in both the biblical verse and the Talmud. The biblical verse enumerates the sovereign's power to tax his constituents, conscript citizens for military service, determine national infrastructure projects, declare and prosecute wars against other nations, and preside over national governance and administration.[33]

Among the sovereign's responsibilities of governance and administration, he is charged with enacting domestic policies and infrastructure projects for the betterment of society.[34] These might include policies relating to healthcare, traffic rules for public safety, funding and administering public goods like public water works, public sewage systems, fire safety regulations, establishing a police force to preserve law and order, and regulating markets and improving commerce. For this reason, the sovereign possesses broad legal powers to prosecute criminals to preserve social order, and he is empowered to assign and redistribute property rights as he deems necessary for the public good (*tikkun ha-medinah*). This includes the right to enact laws that regulate commerce, improve the economy, and advance social welfare.[35]

The Jewish doctrine of the sovereign's law is most lucidly expressed in the writings of Rabbenu Nissim (Ran).[36] He explains that the internal provisions of Jewish law—the laws that comprise most of the Mishnah, Talmud, and later codes—are not designed to yield a complete, self-contained, well-ordered society. They are designed to be complemented and supplemented by the social-economic laws enacted by the political sovereign. The Talmud does not set highway speed limits, the frequency of garbage collection, whether healthcare should be social or private, or how many police officers a city should hire and whether they should be armed. These aspects of social governance and civil administration fall within the purview of the sovereign. The Torah's vision for a fully functioning Jewish society involves the separation of powers between the rabbinic-religious and political-economic branches of government. It envisions an independent religious-*halakhic* branch led by a rabbinic council working alongside an independent political-economic branch led by a political sovereign.[37]

In an ideal Jewish society, the political sovereign would be the rightful Judean monarch, the scion of the Davidic dynasty, who would reign over the Jewish people in the Land of Israel. However, the legal powers conferred by Judaism upon political sovereigns are not limited to a Jewish sovereign. They extend to any political sovereign who exercises legitimate political authority over his constituents. This includes Jewish constituents living in the Diaspora under the political jurisdiction of a Gentile sovereign or government.[38]

The reasons that explain Judaism's recognition of the Jewish sovereign's authority to administer the political economy also explain Judaism's recognition of the political authority of a Gentile sovereign to govern his jurisdiction and enact laws for the public good. For any society to function, there must be some civil administration that ensures safety and security and that regulates commerce. Jewish law delegates and assigns this responsibility to the political sovereign of each society.[39]

Jews living in the Diaspora under the rule of a foreign government are subject to the political authority of the local sovereign, at least for commercial, social, and economic regulations. This arrangement ensures that regardless of where one lives, there is a political entity authorized and tasked by Jewish law to secure and coordinate society's basic needs and best interests: to protect from military invasion, punish crime, pave roads, set speed limits, coordinate public health policy, maintain garbage collection, oversee sewage and water infrastructure, regulate markets, and enforce property rights.

There's a good reason why these social responsibilities are outsourced by Jewish law to the (non-Jewish) political sovereign. These tasks require coordination and cooperation across huge swaths of the citizenry, so they must be orchestrated by a central administration that wields control of the entire population. It would be absurd for a Jewish minority to institute its own speed limits and traffic rules within a network of roads traversed by the general citizenry and maintained and regulated by a Gentile government. Furthermore, coordinating these tasks often requires the threat of coercion, and governments typically hold a monopoly on coercive power.

In summary, the principle of *dina de-malkhuta dina* is grounded in the political authority delegated by Jewish law to the political sovereign (*mishpat ha-melekh*). The Torah has an interest in securing social concord and some measure of economic efficiency. Therefore, it recognizes the authority of sovereigns to govern and legislate within their jurisdiction.[40]

The preceding analysis explains why the sovereign's authority under *dina de-malkhuta dina* is limited to laws that advance the political economy (*tikkun ha-medinah*).[41] Given the *halakhah*'s underlying interest in conferring these legal powers on a sovereign, there is no reason for the sovereign to wield any normative power to affect Jewish ritual law (*issur ve-heter*). A government statute will become valid under Jewish law only if it advances some social good.

Despite its well-founded *halakhic* basis, decisors of Jewish law have been remarkably reluctant to apply *dina de-malkhuta dina* too broadly. This reluctance is twofold. First, it stems from a natural skepticism toward laws legislated by a non-Jewish ("foreign") sovereign often hostile to Jewish constituents.[42] Second, decisors of Jewish law were aware that the laws of the sovereign often clashed with the internal provisions of Jewish law. The more laws Judaism validated from the sovereign, the more it displaced its native laws. Taken to the extreme, all Jewish civil law would be displaced by the law of the jurisdiction. Rashba argued *reductio ad absurdum* that if Judaism were to incorporate all the civil laws of the jurisdiction, Jews should attend Gentile law schools to learn the law of the jurisdiction rather than *yeshivot* to study Talmud.[43]

These considerations led some authorities to impose further limits on *dina de-malkhuta*, even within the domain of commercial law. These authorities ruled that the law of the jurisdiction was valid only in the interstices of Jewish law. That is, the sovereign's law can only apply where there are *halakhic* lacunae, in the gaps where Jewish law has nothing to say. According to this view, the sovereign's law cannot displace or override any internal provision of Jewish law.[44]

Consider the example of bankruptcy. Some authorities held that bankruptcy statutes legislated by the government could not be incorporated into Jewish law through *dina de-malkhuta*. They reason that releasing the debtor from his obligations would violate the creditor's Jewish law entitlement to collect the entirety of the debt. As such, these authorities argue, bankruptcy statutes conflict with the internal provisions of *halakhah* and are therefore not candidates for *dina de-malkhuta*.[45] While this position is not the *halakhic* consensus, it reflects a prominent strain of contemporary *halakhic* jurisprudence wary of *dina de-malkhuta*.

In summary, Judaism delegates to the political sovereign the right to administer political society and regulate commercial and economic life. This applies to the Jewish sovereign as well as to legitimate Gentile governments.[46] This way, Judaism ensures that each society has a designated political leader authorized by Jewish law to coordinate economic activity and governance. *Dina de-malkhuta dina* and the law of the sovereign (*mishpat ha-melekh*) enable Jewish law to interact with the modern marketplace by incorporating the commercial regulations and laws of the jurisdiction. This suggests that *halakhah* envisions economic and commercial regulations as inherently local, both geographically and temporally. This was Rabbenu Nissim's critical insight—that Judaism's vision of a well-ordered society is one where a political-economic branch of government complements and remains separate from the branch of rabbinic-ritual leadership.[47] Thus, rather than prescribing a complete system of immutable and fixed commercial and economic rules, Jewish law delegates the task of political-economic governance to regional governments and recognizes their commercial regulations as *halakhically* binding.

Halakhic authorities over the generations have appealed to *dina de-malkhuta* to incorporate modern commercial laws and regulations into Jewish law. Nevertheless, many decisors continue to express discomfort with recognizing too many laws that originate outside of Judaism. Many are also reluctant to acknowledge non-Jewish law that conflicts with internal provisions of Jewish civil law. There is a prominent camp within *halakhah* that seeks to limit the applicability of *dina de-malkhuta dina*, blunting its utility as an interface between Jewish law and modern commerce.

MERCANTILE CUSTOM

The third principle of incorporation is mercantile custom (*minhag ha-sochrim*). Here Jewish law recognizes the commercial customs and practices of merchants as *halakhically* valid.[48] This principle of incorporation differs from the preceding two. Both rabbinic legislation (*takanah*) and the law of the sovereign (*dina de-malkhuta*) relate to authoritative legal bodies and their laws. Rabbinic legislation works via formal enactments of recognized *halakhic* authorities, and *dina de-malkhuta* validates laws passed by the authoritative political sovereign. By contrast, *minhag ha-sochrim* recognizes the customs and practices of commercial actors without reference to legal authority or promulgated law.

The most prominent example of mercantile custom in the Talmud involves conveying property. Although *halakhah* prescribes rigid rules for transferring property—which types of property can be conveyed by which means (deed, payment, transfer of possession, etc.)—the Talmud recognizes any commercially customary means of conveyance as *halakhically* valid.[49] Thus, the Talmud acknowledges marking wine barrels (*situmta*) as a valid method of conveying them if such is the custom among merchants. Later authorities extend this Talmudic ruling to validate conveyances and contracts involving intangible and future property rights as long as such transfers are commercially customary—even though such interests cannot be transferred under the internal rules of Jewish commercial law.[50]

The Talmud also appeals to commercial custom to govern the terms of contracts. If an employer hires an employee but neglects to specify the terms of the contract, the terms are filled in by custom (*ha-kol ke-minhag ha-medinah*).[51] Industry custom determines the content of vague or incomplete contractual terms, even if Jewish law would otherwise fill them in differently. For example, according to Jewish law, the standard workday begins at sunrise and concludes at nightfall. Therefore, when the parties fail to specify the expected work hours, *halakhah* will typically obligate the worker to work from sunrise to nightfall. However, industry custom overrides the *halakhic* workday. So, if the customary workday is nine to five, and the parties failed to specify work hours in the contract, the nine-to-five workday will govern the agreement, not the sunrise-to-nightfall workday envisioned by the internal provisions of Jewish law. Based on cases such as this, the Jerusalem Talmud formulates the principle that "custom overrides *halakhah*" (*minhag mevatel halakhah*).[52]

In another context, the Talmud articulates a related principle of *minhag ha-sochrim* that courts should give "legal effect to common practice" (*darshinan lashon hedyot*).[53] One of the examples in that discussion involves sharecropper arrangements where a landlord grants a tenant the right to cultivate land in exchange for a percentage of the crop yield. Because the landlord incurs the risk of the tenant leaving the land fallow (resulting in zero profit to the landlord), it was customary to include a provision in the agreement requiring the tenant, should he leave the land fallow, to compensate the landlord "as if it produced a robust yield." Applying the *halakhic* principle granting legal effect to common practice, the Talmud rules that such a provision is deemed to be incorporated into a sharecropping agreement even if the parties did not explicitly do so. Furthermore, the provision becomes enforceable, based on the common practice, even though the internal rules of Jewish law would ordinarily not award expectation damages.[54] *Darshinan lashon hedyot* gives legal recognition to the commercial customs of common people.[55]

For contemporary *halakhic* authorities, *minhag ha-sochrim* has become the most fertile principle through which *halakhah* incorporates external commercial norms. Decisors of Jewish law have appealed to *minhag ha-sochrim* to validate commercially accepted methods of conveyance, conveyances in intangibles and futures, rent control regulations, bankruptcy, arbitration proceedings pursuant to rules of decision governed by industry custom, arbitration before Gentile merchants, equitable distribution of marital property, and corporations. *Minhag ha-sochrim* is perhaps the most prominent contemporary mechanism for enabling *halakhah*'s interface with the modern marketplace.

The normative foundation for *minhag ha-sochrim* resides in the power Judaism confers upon townspeople and tradesmen to collectively adopt local ordinances governing commerce and trade. According to the Talmud and Tosefta, the townspeople are authorized to regulate the price of commodities and wages, they can socialize the ownership of goods that enter their town, they can regulate business and trade hours to ensure efficient competition between businesses, and they can require members of their trade to pay into a collective insurance fund to protect their merchandise and property from loss. In short, the townspeople have the power to collectively adopt commercial regulations and practices that bind members of their town and trade.[56]

The key idea underlying *minhag ha-sochrim* is that a widespread commercial practice across a town or industry has the equivalent *halakhic* status to one formally enacted by it. In other words, the townsmen can vote with their feet rather than their hands. After all, the significance of a formal enactment is that it reflects the community's collective preference to implement a certain ordinance or rule of conduct. Therefore, if the members of a community have adopted a practice through their actual conduct—if that practice has gained widespread support and has become customary—they have effectively enacted it. This interpretation of *minhag ha-sochrim* is perhaps implicit in the Talmudic dictum that courts should "give legal effect to common practice" (*darshinan lashon hedyot*).[57]

It is a striking fact that *halakhic* jurists prefer *minhag ha-sochrim* as a principle of incorporation over *dina de-malkhuta*. Indeed, it is typical for a *halakhic* responsum to decline to incorporate some commercial law qua it being the law but then embrace it qua custom—even where the custom sprouted from compliance with the law. In other words, these decisors would rather incorporate a commercial law because it happens to be the custom of a community or industry to abide by it (*minhag*) rather than because it's the law (*dina de-malkhuta*). This trend is apparent in contemporary responsa involving rent control, bankruptcy, statutes of limitations, and equitable distribution of marital property.[58]

One reason for this trend is that *minhag ha-sochrim* is not subject to the restrictions that constrain *dina de-malkhuta*. As we saw above, some authorities believe that *dina de-malkhuta* has no power to override the internal provisions of Jewish law. But *minhag ha-sochrim* does, as the examples in the Talmud indicate. So, *halakhic* authorities are more comfortable interfacing with the modern economy through *minhag ha-sochrim* than through *dina de-malkhuta*.

The fact that *dina de-malkhuta* is saddled with greater restrictions than *minhag ha-sochrim* requires explanation. One explanation for *halakhah*'s more favorable stance toward *minhag ha-sochrim* may lie in the distinction between law and custom. Law (the object of *dina de-malkhuta dina*) is freighted with the weight of permanence. A law persists until a further legislative act repeals or replaces the law in question. Customs are more temporary and ephemeral. They persist only as long as a given community continues to abide by them. Second, laws are components of comprehensive legal systems. Customs, by contrast, are isolated, free-floating, ad hoc practices. Third, whereas law originates top down from an *authority*, customs evolve bottom up from the ordinary practices of the common people.

These three distinctions may explain why *halakhah* casts a more wary eye toward *dina de-malkhuta*. The permanence, comprehensiveness, and competing source of authority of a foreign legal system present a more formidable challenge to the integrity of *halakhah* as an autonomous system of law. For this reason, *halakhic* authorities are reluctant to embrace *dina de-malkhuta*. At the extreme, too strong an embrace of *dina de-malkhuta* would mean (quasi-)permanently and systematically replacing whole sections of Jewish commercial law with the laws of a competing legal authority.

By contrast, the temporary, ad hoc, and prosaic nature of *minhag ha-sochrim* poses no threat to the integrity of Jewish law. *Minhag ha-sochrim* amounts to nothing more than ad hoc, local, and fleeting accommodations of marketplace practices. The integrity of *halakhah* remains intact even as it allows for local, temporary accommodations of commercial practices that the Jewish community has electively adopted.[59]

This last point merits further elaboration. Because *minhag ha-sochrim* deals with commercial customs, the custom must be practiced by a given Jewish community or industry for it to become valid for them. This means that a practice will not become valid through *minhag ha-sochrim* until the Jewish community in question has adopted it with some regularity. Thus, mercantile customs undergo a vetting process that *dina de-malkhuta* does not. The law of the sovereign is indifferent to the constituents' acceptance of it. So, to the extent that *halakhah* is willing to recognize *dina de-malkhuta* as valid, it cedes to the unilateral will of the political sovereign. Not so for mercantile custom (*minhag ha-sochrim*) where the Jewish community must voluntarily adopt the practice for it to become *halakhically* valid.

This point is doubly significant. Firstly, it implies that the number of norms that will arise as candidates for incorporation through *minhag ha-sochrim* will be far fewer than those that will arise as candidates for incorporation via *dina de-malkhuta*. Second, it means that the Jewish community has had a chance to "vote" on a given norm and has chosen to adopt it.[60] These considerations make *minhag ha-sochrim* a more congenial principle of incorporation than *dina de-malkhuta*.

Jewish Law and Modern Commerce

I have surveyed three mechanisms of Jewish law that enable Judaism's interaction with modern commerce. These mechanisms significantly differ from each other. Rabbinic legislation can be initiated only by a recognized, central rabbinic authority. *Dina de-malkhuta* requires an authoritative political body. *Minhag ha-sochrim* involves nothing more than the practices of townspeople and tradesmen.

The different principles of incorporation can also be distinguished by their scope and duration. Rabbinic legislation binds the entire Jewish people: its scope is unrestricted. A law passed by the rabbinic council becomes part of Jewish law, with the full geographic and temporal reach of Jewish law itself. Thus, a rabbinic enactment designed to facilitate lending in the Land of Israel in the first century of the common era remains good Jewish law in the United States today. *Minhag ha-sochrim* lies at the opposite extreme. The *halakhic* force of commercial practice is geographically and temporally bound to the life of the practice. Practices flit in and out of existence and vary sharply across local community boundaries. *Dina de-malkhuta* falls between these extremes. Its scope is determined by the jurisdiction and duration of the political sovereign authorizing it.

These three principles allow Jewish law to interact with the social, economic, and political norms of any society in any era. Thus, Jewish law can incorporate a range of norms, from specialized trade practices carefully refined by centuries of social evolution to sweeping commercial regulations passed by administrative, regulatory agencies.

Earlier, we saw that the Torah envisions a world with evolving commercial norms and dynamic markets. This makes it impossible to legislate ironclad rules to govern commerce, trade, and the political economy for all time and eternity. Recall Ramban's comment that "it is impossible for the Torah to mention all of man's conduct with his neighbors and fellows, all of his business dealings, and all of the regulations that improve society and civilization." And recall R. Vidal's explanation that this is because commercial practices are dynamic and evolving: "It would have been inappropriate for the Torah to command particular rules on these matters, for the commands of the Torah [must] apply across all time and in each generation and in every context . . . [but] human behavior and conduct is always changing in accordance with the times and the people."

The three principles of incorporation we surveyed above reflect the underlying design of Jewish law as it relates to political economy. Rather than prescribing a fixed set of immutable rules—invariant to era or region—to govern commerce, trade and social coordination, Judaism prescribes *principles* that provide the basis for incorporating or legislating rules of political economy. Recall R. Yosef Albo's claim that "the specific commercial affairs of men are always changing, and no book could detail all the possible circumstances; therefore, Moshe was given at Sinai general principles."

Each principle of incorporation is an internal, native principle of Jewish law. A legal decision grounded in *dina de-malkhuta dina* or *minhag ha-sochrim* or rabbinic legislation is therefore firmly grounded in Jewish law. This point is often missed, for it can feel as though a decision grounded in any of these principles circumvents Jewish law and appeals to external commercial norms. But that is not the case, for the *halakhah* itself prescribes these principles of incorporation as principles of Jewish law. And even though these principles validate practices that originate elsewhere, Jewish law mandates their validation. Thus, a Jewish court that fails to apply any of these principles of incorporation where they *halakhically* govern errs in its application of Jewish law.

An example elucidates the point. Assume for the sake of argument that bankruptcy statutes are validated by *dina de-malkhuta* or *minhag ha-sochrim*. If a Jewish court were to apply the native rule of *hoshen mishpat* that a debtor remains forever obligated to repay his debts, ignoring the bankruptcy statute, it has erred and has applied the wrong principle of Jewish law to the case before it. The Jewish court ought to have applied the Jewish law principle of *dina de-malkhuta dina* or *minhag ha-sochrim*, granting the debtor whatever relief he is entitled to under the bankruptcy statute.

I have argued that Jewish law includes principles of incorporation to enable it to engage with a dynamic marketplace and society. I have also argued that Judaism seeks to validate certain commercial norms and principles of political economy. Several considerations may help explain why it aims to do so.

First, recall Rabbenu Nissim's insight that the internal provisions of Jewish law—the laws that comprise the majority of the Mishnah, Talmud, and later codes—are not designed to yield a complete, self-contained, well-ordered society. They are intended to be complemented by the socioeconomic norms enacted by political society. The idea at the heart of R. Nissim's insight is that Judaism envisions a separation between its rabbinic-religious branch of law and its political-economic branch of law, each of which has its own province. The internal rules of Jewish law generally take no position on broader questions of political economy.[61] For instance, Jewish law makes no decisive claim about whether a Jewish economy should endorse free markets or socialism. It takes no position on the ideal tax brackets for the treasury, the best budget for national defense, social security, whether healthcare should be private or public, the frequency of trash collection, the protection of intellectual property, insurance mandates, and whether shareholders should be shielded from personal liability. Most political economy matters are delegated to local governments to be tailored to society's contingent and changing needs.[62] These governments can be political sovereigns, communal trustees, or direct majoritarianism. In any case, Jewish law will seek to validate the economic and political norms necessary to maintain a well-ordered society through *dina de-malkhuta*, *minhag ha-medinah*, or rabbinic legislation.

Second, the norms of commerce and trade may play a critical role in filling legal gaps within Jewish law. The native, internal rules of Jewish commercial law contain legal gaps—areas where there is no decisive, clear-cut legal rule. For example, Rabad writes that there is no clear-cut Jewish law about whether a borrower can be forced to redeem real property he put up to secure a loan.[63] Likewise, Rabad suggests that there is no clear-cut Jewish law regarding a loan guaranteed by two suretors, whether the lender can sue either suretor to satisfy the whole amount or whether he must sue each suretor pro rata. Intricate questions like these, and thousands of similar ones, inhabit a *halakhic* vacuum.[64] In such cases, Rabad maintains that the *halakhic* vacuum should be filled by external commercial norms.[65] Judaism's desire to incorporate the standards of commerce and political economy may reflect its conviction that legal gaps should be filled.[66] Filling such gaps is crucial for the law to successfully coordinate social activity and for it to be predictable and decisive enough for people to organize their commercial affairs by it. Filling in the interstices of *halakhah* allows Jewish law to guide behavior with greater precision and granularity.

Third, Judaism's incorporation of commercial norms may reflect its commitment to facilitating commerce and promoting greater economic efficiency to enhance communal welfare and improve society.[67] Such is the explicit basis for many pieces of rabbinic legislation, some of which were surveyed earlier. It is also the apparent basis for the authority of the sovereign who is mandated to enhance the welfare of his constituents and to improve society (*tikkun ha-medinah*). Some authorities explicitly connect Judaism's incorporation of mercantile customs with the need to facilitate commerce and improve economic welfare.[68] Thus, Jewish law may validate laws of bankruptcy, copyright, corporate ownership, property rights in intangibles and futures, and the like to displace some of its internal provisions so long as they advance commerce and improve social welfare.

Fourth, Judaism's incorporation of commercial norms and marketplace customs may reflect the equitable principle that law should generally not upend the parties' legitimate commercial expectations. Suppose two people did business together or entered into an agreement with certain expectations, and those expectations were consistent with prevailing commercial practices of the marketplace. In that case, Jewish law should, as long as it doesn't undercut an important value of Judaism, uphold the parties' expectations, even when they diverge from the internal provisions of Jewish law.[69] The idea here is that it would be inequitable to disregard the parties' joint, legitimate commercial expectations—expectations framed by the norms of commerce—and to reconfigure their business dealing into something radically different from what they contemplated and expected.[70]

In summary, the abovementioned principles of incorporation do crucial work for Jewish law. First, they *complement* the internal provisions of Jewish law with principles and rules of political economy (e.g., speed limits, tax brackets, garbage collection, and markets)—a province of social life generally left unregulated by *halakhah*'s native rules. Second, they *fill in* the interstices of *hoshen mishpat* by regulating intricate cases not expressly ruled upon by Jewish law. Third, they *extend* and *update* the rules of commerce to include efficient and economically beneficial trade practices and regulations (e.g., bankruptcy, corporations, intellectual property, ownership of futures, and intangibles). And fourth, they equitably *validate* the legitimate commercial expectations of the parties.

These considerations, coupled with the central insight that commerce and social coordination are inherently dynamic, explain why Jewish law contains principles of incorporation to complement and, at times, displace its native provisions.

Rights, Justice, Efficiency, and *Halakhic* Ontology

Judaism's incorporation of external commercial norms raises a philosophical puzzle. What is the significance of the internal, native rules of Jewish commercial law if external ones can displace them? Why does Judaism prescribe native rules of contract, property, conveyance, debts, and bailments only to validate external commercial norms that may supersede them?

Some rabbinic commentators have suggested that Jewish commercial law is just a set of conventional and reason-based social regulations, fundamentally different from other areas of *halakhah*. According to this view, Judaism's internal commercial rules are not inherently important or special.[71] This approach can explain why Jewish commercial law readily validates external commercial norms. If there is nothing intrinsically privileged about the native provisions of *hoshen mishpat*, there is little presumption against their displacement by a different set of reasonable conventions and regulations via *dina de-malkhuta dina*, *minhag ha-sochrim*, or *takanah*.

The idea that Jewish commercial law is nothing more than reason-based social conventions is problematic. There is little evidence to suggest that the principles of Jewish commercial law are fundamentally different in kind from those of other areas of Jewish law. There is no indication that the duty to comply with the provisions of *hoshen mishpat* is in any way different from the duty to obey Jewish law generally. The Torah and the Talmud present Jewish commercial law as deriving from the same Divine origin as the rest of Jewish law, and the laws of *hoshen mishpat* and *nezikin* feature prominently in the biblical text. And no one has ever suggested that the provisions of *hoshen mishpat* are less worthy of Torah study than other areas of Jewish law.[72]

On the contrary, many authorities explicitly affirm that the provisions of *hoshen mishpat* are endowed with intrinsic value. Rabbenu Nissim, for example, avers that the specific provisions of Jewish commercial law are not conventions to advance social order but prescriptions for "inherently true justice." The significance of this "true justice," Rabbenu Nissim explains, should be understood in terms of the relationship between the Jewish people and the Divine presence. A society of true justice is a society worthy of the Divine presence. So, a society that achieves true justice is a society suffused with the Divine presence.[73]

I believe we can preserve the intrinsic value of *hoshen mishpat*—the idea that it constitutes a system of "true justice"—while explaining Judaism's incorporation of external commercial norms. To do so, let us distinguish between two conceptions of law—between two distinct goals that law may have. One conception of law envisions a system of pure justice. According to this conception, law is determined by the inherent moral rights and duties of each member of society. We can imagine, following Kant, that each person's dignity and moral worth generates a sphere of freedom and protection, a sphere of rights, powers, and entitlements that others are obligated to respect. Each person's intrinsic moral worth generates a sphere of rights and duties in relation to others. These individual spheres of freedoms, powers, obligations, and entitlements aggregate to create the system of law—property, torts, contract, criminal law—that protects, respects, and advances the dignity of each.[74]

A different conception of law envisions a system of regulations that promotes economic efficiency. According to this conception, the law aims to create a more prosperous and wealthy society that maximizes utility quantified in metrics of economic growth and monetary value. According to this approach, the laws of property, torts, contracts, and criminal law are designed to incentivize actions that optimize the production of wealth and increase welfare across society.[75]

Generally, these two conceptions of law are advanced as competing visions for a legal system. However, we need not choose between the two as absolutely disjoint conceptions. We can envision a legal system that unifies these two conceptions. In such a legal system, the law primarily aims at securing the inherent rights of each person—a system of "true justice"—but secondarily encourages economic efficiency and commercial productivity. In such a model, the primary rules of the legal system are aimed at securing the fundamental intrinsic rights of each, but the system would permit innocuous extensions or departures from its primary rules (i.e., deviations that do not disturb the sense of pure justice) to promote greater economic efficiency.[76]

This model can explain the relationship between *halakhah*'s native provisions of *hoshen mishpat* and its principles of incorporation. The native provisions of Jewish commercial law are the set of rules sufficient to secure the basic intrinsic rights, freedoms, and moral powers of individuals—the set of rules sufficient to realize the vision of pure justice—while its principles of incorporation aim at facilitating economic growth and improving the marketplace and society.

Consider the case of bankruptcy in Jewish law. From the perspective of the intrinsic rights of the individuals, an insolvent borrower remains obligated to repay his debt, and his creditor remains entitled to recover it. As a matter of pure justice, the debtor borrowed money and obligated himself, unequivocally and unconditionally, to repay it. Therefore, from the perspective of pure justice, the insolvent debtor remains obligated to satisfy the debt. However, the *halakhah* sees nothing objectionable with society establishing rules of bankruptcy to incentivize borrowers to take investment risks and to offer a fresh economic reset by shifting the risk of loss back to the lender, as long as the bankruptcy rule is prospective, public, and known in advance to the lender. When these conditions are met, the bankruptcy rule does not subvert the regime of true justice. If such a bankruptcy rule promotes greater economic growth and benefits society, then the *halakhah* will permit its incorporation.

Put differently, if we were to examine the intrinsic rights of the individuals, we would find no basis for a bankruptcy-type exemption to grant relief to the borrower. He should remain forever obligated to repay his debt. However, if society chooses to adopt a bankruptcy provision in pursuit of greater economic prosperity or social utility, the *halakhah* will permit and validate such a rule. The bankruptcy provision is innocuous—it does not disturb the underlying order of true justice—as long as the provision is prospective and public and the lender knows before granting the loan that such is the prevailing commercial practice or law.

A similar analysis can be applied to selling and transferring debts. From Jewish law's perspective of intrinsic rights, a debt is a personal relationship between a creditor and a debtor and, therefore, not a commodity transferable to a third party.[77] However, nothing prohibits the Sages from enacting legislation or incorporating commercial practices that permit debt transfers if it is commercially beneficial and practical. The Sages can reconstitute debts into commodities to be transferred and purchased on the open market. And that's exactly what they did in ratifying debt transfers. If the new rules are fair, public, and known to the borrower when he assumes the debt, the enactment does not subvert the system of true justice. The Sages can depart from the existing distribution of intrinsic rights to accommodate commercially beneficial practices if the modification is not harmful to the regime of true justice and the new rules satisfy the criteria of fairness.[78]

Likewise, for conveyances of intangibles and futures. From the perspective of an individual's inherent rights, the *halakhah* finds no basis for ownership and conveyance of intangibles and futures, nor is there a basis for entitlements to intellectual property. But, once again, there is no objection to Judaism recognizing such conveyances and property entitlements where they enhance commerce. And the same can be said for other paradigmatic candidates for *dina de-malkhuta* and *minhag ha-sochrim*, such as bilateral executory contracts, rent control regulations, corporate ownership, and other instruments of modern finance.

This framework offers one way of explaining the significance of *hoshen mishpat*'s native provisions. They are not mere social conventions or regulations. They reflect a system of justice that assigns to each person the legal rights, privileges, and powers that their dignity entitles them. At the same time, we can also appreciate Jewish law's recognition of external commercial norms to increase commercial efficiency and economic welfare.[79] Pure justice does not exhaust the virtues of political economy.

It should also be emphasized that *hoshen mishpat*'s native provisions exist as constitutive parts of Jewish law in a way that the incorporated external norms do not. The native provisions of Jewish commercial law differ in their *halakhic* ontology from the incorporated external norms. Although it is, of course, true that the actual *principles* of incorporation (*dina de-malkhuta dina*, *minhag ha-sochrim*, *takanah*) are native principles internal to Jewish law, the external norms they validate remain external to the corpus of *halakhah*. Studying these external norms would probably not constitute Torah study, whereas studying the internal rules of *hoshen mishpat* and *nezikin*, or the principles of incorporation themselves (e.g., *dina de-malkhuta* or *minhag ha-sochrim*), obviously would.

Further, notice that the native legal provisions of *hoshen mishpat* are never permanently replaced or superseded. Instead, they are only temporarily displaced, ad hoc, by commercial custom (*minhag ha-sochrim*) or local law (*dina de-malkhuta*) until the native provisions reassert themselves. The external norms remain valid only for as long as the underlying commercial practice persists or as long as the local law remains good law. As soon as the underlying practice or law withers, the native provisions of *choshen mishpat* reassert themselves, like a sleeping sovereign reawakened. The native provisions of *halakhah* endure, while the external norms fade out of existence as commercial practices evolve.

In summary, we can explain the significance of Judaism's internal provisions of commercial law while also making sense of its principles of incorporation. I have argued that Judaism's internal provisions of *hoshen mishpat* can be understood as constituting a rights-based system of justice that secures the sphere of inherent rights, powers, and entitlements generated by each person's moral dignity. By contrast, Judaism's principles of incorporation can be understood as efficiency-oriented principles of utility that seek to advance economic prosperity.

I have also argued that the internal provisions of Jewish commercial law differ in their *halakhic* ontology from the incorporated external norms. The external norms, though validated by Jewish law, never become part of the corpus of *halakhah* and, therefore, never become objects of Torah study. Likewise, the external norms are valid only temporarily, until *halakhah*'s internal norms reassert their sovereignty.

Conclusion

This chapter has argued that Jewish commercial law is designed to incorporate external socioeconomic norms through *minhag ha-sochrim*, *dina de-malkhuta*, and rabbinic legislation. Rather than legislating its own immutable, ironclad rules for political economy, Judaism believes that its socioeconomic affairs are best governed by incorporating practices and regulations as they evolve in each era and each locale. In most instances, the incorporated external norms complement *halakhah*'s native rules by filling in *halakhic* gaps otherwise unregulated by Jewish law. In some instances, the incorporated norms temporarily displace the native provisions of Jewish law.

Furthermore, this chapter has argued that the principles of incorporation—*minhag ha-sochrim*, *dina de-malkhuta*, rabbinic legislation—are native provisions of Jewish law. These provisions are as constitutive elements as any other native law of *halakhah*, and a Jewish court is obligated to apply these principles of incorporation where they apply, in the same way it is obligated to apply the other internal provisions of *hoshen mishpat*. However, the external norms that these principles validate—even though they become valid and binding as a matter of Jewish law—remain "external" to the system of *halakhah*, and they remain ontologically distinct from *halakhah*'s internal provisions.

Finally, this chapter has argued that the native provisions of *hoshen mishpat* can be conceptualized as rights-based rules of pure justice that specify the intrinsic rights each person is entitled to. By contrast, the principles of incorporation reflect Judaism's ambition to improve economic and commercial efficiency by incorporating the best practices and norms tailored to the socioeconomic needs of each society. The emerging picture is that of an ancient system of law designed to interface with a dynamic political economy.

Notes

1. See *Shulhan Arukh*, Hoshen Mishpat 209: 4–5.
2. For the distinction between rules and principles, see Ronald Dworkin, *Taking Rights Seriously* (1977).
3. Rambam, *Mishneh Torah*, Mamrim 1:2. The Sages of the rabbinic council wield different types of legal powers. They are charged primarily with interpreting, applying, deriving,

and transmitting biblical law, but they are also tasked with enacting ordinances to protect biblical law and to legislate ad hoc laws as the times may require. In this section, I refer to their legislative power to enact ad hoc laws as needed (*she-hasha'ah tzerikhah*) to improve society (*le-taken ha-'olam*). See Rambam's formulation therein.

4. For a survey of rabbinic *takanot* in the Talmud, see Israel Schepansky, *The Takkanot of Israel* (Jerusalem: Mossad Harav Kook, 1991); Menachem Elon, *Jewish Law: History, Sources, Principles* (Jerusalem: Magnus Press, 1973), 447–546.
5. Rambam *Mishneh Torah*, Mekhirah 6:12; *Tosafot*, Ketubot 85b; Haym Soloveitchik, *Collected Essays I* (Oxford: Littman Library of Jewish Civilization, 2013), 95–96.
6. See Soloveitchik, *Collected Essays I*, 91.
7. See *Rashbam*, Bava Batra 144a s.v. *kanah* and *Rashbam*, Bava Batra 148a s.v. *be-ma'amad* who explains that triple presence was the custom of merchants (*jus mercatorum*) at the time. See also *Rosh*, Gittin 1:17, who characterizes the rabbinic legislation as *takanat ha-shuk* (to improve the marketplace).
8. Soloveitchik, *Collected Essays I*, 95.
9. *Talmud Bavli*, Sanhedrin 3a.
10. *Mishnah*, Shevi'it 10:3.
11. *Talmud Bavli*, Gittin 50a.
12. For the owner to remain entitled to the object, he must not have despaired (*yi'ush*) over retrieving it.
13. *Talmud Bavli*, Bava Kamma 114b–115a; *Meiri*, Bava Kamma 114b.
14. *Ramban*, Commentary on the Torah, Deuteronomy 6:18.
15. Ibid. For a discussion of Ramban's analysis and his use of the biblical verse, see Itamar Rosensweig, "The Biblical Verse as a Source of Law in Ramban's Jurisprudence," *Megadim Journal of Biblical Studies* 61 (2022): 65–67.
16. *Talmud Bavli*, Bava Metzia 108a; *Rambam*, *Mishneh Torah*, Shekhenim 12:15.
17. *Maggid Mishnah*, Shekhenim 14:5.
18. *Sefer Ha-Ikarim*, 3:23.
19. This appears to be Ramban's interpretation of the verse in Deuteronomy 6:18: "[A]nd now the verse states that even on matters that He has not explicitly commanded, be sure to do what is good and right . . . for He loves the good and the right." R. Vidal (*Maggid Mishneh*, Shekhenim 14:5) also follows Ramban on this when he writes, "[T]he intention of the verse is that you should conduct yourself in a manner that is good and rightful with other people." According to their analysis of the verse, the Torah mandates that commerce and social coordination should be organized to achieve *ha-yashar ve-hatov*, and the Sages of each generation are tasked with ensuring that. They are thus charged to enact legislation that is both rightful and beneficial based on the contingent features of their society. So, the Torah mandates the general principle and charges the Sages to formulate rules that best reify the principle in the form of concrete prescriptive norms.

    Based on this mandate to enact legal rules that manifest *yasher* and *tov*, the Sages of the Talmud enacted legislation granting the right of first refusal to the owner of the adjacent property when land is put up for sale. The right of first refusal rule (*dina de-bar metzra*) is designed to be both economically beneficial and morally rightful. It's economically beneficial because it affords property owners the benefit of economies of scale. They can reduce costs by farming contiguous lots. It's also morally rightful because it generally comes at no loss to the outside buyer because he can generally find an equally valuable property elsewhere. To be sure, wherever the right of first refusal is no longer beneficial for society or where it would improperly cause a loss to the seller or prospective buyer, the rule is suspended. See *Talmud Bavli*, Bava Metzia 108a; Rambam, *Mishneh Torah*, Shekhenim 12:15; *Rashi*, Bava Metzia 108a s.v. *ve-asita*; *Rashi* Bava Batra 5a s.v. *arba'ah*; *Sefer Ha-Yasher* (Responsa), no. 32; *Ravya*, no. 996; *Or Zarua*, Bava Metzia 359; Itamar Rosensweig, "When Has a Neighbor Waived His Right to First Refusal," *Jewishprudence* (July 2022).

Another example where the Sages enacted legislation to give concrete legal form to the principle of *ha-yashar ve-hatov* is *gud o a-gud*, the rule that allows one partner to force a buyout of an indivisible partnership. Rashba explains (Responsa I:956; II:141) that under biblical law, the partner would have the right to "split the partnership in half," which would destroy the value of the asset and would cause a loss to both partners. The rabbis therefore created the legal right, under *ha-yashar ve-hatov*, for a partner to force a buyout, which leaves the asset intact. The enactment is both morally proper and economically beneficial compared to the biblical law that would leave each party worse off. See also *Chazon Ish*, Bava Batra 8:1.

R. Vidal's statement that "it is in this sense that they say 'the words of the sages are more beloved than the words of the Torah,'" a nod to the talmudic passage in Avodah Zarah 35a, suggests that rabbinic enactments are "more beloved" because they give clear, precise form to the underlying biblical principle and apply it appropriately to the contemporary circumstance. The Sages' enactments are "more beloved" in this view because the biblical principle depends on the Sages giving it proper form and application to the circumstances of their society.

Further examples where the Sages give precise legal content in the form of rules to a general biblical principle include "you shall love your neighbor as yourself" and the prohibition of labor on the intermediate days of the holidays. For the former, see Lev. 19:18; Rambam, *Mishneh Torah*, Hilkhot De'ot 6:3; Rambam, *Sefer Ha-Mitzvot*, Aseh 206; Rambam, *Mishneh Torah*, Hilkhot Avel 14:1. For the latter example of the Sages' role in prescribing rules of prohibited labor, see *Talmud Bavli*, Chagigah 18a; *Beit Yosef*, Orah Chaim 530.

20. See Rambam's introduction to *Mishneh Torah*.
21. See ibid. For an overview of various attitudes toward the authority of the *Geonim* during the period of the Rishonim, see Itamar Rosensweig, "The Legal Philosophy and Jurisprudence of Rabbi Moshe ben Nahman" (PhD diss., Yeshiva University Press, 2022), 26–176.
22. *Sefer Ha-Hinukh*, no. 495.
23. "Political economy" refers to economic systems of markets and trade and their governance by political institutions, including law and government. Some classic figures associated with the study of political economy include Adam Smith, John Stuart Mill, Karl Marx, and John Maynard Keynes.
24. For the sovereign's authority to collect taxes, see *Talmud Bavli* Nedarim 28a. For the authority to reassign property rights, see *Bava Kamma* 113b. For the authority to regulate commerce and trade, see *Bava Batra* 54b–55a and *Gittin* 10b.
25. *Talmud Bavli* Gittin 10b.
26. See *Responsa Divrei Yosef* (R. David Chazan) no. 21; Shmuel Shilo, *Dina De-Malkhuta Dina: The Law of the State is the Law* (Jerusalem: Jerusalem Academic Press, 1974), 163.
27. See *Responsa Beit Yitzchak*, Yoreh De'ah 2:75; *Responsa Beit Yitzchak*, Hoshen Mishpat Nezikin no. 80. For an overview, see Neil Weinstock Netanel, *From Maimonides to Microsoft: The Jewish Law of Copyright since the Birth of Print* (New York: Oxford University Press, 2016), 232–33.

28. See *Erekh Shai*, Choshen Mishpat 312:5, *Responsa Tzitz Eliezer* 5:30, Shilo, *Dina De-Malkhuta Dina*, 174–77.
29. *Responsa Maharshal*, no. 36. See also *Responsa Rosh*, 13:20.
30. *Shulchan Arukh*, Hoshen Mishpat 207:15, 194:2; *Responsa Sho'el U-Meishiv*, 1:18.
31. *Pitchei Hoshen*, Shutfim 1:33 and n. 65 therein. See also R. Shaul Weingart's position, discussed in *Responsa Minchat Yitzchak*, 3:1. For a survey of the status of a corporation in Jewish law, see Michael Broyde and Steven Resnicoff, "The Corporate Veil and Halakhah: A Still Shrouded Concept," in *Jewish Business Ethics: The Firm and its Stakeholders*, ed. Aaron Levine and Moses Pava (Northvale, NJ: Jason Aronson, 1999).
32. *Derashot Ha-Ran*, no. 11; *Meiri* Avot 3:2.
33. See I Samuel Chapter 8; *Talmud Bavli* Sanhedrin 20b; *Meiri* Sanhedrin 20b; Rambam *Mishneh Torah*, Melakhim Chapter 4.
34. *Derashot Ha-Ran* no. 11; *Responsa Avnei Nezer* 312:50; *Even Ha-Ezel*, Nizkei Mamon 8:5; Gershon German, *Kingship in Israel: The Halachic View of Sovereignty Through History* (Bnei Brak: Moreshet Publishing, 2003), 479–519.
35. For a general overview of the responsibilities and powers of the sovereign, see Gershon German, *Kingship in Israel*; See also *Derashot Ha-Ran*, no. 11.
36. *Derashot Ha-Ran*, no. 11.
37. Scholars debate the scope of Ran's thesis and whether it represents a consensus view. See Chaim Saiman, *Halakhah: The Rabbinic Idea of Law* (2018), 157–62 and n. 21 therein.
38. *Meiri*, Nedarim 28a; *Meiri*, Bava Kamma 113a–b; *Kiryat Sefer* (R. Moshe Trani) Gezelah ch. 5; *Responsa of Geonim*, ed. S. Asaf (5702) nos. 66, 75.
39. See *Mishnah* Avot 3:2; *Talmud Bavli* Avodah Zarah 4a; *Meiri*, Avot 3:2; R. Matityahu Ha-Yitzhari, Avot 3:2; *Markevet Ha-Mishnah* (Alaskhar), Avot 3:2.

    In fact, some commentators identify the authority of the (Gentile) sovereign in Jewish law with the duty incumbent upon all of humanity to establish basic rules of justice (*dinim*). Because Judaism charges each society to implement basic laws of justice, Jewish law recognizes the authority of each sovereign and delegates that responsibility to him. See *Rashi*, Gittin 9b s.v. *hutz*; *Even Ha-Ezel*, Nizkei Mamon 8:5.
40. Some writers point to other legal grounds for *dina de-malkhuta dina*, such as a king's ownership over his territory or social contract theories, claiming that these grounds are distinct from *mishpat ha-melekh*. See Shilo, *Dina De-Malkhuta Dina*, 59–88. I'm skeptical that these alternative grounds are genuinely separable from *mishpat ha-melekh*. And even if they are, the substantive point remains the same: Judaism delegates political authority to a sovereign so that he can exercise proper political power of his constituents.
41. *Rama*, Hoshen Mishpat 369:11, *Meiri*, Bava Kamma 113b. See also *Responsa Avnei Nezer*, Yoreh Deah 312:47.
42. For an example of laws hostile to Jewish constituents, see *Ramban*, Bava Batra 55a.
43. *Responsa Rashba*, 6:254.
44. *Shakh*, Hoshen Mishpat 73:39.
45. *Responsa Chelkat Yaakov*, Hoshen Mishpat no. 32; *Pitchei Hoshen*, Halva'ah ch. 2 n. 63 therein.
46. A sovereign can take many different forms. It can take the form of a parliament or a more complex form of government, such as the one envisioned by the US Constitution. There appears to be no moral reason or basis to limit *dina de-malkhuta* to a reigning monarch. What matters for *dina de-malkhuta* is that some political authority should be tasked with coordinating social activities and overseeing the economy. See, for example, *Meiri*

Sanhedrin 52b; *Responsa Mishpat Kohen*, no. 144; Isaac Herzog, *Techukah Le-Yisrael*, vol. I, 129–30; German, *Kingship in Israel*, 554–71.

47. The ramifications for the *halakhic* legitimacy of the laws passed by the Knesset in the modern State of Israel are quite significant. See, for some discussion, German, *Kingship in Israel*, 554–87; Itzhak Brand, "Secular Law as the King's Law: Zionist Halakhah and Legal Theory" *AJS Review* 43, no. 1 (April 2019): 47–66.
48. For a more comprehensive overview of *minhag ha-sochrim* and a detailed presentation of the examples discussed below, see Itamar Rosensweig, "Minhag Ha-Sochrim: Jewish Law's Incorporation of Mercantile Custom and Marketplace Norms," *Journal of the Beth Din of America* 3 (2023): 35–72.
49. *Talmud Bavli* Bava Metzia 74a.
50. See *Responsa Rosh* 13:21, *Tashbetz Katan* no. 398.
51. *Talmud Bavli* Bava Metzia 83a.
52. *Jerusalem Talmud* Bava Metzia 7:1.
53. *Talmud Bavli* Bava Metzia 104a.
54. Normally such a provision, even if stated explicitly, would be unenforceable under the *halakhic* doctrine of *asmakhta* (speculation). See *Ramban*, Bava Metzia 104a.
55. For this interpretation of *darshinan lashon hedyot*, see *Ramban*, Bava Metzia 104a, *Rashba*, Bava Metzia 104a, *Responsa Rashba* 1:662.
56. See *Talmud Bavli* Bava Batra 8b and *Tosefta* Bava Metzia ch. 11.
57. See Rosensweig, "Minhag Ha-Sochrim," 63–65.
58. For the rent control example, see *Responsa Iggerot Moshe*, Hoshen Mishpat I, 72. For the bankruptcy example, see *Pithei Hoshen*, Halva'ah ch. 2 n. 63 and *Responsa Chelkat Yaakov*, Hoshen Mishpat no. 32. For the example pertaining to the statute of limitations, see *Pithei Hoshen*, Halva'ah Chapter 2 note 72. For the equitable distribution example, see *Responsa Chavalim Be-ne'ima*, vol. 5, Even Ha-Ezer 34; R. Mordechai Willig, "Equitable Distribution and the Enforceability of Choice of Law Clauses in Beit Din," *Journal of the Beth Din of America* 3 (2023): 19–34.
59. This is true even when a Jewish community adopts a practice that coincides with the law. For example, if a Jewish community adopted bankruptcy provisions, the provisions would be binding as *minhag* not as *dina de-malkhuta*. The bankruptcy rules would remain binding, from the perspective of *minhag*, only for as long as the community abides by them.
60. The Jewish community can "vote" in two senses. In one sense, the community votes by either taking up the practice or declining it. In another sense, some authorities believe that communal leaders and scholars can invalidate a practice if they find it improper or foolish. For a discussion of this power to invalidate a custom, see Rosensweig, "Minhag Ha-Sochrim," 55–58.
61. Put more cautiously, we can say that the internal rules of Jewish law take no position on many of the central questions of political economy. The Talmud does, on occasion, provide general principles that might inform, in broad strokes, how the economy should be shaped. For example, the Talmud discusses general principles of market competition and tax collection (whether taxes should be levied proportional to income or as a fixed amount). It is not my intention to claim that the Talmud never engages in discussion of rules that might pertain to political economy. My point, rather, is that Talmud and *halakhah* do not attempt to provide us with a complete or comprehensive system of internal rules that would yield a fully functioning society. Whereas the Talmud engages in systematic and comprehensive

treatments of private law subjects such as the laws of stolen property and the responsibility of bailees, it does not for the principles of political economy.

62. The strongest evidence for this is the fact that the Talmud (Bava Batra 8b) and Tosefta (Bava Metzia Chapter 11) envision local town and trade councils enacting economic regulations for their immediate jurisdictions. R. Yosef Henkin writes that in the absence of centralized Jewish communities with official communal leadership, these powers are outsourced to the government–especially in democratic societies–and are channeled via *dina de-malkhuta dina*. See R. Henkin, *Hapardes* 31, vol. 7; Shilo, *Dina De-Malkhuta Dina*, 147.
63. See *Responsa Rabad*, no. 131.
64. See *Shakh*, Hoshen Mishpat 73:39.
65. See Rabad, *Mishneh Torah*, Malveh ve-Loveh 25:10 and *Responsa Rabad*, no. 131.
66. *Responsa Rabad*, no. 131.
67. For examples of legal decisions that explicitly cite facilitating commerce as a basis for a legal ruling, see *Or Zarua*, Bava Metzia 202 citing Rabbenu Tam; *Or Zarua*, Bava Metzia no. 208; *Tosafot*, Bava Metzia 70b s.v. *tashikh*; *Shita Mekubetzet*, Bava Metzia 71a citing Rashba; *Tosafot*, Avoda Zarah 15a s.v. *Aimur*. For the claim that Judaism is committed to promoting economic efficiency, see Aaron Levine, "Efficiency in Jewish Law," in *Economics and Jewish Law* (New York: Yeshiva University Press, 1987), 159–82. The "*tov*" part of the *ve-asita ha-yashar ve-ha-tov* mandate may imply a duty to enact economically beneficial policies (*tov*). See *Rashi*, Bava Metzia 108a s.v. *ve-asita*; *Tosafot*, Bava Metzia 108b s.v. *ar'a*; Rosensweig, "When Has a Neighbor Waived his Right to First Refusal." For another application of *ve-asita ha-yashar ve-hatov* in this sense of promoting efficiency, see *Responsa Rashba*, 2:141.
68. *Responsa Ba'i Chayai* (Benivesti) Hoshen Mishpat 1:158.
69. This is one way of understanding Ramban and R. Vidal's interpretation of *va-asita ha-yashar ve-hatov*. See supra notes 14 and 17.
70. This appears to be Maharshakh's rationale for applying mercantile custom to decide a case rather than the native provisions of *hoshen mishpat*. See *Responsa Maharshakh* no. 2:229. See also Rosensweig, "Minhag Ha-Sochrim," 3 n. 108.

    Where the parties' joint expectations violate some important principle of Jewish law, *halakhah* may decline to recognize their expectations. Such is the case regarding charging interest (*ribbit*), litigating in Gentile courts (*arka'ot*), and, according to many authorities, inheritance. See, respectively, *Shulhan Arukh* Yoreh De'ah 161, *Shulhan Arukh* Hoshen Mishpat 26; *Pithei Hoshen*, Yerushah 1:2.
71. This view is often attributed to R. Shimon Shkop, *Shaarei Yosher*, Ch. 5. For a discussion of his view, see Shai Wozner, *Legal Thinking in the Lithuanian Yeshivoth: The Heritage and Works of Rabbi Shimon Shkop* (Jerusalem: Magnes Press, 2016), 220–32.
72. In fact, the commercial rules of *hoshen mishpat* are widely seen as ideal Torah study. See Mishnah Bava Batra 10:8; Joseph B. Soloveitchik, *Halakhic Man* (Philadelphia: Jewish Publication Society, 1983), 25–26.
73. *Derashot Ha-Ran*, no. 11. For the connection between justice and the Divine presence, see Talmud Bavli Sanhedrin 7a.
74. There are different ways of conceiving exactly how this works. The basic idea is exemplified by the Kantian tradition in legal and political philosophy, though that tradition is quite diverse. Some of the works that illustrate this approach include John Rawls's *Theory of Justice*, especially his explication of the fundamental rights under his first principle of

justice; Robert Nozick, *Anarchy State and Utopia*; Ernest Weinrib, *The Idea of Private Law*; Arthur Ripstein, *Private Wrongs*; Arthur Ripstein, *Force and Freedom*. For an illustration of this approach applied to property law, see Meir Itamar Rosensweig, "Property and Distributive Justice: A Theory of Moral Property Rights" (PhD diss., University of Pennsylvania, 2022), 121–220.

75. The writings of Ronald Coase, Guido Calabresi, and Richard Posner exemplify this conception of law.

76. For a legal system containing rules based on justice and rules grounded in efficiency, with each set subject to different types of legal protection and enforcement, see Rosensweig, *Property and Distributive Justice*.

By analogy, Rawls's first principle of justice calls for equal basic rights and liberties, recognizing the fundamental moral equality between people. However, his difference principle (the second principle of justice) permits departures from equality for the distribution of income and wealth as long as those departures make everyone better off.

77. See the discussion and sources in Soloveitchik, *Collected Essays I*, 91 and n. 77 therein.

78. It would be helpful if we had criteria to determine when a deviation/modification is harmful to the regime of true justice and when it is innocuous. One way of gauging whether a deviation is harmful is to consider (1) whether the parties could have agreed to that type of modification via the Jewish law mechanism of *tenai* and (2) whether a community could have enacted such a rule as a *takanah*.

79. Rabbenu Nissim already made this insight in Derashot Ha-Ran no. 11. He writes that internal laws aim at true justice while the sovereign is tasked with enacting laws to improve society.

Two qualifications are in order here. First, it is not my intention to claim that *every* rule indigenous to Jewish commercial law needs to be rights-based or that *every* rule that is incorporated must increase welfare. My main objective here is to provide a framework that illustrates how we can distinguish axiologically between Judaism's internal rules of *Hoshen Mishpat* and the external rules it incorporates. The rights-based versus efficiency-based distinction is just one compelling way of capturing why *halakhah* would articulate its own system of internal rules but also allow for the incorporation of external rules. Second, I readily acknowledge that the Talmud contains a handful of rules plausibly understood as efficiency or welfare based. This poses no objection to the thesis suggested in the text. On the contrary, the thesis implies that increasing welfare and efficiency are values internal to Judaism, so it should not surprise us if some of *hoshen mishpat*'s internal rules are efficiency based. There are cases where welfare and efficiency considerations could be so basic that they rise to the level of basic rights and become matters of pure justice.

I should also note the possibility that the Sages may have articulated some rules in the Talmud in their capacity as political leaders of the Jewish community rather than as jurists interpreting the law. We shouldn't be surprised to find, on occasion, the Talmud articulating rules that would ordinarily fall under the jurisdiction of a separate political body to legislate. For large swaths of Jewish history, the Sages functioned as quasi-political leaders in addition to their capacity as interpreters of the Torah. Ran makes this point explicit in his *derashah* (no. 11). This, of course, complicates our ability to discern which rule in the Talmud is an intrinsic rule native to Jewish law and which is a rule legislated by the rabbis or incorporated by them in their capacity as quasi-sovereigns overseeing the social and economic development of their constituents. A rule can be formulated in the Talmud and codified in the *Shulhan Arukh* but nevertheless fail to be an intrinsic rule native to Jewish law.

CHAPTER 26

JEWISH LEGAL RESPONSES TO COVID-19

SHLOMO ZUCKIER

Introduction

The crisis spawned by the rapid spread of COVID-19 beginning in March 2020 and its ramifications spurred an intensive period of *halakhic* innovation unparalleled since the mid-twentieth century. Reactions to the pandemic's medical risks, as well as to the adjustments to daily life it demanded, prompted a massive output of *halakhic* decision-making, both immediately and over the past years, even as the situation became less acute. By May 2021, barely a year since the pandemic's first *halakhic* issues came to the fore, multiple volumes of responsa had been produced, not to mention a bevy of articles—both primary and secondary—treating *halakhic* issues, and more material has appeared since then. This study aims to sketch some of the main issues and novel decisions that have come to the fore, especially those that highlight important questions and may have enduring significance for the history of *halakhah*. These matters have faced various Jewish communities that see *halakhah* as binding, including various Haredi communities in America and Israel, Modern/Centrist Orthodoxy, Dati Leumi, and Conservative Judaism.

Pikkuah Nefesh

Certainly the most urgent issue relating to Jewish Law and COVID was that of how to adopt safety measures in responding to the pandemic, a challenge facing humanity as a whole in 2020–2021 but one that took on particular *halakhic* nuances for these communities. The early *halakhic* sources are clear and authoritative: when a person's life is at risk, one is to violate *halakhah* to save a life,[1] a principle affirming life's value. Leaving aside several exceptional cases (including three particularly severe violations, and attempted coercion and/or desecration of God's name), *halakhah* generally embraces a departure from its strictures in these emergent cases.

Applying *Pikkuah Nefesh* to the Pandemic in Practice

By some point in March 2020, across the developed world, it became clear that the pandemic was life-threatening and was growing exponentially. The only effective response known at the time was minimizing contact through sheltering-in-place orders, or "shutting down," a policy which was summarily put in place across the world, including in areas with large Jewish communities such as the United States and Israel.

Jewish communities worldwide, nearly without exception, heeded these shutdown orders, certainly in the early months of the pandemic, through mid-May 2020.[2] As some noted at the time, this was an unprecedented moment in Jewish history, where essentially all physical Jewish religious institutions worldwide were shuttered. While not all directives to close explicitly cited *Pikkuah Nefesh* as a factor, presumably all would agree that, at least in a case of a high-risk person being directly exposed to an active patient, that category would be operative. Notably, there is actually more room for stringency in this case than in a standard case of *Pikkuah Nefesh*, as this scenario includes both the prospect of endangering oneself and of endangering others, the latter in some ways more severe than the former.[3]

The Broadening of *Pikkuah Nefesh*

With the widely implemented shutdown of religious institutions in the early months of the COVID pandemic, to the extent that communities made these decisions on the basis of *Pikkuah Nefesh*, there was something of a novel development at work. As going about daily life almost necessarily entails risks to one's life, it has always been necessary for *halakhic* decisors to set parameters as to what qualifies as *Pikkuah Nefesh*. Imposing a blanket category of *Pikkuah Nefesh* directing the minimization of communal conduct can thus be seen as a novel ruling.

Classical Talmudic and *halakhic* sources (b.Ta'an 19a and S.A. O.H. 576:2) define the rate of death required to qualify for a pandemic—that is, the definition of *dever* (pestilence), as having three people die over three days for a population of five hundred. Furthermore, the Magen Avraham writes (316:23) that a risk with incidence of less than one in a thousand does not qualify as *Pikkuah Nefesh*. In addition, based on the influential responsum of the Noda Bi-Yehudah (Tinyana, Y.D. 210), standard *halakhic* practice has generally been to calculate dangers based on the standard of *holeh lefanekha*, evaluating the particular person who is ill and their health prospects rather than considering a broad population and the statistical expected value of deaths from any particular cause. On this standard, COVID-19 would not qualify as *Pikkuah Nefesh*, given its relatively lower death rate, particularly when calculated as the risk for attending a single synagogue prayer.

Rabbi Asher Weiss argued against this cluster of points, insisting that the conditions created by COVID-19 would still qualify as *Pikkuah Nefesh* based on precedent.[4] He noted the Talmudic statement that "when a plague is in the city, constrict your feet" (b.BK 60b) as well as other teachings and practices of rabbinic leaders over the years as proof for the need to take precautions in cases such as these.[5]

He similarly asserted an obligation to receive inoculations for common diseases, despite there not being a death rate of more than 1:1,000, because "since we know with certainty that if we do not inoculate children will die, even if only one in several thousand, we have an absolute obligation to prevent this death."[6] The position of the Magen Avraham noted above is contradicted by another position of his, at O.H. 330:3, and R. Weiss argues that the Magen Avraham's settled view is that, while a particular risk one encounters out of *happenstance* has a cutoff of 1:1,000, risks based on *nature* (such as childbirth or infectious disease) are calculated based on the overall population, even if they have a lower than 1:1000 death rate. This view effectively endorses the use of statistical *Pikkuah Nefesh* for these cases.

This approach, noted explicitly by R. Weiss but essentially followed by all who applied *Pikkuah Nefesh* throughout the pandemic,[7] signals a turn away from the focus on *holeh lefanekha*, as under these circumstances one is to calculate not the risk to the individual but to the group as a whole. Not unrelated to this is the conferring upon national health authorities a presumed correlation to *Pikkuah Nefesh* guidelines. As R. Weiss writes, "From this [analysis] we should learn and act even today, to be extremely careful regarding the guidance of authorized medical agencies and for all of the enactments of the [Israeli -SZ] Ministry of Health and not to diverge from them." R. Weiss's ruling allows for leniency in various areas of *halakhah* on the basis of COVID even for those who were not yet known to have contracted or even been exposed to the disease. Others took this approach yet a step further, with multiple decisors ruling that, during more severe periods of the outbreak, no one should observe certain fasts, or should do so with modifications, given the risk that they might have contracted COVID and been at greater risk from the fast.[8]

While this approach builds on pre-COVID *halakhic* developments pertaining to *Pikkuah Nefesh*, such as the ruling requiring inoculation for diseases with less than 1:1,000 death rates noted above,[9] or calculating the risk of fasting to pregnant mothers in their ninth month,[10] it does represent a further move in the direction of considering overall populations rather than the individual in making these decisions. One might speculate on some reasons for the shift:

1. As the medical community has shifted over time to consider public health considerations more directly and to grant government bodies increased authority in implementing them, *halakhic* decisors have similarly moved in a parallel direction.[11]

2. The general, progressive decrease in deaths from disease among the healthy and increase in life expectancy have facilitated a lower trigger point within *halakhah* for what qualifies as *Pikkuah Nefesh*.[12]
3. As communication becomes ever-easier and decisors are consulted for increasingly broad questions with much more extensive data, the framing of the question shifts from the level of localized detail to the systemic and communal plane.

Counterarguments Against Pikkuah Nefesh and Responses

While some novel *halakhic* moves are required to define the situation under COVID-19 as *Pikkuah Nefesh*, once *Pikkuah Nefesh* is invoked, multiple things follow as a direct consequence: One must permit or even require various activities usually prohibited (e.g., Shabbat prohibitions and eating on fast days) and suspend usually required or encouraged behavior (regular prayer in a quorum and attending yeshiva in person).

However, while many adopted and applied *Pikkuah Nefesh*, there were others who rejected its application, at least in some cases. This section will review those *halakhic* arguments largely detached from the context of their application. A later section, "*Halakhah* and the Regulatory State," will explore the political and institutional context for these issues.

The most straightforward objection to applying *Pikkuah Nefesh* is asserting that the risk factor does not rise to the point of *Pikkuah Nefesh*.[13] While this might have been difficult to ascertain in the early stages of the pandemic, and while the cumulative COVID death rate in both America and Israel increased beyond 0.1 percent of the entire population, one might argue that younger populations with less risk might not qualify for *Pikkuah Nefesh*.

Over the course of the pandemic, several additional arguments for why *Pikkuah Nefesh* might not be applicable were raised:

1. One position that has been presented in a variety of contexts and versions argues that studying Torah and/or fulfilling other commandments saves one from the disease, and a shutdown ending organized learning would actually increase the danger. This reasoning was cited in the *New York Times* profile of Rabbi Chaim Kanievsky (then a leading authority in the Haredi community, since deceased) by his grandson and primary spokesman, Yanky Kanievsky. In noting the leading decisor's arguments for keeping boy's *yeshivot* open even as there was significant danger from the pandemic, the grandson explained: "He believes the Torah sustains the world . . . Without Torah learning, we don't have any reason to live. It's written in the Bible—if you stop learning, the world will collapse."[14]

   This account is consistent with a variety of statements made by Rabbi Kanievsky, among similar statements, over the course of the pandemic, asserting that "Torah protects and saves."[15] It is not clear to what degree this is meant literally, as the application of these general statements to practical *halakhah* seems largely unprecedented. Possibly this argument relies on a primary argument that the dangers associated with students returning to school do not rise to the level of *Pikkuah Nefesh* proper, and that the sub-*Pikkuah Nefesh* dangers can be overridden by the salvific powers of Torah.

2. Others have rejected the application of *Pikkuah Nefesh* based on an appeal to God's Divine plan. God predetermines people's health outcomes, and whether one will die of COVID or not is already decided and unrelated to following health regulations. This reasoning is not new; it was raised in a question posed to Rabbi Shlomo ben Shimon Duran (Rashbash, Responsum # 195) during a fifteenth-century epidemic. His response included the idea that while, in some cases, the time of a person's death is predetermined, not everything is decided in advance, and some things are contingent on factors such as the degree to which one follows a healthy lifestyle, as endorsed by the Torah. In particular, he invoked the Talmudic statement "everything is in the hands of Heaven other than cold and hot [*tzinim pahim*],"[16] interpreted as an obligation to take care in extreme weather, and regarding health measures more generally.[17] This argument was endorsed by Rabbi Asher Weiss in his *halakhic* essay on why to follow health regulations.[18]
3. It can conceivably be argued that the government forcing the shutdown of religious institutions qualifies as *shemad*, a governmental antireligious persecutorial decree, which justifies doing dangerous things to avoid submitting to a decree to undermine Jewish practice.[19] Some statements of protest during COVID shutdowns gestured at this sort of argument with language alluding to historical persecution, such as "the government announced and decreed the cancellation of children studying [Torah], public Torah study, and public prayer."[20] Conceptually, such an argument can be headed off if one assumes that the government's goal is not to persecute religious practice but to promote public health, or, in *halakhic* terms, *hana'at atzman* (for their own benefit).[21]
4. Finally, it is possible to argue that a certain degree of risk may be undertaken, if it is part of daily life, under the principle of *shomer peta'im Hashem* (lit. "God protects simpletons") (Ps. 116:6), which justifies taking the minor risks ubiquitous in daily life, and thus going about daily life is permitted despite COVID risks. Furthermore, if one is fulfilling a *mitzvah* there is even less reason to be worried, as "those sent to do a commandment are not harmed" (b.Pesahim 8a). Rabbi Yosef Gavriel Bechhofer argued against this approach, asserting that this category only applies if the relevant danger is "unknown, esoteric, or infrequent," which is not operable here, and that one should always follow doctors who assert that a given situation is dangerous. Similarly, protection for those fulfilling a commandment only applies where there is no prevalent danger, and would not justify a choice to endanger *others*.[22] Rabbi Mayer Twersky, who wrote several strongly worded essays arguing for safety measures above and beyond those recommended by health officials, argued that *shomer peta'im Hashem* only applies in the absence of a public health crisis; as long as the crisis was ongoing and the safety of exposure

unclear, with new data emerging, and vaccines in production, the category was not relevant.[23]

Other relevant *halakhic* arguments besides *Pikkuah Nefesh* include the general obligation to follow governmental regulations (*dina de-malkhuta dina*), if relevant (see section "Relationship between *Halakhic* Communities and the Regulatory State").[24] Additionally, at certain points when COVID-19 was particularly severe and Orthodox communities were seen as noncompliant, some argued that the principle of *eivah*, the goal of minimizing friction with Gentiles, might be operative; to wit, if a nurse thinks that the Jewish community is flouting government regulations, there is a risk that they might offer less than full service for identifiably Jewish patients in the hospital.[25] Finally, there is a possible issue of desecration of God's name (*hillul Hashem*) that might occur if (observant) Jews are seen as flouting the rules and spreading the disease.[26]

Opponents of the Application of *Pikkuah Nefesh*

A small number of rabbis publicly opposed the consensus view of applying *Pikkuah Nefesh* and implementing health measures in response to the pandemic. The materials opposing the idea of a shutdown in principle range widely across genre and style (responsum, *halakhah* article, *pashkevil*/posted open letter) and their full scope and prevalence is difficult to access, given that these views were often unpopular (at the time) and their implementation illegal. A partial list of those expressing these views, which include both *halakhic* and other argumentation, is noted.[27] Their views can be organized into the following groups: (1) rejecting consensus scientific claims such as the death rate upon contracting COVID-19 or rejecting the efficacy of lockdowns or wearing masks for minimizing transmission of COVID-19; (2) arguing that risk factors are too minimal to matter, and thus the relevant death rate does not satisfy the *halakhic* definition of a "plague" and/or a situation of "clear danger" (*bari hezeika*); (3) arguing that there are greater risks in shutdown than in remaining open, given the religious value of prayer/saying *'amen yehei shemeih rabbah*, studying Torah, and/or fulfilling a *mitzvah*, all of which protect people, or even that the fear spread by a shutdown is more deleterious than the disease itself; (4) arguing that, despite the risks, an individual may choose to take risks upon themselves, invoking *shomer peta'im Hashem*.

Various articles and positions did not dispute the relevance of *Pikkuah Nefesh* but diverged on how precisely to apply it. This included those who accepted mask mandates but argued that one should remove their mask during the Amidah prayer,[28] and those who saw hard lockdowns as overly restrictive and ultimately more damaging to the public good than other public health measures.[29] Notably, the extended period of "reopening" running roughly from summer 2020 through summer 2021, and the reimposition of limitations on in-person meeting that occurred with the Omicron (Winter 2021–22) and other waves of the disease, spurred a wide range of views on what should or should not be permitted for synagogue and Jewish school policies. *Halakhic* issues featured at times in these discussions, but the primary frame of these debates was more frequently free exercise of religion.

COVID Anti-Vaxxers

Not unrelated to the emergent opposition to *Pikkuah Nefesh* considerations is the phenomenon of vaccine denial. Interestingly, some leading senior Haredi rabbis who had previously objected to vaccines in general due to (medically unfounded) worries about its potential to cause autism or infertility[30] were more muted in their views, and even denied public proclamations attributing to them anti-COVID vaccine views.[31] Chabad fired a rabbinic representative who had been publicizing anti-vaccine perspectives.[32] At the same time, on a popular level, Haredi communities in both the United States and Israel reflected significantly lower vaccination rates than the general population as worries over risks of infertility were promoted, through WhatsApp and other social media, often invoking these rabbinic figures.[33]

Women's *Mikveh*—The Most Essential Religious Institution?

The one major exception to the closing of all Jewish institutions at the outset of the pandemic was the women's *Mikveh*, the ritual bath in which women immerse following menstruation to allow intimacy with their husbands under Jewish law.[34] While non-Orthodox *Mikva'ot* generally closed, Orthodox women's *Mikv'aot* generally stayed open, in both America and Israel.[35] This can be attributed to a variety of factors: the severity of the prohibition against sexual activity without *Mikveh*;[36] the discrete and limited degree of interpersonal exposure and interaction relevant to *Mikveh* attendance; early indications that COVID was not communicated through water (and certainly not chlorinated/brominated water); and the limited alternatives for women, as well as the unclear forecast as to when a *Mikveh* might reopen if it closed.[37] At the same time, some raised and/or explored alternate means of observing *niddah* laws without resort to a *Mikveh*, including: using lakes as a *Mikveh*; using a pool or bathtub as a *Mikveh*; or allowing for certain types of physical touch between husband and wife without a *Mikveh*, although the last two views faced *halakhic* opposition.[38] In the end, as noted, *Mikva'ot* remained open, although public *halakhic* guidance often urged that women not be expected or pressured to use a *Mikveh* under the circumstances.[39] It is also worth noting that, in this episode, female religious leaders played a major role in determining and communicating policy, in both America and Israel.[40]

Prioritization of Health Care

At two points during the pandemic, both at its outset and when vaccines began to be introduced, the question of prioritization within medical treatment arose, prompting the release of various *halakhic* positions.[41] In the early stages of the pandemic, and particularly in late March and early April in New York, hospitals were running short on medical supplies and especially ventilators, then thought to be the best treatment for advanced-stage COVID.[42] At the time, two Orthodox and two Conservative rabbis produced responsa and/or guidance for how to respond.[43] The basic challenge at hand was how to reconcile the previous, regnant view of Rabbi Moshe Feinstein[44] with the emergent view of triage in hospitals, based on an authoritative *New England Journal of Medicine* (*NEJM*) article.[45] Rabbi Feinstein had argued, based on the rule of *ein dohin nefesh mi-penei nefesh*, "one may not set aside one life for another" (b.San 72b), that it is inappropriate to remove treatment from a patient in favor of another patient with better odds of survival, and that a "first come, first served" policy should be implemented. The *NEJM* criteria argued, instead, that actions should be taken to optimize overall outcomes in terms of life-years saved, even if it meant withdrawing treatment from patients or denying treatment to a patient if it could better be used by someone else. The two Conservative views essentially adopted the opposite extremes, with Rabbi Elliot Dorff permitting any actions necessary to achieve the maximal life-years-saving results and Rabbi Daniel Nevins insisting on holding the line on Rabbi Feinstein's view, even if it meant less than "optimal" results.[46] On the other hand, the two Orthodox responsa tried to walk a fine line between the two approaches, with Rabbi Hershel Schachter ruling that, in a pandemic, with new patients entering the hospital from hour to hour, it is considered as if the next, more viable patient is already present and thus denying treatment to the weaker patient does not violate the "first come first served" rule. Rabbi Jason Weiner, a hospital chaplain presenting treatment guidelines, proposed that hospitals could remove people from life-extending treatments (such as a ventilator) under very limited circumstances, drawing upon an earlier responsum by Rabbi Zalman Nehemiah Goldberg that had been applied in certain contexts in Israel but was not often applied in the United States. These views represented a rare case of explicit treatment of these issues in real time by American rabbis and decisors, and may have shifted the consensus position a step or two away from that of Rabbi Feinstein and toward a more consequentialist approach.[47]

"Hilkhot Zoom"

With the immediate cessation of almost all in-person communal interaction in March 2020, and the shift to Zoom and other remote platforms (for communities willing to use such technologies), a bevy of *halakhic* questions emerged.[48]

Remote *Minyan*

The most immediate and wide-ranging challenge that social distancing raised was that of convening a *Minyan*, or ritual quorum of ten. Such quorums, classically convened in-person, are required in order for prayer groups to (1) recite certain prayers known as *devarim she-be-kedushah* ("matters of holiness"), including *Kaddish*; and (2) qualify the prayer as a communal prayer, which the Talmud says is more likely to be heard than a personal prayer.[49] Additionally, some believe that it is obligatory to attend communal prayer whenever possible.

Porch Minyanim

A variety of solutions for this issue emerged very early on in the pandemic, in March 2020, varying to some degree by geography and community. Across multiple Haredi communities, during the height of the lockdown, *Minyanim* convened (in areas with sufficient population density of observant Jews) across balconies and/or porches, with each person situated on their own property and joining with others in the area. This approach relied on a view, discussed from the medieval period forward, that it is possible to convene a *Minyan*, even if the participants are in different places, as long as they can see one another (*ro'in ellu et ellu*). While somewhat controversial, and receiving some pushback from other decisors,[50] this position was adopted by the overwhelming majority of the Haredi community in America and Israel, as well as by much of the Israeli Dati Leumi community. A significant literature of responsa was produced dealing with various specific issues that came up in this regard—is it possible to convene a porch *Minyan* across a public street and/or private roads? How should the Torah reading be performed—can one be called to the Torah with a "remote" Aliyah? Should one pray as usual in these *Minyanim*, or see them as *halakhically* dubious and thus leave out various prayers as a risk-minimizing hedge?[51] Once absolute lockdown orders ended, backyard or outdoor *Minyanim* picked up as well, often avoiding these complications.

Prayer at Home

For those who found porch *Minyanim* either objectionable in principle or impractical, the only option during the lockdown was to pray individually, at home (*be-yehidut*). Religious organizations produced resources and ran programs geared toward prayer for those at home. Some ran pseudo-*Minyanim* or had singing programs over Zoom not meant to fulfill the technical letter of public prayer but to preserve its spirit. More generally, many synagogues increased their online programming so that people could stay in touch with their religious communities despite not being in physical contact. Additionally, some encouraged people to call in by phone to the rare *Minyanim* taking place in person, in order to qualify for "partial credit" toward praying with a *Minyan*.[52]

Convening a Minyan Over Zoom

Generally, the Orthodox community did not engage with the prospect of convening a *Minyan* quorum over Zoom. However, many within the Conservative movement endorsed that approach to *Minyan* accounting, at least for the duration of the pandemic. In a letter sent on March 17, 2020, which was considered not a formal responsum/Teshuvah but rather temporary guidance, a group of rabbis argued that, given the extenuating circumstances of the pandemic, one may make the following argument: since seeing one another (*ro'in ellu et ellu*) suffices for convening a *Minyan*, if a group of ten can see one another over Zoom, this should count for a *Minyan*.[53] This reversed the prior decision of the movement's Committee on Jewish Law and Standards from 2001 disallowing the convening of a *Minyan* through video camera (but allowing one to virtually join a *Minyan* of ten that had gathered in person).[54] While the new ruling received pushback, a large number of Conservative synagogues made this their standard operating procedure for the duration of the pandemic. On May 13, 2020, the Committee on Jewish Law and Standards (CJLS) offered a formal responsum that did not weigh in directly on the question of convening a virtual *Minyan* but did discuss the possibility of synagogues using Zoom technology over Shabbat, and permitted it with certain limitations.[55] It noted that this was done with an eye to the High Holy Days, where it was clear that synagogues would need to reach a larger audience, despite the prima facie limitations on use of technology on Rosh HaShanah and Yom Kippur.[56]

Kaddish Over Zoom

While no Orthodox community supported the convening of a *Minyan* over Zoom, one major decisor, Rav Eliezer Melamed, permitted saying *Kaddish* (and *Barekhu*) over Zoom.[57] His argument was that, even if a *Minyan* is not constituted, no prohibition is violated by saying this prayer, and including the prayer in memory of a deceased relative is deeply meaningful to people and should be permitted. This practice was adopted by a number of synagogues.[58] Others suggested that in place of the standard *Kaddish*, it would be preferable to recite a different prayer, which would not normally require a *Minyan*, even under normal circumstances.[59]

The Sliding Scale of Halakhic *Exigency Across Communities*

The debates taking place across divergent communities during this crisis reveal each community's values. As communal pressure led to the legitimization of certain rituals utilizing questionable *halakhic* argumentation, one can gain a window into what each community sees as ritually indispensable. For the Haredi community, the indispensable ritual was regular, thrice-daily prayer with a *Minyan*; even if porch *Minyanim* were somewhat problematic to permit, Haredi decisors (including usually stringent ones) found a way to allow them. For segments of the Modern Orthodox and Dati Leumi communities, which have lower rates of daily *Minyan* attendance, the possibility of saying *Kaddish* to honor one's deceased relative was indispensable, which created pressure for a lenient ruling allowing *Kaddish* over Zoom (despite not comprising a *Minyan*), offered by Rabbi Melamed. For the Conservative community, the leniency of allowing Zoom *Minyanim* on Shabbat was presented with an eye toward the essential High Holy Days, once it had become fairly clear that those services would not be taking place in person. In each case, certain rituals were clearly indispensable, on a communal/ sociological level, and decisors were charged with finding a way to permit them within their community's relevant *halakhic* framework.[60]

Is Zoom "Real"?

Beyond the question of convening a quorum over Zoom, the emergence and widespread adoption of virtual technology, as well as similar and even less sophisticated technologies, spurred other *halakhic* questions about virtual seeing, hearing, and presence with regard to both various religious opportunities and prohibitions. While a wide variety of issues arose—reciting blessings (*Ha-Gomel, Birkat Ilanot, Sheva Berakhot*), hearing Megillah by Zoom, and others—the most prominent question surfaced in one particular episode, the controversy over the permissibility of a Zoom Seder for Passover 5780.[61]

The Zoom Seder Controversy

A couple of weeks ahead of Passover 2020, a group of Moroccan rabbis issued a ruling permitting one to set up Zoom to run during the Seder in order to facilitate an intergenerational family experience without physical proximity. This position was met with fierce pushback among Israeli Haredi and Dati Leumi rabbis. One important piece of this debate was the legitimacy of applying the minority position, historically championed by Moroccan and other rabbis, allowing the use of electricity on Yom Tov. While that position should technically be legitimate within the Moroccan community, many raised policy issues, such as the question of the slippery slope, and whether allowing such an activity would undermine "rabbinic unity." Moreover, as argued by Chaim Saiman, the focus of this debate largely not on technical *halakhic* grounds but on issues like whether using Zoom would be improperly "weekday-like" (*uvdin de-hol*), indicates that the current standard for determining the permissibility of technology use on Shabbat and Yom Tov in practice depends on whether technologies "are relatively unavoidable, passive, and discreet" or are "deliberately engaged for real-time responses that command our attention."[62]

The Status of Virtual Interaction in *Halakhah*

The Zoom Seder question raised not just the century-old issue of how *halakhists* should relate to electricity, but also the more complex question of how to relate to virtual reality (VR) technology such as Zoom. It is necessary to decide, for multiple areas of Jewish law, whether virtual sight constitutes seeing, virtual sound counts as hearing, virtual attendance qualifies as presence, and virtual word processing meets the qualifications of writing. The questions are complex, and it is possible to distinguish between different media, various activities, distinct *halakhic* categories and diverse contexts. Fundamentally, though, the question is whether the senses are defined experientially and phenomenologically, and thus VR would qualify as a "real" seeing, hearing, or writing (a *realist view* of VR), or whether the senses are defined formalistically as relating to the actual object itself rather than a projection thereof, a deflationary account of VR in which the transmission of computer data is considered disconnected from its source, not qualifying as seeing or hearing in their formal, *halakhic* sense (a *deflationary view* of VR).

In one interesting case, a decisor argued that transmitting visual images from one computer to another constitutes a violation of the prohibition on "writing" on Sabbaths or holidays—a prohibition understood as extending to drawing, painting, and so forth. However, having one's image appear on one's *own* computer does not violate this prohibition.[63] According to this line of reasoning, the definition of "writing" depends not on whether a computer is *processing* an image but on whether one is *relaying* an image to other parties. Such a realist position, beyond the "stringency" noted immediately above, might also endorse "leniencies" along similar conceptual lines, such as allowing the fulfillment of certain commandments through virtual means, because hearing the Megillah read over Zoom, for example, might still qualify as *actually hearing* the reading of the Megillah.

On the other hand, a deflationary view of VR would assert that whether one is projecting one's image close or far makes no difference—it is no more and no less than the use of electricity in either case. Similarly, one is not truly hearing the Megillah as read over Zoom—one is merely hearing a new set of sound waves projected from one's computer, no different from hearing a recording!

This moment constitutes one of the more engaged discussions on the role of virtual reality in *halakhah*, building on prior *halakhic* discussions largely about virtual hearing. These discussions took place during the pandemic, not because these technologies were new per se (videoconferencing has been around for some time) but because the exigency of the moment precluded decisors from sidestepping or working around these important issues. As the discussion remains relatively young, no consensus has emerged. There is every reason to expect that these questions will continue to emerge as technology becomes more and more central to daily life, and these responsa on the status of Zoom will be an important reference point for ensuing discussions.

Attitude to Technology

Beyond purely *halakhic* issues, the attitude toward technology in observant Jewish communities shifted in various ways, as so many participated in the involuntary experiment of increased reliance on Zoom and other remote technologies. In the Haredi world, despite prior bans of technology,[64] more people began using technology openly, even in communal contexts like schools, while other groups continued and even intensified their objection, doing their best to support less engaging remote teaching by telephone.[65] For communities already using internet and other technologies, the increased effectiveness of Zoom and reliance thereupon promised to shift and complicate the role of technology in *halakhic* contexts going forward. In the Conservative community this has led some to become accustomed to attending *Minyan* online, including on Shabbat, creating a different landscape of synagogue attendance in a post-COVID world.

Other *Halakhic* Issues

Any chapter of this length could not possibly consider the full range of *halakhic* issues that emerged and were treated during the course of the COVID-19 pandemic (beyond those discussed until this point), but it is worth noting some of the more salient topics here:

- Discussions over which additional prayers to recite during the period of crisis—Psalms, Avinu Malkeinu, and the like. In particular, there was a question as to whether some of these prayers could be recited during the month of Nissan, when prayers stemming from and expressing crisis are usually avoided.
- During periods when music is traditionally restricted—*sefirat ha-omer* and the three weeks leading up to Tisha Be'av—some rabbis provided a special permission to listen to music, given the difficulty of isolation and parenting during the pandemic, and others rejected this permission.[66]
- Much *halakhic* ink was spilled over how best to adjudicate cases where contracts were cancelled due to COVID—whether in businesses, schools, or Passover hotels—drawing on both the letter of the law and its spirit of compromise (*pesharah*).[67]
- There was a debate as to what prayer, if any, one might recite upon receiving a COVID vaccination, with main options including *ha-tov ve-ha-metiv*, *shehehiyyanu*, and the usual prayer that a medical procedure be successful (*Berakhot* 60a).[68] One major bone of contention was whether this should change a long-standing practice of not reciting prayers for inoculations.[69]
- Given that nearly all *Minyanim* missed a number of public weekly Torah readings in Spring 2020, there were multiple responsa as to whether and how to "catch up." Given the competing goals of completing the yearly Torah reading as a community and the interest in not imposing too much on community members (*tirha de-tzibbura*) as a multi-hour reading would, many *Minyanim* offered optional "catch-up" readings not during prime prayer times.[70]

Among some of the smaller-scale *halakhic* debates, it is possible distinguish between two attitudes: one that emphasizes the *uniqueness* of the crisis and allows for *novel* rulings, and another that instead emphasizes *routine* and advocates for *standard* legal practices. To a large degree, the approach that "leans in" to the crisis represents Israeli and particularly Dati Leumi approaches, while one that asserts holding the line and continuing prior paradigms aligns better with attitudes of Haredi and American decisors.[71]

Divergent and Shifting Models of *Halakhic* Authority

In different religious communities, the varied responses to COVID-19 revealed divergent and at times shifting models of *halakhic* authority and leadership existing across different communities.

America

On the American scene, major decisions were made by large rabbinic groups and largely accepted by the relevant communities.[72] By contrast, within Haredi American leadership, there was often a leadership vacuum at the top, and local communities and/or individuals were left to make their own decisions. The Moetzes Gedolei ha-Torah, or council of leading American Haredi Sages, rarely weighed in (at least not in a timely fashion) on pressing issues of how to balance safety and ritual during the pandemic, and its affiliated Agudath Israel was not much more prolific. This yielded a situation apparently divergent from the theological principle of *Da'as Torah*, wherein leading rabbinic Sages make the most significant theological decisions. Whereas the Haredi community that usually adheres to *Da'as Torah* (at least on a rhetorical level) had publicized few such positions over the pandemic, the Modern and Centrist Orthodox communities, which stereotypically allow for more local leeway by the religious consumer, actually adopted a top-down religious leadership model for pandemic-related issues, with senior rabbis often leading.

The causes for this inversion include the following factors:

1. Religious communities are organized on a synagogal level, with rabbinic leadership playing a major role to a greater degree within Centrist communities than in Haredi ones. The latter are often much more decentralized, often gathering in small Shtiebels rather than large, membership-based gatherings. Centralized communities are more likely to adopt centralized responses.
2. Non-Haredi communities were much more likely to embrace safety measures than Haredi ones, given attitudes toward science and the prevalence of doctors in their communities (among other reasons), while Haredi followership was much more mixed on the issue. It was thus much easier to lead a Centrist Orthodox community already unified in taking the health risks of COVID seriously than a Haredi community divided on this issue.
3. The Centrist Orthodox communal leadership based their decisions on consultation with medical professionals with experience in epidemiology, in real time. Use of technology, age of rabbinic leadership, and access and prior relationships with doctors may have made this easier to carry out for them than for the Moetzes.

The results for this development have been significant. Within the Haredi community, the leadership gap left by the silence of leading rabbis made space for both broad-scale, commonsense leadership by *gvirim* (major philanthropists), and for anti-governmental and anti-safety measures protests by rabble-rousers like Heshy Tischler,[73] possibly portending a decline in the authority of *Gedolim* (leading decisors) in some communities.[74] As for the Centrist rabbinic leadership, it appears that their proactive pro-safety measures, combined with helpful guidance on how to maintain normalcy amidst the challenges, earned them increased respect both on their "left" (in Open Orthodox communities) and "right" (in moderate Yeshivish communities).

Israel

The parallel question of Israeli rabbinic authority is a complex one, as rabbinic and governmental authority are much more intertwined on the Israeli scene. In broad strokes, the Chief Rabbis generally endorsed governmental health policies and suggestions, although at times more slowly than other rabbinic leaders. Among Hasidic courts, which were each under the authority of their Rebbe, most eschewed safety measures but particular Rebbes, such as the Rebbe of Karlin-Stolin, took the precautions very seriously.[75] As for larger-scale leadership, at several points tensions erupted around the two main *Gedolim* in Israel, Rabbi Chaim Kanievsky and Rabbi Gershon Edelstein (both since deceased). On issues such as opening men's *Mikvaòt* and opening men's yeshivot,[76] among others, there was pressure from some Haredi circles to reopen, against government policies and precautions. (At several points, Israeli Haredi communities had relatively high rates of COVID cases and posed a health risk to Israel as a whole.) Furthermore, in several episodes apparent disagreements emerged between these two *Gedolim*, with Rabbi Kanievsky's camp generally favoring an approach of opening up and Rabbi Edelstein's taking a more cautious approach. While usually resolved behind the scenes while presenting a unified front, these episodes exposed internal divisions within the leadership and the difficulty of offering a single view under the challenging circumstances.[77]

Relationship Between *Halakhic* Communities and the Regulatory State

Regarding shutdowns, alongside the more squarely *halakhic* issues of *Pikkuah Nefesh* discussed in the section "*Pikkuah Nefesh*," *halakhic* decisors and communities had to operate in a context where governments were mandating cessation of synagogal and (religious) school activity, given the pandemic. Would *halakhic* communities adopt the regulations happily, or at least begrudgingly adhere to them out of a sense of legal duty and fear of sanction? Or would they reject the laws outright, defying them privately or even publicly, attitudes which moreover shifted over time? Considering the two interrelated factors of communal attitudes toward the COVID health risks and toward government, this section presents how communities related to governmental health regulations. While explicit opposition to government regulations was not generally publicized, by closely analyzing the different responses of various communities to both the early stages of the pandemic leading to shutdowns as well as to the reverse stage of "starting up" again, it is possible to identify a variety of attitudes to government and COVID risks.

Timing

Focusing on the relative timing of when governmental and religious communities advised shutting down can illuminate divergences among the views of different religious groups. The point at which an institution chose to shut down reflects very clearly on its attitude toward COVID. Some religious groups called for a cessation of religious gatherings *before* the government did so, once it had been clear that this approach was medically recommended. Others waited until shutdowns were mandated or at least formally recommended by the government, essentially following the public at large (despite the increased risk of the disease spreading at religious gatherings). Yet others only ceased their religious gatherings and closed their institutions when there was no choice, when the shutdown was already being enforced; some even attempted to or succeeded in breaking lockdown laws and meeting (surreptitiously) when doing so was illegal.

If we focus on the New York area in mid-March 2020, we can find a range of such views. The first decision by a rabbinical body to close a group of synagogues was made by the Rabbinical Council of Bergen County the night of Wednesday, March 11 (effective March 13),[78] in advance of the New Jersey lockdown order for schools and institutions on March 16.[79] The Modern Orthodox Rabbinical Council of America and Orthodox Union groups issued a general advisory that communities that had confirmed cases of COVID-19 within them should close the afternoon of Friday, March 13,[80] giving communities throughout the New York metropolitan area and the country just enough time to close for Shabbat and avert a potential weekend super-spreader event. The Haredi group Agudath Israel, on Sunday March 15, following Shabbat, recommended "extreme measures . . . including closing shuls and schools" for "strong consideration,"[81] and many Haredi synagogues closed soon after. This coincided closely with the Center for Disease Control's recommendation to not hold gatherings with more than fifty people[82] and New York City's decision to close schools (announced March 15; effective March 16).[83] Still other organizations did not close until they were mandated to do so, or even afterward. An example of this is the Haredi community of Lakewood, which only fully implemented the shutdown on March 20,[84] following several nationwide recommendations to that effect, after a phone call from the White House to New

York Haredi communities,[85] and a day before New Jersey's governor was to make these meetings illegal.

The same logic can be applied in reverse with regard to reopening. Those groups that waited to reopen until sometime after public convenings were permitted made it clear they were being more stringent on safety than governmental organizations. (See, for example, the Rabbinical Council of America/Orthodox Union's recommendation that synagogues open only two weeks *after* they were permitted to do so by local health authorities.[86]) Other groups opened immediately when it was recommended and permitted to do so. And yet other groups either flouted health regulations, criticized them, or lobbied and put forward lawsuits against those regulations.[87] Generally, the same groups that were slow to close were the ones quick to reopen, indicating that there was a consistent approach regarding how to treat government-recommended and mandated health regulations.

Rhetoric

One can also discern the degree of seriousness with which a religious community or leader approached COVID based on the rhetoric they used in connection to the shutdowns. In one impactful quote, Rabbi Asher Weiss of Ramot, Jerusalem quipped that "I believe the [Israeli] Health Ministry is significantly lenient, it is an ignoramus, and we need to be more stringent than it."[88] Along similar lines, Rabbi Uren Reich of Lakewood criticized an attitude that waited until the last minute before closing down. In an impassioned speech given in March 2020, as the number of COVID deaths was climbing, he said:

> I was taken aback when people said to me: "You closed the yeshiva on Tuesday!? The *memshala* [government] only said to close it on Wednesday?" I'm not here to be *yotzei* [merely fulfill] the *memshalah* [government's demands]—that's a minimum! I'm out to be *machmir kefi ha'efshar* [stringent as much as possible] in the *mitzvah* of *pikuach nefesh* and *hatzalas nefashos*, and I'm urging everybody else to do the same."[89]

Indeed, the many rabbinical organizations that invoked *Pikkuah Nefesh* presented an approach to the pandemic that took the risk to life seriously, at times employing greater strictures than the government.

At the same time, there was an alternative view that related to the shutdown orders as an imposition that should be, at best, followed under duress, or else challenged and opposed. This is reflected not only by the views that explicitly critiqued the stay-at-home orders but also by other rhetorical means. One such example is the view critiqued by R. Reich, above, which insisted on closing religious institutions only when absolutely required by the government. A similar formulation was used in the framing of the decision to close Lakewood's Beth Medrash Govoha, the largest yeshiva outside Israel:

> To our great distress, we are forced to comply with an explicit governmental decree, which prohibits us to continue [studying] in open *Battei Midrash* in which the voice of Torah reverberates, out of our absolute obligation to follow all laws that the government imposes upon us.[90]

The announcement notably does not mention the value of *Pikkuah Nefesh* in the decision to close the institution.

As COVID fatigue increased through the summer months of 2020, and as the risks posted by the pandemic became more manageable in light of further knowledge about the disease, much stronger formulations appeared that rejected the relevance and/or value of *Pikkuah Nefesh*.

Israel

While the examples noted to this point were largely taken from the American scene, and particularly the New York area, parallel developments emerged elsewhere, including in Israel. At the outset of the pandemic, while certain Israeli medical-rabbinic figures advised people early on to close down their religious institutions, the Chief Rabbis made explicit calls in that vein only on March 25,[91] and Rav Chaim Kanievsky did so only on March 29,[92] after initial resistance.[93] These views exemplify the alternative approaches of being more stringent, equally stringent, or less stringent than the government on matters of public health.

Following the early stages of the pandemic, the most contentious issue was keeping open boy's Haredi *yeshivot*, where government officials negotiated with Haredi politicians and effectively with Rabbi Chaim Kanievsky and Rabbi Gershon Edelstein, the two leading *Gedolim* in Israel. For all three lockdowns in Israel (March–April 2020, September–October 2020, and January 2021[94]) there were tense negotiations with leading Haredi rabbis to ensure yeshiva compliance,[95] including an unusual semi-public disagreement between the two rabbis.[96]

Conclusion

The incomparable disruption to Jewish religious life posed by the COVID-19 pandemic, and the *halakhic* responses it inspired, had both immediate consequences and an enduring impact that will reverberate for many years ahead. This chapter analyzed the weighty issue of *Pikkuah Nefesh* from a variety of perspectives (*halakhic*, sociological, rabbinic authority) along with several other *halakhic* issues. The magnitude of real-time extensive responses and publications to the exigencies of the moment, a product of the digital age, is unprecedented in the history of Jewish literature. The shifts in application of the principles of *Pikkuah Nefesh* and virtual presence in ritual are likely to have the greatest long-term influence. While it is impossible at this fairly early stage to see their full impact with so little reflective distance, these changes in focus—not gradual but acute, given the needs of the moment—may well have set the stage for further developments in Jewish law and its relation to matters of health and emergent technology.

Acknowledgments

Many thanks to the editors of this volume, as well as to the participants in the June 2021 conference on Jewish law, for their helpful feedback on earlier drafts of this chapter, and to Eliana Diamond for assistance in revising earlier drafts.

Notes

1. See Lev. 18:5, Sifra Aharei Mot 8(13):14, b.Yoma 85b, b.Sanhedrin 74a, Rambam Yesodei ha-Torah 5:1, *Tur* and *Shulhan Arukh* and commentaries, OH 328.
2. "Current Guidelines for Quarantine," *Achiezer Community Resource Center*, March 23, 2020, https://rabbis.org/current-guidelines-for-quarantine/; and Sam Sokol, "Influential Rabbi Claims Ultra-Orthodox More Prone to God's COVID-19 Wrath," *The Times of Israel*, May 6, 2020, https://www.timesofisrael.com/influential-rabbi-claims-ultra-orthodox-more-prone-to-gods-covid-19-wrath/.
3. Some decisors have raised the issue of liability in a case where one spreads the disease to others. See R. Asher Weiss's essays on this matter, at Asher Weiss, *Minhat Asher—Corona I, #14*. (Jerusalem: *Machon Keren Re'eim*, 2021).
4. Aside from making these points in lectures that were disseminated to rabbis across the world, he also published these arguments in his *Minhat Asher—Corona*, as the opening essay in his volume (published online, Nissan 5780, and later in print, pp. 1–6).
5. Note his citations of *Likkutei Amarim*, *Mikhtav* 13, at 19b, of *Shu"t Rashbash* 195, and of Iggerot R. Akiva Eger, #71 on taking health precautions during an epidemic in general, as well as his invocations of Shu"t Hatam Sofer VI:23, Shu"t Mitzpeh Aryeh, OH. 41, and oral rulings by the Sho'el U-Meshiv and R. Israel Salanter regarding leniencies around fasting.
6. Weiss, *Corona I*, at 5.
7. Many dozens of rabbis and rabbinic organizations have invoked *Pikkuah Nefesh* in this context. For one example outside of Orthodoxy (where there was no discernable opposition to the classification of *Pikkuah Nefesh*), see Robert Harris, "Rabbi Robert Harris: Pikuach Nefesh, Social Distancing and a Rabbi's Case for the Need to Protect Life," *Corona Guidance: Religious Norms for Navigating the COVID-19 Pandemic, Colby.edu*, March 12, 2020, https://web.colby.edu/coronaguidance/2020/03/12/harris-social-distancing/.
8. See, for example, this summary of some of the relevant views: Yehuda Lave, "Not Fasting on Tisha B'Av This Year, Because of Corona, Revisited," *The Times of Israel*, July 20, 2020, https://blogs.timesofisrael.com/not-fasting-on-tisha-bav-this-year-because-of-corona-revisited/.
9. Rav Asher Weiss wrote on this topic in *Zikhron Shabtai ve-Aryeh* III, *simanim* 5–7. See also Rabbis J. D. Bleich and Asher Bush: J. David Bleich, "Survey of Recent Halakhic Periodical Literature," *Tradition: A Journal of Orthodox Jewish Thought* 48, nos. 2/3 (2015): 41–64, http://www.jstor.org/stable/44817798; Asher Bush, "Vaccination in Halakhah and

in Practice in the Orthodox Jewish Community," *Hakirah, the Flatbush Journal of Jewish Law and Thought* 13 (2012): 185, https://hakirah.org/Vol13Bush.pdf.

10. See, e.g., Ari Z. Zivotovsky and Alan B. Jotkowitz, "Fetal Risks and Religious Obligations," *The American Journal of Bioethics* 16, no. 2 (2016): 28, https://www.tandfonline.com/doi/full/10.1080/15265161.2015.1120808.
11. For a history of the emergence and growth of public health over the past two centuries, see Institution of Medicine (U.S.) Committee for the Study of the Future of Public Health. "A History of the Public Health System," in *The Future of Public Health* (Washington, DC: National Academies Press [US], National Library of Medicine, 1988), https://www.ncbi.nlm.nih.gov/books/NBK218224/.
12. For a basic history of trends in disease and life expectancy, see Max Rosner, Esteban Ortiz-Ospina, and Hannah Ritchie, "Life Expectancy," *Our World in Data*, 2013; last modified October 2019, https://ourworldindata.org/life-expectancy#:~:text=Globally%20the%20life%20expectancy%20increased,more%20than%20twice%20as%20long.
13. One such view appears to have been asserted by Ohad-Shalom Yishai, "*Odeh Lishmo*," *HebrewBooks*, 2021, https://hebrewbooks.org/pdfpager.aspx?req=64756&st=&pgnum=41&hilite=. He appears to argue that, while doctors should decide how risky certain activities are, they have no place in the realm of policy, where Torah leaders should determine all matters. To that end, in his view, inconsistent application of health guidelines that limited Torah study and prayer but allowed for exercise was illegitimate, deleterious to observant Jews, and comparably evil to an act of Amalek, Israel's ancient enemy.
14. Patrick Kingsley, "He Is Israel's 'Prince of Torah.' But to Some He is the King of COVID," *The New York Times*, January 29, 2021; last modified February 8, 2021, https://www.nytimes.com/2021/01/29/world/israel-virus-rabbi-orthodox.html.
15. This expression is based on b.Sota 21a, which argues that Torah is "*magna umatzla*" (protects and saves). See, e.g., here: Jeremy Sharon, "Rabbi Kanievsky, Who Has COVID, Always Put Torah Study Before Regulations," *The Jerusalem Post*, October 4, 2020, https://www.jpost.com/israel-news/rabbi-kanievsky-who-has-covid-always-put-torah-study-before-regulations-644491.
16. b.Ketubot 30a.
17. Pini Dunner, "Theology in a Pandemic: Is It Your Time to Die?," *Rabbidunner.com*, April 12, 2020, https://rabbidunner.com/theology-in-a-pandemic/.
18. Weiss, *Minhat Asher—Corona #1*, at 1–6.
19. While this was less common in earlier stages of the pandemic, the rioting by Israeli Haredim in January 2021 often touched on this theme. *TOI* Staff, "Ultra-Orthodox Rioters Clash with Police as Some Schools Flout Virus Lockdown," *The Times of Israel*, January 24, 2021, https://www.timesofisrael.com/ultra-orthodox-rioters-clash-with-police-as-some-schools-flout-virus-lockdown/. See also this lecture by R. Avraham Union regarding California's laws in this connection: Avraham Union, "*Din Gezeirat Shemad al Hakikat ha-Korona be-Kalifornia*," *Yeshiva.org.il*, February 23, 2021, yeshiva.org.il/midrash/46924.
20. In April 2020, widely distributed posters across areas with Breslov populations in Israel included this line. See David Cohen, "*Kakh Huhtam Zekan Rabbanei Breslov Neged 'Gezerat' Hatfila Beyahid*," *Kikar.co.il*, April 4, 2020, https://www.kikar.co.il/corona/354684.
21. See b.Sanhedrin 74 and related literature.

22. Yosef Gavriel Bechhofer, "Shomer Pesa'im Hashem ('God Watches the Fools') and the Novel Coronavirus," *The Journal of Halacha and Contemporary Society*, December 2020, https://rygb.blogspot.com/2021/01/shomer-pesaim-hashem-and-novel.html.
23. See his relevant essays: Mayer Twersky, "Go My Nation, Come to Your Rooms: An Essay Concerning the Prohibition at Present to Assemble *Minyanim* or Other Gatherings," https://7d4ab068-0603-408d-89df-fac4580e17c4.filesusr.com/ugd/8b9b1c_52d0b4164 05b423089752234c068204e.pdf; Mayer Twersky, "*Shomer Petaim HaShem*," June 24, 2020, https://7d4ab068-0603-408d-89df-fac4580e17c4.filesusr.com/ugd/8b9b1c_4acd4eb1a 232416a89170d331718fea9.pdf; Mayer Twersky, "*Od Be-Inyan Shomer Petaim HaShem Vesakkanat Harabim*," July 10, 2020, https://7d4ab068-0603-408d-89df-fac4580e17c4.files usr.com/ugd/8b9b1c_edffe98de1e84016a927339ee0a0f00e.pdf; Mayer Twersky, "*Od Be-Inyan Safek Sakkana Vesakkanat Harabim*," July 27, 2020, https://7d4ab068-0603-408d-89df-fac4580e17c4.filesusr.com/ugd/8b9b1c_27641c04152a43f18593d96fd37682d0.pdf; Mayer Twersky, Aug. 7, 2020, https://7d4ab068-0603-408d-89df-fac4580e17c4.filesusr. com/ugd/8b9b1c_9d7569b465ed4185873b5b7aabbda846.pdf.
24. There is little written on the topic, although some have argued that, in cases where governmental policies are irrational and over-reaching, the principle of *dina de-malkhuta* does not apply, as the situation qualifies as the exceptional "*mokhes she'ein lo kitzvah*" (the unbounded and capricious tax-collector). See b.BK 113a, SA H.M. 369.
25. See, for example, this letter to the Lakewood community, which invokes "*Aiva*." "Breaking: Lakewood Poskim Ban All Minyanim, Including on Porches; Visits Within Lakewood also Banned," *The Lakewood Scoop*, April 13, 2020, https://thelakewoodscoop.com/news/break ing-lakewood-poskim-ban-all-minyanim-including-on-porches-visits-within-lakew ood-also-banned/. Notably, this communal ban on porch *Minyanim* was short-lived, indicating a degree of communal pushback to this restriction.
26. See Weiss, *Minhat Asher—Corona #1*, at 33, which invokes this as one reason to oppose undertaking a circumcision that would be illegal under French law.
27. Among the rabbis expressing public views rejecting the application of *Pikkuah Nefesh* factors even at the height of the pandemic are:

    Rabbi Shaul Klein

    Rabbi Shaul Klein, rabbi of the Ohr Hachaim neighborhood of Bnei Brak and of the Ma'ayanei Hayeshuah hospital, in Ysoscher Katz, "*Hahadarah Mibet Hakeneset Beidan Hakorona: Teguvah Lepsak Halakhah Mehagaon R' Moshe Shaul Klein Shlit"a*," September–October 2020. https://drive.google.com/file/d/10AH_hNb1012JOSKItaIZO IAGraUjGzeV/view?fbclid=IwAR3VWEd4uWXRaKLI8DOf9MxZUlKQPsB6z2Tn_ 6kwkp6PVfaqmUAQWB7nwZU. Ariel Bareli, "*Pesika Hilkhatit Hamenugedet Lehoraot Harishmiot*," *Toraland.org.il*, 2020, https://www.toraland.org.il/%D7%9E%D7%90%D7 %9E%D7%A8%D7%99%D7%9D/%D7%9B%D7%9C%D7%9B%D7%9C%D7%94-%D7%95%D7%9E%D7%A9%D7%A4%D7%98/%D7%9E%D7%A9%D7%A4%D7%98-%D7%94%D7%AA%D7%95%D7%A8%D7%94/%D7%A4%D7%A1%D7%99%D7%A7%D7%94-%D7%94%D7%9C%D7%9B%D7%AA %D7%99%D7%AA-%D7%94%D7%9E%D7%A0%D7%95%D7%92%D7%93%D7%AA-%D7%9C%D7%94%D7%95%D7%A8%D7%90%D7%95%D7%AA-%D7%94%D7%A8 %D7%A9%D7%9E%D7%99%D7%95%D7%AA/#_ftn1.

    His article drew responses from Rabbis Natan Slifkin, Ysoscher Katz, and Yosef Gavriel Bechofer; Natan Slifkin, "A Serious Charedi Halachic Responsum on COVID and Torah?," *Rationalist Judaism: Notes on Torah, Science and Society*, October 5, 2020, https://www.rationalistjudaism.com/p/a-serious-charedi-halachic-responsum-on.

Bechhofer, "Shomer Pesa'im Hashem."

Rabbis Moshe Zev Zorger and David Michael Shmidel: Two Israeli Haredi rabbis—Satmar dayyan in Jerusalem, Rabbi Moshe Zev Zorger, and Rabbi David Michael Shmidel of Bnei Brak—spoke out against shutting down synagogues and schools in the early stages of COVID. These views are noted and cited in an article by R. Pini Dunner: Pini Dunner, "Beware of the Golden Calf," *Rabbidunner.com*, April 6, 2020, https://rabbidunner.com/beware-of-the-golden-calf/.

Rabbi Pinchos Frankel: Rabbi Pinchos Frankel, formerly Rabbi of K'hal Igud Avreichem in Flatbush, in a May 2020 speech to that congregation, effectively resigned from his position because they refused to return to synagogue in person.

See a recording and transcription of R. Frankel's speech: Pinchos Frankel, "Rabbi Frankel Resignation Speech," May 2020, https://web.colby.edu/coronaguidance/files/2023/07/Rabbi-Pinchos-Frankel-Resignation-Speech.pdf; Pinchos Frankel, "Rabbi Pinchos Frankel Accusations Against the Agudah and Why Minyonim Should Not Have Been Shut Down," https://drive.google.com/file/d/1GCzhUVNQRloX3C6AEVS_7wxJNkQrrfBa/view.

Rabbi Michoel Green: Rabbi Michoel Green (at the time affiliated with Chabad, which subsequently distanced itself from him) argued against wearing masks, partly on the basis of the pandemic not being *Pikkuah Nefesh*: Shani Bechhofer and Michoel Green, "Point/Counterpoint: To Mask or Not to Mask," *TheJewishPress.com*, October 29, 2020, "https://www.jewishpress.com/indepth/opinions/point-counterpoint-to-mask-or-not-to-mask/2020/10/29/?fbclid=IwAR3IWQmMyRTdy76ezWb7283EaViQ86B5L2yUm-HowFgJwTPUiUqTWn2wFTg.

28. Rabbi Moshe Sternbuch's letter (Parashat Korah, 5780) to this effect is cited in *Heviani Hadarav*, at 16 n. 21.
29. For example, Rabbi Yaakov Epstein wrote a theoretical, retrospective policy article for the "Center for Torah and State" arguing that strong lockdowns had an overall negative effect on well-being in the long run, even as they saved more lives in the short run, and thus Jewish law would have argued for less extreme measures. Yaakov Epstein, "*Kavim Manhim Lenihul Sikunim Leumi*," *Torahmedina.org.il*, https://www.toramedina.org.il/%d7%9e%d7%90%d7%9e%d7%a8%d7%99-%d7%95%d7%a9%d7%99%d7%a2%d7%95%d7%a8%d7%99-%d7%94%d7%9e%d7%a8%d7%9b%d7%96/%d7%9e%d7%9b%d7%aa-%d7%9e%d7%93%d7%99%d7%a0%d7%94-%d7%a7%d7%95%d7%a8%d7%95%d7%a0%d7%94/%d7%a7%d7%95%d7%95%d7%99%d7%9d-%d7%9e%d7%a0%d7%97%d7%99%d7%9d-%d7%9c%d7%a0%d7%99%d7%94%d7%95%d7%9c-%d7%a1%d7%99%d7%9b%d7%95%d7%a0%d7%99%d7%9d-%d7%9c%d7%90%d7%95%d7%9e%d7%99/.
30. "The Vaccine Safety Handbook A4," *P.E.A.C.H. issuu.com*, December 1, 2017, https://issuu.com/peachmoms/docs/the_vaccine_safety_handbook_a4.
31. Dovid Lichtenstein, "Should We Take the COVID Vaccine?," *Halacha Headlines*, December 19, 2020, Podcast, MP3 audio, https://halachaheadlines.com/episodes/should-we-take-the-covid-vaccine/; "Rav Kamenetsky: My Signature on Anti-COVID Vaccine Propaganda Is a Forgery," *Matzav.com*, December 12, 2020, https://matzav.com/rav-kamenetsky-my-signature-on-anti-covid-vaccine-propaganda-is-a-forgery/.
32. Shira Hanau, "Anti-Vaxxer Rabbi Fired by Chabad over Social Media Posts," *The Times of Israel*, February 3, 2021, https://www.timesofisrael.com/anti-vaxxer-rabbi-fired-by-chabad-over-social-media-posts/.

33. "Vaccination Rates in These New Jersey Communities Are Lagging, State Says," ABC7, May 4, 2021, https://abc7ny.com/covid-vaccine-covid-19-nj-appointment-symptoms/10578783/.
34. Both men's *Mikva'ot* and *Mikva'ot* for utensils closed, at least for some period of time, across a wide swath of communities. "*Idkun Hanhayot Sherutei Dat Betzel Negif Hakorona*," *Gov.il*, April. 2, 2020, https://www.gov.il/he/departments/news/corneavirassessments; Avi Ravina, "*Maran Sar HaTorah: 'Lehimana Beyamim Eilu Mitevila Bemikveh Gevarim*," *Kikar.co.il*, March 18, 2020, https://www.kikar.co.il/corona/351786.
35. Hannah Dreyfus, "Why Mikvahs Will Be the 'Very Last Things to Close,'" *NYJewish Week*, *Jewish Telegraphic Agency*, March 23, 2020, https://www.jta.org/2020/03/23/ny/why-mikvahs-will-be-the-very-last-things-to-close. (Contrast Mayyim Hayyim to Orthodox-run *Mikva'ot*.) In Israel there was more concern due to questions of whether protocols were followed; even so, *Mikva'ot* generally remained open: Jeremy Sharon, "Concern Rising over Mikveh Use Amid Coronavirus Epidemic," *The Jerusalem Post*, March 31, 2020, https://www.jpost.com/israel news/amid coronavirus-crisis-religious-zionist-opinions-differ-over-mikveh-use-622150.
36. See, e.g., *Shulhan Arukh*, YD 195.
37. Elana Stein Hain and Mijal Bitton wrote on some of the confusion at the early stages of the pandemic in this connection, when many of these issues were not yet determined. Mijal Bitton and Elana Stein Hain, "The Mikveh Never Closed: What the Pandemic Has Taught Us About Mikveh," *Lehrhaus*, March, 11, 2021, https://thelehrhaus.com/commentary/the-mikveh-never-closed-what-the-pandemic-has-taught-us-about-mikveh/.
38. Rabbi Daniel Sperber permitted certain forms of closeness between a couple who could not use *Mikveh*, and his view was rejected strongly by Rabbi Shmuel Eliyahu: *Kolekh—Forum Nashim Datiyot*, "*Emdat HaRav Daniel Shperber Ba'asher Lenashim . . .*" Facebook, March 20, 2020, https://www.facebook.com/kolech/posts/3150515948294546/; Shmuel Eliyahu, "*HaRav Eliyahu Al 'Hapsak' Shel HaRav Shperber: 'Oy Leoznaim Shekakh Shomot*,'" *Srugim.co.il*, March 22, 2020, https://www.srugim.co.il/432350-%D7%94%D7%A8%D7%91-%D7%90%D7%9C%D7%99%D7%94%D7%95-%D7%A2%D7%9C-%D7%94%D7%A4%D7%A1%D7%A7-%D7%A9%D7%9C-%D7%94%D7%A8%D7%91-%D7%A9%D7%A4%D7%A8%D7%91%D7%A8-%D7%90%D7%95%D7%99-%D7%9C%D7%90%D7%95. Rabbi Haim Amsellem wrote an essay permitting, at least in some scenarios, immersion in bathtubs and pools that were filled by tap water, although that view did not receive much of a positive rabbinic reception: Haim Amsallem, "*Ubaharta BaHayim Mikveh*," *The Zera Israel Foundation*, April 2, 2020, https://fliphtml5.com/irpqa/ofoo/basic.
39. See "COVID-19 and the Mikvah," *Rabbinical Council of America*, April 2, 2020, https://rabbis.org/covid-19-and-the-mikvah/, which reads:

   > Everyone must respect a woman's wish to delay her immersion in the Mikvah and resumption of intimacy until the pandemic has passed. The following is shared for the sake of those who wish to continue to access this sacred resource at this time.

   Several articles presented the difficult situation some women were put in: Sam Sokol, "Women's Ritual Baths Remain Open During the Pandemic, but Fail to Wash Away Fears," *The Times of Israel*, March 31, 2020, https://www.timesofisrael.com/womens-ritual-baths-remain-open-during-pandemic-but-fail-to-wash-away-fears/; Emma Green, "Orthodox Jewish Women Are Facing an Impossible Choice Right Now," *The Atlantic*, April 19, 2020, https://www.theatlantic.com/politics/archive/2020/04/orthodox-jews-mikvah-immersion-covid-19/610204/. Other *halakhic* questions arose as a result of health requirements limiting building access to a minimal number of people, as some decisors weighed in on whether women might be permitted to immerse during the day following their *Mikveh* night and whether they could shower following their dip.

40. "Mikveh Use in the Age of COVID-19: An Open Conversation for Visitors, Volunteers, and Staff," *Rising Tide Open Waters Mikveh Network*, April 1, 2020, Zoom Panel, https://risingtideopenwaters.org/event/mikveh-use-in-the-age-of-covid-19-an-open-conversation-for-visitors-volunteers-and-staff/; Penny Schwartz, "Mikvahs Strive to Provide a Safe, Spiritual Place for Bathers," *Jewish Journal*, October 15, 2020, https://jewishjournal.org/2020/10/15/mikvahs-strive-to-provide-a-safe-spiritual-place-for-bathers/; "Coronavirus Quarantine and Mikveh," *Nishmat's Women's Health and Halacha*, February 29, 2020, https://www.yoatzot.org/questions-and-answers/coronavirus-quarantine-and-mikveh/; "Coronavirus, Mikveh and Taharat Hamishpacha," *Nishmat's Women's Health and Halacha*, https://www.yoatzot.org/health-and-halacha/corona-and-halacha/; Kelsey Osgood, "Is the Mikveh Safe from COVID-19? Some Women opt for the Ocean," *The Forward*, March 29, 2020, https://forward.com/life/442617/is-the-mikveh-safe-from-covid-19-some-women-opt-for-the-ocean/; Tal Meir, "*Mikveh Bizman Korona? HaRabanit Doctor Tirtza Kelman Onah Bere'ayon Ishi*," *Pnima-magazine.co.il*, June 14, 2020, https://pnima-magazine.co.il/%D7%AA%D7%95%D7%A8%D7%AA-%D7%97%D7%99%D7%99%D7%94-%D7%A8%D7%90%D7%99%D7%95%D7%9F-%D7%90%D7%99%D7%A9%D7%99-%D7%A2%D7%9D-%D7%94%D7%A8%D7%91%D7%A0%D7%99%D7%AA-%D7%93%D7%A8-%D7%AA%D7%A8%D7%A6%D7%94/; Riki Rath, "*Neshot Hahalakha Shenotenot Maaneh Leshe'eilot Haregishot Beyoter*," *Makorrishon.co.il*, October 15, 2020, https://www.makorrishon.co.il/magazine/275807/.
41. There is much more literature on this question as it relates to triaging ventilators, although some treatments of the vaccine distribution issue also appeared. Both were largely rendered inoperative based on factors on the ground, as shortages resolved themselves.
42. Andrew Jacobs, "Fears of Ventilator Shortage Unleash a Wave of Innovations," April 17, 2020, https://www.nytimes.com/2020/04/17/health/ventilators-coronavirus.html.
43. Daniel Nevins, "Triage and the Sanctity of Life," *The Rabbinical Assembly*, March 2020, "https://www.rabbinicalassembly.org/sites/default/files/2020-04/Triage%20and%20the%20Sanctity%20of%20Life%20%281%29.pdf"; Elliot Dorff, "Triage in the Time of a Pandemic," *The Rabbinical Assembly*, March 2020, https://www.rabbinicalassembly.org/sites/default/files/2020-03/Triage%20in%20the%20Time%20of%20a%20Pandemic.pdf; Haim Jachter, "Rav Schachter's Landmark Teshuva on Ventilator Triage: The Original Teshuva," *Ou.org*, April 5, 2020, https://www.ou.org/chag/files/2020/05/R-RHS-Teshuva.pdf; and Jason Weiner, "Allocation and Distribution of Scarce Resources Based on Jewish Values," *Rabbiweiner*.com, December 7, 2020, https://rabbiweiner.com/blog/?fbclid=IwAR0HptDeZJz-7lkpmBIJpdoYBgd7FjW7JetcWMn5LBGDYzn6IoAnnb2RdYw. The two Conservative rabbis later settled on a joint, compromise position, attributed to Dorff and with a similar but not identical title to his original piece: Elliot Dorff, "Triage in the Time of a Pandemic: The Sanctity of Saving as Many Lives as Possible," *The Rabbinical Assembly*, May 2020, https://www.rabbinicalassembly.org/sites/default/files/2020-12/Triage%20in%20the%20Time%20of%20a%20Pandemic.12.07.20.docx.
44. R. Moshe Feinstein, *Iggerot Moshe*, Hoshen Mishpat 2 (1964): 73–74.
45. E. J. Emanuel et al., "Fair Allocation of Scarce Medical Resources in the Time of COVID-19," *New England Journal of Medicine*, 382, no. 21 (2020): 2049–55.

46. To some degree, the impetus for R. Nevins's view was to avoid the undertreatment of those with disabilities or others who might be deprioritized in medical contexts, corresponding to critiques made by anti-racist and disability advocates in response to the *NEJM* criteria.
47. See Shlomo Zuckier, *Triaging Medical Treatment Under COVID: Four Recent Views on Halakhah and Medical Ethics* (forthcoming). An as-yet-published work presented at the Society of Jewish Ethics conference in January 2021.
48. For additional accounts of how various Jewish communities responded ritually and otherwise to the lack of in-person interaction during COVID-19, see R. Langer, "Jewish Liturgy During the Early Stages of the COVID-19 Pandemic: Vignettes from Boston Suburbs," *Contemporary Jewry* 41, no. 1 (2021): 23–37; Levi Cooper, "Kaddish During COVID: Mourning Rituals During a Pandemic," *Contemporary Jewry* 41, no. 1 (March 2021): 39–69, https://doi.org/10.1007/s12397-021-09395-x; and Mark L. Trencher, "The Orthodox Jewish Community and the Coronavirus: Halacha Grapples with the Pandemic," *Contemporary Jewry* 41 (2021): 123–39.
49. See, e.g., b.Berakhot 6a, 8a, b.AZ 4b.
50. See Hershel Schachter, "Piskei Corona 14: Forming a Minyan Outside," *YUTorah*, March 31, 2020, https://www.yutorah.org/lectures/lecture.cfm/951048/rabbi-hershel-schachter/piskei-corona-14-forming-a-minyan-outside/; and Yitzhak Yosef, "*Tziruf Leminyan Bemirpesot Vahatzerot, Aniyat Devarim Shebikedushah, Kri'at HaTorah Uvirkat Kohanim*," *Mekhon Hotza'at Hasefarim Tzuf*, April 2020, https://web.colby.edu/coronaguidance/files/2020/07/2020-Heviani-hadarav-Coronavirus-and-Jewish-Law.pdf.
51. See Moshe Sternbuch, *Colby.edu*, [letter on Coronavirus dated 8 Nisan, 5780], April 2, 2020, https://web.colby.edu/coronaguidance/files/2020/04/%D7%92%D7%A8%D7%9E-%D7%A9%D7%98%D7%A8%D7%A0%D7%91%D7%95%D7%9A-%D7%A9%D7%9C%D7%99%D7%98%D7%90-%D7%A2%D7%9C-%D7%9B%D7%9B%D7%9C%D7%99-%D7%94%D7%A6%D7%98%D7%A8%D7%A4%D7%95%D7%AA-%D7%91%D7%9E%D7%A0%D7%99%D7%99%D7%9F-%D7%93%D7%A8%D7%9A-%D7%94%D7%9E%D7%A8%D7%A4%D7%A1%D7%95%D7%AA.pdf.
52. See Yosef, "*Tziruf Leminyan Bemirpesot Vahatzerot*," at 12.
53. "CJLS Guidance for Remote Minyanim in a Time of COVID-19," *The Rabbinical Assembly*, March 17, 2020, https://www.rabbinicalassembly.org/story/cjls-guidance-remote-minyanim-time-covid-19.
54. Avram Israel Reisner, "Wired to the Kadosh Barukh Hu: Minyan via Internet," *Adopted by CJLS*, March 13, 2001, https://www.rabbinicalassembly.org/sites/default/files/public/halakhah/teshuvot/19912000/reisner_internetminyan.pdf.
55. Joshua Heller, "Streaming Services on Shabbat and Yom Tov," approved on May 13, 2020, https://www.rabbinicalassembly.org/sites/default/files/2020-05/Streaming%20on%20Shabbat%20and%20Yom%20Tov%20Heller.pdf.
56. Indeed, the CJLS press release announcing the responsum's adoption emphasized the high holy days as a goal of said responsum: "the Conservative/Masorti movement of Judaism adopted a *teshuvah* (or responsum) this week that could allow for the livestreaming of services on Shabbat and festivals, particularly during the Jewish High Holidays this fall." Cited from "Conservative Rabbis Rule on Streaming Services on Shabbat and Yom Tov," *Rabbinical Assembly*, May 14, 2020, https://www.rabbinicalassembly.org/story/conservative-rabbis-rule-streaming-services-shabbat-and-yom-tov.

57. See also the Hebrew version of Rav Melamed's responsum at Meirav Cohen, "*Harav Eliezer Melamed: 'Mutar Lehagid Kadish Bemifgash Virtuali,'*" *Kipa.co.il*, March 18, 2020, https://www.kipa.co.il/%D7%97%D7%93%D7%A9%D7%95%D7%AA/956904-%D7%94%D7%A8%D7%91-%D7%90%D7%9C%D7%99%D7%A2%D7%96%D7%A8-%D7%9E%D7%9C%D7%9E%D7%93-%D7%9E%D7%95%D7%AA%D7%A8-%D7%9C%D7%94%D7%92%D7%99%D7%93-%D7%A7%D7%93%D7%99%D7%A9-%D7%91%D7%9E%D7%A4%D7%92%D7%A9-%D7%95%D7%99%D7%A8%D7%98%D7%95%D7%90%D7%9C%D7%99/.
58. Benny Lau, "Can Kaddish Be Said in a Virtual Minyan?," *The Times of Israel*, March 26, 2020, https://blogs.timesofisrael.com/can-kaddish-be-said-in-a-virtual-minyan/.
59. For further analysis of *Kaddish* solutions during COVID-19, see Cooper, "Kaddish During COVID."
60. I argue to this effect in my as-yet unpublished paper. Shlomo Zuckier, "*Da Lifnei Mi Ata Omed*: Recent Approaches to Virtual Presence in Jewish Ritual," presented to the Research Group on Law, Halakhah, and Ethics in Conjunction with the Challenges of AI, Hebrew University Law Faculty in April 2021.
61. See the following articles: Chaim Saiman, "In Rejection of the Zoom Seder, What Did Orthodox Jews Affirm?," *Mosaicmagazine.com*, May 4, 2020, https://mosaicmagazine.com/essay/religion-holidays/2020/05/in-rejecting-the-zoom-seder-what-did-orthodox-judaism-affirm/; Shlomo Zuckier, "Does Virtual Seeing Count as Seeing Under Jewish Law?," *Mosaicmagazine.com*, March 21, 2020, https://mosaicmagazine.com/response/religion-holidays/2020/05/does-virtual-seeing-count-as-seeing-under-jewish-law/?print. Shlomo Zuckier, "Making Seder Out of the Zoom Seder Controversy," *The Lehrhaus*, April 7, 2020, https://thelehrhaus.com/timely-thoughts/making-seder-out-of-the-zoom-seder-controversy/.
62. See Saiman, "Rejecting the Zoom Seder."
63. See Hershel Schachter, "Piskei Corona 2: Sick in Isolation," *YUTorah*, March 24, 2020, https://www.yutorah.org/lectures/lecture.cfm/950076/rabbi-hershel-schachter/piskei-corona-2-sick-in-isolation/.
64. Michael M. Grynbaum, "Ultra-Orthodox Jews Hold Rally on Internet at Citi Field," *The New York Times*, May 20, 2012, https://www.nytimes.com/2012/05/21/nyregion/ultra-orthodox-jews-hold-rally-on-internet-at-citi-field.html.
65. Certainly use of technology had been slowly increasing prior to the pandemic as well, but the pressure cooker of having a family at home with no recourse to in-person schooling seems to have sped up that process.
66. For this issue, as well as the one immediately above, see the materials cited in Shlomo Zuckier, "The Pandemic Theology Dilemma: Preserve Normalcy or Embrace Crisis?," *The Lehrhaus*, May 10, 2021, https://thelehrhaus.com/commentary/the-pandemic-theology-dilemma-preserve-normalcy-or-embrace-crisis/.
67. See, for example, a survey of the issues in Shlomo Weissmann, "Contracts and COVID-19," Beth Din of America, April 30, 2020, https://bethdin.org/contracts-and-covid-19/.
68. For some particular views, see Yosef Zvi Rimon, "Birkat Shehehiyanu O Hatov Vehametiv Al Hisun Lekorona," *Yeshiva.org.il*, December 28, 2020, https://www.yeshiva.org.il/midrash/46176; Dov Linzer, "Should I Make a Brakha When Receiving the COVID-19 Vaccine?," *YC Torah Library*, 2020, https://library.yctorah.org/lindenbaum/should-i-make-a-brakha-when-receiving-the-covid-19-vaccine/. For surveys of views, see Shlomo Zuckier, "The Blessing of 2021: Should One Say a Bracha When Receiving the COVID Vaccine?," January 5, 2021, *Youtube*, 1:07:43, https://www.youtube.com/watch?v=2KRX

G90Aycs; Jonathan Muskat, "Bracha on a COVID Vaccine? Rav Rimon, Rav Aviner, Rav Ahser Weiss, Rav Willig and Rav Schachter," *YUTorah*, December 27, 2020, https://www.yutorah.org/lectures/lecture.cfm/982892/rabbi-jonathan-muskat/bracha-on-a-covid-vaccine-rav-rimon-rav-aviner-rav-asher-weiss-rav-willig-and-rav-schachter/. See JLNJ Staff, "Reciting a Bracha on the COVID Vaccine," *Jewish Link*, April 8, 2021, https://jewishlink.news/reciting-a-bracha-on-the-covid-vaccine/; and Laura E. Adkins, "What Blessing Should You Say When You Get the COVID-19 Vaccine? We Asked Rabbis for Their Guidance," *Jewish Telegraphic Agency*, December 23, 2020, https://www.jta.org/2020/12/23/lifestyle/what-blessing-should-you-say-when-you-get-the-covid-19-vaccine-we-asked-rabbis-for-their-guidance.

69. See Shlomo Aviner, "*Tzarikh Levarekh Shehehiyanu Al Hisun Neged Korona?*," *Kipa.co.il*, December 18, 2020, https://www.kipa.co.il/%D7%99%D7%94%D7%93%D7%95%D7%AA/%D7%94%D7%9C%D7%9B%D7%94/1104039-%D7%A6%D7%A8%D7%99%D7%9A-%D7%9C%D7%91%D7%A8%D7%9A-%D7%A9%D7%94%D7%97%D7%99%D7%99%D7%A0%D7%95-%D7%A2%D7%9C-%D7%97%D7%99%D7%A1%D7%95%D7%9F-%D7%A0%D7%92%D7%93-%D7%A7%D7%95%D7%A8%D7%95%D7%A0%D7%94/.
70. Adam Ariel, "*Ein Keva Le-Parshiyot*," *Hakirah* 31 (2022): 5–20; and Hershel Schachter, "Piskei Halacha on Coronavirus Shaylas," *Torahweb.org*, April 23, 2020, 53–55, https://www.torahweb.org/torah/docs/rsch/RavSchachter-Corona-All.pdf.
71. See two independent but complementary discussions of this issue at Avraham Stav, "*Mah Mevarkhim Al Hisun?*," *Makor Rishon*, March 7, 2021, https://www.makorrishon.co.il/judaism/320873/; and Shlomo Zuckier, "The Pandemic Theology Dilemma: Preserve Normalcy or Embrace Crisis?," *The Lehrhaus*, May 10, 2021, https://thelehrhaus.com/commentary/the-pandemic-theology-dilemma-preserve-normalcy-or-embrace-crisis/. See as well this response to Stav: Elli Fischer, "Traditionalism Is Not a Callous Disregard to What is Taking Place" [in Hebrew], *Makor Rishon (Shabbat)*, March 12, 2021, 16.
72. RCBC and OU/RCA are the clearest examples. See nn. 78–81.
73. See Shira Hanau, "'We are at War': Heshy Tischler Is Not Done Stirring Up Orthodox Brooklyn," *New York Magazine*, October 9, 2020, https://nymag.com/intelligencer/2020/10/we-are-at-war-heshy-tischlers-orthodox-populism.html.
74. See Shlomo Zuckier, "American Orthodoxy's Twilight of Authority," *Mosaicmagazine.com*, November 20, 2020, https://mosaicmagazine.com/observation/religion-holidays/2020/11/american-orthodoxys-twilight-of-authority/.
75. Avital Chizhik-Goldschmidt, "More Schools Discouraging COVID-19 Testing in New York, New Jersey Despite Spike," *The Forward*, September 30, 2020, https://forward.com/news/455103/schools-are-not-reporting-covid-cases-among-students-asking-teachers-not/. See also Haisidic (@hasidic_1), "*Beit Midrash Karlin Stalin in Givat Zev*," Twitter, September 15, 2020, https://twitter.com/hasidic_1/status/1305913673215508485.
76. Jacob Magid and *TOI* Staff, "Top Haredi Rabbi Kanievsky Orders Yeshivas Opened; His Colleague Blocks Him–TV," *The Times of Israel*, April 22, 2020, https://www.timesofisrael.com/top-haredi-rabbis-threaten-drastic-steps-if-no-way-found-to-open-yeshivas/; *TOI* Staff, "After Apparent Spat, Top Ultra-Orthodox Rabbis Announce Yeshivas not Reopening," *The Times of Israel*, April 24, 2020, https://www.timesofisrael.com/senior-ultra-orthodox-rabbis-announce-yeshivas-not-reopening/; and "New Letter from Rav Chaim Kanievsky and Rav Gershon Edelstein to Roshei Yeshiva and Mothers," *The Yeshiva World*, April 26, 2020, https://www.theyeshivaworld.com/news/israel-news/1853228/new-letter-from-rav-chaim-kanievsky-and-rav-gershon-edelstein-to-roshei-yeshiva-and-mothers.html; Staff, "Rabbi Kanievsy Orders Haredi Boys Schools to Reopen, then Rescinds

His Decision," *The Times of Israel*, October 11, 2020, https://www.timesofisrael.com/rabbi-kanievsky-suffering-from-covid-revokes-order-to-open-haredi-boys-schools/.

77. On Haredi communities following rabbinic authorities around COVID-19 restrictions, see Sara Zalcberg and S. Z. Block, "COVID-19 Amongst the Ultra-Orthodox Population in Israel: An Inside Look into the Causes of the High Morbidity Rates," *Contemporary Jewry* 41, no. 1 (2021): 99–121, esp. 110–12, https://link.springer.com/article/10.1007/s12397-021-09368-0.
78. "No Shul, Yeshivas, Shabbos Guests, Levayos, Shiva: Vaad Harabanim of Bergen County Releases Letter," *The Yeshiva World*, March 12, 2020, https://www.theyeshivaworld.com/news/featured/1839350/no-shul-yeshivas-shabbos-guests-levayos-shiva-vaad-harabanim-of-bergen-county-releases-letter.html.
79. "Governor Murphy Announces Aggressive Social Distancing Measures to Mitigate Further Spread of COVID-19 in New Jersey," *nj.gov*, March 16, 2020, https://www.nj.gov/governor/news/news/562020/20200316c.shtml. It was later noted that this preemptive decision led to the decision of other religious communities, including those outside the Jewish community, to close down as well. In the opinion of some, this "saved hundreds if not thousands of lives beyond the communities." Chaim Frazer, "Tell Your Rabbis," *Jewish Link*, November 19, 2020, https://jewishlink.news/features/40624-tell-your-rabbis?fbclid=IwARotMlvGrvMXrNrQYILExY89rHc4ttIbIEmjIfAlkoPkLgpjzoPoc9YjBVI.
80. "Orthodox Union Guidance Regarding Coronavirus," *ou.org*, March 17, 2021, https://www.ou.org/covid19/.
81. "Coronavirus: Urgent Update (March 15)," *aguda.org*, March 15, 2020, https://agudah.org/coronavirus-urgent-update/.
82. Alexandra Kerr, "A Historical Timeline of COVID-19 in New York City," *Investopedia.com*, April 5, 2021, https://www.investopedia.com/historical-timeline-of-covid-19-in-new-york-city-5071986.
83. Eliza Shapiro, "New York City Public Schools to Close Due to Coronavirus," *The New York Times*, March 15, 2020, https://www.nytimes.com/2020/03/15/nyregion/nyc-schools-closed.html.
84. Mike Davis and Gustavo Martinez Contreras, "Coronavirus: Orthodox Jewish Leaders Close Lakewood Synagogues Citing 'Mortal Threat,'" *App.com*, March 20, 2020, https://www.app.com/story/news/health/2020/03/20/coronavirus-lakewood-orthodox-jewish-covid-19-shuls-synagogues/2885030001/. There appear to have been some efforts before this point, but they were not as sweeping or as successful. See Shlomo Zuckier, "Rabbis and physicians of the Lakewood community (not the Yeshiva) just announced this, invoking Pikkuach Nefesh . . ." Facebook, March 17, 2020, https://www.facebook.com/photo.php?fbid=1265139147011156&set=p.1265139147011156&type=3.
85. "White House Holds Phone Conference with Admorim, Rabbonim. and Community Activists," *The Yeshiva World*, March 17, 2020, https://www.theyeshivaworld.com/news/featured/1840874/breaking-white-house-holds-phone-conference-with-admorim-rabbonim-and-community-activists.html?fbclid=IwAR3DtbBwFkcL3JCBjfMVpIJkbUisaDn6TRfvkkFP8ZXZBQ_kbRDCnYxNf9A.
86. "Guidance to Shuls and Communities on Reopening," The Orthodox Union, and The Rabbinical Council of America, May 8, 2020, https://res.cloudinary.com/ouwp/images/v1689527459/ouredesign/main/OU-Guidance-To-Shuls-And-Communities-5-8-2020_F-1/OU-Guidance-To-Shuls-And-Communities-5-8-2020_F-1.pdf?_i=AA, 2.
87. See "Agudath Israel of America v. Cuomo," *Becketlaw.org*, October 8, 2020, https://www.becketlaw.org/case/agudath-israel-america-v-cuomo/.

88. Shlomo Zuckier (@ZuckierShlomo), "3.Attitude 3: We Should be *more concerned* about the dangers of COVID-19 than the rest of the population . . ." Twitter, May 21, 2020, https://twitter.com/ZuckierShlomo/status/1264615539592347652.
89. "LISTEN: Hagaon HaRav Uren Reich Regarding Grave Dangers and Chiyuv to Adhere to Medical Guidance," *The Yeshiva World*, March 18, 2020, https://www.theyeshivaworld.com/news/headlines-breaking-stories/1841034/listen-hagaon-harav-uren-reich-regarding-grave-dangers-chiyuv-to-adhere-to-medical-guidance.html.
90. Shlomo Zuckier, "Beth Midrash Gavoha in Lakewood . . ." Facebook, March 19, 2020, https://www.facebook.com/photo/?fbid=1264339967091074&set=a.281862595338821, translated from Hebrew. (The parallel English text featured the weaker formulation, "The Yeshiva is complying with the governor's mandate of a statewide closure of institutions of higher learning.")
91. Jeremy Sharon, "Chief Rabbis Ban Prayer in Synagogues over Coronavirus Crisis," *The Jerusalem Post*, March 25, 2020, https://www.jpost.com/judaism/chief-rabbis-ban-prayer-in-synagogues-over-coronavirus-crisis-622290.
92. "Rav Chaim Kanievski Rules to Daven in Private without a Minyan," *VINnews.com*, March 29, 2020, https://vinnews.com/2020/03/29/rav-chaim-kanievski-rules-to-daven-in-private-without-a-minyan/?fbclid=IwAR2ExEd1vhxE3WDtSibMpAB1xAXWK6mxPdOhWql42zLMgAU_J7qOVGqwsmA.
93. Yanky Katz, "*Maran HaGRa"H Kaniyevsky: Lisgor Heyderim? 'Halila, Zo Sakkana*,'" *Kikar.co.il*, March 13, 2020, https://www.kikar.co.il/corona/351046.
94. "*Magefat HaKorona Beyisrael*," *Wikipedia* (last modified June 6, 2023), https://he.wikipedia.org/wiki/%D7%9E%D7%92%D7%A4%D7%AA_%D7%94%D7%A7%D7%95%D7%A8%D7%95%D7%A0%D7%94_%D7%91%D7%99%D7%A9%D7%A8%D7%90%D7%9C#%D7%A1%D7%92%D7%A8_%D7%A9%D7%A0%D7%99.
95. See note immediately above for the first shutdown and here for the others: "Israel: Ultra-Orthodox Jews Ignore Government Coronavirus Orders, Attend Schools," *Middle East Monitor*, October 19, 2020, https://www.middleeastmonitor.com/20201019-israel-ultra-orthodox-jews-ignore-government-coronavirus-orders-attend-schools/; *TOI* Staff, "Top Ultra-Orthodox Rabbi Orders Schools Shut 'For Several Days' During Lockdown," *The Times of Israel*, September 7, 2021, https://www.timesofisrael.com/top-ultra-orthodox-rabbi-orders-schools-shut-for-several-days-during-lockdown/; *TOI* Staff, "Netanyahu Says Israel May Need to Extend Lockdown, Pleads with Haredim to Comply," *The Times of Israel*, January 18, 2021, https://www.timesofisrael.com/netanyahu-says-israel-may-need-to-extend-lockdown-pleads-with-haredim-to-comply/; *TOI* Staff, "Fresh Clashes in Bnei Brak as Haredi Leaders Blame Police for Violence," *The Times of Israel*, January 24, 2021, https://www.timesofisrael.com/fresh-clashes-in-bnei-brak-as-haredi-leaders-blame-police-for-violence/; *TOI* Staff, "Threatened with Fines, Top Haredi MK Insists Community Won't Shut Down Schools," *The Times of Israel*, October 18, 2020, https://www.timesofisrael.com/threatened-with-fines-top-haredi-mk-says-community-will-not-shut-down-schools/.
96. See Jacob Magid and *TOI* Staff, "Top Haredi Rabbi Kanievsky Orders Yeshivas Opened"; *TOI* Staff, "After Apparent Spat, Top Ultra-Orthodox Rabbis Announce Yeshivas not Reopening"; "New Letter from Rav Chaim Kanievsky and Rav Gershon Edelstein to Roshei Yeshiva and Mothers"; "Rabbi Kanievsy Orders Haredi Boys Schools to Reopen, then Rescinds His Decision."

C

Halakhah *and State*

CHAPTER 27

WHAT IS JEWISH LAW? A CONCEPTUAL VIEW FROM US COURTS

MICHAEL A. HELFAND

INTRODUCTION

IT is far from surprising that Jewish law has made recurring appearances in US courts.[1] Jews and Jewish communities have been features of American life since before the founding.[2] And by and large, when it has come to such cases, US courts have treated Jewish law—and the obligations Jewish law generates for its adherents—as religion. We see this not because Jewish law falls under the conceptual definition of religion as articulated by the American judiciary. To the contrary, courts—following the lead of the First Amendment[3]—have generally avoided providing a definition for religion,[4] leading to a voluminous body of literature attempting to fill this definitional void.[5]

Instead, Jewish law's predominant classification under the rubric of religion draws from how courts treat Jewish legal obligations when it comes to constitutional litigation. For example, when litigants file suit, seeking constitutional protection of Jewish ritual and practices, courts typically analyze such claims under the religion clauses of the First Amendment. In these circumstances, courts treat Jewish legal obligations as religious obligations and, by extension, Jewish law is treated as religion. Importantly, given the prominence of constitutional controversies implicating Jewish rituals and practices, Jewish law has, in the main, been classified as religion both inside and outside the courtroom.

But constitutional controversies do not represent the sum total of instances where Jewish law, and its attendant obligations, become subject to litigation inside American courtrooms. Indeed, at times Jewish law stands at the center of controversies over contracts and torts, where interpretations of obligations and standards for liability are based upon Jewish legal principles and terminology. Constitutional law, under the religious question doctrine, generally forbids courts from resolving disputes if doing so entails addressing matters of religious doctrine, practice, and theology. This constitutional prohibition presents a challenge for litigants whose claims are wrapped up in debates over Jewish law. How should a litigant advance a claim for breach of contract when the breach is a failure to provide the contractually required kosher food? What should a court make of a prenuptial agreement that requires a husband to pay his wife a daily fee as long as the two married in accordance with Jewish law? And how should a jury evaluate a defamation claim when the defamatory statement is phrased using theologically loaded terminology? In each of these cases, if Jewish law is viewed as religion and courts are constitutionally prohibited from resolving the underlying claim, then the underlying claims cannot be adjudicated in court.

For this reason, litigants have adopted over the years different strategies in an attempt to avoid having their claims dismissed on religious question grounds. At their core, such strategies try to reclassify Jewish law not as religion but instead as law or history or sociology. In so doing, litigants hope to avoid the dismissal of their claims as beyond the purview of civil courts. While such strategies have generally proven unsuccessful, they have drawn the legal machinery of US courts into debates over the conceptual nature of Jewish law.

The goal of this chapter is to consider the ways in which such disputes serve as a somewhat surprising venue for debates over the nature of Jewish law. The first part of this chapter begins with a summary of some of the more well-known constitutional controversies implicating Jewish law and how those debates have implicitly framed Jewish law as religion. In so doing, the chapter provides a recap of the big-ticket Jewish law cases that have animated the public perception—both inside and outside the courtroom—of Jewish law and Jewish legal obligations. The discussion then turns to the religious questions doctrine, exploring both its theoretical underpinnings and its doctrinal consequences, especially as it applies to cases involving Jewish law. The next two parts discuss two strategies litigants have used to avoid the religious question doctrine in Jewish law cases: (1) neutral principles of law and (2) the reclassification strategy. The first strategy focuses on how courts might avoid the religious question doctrine by looking to various methods to resolve a dispute that simply bypass the religious question at stake. The second strategy focuses on recasting Jewish law as something other than religion, thereby authorizing the court to resolve the underlying questions because they are not actually religious. While the former strategy has proven successful at times, the latter has proven uniformly unsuccessful.

Jewish Law and the Religious Question Doctrine

Courts have been most clear when Jewish law and legal obligation have been implicated in cases with underlying public law considerations.[6] Maybe the best set of examples come from prominent Supreme Court cases where Jewish litigants have levelled free exercise challenges against government regulations.[7] For example, in 1961, the Supreme Court rejected claims of Orthodox Jewish merchants who had argued—among other claims—that Sunday closing laws violated their religious liberty.[8] Similarly, in 1986, the Supreme Court rejected the religious liberty claims of Simcha Goldman, a commissioned officer and clinical psychologist in the Air Force, who had argued that Air Force regulations prohibiting the wearing of any headgear—including a yarmulke—violated his religious liberty rights.[9] And more recently, in 2020, Agudath Israel of America successfully challenged the constitutionality of Governor Cuomo's COVID public health restrictions on houses of worship, contending that they failed the test of religious neutrality required by the First Amendment.[10] In all these cases, the Court's application of religious liberty doctrine to these Jewish legal obligations—the Sabbath, the yarmulke, and prayer—clearly demonstrated the presumption that these practices were all religious in nature.

As Leora Batnitzky has powerfully argued, viewing Judaism and Jewishness solely through the prism of religion is deeply modern (see Batnitzky, this volume).[11] But given the modern foundations of American law and its approach to religion, it is far from surprising that Jewish legal obligations are typically viewed as—first, foremost and nearly exclusively—religious obligations. And this view is not restricted to the Supreme Court's jurisprudence. In some of the other more frequent areas of religious liberty litigation, lower courts have reached identical conclusions. Thus, for example, numerous courts have been faced with constitutional litigation over the construction of an *eruv*—an enclosure of varying sorts employed by Jewish communities to demarcate public property as (semi-)private property, thereby allowing for the otherwise-prohibited carrying of items on the Jewish Sabbath.[12] Legal controversies over the erection of an *eruv* come in different shapes and sizes, but they typically involve local ordinances prohibiting the placement of signs or items on public telephone poles; because an *eruv* is typically constructed with plastic strips (*lechis*) placed on telephone poles—with thin wires affixed to connect those poles into an unobtrusive enclosure of sorts—local ordinances prohibiting the affixing of items to telephone poles can prevent a community from creating an *eruv*.[13] In such cases, Jewish communities have filed suit, often arguing that such local ordinances have not been consistently applied and therefore the application of such ordinances only to an *eruv* constitutes a form of religious discrimination. Such controversies are often contentious, generating local political clashes between Jewish communities and local town officials. By and large, constitutional claims challenging legal impediments to the construction of an *eruv* have been successful.

Ritual circumcision is another Jewish practice at issue in recurring lower-court legal controversies. Perhaps the most well-known instance involved the proposed, and failed, 2011 San Francisco circumcision ban.[14] The penalty for engaging in the religious ritual of circumcision was "a fine not to exceed $1,000" and/or "imprisonment in the County Jail for a period not to exceed one year."[15] A California court ultimately stuck down the proposed ban—set for a referendum—both on the grounds that municipalities lacked authority to regulate a medical proceeding and because the ban violated the Free Exercise Clause.[16]

A more specific method of ritual circumcision—known as *metzitzah b'peh* (*MBP*)—also became a matter of litigation in New York federal court in 2012.[17] The *MBP* method, practiced primarily by some Hasidic sects of Judaism, requires the ritual circumciser to orally suck blood from the incision; the practice is highly controversial given that it can lead to the transmission of the herpes simplex virus to the baby and thereby—in some cases—causing brain damage or death.[18] The New York City Department of Health and Mental Hygiene attempted to regulate the practice by requiring informed consent of parents to the practice. However, a federal court ultimately struck the regulation down on free exercise grounds, finding in favor of Jewish organizations that had argued the regulation unconstitutionally targeted a religious practice.[19]

While this unremarkable underlying assumption—that Jewish practices qualify as religion—remains consistent in the high-profile landscape of religious liberty litigation, it also has significant consequences for how US courts treat—and don't treat—Jewish law.[20] Modern judicial interpretations of the Establishment Clause prohibit "civil courts [from] adjudicat[ing] disputes turning on church policy and administration or on religious doctrine and practice."[21] This doctrine—typically referred to as the "religious question doctrine"—is generally understood to prohibit courts from resolving cases where there is an "underlying controversy over religious doctrine or practice."[22] Accordingly, courts must "avoid . . . incursions into religious questions that would be impermissible under the [F]irst [A]mendment."[23] And in turn, they cannot "interpret[] ambiguous religious law and usage"[24] or resolve "controversies over religious doctrine and practice."[25] Applied to Jewish law, the religious question doctrine would prohibit courts from analyzing the demands of Jewish law or resolving controversies over Jewish doctrine or practice.

Scholars have long debated the underlying rationale behind the religious question doctrine.[26] For some, courts lack the constitutional competence to address claims that revolve around questions of faith because "[r]eligious experiences . . . may be incomprehensible to others" and are therefore "beyond the ken of mortals."[27] Others have argued that judicial resolution of religious questions might constitute an impermissible endorsement of one religious view over another.[28] And still others have argued, more fundamentally, that courts are constitutionally prohibited from resolving religious questions because such religious disputes remain a province and sovereignty beyond the authority of the state.[29] But regardless of theoretical grounding, the underlying assumption of these accounts is that the Establishment Clause has prohibited—and continues to prohibit—courts from *interrogating* the content of Jewish law; and to the extent a dispute requires that sort of inquiry, a court must dismiss the case pursuant to the religious question doctrine.

As I've argued previously,[30] these more recent assessments of the religious question doctrine appear to ignore judicial treatment of religious questions through the middle of the twentieth century. Indeed, some of the best examples of judicial willingness to evaluate religious questions come from cases involving Jewish law. Consider, for example, a number of early twentieth-century cases where courts adjudicated disputes over the disinterment of a body buried in a Jewish cemetery. The typical fact pattern involves a family seeking to move the body of a relative while the cemetery objects because doing so would, in their view, violate Jewish law. Under modern views of the religious question doctrine, these sorts of claims would likely be beyond the constitutional authority of a court to adjudicate. But early twentieth-century courts were not so reluctant. While they frequently acknowledged that "Ecclesiastical law is not a part of the law of this State, nor are equitable rights to be determined by it,"[31] they still found various ways to assess the content of Jewish law and incorporate that assessment into their final decision.[32] Thus, for example, a New York supreme court considered the petition of a husband to disinter his wife's body—and thereby move it to the family plot—notwithstanding the cemetery's resistance to the disinterment on the grounds that doing so would violate Jewish law.[33] In balancing the equitable consideration in favor of the husband, the court relied, in part, on various affidavits from Jewish law scholars as well as numerous traditional Jewish law sources,[34] concluding that there were legitimate views within Jewish law that the disinterment would not violate Jewish law.[35]

Similarly, another New York supreme court addressed the petition of children to disinter their father's body so that he could be buried alongside other relatives, including his deceased wife. Here the court once again mined Jewish law in reaching its conclusion, although this time it rejected the petition to disinter the body.[36] To be sure, not all courts relied on Jewish law in resolving such disputes. Judicial reluctance to do so did not flow from constitutional worries about resolving a religious question but from the proper scope of equitable principles relevant to adjudicating disputes over disinterment.[37]

Another example of courts addressing Jewish law questions involves early twentieth-century disputes implicating kosher standards. While prevailing constitutional doctrine prohibits courts from interpreting the term "kosher"—to do so would be to resolve a religious question—courts in the first half of the twentieth century unflinchingly interpreted and applied kosher requirements in a variety of contexts. For example, during the early 1900s, numerous states adopted kosher laws, intended to regulate the kosher food industry and thereby protect consumers from kosher fraud.[38] Given that such statutes expressly used the term "kosher" as the relevant category in kosher laws, courts or juries would have had to determine what the category meant as a threshold question to any conviction. And in these early years, numerous courts—including the US Supreme Court—not only did so willingly, but even rejected claims that the word "kosher" was "ambiguous" or "vague" such that conviction under such a statute was unlawful.[39] Similar judicial willingness to resolve claims which implicated the definition of "kosher" occurred in other legal contexts such as claims of slander[40] and breach of contract.[41]

Notwithstanding these examples, however, First Amendment jurisprudence has veered away from such a liberal attitude toward adjudicating religious questions. In more recent years, courts have dismissed such claims as requiring inquiries into the substance of Jewish law and therefore beyond their constitutional authority to resolve. For example, consider the 2012 lawsuit filed against ConAgra, the parent corporation of the Hebrew National brand, for violation of consumer protection laws, breach of contract, and negligence.[42] Hebrew National has long been famous in the United States for its "kosher" hotdogs, which it advertises as being of exceedingly high quality because the company "answers to a higher authority."[43] The plaintiffs highlighted these advertising claims of ConAgra, emphasizing that the company advertises and sells meat products under the Hebrew National label, describing them as "100% kosher" "as defined by the most stringent Jews who follow Orthodox Jewish law."[44] However, the plaintiffs contended that contrary to these representations, Hebrew National meat products did not satisfy these kosher standards.[45] Indeed, according to the complaint, employees informed the kosher certification companies that procedures had "rendered the meat being processed not kosher" and instead of acting on this information, "little or nothing" was done to correct these kosher violations.[46]

But instead of allowing the suit to move forward, two courts concluded that resolving the underlying claim would violate the First Amendment. A Minnesota district court dismissed the plaintiffs' claims, holding that "[t]he definition of the word 'kosher' is intrinsically religious in nature, and this Court may not entertain a lawsuit that will require it to evaluate the veracity of Defendant's representations that its Hebrew National products meet any such religious standard."[47] A Minnesota state court reached an identical conclusion, holding that "It would be unholy, indeed, for this or any other court to substitute its judgment on this purely religious question."[48]

Contemporary application of the religious question doctrine to Jewish law has not been limited to the sale of religious goods. In 2009, the US Court of Appeals for the Second Circuit addressed the lawsuit of a rabbi claiming that she had been wrongfully terminated; the synagogue countered that the rabbi had been justifiably terminated under the terms of the employment agreement for "gross misconduct" and "willful neglect of duty."[49] Normally, this would be the type of dispute where a fact-finder would weigh in by evaluating evidence to determine whether the rabbi's conduct justified the synagogue's decision to terminate employment. But instead, the federal district court hearing the case followed prevailing constitutional doctrine[50] and dismissed the case. The reason: review of the rabbi's claim "in this case would require scrutiny of whether she should have, *inter alia*, read more extensively from the Torah at certain services, prepared students for their Bar or Bat *Mitzvah* more adequately, performed certain pastoral services that were not performed, or followed the Temple's funeral service policies."[51] The court noted that these determinations "would involve impermissible judicial inquiry into religious matters."[52]

In sum, Jewish law—and the attendant expectations it generates—are now viewed by courts as off limits. Once Jewish law is viewed as religious, long gone are the days where courts hear testimony and evidence to determine who is correctly describing the content and demands of Jewish law. Instead, Jewish law—like other forms of religion and religious obligation—have become a black box "beyond the ken of mortals."[53]

So what choices does this leave parties whose disputes require interrogation of Jewish law? Does the modern incarnation of the religious question doctrine simply mean that disputes implicating Jewish law are off limits?

As an initial matter, the consequences for the religious question doctrine help explain one kind of motivation for Jewish litigants (as well as litigants from other faith communities) to enter arbitration agreements submitting matters implicating Jewish law to a *beth din* (rabbinical court).[54] While courts cannot resolve these cases, courts will enforce duly executed arbitration agreements to submit claims to religious arbitration even if they require adjudication of religious questions.[55] And similarly, courts uniformly enforce religious arbitration awards just like any other arbitration award, even where the underlying claims resolved by the arbitrators required adjudication of religious questions.[56] On both counts, the reason flows directly from the requirements of the religious question doctrine; as long as courts are not tasked with resolving religious questions, the constitutional constraints do not apply.[57] For these reasons, the religious question doctrine provides a powerful motivation for parties, with claims implicating Jewish law, to seek redress before a *beth din* thereby moving litigation over Jewish law out of US courts.[58]

But leaving US courts behind is not always palatable to litigants. In such cases, Jewish litigants have pursued strategic alternatives that attempt to recast Jewish legal inquiries in nonreligious terms. If such litigants could recast Jewish law and Jewish practice as a nonreligious affair, they could secure the adjudication and enforcement power of the state. And so, the cost of bringing Jewish law into US courts was to take religion out of Jewish law. The subsequent sections detail two strategic alternatives pursued by litigants. The first is to leverage the neutral principles of law framework, which aims to identify alternative methods to resolve religious disputes that focus solely on "objective, well-established concepts of . . . law familiar to lawyers and judges."[59] The second is what I term the "reclassification strategy," which refers to attempts by litigants to rebrand Jewish law as something other than religion—whether it be law or history or sociology. Of these strategies, the first is sometimes successful, albeit infrequently. The second has, for all intent and purposes, been rejected by courts. And together, the judicial reaction to such strategies demonstrates the powerful consequences of treating Jewish law as religion—and therefore subject to the religious question doctrine.

Jewish Law and Neutral Principles of Law

The classification of Jewish law as religion has, by and large, prevented courts from interrogating the substance of Jewish law. This is the most direct consequence of the First Amendment's religious question doctrine.

With respect to constitutional rights, there has been little attempt to recast Judaism or Jewish law as anything but religion. Although there have been instances where the Supreme Court has described a particular Jewish practice as not fundamentally religious in nature,[60] there has been no resistance to the idea that Jewish law obligations trigger First Amendment constraints with respect to, for example, the free exercise doctrine. In this way, big-ticket constitutional claims implicating Jewish legal obligations have further entrenched the notion of Jewish law as religion.

However, litigants in private law contexts have pursued strategic alternatives that avoid the consequences of the religious question doctrine. Indeed, plaintiffs advancing claims implicating Jewish legal doctrines and practices are incentivized to pursue strategic alternatives; failing to successfully to do so, courts will dismiss their claims pursuant to the religious question doctrine, thereby leaving them without a public forum to provide a legal remedy. In this way, private law claims often present the very opposite set of incentives to plaintiffs as do public law claims. To have your commercial claims adjudicated by a court, Jewish law cannot be religion; to have your constitutional claims heard by a court, Jewish law must be religion. The two operate at conceptual cross-purposes.

One way in which litigants have sought to extricate themselves from this conceptual quagmire is the Supreme Court's neutral principles of law framework. Under such a framework, as long as disputes can be resolved using nonreligious methods and terminology—what the Court described as "objective, well-established concepts of . . . law familiar to lawyers and judges"[61]—courts can adjudicate the claims. Such an approach encourages parties to disentangle religious disputes from religious questions, thereby allowing courts to resolve such disputes without threatening Establishment Clause principles.[62] Accordingly, while courts may not resolve "controversies over religious doctrine and practice"[63] and must "avoid . . . incursions into religious questions,"[64] courts can resolve religious disputes as long as the claims and documents at the heart of dispute can be interpreted and enforced through secular—as opposed to religious—means. In turn, the neutral principles of law framework aims to "free civil courts completely from entanglement in questions of religious doctrine, polity, and practice."[65] Where the stakes of a case are perceived by a court as nonreligious, it would have no need to dismiss claims on First Amendment grounds.

To see how this method has worked in practice—even in the years prior to its formal embrace by the Supreme Court—consider *Fisher v. Congregation B'Nai Yitzchok*, a 1955 case involving a contract between a Jewish congregation and Herman Fisher. According to the contract, Fisher was to officiate at Congregation B'nai Yitchok, a Philadelphia synagogue, as a cantor for the 1950 "high holiday season."[66] However, subsequent to the execution of the agreement, the synagogue—described in its charter as worshiping in accordance with the "faith, discipline, forms and rites of the orthodox Jewish religion"[67]—modified, in part, its practice of separate seating, allowing both men and women to sit together in all but the first eight rows of the sanctuary.[68] This presented a problem for Fisher based on his religious commitments. Accordingly, Fisher informed the synagogue that he could not officiate during their services.[69] Because Fisher learned of these changes to the synagogue shortly before the 1950 Jewish holiday season, Fisher was unable to find other comparable work and therefore filed suit against the synagogue to recoup his lost wages.

A trial court found in favor of Fisher based on the testimony of three rabbis affirming that "Orthodox Judaism required a definite and physical separation of the sexes in the synagogue."[70] This sort of finding, more typical of judicial decisions in the early part of the twentieth century, would seem to run afoul of contemporary interpretations of the religious question doctrine. But an appellate court reviewing the trial court decision ultimately found in favor of Fisher by emphasizing not the substantive content of Orthodox Jewish law and practice but rather the subjective intent of the parties. Thus, the court noted that the rabbi of the congregation had reaffirmed to Fisher at the time they entered the agreement the synagogue's status as an Orthodox Jewish synagogue, that the synagogue had always maintained separate seating, and that this policy would continue in the future.[71] This evidence allowed the court to find in favor of Fisher, concluding that the synagogue had breached the agreement because it violated a shared understanding of the agreement "in the light of custom or immemorial and invariable usage."[72] This methodological shift—away from religious inquiry and toward contract interpretation—represents how courts sometimes, although not often enough,[73] sidestep the religious question doctrine by relying on contextual methods of contract interpretation instead of expert testimony on the content of theological doctrine.

Cases like *Fisher*—where courts analyze disputes through the prism of private law methods such as subjective intent and commercial context—are, in more recent years, infrequent, but not isolated. Consider a more recent example from a Connecticut superior court, *Light v. Light*.[74] In *Light v. Light*, a court was asked to enforce a form prenuptial agreement, conceived of and drafted by a prominent rabbinical court[75]—the Beth Din of America.[76] The goal of the agreement is to provide the wife with financial leverage in the case of a Jewish divorce,[77] counterbalancing the fact that Jewish law grants the husband unilateral authority to initiate a divorce.[78] The key provision of the so-called Jewish prenup at stake in *Light* was the "support provision," which required the husband to support the wife in the amount of $100 per day in the event that the couple remained married under Jewish law, but ceased their domestic residence together.[79] Thus, the longer the husband refused to provide his wife with a Jewish divorce document, the larger his debt grew, thereby undermining the husband's ability to use divorce as a bargaining chip in negotiations related to the dissolution of the marriage.[80]

The husband in *Light* sought to have a Connecticut superior court invalidate the prenuptial agreement on the ground that enforcing such an agreement violated the Establishment Clause, arguing that "the prenuptial agreement refers to and reflects religious doctrine, protocols and ceremonies," and therefore could not be either interpreted or enforced by a civil court.[81] Indeed, if the court had attempted to interpret this provision in light of the substantive requirements of Jewish law and doctrine, it likely would have run afoul of First Amendment constraints.

The court, however, resisted the religious question doctrine and focused instead on intent and context—the kinds of considerations embraced by the neutral principles of law framework: "Determining whether the defendant owes the plaintiff the specified sum of money does not require the court to evaluate the proprieties of religious teachings. Rather, the relief sought by the plaintiff is simply to compel the defendant to perform a secular obligation, i.e., spousal support payments, to which he contractually bound himself."[82] In this way, judicial interpretation of the Jewish prenup stayed true to the religious question doctrine's demand that the black box of Jewish law should remain intact, and still enforced the underlying agreement.

It is important to note that this sort of adjudicative technique—avoiding Jewish law by analyzing contractual intent and context—is not only used to enforce agreements but it can similarly work to support judicial outcomes of nonenforcement. A good set of examples of nonenforcement is the series of court cases addressing *heter iska* (literally, permissible venture) agreements, which restructure loans as joint ventures in order to avoid Jewish law's prohibition against usury.[83] The intended borrower, instead of simply agreeing to pay interest, promises to pay a rate of return on an "investment," typically capped at a rate of return equal to the intended interest rate.[84] While sometimes such *heter iska* agreements will be executed as the sole agreement between the parties, they are often executed alongside some other document—anything from a standard loan agreement to mortgage documents.[85] This device, introduced into the Jewish commercial markets sometime between the twelfth and fourteenth centuries, enables market participants to grant interest-bearing loans—but under a different name—thereby technically avoiding charging interest in violation of Jewish law.[86]

Not surprisingly, courts have been asked on occasion to interpret such *heter iska* agreements in instances where the borrower's venture has failed and the creditor would like his loan repaid.[87] In such circumstances, the borrower will frequently cite the *heter iska* agreement and argue that the creditor bore the risk the venture would fail and therefore there is no remaining debt under the terms of the agreement.[88] In addressing such claims, courts have multiple methodological alternatives. They could simply enforce the agreement according to its terms, ignoring intent, context, and the like. Another option would be for courts to consider the theological underpinnings of the *heter iska* document—how that agreement is interpreted to function in accordance with Jewish law, which would bring a court into conflict with the religious question doctrine. But courts have, in the main, chosen a third alternative, which focuses inquiry on neutral principles of law, such as the subjective intent of the parties, thereby refusing to enforce such agreements where the parties only entered the agreement to satisfy a religious obligation and never intended for the agreements to be contractually binding.[89]

Pushing substantive Jewish law considerations to the background—and reducing them to private law considerations—has also been prevalent in recent court decisions addressing the impact of executing agreements under the specter of a *seruv*—that is, a Jewish contempt order issued by a rabbinical court. Under Jewish law, an individual who refuses to submit a dispute for arbitration before a rabbinical arbitration tribunal will receive a *seruv*, which conveys strong communal disapproval[90] and can carry significant social sanctions.[91] Such contempt orders have periodically made their way into court, with parties arguing that they only signed an arbitration agreement to submit a dispute to a *beth din* because they were threatened with a *seruv*, rendering—in their view—the signing of a *beth din* arbitration agreement as voidable on duress grounds. But courts have not been sympathetic to such claims of duress. As a result, they have painted a picture of Jewish law, practice, and ultimately communal affiliation as simply a form of voluntary association that ought not impact judicial interpretation and enforcement of contracts. As an example, consider a New York appellate court's analysis of a *seruv* and its relevance for enforcing contracts:

> The "threat" of a *siruv*, which entails a type of ostracism from the religious community, and which is prescribed as an enforcement mechanism by the religious law to which the petitioner freely adheres, cannot be deemed duress. . . . The record in the present case does not support a finding that the wife was subjected to any particular coercion greater than that which is intrinsic in the case of any member of a religious community who, as a matter of conscience, feels obligated to obey the laws of his or her religious organization, or to follow the decrees of a religious court, and who consequently exposes himself or herself to the ecclesiastical sanctions available for the enforcement of such decrees or such law.[92]

Other courts have reached similar outcomes, analyzing contempt orders under the private law framework of duress and then rejecting the defense.[93]

Of course, under this same framework, courts might conclude that communal pressure—and threats of social ostracism—might be sufficient under some circumstances to constitute duress and thereby invalidate agreements executed when one party was subject to such pressure.[94] But in doing so, a court would still be cabining analysis of communal enforcement of Jewish law under a private law framework, leveraging such considerations to determine whether the parties manifested sufficient assent to support the enforcement of an agreement. In this way, the *seruv* cases fit within the broader neutral principles of law methodology; Jewish law—and its attendant social consequences—remain a black box in substance, relevant to judicial decision-making only to the extent they generate challenges familiar to lawyers and judges.

Jewish Law and the Reclassification Strategy

Viewing Jewish law through the prism of the neutral principles of law framework is not always an option for courts. And even when it is, courts have often expressed reluctance to do so, falling into standard adjudicatory patterns of non-enforcement on religious question grounds.

It is therefore not surprising that at times litigants attempt to advance more ambitious claims that reclassify Jewish law as something other than religion. In doing so, they hope to avoid the religious question doctrine and open the possibility that courts will resist dismissing their claims on constitutional grounds before ever hearing the underlying merits. However, courts have not been sympathetic to this reclassification strategy. As examples, consider the attempts below to reclassify Jewish law as law, as sociology, and as history. In each case, the conceptual shift away from the religious question doctrine opened the possibility that a court might adjudicate the underlying claims at stake. In the end, however, none of these strategies based on reclassification proved successful.

Jewish Law as Law

One conceptual move to avoid the religious question doctrine is to reclassify Jewish law as law. Indeed, courts regularly adjudicate claims which require analysis of foreign law and, if necessary, supplement their analysis by securing expert testimony interpreting the foreign legal doctrines at stake.[95]

Maybe the most prominent failed attempt to employ this strategy came in the context of litigation over the constitutionality of kosher fraud statutes. Almost half the states in the United States have previously attempted to protect against kosher fraud by incorporating kosher-specific provisions into consumer protection statutes.[96] The perceived need for such statutory protections is not surprising once you consider US history with kosher fraud. Kosher fraud has been a rampant problem in the United States;[97] in fact, in the late nineteenth and early twentieth century, the kosher food business was typified by extortion, intimidation, and physical violence.[98]

But to specifically define and identify "kosher" as an object of consumer protection laws has triggered constitutional litigation. After all, how can courts determine when food is and is not kosher without running afoul of the religious question doctrine? And that is exactly what courts have done. For example, New Jersey enacted a regulation that made it "'an unlawful consumer practice' to sell or attempt to sell food 'which is falsely represented to be Kosher,'" which it defined as food "prepared and maintained in strict compliance with the laws and customs of the Orthodox Jewish religion."[99] The Supreme Court of New Jersey struck down those regulations because they fostered excessive entanglement with religion. The court reasoned that such disputes "would call inescapably on the State to assume a religious role" and to "impose and enforce its own interpretation of Orthodox Jewish doctrine."[100]

When New York faced analogous kosher fraud litigation—challenges to New York's rules focused, in part, on the repeated references to "orthodox Hebrew religious requirements"[101]—a number of rabbinical organizations, among others, intervened in the lawsuit before the Second Circuit, advancing the argument that "kosher" has an objective meaning, shared across Jewish denominations.[102] In their view, instead of capturing religious criteria, the term "kosher" simply "describe[d] the physical characteristics of food—their source, manner of slaughter and preparation."[103] According to this line of reasoning, New York's kosher law did not trigger the religious question doctrine because "the dietary standards are absolutely clear, entirely undisputed, and *remarkably mundane*."[104] If the laws of *kashrut* are mundane, then there can be no constitutional concern; there is no religious question at stake. In other words, as explained by the intervening parties:

> Since the term "kosher" relates to objectively ascertainable qualities of the product being sold—i.e., its ingredients and how it is being processed—this is not a case

> involving a term that has no objective meaning and has only theological significance. This case does not concern descriptive terms pertaining to religion that are amorphous and are definable only in religion terms. The word "kosher" has a well-established objective meaning when applied to the content and preparation of food. Nor is this a case in which enforcing consumer expectations will routinely catapult the state into interpretations of religious doctrine.[105]

Although this argument is pitched specifically in the context of kosher laws, one can easily see how it naturally expands to Jewish law generally. To the extent Jewish law advances rules that are objectively ascertainable, the interpretation and application of those rules do not require "amorphous" or "theological" inquiry. In this way, the nature of Jewish law's rules ought to put it beyond the constraints of the religious question doctrine. Courts should just treat Jewish law as any other form of law.[106]

The Second Circuit, however, explicitly rejected the Jewish law as law argument: "In order to assert that a food article does not conform to kosher requirements, New York must take an official position as to what are the kosher requirements."[107] In so doing, the court rejected the notion that government could interpret and enforce Jewish law without ultimately becoming entangled in religious questions. To enforce kosher law, explained the court, would require government to "either interpret religious doctrine or defer to the interpretations of religious officials in reaching its official position."[108] As it turns out, the Second Circuit was unwilling to reclassify Jewish law as law; to its mind, there was no way to take the religion out of Jewish law.

Jewish Law as History

Recasting Jewish law as law—as opposed to religion—is not the only conceptual alternative deployed in order to avoid the constraints of the religious question doctrine. Another strategy used is to view Jewish law as history. Accordingly, courts ought to be able to interpret and enforce Jewish law terminology because, as objective and ascertainable historical facts, they ought to be susceptible to judicial interpretation and application. Put differently, by reclassifying Jewish law as history—as opposed to religion—litigants can ask courts to interrogate questions of Jewish law because there is no prohibition on judicial inquiry into the past.

Consider, as an example, the case of *Sieger v. Sieger*.[109] In the context of a divorce, the wife's father—Michael Tenenbaum—sought to have a court enforce what he claimed was an arbitration provision that covered disputes between himself and his son-in-law regarding the distribution of shared assets.[110] This purported arbitration provision was located within a larger engagement contract, which the wife, the husband, and Tenenbaum all signed. The text of the provision stated that any disputes between the parties would be settled "in accordance with the 'regulations of Speyer, Worms, and Mainz.'"[111] Tenenbaum submitted the affidavit of an expert in Jewish

Law, which argued that "the engagement contract does in fact contain an arbitration clause" because "the regulations of Speyer, Worms, and Mainz provide that all disputes shall be submitted to a Beth Din for resolution."[112] This tracked the well-known historical fact that Speyer, Worms, and Mainz were the centers for the study and promulgation of Jewish law around the turn of the first millennium.[113] In this argument, the historical record is an objective, verifiable fact. Marshalling the historical record ought not require interrogation of theological content. Instead, parties should simply be required to prove what regulations were promulgated at Speyer, Worms, and Mainz, and if the evidence of such regulations is sufficient, courts should interpret and enforce the provisions as they would any other nonreligious contractual terms.

The court, however, rejected this attempt to reclassify Jewish law. In its view, interpreting and enforcing the purported arbitration provision in the engagement contract would violate the religious question doctrine: "[t]o do so under the circumstances of this case would violate the First Amendment because the engagement contract does not contain a provision that expressly provides for the resolution of disputes before a Beth Din, which would allow the court to decide the issue on neutral principles of contract law, without reference to any religious principles."[114]

Note how the court's invocation of the religious question doctrine relies on the classification of the contractual language as religious and not historical. It is why determining whether the clause "in accordance with the regulations of Speyer, Worms, and Mainz" included a requirement to arbitrate violated the First Amendment: "[t]o permit a party to introduce evidence or offer experts to dispute *an interpretation or application of religious requirements* would place [the court] in the inappropriate role of deciding whether religious law has been violated"[115] By contrast, if the clause had been read by the court as historical, expert testimony would have been well within constitutional bounds. Once again, the conceptual reclassification strategy did not work.[116]

Jewish Law as Sociology

There is one final version of the reclassification strategy—one where litigants encourage courts to view Jewish law not as part of the historical past, but as part of the sociological present. In this version, courts ought to be able to interpret and adjudicate the content of Jewish legal obligations by examining actual social practices. Accordingly, while the religious question doctrine may prohibit courts from interrogating the content of Jewish law, courts could avoid these constitutional prohibitions by simply engaging in a sociological inquiry that fits well within the parameters of the neutral principles of law approach to such questions.

As an example, consider the facts of *Abdelhak v. Jewish Press*.[117] The plaintiff, an Orthodox Jewish doctor specializing in high-risk obstetrics, sued a Jewish newspaper for publishing his name on a list of individuals against whom a rabbinical court had issued an order of contempt. According to the newspaper, this contempt order was for the plaintiff's failure to comply with the rabbinical court's rulings and provide his wife with a *get* (i.e., a Jewish divorce document).[118]

As it turned out, however, the plaintiff had not been issued a contempt order by a rabbinical court.[119] Both parties subsequently agreed that listing the plaintiff's name was a mistake and was based upon misinformation provided by an employee of the rabbinical court.[120] As a result, resolving the plaintiff's claim would not require the court to delve into the truth or falsity of the alleged defamatory statement—an inquiry that surely would run afoul of the religious question doctrine.

But the fact that the parties agreed the defamatory statement was false did not stop the defendant from arguing for dismissal on constitutional grounds. Instead, the defendant focused on the causal nexus between the defamatory statement and the financial consequences for the plaintiff. According to the plaintiff, the defamatory statement had damaged his reputation within the religious community; and, in turn, his medical practice was severely damaged by the newspaper's erroneous report of his religious transgressions. The defendant argued, however, the testing of this claim—that is, allowing the parties to submit evidence supporting this causal nexus—would constitute a violation of the religious question doctrine. After all, how could a court determine the professional consequences of a rabbinical court's contempt order without interrogating religious doctrine?

But this argument appears to paper over important conceptual distinctions that run to the heart of the reclassification strategy. Determining how members of a community would *view* someone against whom a rabbinical court issued a contempt order—in this instance, for refusing to grant his wife a *get*—does not obviously require resolving a religious question. And as a result, the plaintiff argued that the court could resolve the defamation claim without running afoul of the religious question doctrine.[121] In his view, evaluating the degree of damage caused by the defamation ought to be the kind of question susceptible to sociological inquiry—an inquiry that is wholly possible without becoming entangled with theology.

The court, however, rejected any attempt to differentiate between sociology and religion, dismissing the plaintiff's defamation claim on First Amendment grounds.[122] In its view, resolving the defamation claim would impermissibly entangle the court in religious doctrine as it "inevitably requires the application of religious doctrine, practices and belief that the First Amendment forbids."[123] In the court's view, "determin[ing] how much of the decline in plaintiff's income resulted from the defamatory Seruv Listing" would require the "jury . . . to develop a keen understanding of how an Orthodox Jew would view each such event."[124] But this sort of inquiry, according to the court, could not be viewed as secular because Orthodox Jewish perceptions of such an event are inextricable from Jewish law itself. As with the other reclassification strategies, the attempt to treat Jewish law as sociology failed. Jewish law, it seems, can only inhabit one conceptual category: religion.[125]

Conclusion: The Persistence of Jewish Law as Religion

When it comes to US courts, Jewish law is now treated like a black box. This treatment of Jewish law is the result of a relatively straightforward constitutional syllogism. Although courts up until the mid-twentieth century were willing to interrogate the substance of Jewish law, First Amendment jurisprudence—and in particular the religious question doctrine—has put a stop to such inquiries. Accordingly, religion is off limits for courts. And, because Jewish law is viewed as religion, courts will no longer adjudicate claims that require substantive assessment of Jewish law and practice.

That Jewish law is viewed through the singular conceptual category as religion is far from surprising. When it comes to big-ticket constitutional claims—and in particular, religious liberty claims—Jewish claimants have sought First Amendment protection for various Jewish practices. When a Jew wears a yarmulke, keeps the Sabbath, or worships in synagogue, they are engaged in a religious practice worthy of constitutional protection.

But matters become somewhat murkier as Jewish law moves from the realm of public law to private law—from constitutional protection to judicial interpretation. When it comes to commercial litigation, the consequence of subsuming particular Jewish law terms or practices under the umbrella of religion prevents parties in a range of cases from securing redress of legal harms. And so, not surprisingly, plaintiffs have attempted to remove religion from the equation. In some cases, they have done so by using various private law strategies, including an emphasis on subjective intent and commercial context. When such strategies are successful, litigants convince courts that neutral principles of law—as opposed to religious inquiry—provide a methodology sufficient to resolve the dispute without running afoul of the religious question doctrine. However, in many cases, neutral principles of law prove insufficient to resolve a religious dispute without violating the demands of the religious question doctrine. In such cases, parties have advanced an alternative strategy, attempting to conceptually reclassify Jewish law as something other than religion—whether it be law or history or sociology. Courts periodically embrace the neutral principles of law strategy—which presses Jewish law into the background of the litigation—but do so infrequently; the latter strategy—taking the religion out of Jewish law—has been by and large rejected by courts.

It is hard to blame courts for the lockstep classification of Jewish law as religion. As Ethan Leib and Tal Kastner have noted with respect to contract law, "judges and scholars tend to overlook how contract doctrines that are developed in one track creep into another and, in doing so, threaten to undermine the goals of distinctive tracks."[126] Thus, notwithstanding attempts to encourage courts to the contrary, the idea that Jewish law might be treated as religion in some cases but law or history or sociology in other cases appears to be a bridge too far. As a result, given the current jurisprudential trajectory, Jewish law is and will likely continue to be treated as religion whether it be for religious liberty protections under the First Amendment or for purposes of contract interpretation. And all told, Jewish law as a concept—with its multifarious doctrines and disputes—will remain a black box to the American legal system.

Notes

1. Jay M. Zitter, "Application, Recognition, or Consideration of Jewish Law by Court in United States," in *American Law Reports*, vol. 81, 6th ser. (Eagan, MN: Thomson Reuters, 2013), 1–96.
2. Naomi W. Cohen, *Jews in Christian America: The Pursuit of Religious Equality* (Studies in Jewish History) (New York: Oxford University Press, 1992).
3. See, e.g., Note, "Toward a Constitutional Definition of Religion," *Harvard Law Review* 91, no. 5 (March 1978): 1056 (noting that passed Supreme Court opinions addressing the religion clauses of the First Amendment had "enriched our understanding of how the religion clauses should be applied," but that it "failed adequately to define what religion is for first amendment purposes").
4. See, e.g., Eduardo Penalver, "Note. The Concept of Religion," *Yale Law Journal* 107, no. 3 (December 1997): 791–92 (describing the courts' "laissez-faire approach" as "assum[ing] that religion should be used for constitutional purposes in the same way that it is used in everyday language and, further, that its meaning and application are readily apparent").
5. Maybe the most well-known attempt is a *Harvard Law Review* note that suggested varying definitions based upon doctrinal context: Note, "Toward a Constitutional Definition of Religion." For a helpful summary of many such attempts, see Jeffrey L. Oldham, Note, "Constitutional 'Religion': A Survey of First Amendment Definitions of Religion," *Texas Forum on Civil Liberties & Civil Rights* 6, no. 1 (Summer 2001): 117–72.
6. Public law typically stands in opposition to private law. For explanations of this distinction, see John C. P. Goldberg, "Pragmatism and Private Law," *Harvard Law Review* 125, no. 7 (May 2012): 1640 ("Like many legal concepts, 'private law' has recognizable referents yet eludes precise definition. Private law defines the rights and duties of individuals and private entities as they relate to one another. It stands in contrast to public law, which establishes the powers and responsibilities of governments, defines the rights and duties of individuals in relation to governments, and governs relations between and among nations" [footnote omitted]); Gary T. Schwartz, "The Logic of Home Rule and the Private Law Exception," *UCLA Law Review* 20, no. 4 (April 1973): 688 ("Private law consists of the substantive law which establishes legal rights and duties between and among private entities, law that takes effect in lawsuits brought by one private entity against another. The complement of private law is thus 'public law'—the substantive law defining the legal obligations of private individuals or entities to the government, and also establishing their liberties and opportunities in relation to the government" [footnotes omitted]).
7. It is worth noting that Establishment Clause claims advanced by Jewish institution and communities before the Supreme Court have a far more complicated track record. See, e.g., County of Allegheny v. ACLU, 492 U.S. 573, 585 (1989) ("Chanukah, like Christmas, is a cultural event as well as a religious holiday. . . . Indeed, the Chanukah story always has had a political or national, as well as a religious, dimension: it tells of national heroism in addition to Divine intervention. Also, Chanukah, like Christmas, is a winter holiday; according to some historians, it was associated in ancient times with the winter solstice.

Just as some Americans celebrate Christmas without regard to its religious significance, some nonreligious American Jews celebrate Chanukah as an expression of ethnic identity, and as a cultural or national event, rather than as a specifically religious event" (citations and quotation marks omitted)). Leora Batnitzky, *How Judaism Became a Religion: An Introduction to Modern Jewish Thought* (Princeton, NJ: Princeton University Press, 2011), 186–92 (analyzing the Supreme Court's opinion in *Kiryas Joel v. Grumet* and assessing to what extent different Supreme Court Justices viewed Judaism as a religion).

8. Braunfeld v. Brown, 366 U.S. 599 (1961); Gallagher v. Crown Kosher Super Market, Inc., 366 U.S. 617 (1961).
9. Goldman v. Weinberger, 475 U.S. 503 (1986).
10. Roman Catholic Diocese of Brooklyn v. Cuomo, 141 S. Ct. 63 (2020).
11. Leora Batnitzky, *How Judaism Became a Religion: An Introduction to Modern Jewish Thought* (Princeton, NJ: Princeton University Press, 2011), 2 (noting that in the pre-modern period, "Judaism was not a religion, and Jewishness was not a matter of culture or nationality. Rather, Judaism and Jewishness were all these at once: religion, culture and nationality").
12. For a recent collection addressing the various facets of the *eruv*, see Adam Mintz, ed., *It's a Thin Line: Eruv from Talmudic to Modern Culture* (Brooklyn, NY: Ktav, 2014); see also Charlotte E. Fonrobert, "The Political Symbolism of the Eruv," *Jewish Social Studies* 11, no. 3 (Spring–Summer 2005): 9–35; Adam Mintz, "Halakhah in America: The History of City Eruvin, 1894–1962" (PhD diss., New York University, 2011), http://www.rabbimintz.com/wp-content/uploads/Mintz-Dissertation-Final.pdf.
13. As examples of this fact pattern, see Tenafly Eruv Ass'n v. Borough of Tenafly, 309 F.3d 144 (3d Cir. 2002); Bergen Rockland Eruv Ass'n v. Township of Mahwah, 2:17-cv-06054 (D.N.J. Aug. 11, 2017); Friedman v. Borough of Upper Saddle River, 2:17-cv-05512-JMV-CLW (D.N.J. July 27, 2011). Some *eruv* litigation has also focused on Establishment Clause considerations. See, e.g., Jewish People for the Betterment of Westhampton Beach v. Vill. of Westhampton Beach, 778 F.3d 390 (2d Cir. 2015); Smith v. Cmty. Bd. No. 14, 491 N.Y.S.2d 584 (Sup. Ct. 1985).
14. Matthew Hess, "San Francisco MGM Bill," MGMbill.org., accessed May 12, 2021. http://www.mgmbill.org/san-francisco-mgm-bill.html.
15. Ibid.
16. Order Granting Writ of Mandate at 3, Jewish Cmty. Relations Council of S.F. v. Arntz, Case No. CPF-11-511-370 (S.F. Cnty. Super. Ct., Apr. 6, 2012).
17. Cent. Rabbinical Cong. of the U.S. & Can. v. N.Y.C. Dep't of Health & Mental Hygiene, 763 F.3d 183 (2d Cir. 2014).
18. Ibid.; see also Sohail Wahedi, "The Health Law Implications of Ritual Circumcisions," *Quinnipiac Health Law Journal* 22, no. 2 (2019): 209–46.
19. *Cent. Rabbinical Cong.*, 763 F.3d 183.
20. This section addressing the underpinnings of the religious question doctrine draws heavily from Michael A. Helfand, "'The Peculiar Genius of Private-Law Systems': Making Room for Religious Commerce," *Washington University Law Review* 97, no. 6 (2020): 1787–1832.
21. Natal v. Christian & Missionary All., 878 F.2d 1575, 1576 (1st Cir. 1989). For more on the religious question doctrine, see Jared A. Goldstein, "Is There a Religious Question Doctrine? Judicial Authority to Examine Religious Practices and Beliefs," *Catholic University Law Review* 54, no. 2 (Winter 2005): 497–552; Samuel J. Levine, "Rethinking the Supreme Court's Hands-Off Approach to Questions of Religious Practice and Belief," *Fordham*

Urban Law Journal 25, no. 1 (1997–1998): 85–134; Christopher C. Lund, "Rethinking the Religious-Question Doctrine," *Pepperdine Law Review* 41, no. 5 (2014): 1013–28, https://digitalcommons.pepperdine.edu/plr/vol41/iss5/8.

22. Burgess v. Rock Creek Baptist Church, 734 F. Supp. 30, 31 (D.D.C. 1990).
23. Elmora Hebrew Ctr., Inc. v. Fishman, 593 A.2d 726, 730 (N.J. 1991). See, e.g., Serbian E. Orthodox Diocese for U.S. & Can. V. Milivojevich, 426 U.S. 696, 709 (1976); *Natal*, 878 F.2d at 1576; *Burgess*, 734 F. Supp. at 31.
24. *Serbian E. Orthodox Diocese*, 426 U.S. at 708.
25. Presbyterian Church in U.S. v. Mary Elizabeth Blue Hull Mem'l Presbyterian Church, 393 U.S. 440, 450 (1969).
26. For an excellent taxonomy, see Richard W. Garnett, "A Hands-Off Approach to Religious Doctrine: What Are We Talking About?," *Notre Dame Law Review* 84, no. 2 (January 2009): 855–63.
27. United States v. Ballard, 322 U.S. 78, 86–87 (1944); see also Thomas v. Rev. Bd. of the Ind. Emp. Sec. Div., 450 U.S. 707, 716 (1981) ("Courts are not arbiters of scriptural interpretation"). See generally Ira C. Lupu and Robert W. Tuttle, "Courts, Clergy, and Congregations: Disputes between Religious Institutions and Their Leaders," *Georgetown Journal of Law & Public Policy* 7, no. 1 (Winter 2009): 119–64.
28. See, e.g., Laurence H. Tribe, *American Constitutional Law*, 2nd ed. (University Textbook Series) (Mineola, NY: Foundation Press, 1988), §14–11, 1231 (arguing that the prohibition against "doctrinal entanglement in religious issues . . . [m]ore deeply . . . reflects the conviction that government—including the judicial as well as the legislative and executive branches—must never take sides on religious matters"); Christopher L. Eisgruber and Lawrence G. Sager, "Does It Matter What Religion Is?," *Notre Dame Law Review* 84, no. 2 (January 2009): 812 ("If government were to endorse some interpretations of religious doctrine at the expense of others, it would thereby favor some religious persons, sects, and groups over others"); Kent Greenawalt, "Religious Law and Civil Law: Using Secular Law to Assure Observance of Practices with Religious Significance," *Southern California Law Review* 71, no. 4 (May 1998): 804 (worrying that judicial resolution of interdenominational disputes may be perceived as "the possible endorsement of one minority group").
29. Andrew Koppelman, "Corruption of Religion and the Establishment Clause," *William and Mary Law Review* 50, no. 6 (May 2009): 1897–98 ("The legitimate authority of the state does not extend to religious questions" because adjudication of such questions would lead to the "corruption" of religion—that is, "[r]eligious teachings are likely to be altered, in a pernicious way, if the teachers are agents of the state"); Garnett, "A Hands-Off Approach to Religious Doctrine," 861 ("[S]ecular authorities lack the power to answer some questions—religious questions—whose resolution is, under an appropriately pluralistic political theory, left to other institutions" [emphasis omitted]).
30. Michael A. Helfand, "Litigating Religion," *Boston University Law Review* 93, no. 2 (March 2013): 493–562.
31. Cohen v. Congregation, 99 N.Y.S. 732, 734 (App. Div. 1906).
32. See, e.g., Seifer v. Schwimmer, 1 N.Y.S.2d 730, 731–32 (Sup. Ct. 1937) ("This, however, does not mean that religious usages are to be totally disregarded, for as was declared in *Yome v. Gorman* [242 N.Y. 395, 403]: 'Subordinate in importance, and yet at times not wholly to be disregarded, are the sentiments and usages of the religious body which confers the right of burial.' We may not and will not, therefore, entirely discard the religious aspect of the question herein involved and decide it on purely secular grounds").

33. *In re* Katz, 3 N.Y.S.2d 754 (Sup. Ct. 1938).
34. Ibid. (quoting, for example, from both the *Shulchan Aruch* [Code of Jewish Law] and the *Kitzur Shulchan Aruch* [Abridged Code of Jewish Law]).
35. Ibid. at 758 ("If eminent Rabbis differ upon the interpretation of this phrase, one group interpreting it strictly and the other liberally, it seems to me justified for this court of equity to be guided by the liberal point of view, where, as here, all of the nearest of kin of the decedent desire the removal of the body to a family plot").
36. *Seifer*, 1 N.Y.S.2d at 732 (noting that the court's decision gave due consideration to, among other factors, "that part of the Code of Maimonedes concerning the defilement of the dead (Tumas Mais)" and "to that portion of the Schulchan Aruch referring to the burial of the dead, maintenance of the grave, and disinterment").
37. See, e.g., Cohen v. Congregation, 99 N.Y.S. 732, 734 (App. Div. 1906) ("[W]hen a court of equity exercises its powers, it does so only upon equitable principles, irrespective of ecclesiastical or any other law"); see also Friedman v. Agudath Achim N. Shore Congregation, 115 N.E.2d 553, 556 (Ill. App. Ct. 1953) (finding in favor of the cemetery not by "substituting religious tenets and laws for the laws of the State," but by "giving effect to a lawful agreement of the parties and determining their rights thereunder by the standard which they have fixed for that purpose").
38. For some discussion of this approach to kosher regulation in the early twentieth-century, see Timothy D. Lytton, *Kosher: Private Regulation in the Age of Industrial Food* (Cambridge, MA: Harvard University Press, 2013), 27–29.
39. See, e.g., Hygrade Provision Co. v. Sherman, 266 U.S. 497, 502 (1925) ("Furthermore, the evidence, while conflicting, warrants the conclusion that the term 'kosher' has a meaning well enough defined to enable one engaged in the trade to correctly apply it, at least as a general thing. If exceptional cases may sometimes arise where opinions might differ, that is no more than is likely to occur, and does occur, in respect of many criminal statutes either upheld against attack or never assailed as indefinite"); People v. Atlas, 170 N.Y.S. 834, 835–36 (App. Div. 1918) ("It is manifest, however, that the Legislature did not intend to use the word 'kosher' in an indefinite sense, but evidently in the ordinary sense in which it is used in the trade, which is to designate meat as having been prepared under and of a product sanctioned by said religious requirements, and, therefore, as I view it, the Legislature has itself definitely defined the word 'kosher' as used in the statute. This construction leaves the statute sufficiently definite and confines it to those who, with intent to defraud, sell or expose for sale meat or meat preparation and falsely represent the same as having been prepared under and of a product or products sanctioned by the orthodox Hebrew requirements"); Erlich v. Mun. Ct. of Beverly Hills Jud. Dist., 360 P.2d 334 (1961) (citing *Hygrade* and *Atlas*).
40. See, e.g., Cohen v. Eisenberg, 19 N.Y.S.2d 678, 681 (Sup. Ct. 1940) ("This court is unwilling to hold that poultry which would otherwise meet every requirement to make it kosher—requirements that have been established for centuries—and which would be kosher if slaughtered and prepared in any place in the world except the city of New York, would become non-kosher solely because it was slaughtered and prepared in an establishment not maintained under the auspices of an incorporated organization by no means universally accepted as an arbiter by those of the Jewish faith").
41. See, e.g., Berk v. Gordon Johnson Co., 232 F. Supp. 682 (E.D. Mich. 1964) (holding that the contract term "kosher operation" could function as an enforceable express warranty).
42. Class Action Complaint, Wallace v. ConAgra Foods, Inc., 920 F. Supp. 2d 995 (D. Minn. 2013) (No. 0:12-cv-01354-DWF-TNL).

43. Class Action Complaint at 24, *Wallace*, 920 F. Supp. 2d 995 (No. 0:12-cv-01354-DWF-TNL); see also "We Answer to a Higher Authority," Wikipedia, last modified June 6, 2022, https://en.wikipedia.org/wiki/We_answer_to_a_higher_authority.
44. Class Action Complaint at 3, *Wallace*, 920 F. Supp. 2d 995 (No. 0:12-cv-01354-DWF-TNL).
45. Class Action Complaint at 17-21, *Wallace*, 920 F. Supp. 2d 995 (No. 0:12-cv-01354-DWF-TNL).
46. Class Action Complaint at 21, *Wallace*, 920 F. Supp. 2d 995 (No. 0:12-cv-01354-DWF-TNL).
47. Wallace v. ConAgra Foods, Inc., 920 F. Supp. 2d 995, 999 (D. Minn. 2013).
48. Wallace v. ConAgra Foods, Inc., 19HA-CV-12-3237, slip op. at 4 (D. Minn. Oct. 6, 2014).
49. Friedlander v. Port Jewish Ctr., 347 Fed. App'x 654 (2d Cir. 2009).
50. For other similar examples, see Leavy v. Congregation Beth Shalom, 490 F. Supp. 2d 1011, 1026 (N.D. Iowa 2007); Kraft v. Rector, Churchwardens & Vestry of Grace Church, No. 01-CV-7871, 2004 U.S. Dist. LEXIS 4234, at *22–23 (S.D.N.Y. Mar. 15, 2004).
51. *Friedlander*, 347 Fed. App'x at 655.
52. Ibid., 655. This outcome is not unique.
53. United States v. Ballard, 322 U.S. 78, 87 (1944).
54. I have expanded on this point elsewhere. See Michael A. Helfand, "Privatization and Pluralism in Dispute Resolution: Promoting Religious Values through Contract," in *Christianity and Private Law*, ed. Robert F. Cochran, Jr., and Michael P. Moreland (New York: Routledge, 2021): 219–35; Michael A. Helfand, "*Beit Din*'s Gap-Filling Function: Using *Beit Din* to Protect Your Client," *Journal of the Beth Din of America* 2 (2014): 31–47.
55. Meshel v. Ohev Sholom Talmud Torah, 869 A.2d 343, 354 (D.C. 2005) (noting that courts must simply inquire "whether the parties have an enforceable agreement to arbitrate and, if so, whether the underlying dispute between the parties falls within the scope of the agreement").
56. See, e.g., Abd Alla v. Mourssi, 680 N.W.2d 569, 574 (Minn. Ct. App. 2004) (upholding a decision of an Islamic arbitration panel applying Islamic law); Kingsbridge Ctr. of Israel v. Turk, 469 N.Y.S.2d 732, 734 (App. Div. 1983) (confirming a *beth din* decision because the parties consented, through written agreement, to have a *beth din* panel adjudicate the matter); Kovacs v. Kovacs, 633 A.2d 425, 433 (Md. Ct. Spec. App. 1993) (confirming a *beth din* award because the parties "knowingly chose" to participate in arbitration).
57. Helfand, "'The Peculiar Genius of Private-Law Systems,'" 1804–5; Helfand, "Litigating Religion," 506–9.
58. Religious arbitration, however, is not a panacea. For some of the reasons why, see Michael A. Helfand and Barak D. Richman, "The Challenge of Co-Religionist Commerce," *Duke Law Journal* 64, no. 5 (February 2015): 782–83 n. 53.
59. Jones v. Wolf, 443 U.S. 595, 603 (1979).
60. See, e.g., Cnty. of Allegheny v. ACLU, 492 U.S. 573, 585 (1989) ("Just as some Americans celebrate Christmas without regard to its religious significance, some nonreligious American Jews celebrate Chanukah as an expression of ethnic identity, and as a cultural or national event, rather than as a specifically religious event" [citations and quotation marks omitted]); Minkin v. Minkin, 434 A.2d 665, 668 (N.J. Super. Ct. 1981) ("Relying upon credible expert testimony that the acquisition of a get is not a religious act, the court finds that the entry of an order compelling defendant to secure a *get* would have the clear secular purpose of completing a dissolution of the marriage").
61. *Jones*, 443 U.S. at 603.
62. See, e.g., Presbyterian Church in U.S. v. Mary Elizabeth Blue Hull Mem'l Presbyterian Church, 393 U.S. 440, 449 (1969) ("[T]he [First] Amendment therefore commands civil

courts to decide church property disputes without resolving underlying controversies over religious doctrine").

63. Ibid., 449–50 ("But First Amendment values are plainly jeopardized when church property litigation is made to turn on the resolution by civil courts of controversies over religious doctrine and practice").
64. Elmora Hebrew Ctr., Inc. v. Fishman, 593 A.2d 726, 730 (N.J. 1991).
65. Ibid., 730.
66. Fisher v. Congregation B'Nai Yitzhok, 177 Pa. Super. 359 (1955).
67. Ibid., 361.
68. Ibid., 361–62.
69. Ibid., 362.
70. Ibid., 362.
71. Ibid., 364.
72. Ibid., 365.
73. I have criticized judicial reluctance to engage in this sort of contextual or anti-formalist analysis on a number of occasions. See, e.g., Helfand and Richman, "The Challenge of Co-Religionist Commerce"; Helfand, "'The Peculiar Genius of Private-Law Systems.'"
74. Light v. Light, No. NNHFA124051863S, 2012 Conn. Super. LEXIS 2967 (Dec. 6, 2012).
75. Beth Din of America, "Beth Din of America Prenuptial Agreement," https://theprenup.org/the-prenup-forms/.
76. For a discussion of the innovations of the Beth Din of America and for the potential lessons to be gleaned from these innovations, see Michael J. Broyde, "Jewish Law Courts in America: Lessons Offered to Sharia Courts by the Beth Din of America Precedent," *New York Law School Law Review* 57, no. 2 (2012/13): 287–312.
77. Michelle Greenberg-Kobrin, "Civil Enforceability of Religious Prenuptial Agreements," *Columbia Journal Law & Social Problems* 32, no. 4 (Summer 1999): 359–99.
78. This asymmetry has long been an issue of concern within the Jewish community and has been the topic of significant scholarly commentary. See, e.g., Greenawalt, "Religious Law and Civil Law," 811–812; Ayelet Shachar, "The Puzzle of Interlocking Power Hierarchies: Sharing the Pieces of Jurisdictional Authority," *Harvard Civil Rights-Civil Liberties Law Review* 35, no. 2 (Summer 2000): 385–426; Suzanne Last Stone, "The Intervention of American Law in Jewish Divorce: A Pluralist Analysis," *Israel Law Review* 34, no. 2 (Summer 2000): 170–210; Ann Laquer Estin, "Embracing Tradition: Pluralism in American Family Law," *Maryland Law Review* 63, no. 3 (2004): 540–604; Irving Breitowitz, "The Plight of the *Agunah*: A Study in *Halacha*, Contract and the First Amendment," *Maryland Law Review* 51 no. 2 (1992): 312–421; see also Levmore and Gotlib, this volume.

    In response to these issues, New York State has famously adopted two "*Get* Statutes," which attempt to authorize courts to take the failure of a husband to provide his wife with a Jewish divorce document into account when granting a secular divorce and dividing the marital assets: N.Y. Dom. Rel. Law §253 (LEXIS through 2023 released Chapter 1–49); N.Y. Dom. Rel. Law §§236B(5)(h), (6)(d) (LEXIS through 2023 released Chapter 1–49); see also Lisa Zornberg, "Beyond the Constitution: Is the New York *Get* Legislation Good Law?," *Pace Law Review* 15 no. 3 (Spring 1995): 703–86.

    In addition to the so-called Jewish prenup, parties have also sought to secure a husband's agreement to provide a *get* via the *ketuba* or by using settlement agreements, although with somewhat uneven outcomes. In some instances, courts have interpreted contractual instruments, including the *ketuba*, to require a husband to provide his wife with a *get*. See, e.g.,

In re Marriage of Goldman, 554 N.E.2d 1016, 1023 (Ill. App. 1990) (affirming lower court's interpretation of a *ketuba* to require husband to provide a *get*, notwithstanding husband's constitutional objections, because "the trial court merely applied well-established principles of contract law to enforce the agreement made by the parties. The terms of the order were carefully limited to avoid interference with religious doctrine"); Koeppel v. Koeppel, 138 N.Y.S.2d 366, 373 (Sup. Ct. 1954) ("Complying with his agreement would not compel the defendant to practice any religion, not even the Jewish faith to which he still admits adherence"); Minkin v. Minkin, 434 A.2d 665, 668 (N.J. Super. Ct. 1981) ("Relying upon credible expert testimony that the acquisition of a *get* is not a religious act, the court finds that the entry of an order compelling defendant to secure a *get* would have the clear secular purpose of completing a dissolution of the marriage"). In other instances, courts have refused to do so either on contract or constitutional grounds. See, e.g., Victor v. Victor, 866 P.2d 899, 902 (Ariz. Ct. App. 1993) ("If this court were to rule on whether the *ketubah*, given its indefinite language, includes an unwritten mandate that a husband under these circumstances is required to grant his wife a *get*, we would be overstepping our authority and assuming the role of a religious court. This we decline to do. We hold that, in this case, as a matter of law, the *ketubah* does not constitute an enforceable antenuptial agreement"); Tilsen v. Benson, 2019 Conn. Super. LEXIS 2475, at *14 (Super. Ct. Sept. 11, 2019) ("The court concludes that it cannot interpret the 'Torah law' provision of the parties' Ketubah using strictly neutral, secular legal principles").

79. *Light*, 2012 Conn. Super. LEXIS at *3.
80. For further discussion, see Mordechai Willig, "The Prenuptial Agreement: Recent Developments," *Journal of the Beth Din of America* 1 (2012): 12–16; Lang v. Levi, 16 A.3d 980 (Md. App. 2011) (enforcing religious arbitration award modifying amount of payment pursuant to a Jewish prenuptial agreement).
81. *Light*, 2012 Conn. Super. LEXIS at *6–7.
82. Ibid., *19.
83. See Zitter, "Application, Recognition, or Consideration of Jewish Law by Court in United States"; Steven H. Resnicoff, "A Commercial Conundrum: Does Prudence Permit the Jewish 'Permissible Venture?'" *Seton Hall Law Review* 20, no. 1 (1989): 80–85.
84. For further analysis of the Jewish law rules applicable to the *heter iska*, see Yisroel Reisman, *The Laws of Ribbis* (Brooklyn, NY: Mesorah, 1995), 377–407; J. David. Bleich, *Contemporary Halakhic Problems*, vol. 2 (New York: Ktav, 1983), 376–85 (discussing the Jewish legal background to *heter iska* agreements).
85. See, e.g., Heimbinder v. Berkovitz, 670 N.Y.S.2d 301 (Sup. Ct. 1998) (executed alongside loan documents); Edelkind v. Fairmont Funding, Ltd., 539 F. Supp. 2d 449 (D. Mass. 2007) (executed alongside mortgage documents); Barclay Commerce Corp. v. Finkelstein, 205 N.Y.S.2d 551 (App. Div. 1960) (executed alongside a factoring agreement).
86. See Leibovici v. Rawicki, 290 N.Y.S.2d 997, 1000 (Civ. Ct. 1968) ("*Hetter Isske* or *heter 'iska'* was a device developed in the twelfth to fourteenth centuries to overcome the Biblical prohibition against charging interest by one Jew to another"); Bleich, *Contemporary Halakhic Problems*, 376–85 (discussing the Jewish legal background to *heter iska* agreements). For examples of such agreements, see Reisman *The Laws of Ribbis*, 419–24 (providing boilerplate *heter iska* agreements for use in different commercial contexts); Bleich, *Contemporary Halakhic Problems*, 385–388 (same). It is also worth noting that *heter iska* agreements typically incorporate heightened evidentiary requirements to prove the venture's losses, intended to impede the ability of the borrower from avoiding his payments to the lender. Reisman, *The Laws of Ribbis*, 377–407.

87. See, e.g., *Barclay*, 205 N.Y.S.2d 551 (attempting to avoid payment of outstanding debts on the basis of a *heter iska* agreement).
88. Ibid.
89. See, e.g., *Edelkind*, 539 F. Supp. 2d 449; Arnav Indus., Inc. v. Westside Realty Assoc., 579 N.Y.S.2d 382 (App. Div. 1992); *Barclay*, 205 N.Y.S.2d 551; *Leibovici*, 290 N.Y.S.2d 997.
90. See Estin, "Embracing Tradition," 470–72 (discussing sanctions used by religious groups to influence and respond to the choices made by individual group members).
91. See, e.g., *In re* Herman Pachman, No. 09-37475, 2010 WL 1489914 (Bankr. S.D.N.Y. Apr. 14, 2010) (alleging that a *seruv*, issued by a rabbinical court, led other members of the religious community to avoid doing business with the petitioner and to refuse marrying their children to petitioner's children); Abdelhak v. Jewish Press, Inc., 985 A.2d 197 (N.J. Super. Ct. App. Div. 2009) (alleging that plaintiff lost the patronage of his Orthodox Jewish clientele as a result of a *seruv*).
92. Greenberg v. Greenberg, 656 N.Y.S.2d 369, 370 (App. Div. 1997).
93. See Lieberman v. Lieberman, 566 N.Y.S.2d 490, 494 (Sup. Ct. 1991); Mikel v. Scharf, 432 N.Y.S.2d 602, 606 (Sup. Ct. 1980) ("Undoubtedly, pressure was brought to bear to have them participate in the Din Torah, but pressure is not duress. Their decision to acquiesce to the rabbinical court's urgings was made without the coercion that would be necessary for the agreement to be void").
94. Indeed, I have advocated for such an approach on a number of occasions. See Michael A. Helfand, "Arbitration's Counter-Narrative: The Religious Arbitration Paradigm," *Yale Law Journal* 124, no. 8 (June 2015): 2994–3051; Michael A. Helfand, "Religious Arbitration and the New Multiculturalism: Negotiating Conflicting Legal Orders," *New York University Law Review* 86, no. 5 (Nov. 2011): 1231–1305.
95. I have previously advocated for such an approach. See Helfand, "Litigating Religion"; Michael A. Helfand, "Between Law and Religion: Procedural Challenges to Religious Arbitration Awards," *Chicago-Kent Law Review* 90, no. 1 (2015): 141–62.
96. See Barghout v. Bureau of Kosher Meat & Food Control, 66 F.3d 1337, 1340 n. 5 (4th Cir. 1995) (listing twenty-one states that have adopted such laws).
97. Lytton, *Kosher*, 9–35.
98. Ibid., 10.
99. Ran-Dav's Cnty. Kosher, Inc. v. State, 608 A.2d 1353, 1355 (N.J. 1992).
100. Ibid., 1364.
101. Commack Self-Service Kosher Meats, Inc. v. Weiss, 294 F.3d 415, 418 (2d Cir. 2002).
102. Brief for the Intervenor-Appellants at 16, *Commack*, 294 F.3d 415 (No. 00-9116, 00-9118).
103. Ibid., 17, *Commack*, 294 F.3d 415 (No. 00-9116, 00-9118).
104. Ibid., 17, *Commack*, 294 F.3d 415 (No. 00-9116, 00-9118).
105. Ibid., 18, *Commack*, 294 F.3d 415 (No. 00-9116, 00-9118).
106. I have previously expressed similar criticism of the court's opinion for failing to adopt this approach. See, e.g., Michael A. Helfand, "Fighting for the Debtor's Soul: Regulating Religious Commercial Conduct," *George Mason Law Review* 19, no. 1 (Fall 2011): 157–96.
107. *Commack*, 294 F.3d at 427.
108. Ibid., 427.
109. Sieger v. Sieger, 747 N.Y.S.2d 102 (App. Div. 2002).
110. Ibid., 103.
111. Ibid., 103.
112. Ibid., 103.

113. See Menachem Elon, *Jewish Law: History Sources Principles*, vol. 2 (Philadelphia: Jewish Publication Society, 1994), 788 (discussing the enactments of "shum"—the transliteration of the Hebrew acronym for Speyer, Worms and Mainz).
114. *Sieger*, 747 N.Y.S.2d at 104.
115. Ibid., 747 N.Y.S.2d at 105 (citing Lightman v. Flaum, 761 N.E.2d 1027 [N.Y. Ct. App. 2001]) (emphasis added).
116. Sometimes attempts to leverage history can also incorporate questions of geography. What such strategies share is an attempt to have courts interrogate religious questions by arguing that the terms are ascertainable by simply interrogating the past, which in this view is an objective ascertainable fact not subsumed under the religious question doctrine. As another example, see Katz v. Singerman, 127 So. 2d 515, 517–19 (La. 1961) (rejecting an argument that a donor agreement, which required that the donee synagogue operate "worship according to the strict ancient and orthodox forms" and "Orthodox Polish Jewish Ritual," prohibited changing the synagogue's practice from separate sex seating in the sanctuary to mixed seating).
117. Abdelhak v. Jewish Press, Inc., 985 A.2d 197 (N.J. Super. Ct. App. Div. 2009)
118. Ibid., 200–202; see also Greenberg-Kobrin, "Civil Enforceability of Religious Prenuptial Agreements."
119. *Abdelhak*, 985 A.2d at 201–2.
120. Ibid., 201–2.
121. Ibid., 208.
122. Ibid., 211. Similar First Amendment concerns arise in the context of "shunning" in religious communities. See Justin K. Miller, "Comment. Damned if You Do, Damned if You Don't: Religious Shunning and the Free Exercise Clause," *University of Pennsylvania Law Review* 137, no. 1 (November 1988): 272. As examples of this dynamic, see Burgess v. Rock Creek Baptist Church, 734 F. Supp. 30, 34 (D.D.C. 1990); Sands v. Living Word Fellowship, 34 P.3d 955, 959 (Alaska 2001); Anderson v. Watchtower Bible & Tract Soc'y of N.Y., Inc., 2007 Tenn. App. LEXIS 29, 61–62 (2007) ("Shunning is religiously based conduct, a religious practice based on interpretation of scripture, and is subject to the protection of the First Amendment. . . . No tort liability can be imposed for shunning alone"); Grunwald v. Bornfreund, 696 F. Supp. 838, 841 (E.D.N.Y. 1988).
123. *Abdelhak*, 985 A.2d at 210–11.
124. Ibid., 208.
125. I have elsewhere criticized the court's decision in *Abdelhak* for its insistence in applying the religious question doctrine. See, e.g., Helfand, "Fighting for the Debtor's Soul," 193–95; Helfand and Richman, "Challenge of Co-Religionist Commerce," 809–10.
126. Tal Kastner and Ethan J. Leib, "Contract Creep," *Georgetown Law Journal* 107, no. 5 (May 2019): 1279.

[illegible]

the eradication of "shun" [illegible]

Voices and Visions [illegible]

[illegible]

Ibid. [illegible]

[illegible]

Ibid. [illegible]

CHAPTER 28

ISSUR ARKAOT AND *DINA DEMALKHUTA DINA*

Interrelationships between Jewish and Secular Legal Systems

STEVEN H. RESNICOFF

Introduction

In its scope and pervasiveness, Jewish law (*halakhah*) differs significantly from the laws of most religions. Not only does it comprehensively cover devotional practices, holidays, family relations, and life milestones, but it also addresses a broad gamut of private and public matters including crimes, torts, commercial transactions, domestic relations, inheritance, taxation, eminent domain, and extradition. *Halakhic* decisions are primarily rendered by religiously trained rabbis, either individually or as members of a rabbinic court, or through a rabbinically approved dispute resolution process. As discussed elsewhere in this volume, the Talmud is not only Judaism's principal legal text, but it is also its premiere religious text, weaving together discussions regarding law, ethics, and theology.[1] The all-encompassing nature of Jewish law, its dependence on rabbinic authorities, and its profound interrelationship with spiritual teachings suffuse virtually all aspects of Jewish life with religious meaning.

Throughout most of the past two thousand years, however, Jews lived in lands governed by non-Jews. The ideals of reigning non-Jewish legal regimes threatened to displace those of Jewish law, and the power of non-Jewish judicial institutions jeopardized respect for rabbinic authorities and imperiled the commitment to the study of Jewish legal-spiritual literature. In addition, Jewish rejection of non-Jewish laws, especially those of special interest to the government such as its taxing and eminent domain regulations, could deeply offend non-Jewish rulers and arouse them to adopt harsh punitive measures against their Jewish communities.

Two complex and controversial Jewish law principles have blunted these dangers. The first, *Issur Arkaot,* addresses the risk presented by non-Jewish legal institutions. This principle generally forbids Jews from going to non-Jewish courts to adjudicate their disputes, thereby seeking to preserve the status and integrity of rabbinic adjudicatory institutions and processes.

The second principle, *Dina DeMalkhuta Dina* ("the law of the kingdom is the law"), operates in the opposite direction. When it applies, this doctrine transforms non-Jewish law into religiously binding law.[2] A Jew who violates a secular law to which *Dina DeMalkhuta Dina* applies would be guilty of a *halakhic* transgression. Even though it gives effect to some non-Jewish laws, this doctrine plays an important role in preserving Judaism by enhancing relations between the Jewish community and the local government. During some historical periods, *Dina DeMalkhuta Dina* likely helped preserve governmental permission for the Jewish community to enjoy at least partial juridical autonomy and other civil rights.[3]

But too broad an application of *Dina DeMalkhuta Dina* could indicate a lack of appreciation of divinely provided Jewish laws and ingratitude to the Almighty who gifted them to the Jewish people. As a practical matter, the diminished importance of religious law would lead Jews to devote less time, attention, and energy to the study of Jewish religious texts. This would impoverish Jewish knowledge of the legal, ethical, and moral lessons they contain.[4]

Perhaps partly because of the significant consequences of both of these doctrines and the competing considerations underlying them, rabbinic views are sharply divided regarding their proper parameters. The variety of opinions makes the study of these principles an especially fruitful way to examine the Jewish legal process. This chapter begins by briefly describing the religious and historical contexts in which the *Issur Arkaot* and *Dina DeMalkhuta Dina* doctrines developed. It then examines each concept individually, identifying its principal rationales and applications. The chapter concludes by exploring the ways in which the two doctrines remain relevant in modern times.

Contextual Background for *Issur Arkaot* and *Dina DeMalkhuta Dina*

To better understand the critical roles the *Issur Arkaot* and *Dina Demalkhuta Dina* doctrines play, it is necessary to appreciate the centrality of law within Judaism. From a theological perspective, Jewish law reflects the Voice of God who "speaks to [a Jew] from the leaves of the *Gemara* [the Talmud], the paragraphs of the *Shulhan Arukh* [the Code of Jewish Law], and the words of the verses of the Bible."[5] Indeed, "God reveals Himself to anyone who immerses himself in the depths of Torah."[6] Delving into *halakhah* is a "sacramental act" of almost unique significance. It is not only "a means but an end, and not merely an end among ends, but the highest and noblest of human aspirations."[7]

Judaism recognizes God as benevolent, loving, and morally perfect.[8] Consequently, Judaism regards Jewish law[9] and its institutions as incomparably wise and Divine gifts that are to be proudly cherished and tenaciously preserved.[10] Abandoning Jewish courts for non-Jewish courts, and Jewish law for non-Jewish law, demonstrates ungratefulness to God and is deemed a form of heresy and betrayal. Beyond these spiritual concerns, any diminution of their roles could fundamentally alter Jewish life.

The dismantling of the Jewish monarchy over two millenia ago and its replacement by non-Jewish rulers posed precisely this threat. The danger was exacerbated when Jews were dispersed throughout the world and intimately exposed to the diverse practices and juristic structures of their host nations. Several pragmatic considerations arose. One was the need to safeguard the status of Jewish law and to preserve the integrity of Jewish life. Another was to avoid antagonizing non-Jewish rulers and, thereby, preserve Jewish lives. A third was to ensure that Jews could obtain justice in their disputes not only with other Jews but also with non-Jews.[11] *Issur Arkaot* and *Dina DeMalkhuta Dina* are the principal doctrines that address the ways in which the tensions among these concerns are resolved.[12]

The next section initially explores *Issur Arkaot*, beginning with the biblical source and perceived purposes of the doctrine. It then discusses the principal exceptions to the doctrine and examines the two key Talmudic passages upon which some of the exceptions are predicated. This section concludes by exploring whether *Issur Arkaot* applies to persons appearing before the governmental courts of the State of Israel.

Issur Arkaot

The Torah states: "Judges and enforcement officers shall you place for yourself in all of your gates."[13] Numerous Jewish authorities cite this verse as the source for a Torah-based duty to create rabbinic courts in every community[14] for the purposes of enforcing public law and providing forums for people in which to adjudicate their private disputes before erudite rabbinic judges. Typically, a case would be heard by a panel of three such judges.

Another verse, "And these are the laws that you must set before them,"[15] is interpreted as prohibiting the submission of an adjudicative matter to a non-Jewish court. The Talmud explains: "R. Tarfon used to say: Wherever you find [non-Jewish] courts . . ., even though their law is the same as Jewish law, you must not resort to them since it is written, 'These are the judgments [i.e., the laws] that you shall set before them,' that is to say, 'before them' [i.e., Jewish courts] and not before idolaters."[16]

The *Midrash Tanhuma,* a set of rabbinic teachings first compiled in the late eighth or ninth century,[17] treats the resort to non-Jewish courts as a rejection of God and of God's Torah: "Anyone who forsakes Jewish judges and appears between non-Jews has firstly denied God and secondly denied the Torah, as is written, 'For their rock is not as our Rock, and our enemies are judges.'"[18]

This sentiment is also vehemently expressed by Jewish law's principal legal codes and authorities. For instance, the twelfth-century scholar Moses ben Maimon (Maimonides) writes: "Whoever submits a suit for adjudication to non-Jewish judges in their courts, even if the judgment rendered by them is in accord with Jewish law, is a wicked man. It is as though he reviled, blasphemed, and rebelled against the law of Moses, Our Teacher, for it is said, 'These are the ordinances which thou shalt set before them.'[19] 'Before them [i.e., Jewish courts],' not before [the courts of] idolaters . . . ."[20]

As Maimonides explicitly states, this prohibition applies even if it is known that the non-Jewish court would render the same judgment as a rabbinical court.[21] The prohibition also applies even if all of the litigants agree, whether at the outset of a business transaction or after a disagreement arises, to have their dispute tried in a non-Jewish court.[22] This is true even if their agreement to submit to a non-Jewish court is supported by the legal formalities that under Jewish law would otherwise obligate parties to fulfill a contractual promise.[23] This is because *Issur Arkaot* is a "ritual"[24] rule, the violation of which is an offense against the Almighty, similar to a violation of the Sabbath. Jews are not allowed to circumvent ritual rules through private agreements.

To be precise, the texts already cited do not refer to courts of "non-Jews" but to courts of "star-worshippers" or other idolaters. Resorting to such courts is deemed doubly reprehensible: the abandonment of rabbinic courts deeply insults God, while the resort to courts of other faiths appears to endorse those religions, especially if the courtrooms are adorned with their religious images or icons. Nonetheless, Jewish authorities agree that the prohibition applies even to turning to completely secular courts,[25] and even if the judges are Jewish,[26] because these actions also demean Jewish law and exalt secular alternatives. For convenience, non-rabbinic courts will hereafter be referred to as "civil courts."

There are financial consequences for a Jewish plaintiff who wrongfully sues a defendant in civil court. First, even if the plaintiff had a valid *halakhic* claim that would have prevailed in a rabbinic court (*Bet Din*), he is liable under Jewish law for the defendant's costs in having to defend himself in civil court.[27] In addition, if he loses in civil court, and then seeks redress for his valid *halakhic* claim in a *Bet Din*, the *Bet Din* will ordinarily refuse to hear his case.[28] Violators of this rule also face various formal and informal sanctions within the Jewish community.[29]

Exceptions to *Issur Arkaot*

There are least six categories of cases to which *Issur Arkaot* does not apply: (1) resort to a civil court for a purpose other than "adjudication" of a dispute; (2) defense of oneself in a civil court proceeding; (3) participation in certain alternative dispute resolution procedures that are not conducted in civil court; (4) turning to secular court if a rabbinic court wrongfully refuses to exercise jurisdiction over a matter; (5) according to many authorities, filing in civil court when it is legitimately assumed that one's adversary will not submit to rabbinic court; and (6) filing in civil court based on authorization received from a rabbinic court.

The first category of exceptions is predicated on the fact that *Issur Arkaot* prohibits the submission of a dispute for *adjudication* by a civil court. It therefore does not apply to situations in which someone goes to civil court for a nonadjudicative purpose.[30] For example, a person may initiate a civil court proceeding to change her legal name or to become a naturalized citizen. Such proceedings are not brought "against" another party and no "dispute" is presented to be judged.

This category also includes matters filed in civil court that may affect, under civil law, the financial rights of others, provided that the matters are undisputed. Thus, one may submit an uncontested will to probate court,[31] at least if the will is valid under Jewish law,[32] or may obtain a "judgment" regarding an uncontested debt.[33]

Even where there is an actual dispute between Jews, many authorities would permit a party to avail itself of certain forms of civil court relief, provided it does not seek to have the court render a final adjudication. Thus, many would permit a party to file suit in secular court to utilize discovery rights or even to obtain negative injunctive relief to freeze the status quo and avoid imminent loss.[34]

A second category of exceptions comprises cases in which an individual is a defendant in a civil court proceeding. In these cases, the defendant does not submit a matter to the civil court; he or she is dragged there.[35] One may defend oneself in a civil proceeding without violating *Issur Arkaot*, at least if one is unable to convince the plaintiff (whether Jewish or non-Jewish) to resolve the dispute in rabbinic court.

Third, *Issur Arkaot* does not apply to the voluntary submission of financial controversies to arbitration. Jewish law allows arbitrators to consider equitable factors in reaching their decisions and fashioning appropriate relief. Even though the arbitral award may vary from what would otherwise be prescribed by Jewish law, the arbitration is permitted for several reasons. In pecuniary, as opposed to ritual, matters, Jewish law affords a person significant discretion. It permits one to agree to make a gift of one's property, to waive any or all of one's financial rights, to gratuitously incur monetary obligations, and, with the other party's consent, to condition one's contractual liabilities.[36] One draws on these rights when agreeing to abide by a Jewish arbitral award even if it differs from what strict law would require. Moreover, Judaism highly prizes fairness and justice, and these values depend on far too many circumstantial variables than can be neatly incorporated in the text of strict law. In addition, judgments influenced by fairness often constitute a "compromise" that renders neither party a complete loser. By reducing the bitterness of the outcome, this process enhances the prospect that, post-arbitration, the parties will be able to coexist in harmony.

In fact, even when parties submit their disputes to a rabbinic court, rather than to independent arbitrators, they are asked to authorize the court to consider equitable factors rather than issuing a judgment based on strict law.[37] Typically, the parties are asked to authorize issuance of a judgment that is only "near" to what the strict law would prescribe, a standard that ordinarily allows a deviation of no more than one third.[38] For example, suppose a plaintiff would be entitled under strict law to a recovery of $100. A judgment would be considered "near" strict law if it awarded the plaintiff at least $66.67. Similarly, assume that under strict law, a plaintiff asserting a claim for $100 would not be entitled to any recovery. A judgment awarding the plaintiff up to $33.33 would be considered to be near the result under strict law.

Jewish law generally recognizes two principal arbitration processes that may operate outside the purview of a rabbinic court.[39] The most common such process is known as *Zablo*, an acronym based on the Hebrew phrase *Zeh Borer Lo Ehad ve-Zeh Borer Lo Ehad* ("this [party] picks for itself one [arbitrator] and this [party] picks for itself one [arbitrator]").[40] The two arbitrators thus chosen jointly agree to a third. The arbitration then proceeds before this panel of three. Disputants may voluntarily engage in arbitration proceedings without any supervision by an official rabbinic court.

Arbitration before certain non-Jewish panels is similarly permitted. In some trades, professions, or industries, it is customary for disputes to be arbitrated either before fixed arbitration boards that are established for this purpose or before ad hoc panels. Most *halakhic* authorities agree that *Issur Arkaot* does not apply to such arbitration, provided that the arbitrators are supposed to rule according to their "common sense."[41] By contrast, *Issur Arkaot* would apply if the arbitrators are obligated to decide disputes according to either a non-Jewish code of laws or the dictates of a non-Jewish faith.[42] The arbitration exception will be revisited, infra, in evaluating whether *Issur Arkaot* applies to Israel's governmentally established rabbinic courts or whether resort to such courts could be regarded as an acceptable form of arbitration.

A fourth category of exceptions includes cases in which a rabbinic court refuses to exercise jurisdiction over a matter. This might occur, for example, if the court is intimidated by the fact that one's adversary is especially powerful, dangerous, or lawless.[43] If a rabbinic court abstains from such a matter, the plaintiff's turning to civil court in no way reflects any disrespect of Jewish law.

A fifth category of cases to which *Issur Arkaot* does not apply, at least according to many authorities, is where it is legitimately "assumed" that one's adversary will refuse to litigate in rabbinic court.[44] For example, if a Jewish plaintiff wishes to sue a non-Jewish defendant, it is widely believed that the non-Jewish defendant would insist on litigating in civil court due to a lack of familiarity with, or even hostility toward, rabbinic courts. As a result, "in practice, no *Bet Din* issues a summons directing a non-Jew to appear before it for purposes of litigation."[45] Instead, this sort of case is treated as if the rabbinic court had expressly authorized the plaintiff to resort to civil court. Consequently, if the non-Jew is willing to appear before a rabbinic court and obey its decision, it is forbidden to sue him in civil court.[46]

In some cases, a plaintiff's claims, if proved, would be recovered from someone other than the defendant, such as where the defendant's insurance company is responsible for payment. Typically, civil law requires a plaintiff to obtain a judgment against the named insured before allowing the plaintiff to collect from the insurer. Most insurers are legal entities that, it is generally assumed, would not agree to submit themselves to the jurisdiction of a rabbinic court.[47] In such a situation, a Jewish plaintiff may nominally sue the Jewish insured in civil court in order to recover from the insurer. However, some

Jewish law authorities would require that the plaintiff first obligate itself, in a manner valid under Jewish law, to enforce any civil judgment only against the insurer.[48]

A number of authorities argue that it can even be assumed that some Jews, such as those who publicly and routinely violate Jewish law or those who are known to flout the authority of rabbinic courts, would be unwilling to litigate in a *Bet Din*. They argue that one could sue such a person in civil court without first obtaining authorization from a rabbinic court.[49]

A final category of exceptions includes instances in which a rabbinic court explicitly authorizes a person to turn to civil court.[50] A person who relies upon such an authorization cannot be said to deprecate Jewish law or its legal institutions. By initially turning to the rabbinic court and subsequently relying on its permission to sue in civil court, the person clearly demonstrates deference to Jewish law. Nevertheless, in these situations, the question arises as to why the rabbinic court would allow the plaintiff to place the matter before a civil court given that this would appear to be a violation of the law. The next section provides two answers to this question.

Why, and When, Rabbinic Courts May Authorize a Civil Lawsuit: Two Talmudic Passages

Authorities rely on one or both of two Talmudic passages for the authority, in limited situations, to allow a Jew to adjudicate a dispute in civil court. The logic of one passage, appearing in Baba Kamma, seems to provide a broad basis for such authority: "Rava said to Rabbah bar Mari: 'From where do we know this thing that people say, "If you call out your fellow and he does not answer you, lift up a large wall and throw it at him?' He [Rabbah bar Mari] answered, 'Because I tried to cleanse you, but you would not be cleansed, you will never be cleansed of your contamination.'"[51]

Rav Poltoi Gaon (ninth century) explains that Rava refers to a case in which one Jew summons another to rabbinic court, but the second Jew refuses to appear.[52] Rava wants to know why a rabbinic court can "throw a wall" at the defendant by authorizing the plaintiff to seek a remedy in civil court.[53] Rabbah bar Mari responds by saying that the rabbinic court is exercising its inherent power to punish a wrongdoer who refuses to submit to the court's jurisdiction.[54] According to this logic, the rabbinic court appears to be able to authorize the filing of a civil suit even without having actually heard testimony on, or having ruled upon, the merits of the case.

Interestingly, this passage implicitly suggests that a plaintiff who acts upon such authority might even recover more in civil court than that to which she would be entitled under Jewish law. The picturesque expression of "throwing a wall"[55] on the defendant indicates that the authorization is a punishment imposed on the defendant, and a punishment could be in an amount exceeding the defendant's *halakhic* liability.

Indeed, Mordechai Willig, who is associated with the Beth Din of America (BDA), states that when a defendant refuses to appear before a rabbinic court, it is "common practice" for that court to authorize the plaintiff to sue in civil court without first evaluating the validity of the plaintiff's claim. Moreover, he contends that a plaintiff who prevails in secular court and receives a larger judgment than would have been awarded under Jewish law may keep it.[56] The fact that the defendant may suffer a greater loss than would have been the case in the rabbinic proceeding is just part of the penalty imposed on the disobedient party. The extent to which this is the common practice of rabbinical courts other than BDA is unclear. Other authorities, perhaps especially those relying on the second Talmudic commentary, rule that it would be a religious transgression for a party to collect more than his Jewish law entitlement.[57]

The passage is unclear whether plaintiffs must secure permission to turn to civil court on a case-by-case basis. Many authorities find that this is a requirement.[58] Others suggest that the rabbis announced a general "penalty" or "punishment" on the entire class of recalcitrant defendants. As a result, it is unnecessary for individual plaintiffs to apply for and receive authorization to sue individual "no-show" defendants in civil court.[59]

Rabbah bar Mari's reasoning not only applies to a defendant who refuses to litigate in rabbinic court, but also to one who, after litigating and losing, contumaciously refuses to satisfy the judgment against him. Such a refusal also constitutes a flouting of the rabbinic court's authority, warranting the rabbinic court's "throwing a wall at the defendant" by permitting the prevailing party to sue in civil court.

The second of the two Talmudic passages permitting a rabbinic court to authorize resort to a civil court involves a Mishnah discussed in tractate Gittin. This passage is considered by some to be an additional source of this rabbinic court power, while others regard it as merely an alternative, and more restrictive, source: "A divorce decree that was procured by force: If the force was applied by a rabbinic court [until the husband complied, the divorce decree] is valid. But if [the force was applied] by [a court of] idolaters, [the divorce decree] is invalid. [However, even a court] of idolaters, may beat [the husband] and tell him, 'Do what the Jewish [court] tells you to do!' And [if the husband complies, the divorce decree] is valid."[60]

Unlike the passage in Baba Kamma, whose meaning is ambiguous without Rav Poltoi Gaon's interpretation, the context of this Mishnah is clear. It refers to a case in which a rabbinic court has already heard a marital dissolution dispute and ruled that the husband is obligated to give his wife a writ of divorce. Nevertheless, the husband refuses to comply. If, without regard to the rabbinic court decree, a non-Jewish court were to independently order and coerce the husband to give his wife a divorce, the divorce would be invalid under Jewish law. On the other hand, if the civil court ordered and coerced the husband "to comply with the rabbinic court's ruling" (i.e., to give a writ of divorce because the rabbinic court had so ruled), then the divorce would be effective under Jewish law.

Presumably, a civil court would only order the husband to comply with the rabbinic court's ruling after the wife had filed with it a petition for divorce. Yet neither the Mishnah nor the ensuing Talmudic discussion suggests that there would be any impropriety in the wife's filing such a petition. Consequently, many Jewish law authorities interpret this Mishnah as generally allowing someone to file an action in civil court to enforce a rabbinical court judgment, whether the rabbinic judgment involved divorce law or any other matter.[61]

Comparing and Contrasting the Talmudic Passages

In some ways, the passage in *Bava Kamma* provides greater discretion to resort to civil court than does the Mishnah in Gittin. First, as already mentioned, the passage in *Bava Kamma* allows the *Bet Din* to authorize a plaintiff to file a civil court action even before the rabbinic court has ruled on the merits of the case. By contrast, the Mishnah in Gittin only refers to a case in which the *Bet Din* has already issued a ruling, and resort to civil court is merely to enforce that ruling.

Second, by describing the authorization as a punishment against the defendant, the passage in *Baba Kamma* suggests that a plaintiff might be permitted to recover an amount in excess of that to which he is entitled under Jewish law. By contrast, the Mishnah in Gittin only treats as *halakhically* valid a civil court action that enforces a rabbinic court's ruling. It provides no support for the proposition that a plaintiff could recover more in civil court than that which a rabbinic court would award. Many Jewish law authorities limit a plaintiff to recovering only the amount granted by *Bet Din*;[62] they rule that if a plaintiff recovers more than that amount, it is considered as if he had stolen the excess.

Issur Arkaot and the Israeli Court System

Establishment of the State of Israel and its court system in 1948 introduced a new reality: most Israeli judges were Jewish and the laws, to the extent that they deviated from *halakhah*, were adopted or at least embraced by a citizenry that was mostly Jewish. An important question arose as to whether the submission of a dispute to such an Israeli court violated *Issur Arkaot*. At the outset, it is critical to emphasize that the term, "Israeli court," as used in this chapter, does not refer to the independent rabbinic courts within Israel that are unconnected to the government. Such independent courts are typically associated with particular religious organizations or with one or more especially highly regarded rabbis. *Issur Arkaot* certainly does not apply to submission of disputes for adjudication before them.

There are two very different kinds of Israeli governmental courts. The first type involves Israeli "civil" courts. Most disputes fall within the jurisdiction of these courts and are resolved not by the application of *halakhah* but in accordance with secular Israeli law. The second variety consists of Israeli rabbinic courts. These courts enjoy exclusive jurisdiction over a limited number of matters and non-exclusive jurisdiction over a few more. The Israeli rabbinic courts generally resolve issues before them in accordance with *halakhah*. However, there are particular instances in which Israeli secular law seems to require that even these courts apply specified secular law rather than *halakhah*. Whether *Issur Arkaot* applies to Israeli courts may well depend on whether we are asking about Israeli civil courts or Israeli rabbinic courts. Consequently, we will discuss the two types of court separately.

Israeli Civil Courts

Israeli jurist Menahem Elon argued that *Issur Arkaot* did not apply to litigation in Israeli civil courts,[63] contending that those courts were tantamount to an institution referred to in the Talmud as "the courts of [the place known as] Suria."[64] Although the vast majority of Jewish law authorities have rejected this argument, it is instructive to examine the relevant issues.

The persons sitting as judges in the courts of Suria were not experts in Jewish law. However, the citizens of Suria accepted these people to resolve disputes based on their sense of what was proper, rather than on any legal code. Accordingly, resort to the courts of Suria was similar to the type of arbitration identified above as the third category of exceptions to *Issur Arkaot*.

Post-Talmudic Jewish legal sources consistently ruled that where qualified judges were otherwise unavailable, courts like those of Suria could be established. Otherwise, Jews in many small towns that were unable to appoint judges who were expert in Jewish law might submit their controversies to civil courts. The judges so appointed did not need to be *halakhic* scholars, but they did need to be virtuous and God-fearing.[65] In his sixteenth-century gloss on the Code of Jewish Law, Moses Isserles wrote:

> In cities in which there are no sages who are qualified to be judges or in which all of the residents are ignorant about Jewish law and there is a need for judges to adjudicate between them so that they will not go to civil courts, community leaders and the wise among them appoint judges even though [the appointees] are not [really] qualified to be judges. Because the members of the city accept [these people as judges] no one can disqualify them.[66]

Elon argued that Israeli civil courts should be treated as if they were like the courts of Suria, and, by submitting their disputes to these courts, Jewish Israelis would not violate *Issur Arkaot*. Nevertheless, there are several problems with this proposition. First, the post-Talmudic sources cited emphasize that courts such as those in Suria may only be established when it is not possible to adjudicate before courts of judges who are expert in *halakhah*.[67] In Israel, there are many rabbinic courts with expert judges.

Second, as Avraham Yeshaya Karelitz, a leading twentieth-century Israeli authority, argued, the courts of Suria were only permitted because they ruled according to their sense of justice. By resolving disputes in such courts, the litigants were essentially entering into a "compromise," something that Jewish law encourages.[68] The courts of Suria did not apply a specific non-*halakhic* body of law. Had they done so, the Jews going to them would be impermissibly elevating those foreign laws over God's Law. Israeli civil courts apply a non-*halakhic* body of law, the law enacted by the State of Israel.[69]

Third, according to Karelitz, the reality that the Israeli electorate is predominantly Jewish, and that a majority of Israeli court judges are Jewish, does not support Elon. Quite the contrary, the predominant role played by Jews merely accentuates the problem of not following *halakhic* rules. Most prominent Jewish law authorities agree with Karelitz.[70]

Elon did not respond to the first objection, namely, that courts of Suria were only allowed when judges expert in Jewish law were unavailable. He did, however, respond to the second objection. He cited Menachem ben Shlomo (*Meiri*; 1249–1310), who commented, in part, that the courts of Suria "ruled according to their common sense and their *Nimusim*." The word Nimusim can refer to customs and laws. Elon therefore argued that just as the courts of Suria ruled according to Nimusim, it is permissible for Israeli courts to rule according to Israeli law.

Nevertheless, Avraham Sherman, a member of the Great Rabbinical Court in Jerusalem, points out that there is a fundamental distinction between the courts of Suria and Israeli civil courts even according to ben Shlomo. Ben Shlomo does not say that the courts of Suria were "bound" or felt bound to apply local Nimusim. Ben Shlomo simply says that those courts ruled according to such things as their common sense and Nimusim. This might mean that, although the judges "considered" secular laws, they only applied them if and where the results seemed just. By contrast, Israeli civil court judges are legally obligatedto apply Israeli laws and, upon taking office, are required to commit themselves to do so.[71]

Sherman adduces explicit proof that former Israeli Chief Rabbi Isaac ha-Levi Herzog (1888–1959) also interpreted ben Shlomo's statement in this way. Herzog, who cites ben Shlomo without objection, writes that it would be impermissible under Jewish law for the courts of Suria to simply apply local laws. Accordingly, Sherman argues that Herzog must have construed ben Shlomo to mean that the judges in the courts of Suria considered ancient Roman or pre-Roman laws only when they deemed them to be sensible resolutions of cases.[72]

Consequently, according to the overwhelming majority of *halakhic* authorities, it is usually impermissible for a Jew to sue another Jew in an Israeli civil court. As previously discussed, a person may resort to such courts for nonadjudicative purposes, may participate in the courts as a defendant, and may initiate certain out-of-court arbitrations. In addition, a person may affirmatively file suit in such civil courts, according to various authorities if it can be assumed that the defendant would refuse to litigate in rabbinic court; if the rabbinic court refused to exercise jurisdiction over a case; or if the rabbinic court authorized the filing of a civil suit. Furthermore, someone may file suit in a nongovernmental rabbinic court. Alternatively, as the next section illustrates, it may be possible to submit disputes to Israeli rabbinic courts.

Israeli Rabbinic Courts

As already mentioned, Israel has an official, governmentally established rabbinic court system. These courts enjoy essentially exclusive jurisdiction over matters involving marriage and divorce and share jurisdiction with the civil courts as to certain other subjects, including the distribution of marital property, inheritance, and child custody. In light of this, the question arises as to whether the religious doctrine of *Issur Arkaot* applies to filing suit in such courts. The answer depends on whether, under Jewish law, the court is considered "rabbinic" rather than civil.[73]

A court is a "rabbinic" court if: (1) it applies Jewish law, rather than the law of some other country or faith; (2) its judges are proficient in Jewish law; and (3) its judges are Jewish. Israeli rabbinic courts generally satisfy all three conditions. Provided these conditions are satisfied, it does not matter that—as in Israel—the government determines who is eligible to serve as a judge because of the second doctrine addressed in this chapter, *Dina DeMalkhuta Dina*. As discussed shortly, this doctrine provides, *as a matter of Jewish law*, that the ruler or ruling government of every country possesses the authority to enact certain types of laws and to take certain actions that are binding even on Jews within the jurisdiction. One such action is the selection of judges to serve on courts within its territory. This includes the appointment of judges to rabbinic courts, at least if the judges chosen are learned.[74]

Israeli rabbinic courts are almost universally regarded as true "rabbinic courts" because they generally appear to satisfy the three criteria identified above. In one important respect, however, there may be room to question this assumption. The Israeli rabbinic courts are authorized by Israeli law to apply purely Jewish law with respect to certain issues—such as whether someone is regarded as Jewish or whether someone is married or divorced. But as to certain other issues—such as the division of marital property—Israeli rabbinic courts are supposed to follow official Israeli law. The question is whether this requirement prevents the Israeli rabbinic courts from being regarded as "rabbinic courts" when adjudicating such issues.[75]

As demonstrated, the *Issur Arkaot* doctrine deals with the forum in which one may permissibly litigate. The principle of *Dina DeMalkhuta Dina,* on the other hand, focuses on which legal rules, those of *halakhah* or those promulgated by the regnant government, are to be applied by a permitted forum. The following section addresses the doctrine of *Dina DeMalkhuta Dina* comprehensively.

Dina DeMalkhuta Dina

Dina Demalkhuta Dina literally means the "law of the kingdom is [religiously valid] law." Where this principle applies, the law of the non-Jewish government is binding upon Jews, and rabbinical courts are required by Jewish law to apply it. This dictum is first mentioned in the Talmud in the name of Samuel, an authority in the second and third centuries, and is invoked in at least three other passages.[76] Although the Talmud itself offers no specific scriptural source for the doctrine, not a single Talmudic authority questions its validity. Although there are dissenting opinions, it seems that most Jewish law authorities regard *Dina DeMalkhuta Dina* as a biblical doctrine of Divine origin rather than a rule created by the Sages, at least as applied to certain subject matter.[77]

Among the earliest explanations of *Dina DeMalkhuta Dina* was that it was based on the people's "agreement" to be so governed. More modern commentators, however, argue that Jewish law recognizes that a ruler possesses an intrinsic authority to govern, at least as to certain types of matters. Nevertheless, its rationale and scope are subject to substantial controversy with significant practical consequences. The next two sections address these issues.

Implicit Agreement to Follow Non-Jewish Law

One important approach regards *Dina DeMalkhuta Dina* as being based on a social contract to the effect that the residents of a land have agreed to be bound, at least in certain respects, by the ruler's laws. For example, Yom Tov b. Abraham Ishbili (*Rashbam*), who spanned the thirteenth and fourteenth centuries, writes that "All of the inhabitants of the kingdom have taken upon themselves by their own free will the statutes of the king and his laws."[78] This approach, echoed by other authorities,[79] is based on an *implicit* agreement, not an express one.[80]

Authorities suggest various reasons why people would implicitly agree to follow the king's laws. Moshe Sofer (*Hatam Sofer*) posits that they willingly accept the king's law because of various benefits received from the king, including the maintenance of law and order.[81] Among other things, Sofer cites a Mishnah quoting Rebbe Chanina, the assistant High Priest, as saying: "Pray for the welfare of the government. For without fear of it, people would swallow each other alive."[82]

Reuben Gerondi (*Ran*), a fourteenth-century rabbinic authority,[83] appears to offer an alternative explanation. He posits that the king is the ultimate "owner" of all the real property in his jurisdiction. As the "landowner," the king possesses the inherent authority to regulate what is done on his property and the right to expel anyone who refuses to abide by his rules. Gerondi states that, by entering into or remaining upon the king's property, people implicitly agree to obey his laws.

If Gerondi's rationale were the sole basis for *Dina DeMalkhuta Dina*, the doctrine would not apply in the land of Israel. Under Jewish law, all Jews are partners in the ownership of the land of Israel. Therefore, they have the right to reside there, and no government—Jewish or otherwise—possesses the authority—even it does possess the power—to deport Jews from Israel.[84] Indeed, if Gerondi's rationale were the only basis for *Dina DeMalkhuta Dina*, the doctrine might be inapplicable to any country whose government is not regarded as the "owner" of the land[85] or whose government lacks the legitimate authority to exile its citizens.[86] Nevertheless, contemporary *halakhic* authorities reject the categorical premise that *Dina DeMalkhuta Dina* does not apply to Israeli law, although they may recognize restrictions on its scope.[87]

However, several specific objections are often raised in connection with the social contract argument. For example, the theory fails to explain why *Dina DeMalkhuta Dina* binds even those, such as minors, who lack the legal capacity to contract. Second, it fails to justify the doctrine even as to everyone who is legally competent. Consider, for instance, a competent adult Jew who, when first taking up residence in a country, unconditionally declares their unwillingness to agree to the king's authority.[88] How could it be said that this individual has contractually obligated himself or herself to comply with the law of the land? In light of these objections, a number of modern rabbinic authorities integrate the "social contract" argument into a more subtle rationale for *Dina DeMalkhuta Dina*.

Jewish Law's Recognition of a Ruler's Intrinsic Power to Govern

At least two contemporary rabbinic authorities, J. David Bleich and Osher Weiss point to weaknesses regarding the social contract theory.[89] Their argument begins with the fact that Jewish law recognizes that a ruler, whether Jewish or non-Jewish, possesses certain inherent powers to govern. The question then becomes who is to be recognized as the "ruler" for these purposes. Bleich interprets Ishbili's position to be that the people accepted the sovereignty of the monarch. Having done so: "[A]n obligation of obedience flows directly from voluntary acceptance of the authority of the monarch. . . . It is only the sovereign's authority to act as sovereign that requires 'acceptance' on the part of his subjects. Once such acceptance is forthcoming, no further legitimization is required for exercise of the prerogatives enumerated in I Samuel 8:5."[90]

Jewish sources offer at least five bases for the proposition that Jewish law recognizes that a ruler possesses inherent authority to govern. The first basis is offered by the eleventh-century Solomon ben Yitzhaki (*Rashi*), and arises from a Mishnah[91] in the Talmudic tractate Gittin. The Mishnah states that most documents recorded in non-Jewish governmental registries are *halakhically* valid, even if the witnesses who signed them were Gentiles. This is despite the fact that *halakhah* would usually require the witnesses to be Jewish.

Yitzhaki explains these documents are valid "because of *Dina DeMalkhuta Dina*" and this is the case "even though the grantor and the grantee are Jewish." Yitzhaki explains that the reason is because "the children of Noah [i.e., Gentiles] are commanded [by God] to establish laws."[92] Yitzhaki is referring to the basic tenet of Jewish law that, in addition to providing numerous commandments to Jews, God obligates non-Jews to observe seven categories of commandments, one of which is to create and enforce a system of laws.[93] Yitzhaki's point is that because of this Torah-based obligation to promulgate laws, at least some of those laws, as will be discussed, are binding even on Jewish residents.[94]

The Mishnah cites an exception, namely, that divorce decrees in non-Jewish registries are not *halakhically* valid. Yitzhaki explains that this is because Gentiles do not have the same type of legal relationship that is created by a Jewish marriage and ended by a Jewish divorce.[95] In other words, *Dina DeMalkhuta Dina* gives *halakhic* validation only to the types of law that Gentiles need to enact. Because they do not need to enact laws effectuating Jewish divorces, *Dina DeMalkhuta Dina* is inapplicable to the divorce decrees issued by Gentiles regarding Jews.

Sixteenth-century scholar Moses di Trani (*Mabit*) cites the prophet Samuel's description of the powers of a king as a second source for a government's inherent authority to rule.[96] Samuel states:

> [T]he king who will rule over you . . . will take your sons, and appoint them for his chariots and horsemen, and they will run before his chariots. And he will appoint them to him commanders of thousands and commanders of fifties, and to plow his plowing and to reap his harvest . . . . And he will take your daughters for his perfumers, for cooks, and for bakers. And he will take the best of your fields, your vineyards, and your olive trees . . . . And he will tithe your flocks, and you will be his slaves.[97]

Trani and many others state that Samuel is referring to the legitimate, although unpleasant, powers that all kings possess. Some commentators disagree with Trani, contending that Samuel was not referring to the legitimate authority of a king. Instead, Samuel was merely trying to dissuade those demanding appointment of a king by warning them of the illegitimate *power* that a king could potentially wield.[98]

Moshe Sofer offers a third source for a ruler's intrinsic authority to govern. He cites the Talmud's interpretation of the following verse in *Song of Songs*:[99] "My vineyard is before Me. One thousand are for you, Solomon and two hundred for those who guard its fruit."[100] The Talmud explains that all references to "Solomon" in *Song of Songs* actually refer to God.[101] The Talmudic commentator Samuel therefore states that "One thousand for . . . Solomon" means that one thousand of a land's population is "for" the Heavenly Kingdom. Two hundred to "those who guard its fruit" means that two hundred of the population belong to the earthly kingdom (i.e., are for the earthly king's personal benefit). Two hundred people out of a total of twelve hundred constitute one sixth. If the king has the right to demand the lives of up to one sixth of his subjects, then, a fortiori, explains Samuel, he has the right to impose lesser demands upon them through the various laws he promulgates. Interestingly, as discussed, this Samuel is the same person in whose name the Talmud introduces the *Dina DeMalkhuta Dina* doctrine.

Yonah Gerundi, a leading thirteenth-century authority, links *Dina Demalkhuta Dina* to a fourth source, the unusual power of rabbinic courts, under certain circumstances, to expropriate property, rendering it ownerless.[102] Rabbi Abraham Duber Kahana Shapiro (*Devar Avraham*) explains Gerundi's position. He says that the authority for dispossessing a person of property is not "judicial."[103] Instead, it arises from the rabbinic court's mandate to govern, at least in the absence of a Jewish king. Given that secular kings similarly possess authority to govern, they, too, are authorized to exercise exceptional powers that can impinge on people's property rights, such as by dispossessing them of property.

A more recent scholar, Yosef Eliyahu Henkin, offers a fifth approach, connecting the doctrine of *Dina DeMalkhuta Dina* to a different, extraordinary power possessed by a rabbinic court, namely, the authority, when necessary to preserve law and order, to impose punishment, including capital punishment, even when not in strict accordance with the law.[104] A king, too, has such authority,[105] and Henkin adds, the right to promulgate decrees that the populace must obey.[106]

Just as they disagree as to the sources for a ruler's inherent authority to govern, *halakhic* authorities also vigorously debate the scope of *Dina DeMalkhuta Dina*.[107] The broader its scope, the greater the threat that non-Jewish law might completely supplant *halakhah*, dramatically diminishing the study and practical significance of Jewish texts. This would, in turn, result in a drastic reduction in the knowledge of Jewish legal, ethical, and moral teachings. Similarly, a broader scope can undermine the social status of rabbinic authorities and institutions, and deplete the richness of Jewish culture. Many Jewish law authorities cite these types of concerns when explaining limits on the doctrine's reach.

On the other hand, the narrower the doctrine's scope, the greater the danger that Jews would fail to faithfully comply with laws of great importance to the government, possibly causing the government to take umbrage against, and impose disastrously severe sanctions upon, the Jewish community. Although this danger is less frequently mentioned in *halakhic* literature, it seems likely to have influenced some decisions.

The following section briefly addresses several issues concerning the scope of *Dina DeMalkhuta Dina*. It provides some background on those laws to which *Dina DeMalkhuta Dina* applies. In addition, it discusses both the types of government regulations that are regarded as "laws" for purpose of the doctrine and the forms of government to whose laws the doctrine applies.

The Scope of *Dina Demalkhuta Dina*

In determining whether or how *Dina Demalkhuta Dina* applies to a particular law, Jewish law authorities consider various factors, including: (1) whether the law deserves to be treated as "law" or merely as unbridled governmental usurpation; (2) the de facto, rather than the de jure, nature of the law; (3) the subject matter and the motivation underlying the law; and (4) the identity of the issuer of the law.

Law vs. Usurpation

Many *halakhic* decisors declare that *Dina DeMalkhuta Dina* is inapplicable to overly oppressive or intrusive measures that are not regarded as laws but instead, as governmental usurpations. This latter category would include laws that are vindictive or involve invidious discrimination. On the other hand, laws may be legitimate even if they are limited to only some trades, peoples, or practices, provided that these distinctions are supported by reason.[108]

De Facto vs. De Jure Interpretation

For purposes of *Dina DeMalkhuta Dina*, civil laws are construed not merely by how they are written, but also by how they are in fact enforced. Thus, if the custom is that no one receives a speeding ticket unless they exceed the posted speed limit by a minimum of ten miles per hour, then, for *Dina DeMalkhuta Dina* purposes, the law only proscribes driving at ten or more miles per hour over the posted speed. In Israel, there are laws prohibiting the employment of children under the age of fifteen. Nevertheless, because this law is not enforced with respect to temporary jobs during summer vacation from school, one may give such a job to child under fifteen without violating *Dina DeMalkhuta Dina*.[109] Similarly, in Israel it is generally illegal for people to build personal structures on public land. However, it is commonplace for Jews to build on such property temporary structures for the seven-day holiday of Sukkot. Israeli authorities ignore this practice even though it technically violates the law. Consequently, Osher Weiss contends that erecting these buildings does not constitute a violation of *halakhah*.[110]

Subject Matter and Motivation

Virtually all Jewish law scholars agree that *Dina DeMalkhuta Dina* does not religiously validate secular laws that would violate *halakhic* duties owed by man to God, i.e., Jewish "ritual" laws.[111] For example, the doctrine would not apply to a secular law that would require Jews to work on the Sabbath or to consume non-kosher food. But it is not always easy to identify a ritual law. For example, Jewish law prohibits the charging or paying of interest on a loan between Jews. Even if the Jewish borrower and lender voluntarily enter into an interest-bearing loan, believing it to be in their respective best interests, each would be guilty of violating Jewish ritual law.

As to non-ritual laws, an important difference exists between the positions taken by Sephardi authorities (rabbis from Jewish communities in the Middle East and most of the Iberian Peninsula) and Ashkenazi authorities (rabbis from Jewish communities in other parts of Europe, especially Germany and eastern Europe). The dominant Sephardi approach largely restricts *Dina DeMalkhuta Dina* to laws that are of direct benefit to the ruler,[112] such as taxes, immigration, eminent domain,[113] coinage,[114] and military conscription.[115] By contrast, Ashkenazi authorities generally extend *Dina DeMalkhuta Dina* to any laws promulgated to benefit the public.[116] This would include not only bankruptcy,[117] rent control,[118] and tort law, but also health, traffic, and other safety regulations.[119]

Throughout certain historical eras, Jewish communities enjoyed a *Kehillah* (i.e., "corporate") structure in which local rabbinic leaders possessed effective enforcement powers, often with the backing of the jurisdiction's non-Jewish government. During such periods, many *halakhic* authorities held that secular laws regarding transactions between and among Jews fell beyond the scope of the doctrine, because such dealings were of no real consequence either to the secular government or to the people of the land.[120] Some, but a decreasing number, of more modern decisors still hold this opinion.[121] Nevertheless, a number of contemporary authorities argue that, although the scope of *Dina DeMalkhuta Dina* is fairly comprehensive, it does not apply to laws enacted for "ideological" reasons that conflict with essential Jewish values.[122] They point, as an example, to secular laws that mandate equal intestacy rights for a decedent's children irrespective of their gender.[123]

Although this chapter focuses on *Dina DeMalkhuta Dina*, it should be noted that, according to both Sephardi and Ashkenazi authorities, many types of civil laws and business practices are binding on Jews pursuant to two other Jewish law principles. The first principle is known as *Minhog ha-Soharim* (the custom of merchants), similar to *Lex moratoria* (the "Law merchant"). Specifically, when Jews enter into business transactions, it is assumed, unless they explicitly provide to the contrary, that they contract in accordance with local practices. Many authorities rule that such practices are effective under Jewish law even if they developed as a result of compliance with civil laws.[124] Subject to some exceptions, a party's express contractual obligations are enforceable, even by a third-party beneficiary. However, *Minhag ha-Soharim* seems inapplicable to nonconsensual obligations, such as financial liabilities arising from traffic accidents.[125]

The second principle is *halakhah*'s recognition that members of a Jewish community may adopt various sorts of legislation, and that these enactments may be enforced by rabbinic courts.[126] In most places in the world, Jewish communities are no longer sufficiently structured to permit agreement on such rules or, even if rules could be agreed upon, to allow for their enforcement. The most significant exceptions relate to large Hassidic groups who heavily rely on guidance from their respective religious leaders (i.e., their "Rebbes").

A final subject matter issue concerns whether, and if so, how, *Dina DeMalkhuta Dina* applies to non-Jewish criminal laws. According to most Jewish law authorities, secular governments ordinarily possess the right, under Jewish law, to enact criminal laws designed to preserve the peace and welfare of the nation. However, even if the doctrine makes violation of a secular statute a breach of *halakhah*, it does not necessarily authorize a secular ruler to impose statutorily prescribed punishments on Jewish offenders. Of course, this is a question that is only relevant from a Jewish law perspective. The secular government would surely deem itself authorized to impose the same punishment on Jewish and non-Jewish criminals.

Why *Dina DeMalkhuta Dina* might apply differently to criminal law prohibitions than to criminal law punishments is a complex question that exceeds the scope of this chapter. But at least a brief discussion is in order. In medieval times, some countries not only outlawed theft, but made it a capital offense. If *Dina DeMalkhuta Dina* applied to such a statute, a Jew who committed theft would, under Jewish law, be guilty of two offenses.[127] First, she would be guilty of violating Jewish law's own prohibition against theft. This is not a capital offense. Second, she would be guilty under Jewish law of violating the secular law against theft (i.e., for transgressing *Dina DeMalkhuta Dina*), and this, too, is not a capital offense.

Indeed, under *Dina DeMalkhuta Dina*, a secular government's authority to impose a particular punishment on Jewish offenders may depend on whether the punishment is pecuniary or corporal. As has been mentioned before, Jewish law provides considerable flexibility for individuals, communities, and governments to alter laws regarding financial obligations. Consequently, *Dina Demalkhuta Dina* could justify a financial fine. However, the prohibition against causing a person physical harm is a ritual law, and *Dina DeMalkhuta Dina* does not allow secular law to override Jewish ritual law.

This logic might even be applied to punishments involving imprisonment. It is well-known that people who are imprisoned often become helpless victims of severe sexual or other physical abuse. Because of these consequences, imprisonment might also be regarded as violating Jewish ritual law.

The Issuer of the Law

A final issue concerns the issuer of the law. *Dina DeMalkhuta Dina* literally means "the law of the kingdom is law," and, as discussed, according to many authorities, it is based on the inherent authority of kings. Nevertheless, most modern Jewish law authorities extend the principle to include many contemporary forms of government, especially representative democracies, because they stand in the place of kings.[128] In earlier ages, the doctrine did not apply to judgments issued by courts, and some modern authorities adhere to this position.[129] However, In light of the development of *stare decisis*,[130] the partly democratic process of choosing judges, and the formal assignment of governmental authority to courts, other contemporary authorities argue that the doctrine applies to today's courts, at least when they render decisions based on logic rather than the judges' personal, ethical or ideological beliefs.

Conclusion: How These Doctrines Operate in Contemporary Times

In the immediate post-World War II era, neither *Issur Arkaot* nor *Dina Demalkhuta Dina* was of great practical significance. Two-thirds of European Jewry perished and virtually all of its communities and rabbinic structures were destroyed. But, as will be discussed, each of the doctrines has become increasingly relevant in recent decades and the prospect for their further prominence is on the rise.

Those who regard themselves as bound by Jewish law are predominantly Orthodox Jews, and the numbers and percentages of Jews who regard themselves as Orthodox is steadily rising both in the United States and in Israel. Moreover, the number of qualified rabbinic courts, prepared to hear local, national, and international disputes, while once quite small, is growing. In addition, rabbinic judges are increasingly trained not just as to Jewish law but also as to sophisticated financial, commercial, and technological processes, as well as to relevant secular laws to which *Dina DeMalkhuta Dina* applies. A number of rabbinic judges are graduates of prestigious American law schools. Although the Beth Din of America is not a typical example, it is noteworthy that at least five of its *dayanim* are graduates of the Yale or Columbia law schools. [131]

In addition, the number, complexity, and scope of civil law continues to grow, causing Jews to increasingly seek guidance regarding the extent to which *Dina DeMalkhuta*

Dina requires compliance. For example, the diverse health regulations imposed in response to COVID-19, such as mandatory masking, vaccination requirements, and caps on the number of people who could gather together, even for prayer services, raised many questions. Similarly, as secular laws mandating the reporting of certain forms of misconduct have flourished, they have produced a major debate regarding the interaction between *Dina DeMalkhuta Dina* and the Jewish law doctrine known as *Mesirah* ("turning over"). *Mesirah* generally forbids reporting a Jew to non-Jews or to non-Jewish governments, lest they be improperly punished. Decisors disagree as to whether, and if so to what extent, *Mesirah* forbids reporting Jewish criminals to governments that are deemed to have fair criminal justice systems. For instance, *Mesirah* might forbid a Jew from reporting someone who committed property damage, especially if there is no reason to believe he would repeat the crime. On the other hand, as I have argued elsewhere, *Mesirah* does not prevent compliance with a law requiring the reporting of someone who poses a serious, ongoing threat, such as those who sexually abuse children.[132]

In addition to the proliferation of pervasive and intricate government regulation, increased globalization presents challenging *Dina DeMalkhuta Dina* issues. International transactions often implicate the laws of multiple countries, whose forms of governments and legal systems differ.

While religious Jews dwell in lands ruled by secular law, the doctrines *Dina DeMalkhuta Dina* and *Issur Arkaot* will continue to guide their conduct and preserve their traditions and their institutions.

Notes

1. Adin Steinsaltz, *The Essential Talmud*, trans. Chaya Galai (New York: Bantam Books, 1976), 2–5.
2. Jewish law authorities disagree as to whether *Dina DeMalkhuta Dina*, where applicable, integrates secular law into the body of Jewish law or whether the doctrine imposes the secular law upon Jews as an external, supralegal obligation. See Leo Landman, *Jewish Law in the Diaspora: Confrontation and Accommodation* (New York: Shulsinger, 1968), 39; Chaim Povarsky, "The Law of the State: Theories of Accommodation," *Cardozo Law Review* 12 (1991): 941. According to both views, a Jew's obligation to comply is a religious one.
3. Napoleon provides a well-documented example of a secular power's insistence on subordinating not just Jewish law but all religious law to secular law. In 1802, Napoleon enacted Organic Articles of the Catholic Religion, instituting a uniform catechism that established that the church was to serve the state. See Gil Graff, *Dina de-Malkhuta Dina in Jewish Law 750–1848* (Montgomery: University of Alabama Press, 1985), 73. He issued similar articles for Protestants. Napoleon turned to the Jews in 1806, convening an assembly of prominent Jews and posing to it twelve questions for the purpose of "reconciling the belief of the Jews with the duties of Frenchmen, and to make them useful citizens." Graff, *Jewish Law*, 77. Graff argues that "[a] clear symbol of the challenge of the state to the place of religion in the life of the Jews was the insistence that the assembly convene for its first session on Saturday, July 26," even though this fell on the Jewish Sabbath. Graff, *Jewish Law*, 78. For a detailed description of this assembly and its aftermath, see Graff, *Jewish Law*, 77–109.

4. Many early Jewish authorities expressed this concern. See, e.g., the work of thirteenth-century authority Solomon ben Abraham Ibn Aderet (*Rashba*), *Responsa* 6:254.
5. J. David Bleich, *Contemporary Halakhic Problems*, vol. 6 (Hoboken, NJ: KTAV, 2012), xiv.
6. Ibid., xiv–xv.
7. J. David Bleich, *Contemporary Halakhic Problems*, vol. 1 (Hoboken, NJ: KTAV, 1976), xiii.
8. Walter S. Wurzburger, *Ethics of Responsibility: Pluralistic Approaches to Convenantal Ethics* (Philadelphia: Jewish Publication Society, 1994), 3–4 (arguing that these novel beliefs about God were even more innovative than the concept of monotheism).
9. This perception may be limited to biblical law, rather than to the entire body of subsequently added rabbinic rules and customs.
10. Moshe ben Maimon (Maimonides), *Mishneh Torah, Laws of Court* 26:7.
11. Despite the religious rule against litigation in civil courts, and the legal disabilities imposed on Jews in such courts, a considerable amount of such litigation took place, depending on the place and era. Compare, e.g., Ruth Lamdan, "Jewish Encounters in Muslim Courts: The Ottoman Empire, Sixteenth to Seventeen Centuries," in *Jewish Law and Its Interaction with Other Legal Systems*, Hayes and Israel-Vleeschhouwer, eds. (extensive Jewish litigation in Muslim courts) with Landman, *Jewish Law in the Diaspora*, 89 (arguing that from the thirteenth to the end of the sixteenth century, it appears that no individual Jew ever sued another in a German court).
12. Other relevant doctrines, some of which are mentioned *infra*, include, for example, *Minhag ha-Soharim* (the law merchant), *Pikuah Nefesh* (the duty to save a person's life), *Lo Ta'amod Al Dam Re'ekhah* (the obligation to save someone else from harm), *Rodef* (the special obligation to stop a pursuer), and *Mesirah* (the prohibition against turning over a Jew or his property to certain non-Jews).
13. Deut. 16:17.
14. Maimonides, *Sefer ha-Mitzvot, Mizvot Aseh* 176; Moses ben Jacob of Coucy, *Sefer Mizvot Gadol, Mizvot Asein* 87. For a discussion of whether in modern times this remains a biblical obligation or is only a rabbinic obligation, see J. David Bleich, *Contemporary Halakhic Problems*, vol. 4 (Hoboken, NJ: KTAV, 1995), 4 n. 1.
15. Exod. 21:1.
16. b.Gittin 88b.
17. Samuel Berman, *Midrash Tanhuma-Yelammedenu: An English Translation of Genesis and Exodus from the Printed Version of Tanhuma-Yelammedunu with an Introduction, Notes, and Indexes* (Hoboken, NJ: KTAV, 1996), 11–12.
18. Deut. 32:31.
19. Exod. 21:1.
20. Maimonides, *Mishneh Torah, Laws of Court* 26:7.
21. See also Joseph Caro (1488–1575), *Bet Yosef*, HM 26.
22. *Shulhan Arukh*, HM 26:1; Moshe ben Nahman (*Ramban*; 1194–1270), *Commentary on Exodus* 21:1; Hayyim Dovid Azulei, *Birkei Yosef*, HM 26:1.
23. Yehiel Michel Epstein, *Arukh Ha-Shulhan*, HM 26:4 (even if someone took an oath to resolve a dispute before a civil court, it is forbidden for him to do so).
24. "Ritual" is used as an inexact substitute for the Aramaic term *Issura*.
25. Shimon Duran, 4 *Tashbatz* no. 6; Simcha Krauss, "Litigation in Secular Courts," 3 *Journal of Halacha & Contemporary Society* 35 (1982): 37–38 n. 6.
26. Avroham Yeshaya Karelitz (*Hazon Ish*), *Commentary on Sanhedrin*, 15(4); Ovadia Yosef, *Yehave Da'at*, vol. 4, no. 65; Yehoshua Weingarten, *Hilkhat Yo'ev*, 2nd ed., no. 24; Moshe

Sternbuch, *Teshuvot ve-Hanhagot* (Jerusalem: self-published, 1997), vol. 3, no. 441. But see Yaacov Bazak, *The Halachic Status of the Israeli Court System*, Repr., *Crossroads: Halacha and the Modern World*, vol. 2 (Alon Shevut, Israel: Zomet Institute, 1988), 208–9, which argues that Maimonides's words have been mistranslated as prohibiting appearing before non-Jewish *courts* when, in fact, they forbid appearing before non-Jewish *judges*.

27. Epstein, *Arukh Ha-Shulhan*, HM 26:5.
28. Moshe Isserles, *Shulhan Arukh*, HM 26:1; Sternbuch, *Teshuvot ve-Hanhagot*, vol. 3, no. 441 (in Israel, the common practice is not to hear a case from a plaintiff who first sued and lost in civil court).
29. Sanctions might include removal from civil office, withholding of certain religious honors or titles, fines, corporal punishment, and excommunication. See, e.g., Landman, *Jewish Law in the Diaspora*, 88, 90.
30. Moses Sofer, *Shut Hatam Sofer*, HM 3; Chaim Cohn, "Enforcing Arbitral Judgments in Secular Courts," *Divrei Mishpat*, vol. 3, 191 (1997).
31. J. David Bleich, "Litigation and Arbitration before Non-Jews," *Tradition* 34, no. 3 (Fall 2000): 74.
32. As to the validity of secular wills, see Donna Litman and Steven Resnicoff, "Jewish and American Inheritance Law: Commonalities, Clashes, and Estate Planning Consequences," *Jewish Law Association Studies*, vol. 22 (Emerson, NJ: Bridgeport National Bindery, 2012) 166–193 (2012).
33. Mordechai Eliyahu, "The Relationship of Jewish Law to the Laws of the State," 3 *Tehumim* (1981–1982): 242, 244; Shalom Mordechai Shvadron (1835–1911), *Maharsham* 2:252; 3:195; Yaacov Feit, "The Prohibition against Going to Secular Courts," *The Journal of the Beth Din of America* 1 (2012): 36–37.
34. Feit, "Prohibition against Going to Secular Courts," 34 n. 19 (citing authorities). Nevertheless, a party who files a civil complaint, even for a limited purpose, incurs the risk that a *Bet Din* might subsequently refuse to hear the matter. Ibid.
35. Ibid., 32 (citing authorities).
36. Yonah Reiss, *Kanfei Yona, Keren Michoel Sharf Lihotza'at Sefariom Al-Yedei Yeshivat Yitzhak Elhanon* (2017), *simon* 1.
37. Most major Jewish law authorities favor compromise (*psharah*) over strict law. See, e.g., *Shulhan Arukh*, HM 12; Maimonides, *Mishneh Torah*, *Laws of Court*, 24:2. Regarding the different types of psharah, see Itamar Rosensweig, *Psharah vs. Din*, https://bethdin.org/pesharah-vs-din/.
38. Jacob ben Joseph Reischer, *Shevut Yaakov* 2:145.
39. Eugene L. Meyer, "*P'shara* Helps Jews Settle Dispute with Room for Compromise," *The Washington Post*, February 4, 1991. https://www.washingtonpost.com/archive/business/1991/02/04/pshara-helps-jews-settle-disputes-with-room-for-compromise/9aa0adea-9aff-4b0b-9cc6-4b59fb3ed050.
40. *Shulhan Arukh*, HM 13:1; b.Sanhedrin 23a.
41. Cohn, "Enforcing Arbitral Judgments," 188.
42. Arbitration on this basis may be permitted even if there is no prevailing custom regarding it. R. Shabtai Kohen rules that Jews may agree to have their disputes resolved by even a single non-Jew in whose virtue and wisdom they trust. See *Shulhan Arukh,* HM 22:2, *sif koton* 15. Although Yaakov Lorberbaum (1760–1832), *Netivot ha-Mishpat,* HM 22:2, *hiddushim* 22, appears to disagree with *Shakh*, others interpret *Netivot's* position as limited to instances in which the non-Jew is applying some non-Jewish legal system rather

than his own sense of justice. See, e.g., Yehiel Michel Epstein, *Arukh ha-Shulhan*, HM 22:8; J. David Bleich, *BiNitivot ha-Halakhah*, Keren Michoel Sharf Lihotza'at Sefarim Al-Yedei Yeshivat Yitzhak Elhanon (1998), Vol. 2, 170–71.

43. *Shulhan Arukh*, HM 12:1.
44. This reflects the view that the custom or process of receiving permission from rabbinic courts is merely to clearly establish that a defendant is unwilling to submit to *Bet Din* and that this fact can be determined in other ways, including by strong circumstantial evidence. Other authorities appear to believe that obtaining permission from rabbinic court may be a prerequisite. See Ben Yaakov Tzvi Yehuda, "Testimony in Secular Courts," *simon* 24, "Collection of Financial Rulings by Rabbinical Courts," psaki.org./Psakim/File/849 (citing authorities). See also Chaim Aryeh Kahane (1830–1917), *Divrei Geonim*, 52:15 (citing Ahai Gaon [680–752], 3 *Hut Ha-Meshulash* no. 6).
45. J. David Bleich, *Contemporary Halakhic Problems*, vol. 5 (Southfield, MI: Targum Press, 2005), 81–82.
46. Kahane, *Divrei Geonim*. Some *Bet Din* judges occasionally cite rare instances in which non-Jews have agreed to litigate in *Bet Din*, perhaps because such proceedings are speedier and involve lower costs.
47. Ariel bar Ilei, "Suit Against an Insurance Company," Torahland.org.il/50926.
48. Bleich, *Contemporary Halakhic Problems*, vol. 5, 80–81.
49. Avraham David of Buczacz (1770–1840), *Kesef ha-Kodshim*, HM 26:2; Yaakov Lorberbaum, *Netivot ha-Mishpat* HM 26:3; Avraham Shlomo Katz, *Orhot ha-Mishpatim*, cited in Bleich, *Contemporary Halakhic Problems*, vol. 5, 82. For a case relying on a person's collateral conduct as proof that he would not litigate in *Bet Din*, see Shlomo Luria (*Maharshal*), *Yam Shel Shlomo*, *Baba Kamma*, ch. 8, no. 65.
50. See *Shulhan Arukh*, HM 26:2; Maimonides, *Mishneh Torah Laws of Court* 26:7.
51. b.Baba Kamma 92b (citing Ezekiel 24:13).
52. Typically, the defendant has the right to designate a rabbinic court other than the one selected by the plaintiff.
53. This view is cited favorably by many authorities, including Asher ben Yehiel (*Rosh*), *Commentary on b.Bava Kamma* 92b, *simon* 17.
54. *Rosh*, *Commentary on b.Baba Kamma* 92b, *simon* 17.
55. Note the similarity between the Talmudic expression of "throwing the wall" at someone and the American expression of "throwing the book" at a person.
56. Mordechai Willing, "Retaining the Proceeds of Secular Court Judgments," 2 *The Journal of the Beth Din of America* 12 (2014). Willig cites Isaac ben Moses of Vienna (*Ohr Zarua*; *c.* 1200–*c.* 1270) for the proposition that, but for the *Issur Arkaot*, it would be permitted to force a defendant to adjudicate a claim in secular courts, because Judaism recognizes that God commanded non-Jews to establish a judicial system. Willig states that, according to ben Moses, if the two litigants were to voluntarily subject their dispute to a secular court, the judgment would be binding under Jewish law, even though the parties would both be culpable for having violated *Issur Arkaot*. Willig explains this result under the doctrine of *Dina DeMalkhuta Dina*.
57. See Akiva Eiger, *Shulhan Arukh*, HM 26:1; Yehiel Michel Epstein, *Arukh ha-Shulhan*, HM 26:2; Bleich, *Contemporary Halakhic Problems*, vol. 4, 81; Ezra Basri, *Dinei Mamanot*, vol. 1, 346 (2nd ed., Jerusalem: Haktav Institute, 1990) (even if the award was from an Israeli court). Similarly, even if a Jewish defendant prevails in civil court, if he knows that he is liable under Jewish law, he may still be religiously obligated to pay the amount owed. Sternbuch, *Teshuvot ve-Hanhagot*, vol. 3, no. 441.

58. Samuel b. Yitzhak Ha-Sardi, *Sefer ha-Terumot*, gate 62:3.
59. *Rosh* was perhaps the earliest authority to explicate Paltoi's interpretation of the passage in *Baba Kamma*. Subsequent rabbinic authorities disagree as to whether *Rosh* believes that Paltoi requires a plaintiff to receive permission from a *Bet Din* to sue in civil court against a defendant who refuses to submit to *Bet Din*. See Cohn, "Enforcing Arbitral Judgments," 190.
60. b.Gittin 88b.
61. As a practical matter, some secular judiciaries, either because of their own substantive priorities or because of constitutional or other limitations, might be unable or unwilling to issue rulings directing parties to comply with rabbinically issued judgments. Such concerns often arise in connection with enforcement of rabbinical judgments regarding topics such as divorce, child support, or child custody. They are rarely raised with respect to the enforcement of Jewish arbitral awards in other financial or commercial disputes, provided that the arbitration complied with secular concepts of "due process." See generally *Application, Recognition, or Consideration of Jewish Law by Courts in United States*, 81 A.L.R.6th 1 (Jay M. Zitter).
62. See Lorberbaum, *Netivot* 26:2
63. Menahem Elon; *Mishpat Ivri*, vol. 2, 22 n. 20 and 122 n. 147.
64. b.Sanhedrin *23a*.
65. Aderet, *Responsa*, vol. 2, no. 290.
66. Isserles, *Shulhan Arukh*, HM 8:1. This gloss added Ashkenazi viewpoints to the *Shulhan Arukh*, whose principal author was Sephardi.
67. Ibid.; Aderet, *Responsa*, vol. 2, no. 290; Shlomo Goren, *ha-Tzofeh*, 3 Adar I 5708. Repr., *Pi ha-Torah* I, 150–51.
68. *Shulhan Arukh*, HM 12; Maimonides, *Miishneh Torah, Laws of Court* 24:2.
69. Israeli civil law relies principally on pre-1948 law, based on British and Turkish law. But even if were to rely solely on post-1948 laws enacted by the State of Israel, those laws would not necessarily reflect *halakhic* values.
70. See Chaim Jachter, *Gray Matter: Discourses in the Complex Halakhic Issues of Today*, vol. 2 (Brooklyn, NY: Yashar Publications, 2006) 167: "Virtually all authorities accept the *Hazon Ish's* [i.e., Karelitz's] position."
71. See Avraham Sherman, "Parameters of Courts Before Which It Is Prohibited to Appear," *Divrei Mishpat* 3 (1997): 108–9.
72. Ibid. Bleich, *Contemporary Halakhic Problems*, vol. 5, 19–21, explains that Herzog construed Meiri as stating that the courts of Suria permissibly applied rules that they crafted through their intellect (i.e., "judge-made" laws) rather than improperly applying a set of secularly enacted statutes. Bleich himself interprets Meiri's words as stating that the courts of Suria never felt themselves bound to apply secular law but, instead, used their own judgment, considering in part the value, if any, that they saw in the approaches of any legal systems with which they were familiar.
73. As explained in the text, for the purposes of our chapter, a court is not a "rabbinic court" simply because its judges are Jewish and proficient in Jewish law. The court must also apply Jewish law.
74. Isserles, *Shulhan Arukh*, HM 3:4; Maimonides, *Mishneh Torah Laws of Court*, 4:12–16.
75. There are diverse arguments for allowing even these issues to be litigated in Israeli rabbinic courts. Some contend that *Dina Demalkhuta Dina* applies to such laws and makes them religiously binding. Others believe that these laws are not religiously binding, but rely on

the rabbinic judges in those courts to rule according to *halakhah*, while perhaps "framing" their ruling to fit the secular law formula.

76. See generally Rachel Levmore and Steven Gottlieb, this volume, "*Halakhic* Responses to Modernity: Divorce and *Agunah*."
77. Sofer, *Shut Hatam Sofer*, YD 314; Emanuel Quint, *A Restatement of Rabbinic Civil Law*, vol. 9 (New York: Gefen, 2003), 303–4; Samuel Shilo, *Dina DeMalkhuta Dina*, 2nd ed. (Jerusalem: *Difus Akadimi bi-Yerushalayim*, 1995), 85–87.
78. Yom Tov b. Abraham Ishbili (1250–1330), on *b.Bava Basra* 54b, *s.v.*, "*v'ha'mar Shmuel*." This theory is often compared to the "social contract" theory mentioned by Socrates and that Rousseau articulated centuries later.
79. Isaac b. Moses (1180–1250), *Or Zarua* no. 341; *Ramban*, *Shut Ramban* no. 46.
80. R. Israel Isserlein (1390–1460), *Terumath Hadeshen* no. 341; Maimonides, *Mishneh Torah*, *Laws of Theft*, 5:17–18.
81. Sofer, *Shut Hatam Sofer*, OH 208 and HM 44.
82. m.Pirkei Avot 3:2.
83. Nissin b. Reuben Gerondi (1310-137), *Commentary on b.Nedarim* 28a. See also Solomon ben Abraham Ibn Aderet, *Commentary on b.Nedarim* 28a. See also Quint, *Restatement of Rabbinic Civil Law*, vol. 9, 307 (citing this as the view of Eliezer b. Samuel [Eliezer of Metz]).
84. Of course, in extreme cases, it may be permissible under Jewish law to deport a Jew from the land of Israel for reasons other than his violation of Israeli law. See generally Menachem Elon, "Extradition in Jewish Law," and Shaul Yisraeli, "Extradition," in *Crossroads: Halacha and the Modern World*, vol. 3 (Alon Shevut, Israel: Zomet Institute, 1990). A similar argument might be raised against the applicability of *Dina DeMalkhuta Dina* to the laws of any country whose internal rules would not permit it to deport their citizens.
85. Modern political theory does not adopt the perspective that the government owns a nation's property.
86. Even if secular governments outside Israel lack the authority to exile, it is possible for them to change that (e.g., by amending their constitutions to provide such authority). As a matter of Jewish law, however, no government in the land of Israel could acquire such authority.
87. Interestingly, Sofer argues that Gerondi himself would agree that *Dina DeMalkhuta Dina* would apply in Israel pursuant to Ishbili's argument. Sofer, *Shut Hatam Sofer*, OH 208 and HM 44. See also Yosef Eliyahu Henkin (1881–1973), *Kitvei HaGriya Henkin*, vol. 2 (Brooklyn, NY: Ezras Torah Fund, 1989), 175 (arguing that Gerondi really means to cite all the benefits the people receive from living in the land, not merely the king's ownership of the land). But see Osher Weiss (b. 1953), *Shut Minhat Osher*, vol. 2, no. 121:5.
88. This argument, however, might be rebutted by reference to a Jewish law principle known as *Batlah Da'ato*, which provides that, in some instances at least, if an individual's intention is exceedingly eccentric, it is treated as legally meaningless. In such cases, the individual is deemed to have had the intention that a normal person presumably possesses. Thus, if Jewish law authorities believe that a non-eccentric person would agree to accept the king's law, then a particular person's idiosyncratic disagreement is disregarded.
89. Weiss, *Shut Minhat Osher*, vol. 2, no. 121:5. Weiss uses the expression *Kulei Alma* (lit. "the whole world") agrees to this proposition. It is not entirely clear if he intends to refer to all the *halakhic* decisors previously mentioned in his article or only those named in connection with the immediately preceding portion of the article.

90. Bleich, *Contemporary Halakhic Problems*, vol. 4, 67–68. For example, if a people readily buy and sell based on the king's currency, the people accept the king as the sovereign. Bleich contends that this explanation "is echoed" by Maimonides, who identifies specific ways in which a people's acceptance of someone as the sovereign can be established.
91. m.Gittin 1:5.
92. Yitzhaki, on b.Gittin 9b.
93. Steven H. Resnicoff, *Understanding Jewish Law*, 2nd ed. (Durham, NC: Carolina Academic Press, 2019), 47–48, 107–12.
94. Cf. Bleich, *Contemporary Halakhic Problems*, vol. 4, 88–89 (suggesting that Yitzhaki, as well as Maimonides, may posit the need to follow the law of the host country based on *reason* (i.e., the need for law and order, rather than on some other dogmatic principle). See also Weiss, *Shut Minhat Osher*, vol. 2, no. 121:5.
95. Under Jewish law, a marriage between two Jews creates a special relationship—and unique obligations and rights—not mirrored by unions between non-Jews.
96. Kiryat Sefer, *Commentary on Mishneh Torah, Laws of Robbery*, ch. 5. See also Eliyahu of Vilna (Vilna Gaon; 1720–1797), *Commentary to Shulhan Arukh*, HM 369:34.
97. 1 Samuel 8:11–17.
98. Talmudic authorities debate this issue. b.Sanhedrin 20b. See also Yaakov Ariel, *Dina DeMalkhuta Dina*, https://www.yeshiva.org.il/midrash/814#17a (discussing various views, including the opinion that although the Prophet exaggerated a king's powers in order to frighten the people, the Prophet was still basing his message on the true foundation that a king does inherently possess certain powers.)
99. Sofer, *Shut Hatam Sofer*, OH 208 and HM 44; Bleich, *Contemporary Halakhic Problems*, vol. 4, 77–80.
100. Song of Songs 8:12. Sofer also relies on the preceding verse, Song of Sol. 8:11. See Sofer, *Shut Hatam Sofer*, OH 208 and HM 44.
101. b.Shavuot 35b.
102. Bezalel Ashkenazi, *Shittah Mekubetzet, Baba Batra* 54b (citing Yonah Gerundi, 1200–1263); Samuel Shilo, *Dina DeMalkhuta Dina*, 64–65.
103. Rabbi Abraham Duber Kahana Shapiro, *Devar Avraham*, vol. 1, no. 1.
104. For a discussion of this power, see, e.g., *Shulhan Arukh*, HM 2; Resnicoff, *Understanding Jewish Law*, 107–12.
105. Maimonides, *Mishneh Torah, Laws of Murders and the Protection of Life*, 2:4.
106. Henkin, *Kitvei HaGriya Henkin*, vol. 2, 174.
107. Landman argues that the scope of *Dina DeMalkhuta Dina* is in some ways dependent on the theoretical basis on which the principle is predicated. He then contends that the "popularity"—in different places and at different times—of some of the alternative bases depended on the perceived nature of the changing relationship between the people and the government. Landman, *Jewish Law in the Diaspora*, 44–45. Exploring this thesis exceeds this chapter's purview.
108. Henkin, *Kitvei HaGriya Henkin*, vol. 2, 176; *Hokhmat Shelomo*, HM 369:8. However, a minority of authorities maintain that *Dina DeMalkhuta Dina* only applies to a law that applies uniformly across the king's lands and peoples, irrespective of the rationale for the distinction.
109. Uri Sadan, "Child Employment During Summer Vacation," asif.co.il/wpfb-file/1-10-pdf-249/.
110. Weiss, *Shut Minhat Osher*, vol. 2, no. 123.

111. Aaron Rakefet-Rothkoff, "Dina D'Malkhuta Dina—The Law of the Land in Halakhic Perspective," *Tradition* 13, no. 2 (Fall 1972): 6; Simeon ben Zemach Duran (*Tashbetz*; 1361–1444), *Tashbetz*, vol. 1, no. 158; Haim Hezkiyah Medini (834–1904), *Sedei Hemed*, vol. 2, 70, no. 57; Isaac Herzog, I *Main Institutions of Jewish Law* (London: Soncino Press, 1965), vol. 1, 27. We use "ritual laws" as a substitute for the word *issura* used by *halakhic* authorities.
112. Ovadia Yosef, *Yabia Omer*, vol. 2, HM 1 (Israeli domestic relations law, as applied by Israeli courts, did not benefit the Israeli government) and *Yehave Da'at*, vol. 4, no. 65; Yosef ben David Ibn Lev (1505–1580), *Mahari ibn Lev*, vol. 3, no. 109 (law regarding creditors' liens on debtors' real estate did not benefit the government); Samuel diMedina (Turkey; 1506–1580), *Maharshadam*, HM 275.
113. b.Baba Kamma 113b.
114. Samuel b. Isaac Sardi, *Sefer Ha-Terumoth*, gate 46, part 8, para. 1; R. Shabtai Cohen, *Shulhan Arukh*, YD 165:8; Isaac Weiss, *Minhat Yizhak*, vol. 6, no. 161.
115. David Hoffman, *Melamed Lehoil*, vol. 1, OH 42.
116. Isserles, HM 369. See also Quint, *Restatement of Rabbinic Civil Law*, vol. 9, 312 n. 80 (citing numerous authorities). This would include laws involving private transactions between individuals if the laws are intended to promote peace among them. See Aderet, *Responsa*, vol. 2, no. 356; Isserles, *Shulhan Arukh*, HM 259:7, 369:8, 369:11.
117. Weiss, *Shut Minhat Osher*, vol. 2, 123 (discussing conflicting views among decisors and offering his own view that *Dina DeMalkhuta Dina* applies to commercial debts but not to personal debts).
118. Henkin, *Kitvei HaGriya Henkin*, vol. 2, 175.
119. Weiss, *Shut Minhat Osher*, vol. 2, no. 122:5 (applying *Dina DeMalkhuta Dina* to laws requiring schools to have automatic sprinkler systems and laws mandating vaccinations).
120. Yonah Gerondi, *Commentary on b.Nedarim*; Moses Zaccuto, *Remez* no. 37 (*Dina DeMalkhuta Dina* inapplicable to commercial transactions between Jews).
121. Karelitz *Commentary on Sanhedrin*, HM, *likutim* 16:1.
122. See, e.g., Sherman, "Parameters of Courts Before Which It Is Prohibited to Appear," *Divrei Mishpat* 3 (1997): 108–9. Some authorities cite as an example civil intestate laws that require children to inherit equally regardless of their gender. Asher Weiss, *Shut Minhat Asher*, vol. 2, no. 122; Ayel Resnikovitz, "*Dina DeMalkhuta Dina* that Contradicts Jewish Law," asif.co.il/wpfb-file/4_3-pdf-17/.
123. For the proposition that *Dina DeMalkhuta Dina* does not apply to civil intestate law providing for equal rights to the deceased's children regardless of their gender, see, e.g., Weiss, *Shut Minhat Osher*, vol. 2, no. 122; Resnikovitz, "*Dina DeMalkhuta Dina* that Contradicts Jewish Law," asif.co.il/wpfb-file/4_3-pdf-17/.
124. Moshe Feinstein, *Iggerot Moshe*, HM part 1, no. 72.
125. Steven H. Resnicoff, "Bankruptcy Law—A Viable Halachic Option?," *Journal of Halacha & Contemporary Society* 24, no. 5 (Fall 1992): 91–94.
126. Resnicoff, *Understanding Jewish Law*, 91–94.
127. If the underlying conduct prohibited by secular law would not, but for the statute, violate Jewish law, a Jewish offender would be *halakhically* guilty only for violating *Dina DeMalkhuta Dina*.
128. Henkin, *Kitvei HaGriya Henkin*, vol. 2, 174; Weiss, *Shut Minhat Osher*, vol. 2, no. 121:4:9; Moshe Feinstein, *Iggerot Moshe*, HM part 2, 62. Interestingly, few, if any, authorities have examined the possible effects of various electoral scenarios, such as the election of a

government by only a plurality rather than by a majority or the election of a government based on votes cast by non-Jews.

129. Menashe Klein (1924–2011), *Mishne Halachoth*, vol. 9, no. 333(4).
130. *Stare decisis* developed in the mid-nineteenth century. See https://corporatefinanceinstitute.com/resources/wealth-management/stare-decisis/
131. https://bethdin.org/about/
132. Steven H. Resnicoff, "Jewish Law and the Tragedy of Sexual Abuse of Children: The Dilemma within the Orthodox Jewish Community," *Rutgers Journal of Law and Religion* 13, no. 2 (2012): 314–59.

CHAPTER 29

THE RABBINICAL COURTS OF OUR GENERATION

AMIHAI RADZYNER

Introduction

Examination of all the rabbinical courts[1] currently operating in the Jewish world reveals a clear division into two groups. In one group, which contains the absolute majority of the courts, they have no official status in the sense that they do not act on behalf of the state, and the state does not obligate its Jewish citizens to litigate before them. Litigation before these courts is only by virtue of consent of the parties to appear before them, and their power of enforcement is limited to the agreement between the parties and the powers conferred by the state on arbitration institutions, under the arbitration laws of each state. For reasons shown below, in Israel, it is customary to refer to these courts as "private courts."

In the second group are the official courts, that is, those that operate by virtue of an authority granted to them by specific laws of the state. These courts have various powers that are vested only in state courts, for example, to coerce litigants to appear before the court even without their consent, or to enforce court provisions and judgments by various state means of coercion and punishment. In the areas ascribed to them by law, these courts also apply the *halakhah* to Jews who do not consider themselves obligated by it. This group currently includes only the official rabbinical courts of the State of Israel and the rabbinical courts in Morocco.[2] Because Morocco has a very small Jewish community left, the discussion of the second group focuses on the courts in the State of Israel. It is clear that the number of courts in the second group is much smaller than in the first, but the number of litigants and cases in them is much larger, because Israeli citizens are obligated to litigate in matters related to marriage and divorce in these courts. Moreover, the importance of this second group also stems from the fact that many of the innovations in the rabbinical courts in the twentieth century originated from the official courts, and from there moved to some of the private courts. For this reason, I will begin with the review of these courts.

A secondary distinction that can be made between rabbinical courts pertains to their area of practice. There are courts that deal only with the field of civil law (*Dine Mamonot* or *Hoshen Mishpat*), those that deal only with family law (*Even Haezer*), and occasionally with inheritance law and conversion, and there are those that deal with all areas.[3] It appears that in Israel there is a close connection between this division and the status of the court as "official" (i.e., state sponsored) or "private." The official Israeli courts tend to deal more with matters of personal status, whereas private courts with civil matters.

The Official Courts in Israel

It is no exaggeration to say that the official rabbinical courts in Israel are the most significant *halakhic* institutions in the Jewish world today. This is true both with regard to the scope of their authority, which extends over the largest Jewish population, and with regard to their influence on the lives of Jews and Jewish communities in Israel and abroad.

The system of official rabbinical courts was established in the Land of Israel at the beginning of the British Mandate period, with the creation of the Chief Rabbinate of Eretz-Israel as the Supreme Rabbinical Court in 1921,[4] and the delineation of its jurisdiction in mandatory legislation in 1922.[5] Since then, the system has been embedded in Israeli law as an official judicial system of the State, and it has sole jurisdiction in matters of marriage and divorce for all Jewish citizens and residents of Israel (there is no civil marriage or divorce in Israel, except in very rare cases).[6] Moreover, this adjudication is to be carried out strictly in accordance with Orthodox *halakhah*.[7] In recent years, the rabbinical court system has also been granted authority (subject to various conditions) to handle divorce suits involving Jews who are not citizens or residents of Israel. The reason for this is the understanding that only a rabbinical institution that operates by virtue of state law can resolve situations of refusal to grant a divorce and exercise pressure on recalcitrant husbands, using the means placed at its disposal by the State.[8] To a significant degree, Orthodox rabbinical courts abroad are subject to the *halakhic* policy of Israeli rabbinical courts regarding matters of divorce and conversion.[9] This reality, in which a *halakhic* institution operates by virtue of civil law, has far-reaching operational consequences for the rabbinical courts.

There is no doubt that the official system has great advantages, especially in the field of enforcement, and this is the reason its authority has been extended to Jews who do not have an affiliation with the State of Israel. The official courts have a similar authority to that of the courts of law: individuals sued in these courts cannot refuse to appear at a hearing, and the matter is not subject to their consent;[10] the courts can involve state authorities to ensure that their various rulings are complied with; and they have legal tools to put pressure on citizens who do not comply with their rulings. This last point is especially important in the critical issue of refusal to grant a divorce (on this problem in the modern world and the attempts to deal with it, see Eleff, this volume, and Levmore and Gotlieb, this volume): Israeli law provides the courts with many tools, from revoking a driver's license to imprisonment, to obligate a recalcitrant spouse to grant or receive the writ of divorce.[11]

At the same time, alongside the obvious benefits deriving from state recognition of the courts, their becoming official institutions has also led to a dramatic violation of their various powers, which began as early as the Mandate period. The mere fact that the law specified the areas that the rabbinical courts could adjudicate—"matters of marriage and divorce"[12]—left outside its jurisdiction most of the legal issues that rabbinical courts everywhere had adjudicated since time immemorial, namely, civil law cases (*dine mamonot*). Until 2006 these matters were deemed within the rabbinical courts' jurisdiction only where both sides agreed to accept their authority, that is, to adjudicate their matter in accordance with the state's arbitration law (*Arbitration Law*, 5728–1968), which allows the civil courts to interfere with the arbitrator's ruling.[13] Moreover, the rabbinical courts were not given exclusive jurisdiction over many of the issues related to family law, unless both parties agreed to accept their authority.[14]

The State of Israel inherited this situation from the Mandatory government,[15] and from the point of view of the rabbinical courts, made things worse. Although the law made it possible for the rabbinical courts to exercise jurisdiction over matters related to divorce (property, maintenance, etc.), it specified that this authority was contingent on the claim being filed with the rabbinical court before its submission to a civil court, as civil courts also have jurisdiction over such matters.[16] According to many rabbinical judges (*dayanim*), it is *halakhically* problematic for a divorce proceeding to be conducted in parallel by a rabbinical court and a civil court, as they represent quite different legal systems. In other words, it is problematic that divorce proceedings are not in their entirety under the exclusive jurisdiction of the rabbinical courts, and thus not necessarily conducted entirely in accordance with Jewish law.[17] Furthermore, the State of Israel has determined, legislatively and through Supreme Court rulings, that matters pertaining to property are not to be adjudicated in accordance with Jewish law even in the rabbinical courts, unless both sides explicitly agree to it.[18] This is clearly problematic, as it means that the rabbinical court judge is required to divide the parties' property in a manner that does not accord with the rules of Jewish law. Some of the judges actually stated that they could not rule according to the law,[19] but it must be said that most judges in recent years have indeed acted according to the law, even if it was because they had no choice, while offering various *halakhic* justifications for this.[20]

It is not only legislation that has reduced the rabbinical courts' jurisdiction. Over the years, the Supreme Court, in its capacity as High Court of Justice, has handed down various rulings that narrowed the rabbinical courts' powers and directed them to act contrary to what they perceived as binding *halakhah*.[21] This trend culminated in a ruling in 2006 that rabbinical courts are not authorized to engage in arbitration. The significance of this ruling lies in the fact that rabbinical courts have no authority at all to adjudicate monetary issues, including conflicts arising from the execution of divorce agreements after the bill of divorce (*get*) has been granted.[22]

In sum, it can be said that the legal reality in Israel turned the official courts into the most significant *halakhic* institution in our generation, but this is true only in relation to certain parts of family law, especially to matters of personal status. The same official status is also the reason that prevents them from ruling in an area that has occupied a significant part of the legal practice over the generations: civil law or *dine mamonot*.

The transformation of the courts in the Land of Israel into official judicial institutions has also led to significant innovations in the field of *halakhic* procedure. The Mandatory legal system, and then the Israeli system, held that making the rabbinical courts official required the adoption of procedural modifications that were not recognized by the *halakhah*, and perhaps even contrary to it, but were nevertheless necessary in a modern judicial system. Some of these adjustments, stemming from the rules of other legal systems, were imposed on the courts against their will, and the official system of rabbinical courts was forced to accept them. Still, as will be shown below, their acceptance in the official courts has contributed to certain procedural amendments being accepted over the years in some of the private courts as well. The two main procedural innovations appear already during the Mandate period. Namely, in 1921, the British authorities established the Chief Rabbinate of Eretz-Israel, an organization whose main function was to serve as a supreme judicial institution in charge of the rabbinical courts across the country, and to function also as a court of appeals. The establishment of this institution was a significant innovation in the world of *halakhah* in general and in Eretz-Israel in particular, because the main sources of *halakhah* do not recognize the existence of a court of appeals, at least not in the accepted legal sense of this term.[23] Indeed, this innovation, together with the legal institutionalization of the rabbinical courts (which weakened the unofficial rabbinical courts and removed their ability to enforce their rulings), resulted in a great deal of outrage in ultra-Orthodox circles, particularly in Jerusalem. Eventually, it resulted in a rift that remains to this day between extreme ultra-Orthodox circles on one hand and the rabbinate and the other official religious institutions of the State on the other. But the first Ashkenazi Chief Rabbi, R. Abraham I. Kook, gave in to this demand despite ultra-Orthodox opposition.[24]

R. Kook and his successors, R. Isaac Halevi Herzog and R. Benzion Uziel, struggled against additional British demands that required changing traditional *halakhic* procedures and adapting them to modern judicial norms. They eventually gave in to these demands because the authorities warned that the powers that had been granted to the rabbinical courts by law were contingent upon their leaders' willingness to adopt these procedural reforms. The courts were also pressured by the Mandatory authorities and the community of lawyers to publish modern procedural rules practiced by the courts. As a result, two editions of the Rules of Procedure were produced during the Mandate, a compilation reminiscent of the Rules of Procedure of the Civil Courts, and which had no precedent in the history of *halakhah*.[25] The rules of procedure of the official courts have been amended several times since then, and to this day they are binding for the courts and those appearing before them.[26]

A significant change caused by the new rules of procedure was the obligation to write reasoned judgments. According to traditional *halakhah*, the court is not obligated to provide the parties with the reasons for its decision, except in special cases.[27] It is the Rules of Procedure from the Mandate period that for the first time established an obligation to provide justifications to all judgments, for two reasons.[28] First, the establishment of the court of appeals naturally required the regional courts to provide written arguments that could be examined on appeal. Second was the effect of the accepted reality in the case of judgments of the secular courts and the demand that arose from the public of litigants and lawyers for similar transparency in the rulings of rabbinical courts.[29]

The new policy of writing reasoned judgments, even if not always observed by the rabbinical judges,[30] has led to another innovation in the system of official courts: the publication of judgments. Until the second half of the twentieth century, no compendium was published similar in nature to that of the civil court files, and containing the rulings of a particular court.[31] Calls for the publication of official court rulings had already been heard from jurists during the Mandate period,[32] no doubt under the influence of what is customary in the civil court system, but the first collection of court rulings was published only in 1950.[33] In 1954, more volumes of judgments from the regional courts began to appear, and a total of twenty-two volumes were published in this series.[34] Today, most judgments are published electronically[35] and in various dedicated collections,[36] which makes it possible to review thousands of judgments. Even if a significant portion of the official judgments is not yet published, it is difficult to overstate the importance and impact of the published judgments. It is valuable *halakhic* material dealing with most aspects of family law that are common in our generation. In rulings issued up to the first decade of the twenty-first century, when the ability to rule in *dine mamonot* was taken away from the official courts, one can also find extensive material dealing with civil law. In any case, the published judgments make an important contribution both to the theoretical study of *halakhah* and to its application and development.[37] Moreover, the publication of the rulings strengthened the status of the Israeli courts, and many judges abroad also rely on their rulings in various cases.[38]

As discussed in the next section, many of the innovations that emerged in the system of official courts have been adopted also in private courts in Israel and worldwide.

The Private Courts

There are many rabbinical courts throughout the Jewish world.[39] The vast majority of them belong to the Orthodox stream of Judaism, and they are in the focus of the following discussion, although the Conservative movement also has courts dealing mainly with divorce and conversion,[40] and in more liberal streams there are courts that also deal with conversion.[41]

In Israel, too, there are many dozens of private courts, and it seems that their number is constantly growing.[42] The vast majority of these courts deal only with cases concerning monetary law, because in Israeli law matters related to marriage and divorce are adjudicated exclusively by the official courts, and they cannot ostensibly be conducted in a court whose legal status is that of an arbitrator.[43] This point is the most significant distinction between private courts in Israel and abroad.

Private Rabbinical Courts in Israel

The establishment of official rabbinical courts by Israeli law left all other rabbinical courts in Israel in a position to operate strictly by virtue of the consent of the parties (i.e., as arbitrators). As noted, this status allows the rabbinical courts to operate only in the area of civil law, and they cannot deal with issues of personal status.[44] Moreover, as we have seen, the official rabbinical courts have been deprived of the authority to adjudicate in matters of civil law even with the consent of the parties. In any case, Jews who wish to litigate according to Torah law can resort only to private courts.[45] Thus, a clear legal distinction emerged in Israel: only the official rabbinical courts can deal with matters of personal status (and most of their business in this area is divorce lawsuits and divorce arrangements), and only the private courts can deal with civil matters.

This dichotomy is not absolute, however. Although the vast majority of private rabbinical courts in Israel deal exclusively with civil arbitration, there are several institutions, mainly in the ultra-Orthodox sector, that also deal with marriage and divorce.[46] The oldest of these is the rabbinical court of the *Eda haHaredit* community in Jerusalem (*Badatz haEda haHaredit*), which was granted partial autonomy, preserved to this day, during the British Mandate period, because of the opposition of its members in Jerusalem to the Chief Rabbinate and to the official courts under its auspices, for ideological and *halakhic* reasons (e.g., opposition to cooperation with the Zionist establishment and unwillingness to accept the institution of appeal). The *Badatz* handles several dozen divorce cases a year, mainly for members of the *Eda Haredit* itself.[47] The leading private rabbinical court in the number of divorces it arranges is the court established by Rabbi Nissim Karelitz in Bnei Brak, in 1968, in which about 150–200 divorces are arranged per year. Most of those who turn to this rabbinical court belong to the ultra-Orthodox-Lithuanian stream. They litigate in this court for communal and *halakhic* reasons (e.g., the assumption that the writs of divorce arranged in it are *halakhically* more perfect than are those arranged in the official system). Still, some litigants from other sectors turn to the court for economic reasons (e.g., losses that could be incurred if the state knew about their divorce) or ideological ones (opposition to the religious coercion embodied by law in the activities of the official rabbinical court). Note that the official court does not accept the divorces arranged in this rabbinical court, and couples who are nevertheless interested in the official recognition by the state of their divorce must perform another divorce in the official rabbinical court.[48]

Recently, we have witnessed a challenge to the authority of the official rabbinical courts even from the more liberal side of Israeli Orthodoxy. Over the years, there have been repeated claims that the official rabbinical court adopts excessively strict *halakhic* positions or is affected by various political considerations (e.g., the fear of resembling non-Orthodox sects or fear of the reaction of stringent decisors in the ultra-Orthodox world), and therefore refuses to adopt *halakhic* solutions that may at times be controversial, but help release the *agunot* and those who are refused divorce. Because of this perception, attempts have been made in the last decade to release women who are refused divorce, in cases when the official court was not able to resolve their problem, by invalidating their marriage in various ways.[49] The most prominent among these rabbinical courts is the institution established by Rabbi Prof. Daniel Sperber, in 2018, which has since released several women who were denied a divorce.[50] The rulings of this court are not accepted by the official court either, and therefore the woman is still considered married by state authorities.[51] A similar challenge to the official rabbinical system has also arisen in the field of conversion (*giyur*)[52]—especially in light of the emigration to Israel of descendants of Jews from the former Soviet Union, who are not Jewish according to Orthodox *halakhah*[53]—which led to the establishment of an Orthodox rabbinical court that adopted a less strict *halakhic* position regarding the requirements made of converts.[54]

As noted, however, most of the activity of private rabbinical courts in Israel is in the area of civil arbitration according to Torah law, arbitration which is also recognized by Israeli law.[55] Dozens of such rabbinical courts belonging to various religious and ethnic sectors operate in Israel,[56] and in recent years there has even been a significant increase in the number of rabbinical courts dealing with cases concerning monetary law (*dine mamonot*).[57] Some of these, mainly in the religious-Zionist sector, even organized into networks, to create connections between the various courts, transfer information, achieve uniformity in the rules of procedure, to promote courts marketing, and more.[58] Most of the claims are relatively small, but in recent years the rabbinical courts have also dealt with significant financial claims.[59]

The basic justification for the existence of these rabbinical courts is *halakhic*: the fact that the civil courts of law in Israel, although most of their judges are Jewish, are considered by the vast majority of *halakhic* decisors (*poskim*) as "gentile courts" (about the *halakhic* prohibition on litigation in Gentile or secular courts [*Arkaot*], see Resnicoff, this volume). [60] In any case, there is a strict prohibition to turn to them in civil lawsuits, as every effort should be made to litigate in a rabbinical court.[61] At the same time, in recent years, it transpired that some rabbinical courts market themselves as an excellent substitute for the civil court also for reasons of efficiency and convenience: their process is much faster and cheaper (e.g., because in most cases the parties represent themselves and do not need lawyers, unlike the usual situation in civil courts).[62] Obviously, one of the purposes of this marketing method is to increase the numbers of litigants, including those who are not bothered by the *halakhic* prohibition regarding turning to a civil court.[63]

There are considerable differences between the various private rabbinical courts, and without doubt, among the significant factors are the sectoral affiliation of the judges in the various institutions and the target audience on which the rabbinical court focuses. I mention three main issues that distinguish between the rabbinical courts. First, the question of transparency, as expressed in the writing of judgments and their publication.

As noted, classical *halakhah* does not require recording the justifications for judgments, and indeed, many rabbinical courts, especially those operating in the ultra-Orthodox sector, act in accordance with this *halakhah* and do not provide reasoned judgments to the parties, at least not as a matter of routine.[64] By contrast, other rabbinical courts, most of which have been established in the last two decades, realized—as the official rabbinical courts realized many decades ago[65]—that transparency is required today, especially if they want to attract litigants for whom the alternative is to turn to civil courts, where reasoned judgments are a matter of course. Therefore, these courts, many of which belong to the religious-Zionist sector, declare that the default practice for them is to provide reasoned judgments.[66] The differences between the rabbinical courts in the matter of justification and transparency naturally lead to difference in the matter of the publication of rulings. There are rabbinical courts, even those in existence for a long time, for which would be difficult to find any judgments, and their position can be learned, if at all, from the responsa work of the judges who serve in them.[67] At the same time, there are rabbinical courts whose numerous rulings can be easily found, making it possible to learn about their course of action and their views on various legal issues.[68] Most of the judgments that have been published come from rabbinical courts affiliated with religious Zionism, but there is also a rabbinical court affiliated with the ultra-Orthodox sector that has published many of its rulings, probably more than any other private court.[69] In the absence of systematic data, the number of rulings that have been published attests to the fact that over the years there has been an increase in litigation in private rabbinical courts, which is also reflected in the establishment of additional rabbinical courts in recent years.[70]

The second point concerns the existence of established and clear legal procedures and the degree of their innovation. Rabbi Asher Weiss, one of the top decisors in Israel, and a head of a private rabbinical court himself, sent a letter of congratulations to the rabbi who wrote a pamphlet proposing a coordinated and uniform procedure for all rabbinical courts dealing with *dine mamonot* in the ultra-Orthodox sector.[71] According to R. Weiss, all rabbinical courts dealing in *dine mamonot* should strive for uniform rules of procedure, and beyond that, the phenomenon of courts "in which there are no fixed and systematic rules at all . . . and the litigants never know where they are coming and what to expect" should be condemned. According to him, this state of affairs makes litigants prefer to turn to the civil courts over the rabbinical courts. Indeed, only some of the rabbinical courts, especially those that try to expand their "client base" and appeal to the general public, have publicized their rules of procedure. One of the most detailed and comprehensive regulations is that of the *Eretz-Hemda Gazit* network, which is also prominent in the level of innovation reflected in its various regulations.[72] This network does not hide the fact that it strives to model the conduct of the rabbinical court after that of the civil courts, and the fact that both jurists and *halakhic* personalities in the creation of the regulations participated.[73] Indeed, it is clear that the regulations were influenced by procedural rules that originated in the civil courts, and that at times they differ from those of classical *halakhah*.[74] For example, the regulations allow for the possibility of appeal, which is a *halakhic* innovation as mentioned above.[75] It should also be noted that the *Eretz-Hemda Gazit* network has a unique code of ethics, reminiscent of the rules of ethics required of judges and rabbinical judges of the official courts.[76] Naturally, some of the regulations have a basis in *halakhah*, such as the obligation to refrain from "any conduct that may give the impression of giving preference to one of the sides,"[77] or the requirements related to conducting a dignified hearing in court.[78] Still, many rules are influenced by general judicial ethical norms, which are not present in all private rabbinical courts. A striking example of this is found in the extensive restrictions on any political or partisan involvement of the judges.[79]

A third significant difference concerns the substantive rulings of the rabbinical courts that cover all branches of civil law that can be litigated in arbitration. Rabbinical courts operate in a social, economic, and legal reality that is often fundamentally different from that in which courts operated in the past. The need to address this reality is clearly expressed in relation to areas of law where main development happened in recent generations, or those, which *halakhah* has not perceived as subject to human judgment, such as intellectual property,[80] corporations,[81] indirect damages (*grama*),[82] and various aspects of contract law[83] and labor law.[84] Moreover, legal areas that the *halakhic* courts were dealing with for generations, such as physical property and direct and tangible damages, are sometimes regulated differently by Israeli law, and these arrangements usually affect the conduct of the citizens.[85]

Examination of the rulings of the various rabbinical courts makes it possible to see how they deal with topical challenges and informs about the extent to which they are prepared for *halakhic* innovation.[86] For example, whereas some rabbinical courts usually do not award damages that the *halakhah* does not recognize,[87] there are other rabbinical courts in whose arbitration agreement the parties accept the fact that the court has authority to award such damages.[88] There is no doubt that these rabbinical courts understand that today there is room for liability for indirect damages (*grama*) or copyright infringement, partly because most citizens believe that there should be liability for such damages.[89] Refusing litigate and recognize such damages would keep potential litigants away from the rabbinical court and send them to civil courts.[90] At the same time, some rabbinical judges maintain that the rabbinical court must present the position of the "original" Torah law and avoid "foreign influences" that originate in legal conceptions different from those of the *halakhah*.[91]

Significant differences between the various rabbinical courts exist also in their attitude toward Israeli law, and to a large extent (albeit not completely) there is a correlation between the views of rabbinical judges on Zionism and the State and their attitude toward Israeli law. For example, it can be said in general that in the rabbinical courts of the religious Zionist orientation, there is greater willingness to recognize state laws, even if not completely, both by virtue of *dina demalkhuta* and of such laws being "State custom" (*minhag ha-medina*),[92] whereas in the rulings of ultra-Orthodox courts the attitude is much more qualified.[93] Yet, even in the Zionist rabbinical courts we find reservations about accepting the rulings of the civil courts, at times even in cases of binding interpretation according to law.[94]

In sum, the discrepancy between the rulings of different rabbinical courts on similar *halakhic* issues can be quite wide, much wider than the difference between the rulings of different courts in the civil court system.

Rabbinical Courts Outside of Israel

In many Jewish communities, rabbinical courts have been established by the community or by rabbinical bodies, which also confer authority on these courts. In other words, Jews who feel committed to *halakhah* or to the community that expects them to litigate in a religious court will turn to these courts. The situation is clearer regarding issues that concern personal status laws: divorce, *halitza* (release from the levirate obligation), conversion, and so on. Some of these matters are not relevant to civil court proceedings, and others, especially divorce, are carried out in civil courts in a way that has no meaning from the point of view of Jewish law.[95] At the same time, as noted, in financial matters as well, *halakhah* requires a Jew to sue the other in a rabbinical court, and turning to the civil court is perceived as a severe *halakhic* prohibition (see Resnicoff, this volume). Some Jews act on this directive, even if in recent generations there has been a great deal of attrition in this practice.[96]

Rabbinical courts do not report in detail on the scope of their activities, but it seems that the number of cases concerning personal status, especially divorce, is much larger than the number of civil lawsuits (regarding the legal status of Jewish law and rabbinical courts in American law, see Helfand, this volume). For example, the largest court in North America (and almost the only one publishing its rulings), the Beth Din of America (BDA),[97] presents its activities in a wide range of areas:

> Arbitration of commercial, communal and family disputes through the *din Torah* process. The Beth Din handles a wide variety of matters, including cases involving wrongful termination, partnership dissolution, construction litigation, landlord-tenant issues, synagogue governance and matrimonial litigation.[98]

The only number that BDA indicates, however, is that of the divorces it arranges ("the Beth Din arranges approximately 300 *gittin* per year"). Apparently, the number of cases involving civil disputes is about a third to a half of the number of divorces.[99] It appears that abroad, the vast majority of financial disputes between parties who wish to resolve them according to Torah law take place in *zabla* arbitration and not in permanent rabbinical courts.[100]

Legally, these rabbinical courts operate under the arbitration laws of their country, and the consent of the parties to appear before them is required in every case. The various laws also set different restrictions on the activities of the rabbinical courts.[101] As we have seen in the discussion of the private rabbinical courts in Israel, some of the courts abroad, especially those that want to increase the number of litigants who turn to them,[102] have also adopted a modern way of operation that originates in the secular judiciary system. One example of such ways is the transparency reflected in the publication of binding procedures and in the publication, however partial, of judgments.[103]

There is no doubt that different courts may reach different legal results on the same issue. This is due to the fact that Jewish Law is a system in which a judge or arbitrator has a very wide discretion and a relatively large degree of freedom both in choice and in the analysis of the sources used for his ruling.[104] An issue that is particularly relevant in rabbinical courts dealing with civil lawsuits is the attitude toward state law and the ways in which it is customary to act in the commercial space.[105] This question—in particular the relation to the Talmudic principle *Dina deMalkhuta Dina* and to the "merchants' custom" (*minhag haSoharim*) or "state custom" (especially when created by virtue of local law)—has been extensively debated in *halakhic* literature since the Talmudic period, and is still widely debated by contemporary decisors[106] (see also Resnicoff, this volume). As we have seen, Israeli decisors and rabbinical courts consider the question of whether Israeli civil law is *halakhically* binding controversial, but it seems that abroad, especially in the United States, there is a fairly broad consensus that customary civil law should be accepted and acted upon in most cases, certainly when the litigants appearing before the rabbinical court acted in accordance with this law.[107] This is how the matter is described in the BDA guide:[108]

> Cases at the Beth Din of America are decided based on Jewish law, although there are many instances when Jewish law calls for the application of secular law to a case. In deciding a dispute arising under a contract that contains a "choice of law" provision, the Beth Din will respect that provision and apply secular law, except to the extent it runs afoul of a specific Jewish law prohibition (such as the collection of prohibited forms of interest). Even without a written choice of law provision, the Beth Din will apply secular law if it is clear, based on the circumstances and the context of their business dealings, that the parties intended for their transactions to be governed by secular law. In some cases, such as certain bankruptcy matters,[109] the Beth Din will apply secular law under the Jewish law principle of *dina demalchuta dina* (the law of the land is the law) even absent an intent of the parties for secular law to govern their dealings.

The willingness to adopt legal and commercial norms accepted in the United States, as well as many procedural improvements (including the possibility of appeal, however limited),[110] are well demonstrated in the BDA's activities. These have contributed to the BDA becoming the largest and most accepted rabbinical court outside Israel, including in the area of conversion and family law.[111] The way of operation of this rabbinical court—as noted, the only one that publishes its rulings—can be learned from its judgments.[112]

How do rabbinical courts abroad deal with the issue of divorce, which constitutes the bulk of activity for many of them? The problem is that unlike in Israel, the issue of divorce in most countries where Jews live (except, as noted, in Morocco) is regulated by civil law, and the State does not obligate the couple to divorce according to Jewish law.[113] This situation creates a serious problem when the spouses divorced in a civil proceedings, but one of the spouses, in particular the husband, refuses to cooperate with the *halakhic* divorce proceedings. The husband whose wife refuses to accept the divorce bill can apply to a rabbinical court for permission to marry a second wife,[114] but the wife whose husband refuses to divorce her finds herself in a state of *aginut* (chained to him). Her subsequent marriage, which is entirely legitimate under state law, will be *halakhically* invalid and her children from the new spouse (assuming he is Jewish) will have the status of *mamzerim*. This situation forces the rabbinical courts in the Diaspora to find solutions to the problem of *aginut*, which is considered by many as the biggest problem faced by *halakhah* today. In various cases, rabbinical courts, especially in the United States, allow social and religious pressure to be applied to those who refuse to grant or accept a divorce.[115] The main solution proposed in various places and with the encouragement of various rabbinical courts, is the signing of a prenuptial agreement, in which the couples undertake to cooperate with the rabbinical court. The most common and successful agreement is that of the BDA[116] (see also Levmore and Gotlieb, this volume). In this agreement, the husband undertakes that his refusal to grant a divorce—and it does not matter why his wife seeks a divorce—may obligate him to pay substantial sums of money to his wife, which will cause most husbands to agree to grant the divorce. This agreement enjoys a broad consensus, and many couples sign it before their marriage (and occasionally even after it). Yet, it has also been criticized, especially by ultra-Orthodox actors who believe that it has *halakhic* problems and that it makes the divorce process too simple, encouraging family breakdown.[117] For this reason, there have been other agreements proposed, which give the rabbinical court broader discretion in allowing the couple to divorce or which do not include sanctions specified in advance.[118]

At the same time, it is clear that there are quite a few cases of *agunot* who married without such an agreement, and there are cases where the agreement is not helpful (e.g., if the husband disappeared, is ill, and the like). Because of the increasing pressure to find solutions to the problem of *aginut*, in recent years, an Orthodox court in New York (The *International Beit Din*) has been set up to examine options for annulling a marriage without a divorce, in the event that process of obtaining the divorce encounters great difficulties.[119] This rabbinical court has been harshly criticized, among others, by rabbis affiliated with the BDA.[120] Note that the rabbinical court of the Conservative Movement also holds that in cases where a divorce cannot be arranged, the marriage can be annulled in various ways, in particular using conditions that the spouses set at the time of marriage and under which it can be annulled in certain cases.[121]

We began by stating that the official rabbinical court in Israel has a great deal of power in dealing with divorce refusers and putting a lot of pressure on them. This power, however, also causes most rabbinical judges in Israel to oppose the signing of prenuptial agreements, such as that of the BDA. In their opinion, the power given to rabbinical courts by Israeli law obviates the need for solutions originating abroad, and because of disagreement about the *halakhic* "kosherness" of these solutions, their use should be opposed. This matter shows that the power given by the State to the official rabbinical court, which does have its benefits, may also lead to the rejection of *halakhic* solutions that have been proven to be effective. Moreover, the fact that some rabbinical judges and decisors in Israel support the agreement in America but oppose its implementation in Israel indicates that State authority or the absence thereof are a significant factor in the *halakhic* discussion regarding laws of divorce that are supposed to be identical in Israel and abroad.[122]

Conclusion

In this short chapter I have tried to review the main characteristics of the rabbinical courts operating today in the Jewish world, the differences between them, and some of their activities. As we have seen, there are considerable differences between the rabbinical courts, the main one stemming from the status conferred on the court by state law. This distinguishes the official rabbinical courts in Israel from other rabbinical courts in Israel and the Diaspora. The official status of these courts, however, also carries a not-so-simple *halakhic* price tag. Moreover, it is clear that if Israeli law, which requires Jewish citizens of the State to litigate in these courts, changes, their *halakhic* status will also be fatally damaged.

To a large extent, other differences between the way in which the rabbinical courts operate, including their rulings, also derive from their attitude toward state law. It can be concluded that one of the main classification principles of the various rabbinical courts is the degree of their acceptance of state law, as well as the acceptance of procedural characteristics that originate in the rules of civil law, many of which constitute an innovation in the world of *halakhah*. An additional important distinction concerns the areas of rabbinical court discussions. Naturally, the rabbinical court will always be more conservative in relation to family law, and for example, attempts to alleviate the plight of *agunot* will encounter opposition in various rabbinical circles. By contrast, rabbinical courts can afford to be much more dynamic and innovative in the areas of civil law.

Acknowledgments

I would like to thank the editor, Chaim Saiman, and Rachel Levmore for their comments on earlier draft of this chapter.

Notes

1. This section deals only with rabbinical courts that operate on a regular basis, that is, not with courts set up ad hoc for the purpose of clarifying a particular claim, when each party selects a rabbinical judge (*dayan*), and the two together choose a third judge. This procedure is known in *halakhah* as *zabla*, an acronym for *zeh borrer lo ehad* (lit., each party selects one arbitrator). For more information, see Yuval Sinai, "Arbitration as an Ideal Judicial Procedure," *Jewish Law Association Studies* 18 (2008): 279–95.

2. The rabbinical courts in Morocco were given official authority to adjudicate in family and inheritance matters in 1918, six years after the beginning of French Mandate, and the authority exists to this day. See, e.g., Shlomo E. Glicksberg, "The Rabbinical Seminary in Morocco 1950–1967," *Pe'amim: Studies in Oriental Jewry* 131 (2012): 35–41 [Hebrew], and the various sources cited therein; Abdullahi Ahmed An-Naim, *Islamic Family Law in a Changing World: A Global Resource Book* (London: Zed Books, 2002), 179; Daniel J. Schroeter and Joseph Chetrit, "Emancipation and Its Discontents: Jews at the Formative Period of Colonial Rule in Morocco," *Jewish Social Studies* 13 (2006): 170–206. On the status of rabbinical courts after the reforms of family law in the first decade of the twenty-first century, see Laura A. Weingartner, "Family Law & Reform in Morocco—The Mudawana: Modernist Islam and Women's Rights in the Code of Personal Status," *University of Detroit Mercy Law Review* 82 (2004): 692 n. 31. In other Islamic countries, rabbinical courts had had official status in the past, but this was later abolished; see, e.g., regarding Tunisia: Mounira M. Charrad, *States and Women's Rights: The Making of Postcolonial Tunisia, Algeria and Morocco* (Berkeley: University of California Press, 2001), 214, or became irrelevant after there were almost no Jews left.
3. There are also rabbinical courts that deal with areas other than "legal" in the narrow sense of the word, such as in the area of *kashrut* (e.g., *Badatz ha-Edah ha-Haredit* in Israel, or the London Beth Din). I do not deal with these issues in the present article.
4. For the processes that have led to the establishment of the Chief Rabbinate as a supreme judicial institution for Jews in the Land of Israel, see Arie Morgenstern, *The Chief Rabbinate of Palestine* (Netanya: Shorashim, 1973), 56–81 [Hebrew].
5. Palestine Order in Council, 1922, §§51 and 53; about the rabbinical courts that operated in the country during the Ottoman period and their legal status, see Amihai Radzyner, "Jewish Law in Pre-State Palestine," in *The Cambridge Companion to Judaism and Law*, ed. Christine Hayes (New York: Cambridge University Press, 2017), 322–23, and the various sources cited therein.
6. Talia Einhorn, *Private International Law in Israel* (Austin: Wolters Kluwer Law & Business, 2009), 171.
7. *Rabbinical Court Jurisdiction (Marriage and Divorce) Law 5713–1953* [hereinafter *RC Jurisdiction Law*], §§1, 2; Moshe Chigier, *Husband and Wife in Israeli Law* (Jerusalem: Harry Fischel Institute for Research in Talmud and Jurisprudence, 1985), 12–22, 66; see Einhorn, *Private International Law*, 168–70, 212–13.
8. *RC Jurisdiction Law*, §§4a–4b; Einhorn, *Private International Law*, 214–15, 218–20.
9. Not all rabbinical courts that grant divorces and perform conversions are recognized by the Chief Rabbinate of Israel. In its website there are lists of authorized courts for *Gittin* (t.ly/o5fv) and *Giyur* (t.ly/YkNG). To be listed, courts are required to follow the policies of Israeli state rabbinical courts. Those who wish their divorce or conversion to be recognized in Israel must submit a request to the Israeli official rabbinical court system, which does not approve such requests automatically, but rather investigates each procedure to ascertain its conformity with the aforementioned policies.
10. There are several areas where the consent of both spouses is required for a hearing in a rabbinical court to take place; cases where there is such consent are quite rare, however. See *RC Jurisdiction Law*, §9.
11. *RC Jurisdiction Law*, §6; *Rabbinical Courts Law (Enforcement of Divorce Judgements) 5755–1995*.
12. *RC Jurisdiction Law*, §1.

13. See: Amihai Radzyner, "The Impact of Supreme Court Rulings on the Halakhic Status of the Official Rabbinical Courts in Israel," in *Institutionalizing Rights and Religion: Competing Supremacies*, ed. Leora Batnitzky and Hanoch Dagan (New York: Cambridge University Press, 2017), 224–40.
14. See *RC Jurisdiction Law*, §9.
15. Chigier, *Husband and Wife in Israeli Law*, 12–28.
16. *RC Jurisdiction Law*, §3; Chigier, *Husband and Wife in Israeli Law*, 66–67; Einhorn, *Private International Law in Israel*, 188–89.
17. See, e.g., Amihai Radzyner, "Problematic *Halakhah*: Creative *Halakhic* Rulings in Israeli Rabbinical Courts," *Jewish Law Annual* 20 (2013): 103–77; Amihai Radzyner, "Annulment of Divorce in Israeli Rabbinical Court," *Jewish Law Association Studies* 23 (2013): 193–217.
18. See *Financial Relations between Spouses Law*, 5773–1973, § 13(b); HCJ 1000/92, *Bavli v. High Rabbinical Court* (1994), https://t.ly/O8nle; Einhorn, *Private International Law in Israel*, 201–12.
19. R. A. Sherman, a senior rabbinical court judge, contends that it is not possible to divide a divorcing couple's property according to the rules of Israeli law, as they run counter to those of Jewish law; see Avraham Sherman, "The Principle of Joint Property in Light of Torah Law," *Tehumin* 18 (1998): 32–40 [Hebrew]; Avraham Sherman, "Joint Property Is Not Anchored in the *Halakhah*," *Tehumin* 19 (1999): 205–22 [Hebrew].
20. Avishalom Westreich, "Accommodating Religious Law with a Civil Legal System: Lessons from the Jewish Law Experience in Financial Family Matters," *Journal of Law and Religion* 33 (2018): 481–503.
21. For a critical summary of this move, see Ruth Halperin-Kaddari, "Towards Concluding Civil Family Law—Israel Style," *Bar-Ilan Law Studies* 17 (2001): 105–57 [Hebrew]; Shlomo Dichovsky, "Rabbinical and Civil Courts: Insights on the Friction between Them in Family Law Matters," *Moznei Mishpat* [Netanya Academic College Law Review] 4 (2005): 261–302 [Hebrew]; Berachyahu Lifshitz, "The Garden of Illusions in Matters of Marriage and Divorce," *Family in Law Review* 2 (2009): 107–46 [Hebrew].
22. HCJ 8638/03, *Amir v. Rabbinical High Court of Appeal* (2006), https://t.ly/Gz3mo (English translation). In Radzyner, "The Impact of Supreme Court Rulings," I discuss the significance of this ruling and explain why it is perceived by the rabbinical courts as by far the worst blow to its status.
23. J. David Bleich, "The Appeal Process in the Jewish Legal System," *Tradition* 28 (1993): 94–112.
24. Amihai Radzyner, "Rabbi Ouziel, the Tel-Aviv-Jaffa Rabbinate and the Rabbinical Court of Appeal: A Play in Four Acts," *Bar-Ilan Law Studies* 21 (2004): 132–37 [Hebrew].
25. For all that has been said here, see Amihai Radzyner, "On the Beginning of Rabbinical Courts' Procedural Regulations: 'Sidrei Ha-Mishpatim', 1921," *Bar-Ilan Law Studies* 25 (2009): 37–75 [Hebrew]; Amihai Radzyner, "On the Beginning of Rabbinical Courts' Procedural Regulations: 'Takkanot Ha-Diyun', 1943," *Dinei Israel* 25 (2008): 185–260 [Hebrew].
26. For regulations that are currently binding in the official rabbinical courts, see: *The Procedural Regulations in the Rabbinic Courts in Israel*, 1993, https://t.ly/1jm7r.
27. Eliav Shochetman, "The Obligation to State Reasons for Legal Decisions in Jewish Law," *Shenaton ha-Mishpat ha-'Ivri* 6–7 (1979–1980): 326–52 [Hebrew].
28. Ibid., 352–61.
29. See, for example, the words of Rabbi Uziel, Mishpatei Uziel Responsa, part of Hoshen Mishpat (1940), 13, mentioning these two arguments, alongside the duty incumbent on the

rabbinical judge to prove that he is meting out true judgment to the person who appears before him.

30. Shochetman, "Obligation to State Reasons for Legal Decisions in Jewish Law," 361–72; Radzyner, "On the Beginning of Rabbinical Courts' Procedural Regulations: 'Takkanot Ha-Diyun,'" 248–51 and n. 201. The situation has improved over the years, and today it is unusual to find substantive judgments (i.e., not purely procedural decisions) lacking reasoning or sources.
31. Shochetman, "Obligation to State Reasons for Legal Decisions in Jewish Law," 373–74; Zerach Warhaftig, "Precedent in Jewish Law," *Shenaton Hamishpat Haivri* 6–7 (1979–1980): 115–19 [Hebrew]. In their articles, the two authors discuss the differences between the publication of court rulings and the publication—accepted for many generations—of collections of questions and answers.
32. Amihai Radzyner, "'Ma'aseh Bet-Din': Zerach Warhaftig, the Publication of Rabbinical Courts Decisions and Unknown Draft of such Decisions," *Religious Zionism* 5 (2020): 281–89 [Hebrew].
33. Zerach Warhaftig, ed., *Collected Rulings of the Rabbinical High Court of Appeals* (Jerusalem: Ministry of Justice, 1950) [Hebrew]. This is a collection of several dozen rulings given by the Great Rabbinical Court in the years 1943–1947.
34. *Piskei Din shel Batei HaDin HaRabaniim BeIsrael* (Israeli Rabbinical Courts Judgments), vols. 1–22 (1954–2007). In the introduction to the first volume (3), the editor, Zerach Warhaftig, explains how the establishment of the official rabbinical court system during the Mandate period, with an appellate court at its head, led to the need to write reasoned judgments, especially judgments that can be published.
35. See, for example, the website of the rabbinical court system judgments: https://t.ly/AjPMX.
36. Prominent among them is *HaDin veHadayan* which is published by the Rackman Center at Bar-Ilan University Law School: https://t.ly/eADKk.
37. For a notable example of a significant *halakhic* argument that has developed in Israeli rabbinical courts and has become central to many divorce proceedings, see Shay Zilberberg and Amihai Radzyner, "The Revival of the 'Death of Marriage' Cause: R. Jerucham's Opinion in the Rabbinical Courts," *Mishpatim* [Hebrew University Law Journal] 49 (2019): 113–68 [Hebrew]. The great contribution of the publication of the rulings to the expansion of the use of this argument can be seen there.
38. For example, see the quantity of rulings of the Israeli rabbinical court that appears in the index of the books of the New York *dayan* Rabbi Warburg: A. Yehuda (Ronnie) Warburg, *Rabbinic Authority—The Vision and the Reality: Beit Din Decisions in English*, vols. 1–4 (Jerusalem: Urim Publications, 2013–2019).
39. For lists of rabbinical courts dealing with divorce and conversion that are recognized by the Chief Rabbinate of Israel, see t.ly/o5fv and t.ly/YkNG.
40. See, e.g., Phil Lieberman, "What You Need to Know about a Get," https://tinyurl.com/uxfwpow; Mayer E. Rabinowitz, "The Joint Bet Din of the Conservative Movement," in *Hakol Kol Yaakov—The Joel Roth Jubilee Volume*, ed. Robert A. Harris, Robert A. Milgram, and Jonathan S. Milgram (Leiden, The Netherlands: Brill, 2021), 265–77. The position of the Conservative movement is that civil law hearings must take place in the state courts. See Isaac Klein, *A Guide to Jewish Religious Practice* (New York: Jewish Theological Seminary of America, 1979), 23.
41. See, for example, "Reform Giyur," https://t.ly/xdw99.

42. See partial list in *Din Torah* website: http://dintora.org/inner/56. Many of these rabbinical courts have been established in recent years.
43. Amihai Radzyner, "Get under the Supervision of *Badatz*: Divorce Matters in Israeli Unofficial Rabbinical Courts," *Law, Society and Culture* 1 (2018): 73 [Hebrew]. The issue of the status of conversion in the rabbinical courts in Israel that do not belong to the State is a complicated one, and there are various distinctions between the types of converts and between their status in various matters (citizenship, marriage, etc.). For more information, see Yaakov Shapira, "Conversion in Israeli Law," in *Conversion in Israel: Vision, Achievements, and Challenges*, ed. Yedidia Z. Stern and Netanel Fisher (Jerusalem: The Israel Democracy Institute, 2018), 60–119 [Hebrew].
44. Note that these are "personal status" issues, such as the validity of the marriage or the divorce proceedings themselves. There is no reason why the issues related to divorce (property, alimony, etc.), other than the issue of child custody, should not be debated in arbitration with the consent of the parties. See Radzyner, "Get under the Supervision of *Badatz*," 73.
45. There is no doubt that the *Amir* High Court ruling, HCJ 8638/03, *Amir v. Rabbinical High Court of Appeal* (2006), https://t.ly/Gz3mo (English translation), was one of the factors that contributed to the increase in the number of private rabbinical courts and the number of cases they adjudicate. See Adam S. Hofri-Winogradow, "A Plurality of Discontent: Legal Pluralism, Religious Adjudication and the State," *Journal of Law and Religion* 26 (2010): 76–77. This ruling had additional significance: it is also possible from a *halakhic* point of view that the private rabbinical courts now have priority over the official rabbinical courts in *dine mamonot* cases (until a certain point, there were "official" rabbinical judges who continued to hear arbitration cases contrary to the directive of the High Court). See Radzyner, "The Impact of Supreme Court Rulings."
46. For a review of these institutions and their activities, as well as the classification of the litigants and a description of the relationship between them and the official rabbinical courts, see Radzyner, "Get under the Supervision of *Badatz*."
47. Ibid., 75–78.
48. On the rabbinical court of Rabbi Karelitz, see Radzyner, "Get under the Supervision of *Badatz*," 78–86.
49. See, for example, Avishalom Westreich, "The 'Gatekeepers' of Jewish Family Law: Marriage Annulment as a Test Case," *Journal of Law and Religion* 27 (2011–2012): 329–58; Amihai Radzyner, "Jewish Law, State, and Social Reality: Prenuptial Agreements for the Prevention of Divorce Refusal in Israel and the United States," *Journal of Law and Religion* 33 (2018): 61–88.
50. Marissa Newman, "In Rare Move, Private Rabbinical Court Sets 'Chained' Woman Free after 23 Years," *The Times of Israel*, June 5, 2018, t.ly/rd5E; Stuart Winer, "Private Panel of Rabbis Annuls Marriage of Abused Wife Who Sought Divorce," *The Times of Israel*, February 4, 2019, https://t.ly/LfCR6.
51. See, for example, the judgment of the official rabbinical court of Jerusalem, case no. 622918/19 (October 23, 2018), https://t.ly/ZlZPx.
52. In Israel, the conversion process is officially conducted under the supervision of the Chief Rabbinate. See Shapira, "Conversion in Israeli Law."
53. On this issue see, for example, Michal Kravel-Tovi, *When the State Winks: The Performance of Jewish Conversion in Israel* (New York: Columbia University Press, 2017).

54. Giyur K'Halakha Conversion Courts—t.ly/numF. On the legal status of this conversion in Israel, see Shapira, "Conversion in Israeli Law," 93–96.
55. For arbitration law in the State of Israel, see Smadar Ottolenghi, *The Law of Arbitration in Israel* (The Hague: Kluwer Law International, 2001). Arbitration rulings in Israel sometimes require civil court approval, but it is rare for civil courts to overturn a ruling.
56. For a partial list, see https://dintora.org/batei_din.
57. The increase is evident in all sectors: ultra-Orthodox-Ashkenazim, ultra-Orthodox-Sephardic and religious Zionists. Hofri-Winogradow, "Plurality of Discontent," is devoted to analyzing the causes of the increase in the number of rabbinical courts dealing with *dinei mamonot.*
58. The two main networks are the Association of Rabbinical Courts, which contains fifteen courts (https://www.bateidin.org/) and *Eretz-Hemda Gazit* Network, which contains nine courts (https://t.ly/jE3y8).
59. See, for example from *Eretz-Hemda Gazit*, Jerusalem: file 75109, https://t.ly/Jpljv; file 76024 https://t.ly/dEXvL.
60. Maimonides, *Mishneh-Torah*, Hilkhot Sanhedrin 26:7: "When any person has a judgment adjudicated by gentile laws and their courts, he is considered a wicked person. It is as if he disgraced, blasphemed, and lifted up his hand against the Torah of Moses our teacher. This applies even if their laws are the same as the laws of the Jewish people. This is indicated by Exodus 21: 1: 'These are the judgments that you shall place before them:' 'Before them' and not before gentiles; 'before them' and not before ordinary people."
61. For a variety of sources on this issue (as well as for the positions of religious judges in civil courts who oppose seeing Israeli courts as "gentile courts"), see Eliav Shochetman, "The Halachic Status of the Courts of the State of Israel," *Tehumin* 13 (1993): 337–70 [Hebrew]; Hofri-Winogradow, "Plurality of Discontent," 64 n. 21.
62. Hofri-Winogradow, "Plurality of Discontent," 71–73; Tzvi Dorot and Amihai Radzyner, "'Legal Alternative and Social Vision': Procedural Aspects in the Private Rabbinical Courts for Monetary Cases," *Bar-Ilan Law Studies* 33 (2022): 533–91 [Hebrew].
63. For the great weight of efficiency and savings considerations among members of the religious Zionist sector who are considering turning to the private rabbinical courts, see Lilah Amitai-Aplaton, "Rabbinical Authority vs. Legal Authority: The Motives of National Religious Litigants in Selecting a Judicial Setting for Civil Conflicts" (MA thesis, Bar-Ilan University, 2014), esp. 48 [Hebrew].
64. See, for example, the arbitration deeds, in which the parties waive in advance the request for a reasoned judgment: Arbitration agreement of the *Ahavat Shalom* court, https://t.ly/eAGJe; Arbitration agreement of the *Halikhot Olam* court, https://t.ly/xdD6q.
65. See, for example, Mishpatei Uziel Responsa, part of Hoshen Mishpat (1940), 13.
66. See, for example, the Rules of Procedure of the *Eretz Hemda-Gazit* Network from 2016 (https://tinyurl.com/tuvdvdb), ch. 7; Articles of Association of Rabbinical Courts (https://tinyurl.com/v9gr8bo), art. 7.
67. Examples of the use of these books to describe the legal positions of rabbinical judges can be seen, for instance, in Ron S. Kleinman, "The *Halakhic* Validity of Israel's Judicial System among Israeli Ultra-Orthodox *Halakhic* Decisors: The Building Laws and Condominium Housing Laws as a Test Case," *The Review of Rabbinic Judaism* 18 (2015): 227–59.
68. The largest aggregation of judgments can be found on the *Psakim* website, https://www.psakim.org/. See also the Din Torah website, https://dintora.org/articles/1.

69. The court in question is the Jerusalem Rabbinical Court for Financial Disputes, which has published fifteen volumes of judgments to date. Many of them can be viewed at https://t.ly/LeOYV. On this rabbinical court, see Amihai Radzyner, "The Halachic Status of the Israeli Official Rabbinical Courts, and the Influence of the Israeli Supreme Court's Decisions on Them," *Mishpat U-Mimshal* [University of Haifa Law Review] 13 (2011): 327–32 [Hebrew].
70. Additional statistical information on the growing willingness to turn to private courts is available from Amitai-Aplaton, "Rabbinical Authority vs. Legal Authority."
71. Dov Rozman, *Sefer Kelalei HaDiyun* (Jerusalem: Hesed Neurim, 2014) [Hebrew]. The target audience of the pamphlet emerges from the author's introduction and the letters of endorsement he received. The words of Rabbi Asher Weiss appear there in his consent to the publication of the pamphlet, as well as in his book *Responsa Minhat-Asher*, vol. 2 (2014), 329.
72. See the Rules of Procedure of the *Eretz Hemda-Gazit* Network. For a detailed discussion of this document and the innovations it contains: Dorot and Radzyner, "Legal Alternative and Social Vision." Another comprehensive statute is that of the recently established *Shalom veEmet* (Peace and Truth) rabbinical court—https://tinyurl.com/umjvpla.
73. Law and Halakha in Israel—Court of Appeals by the *Eretz-Hemda* Institute, background booklet and rabbinical court documents 5 (5767): https://t.ly/1gyll.
74. For more information, see Dorot and Radzyner, "Legal Alternative and Social Vision." These things are also true of the regulations of hearings in the official rabbinical courts, which have adopted many rules originating in the civil procedures, and which, at least in their first edition, were written by jurists. See Radzyner, "On the Beginning of Rabbinical Courts' Procedural Regulations: 'Takkanot Ha-Diyun.'"
75. The appeal is discussed in section 9 of the Rules of Procedure of the *Eretz Hemda-Gazit* Network. The possibility of appeal exists also in the regulations of other rabbinical courts established in recent years, for example, in that of the Association of Rabbinical Courts (https://tinyurl.com/v9gr8bo). In the older rabbinical courts, which belong to the ultra-Orthodox sector, there is no possibility of appealing to a higher court, because in their opinion it is contrary to *halakhah*. See, e.g., Rozman, *Sefer Kelalei HaDiyun*, 38. Rabbi Sternbuch, head of the rabbinical court of the Eda Haredit community, even believes that the existence of an appellate court constitutes a deviation from the *halakhic* definition of the rabbinical court as judging according to Torah law. See Moshe Sternbuch, *Resp. Teshuvot ve-hanhagot*, vol. 5 (Jerusalem, 2009), 541 and 550.
76. *The Procedural Regulations* of *Eretz-Hemda* courts, https://t.ly/ea_A. For more information: Dorot and Radzyner, "'Legal Alternative and Social Vision.'"
77. Rule 25. Compare, for example, *Shulhan Arukh*, HM 17.
78. Rules 29–32. Compare, for example, *Shulhan Arukh*, HM 8: 2.
79. Rules 21–22.
80. On the problem of finding a *halakhic* basis for the protection of intellectual property in the words of contemporary decisors, see Amihai Radzyner, "The Intellectual Ambivalence: Contemporary *Halakhah* and the Question of Copyright Defenses," in *Interdisciplinary Analysis of Intellectual Property Law*, ed. Miriam Marcowitz-Bitton and Lior Zemer (Sarigim: Nevo, 2015), 169–214 [Hebrew].
81. See, e.g., Michael J. Broyde and Steven H. Resnicoff, "Jewish Law and Modern Business Structures: The Corporate Paradigm," *Wayne Law Review* 43 (1996): 1685–818.
82. See, e.g., Irwin H. Haut, "Causation in Jewish Tort Law," *National Jewish Law Review* 3 (1988): 1–47.

83. In particular, the fact that in order to give effect to most of the obligations, Jewish law requires physical action. See, e.g., Ronnie Warburg, "Breach of Promise to Marry," *Jewish Law Annual* 17 (2007): 267–82.
84. For a *halakhic* approach to innovations in labor law in the twentieth century, see, e.g., Benjamin Brown, "Trade Unions, Strikes, and the Renewal of *Halakhic* Labor Law: Ideologies in the Rulings of Rabbis Kook, Uziel, and Feinstein," in *Contention, Controversy, and Change*, ed. Simcha Fishbane and Eric Levine (Brighton, MA: Academic Studies Press, 2016), 82–118.
85. A prominent example of this is in the field of real estate ownership. Many *halakhic* decisors today would accept the registration of land as the preferred way of acquiring property, even if it is the product of legislation that, owing to the time of its enactment, has no mention in the canonical literature of Jewish law until the nineteenth century (Radzyner, "Jewish Law in Pre-State Palestine," 323–25). See Ron S. Kleinman, *Methods of Acquisition and Commercial Customs in Jewish Law: Theory, Practice and History* (Ramat-Gan: Bar-Ilan University Press, 2013), 211–41 [Hebrew].
86. For a comprehensive study of the rulings of the rabbinical courts in the fields of contracts and torts, and the various directions proposed in them for determining charges that are problematic according to classical *halakhah*, see Tzvi Dorot, "Arka'ot Shel Torah: Contractual, Tortious, and Procedural Aspects of Rulings by the Monetary Rabbinical Courts" (MA thesis, Bar-Ilan University, 2015) [Hebrew].
87. See, for example, the words of Rabbi Asher Weiss, who as a result allowed the plaintiff to turn to the civil court: *Kovetz Darkei Hora'ah* 5 (2006): 99–102 [Hebrew].
88. See, for example, section 6 of the arbitration agreement of the *Eretz-Hemda Gazit* network: https://t.ly/NPqlZ.
89. Regarding the need to recognize and award *grama* damages today, see, for example, Aharon Lichtenstein, *Dina deGarmei* (Alon-Shevut: Yeshivat Har-Etzion, 2000), 200 [Hebrew]; Abraham Shapira, "The Status of Civil Legislation and Halacha," *Techumin* 3 (1982): 238–41 [Hebrew]. For copyright protection, see sources in Radzyner, "The Intellectual Ambivalence," 203–8.
90. Compare *Kovetz Darkei Hora'ah* 5 (2006): 99–102.
91. Regarding the question of copyright protection, see, for example, Radzyner, "The Intellectual Ambivalence," 208–10; regarding the recognition of a contract that most citizens (and naturally, the law) would consider binding, but which is *halakhically* problematic, see Ron S. Kleinman, "Civil Law as Custom: Jewish Law and Secular Law—Do they Diverge or Converge?," *The Review of Rabbinic Judaism* 14 (2011): 26–32. For a position that rejects Israeli law when it originates in a conception that ideologically opposes the *halakhic* arrangement in the same area, see Sherman, "Principle," 35–36.
92. See the position of several rabbinical judges from the religious Zionist stream published under the heading "The Status of State Laws," *Techumin* 29 (2009): 144; Uri Sadan, "The *Halakhic* Status of the Israeli Labor Law," https://t.ly/eAGLO (2020) [Hebrew]. See also the page on the *Eretz-Hemda Gazit* website referring to the various laws that were applied in the rabbinical courts of the network, https://www.beitdin.org.il/Laws.
93. Kleinman, "*Halakhic* Validity of Israel's Judicial System among Israeli Ultra-Orthodox *Halakhic* Decisors"; Ron S. Kleinman, "The Interplay between *Halakhah* and Ideology: Characteristics of Rulings of Israeli Haredi Rabbinical Judges in Monetary Disputes," *Law, Society and Culture* 1 (2018): 107–66 [Hebrew].

94. Sadan, "*Halakhic* Status of the Israeli Labor Law," 21–26, 35–37; Itamar Warhaftig and Iddo Rechnitz, "The Halakhic Status of the Israeli Labor Law," https://t.ly/kgrmD (2017) [Hebrew].
95. According to Jewish law, divorce can be accomplished only through a bill of divorce, and divorce in a civil court does not change the personal status of the spouses. I do not engage here in questions concerning the divorce itself, such as the division of property and the status of the civil court rulings in these matters. For this topic, see, for example, Dichovsky, "Rabbinical and Civil Courts"; Sherman, "Principle"; Sherman, "Joint Property"; Westreich, "Accommodating Religious Law with a Civil Legal System."
96. Menachem Elon, *Jewish Law, History, Sources, Principles*, vol. 4, trans. Bernard Auerbach and Melvin J. Skykes (Philadelphia: Jewish Publication Society, 1994), 1578–86.
97. On this rabbinical court, see Michael J. Broyde, *Sharia Tribunals, Rabbinical Courts, and Christian Panels: Religious Arbitration in America and the West* (New York: Oxford University Press, 2017), 138–71; Chaim Saiman, "Shots Not Fired in the Culture War: Commercial Litigation in Contemporary Rabbinical Courts," in *Democracy, Religion, and Commerce*, ed. Kathleen Flake and Nathan B. Oman (New York: Routledge, 2023), 64–89.
98. *The Journal of the Beth Din of America* 2 (2014): 7, https://tinyurl.com/regpuew.
99. Michael A. Helfand, "Arbitration's Counter-Narrative: The Religious Arbitration Paradigm," *Yale Law Journal* 124 (2015): 3016 n. 86; Michael A. Helfand, "The Future of Religious Arbitration in the United States: Looking through a Pluralist Lens," in *Oxford Legal Handbook on Global Legal Pluralism*, ed. Paul Schiff Berman (New York: Oxford University Press, 2020), 901–28 n. 32; Saiman, "Shots Not Fired in the Culture War," n. 14.
100. About *zabla* see: Sinai, "Arbitration." The information about the fact that most of the hearings in cases concerning monetary law are conducted by *zabla* panels, at least in the greater New York area, was given to me by Rabbi Dr. Ronnie (A. Yehuda) Warburg, himself an active rabbinical judge in this region.
101. For a discussion of the legal status of the rabbinical courts in America and the rulings of the civil courts relating to them, see Helfand "Future of Religious Arbitration in the United States"; Broyde, *Sharia Tribunals, Rabbinical Courts, and Christian Panels*, 115–136. For sources on the law in England, see *THE BETH DIN: Jewish Law in the UK* (2009), https://tinyurl.com/rf8jo8p. See also Nicholas Walter, "Religious Arbitration in the United States and Canada," *Santa Clara Law Review* 52 (2012): 501–69.
102. In Israel and abroad, there are sectoral rabbinical courts of different Hassidic sects and the like, where most of the litigants who come before them belong to the same community. Their turning to the rabbinical court is often the result of internal identification with the community and its institutions, and at times is due to external pressure, by family or community, to turn to "our" institution. Many of these rabbinical courts do not engage in "marketing" to the wider audience.
103. The leading rabbinical court abroad in this area is the BDA. See its rules of procedure, sample judgments, and various guides at https://bethdin.org/forms/. See more about this in Broyde, *Sharia Tribunals, Rabbinical Courts, and Christian Panels*, 137–50. For another rabbinical court that recently adopted Rules of Procedure, see *Vaad Hadin V'Horaah—Rules and Procedures*, https://tinyurl.com/tox7krj.
104. For the absence of a binding precedent in Jewish law, see Warhaftig, "Precedent in Jewish Law."

105. For a discussion of the attitude of *halakhic* decisors on American law in various aspects, see Samuel J. Levine, *Jewish Law and American Law: A Comparative Study*, vol. 1 (New York: Touro College Press, 2018), 230–44.
106. For a broad overview of the development of the central rule regarding relation to state law, see, e.g., Shmuel Shilo, *Dina de-Malkhuta Dina* [The Law of the State is Law] (Jerusalem: Academic Press, 1974) [Hebrew]; Elon, *Jewish Law, History, Sources, Principles*, 132–37; Hershel Schachter, "Dina de-malkhuta Dina: Secular Law as a Religious Obligation," *Journal of Halacha and Contemporary Society* 1 (1981): 103–32. For acknowledgement of the *halakhah* in customs prevailing in the market, see Kleinman, *Methods of Acquisition and Commercial Customs in Jewish Law*; Ron S. Kleinman, "Contemporary *Halakhic* Decisors, Commercial Practices, and Civil Law," *The Review of Rabbinic Judaism* 19 (2016): 78–95.
107. Michael J. Broyde, "Public and Private International Law from the Perspective of Jewish Law," in *The Oxford Handbook of Judaism and Economics*, ed. Aaron Levine (New York: Oxford University Press, 2010), 378–80, and see a dissenting opinion: ibid., 379 n. 78; Warburg, *Rabbinic Authority—The Vision and the Reality*, vol. 2, 130–47. For the difference between Israeli and American decisors regarding the validity of state law in their country, see Kleinman, "*Halakhic* Validity of Israel's Judicial System among Israeli Ultra-Orthodox *Halakhic* Decisors," 32–34.
108. "Arbitration at the Beth Din of America," https://t.ly/xq65q.
109. On the problematic nature of discussion on bankruptcy, both because of the question of whether *halakhah* recognizes this institution at all and because of the limitations imposed by American law on the adjudication in this area, see Broyde, *Sharia Tribunals, Rabbinical Courts, and Christian Panels*, 11–16.
110. Ibid., 146–50.
111. Ibid., 150–71.
112. https://bethdin.org/decisions. Thus, for example, in decision 8 (https://t.ly/8On7o) the court presents the broad discretion conferred on it by the arbitration agreement, and states that in that case New York State law must be acted upon, although it leads to a different result from that reached by some of the decisors on this issue.
113. There are various countries where there may be different legal sanctions against a spouse who prevents the other from divorcing properly. See, e.g., Amihai Radzyner, "'The Essential Thing Is Not Studying, but Deed': *Get* Procedures after Tort Claims and the Publishing Policy of Rabbinical Courts Judgments," *Mishpatim* [Hebrew University Law Journal] 45 (2015): 67–77 [Hebrew], and the references in the footnotes there. For New York law and recent developments there, see Michael J. Broyde, "Prenuptial Agreements and State Regulation as Tools to Avoid Religious Marital Captivity—The Orthodox Jewish Experience in America and Related Legal Developments," In *Marital Captivity: Divorce, Religion and Human Rights*, ed. Susan Rutten, Benedicta Deogratias, and Pauline Kruiniger (The Hague: Eleven International, 2019), 245–52.
114. See, e.g., Rabbi Moshe Feinstein, *Responsa Igrot Moshe*, Even HaEzer 2:2 (1964); David J. Bleich, "A Suggested Antenuptial Agreement: A Proposal in the Wake of Avitzur," *Journal of Halacha and Contemporary Society* 7 (1984): 27.
115. See, e.g., "Rabbinic Endorsements," https://t.ly/O6eLJ.
116. https://theprenup.org/. For a discussion of this agreement and its great success, see Radzyner, "Jewish Law, State, and Social Reality," esp. 63–64, and in the sources cited therein; Broyde, "Prenuptial Agreements and State Regulation as Tools to Avoid Religious Marital Captivity," 243–45, 253–56.

117. Radzyner, "Jewish Law, State, and Social Reality," 67 and 78.
118. See, for example, the agreement of another rabbinical court operating in New York: https://vaadhadinvhoraah.org/forms/; the agreement of the Central Orthodox Court in the United Kingdom: https://t.ly/zylY3.
119. On the operation of the rabbinical court and some of its rulings, see the website: https://www.internationalbeitdin.org/ and more: Masua Sagiv, "A Time to Gather Stones: The International Religious Court for Solving the Jewish *Agunah* Problem" (unpublished draft).
120. See, e.g., "Advising against the Use of the International Beit Din: A Translated Letter from Rabbi Hershel Schachter Shlita," *Jewishlink*, September 3, 2015, https://t.ly/yGkm5.
121. Lieberman, "What You Need to Know about a Get"; Rabinowitz, "The Joint Bet Din of the Conservative Movement."
122. For more information, see Radzyner, "Jewish Law, State, and Social Reality."

D

Halakhah *and Personhood*

CHAPTER 30

JUDAISM AND THE MODERN FAMILY

ZEV ELEFF

Introduction

In 1970, sociologist Charles Liebman theorized about the tensions between "folk religion" and "elite religion" in American Jewish life. By folk religion, Liebman had in mind the popular sensibilities of laypeople within a faith group. In contrast, elite religion represents the rituals and beliefs acknowledged by faith leaders. Folk religion is unencumbered by ideology and doctrine, inspired by intuition and lived practices. Elite religion is driven by personalities and institutions, focused on theology and textual evidence. It desires legitimacy and organized thinking, and typically overcomes folk religion in the long sweep of history. "Therefore," concluded Liebman, "in the eyes of the elite religion, rank-and-file folk religion is not a movement but an error, or a set of errors, shared by many people."[1]

But the neat binary belies the complexities of religious life. Folk and elite forms of religion are not always at odds with one another. Elite religion does not operate in a vacuum, nor has it been so entirely focused on codified texts and hallowed traditions.[2] It is never fully capable of dismissing contemporary culture or, for that matter, folk religion, as mere impulses riddled with "errors." Elite religion, like Liebman's presentation of the folk variety, oftentimes considers popular sentiments to determine the appropriate path of Jewish law and life. The changing contours of the modern family serve as a case in point. On this score, rabbinic elites of all types have treated the modern family as a discrete value that—depending on how it is conceived—can complement or compete against Jewish observance. Owing to this, religious elites have reconsidered or adjusted their positions based on the proclivities of changing popular sentiment of domestic life.

How each of the three major branches of American Judaism has incorporated these factors into their decision-making betokens particular and underappreciated approaches to Jewish law. For instance, Conservative Judaism has aimed to craft a balanced conversation between textual traditions of *halakhah* with the values that stand for the demands of modern life. Its rabbinic leaders—ranging from those who might have described themselves as "semi-Reform" to the "quasi-Orthodox"—have tended to find the most common ground by weighing these two variables (see Kwall, this volume).[3] By contrast, tradition-bound Orthodox Jews have eschewed such jurisprudential alchemy, refusing to offer, at least consciously, such stakeholdership to values and ideas outside the Talmud and codes. Instead, the Orthodox have found less invasive ways to insert modern sensibilities into religious observance. Here, the goal has been to find places in religious life to inject resonance and meaningfulness without upsetting the status quo. Finally, Reform leaders, who do not feel bound by the strictures of Jewish law, have nevertheless felt most comfortable deciding policy by using a *halakhic*-type argumentation while principally privileging the attitudes and values of modern living (see Washofsky, this volume). Withal, family life, a value that has taken on changing forms in the postwar period, provides a prism to better understand these approaches to *halakhah*. The following chapter examines these changes, particularly through the areas of marriage and fertility.

Divorce and the Nuclear Family

In the 1950s, divorce was anathema in most sectors of American life. It was a period marked by an insistence upon family life and, for women, an emphasis on the domestic arena. Divorce rates remained low, compared to the rapid increase in subsequent decades. Nonetheless, worried writers and concerned counselors in this period obtained a prescient intuition of what was in store for American family life. Marriage manuals and lifestyle guidebooks remained reticent about divorced life out of fear of promoting that circumstance to their readers.[4] Christian clergymen—Protestants and Catholics—championed "The family that prays together stays together."[5] In step with this, the American rabbinate felt compelled to do its part to keep marriages intact. To accomplish this, rabbis conceived of creative ways to encourage the stability of the "first marriage" nuclear family through the prism of Jewish law.

Conservative Judaism's engagement with this issue is a prime example of its approach to *halakhah*: to place Jewish jurisprudence and modern sensibilities into conversation and, when possible, on equal footing. Historian Benjamin Steiner has shown that Conservative rabbis in the 1950s sought to preserve marriages by introducing, somewhat counterintuitively, new protocols for religious divorce to support the *agunah*.[6] The "*agunah*" stands at the center of the debate about *halakhic* flexibility (see Gotlieb and Levmore, this volume). The Orthodox feminist Blu Greenberg had this in mind when she coined the phrase: "where there is a rabbinic will, there is a halakhic way."[7] But long before Greenberg, since the 1920s, Conservative rabbinical scholars had channeled the spirit of this notion. They grappled with the *agunah*, the "chained wife," whose unavailable or recalcitrant husband could not or would not issue her a ritual divorce. This posed a presumed insurmountable problem. According to the Talmud's interpretation of Deuteronomy 24:1, only a husband can affect a divorce; his wife passively receives and accepts the writ. Absent a husband's consent to the divorce, the wife would remain tied to the marriage and her future children born out of subsequent relationships would be rendered illegitimate. According to Jewish law, "illegitimate" Jews can only marry other illegitimates. A woman who wished to avoid this situation had little recourse. She was "chained" to her religiously unfinalized marriage.

Solving the *agunah* dilemma was paramount for Conservative leaders who believed that their Movement could, more than its counterparts, successfully straddle Jewish law and the exigencies of modern living.[8] Ensuring that women could regain their familial footing after obtaining a divorce was directly aligned with this mission. Earlier attempts by Rabbi Louis Epstein and then Rabbi Michael Higger called for the husband at the time of the nuptials to designate a rabbinical court to execute the divorce on his behalf, if such a need arose. But internally, the Conservative Movement struggled with these formulations, fearing that Epstein and Higger had removed too much of the husband's authority to issue the divorce bill, per the Bible's directive. It did not sufficiently negotiate *halakhah* and modern life, conceding far too much on the former to satisfy the latter.

The mid-1950s iteration of this effort was different. First, the practical *halakhic* mechanics were no longer so sacrosanct. By then, Conservative leaders did not feel as threatened by the *agunah* problem. One Conservative pundit put it plainly that these chained women "don't exist."[9] Other realms of *halakhic* discourse fulfilled the Conservative Movement's need to showcase its place in American religious life. Through modifications to standard liturgy and the Sabbath laws, Conservative leaders had identified other significant ways to demonstrate its fidelity to "tradition" and "change."[10]

Second, the so-called Lieberman Clause, this latest incarnation of the *agunah* solution, transformed the narrative from "divorce" to "marriage." The *halakhic* tool was a prenuptial agreement embedded in the *ketubah*, the traditional marriage document. It was legislated and guided by Rabbi Saul Lieberman of the Jewish Theological Seminary (JTS). The amendment stipulated that if a husband refused to provide a writ of divorce to his wife, the couple would be compelled (under an unstipulated but severe financial penalty) to appear before a Conservative rabbinical court empowered to arbitrate a ritual divorce. If the husband still refused, the court could impose an unspecified financial penalty on the recalcitrant spouse.[11] The Conservative's Rabbinical Assembly (RA) agreed that this appropriately pressured the recalcitrant husband while preserving his authority to authorize the divorce. This, however, was not the only reason the Lieberman Clause was agreeable to Conservative rabbis. As Steiner writes, the architects of the Lieberman Clause "worried more about the dignity of marriage than the practical efficacy of the document."[12] Conservative leaders envisioned that the document, approved in 1954, would provide an impetus for rabbis to connect with their congregants and help them work through marital challenges before matters became permanently irreconcilable. This dual purpose made the marriage amendment that much more appealing and in keeping with Conservative Judaism's perspective on Jewish law.

The value of sustainable married life was placed front and center in the discourse surrounding the Lieberman Clause. JTS leaders declared that the purpose was to "preserv[e] the integrity of family life and of strengthening family relations in accordance with the standards of the Jewish law and tradition."[13] The RA downplayed "divorce" in its deliberations, instead favoring elements in the policy that would help sustain the nuclear family instead of dissolving it. The Lieberman Clause stressed the rabbinic role in dissolving a broken marriage but also socialized families to the place of the rabbinate in sustaining home life. Conservative rabbis believed that the Lieberman Clause provided them with better access to counsel engaged couples and spouses encountering marital discord. One earlier draft of the Lieberman Clause emphasized that the couple should "seek the counsel of their rabbi to guide them to harmony and reconciliation, in accordance with the tradition of Judaism, before taking steps which might lead to a conviction of differences."[14] The purpose was evident. Orthodox opponents understood what undergirded Conservative rabbis' point of view. But contrary to the effort on behalf of keeping families intact, Lieberman's prenuptial posturing, alleged Rabbi Norman Lamm, would be "forcing an unwilling spouse to consent to divorce, not preventing one."[15]

The Lieberman Clause, then, provided a vehicle that the Conservative Movement had sought to stabilize the Jewish nuclear families of first marriages. In 1951, together with the United Synagogue, the Rabbinical Assembly established the Commission on Marriage and the Family.[16] The Commission's goal was to support Conservative clergymen. Part of a wider counseling effort, the Conservative Movement launched a series of rabbinic workshops on pastoral counseling and distributed pamphlets on family life because "most of our men had not received sufficient background in their college and Seminary studies to understand the dynamics of the marriage relationship."[17] While the Commission's programs were "sparsely attended," this group was successful in lobbying JTS to introduce a course in pastoral psychology for rabbinical students, the future leaders of the Movement.[18] The Lieberman Clause offered a far more substantial avenue for the Commission and its partner, the Committee of Jewish Law and Standards (CJLS), to formalize a plan to bring rabbis and couples together for the sake of familial stability.

The other sectors of American Judaism reacted differently to the *agunah* problem. These stances were emblematic of their respective approaches to Jewish law and life. The Reform Movement did not hold a market share in the American Jewish *agunah* angst. Since the late-1860s, the Reform rabbinate in the United States had resolved that a divorce "should be recognized as an act emanating solely from the judicial authorities of the State."[19] This meant that the *agunah* was a plight "which happily Reform Judaism abrogated."[20] By deferring to civil authorities to gatekeep divorce, the Reform-aligned Central Conference of American Rabbis (CCAR) possessed relatively little power to protect first marriages and the nuclear family as their Conservative counterparts had done with the introduction of the Lieberman Clause.

But preserving marriages was a shared agenda. The Reform Movement instituted measures to defend against the "divorce contagion." The CCAR established a Committee on Marriage, Family and the Home in the 1930s to "aid the members of the CCAR in their efforts to safeguard marriage and conserve the family."[21] In the postwar period, the Reform rabbinate was the most prepared to embrace pastoral work, relative to the other branches of American Judaism, and to shepherd its married flock.[22] For this very reason, one Reform rabbi averred that "there has been less divorce proportionately in the modern Jewish home is in no small measure related to the healthier Jewish attitude toward sex, to the very fact of Jewish permissiveness with reference to divorce, and particularly to Judaism's high evaluation of marriage."[23]

Orthodox leaders also articulated concern for the first-marriage nuclear family. Much more like their Conservative counterparts than the Reform group, the Orthodox's solutions engaged *halakhic* measures. Yet, Orthodox rabbis, unlike Conservative leaders, resisted the use of ritual divorce as a vehicle to protect it. A preliminary plan for Orthodox and Conservative rabbis to cooperate based on the Lieberman Clause was, for the Orthodox, untenable. The "gap" between the two groups was "wide and unbridgeable."[24] Moreover, the overt confluence of Talmud learning and the values attached to modern living was not a discourse that Orthodox scholars could support. To be sure, in the 1960s, Orthodox scholars such as Rabbi Melech Schachter vexed frustration over the *agunah* problem and declared that a recalcitrant husband was "most contemptible and deserves utter condemnation."[25] Still, Schachter would not yield on his fidelity to traditional norms and interpretations of *halakhah*. Perhaps with the rhetoric surrounding the Lieberman Clause in mind, Schachter expressed bemusement over the "shocking present-day frequency of divorce" but explained that he felt unable, no matter how sympathetic, to take measures to prevent the increase rate of broken marriages and *agunah* cases.[26] Along these lines, the Orthodox rabbinate, although not a centralized group compared to the Conservative's RA or the Reform's CCAR, rejected attempts by leading figures such as Rabbis Emanuel Rackman and Eliezer Berkovits to solve the *agunah* problem. The Orthodox opponents to these rabbinic endeavors feared that the proposals appeared too much like the Conservative formulations.[27]

The Orthodox's principal issue, on a *halakhic* matter, was that the rabbinate could not play as central a role in marriage as the Lieberman Clause, in the Orthodox's interpretation of it, had alleged. Orthodox rabbis rejected the RA's textual changes to the traditional *ketubah* on the grounds that it failed to enfranchise the husband's role to autonomously deliver the divorce writ. They also pointed out that the Lieberman Clause did not indicate the amount of the fine for recalcitrancy. The lack of the specificity for the financial penalty appeared to violate the Talmud's rule of *asmakhta* and rendered the document unbinding and invalid.[28]

Orthodox pundits were also unconvinced by the Lieberman Clause's concern for family values. Orthodox rabbis flouted the RA's attempt to inject modern values into the Conservative marriage contract. These opponents openly doubted whether the Conservative Movement truly cared about it and its implications for *agunot*. "We contend that behind the mask of religious verbiage employed by the Conservative Rabbis," wrote Rabbi Fabian Schoenfeld about the Lieberman Clause, "there lies an underlying sense of insincerity and outright chicanery."[29] Rabbi Chaim David Regensberg of Chicago's Hebrew Theological College was just as suspecting but even pithier than

Schoenfeld: "It's a farce!"[30] Furthermore, Orthodox rabbis were unmoved by the opportunity afforded, in theory, by the Lieberman Clause to counsel couples and preserve their marriages. The Orthodox rabbinate was far less sanguine in the postwar period about its role in pastoral life.[31] Rabbi Melech Schachter, in the above-cited article on divorce and the role of the rabbinate, disagreed with Conservative and Reform leaders who placed much of their faith in marriage counselors. Schachter opined that these "self-proclaimed" experts tend to "prompt the decision that divorce is necessary" rather than attempt to preserve the matrimony.[32]

Orthodox leaders remained concerned about the *agunah* problem and the Jewish family, even as they demurred at the Lieberman Clause. Their direction needed to remain outside the sphere of ritual and existing *halakhic* practice. The Orthodox efforts to solve the *agunah* problem focused on irreparable marriages and for the sake of the chained wife's future relationships, not to repair her present one. For instance, in the 1930s the newly established Rabbinical Council of America (RCA) unsuccessfully lobbied American courts to deny Jewish couples the right to a divorce unless they "first obtain separation from their religious authorities."[33] Here, the emphasis was on women and men who had already decided to break up their marriages. Later Orthodox attempts to support the *agunah* emerged in the final third of the century when divorce was far more common and accepted in American life. In 1983, the Agudath Israel pushed New York State to approve the so-called Get Law that required couples to finalize religious divorce proceedings before applying for a civil divorce (see Helfand, this volume).[34]

In the 1980s and more successfully in the 1990s, the RCA furnished premarital contracts designed to encourage a recalcitrant husband to offer his wife a divorce by threatening to fine him for refusing her request for it.[35] The goal in each attempt was to "rid Jewish society of this scourge which now afflicts our moral condition as a people"—the ability to protect the future marriages, not preserve the first.[36] The RCA's prenuptial agreement did not replace existing Jewish ritual or texts. The "prenup" did not alter the husband's authority to deliver the divorce writ. It was not embedded in the *ketubah* and therefore did not threaten to revise Jewish practice based on in vogue popular sentiment.

The Orthodox rabbinate found other ways to help reinforce Jewish family life, on par with the broader American concerns for domestic life. Take, for example, the family purity laws. Here, Orthodox leaders did not change Jewish law to fill a need. Rather, their goal was to recalibrate the intentions to provide renewed meaning to the Orthodox rank and file. Traditional interpretations of *halakhah* demand that a couple practice abstinence during the wife's menstruation period. The couple is permitted to resume their sexual relationship once the woman immerses in a mikvah, a ritual bath. In 1941, the Orthodox Union's Women's Branch promoted adherence in a five-point campaign that deployed rather harsh tones. Here are the Orthodox Union's top two reasons for observance of the family purity laws:

1. THE TORAH COMMANDS IT. Any Jewish woman who violates Taharath Hamishpachah (family purity) by neglecting to observe the ritual of Mikvah transgresses one of the fundamental precepts of the Torah. *This violation is as serious as eating on Yom Kippur.*

2. FOR YOUR CHILDREN'S SAKE. The future spiritual destiny of your children demands it. Born in traditional purity your children will be afforded spiritual recognition, a life of health and G-d-given immunity from disease which will ultimately lead them to love you and regard you with devoted honor and respect.[37]

Postwar Orthodoxy required a more compelling, family-oriented approach to this area of *halakhah*. In 1966, Rabbi Norman Lamm published a manual on sexuality and married life that rebranded observance of family purity laws. Lamm's popular book—it went through at least six printings and was translated into Hebrew and Portuguese—argued that observance of the family purity laws helped protect marriages.[38] The manual provided an explicit sexual and marital ethic to the observance of Jewish law. Lamm claimed that Jewish law was a better source for this than a learned theological treatise. "No philosophy of sex, no matter how well and cogently articulated, can ever be as psychologically meaningful and compelling as the observance of Family Purity," wrote Lamm. "Only the actual practice of these laws can successfully inculcate Judaism's values and insights into this immensely significant and delicate area of life."[39]

"Divorce" loomed in the background of Lamm's book, even as he endeavored to avoid explicit reference to the word. Lamm included a chapter titled "Staying Married" in which he relied on anecdotal evidence of "domestic happiness characteristic of Orthodox Jewish homes even in the midst of an environment where the breakdown of family life becomes more shocking with each year."[40] The secret of Orthodox marital bliss, Lamm concluded, was adherence to the separation period demanded of married couples by *halakhah*. "For marriage to thrive," he theorized, "the attractiveness of wife and husband for each other that prevailed during the early period of the marriage must be preserved and even enhanced. And it is the abstinence enjoined by Family Purity that helps keep that attraction and longing fresh and youthful."[41]

Orthodox Judaism's attempt to protect first marriages and the nuclear family found its way into other areas of the *halakhic* frontier. One example is Rabbi Moshe Feinstein's position on artificial insemination. Contrary to the Talmud's statement (Yevamot 65b), Feinstein did not believe it was advisable for a sterile husband to grant his wife a divorce so that she may pursue a childbearing marriage with another man. Conditions had changed: with the advance of modern gynecological science, Feinstein recommended in vitro fertilization.[42] Orthodox opponents—most notably Rabbi Yoel Teitelbaum—attacked Feinstein, claiming that the process (if done with a donor's sperm rather than the husband's) was adulterous. That most donors would have been Gentile men (in fact, Feinstein recommended Gentile rather than Jewish donors) also compromised the "purity" and "holiness" of the Jewish people.[43]

However, Feinstein dismissed his vituperative critics (several issued death threats), claiming that his ruling, unlike theirs, had only considered the sources and no "ulterior factors."[44] He rejected Teitelbaum's claims that a woman undergoing artificial insemination was committing adultery and her children were therefore illegitimate. Marshalling many rabbinic texts, Feinstein held that adultery required sexual intercourse and there was none in the case of artificial insemination. In another responsum,

Feinstein reaffirmed his position on artificial insemination and added that his ruling eliminated a wife's "great frustration toward her husband."[45] While Feinstein felt that his ruling stood on solid textual footing, he also advocated his position on the grounds that it supported Jewish couples is an important feature of the *halakhah*'s consideration of modern families.

Feinstein was also involved in Orthodox discussions about screening for Tay-Sachs disease. Much discussed in the late 1960s, Tay-Sachs disease is a fatal genetic disorder, prevalent among Ashkenazic Jews. In 1973, Feinstein wrote on how to defend against Tay-Sachs. He supported discrete genetic testing of marriageable-aged couples. Feinstein opposed testing of young children on the grounds that it would create a stigma against them and feared for the psychological trauma heaped upon these young people who were not yet prepared to consider specific marriage partners.[46]

Feinstein's position did not address Jewish family life. However, it quickly became interpreted through that domestic lens and the efforts of his son-in-law, Rabbi Moshe Tendler. Tendler circulated Feinstein's ruling and, as president of the Association of Orthodox Jewish Scientists (Tendler held a PhD in biology from Columbia University and a professorial appointment at Yeshiva University), adopted Feinstein's position on behalf of that then-influential organization.[47] He also spoke and wrote about his and his father-in-law's shared position on Tay-Sachs screening. In these forums, Tendler encouraged Tay-Sachs testing—in addition and primarily to halting the spread of the disease—to prevent potential divorce.[48] Others within the Orthodox camp disagreed with Tendler's approach and were willing to take issue with him since, by virtue of its focus on values rather than *halakhic* text, this was a matter of public policy and not inherent to the technical mechanics of *halakhah*.[49]

"Intramarriage" and "Intermarriage"

The openness of American life also tasked the rabbinate to respond to various forms of mixed marriages. The most pressing issue for the Orthodox was how to accept children of Conservative and Reform families. With the rise of divorce in the United States, the Orthodox might have been faced with increased possibilities of children born into *halakhically* "problematic" second marriages, at least according to the Orthodox standard. This issue was the core of the *agunah* dilemma and emerged as a paramount challenge as more Jewish couples separated from each other without an Orthodox-authenticated ritual divorce. The Orthodox rabbinate did not approve of the Reform Movement's decision to recognize civil divorce as religiously binding, nor did it endorse the Conservative Movement's change in divorce proceedings. As a result, Rabbi Yosef Henkin ruled that children born into these circumstances were "illegitimate" and prohibited to wed.[50] Henkin's was not the only word on the matter, however. In 1957, Rabbi Feinstein ruled against Henkin on the grounds that neither Conservative nor Reform nuptials were religiously binding. Therefore, a writ of divorce, secured by the substantial weight of Feinstein's reputation and reasoning, was therefore unneeded.[51]

The lenient ruling for Orthodox Jews offended others. Feinstein's attitude frustrated non-Orthodox rabbis, to say the least. Reform Judaism's leading authority on *halakhah* penned a learned response in opposition to "Orthodox aspersions against Reform marriages" in 1963.[52] In addition, the Rabbinical Assembly's Committee on Jewish Law and Standards acknowledged that Feinstein's stance on conversion made matters difficult for its Conservative community but ultimately refused to augment its policies.[53] Conservative leaders revealed heightened irritation in the 1970s. After a review of Feinstein's rulings, a Conservative writer asked: "what do his responsa do for the sanctity of marriage and unity of the Jewish people?"[54] Another leading Conservative *halakhist* applauded that sentiment and hoped that others would respond in kind to Feinstein's "rather harsh" decisions.[55]

The debate betokened the fraying unity of the American Jewish community. Religious leaders had already engaged in fraught conversations around conversion and who was an acceptable authority to "make" someone into a Jew.[56] The question of acceptable marriage and divorce standards moved that anxiety-filled conversation over Jewish identity and status into the Jewish home a hot-button item within the religiously liberal quarters of American Judaism.[57] The Orthodox refused to adjust its *halakhic* posturing for the sake of an existential threat to Jewish status and peoplehood, core values to the American Jewish enclaves.

Foremost, family life and Jewish peoplehood was the major concern of the Reform Movement in the final quarter of the twentieth century. Reform rabbis were impelled to act in the realms of marriage and divorce due to major criticisms related to intermarriage. In the 1960s, sociologists sounded an alarm that the "rate of Jewish intermarriage is higher than has been generally assumed and is rising."[58] Scholars of American Jewish life worried over the implications for, as they described it, "Jewish continuity," but were also heartened "that this community may at last be preparing to recognize that a problem does exist."[59]

American Jews reasoned that intermarriage would promote assimilation and a thinning of Jewish identity. Some also cautioned that intermarriage was a formula for domestic discord and divorce.[60] Writing in 1970, one observer phrased the conversations connecting intermarriage to divorce as follows:

> Divorce has for long been the workhorse argument of those who would discourage intermarriage. Under the best circumstances, the argument runs, marriage requires a difficult adjustment and accommodation between two very different individuals. The introduction of religious differences only complicates the marital adjustment, causing additional conflict and unhappiness. Intermarriage, the argument continues, is most likely to end in divorce.[61]

Sociological research determined that Jews were far better off marrying coreligionists who would help foster a more stable home environment. In turn, the rabbinate made ample use of this literature but struggled—untrained and passive—to assert its voice into the discussion. Intermarriage was perceived as a destabilizer of the nuclear family and Jewish continuity.[62] According to traditional interpretations of *halakhah*, based on the Talmud's comments in Kiddushin 66a, an individual was Jewish if her or his mother was Jewish (matrilineal descent), or if that person had converted to Judaism. The children of a Jewish man and non-Jewish woman were not, according to *halakhah*, considered Jewish. Still, Jewish pundits worried about their daughters as well as their sons marrying out of their faith since it engendered a culture of religious volatility and domestic intranquility.

Reform Judaism faced the lion's share of the intermarriage criticism. In September 1963, Milton Himmelfarb wrote about "The Vanishing Jews" in the United States who faced an accelerating intermarriage rate and a dropping birthrate. He placed much of the blame on the Reform rabbinate and the "consequences of its anti-legalism."[63] Less than a year later, Himmelfarb's editorial inspired the title of journalist Thomas Morgan's exposé, "The Vanishing American Jew," in the pages of the then-popular *Look* magazine.[64] Although he did not cast blame to a particular subset of American Jewry, Morgan drew the bulk of his quotations and examples from Reform instances.

At that time, the Reform Movement did not sanction intermarriage. However, it was an open secret that an increasing number of Reform rabbis were performing mixed-faith nuptials. For many years, Rabbi David Eichhorn, who chaired the CCAR Committee on the Unaffiliated, appealed to the "liberal" nature of Reform Judaism to recognizing this trend and embrace intermarriage.[65] Eichhorn called into question the "Reform" bona fides of any rabbi who followed the "letter of an outmoded Judaism and not the spirit of a liberal Judaism." Similarly, Rabbi Allan Tarshish reprimanded some Reform colleagues who he charged had "lost sight of the very nature of Reform, the mainspring of our being, our reason for existence: that we are liberals."[66] Their view matched several leading Protestant groups such as the National Council of Churches of Christ and even a few liberal Catholic theologians such as Hans Küng who advocated for more accommodating stances toward intermarried couples who came of age in the post-World War II Tri-Faith America.[67]

Things started to change in the 1970s. Several influential Reform leaders such as Rabbis Roland Gittleson and David Polish refused to countenance intermarriage, fearing that the repercussions of religious exogamy would lead to an irrevocable breakdown of Jewish identity and continuity. Yet, the majority of the CCAR voted down the Gittleson-Polish amendment in 1972, thereby granting tacit approval to its members to perform interfaith weddings. The prevailing feeling was that allying with interfaith couples and supporting their marriages was the best way to ensure that Judaism played a pivotal part of these families' lives.[68] Throughout the balance of the 1970s, no one was sure which side was more correct about the Jewishness of interfaith families. Most agreed, however, that the core issue was the dubious religious classification of the children. Everyone agreed at this juncture that the daughters and sons of a Jewish father and non-Jewish mother required conversion. Without it, religious leaders and institutions did not know exactly how to fully engage these mixed families in their synagogues, schools, or elsewhere.

The Reform Movement's solution was to change the definitions of Jewishness to fit the complexities and religious fragmentations of American family life. This, they reckoned, would best set in place those "fractured" families. In December 1979, Rabbi Alexander Schindler, president of the Union of American Hebrew Congregations, called for Reform to welcome the non-Jewish spouses and children of interfaith couples.[69] "The status of Jew," declared Schindler, "should be conferred on any child, either of whose parents is Jewish, provided they both agree to raise their child Jewishly and do so."[70] In 1983, the CCAR, after much debate, finally ratified Schindler's proposal:

> The Central Conference of American Rabbis declares that the child of one Jewish parent is under the presumption of Jewish descent. This presumption of the Jewish status of the offspring of any mixed marriage is to be established through appropriate and timely public and formal acts of identification with the Jewish faith and people. The performance of these mitzvot serves to commit those who participate in them, both parent and child, to Jewish life.
>
> Depending on circumstances, mitzvot leading toward a positive and exclusive Jewish identity will include entry into the covenant, acquisition of a Hebrew name, Torah study, Bar/Bat Mitzvah, and Kabbalat Torah (Confirmation). For those beyond childhood claiming Jewish identity, other public acts or declarations may be added or substituted after consultation with their rabbi.[71]

Although the Reform Movement did not subscribe to the bindingness of *halakhah*, its leaders recognized that its rabbinic community required a jurisprudential framework to its decision-making. After all, the resolution changed the dynamics of Jewish status and the religious responsibilities of Reform families. The Orthodox and Conservative groups defined Jewish status through the lens of *halakhah*, as determined by matrilineal descent. Reform rabbis suggested that this was not a sufficiently expansive definition. Instead, in quasi-*halakhic* logic, the CCAR offered a "presumption" of Jewishness to anyone with a Jewish mother or father. However, Reform leaders also required an affirmative declaration by way of "formal acts of identification with the Jewish faith and people." Some within the Reform camp criticized the decision to include a proactive requirement to Jewish identity. However, a spokesman for the majority position was unmoved. "What are we uneasy about—being *machmirim*?" chided Rabbi Jerome Malino, seizing upon the Hebrew word for "stringent." "We have been condemned over and over again because we have taken the easy way out or have seemed to take the easy way out."[72]

The use of traditional and rabbinic language in the CCAR's so-called patrilineal descent decision—some preferred the more accurately phrased "non-lineal" decision—signaled an oft-overlooked feature of the Reform Movement's intentions. The Reform rabbinate understood the import of its ruling: that it created disparate formulations of Jewish status and identity within American Judaism. To defend their position, Reform leaders furnished a juridical argument that meant to compete with the traditional *halakhah*. "The *chidush* [*halakhic* novelty] of this report is that we now believe that we can no longer assume," explained Rabbi Peter Knobel in his introductory remarks on behalf of the Patrilineal Descent Committee, "as the Halacha does, that biological descent alone is sufficient for the child of a Jewish mother and insufficient in the case of the child of a Jewish father."[73]

Patrilineal decent advocates appreciated that its champions made a case for a "biblical understanding" of Jewish status that privileged the father's faith rather than the mothers. This position argued that a "Rabbinical Judaism" had replaced patrilineal descent with matrilineal descent, either in the age of Ezra or several centuries afterward. Schindler singled out Rabbi Bernard Zlotowitz for his "research on the matter of patrilineal descent" and "excellent background in Halachah."[74] The son of an Orthodox rabbi, Zlotowitz encouraged Schindler's campaign to "restore" the Jewishness of mixed marriages. Zlotowitz reported to Schindler that "the Jewish law of determining the status of the child on the basis of the mother's religion is a rabbinic innovation and does not follow biblical practice or observance. A careful study of the Bible points up unmistakably that the child followed the status of the father and rarely the mother."[75] The handful of lineage lists in the Bible as well as the stories of the patriarchs suggested to him that Jewish status was defined by the father's religious affiliation. The biblical narrative of Ezra's banishment of his people's non-Jewish wives and children after the Babylonian exile was an indication of a redefinition of religious status, he claimed. According to Zlotowitz's reading of the sources, then, it was the Orthodox and Conservative who preserved a "reformed" version of Jewish status. Zlotowitz concluded that his Reform camp's openness to both matrilineal and patrilineal descent was the fairest interpretation.

Owing to his appreciation for *halakhah*, Zlotowitz was in favor of the CCAR's additional requirements to demonstrate one's Jewish identity through Jewish ritual and practice. The CCAR's requirement for "participation in Jewish life" was, offered Zlotowitz, the "surest" manner to maintain Jewish continuity, in keeping with the spirit of the Bible.[76] Others demurred, sensing that the new requirements for Jewish status would "will act as if it were Halacha." These sorts of legalisms and jurisprudence, warned Rabbi Bruce Goldwasser, do not "exist in our movement." Speaking on behalf of the minority opinion, Goldwasser told the CCAR that "Our movement is not bound by Halacha."[77] However, most CCAR members approved of the *halakhic*-like formulation of Jewish status, given the import of the patrilineal descent resolution.

The Orthodox and Conservative rabbinates disagreed with the CCAR's decision. Neither could square it with their *halakhic* sources. The Reform's Committee on Patrilineal Descent anticipated Orthodox and Conservative backlash but recommended that there was no recourse other than to move forward in the face of opposition and rejection: "While our adoption of this report may cause us some difficulty with our Orthodox and Conservative colleagues," explained the committee chairman, "I believe many will greet it with understanding, if not agreement. It is clear that those who differ from us need no new excuses."[78]

Of course, mixed marriages and families were not specific to Reform. Intermarriage had been on the Conservative Movement's religious radar since the 1960s. To defend his group's stance against charges of insularism and racism, Rabbi Louis Finkelstein stated that "Jews are not hostile to intermarriage with people of another race, if they are Jews." Finkelstein explained that it was a matter of family life:

> The basic doctrine here is that the home is a sanctuary. It cannot be so maintained if either the high priest or the high priestess, so to speak, belongs to another faith. That is something Jews do not like—marriage outside of their fold—because it means the children will not be Jews, or will be only half-Jews.[79]

In 1964, Rabbi Albert Gordon shared his research on Jewish mixed marriages in a paper delivered before the Rabbinical Assembly. Gordon warned that in the United States, while "we cannot recreate the ghetto" it was possible to "recreate the mood of appreciation and respect for the uniqueness of Judaism as a religion with certain standards and certain values that differentiate it from other religions." Though he stopped short of offering concrete suggestions, Gordon was clear in subsequent discussions that Jewish education was no vaccination to this problem. "Intermarriage," averred Gordon in a room full of the best educated men in Conservative Judaism, "occurs also within the families of rabbis."[80] In the same meetings, the Committee on Jewish Law and Standards voted in favor of synagogue standards that would prevent intermarried Jews from obtaining membership to Conservative congregations. The committee strongly encouraged rabbis to preach conversion and agreed that existing synagogue members should not be expelled for marrying non-Jews. The committee also voted down a dissenting view that called for Conservative congregations to expel any and all members who intermarried and whose spouse subsequently refused to convert after a period of five years.[81]

The Conservative rabbinate reaffirmed its position in the wake of the CCAR's patrilineal decent decision, but not without some internal debate. Chancellor Gerson Cohen of the Jewish Theological Seminary anticipated that his Conservative colleagues would reconsider its stance on the determinants of religious status.[82] Cohen was encouraged by the work of Shaye Cohen (no relation), a then-JTS professor, whose research on Judaism and matrilineal descent had informed Bernard Zlotowitz's and other Reform scholars' justifications for patrilineality. This, even though Shaye Cohen had made clear that he disagreed with those who contended that his work held "Halakic implications."[83]

RA President Rabbi Alexander Shapiro agreed with the latter. "Our path," said Shapiro, "must remain that of matrilinealism, motivated as we all are by our concern for klal yisrael," Jewish peoplehood.[84] Shapiro rejected Gerson Cohen's plea as misguided and too concerned with refashioning Jewish status to fit the porousness of contemporary family life rather than the other way around. In other words, an embrace of patrilineal descent would not satisfactorily blend Jewish law and modern values. In a March 1985 vote at the RA's annual convention, Shapiro's supporters handedly defeated Gerson Cohen's group, 49–21. The issue was brought to a vote a year later before a much larger presidium and was defeated by a tally of 235–292.[85] Cohen stepped down from the JTS chancellorship in 1986 and was replaced by Ismar Schorsch who declared he was "opposed" to a redefinition of Jewish status. "I do not think that is the direction in which the

Conservative movement ought to go."[86] But for many within the Conservative ranks this remained an open question. As recently as 2017, JTS has had to publicly uphold its policy against interfaith weddings as some of its alumni have defied its stance and officiated at mixed marriages.[87] The enduring tensions reflect the challenges and limits of the Conservative Movement's willingness to place traditional texts and modern values so directly into *halakhic* conversation.

Gay Marriage

That Reform Judaism's embrace of interfaith families was tied to Jewish continuity as an inherent value of Jewish practice was evident in another decision rendered by its Responsa Committee in October 1985. On this occasion, Reform leaders were petitioned to weigh in on whether their colleagues could perform a religious marriage for gay partners. The source banning homosexual relationships is stated in Scripture: "You shall not lie with a man as with a woman; it is an abomination" (Leviticus 18:22). Some Reform rabbis had called on their colleagues to ally with the Gay Rights Movement and disavow the Bible's condemnation. They were unsatisfied with the CCAR's resolution in 1977 that supported the "decriminalization" of homosexuality. However, most agreed with Rabbi Solomon Freehof that Reform could not budge beyond the "civil rights" posturing. "It may well be that we do not consider ourselves bound by all the ritual and ceremonial laws of Scripture, but we certainly revere the ethical attitudes and judgments of the Bible."[88] Likewise, Rabbi Walter Jacob voted against admitting an openly gay individual to Reform's rabbinical ranks. "We cannot recommend such an individual as a role model nor should he/she be placed in a position of leadership or guidance for children of any age."[89]

Religion scholars Samira Mehta and Brett Krutzsch are certainly correct about the Reform Movement that "as the national temperature shifted on same-gender relationships, American Jews shifted with those trends."[90] Or, as the legal scholar Roberta Kwall has put it, all religious movements needed to grapple with the "cultural" and "*halakhic*" realities that tested American Judaism's fidelity to a *halakhic* system and their social suitability within modern life.[91] Much of the stigma had been purged from Reform ranks by the 1980s. Still, many out-of-the-closet Reform Jews belonged to self-described "gay congregations" rather than the more mainstream temples. These individuals called on Reform leaders to embrace homosexual lifestyles more fully.[92] Yet, The CCAR could not dismiss the implications of gay rights for then-normative domestic life. The Responsa Committee's negative response was based on its conception and purpose of the Jewish family:

> Judaism places great emphasis on family, children and the future, which is assured by a family. However we may understand homosexuality, whether as an illness, as a genetically based dysfunction or as a sexual preference and lifestyle—we cannot

> accommodate the relationship of two homosexuals as a "marriage" within the context of Judaism, for none of the elements of *qiddushin* (sanctification) normally associated with marriage can be invoked for this relationship.[93]

Several years later, an Ad Hoc Committee on Homosexuality and the Rabbinate simultaneously ruled that a gay women and men may serve in the rabbinate but reaffirmed its position that "procreative marriage is the ideal human relationship." On the matter of gay rabbis, Reform leaders reasoned that the scientific community had not reached a consensus on whether homosexuality was determined by nature or nurture. In lieu of this, the CCAR resolved that another salient Jewish value trumped this unresolved matter: namely, that all people were created in God's image. However, the Reform jurists remained aligned with "Jewish tradition" and the nuclear family. "There are some people for whom heterosexual, monogamous, procreative marriage is not a viable option or possibility," offered the Committee. Even so, continued the decision, "the majority of the committee reaffirms unequivocally the centrality of this ideal and its special status as kiddushin. To the extent that sexual orientation is a matter of choice, the majority of the committee affirms that heterosexuality is the only appropriate Jewish choice for fulfilling one's covenantal obligations."[94] The dominant view of the American family unit, then, still conformed to the traditional interpretation of the Bible and *halakhah*.

Reform finally changed course in step with liberal America. In the mid-1990s, Republicans and Democrats debated the Defense of Marriage Act (DOMA) and the federal definition of matrimony. In March 1996, the CCAR adopted the liberal position and resolved to "support the right of gay and lesbian couples to share fully and equally in the rights of civil marriage."[95] To be sure, not everyone within the CCAR's agreed on how far to take this reversal. Some wished to extend the ritual marriage ceremony meant for a husband and a wife to homosexual couples. However, most were not prepared for this. One insider admitted that "in trying to talk to each other about this question, we discovered that we as a Committee had ceased to share the most elemental kinds of assumptions necessary for a common religious conversation."[96] Once again, it was changed popular sentiment that reunited disparate views in American Reform. By 2000, progressives had taken on gay marriage as a major plank of their political liberalism. The Reform rabbinate agreed, authorizing its group to officiate at gay marriage in the same manner that it would a heterosexual couple. Importantly, the reasoning was based in a reconceptualization of the modern family structure, that both straight and gay couples could stand as the "foundation of stable Jewish families, thus adding strength to the Jewish community."[97]

The Conservative Movement's encounter with gay marriage also conformed with how this group has considered the relationship of Jewish law and modern family values. In the 1970s, most members of the RA would have in all probability agreed with their colleague who remarked at a national convention "How wonderful it would be if the Conservative movement, with its interest in improving the quality of the world, would become a pioneer in welcoming all the lonely and isolated of our people into our midst" but also cautioned that "we must make it clear that we cannot legitimize homosexuality as an alternative lifestyle."[98]

Perspective changed along with American political sentiment. In January 1989, The RA's Committee on Jewish Law and Standards solicited two responsa on the issue. In one, Rabbi Steven Saltzman advised that Conservative Judaism could not renegotiate gay relationships because it placed too high a principle on procreation and the Jewish family. In the other, Rabbi Bradley Shavit Artson urged a reconsideration of Scripture on the grounds that family structures had changed. Artson argued that the Bible had outlawed coercive homosexual relationships, the only type of gay relationship, according to the scholarship Artson marshalled, of which the ancients were aware. Artson therefore held that the Torah would—and Jewish authorities should—sanction any committed relationship. Artson agreed that the Jewish ideal was for individuals to be a part of a stable family life. But "to posit a norm without providing a means for all people to attain that norm is an act of shortsighted cruelty."[99] Wrote Artson: "Homosexuals are able to adopt children, to utilize in vitro fertilization, artificial insemination, even surrogate motherhood. Just as with other couples who are infertile, homosexual couples now have the possibility to bring children into their homes and to sanctify their homes with the job and responsibilities of raising a family."[100] In step with American liberal culture, Artson favored a covenant ceremony for gay Jews, different from traditional heterosexual matrimony:

> By developing a public ceremony to mark the beginning and the termination of an exclusive, committed homosexual relationship, the traditional Jewish standards would be clear and enforceable. In fact, by extending those standards to include responsible gay and lesbian love, we would simultaneously strengthen our resolve to place sexual expression within the confines of commitment and fidelity for heterosexuals as well—applying one clear and moral standard to all.[101]

However, the traditionalists among the Conservative Movement could not support Artson's formulation. They believed that Artson's method had imposed modern values to unbind their community's allegiance to traditional Jewish law, blurring the lines in fact and in form "separating Conservative and Reform."[102] In 1992, Rabbi Joel Roth led a movement to approve of the traditionalist position. Roth went so far as to distribute photocopies of scholarship, contrary to Artson, that "demonstrate that long-term homosexual relationships did indeed exist in antiquity"—that led to a Consensus Statement on Homosexuality that outlawed gay commitment ceremonies and acceptance of gay individuals to Conservative rabbinical schools. Roth and others were heartened that Conservative groups had denounced bigotry and violence against homosexuals but could not support further religious inclusion.[103]

The majority of the Conservative Movement finally embraced gay marriage in December 2006. Roth resubmitted a revised version of his position. He continued to advise against gay religious marriage and the ordination of gay rabbis in the Conversative movement. The CJLS voted to approve Roth's position and another contradictory ruling (in fact, it was officially three decisions, in the end). "When the ballots were tallied," wrote historian Jack Wertheimer of the debate within the CJLS, "it emerged that, on the issue of gay ordination, equal numbers had voted in favor and against, enough in each case to leave both as equally valid positions for Conservative Jews."[104] One CJLS member who sided with Artson and not Roth, wrote that Scripture's descriptive word, "abomination," no longer applied to homosexuals. The sin, then, only applied to a time and place in which homosexuality was regarded as such. Another Conservative *halakhah* writer argued that new scientific knowledge should trump traditional understandings of the Bible while a third responsum contended that anything less than a reversal from the biblical ban on homosexuality would threaten the mental health of LGBTQ members of the Conservative Movement.

Wertheimer and others point out that the CJLS's open-mindedness was more "confusing" than "helpful."[105] It was also clear where most Conservative Jewish leaders outside the CJLS stood on the matter. That the Conservative-affiliated American Jewish University in Los Angeles soon after decided to admit gay women and men into its rabbinical school reflected a sea change in the Movement. In time, JTS in New York and the Schechter Institute of Jewish Studies in Israel also changed their policies. The moves suggested to some that Conservative Judaism had cast off its unique attachment to *halakhah*. Others, however, felt comfortable in how the Movement and negotiated the tenets of Jewish law and contemporary values.[106]

Finally, homosexuality demonstrates the steadfastness of Orthodox Judaism to traditional interpretations of *halakhah* in the face of changing family values. Reflecting on this, Rabbi Norman Lamm poignantly defined his community as "Jews who retain their first loyalty to Judaism and Halachah, rather than to the newest canons of contemporary liberalism."[107] Concurrent to the rise of writing on the subject within Conservative and Reform circles, the Orthodox were noticeably reticent.[108] This was a point not lost on outsiders, who called on Orthodox rabbis—the ones who were not, it was so alleged, "bigoted" and "biased"—to take deliberate and actionable steps to effect change in their tradition-bound enclave.[109] However, Orthodox scholars, when they deigned to broach the subject, tended to couch their statements in theoretical and tentative language. In one example, a presenter at a conference of Orthodox scientists framed his remarks in a circumspective fashion, suggesting that a more concrete approach to homosexuality within his community "awaits a full response on the topic by recognized halakhic authorities."[110]

The Orthodox rabbinate sensed that theirs was a no-win proposition. In the 1980s, one Orthodox rabbi preached resolute fidelity to the biblical text to withstand the "media's continuing portrayal of homosexuals as positive role models and the increasing acceptance of the homosexual as a minority group with 'legitimate' civil rights."[111] Others were more congenial about the predicament. In December 1992, Rabbi Reuven Bulka expressed "sympathy" with homosexuals who wished to live an Orthodox life. On the other hand, Bulka was incorrigible about the *halakhic* implications. To him, the plain meaning of the Bible's view on homosexual relations was immutable. Bulka also reasoned that homosexuals led lives that were less in sync with Jewish continuity.

"The homosexual lifestyle," wrote Bulka, "since it cannot result in childbirth, is more alluring to those who would like to avoid such responsibilities."[112]

Still, most Orthodox rabbis just preferred to stay silent. When the Yeshiva University-trained rabbi, Steven Greenberg, recalled publicly acknowledging his sexuality in the late 1990s, he wrote that "my coming out was largely ignored by the organized Orthodox community."[113] Most public discussion within the Orthodox fold was concentrated on muting the conversation. In December 2009, Yeshiva University (YU) students held a panel on "Being Gay in the Modern Orthodox World." Leading members of the YU faculty disapproved, reprimanding that "publicizing or seeking legitimization even for the homosexual orientation one feels, runs contrary to Torah."[114] However, their call went by and large unheeded. The event attracted eight hundred students and interested listeners. It was hailed as a watershed moment for this faith community, even though the rabbinic moderator "stressed that the discussion was not meant to be a debate about halacha."[115]

Another example reflects the rabbinic desire to avoid discussion. In September 2010, a Jewish weekly in New Jersey included an engagement notice.[116] The editors nonchalantly reported the short note of a gay couple in its "lifecycles" section, opting to keep it understated without mention that it was a "first" for its paper. The decision sparked outrage from the Orthodox rabbinate. The editors therefore issued a statement in its following edition:

> We set off a firestorm last week by publishing a same-sex couple's announcement of their intent to marry. Given the tenor of the times, we did not expect the volume of comments we have received, many of them against our decision to run the announcement, but many supportive as well.
>
> A group of rabbis has reached out to us and conveyed the deep sensitivities within the traditional/Orthodox community to this issue. Our subsequent discussions with representatives from that community have made us aware that publication of the announcement caused pain and consternation, and we apologize for any pain we may have caused.[117]

The notice exacerbated the situation. The pluralistic North Jersey Board of Rabbis and a host of other liberal Jews and organizations wrote to the newspaper to express their frustration in what they perceived as too much cajoling to the Orthodox establishment.[118] Orthodox Judaism and homosexuality proved too hot to handle—for all parties involved. In February 2013, a teacher at Maimonides School in Brookline, Massachusetts, had planned to introduce a unit on the Gay Rights Movement in her twelfth-grade history class. The school administration permitted it, as long as a Jewish studies faculty member could also present the "gay issue from a Torah perspective." This was similar, the School Committee explained, to how the school taught evolution in biology class. The teacher demurred, electing to strike the unit out of her curriculum since "she could no longer teach an unbiased history."[119] In 2021, a small group of Yeshiva University students and alumni filed a discrimination lawsuit against school leaders for repeatedly refusing to allow an LGBTQ club in 2019 and 2020.[120] In March 2025, Yeshiva settled the protracted legal case with the students. YU agreed to recognize the LGBTQ club "Hareni," and provide it access to school funding, while under the guidance of its senior rabbis.

Like intermarriage, homosexuality may be beyond the outer limit of Orthodox Judaism's ability to find room for all modern conceptions of family. One attempt to make space was led by Rabbi Nathaniel Helfgot. In July 2010, Helfgot published a "Statement of Principles on the Place of Jews with a Homosexual Orientation in Our Community." The twelve-plank text was signed by hundreds of rabbis and communal leaders from all sectors within the Modern Orthodox fold. The Statement of Principles condemned hostility toward homosexuals and acknowledged a range of scientific perspectives on the nature of "choice" within sexuality. The text straddled a hard-line position on homosexuality and an attempt to establish a division between individuals and their sexual orientation: "Halakhah sees heterosexual marriage as the ideal model and sole legitimate outlet for human sexual expression. The sensitivity and understanding we properly express for human beings with other sexual orientations does not diminish our commitment to that principle."[121]

Helfgot's text did not avoid the tensions of Jewish law and modern living. Speaking on behalf of "Halakhic Judaism," his online statement was clear that it "cannot give its blessing and imprimatur to Jewish religious same-sex commitment ceremonies and weddings" while calling for homosexuals to be "welcomed as full members of the synagogue and school community." What is more, the Statement of Principles urged for a "full embrace of the adopted or biological children of homosexually active Jews."[122] This was a gesture that fell well short of the integrationist position of the Conservative Movement or the liberal agenda of the Reform rabbinate. Yet, it bespoke the inescapable interaction between folk religion and elite religion. All these cases suggest that it is not the case that elite religion, given time, defeats the misguided tendencies proffered by folk religion. To the contrary, theirs is a complex relationship and yields variegated expressions of Jewish observance on all ends of the religious spectrum of modern Jewish life.

Conclusion

The myriad sociological, political, and scientific forces on the modern family are dizzying when placed in historical perspective. Changing attitudes and medical advances in the area of transgender, not covered above, demonstrate the vastness of this important topic and its relationship to Jewish law. The challenge to keep up with the quick-paced transformations in American family life is not unique to Judaism. Catholicism in the 1960s struggled to keep all adherents content after Pope Paul VI published *Humanae vitae* that reaffirmed this faith community's religious-legal perspective on birth control.[123]

It is also the case that sectors of American society got a late jump on the issues. Until the twenty-first century, few groups deigned to reconsider their public and private stances on divorce, fertility, and gay marriage. They liked to think about an idealized status quo. As historian Stephanie Coontz makes clear, it was near-impossible for Americans of all kinds to detach themselves, no matter the facts on the ground, from the "idyllic" 1950s that is mythologized and remembered by the rise of television programs that stress middle class, tradition family values such as *Father Knows Best, The Adventures of Ozzie and Harriet, Leave It to Beaver, Make Room for Daddy,* and *The Donna Reed Show.*[124] Recent political upheaval no longer permits such tentativeness to decision-making. Whether American Jews have been emboldened, have been infuriated, or had their minds altogether changed by how it has manifested in the recent discussions, there is no question of the paramount importance of American Judaism's continued confrontation with the modern family.

Notes

1. Charles S. Liebman, "Reconstructionism in American Jewish Life," *American Jewish Yearbook* 71 (1970): 91. Soon after, Liebman presented a more extended version of this binary. See Charles S. Liebman, *The Ambivalent American Jew: Politics, Religion, and Family in American Jewish Life* (Philadelphia: Jewish Publication Society of America, 1973), 42–87.
2. See Haym Soloveitchik, *Collected Essays*, vol. 3 (London: Littman Library, 2020), 407–21.
3. See Zev Eleff, "The Origins of the Young Israel of Brookline and the Contest for 'Modern Orthodoxy,'" *Me'orei Ha'eish* 1 (2017): 141–63.
4. Glenda Riley, *Divorce: An American Tradition* (New York: Oxford University Press, 1991), 174–78.
5. On the origins and popularization of this adage, see Richard Gribble, "'Family Theater of the Air': The Radio Ministry of Father Patrick Peyton, C.S.C., 1945–1952," *U.S. Catholic Historian* 19 (Summer 2001): 51–66.
6. Benjamin Steiner, "The Lieberman Clause Revisited," *American Jewish Archives Journal* 69, no. 1 (2017): 41–70.
7. See Blu Greenberg, *On Woman and Judaism: A View from Tradition* (Philadelphia: Jewish Publication Society of America, 1981), 44–47.
8. See Michael R. Cohen, *The Birth of Conservative Judaism: Solomon Schechter's Disciples and the Creation of an American Religious Movement* (New York: Columbia University Press, 2012), 124–31.
9. Steiner, "Lieberman Clause Revisited," 61.
10. See Mordecai Waxman, "Conservative Judaism—A Survey," in *Tradition and Change: The Development of Conservative Judaism*, ed. Mordecai Waxman (New York: Rabbinical Assembly of America, 1958), 3–37.
11. See Solomon Gutstein, "Civil Enforceability of Religious Antenuptial Agreements," *University of Chicago Law Review* 23 (1955): 122–32.
12. Steiner, "Lieberman Clause Revisited," 52.
13. Ibid.
14. "Report on the Joint Law Conference," *Proceedings of the Rabbinical Assembly* 17 (1953): 77.
15. Norman Lamm, "Recent Additions to the Ketubah: A Halakhic Critique," *Tradition* 2 (Fall 1959): 98.
16. "Commission on Marriage and the Family," *Proceedings of the Rabbinical Assembly* 15 (1951): 64.

17. Reuben M. Katz, "Commission on Marriage and the Family," *Proceedings of the Rabbinical Assembly* 19 (1955): 50. On the development of pastoral work in the Conservative Movement, see Benjamin Steiner, "That Judaism Might Yet Live: Pastoral Care and the Making of the Post-Holocaust Conservative Rabbinate," *American Jewish History* 101 (April 2017): 265–86.
18. Ibid.
19. *The New World of Reform: Containing the Proceedings of the Conference of Reform Rabbis Held in Philadelphia in November 1869*, trans. Sefton D. Temkin (London: Leo Baeck College, 1971), 118.
20. Henry E. Kagan, "The Jewish Family," *CCAR Journal* 7 (October 1954): 13.
21. See Robert P. Jacobs, "Report of the Committee on Marriage, Family and the Home," *CCAR Yearbook* 69 (1959): 97–98; and Albert M. Shulman, "Report of the Committee on Marriage, Family and the Home," *CCAR Yearbook* 73 (1963): 72–75.
22. See "Report of the Committee on Marriage, Family and the Home," *CCAR Yearbook* 67 (1957): 69.
23. Henry E. Kagan, "The Jewish Family," *CCAR Journal* 7 (October 1954): 13.
24. Louis Bernstein, *Challenge and Mission: The Emergence of the English Speaking Orthodox Rabbinate* (New York: Shengold, 1982), 69.
25. Melech Schachter, "The Divorce Problem," *Jewish Life* 31 (May–June 1964): 22.
26. Ibid., 19.
27. See David Singer, "Emanuel Rackman: Gadfly of Modern Orthodoxy," *Modern Judaism* 28 (May 2008): 134–48; and Marc B. Shapiro, *Between the Yeshiva World and Modern Orthodoxy: The Life and Works of Rabbi Jehiel Jacob Weinberg* (Portland, OR: Littman Library, 1999), 190–92.
28. Avraham Weiss, "The Modern Day *Agunah*: In Retrospect and Prospect," in *The Prenuptial Agreement: Halakhic and Pastoral Considerations*, ed. Kenneth Auman and Basil Herring (Northvale, NJ: Jason Aronson, 1996), 10–12.
29. Fabian Schoenfeld, "Sincerity behind the Conservative Beth-Din," *Young Israel Viewpoint* 43 (November–December 1954): 28.
30. "New Kesuba Introduced by Conservatives," *The Scribe* 6 (December 27, 1954): 8.
31. See Zev Eleff, "From Teacher to Scholar to Pastor: The Evolving Postwar Modern Orthodox Rabbinate," *American Jewish History* 98 (October 2014): 289–313.
32. Schachter, "Divorce Problem," 19.
33. "Rabbinical Tampering with Divorce Laws," *Jewish Exponent*, July 17, 1936, 4.
34. Larry Yudelson, "The New York State Get Law: For Better or for Worse," *Hamevaser*, December 2, 1983, 1.
35. See Larry Cohler, "RCA Suspends Orthodox Pre-Nuptial Agreement," *Jewish World*, November 23, 1984, 12.
36. Saul J. Berman, "Why Orthodox Rabbis Should Insist on a Prenuptial Agreement," *Rabbinics Today* 2 (December 1993): 1.
37. Mrs. Isidor Freedman, "A Chanukah Message," Orthodox Union (Chanukah 1941): 13
38. See Jonah Steinberg, "From a 'Pot of Filth' to a 'Hedge of Roses' (and Back): Changing Theorizations of Menstruation in Judaism," *Journal of Feminist Studies in Religion* 13 (Fall 1997): 5–26. Lamm's teachings on marriage and *halakhah* were persuasive and pervasive. His manual emerged as the standard premarital text for young women and men in the religiously moderate Orthodox camp as well as those situated in the more "rightist" portion of the community. See Norman Lamm, "Love and Law," *Jewish Observer* 5 (May 1969): 7–10.

39. Norman Lamm, *A Hedge of Roses: Jewish Insights into Marriage and Married Life* (New York: Philipp Feldheim, 1966), 37–38.
40. Ibid., 51.
41. Ibid., 56.
42. Moshe Feinstein, *Iggerot Moshe*, vol. 3 (EH 1:10), 12.
43. See, for example, Shlomo Halberstam, "Kuntres Le-Hatzalat Kedushat ve-Yihus Yisrael," *Hamaor* 14 (October–November 1964): 5–20.
44. Moshe Feinstein, *Iggerot Moshe*, vol. 4 (EH 1:11), 322.
45. Moshe Feinstein, *Iggerot Moshe*, vol. 7 (EH 4:32), 75.
46. Ibid. (EH 1:10), 21.
47. See Fred Rosner, "Tay-Sachs Disease: To Screen or Not to Screen?," *Journal of Religion and Health* 15 (October 1976): 277.
48. See Alan S. Kaplan, "Dr. Tendler Opposes Tay-Sachs Screening," *The Commentator*, February 28, 1973, 5; and Moshe David Tendler, *Pardes Rimonim: A Marriage Manual for the Jewish Family* (New York: Judaica Press, Inc., 1977), 83.
49. See Zev Eleff, *Modern Orthodox Judaism: A Documentary History* (Lincoln: University of Nebraska Press, 2016), 312–16.
50. Adam S. Ferziger, "'And Who Even Knows What It Is?': The Role of Reform in the Rulings of Rabbi Yosef Eliyahu Henkin," in *"In the Dwelling of a Sage Lie Precious Treasures": Essays in Jewish Studies in Honor of Shnayer Z. Leiman*, ed. Yitzhak Berger and Chaim Milikowsky (New York: Yeshiva University Press, 2020), 323–39.
51. Moshe Feinstein, *Iggerot Moshe*, vol. 3 (EH 3:76), 177–178. See also Moshe Feinstein, *Iggerot Moshe*, vol. 7 (EH 4:13), 25–29.
52. Solomon B. Freehof, *Recent Reform Responsa* (Cincinnati: Hebrew Union College Press, 1963), 194–203.
53. "Converts of Questionable Status," *Proceedings of the Rabbinical Assembly* 30 (1966): 105–10.
54. David Novak, *Law and Theology in Judaism* (New York: KTAV, 1974), 37.
55. Isaac Klein, "Book Reviews," *Conservative Judaism* 29 (Summer 1975): 89. For a later assessment and lament, see Jacob Chinitz, "Reb Moshe and the Conservatives," *Conservative Judaism* 41 (Spring 1989): 5–15.
56. David Ellenson and Daniel Gordis, *Pledges of Jewish Allegiance: Conversion, Law, and Policymaking in Nineteenth- and Twentieth-Century Orthodox Responsa* (Stanford, CA: Stanford University Press, 2012), 103–5.
57. See Zev Eleff, "Reform Judaism's Patrilineal Descent and the Shaping of Intermarriage Discourse in American Judaism," *Zeramim* 3 (Fall 2018): 27–38
58. Milton Himmelfarb, "The Vanishing Jews," *Commentary* 36 (September 1963): 249.
59. "Marshall Sklare, "Intermarriage and the Jewish Future," *Commentary* 37 (April 1964): 47.
60. Edgar E. Suskin, "Jewish Survival and Jewish Identity," *CCAR Yearbook* 74 (1964): 133–34.
61. See Arnold Schwartz, "Intermarriage in the United States," *American Jewish Year Book* 71 (1970): 113.
62. See Lila Corwin Berman, *Speaking of Jews: Rabbis, Intellectuals, and the Creation of an American Public Identity* (Berkeley: University of California Press, 2009), 53–72.
63. Himmelfarb, "Vanishing Jews," 251.
64. Thomas B. Morgan, "The Vanishing American Jew," *Look* 28 (May 5, 1964): 43–46
65. David Max Eichhorn, "Conversion and Marriage—A New Look," *Jewish Digest* 3 (March 1958): 3.

66. Allan Tarshish, "How 'Central' Is the CCAR?" *CCAR Journal* 7 (January 1960): 32.
67. See Kevin M. Schultz, *Tri-Faith America: How Catholics and Jews Held Postwar America to Its Protestant Promise* (Oxford: Oxford University Press, 2011), 87–89.
68. See Samira K. Mehta, *Beyond Chrismukkah: The Christian-Jewish Interfaith Family in the United States* (Chapel Hill: University of North Carolina Press, 2018), 21–22.
69. See Marjorie Hyer, "Change Proposed in Parental Link to Jews' Lineage," *Washington Post*, December 8, 1979, A4.
70. Ibid., A1.
71. "Report of the Committee on Patrilineal Descent on the Status of Children of Mixed Marriages," *CCAR Year Book* 93 (1983): 160.
72. Ibid., 153–54.
73. Ibid., 144–45.
74. Alexander M. Schindler to Jerome Malino, October 14, 1980, Box 31, Folder 2, Jerome R. Malino Papers, MS-729, The Jacob Rader Marcus Center of the American Jewish Archives, Cincinnati, OH.
75. Phil Hiat and Bernard Zlotowitz to Alexander M. Schindler, June 1, 1982, Box 12, Folder 4, Alexander M. Schindler Papers, MS-630, AJA.
76. Bernard M. Zlotowitz, "A Perspective on Patrilineal Descent," *Judaism* 34 (Winter 1985): 135.
77. "Report of the Committee on Patrilineal Descent on the Status of Children of Mixed Marriages," 151.
78. Peter S. Knobel, "Presentation," *CCAR Year Book* 93 (1983): 145.
79. See Albert I. Gordon, *Intermarriage: Interfaith, Interracial, Interethnic* (Boston: Beacon Press, 1964), 187.
80. Albert I. Gordon, "Intermarriage," *Proceedings of the Rabbinical Assembly* 28 (1964): 172–73.
81. See Max J. Routtenberg, "The Jew Who Has Intermarried," *Proceedings of the Rabbinical Assembly* 28 (1964): 244–48; and Wilfred Shuchat, "The Intermarried Jew and Synagogue Membership: A Dissenting Opinion," *Proceedings of the Rabbinical Assembly* 28 (1964): 249–54.
82. "Conservatism Studies Patrilineal Descent," *National Jewish Post and Opinion*, February 13, 1985, 27.
83. Shaye J. D. Cohen, "The Matrilineal Principle in Historical Perspective," *Judaism* 34 (Winter 1985): 13.
84. Ari L. Goldman, "Conservatives Reaffirm Rule on Determining Jewishness," *New York Times*, March 12, 1985, A29.
85. Joseph Berger, "Conservative Rabbis Affirm Mother Alone Is Identity Key," *New York Times*, May 22, 1986, B4.
86. Sheldon Engelmayuer, "New JTS Chancellor Seeks to Be Healer," *Jewish Exponent*, March 14, 1986, 5.
87. Yair Ettinger, "Will Conservatives' Interfaith Wedding Ban Make a Difference?," *Jerusalem Post*, October 27, 2017, 1.
88. Solomon B. Freehof, "Judaism and Homosexuality," in *American Reform Responsa: Jewish Questions, Rabbinic Answers*, ed. Walter Jacob (New York: Central Conference of American Rabbis, 1983), 50.
89. Walter Jacob, "Homosexuals in Leadership Positions," in *American Reform Responsa: Jewish Questions, Rabbinic Answers*, ed. Walter Jacob (New York: Central Conference of American Rabbis, 1983), 54.

90. Samira K. Mehta and Brett Krutzsch, "The Changing Jewish Family: Jewish Communal Responses to Interfaith and Same-Sex Marriage," *American Jewish History* 104 (October 2020): 555.
91. Roberta Rosenthal Kwall, *The Myth of the Cultural Jew: Culture and Law in Jewish Tradition* (Oxford: Oxford University Press, 2015), 157–92.
92. John E. Hirsch, "Don't Ghettoize Gays," *Reform Judaism* 16 (Spring 1988): 14–15.
93. Walter Jacobs, *Contemporary American Reform Responsa* (New York: Central Conference of American Rabbis, 1987), 298.
94. Arthur Hertzberg, *Judaism: The Key Spiritual Writings of the Jewish Tradition* (New York: Free Press, 1991), 136–37.
95. E. J. Kessler, "Reform Mulls Gay Marriage," *Forward*, July 11, 1997, 14.
96. Joan S. Friedman, *"Guidance, Not Governance": Rabbi Solomon B. Freehof and Reform Responsa* (Cincinnati, OH: Hebrew Union College Press, 2013), 255.
97. "Reform Rabbis Offer Alternative Stance to a Resolution in Support of Gay Vows," *Forward*, February 11, 2000, 1.
98. Barry Dov Schwartz, "Judaism and Homosexuality," *Proceedings of the Rabbinical Assembly* 40 (1978): 113–14.
99. Bradley Shavit Artson, "Enfranchising the Monogamous Homosexual: A Legal Possibility, a Moral Imperative," *S'vara* 3 (1993): 25.
100. Bradley S. Artson, "Gay and Lesbian Jews: An Innovative Jewish Legal Position," *Jewish Spectator* (Winter 1990–1991): 9.
101. Artson, "Enfranchising the Monogamous Homosexual," 25.
102. Cited in Mehta and Krutzsch, "Changing Jewish Family," 570.
103. "Conservative Branch Rejects Proposal to Allow Gay Rabbis," *New York Times*, March 29, 1992, 34.
104. Jack Wertheimer, *The New American Judaism: How Jews Practice Their Religion Today* (Princeton, NJ: Princeton University Press, 2018), 122.
105. Ibid., 123.
106. Elliot N. Dorff, *Modern Conservative Judaism: Evolving Thought and Practice* (Lincoln: University of Nebraska Press, 2018), 291–96
107. Norman Lamm, "The New Dispensation on Homosexuality: A Jewish Reaction to a Developing Christian Attitude," *Jewish Life* 34 (January–February 1968): 15.
108. Lamm was therefore an exception. See also Norman Lamm, "Judaism and the Modern Attitude to Homosexuality," *Encyclopedia Judaica Year Book* (1974): 194–205.
109. See Abram Vossen Goodman, "The Homosexual and Jewish Tradition," *Reform Judaism* 13 (Winter 1984–85): 16; and C. Parens, Letter to the Editor, *Midstream* 39 (April 1993): 48.
110. Moshe Halevi Spero, "Homosexuality: Clinal and Halakhic Challenges," *Proceedings of the Association of Orthodox Jewish Scientists* 6 (1980): 187.
111. B. Freundel, "Homosexuality and Judaism," *Journal of Halacha and Contemporary Society* 11 (Spring 1986): 87.
112. Reuven P. Bulka, "Is Homosexuality Religiously Legitimate?" *Midstream* 38 (December 1992): 26.
113. Steven Greenberg, *Wrestling with God and Men: Homosexuality in the Jewish Tradition* (Madison: University of Wisconsin Press, 2004), 12.
114. Zvi Schachter et al., Public Letter, December 22, 2009, a copy in the possession of the author.

115. E. B. Solomont, "YU Conducts Public Discussion on Homosexuality in the Orthodox World," *Jerusalem Post*, December 24, 2009, 1. For a reflection on the program's impact, see Hannah Dreyfus, "Yeshiva U. Students Hold LGBTQ Event," *Jewish Exponent*, December 24, 2020, 6.
116. For the background of this brief affair, see Steve Lipman, "N.J. Newspaper Controversy Pits Gays Against Orthodox," *Jewish Week*, October 8, 2010, 17; and Gary Rosenblatt, "Tolerance, Tradition Collide in Same-Sex Union Row," *Jewish Week*, October 15, 2010, 1.
117. "A Statement from the Jewish Standard," *Jewish Standard*, October 1, 2010, 14.
118. "The Community Responds," *Jewish Standard*, October 8, 2010, 16.
119. Yoni Schoenberg, "Gay Rights Unit Stopped in Minority Experience Class," *Spectrum*, April 2013, 1.
120. Sruli Fruchter, "YU and Administrators Sued for LGBTQ Discrimination by YU Pride Alliance, Students and Alumni," *The Commentator*, May 5, 2021, 6.
121. See Eleff, *Modern Orthodox Judaism*, 416.
122. Ibid., 417–19.
123. See Leslie Woodcock Tentler, *Catholics and Contraception: An American History* (Ithaca, NY: Cornell University Press, 2004), 204–63.
124. See Stephanie Coontz, *The Way We Never Were: American Families and the Nostalgia Trap* (New York: Basic Books, 2016), 24.

CHAPTER 31

FETICIDE IN *HALAKHAH*

Attitudes, Approaches, and Application

ELLI FISCHER

Introduction

Every legal, ethical, and moral system must explicitly or implicitly answer a question that has been asked since human beings first began reflecting on their own condition: what is human life? Different systems offer different answers to this metaphysical question. Each system develops empirical criteria to determine what constitutes being alive and human, but those criteria are necessarily predicated on metaphysical assumptions about what constitutes life. Consequently, since systems differ about those metaphysical assumptions, there will be actions that one system deems permissible, and even necessary, while other systems consider the same act to be an unwarranted destruction of human life. Thus, when different systems vie for the authority to govern, or opinions based on different metaphysical assumptions compete for supremacy within a single system, it can cause an acute crisis, as matters of life and death are at stake.

The most acute dilemmas involve the liminal moments of the beginning and end of life. This volume's chapter on brain death and organ donation addresses when life ends (see Berkowitz, this volume). This chapter addresses the question of when human life begins—or, stated differently, at what point does the destruction of a developing human being constitute homicide.

Halakhic opinion is all but unanimous that unwarranted feticide is not permitted. However, as is characteristic of *halakhah*, when it comes to defining the parameters of this prohibition in practice, there is considerable debate and disagreement surrounding questions such as the following: What actions are considered "warranted?" Does the prohibition apply from conception, or from a different stage of fetal development? Is feticide murder or a different transgression? Does the method of feticide matter?

Moreover, *halakhah* itself is multivocal, and the relationship between its different "voices" is dynamic. In one era or locale, a specific voice may dominate, even as another voice dictates attitudes and practices elsewhere. Sometimes the different voices are sounded at the same time, but while one is shouted, the other is whispered; one voice can express an overarching value, another may utter a general rule, while a third registers exceptions. This feature, this peculiar type of multivocality, applies to many areas of *halakhah*, and it is a particularly effective rubric for understanding *halakhic* treatments of feticide.

The first three parts of this chapter trace the development of *halakhic* attitudes toward feticide by following, to the extent possible, the structure of the first section of this volume. The first part of this chapter examines how the early rabbis understood and derived laws from biblical verses. The second part explores how authorities from the late first millennium through the sixteenth century interpreted the earlier rabbinic texts. The third part focuses on how later authorities, from early modernity until today, interpreted the medieval authorities and reached practical rulings.

The fourth and final part of this chapter explores some distinct features of the *halakhic* tradition and its interactions with the prevailing sociopolitical environment in the context of feticide. In the United States, home to almost half of world Jewry, the question of feticide is a major dividing line between the politically conservative, right-wing, "pro-life" camp, and the politically liberal, left-wing, "pro-choice" camp. *halakhah* does not fit neatly into either of these camps. The discussion examines how *halakhah* interacts with political and cultural circumstances and how the pressure to form coalitions and alliances affects the rhetoric of *halakhah* and the articulation of its values. This in turn leads to reflection on a critical distinction between what will be termed "wholesale" and "retail" *halakhah*, where the former relates to the articulation of general principles and the latter to individual circumstances. Significantly, this distinction is indicative of how *halakhah* functions in other areas as well.

Early Rabbinic Understandings of Torah Law on Feticide

The Torah nowhere explicitly states whether feticide is prohibited or permitted. However, several verses and passages served as prooftexts from which the rabbis extrapolated laws:

1. "One who sheds the blood of man, through man shall his blood be shed."[1]
2. "When men fight, and one of them pushes a pregnant woman and a miscarriage results, but there is no *ason*, the one responsible shall be fined according as the woman's husband may exact from him, the payment to be based on reckoning. But if there is *ason*, the penalty shall be life for life."[2]
3. "If a man strikes down any human life, he shall be put to death."[3]

The first prooftext is addressed to Noah—and thus, according to the rabbis, all of humanity, his descendants—in the immediate aftermath of the Deluge. *Halakhah*, by and large, refers to the web of norms, laws, and practices addressed to the Jewish people. There is, however, a corpus known as the "Seven Noahide Commandments," which, according to *halakhah*, applies to all of humanity and, indeed, may correspond to a rabbinic idea of "natural law."[4] The verse in question avers that one who commits homicide, who "sheds the blood of man," shall be put to death by fellow human beings.

The Talmud,[5] as is typical, expounds this verse to deduce the parameters of the homicide prohibition and infers that it includes feticide: "It was said in the name of Rabbi Yishmael: [They are liable to be put to death] even for [killing] a fetus . . . as it is written, 'One who sheds the blood of man, through man (*ba-adam*) shall his blood be shed.' What man is inside man (*ba-adam*)? You must say that this is a fetus in its mother's womb." Rabbi Yishmael's derivation is based on the fact that this verse can be parsed in two ways. The plain meaning is that homicide is punishable by death at the hands of human beings. But the verse can also be read as: "One who sheds the blood of man within man, his blood shall be shed." "Man within man" is taken to refer to a fetus, which is thus included in the prohibition on homicide. Accordingly, feticide is understood by Rabbi Yishmael to be a universal, capital offense that at the very least falls under the broader rubric of homicide. While no dissenting view is recorded explicitly, the Talmud's ensuing discussion takes for granted that Rabbi Yishmael, whose ruling appears at the end of a series of unattributed rulings, disagrees with the anonymous first "speaker" of these rulings, who maintains that feticide is not a form of homicide under Noahide law.

The second source, from Exodus, introduces a case of inadvertent destruction of a fetus. The interpretation of the passage, which introduces the Bible's well-known doctrine of *lex talionis*, or "an eye for an eye," hinges on the meaning of the relatively rare term "*ason*." The Septuagint, the Greek translation of the Bible from the third century BCE, renders this term as "formed." Philo of Alexandria, writing in the first century CE, echoes this interpretation when he distinguishes between an unformed fetus and one that has taken shape.[6] According to this interpretation, the key distinction raised by the Exodus passage is between a formed fetus and an as-yet-unformed embryo. Killing an unformed embryo incurs a monetary penalty and is thus viewed as a tort, whereas a fully formed fetus is deemed a person, the killing of whom constitutes homicide and incurs the death penalty.[7]

Other early traditions of interpretation, including the entirety of the rabbinic tradition and its antecedents,[8] interpret "*ason*" to mean "damage" or "calamity," referring to the death of the pregnant woman. That is, if the fight results in a miscarriage, but the mother lives, then the penalty is monetary. But if the pregnant woman dies, then the penalty is death, not remuneration. In other words, within Rabbinic Judaism, the killing of a fetus is classified as a tort, not a capital crime, as one who commits a capital crime is put to death but exempted from monetary damages, so if feticide were considered a capital crime like homicide, there would be no monetary payment.

The third source, like the first, presents the punishment for homicide. But whereas Rabbi Yishmael read the first verse so as to *include* feticide in the rubric of homicide, in the case of the third source, the rabbis read the verse to *exclude* feticide. The context is a Mishnah that lists the various status changes that accrue to a child immediately upon birth.[9] Specifically, the child has the status to inherit, bequeath, contract certain forms of ritual impurity, and "one who kills him is liable [for murder]." The Talmud cites a biblical prooftext for this latter ruling: "For it is written, 'If a man strikes down any human life'—in any case."[10] The homicide prohibition applies to "any human life" (*kol nefesh adam*),[11] even one just born. By implication, one who kills an unborn fetus is not liable for murder.

Several rabbinic texts also address the issue of feticide, both explicitly and implicitly, without reference to sources from the Bible. Perhaps the best-known of these is from m.Ohalot:[12] "[If] a woman was having trouble giving birth, they cut up the fetus inside her and take it out limb by limb, because her life comes before its life. If most of it had come out already, they do not touch it, because we do not push off one life for another." This Mishnah explicitly permits (or requires) the destruction of the fetus to save the mother's life. However, once the baby has mostly emerged, one may not kill it, even to save the mother.

Another Mishnah makes a similar distinction in a case of a pregnant woman sentenced to be executed: "If a woman is about to be executed, they do not delay until she gives birth. But if she is already sitting on the birthstool, they wait for her until she gives birth."[13] Commenting on this Mishnah, the Talmud asks: "Isn't this obvious?"[14] That is, it is obvious to the Talmud's anonymous editors that the execution should not be stayed for the fetus's sake. The Talmud answers that one might have thought that the execution should be delayed because of the value of the fetus to the father; the *Mishnah* must therefore clarify that this is not the case, and the fetus suffers its mother's fate despite the father's interests.

The Talmud then goes on to explain that the executioners actually kill the fetus before executing the woman, out of respect for the dignity of the executed woman, whose body would suffer degradation if the fetus were to be alive at the time of execution. The execution of the woman is preceded by, or begins with, the killing of her fetus, implying that the fetus is treated as part of the mother. The Talmud explains why the fetus is spared once the birthing process has begun: "Once [the fetus] is detached [lit: 'uprooted,' from the womb], it is a separate body (*gufa aharina*)." In this context, the Talmud cites an associated ruling: "Rabbi Nahman said in the name of Shmuel: If a woman was sitting on the birthing stool and died on the Sabbath, one brings a knife, tears open her belly, and removes the fetus." The ensuing discussion clarifies that even Torah-level Sabbath prohibitions are set aside to save the fetus, and even if there is uncertainty whether the fetus is viable.

The three mishnaic passages discussed above[15] indicate that a fetus attains personhood, with implications for the permissibility of killing it at, or just prior to, birth. But at least three other concepts from the rabbinic corpus also have direct and indirect bearing on the question of feticide. Although the classical rabbinic literature does not invoke the concepts discussed below specifically in the context of feticide, all are germane to the discussion and are raised in this context by later authorities. One such concept is "*ubar yerekh imo*" (the fetus is a limb [lit., "thigh"] of its mother), the rabbinic analogue of the Latin *pars viscera matris*. The Talmud[16] invokes this concept in several contexts, for instance, when discussing the status of a fetal calf whose mother was consecrated for sacrifice or perpetrated damages, the status of a child born to a mother who converted to Judaism while pregnant with this child, and whether a master can manumit a slave woman while retaining ownership of her unborn fetus. Prima facie, it seems that according to this concept, a fetus is indeed part of the mother, it should not be considered a separate person, and feticide should be considered a form of mutilation of the mother, but not murder. However, the Talmud considers the concept of *ubar yerekh imo* to be subject to dispute, and the view that a fetus has an identity independent of the mother's remains relevant.

A second concept concerns the prohibition against wasteful seminal emission (*hashhatat zera*, lit., "wasting of seed"), which the Talmud likens to each of the three cardinal sins of bloodshed, idolatry, and adultery.[17] Presumably, if the destruction of viable semen can be compared to bloodshed, then certainly the destruction of a fetus, which is much further along the path to human life, can be so compared.

A third concept is the Talmud's view that until the fortieth day after conception, a fetus is considered insubstantial—"mere water" (*maya be-alma*). This has normative implications. For instance, the commandment to redeem a firstborn son (*pidyon ha-ben*) does not apply if his mother had a prior abortion or miscarriage. However, if the earlier pregnancy was terminated within forty days of conception, the obligation to redeem remains in force.[18] Additionally, the Talmud records a view that it is permissible to pray for a child to be of a particular sex only during the first forty days of pregnancy; afterward, such a prayer is deemed to be in vain.[19]

The sources discussed in this section address a variety of cases that concern the status of a fetus. Rabbi Yishmael expressly links feticide to homicide and considers it punishable by death under Noahide law. No other source directly prohibits feticide, and Rabbi Yishmael's view is itself disputed in the Talmud. Several sources clearly indicate that a fetus is not yet considered a person and that there are situations in which fetal life is terminated to save the mother's life, or even her dignity. None of these sources explicitly prohibits feticide under Jewish law (in contrast to Noahide law), and some appear to diminish the value of fetal life, but at least one source likens the waste of seed, and presumably feticide *a fortiori*, to cardinal sins. Though comparing two things does not imply equating them, there is no doubt that comparing a specific act to murder, idolatry, and adultery clearly expresses how terrible the act is considered to be.

Discussion of Feticide in Medieval Rabbinic Writings

The sources discussed thus far are scattered across several talmudic tractates and address different cases. Although the Talmud is far from an organized legal code, it has been accepted as the authoritative source of *halakhah*. The medieval Sages (*Rishonim*) undertook the tasks of organizing, categorizing, harmonizing, and clarifying the vast talmudic corpus into a functional legal source (see Kanarfogel, this volume). Therefore, this section examines how these authorities interpreted and harmonized the passages addressed in the previous section.

"It Is Not a 'Life'": The Question of Fetal Personhood

The *Rishonim* explain why it is permissible to destroy a fetus to save the mother's life. Rashi, the great eleventh-century exegete, states, "as long as it has not emerged into the world, it is not a life (*nefesh*), and it may be killed to save its mother."[20] Similar statements about a fetus not being a "life" are found in the writings of several other *Rishonim*, and this seems to be the standard view.[21]

The question of violating another prohibition to save a fetus would seem to be a good test case for this view. Almost every prohibition in the Torah is set aside to save a life. The rabbis inferred this from verse, "You shall keep My laws and My rules, by which a *person* shall live,"[22] which they understood to mean, "'A person (*adam*) shall live' by them and not die by them."[23] It would, therefore, seem that if one may set aside a Torah prohibition to save a fetus, the fetus is indeed considered a "person." But if one does not set aside a Torah prohibition to save a fetus, this would be clear evidence that a fetus is not considered a person.

We have already seen that the Talmud permits the violation of the Sabbath to remove a living fetus from its dead mother.[24] However, in that case, the mother was already "sitting on the birthing stool," and the fetus is already considered a "separate body." The more relevant question is whether it is permissible to violate the Sabbath to save a fetus that is not nearing full term, or whether a mother may violate the Yom Kippur by eating to save such a fetus. There are three distinct views on this issue, all of which support the idea that a fetus has not reached personhood.

The first view, articulated in a responsum from the *geonic* era (spanning the eighth through tenth centuries), states that we make no effort to save the fetus, even when it is not the Sabbath: "Question: A woman died on the birthing stool, and the fetus is still moving in her belly: Do we tear open her belly to take out the baby, or not? Answer: We do not tear her open. Rather, we leave her and place a stone over her belly until the baby dies, and then we bury her."[25]

A second view, cited by several leading rabbis of late medieval Spain,[26] maintains that it is not permissible to violate the Sabbath (or to eat on Yom Kippur) to save the fetus, but only to save the mother, unless the mother had already died, in which case the still-living fetus attains personhood (and is no longer a limb of its mother), and one may violate the Sabbath to save the fetus.[27]

The third view, representing the wide majority of *halakhic* opinion, dates to the ninth-century compendium *Halakhot Gedolot* and states: "A pregnant woman about whom we know that if she does not eat will miscarry, even if we say it is uncertain whether it will live or die, it is fine to give her what to eat [on Yom Kippur]."[28] Several medieval commentators, beginning with Nahmanides in the thirteenth century, point out that this permissive ruling is not based on the general principle of "by which a person shall live," but the different principle: "Violate one Sabbath in order to observe many Sabbaths."[29] In other words, even if feticide is not considered taking a life, and saving a fetus is not considered saving a life, one may nevertheless violate the Sabbath to save a fetus, as a fetus potentially will "observe many Sabbaths" in the future. Therefore, Nahmanides concludes, "even to save a fetus less than forty days [after conception], which is not living at all, one may desecrate [the Sabbath]."[30] Even though he permits the desecration of the Sabbath to save a fetus, Nahmanides explicitly precludes the implication that a fetus has reached personhood. Like the other two views, this view, too, is compatible with the basic consensus that a fetus has not reached personhood.

"There Is Nothing Forbidden to a Gentile That Is Permitted to Israel"

As previously mentioned,[31] Rabbi Yishmael maintains that feticide is forbidden to Gentiles under Noahide law. While this may suggest that the prohibition does not apply to Jews, only two folios later the Talmud avers, with respect to Noahide law, that, "There is nothing forbidden to a gentile that is permitted to Israel."[32] The Tosafists, a cadre of Talmudic scholars who flourished in northern France and the Rhineland in the twelfth and thirteenth centuries and produced a very influential Talmud commentary, apply this principle to feticide. On two occasions, they contend that it is forbidden to both Jews and non-Jews, and that, conversely, killing a fetus to save the mother's life is permitted to Jews and non-Jews.[33] This statement by the Tosafists provides the earliest explicit ruling that forbids feticide to Jews.[34]

On a third occasion,[35] however, the Tosafists appear to articulate a different view, stating in the course of discussion that feticide is permitted. Nevertheless, the context suggests that "permitted" means only that feticide is not punishable as an act of homicide, but not that it is outright permissible.

In sum, the views articulated by the *Rishonim* that we have encountered thus far suggest that the prevailing view is that the life of a fetus is not yet human life, and that consequently, its destruction is not a capital offense and, indeed, under certain circumstances, destruction is permitted and perhaps even required. At the same time, the majority view, notwithstanding the inferior status of the life of a fetus, is that one may violate the Sabbath to save a fetus. The implication here is that if saving a fetus overrides severe transgressions, then certainly a fetus must not be destroyed without a compelling reason. The Tosafists forbid feticide based on the principle that if something is forbidden to Gentiles, it must also be forbidden to Jews As the next section illustrates, Maimonides invokes the *rodef* principle in this context, implying that at the very least, feticide is generally prohibited and is only permitted in an extraordinary case, like when the mother's life is in jeopardy.

Maimonides: The Fetus as a "Pursuer"

In his monumental twelfth-century *halakhic* work, *Mishneh Torah*, Maimonides codifies the law of the fetus that threatens its mother's life:

> We are commanded not to show compassion to a pursuer (*rodef*).[36] Therefore, the Sages teach that if a pregnant woman is having a dangerously difficult birth, it is permissible to destroy the fetus inside her, whether with drugs or a knife, since it is like a pursuer trying to kill her. However, once its head has emerged, we do not harm him, for one life does not supersede another, and this is the nature of the world.[37]

The law of *rodef* permits neutralizing and even killing a would-be killer or rapist. This applies even to an inadvertent killer. The Talmud, in its discussion of m.Ohalot,[38] indeed asks why the permissibility of killing the fetus to save the mother ends once the baby's head has emerged into the world. Shouldn't a baby who threatens his mother's life have the status of a *rodef*? The Talmud answers rather cryptically that it is not the baby who pursues the mother, but rather, "she is being pursued by heaven." In other words, the threat to the mother's life is an act of God, not an act of the newborn. As Maimonides paraphrases, "this is the nature of the world."

Clearly, Maimonides's ruling purports to codify the Talmudic passage. However, the Talmud only invokes the law of *rodef* in asking why it does not justify killing the emerging baby; it does *not* invoke the law of the *rodef* to explain the permissibility of killing an *unborn* fetus that threatens its mother's life, and we have seen that most commentators explain that this is permitted because a fetus has not reached personhood. Maimonides, however, invokes the concept of *rodef* as the rationale for the permissibility of killing a fetus that threatens its mother's life—even as he states that once the child is born it no longer is considered a *rodef* because "this is the nature of the world."

The implication of Maimonides's ruling is that absent the justification of *rodef*, feticide is prohibited. Whereas the *Mishnah* states that a fetus may (or must) be killed even just prior to birth to save the mother's life, Maimonides seems to imply the corollary: a fetus may *only* be killed to save the mother's life. Only the *rodef* principle justifies the destruction of a fetus, and only until the baby's head emerges, whereupon it is not the baby but "the nature of the world" that threatens the mother's life. This ruling is surprising in two ways: first because Maimonides does not explain why a fetus is considered a *rodef* but not a baby whose head has emerged; and second because it seems to contravene the plain meaning of the Talmud.

Discussions of Feticide in the Modern Era

Given Maimonides's stature as the author of the greatest medieval *halakhic* code, there have been numerous attempts to explain his ruling. Therefore, this section concerning the modern period begins with a discussion of interpretations of Maimonides's seminal ruling. It then explores different views concerning the nature of the feticide prohibition, and concludes with a survey of "case law" from recent times.

Interpretations of Maimonides's Ruling

One common interpretation of Maimonides's position acknowledges that feticide, while not murder, is nevertheless forbidden and cannot be performed without justification. In other words, it is only because of the fetus's lack of personhood that the *rodef* principle can be applied to save the mother.[39] Others explain that Maimonides *compares* but does not *equate* the fetus with a *rodef*; his specific language is that the fetus is "*like* a pursuer" (*ke-rodef*).[40] That is, there are similarities between the status of the fetus that threatens its mother's life and a person pursuing another person with murderous intent. For instance, just as one need not consider whether a *rodef* needs to be killed or merely disabled, because it is permissible to save the potential victim using any means necessary, so too one may destroy a fetus that threatens its mother's life in any way possible.[41]

In the early nineteenth century, Rabbi Akiva Eger wrote that while feticide is not considered homicide for Jews, under Noahide law it falls under the rubric of murder. Accordingly, Maimonides invoked the law of *rodef* to establish that it is permissible even for non-Jews to destroy a fetus when the mother's life is at stake.[42] Rabbi Hayim Ozer Grodzinski, the leading Lithuanian *halakhist* of the early twentieth century, argued that this entire discussion applies only after parturition has begun. In such a case, since the fetus has already begun to detach from its mother, it has attained a degree of personhood, and the *rodef* principle must be invoked. Prior to the onset of labor, however, he believes that even Maimonides would agree that "the fetus is a limb of its mother," and there are instances where the destruction of the fetus would be permitted even if it does not have the status of *rodef*.[43]

Also in the twentieth century, two extremely influential rabbinic authorities took Maimonides's invocation of *rodef* to mean that feticide is a form of murder, permitted only when the fetus poses a threat to the mother's life. The first is Rabbi Hayim Soloveichik of Brisk (Brest-Litovsk), whose collection of novellae on Maimonides's *Mishneh Torah* is a key exemplar of the Lithuanian-style of analysis that came to dominate *yeshivot* all over the world in the twentieth century. In his reading, the mandate to save a life applies equally to the mother and to the fetus.[44] In other words, the mother's life would not take precedence over the life of the fetus if not for the fact that the fetus is a *rodef*, and the Torah considers a *rodef* to have forfeited his right to life. This position was also espoused by R. Hayim's illustrious grandson, Rabbi Joseph B. Soloveitchik (1903–1993), whose writings formed a linchpin of twentieth-century Orthodox thought.

Another major authority who interprets Maimonides to mean that feticide is murder is Rabbi Moshe Feinstein (1895–1986),[45] the leading *halakhist* in the United States during the latter half of the twentieth century. He concludes that feticide is permitted only when the fetus will almost certainly cause its mother's death, arguing vehemently against any interpretation that denies that Maimonides equates feticide with murder or rules against Maimonides.

An ancillary disagreement regarding modern interpretations of Maimonides's *rodef* theory that consider feticide homicide relates to the point of development when the fetus achieves personhood. The most prohibitive view seems to be that of Rabbi Menasheh Klein (1924–2011), who maintains that the prohibition of feticide begins from the moment of conception, based on the Talmud's statement that a fetus is endowed with a soul from conception.[46] He therefore prohibits the use of intrauterine devices (IUDs), which can prevent fertilized eggs from becoming implanted in the uterus, thereby resulting in their destruction. In contrast, Rabbi Aharon Lichtenstein (1933–2015) notes that some maintain that the relevant stage is when the fetus reaches "the point of independent viability," a cutoff that varies with the accessibility of medical techniques. Other authorities set the relevant cutoff at forty days, until which, as we have seen, the Talmud deems an embryo "mere water."[47]

In sum, according to most interpretations of Maimonides's ruling, he does not equate feticide with homicide and does necessarily not limit the permissibility of feticide to cases where the mother's life is endangered. However, two enormously influential twentieth-century authorities adopted the view that Maimonides equates feticide with murder.[48]

Discussions of the Nature of the Prohibition

There is broad agreement among rabbis of the modern era (the *Aharonim*) that feticide is prohibited. However, as we have seen, there is disagreement about whether it constitutes homicide. This question, in turn, has practical implications for the circumstances in which the prohibition may be abrogated.

There are several opinions about the source and reason for the prohibition of feticide. Some maintain that it is forbidden by rabbinic decree, not biblical mandate; others maintain that it constitutes a dereliction of one's duty to procreate; several others deem it a form of destruction, mutilation, or even the taking of a subhuman or quasi-human life; finally, there are those who maintain that it is indeed a form of homicide. Although there is universal agreement that abortion is forbidden in general, the question of the source of the prohibition is very important for understanding what might constitute an exception. Generally speaking, the more serious the nature of the prohibition, the more dire the circumstances that warrant abortion must be.

Rabbi Yosef di Trani (known as Maharit), writing in early seventeenth-century Safed,[49] argues based on the verses in Exodus 22 (concerning a pregnant woman suffering a miscarriage as a by-product of men fighting)[50] that destroying a fetus is akin to inflicting bodily harm on someone. This prohibition, which includes self-mutilation, mandates that it is forbidden for a woman to have an abortion just as it is forbidden for someone to have a limb amputated. However, when a person's overall health requires the amputation of a limb, even when the person's life is not in jeopardy, such an operation would be permitted. Consequently, according to Maharit, an abortion may be permitted in the interest of the mother's overall health, even when there is no risk to her life.

Toward the end of the seventeenth century, Rabbi Yair Hayim Bacharach, living in the Rhineland, was asked about the permissibility of terminating a pregnancy that would result in an illegitimate child (*mamzer*). He discusses the theoretical possibility of aborting in the early stages of pregnancy, but he ultimately prohibits it. His primary reason for prohibiting in the case before him is preexisting custom, rooted in public policy of both Jewish and Christian society; treating abortion as a prohibition would compel the pregnant mother to bear the illegitimate child and consequently discourage promiscuity. He then adds another reason for prohibiting: abortion is certainly no less severe than "wasting seed," which is prohibited and also entails the destruction of potential life.[51]

In the early twentieth century, Rabbi Meir Ben-Zion Uziel, the first Sephardic Chief Rabbi of the State of Israel, cites a discussion in the Talmud[52] that criticizes one who fails to engage in procreation. He concludes: "If these words were said of one who does not engage in procreation, who makes no active effort, then certainly they apply to one who takes action that excludes the possibility that this one Jewish soul will exist and grow."[53] Not only is abortion a failure to uphold the obligation to procreate, but it actively prevents procreation. While he does not link abortion to a specific transgression, Rabbi Uziel sees it as a direct contravention of *halakhic* norms.

Other *Aharonim* conclude that feticide is a rabbinic prohibition, not a biblical prohibition,[54] or that the question of whether the prohibition is biblical or rabbinic is itself a matter of dispute among the *Rishonim*.[55] A relatively large cluster of *Aharonim* maintain with certainty that although feticide is forbidden, it should not be considered homicide, murder, or a derivative thereof.[56]

A significant group of later *Aharonim* link feticide to murder, albeit as a lesser prohibition than actual homicide. Thus, late nineteenth-century Hungarian Rabbi Moshe Schick states that a fetus is "like a partial life," and feticide is "like a half measure" (*ke-hatzi shi'ur*), "ancillary to homicide." He concludes that feticide is forbidden by the

Torah, and one must even give up their own life to avoid committing feticide.[57] A similar view was taken in the mid-twentieth century by Rabbi Isser Yehudah Unterman, the Ashkenazic Chief Rabbi of Israel. He was asked whether a pregnant woman who contracted rubella, a disease that can have significant adverse physical and mental effects on fetal development, may have the pregnancy aborted. In his answer, he refers to feticide several times as "ancillary to murder" and "quasi-murder." He ultimately forbids the abortion even if it is known for certain that the baby will have mental or physical defects.[58] A contemporary of Rabbi Unterman, Syrian-born Rabbi Ovadiah Hedaya, likewise refers to feticide as a "branch" or derivative of murder.[59] This group of rabbis stops short of equating feticide with actual murder, but it is clear from their formulations that they regard it as something "murder-like" and therefore, they tend to prohibit feticide even if the baby will be born with severe defects.

Finally, there is a group of *Aharonim* who explicitly take the position that feticide is a form of bona fide murder. The first to articulate this view was Rabbi Eliyahu Mizrahi of Constantinople in the early sixteenth century. In his supercommentary to Rashi's Torah commentary,[60] he contends that feticide is not punishable by death only due to the technicality that the viability of an unborn fetus is uncertain.[61] In the twentieth century, we have seen that the view that feticide is indeed murder was espoused by a significant group of rabbinic authorities, especially from within the intellectual milieu of Greater Lithuania, home to a vibrant Jewish legal community prior to the Holocaust. These authorities had a critical influence over twentieth-century Orthodox Judaism.[62]

Feticide in Twentieth-and Twenty-First-Century Rabbinic Case Law

Advances in diagnostic and reproductive technology, cultural changes pertaining to sexuality and the status of women, the wide availability of medical procedures that could terminate a pregnancy without compromising the health of the mother, and decriminalization (at least until recently in the United States) all contributed to the production of a voluminous *halakhic* literature, addressing a wide variety of cases. As we have seen, there is a *halakhic* consensus that feticide is generally prohibited, but that there are circumstances that override the prohibition. The key question, therefore, is which circumstances warrant abortion. The answers reveal subtle distinctions and disagreements.

The cases addressed in the *halakhic* literature tend to have certain features in common. If the mother's life is in danger, abortion is permitted by all *halakhic* authorities. But even the more permissive *halakhic* authorities limit abortion to cases where its effects are deemed therapeutic such as saving the mother injury, pain, or anguish; protecting the health and well-being of others (for instance, an older sibling who demands special care); or sparing the fetus from a life that would be compromised by significant defects. There is no support for allowing abortion "on demand" or as a means of birth control.

This basic rubric applies to the *halakhic* interpretations of every major American Jewish denomination. The Conservative movement has consistently taken the view that abortion is not murder but is nevertheless impermissible except when "continuation of a pregnancy might cause severe physical or psychological harm, or where the fetus is judged by competent medical opinion as severely defective."[63] Reform rabbinic responses to individual questions invoke the same *halakhic* considerations as their Conservative (and some Orthodox) counterparts.[64] The Reform movement stands apart from the other movements, however, in granting the ultimate autonomy over the decision to abort to the mother or family: "In any decision whether or not to terminate a pregnancy, the individual family or woman must weigh the tradition as they struggle to formulate their own religious and moral criteria to reach their own personal decision" (see Washofsky, this volume).[65]

The bulk of the literature and the greatest divergence of opinion is represented within Orthodox Judaism, primarily in the United States and Israel. A full survey of the cases addressed in this literature would (and does) fill several books. The manifold dilemmas addressed therein include topics such as the permissibility of abortion to save the mother from a severe but non-life-threatening condition;[66] abortion by a nursing mother whose pregnancy adversely affects her milk supply and threatens the health of an older child;[67] fetal reduction in the case of multiple fetuses, in which destruction of some is recommended to ensure the survival of others; abortion in cases where there is concern that the mother's infection with rubella[68] or exposure to thalidomide[69] during pregnancy may result in mental and/or physical deformities to the fetus; and termination of pregnancy where the child either may or certainly will be born with a condition like epilepsy[70] or Down syndrome.[71]

The best-known and most contentious debate concerns the abortion of fetuses diagnosed *in utero* with the genetic defect that results in Tay-Sachs disease, a terrible, painful, and incurable disease that results in the child's death, usually by the age of four. The primary disputants in the debate, all of whom were late twentieth-century Orthodox *halakhic* heavyweights, were Rabbi Moshe Feinstein, who prohibited abortion,[72] Rabbi Eliezer Waldenberg, who permitted it,[73] and Rabbi Shlomo Zalman Auerbach, who ruled that a Tay-Sachs fetus may be aborted within forty days of conception.[74]

It is important to note that the *halakhists* who permit abortions in cases of fetal defects do so on the grounds that the mother is suffering in the present, not out of pity for the unborn child who will face unknown difficulties. As one mid-twentieth-century *halakhist*, Rabbi David Sperber of Romania, expressed when considering (and rejecting) the possibility of aborting a defective child: "this seems to me very much like the laws of Lycurgus, King of Sparta, according to which every blemished child was to be put to death."[75]

Another set of cases in which the permissibility of abortion is discussed pertains to fetuses conceived through adultery, incest, and rape, or where the pregnancy causes profound shame to the mother and her family. Writing at the turn of the twentieth century, Rabbi Yosef Hayim of Baghdad addressed the case of a woman who became pregnant through adultery, and in her sixth month, wishes to drink an abortifacient.[76] The rabbi does not definitively answer the question, writing: "I do not wish to respond to this issue by giving instructions, neither to forbid nor to permit." However, he cites three earlier opinions—Maharit, *Havot Ya'ir*, and Rabbi Yaakov Emden—and concludes: "I am not revealing my opinion; rather, I presented the aforementioned to the questioner, who will show my words to a sage [i.e., rabbi], who will instruct him what to do." We have already seen that neither Maharit nor *Havot Ya'ir* equates feticide with murder,[77] and the same can be said for Rabbi Emden, of eighteenth-century Germany, who maintains that it is permissible, and perhaps even required, to abort a fetus conceived through adultery.[78] Rabbi Yosef Hayim, even while referring the case to a local scholar, sets the terms of the debate: there are grounds to permit the abortion, and even if it is prohibited, it is not murder.

Later in the century, Rabbi Uziel was asked about a married woman who conceived through adultery, and he ruled that the parents of the fetus could induce an abortion, to spare it (and themselves) from living with the taint of *mamzer*. On the other hand, he prohibited abortion in the case of an unwed mother, since the child would carry no such taint.[79] Rabbi Waldenberg argued more broadly for permissiveness in cases of unwed and adulterous mothers, to relieve their anguish.[80]

Significantly, the permissive rulings cited in this section are predicated on the view that abortion is not a form of murder. Authorities who view abortion as a form of murder are unwilling to permit it to save the mother from shame, physical pain, injury, psychological anguish, or indeed for any reason short of saving the mother's life.[81] Moreover, even some authorities who do not equate feticide with homicide adopt strict views on the matter. For instance, Rabbi Shmuel Wosner of Bnei Brak rejects Rabbi Feinstein's reasoning and concludes that abortion does not even smack of murder. Still, while this view yields a more permissive ruling in certain cases, he is reluctant to permit abortion based on doctors' assessments of the mother's psychological state on the grounds that doctors tend to overstate psychological risks, especially in an era characterized by what he considered to be a flippant attitude toward the lives of fetuses.[82]

Conclusion: Some Considerations of How *Halakhah* Functions

Notwithstanding the variety of abortion questions addressed in rabbinic literature over the past century, the range of cases in which there is disagreement is relatively narrow. Orthodox and Conservative *halakhic* authorities are all but unanimous in prohibiting abortion for financial reasons or as a form of birth control, and permitting or requiring it in a case where the mother's life is threatened. The clear consensus of *halakhic* authorities is that abortion is unlawful and morally wrong, except in a delimited set of circumstances. No authorities grant blanket permission to commit feticide. Indeed, the public *halakhic* rhetoric emphasizes the unlawfulness and wrongfulness of abortion. As Rabbi Feinstein wrote in 1977:

> I wrote all this concerning the great breach in the world, whereby the governments of many countries permitted killing fetuses, including the heads of the State of Israel. Innumerable fetuses have already been killed. Thus, nowadays it is necessary to erect safeguards for the Torah and certainly not create leniencies in the most severe prohibition of murder.[83]

Although limited but significant leeway is brought to bear on individual cases, these cases, due to their sensitive nature, tend to remain out of the spotlight.[84] This results in an incongruity, particularly in Orthodox circles, between the public-facing, "wholesale" *halakhah*, which emphasizes the wrongness of abortion, and a more secretive, individuated "retail" *halakhah*, where there may be grounds to permit abortion.[85]

There are other *halakhic* realms in which the wholesale/retail divide is evident. The laws of *mamzerut*, for example, dictate that a child of incest or adultery is a *mamzer* and severely restricted in who he or she can marry. Clearly, these laws have the effect of deterring adulterous or incestuous behavior that can result in a stigmatized child. Yet, when the plight of an individual *mamzer* comes before a rabbinical court or *halakhic* authority, often the grounds to release the *mamzer* from these restrictions—which were, after all, the result of the parents' behavior, rather than the child's—will be found.[86]

Another salient example is *agunah*, a woman whose husband has gone missing. Throughout history, the *halakhic* system has demonstrated a clear preference for permitting the woman to remarry on a case-by-case basis rather than developing broad remedies that would trigger the automatic termination or annulment of the marital bonds if certain conditions are met (see Gotlib and Levmore, this volume). Conversion is yet another example. At the wholesale level, conversion to Judaism requires commitment to a life of *halakhic* observance; at the retail level, conversions are performed under a variety of mitigating circumstances without a full or sincere commitment to observance.[87]

The common denominator between these areas of *halakhah* is that the wholesale ruling expresses an overarching cultural value—the sanctity of the marital bond, the centrality of observance, and the importance of fetal life—while the retail rulings are geared toward real-world scenarios that are often quite messy. By maintaining the wholesale/retail divide, *halakhists* can convey important principles and create a public perception that frowns upon and deters certain behavior, or lends certain decisions a degree of gravitas, while also ensuring that individuals facing difficult circumstances have their concerns addressed with the requisite sensitivity. Thus, it is not surprising to find rhetorical opposition to abortion, especially when the issue is at the fore of political discourse, alongside permissive dispensations on an individual basis. The central message remains: it is generally forbidden, it violates a cardinal value, and it should never be taken lightly.

The wholesale/retail structure regarding abortion plays out in other interesting ways. We have seen that there is a range of *halakhic* opinion about abortion "on the books," but that range is not necessarily represented evenly in practice. Since there is no formal judiciary hierarchy for deciding matters of *halakhah*, women and families facing dilemmas are likely to gravitate toward authorities who, on one hand, have developed a reputation for *halakhic* reliability and expertise, and, on the other hand, demonstrate willingness to at least consider a permissive ruling. The result is that the *halakhah* as codified and publicized—the "written tradition"—more closely resembles the wholesale attitude, while the "oral tradition" of individual decisions tend to exemplify retail attitudes.[88]

We have already seen a case where Rabbi Yosef Hayim of Baghdad expressed reluctance to articulate his view explicitly but intimated that there are ample grounds on which to base a lenient ruling.[89] A more surprising dimension of this trend is exemplified in a story about Rabbi Shlomo Zalman Auerbach.[90] Presented with the emotionally difficult case in which he maintained that feticide was forbidden, he advised the physician to tell the pregnant woman that Rabbi Eliezer Waldenberg rules permissively; he felt that the woman was not required to follow his (restrictive) ruling but could follow a different legitimate view.

The phenomenon of *halakhic* authorities referring questioners to more permissive authorities, while remaining silent about their personal views, is hard to conceptualize within secular legal contexts. Litigants might venue shop, but the judges themselves can hardly recommend a different venue to obtain a ruling that they would not themselves issue or approve. How can one maintain, and even publicly espouse, the view that feticide constitutes an unlawful destruction of life, perhaps even murder, and then refer a petitioner to someone who will permit the termination of that fetal life?

It seems clear that this phenomenon is grounded in a strong conception of *halakhic* pluralism, wherein multiple legitimate *halakhic* opinions coexist. One whose understanding of the *halakhic* issue mitigates toward a restrictive view must act and rule consistently with that understanding. Yet, such an authority may still acknowledge the existence and integrity of an opposing permissive view, and even, in some circumstances, recommend consulting an authority who espouses it.

Perhaps we may also posit a gap between formal prohibitions and more lenient situational choices. That is, a *halakhist* may believe that abortion is the morally correct course of action in a specific case yet refrain from permitting it on formal grounds. In such an instance, we can understand the impetus for recommending a different authority, one whose reading of the relevant sources yields a ruling that better aligns with the moral judgment of the initial *halakhic* consultant. Also, although in most cases a rabbi's moral judgment may align with the formal *halakhah* that prohibits abortion, in reality there is an internalization of the wholesale/retail structure of *halakhah* concerning abortion. As such, a *halakhist* might experience no dissonance between taking a public stance against abortion while demonstrating a more nuanced position in specific cases.

The wholesale/retail gap adds another dimension to the reluctance of certain *halakhists* to publicize rulings. Once an opinion is published in writing (or merely made public), there is a risk that a retail ruling will be applied wholesale. In cases where the mother's anguish is the potential grounds for abortion, the ruling will depend, to a very large degree, on an honest assessment of the danger to her mental and physical health. The risk of misapplication to other cases tends to be high, and the stakes of every such decision is momentous: potential life and an individual's long-term health are both at risk. For this reason, statements like Rabbi Yosef Hayim of Baghdad's "I do not wish to respond to this issue by giving instructions, neither to forbid nor to permit" are entirely understandable.

Another effect of the wholesale/retail layering of *halakhah* is that it induces people to seek the guidance of a *halakhic* authority and, by implication, constrains their personal autonomy. As a general matter, it is necessary to obtain a rabbinic dispensation to undergo a procedure that is normally prohibited because a person's responsibilities toward his or her physical health is ordained by the Torah—by God. Therefore, requiring a *halakhic* imprimatur for an abortion signifies that even in cases where *halakhah* permits abortion, it is not because women have bodily autonomy.

In this way, the theory of Jewish law is at odds with the concept of personal autonomy that has played a significant role in the abortion debate in the United States.[91] The centrality of rabbis in the decision-making process, even when they permit abortion, demonstrates that *halakhah* cannot accept the notion of "my body, my choice."[92] Our bodies, according to *halakhah*, are not ours to do with as we please. They are, rather, instruments given to us by God and subject to His commandments and strictures.

Notes

1. Gen. 9:6.
2. Exod. 21:22–23, based on the NJPS (Jewish Publication Society, formerly NJV, or New Jewish Version) Tanakh translation. The word "*ason*" was left untranslated for reasons that will become clear below.
3. Lev. 24:17. According to some scholars, the potion administered to a woman suspected of adultery, described in Numbers 5:11–31, was an abortifacient. See, for instance, Nissim Amzallag and Shamir Yona, "The Kenite Origin of the Sotah Prescription (Numbers 5:11–31)," *Journal for the Study of the Old Testament* 41, no. 4 (2017): 393–96. Given that this interpretation was never entertained by the rabbis, according to whom the potion resulted in death if the woman was indeed guilty, it does not factor into *halakhic* discussions of feticide.
4. See, e.g., Aaron Lichtenstein, *The Seven Laws of Noah* (New York: Rabbi Jacob Joseph School Press, 1981).
5. b.Sanhedrin 57b.
6. Philo of Alexandria, *The Special Laws* III:XIX:108–9. See also Philo of Alexandria, *On Mating, with the Preliminary Studies* XXIV:137.
7. This interpretation was likewise preserved in the practice of the Samaritan and Karaite communities. The Church Fathers largely accepted the equation of feticide and homicide, though some applied this to all forms of abortion, whereas others, following Augustine, accepted the Septuagint's distinction between a formed and unformed fetus. See David M. Feldman, *Marital Relations, Birth Control, and Abortion in Jewish Law* (New York: Schocken Books, 1987), 257–58, 268–71; Victor Aptowitzer, "Observations on the Criminal Law of the Jews," *Jewish Quarterly Review* 15 (1924): 85–91.

8. Among the earliest rabbinic sources, Onkelos (first–second century CE) renders "*ason*" as *mota* ("death"), referring to the mother's death. *Mekhilta de-Rabbi Yishmael* and *Mekhilta De-Rabbi Shimon bar Yohai*, third-century *midrashim* on Exodus, both explicitly interpret "*ason*" as the death of the pregnant woman. Josephus (*Antiquities* 4:278) likewise states that the key distinction made by the verses is between a case where the woman miscarries and a case where the woman dies.
9. m.Niddah 5:3.
10. b.Niddah 44b, citing Leviticus 24:17.
11. The literal sense of the word "*nefesh*" is not "life" but "breath." It seems that the Talmud's derives from this word that human life begins with the newborn's first breaths.
12. m.Ohalot 7:6, also cited and discussed in b.Sanhedrin 72b.
13. m.Arakhin 1:4.
14. b.Arakhin 7a–b.
15. m.Niddah 5:3, m.Arakhin 1:4, and m.Ohalot 7:6.
16. b.Yevamot 78a; b.Temurah 25b and 30b; and elsewhere.
17. b.Niddah 13a–b.
18. m.Bekhorot 8:1.
19. b.Berakhot 60a. A related, albeit theoretical discussion between Rabbi Yehudah the Prince and the Roman Emperor Antoninus appears in b.Sanhedrin 91a regarding the moment of "ensoulment"—when a fetus is endowed with a soul. Rabbi Yehudah maintains that it occurs at the moment of "formation" (*yetzirah*), whereas Antoninus claims that it occurs at the moment of conception. Rabbi Yehudah later changed his view and conceded to Antoninus.

    This debate is reminiscent of debates about feticide in the early Church. Augustine maintained that the soul is endowed, and feticide becomes prohibited, at the moment of "formation," which Aristotle, and Roman jurisprudence in his wake, specify occurs at forty days. Tertullian, on the other hand, accepts the Pythagorean view that the soul is endowed at conception and concludes that feticide is prohibited from that moment. See Aptowitzer, "Observations on the Criminal Law of the Jews," 115–18; Feldman, *Marital Relations, Birth Control, and Abortion*, 266–69.

    Though rabbinic sources address the moment of the soul's endowment, they do not link it with feticide or the more general question of fetal personhood. Nevertheless, see the view of Rabbi Menasheh Klein in *Mishneh Halakhot* 9:328, s.v. "*u-me'atah yesh lomar*," which is discussed below in the section titled "Discussions of Maimonides's Ruling."
20. b.Sanhedrin 72b, s.v. "*yatza*."
21. Other *Rishonim* who express such a view include: Rabbi Meir Abulafiah (*Yad Ramah* to b.Sanhedrin 72b, s.v. "*amar*"); Rabbi Menahem Meiri to b.Shabbat 107b ("it is inappropriate to speak of 'taking the life' of something that has not been born"); Rabbi Shimshon of Sens, commentary to *Sifre Tazri'a, Nega'im* 1.
22. Lev. 18:5.
23. b.Yoma 85b, b.Sanhedrin 74a, and elsewhere.
24. b.Arakhin 7b.
25. *She'elot U-Teshuvot Ha-Ge'onim* (Istanbul: David Kashti, 1575), 36b (§248). The editor of the Prague, 1590 edition of the same work notes the contradiction between this responsum and the ruling in b.Arakhin 7b and attempts to reconcile them.
26. First cited in Nahmanides, *Torat Ha-Adam*, Chavel (Jerusalem: Mossad Harav Kook, 1964), 28–29; thereafter cited by Rabbi Asher ben Yehiel (Rosh), Yoma 8:13, and Rabbi

Nissim Gerondi (Ran), Yoma 3b in the Alfasi pagination. See also *Tosafot* to b.Niddah 44a, s.v. "*ihu*," which may be the source of this opinion.

27. Rabbi Asher ben Yehiel (Rosh), Yoma 8:13, and Rabbi Nissim Gerondi (Ran), Yoma 3b in the Alfasi pagination, assert that the distinction between danger to the mother and danger to the fetus is largely academic, as "it is uncommon for the fetus to be endangered without the mother being endangered, nor for the mother to be endangered without the fetus being endangered," so in any case the violation of the Sabbath would be permitted.
28. *Halakhot Gedolot*, ed. Ezriel Hildesheimer (Jerusalem: Mekitze Nirdamim, 1971), 1:319 (Laws of Yom Kippur).
29. b.Yoma 85b.
30. Nahmanides, *Torat Ha-Adam*. See also the commentaries of Nahmanides, Ran, Rabbi Shlomo Ibn Adret (Rashba), and Rabbi Yom Tov Ibn Ashvili (Ritva) to b.Niddah 44a–b; Rosh, Yoma 8:13.
31. b.Sanhedrin 57a.
32. b.Sanhedrin 59a.
33. *Tosafot* to b.Sanhedrin 59a, s.v. "*leika*"; to b.Hullin 33a, s.v. "*ehad*."
34. It is also noting that the principle that "there is nothing forbidden to a gentile that is permitted to Israel" does not necessarily imply that the prohibition for Jews is substantively linked to the Noahide prohibition.
35. *Tosafot* to b.Niddah 44a, s.v. "*ihu*."
36. The law of the *rodef* permits the neutralizing of a would-be killer (or rapist), even at the expense of his life.
37. Laws of Murderers and the Protection of Life 1:9. See also *Sefer Mitzvot Gadol*, Negative Commandment 164 and *Sefer Ha-Hinukh* §600, which echo the formulation of Maimonides.
38. b.Sanhedrin 72b, discussion m.Ohalot 7:6.
39. Rabbi Yair Hayim Bacharach, *Responsa Havot Ya'ir* §31; Rabbi Yehezkel Landau, *Responsa Noda Bi-Yehuda*, vol. 2, HM 59; Rabbi Moshe Schick, *Responsa Maharam Schick*, YD 155; Rabbi Avraham Yitzhak Kook, *Responsa Ezrat Kohen*, omissions §1: 397–98; Rabbi Isser Zalman Meltzer, *Even Ha-Ezel* to *Mishneh Torah*, Laws of Murderers and the Protection of Life 1:9.
40. Rabbi Joseph Teomim, *Peri Megadim*, *Mishbetzot Zahav* to *Shulhan Arukh*, OH 328:1; Rabbi Shneur Zalman Fradkin of Lublin, *Responsa Torat Hesed* 2:42; Rabbi Nachum Rabinovitch, *Yad Peshutah* to *Mishneh Torah*, Laws of Murderers and the Protection of Life 1:9. The latter two invoke another ruling of Maimonides (Laws of Injury and Tort 8:15) that invokes the pursuer principle—likewise with the modifier "like a pursuer"—with respect to cargo that must be jettisoned from a sinking ship. The rationale is that nonhuman cargo may be cast overboard to save human cargo, though human cargo obviously must not be cast overboard. This is entirely analogous to the case of the fetus in that it has the status of being "like a pursuer" only as long as it has not attained human status.
41. Variations on this idea are suggested by Rabbi Yitzhak Schorr, *Responsa Ko'ah Shor* §20; Rabbi Yaakov Schorr, *Responsa Ge'onim Batrai* §45; Rabbi Yekutiel Teitelbaum, *Responsa Avnei Tzedek*, HM 19; Rabbi Yehiel Yaakov Weinberg, *Seridei Esh*, HM 162:12.
42. *Tosafot Rabbi Akiva Eger* to m.Ohalot 7:6.
43. *Responsa Ahiezer* 3:72:3.
44. *Hiddushei Rabbenu Hayim Ha-Levi al ha-Rambam* to *Mishneh Torah*, Laws of Murderers and the Protection of Life 1:9.

45. *Igrot Moshe*, HM 2:69 and elsewhere.
46. *Mishneh Halakhot* 9:328, s.v. "*u-me'atah yesh lomar*."
47. See Rabbi Ovadiah Yosef, *Responsa Yabia Omer*, EH 4:1.
48. A fuller treatment of the various interpretations of Maimonides, including references to secondary literature, appear in Feldman, *Marital Relations, Birth Control, and Abortion*, 277–81; Maor Cayam, *Harhavot Le-simhat Ha-bayit U-virkhato* (Har Bracha: Machon Har Bracha, 2015): 444–47.
49. *Responsa Maharit* 1:97 and 99.
50. Exod. 21:22–23, based on the NJPS (Jewish Publication Society, formerly NJV, or New Jewish Version) Tanakh translation.
51. *Responsa Havot Ya'ir* 31.
52. b.Yevamot 63b–64a. *Zohar* to Exodus 3:2 makes similar statements about the destruction of a fetus. Although it is not generally cited in the *halakhic* literature, *Zohar* was an influential work that certainly shaped *halakhic* attitudes.
53. *Responsa Mishpetei Uziel* 4, HM 46
54. *Responsa Tzitz Eliezer* 9:51:3 cites Rabbi Shlomo Kluger and *Responsa Emunat Shmuel* §14 as maintaining this view.
55. *Responsa Torat Hesed* 2:42; *Responsa Ahiezer* 3:65:14; *Responsa Yabi'a Omer* 4, EH 1; Rabbi Shmuel Engel, cited in *Responsa Tzitz Eliezer* 9:51:3.
56. This extensive list includes *Responsa Radbaz* 3:695 and 8:22; Maharal of Prague, *Gur Aryeh* to Exodus 21:22; *Responsa Maharit* 1:99; *Me'irat Eynayim* to *Shulhan Arukh*, HM 425:8; *Magen Avraham* to *Shulhan Arukh*, OH 128:53 (citing Rabbi Levi Ibn Habib); *Arukh Ha-Shulhan*, HM 30:29; and *Tosafot Yom Tov*, *Tosafot Rabbi Akiva Eger*, and *Tiferet Yisrael* to m.Ohalot 7:6. Rabbi Yehiel Yaakov Weinberg (*Responsa Seridei Esh*, HM 162:12) concludes: "We still do not know the source of this prohibition."
57. *Responsa Maharam Schick*, YD 155.
58. *Responsa Shevet Mi-Yehudah*, 26ff.
59. *Responsa Yaskil Avdi* 6, YD 85
60. Exodus 21:22.
61. This was apparently the view of the eighteenth-century Rabbi Isaiah (Pick) Berlin of Breslau as well. See *Responsa Noda Bi-Yehuda*, vol. 2, HM 59 and *Responsa Tiferet Tzvi* §14.
62. Rabbi Joseph Rosin (the Rogachover Gaon), *Responsa Tzofnat Pa'ane'ah* 59; Rabbi Meir Simcha HaKohen of Dvinsk, *Meshekh Hokhmah* to Exodus 32:5 (tentatively); Rabbi Hayim Soloveichik and Rabbi Moshe Feinstein (who espouse this view following their respective interpretations of Maimonides, discussed in the section titled "Interpretations of Maimonides's Ruling"), and Rabbi Aharon Lichtenstein, "Abortion: A *Halakhic* Perspective," *Tradition* 25, no. 4 (1991): 3–12.
63. This quote has appeared in several statements of the Rabbinical Assembly, most recently on June 24, 2022. See Rabbinical Assembly, "Conservative Rabbis Strongly Condemn U.S. Supreme Court Decision to Overturn Abortion Rights," https://www.wlcj.org/2022/06/conservative-rabbis-strongly-condemn-u-s-supreme-court-decision-to-overturn-abortion-rights/.

    The baseline attitude of the Rabbinical Assembly was articulated in 1959 in Rabbi Isaac Klein, "A Teshuvah on Abortion," https://www.rabbinicalassembly.org/sites/default/files/assets/public/halakhah/teshuvot/20012004/06.pdf. Rabbi Klein concluded that abortion is "morally wrong" and "permitted only for therapeutic reasons." It was adopted as the majority position of the Rabbinical Assembly's Committee on Jewish Laws and Standards in 1983, alongside several resolutions that reached the same basic conclusion regarding acceptable reasons for permitting abortion. See, specifically, David M. Feldman, "Abortion: The Jewish View," https://www.rabbinicalassembly.org/sites/default/files/assets/public/halakhah/teshuvot/19861990/feldman_abortion.pdf; Kassel Abelson, "Prenatal Testing and Abortion," https://www.rabbinicalassembly.org/sites/default/files/assets/public/halakhah/teshuvot/20012004/03.pdf; Ben Zion Bokser and Kassel Abelson, "A Statement on the Permissibility of Abortion." https://www.rabbinicalassembly.org/sites/default/files/public/halakhah/teshuvot/20012004/07.pdf.

64. See "Abortion to Save Sibling from Suffering (5755.13)," in *Teshuvot for the Nineties*, ed. Gunther Plaut and Mark Washofsky (New York: CCAR Press, 1997), 171–76, https://www.ccarnet.org/ccar-responsa/tfn-no-5755-13-171-176/. After citing several precedents, the respondent concludes: "all the Reform responsa concerning this subject are careful to couch their lenient rulings within the general traditional understanding of the importancc of alleviating 'great pain' to the mother. None of them suggest that Judaism should countenance any other reason as a valid basis for abortion."
65. "Resolution on Abortion, Adopted by the Central Conference of American Rabbis, 1975," https://www.ccarnet.org/ccar-resolutions/abortion-1975/.
66. Rabbi Meir Ben-Zion Uziel, *Responsa Mishpetei Uziel* 4, HM 46, addresses a case where continuing the pregnancy threatened the mother with permanent deafness.
67. Rabbi Yitzhak Oelbaum, *Responsa She'ilat Yitzhak* §64.
68. Rabbi Isser Yehudah Unterman, *Responsa Shevet Mi-Yehudah*, 26ff.; see also Solomon. Freehof, "Abortion," in *American Reform Responsa*, ed. Walter Jacob (New York: CCAR Press, 1983), 541–43, https://www.ccarnet.org/ccar-responsa/arr-541-543/.
69. Rabbi Shaul Yisraeli, *Amud Ha-yemini* §32.
70. Rabbi David Sperber, *Responsa Afarkasta De-anya* 1:169.
71. Israeli Chief Rabbi Shlomo Goren (*Torat Ha-Refu'ah*, 192–94) forbids the abortion of a fetus diagnosed with Down syndrome. Rabbis Shaul Yisraeli (*Amud Ha-yemini* §32) and Eliezer Waldenberg (*Responsa Tzitz Eliezer* 14:101) permit abortion if having a baby with Down syndrome will cause the parents extreme anguish. (Rabbi Waldenberg addresses the case of parents who already had two children with Down syndrome and who died very young.)
72. Rabbi Moshe Feinstein, *Igrot Moshe*, HM 2:69. Rabbi Feinstein even advised Torah-observant physicians not to test for Tay-Sachs, as there are no grounds to permit abortion when the mother's life is not in danger and finding out about the disease would only cause extra anguish.
73. Rabbi Eliezer Waldenberg, *Responsa Tzitz Eliezer* 13:102; 14:100; 20:56. This is also the view of Rabbis Yisraeli and Goren.
74. Cited in *Nishmat Avraham*, HM 425:12 and 18.
75. Rabbi David Sperber, *Responsa Afarkasta De-anya* 1:169. This is quoted in Reform, Conservative, and Orthodox responsa. Nevertheless, it should be noted that Rabbis Yisraeli and Unterman indicate that the interest of the unborn fetus is indeed taken into consideration.
76. Rabbi Yosef Hayim, *Responsa Rav Pe'alim*, EH 1:4.
77. See the section titled "Discussions of the Nature of the Prohibition."
78. *Responsa She'elat Ya'avetz* 1:43. Rabbi Emden takes what is perhaps the most idiosyncratic view of abortion in early modern rabbinic literature. He argues his permissive view

vis-à-vis a fetus conceived through adultery on the grounds that the mother forfeited her own life through an act that, according to the Torah, is a capital offense. Aborting the fetus, which is a part of its mother, is thus warranted. This ruling differentiates between a fetus conceived in an adulterous relationship and the fetus of an unwed mother or a married victim of rape; termination of the former is permitted, but the latter are not. However, he concludes his discussion by adding that abortion is also permitted to spare its mother from great pain.

79. *Responsa Mishpetei Uziel* 4, HM 47.
80. *Tzitz Eliezer* 9:51:3:8.
81. There are, however, credible reports that Rabbis Yosef Shalom Elyashiv and Joseph B. Soloveitchik, who took the view that equates feticide with homicide, permitted abortions in certain cases in order to spare the mother extreme, albeit not directly life-threatening anguish.
82. *Responsa Shevet Ha-Levi* 7:208 and 9:266. Rabbi Shlomo Zalman Auerbach likewise espoused the restrictive approach even though he did not consider abortion to be murder. See *Nishmat Avraham*, HM 425:1:1, pp. 134–5.
83. *Igrot Moshe*, HM 2:69. The date of the responsum, four years after *Roe v. Wade*, cannot be ignored. Though public *halakhic* rhetoric concerning abortion emphasizes its wrongfulness, this rhetoric seems to reach a higher pitch when the norms and attitudes of the prevailing society are (or are perceived to be) more permissive than the *halakhic* view. We saw another example of this in Rabbi Wosner's *Responsa Shevet Ha-Levi* 7:208 and 9:266. See also Feldman, "Abortion," 805–6. See also Yaakov Jacobs, *Be-Mehitzat Rabbenu* (Jerusalem: Feldheim, 2005), 133. Jacobs cites a homily delivered by Rabbi Yaakov Kamenetsky when an abortion clinic opened in Monsey, New York, in 1970, in which he lamented the fact that we have become habituated and desensitized to killing.
84. See Avital Chizhik-Goldschmidt, "'My Dark Secret': Orthodox Women Reveal Their Abortion Stories," *The Forward*, August 1, 2018, https://forward.com/life/406674/orthodox-jewish-women-abortion-stories/.
85. I am thankful to Rabbi Aryeh Klapper for introducing me to this useful heuristic and terminology.
86. For a survey of innovative methods for cleansing the taint of *mamzerut*, see Amihai Radzyner, "'There Is a *Mamzer* from the Torah Only if His Parents Were Imprisoned Together': Innovative Solutions for Purifying *Mamzerim* in Israel Rabbinical Courts," *Jewish Studies Internet Journal* 20 (2021): 1–59 [Hebrew]. http://jewish-faculty.biu.ac.il/files/jewish-faculty/shared/JSIJ20/radzyner.pdf.
87. By its very nature, it is hard to find hard evidence of insincere conversion, even if, empirically, it can be shown that, in certain eras in particular, conversion did not often result in an observant lifestyle. On the contemporary Israeli context, see Michal Kravel-Tovi, *When the State Winks: The Performance of Jewish Conversion in Israel* (New York: Columbia University Press, 2017), 10–17.
88. Due to the sensitive nature of the topic, the reluctance of many *halakhists* to commit permissive views in writing less they be misused, and the transmission of such stories by hearsay, it is hard to document this trend. However, see Chizhik-Goldschmidt, "'My Dark Secret.'"
89. *Responsa Rav Pe'alim*, EH 1:4.
90. Rabbi Hershel Schachter of Yeshiva University (b. 1941), a leading contemporary American *halakhist*, recounts this story in several public lectures on abortion in *halakhah*,

for example: https://www.yutorah.org/lectures/lecture.cfm/1021843/rabbi-hershel-schachter/abortion-in-halacha/, minutes 20–23.

91. See Dobbs v. Jackson Women's Health Organization, No. 19-1392 (2022), especially the summary of the dissenting opinion on 38–40.

92. Interestingly, Israeli law reflects this heteronomous structure. Abortion is legal in Israel, but in order to be covered by the national health insurance, a woman who wants an abortion must appear before a panel that includes representatives of the medical establishment and the state rabbinate. These panels approve the abortions in almost all cases, but the fact that the woman must appear before the panel signifies that the state and *halakhah* are also stakeholders in the decision to keep or terminate a pregnancy. The choice is not one person's alone.

CHAPTER 32

ORGAN DONATION AND BRAIN DEATH

ADENA BERKOWITZ

Introduction

For almost two thousand years, rabbinic sources reveal that the classic definition of death according to *halakhah* (Jewish law) was understood to be cessation of a heartbeat. The scientific acceptance around the late 1960s of a second criteria of death—brain stem death (hereinafter "brain death")—immediately posed a challenge to this traditional understanding of the end of life. Coupled with the ability of doctors to perform heart transplants, *poskim* (decisors of Jewish law) were faced with the dual question of *halakhic* acceptance of brain death and the acceptability of human organ donation and transplantation. For more than fifty years, different rabbinic authorities have taken different approaches. The lack of a uniform response is also a reminder of the controversial nature of this topic.

To understand the intertwined question of brain death and postmortem organ donation, and its acceptability according to *halakhah*, this chapter initially discusses the historical development of human organ transplantation. This part delves into how postmortem organ donations became a reality, specifically focusing on the United States. It provides insight as to the moral and legal questions that arose early on and examines how this history ultimately impacts modern-day views of *halakhah*.

The next part reviews the *halakhic* approach to death and the primary sources that lay the foundation for future discussions. How *poskim* accept living organ donations is a fundamental starting point, from which the debate surrounding deceased organ donation stems. A natural next step considers organ donation from a deceased donor. The discussion analyzes the split between Orthodox *poskim* that define death as the cessation of heartbeats and those that define death as the cessation of all bodily functions. It also examines additional Orthodox approaches to this issue as well as the positions of the Reform and Conservative movements.

The chapter concludes by addressing the question of where we are headed when it comes to post deceased organ donation. It considers ways that Judaism, and the world, is increasing organ donations and longer-term possibilities, and explores how incentives to increase donations and new technologies may impact organ donation. It also raises, but leaves unanswered, whether the entire *halakhic*, moral, and political conversation surrounding deceased organ donations will eventually become moot in light of technological advances.

History of Organ Transplants and Definition of Death in the United States

In the modern era, cornea and kidney transplants from living donors were the forerunners in developments of human organ transplantation.[1] The first successful human cornea transplant was performed in 1905,[2] and forty-nine years later, the first successful kidney transplant took place, marking the major milestone of solid organ donation.[3] These transplants saved lives, leading physicians and researchers to work on ways to allow for the transplantation of other organs.

An important turning point in transplant research took place in the 1950s, when mechanical ventilators were developed, allowing physicians to keep "people alive who had very severe brain injury who would otherwise have died from respiratory arrest."[4] This development made possible the concept of deceased organ donation. On December 3, 1967, startling news came out of Cape Town, South Africa. Dr. Christiaan Neethling Barnard performed the first interhuman heart transplant.[5] This was followed just days later in the United States by Dr. Adrian Kantrowitz, whose transplant case was pediatric.[6] About a month later, Dr. Norman Shumway attempted the first American adult interhuman heart transplant.[7] Science writer Tracie White highlighted the enormous weight this moment carried, pointing to the question that Dr. Edward Stinson asked his mentor Dr. Shumway as he tried to save his patient by removing another's heart: "'Do you think this is really legal?' Stinson asked Shumway. 'I guess we'll see,' Shumway said."[8] The question here was whether the donor was dead before the transplant arose since their brain had already stopped working, or if the cessation of heartbeats alone marks death. The answer raises serious legal implications because it determines whether a physician performing a deceased organ donation takes an organ from a deceased person, or whether by taking the organ, the physician actually kills a patient by stopping their heart from beating.

Unfortunately, physicians were not able to keep recipients alive due to organ rejection. High death rates of recipients, coupled with the pressure of lawsuits, raised the same legal and moral question of how to define death.[9] Prior to these transplants, death was defined as the cessation of heartbeats, but now physicians were keeping hearts beating through machines, calling donors "dead" based on a different set of criteria, namely, brain death.

Two clear problems emerged. First, the law recognized one definition of death (cessation of heartbeats), but physicians were following a different definition of death in order to perform transplants (brain death). Second, so many patients were dying after receiving organs due to organ rejection, which caused major concern and heightened the controversy. A change definitionally needed to be made to allow the groundwork for advancing the transplant field. Transplant surgery also needed to improve the odds of survival of recipients. Both things happened somewhat simultaneously.

In 1968, Harvard Medical School developed a new definition of death.[10] An ad hoc committee defined death as when patients reach an "irreversible coma" state, where they have a "permanently non-functioning brain."[11] Harvard's definition involved this new approach, now referred to as "brain death." This was more of a recommendation than a legally binding mandate, so Harvard urged America's legal system to create laws that supported this recommendation instead of treating "the question of human death as a question of fact to be decided in every case," thereby leaving room for inconsistency among the states.[12]

As states began legally adopting Harvard's definition of death, the legal system responded.[13] But some states did not adopt this definition, which made it possible to be declared dead in one state and alive in another. The President's Commission for the Study of Ethical Problems in Medicine and Biomedical and Behavioral Research concluded that death is when a person experiences either "irreversible cessation of circulatory and respiratory functions," or "irreversible cessation of all functions of the entire brain, including the brain stem."[14] In 1981, based on the President Commission's definition, the Uniform Determination of Death Act became the legal standard in the United States, thus ending the different standards in different states This definition has now been adopted both by state legislatures and by the American Academy of Neurology (AAN).[15]

Although the legal definition of death was thus settled with respect to American law, the application of *halakhah* is an entirely different matter. The definition used in the United States was not adopted by all *poskim*. If brain death is not an acceptable standard within Jewish law, then it is forbidden for someone to be an organ donor, and a doctor would be committing murder by retrieving organs from a brain dead patient for donation. On the other hand, if brain death is deemed acceptable, Jewish individuals can—and maybe even should—elect to donate their organs. The following section demonstrates that the *halakhic* opinions are split into two main categories of thought: defining death as the cessation of breathing versus defining death as the cessation of all bodily functions.

Halakhic Responses to Defining Death and Organ Donation

Prior to dealing with questions pertaining to postmortem organ donation and brain death, rabbinic decisors addressed preliminary issues that laid the groundwork for the *halakhic* acceptability of deceased organ donations. Already in the eighteenth century, Rabbi Yaakov Emden, a leading *halakhic* authority of the time, ruled that autopsies would be permitted if there was a very ill patient present who could benefit from one immediately. This opinion worked around the prohibitions of benefiting from the dead and defiling the dead, as well as the obligation to bury the dead and the body whole.[16] The same considerations, in the context of cornea donations, led to certain *responsa* (opinions) that set a precedent for allowing such donations for the purpose of curing someone of blindness through corneal transplants. Here too, *poskim* weighed the challenges against the benefits that such donations would offer.[17]

Poskim have historically made decisions related to conflicts that arise in the biomedical world. Therefore, the *halakhic* response to living organ donations, in particular blood and bone marrow donations, were not controversial.[18] But deceased organ donation (hereinafter "organ donation") is more *halakhically* challenging, as it rests on conflicting definitions of death.

Primary Sources Defining Death

At the core of traditional Jewish theology, Jewish law originates from the Torah (Written) and the Oral Law, given to the Jewish people by G-d (see Lifshitz, this volume). The Oral Law, starting with the Mishnah and the Talmud, serves as the starting point for the later codification of the *Shulhan Arukh* (the Code of Jewish Law), which has been further elucidated and explained through questions (*sheilot*) that Jews or Jewish communities asked their rabbis, and the answers (*teshuvot*) given that serve as precedents until today (see Morsel-Eisenberg, this volume).[19]

When it comes to defining death, *poskim* across the generations have been divided, a reality that contributed to the current *halakhic* differences in defining death, and the resulting acceptability, or lack thereof, of donating organs. Most of the time, defining death comes back to two primary sources: Mishnah Oholot and Talmud Yoma. All the Orthodox *poskim*, and most of the non-Orthodox decisors, invoke these two sources when defining death, as they are the earliest sources in codified Jewish law that discuss the issue.

Mishnah Oholot reads: "A person does not defile [as a corpse] until he dies . . . Similarly in the case of cattle or wild animals, they do not defile until they die. If their heads have been cut off, even though they are moving convulsively, they are unclean, like a lizard's tail, which moves convulsively."[20] For the purposes of defining death, the main consideration in Mishnah Oholot revolves around postmortem spontaneous spasmic movement. By explaining that a lizard is still dead even though it may move after its head is cut off, this Mishnah provides a helpful context for defining death as brain death. A finding that spontaneous spasmic movements postmortem indicate that a person is still alive would create a serious burden in arguing that brain death is an acceptable standard of death *halakhically*. This Mishnah, however, states clearly that movement does not preclude a finding of death.

In the Talmud *Bavli*, Yoma discusses a case in which a person is buried under a collapsed building and raises the question of how far to check to see whether they are still alive during Shabbat (thus violating Shabbat by digging and performing other actions): "The Rabbis taught: . . . until what point does one check to clarify whether the victim is still alive? Until what point is he allowed to continue clearing the debris? They said: One clears until the victim's nose. If there is no sign of life, i.e., if he is not breathing, he is certainly dead. And some say: One clears until the victim's heart to check for a heartbeat."[21] This text shows the complexity in defining death by expounding upon two opinions. The first opinion does not depend on heartbeat and rules that a lack of breathing is enough to label the person as dead. The latter opinion is that even if a person is buried and not breathing, the person may still be alive if the heart is beating.

Both texts indicate that even in the primary sources themselves, there is conflict about the definition of death. The sources contain several different opinions: first, postmortem movement being irrelevant; second, the discontinuation of breathing being enough to define death; and third (and most extreme), even a body that has been buried by debris and is not breathing would still be alive if there is any sign of a heartbeat. As the following part illustrates, the subsequent interpretation and utilization of these sources by the *poskim* impacts the modern Jewish definition of death.

Discourse among Orthodox Authorities

How *poskim* define death depends on whether they interpret Yoma and Oholot as determining that brain death constitutes death from a *halakhic* standpoint. The *poskim* can be broken down into two categories: those that define death as the cessation of breathing (encompassed by the definition of "brain death," which is when irreversible brain damage occurs causing the end of independent respiration), and those that define death as the cessation of all bodily functions, which includes one's heart. The first category is represented mainly by Rabbi Moshe Tendler[22] and the Israeli Chief Rabbinate. The second category is represented by Rabbi J. David Bleich, a Rosh Yeshiva of the Rabbi Isaac Elchanan Theological Seminary (RIETS).[23]

The main split between these authorities comes down to whether cessation of breathing is the criteria for defining death, or cessation of breathing *and* heartbeat defines death. But as this discussion below reveals, there are also notable Orthodox opinions that provide even more nuance to this discussion by taking more lenient or stringent approaches, as well as middle-ground stances. In addition, the positions of leading rabbinic organizations also vary, leading to a non-uniform view of defining death within the Orthodox framework.

When the brain death standard was introduced, Rabbi Moshe Feinstein was adamantly opposed to accepting brain death as an additional *halakhic* definition of death.[24] In fact, he went so far as to refer to organ donation as double murder.[25] However, in his last writing on the subject, Rabbi Feinstein expressed support for organ donation based on a change in key scientific circumstances.[26]

Rabbi Moshe Tendler's argument in fervent support of defining brain death and cessation of breathing as acceptable was largely rooted in his father-in-law's last writings on the topic and verbal exchanges with him. He regularly argued in support of these concepts and is known as the main defender of this approach. Those that dislike the fact that Rabbi Feinstein changed his *halakhic* approach so late in life therefore also disagree with the premise of Rabbi Tendler's argument.[27]

When discussing Oholot, Rabbi Tendler argued that when a person is "brain dead," their brain is no longer part of their bodily functions, and therefore any spasmatic movements afterward are exactly as described in the Mishnah.[28] Much like the lizard that still moves after decapitation but is not classified as alive, brain death can be seen as "physiological decapitation." Many other *poskim* have taken the same approach, even applying it to heartbeats post "brain death."[29]

As will be discussed below, in 1991, the Rabbinical Council of America (RCA), the main rabbinic organization of Modern Orthodox rabbis, adopted a resolution at their annual convention supporting the dissemination of a *halakhic* healthcare proxy.[30] This form was prepared by Rabbi Tendler, who was the chairman of the RCA's Medical Ethics Commission. In terms of organ donation, this document reads: "Upon my death I wish to donate life-saving organs such as my cornea(s), kidney(s), heart, lung(s), liver and pancreas for the sole purpose of transplantation."[31] This language is based on the resolution that there are "no halachic barriers" prohibiting organ donation.[32] However, this resolution was ultimately retracted despite receiving acceptance at the time it was drafted.[33]

Some major *poskim* follow Rabbi Tendler's approach, perhaps the most notable being the Israeli Chief Rabbinate ("the Rabbinate"). The Rabbinate published a formal opinion defining brain death as *halakhically* acceptable as medical history was being made in Israel. Israel's first two liver transplants (and first deceased organ transplant) took place in October 1986, before any ruling had been issued supporting brain death as a valid *halakhic* definition of death in Israel.[34] Just one week later, before the special committee the Rabbinate convened to discuss the issue, former Ashkenazic Chief Rabbi Shlomo Goren publicly expressed his support for organ donation, claiming it is "not only permissible under religious law but [constitutes] a mitzvah."[35] The Rabbinate endorsed this approach, and preparations for the first heart transplant began immediately in the Hadassah Medical Center.[36] The third interhuman heart transplant in Israel took place less than a year later.[37] The Rabbinate's unanimous confirmation that "brain death was confirmatory of irreversible cessation of respiration" was based on its interpretation of Yoma.[38] Furthermore, the Rabbinate explained that the earlier rulings of Rabbi Feinstein and Rabbi Unterman prohibiting organ donor transplants took place before medical advancements of the modern era.[39] Finally, the Rabbinate felt that because enough rabbis were already allowing transplants, its ruling was not controversial.[40]

Other authorities oppose defining brain death as acceptable for organ donation. This position is represented by Rabbi Bleich: "Let me clearly and unequivocally state that a so-called 'brain-dead' patient is alive for all purposes of *halakhah*."[41] Rabbi Bleich's main argument pertains to Oholot. He argues that brain death is not the same as the "physiological decapitation" expressed in the Mishnah, claiming that heartbeats cannot be spontaneous or postmortem.[42] Therefore, Rabbi Bleich claims that in brain dead patients, some parts of the brain continue to work to the extent that the patient cannot be deemed dead.[43] Despite the Rabbinate's approach, many leading *poskim* in Israel did not accept brain death as a *halakhically* acceptable definition of death.[44]

Significantly, Rabbi Bleich does not view *accepting* organs from someone who was brain dead as problematic, even though he believes that *donating* an organ while brain dead is prohibited.[45] In other words, you cannot give, but you can take. He bases this argument on the fact that since such a long list of recipients exists for transplants, the same organ transplant process would be followed regardless of whether one specific individual was, or was not, on the list. Furthermore, "should a prospective recipient decline a transplant, the organs will immediately be given to another . . . with no delay whatsoever."[46] However, as discussed below, his approach raises profound ethical and meta-*halakhic* questions, and is not well-received by many.

In addition to the primary two positions of the *halakhic* definition of death discussed above, several *poskim* have contributed slightly nuanced approaches. Rabbi Breitowitz summarizes several authorities embracing this approach.[47] He quotes Rabbi Ahron Soloveichik,[48] for example, as going a step further than requiring cessation of breathing and heartbeats by holding that "the patient is alive if there is some detectable electrical activity in the brain."[49] On the other hand, Rabbi Hershel Schachter, Rosh Yeshiva at RIETS, brings an entirely new element to the conversation and concedes that the concept of brain death may find *halakhic* support in the later decisions of Rabbi Feinstein. Nonetheless, Rabbi Schachter did not accept Rabbi Feinstein's revised opinion and instead sees the person as a "doubtful life (*safek chai; safek met*)." Removing organs, he says, would still be prohibited as "possible murder."[50]

On the other hand, some *poskim* in Israel have taken a middle-ground approach. They have encouraged their students to sign organ donor cards specifying that brain death warrants organ donation.[51] However, the card also states that the donor requests that a rabbi who is knowledgeable in the medical field should participate in determining brain death. This position is due to skepticism of the medical community. That said, this middle ground approach gives room for a more thoughtful position than the hard-line stances discussed above. Instead of treating brain death as a black-or-white distinction, this type of approach allows for decisions to be made on a case-by-case basis.

In 1991, the RCA adopted a resolution at its annual convention supporting the dissemination of a *halakhic* healthcare proxy.[52] This resolution received significant attention and accepted brain death as *halakhic* death, redirecting the entire conversation from defining death to focusing on the ability to save lives. However, this resolution did not stand the test of time. In conjunction with a study released in 2010 by the Vaad Halacha, the *halakhah* committee of the RCA,[53] addressing concerns regarding the lack of *halakhic* support of the brain death definition of death, the RCA chose not to support brain death as explicitly as the earlier resolution and proxy.[54] In the document that supplemented the new proxy, the RCA described the updated stance: "The halachic approach to organ donation is varied and complex, and beyond the scope of this document. Questions about organ donation both before and after death should be posed to a halachic authority."[55] This approach in the revised proxy contrasts sharply Rabbi Tendler's 1991 proxy, which clearly accepted brain death as *halakhic* death. Reaction to this revision was mixed, with a number of Modern Orthodox rabbis not pleased with the change.[56]

A more liberal approach to organ donation, first raised in 1992, is Donation after Cardiac Death/Donation after Circulatory Death (DCD), organ donation before brain death but after catastrophic and nonreversible brain injury.[57] This approach aimed at expanding the number of possible organ donations. By this standard, once it is determined that a patient would not recover, the patient is brought to the operating room for their organs to be retrieved. Rabbi Asher Lopatin, the former President of Yeshivat Chovevei Torah, suggested a *halakhic* way to endorse this approach. According to Rabbi Lopatin, withdrawing life support, the controversial aspect of DCD, "involve[s] only an abstention from the *mitzvah* of saving a life," rather than committing active or passive murder.[58] Viewed in this way, withdrawal of life support would then be offset by the commandment to save a life, as the organs used would save the life of the recipient. To encourage this approach, Rabbi Lopatin advises patients to use directives to transfer "all rights of use of the respirator" to doctors *in advance*, so that the patient does not have an obligation to save their own life.[59] According to Rabbi Lopatin, even Rabbi Ahron Soloveichik's strict definition of death would work within the framework of DCD.[60]

In sum, while there are varying views by Orthodox poskim defining death, the majority of individual opinions and organizations fall into the two main categories. First, those viewing brain death as the definition of death based on the cessation of breathing, thereby making room for the possibility of organ donation, and even encouraging this option. Second, and in contrast, those defining death as the cessation of all bodily functions, and thus leaving little room for interhuman organ donations. As the following section illustrates, other Jewish denominations have a much more uniform stance favoring donation based on the value of saving human life.

Other Jewish Denominations

In contrast to Orthodox Judaism, the Conservative and Reform movements have accepted brain death across the board as *halakhic* death. In 1995, the Conservative Movement's Committee on Jewish Law and Standards (CJLS), which sets *halakhic* policy for the movement, issued a responsum.[61] This paper argues that organ donation is not only permissible but also religiously obligatory (a *chiyuv*) given that the demand for such organs outweighs their supply, and that as a result there are "thousands of desperate, specific, life threatening situations."[62] This approach is deeply rooted in the religious obligation of saving a life (*pikuach nefesh*). The responsum states that this obligation extends to individuals as well as those empowered to make healthcare decisions on behalf of others.

The paper responds to several potential objections, including desecrating the dead, by indicating that the importance of saving lives supersedes even the "most sacred" practices of Judaism. Postmortem organ donation, according to this view, is not a general concept but rather one that involves specific people, and that refraining from saving those specific lives is a violation of *halakhah*. In short, prohibiting donation "violates the Torah's prohibition of *al taamod al dam raiecha* (do not stand idly by while the blood of your fellow is shed), as well as the prescriptive obligation to preserve human life."[63]

In 2010, the CJLS endorsed DCD as a *halakhically* acceptable option for postmortem organ donation.[64] In seeking *halakhic* support for DCD, Rabbi Leonard Sharzer, M.D., looked at both Yoma and Oholot. He explained that in DCD, death is declared when both respiratory and cardiac activity cease, and that this definition falls under the framework set forth in the sources.[65] Furthermore, in his view, Oholot actually strengthens the idea that even in cases in which there is "some return of spontaneous resuscitation following CPR," in a patient, they can still be declared dead via the DCD approach.[66]

Rabbi Sharzer addressed several relevant concerns in his responsum. According to *halakhah*, one cannot touch someone who is in a dying state out of concern for hastening their death, versus someone who has already been declared dead. In order to deal with this issue, Rabbi Sharzer posits that a person should be regarded as actively dying "only after discontinuation of the ventilator."[67] Further, regarding whether restarting a heart means that cessation of heartbeats was not really irreversible, Rabbi Sharzer clarifies that in terms of Jewish law, the consideration should be "the death of the organ donor, not the death of the organ," making the concern irrelevant.[68] Rabbi Sharzer goes into great detail to create criteria to allow for this approach.[69] Then and only then does Rabbi Sharzer support DCD as acceptable to begin an interhuman organ transplant, and thereby expanding the potential pool of donors.

The Reform Movement relies on the same sources as the Conservative Movement when discussing brain death and organ donation.[70] The Reform Movement's Central Conference of American Rabbis (CCAR) (see Washofsky, this volume) carefully weighed the desire to save human life, as balanced against the prohibition of hastening death.[71] Ultimately, it endorsed brain death as a proper standard for determining death, concluding that brain death does not replace the cardiopulmonary criteria but instead confirms it.[72] Interestingly, unlike the Conservative Movement, the CCAR refuses to adopt the DCD standard. They explain that implementing the Pittsburgh protocol or other alternative to the accepted criteria for death involves retrieving organs from persons who, in the eyes of Jewish tradition, are likely still alive.[73]

As the foregoing discussion illustrates, while drawing the line with newer approaches that fall short of brain death, the Conservative and Reform movements differ from Orthodox Judaism in that they fully endorse brain death as *halakhic* death. Both movements discuss the topic with a very sharp focus on the value of saving human life whenever possible. As the next section demonstrates, however, the future may hold other options that accomplish saving human lives without depending on interhuman organ donations.

Where Are We Headed?

The speed of the development of new technologies continues to accelerate, raising the question of where we are headed when it comes to organ donation. This section covers the short-term issue of religious exemptions to the current American law, and then concentrates on how incentives to donation and technology might impact the sphere of organ donation long term. It remains to be seen whether any of this discussion will be relevant in years to come.

The opposition of some within the Orthodox community to the currently accepted legal definition of death as brain death has led to court challenges.[74] New Jersey is the only state that currently allows religious objection to the diagnosis of brain death.[75] California, New York, and Illinois "require 'reasonable accommodation' for religious beliefs," but these accommodations are vague and generally determined by individual hospitals.[76] In 2017, a legal challenge to brain death in New York involved an Orthodox Jew whose family did not accept taking their relative off life support.[77] The court sided with the family based on the argument that the hospital did not provide a reasonable accommodation "by not delaying the declaration of death until the family's concerns had been addressed."[78] As only a handful of state legislatures require such an accommodation, the question remains whether this will continue to be the case, or whether new lawsuits will force more legislatures to reexamine religious circumstances of organ donation.

Another issue, based on anecdotal evidence going back to the 1990s, is that some transplant surgeons were resentful of so many within the Orthodox Jewish community willing to accept organs but not serve as donors.[79] Some Jewish medical leaders have called out this contradictory approach as well.[80] According to LiveOnNY, a nonprofit that oversees deceased organ donations in the New York area, while the national consent rate in the United States is around 75 percent, Jews in the New York City area agree to donate only 23 percent of the time. Yet, according to Rabbi Ari Perl, Vice President for Jewish Community Engagement at LiveOnNY, this rate is based on "responses from Jews across the ideological spectrum—Modern Orthodox, liberal and secular, thereby debunking the myth that the Jewish consent rate is suppressed by the Ultra-Orthodox communities rejection of deceased donation."[81] In addition, in Israel, the rate of organ donations has historically been lower than in most Western countries, but is now rising steadily, even among Orthodox Jews.[82] For example, Israel was rated by the World Health Organization as having the largest number per capita of live kidney donations.[83]

One organization that worked to encourage not only Israelis but Jews around the world to donate organs is the Halachic Organ Donor Society (HODS), now integrated into Ematai.[84] Although HODS, founded in 2001, certainly endorsed brain death as a *halakhically* acceptable definition of death, it allowed people who sign up to be organ donors to choose whether their organs will be donated based on brain death or after cardiac death. The society educates Jews around the world about organ donation, publicizes rabbinic opinions that endorse organ donation, and even publishes a list of rabbis who have agreed to make their own organ donation commitment public.[85] Ematai's organ donation initiative is called "Option 18," focusing on patient choice and encouraging patients to donate their organs based on *halakhah*.[86] Ematai also recently launched an Advance Healthcare Directive and Conversation Guide, titled "Netivot," which directs proxies to consult with a designated "rabbi or religious institution" prior to making decisions.[87] Notably, instead of endorsing *halakhic* brain death for all Jews, Ematai focuses on respecting the different approaches of *poskim* within the various Orthodox communities.[88]

Another organization that promotes organ donation in general is Renewal (https://www.renewal.org/whowea), which focuses on living organ donations and specifically kidney transplants. Due to this focus, Renewal has avoided the *halakhic* issues that can arise in the framework of deceased organ donation. This organization encourages Jews to donate kidneys to total strangers around the world, oftentimes strangers who are not even Jewish. In Israel, ultra-Orthodox Rabbi Avraham Yeshayahu Heber founded in 2009 another organization by the name of *Matnat Chaim* (Gift of Life). Rabbi Heber was a kidney recipient and decided to establish this organization to recruit volunteers to become living kidney donors. As of September 2022, *Matnat Chaim* has recruited 1,300 donors.[89]

Although these organizations have focused on Jewish communities, many efforts are being made more generally to focus on expanding organ donation. Although organ donation, both living and deceased, has increased dramatically over the decades, the reality remains that there are tens of thousands of people on waiting lists for many different organs. According to the United Network for Organ Sharing (UNOS), about 104,000 people need an organ transplant to save their lives.[90] In terms of the average deaths, the American Transplant Foundation shares that about sixteen people die each day due to a lack of available organ transplants.[91] This, coupled with the fact that one deceased donor alone "can save up to eight lives" and enhance over one hundred lives,[92] warrants an examination of the realities of accepting or rejecting brain death as a *halachically* viable option. The ramifications are not just technical; the consequences result in lives being saved.

To combat low organ donation rates, Israel became among the first countries to implement the "donor-priority rule," which had dramatic effects on elevating the organ donation rates there.[93] This rule encourages people to opt into being organ donors by incentivizing them to be bumped up on the recipient list should they need a transplant in the future. In theory, donors could not have the highest medical criteria for getting an organ, but will still get priority because they had agreed to be a donor if needed.[94] Although less effective than an opt-out system, in which people must specifically designate that they do not want to be donors in order to be excluded, this idea is both effective and realistic in countries where the topic of organ donation is complicated due to religious objections.

Although we are still a long way away from reaching a reality in which there is no such thing as brain death, or a need for organ donation, technological and medical advances could realistically get us there at some point in time, making the *halakhic*, moral, and legal conversation moot. For example, Elon Musk's technology Neuralink currently focuses on implanting a chip in a patient's brain in order to "help solve an array of brain and spine problems, including paralysis, extreme pain, memory loss, blindness, hearing loss, depression, insomnia, seizures and addiction."[95] Already implanted in animals in trials, it seems this technology is well on its way to success.[96] Who is to say that actual brain damage, if not brain death, will not be next on the list of issues this technology can treat?[97]

Other potential advancements that can change the face of organ donation include finding different sources for organ transplants. One such possibility is using animals such as piglets as a source of organ donors instead of humans. Genetic engineering may allow for the complete removal of the infection and immunological concerns that arise in human to human organ transplants.[98] This could completely eliminate the need for human to human organ transplantation.[99] Another possibility lies in actual technology: using an artificial heart pump to prevent heart failure.[100] Scientists working on such a pump hope to prevent heart failure "within a decade," possibly even completely healing hearts and preventing the need for heart transplants.[101]

One of the most impressive recent advancements is the printing of the first 3-D heart in the world, "complete with blood vessels using personalized 'ink' made of collagen, a protein that supports the cell structures, and other biological molecules."[102] This technology is being developed by Israeli scientists who project having them in use within a decade. They also hope to expand their use to include other organs and tissues in order to eliminate the organ rejection rates by moving away from interhuman organ transplants.[103]

Conclusion

The recent scientific advancements are incredibly exciting and even inspiring. Each day brings about new developments that will hopefully provide help to so many who are in desperate need of organs. In the meantime, however, the reality of long waiting lists and real human beings waiting for their lives to be saved by donors remains. Until such a time as human-to-human organ donation will become obsolete, we cannot ignore the difficult current situation of great need. Legal arguments as to what *halakhah* does permit have substantial real-life ramifications in this context. The interconnection between organ donation, *halakhah*, medical science, and our care and concern for all members of both Jewish and general communities requires the entire spectrum of the Jewish community to redouble efforts to draw attention to this pressing medical and moral situation. May we all be blessed with long and healthy lives, and at the same time, may all Jews—based on *halakhah* and meta-*halakhic* reasons—opt to become (both living and deceased) organ donors.

Acknowledgment

I would like to acknowledge the invaluable assistance of my research fellow Shanee Markovitz Kay (Harvard Law School, Class of 2026) in the preparation of this chapter.

Notes

1. A living-donor transplant involves placing an organ from a living donor into the body of another person. In the case of a kidney transplant, for example, a person can donate one of their two kidneys and continue functioning normally with the remaining kidney. Mayo Clinic, "Living-Donor Transplant," Mayo Foundation for Medical Education and Research, April 27, 2021, www.mayoclinic.org/tests-procedures/living-donor-transplant/about/pac-20384787.
2. Eduard Zirm completed the first transplant near Prague. Alois Glogar was the forty-five-year-old recipient, a farmer laborer "who had sustained severe bilateral alkali burns while cleaning out a chicken coop with lime." His donor was an eleven-year-old boy whose eye was removed after it was blinded by an object that penetrated it. The operation significantly improved Glogar's vision in his left eye. Alexandra Z. Crawford et al., "A Brief History Of Corneal Transplantation: From Ancient to Modern," *Oman Journal of Ophthalmology* 6, Suppl. 1 (2013): S12–S17, https://doi.org/10.4103/0974-620X.122289.
3. A kidney was transplanted successfully in Boston in 1954 between identical twins, which may be the reason immune response was not an issue. Josep M. Grinyó, "Why Is Organ Transplantation Clinically Important?," *Cold Spring Harbor Perspectives in Medicine* 3, no. 6 (2013): a014985, https://www.ncbi.nlm.nih.gov/pmc/articles/PMC3662355/. See also Alvin Powell, "Death Is Universal, but Sometimes Murky," *Harvard Gazette*, July 7, 2018, news.harvard.edu/gazette/story/2018/07/harvard-ethicist-robert-truog-on-why-brain-death-remains-controversial/.
4. https://news.harvard.edu/gazette/story/2018/07/harvard-ethicist-robert-truog-on-why-brain-death-remains-controversial/#:~:text=TRUOG%3A%20In%20the%2019 50s%2C%20medicine,have%20died%20from%20respiratory%20arrest.
5. The recipient, Louis Washkansky, was diagnosed with "end stage ischemic cardiomyopathy." He received Denise Darvall's heart after she was hit by a drunk driver. "They stopped ventilation, waited for cardiac arrest and then cardiopulmonary bypass was initiated to resuscitate the heart." Although Washkansky initially did well, he died eighteen days later. See Noedir A. G. Stolf, "History of Heart Transplantation: A Hard and Glorious Journey," *Brazilian Journal of Cardiovascular Surgery* 32, no. 5 (2017): 423–27, https://doi.org/10.21470/1678-9741-2017-0508. Prior to this period, surgeons performed heart transplants using dogs. Dr. Vladimir P. Demikhov looked for causes that could account for the lack of successful transplants, finally considering "technical factors." Ibid.
6. Noedir A. G. Stolf "History of Heart Transplantation: A Hard and Glorious Journey," *Brazilian Journal of Cardiovascular Surgery* 32, no. 5 (2017): 423–27. doi:10.21470/1678-9741-2017-0508. Dr. Kantrowitz's transplant case was a donor "anencephalic baby and the recipient was [an] 18-day-old child with Ebstein anomaly." The patient died that day.
7. "In the race to be the first to transplant the human heart . . . Shumway . . . was considered the leader of the pack." Tracie White, "Magical Moment: The Enormity of the First U.S. Adult Heart Transplant" (Winter 2018); He also helped develop the current "standard surgical

technique for heart transplantation," which involves placing the donor heart in an ice-cold saltwater solution, reducing its metabolism and combating rejection response. Ibid.

8. Ibid.
9. For example, *The New York Times* reported on the 1974 murder trial of Andrew Lyons, who was charged with murder for shooting one of Shumway's heart donors. The question in the trial was "whether the removal of the victim's heart, while still beating, for use in a transplant operation means that death was caused by the operation rather than by a gunshot wound." Dr. Shumway's argument that the victim was dead before the transplant prevailed. "How to Define Death Is the Issue in Murder Trial," *New York Times*, May 20, 1974, p. 23, https://www.nytimes.com/1974/05/20/archives/how-to-define-death-is-the-issue-in-murder-trial-transplanted-sept.html.
10. "A Definition of Irreversible Coma—Report of the Ad Hoc Committee of the Harvard Medical School to Examine the Definition of Brain Death," *University of San Francisco Law Review* 5, no. 2 (1971): 283–90 (hereinafter "Harvard's Definition").
11. Ibid., 283.
12. Ibid., 286.
13. In 1970, the American Heart Association and medical establishment agreed to halt heart transplants due to the high death rates, yet in Stanford, Dr. Shumway continued to work on research that led to the introduction of cyclosporine, a drug that combats rejection in organ transplant. Robert D. Truog et al., "Brain Death at Fifty: Exploring Consensus, Controversy, and Contexts," special report, *Defining Death: Organ Transplantation and the Fifty-Year Legacy of the Harvard Report on Brain Death, Hastings Center Report* 48, no. 6 (2018): S2–S5, https://doi.org/10.1002/hast.942.
14. President's Commission for the Study of Ethical Problems in Medicine and Biomedical and Behavioral Research, *Defining Death: Medical, Legal, and Ethical Issues in the Determination of Death* (1981).
15. Sarang Biel and Julia Durrant, "Controversies in Brain Death Declaration: Legal and Ethical Implications in the ICU," *Current Treatment Options in Neurology* 22, no. 4 (2020): 12, https://doi.org/10.1007/s11940-020-0618-6. It is important to point out that those in a persistent vegetative state do not fall into the category of being brain dead.
16. Furthermore, Rabbi Yechezkel Landau, another leading *posek*, had ruled against performing autopsies for the purpose of procuring medical information that would be helpful in the future. However, he too saw room for leniency in the face of an immediate life-threatening situation. He thus allowed doctors to perform autopsies on cholera victims, in the hopes it would help find a cure for so many who were deathly ill.
17. Thus, in the twentieth century, a major *posek*, Rabbi Yechiel Yaakov Weinberg (1884–1966), allowed corneal transplants, as he saw it averting a present life-threatening situation. He wrote that a blind person could trip over something or fall into a pit which could lead to death. The former Ashkenazi Chief Rabbi of Israel, Rabbi Isser Yehuda Unterman (1886–1976), approached the prohibition of benefiting from the dead in an equally novel fashion. He said that when an organ was transplanted from someone dead to the living, it was in a sense "resurrected." As such, it no longer needed burial and thus using it would no longer be considered benefiting from the dead. Shevet MiYehuda, 312–22.
18. Rabbi Shlomo M. Brody analyzed the question not of whether it is permissible to donate, but rather whether one is obligated to do so. Shlomo Brody, *A Guide to the Complex*, 1st ed. (Jerusalem: Maggid Books, 2014), 27–29. Rabbi Brody quotes Rabbi Shmuel HaLevi

Wosner (Shevet HaLevi 5:219) (written in 1974) and Rabbi J. David Bleich (Tradition 27:3) as obligating blood donation and other donations in an emergency. If it poses no harm to the donor and saves lives, why would it not be required to donate blood and bone marrow? Donating a kidney, however, involves some level of danger for the donor, in the event that the remaining kidney gets damaged, so there is less consensus amongst the *poskim*, but still most mainstream rabbis permit the donation and some require it. Ibid., 30–32. See Shlomo Minkowitz, "Organ Donation in Judaism," https://www.chabad.org/library/article_cdo/aid/4291387/jewish/Organ-Donation-in-Judaism.htm#footnoteRef29a4291387, quoting *Igrot Moshe, Yoreh Deah*, vol. 2, 174:4; and *Tzitz Eliezer*, vol. 10, 25:7. R' Ovadiah Yosef (Dinei Yisrael 7 [5736]: 25–43).

19. See Elana Stein Hain, *The Legal Parameters and Tools of Talmudic and Rabbinic Interpretation*; Shlomo Pill, *The Role of Humrah, Kula, and Safek in Halakhic Rulings and Practices*; and Joseph Davis, *Consensus in Halakhic Decision Making and the Canonization of Authority*.
20. Mishnah Oholot 1:6, trans. Joshua Kulpt, *Sefaria*, www.sefaria.org/sheets/327127.1?lang=bi&with=Translations&lang2=en (hereinafter "Oholot").
21. "Yoma 85a:9," trans. William Davidson, *Sefaria*, iwww.sefaria.org/Yoma.85a.9?lang=bi&with=Translations&lang2=en (hereinafter "Yoma"). The debate continues among the scholars, who ultimately conclude that when searching from the head down, checking until the nose is sufficient. When searching up from the feet, there is not a consensus of where to stop.
22. Notably, Rabbi Tendler (1926–2021; former Rosh Yeshiva and Professor of Biology at Yeshiva University) relied on his father-in-law, Rabbi Moshe Feinstein (1895–1986; one of the most notable twentieth-century *halakhic* authorities).
23. The debate is often referred to as the Bleich vs. Tendler debate, though Rabbi Feinstein's statements majorly contributed to the latter's approach.
24. See Responsa of Rav Moshe Feinstein, *Igrot Moshe, Yoreh Deah*, vol. 2, 174: "Concerning Heart Transplants for Sick Patients" (written in 1968 to the Gaon Rav Yitzchok Yaakov Weiss).
25. Ibid. The explanation for "double murder" is hastening the death of the recipient and causing the death of the donor, each counting as a murder.
26. Responsum of Rav Moshe Feinstein, *Igrot Moshe, Yoreh Deah*, Part 3, no. 132, vol. 4, no. 54, dated May 1976 and published 1982. Rabbi Moshe Feinstein's later-in-life approach to organ donation has been viewed by some as controversial. It is important to note that the first responses to the question of defining death that Rabbi Feinstein answered were dated in the late 1960s, at a time when organ donation was unsuccessful. His last statement is dated after the introduction of cyclosporine and other advances that drastically improved the likelihood of organ donation succeeding. Nonetheless, critics questioned Rabbi Feinstein's new approach to brain death toward the very end of his life and hesitated to adopt it.
27. Rabbi Tendler did not shy away from explaining Rabbi Feinstein's prior disapproval of defining *halakhic* death as brain death. See also Brody, *A Guide to the Complex*, 34."Rabbi Feinstein's family has affirmed that such was indeed his opinion (Assia 7)." Ibid., 35. For a different approach, see Rabbi Yitzchak Breitowitz's summary. Yitzchak A. Breitowitz, "The Brain Death Controversy in Jewish Law," *Jewish Law*, www.jlaw.com/Articles/brain.html. Rabbi Breitowitz, born in 1954, is the Rabbi Emeritus of Woodside Synagogue and a graduate of Harvard Law School.

28. Jason Weiner, "Death vs. Brain Death in Judaism," *My Jewish Learning*, March 7, 2019, www.myjewishlearning.com/article/defining-death-in-jewish-law/. See Rabbi Moshe Feinstein, *Igrot Moshe, Yoreh Deah*, vol. 3, 132, and Rabbi Tendler's letter in *The Jewish Observer*, October 1991.
29. Ibid.
30. Rabbinical Council of America, *Resolutions Adopted at the Annual Convention* (June 1991), https://hods.org/pdf/Living%20Will%20RCA.pdf.
31. Ibid.
32. Ibid.
33. As the Jewish Telegraphic Agency reported, the RCA focused on the concept of saving a life. Statements in the resolution such as "the saving of a life takes precedence over all but three halachic imperatives—murder, idolatry and adultery" and "since organs that can be life-saving may be donated, the family urged do so. When human life can be saved, it must be saved," support this focus. Debra Nussbaum Cohen, "Organ Donations Authorized by Orthodox Rabbinic Group," *Daily News Bulletin* (Jewish Telegraphic Agency), June 17, 1991, pdfs.jta.org/1991/1991-06-17_114.pdf?_ga=2.27188349.1778294660.1622591165-1299835090.1622377593.
34. The patient, Mira Schichmanter, "suffered from a chronic liver ailment for seven years" and was dying when Rivital Brandt died from a car accident and became her organ donor. Despite prior religious objections, newly appointed Health Minister Shoshana Arbeli-Amoslina gave the surgeon, Dr. Kam, special permission to conduct the surgery. The Rabbinate quickly put together a committee to discuss precisely this issue. David Landau and Hugh Orgel, "Israel's First Liver Transplant Patient Reported in Critical but Stable Condition in Rambam Hospital," *Daily News Bulletin* (Jewish Telegraphic Agency), October 23, 1986, www.jta.org/1986/10/23/archive/israels-first-liver-transplant-patient-reported-in-critical-but-stable-condition-in-rambam-hospital.
35. David Landau, "Israel's Two Liver Transplant Patients Show 'Some Slight Stability,'" *Daily News Bulletin* (Jewish Telegraphic Agency), November 3, 1986, www.jta.org/1986/11/03/archive/israels-two-liver-transplant-patients-show-some-slight-stability.
36. David Landau, "Chief Rabbinate Council Rules That Heart Transplants Are Permissible Under Certain Conditions of Jew," *Daily News Bulletin* (Jewish Telegraphic Agency), November 5, 1986, https://www.jta.org/archive/chief-rabbinate-council-rules-that-heart-transplants-are-permissable-under-certain-conditions-of-jew.
37. Landau, David. "Heart Transplant Patient Doing Well." *Daily News Bulletin* (Jewish Telegraphic Agency), September 11, 1987, www.jta.org/1987/09/11/archive/heart-transplant-patient-doing-well. The first two heart transplants were performed in Israel nearly twenty years prior.
38. Yoel Jakobovits, "Brain Death and Heart Transplants: The [Israeli] Chief Rabbinate's Directives," *Tradition: A Journal of Orthodox Jewish Thought* 24, no. 4 (1989): 1–14, accessed May 31, 2021, www.jstor.org/stable/23260715.
39. Ibid.
40. Ibid.
41. J. David Bleich, "Halakha and Brain Death: A Response by Rabbi J. David Bleich," *The Jewish Review* 3, no. 4 (March 1990), https://thejewishreview.org/articles/?id=117. "Accordingly: A *kohen* may enter the patient's room . . . unless the patient is deemed to be a *gosses* . . . Sabbath restrictions are suspended in the treatment . . . [and the] patient's wife has no capacity to contract a marriage." Ibid.

42. Ibid. Rabbi Bleich specifically highlights the fact that several "brain dead" women continued gestation and delivered living babies.
43. Ibid.
44. For example, Rabbi Shlomo Zalman Auerbach in *Nishmat Avraham* EH 80:1 (1910–1995; Rosh Yeshiva of the Kol Torah Yeshiva of Jerusalem); and Rabbi Yosef Elyashiv (1910–2012; a leading *posek* in the *Hareidi* community).
45. Bleich, "Halakha and Brain Death."
46. Ibid.
47. Breitowitz, "Brain Death Controversy in Jewish Law."
48. 1917–2001; a major Torah scholar who headed the Hebrew Theological Seminary in Skokie and later Yeshivas Brisk in Chicago.
49. Ibid. Rabbi Soloveichik does point out that this "phenomenon" has never actually been documented as having occurred.
50. Ibid. This approach places even more *halakhic* limitations. A person may be dead, so a *Kohen* would not be allowed to enter the room. Yet the person may also be alive, so donating their organs would be equivalent to murder.
51. Rabbi Eliezer Melamed, "Sign the New Organ Donor Card," *Yeshiva Har Bracha* 29 (December 2017), https://en.yhb.org.il/sign-the-new-organ-donor-card/. Rabbi Melamed (born 1961) is a Rosh Yeshiva of Yeshivat Har Bracha and author of the book series Peninei Halakha.
52. RCA, *Resolutions Adopted.*
53. Vaad Halacha of the Rabbinical Council of America, "Halachic Issues in the Determination of Death and in Organ Transplantation" (June 2010), www.rabbis.org/pdfs/Halachi_%20Issues_the_Determination.pdf.
54. The Rabbinical Council of America, "Halachic Health Care Proxy" (August 2009), hods.org/pdf/RCA%20Health%20Care%20Proxy%202010.pdf.
55. The Rabbinical Council of America, "Halachic Guidelines to Assist Patients and Their Families in Making 'End-of-Life' Medical Decisions" (August 10, 2009), images.shulcloud.com/590/uploads/Forms/advanceddirectivesmerged.pdf.
56. An example can be found in one of several responses written following the new proxy's release, undersigned by many rabbis both in the United States and in Israel. "Rabbinic Statement Regarding Organ Donation" (January 7, 2011), www.internationalrabbinicfellowship.org/news/rabbinic-statement-regarding-organ-donation. (See the list of signers on the bottom of the letter.) The letter contains sharp language endorsing brain death as *halakhic* death. ("It is both *halachically* permissible and desirable and ethically mandated for every Jew to be an organ donor consistent with his or her definition of halakhic death . . . To adopt a restrictive position regarding donating organs and a permissive position regarding receiving organs is morally untenable." Ibid.)
57. Otherwise known as Non-Heart Beating Donation (NHBC). This was originally known as the Pittsburgh protocol developed by the University of Pittsburgh Medical Center to allow for "planned" organ retrieval. A patient or their surrogate could make a legal and ethical decision to withdraw life support. The patient would then be weaned from the ventilator and prepared for organ retrieval. The patient's pulse would be monitored by a femoral catheter, and the heart's electrical activity measured by electrocardiogram (EKG). When these would show a total absence of a pulse and cardiac activity for a period of two minutes, the patient would be pronounced dead and organ retrieval may proceed. If the patient spontaneously resumed breathing after the removal of the ventilator they would be returned to the intensive care unit.

58. Asher Lopatin, "Non-Heart-Beating Donation from Brain Dead Patients: Rav Ahron Soloveichik's Solution," Science & Medical Ethics, YC Torah Library, September 22, 2016, library.yctorah.org/2016/09/non-heart-beating-donation-from-brain-dead-patients-rav-ahron-soloveichiks-solution/.
59. "If the patient no longer has rights to the respirator, because he has transferred them to the hospital . . . a doctor's assigning the machine to someone else is only an avoidance of the obligation of saving life. Such an act is offset by the need to save someone else." Ibid.
60. Ibid.
61. Rabbi Joseph Prouser, "Hesed or Hiyuv? The Obligation to Preserve Life and the Question of Postmortem Organ Donation," in *Responsa of the CTLS 1999–2000, Visiting the Sick and Medicine*, https://www.rabbinicalassembly.org/sites/default/files/assets/public/halakhah/teshuvot/19912000/prouser_chesed.pdf.
62. Ibid., 189.
63. Ibid., 190.
64. Leonard A. Sharzer, "Organ Donation after Cardiac Death," *YD* 370, no. 1 (2010). The Rabbinical Assembly, February 2, 2010, https://www.rabbinicalassembly.org/sites/default/files/assets/public/halakhah/teshuvot/20052010/dcd_teshuvah_final%2002-10.pdf.
65. Ibid.
66. Ibid., 16.
67. Ibid., 15.
68. Ibid., 24.
69. This includes having a physician conclude that the procedure would not hasten the death of the donor, incorporating an observation period, getting donor consent, requiring standard end-of-life care, and treating the deceased donor with dignity. Ibid.
70. Central Conference of American Rabbis, "Hastening the Death of a Potential Organ Donor," NYP No. 5763.3 2010, https://www.ccarnet.org/ccar-responsa/nyp-no-5763-3/.
71. Ibid.
72. Ibid.
73. "The prospect of killing NHBDs may not trouble those who do not share the Jewish conception of the sanctity of human life. But those of us who do, who participate in a tradition that regards human life as inviolate and beyond our power to destroy even for beneficial purposes, find it a chilling thought indeed." Ibid.
74. It should also be emphasized that the *halakhic* validity of brain death does not include those in persistent vegetative state. Yet, cases in which a patient is reported incorrectly as brain dead but is actually in a persistent vegetative state, and ultimately wakes up, have caused controversy and led to misconceptions that a brain dead person is not really dead. In Truog, "Brain Death at Fifty," the authors address this phenomenon and claim that each story of someone brain dead waking up is false. Ibid. They urge brain death to not be used as a colloquial label for any type of brain injury to avoid "public misunderstanding." Ibid. It follows logically that using the term only when medically appropriate would avoid the argument made in opposition to organ donation based on the theory that a patient could recover after being declared brain dead.
75. Rachel Son and Susan Setta, "Frequency of Use of the Religious Exemption in New Jersey Cases of Determination of Brain Death," *BMC Medical Ethics*19 (2018): Article 76. https://doi.org/10.1186/s12910-018-0315-0. The State of Florida signed into law Senate Bill 1580 in May 2023. This bill generally provides protections to healthcare providers and payers from engaging in medical care that they do not believe in "on the basis of conscience-based objection," including moral, ethical, and religious objections. How this bill may impact areas

of medicine and whether it will affect the involvement of healthcare providers in post-mortem organ donation remains to be seen.

76. Sarang Biel and Julia Durrant, "Controversies in Brain Death Declaration: Legal and Ethical Implications in the ICU," *Current Treatment Options in Neurology* 22, no. 4 (2020): 12, https://doi.org/10.1007/s11940-020-0618-6, citing California Health and Safety Code § 1254.4 (2008); Illinois Anatomical Gift Act, 755 ILCS 50 (2004); and New York Codes, Rules, and Regulations §§400.16 (2011).
77. Despite his family's resistance, physicians determined that Yechezkel Nakar was brain dead during a Jewish holiday, while his family was absent. His wife ultimately won her petition to nullify Nakar's death certificate, which she did "in order for medical insurance coverage to continue during the three weeks he remained on cardiopulmonary support before circulatory arrest." Nakar v. NY Presbyterian Hospital (N.Y. Kings County Sup. Ct. 2019).
78. Ibid.
79. Adena K. Berkowitz, "All Take and No Give?," *Moment Magazine*, August 1995, 32–59.
80. Following the RCA's updated proxy, for example, Dr. Kenneth Prager and Dr. Neil W. Schluger publicly expressed discontent with the RCA and the Vaad. "To the public at large, the willingness of Jews to use organs that halakha indicates were obtained by murder, coupled with their refusal to donate organs of brain-dead relatives, will be viewed as morally repugnant . . . If the Vaad cannot accept brain death as death, it should not hide behind a halakhic smokescreen to permit Jews to benefit from the organs obtained from brain-dead donors." Kenneth Prager and Neil W. Schluger, "RCA And Brain Death," *The New York Jewish Week*, December 7, 2010, jewishweek.timesofisrael.com/rca-and-brain-death/. See also Ari Perl, "The Iniquity of Inequity," *Lehrhaus* (September 16, 2020) While acknowledging that "Declining the opportunity to donate organs is a personal choice that must be respected . . . especially if the decision is rooted in a principled halakhic position. . . . (But) a principled halakhic position must have integrity . . .; it must be an *equitable* one that affirms the value of every human life. Anyone who declines the opportunity to save a life through organ donation—*especially* if he or she considers it to be murderous—should be prepared to decline a donated organ that could save them or their loved one. Likewise, anyone who is prepared to accept the beneficent gift of a donated organ should be prepared to donate organs to save the life of a fellow human being." Even if a technical *halakhic* argument can be made in support of receiving organs but not donating, such a position epitomizes R. Aharon Lichtenstein's scenario where "the fulfillment of explicit halakhic duty could fall well short of exhausting clearly felt moral responsibility . . . [and] the full discharge of one's formal duty as defined by *din* often appears palpably insufficient." *Does Jewish Tradition Recognize an Ethic Independent of Halakha?*, https://thelehrhaus.com/commentary/iniquity-inequity/.
81. See Ari Perl, "Uvacharta VaChayim: 'And you Shall Choose Life,'" *The Times of Israel*, February 25, 2020, https://blogs.timesofisrael.com/uvacharta-vachayim-and-you-shall-choose-life/.
82. Tamar Ashkenazi et al., "Organ donation in Israel—Achievements and Challenges," *Transplantation* 99, no. 2 (2015): 265–66, https://doi.org/10.1097/TP.0000000000000591.
83. Jerusalem Post Staff, "Israel Becomes World Leader in Live Donor Kidney Donations—WHO," *The Jerusalem Post*, January 23, 2022, https://www.jpost.com/health-and-wellness/article-694257. In addition to organizational work, several nationwide stories have inspired Israelis and Jews around the world to donate organs. When Alisa Flatow was killed in a terrorist attack nearly three decades ago, her father said that donating her organs postmortem to six people were Alisa's "lasting contribution to the people of Israel." Robert Hanley, "Father

Says U.S. Victim Loved Israel," *The New York Times*, April 11, 1995, 10, https://www.nytimes.com/1995/04/11/world/father-says-us-victim-loved-israel.html. More recently, Lucy Dee's organ donations captured the attention of Jews around the world. Videos of the surviving Dee family members listening to their mother's heartbeat inside the body of a woman she saved circulated and raised questions about *halakhic* death and the significance of saving lives via organ donation. See Shlomo Brody, "Judaism and Organ Donation: Is Respiratory Brain Death Considered Death?," *The Jerusalem Post*, May 26, 2023, https://www.jpost.com/judaism/article-744079. See also "'Like I'm with her': Terror Victim Lucy Dee's family Visits Recipients of Her Organs," *The Times of Israel*, May 2, 2023, https://www.timesofisrael.com/like-im-with-her-terror-victim-lucy-dees-family-visits-recipients-of-her-organs/.

84. See the HODS archives at https://hods.org, relaunched as Ematai in 2023 with a new mission of enabling Jewish families "to navigate an increasingly complex healthcare journey, particularly in the dilemmas of aging and end-of-life treatment." https://www.ematai.org/about-us/.
85. Halachic Organ Donor Society, "Hundreds of Orthodox Rabbis Carry Organ Donor Cards," hods.org/about-hods/orthodox-rabbis/?selCountry=USA.
86. "Organ Donation Registration," Ematai, https://www.ematai.org/learn/organ-donation/organ-donation-registration-2/.
87. See "Advance Directive," Ematai, https://www.ematai.org/plan-ahead/living-will/advance-directive-conversation-guide/.
88. Michael Feldstein, "If Not Now, When? An Interview with Rabbi Dr. Shlomo Brody," *Jewish Link*, May 24, 2023, https://jewishlink.news/if-not-now-when-an-interview-with-rabbi-dr-shlomo-brody/. "There is a major halachic debate on the criterion of respiratory brain-death. Ematai's policy follows the lead of mainstream rabbis within the given area. Within the religious Zionist community in Israel, every single major Ashkenazic and Sephardic *posek* living today, following the lead of the Chief Rabbinate, supports posthumous organ donation after the determination of respiratory brain death. Rav Yaakov Ariel, Rav Shlomo Aviner, Rav Yosef Rimon, Rav Aryeh Stern, Rav Shlomo Amar, Rav Shmuel Eliyahu, Rabbi Dov Lior, Rabbi Yosef Carmel, and Rabbi Re'em Hacohen all support organ donation. So we strongly encourage it within that community. No contemporary Haredi posek in Israel supports it, and so we wouldn't push for it within that community. In Diaspora communities, there's a deep divide on this issue and the matter became contentious. Ematai's policy respects all sides." Ibid.
89. Hagai Boas, "The Paradox of Organ Donations among Ultra-Orthodox Jews in Israel," September 29, 2022, https://divinity.uchicago.edu/sightings/articles/paradox-organ-donations-among-ultra-orthodox-jews-israel.
90. "Transplant Trends," *UNOS*, unos.org/data/transplant-trends/#OPTNData. This number is accurate as of July 27, 2023, at 12:45 PM; the data update constantly. https://www.organdonor.gov/learn/organ-donation-statistics.
91. American Transplant Foundation, "Facts and Myths about Transplants," www.americantransplantfoundation.org/about-transplant/facts-and-myths/.
92. Ibid.
93. In 2020, in the New York area, more than one thousand members of the Jewish community were on the UNOS waiting list. Jerusalem Post Staff, "Israel Becomes World Leader in Live Donor Kidney Donations." See Centre for Public Impact, "Legislating to encourage organ donation in Israel," *BCG Foundation* (March 8, 2016), https://www.centreforpublicimpact.org/case-study/organ-donation-israel#:~:text=The%20government%20passed%20two%20laws,legal%20organ%20donation%20in%20Israel. See also J. Zaltzman, "Ten Years of Israel's Organ Transplant Law: Is It on the Right Track?," *Israel Journal of Health Policy Research*, 7, no. 45 (2018), https://doi.org/10.1186/s13584-018-0232-1.

94. This only applies when all medical circumstances are equal among recipients on a list. Other countries have developed differing approaches. In Singapore, for example, everyone above the age of twenty-one is automatically registered as an organ donor. Opting out from this results in being put at the very bottom of the organ priority list, should you need an organ transplantation. Daisy Phillipson, "People Praise Singapore's Controversial Organ Donation Rules," *UNILAND*, March 24, 2022, https://www.unilad.com/news/people-praise-singapore-controversial-organ-donation-rule-20220324. In the United States, living kidney donors have organ priority status should they need it. See Zaltzman, "Ten Years of Israel's Transplant Law." Chile amended the Organ Donor Act with Law 20673 in October 2013, requiring individuals wishing to become nondonors to submit a notarized statement to the nondonor registry and also asserts that "all else being equal," those who are registered as donors get priority for donations should they need them over those who are registered as nondonors. Alejandra Zúñiga-Fajuri, "Increasing Organ Donation by Presumed Consent and Allocation Priority: Chile," *Bulletin of the World Health Organization* 93, no. 3 (2015): 199–202, https://doi.org/10.2471/BLT.14.139535.
95. Renuka Kennedy, "What Is Neuralink? How Does the Technology Work and What Can a Person Do with It?," *Republic World*, April 17, 2021, www.republicworld.com/technology-news/other-tech-news/what-is-neuralink-how-does-the-technology-work-and-what-can-a-person-do-with-it.html. See also Brandon Lingle, "With Brain Implants, the 'Future's Gonna Be Weird,'" *MySanAntonio*, May 4, 2021, www.mysanantonio.com/sa-inc/article/Brain-implants-will-make-for-a-weird-future-16146961.php.
96. Musk's Neuralink has recently received FDA approval to be studied in human brains. Mike Snider, "Elon Musk's Neuralink Has FDA Approval To Put Chips In Humans' Brains. Here's What's Next," *USA Today*, June 9, 2023, https://www.usatoday.com/story/tech/2023/06/09/musk-neuralink-brain-chips-fda-human-trials/70299875007/. See also https://www.nytimes.com/2023/05/24/science/paralysis-brain-implants-ai.html, where a paralyzed man walked after having a chip put in his brain.
97. Danny Schiff, *Judaism in a Digital Age: An Ancient Tradition Confronts a Transformative Era*, 1st ed. (London: Palgrave Macmillan, 2023).
98. Ibid.
99. It seems that this may be a reality not too far into the future. NYU Langone Health/NYU Grossman School of Medicine, "Successful Heart Xenotransplant Experiments Set Protocol for Pig-to-Human Organ Transplantation," *ScienceDaily*, July 12, 2022, www.sciencedaily.com/releases/2022/07/220712141355.htm.
100. Engineering.com Staff, "3D-Printed Pump Could Make Heart Transplants Obsolete by Staff," Engineering.com, January 26, 2017, www.engineering.com/story/3d-printed-pump-could-make-heart-transplants-obsolete.
101. Ibid.
102. Ido Efrati, "Israeli Scientists Print World's First 3-D Heart," *Science & Health*, Haaretz, April 15, 2019, www.haaretz.com/science-and-health/.premium-israeli-scientists-print-world-s-first-3-d-heart-1.7124321.
103. Ibid.

Index

For the benefit of digital users, indexed terms that span two pages (e.g., 52–53) may, on occasion, appear on only one of those pages.